Craftsman

2021 NATIONAL CONSTRUCTION ESTIMATOR

69th Edition

Edited by Richard Pray

Includes inside the back cover:

Inside the back cover of this book you'll find a software download certificate. To access the download, follow the instructions printed there. The download includes the National Estimator, an easy to-use estimating program with all the cost estimates in this book. The software will run on PCs using Windows XP, Vista, 7, 8, or 10 operating systems.

Quarterly price updates on the Web are free and automatic all during 2021. You'll be prompted when it's time to collect the next update. A connection to the Web is required.

Download all of Craftsman's most popular costbooks for one low price with the Craftsman Site License. http://CraftsmanSiteLicense.com

Craftsman

Craftsman Book Company
6058 Corte del Cedro, Carlsbad, CA 92011

Contents

A complete index begins on page 640

 ISBN 978-1-57218-363-6 1st printing October 2020 for the year 2021

This Book Is an Encyclopedia of 2021 Building Costs

The 2021 National Construction Estimator lists estimated construction costs to general contractors performing the work with their own crews, as of mid-2021. Overhead & profit are not included.

This Manual Has Two Parts; the Residential Construction Division begins on page 17. Use the figures in this division when estimating the cost of homes and apartments with a wood, steel or masonry frame. The Industrial and Commercial Division begins on page 308 and can be used to estimate costs for nearly all construction not covered by the Residential Division.

The Residential Construction Division is arranged in alphabetical order by construction trade and type of material. The Industrial and Commercial Division follows MasterFormat™ 2004. A complete index begins on page 640.

National Estimator Inside the back cover of this book you'll find a software download certificate. To access the download, follow the instructions printed there. The download includes an easy to-use estimating program with all the cost estimates in this book. The software will run on PCs using Windows XP, Vista, 7, 8, or 10 operating systems.

When the National Estimator program has been installed, click Help on the menu bar to see a list of topics that will get you up and running. Or go online to www.craftsman-book.com, click on "Support", then click on "Tutorials" to view an interactive video for National Estimator.

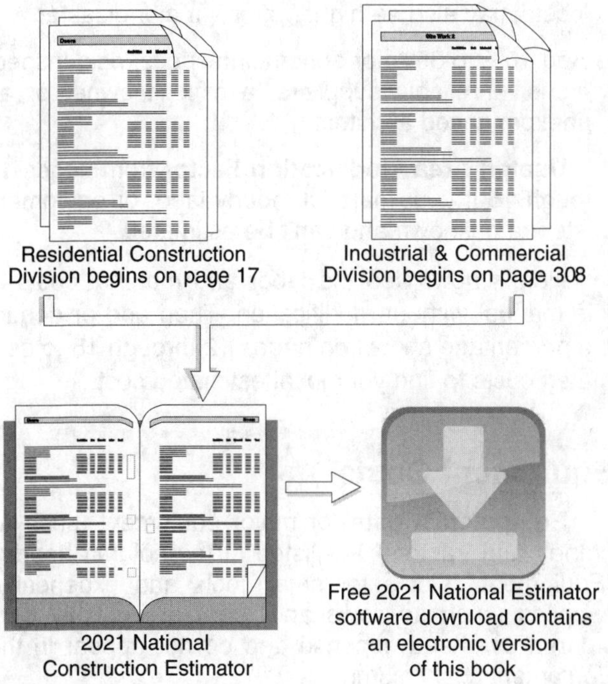

Material Costs

Material Costs for each item are listed in the column headed "Material." These are neither retail nor wholesale prices. They are estimates of what most contractors who buy in moderate volume will pay suppliers as of mid-2021. Discounts may be available for purchases in larger volume.

Quarterly prices updates on the Web are free and automatic all during 2021. You'll be prompted when it's time to collect the next update. A connection to the Web is required.

Add Delivery Expense to the material cost for other than local delivery of reasonably large quantities. Cost of delivery varies with the distance from source of supply, method of transportation, and quantity to be delivered. But most material dealers absorb the delivery cost on local delivery (5 to 15 miles) of larger quantities to good customers. Add the expense of job site delivery when it is a significant part of the material cost.

Add Sales Tax when sales tax will be charged to the contractor buying the materials.

Waste and Coverage loss is included in the installed material cost. The cost of many materials per unit after installation is greater than the purchase price for the same unit because of waste, shrinkage or coverage loss during installation. For example, about 120 square feet of nominal 1" x 4" square edge boards will be needed to cover 100 square feet of floor or wall. There is no coverage loss with plywood sheathing, but waste due to cutting and fitting will average about 6%.

Costs in the "Material" column of this book assume normal waste and coverage loss. Small and irregular jobs may require a greater waste allowance. Materials priced without installation (with no labor cost) do not include an allowance for waste and coverage except as noted.

Labor Costs

Labor Costs for installing the material or doing the work described are listed in the column headed "Labor." The labor cost per unit is the labor cost per hour multiplied by the manhours per unit shown after the @ sign in the "Craft@Hours" column. Labor cost includes the basic wage, the employer's contribution to welfare, pension, vacation and apprentice funds and all tax and insurance charges based on wages. Hourly labor costs for the various crafts are listed on page 10 (for the Residential Division) and page 309 (for the Industrial and Commercial Division).

Hourly labor costs used in the Industrial and Commercial Division are higher than those used in the

Residential Division, reflecting the fact that craftsmen on industrial and commercial jobs are often paid more than craftsmen on residential jobs.

Supervision Expense to the general contractor is not included in the labor cost. The cost of supervision and non-productive labor varies widely from job to job. Calculate the cost of supervision and non-productive labor and add this to the estimate.

Payroll Taxes and Insurance included in the labor cost are itemized in the sections beginning on pages 185 and 285.

Manhours per Unit and the Craft performing the work are listed in the "Craft@Hrs" column. Pages 7 through 9 explain the "Craft@Hrs" column. To find the units of work done per man in an 8-hour day, divide 8 by the manhours per unit. To find the units done by a crew in an 8-hour day, multiply the units per man per 8-hour day by the number of crew members.

Manhours Include all productive labor normally associated with installing the materials described. This will usually include tasks such as:

- Unloading and storing construction materials, tools and equipment on site.
- Moving tools and equipment from a storage area or truck on site at the beginning of the day.
- Returning tools and equipment to a storage area or truck on site at the end of the day.
- Normal time lost for work breaks.
- Planning and discussing the work to be performed.
- Normal handling, measuring, cutting and fitting.
- Keeping a record of the time spent and work done.
- Regular cleanup of construction debris.
- Infrequent correction or repairs required because of faulty installation.

Adjust the Labor Cost to the job you are figuring when your actual hourly labor cost is known or can be estimated. The labor costs listed on pages 10 and 309 will apply within a few percent on many jobs. But labor costs may be much higher or much lower on the job you are estimating.

If the hourly wage rates listed on page 10 or page 309 are not accurate, divide your known or estimated cost per hour by the listed cost per hour. The result is your adjustment for any figure in the "Labor" column for that craft. See page 11 for more information on adjusting labor costs.

Adjust for Unusual Labor Productivity. Costs in the labor column are for normal conditions: experienced craftsmen working on reasonably well planned and managed new construction with fair to good productivity. Labor estimates assume that materials are standard grade, appropriate tools are on hand, work done by other crafts is adequate, layout and installation are relatively uncomplicated, and working conditions don't slow progress.

Working conditions at the job site have a major effect on labor cost. Estimating experience and careful analysis can help you predict the effect of most changes in working conditions. Obviously, no single adjustment will apply on all jobs. But the adjustments that follow should help you produce more accurate labor estimates. More than one condition may apply on a job.

- Add 10% to 15% when working temperatures are below 40 degrees or above 95 degrees.
- Add 15% to 25% for work on a ladder or a scaffold, in a crawl space, in a congested area or remote from the material storage point.
- Deduct 10% when the work is in a large open area with excellent access and good light.
- Add 1% for each 10 feet that materials must be lifted above ground level.
- Add 5% to 50% for tradesmen with below average skills. Deduct 5% to 25% for highly motivated, highly skilled tradesmen.
- Deduct 10% to 20% when an identical task is repeated many times for several days at the same site.
- Add 30% to 50% on small jobs where fitting and matching of materials is required, adjacent surfaces have to be protected and the job site is occupied during construction.
- Add 25% to 50% for work done following a major flood, fire, earthquake, hurricane or tornado while skilled tradesmen are not readily available. Material costs may also be higher after a major disaster.
- Add 10% to 35% for demanding specs, rigid inspections, unreliable suppliers, a difficult owner or an inexperienced architect.

Use an Area Modification Factor from pages 12 through 15 if your material, hourly labor or equipment costs are unknown and can't be estimated.

Here's how: Use the labor and material costs in this manual without modification. Then add or deduct the percentage shown on pages 12 through 15 to estimated costs to find your local estimated cost.

Equipment Costs

Equipment Costs for major equipment (such as cranes and tractors) are listed in the column headed "Equipment." Costs for small tools and expendable supplies (such as saws and tape) are usually considered overhead expense and do not appear in the Equipment cost column.

Equipment costs are based on rental rates listed in the section beginning on page 320 and assume that the equipment can be used productively for an entire 8-hour day. Add the cost of moving equipment on and off the site. Allow for unproductive time when equipment can't be used for the full rental period. For example, the equipment costs per unit of work completed will be higher when a tractor is used for 4 hours during a day and sits idle for the remaining 4 hours. Generally, an 8-hour day is the minimum rental period for most heavy equipment. Many sections describe the equipment being used, the cost per hour and a suggested minimum job charge.

Subcontracted Work

Subcontractors do most of the work on construction projects. That's because specialty contractors can often get the work done at competitive cost, even after adding overhead and profit.

Many sections of this book cover work usually done by subcontractors. If you see the word "subcontract" in a section description, assume that costs are based on quotes by subcontractors and include typical subcontractor markup (about 30% on labor and 15% on material). Usually no material or labor costs will appear in these sections. The only costs shown will be in the "Total" column and will include all material, labor and equipment expense.

If you don't see the word "subcontract" in a section description, assume that costs are based on work done by a general contractor's crew. No markup is included in these costs. If the work is done by a subcontractor, the specialty contractor may be able to perform the work for the cost shown, even after adding overhead and profit.

Markup

The General Contractor's Markup is not included in any costs in this book. On page 208 we suggest a 20% markup on the contract price for general contractors handling residential construction. Apply this markup or some figure you select to all costs, including both subcontract items and work done by your own crews.

To realize a gross profit of 20% on the contract price, you'll have to mark up costs by 25%. See page 208 for an example of how markup is calculated. Markup includes overhead and profit and may be the most difficult item to estimate.

Keep In Mind

Labor and Material Costs Change. Costs were compiled in the fall of 2020 and projected to mid-2021 based on recent price trends. These estimates will be accurate for some materials and inaccurate for others. No one can predict every change in material prices.

How Accurate Are These Figures? As accurate as possible considering that the estimators who wrote this book don't know your subcontractors or material suppliers, haven't seen the plans or specifications, don't know what building code applies or where the job is, had to project material costs at least 6 months into the future, and had no record of how much work the crew that will be assigned to the job can handle.

You wouldn't bid a job under those conditions. And we don't claim that all construction is done at these prices.

Estimating Is an Art, not a science. On many jobs the range between high and low bid will be 20% or more. There's room for legitimate disagreement on what the correct costs are, even when complete plans and specifications are available, the date and site are established, and labor and material costs are identical for all bidders.

No cost fits all jobs. Good estimates are custom made for a particular project and a single contractor through judgment, analysis and experience.

This book is not a substitute for judgment, analysis and sound estimating practice. It's an aid in developing an informed opinion of cost. If you're using this book as your sole cost authority for contract bids, you're reading more into these pages than the editors intend.

Use These Figures to compile preliminary estimates, to check your costs and subcontract bids and when no actual costs are available. This book will reduce the chance of error or omission on bid estimates, speed "ball park" estimates, and be a good guide when there's no time to get a quote.

Where Do We Get These Figures? From the same sources all professional estimators use: contractors and subcontractors, architectural and engineering firms, material suppliers, material price services, analysis of plans, specifications, estimates and completed project costs, and both published and unpublished cost studies. In addition, we conduct nationwide mail and phone surveys and have the use of several major national estimating databases.

We'll Answer Your Questions about any part of this book and explain how to apply these costs.

Free telephone assistance is available from 8 a.m. until 5 p.m. California time Monday through Friday except holidays. Phone 760-438-7828 x 2.

We don't accept collect calls and won't estimate the job for you. But if you need clarification on something in this manual, we can help.

Abbreviations

AASHO	American Assn. of State Highway Officials
ABS	acrylonitrile butadiene styrene
AC	alternating current
AISC	American Institute of Steel Construction Inc.
APP	attactic polypropylene
ASHRAE	American Society of Heating, Refrigerating and Air Conditioning Engineers
ASME	American Society of Mechanical Engineers
ASTM	American Society for Testing Materials
AWPA	American Wood Products Association
AWWA	American Water Works Association
Ba	bay
Bdle	bundle
BF	board foot
BHP	boiler horsepower
Btr	better
Btu	British thermal unit
B & W	black & white
C	thermal conductance
C	one hundred
CF	cubic foot
CFM	cubic feet per minute
CLF	100 linear feet
cm	centimeter
CPE	chlorinated polyethylene
CPM	cycles per minute
CPVC	chlorinated polyvinyl chloride
CSPE	chloro sulphinated polyethylene
CSF	100 square feet
CSY	100 square yards
CY	cubic yard
d	penny
D	depth
DC	direct current
dia	diameter
DSB	double strength B quality glass
DWV	drain, waste, vent piping
Ea	each
EMT	electric metallic tube
EPDM	ethylene propylene diene monomer
equip.	equipment
exp.	exposure
F	Fahrenheit
FAA	Federal Aviation Administration
FICA	Federal Insurance Contributions Act (Social Security, Medicare tax)
FOB	freight on board
FPM	feet per minute
FRP	fiberglass reinforced plastic
FS	Federal Specification
ft-lbs	foot pounds
FUTA	Federal Unemployment Compensation Act Tax
Gal	gallon
GFCI	ground fault circuit interruptor
GPH	gallon(s) per hour
GPM	gallon(s) per minute
H	height
HP	horsepower
Hr(s)	hour(s)
IMC	intermediate metal conduit
ID	Inside diameter
KD	kiln dried or knocked down
KSI	kips per square inch
KV	kilovolt(s)
KVA	1,000 volt amps
kw	kilowatt(s)
kwh	kilowatt hour
L	length
Lb(s)	pound(s)
LF	linear foot
LP	liquified propane
LS	lump sum
M	one thousand
Mb	million bytes (characters)
MBF	1,000 board feet
MBtu	1,000 British thermal units
MCM	1,000 circular mils
MDO	medium density overlaid
MH	manhour
Mi	mile
MLF	1,000 linear feet
MPH	miles per hour
mm	millimeter(s)
Mo	month
MSF	1,000 square feet
NEMA	National Electrical Manufacturer's Association
NFPA	National Fire Protection Association
No.	number
NRC	noise reduction coefficient
OC	spacing from center to center
OD	outside diameter
OS & Y	outside screw & yoke
oz	ounce
perf	perforated
Pr	pair
PSF	pounds per square foot
PSI	pounds per square inch
PV	photovoltaic
PVC	polyvinyl chloride
Qt	quart
R	thermal resistance
R/L	random length(s)
R/W/L	random widths and lengths
RPM	revolutions per minute
RSC	rigid steel conduit
S1S2E	surfaced 1 side, 2 edges
S2S	surfaced 2 sides
S4S	surfaced 4 sides
Sa	sack
SBS	styrene butyl styrene
SDR	size to diameter ratio
SF	square foot
SFCA	square feet of form in contact with concrete
Sq	100 square feet
SSB	single strength B quality glass
STC	sound transmission class
Std	standard
SY	square yard
T	thick
T&G	tongue & groove edge
TV	television
UBC	Uniform Building Code
UL	Underwriter's Laboratory
USDA	United States Dept. of Agriculture
VLF	vertical linear foot
W	width
Wk	week
W/	with
x	by or times

Symbols

/	per
—	through or to
@	at
%	per 100 or percent
$	U.S. dollars
'	feet
"	inches
#	pound or number

Craft Codes, Hourly Costs and Crew Compositions

Both the Residential Division and Commercial and Industrial Division of this book include a column titled Craft@Hrs. Letters and numbers in this column show our estimates of:

- Who will do the work (the craft code)
- An @ symbol which means at
- How long the work will take (manhours).

For example, on page 51 you'll find estimates for installing BC plywood wall sheathing by the square foot. The Craft@Hrs column opposite ½" plywood wall sheathing shows:

B1@.016

That means we estimate the installation rate for crew B1 at .016 manhours per square foot. That's the same as 16 manhours per 1,000 square feet.

The table that follows defines each of the craft codes used in this book. Notice that crew B1 is composed of two craftsmen: one laborer and one carpenter. To install 1,000 square feet of ½" BC wall sheathing at .016 manhours per square foot, that crew would need 16 manhours (one 8-hour day for a crew of two).

Notice also in the table below that the cost per manhour for crew B1 is listed as $33.85. That's the average for a residential laborer (listed at $30.31 per hour on page 10) and a residential carpenter (listed at $37.38 per hour): $30.31 plus $37.38 is $67.69. Divide by 2 to get $33.845 (rounded up to $33.85), the average cost per manhour for crew B1.

In the table below, the cost per manhour is the sum of hourly costs of all crew members divided by the number of crew members. That's the average cost per manhour.

Costs in the Labor column in this book are the installation time (in manhours) multiplied by the cost per manhour. For example, on page 51 the labor cost listed for ½" BC wall sheathing is $0.54 per square foot. That's the installation time (.016 manhours per square foot) multiplied by $33.85, the average cost per manhour for crew B1.

Residential Division

Craft Code	Cost Per Manhour	Crew Composition
B1	$33.85	1 laborer and 1 carpenter
B2	$35.02	1 laborer, 2 carpenters
B3	$32.67	2 laborers, 1 carpenter
B4	$37.45	1 laborer 1 operating engineer 1 reinforcing iron worker
B5	$37.06	1 laborer, 1 carpenter 1 cement mason 1 operating engineer 1 reinforcing iron worker
B6	$32.93	1 laborer, 1 cement mason
B7	$30.72	1 laborer, 1 truck driver
B8	$36.51	1 laborer 1 operating engineer
B9	$33.06	1 bricklayer 1 bricklayer's helper
BB	$37.97	1 bricklayer
BC	$37.38	1 carpenter
BE	$40.63	1 electrician
BF	$34.28	1 floor layer
BG	$36.13	1 glazier
BH	$28.15	1 bricklayer's helper
BL	$30.31	1 laborer

Craft Code	Cost Per Manhour	Crew Composition
BR	$35.97	1 lather
BS	$33.27	1 marble setter
CF	$35.55	1 cement mason
CT	$35.35	1 mosaic & terrazzo worker
D1	$36.54	1 drywall installer 1 drywall taper
DI	$36.47	1 drywall installer
DT	$36.60	1 drywall taper
HC	$29.39	1 plasterer helper
OE	$42.71	1 operating engineer
P1	$36.89	1 laborer, 1 plumber
PM	$43.47	1 plumber
PP	$34.27	1 painter, 1 laborer
PR	$37.46	1 plasterer
PT	$38.22	1 painter
R1	$35.99	1 roofer, 1 laborer
RI	$39.33	1 reinforcing iron worker
RR	$41.66	1 roofer
SW	$42.16	1 sheet metal worker
T1	$32.99	1 tile layer, 1 laborer
TL	$35.66	1 tile layer
TR	$31.13	1 truck driver

Commercial and Industrial Division

Craft Code	Cost Per Manhour	Crew Composition
A1	$51.10	1 asbestos worker 1 laborer
AT	$44.09	1 air tool operator
AW	$60.94	1 asbestos worker
BM	$61.69	1 boilermaker
BT	$41.41	1 bricklayer tender
C1	$42.18	4 laborers, 1 truck driver
C2	$49.53	1 laborer, 2 truck drivers 2 tractor operators
C3	$48.15	1 laborer, 1 truck driver 1 tractor operator
C4	$42.81	2 laborers, 1 truck driver
C5	$46.43	2 laborers, 1 truck driver 1 tractor operator
C6	$45.39	6 laborers, 2 truck drivers 2 tractor operators
C7	$47.86	2 laborers , 3 truck drivers 1 crane operator 1 tractor operator
C8	$47.14	1 laborer, 1 carpenter
C9	$49.38	1 laborer, 1 crane operator
CB	$54.06	1 bricklayer
CC	$53.02	1 carpenter
CD	$52.29	1 drywall Installer
CE	$60.41	1 electrician
CG	$55.53	1 glazier
CL	$41.25	1 laborer
CM	$51.35	1 cement mason
CO	$57.50	1 crane operator
CV	$57.20	1 elevator constructor
D2	$46.77	1 drywall installer 1 laborer
D3	$53.77	1 laborer, 1 iron worker (structural), 1 millwright
D4	$47.56	1 laborer, 1 millwright
D5	$51.47	1 boilermaker, 1 laborer
D6	$55.01	2 millwrights 1 tractor operator
D7	$47.25	1 painter, 1 laborer
D9	$49.66	2 millwrights, 1 laborer
E1	$52.12	2 electricians, 2 laborers 1 tractor operator
E2	$50.83	2 electricians, 2 laborers
E3	$51.56	2 electricians, 2 laborers 2 carpenters
E4	$50.83	1 electrician, 1 laborer
F5	$48.31	3 carpenters, 2 laborers
F6	$49.16	2 carpenters, 2 laborers 1 tractor operator
F7	$51.14	2 carpenters, 1 laborer 1 tractor operator
F8	$51.73	2 plasterers 1 plasterer's helper
F9	$46.32	1 laborer, 1 floor layer
FL	$51.39	1 floor layer
G1	$48.39	1 glazier, 1 laborer
H1	$54.44	1 carpenter, 1 laborer 1 iron worker (structural) 1 tractor operator
H2	$51.71	1 crane operator 1 truck driver
H3	$46.70	1 carpenter, 3 laborers 1 crane operator 1 truck driver
H4	$62.57	1 crane operator 6 iron workers (structural) 1 truck driver
H5	$54.48	1 crane operator 2 iron workers (structural) 2 laborers
H6	$53.72	1 iron worker (structural) 1 laborer
H7	$62.29	1 crane operator 2 iron workers (structural)
H8	$61.36	1 crane operator 4 iron workers (structural) 1 truck driver
H9	$60.54	1 electrician 1 sheet metal worker
IW	$66.19	1 iron worker (structural)
LA	$47.97	1 lather
M1	$47.74	1 bricklayer 1 bricklayer's tender
M2	$45.17	1 carpenter, 2 laborers
M3	$50.13	1 plasterer 1 plasterer's helper
M4	$47.72	1 laborer, 1 marble setter
M5	$51.86	1 pipefitter, 1 laborer,
M6	$54.89	1 asbestos worker 1 laborer, 1 pipefitter
M8	$57.17	3 pipefitters, 1 laborer
M9	$61.44	1 electrician, 1 pipefitter
MI	$55.40	2 pipefitters, 1 laborer
MS	$54.18	marble setter
MT	$51.11	mosaic & terrazzo worker
MW	$53.87	millwright

Commercial and Industrial Division

Craft Code	Cost Per Manhour	Crew Composition
P5	$45.39	3 laborers 1 tractor operator 1 truck driver
P6	$52.39	1 laborer, 1 plumber
P8	$46.30	1 laborer, 1 cement mason
P9	$48.54	1 carpenter, 1 laborer 1 cement mason
PA	$53.25	1 painter
PD	$56.97	1 pile driver
PF	$62.47	1 pipefitter
PH	$45.32	1 plasterer's helper
PL	$63.52	1 plumber
PS	$54.94	1 plasterer
R3	$46.76	2 roofers, 1 laborer
RB	$65.21	1 reinforcing iron worker
RF	$49.52	1 roofer
S1	$49.27	1 laborer 1 tractor operator
S3	$51.60	1 truck driver 1 tractor operator
S4	$41.25	3 laborers
S5	$44.24	5 laborers 1 crane operator 1 truck driver
S6	$46.59	2 laborers 1 tractor operator
S7	$49.27	3 laborers 3 tractor operators
S8	$51.02	2 pile drivers, 2 laborers 1 truck driver 1 crane operator 1 tractor operator
S9	$48.53	1 pile driver, 2 laborers 1 tractor operator 1 truck driver
SM	$60.67	1 sheet metal worker
SP	$64.82	1 sprinkler fitter
SS	$51.94	1 laborer 2 tractor operators
T2	$53.16	3 laborers, 3 carpenters 3 iron workers (structural) 1 crane operator 1 truck driver
T3	$53.23	1 laborer 1 reinforcing iron worker
T4	$46.18	1 laborer, 1 mosaic worker
T5	$50.96	1 sheet metal worker 1 laborer
T6	$54.20	2 sheet metal workers 1 laborer
TD	$45.92	1 truck driver
TO	$57.28	1 tractor operator
U1	$50.83	1 plumber, 2 laborers 1 tractor operator
U2	$48.67	1 plumber, 2 laborers

Residential Division

	1	2	3	4	5	6
Craft	**Base wage per hour**	**Taxable fringe benefits (@5.56% of base wage)**	**Insurance and employer taxes (%)**	**Insurance and employer taxes ($)**	**Non-taxable fringe benefits (@4.91% of base wage)**	**Total hourly cost used in this book**
Bricklayer	$27.76	$1.54	24.94%	$7.31	$1.36	$37.97
Bricklayer's Helper	20.58	1.14	24.94	5.42	1.01	28.15
Building Laborer	21.00	1.17	32.07	7.11	1.03	30.31
Carpenter	26.11	1.45	30.97	8.54	1.28	37.38
Cement Mason	26.40	1.47	22.89	6.38	1.30	35.55
Drywall installer	27.02	1.50	23.22	6.62	1.33	36.47
Drywall Taper	27.11	1.51	23.22	6.65	1.33	36.60
Electrician	30.97	1.72	19.65	6.42	1.52	40.63
Floor Layer	25.34	1.41	23.52	6.29	1.24	34.28
Glazier	26.34	1.46	25.34	7.04	1.29	36.13
Lather	27.11	1.51	21.05	6.02	1.33	35.97
Marble Setter	25.06	1.39	21.13	5.59	1.23	33.27
Millwright	26.56	1.48	21.02	5.89	1.30	35.23
Mosiac & Terrazzo Worker	26.62	1.48	21.13	5.94	1.31	35.35
Operating Engineer	31.25	1.74	24.83	8.19	1.53	42.71
Painter	28.02	1.56	24.55	7.26	1.38	38.22
Plasterer	26.74	1.49	28.05	7.92	1.31	37.46
Plasterer Helper	20.98	1.17	28.05	6.21	1.03	29.39
Plumber	32.01	1.78	24.00	8.11	1.57	43.47
Reinforcing Ironworker	28.06	1.56	28.12	8.33	1.38	39.33
Roofer	26.73	1.49	43.00	12.13	1.31	41.66
Sheet Metal Worker	30.66	1.70	25.62	8.29	1.51	42.16
Sprinkler Fitter	31.46	1.75	24.76	8.22	1.55	42.98
Tile Layer	26.86	1.49	21.13	5.99	1.32	35.66
Truck Driver	22.60	1.26	25.83	6.16	1.11	31.13

Hourly Labor Cost

The labor costs shown in Column 6 were used to compute the manhour costs for crews on page 7 and the figures in the "Labor" column of the Residential Division of this manual. Figures in the "Labor" column of the Industrial and Commercial Division of this book were computed using the hourly costs shown on page 309. All labor costs are in U.S. dollars per manhour.

It's important that you understand what's included in the figures in each of the six columns above. Here's an explanation:

Column 1, the base wage per hour, is the craftsman's hourly wage. These figures are representative of what many contractors will be paying craftsmen working on residential construction in 2021.

Column 2, taxable fringe benefits, includes vacation pay, sick leave and other taxable benefits. These fringe benefits average 5.56% of the base wage for many construction contractors. This benefit is in addition to the base wage.

Column 3, insurance and employer taxes in percent, shows the insurance and tax rate for construction trades. The cost of insurance in this column includes workers' compensation and contractor's casualty and liability coverage. Insurance rates vary widely from state to state and depend on a contractor's loss experience. Typical rates are shown in the Insurance section of this manual beginning on page 185. Taxes are itemized in the section on page 285. Note that taxes and insurance increase the hourly labor cost by 30 to 35% for most trades. There is no legal way to avoid these costs.

Column 4, insurance and employer taxes in dollars, shows the hourly cost of taxes and insurance for each construction trade. Insurance and taxes are paid on the costs in both columns 1 and 2.

Column 5, non-taxable fringe benefits, includes employer paid non-taxable benefits such as medical coverage and tax-deferred pension and profit sharing plans. These fringe benefits average 4.91% of the base wage for many construction contractors. The employer pays no taxes or insurance on these benefits.

Column 6, the total hourly cost in dollars, is the sum of columns 1, 2, 4, and 5.

These hourly labor costs will apply within a few percent on many jobs. But wage rates may be much higher or lower in some areas. If the hourly costs shown in column 6 are not accurate for your work, develop modification factors that you can apply to the labor costs in this book. The following paragraphs explain the procedure.

Adjusting Labor Costs

Here's how to customize the labor costs in this book if your wage rates are different from the wage rates shown on page 10 or 309.

Start with the taxable benefits you offer. Assume craftsmen on your payroll get one week of vacation each year and one week of sick leave each year. Convert these benefits into hours. Your computation might look like this:

40 vacation hours
+ 40 sick leave hours
80 taxable leave hours

Then add the regular work hours for the year:

2,000 regular hours
+ 80 taxable benefit hours
2,080 total hours

Multiply these hours by the base wage per hour. If you pay carpenters $10.00 per hour, the calculation would be:

2,080 hours
x $10.00 per hour
$20,800 per year

Next, determine the tax and insurance rate for each trade. If you know the rates that apply to your jobs, use those rates. If not, use the rates in column 3 on page 10.

Continuing with our example, we'll use 30.97%, the rate for carpenters in column 3 on page 10. To increase the annual taxable wage by 30.97%, we'll multiply by 1.3097:

$20,800 per year
x 1.3097 tax & insurance rate
$27,242 annual cost

Then add the cost of non-taxable benefits. Suppose your company has no pension or profit sharing plan but does provide medical insurance for employees. Assume that the cost for your carpenter is $343.67 per month or $4,124 per year.

$4,124 medical plan
+ 27,242 annual cost
$31,366 total annual cost

Divide this total annual cost by the actual hours worked in a year. This gives the contractor's total hourly labor cost including all benefits, taxes and insurance. Assume your carpenter will work 2,000 hours a year:

$$\frac{\$31{,}366}{2{,}000} = \$15.68 \text{ per hour}$$

Finally, find your modification factor for the labor costs in this book. Divide your total hourly labor cost by the total hourly labor cost shown on page 10. For the carpenter in our example, the figure in column 6 is $37.38.

$$\frac{\$15.68}{\$37.38} = .419$$

Your modification factor is 41.9%. Multiply any building carpenter (Craft Code BC) labor costs in the Residential Division of this book by .419 to find your estimated cost. For example, on page 24 the labor cost for installing an 18" long towel bar is $10.50 per each bar. If installed by your carpenter working at $10.00 per hour, your estimated cost would be 41.9% of $10.50 or $4.40. The manhours would remain the same @.280, assuming normal productivity.

If the Labor Rate Is Unknown

On some estimates you may not know what labor rates will apply. In that case, use both labor and material figures in this book without making any adjustment. When all labor, equipment and material costs have been compiled, add or deduct the percentage shown in the area modification table on pages 12 through 15.

Adjusting the labor costs in this book will make your estimates much more accurate.

Area Modification Factors

Construction costs are higher in some areas than in other areas. Add or deduct the percentages shown on the following pages to adapt the costs in this book to your job site. Adjust your cost estimate by the appropriate percentages in this table to find the estimated cost for the site selected. Where 0% is shown, it means no modification is required.

Modification factors are listed alphabetically by state and province. Areas within each state are listed alphabetically. For convenience, one representative city is identified in each three-digit zip or range of zips. Percentages are based on the average of all data points in the table. Factors listed for each state and province are the average of all data points in that state or province. Figures for three-digit zips are the average of all five-digit zips in that area. Figures in the Total column are the weighted average of factors for Labor, Material and Equipment.

The National Estimator program will apply an area modification factor for any five-digit zip you select. Click Utilities. Click Options. Then select the Area Modification Factors tab.

These percentages are composites of many costs and will not necessarily be accurate when estimating the cost of any particular part of a building. But when used to modify costs for an entire structure, they should improve the accuracy of your estimates.

Location	Zip	Mat.	Lab.	Equip.	Total Wtd. Avg.
Alabama Average		**-1**	**-7**	**0**	**-4%**
Anniston	362	0	-13	-1	-6%
Auburn	368	-1	-8	0	-4%
Bellamy	369	-2	13	-1	5%
Birmingham	350-352	-3	8	-1	2%
Dothan	363	-1	-13	0	-7%
Evergreen	364	-2	-20	-1	-10%
Gadsden	359	-4	-15	-1	-9%
Huntsville	358	1	-3	0	-1%
Jasper	355	-2	-16	-1	-8%
Mobile	365-366	-1	-3	0	-2%
Montgomery	360-361	-1	-3	0	-2%
Scottsboro	357	0	-8	0	-4%
Selma	367	-1	-10	0	-5%
Sheffield	356	-1	1	0	0%
Tuscaloosa	354	1	-9	0	-4%
Alaska Average		**14**	**33**	**4**	**23%**
Anchorage	995	16	38	5	26%
Fairbanks	997	16	40	5	27%
Juneau	998	18	20	6	19%
Ketchikan	999	3	36	1	18%
King Salmon	996	16	32	5	23%
Arizona Average		**1**	**-9**	**0**	**-4%**
Chambers	865	1	-19	0	-8%
Douglas	855	0	-18	0	-8%
Flagstaff	860	2	-17	1	-7%
Kingman	864	1	-11	0	-5%
Mesa	852	1	5	0	3%
Phoenix	850	1	6	0	3%
Prescott	863	3	-16	1	-6%
Show Low	859	2	-18	1	-7%
Tucson	856-857	0	-10	0	-5%
Yuma	853	0	5	0	2%
Arkansas Average		**-2**	**-13**	**0**	**-7%**
Batesville	725	0	-20	0	-9%
Camden	717	-4	1	-1	-2%
Fayetteville	727	0	-8	0	-4%
Fort Smith	729	-1	-14	0	-7%
Harrison	726	-1	-25	0	-12%
Hope	718	-3	-15	-1	-8%
Hot Springs	719	-2	-25	-1	-13%
Jonesboro	724	-1	-18	0	-9%
Little Rock	720-722	-1	-6	0	-3%
Pine Bluff	716	-4	-19	-1	-11%
Russellville	728	0	-9	0	-4%
West Memphis	723	-3	-1	-1	-2%
California Average		**2**	**16**	**1**	**9%**
Alhambra	917-918	3	15	1	8%
Bakersfield	932-933	1	4	0	2%
El Centro	922	1	-1	0	0%
Eureka	955	1	13	0	7%
Fresno	936-938	0	-5	0	-2%
Herlong	961	2	17	1	9%
Inglewood	902-905	3	16	1	9%
Irvine	926-927	3	24	1	13%
Lompoc	934	3	2	1	3%

Location	Zip	Mat.	Lab.	Equip.	Total Wtd. Avg.
Long Beach	907-908	3	17	1	9%
Los Angeles	900-901	3	13	1	8%
Marysville	959	1	18	0	9%
Modesto	953	1	2	0	1%
Mojave	935	0	11	0	5%
Novato	949	3	36	1	18%
Oakland	945-947	3	48	1	24%
Orange	928	3	22	1	12%
Oxnard	930	3	1	1	2%
Pasadena	910-912	4	16	1	9%
Rancho Cordova	956-957	2	6	1	4%
Redding	960	1	-8	0	-3%
Richmond	948	2	35	1	17%
Riverside	925	1	7	0	4%
Sacramento	958	1	6	0	3%
Salinas	939	3	-1	1	1%
San Bernardino	923-924	0	4	0	2%
San Diego	919-921	3	13	1	8%
San Francisco	941	3	55	1	27%
San Jose	950-951	3	33	1	17%
San Mateo	943-944	4	40	1	21%
Santa Barbara	931	3	11	1	7%
Santa Rosa	954	3	32	1	16%
Stockton	952	2	7	1	4%
Sunnyvale	940	3	39	1	20%
Van Nuys	913-916	3	14	1	8%
Whittier	906	3	14	1	8%
Colorado Average		**2**	**1**	**1**	**1%**
Aurora	800-801	3	11	1	7%
Boulder	803-804	3	5	1	4%
Colorado Springs	808-809	2	-3	1	0%
Denver	802	3	13	1	8%
Durango	813	1	-3	0	-1%
Fort Morgan	807	2	-6	1	-2%
Glenwood Springs	816	2	6	1	4%
Grand Junction	814-815	1	-1	0	0%
Greeley	806	3	8	1	5%
Longmont	805	3	1	1	2%
Pagosa Springs	811	0	-9	0	-4%
Pueblo	810	-1	2	0	0%
Salida	812	2	-15	1	-6%
Connecticut Average		**1**	**16**	**0**	**8%**
Bridgeport	066	0	13	0	6%
Bristol	060	1	24	0	12%
Fairfield	064	2	17	1	9%
Hartford	061	0	23	0	11%
New Haven	065	1	15	0	7%
Norwich	063	0	7	0	3%
Stamford	068-069	4	21	1	12%
Waterbury	067	1	12	0	6%
West Hartford	062	1	9	0	5%
Delaware Average		**1**	**3**	**0**	**2%**
Dover	199	1	-9	0	-4%
Newark	197	2	10	1	6%
Wilmington	198	0	9	0	4%

Location	Zip	Mat.	Lab.	Equip.	Total Wtd. Avg.
District of Columbia Average					
Washington	200-205	2	23	1	12%
Florida Average		**0**	**-10**	**0**	**-5%**
Altamonte Springs	327	-1	-6	0	-3%
Bradenton	342	0	-12	0	-6%
Brooksville	346	0	-16	0	-7%
Daytona Beach	321	-2	-18	-1	-9%
Fort Lauderdale	333	3	1	1	2%
Fort Myers	339	0	-12	0	-6%
Fort Pierce	349	-2	-20	-1	-10%
Gainesville	326	-1	-18	0	-9%
Jacksonville	322	-1	-3	0	-2%
Lakeland	338	-3	-13	-1	-8%
Melbourne	329	-2	-15	-1	-8%
Miami	330-332	2	-1	1	1%
Naples	341	3	-8	1	-2%
Ocala	344	-3	-23	-1	-12%
Orlando	328	0	2	0	1%
Panama City	324	-2	-21	-1	-11%
Pensacola	325	-1	-17	0	-8%
Saint Augustine	320	-1	-4	0	-2%
Saint Cloud	347	0	-5	0	-2%
St Petersburg	337	0	-12	0	-6%
Tallahassee	323	0	-13	0	-6%
Tampa	335-336	-1	-1	0	-1%
West Palm Beach	334	1	-5	0	-2%
Georgia Average		**-1**	**-7**	**0**	**-4%**
Albany	317	-2	-10	-1	-6%
Athens	306	0	-11	0	-5%
Atlanta	303	3	23	1	12%
Augusta	308-309	-2	-2	-1	-2%
Buford	305	0	-5	0	-2%
Calhoun	307	-1	-19	0	-9%
Columbus	318-319	-1	-6	0	-3%
Dublin/Fort Valley	310	-3	-13	-1	-8%
Hinesville	313	-2	-11	-1	-6%
Kings Bay	315	-2	-19	-1	-10%
Macon	312	-2	-7	-1	-4%
Marietta	300-302	1	8	0	4%
Savannah	314	-1	-7	0	-4%
Statesboro	304	-2	-21	-1	-11%
Valdosta	316	-1	-1	0	-1%
Hawaii Average		**17**	**25**	**6**	**20%**
Aliamanu	968	17	29	6	22%
Ewa	967	17	23	6	20%
Halawa Heights	967	17	23	6	20%
Hilo	967	17	23	6	20%
Honolulu	968	17	29	6	22%
Kailua	968	17	29	6	22%
Lualualei	967	17	23	6	20%
Mililani Town	967	17	23	6	20%
Pearl City	967	17	23	6	20%
Wahiawa	967	17	23	6	20%
Waianae	967	17	23	6	20%
Wailuku (Maui)	967	17	23	6	20%

Area Modification Factors

Location	Zip	Mat.	Lab.	Equip.	Total Wtd. Avg.
Idaho Average		**0**	**-19**	**0**	**-9%**
Boise	837	1	-12	0	-5%
Coeur d'Alene	838	0	-21	0	-10%
Idaho Falls	834	-1	-19	0	-9%
Lewiston	835	0	-24	0	-11%
Meridian	836	0	-19	0	-9%
Pocatello	832	-1	-20	0	-10%
Sun Valley	833	0	-18	0	-8%
Illinois Average		**-1**	**9**	**0**	**4%**
Arlington Heights	600	1	29	0	14%
Aurora	605	2	28	1	14%
Belleville	622	-2	2	-1	0%
Bloomington	617	1	-4	0	-1%
Carbondale	629	-3	-6	-1	-4%
Carol Stream	601	2	28	1	14%
Centralia	628	-3	-3	-1	-3%
Champaign	618	-1	-3	0	-2%
Chicago	606-608	2	31	1	15%
Decatur	623	-2	-13	-1	-7%
Galesburg	614	-2	-6	-1	-4%
Granite City	620	-3	11	-1	3%
Green River	612	-1	12	0	5%
Joliet	604	0	29	0	13%
Kankakee	609	-2	-4	-1	-3%
Lawrenceville	624	-4	-9	-1	-6%
Oak Park	603	3	35	1	18%
Peoria	615-616	-1	15	0	6%
Peru	613	0	4	0	2%
Quincy	602	3	31	1	16%
Rockford	610-611	-2	8	-1	3%
Springfield	625-627	-2	2	-1	0%
Urbana	619	-3	-6	-1	-4%
Indiana Average		**-2**	**-3**	**-1**	**-3%**
Aurora	470	-1	-9	0	-5%
Bloomington	474	1	-6	0	-2%
Columbus	472	0	-9	0	-4%
Elkhart	465	-2	-7	-1	-4%
Evansville	476-477	-2	12	-1	4%
Fort Wayne	467-468	-3	1	-1	-1%
Gary	463-464	-4	23	-1	8%
Indianapolis	460-462	-1	10	0	4%
Jasper	475	-2	-14	-1	-8%
Jeffersonville	471	0	-11	0	-5%
Kokomo	469	-2	-15	-1	-8%
Lafayette	479	-2	-9	-1	-5%
Muncie	473	-4	-13	-1	-8%
South Bend	466	-4	0	-1	-2%
Terre Haute	478	-4	-2	-1	-3%
Iowa Average		**-2**	**-4**	**-1**	**-3%**
Burlington	526	0	2	0	1%
Carroll	514	-3	-20	-1	-11%
Cedar Falls	506	-1	-7	0	-4%
Cedar Rapids	522-524	0	5	0	2%
Cherokee	510	-2	4	-1	1%
Council Bluffs	515	-2	1	-1	-1%
Creston	508	-3	6	-1	1%
Davenport	527-528	-1	3	0	1%
Decorah	521	-2	-14	-1	-8%
Des Moines	500-503	-2	13	-1	5%
Dubuque	520	-2	-7	-1	-4%
Fort Dodge	505	-2	-5	-1	-3%
Mason City	504	0	-6	0	-3%
Ottumwa	525	0	-13	0	-6%
Sheldon	512	0	-15	0	-7%
Shenandoah	516	-3	-26	-1	-14%
Sioux City	511	-2	14	-1	5%
Spencer	513	-1	-14	0	-7%
Waterloo	507	-4	-1	-1	-3%
Kansas Average		**-2**	**2**	**-1**	**0%**
Colby	677	-1	-17	0	-8%
Concordia	669	-1	-25	0	-12%
Dodge City	678	-2	-7	-1	-4%
Emporia	668	-3	20	-1	8%
Fort Scott	667	-2	-11	-1	-6%
Hays	676	-2	-26	-1	-13%

Location	Zip	Mat.	Lab.	Equip.	Total Wtd. Avg.
Hutchinson	675	-3	-9	-1	-6%
Independence	673	-3	67	-1	29%
Kansas City	660-662	0	10	0	5%
Liberal	679	-2	33	-1	14%
Salina	674	-3	-11	-1	-7%
Topeka	664-666	-3	2	-1	-1%
Wichita	670-672	-2	-6	-1	-4%
Kentucky Average		**-1**	**-8**	**0**	**-4%**
Ashland	411-412	-4	-5	-1	-4%
Bowling Green	421	0	-11	0	-5%
Campton	413-414	-1	-23	0	-11%
Covington	410	-1	5	0	2%
Elizabethtown	427	-1	-20	0	-10%
Frankfort	406	1	13	0	7%
Hazard	417-418	-2	-19	-1	-10%
Hopkinsville	422	-2	-9	-1	-5%
Lexington	403-405	1	1	0	1%
London	407-409	-1	-13	0	-7%
Louisville	400-402	-1	5	0	2%
Owensboro	423	-2	-6	-1	-4%
Paducah	420	-2	2	-1	0%
Pikeville	415-416	-3	-14	-1	-8%
Somerset	425-426	0	-23	0	-11%
White Plains	424	-3	-6	-1	-4%
Louisiana Average		**-1**	**7**	**-1**	**2%**
Alexandria	713-714	-3	13	-1	4%
Baton Rouge	707-708	0	21	0	10%
Houma	703	-2	11	-1	4%
Lafayette	705	0	18	0	8%
Lake Charles	706	-2	30	-1	13%
Mandeville	704	-1	-5	0	-3%
Minden	710	-2	-8	-1	-5%
Monroe	712	-2	-14	-1	-8%
New Orleans	700-701	0	5	0	2%
Shreveport	711	-2	-6	-1	-4%
Maine Average		**0**	**-10**	**0**	**-5%**
Auburn	042	-1	-7	0	-4%
Augusta	043	-1	-9	0	-5%
Bangor	044	-1	-11	0	-6%
Bath	045	1	-15	0	-6%
Brunswick	039-040	1	-3	0	-1%
Camden	048	-1	-21	0	-10%
Cutler	046	-1	-15	0	-7%
Dexter	049	-1	-8	0	-4%
Northern Area	047	-2	-16	-1	-8%
Portland	041	2	2	1	2%
Maryland Average		**1**	**3**	**0**	**2%**
Annapolis	214	4	13	1	8%
Baltimore	210-212	-1	16	0	7%
Bethesda	208-209	3	24	1	13%
Church Hill	216	2	-10	1	-4%
Cumberland	215	-4	-12	-1	-8%
Elkton	219	2	-14	1	-5%
Frederick	217	1	13	0	7%
Laurel	206-207	2	15	1	8%
Salisbury	218	1	-14	0	-6%
Massachusetts Average		**2**	**23**	**1**	**12%**
Ayer	015-016	1	11	0	6%
Bedford	017	3	30	1	15%
Boston	021-022	3	77	1	37%
Brockton	023-024	3	41	1	20%
Cape Cod	026	2	6	1	4%
Chicopee	010	1	14	0	7%
Dedham	019	2	36	1	18%
Fitchburg	014	2	21	1	11%
Hingham	020	3	37	1	19%
Lawrence	018	2	28	1	14%
Nantucket	025	3	16	1	9%
New Bedford	027	1	12	0	6%
Northfield	013	2	3	1	2%
Pittsfield	012	1	0	0	1%
Springfield	011	-1	18	0	8%

Location	Zip	Mat.	Lab.	Equip.	Total Wtd. Avg.
Michigan Average		**-2**	**3**	**-1**	**1%**
Battle Creek	490-491	-3	1	-1	-1%
Detroit	481-482	0	15	0	7%
Flint	484-485	-3	-5	-1	-4%
Grand Rapids	493-495	-2	4	-1	1%
Grayling	497	1	-17	0	-7%
Jackson	492	-3	1	-1	-1%
Lansing	488-489	-1	1	0	0%
Marquette	498-499	-1	7	0	3%
Pontiac	483	-3	29	-1	12%
Royal Oak	480	-2	18	-1	7%
Saginaw	486-487	-2	-9	-1	-5%
Traverse City	496	-1	-4	0	-2%
Minnesota Average		**0**	**-1**	**0**	**-1%**
Bemidji	566	-1	-11	0	-6%
Brainerd	564	0	-6	0	-3%
Duluth	556-558	-2	7	-1	2%
Fergus Falls	565	-1	-20	0	-10%
Magnolia	561	0	-18	0	-8%
Mankato	560	0	-8	0	-4%
Minneapolis	553-555	1	28	0	13%
Rochester	559	0	-3	0	-1%
St Cloud	563	-1	6	0	2%
St Paul	550-551	1	26	0	12%
Thief River Falls	567	0	-5	0	-2%
Willmar	562	-1	-11	0	-6%
Mississippi Average		**-2**	**-11**	**-1**	**-6%**
Clarksdale	386	-3	-16	-1	-9%
Columbus	397	-1	1	0	0%
Greenville	387	-4	-26	-1	-14%
Greenwood	389	-3	-18	-1	-10%
Gulfport	395	-2	-11	-1	-6%
Jackson	390-392	-3	-2	-1	-3%
Laurel	394	-3	-11	-1	-7%
McComb	396	-2	-22	-1	-11%
Meridian	393	-2	8	-1	3%
Tupelo	388	-1	-13	0	-7%
Missouri Average		**-1**	**-5**	**0**	**-3%**
Cape Girardeau	637	-2	-8	-1	-5%
Caruthersville	638	-1	-15	0	-7%
Chillicothe	646	-2	-7	-1	-4%
Columbia	652	1	-9	0	-4%
East Lynne	647	-1	10	0	4%
Farmington	636	-3	-15	-1	-8%
Hannibal	634	0	-4	0	-2%
Independence	640	-1	13	0	5%
Jefferson City	650-651	1	-11	0	-5%
Joplin	648	-2	-10	-1	-6%
Kansas City	641	-2	15	-1	6%
Kirksville	635	0	-33	0	-15%
Knob Noster	653	0	7	0	3%
Lebanon	654-655	-2	-23	-1	-12%
Poplar Bluff	639	-1	-21	0	-10%
Saint Charles	633	1	2	0	1%
Saint Joseph	644-645	-3	2	-1	-1%
Springfield	656-658	-2	-15	-1	-8%
St Louis	630-631	-2	20	-1	8%
Montana Average		**0**	**-7**	**0**	**-3%**
Billings	590-591	0	-4	0	-2%
Butte	597	1	-7	0	-3%
Fairview	592	-1	27	0	12%
Great Falls	594	-1	-11	0	-6%
Havre	595	-1	-19	0	-9%
Helena	596	0	-4	0	-2%
Kalispell	599	1	-15	0	-6%
Miles City	593	-1	-15	0	-7%
Missoula	598	1	-14	0	-6%
Nebraska Average		**-1**	**-17**	**0**	**-8%**
Alliance	693	-1	-21	0	-10%
Columbus	686	-1	-15	0	-7%
Grand Island	688	0	-18	0	-8%
Hastings	689	0	-20	0	-9%
Lincoln	683-685	0	-9	0	-4%

Area Modification Factors

Location	Zip	Mat.	Lab.	Equip.	Total Wtd. Avg.
McCook	690	1	-21	0	-9%
Norfolk	687	-3	-19	-1	-10%
North Platte	691	0	-14	0	-6%
Omaha	680-681	-1	1	0	0%
Valentine	692	-2	-31	-1	-15%
Nevada Average		**2**	**0**	**1**	**1%**
Carson City	897	2	-12	1	-4%
Elko	898	1	19	0	9%
Ely	893	2	-8	1	-3%
Fallon	894	2	-2	1	0%
Las Vegas	889-891	2	5	1	3%
Reno	895	2	-4	1	-1%
New Hampshire Average		**1**	**-4**	**0**	**-1%**
Charlestown	036	1	-11	0	-5%
Concord	034	1	-7	0	-3%
Dover	038	1	1	0	1%
Lebanon	037	2	-8	1	-3%
Littleton	035	-1	-12	0	-6%
Manchester	032-033	0	4	0	2%
New Boston	030-031	1	5	0	3%
New Jersey Average		**1**	**20**	**0**	**9%**
Atlantic City	080-084	-2	12	-1	4%
Brick	087	2	2	1	2%
Dover	078	1	19	0	9%
Edison	088-089	1	28	0	13%
Hackensack	076	3	18	1	10%
Monmouth	077	3	22	1	12%
Newark	071-073	1	23	0	11%
Passaic	070	2	23	1	12%
Paterson	074-075	2	13	1	7%
Princeton	085	-2	23	-1	10%
Summit	079	3	32	1	16%
Trenton	086	-3	19	-1	7%
New Mexico Average		**0**	**-17**	**0**	**-8%**
Alamogordo	883	-1	-22	0	-11%
Albuquerque	870-871	2	-8	1	-3%
Clovis	881	-2	-22	-1	-11%
Farmington	874	2	-4	1	-1%
Fort Sumner	882	-3	0	-1	-2%
Gallup	873	1	-17	0	-7%
Holman	877	2	-24	1	-10%
Las Cruces	880	-1	-17	0	-8%
Santa Fe	875	3	-20	1	-8%
Socorro	878	1	-32	0	-14%
Truth or Consequences	879	-2	-15	-1	-8%
Tucumcari	884	-1	-17	0	-8%
New York Average		**0**	**13**	**0**	**6%**
Albany	120-123	-1	16	0	7%
Amityville	117	2	18	1	9%
Batavia	140	-3	5	-1	1%
Binghamton	137-139	-3	0	-1	-2%
Bronx	104	2	19	1	10%
Brooklyn	112	3	12	1	7%
Buffalo	142	-4	7	-1	1%
Elmira	149	-4	-1	-1	-3%
Flushing	113	3	30	1	15%
Garden City	115	3	29	1	15%
Hicksville	118	3	27	1	14%
Ithaca	148	-4	-6	-1	-5%
Jamaica	114	3	27	1	14%
Jamestown	147	-4	-11	-1	-7%
Kingston	124	0	-8	0	-4%
Long Island	111	3	62	1	30%
Montauk	119	1	15	0	7%
New York (Manhattan)	100-102	3	64	1	31%
New York City	100-102	3	64	1	31%
Newcomb	128	-1	2	0	0%
Niagara Falls	143	-4	-8	-1	-6%
Plattsburgh	129	1	-3	0	-1%
Poughkeepsie	125-126	1	2	0	1%
Queens	110	4	33	1	17%

Location	Zip	Mat.	Lab.	Equip.	Total Wtd. Avg.
Rochester	144-146	-3	8	-1	2%
Rockaway	116	3	18	1	10%
Rome	133-134	-3	-6	-1	-4%
Staten Island	103	3	15	1	8%
Stewart	127	-1	-9	0	-5%
Syracuse	130-132	-3	7	-1	2%
Tonawanda	141	-4	2	-1	-1%
Utica	135	-4	-8	-1	-6%
Watertown	136	-2	0	-1	-1%
West Point	109	1	11	0	6%
White Plains	105-108	3	27	1	14%
North Carolina Average		**1**	**-9**	**0**	**-4%**
Asheville	287-289	1	-16	0	-7%
Charlotte	280-282	1	15	0	7%
Durham	277	2	-3	1	0%
Elizabeth City	279	1	-18	0	-8%
Fayetteville	283	-1	-12	0	-6%
Goldsboro	275	1	-2	0	0%
Greensboro	274	1	-7	0	-3%
Hickory	286	-1	-17	0	-8%
Kinston	285	-1	-19	0	-9%
Raleigh	276	3	2	1	3%
Rocky Mount	278	-1	-14	0	-7%
Wilmington	284	1	-14	0	-6%
Winston-Salem	270-273	0	-10	0	-5%
North Dakota Average		**-1**	**10**	**0**	**4%**
Bismarck	585	0	6	0	3%
Dickinson	586	-1	34	0	15%
Fargo	580-581	0	1	0	0%
Grand Forks	582	0	-3	0	-1%
Jamestown	584	-1	-7	0	-4%
Minot	587	-1	21	0	9%
Nekoma	583	-1	-20	0	-10%
Williston	588	-1	47	0	21%
Ohio Average		**-2**	**2**	**-1**	**0%**
Akron	442-443	-2	4	-1	1%
Canton	446-447	-2	-3	-1	-2%
Chillicothe	456	-2	-3	-1	-2%
Cincinnati	450-452	-1	7	0	3%
Cleveland	440-441	-3	11	-1	3%
Columbus	432	0	11	0	5%
Dayton	453-455	-3	6	-1	1%
Lima	458	-3	-8	-1	-5%
Marietta	457	-2	-8	-1	-5%
Marion	433	-3	-9	-1	-6%
Newark	430-431	-1	8	0	3%
Sandusky	448-449	-1	-5	0	-3%
Steubenville	439	-3	6	-1	1%
Toledo	434-436	-1	16	0	7%
Warren	444	-4	-6	-1	-5%
Youngstown	445	-5	-1	-2	-3%
Zanesville	437-438	-2	0	-1	-1%
Oklahoma Average		**-3**	**-7**	**-1**	**-5%**
Adams	739	-2	-20	-1	-10%
Ardmore	734	-3	1	-1	-1%
Clinton	736	-3	-2	-1	-3%
Durant	747	-4	-20	-1	-11%
Enid	737	-4	-4	-1	-4%
Lawton	735	-3	-15	-1	-8%
McAlester	745	-4	-10	-1	-7%
Muskogee	744	-2	-16	-1	-8%
Norman	730	-2	-6	-1	-4%
Oklahoma City	731	-2	-4	-1	-3%
Ponca City	746	-3	1	-1	-1%
Poteau	749	-2	-13	-1	-7%
Pryor	743	-2	-11	-1	-6%
Shawnee	748	-4	-13	-1	-8%
Tulsa	740-741	-1	1	0	0%
Woodward	738	-4	15	-1	5%
Oregon Average		**1**	**-9**	**1**	**-3%**
Adrian	979	-1	-24	0	-12%
Bend	977	1	-11	0	-5%
Eugene	974	2	-9	1	-3%

Location	Zip	Mat.	Lab.	Equip.	Total Wtd. Avg.
Grants Pass	975	2	-13	1	-5%
Klamath Falls	976	2	-19	1	-8%
Pendleton	978	0	-7	0	-3%
Portland	970-972	2	19	1	10%
Salem	973	2	-7	1	-2%
Pennsylvania Average		**-3**	**0**	**-1**	**-1%**
Allentown	181	-2	8	-1	3%
Altoona	166	-3	-14	-1	-8%
Beaver Springs	178	-3	-8	-1	-5%
Bethlehem	180	-1	10	0	4%
Bradford	167	-4	-13	-1	-8%
Butler	160	-4	1	-1	-2%
Chambersburg	172	-1	-13	0	-7%
Clearfield	168	2	-8	1	-3%
DuBois	158	-2	-19	-1	-10%
East Stroudsburg	183	0	-11	0	-5%
Erie	164-165	-3	-10	-1	-6%
Genesee	169	-4	-5	-1	-4%
Greensburg	156	-4	-5	-1	-4%
Harrisburg	170-171	-2	8	-1	3%
Hazleton	182	-3	-3	-1	-3%
Johnstown	159	-4	-16	-1	-9%
Kittanning	162	-4	-9	-1	-6%
Lancaster	175-176	-2	1	-1	-1%
Meadville	163	-4	-16	-1	-9%
Montrose	188	-3	-6	-1	-4%
New Castle	161	-4	-1	-1	-3%
Philadelphia	190-191	-3	27	-1	11%
Pittsburgh	152	-4	17	-1	6%
Pottsville	179	-4	-12	-1	-8%
Punxsutawney	157	-4	-1	-1	-3%
Reading	195-196	-4	9	-1	2%
Scranton	184-185	-2	4	-1	1%
Somerset	155	-4	-16	-1	-9%
Southeastern	193	0	18	0	8%
Uniontown	154	-4	-9	-1	-6%
Valley Forge	194	-3	27	-1	11%
Warminster	189	-1	24	0	11%
Warrendale	150-151	-4	16	-1	5%
Washington	153	-4	23	-1	8%
Wilkes Barre	186-187	-3	2	-1	-1%
Williamsport	177	-3	-1	-1	-2%
York	173-174	-3	2	-1	-1%
Rhode Island Average		**1**	**10**	**0**	**5%**
Bristol	028	1	9	0	5%
Coventry	028	1	9	0	5%
Cranston	029	1	12	0	6%
Davisville	028	1	9	0	5%
Narragansett	028	1	9	0	5%
Newport	028	1	9	0	5%
Providence	029	1	12	0	6%
Warwick	028	1	9	0	5%
South Carolina Average		**-1**	**-2**	**0**	**-1%**
Aiken	298	0	9	0	4%
Beaufort	299	-1	-4	0	-2%
Charleston	294	-1	0	0	-1%
Columbia	290-292	0	-4	0	-2%
Greenville	296	0	17	0	8%
Myrtle Beach	295	0	-17	0	-8%
Rock Hill	297	-1	-11	0	-6%
Spartanburg	293	-2	-6	-1	-4%
South Dakota Average		**-1**	**-12**	**0**	**-6%**
Aberdeen	574	-1	-15	0	-7%
Mitchell	573	-1	-11	0	-6%
Mobridge	576	-2	-18	-1	-9%
Pierre	575	-2	-20	-1	-10%
Rapid City	577	-2	-14	-1	-8%
Sioux Falls	570-571	0	-2	0	-1%
Watertown	572	-1	-7	0	-4%
Tennessee Average		**0**	**-5**	**0**	**-2%**
Chattanooga	374	-1	5	0	2%
Clarksville	370	1	2	0	1%
Cleveland	373	-1	-1	0	-1%

Area Modification Factors

Location	Zip	Mat.	Lab.	Equip.	Total Wtd. Avg.
Columbia	384	-1	-14	0	-7%
Cookeville	385	0	-18	0	-8%
Jackson	383	-1	-3	0	-2%
Kingsport	376	0	-11	0	-5%
Knoxville	377-379	-1	-3	0	-2%
McKenzie	382	-1	-16	0	-8%
Memphis	380-381	-1	3	0	1%
Nashville	371-372	1	4	0	2%
Texas Average		**-2**	**12**	**-1**	**5%**
Abilene	795-796	-4	0	-1	-2%
Amarillo	790-791	-2	-2	-1	-2%
Arlington	760	-1	4	0	1%
Austin	786-787	1	24	0	12%
Bay City	774	-1	86	0	39%
Beaumont	776-777	-3	43	-1	18%
Brownwood	768	-3	-14	-1	-8%
Bryan	778	0	18	0	8%
Childress	792	-3	-28	-1	-14%
Corpus Christi	783-784	-2	41	-1	18%
Dallas	751-753	-1	15	0	6%
Del Rio	788	-3	4	-1	0%
El Paso	798-799	-3	-12	-1	-7%
Fort Worth	761-762	-1	5	0	2%
Galveston	775	-3	55	-1	24%
Giddings	789	0	13	0	6%
Greenville	754	-3	9	-1	3%
Houston	770-772	-1	58	0	26%
Huntsville	773	-2	59	-1	26%
Longview	756	-2	4	-1	1%
Lubbock	793-794	-3	-11	-1	-7%
Lufkin	759	-3	20	-1	8%
McAllen	785	-3	-9	-1	-6%
Midland	797	-3	25	-1	10%
Palestine	758	-2	7	-1	2%
Plano	750	0	15	0	7%
San Angelo	769	-3	-9	-1	-6%
San Antonio	780-782	-2	19	-1	8%
Texarkana	755	-3	-15	-1	-8%
Tyler	757	-1	-15	0	-7%
Victoria	779	-2	29	-1	12%
Waco	765-767	-3	-2	-1	-3%
Wichita Falls	763	-3	-16	-1	-9%
Woodson	764	-3	-3	-1	-3%
Utah Average		**1**	**-9**	**1**	**-3%**
Clearfield	840	2	-3	1	0%
Green River	845	1	-7	0	-3%
Ogden	843-844	0	-19	0	-9%
Provo	846-847	2	-16	1	-6%
Salt Lake City	841	2	-1	1	1%
Vermont Average		**1**	**-11**	**0**	**-5%**
Albany	058	1	-16	0	-7%
Battleboro	053	1	-9	0	-4%
Beecher Falls	059	1	-19	0	-8%
Bennington	052	-1	-12	0	-6%
Burlington	054	3	5	1	4%
Montpelier	056	2	-10	1	-4%
Rutland	057	-1	-13	0	-7%
Springfield	051	-1	-11	0	-6%
White River Junction	050	1	-12	0	-5%
Virginia Average		**0**	**-8**	**0**	**-4%**
Abingdon	242	-2	-18	-1	-9%
Alexandria	220-223	3	18	1	10%

Location	Zip	Mat.	Lab.	Equip.	Total Wtd. Avg.
Charlottesville	229	1	-15	0	-6%
Chesapeake	233	0	-8	0	-4%
Culpeper	227	1	-12	0	-5%
Farmville	239	-2	-24	-1	-12%
Fredericksburg	224-225	1	-11	0	-5%
Galax	243	-2	-20	-1	-10%
Harrisonburg	228	1	-14	0	-6%
Lynchburg	245	-2	-17	-1	-9%
Norfolk	235-237	0	-4	0	-2%
Petersburg	238	-2	-5	-1	-3%
Radford	241	-1	-18	0	-9%
Reston	201	3	12	1	7%
Richmond	232	-1	5	0	2%
Roanoke	240	-1	-18	0	-9%
Staunton	244	0	-15	0	-7%
Tazewell	246	-3	-10	-1	-6%
Virginia Beach	234	0	-6	0	-3%
Williamsburg	230-231	0	-6	0	-3%
Winchester	226	0	9	0	4%
Washington Average		**1**	**-2**	**1**	**0%**
Clarkston	994	0	-18	0	-8%
Everett	982	2	2	1	2%
Olympia	985	2	-6	1	-2%
Pasco	993	0	2	0	1%
Seattle	980-981	3	21	1	11%
Spokane	990-992	0	-7	0	-3%
Tacoma	983-984	2	3	1	2%
Vancouver	986	2	4	1	3%
Wenatchee	988	1	-14	0	-6%
Yakima	989	0	-10	0	-5%
West Virginia Average		**-2**	**-8**	**-1**	**-5%**
Beckley	258-259	1	-11	0	-5%
Bluefield	247-248	-1	2	0	0%
Charleston	250-253	1	8	0	4%
Clarksburg	263-264	-3	-11	-1	-7%
Fairmont	266	0	-24	0	-11%
Huntington	255-257	-1	-7	0	-4%
Lewisburg	249	-2	-29	-1	-14%
Martinsburg	254	-1	-10	0	-5%
Morgantown	265	-3	-6	-1	-4%
New Martinsville	262	-2	-18	-1	-9%
Parkersburg	261	-3	5	-1	1%
Romney	267	-4	-10	-1	-7%
Sugar Grove	268	-3	-14	-1	-8%
Wheeling	260	-3	14	-1	5%
Wisconsin Average		**-1**	**1**	**0**	**0%**
Amery	540	0	-3	0	-1%
Beloit	535	0	10	0	5%
Clam Lake	545	-1	-17	0	-8%
Eau Claire	547	-1	-4	0	-2%
Green Bay	541-543	0	6	0	3%
La Crosse	546	-2	3	-1	0%
Ladysmith	548	-2	-1	-1	-2%
Madison	537	2	14	1	8%
Milwaukee	530-534	0	12	0	6%
Oshkosh	549	-1	9	0	4%
Portage	539	0	0	0	0%
Prairie du Chien	538	-2	-12	-1	-7%
Wausau	544	-1	-6	0	-3%
Wyoming Average		**0**	**-1**	**0**	**-1%**
Casper	826	-1	4	0	1%
Cheyenne/ Laramie	820	1	-6	0	-2%

Location	Zip	Mat.	Lab.	Equip.	Total Wtd. Avg.
Gillette	827	-1	7	0	3%
Powell	824	0	-7	0	-3%
Rawlins	823	0	17	0	8%
Riverton	825	-1	-12	0	-6%
Rock Springs	829-831	0	2	0	1%
Sheridan	828	1	-8	0	-3%
Wheatland	822	0	-7	0	-3%
UNITED STATES TERRITORIES					
Guam		53	-21	-5	18%
Puerto Rico		2	-47	-5	-21%
VIRGIN ISLANDS					
St. Croix		18	-15	-4	2%
St. John		52	-15	-4	20%
St. Thomas		23	-15	-4	5%
CANADIAN AREA MODIFIERS					
These figures assume an exchange rate of $1.00 Canadian to $0.76 U.S.					
Alberta Average		**26**	**-1**	**7**	**13%**
Calgary		26	1	7	14%
Edmonton		25	2	7	14%
Fort McMurray		28	-7	7	12%
British Columbia Average		**26**	**-15**	**7**	**7%**
Fraser Valley		26	-16	7	6%
Okanagan		27	-18	7	6%
Vancouver		26	-11	7	9%
Manitoba Average		**20**	**-22**	**5**	**0%**
North Manitoba		20	-22	5	0%
Selkirk		20	-22	5	0%
South Manitoba		20	-22	5	0%
Winnipeg		20	-22	5	0%
New Brunswick		**16**	**-47**	**3**	**-13%**
Moncton		16	-47	3	-13%
Newfoundland/ Labrador		**19**	**-29**	**4**	**-3%**
Nova Scotia Average		**17**	**-36**	**4**	**-8%**
Amherst		16	-36	3	-8%
Nova Scotia		17	-35	4	-7%
Sydney		17	-37	4	-8%
Ontario Average		**22**	**-11**	**5**	**7%**
London		22	-10	5	7%
Thunder Bay		24	-14	6	6%
Toronto		21	-9	5	7%
Quebec Average		**19**	**-24**	**4**	**-1%**
Montreal		19	-24	4	-1%
Quebec City		19	-24	4	-1%
Saskatchewan Average		**23**	**-18**	**5**	**4%**
La Ronge		24	-21	6	3%
Prince Albert		22	-20	5	2%
Saskatoon		22	-14	5	5%

Credits and Acknowledgments

This book has over 30,000 cost estimates for 2021. To develop these estimates, the editors relied on information supplied by hundreds of construction cost authorities. We offer our sincere thanks to the contractors, engineers, design professionals, construction estimators, material suppliers and manufacturers who, in the spirit of cooperation, have assisted in the preparation of this Sixty-ninth Edition of the National Construction Estimator. Many of the cost authorities who supplied information for this volume are listed below.

AFCO Roofing Supply, John Ording
Amerec Products, Jim Haas
American Arbitration Assoc., Kerstin Norlin
Anthem Contracting, Joe Caronna
Bell Blueprint, Paul Moore
Cement Cutting, Inc., Matt Becker
Dial One, Charlie Gindele
Fiorentine Company, Tom Forsyth
Groundwater Data, Inc., John Kratz
H&H Specialties, Reid Neslage
Iron-A-Way Company, Reg Smidt
J.H. Baxter, Inc., Dean Rogers
KEL-EEZ Weatherstripping, James Adams
Marbleworks of San Diego, Charlene Butler
Mel-Northey Co., Mel Northey
On Time Appraisal, Ralph Kinney
Prof. Photographic Service, Larry Hoagland
RCP Block & Brick Co., Gina Adams
San Diego Gas & Electric, Don Altevers
Superior Rock Products, John Knieff
U. S. Gypsum Company, Roger Merchet
West Coast Lumber Inspect. Bur., Jim Kneaper
Weyerhauser Company, Doug Barkee
York Spiral Stair, Jim A. Guerette
Daniel Atcheson

A special thanks to the following people. Special assistants to the editors: Ray Hicks, James Thomson.
Layout & Images: Christine Pray. Software production: Bilandra Chase.

Cover design: Jennifer Johnson

Photos: iStock by Getty Images™

Adhesives See also, Caulking, Flooring, Roofing and Tile in the Residential Division

Panel adhesives Better quality, gun applied in continuous bead to wood or metal framing or furring members, material only, add labor below. Per 100 SF of wall, floor, or ceiling including 6% waste.

		Bead diameter			
	Unit	**1/8"**	**1/4"**	**3/8"**	**1/2"**
Subfloor adhesive, on floors					
12" OC members	CSF	2.70	10.80	24.20	43.10
16" OC members	CSF	2.02	8.08	18.20	32.30
20" OC members	CSF	1.62	6.46	14.50	25.90
24" OC members	CSF	1.35	5.39	12.10	21.60
Wall sheathing or shear panel adhesive, on walls					
16" OC members	CSF	2.63	10.90	24.60	43.70
20" OC members	CSF	2.11	8.74	19.70	35.00
24" OC members	CSF	1.76	7.28	16.40	29.10
Polystyrene or polyurethane foam panel adhesive, on walls					
12" OC members	CSF	3.43	14.30	32.20	57.20
16" OC members	CSF	2.57	10.70	24.10	42.90
20" OC members	CSF	2.06	8.58	19.30	34.30
24" OC members	CSF	1.72	7.15	16.10	28.60
Gypsum drywall adhesive					
12" OC members	CSF	1.39	5.65	12.70	22.60
16" OC members	CSF	1.04	4.24	9.54	17.00
20" OC members	CSF	.83	3.39	7.63	13.60
24" OC members	CSF	.69	2.83	6.36	11.30
Hardboard or plastic panel adhesive, on walls					
12" OC members	CSF	4.00	14.30	32.20	57.20
16" OC members	CSF	3.00	10.70	24.10	42.90
20" OC members	CSF	2.40	8.58	19.30	34.30
24" OC members	CSF	2.00	7.15	16.10	28.60

	Craft@Hrs	**Unit**	**Material**	**Labor**	**Total**
Labor to apply adhesive to framing members, 1/8" to 1/2" bead diameter, no material included					
Floor or ceiling joists					
12" OC members	BC@.075	CSF	—	2.80	2.80
16" OC members	BC@.056	CSF	—	2.09	2.09
20" OC members	BC@.052	CSF	—	1.94	1.94
24" OC members	BC@.042	CSF	—	1.57	1.57
Interior and exterior wall members					
12" OC members	BC@.100	CSF	—	3.74	3.74
16" OC members	BC@.090	CSF	—	3.36	3.36
20" OC members	BC@.084	CSF	—	3.14	3.14
24" OC members	BC@.084	CSF	—	3.14	3.14
Special purpose adhesives					
Construction adhesive, for counters, cabinets, paneling, brick veneer, ceramic fixtures, shelving, sets in 10 minutes, 10.5 oz. cartridge	—	Ea	1.65	—	1.65
Epoxy-tie adhesive, bonds concrete, fills cracks to 3/4", seals doors and windows, anchor grouting, non-shrink, 22 oz. cartridge	—	Ea	28.90	—	28.90
Gypsum drywall adhesive, waterproof, bonds to wood, metal, masonry, concrete, 29 oz. cartridge	—	Ea	4.70	—	4.70

	Craft@Hrs	Unit	Material	Labor	Total
Latex FRP adhesive, indoor, bonds wood, concrete, drywall, foamboard, trowel grade, gallon	—	Ea	20.70	—	20.70
Panel insulation adhesive, waterproof, for polyurethane & polystyrene panels, bonds to wood, metal, masonry, concrete, 4.5 lbs.	—	Ea	37.20	—	37.20
Marine adhesive/sealant, 10 oz.	—	Ea	25.00	—	25.00
Project adhesive, rubber-based, bonds plywood, hardboard fiberglass, drywall, foam board, shelving, ceramic fixtures, 10 minute work time, 10.5 oz. cartridge	—	Ea	3.85	—	3.85

	Unit	1 quart can	1 gallon can
General purpose adhesives			
Acoustic tile adhesive, solvent base, waterproof, sound deadening type	Ea	—	14.30
Aliphatic resin woodworking glue	Ea	14.00	35.00
Carpet cement, outdoor	Ea	25.30	—
Professional carpenter's glue, multi-purpose	Ea	11.00	33.00
Contact cement, rubber based, waterproof, bonds veneers to plywood, particleboard, wallboard	Ea	16.80	40.00
Gel contact cement	Ea	16.50	—
Resilient flooring adhesive, latex base, adheres to concrete, plywood, felt, sheet flooring	Ea	6.15	26.20
Tile cement, solvent base, ceramic/stone, interior	Ea	18.60	23.50

	Craft@Hrs	Unit	Material	Labor	Total
Aggregate Typical prices, 5 mile haul, 24 ton minimum. See also Roofing, Built-up					
Crushed stone (1.4 tons per CY)					
3/8" stone	—	Ton	30.80	—	30.80
3/4" (Number 3)	—	Ton	29.40	—	29.40
1-1/2" (Number 2)	—	Ton	30.80	—	30.80
Crushed slag, typical prices where available					
3/4" slag	—	Ton	19.80	—	19.80
1-1/2"	—	Ton	20.20	—	20.20
Washed gravel (1.4 tons per CY)					
3/4" gravel	—	Ton	30.80	—	30.80
1-1/2"	—	Ton	31.00	—	31.00
Fill sand (1.35 tons per CY)	—	Ton	14.30	—	14.30
Add per ton less than 24 tons	—	Ton	8.00	—	8.00
Add for delivery over 5 miles, one way	—	Mile	10.00	—	10.00

Appraisal Fees Costs for determining the value of existing buildings, land, and equipment. Actual fee charged is based on the level of difficulty and the time spent on appraisal plus travel to location and cost of support services, if any. Costs include research and report by a professional state licensed appraiser. Client may request an appraisal on a "fee not to exceed" basis. Fees shown are averages and are not quoted as a percentage of value or contingent on value. The fee for cancelling an appraisal after the inspection is equal to the original appraisal fee.

	Craft@Hrs	Unit	Material	Labor	Total
Single family residences, condominiums, planned unit developments (PUDs). Fees for complex, expensive (over $1 million) or atypical properties or those that require higher licensure than a state license are usually negotiated. Based on square feet of gross living area (excluding the garage).					
To 2,500 square feet	—	LS	—	—	389.00
Over 2,500 SF to 3,500 SF	—	LS	—	—	441.00
Over 3,500 SF to 5,000 SF	—	LS	—	—	544.00
Over 5,000 SF	—	LS	—	—	803.00
Small residential income properties (duplex, triplex, quadriplex)					
2 to 4 units	—	LS	—	—	700.00
Apartment houses, commercial and industrial buildings					
To $300,000 valuation	—	LS	—	—	3,370.00
Over $300,000 to $1,000,000 valuation	—	LS	—	—	4,410.00
Over $1,000,000 to $3,000,000 valuation	—	LS	—	—	4,920.00
Over $3,000,000 to $5,000,000 valuation	—	LS	—	—	6,220.00
Other services					
Additional photograph (each)	—	LS	—	—	28.50
Outlying area fee	—	LS	—	—	57.00
Satisfactory Completion (old Form 442 / new Form 1004d)	—	LS	—	—	156.00
Appraisal Update same comps (Form 1004d)	—	LS	—	—	311.00
Operating Income Statement (FNMA 216)	—	LS	—	—	82.90
SFR Rental Survey (FNMA 1007)	—	LS	—	—	82.90
Appraisal review (desk)	—	LS	—	—	181.00
Appraisal review (field)	—	LS	—	—	389.00
Drive-by appraisal (Form 2055) starting at	—	LS	—	—	285.00
Drive-by appraisal (Form 2070/2075)	—	LS	—	—	233.00
Machinery (Fee is based on total value of equipment appraised) Additional charges for travel and lodging may be required					
To $30,000 valuation	—	LS	—	—	643.00
Over $30,000 to $100,000 valuation	—	LS	—	—	860.00
Over $100,000 to $500,000 valuation	—	LS	—	—	1,450.00
Over $500,000 to $1,000,000 valuation	—	LS	—	—	1,970.00
Over $1,000,000 to $5,000,000 valuation	—	LS	—	—	3,370.00
Court testimony (excluding preparation)	—	Day	—	—	1,560.00
Consulting fees are billed at an hourly rate	—	Hour	—	—	197.00

Outside of office meetings or court appearance are billed including travel time and expenses round trip, minimum 4 hours.

Arbitration and Mediation Fees These are administrative fees paid to the American Arbitration Association (AAA). Rules and fees are subject to change. The AAA's web site at www.adr.org has current rules and fee information. Fees charged by Construction Dispute Resolution Services (http://www.constructiondisputes-cdrs.com) will usually be less. Arbitrators are chosen from the National Roster of Construction Arbitrators and are paid a fee by the parties. Legal representation, if desired (although not necessary), is at the expense of each party. These fees do not include rental of a hearing room. An initial filing fee is payable in full by a filing party when a claim, counterclaim or additional claim is filed. A case service fee is payable at the time the first hearing is scheduled. This fee will be refunded at the conclusion of the case if no hearings have occurred so long as the Association was notified of cancellation at least 24 hours before the first scheduled hearing. The minimum AAA filing fee for any case having three or more arbitrators is $2,750 plus a $1,000 case service fee.

Arbitration and Mediation Fees

	Unit	Initial Filing Fee	Case Service Fee
Claims to $75,000	LS	750.00	800.00
Claims over $75,000 to $150,000	LS	1,750.00	1,250.00
Claims over $150,000 to $300,000	LS	2,650.00	2,000.00
Claims over $300,000 to $500,000	LS	4,000.00	3,500.00
Claims over $500,000 to $1,000,000	LS	5,000.00	6,200.00
Claims over $1,000,000 to $10,000,000	LS	7,000.00	7,700.00
Claims over $10,000,000 *	LS	*	12,500.00
No Amount Stated **	LS	7,000.00	7,700.00

* $10 million and above – Base fee is $10,000 plus .01% of the amount of claim above $10 million. Filing fees are capped at $65,000.

**This fee is applicable when a claim or counterclaim is not for a monetary amount. Where a monetary claim is not known, parties will be required to state a range of claims or be subject to the highest possible filing fee.

*** Fees above based upon a 'Standard Fee Schedule' For 'Flexible Fee Schedule' costs, add 10% to the total of Initial and Case Service Fees.

	Craft@Hrs	Unit	Material	Labor	Total

Mediation, mobile Generally will meet at the offices of the attorneys involved in the dispute. Does not replace legal counsel but is used to maintain equity between the mediating parties. Typical fees.

	Craft@Hrs	Unit	Material	Labor	Total
Nonrefundable retainer (half from each party)	—	Ea	—	—	369.00
Weekday sessions after the initial consultation	—	Hr	—	—	185.00
Nonrefundable retainer for weekend mediation	—	Ea	—	—	446.00
Weekend mediation sessions	—	Hr	—	—	279.00

Architectural Illustrations Full color painting on watercolor board with matted frame with title and credit on matte. Glass and elaborate framing are extra. Costs for pen and ink illustrations with color Mylar overlay are similar to cost for watercolor illustrations. Typical fees.

	Craft@Hrs	Unit	Material	Labor	Total
Custom home, eye level view					
Simple rendering	—	LS	—	—	1,00.00
Complex rendering	—	LS	—	—	1,480.00
Custom home, bird's eye view					
Simple rendering	—	LS	—	—	1,210.00
Complex rendering	—	LS	—	—	1,740.00
Tract homes in groups of five or more (single floor plans, multiple elevations), eye level view					
Simple rendering	—	LS	—	—	595.00
Complex rendering	—	LS	—	—	819.00
Tract homes in groups of five or more (single floor plans, multiple elevations), bird's eye view					
Simple rendering	—	LS	—	—	766.00
Complex rendering	—	LS	—	—	1,240.00
Tract homes or condominium project, overall bird's eye view					
10-25 homes or living units	—	LS	—	—	3,790.00
Typical commercial structure					
Eye level view	—	LS	—	—	1,700.00
Bird's eye view	—	LS	—	—	1,910.00
Complex commercial structure					
Eye level view	—	LS	—	—	2,510.00
Bird's eye view	—	LS	—	—	3,240.00

	Craft@Hrs	Unit	Material	Labor	Total
Deduct for pen and ink drawings (no color)	—	%	—	—	−33.0
Computer generated perspective drawings using CAD system for design studies					
Custom home	—	LS	—	—	643.00
Large condo or apartment projects	—	LS	—	—	1,620.00
Tract homes	—	LS	—	—	404.00
Commercial structure, line drawing	—	LS	—	—	1,210.00

Awnings and Canopies for Doors and Windows All hardware included. For commercial grade awnings, see the Industrial and Commercial Division section 12, Furnishings.

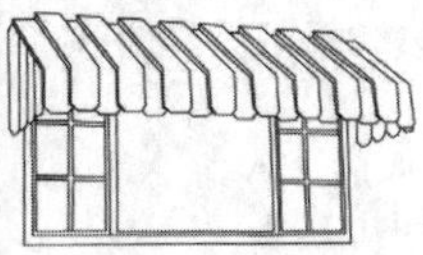

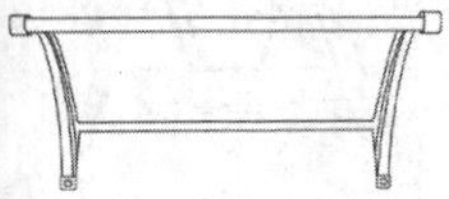

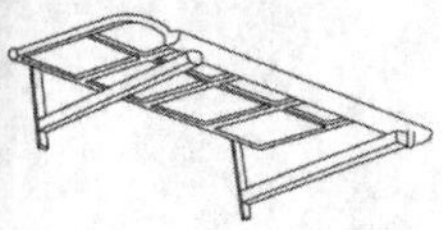

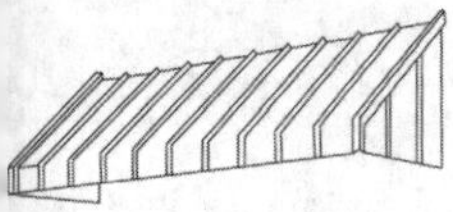

	Craft@Hrs	Unit	Material	Labor	Total
Aluminum pan-type window or door awnings, 025 gauge roof and pans, .040 gauge supports					
42" wide x 24" projection, 18" drop	SW@2.17	Ea	390.00	91.50	481.50
60" wide x 30" projection, 20" drop	SW@2.79	Ea	565.00	118.00	683.00
78" wide x 36" projection, 24" drop	SW@3.11	Ea	780.00	131.00	911.00
88" wide x 42" projection, 26" drop	SW@3.41	Ea	930.00	144.00	1,074.00
Polycarbonate door awnings, clear or tinted curved poly sheet in aluminum frame, 39" projection, 12" drop					
46" wide	SW@2.18	Ea	200.00	91.90	291.90
90" wide	SW@4.36	Ea	280.00	184.00	464.00
134" wide	SW@6.54	Ea	359.00	276.00	635.00
178" wide	SW@8.72	Ea	510.00	368.00	878.00
222" wide	SW@10.9	Ea	600.00	460.00	1,060.00
Roll-up aluminum awnings with hinged support arms and pull cord assembly					
36" wide x 18" projection, 27" drop	SW@2.28	Ea	290.00	96.10	386.10
48" wide x 24" projection, 34" drop	SW@2.91	Ea	330.00	123.00	453.00
54" wide x 30" projection, 39" drop	SW@3.29	Ea	340.00	139.00	479.00
60" wide x 35" projection, 44" drop	SW@3.50	Ea	355.00	148.00	503.00
72" wide x 42" projection, 51" drop	SW@4.20	Ea	420.00	177.00	597.00
Curved top door or window canopy, rigid aluminum frame with tinted or clear polycarbonate inserts.					
59" wide x 46" projection, 16" drop	BC@3.40	Ea	530.00	127.00	657.00
84" wide x 46" projection, 16" drop	BC@5.10	Ea	740.00	191.00	931.00
120" wide x 57" projection, 16" drop	BC@6.80	Ea	1,310.00	254.00	1,564.00
Mansard window or door awnings, 24 gauge 18"-wide standing seam steel panels, aluminum frame					
54" wide x 36" projection, 36" drop	BC@3.40	Ea	1,410.00	127.00	1,537.00
72" wide x 36" projection, 36" drop	BC@4.50	Ea	1,640.00	168.00	1,808.00
90" wide x 36" projection, 36" drop	BC@5.60	Ea	1,900.00	209.00	2,109.00
108" wide x 48" projection, 48" drop	BC@6.70	Ea	2,700.00	250.00	2,950.00
Fabric door awning, with waterproof, acrylic duck, colorfast fabric, double stitched seams, tubular aluminum frame					
36" wide x 26" projection	SW@1.45	Ea	260.00	61.10	321.10
40" wide x 36" projection	SW@1.86	Ea	290.00	78.40	368.40
48" wide x 40" projection	SW@2.07	Ea	365.00	87.30	452.30
72" wide x 46" projection	SW@2.27	Ea	410.00	95.70	505.70
Cloth retractable patio awning, folding spring loaded aluminum arm, dual cable manual operation.					
16' wide x 12' projection	BC@3.05	Ea	3,700.00	114.00	3,814.00
20' wide x 12' projection	BC@3.40	Ea	4,300.00	127.00	4,427.00

Barricades, Construction Safety

Barricades, Construction Safety Purchase prices except as noted. See also Equipment Rental in the index.

	Craft@Hrs	Unit	Material	Labor	Total
Heavy Duty Plastic Type I barricade, Engineer Grade Reflectivity, 8" height Top Panel					
Quantities from 1 - 15 units	—	Ea	45.00	—	45.00
Quantities from 16 - 31 units	—	Ea	42.50	—	42.50
Pallet quantities, multiples of 32 units	—	Ea	40.30	—	40.30
Reflectorized injected plastic barricade, NCHRP-350 certified meets M.U.T.C.D. specifications 8" to 12" wide rail, 4" to 6" wide stripes, 40" legs, no light					
Type I, 2' wide, 3' high, Top panel 12" height, 1 reflectorized rail each side					
Quantities from 1 - 15 units	—	Ea	53.90	—	53.90
Quantities from 16 - 31 units	—	Ea	50.90	—	50.90
Pallet quantities, multiples of 32 units	—	Ea	48.30	—	48.30
Type II, 2' wide, 3' high, Top panel 8" height, 1 reflectorized rail each side					
Quantities from 1 - 15 units	—	Ea	59.70	—	59.70
Quantities from 16 - 31 units	—	Ea	56.40	—	56.40
Pallet quantities, multiples of 32 units	—	Ea	53.50	—	53.50
Type III, 4' wide, 5' high, 3 reflectorized rails each side, wood & steel legs					
Quantities from 1 - 15 units	—	Ea	149.00	—	149.00
Quantities from 16 - 31 units	—	Ea	146.00	—	146.00
Pallet quantities, multiples of 32 units	—	Ea	143.00	—	143.00
Add for lighted units without batteries (batteries last 2 months)					
Amber lens	—	Ea	19.40	—	19.40
Red lens	—	Ea	19.40	—	19.40
Batteries, 6 volt (2 needed)	—	Ea	10.50	—	10.50

Utility barricade lights, solar powered Utility barricade solar powered lights, compliant with M.U.T.C.D. Specification 6E-5 and ITE Specifications for Flashing / Steady Burn warning light, 180 degree swivel base axis.

	Craft@Hrs	Unit	Material	Labor	Total
Utility barricade solar powered lights	—	Ea	44.60	—	44.60

Miscellaneous signage/traffic control

	Craft@Hrs	Unit	Material	Labor	Total
"Road Closed", reflectorized, 30" x 48", Engineer Grade	—	Ea	92.50	—	92.50
"Construction Zone", 4' x 4' high intensity grade	—	Ea	253.00	—	253.00
High-rise tripod with 3 orange flags	—	Ea	207.00	—	207.00
Flags	—	Ea	3.92	—	3.92
Traffic cones, PVC					
Non-reflectorized type					
18" high	—	Ea	6.40	—	6.40
28" high	—	Ea	10.00	—	10.00
Reflectorized type					
18" high	—	Ea	10.00	—	10.00
28" high	—	Ea	16.80	—	16.80
36" high	—	Ea	21.80	—	21.80
Lane delineator, 42" orange plastic cylinder with 2 reflectors on a 12 pound rubber base	—	Ea	21.80	—	21.80
Mesh signs, orange, 48" x 48", includes brace and clamp	—	Ea	70.00	—	70.00
Hand-held traffic paddles, "Stop" and "Slow"	—	Ea	25.50	—	25.50

	Craft@Hrs	Unit	Material	Labor	Total
Orange plastic safety fencing					
Budget, 4' x 50' roll, mesh opening 3" x 1.25"	—	Ea	26.70	—	26.70
Square mesh, 4' x 50' roll, opening 1.5" x 1.25"	—	Ea	27.00	—	27.00
Heavy Duty, 4' x 50' roll, opening 1.25" x 1.25"	—	Ea	51.90	—	51.90
Medium Weight 4' x 100', opening 2" x 2.5"	—	Ea	48.40	—	48.40
Barricade tape for marking construction sites, landscaping, wet paint					
Yellow plastic 3" x 1,000', "Caution"	—	Ea	10.00	—	10.00
Various colors, 3" x 200', "Danger"	—	Ea	6.00	—	6.00
Utility Highway Barricade Rental					
Lighted units, rental, per day	—	Ea	11.00	—	11.00
Unlighted units, rental per day	—	Ea	8.00	—	8.00
Add for pickup and delivery, per trip	—	Ea	50.00	—	50.00
Typical labor cost, place and remove any barricade					
Per use	BL@.160	Ea	—	4.85	4.85

Basement Doors Good quality 12 gauge primed steel, center opening basement doors. Costs include assembly and installation hardware. No concrete, masonry, anchor placement or finish painting included.

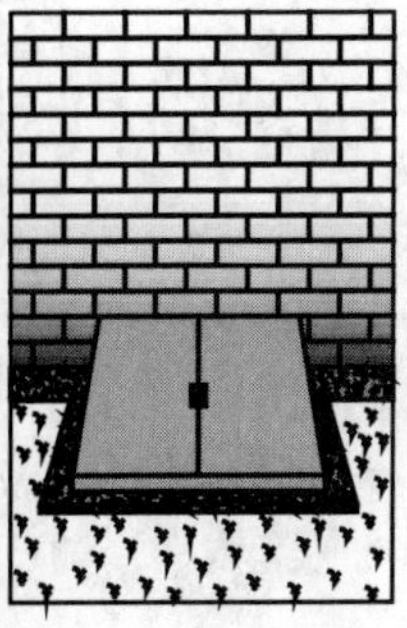

	Craft@Hrs	Unit	Material	Labor	Total
Doors (overall dimensions)					
Classic Series standard, all sizes	BC@3.41	Ea	729.00	127.00	856.00
SLW Series standard, all sizes	BC@3.41	Ea	736.00	127.00	863.00
Add for powder coating	—	%	28.2	—	—
Ultra Series, polyethylene, all sizes	BC@3.41	Ea	1,110.00	127.00	1,237.00
Add for keyed lock	BC@.160	Ea	77.80	5.98	83.78
Door extensions (available for 19-1/2"H, 55"W, 72"L door only)					
6" deep	BC@1.71	Ea	196.00	63.90	259.90
12" deep	BC@1.71	Ea	246.00	63.90	309.90
18" deep	BC@1.71	Ea	309.00	63.90	372.90
Stair stringers, steel, pre-cut for 2" x 10" wood treads (without treads). Price is for a pair, or set of two stringers with hardware.					
32" to 39" stair height	BC@1.71	Pr	150.00	63.90	213.90
48" to 55" stair height	BC@1.71	Pr	190.00	63.90	253.90
56" to 64" stair height	BC@1.71	Pr	256.00	63.90	319.90
65" to 72" stair height	BC@1.71	Pr	249.00	63.90	312.90
73" to 78" stair height	BC@1.71	Pr	349.00	63.90	412.90
81" to 88" stair height	BC@1.71	Pr	377.00	63.90	440.90
89" to 97" stair height	BC@1.71	Pr	404.00	63.90	467.90

Bathroom Accessories Average quality. Better quality brass accessories cost 75% to 100% more. See also Medicine Cabinets and Vanities

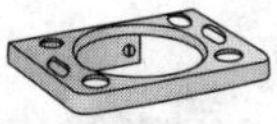

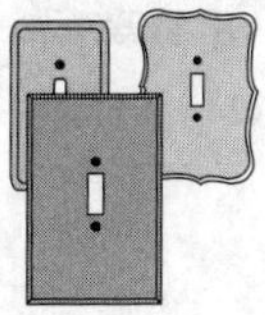

	Craft@Hrs	Unit	Material	Labor	Total
Cup and toothbrush holder, chrome	BC@.258	Ea	13.30	9.64	22.94
Cup holder, porcelain, surface mounted	BC@.258	Ea	9.31	9.64	18.95
Cup, toothbrush & soap holder, recessed	BC@.258	Ea	35.30	9.64	44.94
Cup, toothbrush holder, polished brass	BC@.258	Ea	18.80	9.64	28.44
Electrical plates, chrome plated					
Switch plate, single	BE@.154	Ea	4.94	6.26	11.20
Switch plate, double	BE@.154	Ea	6.51	6.26	12.77
Duplex receptacle plate	BE@.154	Ea	4.94	6.26	11.20
Duplex receptacle and switch	BE@.154	Ea	6.49	6.26	12.75

Bathroom Accessories

	Craft@Hrs	Unit	Material	Labor	Total
Grab bars					
Tubular chrome plated, with anchor plates					
Straight bar, 16"	BC@.414	Ea	28.90	15.50	44.40
Straight bar, 24"	BC@.414	Ea	35.30	15.50	50.80
Straight bar, 32"	BC@.414	Ea	38.10	15.50	53.60
"L"- shaped bar, 16" x 32"	BC@.620	Ea	88.60	23.20	111.80
Stainless steel, with anchor plates					
Straight bar, 16"	BC@.414	Ea	43.70	15.50	59.20
Straight bar, 24"	BC@.414	Ea	52.60	15.50	68.10
Straight bar, 32"	BC@.414	Ea	57.30	15.50	72.80
"L"- shaped bar, 16" x 32"	BC@.620	Ea	123.00	23.20	146.20
Mirrors, stainless steel framed, surface mount, no light or cabinet					
16" high x 20" wide	BG@.420	Ea	69.00	15.20	84.20
18" high x 24" wide	BG@.420	Ea	80.10	15.20	95.30
18" high x 36" wide	BG@.420	Ea	122.00	15.20	137.20
24" high x 36" wide	BG@.420	Ea	143.00	15.20	158.20
48" high x 24" wide	BG@.420	Ea	177.00	15.20	192.20
Mirrors, wood framed, surface mount, better quality					
18" x 29" rectangular	BG@.420	Ea	85.60	15.20	100.80
20" x 27" oval, oak	BG@.420	Ea	121.00	15.20	136.20
Robe hook					
Chrome	BC@.258	Ea	26.00	9.64	35.64
Double, solid brass	BC@.258	Ea	25.00	9.64	34.64
Shower curtain rods, chrome plated					
60", recessed	BC@.730	Ea	30.40	27.30	57.70
66", recessed	BC@.730	Ea	33.40	27.30	60.70
Soap holder, surface mounted, with drain holes					
Williamsburg, satin chrome	BC@.258	Ea	61.90	9.64	71.54
Polished brass	BC@.258	Ea	20.20	9.64	29.84
Facial tissue holder, stainless steel, recessed	BC@.258	Ea	41.70	9.64	51.34
Toilet tissue roll holder, chrome, recessed	BC@.258	Ea	19.40	9.64	29.04
Toothbrush holder, chrome, surface mount	BC@.258	Ea	7.18	9.64	16.82
Towel bars, 3/4" bar					
18" long, chrome	BC@.280	Ea	15.90	10.50	26.40
24" long, chrome	BC@.280	Ea	18.90	10.50	29.40
30" long, chrome	BC@.280	Ea	22.40	10.50	32.90
36" long, chrome	BC@.280	Ea	25.50	10.50	36.00
18" long, solid brass	BC@.280	Ea	51.80	10.50	62.30
24" long, solid brass	BC@.280	Ea	54.50	10.50	65.00
Towel rack, swing-arm, chrome, 3 bars, 12" L	BC@.280	Ea	18.10	10.50	28.60
Towel rings					
Williamsburg chrome and brass	BC@.280	Ea	49.10	10.50	59.60
Williamsburg chrome and porcelain	BC@.280	Ea	46.90	10.50	57.40
Towel shelf, chrome, 24" L with bar below	BC@.280	Ea	45.90	10.50	56.40
Heated towel racks, 16" and 24" width, mounted on wall with brackets. Direct wire connection, 700 watt output. Add for electrical work					
26" high, 16" wide, standard colors	BE@.850	Ea	792.00	34.50	826.50
26" high, 24" wide, standard colors	BE@.850	Ea	846.00	34.50	880.50
26" high, 24" wide, chrome finish	BE@.850	Ea	2,610.00	34.50	2,644.50

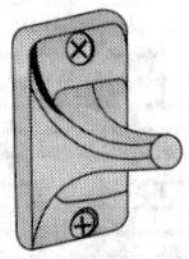

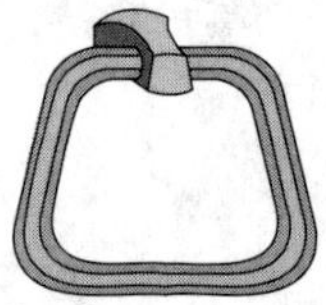

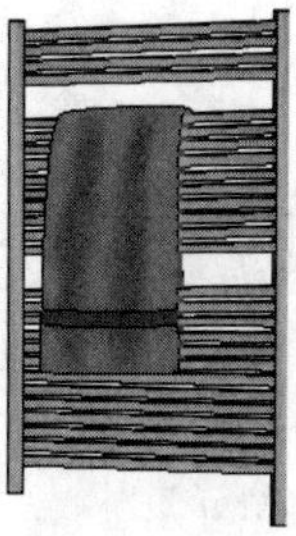

	Craft@Hrs	Unit	Material	Labor	Total
35" high, 16" wide, standard colors	BE@1.00	Ea	990.00	40.60	1,030.60
35" high, 24" wide, standard colors	BE@1.00	Ea	940.00	40.60	980.60
35" high, 24" wide, chrome finish	BE@1.00	Ea	3,150.00	40.60	3,190.60
44" high, 16" wide, standard colors	BE@1.10	Ea	990.00	44.70	1,034.70
44" high, 24" wide, standard colors	BE@1.10	Ea	1,040.00	44.70	1,084.70
44" high, 24" wide, chrome finish	BE@1.10	Ea	3,450.00	44.70	3,494.70
Add for direct wire w/ control panel	BE@.100	Ea	218.00	4.06	222.06
Add for wall plug in	BE@.100	Ea	292.00	4.06	296.06
Heated towel rack accessories					
Programmable control panel	BE@.250	Ea	284.00	10.20	294.20
Pull out drying racks	BE@.250	Ea	79.60	10.20	89.80
Robe knobs	BE@.150	Ea	51.20	6.09	57.29
Towel bar accents with standard colors	BE@.150	Ea	102.00	6.09	108.09
Towel bar accents with chrome finish	BE@.150	Ea	137.00	6.09	143.09
Robe knob accents (all styles)	BE@.150	Ea	238.00	6.09	244.09
Tub or shower chairs					
Wall-hung elevated fixed seat	BE@.750	Ea	37.60	30.50	68.10
White adjustable seat	BE@.750	Ea	70.10	30.50	100.60

Beds, Folding Concealed-in-wall type. Steel framed, folding wall bed system. Bed requires 18-5/8" or 22" deep recess. Includes frame, lift mechanism, all hardware. Installed in framed opening. Padded vinyl headboard. Bed face panel accepts paint, wallpaper, vinyl or laminate up to 1/4" thick. Box spring and mattress not included. Murphy Wall Beds

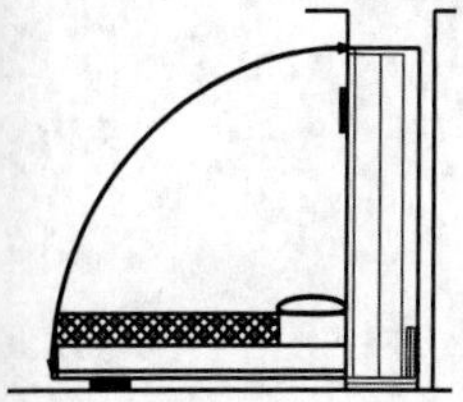

	Craft@Hrs	Unit	Material	Labor	Total
Twin, frames and mechanisms	B1@5.41	Ea	835.00	183.00	1,018.00
Double, frames and mechanisms	B1@5.41	Ea	875.00	183.00	1,058.00
Queen, frames and mechanisms	B1@5.41	Ea	914.00	183.00	1,097.00
King, frames and mechanisms	B1@5.41	Ea	1,000.00	183.00	1,183.00
Add for wood-tone melamine cabinet	—	LS	1,480.00	—	1,480.00
Add for white melamine cabinet	—	LS	1,320.00	—	1,320.00

Blueprinting (Reproduction only) Assumes original is on semi-transparent drafting paper or film. See also Architectural Illustration and Drafting. Cost per square foot reproduced except as noted. Stapled edge and binder included.

	Craft@Hrs	Unit	Material	Labor	Total
Blueline or blackline prints					
1-100 SF	—	SF	—	—	.21
101-1,000 SF	—	SF	—	—	.19
1,001-2,000 SF	—	SF	—	—	.18
2,001-to 3,000 SF	—	SF	—	—	.16
3,001-4,000 SF	—	SF	—	—	.09
4,001 SF and higher	—	SF	—	—	.08
Presentation blackline (heavy paper)	—	SF	—	—	.56
Sepia	—	SF	—	—	.83
Mylar	—	SF	—	—	2.77
Xerographic prints					
Vellum	—	SF	—	—	1.10
Erasable vellum	—	SF	—	—	1.39
Mylar	—	SF	—	—	2.77
Enlargements (bond)	—	SF	—	—	.66
Reductions (bond, per sheet)	—	Ea	—	—	2.76

Building Inspection Service

	Craft@Hrs	Unit	Material	Labor	Total
Plotting prints					
Translucent bond	—	SF	—	—	1.67
Vellum	—	SF	—	—	1.93
Erasable vellum	—	SF	—	—	2.75
Mylar	—	SF	—	—	2.77
Photo prints					
Mylar	—	SF	—	—	6.21
Add for local pickup and delivery, round trip	—	LS	—	—	20.00

Building Inspection Service (Home inspection service) Inspection of all parts of building by qualified engineer or certified building inspection technician. Includes written report covering all doors and windows, electrical system, foundation, heating and cooling system, insulation, interior and exterior surface conditions, landscaping, plumbing system, roofing, and structural integrity.

	Craft@Hrs	Unit	Material	Labor	Total
Single-family residence					
Base fee (up to 2,500 SF)	—	LS	—	—	348.00
Add for additional 1,000 SF or fraction	—	LS	—	—	106.00
Add for out buildings (each)	—	LS	—	—	53.50
Add for houses over 50 years old	—	LS	—	—	80.20
Add per room for houses with over 10 rooms	—	Ea	—	—	64.20
Add per room for houses with over 15 rooms	—	Ea	—	—	69.60
Add for swimming pool, spa or sauna	—	LS	—	—	212.00
Add for soil testing (expansive soil only)	—	LS	—	—	214.00
Add for water testing (coliform only)	—	LS	—	—	75.00
Add for warranty protection					
Houses to 10 rooms & 50 years old	—	LS	—	—	267.00
Houses over 50 years old	—	LS	—	—	287.00
Houses over 10 rooms	—	LS	—	—	289.00
Multi-family structures					
Two family residence base fee	—	LS	—	—	483.00
Apartment or condominium base fee	—	LS	—	—	267.00
Warranty protection (base cost)	—	LS	—	—	267.00
Add for each additional unit	—	LS	—	—	53.60
Add for each family living unit					
Standard inspection	—	LS	—	—	53.50
Detailed inspection	—	LS	—	—	79.60
Add for swimming pool, spa, sauna	—	LS	—	—	80.20
Add for potable water quality testing	—	LS	—	—	241.00
Add for water quantity test, per well	—	LS	—	—	161.00
Add for soil testing (EPA toxic)	—	LS	—	—	1,610.00
Add for soil testing (lead)	—	LS	—	—	48.30
Add for lead paint testing, full analysis, per room	—	LS	—	—	42.80
Hazards testing for single and multi-family dwellings					
Urea-formaldehyde insulation testing	—	LS	—	—	187.00
Asbestos testing	—	LS	—	—	189.00
Radon gas testing	—	LS	—	—	135.00
Geotechnical site examination, typical price	—	LS	—	—	430.00

	Craft@Hrs	Unit	Material	Labor	Total
Building Paper See also Roofing for roof applications and Polyethylene Film. Costs include 7% coverage allowance for 2" lap and 5% waste allowance. See installation costs at the end of this section.					
Asphalt felt, 36" wide					
15 lb., ASTM F45 (432 SF roll)	—	SF	.06	—	.06
15 lb., F40 (432 SF roll)	—	SF	.05	—	.05
30 lb. (216 SF roll)	—	SF	.12	—	.12
Asphalt shake felt, 18" x 72"					
30 lb. (108 SF roll)	—	SF	.18	—	.18
Building paper, 40" wide					
Single ply, black (1,078 SF roll)	—	SF	.05	—	.05
Two ply (539 SF roll)	—	SF	.07	—	.07
Aquabar™, two layer, laminated with asphalt, Fortifiber™ products					
Class A, 36" wide, 30-50-30 (1,000 SF roll)	—	SF	.05	—	.05
Class B, 36" wide, 30-30-30 (500 SF roll)	—	SF	.07	—	.07
Ice and water shield, self-adhesive rubberized asphalt and poly					
225 SF roll	—	SF	.95	—	.95
High temperature, 225 SF roll	—	SF	1.04	—	1.04
"Jumbo Tex" gun grade sheathing paper, 40" wide, asphalt saturated (324 SF roll)	—	SF	.07	—	.07
"Jumbo Tex" black building paper, 36", 40" wide, asphalt saturated (500 SF roll)	—	SF	.10	—	.10
"Super Jumbo Tex" two-ply, 60 minute, asphalt saturated Kraft (162 SF roll)	—	SF	.11	—	.11
Red rosin sized sheathing (duplex sheathing) 36" wide (501 SF roll)	—	SF	.03	—	.03
Bruce rosin paper, floor underlay (500 SF roll)	—	SF	.04	—	.04
Moistop flashing paper, Fortifiber™, 12" wide x 300' long (300 SF roll)	—	SF	.15	—	.15
Vycor window and door flashing, self adhesive, Grace					
6" x 75' roll, 25 mil thickness	—	SF	1.78	—	1.78
Vycor deck protector, self adhesive joist flashing, Grace					
4" x 75' roll, Roll covers 66 LF of joist	—	LF	1.79	—	1.79
Plasterkraft grade D weather-resistive sheathing paper, 40" wide					
Super 60 minute (500 SF roll)	—	SF	.04	—	.04
Ten minute 2-ply (500 SF roll)	—	SF	.03	—	.03
Roof flashing paper, seals around skylights, dormers, vents, valleys and eaves, rubberized, fiberglass reinforced, self-adhesive					
GAF StormGuard™ Roll covers 200 SF	—	SF	.54	—	.54
Roof underlay, for use under shingles, granular surface					
Weatherlock® 200 SF roll	—	SF	.53	—	.53
Tri-Flex roof underlay, for use under shingles, tile, slate or metal roofing					
48" x 250', 1,000 SF roll	—	SF	.13	—	.13
Below grade vapor barrier, Fortifiber™ Moistop (fiberglass reinforced Kraft between 2 layers of polyethylene)					
8' x 250' roll (2,000 SF roll)	—	SF	.19	—	.19

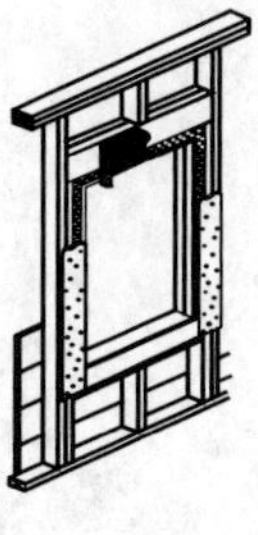

Building Permit Fees

	Craft@Hrs	Unit	Material	Labor	Total
Concrete curing papers, Fortifiber™					
Orange Label Sisalkraft (fiberglass and adhesive between 2 layers of Kraft), 4.8 lbs. per CSF					
48" x 125' roll, (500 SF roll)	—	SF	.25	—	.25
Sisalkraft SK-10, economy papers, fiberglass and adhesive between 2 layers of Kraft, 4.2 lbs. per CSF					
48" x 300' roll (1,200 SF roll)	—	SF	.08	—	.08
Protective paper, Fortifiber™ Seekure (fiberglass reinforcing strands and nonstaining adhesive between 2 layers of Kraft)					
8" x 300' roll, (2,400 SF)	—	SF	.09	—	.09
House wrap membrane, aka Tyvek™ HomeWrap by DuPont					
Air/moisture infiltration barrier (high-density polyethylene fibers in sheet form)					
3' x 100' rolls or 9' x 150' rolls	—	SF	.13	—	.13
House wrap tape, 2" x 165'	—	LF	.09	—	.09
Labor to install building papers					
Felts, vapor barriers, infiltration barriers, building papers on walls					
Tack stapled, typical	BC@.002	SF	—	.07	.07
Heavy stapled, typical	BC@.003	SF	—	.11	.11
Felts, vapor barriers, infiltration barriers, building papers on ceilings and roofs					
Tack stapled, typical	BC@.004	SF	—	.15	.15
Heavy stapled, typical	BC@.006	SF	—	.22	.22
Self-adhesive, typical	BC@.006	SF	—	.22	.22
Curing papers, protective papers and vapor barriers, minimal fasteners	BC@.001	SF	—	.04	.04
Flashing papers, 6" to 8" wide	BC@.010	LF	—	.37	.37

Building Permit Fees Fees are set by each jurisdiction and are based on the type of construction and the square foot area. Most building departments either publish a fee schedule or offer a Web-based fee calculator. The permit fee will usually be doubled when work is started without a permit. When the valuation of the proposed construction exceeds $1,000, plans are usually required. For most residential construction, building permit will be about 1% of the construction cost (with a $200 minimum) based on a table of values published by the International Code Council at:
https://www.iccsafe.org/products-and-services/i-codes/code-development-process/building-valuation-data/
Most wood-frame residences are Group R3 and Type VB. This estimate of 1% includes the plan check fee, building, plumbing, HVAC and electrical permits, GIS mapping and issuance of a certificate of occupancy. Permits required by planning authorities will be extra. Estimate the fee for reinspection at $145 per hour. Inspections outside normal business hours are about $145 per hour with a two-hour minimum. Estimate the fee for additional plan review required by changes, additions or revisions to approved plans at $155 per hour with a one-half hour minimum.

	Craft@Hrs	Unit	Material	Labor	Total
Minimum building permit fee	—	LS	200.00	—	200.00
Typical fee based on estimated total construction cost	—	%	1.0	—	—

	Craft@Hrs	Unit	Material	Labor	Total

Cabinets, Kitchen See also Vanities. Good quality mill-made modular units with solid hardwood face frames, hardwood door frames and drawer fronts, hardwood veneer on raised door panels (front and back), glued mortise, dowel, and dado joint construction, full backs (1/8" vinyl laminated plywood), vinyl laminated cabinet interiors, vinyl laminated composition drawer bodies with nylon and metal guides. Includes self-closing hinges, door and drawer pulls, mounting hardware and adjustable shelves. See illustrations for unit types. See the price adjustments below for pricing of other units. No countertops included. See Countertops, page 96.

Kitchen cabinet costs vary widely. The prices listed in this section are for standard grade residential cabinets. Add 65% to material costs for premium grade cabinets with solid hardwood fronts and frames, mitered corners and solid wood drawer bodies with steel guides and ball bearings. Deduct 45% from material costs for economy grade cabinets, laminated plastic on particleboard.

Cabinets, Rule of Thumb Cabinet cost per running foot of cabinet installed. These figures are based on a set of mill-fabricated and assembled kitchen cabinets including a sink base cabinet, one 3-drawer base cabinet and six door base cabinets. Per linear foot of front or back edge, whichever is longer.

	Craft@Hrs	Unit	Material	Labor	Total
Base cabinets, 34-1/2" high, 24" deep	BC@.521	LF	173.00	19.50	192.50
Wall cabinets, 30" high, 12" deep	BC@.340	LF	90.50	12.70	103.20

Cabinets, Kitchen (See the note above on cabinet costs.)

	Craft@Hrs	Unit	Material	Labor	Total
One door base cabinets, 34-1/2" high, 24" deep					
9" wide, tray divider	BC@.461	Ea	163.00	17.20	180.20
12" wide, 1 door, 1 drawer	BC@.461	Ea	218.00	17.20	235.20
15" wide, 1 door, 1 drawer	BC@.638	Ea	233.00	23.80	256.80
18" wide, 1 door, 1 drawer	BC@.766	Ea	245.00	28.60	273.60
21" wide, 1 door, 1 drawer	BC@.766	Ea	267.00	28.60	295.60
24" wide, 1 door, 1 drawer	BC@.911	Ea	273.00	34.10	307.10
Drawer base cabinets, 34-1/2" high, 24" deep					
15" wide, 4 drawers	BC@.638	Ea	239.00	23.80	262.80
18" wide, 4 drawers	BC@.766	Ea	254.00	28.60	282.60
24" wide, 4 drawers	BC@.911	Ea	295.00	34.10	329.10
Sink base cabinets, 34-1/2" high, 24" deep					
24" wide, 1 door, 1 drawer front	BC@.740	Ea	233.00	27.70	260.70
30" wide, 2 doors, 2 drawer fronts	BC@.766	Ea	280.00	28.60	308.60
33" wide, 2 doors, 2 drawer fronts	BC@.766	Ea	295.00	28.60	323.60
36" wide, 2 doors, 2 drawer fronts	BC@.766	Ea	302.00	28.60	330.60
42" wide, 2 doors, 2 drawer fronts	BC@.911	Ea	333.00	34.10	367.10
48" wide, 2 doors, 2 drawer fronts	BC@.911	Ea	366.00	34.10	400.10
Two door base cabinets, 34-1/2" high, 24" deep					
27" wide, 2 door, 2 drawer front	BC@1.25	Ea	360.00	46.70	406.70
30" wide, 2 doors, 2 drawer fronts	BC@1.25	Ea	380.00	46.70	426.70
33" wide, 2 doors, 2 drawer fronts	BC@1.25	Ea	398.00	46.70	444.70
36" wide, 2 doors, 2 drawer fronts	BC@1.35	Ea	419.00	50.50	469.50
42" wide, 2 doors, 2 drawer fronts	BC@1.50	Ea	436.00	56.10	492.10
48" wide, 2 doors, 2 drawer fronts	BC@1.71	Ea	485.00	63.90	548.90
Blind corner base cabinets, 34-1/2" high					
Minimum 36", maximum 39" at wall	BC@1.39	Ea	267.00	52.00	319.00
Minimum 39", maximum 42" at wall	BC@1.50	Ea	287.00	56.10	343.10
Corner base cabinet, revolving shelves					
34-1/2" high x 36" wide at walls	BC@2.12	Ea	413.00	79.20	492.20

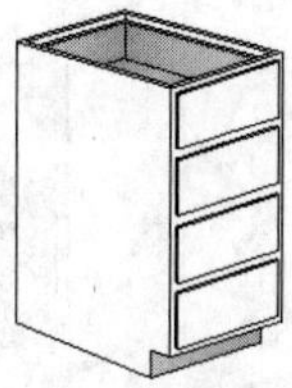
DRAWER BASE

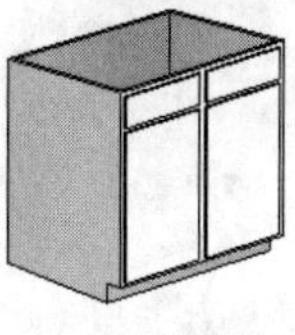
SINK BASE

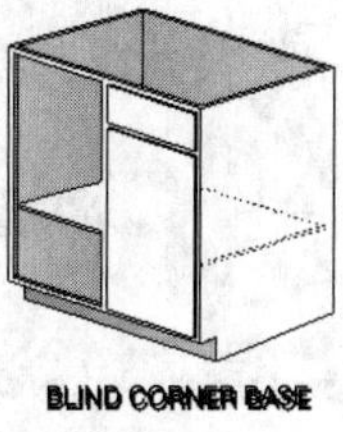
BLIND CORNER BASE

Cabinets, Kitchen

	Craft@Hrs	Unit	Material	Labor	Total
Corner sink front, 34-1/2" high					
40" wide at walls	BC@2.63	Ea	233.00	98.30	331.30
Wall cabinets, adjustable shelves, 30" high, 12" deep					
9" wide, 1 door	BC@.461	Ea	147.00	17.20	164.20
12" wide or 15" wide, 1 door	BC@.461	Ea	160.00	17.20	177.20
18" wide, 1 door	BC@.638	Ea	189.00	23.80	212.80
21" wide, 1 door	BC@.638	Ea	195.00	23.80	218.80
24" wide, 1 door	BC@.766	Ea	209.00	28.60	237.60
27" wide, 2 doors	BC@.766	Ea	245.00	28.60	273.60
30" wide, 2 doors	BC@.911	Ea	245.00	34.10	279.10
33" wide, 2 doors	BC@.911	Ea	267.00	34.10	301.10
36" wide, 2 doors	BC@1.03	Ea	281.00	38.50	319.50
42" wide, 2 doors	BC@1.03	Ea	302.00	38.50	340.50
48" wide, 2 doors	BC@1.16	Ea	326.00	43.40	369.40
Above-appliance wall cabinets, 12" deep					
12" high, 30" wide, 2 doors	BC@.461	Ea	155.00	17.20	172.20
15" high, 30" wide, 2 doors	BC@.461	Ea	177.00	17.20	194.20
15" high, 33" wide, 2 doors	BC@.537	Ea	190.00	20.10	210.10
15" high, 36" wide, 2 doors	BC@.638	Ea	195.00	23.80	218.80
18" high, 18" wide, 2 doors	BC@.537	Ea	147.00	20.10	167.10
18" high, 30" wide, 2 doors	BC@.766	Ea	195.00	28.60	223.60
18" high, 36" wide, 2 doors	BC@.911	Ea	215.00	34.10	249.10
Corner wall cabinets, 30" high, 12" deep					
24" at each wall, fixed shelves	BC@1.03	Ea	267.00	38.50	305.50
24" at each wall, revolving shelves	BC@1.03	Ea	358.00	38.50	396.50
Blind corner wall cabinets, 30" high					
24" minimum, 1 door	BC@1.03	Ea	202.00	38.50	240.50
36" minimum, 1 door	BC@1.32	Ea	245.00	49.30	294.30
42" minimum, 2 doors	BC@1.20	Ea	308.00	44.90	352.90
Utility cabinets, 66" high, 12" deep, no shelves					
18" wide	BC@1.32	Ea	308.00	49.30	357.30
24" wide	BC@1.71	Ea	352.00	63.90	415.90
Utility cabinets, 66" high, 24" deep, add shelf cost below					
18" wide	BC@1.24	Ea	326.00	46.40	372.40
24" wide	BC@1.71	Ea	387.00	63.90	450.90
Add for utility cabinet revolving shelves, includes mounting hardware					
18" wide x 24" deep	BC@.360	Ea	280.00	13.50	293.50
24" wide x 24" deep	BC@.360	Ea	328.00	13.50	341.50
Add for utility cabinet plain shelves					
18" wide x 24" deep	BC@.541	Ea	94.70	20.20	114.90
24" wide x 24" deep	BC@.541	Ea	99.20	20.20	119.40
Oven cabinets, 66" high, 24" deep					
27" wide, single oven	BC@2.19	Ea	391.00	81.90	472.90
27" wide, double oven	BC@2.19	Ea	296.00	81.90	377.90

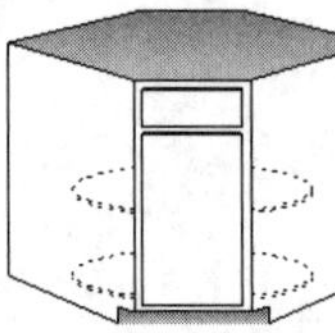
45 DEGREE CORNER BASE CABINET

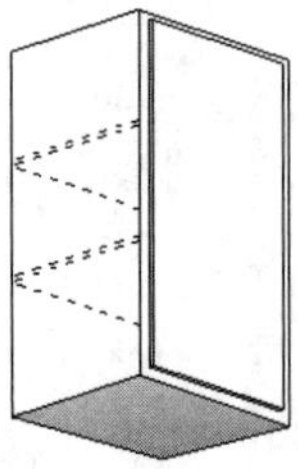
1 DOOR WALL CABINET

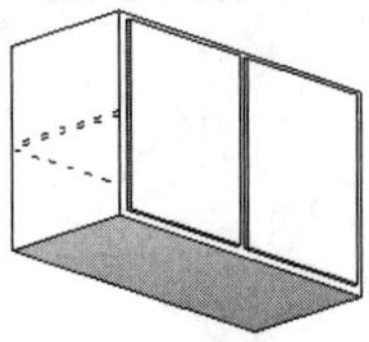
ABOVE-APPLIANCE WALL CABINET

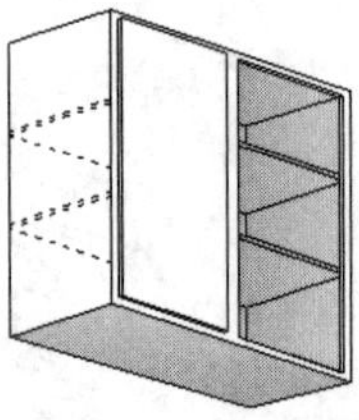
BLIND CORNER WALL CABINET

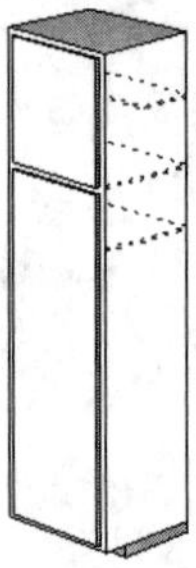
UTILITY

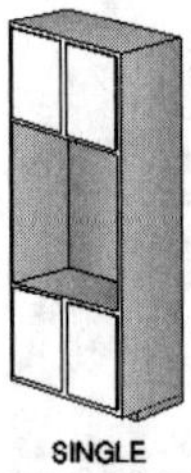
SINGLE OVEN CABINET

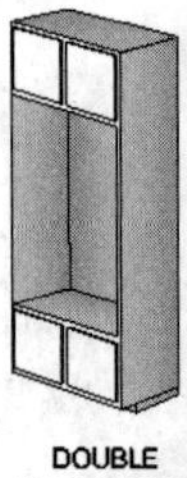
DOUBLE OVEN CABINET

	Craft@Hrs	Unit	Material	Labor	Total
Microwave cabinet, with trim,					
21" high, 20" deep, 30" wide	BC@.986	Ea	235.00	36.90	271.90
Additional labor costs for cabinets					
Tall utility, pantry, or oven cabinets	BC@2.00	Ea	—	74.80	74.80
Tall wall cabinet to counter level	BC@1.50	Ea	—	56.10	56.10
Hood cabinet over a range with vent cutout	BC@1.50	Ea	—	56.10	56.10
3/4" raised end panels applied to cabinet ends	BC@.250	Ea	—	9.35	9.35
Refrigerator end panels, cut, fit, install	BC@.500	Ea	—	18.70	18.70
Cabinet end panels, most sizes, per panel					
Refrigerator end panels	BC@.557	Ea	—	20.80	20.80
Refrigerator end panels with return	BC@1.00	Ea	—	37.40	37.40
Applied decorative end panels	BC@.334	Ea	—	12.50	12.50
Mitered island end or back panels	BC@.667	Ea	—	24.90	24.90
Dishwasher return panels	BC@.667	Ea	—	24.90	24.90
Precut filler panels installed between cabinets, per panel					
Most base or wall fillers	BC@.200	Ea	—	7.48	7.48
Most base or wall fillers with overlays	BC@.400	Ea	—	15.00	15.00
Tall filler panels over 36"	BC@.268	Ea	—	10.00	10.00
Tall filler panels over 36" with overlays	BC@.535	Ea	—	20.00	20.00
Corner filler panels	BC@.224	Ea	—	8.37	8.37
Corner fillers panels with overlays	BC@.448	Ea	—	16.70	16.70
Angled corner filler panels	BC@.268	Ea	—	10.00	10.00
Angled corner filler panels with overlays	BC@.536	Ea	—	20.00	20.00
Moldings and trim for cabinet work					
Scribe molding, per 8' length	BC@.224	Ea	—	8.37	8.37
Scribe molding, per linear foot	BC@.028	LF	—	1.05	1.05
Crown molding, per 8' length, miter cut	BC@.448	Ea	—	16.70	16.70
Crown molding, per 8' length, butt joint	BC@.180	Ea	—	6.73	6.73
Crown plate and riser, per miter cut	BC@.180	Ea	—	6.73	6.73
Crown plate and riser, per straight cut	BC@.112	Ea	—	4.19	4.19
Applied molding, per miter cut	BC@.112	Ea	—	4.19	4.19
Applied molding, per straight cut	BC@.067	Ea	—	2.50	2.50
Light rail molding, per miter cut	BC@.224	Ea	—	8.37	8.37
Light rail molding, per straight cut	BC@.067	Ea	—	2.50	2.50
Furniture toe kick, per 8' length	BC@.334	Ea	—	12.50	12.50
Furniture toe kick, per linear foot	BC@.042	LF	—	1.57	1.57
Valance, straight, per 8' length	BC@.334	Ea	—	12.50	12.50
Valance, with side returns or cap, 8' length	BC@.667	Ea	—	24.90	24.90
Mantle or hood molding, length to 8'	BC@.800	Ea	—	29.90	29.90
Corbels, plain	BC@.224	Ea	—	8.37	8.37
Corbels, on uprights	BC@.334	Ea	—	12.50	12.50
Enkeboll molding, miter cut, 8' length	BC@.667	Ea	—	24.90	24.90
Enkeboll molding, straight cut, 8' length	BC@.180	Ea	—	6.73	6.73
Posts, to 8' length	BC@.500	Ea	—	18.70	18.70
Pilasters	BC@.334	Ea	—	12.50	12.50
Cabinet feet, per cabinet	BC@.334	Ea	—	12.50	12.50
Cabinet extras					
Scribing in wood tops	BC@.133	LF	—	4.97	4.97
Job built 2 x 4 support wall to 42" high	BC@.334	LF	—	12.50	12.50
Framing for range support or sink cutout	BC@.667	Ea	—	24.90	24.90

	Craft@Hrs	Unit	Material	Labor	Total

Carpentry See also carpentry items in other sections: Carpentry Steel Framing, Cabinets, Ceilings, Closet Door Systems, Countertops, Cupolas, Doors, Entrances, Flooring, Framing Connectors, Hardboard, Hardware, Lumber, Molding, Paneling, Shutters, Siding, Skylights, Soffits, Stairs, Thresholds, and Weatherstripping.

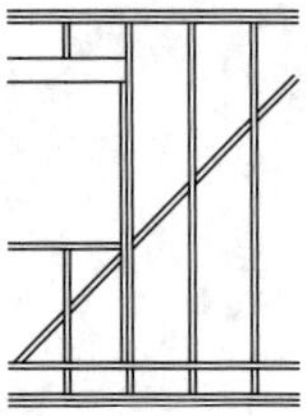

Carpentry Rule of Thumb Typical rough carpentry (framing) cost per square foot of floor in living area. These figures will apply on many residential jobs where joists, studs and rafters are 16" on center. Unconventional designs and complex framing plans will cost more. See detailed cost breakdowns in the next section.

	Craft@Hrs	Unit	Material	Labor	Total
Using framing lumber at	—	MBF	816.00	—	816.00
Using 1/2" OSB sheathing at	—	MSF	530.00	—	530.00
Using 7/16" OSB sheathing at	—	MSF	384.00	—	384.00
Using 5/8" OSB sheathing at	—	MSF	549.00	—	549.00
Using 1/2" CDX sheathing at	—	MSF	726.00	—	726.00
Using 5/8" CDX sheathing at	—	MSF	1,130.00	—	1,130.00
Single story, conventional foundation	B1@.237	SF	6.20	8.02	14.22
Single story, concrete slab foundation	B1@.180	SF	4.24	6.09	10.33
First of two floors, conventional foundation	B1@.203	SF	4.90	6.87	11.77
First of two floors, concrete slab foundation	B1@.146	SF	2.94	4.94	7.88
Second floor of a two-story residence	B1@.191	SF	4.87	6.46	11.33
Add for plywood sheathing	—	%	13.7	—	—

Framing a single story residence, conventional crawl-space foundation

	Craft@Hrs	Unit	Material	Labor	Total
Sills, pier blocks, floor beams (145 BF per 1,000 SF)	B1@.018	SF	.12	.61	.73
Floor joists, doublers, blocking, bridging (1,480 BF per 1,000 SF)	B1@.028	SF	1.21	.95	2.16
Subflooring, 5/8" OSB (1,150 SF per 1,000 SF)	B1@.011	SF	.63	.37	1.00
Layout, studs, sole plates, top plates, header and end joists, backing, blocking, bracing and framing for openings (2,250 BF per 1,000 SF)	B1@.093	SF	1.84	3.15	4.99
Ceiling joists, header and end joists, backing, blocking and bracing (1,060 BF per 1,000 SF)	B1@.045	SF	.87	1.52	2.39
Rafters, braces, collar beams, ridge boards, 2" x 8" rafters 16" OC, (1,340 BF per 1000 SF)	B1@.032	SF	1.09	1.08	2.17
Roof sheathing, 7/16" OSB (1,150 SF per 1,000 SF)	B1@.010	SF	.44	.34	.78
Total framing, single story, conventional foundation	B1@.237	SF	6.20	8.02	14.22
Add for plywood sheathing	—	%	17.1	—	—

Framing a single story residence, concrete slab foundation

	Craft@Hrs	Unit	Material	Labor	Total
Layout, sole plates, anchors, studs, top plates, header and end joists, backing, blocking, bracing and framing for openings (2,250 BF per 1,000 SF)	B1@.093	SF	1.84	3.15	4.99
Ceiling joists, header and end joists, backing, blocking and bracing (1,060 BF per 1,000 SF)	B1@.045	SF	.87	1.52	2.39
Rafters, braces, collar beams, ridge boards, 2" x 8" rafters 16" OC, (1,340 BF per 1,000 SF)	B1@.032	SF	1.09	1.08	2.17
Roof sheathing, 7/16" OSB (1,150 SF per 1,000 SF)	B1@.010	SF	.44	.34	.78
Total framing, single story, concrete slab foundation	B1@.180	SF	4.24	6.09	10.33
Add for plywood sheathing	—	%	9.3	—	—

	Craft@Hrs	Unit	Material	Labor	Total
Framing the first of two floors, conventional crawl-space foundation					
Sills, pier blocks, floor beams (145 BF per 1,000 SF)	B1@.018	SF	.12	.61	.73
Floor joists, doublers, blocking, bridging (1,480 BF per 1,000 SF)	B1@.028	SF	1.21	.95	2.16
Subflooring, 5/8" OSB (1,150 SF per 1,000 SF)	B1@.011	SF	.63	.37	1.00
Layout, studs, sole plates, top plates, header and end joists, backing, blocking, bracing and framing for openings (2,250 BF per 1,000 SF)	B1@.093	SF	1.84	3.15	4.99
Rough stairway, 15 risers and landing (96 BF of dimension lumber and 128 SF of plywood per 1,000 SF)	B1@.008	SF	.23	.27	.50
Ceiling joists, header and end joists, backing, blocking and bracing (1,060 BF per 1,000 SF)	B1@.045	SF	.87	1.52	2.39
Total framing, 1st of 2 floors, crawl-space foundation	**B1@.203**	**SF**	**4.90**	**6.87**	**11.77**
Add for plywood sheathing	—	%	13.6	—	—
Framing the first of two floors, concrete slab foundation					
Layout, sole plates, anchors, studs, top plates, header and end joists, backing, blocking, bracing and framing for openings (2,250 BF per 1,000 SF)	B1@.093	SF	1.84	3.15	4.99
Rough stairway, 15 risers and landing (96 BF of dimension lumber and 128 SF of plywood per 1,000 SF)	B1@.008	SF	.87	.27	1.14
Ceiling joists, header and end joists, backing, blocking and bracing (1,060 BF per 1,000 SF)	B1@.045	SF	.23	1.52	1.75
Total framing, first of two floors, concrete foundation	**B1@.146**	**SF**	**2.94**	**4.94**	**7.88**
Framing the second story of a residence					
Subflooring, 5/8" OSB (1,150 SF per 1,000 SF)	B1@.011	SF	.63	.37	1.00
Layout, studs, sole plates, top plates, header and end joists, backing, blocking, bracing and framing for openings (2,250 BF per 1,000 SF)	B1@.093	SF	1.84	3.15	4.99
Ceiling joists, header and end joists, backing, blocking and bracing (1,060 BF per 1,000 SF)	B1@.045	SF	.87	1.52	2.39
Rafters, braces, collar beams, ridge boards, 2" x 8" rafters 16" OC (1,340 BF per 1,000 SF)	B1@.032	SF	1.09	1.08	2.17
Roof sheathing, 7/16" OSB (1,150 SF per 1,000 SF)	B1@.010	SF	.44	.34	.78
Total framing, second floor of a two-story residence	**B1@.191**	**SF**	**4.87**	**6.46**	**11.33**
Add for plywood sheathing	—	%	21.2	—	—

Floor Assemblies Costs for wood framed floor joists with subflooring and R-19 insulation. These costs include the floor joists, subflooring as described, blocking, nails and 6-1/4" thick R-1.9 fiberglass insulation between the floor joists. Figures include box or band joists and typical double joists. No beams included. Planked subflooring is based on 1.24 BF per square foot of floor. Costs shown are per square foot of area covered and include normal waste. Deduct for openings over 25 SF.

	Craft@Hrs	Unit	Material	Labor	Total
Using framing lumber at	—	MBF	816.00	—	816.00
Using 5/8" CDX plywood subfloor at	—	MSF	1,130.00	—	1,130.00
Using 3/4" CDX plywood subfloor at	—	MSF	847.00	—	847.00
Using 7/16" OSB subfloor at	—	MSF	384.00	—	384.00
Using 5/8" OSB subfloor at	—	MSF	549.00	—	549.00
Using 3/4" OSB T&G subfloor at	—	MSF	677.00	—	677.00

	Craft@Hrs	Unit	Material	Labor	Total
Floor joists 16" OC, R-19 insulation and OSB subflooring					
7/16" OSB subfloor					
2" x 6" joists	B1@.040	SF	2.26	1.35	3.61
2" x 8" joists	B1@.041	SF	2.68	1.39	4.07
2" x 10" joists	B1@.043	SF	3.12	1.46	4.58
2" x 12" joists	B1@.044	SF	3.79	1.49	5.28
Floor joists 16" OC, R-19 insulation and OSB subflooring					
5/8" OSB subfloor					
2" x 6" joists	B1@.040	SF	2.43	1.35	3.78
2" x 8" joists	B1@.041	SF	2.85	1.39	4.24
2" x 10" joists	B1@.043	SF	3.29	1.46	4.75
2" x 12" joists	B1@.044	SF	3.95	1.49	5.44
3/4" OSB subfloor					
2" x 6" joists	B1@.042	SF	2.56	1.42	3.98
2" x 8" joists	B1@.043	SF	2.97	1.46	4.43
2" x 10" joists	B1@.045	SF	3.42	1.52	4.94
2" x 12" joists	B1@.046	SF	4.08	1.56	5.64
Floor joists 16" OC, R-19 insulation and plywood subflooring					
5/8" plywood subfloor					
2" x 6" joists	B1@.040	SF	2.62	1.35	3.97
2" x 8" joists	B1@.041	SF	3.03	1.39	4.42
2" x 10" joists	B1@.043	SF	3.47	1.46	4.93
2" x 12" joists	B1@.044	SF	4.14	1.49	5.63
3/4" plywood subfloor					
2" x 6" joists	B1@.042	SF	2.73	1.42	4.15
2" x 8" joists	B1@.043	SF	3.14	1.46	4.60
2" x 10" joists	B1@.045	SF	3.59	1.52	5.11
2" x 12" joists	B1@.046	SF	4.25	1.56	5.81
For different type insulation					
Fiberglass batts					
10" thick R-30, add	—	SF	.40	—	.40
12" thick R-38, add	—	SF	1.01	—	1.01

Wall Assemblies Costs for wood framed stud walls with wall finish treatment on both sides. These costs include wall studs at 16" center to center, double top plates, single bottom plates, fire blocking, nails and wall finish treatment as described. No headers or posts included. All lumber is Std & Btr. 2" x 4" walls have 1.12 BF per SF of wall and 2" x 6" walls have 1.68 BF per SF of wall. Costs shown are per SF or LF of wall measured on one face and include normal waste.

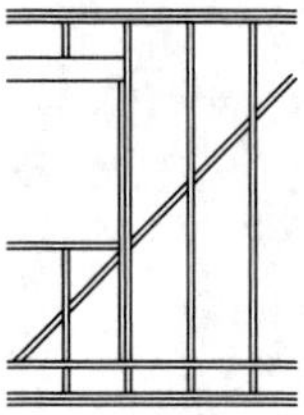

	Craft@Hrs	Unit	Material	Labor	Total
Using 2 x 4 lumber at	—	MBF	777.00	—	777.00
Using 2 x 6 lumber at	—	MBF	756.00	—	756.00
Using 1/2" gypsum wallboard at	—	SF	.42	—	.42
Using 5/8" gypsum wallboard at	—	SF	.41	—	.41
Interior wall assemblies					
2" x 4" stud walls with 1/2" gypsum drywall both sides, ready for painting					
Cost per square foot of wall	B1@.064	SF	1.48	2.17	3.65
Cost per running foot, for 8' high walls	B1@.512	LF	11.90	17.30	29.20
2" x 4" stud walls with 1/2" gypsum drywall one side, ready for painting					
Cost per square foot of wall	B1@.046	SF	1.07	1.56	2.63
Cost per running foot, for 8' high walls	B1@.368	LF	8.55	12.50	21.05
2" x 4" stud walls with 5/8" gypsum fire rated drywall both sides, ready for painting					
Cost per square foot of wall	B1@.068	SF	1.48	2.30	3.78
Cost per running foot, for 8' high walls	B1@.544	LF	11.80	18.40	30.20

	Craft@Hrs	Unit	Material	Labor	Total
2" x 4" stud walls with 5/8" gypsum fire rated drywall one side, ready for painting					
Cost per square foot of wall	B1@.048	SF	1.06	1.62	2.68
Cost per running foot, for 8' high walls	B1@.384	LF	8.52	13.00	21.52
2" x 6" stud walls with 1/2" gypsum drywall both sides, ready for painting					
Cost per square foot of wall	B1@.072	SF	1.81	2.44	4.25
Cost per running foot, for 8' high walls	B1@.576	LF	14.40	19.50	33.90
2" x 6" stud walls with 1/2" gypsum drywall one side, ready for painting					
Cost per square foot of wall	B1@.054	SF	1.39	1.83	3.22
Cost per running foot, for 8' high walls	B1@.432	LF	11.10	14.60	25.70
2" x 6" stud walls with 5/8" gypsum fire rated drywall both sides, ready for painting					
Cost per square foot of wall	B1@.076	SF	1.80	2.57	4.37
Cost per running foot, for 8' high walls	B1@.608	LF	14.40	20.60	35.00
2" x 6" stud walls with 5/8" gypsum fire rated drywall one side, ready for painting					
Cost per square foot of wall	B1@.056	SF	1.39	1.90	3.29
Cost per running foot, for 8' high walls	B1@.448	LF	11.10	15.20	26.30
Exterior wall assemblies					
2" x 4" stud walls with drywall interior, wood siding exterior, 1/2" gypsum drywall inside face ready for painting, over 3-1/2" R-13 insulation with 5/8" thick rough sawn T-1-11 exterior grade plywood siding on the outside face.					
Using 5/8" rough sawn T-1-11 siding at	—	MSF	1,130.00	—	1,130.00
Cost per square foot of wall	B1@.068	SF	2.72	2.30	5.02
Cost per running foot, for 8' high walls	B1@.544	LF	21.80	18.40	40.20
2" x 6" stud walls with drywall interior, wood siding exterior, same construction as above, except with 6-1/4" R-19 insulation					
Cost per square foot of wall	B1@.077	SF	3.26	2.61	5.87
Cost per running foot, for 8' high walls	B1@.616	LF	26.10	20.90	47.00
2" x 4" stud walls with drywall interior, 1/2" gypsum drywall on inside face ready for painting, over 3-1/2" R-11 insulation with 1" x 6" southern yellow pine drop siding, D grade, 1.19 BF per SF at 5-1/4" exposure on the outside face.					
Using D grade yellow pine drop siding at	—	MSF	2,910.00	—	2,910.00
Cost per square foot of wall	B1@.074	SF	4.50	2.50	7.00
Cost per running foot, for 8' high wall	B1@.592	LF	36.00	20.00	56.00
2" x 6" stud walls with drywall interior, 1" x 6" drop siding exterior, same construction as above, except with 6-1/4" R-19 insulation					
Cost per square foot of wall	B1@.083	SF	5.04	2.81	7.85
Cost per running foot, for 8' high wall	B1@.664	LF	40.30	22.50	62.80
2" x 4" stud walls with drywall interior, stucco exterior, 1/2" gypsum drywall on inside face ready for painting, over 3-1/2" R-11 insulation and a three-coat exterior plaster (stucco) finish with integral color on the outside face					
Cost per square foot of wall	B1@.050	SF	4.74	1.69	6.43
Cost per running foot, for 8' high wall	B1@.400	LF	37.90	13.50	51.40
2" x 6" stud walls with drywall interior, stucco exterior, same construction as above, except with 6-1/4" R-19 insulation					
Cost per square foot of wall	B1@.059	SF	5.28	2.00	7.28
Cost per running foot, for 8' high wall	B1@.472	LF	42.20	16.00	58.20
Add for different type gypsum board					
1/2" or 5/8" moisture resistant greenboard					
Cost per SF, greenboard per side, add	—	SF	.13	—	.13
1/2" or 5/8" moisture resistant greenboard					
Cost per running foot per side 8' high	—	LF	1.01	—	1.01
5/8" thick fire rated type X gypsum drywall					
Cost per SF, per side, add	—	SF	.08	—	.08
5/8" thick fire rated type X gypsum drywall					
Cost per running foot per side 8' high	—	LF	.60	—	.60

	Craft@Hrs	Unit	Material	Labor	Total

Ceiling Assemblies Costs for wood framed ceiling joists with ceiling finish and fiberglass insulation, based on performing the work at the construction site. These costs include the ceiling joists, ceiling finish as described, blocking, nails and 3-1/2" thick R-11 fiberglass insulation batts between the ceiling joists. Figures in parentheses indicate board feet per square foot of ceiling framing including end joists and typical header joists. No beams included. Ceiling joists and blocking are based on standard and better grade lumber. Costs shown are per square foot of area covered and include normal waste. Deduct for openings over 25 SF.

	Craft@Hrs	Unit	Material	Labor	Total
Ceiling joists with 5/8" regular gypsum drywall taped and sanded smooth finish, ready for paint					
Using 2" x 4" at	—	MBF	777.00	—	777.00
Using 2" x 6" at	—	MBF	759.00	—	759.00
Using 2" x 8" at	—	MBF	776.00	—	776.00
2" x 4" ceiling joists at 16" on center (.59 BF per SF), with insulation and 1/2" gypsum drywall	B1@.053	SF	1.64	1.79	3.43
2" x 6" ceiling joists at 16" on center (.88 BF per SF), with insulation and 1/2" gypsum drywall	B1@.055	SF	1.97	1.86	3.83
2" x 8" ceiling joists at 16" on center (1.17 BF per SF), with insulation and 1/2" gypsum drywall	B1@.057	SF	2.34	1.93	4.27
For spray applied plaster finish (sometimes called "popcorn" or "cottage cheese" texture)					
Add for ceiling texture	DT@.011	SF	.02	.40	.42
For different type gypsum drywall with taped and sanded smooth finish, ready for paint					
5/8" moisture resistant greenboard, add	—	SF	.10	—	.10
5/8" ultralight, add	—	SF	.02	—	.02
5/8" fire rated "C", add	—	SF	.08	—	.08
For different ceiling joist center to center dimensions					
2" x 4" ceiling joists					
12" on center, add	B1@.004	SF	.15	.14	.29
20" on center, deduct	—	SF	-.09	-.07	-.16
24" on center, deduct	—	SF	-.13	-.10	-.23
2" x 6" ceiling joists					
12" on center, add	B1@.006	SF	.20	.20	.40
20" on center, deduct	—	SF	-.12	-.07	-.19
24" on center, deduct	—	SF	-.19	-.10	-.29
2" x 8" ceiling joists					
12" on center, add	B1@.006	SF	.28	.20	.48
20" on center, deduct	—	SF	-.16	-.07	-.23
24" on center, deduct	—	SF	-.26	-.10	-.36
For different type insulation					
Fiberglass batts					
6-1/4" thick R-19, add	—	SF	.29	—	.29
10" thick R-30, add	—	SF	.31	—	.31
Blown-in fiberglass					
8" thick R-19, add	—	SF	.38	—	.38

Roofing Assemblies Costs for wood framed roof assemblies with roof finish material as shown based on performing the work at the construction site. Costs shown include all material and labor required above the top plate or ledger on the supporting walls. These costs assume the supporting wall structure is in-place and suitable for the assembly described.

	Craft@Hrs	Unit	Material	Labor	Total
Flat roof assembly Based on using 2" x 12" joists Std & Btr grade at 16" on center including blocking, ripped strips and normal waste. The roof surface is built-up 3 ply asphalt consisting of 2 plies of 15 lb. felt hot mopped with a 90 lb. mineral-coated cap sheet.					
Using 2" x 12" joists at	—	MBF	881.00	—	881.00
Using 2" x 8" joists at	—	MBF	776.00	—	776.00
Using 1/2" CDX plywood at	—	MSF	726.00	—	726.00
Using 7/16" OSB at	—	MSF	384.00	—	384.00
Flat roof assembly as described above					
Framing, with plywood sheathing	B1@5.00	Sq	295.00	169.00	464.00
Framing, with OSB sheathing	B1@5.00	Sq	260.00	169.00	429.00
Built-up roofing, 3-ply and gravel	R1@2.15	Sq	107.00	77.40	184.40
Conventionally framed roof assemblies Based on straight gable type roof (no hips, valleys, or dormers) with 6" in 12" rise or less. Cost per 100 square feet of plan area under the roof, not actual roof surface area. Framing includes 2" x 8" common rafters Std & Btr grade at 24" on center. Cost includes blocking, ridge and normal bracing. Roof sheathing is either 7/16" OSB (oriented strand board) or 1/2" CDX plywood.					
Conventionally framed roof assembly. Select roof finish from below					
Framing, with plywood sheathing	B1@4.10	Sq	166.00	139.00	305.00
Framing, with OSB sheathing	B1@4.10	Sq	130.00	139.00	269.00
Add for built-up 3-ply finish roofing	R1@1.25	Sq	99.00	45.00	144.00
Add for composition shingle (Class C) roofing	R1@1.83	Sq	392.00	65.90	457.90
Add for asphalt shingle (Class A) roofing	R1@1.83	Sq	147.00	65.90	212.90
Framing, with no sheathing	B1@2.80	Sq	89.50	94.80	184.30
Add for 26 gauge steel roofing	R1@2.70	Sq	159.00	97.20	256.20
Add for gable studs					
2" x 4" spaced 16" OC (.54 BF per SF)	B1@.023	SF	.42	.78	1.20
Add for purlins (purling), Std & Btr, installed below roof rafters. Figures in parentheses indicate board feet per LF including 5% waste					
Using 2" x 8" joists at	—	MBF	776.00	—	776.00
2" x 8" (1.40 BF per LF)	B1@.023	LF	1.09	.78	1.87

Piecework, Rough Carpentry Rough carpentry on residential tracts is usually done by framing subcontractors who bid at piecework rates (such as per square foot of floor). The figures below list typical piecework rates for repetitive framing work and assume all materials are supplied to the framing subcontractor. No figures appear in the Craft@Hrs column because the work is done for a fixed price per square foot and the labor productivity can be expected to vary widely.

	Craft@Hrs	Unit	Material	Labor	Total
Layout and plating Piecework rates Lay out wall plates according to the plans (snap chalk lines for wall plates, mark location for studs, windows, doors and framing details), cut top and bottom plates and install bottom plates. Costs per square foot of floor (excluding garage).					
Custom or more complex jobs	—	SF	—	.27	.27
Larger job, longer runs	—	SF	—	.18	.18

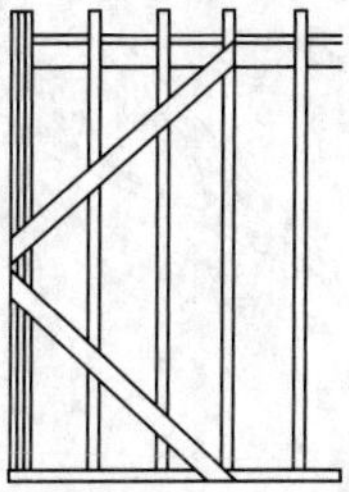

	Craft@Hrs	Unit	Material	Labor	Total
Wall framing Piecework rates Measure, cut, fit, assemble, and tip up walls, including studs, plates, cripples, let-in braces, trimmers and blocking. Costs per square foot of floor.					
Complex job, radius walls, rake walls	—	SF	—	.75	.75
Larger job, 8' high walls, fewer partitions	—	SF	—	.27	.27

	Craft@Hrs	Unit	Material	Labor	Total
Plumb and align framed walls Piecework rates					
Force walls into alignment. Adjust walls to vertical and install temporary wood braces as needed. Bracing plates includes shooting powder driven fasteners through wall plates. Based on accuracy to 3/16". Includes re-checking plumb and alignment when framing is done. Costs per square foot of floor.					
Small or complex job, brace walls and plates	—	SF	—	.24	.24
Larger job, fewer braces, walls only	—	SF	—	.14	.14
Sheathed walls, squared before lifting	—	SF	—	.08	.08
Floor joists or ceiling joists Piecework rates					
Lay out, cut and install floor or ceiling joists, including rim joists, doubled joists, straps, joist hangers, blocking at 8' OC and ceiling backing for drywall. Based on larger jobs with simple joist layouts set 16" OC and pre-cut blocking supplied by the general contractor. Add the cost of floor beams, if required. Costs per square foot of horizontal joist area. More complex jobs with shorter runs may cost 50% more.					
2" x 8" ceiling or floor joists	—	SF	—	.21	.21
2" x 10" ceiling or floor joists	—	SF	—	.24	.24
2" x 12" ceiling or floor joists	—	SF	—	.26	.26
2" x 14" ceiling or floor joists	—	SF	—	.30	.30
Add for 12" OC spacing	—	SF	—	.09	.09
Deduct for 20" OC spacing	—	SF	—	–.03	–.03
Deduct for 24" OC spacing	—	SF	—	–.06	–.06
Floor sheathing Piecework rates					
Lay out, cut, fit and install 5/8" or 3/4" tongue and groove plywood floor sheathing, including blocking as required. Based on nailing done with a pneumatic nailer and nails supplied by the general contractor. Costs per square foot of sheathing installed					
Smaller, cut-up job	—	SF	—	.24	.24
Larger job, longer runs	—	SF	—	.18	.18
Add for 1-1/8" sheathing	—	SF	—	.08	.08
Stair framing Piecework rates					
Lay out, cut, fit and install straight, "U"- or "L"-shaped 30" to 36" wide stairs made from plywood and 2" x 12" stringers set 16" OC. These costs include blocking in the adjacent stud wall and a 1" skirt board. Costs per 7-1/2" riser. Framing more complex stairs may cost up to $500 per flight.					
Small job, short runs	—	Ea	—	17.50	17.50
Larger job, longer runs	—	Ea	—	13.20	13.20
Add per 3' x 3' landing, including supports	—	Ea	—	45.10	45.10
Add for larger landings, including supports	—	Ea	—	112.00	112.00
Shear panels Piecework rates					
Lay out, cut, fit and install structural 3/8" or 1/2" OSB or plywood wall panels. These figures assume shear studs were set correctly by others and that panel nails are driven at 4" OC with a pneumatic nailer. Not including hold-down straps, posts, shear blocking or extra studs. Costs per 4' x 9' panel installed.					
Small job, many openings, 2nd floor	—	Ea	—	12.10	12.10
Larger job, few openings, 1st floor	—	Ea	—	7.46	7.46
Roof trusses Piecework rates					
Setting and nailing engineered gable and hip roof trusses 24" OC on prepared wall plates. These figures assume that lifting equipment is provided by the general contractor and that the truss supplier provides a fill package, spreader blocks for each plate and the ridge and jack rafters (if required). Includes installation of ceiling backing where required and catwalks at the bottom chord. Costs per square foot of plan area under the truss.					
Small job assumes multiple California fill between roof surfaces and understacking					
Small job, rake fill above a partition wall	—	SF	—	.65	.65
Larger job, little or no fill or understacking	—	SF	—	.36	.36

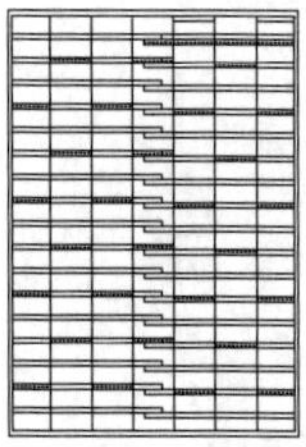
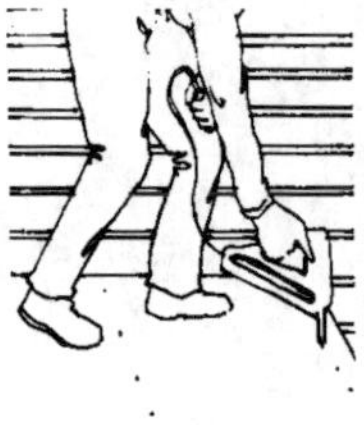
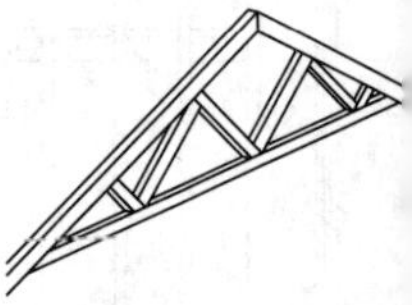

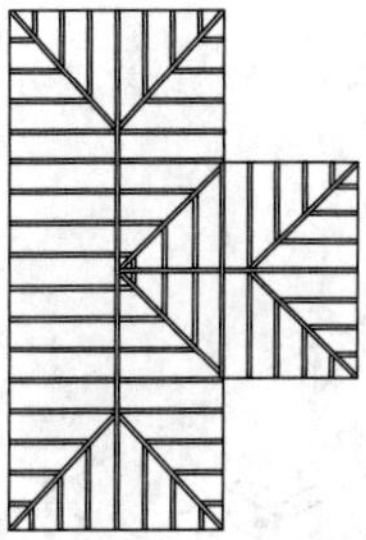

Conventional roof framing Piecework rates

Calculate lengths, lay out, cut and install 2" x 10" or 2" x 12" common, hip, valley and jack rafters on parallel and horizontal plates. Costs per square foot of plan area under the roof.

	Craft@Hrs	Unit	Material	Labor	Total
Small job, cut-up roof, few common rafters					
Rafters 12" OC	—	SF	—	1.35	1.35
Rafters 16" OC	—	SF	—	1.14	1.14
Rafters 20" OC	—	SF	—	.90	.90
Rafters 24" OC	—	SF	—	.65	.65
Larger job, longer runs, nearly all common rafters					
Rafters 12" OC	—	SF	—	.65	.65
Rafters 16" OC	—	SF	—	.58	.58
Rafters 20" OC	—	SF	—	.45	.45
Rafters 24" OC	—	SF	—	.37	.37
Add for slope over 6 in 12	—	SF	—	.22	.22
Deduct for 2" x 6" or 2" x 8" rafters	—	SF	—	-.08	-.08

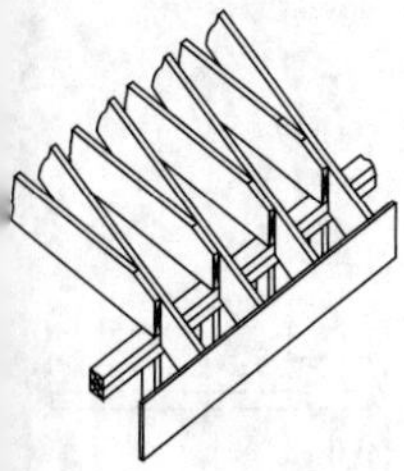

Fascia Piecework rates

Applied to rafter tails and as a barge rafter on gable ends. Includes trimming the rafter tails to the correct length and installing outlookers at gable ends. Costs per linear foot of 2" x 8" fascia installed.

	Craft@Hrs	Unit	Material	Labor	Total
Small job, short runs, with molding	—	LF	—	2.91	2.91
Larger job, longer runs	—	LF	—	1.67	1.67

Roof sheathing Piecework rates

Lay out, cut, fit and install 1/2" or 5/8" OSB or plywood roof sheathing, including blocking and 1" x 8" starter board on overhangs as required. Based on nailing done with a pneumatic nailer and nails supplied by the general contractor. Costs per square foot of sheathing installed.

	Craft@Hrs	Unit	Material	Labor	Total
Smaller, cut-up hip and valley job	—	SF	—	.25	.25
Larger job, longer runs	—	SF	—	.19	.19
Add for slope over 6 in 12	—	SF	—	.12	.12

Carpentry Cost, Detailed Breakdown This section is arranged in the order of construction. Material costs shown here can be adjusted to reflect your actual lumber cost: divide your actual lumber cost (per MBF) by the cost listed (per MBF). Then multiply the cost in the material column by this adjustment factor. No waste included.

Lally columns (Residential adjustable basement column) 7' 9" to 8' 1", steel tube

	Craft@Hrs	Unit	Material	Labor	Total
Column installation, to 12' high	B1@.458	Ea	185.00	15.50	200.50

Precast pier blocks Posts set on precast concrete pier block, including pier block with anchor placed on existing grade, temporary reusable 1" x 6" bracing (8 LF) and stakes (2). Cost is for each post set. Add for excavation if required

	Craft@Hrs	Unit	Material	Labor	Total
Heights to 8', cost of post not included	BL@.166	Ea	7.93	5.03	12.96

Pier pads 2" x 6", treated, #2 & Btr

	Craft@Hrs	Unit	Material	Labor	Total
Using #2 & Btr treated lumber at	—	MBF	1,160.00	—	1,160.00
1.10 BF per LF	B1@.034	LF	1.28	1.15	1.15

Posts 4" x 4", material costs include 10% waste (1.47 BF per LF). See also Lally columns above and Posts in the Lumber section

	Craft@Hrs	Unit	Material	Labor	Total
Fir, rough Std & Btr, K.D.	—	MBF	950.00	—	950.00
Fir, rough Std & Btr, K.D. 4" x 4"	—	LF	1.40	—	1.40
Red cedar, rough green constr.	—	MBF	2,810.00	—	2,810.00
Red cedar, rough green constr.	—	LF	4.13	—	4.13
Redwood, S4S construction heart	—	MBF	2,520.00	—	2,520.00

	Craft@Hrs	Unit	Material	Labor	Total
Redwood, S4S construction heart	—	LF	3.71	—	3.71
Southern yellow pine #2, pressure treated	—	MBF	1,250.00	—	1,250.00
Southern yellow pine #2, pressure treated	—	LF	1.84	—	1.84

Girders Standard and better lumber, first floor work. Figures in parentheses show board feet per linear foot of girder, including 7% waste

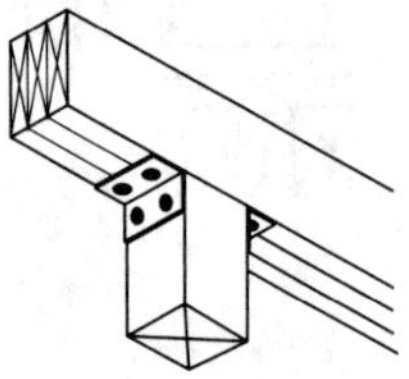

	Craft@Hrs	Unit	Material	Labor	Total
4" x 6", per MBF	—	MBF	918.00	—	918.00
4" x 8", 10", 12", per MBF	—	MBF	965.00	—	965.00
6" x 6", per MBF	—	MBF	1,680.00	—	1,680.00
6" x 8", 10", 12", 8" x 8", per MBF	—	MBF	1,680.00	—	1,680.00
4" x 6" (2.15 BF per LF)	B1@.034	LF	1.97	1.15	3.12
4" x 8" (2.85 BF per LF)	B1@.045	LF	2.75	1.52	4.27
4" x 10" (3.58 BF per LF)	B1@.057	LF	3.45	1.93	5.38
4" x 12" (4.28 BF per LF)	B1@.067	LF	4.13	2.27	6.40
6" x 6" (3.21 BF per LF)	B1@.051	LF	5.39	1.73	7.12
6" x 8" (4.28 BF per LF)	B1@.067	LF	7.18	2.27	9.45
6" x 10" (5.35 BF per LF)	B1@.083	LF	8.98	2.81	11.79
6" x 12" (6.42 BF per LF)	B1@.098	LF	10.80	3.32	14.12
8" x 8" (5.71 BF per LF)	B1@.088	LF	9.60	2.98	12.58

Sill plates (At foundation) SYP #2 pressure treated lumber, drilled and installed with foundation bolts at 48" OC, no bolts, nuts or washers included. See also plates in this section. Figures in parentheses indicate board feet per LF of foundation, including 5% waste and wolmanized treatment.

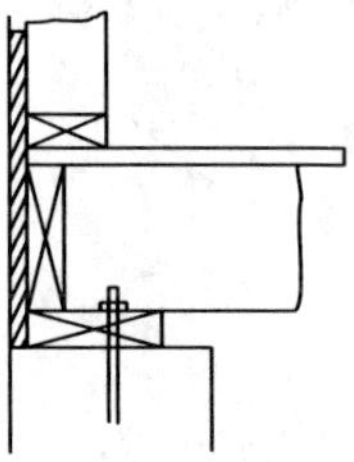

	Craft@Hrs	Unit	Material	Labor	Total
Sill plates, per MBF	—	MBF	1,050.00	—	1,050.00
2" x 3" (.53 BF per LF)	B1@.020	LF	.48	.68	1.16
2" x 4" (.70 BF per LF)	B1@.023	LF	.81	.78	1.59
2" x 6" (1.05 BF per LF)	B1@.024	LF	1.07	.81	1.88
2" x 8" (1.40 BF per LF)	B1@.031	LF	1.36	1.05	2.41

Floor joists Per SF of area covered. Figures in parentheses indicate board feet per square foot of floor including box or band joist, typical double joists, and 6% waste. No beams, blocking or bridging included. Deduct for openings over 25 SF. Costs shown are based on a job with 1,000 SF of area covered. For scheduling purposes, estimate that a two-man crew can complete 750 SF of area per 8-hour day for 12" center to center framing; 925 SF for 16" OC; 1,100 SF for 20" OC; or 1,250 SF for 24" OC.

	Craft@Hrs	Unit	Material	Labor	Total
2" x 6" Std & Btr					
2" x 6" floor joists, per MBF	—	MBF	759.00	—	759.00
12" centers (1.28 BF per SF)	B1@.021	SF	.97	.71	1.68
16" centers (1.02 BF per SF)	B1@.017	SF	.77	.58	1.35
20" centers (.88 BF per SF)	B1@.014	SF	.67	.47	1.14
24" centers (.73 BF per SF)	B1@.012	SF	.55	.41	.96
2" x 8" Std & Btr					
2" x 8" floor joists, per MBF	—	MBF	776.00	—	776.00
12" centers (1.71 BF per SF)	B1@.023	SF	1.33	.78	2.11
16" centers (1.36 BF per SF)	B1@.018	SF	1.06	.61	1.67
20" centers (1.17 BF per SF)	B1@.015	SF	.91	.51	1.42
24" centers (1.03 BF per SF)	B1@.013	SF	.80	.44	1.24
2" x 10" Std & Btr					
2" x 10" floor joists, per MBF	—	MBF	794.00	—	794.00
12" centers (2.14 BF per SF)	B1@.025	SF	1.70	.85	2.55
16" centers (1.71 BF per SF)	B1@.020	SF	1.36	.68	2.04
20" centers (1.48 BF per SF)	B1@.016	SF	1.17	.54	1.71
24" centers (1.30 BF per SF)	B1@.014	SF	1.03	.47	1.50

	Craft@Hrs	Unit	Material	Labor	Total
2" x 12" Std & Btr					
2" x 12" floor joists, per MBF	—	MBF	881.00	—	881.00
12" centers (2.56 BF per SF)	B1@.026	SF	2.25	.88	3.13
16" centers (2.05 BF per SF)	B1@.021	SF	1.81	.71	2.52
20" centers (1.77 BF per SF)	B1@.017	SF	1.56	.58	2.14
24" centers (1.56 BF per SF)	B1@.015	SF	1.37	.51	1.88

Floor joist wood, TJI truss type Suitable for residential use, 50 PSF floor load design. Costs shown are per square foot (SF) of floor area, based on joists at 16" OC, for a job with 1,000 SF of floor area. Figure 1.22 SF of floor area for each LF of joist. Add the cost of beams, supports and blocking. For scheduling purposes, estimate that a two-man crew can install 900 to 950 SF of joists in an 8-hour day.

	Craft@Hrs	Unit	Material	Labor	Total
9-1/2" TJI/15	B1@.017	SF	2.74	.58	3.32
11-7/8" TJI/15	B1@.017	SF	3.01	.58	3.59
14" TJI/35	B1@.018	SF	4.39	.61	5.00
16" TJI/35	B1@.018	SF	4.78	.61	5.39

Bridging or blocking Installed between 2" x 6" thru 2" x 12" joists. Costs shown are per each set of cross bridges or per each block for solid bridging, and include normal waste. The spacing between the bridging or blocking, sometimes called a "bay," depends on job requirements. Labor costs assume bridging is cut to size on site.

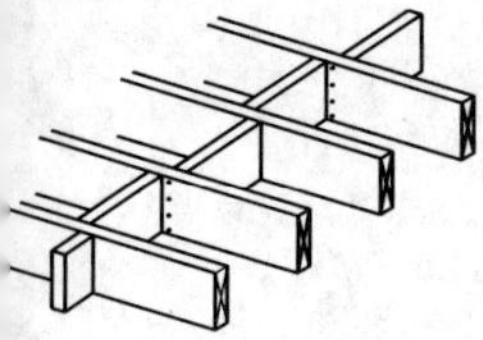

	Craft@Hrs	Unit	Material	Labor	Total
1" x 4" cross					
Joist bridging, per MBF	—	MBF	2,020.00	—	2,020.00
Joists on 12" centers	B1@.034	Ea	1.01	1.15	2.16
Joists on 16" centers	B1@.034	Ea	1.38	1.15	2.53
Joists on 20" centers	B1@.034	Ea	1.75	1.15	2.90
Joists on 24" centers	B1@.034	Ea	2.13	1.15	3.28
2" x 6" solid, Std & Btr					
2" x 6" blocking, per MBF	—	MBF	759.00	—	759.00
Joists on 12" centers	B1@.042	Ea	.83	1.42	2.25
Joists on 16" centers	B1@.042	Ea	1.11	1.42	2.53
Joists on 20" centers	B1@.042	Ea	1.39	1.42	2.81
Joists on 24" centers	B1@.042	Ea	1.67	1.42	3.09
2" x 8" solid, Std & Btr					
2" x 8" blocking, per MBF	—	MBF	776.00	—	776.00
Joists on 12" centers	B1@.042	Ea	1.14	1.42	2.56
Joists on 16" centers	B1@.042	Ea	1.52	1.42	2.94
Joists on 20" centers	B1@.042	Ea	1.90	1.42	3.32
Joists on 24" centers	B1@.042	Ea	2.28	1.42	3.70
2" x 10" solid, Std & Btr					
2" x 10" blocking, per MBF	—	MBF	794.00	—	794.00
Joists on 12" centers	B1@.057	Ea	1.45	1.93	3.38
Joists on 16" centers	B1@.057	Ea	1.94	1.93	3.87
Joists on 20" centers	B1@.057	Ea	2.42	1.93	4.35
Joists on 24" centers	B1@.057	Ea	2.91	1.93	4.84

	Craft@Hrs	Unit	Material	Labor	Total
2" x 12" solid, Std & Btr					
2" x 12" blocking, per MBF	—	MBF	881.00	—	881.00
Joists on 12" centers	B1@.057	Ea	1.94	1.93	3.87
Joists on 16" centers	B1@.057	Ea	2.58	1.93	4.51
Joists on 20" centers	B1@.057	Ea	3.23	1.93	5.16
Joists on 24" centers	B1@.057	Ea	3.88	1.93	5.81
Steel, no nail type, cross					
Snap-on joist bridging	B1@.020	Ea	2.30	.68	2.98

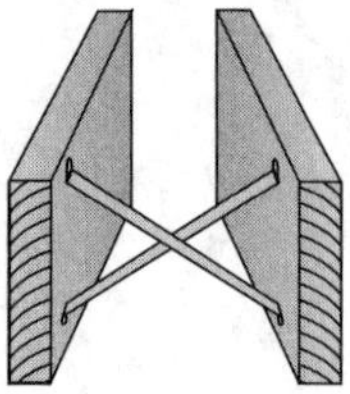

Subflooring

	Craft@Hrs	Unit	Material	Labor	Total
Board sheathing, 1" x 6" #3 & Btr (1.18 BF per SF)					
Board sheathing, per MBF	—	MBF	2,930.00	—	2,930.00
With 12% shrinkage, 5% waste & nails	B1@.020	SF	3.46	.68	4.14
Add for diagonal patterns	B1@.001	SF	.35	.03	.38
Plywood sheathing, CD standard exterior grade. Material costs shown include 5% for waste & fasteners					
3/8"	B1@.011	SF	.46	.37	.83
1/2"	B1@.012	SF	.76	.41	1.17
5/8"	B1@.012	SF	.77	.41	1.18
3/4"	B1@.013	SF	.89	.44	1.33
OSB sheathing, Material costs shown include 5% for waste & fasteners					
3/8"	B1@.011	SF	.43	.37	.80
7/16"	B1@.011	SF	.40	.37	.77
1/2"	B1@.012	SF	.56	.41	.97
5/8"	B1@.012	SF	.58	.41	.99
3/4"	B1@.014	SF	.71	.47	1.18
7/8"	B1@.014	SF	1.40	.47	1.87
1"	B1@.015	SF	2.04	.51	2.55
Engineered floating subfloor, 2' x 2' panels, trade name DRIcore, resilient engineered wood core with a water-resistant polyethylene membrane on the underside. www.dricore.com					
Per SF costs including 10% for waste	B1@.020	SF	1.86	.68	2.54

Plates (Wall plates) Std & Btr, untreated. For pressure treated plates, see also Sill Plates in this section. Figures in parentheses indicate board feet per LF. Costs shown include 10% for waste and nails

	Craft@Hrs	Unit	Material	Labor	Total
2" x 3" wall plates, per MBF	—	MBF	912.00	—	912.00
2" x 4" wall plates, per MBF	—	MBF	777.00	—	777.00
2" x 6" wall plates, per MBF	—	MBF	759.00	—	759.00
2" x 8" wall plates, per MBF	—	MBF	776.00	—	776.00
2" x 3" (.55 BF per LF)	B1@.010	LF	.55	.34	.89
2" x 4" (.73 BF per LF)	B1@.012	LF	.62	.41	1.03
2" x 6" (1.10 BF per LF)	B1@.018	LF	.92	.61	1.53
2" x 8" (1.40 BF per LF)	B1@.020	LF	1.19	.68	1.87

Studding Per square foot of wall area. Do not subtract for openings less than 16' wide. Figures in parentheses indicate typical board feet per SF of wall area, measured on one side, and include normal waste. Add for each corner and partition from below. Costs include studding, nails. Add for plates from the section above and also, door and window opening framing, backing, let-in bracing, fire blocking, and sheathing for shear walls from the sections that follow. Labor includes layout, plumb and align.

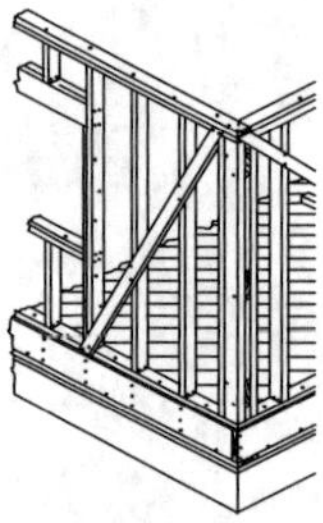

	Craft@Hrs	Unit	Material	Labor	Total
2" x 3", Std & Btr					
2" x 3" studs, 16" centers, per MBF	—	MBF	912.00	—	912.00
12" centers (.55 BF per SF)	B1@.024	SF	.50	.81	1.31

	Craft@Hrs	Unit	Material	Labor	Total
16" centers (.41 BF per SF)	B1@.018	SF	.37	.61	.98
20" centers (.33 BF per SF)	B1@.015	SF	.30	.51	.81
24" centers (.28 BF per SF)	B1@.012	SF	.26	.41	.67
Add for each corner or partition	B1@.083	Ea	11.80	2.81	14.61
2" x 4", Std & Btr					
2" x 4" studs, 16" centers, per MBF	—	MBF	777.00	—	777.00
12" centers (.73 BF per SF)	B1@.031	SF	.57	1.05	1.62
16" centers (.54 BF per SF)	B1@.023	SF	.42	.78	1.20
20" centers (.45 BF per SF)	B1@.020	SF	.35	.68	1.03
24" centers (.37 BF per SF)	B1@.016	SF	.29	.54	.83
Add for each corner or partition	B1@.083	Ea	13.20	2.81	16.01
2" x 6", Std & Btr					
2" x 6" studs, 24" centers, per MBF	—	MBF	759.00	—	759.00
12" centers (1.10 BF per SF)	B1@.044	SF	.83	1.49	2.32
16" centers (.83 BF per SF)	B1@.033	SF	.63	1.12	1.75
20" centers (.67 BF per SF)	B1@.027	SF	.51	.91	1.42
24" centers (.55 BF per SF)	B1@.022	SF	.42	.74	1.16
Add for each corner or partition	B1@.083	Ea	18.10	2.81	20.91
4" x 4", Std & Btr					
Installed in wall framing, with 10% waste	B1@.064	LF	1.39	2.17	3.56

Door opening framing In wall studs, based on walls 8' in height. Costs shown are per each door opening and include header of appropriate size, double vertical studs each side of the opening less than 8' wide (triple vertical studs each side of openings 8' wide or wider), cripples, blocking, nails and normal waste. Width shown is size of finished opening. Figures in parentheses indicate header size

	Craft@Hrs	Unit	Material	Labor	Total
2" x 4" wall studs, Std & Btr, opening size as shown					
2" x 4" wall studs, per MBF	—	MBF	777.00	—	777.00
4" x 4" and 4" x 6" headers, per MBF	—	MBF	950.00	—	950.00
4" x 8", 10", 12" and 14" headers, per MBF	—	MBF	965.00	—	965.00
To 3' wide (4" x 4" header)	B1@.830	Ea	23.20	28.10	51.30
Over 3' to 4' wide (4" x 6" header)	B1@1.11	Ea	28.20	37.60	65.80
Over 4' to 5' wide (4" x 6" header)	B1@1.39	Ea	30.90	47.10	78.00
Over 5' to 6' wide (4" x 8" header)	B1@1.66	Ea	37.20	56.20	93.40
Over 6' to 8' wide (4" x 10" header)	B1@1.94	Ea	57.90	65.70	123.60
Over 8' to 10' wide (4" x 12" header)	B1@1.94	Ea	72.00	65.70	137.70
Over 10' to 12' wide (4" x 14" header)	B1@2.22	Ea	88.20	75.10	163.30
Add per foot of height for 4" walls over 8' in height	—	LF	3.11	—	3.11
2" x 6" wall studs, Std & Btr, opening size as shown					
2" x 6" wall studs, per MBF	—	MBF	759.00	—	759.00
6" x 4" headers, per MBF	—	MBF	918.00	—	918.00
6" x 8", 10", 12" and 14" headers, per MBF	—	MBF	1,680.00	—	1,680.00
To 3' wide (6" x 4" header)	B1@1.11	Ea	35.70	37.60	73.30
Over 3' to 4' wide (6" x 6" header)	B1@1.39	Ea	46.30	47.10	93.40
Over 4' to 5' wide (6" x 6" header)	B1@1.66	Ea	52.10	56.20	108.30
Over 5' to 6' wide (6" x 8" header)	B1@1.94	Ea	67.90	65.70	133.60
Over 6' to 8' wide (6" x 10" header)	B1@2.22	Ea	108.00	75.10	183.10
Over 8' to 10' wide (6" x 12" header)	B1@2.22	Ea	143.00	75.10	218.10
Over 10' to 12' wide (6" x 14" header)	B1@2.50	Ea	184.00	84.60	268.60
Add per foot of height for 6" walls over 8' in height	—	LF	4.55	—	4.55

Window opening framing In wall studs, based on walls 8' in height. Costs shown are per window opening and include header of appropriate size, sub-sill plate (double sub-sill if opening is 8' wide or wider), double vertical studs each side of openings less than 8' wide (triple vertical studs each side of openings 8' wide or wider), top and bottom cripples, blocking, nails and normal waste. Figures in parentheses indicate header size.

	Craft@Hrs	Unit	Material	Labor	Total
2" x 4" wall studs, Std & Btr, opening size shown is width of finished opening					
2" x 4" wall studs, per MBF	—	MBF	777.00	—	777.00
4" x 4" and 4" x 6" headers, per MBF	—	MBF	918.00	—	918.00
4" x 8", 10", 12" and 14" headers, per MBF	—	MBF	965.00	—	965.00
To 2' wide (4" x 4" header)	B1@1.00	Ea	21.10	33.90	55.00
Over 2' to 3' wide (4" x 4" header)	B1@1.17	Ea	26.20	39.60	65.80
Over 3' to 4' wide (4" x 6" header)	B1@1.45	Ea	32.10	49.10	81.20
Over 4' to 5' wide (4" x 6" header)	B1@1.73	Ea	35.80	58.60	94.40
Over 5' to 6' wide (4" x 8" header)	B1@2.01	Ea	43.40	68.00	111.40
Over 6' to 7' wide (4" x 8" header)	B1@2.29	Ea	55.30	77.50	132.80
Over 7' to 8' wide (4" x 10" header)	B1@2.57	Ea	66.10	87.00	153.10
Over 8' to 10' wide (4" x 12" header)	B1@2.57	Ea	82.30	87.00	169.30
Over 10' to 12' wide (4" x 14" header)	B1@2.85	Ea	107.00	96.50	203.50
Add per foot of height for walls over 8' high	—	LF	3.11	—	3.11
2" x 6" wall studs, Std & Btr, opening size as shown					
2" x 6" wall studs, per MBF	—	MBF	759.00	—	759.00
4" x 4" and 6" x 4" headers, per MBF	—	MBF	918.00	—	918.00
6" x 6", 8", 10", 12" and 14" headers, per MBF	—	MBF	1,680.00	—	1,680.00
To 2' wide (4 x 4)	B1@1.17	Ea	26.10	39.60	65.70
Over 2' to 3' wide (6" x 4" header)	B1@1.45	Ea	33.20	49.10	82.30
Over 3' to 4' wide (6" x 6" header)	B1@1.73	Ea	50.40	58.60	109.00
Over 4' to 5' wide (6" x 6" header)	B1@2.01	Ea	59.90	68.00	127.90
Over 5' to 6' wide (6" x 8" header)	B1@2.29	Ea	74.00	77.50	151.50
Over 6' to 8' wide (6" x 10" header)	B1@2.85	Ea	116.00	96.50	212.50
Over 8' to 10' wide (6" x 12" header)	B1@2.85	Ea	158.00	96.50	254.50
Over 8' to 12' wide (6" x 14" header)	B1@3.13	Ea	203.00	106.00	309.00
Add per foot of height for 6" walls over 8' high	—	LF	4.55	—	4.55

Bracing See also sheathing for plywood bracing and shear panels

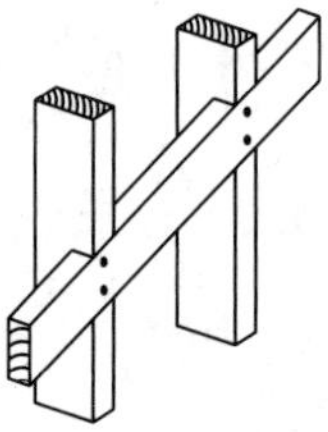

	Craft@Hrs	Unit	Material	Labor	Total
Let-in wall bracing, using standard and better lumber					
1" x 4"	B1@.021	LF	.77	.71	1.48
1" x 6"	B1@.027	LF	1.12	.91	2.03
2" x 4"	B1@.035	LF	.52	1.18	1.70
Steel strap bracing, 1-1/4" wide					
9'6" or 11'6" lengths	B1@.010	LF	.68	.34	1.02
Steel "V" bracing, 3/4" x 3/4"					
9'6" or 11'6" lengths	B1@.010	LF	1.04	.34	1.38
Temporary wood frame wall bracing, assumes salvage at 50% and 3 uses					
1" x 4" Std & Btr	B1@.006	LF	.19	.20	.39
1" x 6" Std & Btr	B1@.010	LF	.28	.34	.62
2" x 4" utility	B1@.012	LF	.13	.41	.54
2" x 6" utility	B1@.018	LF	.19	.61	.80

	Craft@Hrs	Unit	Material	Labor	Total
Fireblocks Installed in wood frame walls, per LF of wall to be blocked. Figures in parentheses indicate board feet of fire blocking per linear foot of wall including 10% waste. See also Bridging and Backing and Nailers in this section					
2" x 3" blocking, Std & Btr					
2" x 3" fireblocks, 16" centers, per MBF	—	MBF	912.00	—	912.00
12" OC members (.48 BF per LF)	B1@.016	LF	.44	.54	.98
16" OC members (.50 BF per LF)	B1@.015	LF	.46	.51	.97
20" OC members (.51 BF per LF)	B1@.012	LF	.47	.41	.88
24" OC members (.52 BF per LF)	B1@.010	LF	.47	.34	.81
2" x 4" blocking, Std & Btr					
2" x 4" fireblocks, 16" centers, per MBF	—	MBF	777.00	—	777.00
12" OC members (.64 BF per LF)	B1@.020	LF	.50	.68	1.18
16" OC members (.67 BF per LF)	B1@.015	LF	.52	.51	1.03
20" OC members (.68 BF per LF)	B1@.012	LF	.53	.41	.94
24" OC members (.69 BF per LF)	B1@.010	LF	.54	.34	.88
2" x 6" blocking, Std & Btr					
2" x 6" fireblocks, 24" centers, per MBF	—	MBF	759.00	—	759.00
12" OC members (.96 BF per LF)	B1@.021	LF	.73	.71	1.44
16" OC members (1.00 BF per LF)	B1@.016	LF	.76	.54	1.30
20" OC members (1.02 BF per LF)	B1@.012	LF	.77	.41	1.18
24" OC members (1.03 BF per LF)	B1@.010	LF	.78	.34	1.12
Beams Std & Btr. Installed over wall openings and around floor, ceiling and roof openings or where a flush beam is called out in the plans, including 10% waste. Do not use these beams for door or window headers in framed walls, use door or window opening framing assemblies.					
2" x 6" beams, per MBF	—	MBF	759.00	—	759.00
2" x 8" beams, per MBF	—	MBF	776.00	—	776.00
2" x 10" beams, per MBF	—	MBF	794.00	—	794.00
2" x 12" beams, per MBF	—	MBF	881.00	—	881.00
4" x 6" beams, per MBF	—	MBF	918.00	—	918.00
4" x 8", 10", 12", 14" beams, per MBF	—	MBF	965.00	—	965.00
6" x 6", 8", 10", 12", 14" beams, per MBF	—	MBF	1,680.00	—	1,680.00
2" x 6" (1.10 BF per LF)	B1@.028	LF	.83	.95	1.78
2" x 8" (1.47 BF per LF)	B1@.037	LF	1.14	1.25	2.39
2" x 10" (1.83 BF per LF)	B1@.046	LF	1.45	1.56	3.01
2" x 12" (2.20 BF per LF)	B1@.057	LF	1.94	1.93	3.87
4" x 6" (2.20 BF per LF)	B1@.057	LF	2.02	1.93	3.95
4" x 8" (2.93 BF per LF)	B1@.073	LF	2.83	2.47	5.30
4" x 10" (3.67 BF per LF)	B1@.094	LF	3.54	3.18	6.72
4" x 12" (4.40 BF per LF)	B1@.112	LF	4.24	3.79	8.03
4" x 14" (5.13 BF per LF)	B1@.115	LF	4.95	3.89	8.84
6" x 6" (3.30 BF per LF)	B1@.060	LF	5.54	2.03	7.57
6" x 8" (4.40 BF per LF)	B1@.080	LF	7.39	2.71	10.10
6" x 10" (5.50 BF per LF)	B1@.105	LF	9.23	3.55	12.78
6" x 12" (6.60 BF per LF)	B1@.115	LF	11.10	3.89	14.99
6" x 14" (7.70 BF per LF)	B1@.120	LF	12.90	4.06	16.96
Posts S4S, green. Posts not in wall framing. Material costs include 10% waste. For scheduling purposes, estimate that a two-man crew can complete 100 to 125 LF per 8-hour day.					
4" x 4", 4" x 6" posts, per MBF	—	MBF	950.00	—	950.00
4" x 8" to 4" x 12" posts, per MBF	—	MBF	965.00	—	965.00
6" x 6" to 8" x 12" posts, per MBF	—	MBF	1,680.00	—	1,680.00

	Craft@Hrs	Unit	Material	Labor	Total
4" x 4" per LF	B1@.110	LF	1.39	3.72	5.11
4" x 6" per LF	B1@.120	LF	2.09	4.06	6.15
4" x 8" per LF	B1@.140	LF	2.83	4.74	7.57
4" x 10" per LF	B1@.143	LF	3.54	4.84	8.38
4" x 12" per LF	B1@.145	LF	4.24	4.91	9.15
6" x 6" per LF	B1@.145	LF	5.54	4.91	10.45
6" x 8" per LF	B1@.145	LF	6.10	4.91	11.01
6" x 10" per LF	B1@.147	LF	9.23	4.98	14.21
6" x 12" per LF	B1@.150	LF	11.10	5.08	16.18
8" x 8" per LF	B1@.150	LF	9.85	5.08	14.93
8" x 10" per LF	B1@.155	LF	12.30	5.25	17.55
8" x 12" per LF	B1@.166	LF	14.80	5.62	20.42

Ceiling joists and soffits Per SF of area covered. Figures in parentheses indicate board feet per square foot of ceiling including end joists, header joists, and 5% waste. No beams, bridging, blocking, or ledger strips included. Deduct for openings over 25 SF. Costs shown are based on a job with 1,000 SF of area covered. For scheduling purposes, estimate that a two-man crew can complete 650 SF of area per 8-hour day for 12" center to center framing; 800 SF for 16" OC; 950 SF for 20" OC; or 1,100 SF for 24" OC.

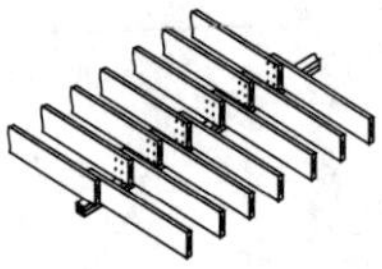

	Craft@Hrs	Unit	Material	Labor	Total
2" x 4", Std & Btr grade					
2" x 4" ceiling joists, per MBF	—	MBF	777.00	—	777.00
12" centers (.78 BF per SF)	B1@.026	SF	.61	.88	1.49
16" centers (.59 BF per SF)	B1@.020	SF	.46	.68	1.14
20" centers (.48 BF per SF)	B1@.016	SF	.37	.54	.91
24" centers (.42 BF per SF)	B1@.014	SF	.33	.47	.80
2" x 6", Std & Btr grade					
2" x 6" ceiling joists, per MBF	—	MBF	759.00	—	759.00
12" centers (1.15 BF per SF)	B1@.026	SF	.88	.87	1.75
16" centers (.88 BF per SF)	B1@.020	SF	.67	.68	1.35
20" centers (.72 BF per SF)	B1@.016	SF	.55	.54	1.09
24" centers (.63 BF per SF)	B1@.014	SF	.48	.47	.95
2" x 8", Std & Btr grade					
2" x 8" ceiling joists, per MBF	—	MBF	776.00	—	776.00
12" centers (1.53 BF per SF)	B1@.028	SF	1.19	.95	2.14
16" centers (1.17 BF per SF)	B1@.022	SF	.91	.74	1.65
20" centers (.96 BF per SF)	B1@.018	SF	.74	.61	1.35
24" centers (.84 BF per SF)	B1@.016	SF	.65	.54	1.19
2" x 10", Std & Btr grade					
2" x 10" ceiling joists, per MBF	—	MBF	794.00	—	794.00
12" centers (1.94 BF per SF)	B1@.030	SF	1.54	1.02	2.56
16" centers (1.47 BF per SF)	B1@.023	SF	1.17	.78	1.95
20" centers (1.21 BF per SF)	B1@.019	SF	.96	.64	1.60
24" centers (1.04 BF per SF)	B1@.016	SF	.83	.54	1.37
2" x 12", Std & Btr grade					
2" x 12" ceiling joists, per MBF	—	MBF	881.00	—	881.00
12" centers (2.30 BF per SF)	B1@.033	SF	2.03	1.12	3.15
16" centers (1.76 BF per SF)	B1@.025	SF	1.55	.85	2.40
20" centers (1.44 BF per SF)	B1@.020	SF	1.27	.68	1.95
24" centers (1.26 BF per SF)	B1@.018	SF	1.11	.61	1.72

Catwalks 1" x 6" solid planking walkway, #2 & Btr grade

	Craft@Hrs	Unit	Material	Labor	Total
(0.50 BF per SF)	B1@.017	SF	1.47	.58	2.05

	Craft@Hrs	Unit	Material	Labor	Total

Backing and nailers Std & Btr, for wall finishes, "floating" backing for drywall ceilings, trim, z-bar, appliances and fixtures, etc. See also Bridging and Fireblocking in this section. Figures in parentheses show board feet per LF including 10% waste.

	Craft@Hrs	Unit	Material	Labor	Total
1" x 4" (.37 BF per LF)	B1@.011	LF	.75	.37	1.12
1" x 6" (.55 BF per LF)	B1@.017	LF	1.19	.58	1.77
1" x 8" (.73 BF per LF)	B1@.022	LF	1.58	.74	2.32
1" x 10" (.92 BF per LF)	B1@.027	LF	1.73	.91	2.64
1" x 12" (1.10 BF per LF)	B1@.030	LF	2.73	1.02	3.75
2" x 4" (.73 BF per LF)	B1@.023	LF	.57	.78	1.35
2" x 6" (1.10 BF per LF)	B1@.034	LF	.83	1.15	1.98
2" x 8" (1.47 BF per LF)	B1@.045	LF	1.14	1.52	2.66
2" x 10" (1.83 BF per LF)	B1@.057	LF	1.45	1.93	3.38
3" x 10" (2.76 BF per LF)	B1@.064	LF	2.74	2.17	4.91
1" x 8" Azec core	B1@.042	LF	3.87	1.42	5.29

Ledger strips Std & Btr, nailed to faces of studs, beams, girders, joists, etc. See also Ribbons in this section for let-in type. Figures in parentheses indicate board feet per LF including 10% waste.

	Craft@Hrs	Unit	Material	Labor	Total
1" x 2", 3" or 4" ledger, per MBF	—	MBF	2,020.00	—	2,020.00
2" x 2", 3" or 4" ledger, per MBF	—	MBF	777.00	—	777.00
1" x 2" (.18 BF per LF)	B1@.010	LF	.36	.34	.70
1" x 3" (.28 BF per LF)	B1@.010	LF	.57	.34	.91
1" x 4" (.37 BF per LF)	B1@.010	LF	.75	.34	1.09
2" x 2" (.37 BF per LF)	B1@.010	LF	.29	.34	.63
2" x 3" (.55 BF per LF)	B1@.010	LF	.43	.34	.77
2" x 4" (.73 BF per LF)	B1@.010	LF	.57	.34	.91

Ribbons (Ribbands) Let in to wall framing. See also Ledgers in this section. Figures in parentheses indicate board feet per LF including 10% waste.

	Craft@Hrs	Unit	Material	Labor	Total
1" x 3", 4" or 6" ribbon, per MBF	—	MBF	2,020.00	—	2,020.00
2" x 3", 4" ribbon, per MBF	—	MBF	777.00	—	777.00
2" x 6" ribbon, per MBF	—	MBF	759.00	—	759.00
2" x 8" ribbon, per MBF	—	MBF	776.00	—	776.00
1" x 3", Std & Btr (.28 BF per LF)	B1@.020	LF	.57	.68	1.25
1" x 4", Std & Btr (.37 BF per LF)	B1@.020	LF	.75	.68	1.43
1" x 6", Std & Btr (.55 BF per LF)	B1@.030	LF	1.11	1.02	2.13
2" x 3", Std & Btr (.55 BF per LF)	B1@.041	LF	.43	1.39	1.82
2" x 4", Std & Btr (.73 BF per LF)	B1@.041	LF	.57	1.39	1.96
2" x 6", Std & Btr (1.10 BF per LF)	B1@.045	LF	.83	1.52	2.35
2" x 8", Std & Btr (1.47 BF per LF)	B1@.045	LF	1.14	1.52	2.66

Rafters Flat, shed, or gable roofs, up to 5 in 12 slope (5/24 pitch), maximum 25' span. Figures in parentheses indicate board feet per SF of actual roof surface area (not roof plan area), including rafters, ridge boards, collar beams and normal waste, but no blocking, bracing, purlins, curbs, or gable walls.

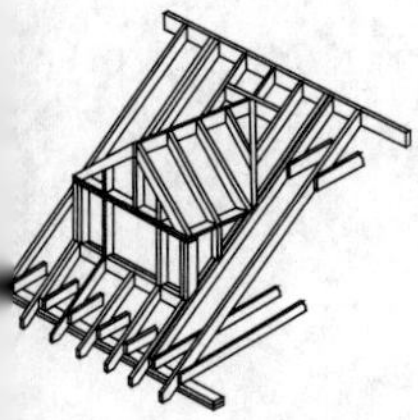

	Craft@Hrs	Unit	Material	Labor	Total
2" x 4", Std & Btr					
2" x 4" rafters, per MBF	—	MBF	777.00	—	777.00
12" centers (.89 BF per SF)	B1@.021	SF	.69	.71	1.40
16" centers (.71 BF per SF)	B1@.017	SF	.55	.58	1.13
24" centers (.53 BF per SF)	B1@.013	SF	.41	.44	.85

	Craft@Hrs	Unit	Material	Labor	Total
2" x 6", Std & Btr					
2" x 6" rafters, per MBF	—	MBF	759.00	—	759.00
12" centers (1.29 BF per SF)	B1@.029	SF	.98	.98	1.96
16" centers (1.02 BF per SF)	B1@.023	SF	.77	.78	1.55
24" centers (.75 BF per SF)	B1@.017	SF	.57	.58	1.15
2" x 8", Std & Btr					
2" x 8" rafters, per MBF	—	MBF	776.00	—	776.00
12" centers (1.71 BF per SF)	B1@.036	SF	1.33	1.22	2.55
16" centers (1.34 BF per SF)	B1@.028	SF	1.04	.95	1.99
24" centers (1.12 BF per SF)	B1@.024	SF	.87	.81	1.68
2" x 10", Std & Btr					
2" x 10" rafters, per MBF	—	MBF	794.00	—	794.00
12" centers (2.12 BF per SF)	B1@.039	SF	1.68	1.32	3.00
16" centers (1.97 BF per SF)	B1@.036	SF	1.56	1.22	2.78
24" centers (1.21 BF per SF)	B1@.022	SF	.96	.74	1.70
2" x 12", Std & Btr					
2" x 12" rafters, per MBF	—	MBF	881.00	—	881.00
12" centers (2.52 BF per SF)	B1@.045	SF	2.22	1.52	3.74
16" centers (1.97 BF per SF)	B1@.035	SF	1.74	1.18	2.92
24" centers (1.43 BF per SF)	B1@.026	SF	1.26	.88	2.14
Add for hip roof	B1@.007	SF	—	.24	.24
Add for slope over 5 in 12	B1@.015	SF	—	.51	.51

Trimmers and curbs At stairwells, skylights, dormers, etc. Figures in parentheses show board feet per LF, Std & Btr grade, including 10% waste.

	Craft@Hrs	Unit	Material	Labor	Total
2" x 4" (.73 BF per LF)	B1@.018	LF	.57	.61	1.18
2" x 6" (1.10 BF per LF)	B1@.028	LF	.83	.95	1.78
2" x 8" (1.47 BF per LF)	B1@.038	LF	1.14	1.29	2.43
2" x 10" (1.83 BF per LF)	B1@.047	LF	1.45	1.59	3.04
2" x 12" (2.20 BF per LF)	B1@.057	LF	1.94	1.93	3.87

Collar beams & collar ties Std & Btr grade, including 10% waste

	Craft@Hrs	Unit	Material	Labor	Total
Collar beams, 2" x 6"	B1@.013	LF	.83	.44	1.27
Collar ties, 1" x 6"	B1@.006	LF	1.19	.20	1.39

Purlins (Purling) Std & Btr, installed below roof rafters. Figures in parentheses indicate board feet per LF including 5% waste.

	Craft@Hrs	Unit	Material	Labor	Total
2" x 4" (.70 BF per LF)	B1@.012	LF	.54	.41	.95
2" x 6" (1.05 BF per LF)	B1@.017	LF	.80	.58	1.38
2" x 8" (1.40 BF per LF)	B1@.023	LF	1.09	.78	1.87
2" x 10" (1.75 BF per LF)	B1@.027	LF	1.39	.91	2.30
2" x 12" (2.10 BF per LF)	B1@.030	LF	1.85	1.02	2.87
4" x 6" (2.10 BF per LF)	B1@.034	LF	1.93	1.15	3.08
4" x 8" (2.80 BF per LF)	B1@.045	LF	2.35	1.52	3.87

Dormer studs Std & Btr, per square foot of wall area, including 10% waste

	Craft@Hrs	Unit	Material	Labor	Total
2" x 4" (.84 BF per SF)	B1@.033	SF	.65	1.12	1.77

Roof trusses 24" OC, any slope from 3 in 12 to 12 in 12, total height not to exceed 12' high from bottom chord to highest point on truss. Prices for trusses over 12' high will be up to 100% higher. Square foot (SF) costs, where shown, are per square foot of area to be covered.

	Craft@Hrs	Unit	Material	Labor	Total
Scissor truss					
2" x 4" top and bottom chords					
Up to 38' span	B1@.022	SF	3.91	.74	4.65
40' to 50' span	B1@.028	SF	4.88	.95	5.83

	Craft@Hrs	Unit	Material	Labor	Total
Fink truss "W" (conventional roof truss)					
2" x 4" top and bottom chords					
Up to 38' span	B1@.017	SF	3.39	.58	3.97
40' to 50' span	B1@.022	SF	4.10	.74	4.84
2" x 6" top and bottom chords					
Up to 38' span	B1@.020	SF	4.21	.68	4.89
40' to 50' span	B1@.026	SF	5.05	.88	5.93
Truss with gable fill at 16" OC					
28' span, 5 in 12 slope	B1@.958	Ea	282.00	32.40	314.40
32' span, 5 in 12 slope	B1@1.26	Ea	347.00	42.70	389.70
40' span, 5 in 12 slope	B1@1.73	Ea	488.00	58.60	546.60
Fascia Material column includes 10% waste					
White Wood, #3 & Btr					
1" x 4", per MBF	—	MBF	2,480.00	—	2,480.00
1" x 6", per MBF	—	MBF	2,670.00	—	2,670.00
1" x 8", per MBF	—	MBF	2,710.00	—	2,710.00
1" x 4", per LF	B1@.044	LF	.91	1.49	2.40
1" x 6", per LF	B1@.044	LF	1.47	1.49	2.96
1" x 8", per LF	B1@.051	LF	1.99	1.73	3.72
Hem-fir, S4S, dry, Std and Btr					
2" x 6", per MBF	—	MBF	440.00	—	440.00
2" x 8", per MBF	—	MBF	577.00	—	577.00
2" x 10", per MBF	—	MBF	751.00	—	751.00
2" x 6", per LF	B1@.044	LF	.48	1.49	1.97
2" x 8", per LF	B1@.051	LF	.85	1.73	2.58
2" x 10", per LF	B1@.051	LF	1.38	1.73	3.11
Redwood, S4S kiln dried, clear					
1" x 4", per MBF	—	MBF	2,880.00	—	2,880.00
1" x 6", per MBF	—	MBF	4,240.00	—	4,240.00
1" x 8", per MBF	—	MBF	2,860.00	—	2,860.00
2" x 4", per MBF	—	MBF	2,110.00	—	2,110.00
2" x 6", per MBF	—	MBF	2,010.00	—	2,010.00
2" x 8", per MBF	—	MBF	2,220.00	—	2,220.00
1" x 4", per LF	B1@.044	LF	1.06	1.49	2.55
1" x 6", per LF	B1@.044	LF	2.33	1.49	3.82
1" x 8", per LF	B1@.051	LF	2.10	1.73	3.83
2" x 4", per LF	B1@.044	LF	1.55	1.49	3.04
2" x 6", per LF	B1@.044	LF	2.21	1.49	3.70
2" x 8", per LF	B1@.051	LF	3.25	1.73	4.98
Sheathing, roof Per SF of roof surface including 10% waste					
CDX plywood sheathing, rough					
1/2"	B1@.013	SF	.68	.44	1.12
1/2", 4-ply	B1@.013	SF	.80	.44	1.24
1/2", 5-ply	B1@.013	SF	1.07	.44	1.51
5/8", 4-ply	B1@.013	SF	.81	.44	1.25
5/8", 5-ply	B1@.013	SF	1.24	.44	1.68
3/4"	B1@.013	SF	.93	.44	1.37
OSB sheathing					
7/16"	B1@.013	SF	.42	.44	.86
1/2"	B1@.013	SF	.58	.44	1.02
5/8"	B1@.013	SF	.60	.44	1.04
3/4"	B1@.014	SF	.74	.47	1.21

	Craft@Hrs	Unit	Material	Labor	Total
7/8"	B1@.014	SF	1.47	.47	1.94
1-1/8"	B1@.015	SF	2.13	.51	2.64
Add for hip roof	B1@.007	SF	—	.24	.24
Add for steep pitch or cut-up roof	B1@.015	SF	—	.51	.51
Board sheathing, 1" x 6" or 1" x 8" utility T&G laid diagonal					
1" utility T&G lumber, per MBF	—	MBF	2,390.00	—	2,390.00
(1.13 BF per SF)	B1@.026	SF	2.96	.88	3.84
Add for hip roof	B1@.007	SF	—	.24	.24
Add for steep pitch or cut-up roof	B1@.015	SF	—	.51	.51

Roof decking Std & Btr grade. See also Sheathing in this section. Flat, shed, or gable roofs to 5 in 12 slope (5/24 pitch). Figures in parentheses indicate board feet per SF of actual roof area (not roof plan area), including 5% waste.

	Craft@Hrs	Unit	Material	Labor	Total
2" x 6", per MBF	—	MBF	759.00	—	759.00
2" x 8", per MBF	—	MBF	776.00	—	776.00
3" x 6", per MBF	—	MBF	854.00	—	854.00
2" x 6" (2.28 BF per SF)	B1@.043	SF	1.73	1.46	3.19
2" x 8" (2.25 BF per SF)	B1@.043	SF	1.77	1.46	3.23
3" x 6" (3.43 BF per SF)	B1@.047	SF	2.91	1.59	4.50
Add for steep pitch or cut-up roof	B1@.019	SF	—	.64	.64

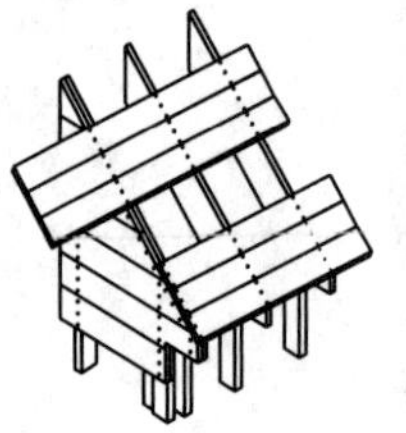

Cant strips Std & Btr grade lumber

	Craft@Hrs	Unit	Material	Labor	Total
2" x 4" beveled	B1@.020	LF	.85	.68	1.53
For short or cut-up runs	B1@.030	LF	.85	1.02	1.87

Furring Per SF of surface area to be covered. Figures in parentheses show coverage including 7% waste, typical job.

	Craft@Hrs	Unit	Material	Labor	Total
1" furring, per MBF	—	MBF	2,020.00	—	2,020.00
Over masonry, Utility grade					
12" OC, 1" x 2" (.24 BF per SF)	B1@.025	SF	.49	.85	1.34
16" OC, 1" x 2" (.20 BF per SF)	B1@.020	SF	.40	.68	1.08
20" OC, 1" x 2" (.17 BF per SF)	B1@.018	SF	.34	.61	.95
24" OC, 1" x 2" (.15 BF per SF)	B1@.016	SF	.30	.54	.84
12" OC, 1" x 3" (.36 BF per SF)	B1@.025	SF	.73	.85	1.58
16" OC, 1" x 3" (.29 BF per SF)	B1@.020	SF	.59	.68	1.27
20" OC, 1" x 3" (.25 BF per SF)	B1@.018	SF	.51	.61	1.12
24" OC, 1" x 3" (.22 BF per SF)	B1@.016	SF	.45	.54	.99
Over wood frame, Utility grade					
12" OC, 1" x 2" (.24 BF per SF)	B1@.016	SF	.49	.54	1.03
16" OC, 1" x 2" (.20 BF per SF)	B1@.013	SF	.40	.44	.84
20" OC, 1" x 2" (.17 BF per SF)	B1@.011	SF	.34	.37	.71
24" OC, 1" x 2" (.15 BF per SF)	B1@.010	SF	.30	.34	.64
12" OC, 1" x 3" (.36 BF per SF)	B1@.016	SF	.73	.54	1.27
16" OC, 1" x 3" (.29 BF per SF)	B1@.013	SF	.59	.44	1.03
20" OC, 1" x 3" (.25 BF per SF)	B1@.011	SF	.51	.37	.88
24" OC, 1" x 3" (.22 BF per SF)	B1@.010	SF	.45	.34	.79
Over wood subfloor, Utility grade					
12" OC, 1" x 2" (.24 BF per SF)	B1@.033	SF	.49	1.12	1.61
16" OC, 1" x 2" (.20 BF per SF)	B1@.028	SF	.40	.95	1.35
20" OC, 1" x 2" (.17 BF per SF)	B1@.024	SF	.34	.81	1.15
24" OC, 1" x 2" (.15 BF per SF)	B1@.021	SF	.30	.71	1.01

	Craft@Hrs	Unit	Material	Labor	Total
2" furring, per MBF	—	MBF	777.00	—	777.00
12" OC, 2" x 2" Std & Btr (.48 BF per SF)	B1@.033	SF	.37	1.12	1.49
16" OC, 2" x 2" Std & Btr (.39 BF per SF)	B1@.028	SF	.30	.95	1.25
20" OC, 2" x 2" Std & Btr (.34 BF per SF)	B1@.024	SF	.26	.81	1.07
24" OC, 2" x 2" Std & Btr (.30 BF per SF)	B1@.021	SF	.23	.71	.94

Grounds Screeds for plaster or stucco, #3, 1" x 2" lumber. Based on .18 BF per LF including 10% waste.

	Craft@Hrs	Unit	Material	Labor	Total
1" grounds, per MBF	—	MBF	2,020.00	—	2,020.00
Over masonry	B1@.047	LF	.36	1.59	1.95
Over wood	B1@.038	LF	.36	1.29	1.65

Sheathing, wall Per SF of wall surface, including 5% waste

	Craft@Hrs	Unit	Material	Labor	Total
BC plywood sheathing, plugged and touch sanded, interior grade					
1/4"	B1@.013	SF	.83	.44	1.27
3/8"	B1@.015	SF	.82	.51	1.33
1/2"	B1@.016	SF	1.06	.54	1.60
5/8"	B1@.018	SF	1.00	.61	1.61
3/4"	B1@.020	SF	1.13	.68	1.81
AB marine grade Douglas fir plywood					
1/2", 5-ply	B1@.016	SF	2.00	.54	2.54
3/4", 7-ply	B1@.020	SF	2.65	.68	3.33
OSB sheathing					
1/4"	B1@.013	SF	.30	.44	.74
3/8"	B1@.015	SF	.43	.51	.94
7/16"	B1@.015	SF	.40	.51	.91
1/2"	B1@.016	SF	.56	.54	1.10
5/8"	B1@.018	SF	.58	.61	1.19
3/4"	B1@.018	SF	.71	.61	1.32
7/8"	B1@.020	SF	1.40	.68	2.08
1-1/8"	B1@.020	SF	2.04	.68	2.72
Board sheathing 1" x 6" or 1" x 8" utility T&G					
1" x 6" or 8" utility T&G, per MBF	—	MBF	2,170.00	—	2,170.00
(1.13 BF per SF)	B1@.020	SF	2.45	.68	3.13
Add for diagonal patterns	B1@.006	SF	—	.20	.20

Sleepers Std & Btr pressure treated lumber, including 5% waste, laid flat 16" OC over a waterproof membrane spread on a concrete slab and set with shot fasteners

	Craft@Hrs	Unit	Material	Labor	Total
2" x 4" sleepers, per MBF	—	MBF	1,160.00	—	1,160.00
2" x 4" sleepers, per LF	B1@.017	LF	1.22	.58	1.80
2" x 4" sleepers, per SF of floor slab	B1@.017	SF	.72	.58	1.30
Add for waterproof membrane	B1@.002	SF	.08	.07	.15
Add for shot fasteners, 24" OC, per SF of slab	B1@.009	SF	.11	.30	.41
Add for taper cuts on sleepers, per cut	B1@.009	Ea	—	.30	.30

Finish Carpentry These figures assume all materials to be installed are supplied by others. Labor costs assume good quality stain-grade work up to 9 feet above floor level. Paint-grade work will cost from 20% to 33% less. Add the cost of scaffolding, staining or painting, if required.

Blocking and backing Installation before drywall is hung. Cost per piece of blocking or backing set

	Craft@Hrs	Unit	Material	Labor	Total
2" x 4" backing or blocking	BC@.040	Ea	—	1.50	1.50
2" x 4" strongback 10' to 16' long					
screwed to ceiling joists	BC@.350	Ea	—	13.10	13.10

	Craft@Hrs	Unit	Material	Labor	Total
Furring Nailed over studs and adjusted with shims to bring the wall surface flush. Costs will be higher if the wall plane is very uneven or if the furred wall has to be exceptionally even.					
Cost per linear foot of furring installed					
1" x 4" furring, few shims required	BC@.010	LF	—	.37	.37
Straightening wall studs Costs per stud straightened					
Cut saw kerf and drive shim or screw into the kerf					
reinforce with a plywood scab	BC@.300	Ea	—	11.20	11.20
Remove and replace a badly warped stud	BC@.300	Ea	—	11.20	11.20
Cased openings Install jambs only. See costs for casing below. Costs per opening cased					
Opening to 4' wide	BC@.800	Ea	—	29.90	29.90
Openings over 4' wide	BC@1.05	Ea	—	39.20	39.20
Exterior doors Based on hanging doors in prepared openings. No lockset, or casing included. See the sections that follow. Costs will be higher if the framing has to be adjusted before the door can be set.					
Hang a new door in an existing jamb					
Cut door, set butt hinges, install door	BC@1.46	Ea	—	54.60	54.60
Prehung flush or panel 1-3/4" thick solid core single doors, with felt insulation, based on an adjustable metal sill					
Up to 3' wide	BC@.750	Ea	—	28.00	28.00
Over 3' wide	BC@1.25	Ea	—	46.70	46.70
Add for door with sidelights	BC@.750	Ea	—	28.00	28.00
Sliding glass doors, opening to 8' wide	BC@1.75	Ea	—	65.40	65.40
French doors, 1-3/4" thick, to 6' wide	BC@1.75	Ea	—	65.40	65.40
Interior doors Based on hanging 1-3/8" hollow core doors in prepared openings. No locksets or casing included. See the sections that follow.					
Prehung interior doors	BC@.500	Ea	—	18.70	18.70
Add for assembling a factory-cut					
mortised and rabbeted jamb	BC@.200	Ea	—	7.48	7.48
Pocket doors					
Assemble and install the door frame	BC@.981	Ea	—	36.70	36.70
Install door and valances in existing frame	BC@.500	Ea	—	18.70	18.70
Bifold doors installed in cased openings. See costs for cased openings above					
Single bifold door to 4' wide	BC@.700	Ea	—	26.20	26.20
Double bifold door to 8' wide, pair of doors	BC@1.20	Pr	—	44.90	44.90
Bypass closet doors installed on a track in a cased opening. See cased opening manhours above					
Double doors, per opening	BC@.660	Ea	—	24.70	24.70
Triple doors, per opening	BC@1.00	Ea	—	37.40	37.40
Rehang most hollow core doors in an existing opening,					
re-shim jamb and plane door, per door	BC@1.50	Ea	—	56.10	56.10
Rehang large or heavy solid core doors in an existing opening,					
re-shim jamb and plane door, per door	BC@1.75	Ea	—	65.40	65.40
Correcting a sagging door hinge. Remove door from the jamb, remove hinge leaf,					
deepen the mortise and rehang the door	BC@.600	Ea	—	22.40	22.40
Hang a new door in an existing jamb. Mark the door to fit opening, cut the door, set butt hinges, install door in the jamb, install door hardware					
Per door hung	BC@1.75	Ea	—	65.40	65.40
Prehanging doors off site. Cost per door hung, excluding door cost					
Make and assemble frame, cost per frame	BC@.750	Ea	—	28.00	28.00

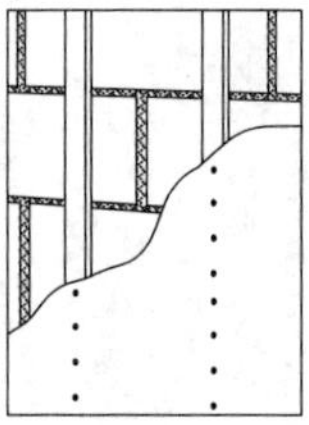

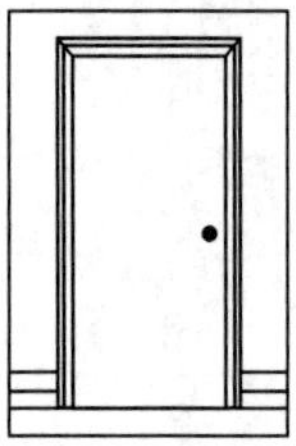

	Craft@Hrs	Unit	Material	Labor	Total
Set hinge on door and frame, panel or flush door, per hinge					
Using jigs and router	BC@.160	Ea	—	5.98	5.98
Using hand tools	BC@.500	Ea	—	18.70	18.70
Add for French doors, per door	BC@.250	Ea	—	9.35	9.35

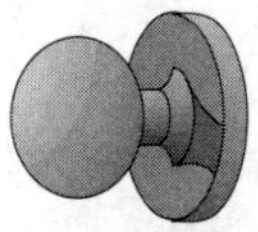

Lockset installation Set in either a solid core or hollow core door, includes setting the strike plate

	Craft@Hrs	Unit	Material	Labor	Total
Costs per lockset					
Standard 2-1/8" bore, factory bored	BC@.160	Ea	—	5.98	5.98
Standard 2-1/8" bore, site bored	BC@1.00	Ea	—	37.40	37.40
Mortise type lockset, using a boring machine	BC@1.50	Ea	—	56.10	56.10
Mortise type lockset, using hand tools	BC@3.00	Ea	—	112.00	112.00
Pocket door hardware					
Privacy latch	BC@.500	Ea	—	18.70	18.70
Passage latch	BC@.300	Ea	—	11.20	11.20
Edge pull	BC@.300	Ea	—	11.20	11.20

Setting door stop molding Set at the head and on two sides. Costs per opening

	Craft@Hrs	Unit	Material	Labor	Total
Panel or flush door	BC@.250	Ea	—	9.35	9.35
French door	BC@.330	Ea	—	12.30	12.30
Pocket door	BC@.250	Ea	—	9.35	9.35

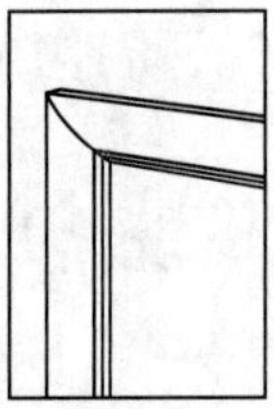

Set casing around a framed opening Mitered or butted molding corners. Costs per opening, per side, using a pneumatic nail gun

	Craft@Hrs	Unit	Material	Labor	Total
Opening to 4' wide using casing to 2-1/4" wide	BC@.250	Ea	—	9.35	9.35
Opening over 4' wide to 8' wide					
using casing up to 2-1/4" wide	BC@.300	Ea	—	11.20	11.20
Add for casing over 2-1/4" wide to 4" wide	BC@.160	Ea	—	5.98	5.98
Add for block and plinth door casing	BC@.300	Ea	—	11.20	11.20
Add for hand nailing	BC@.275	Ea	—	10.30	10.30

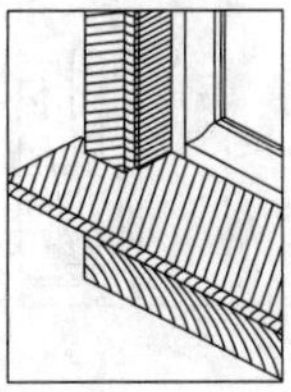

Window trim Based on trim set around prepared openings. Costs per window opening on square windows. Extra tall or extra wide windows will cost more.

	Craft@Hrs	Unit	Material	Labor	Total
Extension jambs cut, assembled, shimmed and installed					
Up to 3/4" thick, 3 or 4 sides, per window	BC@.330	Ea	—	12.30	12.30
Over 3/4" thick, per LF of extension jamb	BC@.100	LF	—	3.74	3.74
Window stool					
Set to sheetrock wraps					
nailed directly on framing	BC@.500	Ea	—	18.70	18.70
When stool has to be shimmed up from framing					
Add per LF of stool	BC@.050	LF	—	1.87	1.87
Stool set to wooden jambs, per opening	BC@.400	Ea	—	15.00	15.00
When stool has to be shimmed up from jambs					
Add per LF of stool	BC@.050	LF	—	1.87	1.87
Add for mitered returns on horns					
Per opening	BC@.500	Ea	—	18.70	18.70
Window apron molding without mitered returns					
Per opening	BC@.160	Ea	—	5.98	5.98
Window apron molding with mitered returns					
Per opening	BC@.320	Ea	—	12.00	12.00

	Craft@Hrs	Unit	Material	Labor	Total
Window casing, straight casing with square corners, per opening					
3 sides (stool and apron), up to 5' on any side	BC@.330	Ea	—	12.30	12.30
4 sides (picture frame), up to 5' on any side	BC@.500	Ea	—	18.70	18.70
Add for any side over 5' long, per side	BC@.090	Ea	—	3.36	3.36
Add for angle corners (trapezoid or triangle)					
Per corner	BC@.250	Ea	—	9.35	9.35
Installing a pre-manufactured arched top casing only, per opening					
To 4' wide set against rosettes	BC@.330	Ea	—	12.30	12.30
To 4' wide, mitered corners	BC@.500	Ea	—	18.70	18.70
Over 4' wide set against rosettes	BC@.660	Ea	—	24.70	24.70
Over 4' wide, mitered corners	BC@1.00	Ea	—	37.40	37.40

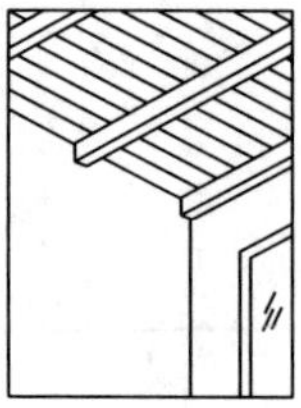

Ceiling treatments All figures assume a wall height not over 9' with work done from scaffolding. Add the cost of scaffolding

	Craft@Hrs	Unit	Material	Labor	Total
Set up and dismantle scaffolding, based on a typical 10' x 16' room					
Per room	BC@1.75	Ea	—	65.40	65.40
Wood strip ceiling, T&G or square edged, applied wall to wall with no miters					
Per square foot of ceiling	BC@.050	SF	—	1.87	1.87
Plywood panel ceiling					
Screwed in place, molding strips nailed with a pneumatic nailer, including normal layout					
Per square foot of ceiling covered	BC@.160	SF	—	5.98	5.98
Applied beams, including building up the beam, layout and installation on a flat ceiling					
Per LF of beam applied	BC@.310	LF	—	11.60	11.60
Additional costs for ceiling treatments					
Add for each joint or beam scribed to the wall	BC@.660	Ea	—	24.70	24.70
Add for each corbel	BC@.400	Ea	—	15.00	15.00
Add for each knee brace	BC@.600	Ea	—	22.40	22.40

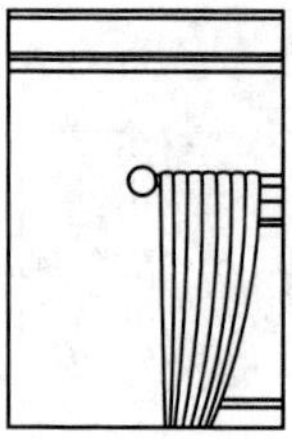

Cornice or crown molding Including layout and coped joints, per LF of molding

	Craft@Hrs	Unit	Material	Labor	Total
Up to 2-1/4" wide	BC@.050	LF	—	1.87	1.87
Over 2-1/4" wide to 3-1/2" wide	BC@.060	LF	—	2.24	2.24
Over 3-1/2" wide	BC@.070	LF	—	2.62	2.62

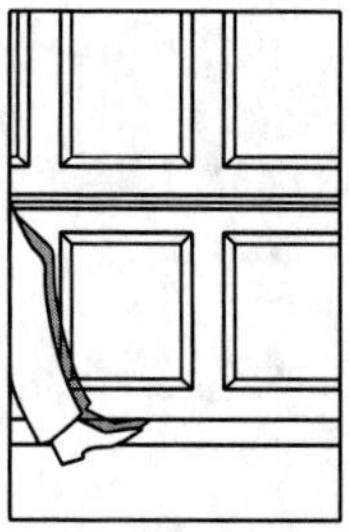

Wall paneling No molding included. See molding below. Costs per square foot of wall covered

	Craft@Hrs	Unit	Material	Labor	Total
Board wainscot or paneling, 3-1/2" to 5-1/2" wide tongue and groove					
Per square foot of wall covered	BC@.080	SF	—	2.99	2.99
Frame and panel wainscot. Installation only. Add for fabricating the frames and panels					
Per square foot of wall covered	BC@.090	SF	—	3.36	3.36
Add for frame attached with screws and covered with wood plugs	BC@.010	SF	—	.37	.37
Hardwood sheet paneling installed on wood frame or masonry walls					
Per square foot of wall covered	BC@.040	SF	—	1.50	1.50
Add for running molding if required	BC@.040	SF	—	1.50	1.50
Add if vapor barrier must be installed with mastic over a masonry wall	BC@.010	SF	—	.37	.37
Add when 1" x 4" furring is nailed on a masonry wall with a powder-actuated nail gun					
No shimming or straightening included	BC@.020	SF	—	.75	.75
Add if sheet paneling is scribed around stone veneer					
Per linear foot scribed	BC@.150	LF	—	5.61	5.61
Minimum time for scribing sheet paneling	BC@.500	Ea	—	18.70	18.70

Running moldings Single piece mitered installations nailed by hand. Add 100% for two-piece molding. Costs per LF of molding

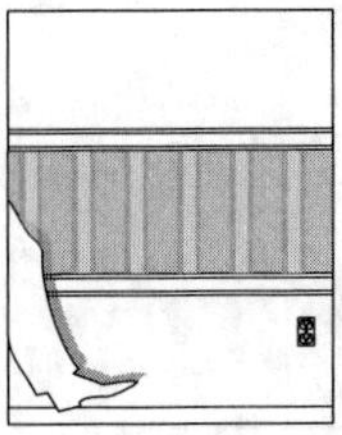

	Craft@Hrs	Unit	Material	Labor	Total
Picture rail	BC@.050	LF	—	1.87	1.87
Chair rail	BC@.040	LF	—	1.50	1.50
Wainscot cap or bed molding	BC@.040	LF	—	1.50	1.50
Baseboard	BC@.040	LF	—	1.50	1.50
Kneewall cap up to 8" wide and 1-1/2" thick. Complex job layout and bed molding will increase costs					
Kneewall cap	BC@.160	LF	—	5.98	5.98

Closet poles and shelving Including layout and installation

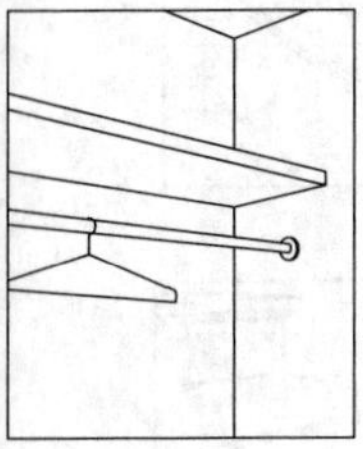

	Craft@Hrs	Unit	Material	Labor	Total
1-1/4" closet pole supported with a metal bracket every 32"					
Per LF of pole	BC@.040	LF	—	1.50	1.50
Add for mitered corner joints, per corner	BC@.300	Ea	—	11.20	11.20
3/4" x 12" hat shelf supported with a metal shelf bracket every 32"					
Per LF of shelf	BC@.100	LF	—	3.74	3.74
Add for mitered corner joint, per corner	BC@.300	Ea	—	11.20	11.20
Site-built closet storage unit with drawers using plate biscuit joiners and 3/4" board or plywood stock, including fabrication, layout, assembly and installation					
Per square foot of storage unit face	BC@.680	SF	—	25.40	25.40
Add for each drawer	BC@.850	Ea	—	31.80	31.80

Cabinet installation Including layout, leveling and installation. No fabrication, assembly or countertops included. Costs per cabinet

	Craft@Hrs	Unit	Material	Labor	Total
Base cabinets					
Cabinets to 36" wide	BC@.766	Ea	—	28.60	28.60
Cabinets over 36" wide	BC@.911	Ea	—	34.10	34.10
Wall cabinets					
Cabinets to 18" wide	BC@.638	Ea	—	23.80	23.80
Cabinets over 18" to 36" wide	BC@.766	Ea	—	28.60	28.60
Cabinets over 36" wide	BC@1.03	Ea	—	38.50	38.50
Oven or utility cabinets, 70" high, to 30" wide	BC@1.71	Ea	—	63.90	63.90
Filler strip between cabinets, measured, cut, fit and installed					
Per strip installed	BC@.200	Ea	—	7.48	7.48

Fireplace surrounds and mantels Costs will be higher when a mantel or molding must be scribed around irregular masonry surfaces

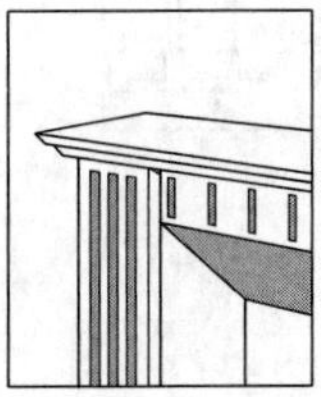

	Craft@Hrs	Unit	Material	Labor	Total
Layout, cutting, fitting, assembling and installing a vertical pilaster on two sides and a horizontal frieze board above the pilasters. Additional moldings will take more time					
Costs per linear foot of pilaster and frieze	BC@.350	LF	—	13.10	13.10
Mantel shelf attached to masonry, including cutting, fitting and installation					
Per mantel	BC@.750	Ea	—	28.00	28.00
Installing a prefabricated mantel and fireplace surround					
Per mantel and surround installed	BC@1.50	Ea	—	56.10	56.10

Wood flooring Including layout, vapor barrier and installation with a power nailer. Add for underlayment, sanding and finishing. Borders, feature strips and mitered corners will increase costs. Costs per square foot of floor covered

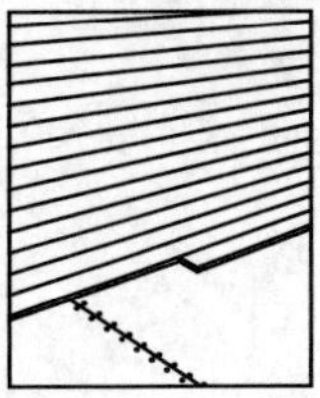

	Craft@Hrs	Unit	Material	Labor	Total
Tongue & groove strip flooring					
3/4" x 2-1/4" strips	BF@.036	SF	—	1.23	1.23

	Craft@Hrs	Unit	Material	Labor	Total
Straight edge plank flooring, 3/4" x 6" to 12" wide					
Set with biscuit joiner plates	BF@.055	SF	—	1.89	1.89
Add for plank flooring					
set with screws and butterfly plugs	BF@.010	SF	—	.34	.34
Filling and sanding a wood floor with drum and disc sanders					
3 passes (60, 80, 100 grit), per square foot	BF@.023	SF	—	.79	.79
Finishing a wood floor, including filler, shellac,					
polyurethane or waterborne urethane	BF@.024	SF	—	.82	.82

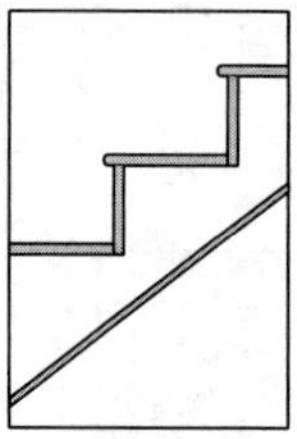

Skirt boards for stairways Including layout, fitting, assembly and installation. Based on a 9' floor-to-floor rise where the stair carriage has already been installed by others. Costs will be higher if re-cutting, shimming, or adjusting of an existing stair carriage is required.

	Craft@Hrs	Unit	Material	Labor	Total
Cutting and installing a skirt board on the closed side of a stairway. Costs per skirt board					
Treads and risers butted against skirt boards,					
no dadoes	BC@2.00	Ea	—	74.80	74.80
Treads and risers set in dadoes	BC@3.75	Ea	—	140.00	140.00
Cutting and installing a skirt board on the open side of a stairway					
Risers miter-jointed into the board	BC@5.50	Ea	—	206.00	206.00

Treads and risers for stairs Including layout, cutting, fitting, and installation of treads, risers and typical molding under the tread nosing. Includes a miter return on one side of each tread. Cost per 9' rise of 14 treads and 15 risers

	Craft@Hrs	Unit	Material	Labor	Total
9' rise stairway	BC@2.50	Ea	—	93.50	93.50

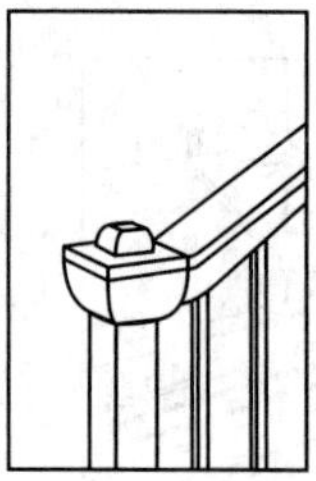

Handrail for stairs Including layout, cutting, fitting and installation. Based on milled hardwood rail, posts and fittings

	Craft@Hrs	Unit	Material	Labor	Total
Setting newel posts, costs per post	BC@2.50	Ea	—	93.50	93.50
Setting post-to-post handrail					
Costs per 10 linear feet of rail	BC@1.50	Ea	—	56.10	56.10
Setting over-the-post handrail					
Costs per 10 linear feet of rail	BC@2.50	Ea	—	93.50	93.50
Add for each transition fitting					
Turn, easing or gooseneck	BC@1.75	Ea	—	65.40	65.40

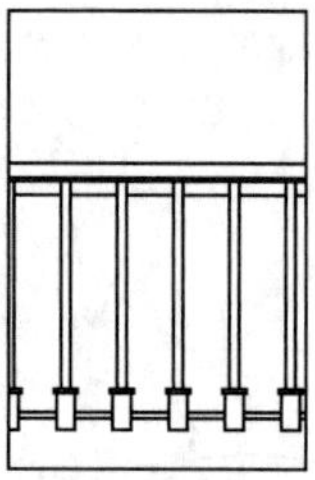

Balusters for stair railing Including layout, cutting, fitting and installation. Based on mill-made hardwood balusters. Cost per baluster

	Craft@Hrs	Unit	Material	Labor	Total
Balusters with round top section	BC@.330	Ea	—	12.30	12.30
Balusters with square top section	BC@.750	Ea	—	28.00	28.00

Steel Framing, Rule of Thumb Light-gauge steel framing cost per square foot of living area. These figures will apply on most crawl space and basement homes. Labor and material cost will be about 30% less for framing over a slab on grade. Complex framing jobs will cost more. The seven lines of cost data under "Steel framing rule of thumb cost breakdown" below show the cost breakdown for framing a house including steel framing, sheathing and blocking. Add $1.50 to $3.00 per SF of floor if engineer approval is required (plans not based on code tables). Material costs in this section assume that (1) precut materials are fastened with screws and that (2) tariffs imposed on imported sheet steel in 2018 remain in place during 2021. Labor cost includes layout, assembly, plumb and align.

	Craft@Hrs	Unit	Material	Labor	Total
Low cost house	B1@.223	SF	9.76	7.55	17.31
Medium cost house	B1@.268	SF	11.10	9.07	20.17
Better quality house	B1@.355	SF	15.20	12.00	27.20

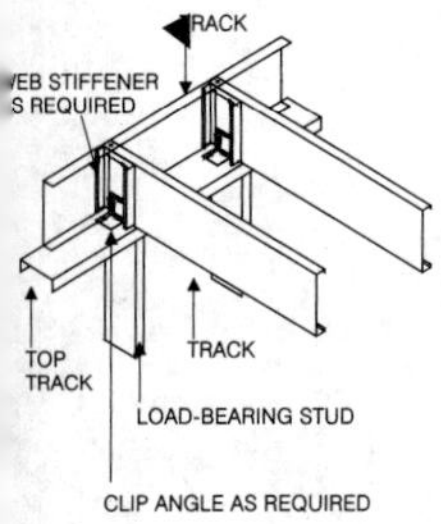

	Craft@Hrs	Unit	Material	Labor	Total
Steel framing rule of thumb cost breakdown Costs per square foot of living area. These figures were used to compile the framing cost for a medium cost home in the section immediately above.					
Using light-gauge steel framing materials at	—	Lb	1.14	—	1.14
Using 1/2" OSB subfloor at	—	MSF	530.00	—	530.00
Using 7/16" OSB roof sheathing at	—	MSF	384.00	—	384.00
Using 5/8" CDX plywood subfloor at	—	MSF	735.00	—	735.00
Using 1/2" CDX plywood roof sheathing at	—	MSF	726.00	—	726.00
Sills, pier blocks, floor beams (270 Lb per 1,000 SF of floor)	B1@.020	SF	.31	.68	.99
Floor joists, doublers, blocking, bridging (2,200 Lb per 1,000 SF of floor)	B1@.031	SF	2.51	1.05	3.56
Subflooring, 1/2" OSB sheathing (1,150 SF per 1,000 SF)	B1@.011	SF	.61	.37	.98
Subfloor, 5/8" CDX plywood (1,150 SF per 1,000 SF of floor)	B1@.012	SF	.85	.41	1.26
Layout, studs, top and bottom track, headers, backing, blocking, bracing and framing for openings (2,230 Lb per 1,000 SF of floor)	B1@.102	SF	2.55	3.45	6.00
Ceiling joists, header and end joists, backing, blocking and bracing (1,810 Lb per 1,000 SF of floor)	B1@.050	SF	2.07	1.69	3.76
Rafters, braces, collar beams, ridge members, 8" rafters, 24" OC (2,300 Lb per 1000 SF of roof)	B1@.042	SF	2.62	1.42	4.04
Roof sheathing, 1/2" CDX plywood (1,150 SF per 1,000 SF of roof)	B1@.011	SF	.83	.37	1.20
Roof sheathing, 7/16" OSB sheathing (1,150 SF per 1,000 SF)	B1@.010	SF	.44	.34	.78
Steel lally columns Residential basement columns, 3-1/2" diameter, steel tube					
Material only	—	LF	14.20	—	14.20
Add for base or cap plate	—	Ea	5.83	—	5.83
Add for installation, per column to 12' high	B1@.458	Ea	—	15.50	15.50
Wood sill plates for steel framing (At foundation) SYP #2 pressure treated lumber, drilled and installed with foundation bolts at 48" OC, no bolts, nuts or washers included. See also wood plates in this section. Figures in parentheses indicate board feet per LF of foundation, including 5% waste and Wolmanized treatment.					
2" x 3" sill plates, per MBF	—	MBF	907.00	—	907.00
2" x 4" sill plates, per MBF	—	MBF	1,160.00	—	1,160.00
2" x 6" sill plates, per MBF	—	MBF	1,020.00	—	1,020.00
2" x 8" sill plates, per MBF	—	MBF	974.00	—	974.00
2" x 3" (.53 BF per LF)	B1@.020	LF	.48	.68	1.16
2" x 4" (.70 BF per LF)	B1@.023	LF	.81	.78	1.59
2" x 6" (1.05 BF per LF)	B1@.024	LF	1.07	.81	1.88
2" x 8" (1.40 BF per LF)	B1@.031	LF	1.36	1.05	2.41

	Craft@Hrs	Unit	Material	Labor	Total
Foundation anchors Set and aligned in forms before concrete is placed. Equivalent Simpson Strong-Tie Co. model numbers are shown in parentheses					
Mud sill anchors, embedded in concrete, folded over the track and screw fastened					
(MASA)	B1@.051	Ea	1.54	1.73	3.27
Anchor bolts, including bolts, nuts and washers as required					
5/8" x 17" (SSTB16)	B1@.157	Ea	5.17	5.31	10.48
5/8" x 21" (SSTB20)	B1@.158	Ea	8.96	5.35	14.31
5/8" x 25" (SSTB24)	B1@.159	Ea	6.41	5.38	11.79
7/8" x 34" (SSTB34)	B1@.164	Ea	18.30	5.55	23.85
7/8" x 36" (SSTB36)	B1@.167	Ea	23.60	5.65	29.25
Hold down brackets (one per anchor bolt to distribute pull-out forces over a greater area)					
24-1/8" x 10" x 6-1/4" (STHD14)	B1@.165	Ea	20.90	5.59	26.49
24-1/8" x 14" x 6-1/4" (S/HPAHD22)	B1@.169	Ea	12.80	5.72	18.52
13-7/8" x 2-1/2" x 1-1/2" (S/HD8)	B1@.650	Ea	33.70	22.00	55.70
16-1/8" x 2-1/2" x 1-1/2" (S/HD10)	B1@.655	Ea	42.71	22.20	64.91

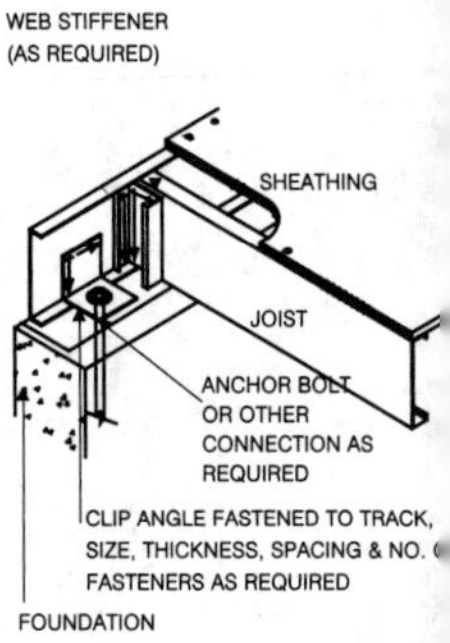

Steel first floor joists Per SF of area covered. Includes joists and rim joists, typical screws, stiffeners, splices, blocking and strapping. Add the cost of support beams, bridging, trimmer joists and sheathing. See the beam, bridging, trimmer joist and sheathing costs below. Deduct for openings over 25 SF. Figures in parentheses show weight of steel per square foot of floor. Assumes minimal waste.

	Craft@Hrs	Unit	Material	Labor	Total
Using light-gauge steel framing materials at	—	Lb	1.14	—	1.14
Deduct for multiple spans (supported at midpoint)	—	%	-6.0	—	—
6" steel floor joists 16" OC, 2" flange					
600S200-33 (20 gauge, 1.22 Lbs./SF)	B1@.019	SF	1.39	.64	2.03
600S200-43 (18 gauge, 1.57 Lbs./SF)	B1@.019	SF	1.79	.64	2.43
600S200-54 (16 gauge, 1.96 Lbs./SF)	B1@.021	SF	2.24	.71	2.95
600S200-68 (14 gauge, 2.42 Lbs./SF)	B1@.023	SF	2.76	.78	3.54
600S200-97 (12 gauge, 3.37 Lbs./SF)	B1@.025	SF	3.85	.85	4.70
6" steel floor joists 24" OC, 1-5/8" flange					
600S162-33 (20 gauge, .78 Lbs./SF)	B1@.013	SF	.89	.44	1.33
600S162-43 (18 gauge, 1.01 Lbs./SF)	B1@.013	SF	1.15	.44	1.59
600S162-54 (16 gauge, 1.25 Lbs./SF)	B1@.014	SF	1.43	.47	1.90
600S162-68 (14 gauge, 1.55 Lbs./SF)	B1@.016	SF	1.77	.54	2.31
600S162-97 (12 gauge, 2.15 Lbs./SF)	B1@.018	SF	2.45	.61	3.06
6" steel floor joists 24" OC, 2" flange					
600S200-33 (20 gauge, .86 Lbs./SF)	B1@.013	SF	.98	.44	1.42
600S200-43 (18 gauge, 1.11 Lbs./SF)	B1@.013	SF	1.27	.44	1.71
600S200-54 (16 gauge, 1.38 Lbs./SF)	B1@.014	SF	1.57	.47	2.04
600S200-68 (14 gauge, 1.71 Lbs./SF)	B1@.016	SF	1.95	.54	2.49
600S200-97 (12 gauge, 2.37 Lbs./SF)	B1@.018	SF	2.70	.61	3.31
8" steel floor joists 12" OC, 1-5/8" flange					
800S162-33 (20 gauge, 1.47 Lbs./SF)	B1@.025	SF	1.68	.85	2.53
800S162-43 (18 gauge, 2.24 Lbs./SF)	B1@.025	SF	2.56	.85	3.41
800S162-54 (16 gauge, 2.78 Lbs./SF)	B1@.028	SF	3.17	.95	4.12
800S162-68 (14 gauge, 3.44 Lbs./SF)	B1@.031	SF	3.93	1.05	4.98
800S162-97 (12 gauge, 4.79 Lbs./SF)	B1@.034	SF	5.47	1.15	6.62

	Craft@Hrs	Unit	Material	Labor	Total
8" steel floor joists 12" OC, 2" flange					
800S200-33 (20 gauge, 1.87 Lbs./SF)	B1@.025	SF	2.13	.85	2.98
800S200-43 (18 gauge, 2.42 Lbs./SF)	B1@.025	SF	2.76	.85	3.61
800S200-54 (16 gauge, 3.00 Lbs./SF)	B1@.028	SF	3.42	.95	4.37
800S200-68 (14 gauge, 3.74 Lbs./SF)	B1@.031	SF	4.27	1.05	5.32
800S200-97 (12 gauge, 5.20 Lbs./SF)	B1@.034	SF	5.93	1.15	7.08
8" steel floor joists 16" OC, 1-5/8" flange					
800S162-33 (20 gauge, 1.35 Lbs./SF)	B1@.020	SF	1.54	.68	2.22
800S162-43 (18 gauge, 1.73 Lbs./SF)	B1@.020	SF	1.97	.68	2.65
800S162-54 (16 gauge, 2.14 Lbs./SF)	B1@.022	SF	2.44	.74	3.18
800S162-68 (14 gauge, 2.66 Lbs./SF)	B1@.024	SF	3.04	.81	3.85
800S162-97 (12 gauge, 3.70 Lbs./SF)	B1@.026	SF	4.22	.88	5.10
8" steel floor joists 16" OC, 2" flange					
800S200-33 (20 gauge, 1.45 Lbs./SF)	B1@.020	SF	1.65	.68	2.33
800S200-43 (18 gauge, 1.87 Lbs./SF)	B1@.020	SF	2.13	.68	2.81
800S200-54 (16 gauge, 2.32 Lbs./SF)	B1@.022	SF	2.65	.74	3.39
800S200-68 (14 gauge, 2.89 Lbs./SF)	B1@.024	SF	3.30	.81	4.11
800S200-97 (12 gauge, 4.01 Lbs./SF)	B1@.026	SF	4.58	.88	5.46
8" steel floor joists 24" OC, 1-5/8" flange					
800S162-33 (20 gauge, .95 Lbs./SF)	B1@.014	SF	1.08	.47	1.55
800S162-43 (18 gauge, 1.22 Lbs./SF)	B1@.014	SF	1.39	.47	1.86
800S162-54 (16 gauge, 1.51 Lbs./SF)	B1@.016	SF	1.72	.54	2.26
800S162-68 (14 gauge, 1.87 Lbs./SF)	B1@.017	SF	2.13	.58	2.71
800S162-97 (12 gauge, 2.61 Lbs./SF)	B1@.019	SF	2.98	.64	3.62
8" steel floor joists 24" OC, 2" flange					
800S200-33 (20 gauge, 1.02 Lbs./SF)	B1@.014	SF	1.16	.47	1.63
800S200-43 (18 gauge, 1.32 Lbs./SF)	B1@.014	SF	1.51	.47	1.98
800S200-54 (16 gauge, 1.63 Lbs./SF)	B1@.016	SF	1.86	.54	2.40
800S200-68 (14 gauge, 2.03 Lbs./SF)	B1@.017	SF	2.32	.58	2.90
800S200-97 (12 gauge, 2.83 Lbs./SF)	B1@.019	SF	3.23	.64	3.87
10" steel floor joists 12" OC, 1-5/8" flange					
1000S162-43 (18 gauge, 2.62 Lbs./SF)	B1@.028	SF	2.99	.95	3.94
1000S162-54 (16 gauge, 3.24 Lbs./SF)	B1@.030	SF	3.70	1.02	4.72
1000S162-68 (14 gauge, 4.04 Lbs./SF)	B1@.033	SF	4.61	1.12	5.73
1000S162-97 (12 gauge, 5.63 Lbs./SF)	B1@.037	SF	6.43	1.25	7.68
10" steel floor joists 12" OC, 2" flange					
1000S200-43 (18 gauge, 2.81 Lbs./SF)	B1@.028	SF	3.21	.95	4.16
1000S200-54 (16 gauge, 3.48 Lbs./SF)	B1@.030	SF	3.97	1.02	4.99
1000S200-68 (14 gauge, 4.32 Lbs./SF)	B1@.033	SF	4.93	1.12	6.05
1000S200-97 (12 gauge, 6.05 Lbs./SF)	B1@.037	SF	6.90	1.25	8.15
10" steel floor joists 16" OC, 1-5/8" flange					
1000S162-43 (18 gauge, 2.02 Lbs./SF)	B1@.022	SF	2.31	.74	3.05
1000S162-54 (16 gauge, 2.50 Lbs./SF)	B1@.024	SF	2.85	.81	3.66
1000S162-68 (14 gauge, 3.12 Lbs./SF)	B1@.027	SF	3.56	.91	4.47
1000S162-97 (12 gauge, 4.35 Lbs./SF)	B1@.029	SF	4.96	.98	5.94
10" steel floor joists 16" OC, 2" flange					
1000S200-43 (18 gauge, 2.17 Lbs./SF)	B1@.022	SF	2.48	.74	3.22
1000S200-54 (16 gauge, 2.69 Lbs./SF)	B1@.024	SF	3.07	.81	3.88
1000S200-68 (14 gauge, 3.34 Lbs./SF)	B1@.027	SF	3.81	.91	4.72
1000S200-97 (12 gauge, 4.67 Lbs./SF)	B1@.029	SF	5.33	.98	6.31

	Craft@Hrs	Unit	Material	Labor	Total
10" steel floor joists 24" OC, 1-5/8" flange					
1000S162-43 (18 gauge, 1.42 Lbs./SF)	B1@.015	SF	1.62	.51	2.13
1000S162-54 (16 gauge, 1.76 Lbs./SF)	B1@.017	SF	2.01	.58	2.59
1000S162-68 (14 gauge, 2.20 Lbs./SF)	B1@.019	SF	2.51	.64	3.15
1000S162-97 (12 gauge, 3.06 Lbs./SF)	B1@.020	SF	3.49	.68	4.17
10" steel floor joists 24" OC, 2" flange					
1000S200-43 (18 gauge, 1.52 Lbs./SF)	B1@.015	SF	1.73	.51	2.24
1000S200-54 (16 gauge, 1.89 Lbs./SF)	B1@.017	SF	2.16	.58	2.74
1000S200-68 (14 gauge, 2.35 Lbs./SF)	B1@.019	SF	2.68	.64	3.32
1000S200-97 (12 gauge, 3.29 Lbs./SF)	B1@.020	SF	3.75	.68	4.43
12" steel floor joists 12" OC, 1-5/8" flange					
1200S162-54 (16 gauge, 3.72 Lbs./SF)	B1@.029	SF	4.25	.98	5.23
1200S162-68 (14 gauge, 4.63 Lbs./SF)	B1@.032	SF	5.28	1.08	6.36
1200S162-97 (12 gauge, 6.47 Lbs./SF)	B1@.035	SF	7.38	1.18	8.56
12" steel floor joists 12" OC, 2" flange					
1200S200-54 (16 gauge, 3.95 Lbs./SF)	B1@.029	SF	4.51	.98	5.49
1200S200-68 (14 gauge, 4.92 Lbs./SF)	B1@.032	SF	5.62	1.08	6.70
1200S200-97 (12 gauge, 6.88 Lbs./SF)	B1@.035	SF	7.85	1.18	9.03
12" steel floor joists 16" OC, 1-5/8" flange					
1200S162-54 (16 gauge, 2.88 Lbs./SF)	B1@.023	SF	3.29	.78	4.07
1200S162-68 (14 gauge, 3.57 Lbs./SF)	B1@.025	SF	4.07	.85	4.92
1200S162-97 (12 gauge, 4.99 Lbs./SF)	B1@.028	SF	5.70	.95	6.65
12" steel floor joists 16" OC, 2" flange					
1200S200-54 (16 gauge, 3.05 Lbs./SF)	B1@.023	SF	3.48	.78	4.26
1200S200-68 (14 gauge, 3.80 Lbs./SF)	B1@.025	SF	4.34	.85	5.19
1200S200-97 (12 gauge, 5.31 Lbs./SF)	B1@.028	SF	6.06	.95	7.01
12" steel floor joists 24" OC, 1-5/8" flange					
1200S162-54 (16 gauge, 2.03 Lbs./SF)	B1@.017	SF	2.32	.58	2.90
1200S162-68 (14 gauge, 2.52 Lbs./SF)	B1@.018	SF	2.88	.61	3.49
1200S162-97 (12 gauge, 3.52 Lbs./SF)	B1@.020	SF	4.02	.68	4.70
12" steel floor joists 24" OC, 2" flange					
1200S200-54 (16 gauge, 2.15 Lbs./SF)	B1@.017	SF	2.45	.58	3.03
1200S200-68 (14 gauge, 2.68 Lbs./SF)	B1@.018	SF	3.06	.61	3.67
1200S200-97 (12 gauge, 3.75 Lbs./SF)	B1@.020	SF	4.28	.68	4.96

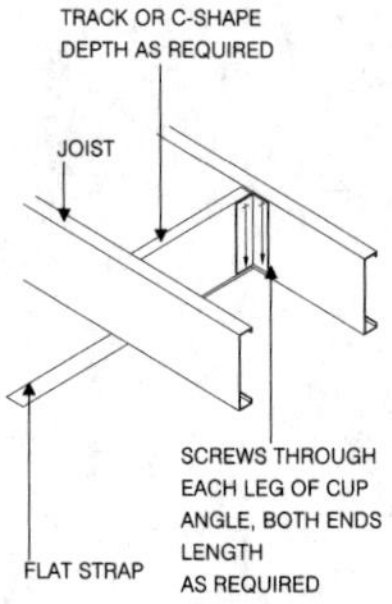

Built-up steel support beams and girders Box or back-to-back beams made from 1-5/8" flange C-shaped sections. Includes typical fasteners and minimal waste.

	Craft@Hrs	Unit	Material	Labor	Total
Using built-up steel sections at	—	Lb	1.14	—	1.14
6" beams and girders built-up from two members					
2-600S162-43 (18 gauge, 3.04 Lbs./LF)	B1@.037	LF	3.47	1.25	4.72
2-600S162-54 (16 gauge, 3.78 Lbs./LF)	B1@.038	LF	4.31	1.29	5.60
2-600S162-68 (14 gauge, 4.72 Lbs./LF)	B1@.039	LF	5.39	1.32	6.71
2-600S162-97 (12 gauge, 6.58 Lbs./LF)	B1@.041	LF	7.51	1.39	8.90
8" beams and girders built-up from two members					
2-800S162-43 (18 gauge, 3.66 Lbs./LF)	B1@.049	LF	4.18	1.66	5.84
2-800S162-54 (16 gauge, 4.56 Lbs./LF)	B1@.050	LF	5.20	1.69	6.89
2-800S162-68 (14 gauge, 5.68 Lbs./LF)	B1@.051	LF	6.48	1.73	8.21
2-800S162-97 (12 gauge, 7.96 Lbs./LF)	B1@.053	LF	9.08	1.79	10.87

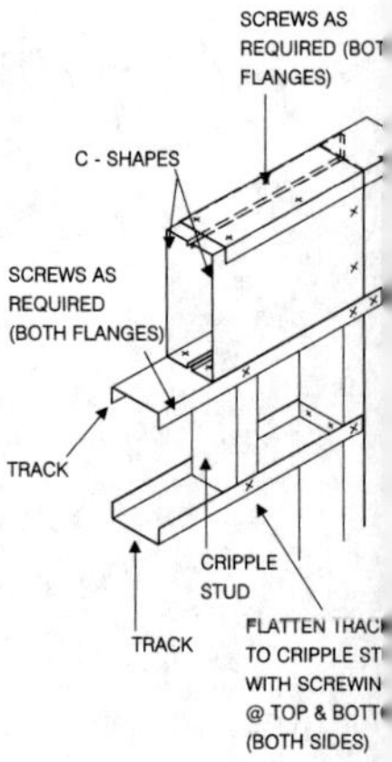

	Craft@Hrs	Unit	Material	Labor	Total
10" beams and girders built-up from two members					
2-1000S162-43 (18 gauge, 4.26 Lbs./LF)	B1@.063	LF	4.86	2.13	6.99
2-1000S162-54 (16 gauge, 5.23 Lbs./LF)	B1@.064	LF	6.07	2.17	8.24
2-1000S162-68 (14 gauge, 6.66 Lbs./LF)	B1@.065	LF	7.60	2.20	9.80
2-1000S162-97 (12 gauge, 9.34 Lbs./LF)	B1@.069	LF	10.70	2.34	13.04
12" beams and girders built-up from two members					
2-1200S162-54 (16 gauge, 6.10 Lbs./LF)	B1@.073	LF	6.96	2.47	9.43
2-1200S162-68 (14 gauge, 7.62 Lbs./LF)	B1@.075	LF	8.70	2.54	11.24
2-1200S162-97 (12 gauge, 10.72 Lbs./LF)	B1@.079	LF	12.20	2.67	14.87

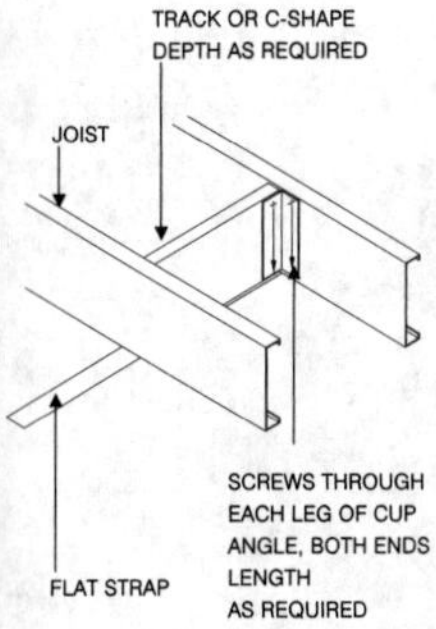

Steel joist solid blocking Installed between 6" thru 12" joists. 18 gauge, C-shape, with angle. Including typical screws, stiffeners and minimal waste.

	Craft@Hrs	Unit	Material	Labor	Total
Using light-gauge steel framing materials at	—	Lb	1.14	—	1.14
Blocking for 6" steel joists					
Joists on 12" centers	B1@.042	Ea	1.87	1.42	3.29
Joists on 16" centers	B1@.042	Ea	2.49	1.42	3.91
Joists on 20" centers	B1@.042	Ea	3.15	1.42	4.57
Joists on 24" centers	B1@.042	Ea	3.77	1.42	5.19
Blocking for 8" steel joists					
Joists on 12" centers	B1@.050	Ea	2.83	1.69	4.52
Joists on 16" centers	B1@.050	Ea	3.77	1.69	5.46
Joists on 20" centers	B1@.050	Ea	4.70	1.69	6.39
Joists on 24" centers	B1@.050	Ea	5.64	1.69	7.33
Blocking for 10" steel joists					
Joists on 12" centers	B1@.057	Ea	3.29	1.93	5.22
Joists on 16" centers	B1@.057	Ea	4.39	1.93	6.32
Joists on 20" centers	B1@.057	Ea	5.50	1.93	7.43
Joists on 24" centers	B1@.057	Ea	6.54	1.93	8.47
Blocking for 12" steel joists					
Joists on 12" centers	B1@.064	Ea	3.80	2.17	5.97
Joists on 16" centers	B1@.064	Ea	5.04	2.17	7.21
Joists on 20" centers	B1@.064	Ea	6.30	2.17	8.47
Joists on 24" centers	B1@.064	Ea	7.54	2.17	9.71

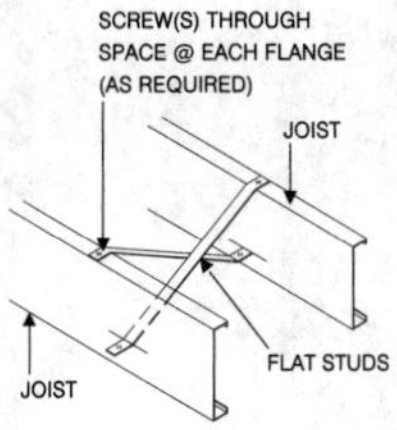

Steel cross bridging for steel floor joists Using strap material or manufactured straps installed between 6" thru 12" joists, cost per pair of straps including typical fasteners.

	Craft@Hrs	Unit	Material	Labor	Total
Joists on 12" centers	B1@.025	Pr	5.10	.85	5.95
Joists on 16" centers	B1@.025	Pr	5.26	.85	6.11
Joists on 20" centers	B1@.025	Pr	5.36	.85	6.21
Joists on 24" centers	B1@.025	Pr	5.51	.85	6.36

Board sheathing subfloor 1" x 6" #3 & Btr (1.28 BF per SF), screwed or pinned to steel floor joists, including fasteners.

	Craft@Hrs	Unit	Material	Labor	Total
Board sheathing, per MBF	—	MBF	2,930.00	—	2,930.00
With 12% shrinkage, 5% waste & screws	B1@.022	SF	3.46	.74	4.20
Add for diagonal patterns	B1@.001	SF	.35	.03	.38

Plywood subfloor CD standard exterior grade. Material costs shown include 5% for waste, screwed or pinned to steel floor joists, including fasteners

	Craft@Hrs	Unit	Material	Labor	Total
3/8"	B1@.012	SF	.46	.41	.87
1/2"	B1@.013	SF	.76	.44	1.20
5/8"	B1@.013	SF	.77	.44	1.21
3/4"	B1@.014	SF	.89	.47	1.36

	Craft@Hrs	Unit	Material	Labor	Total
OSB sheathing, Material costs shown include 5% for waste & fasteners					
7/16"	B1@.011	SF	.40	.37	.77
1/2"	B1@.012	SF	.56	.41	.97
5/8"	B1@.012	SF	.58	.41	.99
3/4" tongue and groove	B1@.014	SF	.71	.47	1.18

Steel interior wall studs Per square foot of partition wall area measured one side. Do not subtract for openings less than 16' wide. Costs include studs, top and bottom track, screws and splices. Add for each corner or wall junction as indicated below. Add the cost of wood plates (if used), support beams, door opening framing and corners from below. All studs with 1-1/4" flange are assumed to have a 3/16" stiffening lip. Labor includes layout, assembly, plumb and align. Figures in parentheses show weight of steel per square foot of wall measured one side. Assumes minimal waste. See the following section for exterior wall estimates.

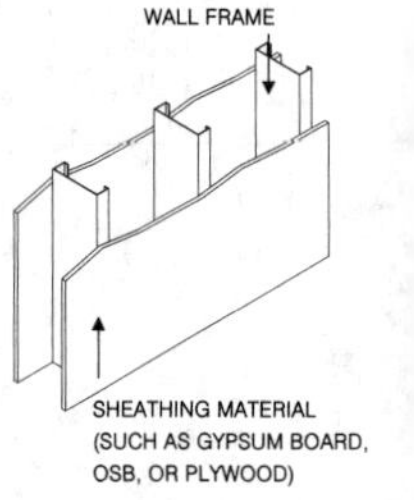

	Craft@Hrs	Unit	Material	Labor	Total
Using light-gauge steel framing materials at	—	Lb	1.14	—	1.14
2-1/2" steel interior wall framing, 16" OC, 1-1/4" flange					
250S125-18 (25 gauge, .33 Lbs./SF)	B1@.018	SF	.38	.61	.99
250S125-27 (22 gauge, .49 Lbs./ SF)	B1@.018	SF	.56	.61	1.17
250S125-30 (20DW gauge, .54 Lbs./SF)	B1@.019	SF	.62	.64	1.26
250S125-33 (20 gauge, .60 Lbs./SF)	B1@.020	SF	.68	.68	1.36
2-1/2" steel interior wall framing, 24" OC, 1-1/4" flange					
250S125-18 (25 gauge, .25 Lbs./SF)	B1@.017	SF	.29	.58	.87
250S125-27 (22 gauge, .37 Lbs./SF)	B1@.017	SF	.42	.58	1.00
250S125-30 (20DW gauge, .41 Lbs./SF)	B1@.018	SF	.47	.61	1.08
250S125-33 (20 gauge, .45 Lbs./SF)	B1@.019	SF	.51	.64	1.15
Add for each 2-1/2" corner or wall junction	B1@.091	Ea	5.15	3.08	8.23
3-1/2" steel interior wall framing, 16" OC, 1-1/4" flange					
350S125-18 (25 gauge, .39 Lbs./SF)	B1@.023	SF	.45	.78	1.23
350S125-27 (22 gauge, .59 Lbs./SF)	B1@.023	SF	.67	.78	1.45
350S125-30 (20DW gauge, .65 Lbs./SF)	B1@.024	SF	.74	.81	1.55
350S125-33 (20 gauge, .72 Lbs./SF)	B1@.025	SF	.82	.85	1.67
3-1/2" steel interior wall framing, 24" OC, 1-1/4" flange					
350S125-18 (25 gauge, .29 Lbs./SF)	B1@.020	SF	.33	.68	1.01
350S125-27 (22 gauge, .44 Lbs./SF)	B1@.020	SF	.50	.68	1.18
350S125-30 (20DW gauge, .49 Lbs./SF)	B1@.022	SF	.56	.74	1.30
350S125-33 (20 gauge, .54 Lbs./SF)	B1@.023	SF	.62	.78	1.40
Add for each 3-1/2" corner or wall junction	B1@.091	Ea	5.49	3.08	8.57
3-5/8" steel interior wall framing, 16" OC, 1-1/4" flange					
362S125-18 (25 gauge, .40 Lbs./SF)	B1@.023	SF	.46	.78	1.24
362S125-27 (22 gauge, .60 Lbs./SF)	B1@.023	SF	.68	.78	1.46
362S125-30 (20DW gauge, .66 Lbs./SF)	B1@.024	SF	.75	.81	1.56
362S125-33 (20 gauge, .73 Lbs./SF)	B1@.025	SF	.83	.85	1.68
3-5/8" steel interior wall framing, 24" OC, 1-1/4" flange					
362S125-18 (25 gauge, .30 Lbs./SF)	B1@.021	SF	.34	.71	1.05
362S125-27 (22 gauge, .45 Lbs./SF)	B1@.021	SF	.51	.71	1.22
362S125-30 (20DW gauge, .50 Lbs./SF)	B1@.022	SF	.57	.74	1.31
362S125-33 (20 gauge, .55 Lbs./SF)	B1@.023	SF	.63	.78	1.41
Add for each 3-5/8" corner or wall junction	B1@.091	Ea	5.49	3.08	8.57

	Craft@Hrs	Unit	Material	Labor	Total
5-1/2" steel interior wall framing, 16" OC, 1-1/4" flange					
550S125-18 (25 gauge, .52 Lbs./SF)	B1@.029	SF	.59	.98	1.57
550S125-27 (22 gauge, .78 Lbs./SF)	B1@.029	SF	.89	.98	1.87
550S125-30 (20DW gauge, .86 Lbs./SF)	B1@.030	SF	.98	1.02	2.00
550S125-33 (20 gauge, .95 Lbs./SF)	B1@.032	SF	1.08	1.08	2.16
5-1/2" steel interior wall framing, 24" OC, 1-1/4" flange					
550S125-18 (25 gauge, .39 Lbs./SF)	B1@.028	SF	.45	.95	1.40
550S125-27 (22 gauge, .59 Lbs./SF)	B1@.028	SF	.67	.95	1.62
550S125-30 (20DW gauge, .65 Lbs./SF)	B1@.029	SF	.74	.98	1.72
550S125-33 (20 gauge, .71 Lbs./SF)	B1@.030	SF	.81	1.02	1.83
Add for each 5-1/2" corner or wall junction	B1@.091	Ea	7.18	3.08	10.26
6" steel interior wall framing, 16" OC, 1-1/4" flange					
600S125-18 (25 gauge, .55 Lbs./SF)	B1@.028	SF	.63	.95	1.58
600S125-27 (22 gauge, .83 Lbs./SF)	B1@.029	SF	.95	.98	1.93
600S125-30 (20DW gauge), .91 Lbs./SF	B1@.030	SF	1.04	1.02	2.06
600S125-33 (20 gauge, 1.01 Lbs./SF)	B1@.032	SF	1.15	1.08	2.23
6" steel interior wall framing, 24" OC, 1-1/4" flange					
600S125-18 (25 gauge, .41 Lbs./SF)	B1@.027	SF	.47	.91	1.38
600S125-27 (22 gauge, .62 Lbs./SF)	B1@.027	SF	.71	.91	1.62
600S125-30 (20DW gauge, .68 Lbs./SF)	B1@.028	SF	.78	.95	1.73
600S125-33 (20 gauge, .76 Lbs./SF)	B1@.030	SF	.87	1.02	1.89
Add for each 6" corner or wall junction	B1@.091	Ea	7.66	3.08	10.74

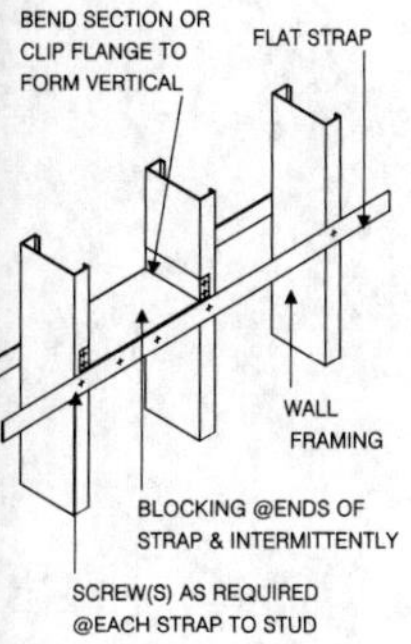

Steel exterior wall studs Per square foot of wall area measured one side. Do not subtract for openings less than 16' wide. Add for each corner and partition from below. Costs include studs, top and bottom track, screws and splices. Add for door and window opening framing, backing, cross-bracing and sheathing for shear walls from the sections that follow. Add the cost of wood plates (if used), support beams, door opening framing, corners and wall junctions from below. All studs with 1-5/8" flange are assumed to have a 1/2" stiffening lip. Labor includes layout, assembly, plumb and align. Figures in parentheses show weight of steel per square foot of wall measured one side. Assumes minimal waste. See the previous section for interior (partition) wall estimates.

	Craft@Hrs	Unit	Material	Labor	Total
Using light-gauge steel framing materials at	—	Lb	1.14	—	1.14
3-1/2" steel exterior wall framing, 12" OC, 1-5/8" flange					
350S162-33 (20 gauge, 1.10 Lbs./SF)	B1@.026	SF	1.26	.88	2.14
350S162-43 (18 gauge, 1.43 Lbs./SF)	B1@.026	SF	1.63	.88	2.51
350S162-54 (16 gauge, 1.76 Lbs./SF)	B1@.028	SF	2.01	.95	2.96
350S162-68 (14 gauge, 2.19 Lbs./SF)	B1@.029	SF	2.50	.98	3.48
3-1/2" steel exterior wall framing, 16" OC, 1-5/8" flange					
350S162-33 (20 gauge, .88 Lbs./SF)	B1@.025	SF	1.00	.85	1.85
350S162-43 (18 gauge, 1.14 Lbs./SF)	B1@.025	SF	1.30	.85	2.15
350S162-54 (16 gauge, 1.41 Lbs./SF)	B1@.028	SF	1.61	.95	2.56
350S162-68 (14 gauge, 1.75 Lbs./SF)	B1@.029	SF	2.00	.98	2.98
3-1/2" steel exterior wall framing, 24" OC, 1-5/8" flange					
350S162-33 (20 gauge, .66 Lbs./SF)	B1@.023	SF	.75	.78	1.53
350S162-43 (18 gauge, .86 Lbs./SF)	B1@.023	SF	.98	.78	1.76
350S162-54 (16 gauge, 1.06 Lbs./SF)	B1@.025	SF	1.21	.85	2.06
350S162-68 (14 gauge, 1.31 Lbs./SF)	B1@.026	SF	1.50	.88	2.38
Add for each 3-1/2" corner or partition (33 mil)	B1@.091	Ea	6.74	3.08	9.82

	Craft@Hrs	Unit	Material	Labor	Total
3-5/8" steel exterior wall framing, 12" OC, 1-5/8" flange					
362S162-33 (20 gauge, 1.11 Lbs./SF)	B1@.026	SF	1.27	.88	2.15
362S162-43 (18 gauge, 1.45 Lbs./SF)	B1@.026	SF	1.65	.88	2.53
362S162-54 (16 gauge, 1.80 Lbs./SF)	B1@.028	SF	2.05	.95	3.00
362S162-68 (14 gauge, 2.23 Lbs./SF)	B1@.029	SF	2.55	.98	3.53
3-5/8" steel exterior wall framing, 16" OC, 1-5/8" flange					
362S162-33 (20 gauge, .89 Lbs./SF)	B1@.025	SF	1.02	.85	1.87
362S162-43 (18 gauge, 1.16 Lbs./SF)	B1@.025	SF	1.32	.85	2.17
362S162-54 (16 gauge, 1.44 Lbs./SF)	B1@.028	SF	1.64	.95	2.59
362S162-68 (14 gauge, 1.78 Lbs./SF)	B1@.029	SF	2.03	.98	3.01
3-5/8" steel exterior wall framing, 24" OC, 1-5/8" flange					
362S162-33 (20 gauge, .67 Lbs./SF)	B1@.023	SF	.76	.78	1.54
362S162-43 (18 gauge, .87 Lbs./SF)	B1@.023	SF	.99	.78	1.77
362S162-54 (16 gauge, 1.08 Lbs./SF)	B1@.025	SF	1.23	.85	2.08
362S162-68 (14 gauge, 1.34 Lbs./SF)	B1@.026	SF	1.53	.88	2.41
Add for each 3-5/8" corner or partition (33 mil)	B1@.091	Ea	6.92	3.08	10.00
5-1/2" steel exterior wall framing, 12" OC, 1-5/8" flange					
550S162-33 (20 gauge, 1.39 Lbs./SF)	B1@.035	SF	1.59	1.18	2.77
550S162-43 (18 gauge, 1.80 Lbs./SF)	B1@.036	SF	2.05	1.22	3.27
550S162-54 (16 gauge, 2.25 Lbs./SF)	B1@.039	SF	2.57	1.32	3.89
550S162-68 (14 gauge, 2.80 Lbs./SF)	B1@.041	SF	3.20	1.39	4.59
5-1/2" steel exterior wall framing, 16" OC, 1-5/8" flange					
550S162-33 (20 gauge, 1.11 Lbs./SF)	B1@.032	SF	1.27	1.08	2.35
550S162-43 (18 gauge, 1.44 Lbs./SF)	B1@.033	SF	1.64	1.12	2.76
550S162-54 (16 gauge, 1.80 Lbs./SF)	B1@.035	SF	2.05	1.18	3.23
550S162-68 (14 gauge, 2.24 Lbs./SF)	B1@.037	SF	2.56	1.25	3.81
5-1/2" steel exterior wall framing, 20" OC, 1-5/8" flange					
550S162-33 (20 gauge, .94 Lbs./SF)	B1@.031	SF	1.07	1.05	2.12
550S162-43 (18 gauge, 1.22 Lbs./SF)	B1@.032	SF	1.39	1.08	2.47
550S162-54 (16 gauge, 1.53 Lbs./SF)	B1@.034	SF	1.75	1.15	2.90
550S162-68 (14 gauge, 1.90 Lbs./SF)	B1@.036	SF	2.17	1.22	3.39
5-1/2" steel exterior wall framing, 24" OC, 1-5/8" flange					
550S162-33 (20 gauge, .83 Lbs./SF)	B1@.030	SF	.95	1.02	1.97
550S162-43 (18 gauge, 1.08 Lbs./SF)	B1@.031	SF	1.23	1.05	2.28
550S162-54 (16 gauge, 1.35 Lbs./SF)	B1@.033	SF	1.54	1.12	2.66
550S162-68 (14 gauge, 1.68 Lbs./SF)	B1@.035	SF	1.92	1.18	3.10
Add for each 5-1/2" corner or partition (43 mil)	B1@.091	Ea	8.58	3.08	11.66
6" steel exterior wall framing, 12" OC, 1-5/8" flange					
600S162-33 (20 gauge, 1.46 Lbs./SF)	B1@.035	SF	1.67	1.18	2.85
600S162-43 (18 gauge, 1.90 Lbs./SF)	B1@.036	SF	2.17	1.22	3.39
600S162-54 (16 gauge, 2.36 Lbs./SF)	B1@.039	SF	2.69	1.32	4.01
600S162-68 (14 gauge, 2.95 Lbs./SF)	B1@.041	SF	3.37	1.39	4.76
600S162-97 (12 gauge, 4.11 Lbs./SF)	B1@.043	SF	4.69	1.46	6.15
6" steel exterior wall framing, 16" OC, 1-5/8" flange					
600S162-33 (20 gauge, 1.17 Lbs./SF)	B1@.032	SF	1.34	1.08	2.42
600S162-43 (18 gauge, 1.52 Lbs./SF)	B1@.033	SF	1.73	1.12	2.85
600S162-54 (16 gauge, 1.89 Lbs./SF)	B1@.035	SF	2.16	1.18	3.34
600S162-68 (14 gauge, 2.36 Lbs./SF)	B1@.037	SF	2.69	1.25	3.94
600S162-97 (12 gauge, 3.29 Lbs./SF)	B1@.039	SF	3.75	1.32	5.07

	Craft@Hrs	Unit	Material	Labor	Total
6" steel exterior wall framing, 20" OC, 1-5/8" flange					
600S162-33 (20 gauge, .99 Lbs./SF)	B1@.031	SF	1.13	1.05	2.18
600S162-43 (18 gauge, 1.29 Lbs./SF)	B1@.032	SF	1.47	1.08	2.55
600S162-54 (16 gauge, 1.60 Lbs./SF)	B1@.034	SF	1.83	1.15	2.98
600S162-68 (14 gauge, 2.00 Lbs./SF)	B1@.036	SF	2.28	1.22	3.50
600S162-97 (12 gauge), 2.79 Lbs./SF	B1@.038	SF	3.18	1.29	4.47
6" steel exterior wall framing, 24" OC, 1-5/8" flange					
600S162-33 (20 gauge, .88 Lbs./SF)	B1@.030	SF	1.00	1.02	2.02
600S162-43 (18 gauge, 1.14 Lbs./SF)	B1@.031	SF	1.30	1.05	2.35
600S162-54 (16 gauge, 1.42 Lbs./SF)	B1@.033	SF	1.62	1.12	2.74
600S162-68 (14 gauge, 1.77 Lbs./SF)	B1@.035	SF	2.02	1.18	3.20
600S162-97 (12 gauge, 2.47 Lbs./SF)	B1@.037	SF	2.82	1.25	4.07
Add for each 6" corner or partition (43 mil)	B1@.091	Ea	8.99	3.08	12.07
8" steel exterior wall framing, 16" OC, 1-5/8" flange					
18 gauge	B1@.044	SF	2.66	1.49	4.15
16 gauge	B1@.046	SF	2.97	1.56	4.53

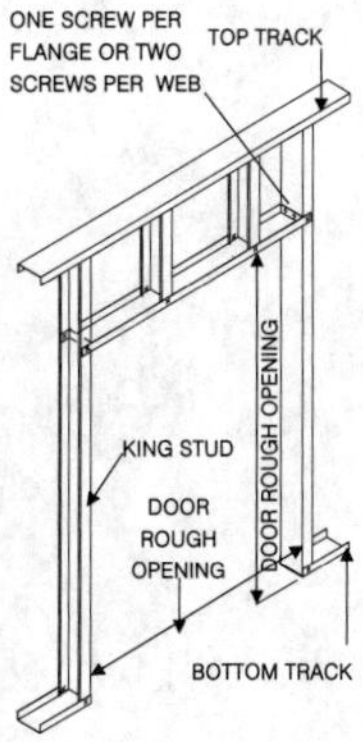

Door opening steel framing In wall studs, based on walls 8' high. Costs shown are per each door opening and include header of appropriate size, double king studs each side of the opening for doors greater than 3' wide, double trimmer studs each side of the opening for doors greater than 8' wide, cripples, blocking, screws and normal waste. Width shown is size of finished opening. Figures in parentheses indicate header size.

	Craft@Hrs	Unit	Material	Labor	Total
Using wall studs and headers, per Lb	—	Lb	1.14	—	1.14
Door opening steel framing in 3-1/2" wall, 20 gauge (33 mil) stud wall, opening size as shown					
To 3' wide, 6" header, 18 gauge, two 600S162-43, 40.05 Lbs	B1@1.00	Ea	45.70	33.90	79.60
Over 3' to 4' wide, 6" header, 16 gauge, two 600S162-54, 56.48 Lbs	B1@1.33	Ea	64.50	45.00	109.50
Over 4' to 5' wide, 8" header, 16 gauge, two 800S162-54, 63.85 Lbs	B1@1.67	Ea	72.90	56.50	129.40
Over 5' to 6' wide, 8" header, 16 gauge, two 800S162-54, 68.43 Lbs	B1@1.99	Ea	78.10	67.40	145.50
Over 6' to 8' wide, 10" header, 14 gauge, two 1000S162-68, 107.25 Lbs	B1@2.33	Ea	122.00	78.90	200.90
Over 8' to 10' wide, 12" header, 14 gauge, two 1200S162-68, 130.15 Lbs	B1@2.33	Ea	149.00	78.90	227.90
Over 10' to 12' wide, 12" header, 12 gauge, two 1200S162-97, 182.60 Lbs	B1@2.67	Ea	208.00	90.40	298.40
Add per foot of height for 3-1/2" walls over 8' in height	—	LF	6.57	—	6.57
Door opening steel framing in 5-1/2" wall, 18 gauge (43 mil) stud wall, opening size as shown					
To 3' wide, 6" header, 18 gauge, two 600S162-43, 53.75 Lbs	B1@1.00	Ea	61.30	33.90	95.20
Over 3' to 4' wide, 6" header, 16 gauge, two 600S162-54, 82.80 Lbs	B1@1.33	Ea	94.50	45.00	139.50
Over 4' to 5' wide, 8" header, 16 gauge, two 800S162-54, 90.00 Lbs	B1@1.67	Ea	103.00	56.50	159.50
Over 5' to 6' wide, 8" header, 16 gauge, two 800S162-54, 94.55 Lbs	B1@1.99	Ea	108.00	67.40	175.40
Over 6' to 8' wide, 10" header, 14 gauge, two 1000S162-68, 120.00 Lbs	B1@2.33	Ea	137.00	78.90	215.90
Over 8' to 10' wide, 12" header, 14 gauge, two 1200S162-68, 162.60 Lbs	B1@2.33	Ea	186.00	78.90	264.90

	Craft@Hrs	Unit	Material	Labor	Total
Over 10' to 12' wide, 12" header, 12 gauge, two 1200S162-97, 215.05 Lbs	B1@2.67	Ea	245.00	90.40	335.40
Add per foot of height for 5-1/2" walls over 8' in height	—	LF	10.70	—	10.70

Window opening steel framing In wall studs, based on walls 8' high. Costs shown are per window opening and include header of appropriate size, sill track, double king studs each side of the opening for windows greater than 3' wide, double trimmer studs each side of the opening for windows greater than 8' wide, top and bottom cripples, blocking, screws and normal waste. Width shown is size of finished opening.

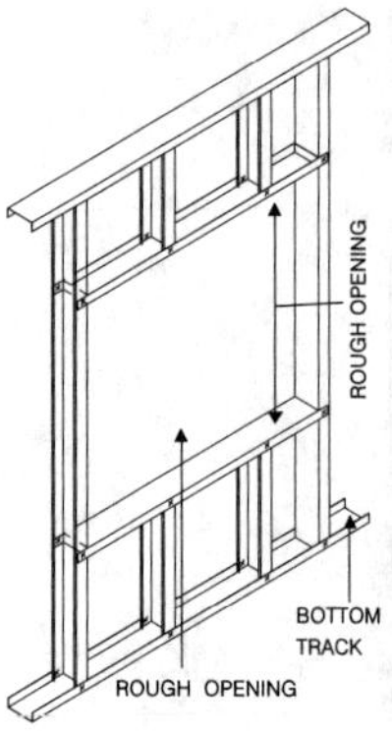

	Craft@Hrs	Unit	Material	Labor	Total
Using steel framing materials at	—	Lb	1.14	—	1.14
Window opening steel framing in 3-1/2" wall, 20 gauge (33 mil) stud wall, opening size shown					
To 2' wide, 4" header, 18 gauge, two 400S162-43, 35.18 Lbs	B1@1.20	Ea	40.20	40.60	80.80
Over 2' to 3' wide, 6" header, 18 gauge, two 600S162-43, 40.48 Lbs	B1@1.40	Ea	46.20	47.40	93.60
Over 3' to 4' wide, 6" header, 16 gauge, two 600S162-54, 61.85 Lbs	B1@1.74	Ea	70.60	58.90	129.50
Over 4' to 5' wide, 8" header, 16 gauge, two 800S162-54, 71.45 Lbs	B1@2.08	Ea	81.60	70.40	152.00
Over 5' to 6' wide, 8" header, 16 gauge, two 800S162-54, 77.55 Lbs	B1@2.41	Ea	88.50	81.60	170.10
Over 6' to 7' wide, 8" header, 14 gauge, two 800S162-68, 91.45 Lbs	B1@2.75	Ea	104.00	93.10	197.10
Over 7' to 8' wide, 10" header, 14 gauge, two 1000S162-68, 106.23 Lbs	B1@3.08	Ea	121.00	104.00	225.00
Over 8' to 10' wide, 12" header, 14 gauge, two 1200S162-68, 144.20 Lbs	B1@3.08	Ea	165.00	104.00	269.00
Over 10' to 12' wide, 12" header, 12 gauge, two 1200S162-97, 199.68 Lbs	B1@3.42	Ea	228.00	116.00	344.00
Add per foot of height for 3-1/2" walls over 8' high	—	LF	6.57	—	6.57
Window opening steel framing in 5-1/2" wall, 18 gauge, 43 mil stud wall, opening size as shown					
To 2' wide, 4" header, 18 gauge, two 400S162-43, 55.00 Lbs	B1@1.20	Ea	62.80	40.60	103.40
Over 2' to 3' wide, 6" header, 18 gauge, two 600S162-43, 61.18 Lbs	B1@1.40	Ea	69.80	47.40	117.20
Over 3' to 4' wide, 6" header, 16 gauge, two 600S162-54, 92.62 Lbs	B1@1.74	Ea	106.00	58.90	164.90
Over 4' to 5' wide, 8" header, 16 gauge, two 800S162-54, 103.15 Lbs	B1@2.08	Ea	118.00	70.40	188.40
Over 5' to 6' wide, 8" header, 16 gauge, two 800S162-54, 110.30 Lbs	B1@2.41	Ea	126.00	81.60	207.60
Over 6' to 8' wide, 10" header, 14 gauge, two 1000S162-68, 140.95 Lbs	B1@3.08	Ea	161.00	104.00	265.00
Over 8' to 10' wide, 12" header, 14 gauge, two 1200S162-68, 188.78 Lbs	B1@3.08	Ea	215.00	104.00	319.00
Over 8' to 12' wide, 12" header, 12 gauge, two 1200S162-97, 246.43 Lbs	B1@3.42	Ea	281.00	116.00	397.00
Add per foot of height for 5-1/2" walls over 8' high	—	LF	10.70	—	10.70

Steel wall bracing See also sheathing for plywood bracing and shear panels.

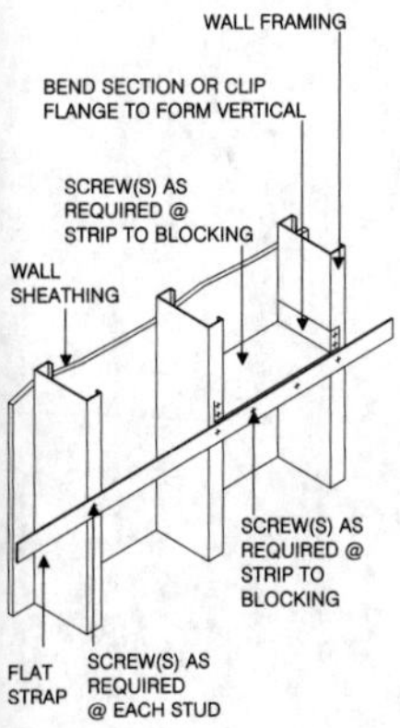

	Craft@Hrs	Unit	Material	Labor	Total
Steel strap bracing					
4" wide 33 mil with gusset plates	B1@.015	LF	.44	.51	.95
4" wide 43 mil with gusset plates	B1@.015	LF	.57	.51	1.08
8.8" wide 33 mil	B1@.015	LF	.89	.51	1.40
8.8" wide 43 mil	B1@.015	LF	1.16	.51	1.67
8.8" wide 54 mil	B1@.015	LF	1.46	.51	1.97
Intermediate bracing 3-1/2", 33 mil studs or track					
350S162-33 (0.80 Lbs./LF)	B1@.019	LF	1.09	.64	1.73
Temporary wood bracing for walls, assumes salvage at 50% and 3 uses					
1" x 4" Std & Btr	B1@.006	LF	.19	.20	.39
1" x 6" Std & Btr	B1@.010	LF	.28	.34	.62
2" x 4" utility	B1@.012	LF	.13	.41	.54
2" x 6" utility	B1@.018	LF	.19	.61	.80

Wood wall plates Std & Btr, untreated. For pressure treated plates, see Wood sill plates for steel framing previously in this section. Figures in parentheses indicate board feet per LF. Costs shown include 10% waste.

	Craft@Hrs	Unit	Material	Labor	Total
2" x 3" wall plates, per MBF	—	MBF	912.00	—	912.00
2" x 4" wall plates, per MBF	—	MBF	777.00	—	777.00
2" x 6" wall plates, per MBF	—	MBF	759.00	—	759.00
2" x 8" wall plates, per MBF	—	MBF	776.00	—	776.00
2" x 3" (.55 BF per LF)	B1@.010	LF	.55	.34	.89
2" x 4" (.73 BF per LF)	B1@.012	LF	.62	.41	1.03
2" x 6" (1.10 BF per LF)	B1@.018	LF	.92	.61	1.53
2" x 8" (1.10 BF per LF)	B1@.018	LF	1.20	.61	1.81

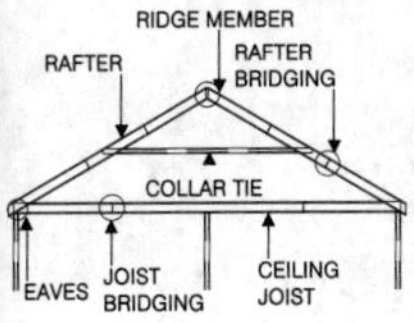

Steel ceiling joists and soffits Per SF of area covered. Including typical stiffeners, splices, bracing, rim joists and screws. Add the cost of beams, bridging, blocking, ledger strips and trimmers as required. See costs for beams, bridging, backing, blocking and trimmers elsewhere in this section. Deduct for openings over 25 SF. Labor includes layout, assembly and alignment. Figures in parentheses show weight of steel per square foot of ceiling. Assumes minimal waste.

	Craft@Hrs	Unit	Material	Labor	Total
Using light-gauge steel framing materials at	—	Lb	1.14	—	1.14
3-1/2" steel ceiling joists, 16" OC, 1-5/8" flange					
350S162-33 (20 gauge, .88 Lbs./SF)	B1@.022	SF	1.00	.74	1.74
350S162-43 (18 gauge), 1.11 Lbs./SF	B1@.024	SF	1.27	.81	2.08
350S162-54 (16 gauge, 1.35 Lbs./SF)	B1@.027	SF	1.54	.91	2.45
350S162-68 (14 gauge, 1.65 Lbs./SF)	B1@.029	SF	1.88	.98	2.86
3-1/2" steel ceiling joists, 24" OC, 1-5/8" flange					
350S162-33 (20 gauge, .63 Lbs./SF)	B1@.015	SF	.72	.51	1.23
350S162-43 (18 gauge, .79 Lbs./SF)	B1@.017	SF	.90	.58	1.48
350S162-54 (16 gauge, .96 Lbs./SF)	B1@.019	SF	1.10	.64	1.74
350S162-68 (14 gauge, 1.17 Lbs./SF)	B1@.020	SF	1.34	.68	2.02
4" steel ceiling joists, 16" OC, 1-5/8" flange					
400S162-33 (20 gauge, .93 Lbs./SF)	B1@.022	SF	1.06	.74	1.80
400S162-43 (18 gauge), 1.17 Lbs./SF	B1@.024	SF	1.34	.81	2.15
400S162-54 (16 gauge, 1.44 Lbs./SF)	B1@.027	SF	1.64	.91	2.55
400S162-68 (14 gauge, 1.76 Lbs./SF)	B1@.029	SF	2.01	.98	2.99

	Craft@Hrs	Unit	Material	Labor	Total
4" steel ceiling joists, 24" OC, 1-5/8" flange					
400S162-33 (20 gauge, .67 Lbs./SF)	B1@.015	SF	.76	.51	1.27
400S162-43 (18 gauge, .84 Lbs./SF)	B1@.017	SF	.96	.58	1.54
400S162-54 (16 gauge, 1.02 Lbs./SF)	B1@.019	SF	1.16	.64	1.80
400S162-68 (14 gauge, 1.25 Lbs./SF)	B1@.020	SF	1.43	.68	2.11
5-1/2" steel ceiling joists, 12" OC, 1-5/8" flange					
550S162-33 (20 gauge, 1.41 Lbs./SF)	B1@.029	SF	1.61	.98	2.59
550S162-43 (18 gauge, 1.79 Lbs./SF)	B1@.032	SF	2.04	1.08	3.12
550S162-54 (16 gauge, 2.21 Lbs./SF)	B1@.035	SF	2.52	1.18	3.70
550S162-68 (14 gauge, 2.72 Lbs./SF)	B1@.038	SF	3.10	1.29	4.39
5-1/2" steel ceiling joists, 16" OC, 1-5/8" flange					
550S162-33 (20 gauge, 1.09 Lbs./SF)	B1@.022	SF	1.24	.74	1.98
550S162-43 (18 gauge, 1.39 Lbs./SF)	B1@.024	SF	1.59	.81	2.40
550S162-54 (16 gauge, 1.71 Lbs./SF)	B1@.027	SF	1.95	.91	2.86
550S162-68 (14 gauge, 2.10 Lbs./SF)	B1@.029	SF	2.40	.98	3.38
5-1/2" steel ceiling joists, 24" OC, 1-5/8" flange					
550S162-33 (20 gauge, .78 Lbs./SF)	B1@.016	SF	.89	.54	1.43
550S162-43 (18 gauge, .99 Lbs./SF)	B1@.018	SF	1.13	.61	1.74
550S162-54 (16 gauge, 1.21 Lbs./SF)	B1@.020	SF	1.38	.68	2.06
550S162-68 (14 gauge, 1.48 Lbs./SF)	B1@.022	SF	1.69	.74	2.43
6" steel ceiling joists, 12" OC, 1-5/8" flange					
600S162-33 (20 gauge, 1.48 Lbs./SF)	B1@.029	SF	1.69	.98	2.67
600S162-43 (18 gauge, 1.89 Lbs./SF)	B1@.032	SF	2.16	1.08	3.24
600S162-54 (16 gauge, 2.32 Lbs./SF)	B1@.035	SF	2.65	1.18	3.83
600S162-68 (14 gauge, 2.86 Lbs./SF)	B1@.038	SF	3.26	1.29	4.55
6" steel ceiling joists, 16" OC, 1-5/8" flange					
600S162-33 (20 gauge, 1.15 Lbs./SF)	B1@.022	SF	1.31	.74	2.05
600S162-43 (18 gauge, 1.46 Lbs./SF)	B1@.024	SF	1.67	.81	2.48
600S162-54 (16 gauge, 1.79 Lbs./SF)	B1@.027	SF	2.04	.91	2.95
600S162-68 (14 gauge, 2.21 Lbs./SF)	B1@.029	SF	2.52	.98	3.50
6" steel ceiling joists, 24" OC, 1-5/8" flange					
600S162-33 (20 gauge, .82 Lbs./SF)	B1@.016	SF	.94	.54	1.48
600S162-43 (18 gauge, 1.04 Lbs./SF)	B1@.018	SF	1.19	.61	1.80
600S162-54 (16 gauge, 1.27 Lbs./SF)	B1@.020	SF	1.45	.68	2.13
600S162-68 (14 gauge, 1.56 Lbs./SF)	B1@.022	SF	1.78	.74	2.52
8" steel ceiling joists, 12" OC, 1-5/8" flange					
800S162-33 (20 gauge, 1.78 Lbs./SF)	B1@.031	SF	2.03	1.05	3.08
800S162-43 (18 gauge, 2.26 Lbs./SF)	B1@.034	SF	2.58	1.15	3.73
800S162-54 (16 gauge, 2.79 Lbs./SF)	B1@.037	SF	3.18	1.25	4.43
800S162-68 (14 gauge, 3.44 Lbs./SF)	B1@.041	SF	3.93	1.39	5.32
800S162-97 (12 gauge, 4.76 Lbs./SF)	B1@.049	SF	5.43	1.66	7.09
8" steel ceiling joists, 16" OC, 1-5/8" flange					
800S162-33 (20 gauge, 1.38 Lbs./SF)	B1@.024	SF	1.57	.81	2.38
800S162-43 (18 gauge, 1.75 Lbs./SF)	B1@.027	SF	2.00	.91	2.91
800S162-54 (16 gauge, 2.15 Lbs./SF)	B1@.029	SF	2.45	.98	3.43
800S162-68 (14 gauge, 2.65 Lbs./SF)	B1@.032	SF	3.02	1.08	4.10
800S162-97 (12 gauge, 3.67 Lbs./SF)	B1@.039	SF	4.19	1.32	5.51
8" steel ceiling joists, 20" OC, 1-5/8" flange					
800S162-33 (20 gauge, 1.14 Lbs./SF)	B1@.020	SF	1.30	.68	1.98
800S162-43 (18 gauge, 1.44 Lbs./SF)	B1@.022	SF	1.64	.74	2.38
800S162-54 (16 gauge, 1.77 Lbs./SF)	B1@.024	SF	2.02	.81	2.83
800S162-68 (14 gauge, 2.18 Lbs./SF)	B1@.026	SF	2.49	.88	3.37
800S162-97 (12 gauge, 3.01 Lbs./SF)	B1@.032	SF	3.44	1.08	4.52

	Craft@Hrs	Unit	Material	Labor	Total
8" steel ceiling joists, 24" OC, 1-5/8" flange					
800S162-33 (20 gauge, .98 Lbs./SF)	B1@.018	SF	1.12	.61	1.73
800S162-43 (18 gauge, 1.24 Lbs./SF)	B1@.019	SF	1.42	.64	2.06
800S162-54 (16 gauge, 1.52 Lbs./SF)	B1@.021	SF	1.73	.71	2.44
800S162-68 (14 gauge, 1.87 Lbs./SF)	B1@.023	SF	2.13	.78	2.91
800S162-97 (12 gauge, 2.57 Lbs./SF)	B1@.028	SF	2.93	.95	3.88
10" steel ceiling joists, 12" OC, 1-5/8" flange					
1000S162-43 (18 gauge, 2.63 Lbs./SF)	B1@.033	SF	3.00	1.12	4.12
1000S162-54 (16 gauge, 3.24 Lbs./SF)	B1@.036	SF	3.70	1.22	4.92
1000S162-68 (14 gauge, 4.02 Lbs./SF)	B1@.040	SF	4.59	1.35	5.94
1000S162-97 (12 gauge, 5.58 Lbs./SF)	B1@.048	SF	6.37	1.62	7.99
10" steel ceiling joists, 16" OC, 1-5/8" flange					
1000S162-43 (18 gauge, 2.03 Lbs./SF)	B1@.025	SF	2.32	.85	3.17
1000S162-54 (16 gauge, 2.50 Lbs./SF)	B1@.028	SF	2.85	.95	3.80
1000S162-68 (14 gauge, 3.10 Lbs./SF)	B1@.031	SF	3.54	1.05	4.59
1000S162-97 (12 gauge, 4.29 Lbs./SF)	B1@.037	SF	4.90	1.25	6.15
10" steel ceiling joists, 20" OC, 1-5/8" flange					
1000S162-43 (18 gauge, 1.67 Lbs./SF)	B1@.022	SF	1.91	.74	2.65
1000S162-54 (16 gauge, 2.06 Lbs./SF)	B1@.024	SF	2.35	.81	3.16
1000S162-68 (14 gauge, 2.54 Lbs./SF)	B1@.027	SF	2.90	.91	3.81
1000S162-97 (12 gauge, 3.52 Lbs./SF)	B1@.032	SF	4.02	1.08	5.10
10" steel ceiling joists, 24" OC, 1-5/8" flange					
1000S162-43 (18 gauge, 1.44 Lbs./SF)	B1@.019	SF	1.64	.64	2.28
1000S162-54 (16 gauge, 1.76 Lbs./SF)	B1@.021	SF	2.01	.71	2.72
1000S162-68 (14 gauge, 2.18 Lbs./SF)	B1@.023	SF	2.49	.78	3.27
1000S162-97 (12 gauge, 3.01 Lbs./SF)	B1@.027	SF	3.44	.91	4.35
12" steel ceiling joists, 12" OC, 1-5/8" flange					
1200S162-54 (16 gauge, 3.71 Lbs./SF)	B1@.034	SF	4.23	1.15	5.38
1200S162-68 (14 gauge, 4.60 Lbs./SF)	B1@.038	SF	5.25	1.29	6.54
1200S162-97 (12 gauge, 6.39 Lbs./SF)	B1@.045	SF	7.29	1.52	8.81
12" steel ceiling joists, 16" OC, 1-5/8" flange					
1200S162-54 (16 gauge, 2.86 Lbs./SF)	B1@.028	SF	3.26	.95	4.21
1200S162-68 (14 gauge, 3.54 Lbs./SF)	B1@.030	SF	4.04	1.02	5.06
1200S162-97 (12 gauge, 4.92 Lbs./SF)	B1@.036	SF	5.62	1.22	6.84
12" steel ceiling joists, 20" OC, 1-5/8" flange					
1200S162-54 (16 gauge, 2.35 Lbs./SF)	B1@.022	SF	2.68	.74	3.42
1200S162-68 (14 gauge, 2.90 Lbs./SF)	B1@.024	SF	3.31	.81	4.12
1200S162-97 (12 gauge, 4.03 Lbs./SF)	B1@.029	SF	4.60	.98	5.58
12" steel ceiling joists, 24" OC, 1-5/8" flange					
1200S162-54 (16 gauge, 2.01 Lbs./SF)	B1@.020	SF	2.29	.68	2.97
1200S162-68 (14 gauge, 2.49 Lbs./SF)	B1@.022	SF	2.84	.74	3.58
1200S162-97 (12 gauge, 3.45 Lbs./SF)	B1@.026	SF	3.94	.88	4.82

Backing for drywall ceiling Floating backing for drywall ceilings, trim, appliances, fixtures, etc.

	Craft@Hrs	Unit	Material	Labor	Total
1-1/2" x 1-1/2" (.54 Lbs./LF)	B1@.012	LF	.62	.41	1.03

Steel rafters Shed or gable roof with spans from 7'0" to 38'0" and pitch of 3 in 12 to 12 in 12 as published in light-gauge steel framing span tables. Costs per square foot of roof surface. Includes rafters, bracing, screws and minimal waste but no blocking, purlins, ridge boards, collar beams, or gable walls. See costs for blocking, purlins, ridgeboards and collar beams elsewhere in this section. Labor includes layout, assembly, and alignment. Figures in parentheses show weight of steel per square foot of roof.

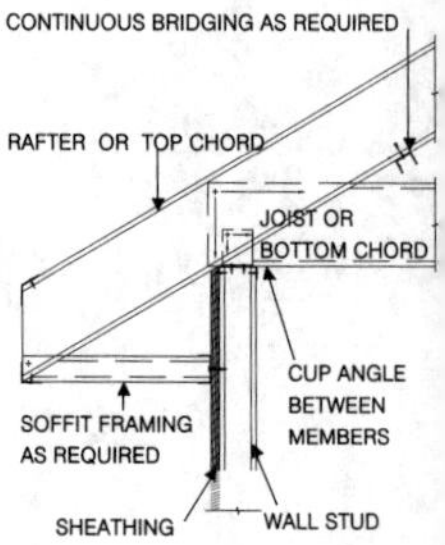

	Craft@Hrs	Unit	Material	Labor	Total
Using light gauge steel rafters at	—	Lb	1.14	—	1.14
Add for hip roof	B1@.009	SF	—	.30	.30
5-1/2" steel rafters, 12" OC, 1-5/8" flange					
550S162-33 (20 gauge, 1.18 Lbs./SF)	B1@.037	SF	1.35	1.25	2.60
550S162-43 (18 gauge, 1.51 Lbs./SF)	B1@.041	SF	1.72	1.39	3.11
550S162-54 (16 gauge, 1.87 Lbs./SF)	B1@.045	SF	2.13	1.52	3.65
550S162-68 (14 gauge, 2.31 Lbs./SF)	B1@.050	SF	2.64	1.69	4.33
5-1/2" steel rafters, 16" OC, 1-5/8" flange					
550S162-33 (20 gauge, .90 Lbs./SF)	B1@.031	SF	1.03	1.05	2.08
550S162-43 (18 gauge, 1.15 Lbs./SF)	B1@.034	SF	1.31	1.15	2.46
550S162-54 (16 gauge, 1.42 Lbs./SF)	B1@.037	SF	1.62	1.25	2.87
550S162-68 (14 gauge, 1.75 Lbs./SF)	B1@.041	SF	2.00	1.39	3.39
5-1/2" steel rafters, 24" OC, 1-5/8" flange					
500S162-33 (20 gauge, .63 Lbs./SF)	B1@.024	SF	.72	.81	1.53
500S162-43 (18 gauge, .79 Lbs./SF)	B1@.026	SF	.90	.88	1.78
500S162-54 (16 gauge, .97 Lbs./SF)	B1@.029	SF	1.11	.98	2.09
500S162-68 (14 gauge, 1.19 Lbs./SF)	B1@.032	SF	1.36	1.08	2.44
8" steel rafters, 12" OC, 1-5/8" flange					
800S162-33 (20 gauge, 1.48 Lbs./SF)	B1@.048	SF	1.69	1.62	3.31
800S162-43 (18 gauge, 1.90 Lbs./SF)	B1@.053	SF	2.17	1.79	3.96
800S162-54 (16 gauge, 2.35 Lbs./SF)	B1@.058	SF	2.68	1.96	4.64
800S162-68 (14 gauge, 2.91 Lbs./SF)	B1@.064	SF	3.32	2.17	5.49
800S162-97 (12 gauge, 4.05 Lbs./SF)	B1@.070	SF	4.62	2.37	6.99
8" steel rafters, 16" OC, 1-5/8" flange					
800S162-33 (20 gauge, 1.13 Lbs./SF)	B1@.040	SF	1.29	1.35	2.64
800S162-43 (18 gauge, 1.44 Lbs./SF)	B1@.044	SF	1.64	1.49	3.13
800S162-54 (16 gauge, 1.78 Lbs./SF)	B1@.048	SF	2.03	1.62	3.65
800S162-68 (14 gauge, 2.20 Lbs./SF)	B1@.053	SF	2.51	1.79	4.30
800S162-97 (12 gauge, 3.06 Lbs./SF)	B1@.058	SF	3.49	1.96	5.45
8" steel rafters, 24" OC, 1-5/8" flange					
800S162-33 (20 gauge, .78 Lbs./SF)	B1@.032	SF	.89	1.08	1.97
800S162-43 (18 gauge, .99 Lbs./SF)	B1@.035	SF	1.13	1.18	2.31
800S162-54 (16 gauge, 1.21 Lbs./SF)	B1@.039	SF	1.38	1.32	2.70
800S162-68 (14 gauge, 1.49 Lbs./SF)	B1@.043	SF	1.70	1.46	3.16
800S162-97 (12 gauge, 2.06 Lbs./SF)	B1@.047	SF	2.35	1.59	3.94
10" steel rafters, 12" OC, 1-5/8" flange					
1000S162-43 (18 gauge, 2.20 Lbs./SF)	B1@.060	SF	2.51	2.03	4.54
1000S162-54 (16 gauge, 2.73 Lbs./SF)	B1@.066	SF	3.12	2.23	5.35
1000S162-68 (14 gauge, 3.40 Lbs./SF)	B1@.072	SF	3.88	2.44	6.32
1000S162-97 (12 gauge, 4.74 Lbs./SF)	B1@.080	SF	5.41	2.71	8.12
10" steel rafters, 16" OC, 1-5/8" flange					
1000S162-43 (18 gauge, 1.67 Lbs./SF)	B1@.048	SF	1.91	1.62	3.53
1000S162-54 (16 gauge, 2.07 Lbs./SF)	B1@.053	SF	2.36	1.79	4.15
1000S162-68 (14 gauge, 2.57 Lbs./SF)	B1@.058	SF	2.93	1.96	4.89
1000S162-97 (12 gauge, 3.57 Lbs./SF)	B1@.064	SF	4.07	2.17	6.24

	Craft@Hrs	Unit	Material	Labor	Total
10" steel rafters, 24" OC, 1-5/8" flange					
1000S162-43 (18 gauge, 1.14 Lbs./SF)	B1@.039	SF	1.30	1.32	2.62
1000S162-54 (16 gauge, 1.40 Lbs./SF)	B1@.042	SF	1.60	1.42	3.02
1000S162-68 (14 gauge, 1.74 Lbs./SF)	B1@.047	SF	1.99	1.59	3.58
1000S162-97 (12 gauge, 2.41 Lbs./SF)	B1@.051	SF	2.75	1.73	4.48
12" steel rafters, 12" OC, 1-5/8" flange					
1200S162-54 (16 gauge, 3.12 Lbs./SF)	B1@.066	SF	3.56	2.23	5.79
1200S162-68 (14 gauge, 3.88 Lbs./SF)	B1@.073	SF	4.43	2.47	6.90
1200S162-97 (12 gauge, 5.43 Lbs./SF)	B1@.080	SF	6.20	2.71	8.91
12" steel rafters, 16" OC, 1-5/8" flange					
1200S162-54 (16 gauge, 2.36 Lbs./SF)	B1@.053	SF	2.69	1.79	4.48
1200S162-68 (14 gauge, 2.93 Lbs./SF)	B1@.059	SF	3.34	2.00	5.34
1200S162-97 (12 gauge, 4.09 Lbs./SF)	B1@.064	SF	4.67	2.17	6.84
12" steel rafters, 24" OC, 1-5/8" flange					
1200S162-54 (16 gauge, 1.60 Lbs./SF)	B1@.043	SF	1.83	1.46	3.29
1200S162-68 (14 gauge, 1.98 Lbs./SF)	B1@.047	SF	2.26	1.59	3.85
1200S162-97 (12 gauge, 2.75 Lbs./SF)	B1@.052	SF	3.14	1.76	4.90

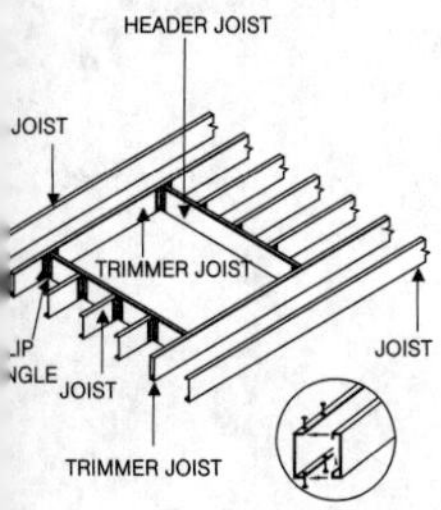

Steel trimmers At floor openings, stairwells, skylights, dormers, etc. Consists of one C-shaped member nested in same size track. Labor includes layout, assembly and alignment. Figures in parentheses show weight of steel per linear foot of trimmer. Includes screws and minimal waste.

	Craft@Hrs	Unit	Material	Labor	Total
Using light-gauge steel framing materials	—	Lb	1.14	—	1.14
3-1/2" steel trimmers, 1-5/8" flange					
350S162-33 (20 gauge, 1.76 Lbs./LF)	B1@.020	LF	2.01	.68	2.69
350S162-43 (18 gauge, 2.29 Lbs./LF)	B1@.020	LF	2.61	.68	3.29
350S162-54 (16 gauge, 2.85 Lbs./LF)	B1@.022	LF	3.25	.74	3.99
350S162-68 (14 gauge, 3.60 Lbs./LF)	B1@.023	LF	4.11	.78	4.89
5-1/2" steel trimmers, 1-5/8" flange					
550S162-33 (20 gauge, 2.23 Lbs./LF)	B1@.031	LF	2.55	1.05	3.60
550S162-43 (18 gauge, 2.90 Lbs./LF)	B1@.031	LF	3.31	1.05	4.36
550S162-54 (16 gauge, 3.63 Lbs./LF)	B1@.034	LF	4.14	1.15	5.29
550S162-68 (14 gauge, 4.54 Lbs./LF)	B1@.035	LF	5.18	1.18	6.36
8" steel trimmers, 1-5/8" flange					
800S162-33 (20 gauge, 2.82 Lbs./LF)	B1@.042	LF	3.22	1.42	4.64
800S162-43 (18 gauge, 3.67 Lbs./LF)	B1@.042	LF	4.19	1.42	5.61
800S162-54 (16 gauge, 4.59 Lbs./LF)	B1@.046	LF	5.24	1.56	6.80
800S162-68 (14 gauge, 5.75 Lbs./LF)	B1@.047	LF	6.56	1.59	8.15
800S162-97 (12 gauge, 8.13 Lbs./LF)	B1@.048	LF	9.28	1.62	10.90
10" steel trimmers, 1-5/8" flange					
1000S162-43 (18 gauge, 4.28 Lbs./LF)	B1@.052	LF	4.88	1.76	6.64
1000S162-54 (16 gauge, 5.35 Lbs./LF)	B1@.052	LF	6.11	1.76	7.87
1000S162-68 (14 gauge, 6.72 Lbs./LF)	B1@.057	LF	7.67	1.93	9.60
1000S162-97 (12 gauge, 9.51 Lbs./LF)	B1@.058	LF	10.90	1.96	12.86
12" steel trimmers, 1-5/8" flange					
1200S162-54 (16 gauge, 6.13 Lbs./LF)	B1@.063	LF	7.00	2.13	9.13
1200S162-68 (14 gauge, 7.69 Lbs./LF)	B1@.066	LF	8.78	2.23	11.01
1200S162-97 (12 gauge, 10.89 Lbs./LF)	B1@.069	LF	12.40	2.34	14.74

Carpentry, Steel Framing

	Craft@Hrs	Unit	Material	Labor	Total
Steel collar beams Cost per linear foot of collar beam or rafter brace, including screws.					
350S162-33 (3-1/2", 33 mil, 20 gauge)	B1@.007	LF	.76	.24	1.00
550S162-43 (5-1/2", 43 mil, 18 gauge)	B1@.014	LF	1.31	.47	1.78
Steel purlins Purlins or "perling" installed below roof rafters.					
350S162-33 (3-1/2", 33 mil, 20 gauge)	B1@.013	LF	1.00	.44	1.44
350S162-43 (3-1/2", 43 mil, 18 gauge)	B1@.019	LF	.76	.64	1.40
Steel dormer studs Per square foot of wall area					
350S162-33 (3-1/2", 33 mil, 20 gauge)	B1@.036	SF	.97	1.22	2.19

Steel ridgeboard Horizontal support at top of rafter ends. Consists of one C-shaped member nested in same size track. Labor includes layout, assembly and alignment. Figures in parentheses show weight of steel per linear foot of ridgeboard. Includes screws and minimal waste.

	Craft@Hrs	Unit	Material	Labor	Total
Using light-gauge steel framing materials	—	Lb	1.14	—	1.14
5-1/2" steel ridgeboard, 1-5/8" flange					
550S162-33 (20 gauge, 2.23 Lbs./LF)	B1@.031	LF	2.55	1.05	3.60
550S162-43 (18 gauge, 2.90 Lbs./LF)	B1@.031	LF	3.31	1.05	4.36
550S162-54 (16 gauge, 3.63 Lbs./LF)	B1@.034	LF	4.14	1.15	5.29
550S162-68 (14 gauge, 4.54 Lbs./LF)	B1@.035	LF	5.18	1.18	6.36
8" steel ridgeboard, 1-5/8" flange					
800S162-33 (20 gauge, 2.82 Lbs./LF)	B1@.042	LF	3.22	1.42	4.64
800S162-43 (18 gauge, 3.67 Lbs./LF)	B1@.042	LF	4.19	1.42	5.61
800S162-54 (16 gauge, 4.59 Lbs./LF)	B1@.046	LF	5.24	1.56	6.80
800S162-68 (14 gauge, 5.75 Lbs./LF)	B1@.047	LF	6.56	1.59	8.15
800S162-97 (12 gauge, 8.13 Lbs./LF)	B1@.048	LF	9.28	1.62	10.90
10" steel ridgeboard, 1-5/8" flange					
1000S162-43 (18 gauge, 4.28 Lbs./LF)	B1@.052	LF	4.88	1.76	6.64
1000S162-54 (16 gauge, 5.35 Lbs./LF)	B1@.052	LF	6.11	1.76	7.87
1000S162-68 (14 gauge, 6.72 Lbs./LF)	B1@.057	LF	7.67	1.93	9.60
1000S162-97 (12 gauge, 9.51 Lbs./LF)	B1@.058	LF	10.90	1.96	12.86
12" steel ridgeboard, 1-5/8" flange					
1200S162-54 (16 gauge, 6.13 Lbs./LF)	B1@.063	LF	7.00	2.13	9.13
1200S162-68 (14 gauge, 7.69 Lbs./LF)	B1@.066	LF	8.78	2.23	11.01
1200S162-97 (12 gauge, 10.89 Lbs./LF)	B1@.069	LF	12.40	2.34	14.74

Steel roof trusses Site-fabricated and set by hand 24" OC for any roof slope from 3 in 12 to 12 in 12 so long as the total truss height does not exceed 12' from bottom chord to highest point on truss. Trusses over 12' high may cost up to 100% more. Costs are per square foot (SF) of horizontal area covered.

	Craft@Hrs	Unit	Material	Labor	Total
Using light-gauge steel framing materials at	—	Lb	1.14	—	1.14
4" C-shaped top and bottom chords, members unpunched					
Up to 38' span	B1@.029	SF	5.26	.98	6.24
40' to 50' span	B1@.037	SF	6.57	1.25	7.82
Fink truss "W" (conventional roof truss). 4" C-shaped top and bottom chords					
Up to 38' span	B1@.023	SF	4.60	.78	5.38
40' to 50' span	B1@.029	SF	5.43	.98	6.41
6" C-shaped top and bottom chords, members unpunched					
Up to 38' span	B1@.027	SF	5.53	.91	6.44
40' to 50' span	B1@.035	SF	6.67	1.18	7.85

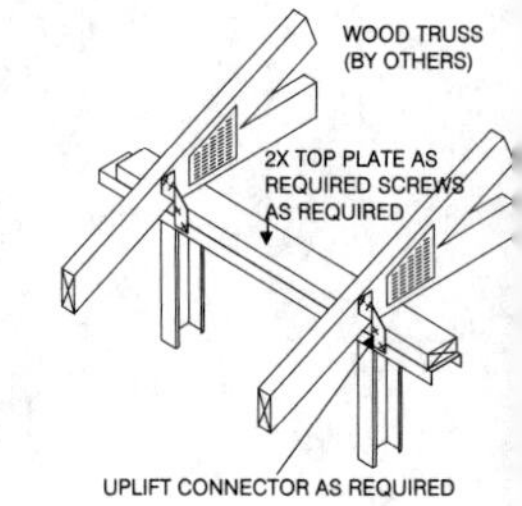

	Craft@Hrs	Unit	Material	Labor	Total
Truss with gable fill at 16" OC					
28' span, 5 in 12 slope	B1@1.27	Ea	374.00	43.00	417.00
32' span, 5 in 12 slope	B1@1.68	Ea	463.00	56.90	519.90
40' span, 5 in 12 slope	B1@2.30	Ea	647.00	77.90	724.90

Piecework Steel Framing Steel framing on residential tracts is sometimes done by subcontractors who bid at piecework rates (such as per square foot of floor). The figures below list typical piecework rates for repetitive framing and assume all materials are supplied to the framing subcontractor. No figures appear in the Craft@Hrs column because the work is done for a fixed price per square foot and the labor productivity can be expected to vary widely.

Steel frame layout and bottom track Piecework rates
Lay out wall track according to the plans (snap chalk lines for wall track, mark location for studs, windows, doors and framing details), cut top and bottom track and install bottom track. Costs per square foot of floor (excluding garage).

	Craft@Hrs	Unit	Material	Labor	Total
Custom or more complex jobs	—	SF	—	.29	.29
Larger job, longer runs	—	SF	—	.19	.19

Steel exterior wall framing Piecework rates
Measure, cut, fit, assemble, and tip up walls, including studs, track, cripples, x-bracing, trimmers and blocking. Costs per square foot of floor.

	Craft@Hrs	Unit	Material	Labor	Total
Complex job, radius walls, rake walls	—	SF	—	.84	.84
Larger job, 8' high walls, fewer partitions	—	SF	—	.29	.29

Plumb and align steel framed walls Piecework rates
Align walls, adjust walls to vertical and install temporary braces as needed, fasten nuts on anchor bolts or shoot power driven fasteners through wall track into the slab. Based on accuracy to 3/16". Costs per square foot of floor are shown below.

	Craft@Hrs	Unit	Material	Labor	Total
Small or complex job, many braces	—	SF	—	.28	.28
Larger job, fewer braces	—	SF	—	.17	.17

Install steel floor or ceiling joists Piecework rates
Lay out, cut and install floor or ceiling joists, including rim track, doubled joists, straps, joist hangers, blocking at 12' OC and ceiling backing for drywall. Based on larger jobs with simple joist layouts set 24" OC and pre-cut blocking supplied by the general contractor. Add the cost of floor beams, if required. Costs per square foot of horizontal joist area. More complex jobs with shorter runs may cost 50% more.

	Craft@Hrs	Unit	Material	Labor	Total
Install 6" ceiling or floor joists 24" OC					
600S200-33 (2" flange, 20 gauge)	—	SF	—	.20	.20
600S200-43 (2" flange, 18 gauge)	—	SF	—	.20	.20
600S200-54 (2" flange, 16 gauge)	—	SF	—	.21	.21
600S200-68 (2" flange, 14 gauge)	—	SF	—	.22	.22
Install 8" ceiling or floor joists 24" OC					
800S200-43 (2" flange, 18 gauge)	—	SF	—	.20	.20
800S200-54 (2" flange, 16 gauge)	—	SF	—	.21	.21
800S200-68 (2" flange, 14 gauge)	—	SF	—	.22	.22
800S200-97 (2" flange, 12 gauge)	—	SF	—	.24	.24

	Craft@Hrs	Unit	Material	Labor	Total
Install 10" ceiling or floor joists 24" OC					
1000S200-43 (2" flange, 18 gauge)	—	SF	—	.21	.21
1000S200-54 (2" flange, 16 gauge)	—	SF	—	.22	.22
1000S200-68 (2" flange, 14 gauge)	—	SF	—	.23	.23
1000S200-97 (2" flange, 12 gauge)	—	SF	—	.25	.25
Install 12" ceiling or floor joists 24" OC					
1200S200-54 (2" flange, 16 gauge)	—	SF	—	.23	.23
1200S200-68 (2" flange, 14 gauge)	—	SF	—	.24	.24
1200S200-97 (2" flange, 12 gauge)	—	SF	—	.26	.26
Add for other than 24" joist spacing					
Add for 12" OC spacing	—	SF	—	.16	.16
Add for 16" OC spacing	—	SF	—	.06	.06
Add for 20" OC spacing	—	SF	—	.03	.03

Install plywood floor sheathing on steel joists Piecework rates
Lay out, cut, fit and install 5/8" or 3/4" tongue and groove plywood floor sheathing, including blocking as required. Based on nailing done with a pneumatic nailer and pins supplied by the general contractor, or screwing done with a collated screw gun and screws supplied by the general contractor. Costs per square foot of sheathing installed.

	Craft@Hrs	Unit	Material	Labor	Total
Smaller, cut-up job	—	SF	—	.26	.26
Larger job, longer runs	—	SF	—	.21	.21
Add for 1-1/8" sheathing	—	SF	—	.06	.06

Install structural shear panels on steel studs Piecework rates
Lay out, cut, fit and install structural 3/8" or 1/2" plywood wall panels. These figures assume steel shear studs were set correctly by others and that panel nails or screws are driven at 4" OC with a pneumatic nailer or collated screwgun. Not including hold-down straps, posts, shear blocking or extra studs. Costs per 4' x 9' panel installed.

	Craft@Hrs	Unit	Material	Labor	Total
Small job, many openings, 2nd floor	—	Ea	—	13.50	13.50
Larger job, few openings, 1st floor	—	Ea	—	8.33	8.33

Steel roof trusses Piecework rates
Setting and anchoring engineered gable and hip steel roof trusses 24" OC on prepared wall top track. These figures assume that lifting equipment is provided by the general contractor (if required) and that the truss supplier provides a fill package, spreader blocks for each plate and the ridge and jack rafters (if required). Includes installation of ceiling backing where required and rat runs at the bottom chord. Costs per square foot of plan area under the truss. Small job assumes multiple California fill between roof surfaces and understacking.

	Craft@Hrs	Unit	Material	Labor	Total
Small job, rake fill above a partition wall	—	SF	—	.90	.90
Larger job, little or no fill or understacking	—	SF	—	.51	.51

Conventional roof framing Piecework rates
Calculate lengths, lay out, cut and install steel 8", 10" or 12" common, hip, valley and jack rafters on parallel and horizontal top track. Costs per square foot of plan area under the roof. Slope to 6 in 12.

	Craft@Hrs	Unit	Material	Labor	Total
Add for slope over 6 in 12	—	SF	—	.29	.29
Steel rafters 12" OC, small job, cut-up roof, few common rafters					
800S162-33 (8", 1-5/8" flange, 20 gauge)	—	SF	—	1.81	1.81
800S162-43 (8", 1-5/8" flange, 18 gauge)	—	SF	—	1.83	1.83
800S162-54 (8", 1-5/8" flange, 16 gauge)	—	SF	—	1.86	1.86
800S162-68 (8", 1-5/8" flange, 14 gauge)	—	SF	—	1.94	1.94
800S162-97 (8", 1-5/8" flange, 12 gauge)	—	SF	—	2.04	2.04
1000S162-43 (10", 1-5/8" flange, 18 gauge)	—	SF	—	1.88	1.88

	Craft@Hrs	Unit	Material	Labor	Total
1000S162-54 (10", 1-5/8" flange, 16 gauge)	—	SF	—	1.90	1.90
1000S162-68 (10", 1-5/8" flange, 14 gauge)	—	SF	—	1.98	1.98
1000S162-97 (10", 1-5/8" flange, 12 gauge)	—	SF	—	2.10	2.10
1200S162-54 (12", 1-5/8" flange, 16 gauge)	—	SF	—	1.96	1.96
1200S162-68 (12", 1-5/8" flange, 14 gauge)	—	SF	—	2.03	2.03
1200S162-97 (12", 1-5/8" flange, 12 gauge)	—	SF	—	2.16	2.16
Steel rafters 16" OC, small job, cut-up roof, few common rafters					
800S162-33 (8", 1-5/8" flange, 20 gauge)	—	SF	—	1.53	1.53
800S162-43 (8", 1-5/8" flange, 18 gauge)	—	SF	—	1.54	1.54
800S162-54 (8", 1-5/8" flange, 16 gauge)	—	SF	—	1.56	1.56
800S162-68 (8", 1-5/8" flange, 14 gauge)	—	SF	—	1.64	1.64
800S162-97 (8", 1-5/8" flange, 12 gauge)	—	SF	—	1.74	1.74
1000S162-43 (10", 1-5/8" flange, 18 gauge)	—	SF	—	1.59	1.59
1000S162-54 (10", 1-5/8" flange, 16 gauge)	—	SF	—	1.60	1.60
1000S162-68 (10", 1-5/8" flange, 14 gauge)	—	SF	—	1.67	1.67
1000S162-97 (10", 1-5/8" flange, 12 gauge)	—	SF	—	1.79	1.79
1200S162-54 (12", 1-5/8" flange, 16 gauge)	—	SF	—	1.66	1.66
1200S162-68 (12", 1-5/8" flange, 14 gauge)	—	SF	—	1.74	1.74
1200S162-97 (12", 1-5/8" flange, 12 gauge)	—	SF	—	1.82	1.82
Steel rafters 24" OC, small job, cut-up roof, few common rafters					
800S162-33 (8", 1-5/8" flange, 20 gauge)	—	SF	—	.91	.91
800S162-43 (8", 1-5/8" flange, 18 gauge)	—	SF	—	.92	.92
800S162-54 (8", 1-5/8" flange, 16 gauge)	—	SF	—	.93	.93
800S162-68 (8", 1-5/8" flange, 14 gauge)	—	SF	—	.97	.97
800S162-97 (8", 1-5/8" flange, 12 gauge)	—	SF	—	1.03	1.03
1000S162-43 (10", 1-5/8" flange, 18 gauge)	—	SF	—	.94	.94
1000S162-54 (10", 1-5/8" flange, 16 gauge)	—	SF	—	.95	.95
1000S162-68 (10", 1-5/8" flange, 14 gauge)	—	SF	—	.99	.99
1000S162-97 (10", 1-5/8" flange, 12 gauge)	—	SF	—	1.06	1.06
1200S162-54 (12", 1-5/8" flange, 16 gauge)	—	SF	—	.98	.98
1200S162-68 (12", 1-5/8" flange, 14 gauge)	—	SF	—	1.03	1.03
1200S162-97 (12", 1-5/8" flange, 12 gauge)	—	SF	—	1.10	1.10
Steel rafters 12" OC, larger job, longer runs, nearly all common rafters					
800S162-33 (8", 1-5/8" flange, 20 gauge)	—	SF	—	.91	.91
800S162-43 (8", 1-5/8" flange, 18 gauge)	—	SF	—	.92	.92
800S162-54 (8", 1-5/8" flange, 16 gauge)	—	SF	—	.93	.93
800S162-68 (8", 1-5/8" flange, 16 gauge)	—	SF	—	.97	.97
800S162-97 (8", 1-5/8" flange, 12 gauge)	—	SF	—	1.03	1.03
1000S162-43 (10", 1-5/8" flange, 18 gauge)	—	SF	—	.94	.94
1000S162-54 (10", 1-5/8" flange, 16 gauge)	—	SF	—	.95	.95
1000S162-68 (10", 1-5/8" flange, 14 gauge)	—	SF	—	.99	.99
1000S162-97 (10", 1-5/8" flange, 12 gauge)	—	SF	—	1.06	1.06
1200S162-54 (12", 1-5/8" flange, 16 gauge)	—	SF	—	.98	.98
1200S162-68 (12", 1-5/8" flange, 14 gauge)	—	SF	—	1.03	1.03
1200S162-97 (12", 1-5/8" flange, 12 gauge)	—	SF	—	1.10	1.10
Steel rafters 16" OC, larger job, longer runs, nearly all common rafters					
800S162-33 (8", 1-5/8" flange, 20 gauge)	—	SF	—	.82	.82
800S162-43 (8", 1-5/8" flange, 18 gauge)	—	SF	—	.82	.82
800S162-54 (8", 1-5/8" flange, 16 gauge)	—	SF	—	.83	.83
800S162-68 (8", 1-5/8" flange, 16 gauge)	—	SF	—	.87	.87
800S162-97 (8", 1-5/8" flange, 12 gauge)	—	SF	—	.90	.90

	Craft@Hrs	Unit	Material	Labor	Total
1000S162-43 (10", 1-5/8" flange, 18 gauge)	—	SF	—	.84	.84
1000S162-54 (10", 1-5/8" flange, 16 gauge)	—	SF	—	.86	.86
1000S162-68 (10", 1-5/8" flange, 14 gauge)	—	SF	—	.88	.88
1000S162-97 (10", 1-5/8" flange, 12 gauge)	—	SF	—	.92	.92
1200S162-54 (12", 1-5/8" flange, 16 gauge)	—	SF	—	.88	.88
1200S162-68 (12", 1-5/8" flange, 14 gauge)	—	SF	—	.90	.90
1200S162-97 (12", 1-5/8" flange, 12 gauge)	—	SF	—	.94	.94
Steel rafters 24" OC, larger job, longer runs, nearly all common rafters					
800S162-33 (8", 1-5/8" flange, 20 gauge)	—	SF	—	.52	.52
800S162-43 (8", 1-5/8" flange, 18 gauge)	—	SF	—	.53	.53
800S162-54 (8", 1-5/8" flange, 16 gauge)	—	SF	—	.53	.53
800S162-68 (8", 1-5/8" flange, 16 gauge)	—	SF	—	.55	.55
800S162-97 (8", 1-5/8" flange, 12 gauge)	—	SF	—	.58	.58
1000S162-43 (10", 1-5/8" flange, 18 gauge)	—	SF	—	.54	.54
1000S162-54 (10", 1-5/8" flange, 16 gauge)	—	SF	—	.54	.54
1000S162-68 (10", 1-5/8" flange, 14 gauge)	—	SF	—	.57	.57
1000S162-97 (10", 1-5/8" flange, 12 gauge)	—	SF	—	.59	.59
1200S162-54 (12", 1-5/8" flange, 16 gauge)	—	SF	—	.55	.55
1200S162-68 (12", 1-5/8" flange, 14 gauge)	—	SF	—	.58	.58
1200S162-97 (12", 1-5/8" flange, 12 gauge)	—	SF	—	.60	.60

Fascia, wood Piecework rates

Applied to rafter tails and as a barge rafter on gable ends. Includes trimming the rafter tails to the correct length and installing outlookers at gable ends. Costs per linear foot of 2" x 8" fascia installed.

	Craft@Hrs	Unit	Material	Labor	Total
Small job, short runs, with molding	—	LF	—	3.00	3.00
Larger job, longer runs	—	LF	—	1.63	1.63

Install roof sheathing on steel rafters Piecework rates

Lay out, cut, fit and install 1/2" or 5/8" plywood roof sheathing, including blocking and 1" x 8" starter board on overhangs as required. Based on nailing done with a pneumatic nailer and nails or collated screwgun and screws supplied by the general contractor. Slope to 6 in 12. Costs per square foot of sheathing installed.

	Craft@Hrs	Unit	Material	Labor	Total
Smaller, cut-up hip and valley job	—	SF	—	.27	.27
Larger job, longer runs	—	SF	—	.21	.21
Add for slope over 6 in 12	—	SF	—	.11	.11

Carpeting, Subcontract Costs listed are typical for a complete residential job and include consultation, measurement, pad, carpet, and professional installation of pad and carpet using tack strips and hot melt tape on seams. Prices for brand name (specification grade) carpet will be up to 50% higher.

	Craft@Hrs	Unit	Material	Labor	Total
Minimum quality, 25 to 28 oz. olefin (polypropylene) carpet					
Including a 1/2" (4 lb density) rebond pad	—	SY	—	—	24.10
Minimum quality, 25 to 35 oz. face weight nylon carpet					
Including a 1/2" (4 lb density) rebond pad	—	SY	—	—	31.10
Good quality, 35 to 50 oz. face weight nylon carpet					
Including a 1/2" (6 lb density) rebond pad	—	SY	—	—	44.10
Better quality, 50 (plus) oz. face weight nylon carpet					
Including a 1/2" (6 lb density) rebond pad	—	SY	—	—	61.10
Wool tufted carpet	—	SY	—	—	81.10
Installation cost alone (residential)	—	SY	—	—	7.34
Installation cost alone (commercial)	—	SY	—	—	6.22
Add for typical furniture moving	—	SY	—	—	2.26
Add for waterfall (box steps) stairways	—	Riser	—	—	8.67

	Craft@Hrs	Unit	Material	Labor	Total
Add for wrapped steps (open riser), sewn	—	Step	—	—	11.50
Add for sewn edge treatment on one side	—	Riser	—	—	13.90
Add for circular stair steps, costs vary depending on frame					
Add for circular stairs, typical cost	—	Step	—	—	18.60

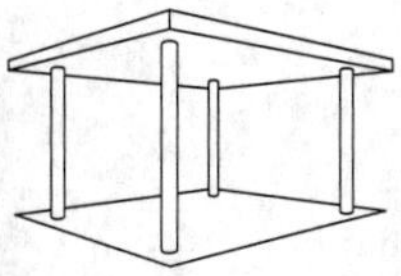

Carports Material costs include all hardware. Labor is based on bolting posts to an existing concrete slab. Steel frame, 4" x 4" galvanized 14 gauge posts, 14 gauge purlins, 26 gauge rib metal roofing, 90 MPH wind load.

	Craft@Hrs	Unit	Material	Labor	Total
18' wide x 18' long x 8' high, four posts, 20 PSF snow load					
Natural zinc finish	B1@8.00	Ea	2,080.00	271.00	2,351.00
White enamel finish	B1@8.00	Ea	2,290.00	271.00	2,561.00
18' wide x 18' long x 8' high, six posts, 40 PSF snow load					
Natural zinc finish	B1@9.00	Ea	2,560.00	305.00	2,865.00
White enamel finish	B1@9.00	Ea	2,770.00	305.00	3,075.00
36' wide x 18' long x 8' high, six posts, 20 PSF snow load					
Natural zinc finish	B1@10.0	Ea	3,190.00	339.00	3,529.00
White enamel finish	B1@10.0	Ea	3,620.00	339.00	3,959.00
36' wide x 18' long x 8' high, nine posts, 40 PSF snow load					
Natural zinc finish	B1@11.5	Ea	3,980.00	389.00	4,369.00
White enamel finish	B1@11.5	Ea	4,410.00	389.00	4,799.00
15' wide x 35' long x 15' high, ten posts, 40 PSF snow load					
Natural zinc finish	B1@13.0	Ea	3,940.00	440.00	4,380.00
White enamel finish	B1@13.0	Ea	4,510.00	440.00	4,950.00

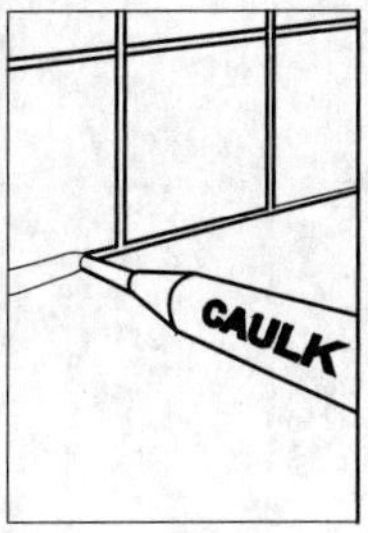

Caulking Material costs are typical costs for bead diameter listed. Figures in parentheses indicate approximate coverage including 5% waste. Labor costs are for good quality application on smooth to slightly irregular surfaces. Per LF of bead length.

	Craft@Hrs	Unit	Material	Labor	Total
Concrete sealant with polyurethane					
Concrete sealant, per ounce	—	Oz	.70	—	.70
1/4" (2.91 LF per fluid oz.)	BC@.025	LF	.24	.93	1.17
3/8" (1.29 LF per fluid oz.)	BC@.030	LF	.55	1.12	1.67
1/2" (.728 LF per fluid oz.)	BC@.033	LF	.97	1.23	2.20
Acoustical caulk, flexible, sound deadening					
Acoustical caulk, per ounce	—	Oz	.34	—	.34
1/8" (11.6 LF per fluid oz.)	BC@.018	LF	.03	.67	.70
1/4" (2.91 LF per fluid oz.)	BC@.025	LF	.12	.93	1.05
3/8" (1.29 LF per fluid oz.)	BC@.030	LF	.26	1.12	1.38
1/2" (.728 LF per fluid oz.)	BC@.033	LF	.46	1.23	1.69
Acrylic latex caulk, premium quality, 35 year life expectancy					
Acrylic latex caulk, per ounce	—	Oz	.24	—	.24
1/8" (11.6 LF per fluid oz.)	BC@.018	LF	.02	.67	.69
1/4" (2.91 LF per fluid oz.)	BC@.025	LF	.08	.93	1.01
3/8" (1.29 LF per fluid oz.)	BC@.030	LF	.19	1.12	1.31
1/2" (.728 LF per fluid oz.)	BC@.033	LF	.33	1.23	1.56
Painter's acrylic latex caulk, paintable in 30 minutes					
Painter's acrylic latex caulk, per ounce	—	Oz	.17	—	.17
1/8" (11.6 LF per fluid oz.)	BC@.018	LF	.01	.67	.68
1/4" (2.91 LF per fluid oz.)	BC@.025	LF	.06	.93	.99
3/8" (1.29 LF per fluid oz.)	BC@.030	LF	.13	1.12	1.25
1/2" (.728 LF per fluid oz.)	BC@.033	LF	.23	1.23	1.46

Caulking

	Craft@Hrs	Unit	Material	Labor	Total
Elastomeric latex sealant. Clearer than silicone					
Elastomeric latex sealant, per ounce	—	Oz	.77	—	.77
1/8" (11.6 LF per fluid oz.)	BC@.018	LF	.07	.67	.74
1/4" (2.91 LF per fluid oz.)	BC@.025	LF	.26	.93	1.19
3/8" (1.29 LF per fluid oz.)	BC@.030	LF	.60	1.12	1.72
1/2" (.728 LF per fluid oz.)	BC@.033	LF	1.06	1.23	2.29
Tub & tile caulk, for tubs, showers and sinks					
Tub & tile caulk, per ounce	—	Oz	.86	—	.86
1/8" (11.6 LF per fluid oz.)	BC@.018	LF	.07	.67	.74
1/4" (2.91 LF per fluid oz.)	BC@.025	LF	.29	.93	1.22
3/8" (1.29 LF per fluid oz.)	BC@.030	LF	.66	1.12	1.78
1/2" (.728 LF per fluid oz.)	BC@.033	LF	1.18	1.23	2.41
Fire barrier latex caulk, four hour fire rating for pipes up to 30 inches					
Fire barrier latex caulk, per ounce	—	Oz	1.25	—	1.25
1/8" (11.6 LF per fluid oz.)	BC@.018	LF	.11	.67	.78
1/4" (2.91 LF per fluid oz.)	BC@.022	LF	.43	.82	1.25
3/8" (1.29 LF per fluid oz.)	BC@.027	LF	.97	1.01	1.98
1/2" (.728 LF per fluid oz.)	BC@.030	LF	1.72	1.12	2.84
Silicone caulk					
Siliconized acrylic caulk, per ounce	—	Oz	.72	—	.72
1/8" (11.6 LF per fluid oz.)	BC@.018	LF	.06	.67	.73
1/4" (2.91 LF per fluid oz.)	BC@.025	LF	.25	.93	1.18
3/8" (1.29 LF per fluid oz.)	BC@.030	LF	.56	1.12	1.68
1/2" (.728 LF per fluid oz.)	BC@.033	LF	.99	1.23	2.22
Marine adhesive/sealant, premium quality					
Silicon rubber sealant, per ounce	—	Oz	2.47	—	2.47
1/8" (11.6 LF per fluid oz.)	BC@.043	LF	.21	1.61	1.82
1/4" (2.91 LF per fluid oz.)	BC@.048	LF	.85	1.79	2.64
3/8" (1.29 LF per fluid oz.)	BC@.056	LF	1.92	2.09	4.01
1/2" (.728 LF per fluid oz.)	BC@.060	LF	3.40	2.24	5.64
Anti-algae and mildew-resistant tub caulk, premium quality white or clear silicone					
Anti-algae tub caulk, per ounce	—	Oz	.64	—	.64
1/8" (11.6 LF per fluid oz.)	BC@.018	LF	.06	.67	.73
1/4" (2.91 LF per fluid oz.)	BC@.022	LF	.22	.82	1.04
3/8" (1.29 LF per fluid oz.)	BC@.027	LF	.50	1.01	1.51
1/2" (.728 LF per fluid oz.)	BC@.030	LF	.88	1.12	2.00
Vinyl window and siding sealant, permanently flexible, paintable					
Vinyl window and siding sealant, per ounce	—	Oz	.73	—	.73
1/8" (11.6 LF per fluid oz.)	BC@.018	LF	.06	.67	.73
1/4" (2.91 LF per fluid oz.)	BC@.022	LF	.25	.82	1.07
3/8" (1.29 LF per fluid oz.)	BC@.027	LF	.57	1.01	1.58
1/2" (.728 LF per fluid oz.)	BC@.030	LF	1.01	1.12	2.13
Gutter and flashing sealant for gutters, downspouts, lap joints, flashing, vents, aluminum siding, and other metal joints. Meets ASTM C-1085					
Gutter and flashing sealant, per ounce	—	Oz	.77	—	.77
1/8" (11.6 LF per fluid oz.)	BC@.018	LF	.07	.67	.74
1/4" (2.91 LF per fluid oz.)	BC@.022	LF	.26	.82	1.08
3/8" (1.29 LF per fluid oz.)	BC@.027	LF	.60	1.01	1.61
1/2" (.728 LF per fluid oz.)	BC@.030	LF	1.06	1.12	2.18
Polyurethane door, window & siding sealant, for installing or repairing door and window frames					
Gutter and flashing sealant, per ounce	—	Oz	.63	—	.63
1/8" (11.6 LF per fluid oz.)	BC@.018	LF	.05	.67	.72
1/4" (2.91 LF per fluid oz.)	BC@.022	LF	.22	.82	1.04

	Craft@Hrs	Unit	Material	Labor	Total
3/8" (1.29 LF per fluid oz.)	BC@.027	LF	.49	1.01	1.50
1/2" (.728 LF per fluid oz.)	BC@.030	LF	.86	1.12	1.98
Sanded caulk, comes in a variety of colors to match colored grout					
Sanded caulk, per ounce	—	Oz	.77	—	.77
1/8" (11.6 LF per fluid oz.)	BC@.018	LF	.07	.67	.74
1/4" (2.91 LF per fluid oz.)	BC@.022	LF	.27	.82	1.09
3/8" (1.29 LF per fluid oz.)	BC@.027	LF	.60	1.01	1.61
1/2" (.728 LF per fluid oz.)	BC@.030	LF	1.06	1.12	2.18
Tub and wall caulk strip, white, 1-5/8" x 11'					
Tub and wall sealant, per LF	BC@.025	LF	.43	.93	1.36
Caulking gun, professional type, heavy duty					
Cordless caulk gun	—	Ea	195.00	—	195.00
"Caulk Master" caulking gun	—	Ea	60.00	—	60.00
Caulking gun, economy grade					
1/10 gallon tube, ratchet rod	—	Ea	10.00	—	10.00
Quart capacity, smooth rod	—	Ea	22.00	—	22.00

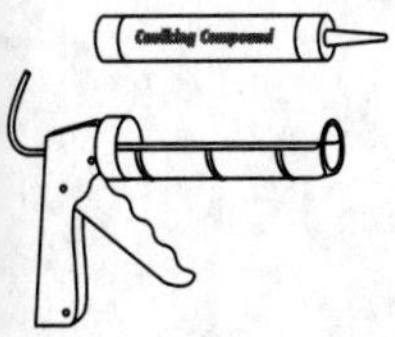

Cedar Closet Lining Material costs are per SF covered including 7% waste. Labor is for good quality installation in typical residential closet over studs or gypsum wallboard.

	Craft@Hrs	Unit	Material	Labor	Total
Solid cedar planks					
15 SF package	BC@.060	SF	2.27	2.24	4.51
35 SF package	BC@.060	SF	1.70	2.24	3.94

Ceiling Domes Complete ceiling dome kits, includes grid, hardware, panels and crating, from flat to 30 degree pitch in 5 degree increments. Prices shown are for best quality. Prices may be as much as 40% lower depending on the requirements. Envel Design Corp.

	Craft@Hrs	Unit	Material	Labor	Total
9' diameter	B1@10.7	Ea	5,250.00	362.00	5,612.00
10' diameter	B1@10.7	Ea	7,200.00	362.00	7,562.00
11' diameter	B1@17.2	Ea	9,480.00	582.00	10,062.00
UV stabilized commercial grade acrylic with decorative patterns (Costs vary from $3.90 to $6.50 per SF)					
Typical cost per SF	B1@.100	SF	5.58	3.39	8.97
Custom, dimensional Envelex™ Designs					
Standard sizes and patterns (2' x 2', 2' x 4')	B1@.006	SF	34.90	.20	35.10
Irregular shapes					
Oversize and custom designs	B1@.006	SF	40.90	.20	41.10
Add for cutting panels	B1@.033	Ea	—	1.12	1.12

Ceiling Panel Suspension Grids Typical costs, 15/16" flange, plain white. Add panel costs below.

	Craft@Hrs	Unit	Material	Labor	Total
Main runner, 12' long	—	Ea	8.33	—	8.33
Main runner, 12' long	—	LF	.69	—	.69
Cross tee, 2' long	—	Ea	1.49	—	1.49
Cross tee, 2' long	—	LF	.75	—	.75
Cross tee, 4' long	—	Ea	2.86	—	2.86
Cross tee, 4' long	—	LF	.71	—	.71
Wall mold, 12' long	—	Ea	4.90	—	4.90
Wall mold, 12' long	—	LF	.41	—	.41
Add for colored	—	%	10.0	—	—
Add for fire-rated white	—	%	100.0	—	—
Add for chrome or gold color grid	—	%	40.0	—	—
Suspension grid system including runners, tees, wall mold, hooks and hanging wire (but no tile or lighting fixtures)					
2' x 2' grid with wire suspension, per square foot					
15/16" flange	BC@.017	SF	.85	.64	1.49
9/16" flange	BC@.015	SF	1.02	.56	1.58

Ceiling Panel Suspension Grids

	Craft@Hrs	Unit	Material	Labor	Total
15/16" flange, shadow molding	BC@.019	SF	.96	.71	1.67
9/16" flange, shadow molding	BC@.017	SF	1.11	.64	1.75
2' x 2' grid suspended from black iron and pencil rod, per square foot					
15/16" flange	BC@.030	SF	1.44	1.12	2.56
9/16" flange	BC@.028	SF	1.61	1.05	2.66
15/16" flange, shadow molding	BC@.030	SF	1.46	1.12	2.58
9/16" flange, shadow molding	BC@.028	SF	1.65	1.05	2.70
2' x 4' grid with wire suspension, per square foot					
15/16" flange	BC@.015	SF	.86	.56	1.42
9/16" flange	BC@.014	SF	1.02	.52	1.54
15/16" flange, shadow molding	BC@.017	SF	.96	.64	1.60
2' x 4' grid suspended from black iron and pencil rod, per square foot					
15/16" flange	BC@.028	SF	1.34	1.05	2.39
9/16" flange	BC@.026	SF	1.51	.97	2.48
4' x 4' grid with wire suspension, per square foot					
15/16" flange	BC@.012	SF	.66	.45	1.11
Sheetrock grid system, wire suspended	BC@.015	SF	1.08	.56	1.64
Las Vegas code sublid grid	BC@.080	SF	1.14	2.99	4.13
Sub-ceiling grid suspended from black iron, Pencil rod and hat channel	BC@.020	SF	1.08	.75	1.83
Additional costs for suspension grid systems					
2-1/4" Compasso free form edge trim	BC@.050	LF	13.50	1.87	15.37
8" Axiom edge trim	BC@.060	LF	25.70	2.24	27.94
2" Axiom edge trim	BC@.060	LF	12.10	2.24	14.34
"L" trim	BC@.025	LF	1.21	.93	2.14
Add for small or irregular rooms	BC@.007	SF	—	.26	.26
Add for hold down clips	BC@.005	SF	.12	.19	.31
Serpentina wave curved grid	BC@3.00	SF	32.30	112.00	144.30
Troffer lighting fixtures for ceiling suspension grid, includes installation, connection, lens and tubes					
2 tube 2' x 2' fixture	BE@1.00	Ea	40.80	40.60	81.40
2 tube 2' x 4' fixture	BE@1.00	Ea	52.90	40.60	93.50
3 tube 2' x 4' fixture	BE@1.00	Ea	51.60	40.60	92.20
4 tube 2' x 4' fixture	BE@1.00	Ea	60.60	40.60	101.20
Light-diffusing panels for installation in suspension system under fluorescent lighting. Reduce per unit price by 10% for volume purchases.					
Styrene, assuming minimum quantity of 10					
.065" thick, cracked ice, 2' x 2', white	BC@.020	Ea	6.55	.75	7.30
.065" thick, cracked ice, 2' x 4', white	BC@.029	Ea	13.10	1.08	14.18
.095" thick, prismatic, 2' x 2', clear	BC@.020	Ea	8.09	.75	8.84
.095" thick, prismatic, 2' x 2', white	BC@.020	Ea	6.55	.75	7.30
.095" thick, prismatic, 2' x 4', clear	BC@.029	Ea	16.20	1.08	17.28
.095" thick, prismatic, 2' x 4', white	BC@.029	Ea	13.10	1.08	14.18
.095" thick, Victorian pattern 2' x 4'	BC@.029	Ea	38.50	1.08	39.58
Egg crate louvers, 1/2" x 1/2" x 3/8" cell size					
Frost	BC@.188	Ea	13.70	7.03	20.73
White styrene	BC@.188	Ea	19.10	7.03	26.13
Silver finish	BC@.188	Ea	64.70	7.03	71.73
Metallic styrene	BC@.188	Ea	73.20	7.03	80.23
Anodized aluminum	BC@.188	Ea	82.00	7.03	89.03

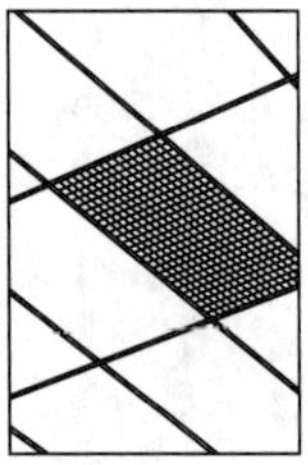

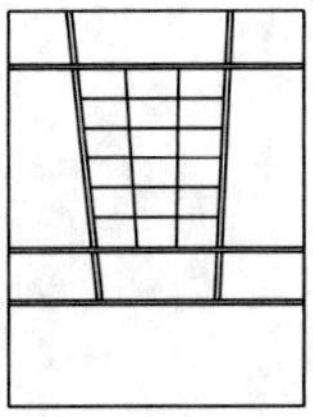

	Craft@Hrs	Unit	Material	Labor	Total
Parabolic louvers, 5/8" x 5/8" x 7/16" cell size					
Silver styrene	BC@.188	Ea	29.50	7.03	36.53
Gold styrene	BC@.188	Ea	31.10	7.03	38.13
Silver acrylic	BC@.188	Ea	50.30	7.03	57.33
Gold acrylic	BC@.188	Ea	50.30	7.03	57.33
Stained glass look, one dimension, 2' x 2'					
Standard colors	BC@.033	Ea	34.90	1.23	36.13
Antiqued colors	BC@.035	Ea	46.60	1.31	47.91

Ceiling Panels, Lay-in Type Costs per SF of ceiling area covered. No waste included. Add suspension grid system cost from preceding pages.

	Craft@Hrs	Unit	Material	Labor	Total
Acoustical rated suspended ceiling panels					
2' x 2' suspended ceiling panels					
Non directional tegular, dining	BC@.012	SF	1.30	.45	1.75
Random texture "A" fire rated	BC@.012	SF	1.87	.45	2.32
Armstrong Cortega™ #770 tegular	BC@.012	SF	.82	.45	1.27
Armstrong, random textured	BC@.012	SF	1.59	.45	2.04
Armstrong "A" fire rated, Sahara	BC@.012	SF	2.65	.45	3.10
Armstrong Ultima™ #1911 tegular	BC@.012	SF	3.30	.45	3.75
Armstrong Ultima™ #1912 tegular	BC@.012	SF	3.30	.45	3.75
Armstrong Minnetone 2nd look™ #704 tegular	BC@.012	SF	1.28	.45	1.73
Armstrong Cirrus #556 tegular	BC@.012	SF	2.05	.45	2.50
Armstrong Ultima open beveled tegular #1942	BC@.012	SF	2.22	.45	2.67
Armstrong Dune tegular FR	BC@.012	SF	3.93	.45	4.38
Armstrong Dune tegular #1775	BC@.012	SF	1.35	.45	1.80
Armstrong Dune #1774	BC@.012	SF	1.94	.45	2.39
Armstrong Bravada II	BC@.012	SF	3.60	.45	4.05
Armstrong Classic	BC@.012	SF	3.60	.45	4.05
Armstrong Optima tegular	BC@.012	SF	3.76	.45	4.21
Armstrong Tincraft Circles	BC@.025	SF	9.34	.93	10.27
5/8" Armstrong #1713 School Zone	BC@.012	SF	1.97	.45	2.42
3/4" Armstrong Optima #3250	BC@.015	SF	5.76	.56	6.32
3/4" Armstrong Optima #3251	BC@.015	SF	5.90	.56	6.46
"A" fire rated with Bioguard™	BC@.012	SF	2.53	.45	2.98
Shadow Line tegular USG#86985	BC@.012	SF	3.06	.45	3.51
Sandstone Fine Fissure tegular, Certainteed	BC@.012	SF	3.19	.45	3.64
Eclipse Clima Plus	BC@.012	SF	3.63	.45	4.08
5/8" Millinia Clima Plus, square edge	BC@.012	SF	3.45	.45	3.90
5/8" USG 5th Avenue	BC@.012	SF	.99	.45	1.44
5/8" USG slant edge, Alpine	BC@.012	SF	1.79	.45	2.24
5/8" USG square edge, Astro	BC@.012	SF	2.14	.45	2.59
3/4" USG foil back Cheyenne	BC@.007	SF	3.22	.26	3.48
3/4" USG Luna, fine textured	BC@.007	SF	3.26	.26	3.52
3/4" USG Sandrift Clima-Plus, #808 tegular	BC@.007	SF	3.44	.26	3.70
2' x 4' suspended ceiling panels					
Textured	BC@.007	SF	.99	.26	1.25
Square edge, scored	BC@.007	SF	1.23	.26	1.49
#860 Armatuff square edge	BC@.007	SF	2.87	.26	3.13
Armstrong Ultima #1915, Humiguard Plus	BC@.007	SF	2.22	.26	2.48
Armstrong Second Look, tegular	BC@.007	SF	1.26	.26	1.52
5/8" fissured fire code, Humiguard Plus	BC@.007	SF	1.67	.26	1.93
Armstrong Second Look, fire rated, tegular	BC@.007	SF	2.20	.26	2.46
Textured class "A", fire rated	BC@.007	SF	1.03	.26	1.29
5/8" fissured fire code	BC@.007	SF	1.55	.26	1.81
Cortega	BC@.007	SF	.65	.26	.91

	Craft@Hrs	Unit	Material	Labor	Total
Mars Clima Plus #88185	BC@.007	SF	3.30	.26	3.56
Dune square edge, #1776	BC@.007	SF	1.18	.26	1.44
Fiberglass class "A" fire rated	BC@.007	SF	1.48	.26	1.74
5/8" "A" fire rated USG 5th Avenue	BC@.007	SF	1.21	.26	1.47
5/8" perforated, USG Tabaret	BC@.007	SF	1.49	.26	1.75
Fiberglass reinforced 24" x 24" gypsum panels for T-bar systems. Weight is 3 to 4 pounds each, depending on pattern					
White painted finish	BC@.015	Ea	12.50	.56	13.06
Wood grain finish	BC@.020	Ea	24.90	.75	25.65

Ceiling Pans, Metal Flat, 2' x 2' pans

	Craft@Hrs	Unit	Material	Labor	Total
Aluminum with concealed grid					
2' x 2' painted	BC@.083	SF	7.52	3.10	10.62
2' x 2' polished	BC@.083	SF	11.00	3.10	14.10
Stainless steel with concealed grid					
2' x 2', polished clear mirror	BC@.097	SF	18.20	3.63	21.83
Stainless steel with exposed grid					
2' x 2', polished clear mirror	BC@.074	SF	10.40	2.77	13.17

Ceiling Tile Class "C" panels for non-acoustical and non-fire rated applications. Tongue and groove 12" x 12" tile nailed or stapled to ceilings. Costs per SF of ceiling area covered including fasteners, trim and typical waste.

	Craft@Hrs	Unit	Material	Labor	Total
12" x 12", Washable, White	BC@.035	SF	1.36	1.31	2.67
12" x 12", Armstrong "Grenoble"	BC@.036	SF	1.85	1.35	3.20
12" x 12", USG lace wood fiber	BC@.035	SF	1.50	1.31	2.81
12" x 12", USG white wood fiber	BC@.035	SF	1.70	1.31	3.01
12" x 12", USG "Tivoli"	BC@.035	SF	1.69	1.31	3.00
12" x 12", Armstrong "Glenwood"	BC@.035	SF	1.46	1.31	2.77
12" x 12", Armstrong tin ceiling design	BC@.035	SF	2.84	1.31	4.15
6" x 48", Armstrong classic plank	BC@.054	SF	2.42	2.02	4.44

Ceilings, Tin look Various patterns

	Craft@Hrs	Unit	Material	Labor	Total
Embossed panels					
2' x 2' square panels, cost each, unfinished	B1@.147	Ea	8.13	4.98	13.11
2' x 2' square panels, cost each, white	B1@.147	Ea	14.20	4.98	19.18
2' x 2' square panels, cost each, copper/gold	B1@.147	Ea	24.40	4.98	29.38
2' x 2' square panels, cost each, silver	B1@.147	Ea	20.30	4.98	25.28
2' x 2' square panels, cost each, faux	B1@.147	Ea	42.70	4.98	47.68
Embossed plates					
12" x 12" plates, cost per SF	B1@.042	SF	2.28	1.42	3.70
12" x 24" plates, cost per SF	B1@.040	SF	2.60	1.35	3.95
24" x 24" plates, cost per SF	B1@.037	SF	3.64	1.25	4.89
24" x 48" plates, cost per SF	B1@.035	SF	3.42	1.18	4.60

Cement See also Adhesives, Aggregates, and Concrete

	Craft@Hrs	Unit	Material	Labor	Total
Portland cement, type I and II, 94 lb sack	—	Sa	12.60	—	12.60
Plastic cement, 94 lb sack	—	Sa	13.10	—	13.10
High early strength cement, 80 lb sack	—	Sa	6.18	—	6.18
White cement, 94 lb sack	—	Sa	29.20	—	29.20
Concrete mix, fast setting, 50 lb sack	—	Sa	5.43	—	5.43
Light-weight concrete, 2/3 CF sack	—	Sa	4.87	—	4.87
Masonry cement, type N, 70 lb sack	—	Sa	12.60	—	12.60
Mortar mix, 60 lb sack	—	Sa	6.05	—	6.05

	Craft@Hrs	Unit	Material	Labor	Total
Non-shrink construction grout, 50 lb sack	—	Sa	16.50	—	16.50
Fiber-reinforced stucco mix, 90 lb sack	—	Sa	21.60	—	21.60
Plaster patch, 25 lb sack	—	Sa	15.40	—	15.40
Blacktop cold patch mix, 50 lb sack	—	Sa	13.10	—	13.10
Sand, 60 lb sack	—	Sa	5.44	—	5.44
Deduct for pallet quantities	—	%	–15.0	—	—

Cleaning, Final Interior surfaces, plumbing fixtures and windows. Includes removing construction debris and grime. Add for removing paint splatter or mastic. Work performed using hand tools and commercial non-toxic cleaning products or solvent. Use $80.00 as a minimum job charge.

	Craft@Hrs	Unit	Material	Labor	Total
Cabinets, per linear foot of cabinet face. Wall or base cabinet, (bathroom, kitchen or linen)					
Cleaned inside and outside	BL@.048	LF	.09	1.45	1.54
Add for polish, exposed surface only	BL@.033	LF	.07	1.00	1.07
Countertops, per linear foot of front, bathroom, family room or kitchen					
Marble, granite, laminated or composition	BL@.012	LF	.07	.36	.43
Tile, including grouted joints	BL@.020	LF	.09	.61	.70
Painted surfaces, wipe down by hand					
Base board, trim or molding	BL@.003	LF	.05	.09	.14
Cased openings, per side cleaned	BL@.060	Ea	.04	1.82	1.86
Ceilings, painted	BL@2.00	MSF	6.00	60.60	66.60
Walls, painted or papered	BL@1.50	MSF	6.00	45.50	51.50
Window sills	BL@.004	LF	.03	.12	.15
Doors, painted or stained					
Cleaned two sides, including casing	BL@.150	Ea	.11	4.55	4.66
Floors					
Hardwood floor, clean, wax and polish	BL@5.50	MSF	7.50	167.00	174.50
Mop floor	BL@1.25	MSF	.51	37.90	38.41
Vacuum carpet or sweep floor	BL@.650	MSF	—	19.70	19.70
Shampoo carpet	BL@3.30	MSF	4.50	100.00	104.50
Plumbing fixtures					
Bar sink, including faucet	BL@.285	Ea	.17	8.64	8.81
Bathtubs, including faucets & shower heads	BL@.560	Ea	.33	17.00	17.33
Kitchen sink, including faucets	BL@.375	Ea	.17	11.40	11.57
Lavatories, including faucets	BL@.375	Ea	.17	11.40	11.57
Toilets, including seat and tank	BL@.450	Ea	.17	13.60	13.77
Shower stalls, including walls, floor, ceiling, controls and shower head					
Three-sided	BL@1.80	Ea	.27	54.60	54.87
Add for glass doors	BL@.500	Ea	.09	15.20	15.29
Sliding glass doors, clean and polish both sides including cleaning of track and screen					
Up to 8' wide	BL@.650	Ea	.09	19.70	19.79
Over 8' wide	BL@.750	Ea	.14	22.70	22.84
Windows, clean and polish, inside and outside, first or second floors, per SF cleaned					
Sliding, casement or picture windows	BL@.003	SF	.02	.09	.11
Jalousie type	BL@.004	Ea	.02	.12	.14
Remove window screen, hose wash, replace	BL@.100	Ea	—	3.03	3.03
Typical final cleanup for new residential construction					
Per SF of floor (no glass cleaning)	BL@.004	SF	.13	.12	.25

	Craft@Hrs	Unit	Material	Labor	Total
Clothesline Units					
Retractable type, 5-line, indoor-outdoor, one end is wall-mounted, lines retract into aluminum case					
Cost per unit as described	B1@.860	Ea	67.30	29.10	96.40
Two "T"-shaped galvanized steel pole, set in concrete					
4 prong (not including cost of concrete)	BL@1.91	Ea	185.00	57.90	242.90
Concrete mix, 60 lb sack	—	Sa	5.25	—	5.25
Umbrella-type, 8' galvanized steel center post, requires 10' x 10' area, folds for storage					
One post, set in concrete	BL@.885	Ea	60.00	26.80	86.80
Concrete mix, 60 lb sack	—	Sa	5.25	—	5.25
Columns and Porch Posts					
Colonial style round wood, standard cap and base, hemlock/pine.					
8" x 8'	B1@2.00	Ea	127.00	67.70	194.70
10" x 10'	B1@2.00	Ea	163.00	67.70	230.70
Add for fluted wood, either of above	—	Ea	25.00	—	25.00
Round aluminum, standard cap and base					
8" x 9'	B1@2.00	Ea	165.00	67.70	232.70
10" x 10'	B1@2.00	Ea	255.00	67.70	322.70
12" x 12'	B1@3.00	Ea	473.00	102.00	575.00
Add for ornamental wood cap, typical price	—	Ea	86.20	—	86.20
Add for ornamental aluminum cap, typical	—	Ea	62.30	—	62.30
Turncraft poly round columns					
8" x 8' fluted	B1@2.00	Ea	215.00	67.70	282.70
8" x 8' plain	B1@2.00	Ea	168.00	67.70	235.70
10" x 10' plain	B1@2.00	Ea	247.00	67.70	314.70
10" x 12' plain	B1@3.00	Ea	288.00	102.00	390.00
Add for cap	—	Ea	18.20	—	18.20
Add for base	—	Ea	23.40	—	23.40
Porch posts, clear laminated west coast hemlock, solid turned.					
3-1/4" x 8'	B1@1.04	Ea	85.00	35.20	120.20
4-1/4" x 8'	B1@1.18	Ea	134.00	39.90	173.90
5-1/4" x 8'	B1@1.28	Ea	174.00	43.30	217.30

Concrete Ready-mix delivered by truck. Typical prices for most cities. Includes delivery up to 20 miles for 10 CY or more, 3" to 4" slump. Material cost only, no placing or pumping included. See forming and finishing costs on the following pages.

	Craft@Hrs	Unit	Material	Labor	Total
Footing and foundation concrete, 1-1/2" aggregate					
2,000 PSI, 4.8 sack mix	—	CY	123.00	—	123.00
2,500 PSI, 5.2 sack mix	—	CY	126.00	—	126.00
3,000 PSI, 5.7 sack mix	—	CY	128.00	—	128.00
3,500 PSI, 6.3 sack mix	—	CY	132.00	—	132.00
4,000 PSI, 6.9 sack mix	—	CY	136.00	—	136.00
Slab, sidewalk, and driveway concrete, 1" aggregate					
2,000 PSI, 5.0 sack mix	—	CY	125.00	—	125.00
2,500 PSI, 5.5 sack mix	—	CY	128.00	—	128.00
3,000 PSI, 6.0 sack mix	—	CY	130.00	—	130.00
3,500 PSI, 6.6 sack mix	—	CY	132.00	—	132.00
4,000 PSI, 7.1 sack mix	—	CY	135.00	—	135.00

	Craft@Hrs	Unit	Material	Labor	Total
Pea gravel pump mix / grout mix, 3/8" aggregate					
2,000 PSI, 6.0 sack mix	—	CY	135.00	—	135.00
2,500 PSI, 6.5 sack mix	—	CY	136.00	—	136.00
3,000 PSI, 7.2 sack mix	—	CY	141.00	—	141.00
3,500 PSI, 7.9 sack mix	—	CY	145.00	—	145.00
5,000 PSI, 8.5 sack mix	—	CY	154.00	—	154.00
Fiber mesh integral concrete reinforcing, polypropylene fiber, add per cubic yard of concrete					
Short fiber polypropylene (slabs)	—	CY	6.50	—	6.50
Long fiber polypropylene (structural)	—	CY	9.13	—	9.13
Extra delivery costs for ready-mix concrete					
Add for delivery over 20 miles	—	Mile	9.95	—	9.95
Add for standby charge in excess of 5 minutes per CY delivered per minute of extra time	—	Ea	3.11	—	3.11
Add for less than 10 CY per load delivered	—	CY	54.50	—	54.50
Add for Saturday delivery, per CY	—	CY	8.72	—	8.72
Extra costs for non-standard aggregates					
Add for lightweight aggregate, typical	—	CY	57.20	—	57.20
Add for lightweight aggregate, pump mix	—	CY	59.80	—	59.80
Add for granite aggregate, typical	—	CY	8.97	—	8.97
Extra costs for non-standard mix additives					
High early strength 5 sack mix	—	CY	16.20	—	16.20
High early strength 6 sack mix	—	CY	21.50	—	21.50
Add for white cement (architectural)	—	CY	74.00	—	74.00
Add for 1% calcium chloride	—	CY	2.08	—	2.08
Add for chemical compensated shrinkage	—	CY	27.30	—	27.30
Add for super plasticized mix, 7" - 8" slump	—	%	8.0	—	—

Add for colored concrete, typical prices. The ready-mix supplier charges for cleanup of the ready-mix truck used for delivery of colored concrete. The usual practice is to provide one truck per day for delivery of all colored concrete for a particular job. Cost will be based on the quantity of pigment required. Pastels require one to two pounds of pigment per sack of cement. Greater color density may require up to five pounds of pigment per cubic yard. Cost per cubic yard based on a 5-sack mix and one pound of color per sack.

	Craft@Hrs	Unit	Material	Labor	Total
Most colors (tan, brown, gray, beige)	—	CY	32.00	—	32.00
Green (requires white cement)	—	CY	58.10	—	58.10
Blue (requires white cement)	—	CY	176.00	—	176.00
White concrete pigment	—	CY	44.80	—	44.80
Colored concrete, truck cleanup, per day	—	LS	98.90	—	98.90

Concrete Expansion Joints Fiber or asphaltic-felt sided. Per linear foot

Wall (thickness)

Depth	**1/4"**	**3/8"**	**1/2"**
3" deep	.13	.19	.29
3-1/2" deep	.14	.24	.36
4" deep	.17	.26	.39
6" deep	.19	.32	.44

	Craft@Hrs	Unit	Material	Labor	Total
Labor to install concrete expansion joints					
3" to 6" width, 1/4" to 1/2" thick	B1@.030	LF	—	1.02	1.02

	Craft@Hrs	Unit	Material	Labor	Total
Concrete Snap Ties Short end ties, price each based on cartons of 200.					
6" form	—	Ea	.45	—	.45
8" form	—	Ea	.73	—	.73
10" form	—	Ea	.59	—	.59
12" form	—	Ea	.62	—	.62
14" form	—	Ea	.66	—	.66
16" form	—	Ea	.70	—	.70
18" form	—	Ea	.72	—	.72
24" form	—	Ea	.82	—	.82
6" wedge form tie	—	Ea	.45	—	.45
8" wedge form tie	—	Ea	.47	—	.47
10" wedge form tie	—	Ea	.56	—	.56
12" wedge form tie	—	Ea	.67	—	.67
14" wedge form tie	—	Ea	.78	—	.78
16" wedge form tie	—	Ea	.48	—	.48
24" wedge form tie	—	Ea	2.50	—	2.50
Add for long end ties	—	%	12.0	—	—

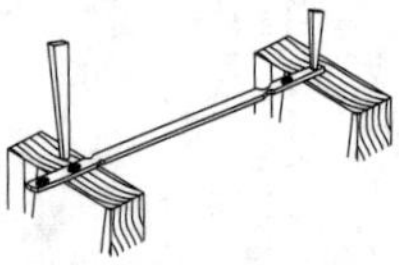

	Craft@Hrs	Unit	Material	Labor	Total
Concrete Form Stakes Steel, 3/8" thick x 1-1/2" wide. Costs per stake.					
18" x 1", flat	—	Ea	3.50	—	3.50
24" x 1", flat	—	Ea	3.73	—	3.73
30" x 1", flat	—	Ea	4.64	—	4.64
48" x 1", flat	—	Ea	7.14	—	7.14
12" x 1-1/2", flat	—	Ea	2.12	—	2.12
18" x 1-1/2", flat	—	Ea	3.80	—	3.80
24" x 1-1/2", flat	—	Ea	4.49	—	4.49
30" x 1-1/2", flat	—	Ea	4.60	—	4.60
36" x 1-1/2", flat	—	Ea	6.00	—	6.00
42" x 1-1/2", flat	—	Ea	5.18	—	5.18
48" x 1-1/2", flat	—	Ea	6.83	—	6.83
12" x 3/4", round	—	Ea	2.58	—	2.58
36" x 3/4", round	—	Ea	5.62	—	5.62
42" x 3/4", round	—	Ea	5.42	—	5.42
18" x 5/8", square	—	Ea	2.52	—	2.52
24" x 3/4", square	—	Ea	3.19	—	3.19
30" x 5/8", square	—	Ea	5.61	—	5.61
36" x 5/8", square	—	Ea	7.20	—	7.20
48" x 3/4", square	—	Ea	8.11	—	8.11

Insulated Concrete Forms (ICFs) Expanded polystyrene (EPS) forms for residential and commercial reinforced concrete walls 4", 6" or 8" thick. Based on standard sized block connected with plastic clips and reinforced with steel bars before cores are filled with concrete. Costs assume forms are left in place as wall insulation and that no concrete finishing is required. See www.eco-block.com. The crew is a carpenter and a laborer. Material costs include EPS forms and connectors as described but no concrete or rebar.

	Craft@Hrs	Unit	Material	Labor	Total
Standard block, 5.3 SF per block					
16" H, 48" L, with 12 panel connectors	—	Ea	20.30	—	20.30

	Craft@Hrs	Unit	Material	Labor	Total
Corner blocks, each includes 8 panel connectors					
4" cavity, 16" H, 32" L	—	Ea	20.20	—	20.20
6" cavity, 16" H, 32" L	—	Ea	20.20	—	20.20
8" cavity, 16" H, 32" L	—	Ea	17.80	—	17.80
Connectors					
4" connectors, per box of 1000	—	Ea	209.00	—	209.00
6" connectors, per box of 500	—	Ea	105.00	—	105.00
8" connectors, per box of 500	—	Ea	105.00	—	105.00
10" connectors, per box of 500	—	Ea	105.00	—	105.00
Splice connectors, per box of 1000	—	Ea	94.30	—	94.30
Brick ledge rails, per box of 50 rails	—	Ea	47.40	—	47.40
1" extension "Texas T", per box of 500	—	Ea	43.30	—	43.30
16" 90 degree panel connectors, per box of 40	—	Ea	139.00	—	139.00
24" 90 degree panel connectors, per box of 40	—	Ea	174.00	—	174.00
16" 45 degree panel connectors, per box of 40	—	Ea	139.00	—	139.00
24" 45 degree panel connectors, per box of 40	—	Ea	174.00	—	174.00

Material and labor for EPS forms. These figures assume footings or concrete slab are in place and ready to accept the first course of forms. Material includes forms, connectors, rebar and concrete for a 6" wall. Labor includes erecting forms, setting rebar and pouring concrete in walls to 8' high. Assume that each square foot of wall requires 1 linear foot of #4 rebar.

	Craft@Hrs	Unit	Material	Labor	Total
Per square foot of wall, below grade	B1@.060	SF	5.55	2.03	7.58
Per standard block (5.3 SF), below grade	B1@.318	Ea	29.40	10.80	40.20
Per square foot of wall, above grade	B1@.080	SF	5.55	2.71	8.26
Per standard block (5.3 SF), above grade	B1@.424	Ea	29.40	14.40	43.80
Add for 8" walls	—	%	12.0	5.0	—
Deduct for 4" walls	—	%	–8.0	–5.0	—

Cement and expanded polystyrene forms Similar to EPS forms above but with cement added to the mix: Recycled polystyrene (85%) and concrete (15%) building blocks with a grid of internal chambers designed to be placed either horizontally or vertically. Available brands are Rastra Block and Grid-WALL. Once the panels are in place they are filled with concrete providing a high strength, fireproof structural grid. Includes cement filling and grouting. When cut for odd sizes use per sq ft pricing.

	Craft@Hrs	Unit	Material	Labor	Total
Material unit costs for Grid-WALL systems					
Standard wall block, 5.3 SF per block					
48" L, 16" H,	—	Ea	30.10	—	30.10

Labor and material for wall construction

Material includes cost of Grid-WALL but not concrete or rebar. Labor includes stacking, leveling, adding rebar, bracing and prepping the wall but not the concrete pour.

	Craft@Hrs	Unit	Material	Labor	Total
Per square foot of wall	B1@.058	SF	5.71	1.96	7.67
Per standard block (5.3 SF)	B1@.313	Ea	30.10	10.60	40.70
Add to labor if concrete pour included	—	%	—	20.0	—

Use to calculate concrete and rebar costs:

1.1 cubic yards of concrete are required to fill 100 square feet of Grid-WALL.

1 Grid-WALL block will take 8 ft. of rebar, unless engineered otherwise.

Concrete Formwork Multiple use of forms assumes that forms can be removed, partially disassembled and cleaned and that 75% of the form material can be reused. Costs include assembly, oiling, setting, stripping and cleaning. Material costs in this section can be adjusted to reflect your actual cost of lumber. Here's how: Divide your actual lumber cost per MBF by the assumed cost (listed in parentheses). Then multiply the cost in the material column by this adjustment factor. For expanded coverage of concrete and formwork, see the *National Concrete & Masonry Estimator* at http://CraftsmanSiteLicense.com.

Concrete Formwork

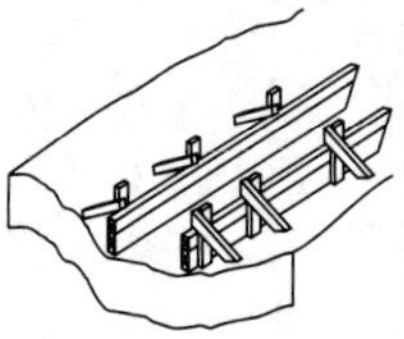

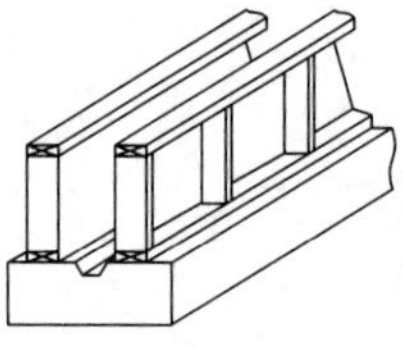

Board forming and stripping For wall footings, grade beams, column footings, site curbs and steps. Includes 5% waste. Per SF of contact area. When forms are required on both sides of the concrete, include the contact surface for each side.

	Craft@Hrs	Unit	Material	Labor	Total
2" thick forms and bracing, using 2.85 BF of form lumber per SF. Includes nails, ties, and form oil					
Using 2" lumber, per MBF	—	MBF	768.00	—	768.00
Using nails, ties and form oil, per SF	—	SF	.22	—	.22
1 use	B2@.115	SF	2.50	4.03	6.53
3 use	B2@.115	SF	1.18	4.03	5.21
5 use	B2@.115	SF	.92	4.03	4.95
Add for keyway beveled on two edges, one use. No stripping included					
2" x 4"	B2@.027	LF	.54	.95	1.49
2" x 6"	B2@.027	LF	.80	.95	1.75

Driveway and walkway edge forms Material costs include stakes, nails, and form oil and 5% waste. Per LF of edge form. When forms are required on both sides of the concrete, include the length of each side plus the end widths.

	Craft@Hrs	Unit	Material	Labor	Total
2" x 4" edge form					
Using 2" x 4" lumber, .7 BF per LF	—	MBF	777.00	—	777.00
Using nails, ties and form oil, per LF	—	LF	.22	—	.22
1 use	B2@.050	LF	.70	1.75	2.45
3 use	B2@.050	LF	.40	1.75	2.15
5 use	B2@.050	LF	.34	1.75	2.09
2" x 6" edge form					
Using 2" x 6" lumber, 1.05 BF per LF	—	MBF	759.00	—	759.00
1 use	B2@.050	LF	.96	1.75	2.71
3 use	B2@.050	LF	.52	1.75	2.27
5 use	B2@.050	LF	.42	1.75	2.17
2" x 8" edge form					
Using 2" x 8" lumber, 1.4 BF per LF	—	MBF	776.00	—	776.00
1 use	B2@.055	LF	1.31	1.93	3.24
3 use	B2@.055	LF	.68	1.93	2.61
5 use	B2@.055	LF	.54	1.93	2.47
2" x 10" edge form					
Using 2" x 10" lumber, 1.75 BF per LF	—	MBF	794.00	—	794.00
1 use	B2@.055	LF	1.55	1.93	3.48
3 use	B2@.055	LF	.79	1.93	2.72
5 use	B2@.055	LF	.62	1.93	2.55
2" x 12" edge form					
Using 2" x 12" lumber, 2.1 BF per LF	—	MBF	881.00	—	881.00
1 use	B2@.055	LF	2.01	1.93	3.94
3 use	B2@.055	LF	.99	1.93	2.92
5 use	B2@.055	LF	.77	1.93	2.70

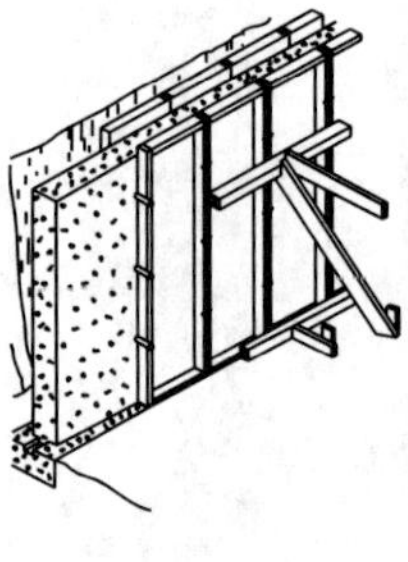

Plywood forming For foundation walls, building walls and retaining walls, using 3/4" plyform with 10% waste and 2" bracing with 20% waste. All material costs include nails, ties, clamps, form oil and stripping. Costs shown are per SF of contact area. When forms are required on both sides of the concrete, include the contact surface area for each side.

	Craft@Hrs	Unit	Material	Labor	Total
Using 3/4" plyform, per MSF	—	MSF	1,290.00	—	1,290.00
Using 2" bracing, per MBF	—	MBF	768.00	—	768.00
Using nails, ties, clamps & form oil, per SF	—	SFCA	.22	—	.22

	Craft@Hrs	Unit	Material	Labor	Total
Walls up to 4' high (1.10 SF of plywood and .42 BF of bracing per SF of form area)					
1 use	B2@.051	SFCA	1.96	1.79	3.75
3 use	B2@.051	SFCA	1.01	1.79	2.80
5 use	B2@.051	SFCA	.80	1.79	2.59
Walls 4' to 8' high (1.10 SF of plywood and .60 BF of bracing per SF of form area)					
1 use	B2@.060	SFCA	2.10	2.10	4.20
3 use	B2@.060	SFCA	1.07	2.10	3.17
5 use	B2@.060	SFCA	.84	2.10	2.94
Walls 8' to 12' high (1.10 SF of plywood and .90 BF of bracing per SF of form area)					
1 use	B2@.095	SFCA	2.33	3.33	5.66
3 use	B2@.095	SFCA	1.17	3.33	4.50
5 use	B2@.095	SFCA	.92	3.33	4.25
Walls 12' to 16' high (1.10 SF of plywood and 1.05 BF of bracing per SF of form area)					
1 use	B2@.128	SFCA	2.45	4.48	6.93
3 use	B2@.128	SFCA	1.22	4.48	5.70
5 use	B2@.128	SFCA	.96	4.48	5.44
Walls over 16' high (1.10 SF of plywood and 1.20 BF of bracing per SF of form area)					
1 use	B2@.153	SFCA	2.56	5.36	7.92
3 use	B2@.153	SFCA	1.27	5.36	6.63
5 use	B2@.153	SFCA	.99	5.36	6.35

Form stripping Labor to remove forms and bracing, clean, and stack on the job site.

	Craft@Hrs	Unit	Material	Labor	Total
Board forms at wall footings, grade beams and column footings. Per SF of contact area					
1" thick lumber	BL@.010	SFCA	—	.30	.30
2" thick lumber	BL@.012	SFCA	—	.36	.36
Keyways, 2" x 4" and 2" x 6"	BL@.006	LF	—	.18	.18
Slab edge forms. Per LF of edge form					
2" x 4" to 2" x 6"	BL@.012	LF	—	.36	.36
2" x 8" to 2" x 12"	BL@.013	LF	—	.39	.39
Walls, plywood forms. Per SF of contact area stripped					
To 4' high	BL@.017	SFCA	—	.52	.52
Over 4' to 8' high	BL@.018	SFCA	—	.55	.55
Over 8' to 12' high	BL@.020	SFCA	—	.61	.61
Over 12' to 16' high	BL@.027	SFCA	—	.82	.82
Over 16' high	BL@.040	SFCA	—	1.21	1.21

Concrete Reinforcing Steel Steel reinforcing bars (rebar), ASTM A615 Grade 60. Material costs are for deformed steel reinforcing rebars, including 10% lap allowance, cutting and bending. These costs also include detailed shop drawings and delivery to jobsite with identity tags per shop drawings. Add for epoxy or galvanized coating of rebars, chairs, splicing, spiral caissons and round column reinforcing, if required, from the sections following the data below. Costs per pound (Lb) and per linear foot (LF) including tie wire and tying.

	Craft@Hrs	Unit	Material	Labor	Total
Reinforcing steel placed and tied in footings and grade beams					
1/4" diameter, #2 rebar	RI@.015	Lb	1.29	.59	1.88
1/4" diameter, #2 rebar (.17 Lb per LF)	RI@.003	LF	.22	.12	.34
3/8" diameter, #3 rebar	RI@.011	Lb	.88	.43	1.31
3/8" diameter, #3 rebar (.38 Lb per LF)	RI@.004	LF	.33	.16	.49
1/2" diameter, #4 rebar	RI@.010	Lb	.76	.39	1.15
1/2" diameter, #4 rebar (.67 Lb per LF)	RI@.007	LF	.51	.28	.79
5/8" diameter, #5 rebar	RI@.009	Lb	.81	.35	1.16

	Craft@Hrs	Unit	Material	Labor	Total
5/8" diameter, #5 rebar (1.04 Lb per LF)	RI@.009	LF	.84	.35	1.19
3/4" diameter, #6 rebar	RI@.008	Lb	.68	.31	.99
3/4" diameter, #6 rebar (1.50 Lb per LF)	RI@.012	LF	1.02	.47	1.49
7/8" diameter, #7 rebar	RI@.008	Lb	.83	.31	1.14
7/8" diameter, #7 rebar (2.04 Lb per LF)	RI@.016	LF	1.69	.63	2.32
1" diameter, #8 rebar	RI@.008	Lb	.70	.31	1.01
1" diameter, #8 rebar (2.67 Lb per LF)	RI@.021	LF	1.88	.83	2.71
Reinforcing steel placed and tied in structural slabs					
1/4" diameter, #2 rebar	RI@.014	Lb	1.29	.55	1.84
1/4" diameter, #2 rebar (.17 Lb per LF)	RI@.002	LF	.22	.08	.30
3/8" diameter, #3 rebar	RI@.010	Lb	.88	.39	1.27
3/8" diameter, #3 rebar (.38 Lb per LF)	RI@.004	LF	.33	.16	.49
1/2" diameter, #4 rebar	RI@.009	Lb	.76	.35	1.11
1/2" diameter, #4 rebar (.67 Lb per LF)	RI@.006	LF	.51	.24	.75
5/8" diameter, #5 rebar	RI@.008	Lb	.81	.31	1.12
5/8" diameter, #5 rebar (1.04 Lb per LF)	RI@.008	LF	.84	.31	1.15
3/4" diameter, #6 rebar	RI@.007	Lb	.68	.28	.96
3/4" diameter, #6 rebar (1.50 Lb per LF)	RI@.011	LF	1.02	.43	1.45
7/8" diameter, #7 rebar	RI@.007	Lb	.83	.28	1.11
7/8" diameter, #7 rebar (2.04 Lb per LF)	RI@.014	LF	1.69	.55	2.24
1" diameter, #8 rebar	RI@.007	Lb	.70	.28	.98
1" diameter, #8 rebar (2.67 Lb per LF)	RI@.019	LF	1.88	.75	2.63
Reinforcing steel placed and tied in walls					
1/4" diameter, #2 rebar	RI@.017	Lb	1.29	.67	1.96
1/4" diameter, #2 rebar (.17 Lb per LF)	RI@.003	LF	.22	.12	.34
3/8" diameter, #3 rebar	RI@.012	Lb	.88	.47	1.35
3/8" diameter, #3 rebar (.38 Lb per LF)	RI@.005	LF	.33	.20	.53
1/2" diameter, #4 rebar	RI@.011	Lb	.76	.43	1.19
1/2" diameter, #4 rebar (.67 Lb per LF)	RI@.007	LF	.51	.28	.79
5/8" diameter, #5 rebar	RI@.010	Lb	.81	.39	1.20
5/8" diameter, #5 rebar (1.04 Lb per LF)	RI@.010	LF	.84	.39	1.23
3/4" diameter, #6 rebar	RI@.009	Lb	.68	.35	1.03
3/4" diameter, #6 rebar (1.50 Lb per LF)	RI@.014	LF	1.02	.55	1.57
7/8" diameter, #7 rebar	RI@.009	Lb	.83	.35	1.18
7/8" diameter, #7 rebar (2.04 Lb per LF)	RI@.018	LF	1.69	.71	2.40
1" diameter, #8 rebar	RI@.009	Lb	.70	.35	1.05
1" diameter, #8 rebar (2.67 Lb per LF)	RI@.024	LF	1.88	.94	2.82

Add for reinforcing steel coating. Coating applied prior to shipment to the job site. Labor for placing coated rebar is the same as that shown for plain rebar above. Cost per pound of reinforcing steel.

	Craft@Hrs	Unit	Material	Labor	Total
Epoxy coating					
Any size rebar, add	—	Lb	.39	—	.39
Galvanized coating					
Any #2 rebar, #3 rebar or #4 rebar, add	—	Lb	.51	—	.51
Any #5 rebar or #6 rebar, add	—	Lb	.48	—	.48
Any #7 rebar or #8 rebar, add	—	Lb	.45	—	.45

Add for reinforcing steel chairs. Labor for placing rebar shown above includes time for setting chairs.

	Craft@Hrs	Unit	Material	Labor	Total
Chairs, individual type, cost each					
3" high					
Steel	—	Ea	.75	—	.75
Plastic	—	Ea	.30	—	.30
Galvanized steel	—	Ea	1.37	—	1.37

	Craft@Hrs	Unit	Material	Labor	Total
5" high					
Steel	—	Ea	1.15	—	1.15
Plastic	—	Ea	.79	—	.79
Galvanized steel	—	Ea	1.80	—	1.80
8" high					
Steel	—	Ea	2.44	—	2.44
Plastic	—	Ea	1.60	—	1.60
Galvanized steel	—	Ea	3.86	—	3.86
Chairs, continuous type, with legs 8" OC, cost per linear foot					
3" high					
Steel	—	LF	1.05	—	1.05
Plastic	—	LF	.65	—	.65
Galvanized steel	—	LF	1.60	—	1.60
6" high					
Steel	—	LF	1.44	—	1.44
Plastic	—	LF	.90	—	.90
Galvanized steel	—	LF	2.26	—	2.26
8" high					
Steel	—	LF	2.20	—	2.20
Plastic	—	LF	1.66	—	1.66
Galvanized steel	—	LF	3.17	—	3.17
Waterstop, 3/8", adhesive not included.					
Rubber, 6"	B2@.059	LF	1.57	2.07	3.64
Rubber, 9"	B2@.059	LF	3.39	2.07	5.46

Spiral caisson and round column reinforcing 3/8" diameter hot rolled steel spirals with main vertical bars as shown. Costs include typical engineering and shop drawings. Based on shop fabricated spirals delivered, tagged, ready to install. Cost per vertical linear foot (VLF)

	Craft@Hrs	Unit	Material	Labor	Total
16" diameter with 6 #6 bars, 16.8 Lbs per VLF	RI@.041	VLF	34.70	1.61	36.31
24" diameter with 6 #6 bars, 28.5 Lbs per VLF	RI@.085	VLF	59.60	3.34	62.94
36" diameter with 8 #10 bars, 51.2 Lbs per VLF	RI@.176	VLF	108.00	6.92	114.92

Welded wire mesh Steel, electric weld, including 15% waste and overlap

	Craft@Hrs	Unit	Material	Labor	Total
2" x 2" W.9 x W.9 (#12 x #12), slabs	RI@.004	SF	1.20	.16	1.36
2" x 2" W.9 x W.9 (#12 x #12), beams and columns	RI@.020	SF	1.20	.79	1.99
4" x 4" W1.4 x W1.4 (#10 x #10), slabs	RI@.003	SF	.58	.12	.70
4" x 4" W2.0 x W2.0 (#8 x #8), slabs	RI@.004	SF	.67	.16	.83
4" x 4" W2.9 x W2.9 (#6 x #6), slabs	RI@.005	SF	.75	.20	.95
4" x 4" W4.0 x W4.0 (#4 x #4), slabs	RI@.006	SF	1.00	.24	1.24
6" x 6" W1.4 x W1.4 (#10 x #10), slabs	RI@.003	SF	.25	.12	.37
6" x 6" W2.0 x W2.0 (#8 x #8), slabs	RI@.004	SF	.44	.16	.60
6" x 6" W2.9 x W2.9 (#6 x #6), slabs	RI@.004	SF	.51	.16	.67
6" x 6" W4.0 x W4.0 (#4 x #4), slabs	RI@.005	SF	.70	.20	.90
Add for lengthwise cut, LF of cut	RI@.002	LF	—	.08	.08
Welded wire mesh, galvanized steel, electric weld, including 15% waste and overlap					
2" x 2" W.9 x W.9 (#12 x #12), slabs	RI@.004	SF	2.43	.16	2.59
4" x 4" W1.4 x W1.4 (#10 x #10), slabs	RI@.003	SF	1.13	.12	1.25
4" x 4" W2.0 x W2.0 (#8 x #8), slabs	RI@.004	SF	1.36	.16	1.52
4" x 4" W2.9 x W2.9 (#6 x #6), slabs	RI@.005	SF	1.50	.20	1.70
4" x 4" W4.0 x W4.0 (#4 x #4), slabs	RI@.006	SF	1.96	.24	2.20
6" x 6" W1.4 x W1.4 (#10 x #10), slabs	RI@.003	SF	.64	.12	.76

	Craft@Hrs	Unit	Material	Labor	Total
6" x 6" W2.0 x W2.0 (#8 x #8), slabs	RI@.004	SF	.78	.16	.94
6" x 6" W2.9 x W2.9 (#6 x #6), slabs	RI@.004	SF	1.00	.16	1.16
6" x 6" W4.0 x W4.0 (#4 x #4), slabs	RI@.005	SF	1.43	.20	1.63
Add for lengthwise cut, LF of cut	RI@.002	LF	—	.08	.08
Welded wire mesh, epoxy coated steel, electric weld, including 15% waste and overlap					
2" x 2" W.9 x W.9 (#12 x #12), slabs	RI@.004	SF	4.99	.16	5.15
4" x 4" W1.4 x W1.4 (#10 x #10), slabs	RI@.003	SF	4.46	.12	4.58
4" x 4" W2.0 x W2.0 (#8 x #8), slabs	RI@.004	SF	4.43	.16	4.59
4" x 4" W2.9 x W2.9 (#6 x #6), slabs	RI@.005	SF	4.50	.20	4.70
4" x 4" W4.0 x W4.0 (#4 x #4), slabs	RI@.006	SF	4.73	.24	4.97
6" x 6" W1.4 x W1.4 (#10 x #10), slabs	RI@.003	SF	4.06	.12	4.18
6" x 6" W2.0 x W2.0 (#8 x #8), slabs	RI@.004	SF	4.15	.16	4.31
6" x 6" W2.9 x W2.9 (#6 x #6), slabs	RI@.004	SF	4.22	.16	4.38
6" x 6" W4.0 x W4.0 (#4 x #4), slabs	RI@.005	SF	4.46	.20	4.66
Add for lengthwise cut, LF of cut	RI@.002	LF	—	.08	.08

Concrete Walls Cast-in-place concrete walls for buildings or retaining walls. Material costs for concrete placed direct from chute are based on 2,000 PSI, 5.0 sack mix, with 1" aggregate, including 5% waste. Pump mix costs include an additional $15.00 per CY for the pump. Labor costs are for placing only. Add the cost of excavation, formwork, steel reinforcing, finishes and curing. Square foot costs are based on SF of wall measured on one face only. Costs do not include engineering, design or foundations. For expanded coverage of concrete and formwork, see the *National Concrete & Masonry Estimator* at http://CraftsmanSiteLicense.com

	Craft@Hrs	Unit	Material	Labor	Total
Using concrete (before 5% waste allowance)	—	CY	125.00	—	125.00
4" thick walls (1.23 CY per CSF)					
To 4' high, direct from chute	B1@.013	SF	1.61	.44	2.05
4' to 8' high, pumped	B3@.015	SF	1.80	.49	2.29
8' to 12' high, pumped	B3@.017	SF	1.80	.56	2.36
12' to 16' high, pumped	B3@.018	SF	1.80	.59	2.39
16' high, pumped	B3@.020	SF	1.80	.65	2.45
6" thick walls (1.85 CY per CSF)					
To 4' high, direct from chute	B1@.020	SF	2.42	.68	3.10
4' to 8' high, pumped	B3@.022	SF	2.70	.72	3.42
8' to 12' high, pumped	B3@.025	SF	2.70	.82	3.52
12' to 16' high, pumped	B3@.027	SF	2.70	.88	3.58
16' high, pumped	B3@.030	SF	2.70	.98	3.68
8" thick walls (2.47 CY per CSF)					
To 4' high, direct from chute	B1@.026	SF	3.24	.88	4.12
4' to 8' high, pumped	B3@.030	SF	3.61	.98	4.59
8' to 12' high, pumped	B3@.033	SF	3.61	1.08	4.69
12' to 16' high, pumped	B3@.036	SF	3.61	1.18	4.79
16' high, pumped	B3@.040	SF	3.61	1.31	4.92
10" thick walls (3.09 CY per CSF)					
To 4' high, direct from chute	B1@.032	SF	4.05	1.08	5.13
4' to 8' high, pumped	B3@.037	SF	4.51	1.21	5.72
8' to 12' high, pumped	B3@.041	SF	4.51	1.34	5.85
12' to 16' high, pumped	B3@.046	SF	4.51	1.50	6.01
16' high, pumped	B3@.050	SF	4.51	1.63	6.14
12" thick walls (3.70 CY per CSF)					
To 4' high, placed direct from chute	B1@.040	SF	4.85	1.35	6.20
4' to 8' high, pumped	B3@.045	SF	5.40	1.47	6.87
8' to 12' high, pumped	B3@.050	SF	5.40	1.63	7.03
12' to 16' high, pumped	B3@.055	SF	5.40	1.80	7.20
16' high, pumped	B3@.060	SF	5.40	1.96	7.36

Concrete Footings, Grade Beams and Stem Walls Use the figures below for preliminary estimates. Concrete costs are based on 2,000 PSI, 5.0 sack mix with 1" aggregate placed directly from the chute of a ready-mix truck. Figures in parentheses show the cubic yards of concrete per linear foot of foundation (including 5% waste). Costs shown include concrete, 60 pounds of reinforcing per CY of concrete, and typical excavation using a 3/4 CY backhoe with excess backfill spread on site.

Footings and grade beams Cast directly against the earth, no forming or finishing required. These costs assume the top of the foundation will be at finished grade. For scheduling purposes estimate that a crew of 3 can lay out, excavate, place and tie the reinforcing steel and place 13 CY of concrete in an 8-hour day. Use $900.00 as a minimum job charge.

	Craft@Hrs	Unit	Material	Labor	Equipment	Total
Using 2,000 PSI concrete, per CY	—	CY	125.00	—	—	125.00
Using #4 reinforcing bars, per pound	—	Lb	.77	—	—	.77
Typical cost per CY	B4@1.80	CY	171.00	67.40	26.30	264.70
12" W x 6" D (0.019 CY per LF)	B4@.034	LF	3.24	1.27	.50	5.01
12" W x 8" D (0.025 CY per LF)	B4@.045	LF	4.27	1.69	.66	6.62
12" W x 10" D (0.032 CY per LF)	B4@.058	LF	5.46	2.17	.85	8.48
12" W x 12" D (0.039 CY per LF)	B4@.070	LF	6.66	2.62	1.02	10.30
12" W x 18" D (0.058 CY per LF)	B4@.104	LF	9.90	3.89	1.52	15.31
16" W x 8" D (0.035 CY per LF)	B4@.063	LF	5.98	2.36	.92	9.26
16" W x 10" D (0.043 CY per LF)	B4@.077	LF	7.34	2.88	1.13	11.35
16" W x 12" D (0.052 CY per LF)	B4@.094	LF	8.88	3.52	1.37	13.77
18" W x 8" D (0.037 CY per LF)	B4@.067	LF	6.32	2.51	.98	9.81
18" W x 10" D (0.049 CY per LF)	B4@.088	LF	8.37	3.30	1.29	12.96
18" W x 24" D (0.117 CY per LF)	B4@.216	LF	20.00	8.09	3.16	31.25
20" W x 12" D (0.065 CY per LF)	B4@.117	LF	11.10	4.38	1.71	17.19
24" W x 12" D (0.078 CY per LF)	B4@.140	LF	13.30	5.24	2.05	20.59
24" W x 24" D (0.156 CY per LF)	B4@.281	LF	26.60	10.50	4.11	41.21
24" W x 30" D (0.195 CY per LF)	B4@.351	LF	33.30	13.10	5.13	51.53
24" W x 36" D (0.234 CY per LF)	B4@.421	LF	40.00	15.80	6.16	61.96
30" W x 36" D (0.292 CY per LF)	B4@.526	LF	49.90	19.70	7.69	77.29
30" W x 42" D (0.341 CY per LF)	B4@.614	LF	58.20	23.00	8.98	90.18
36" W x 48" D (0.467 CY per LF)	B4@.841	LF	79.70	31.50	12.30	123.50

Tricks of the trade: To estimate the cost of footing or grade beam sizes not shown, multiply the width in inches by the depth in inches and divide the result by 3700. This is the CY of concrete per LF of footing including 5% waste. Multiply by the "Typical cost per CY" in the prior table to find the cost per LF.

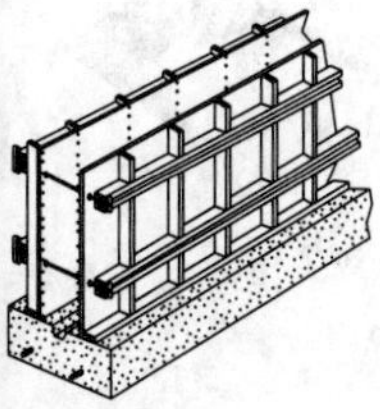

Continuous concrete footing with foundation stem wall These figures assume the foundation stem wall projects 24" above the finished grade and extends into the soil 18" to the top of the footing. Costs shown include typical excavation using a 3/4 CY backhoe with excess backfill spread on site, forming both sides of the foundation wall and the footing, based on three uses of the forms and 2 #4 rebar. Use $1,200.00 as a minimum cost for this type work.

	Craft@Hrs	Unit	Material	Labor	Equipment	Total
Typical cost per CY	B5@7.16	CY	193.00	265.00	62.80	520.80
Typical single story structure, footing 12" W x 8" D, wall 6" T x 42" D (.10 CY per LF)	B5@.716	LF	19.30	26.50	6.28	52.08
Typical two story structure, footing 18" W x 10" D, wall 8" T x 42" D (.14 CY per LF)	B5@1.00	LF	27.00	37.10	8.77	72.87
Typical three story structure, footing 24" W x 12" D, wall 10" T x 42" D (.19 CY per LF)	B5@1.36	LF	36.70	50.40	11.90	99.00

Concrete Slabs

	Craft@Hrs	Unit	Material	Labor	Total
Column Footings Concrete material and placing only. Material costs are for 3,000 PSI, 5.7 sack mix, with 1-1/2" aggregate with 5% waste included. Labor cost is for placing concrete in an existing form. Add for excavation, board forming and steel reinforcing.					
Using concrete (before waste allowance)	—	CY	130.00	—	130.00
Typical cost per CY	B1@.875	CY	136.00	29.60	165.60
Slabs, Walks and Driveways Typical costs for reinforced concrete slabs-on-grade including fine grading, slab base, forms, vapor barrier, wire mesh, 3,000 PSI concrete, finishing and curing. For expanded coverage of concrete and formwork, see the *National Concrete & Masonry Estimator* at http://CraftsmanSiteLicense.com. For thickened edge slabs, add the area of the thickened edge. Use 500 square feet as a minimum.					
2" thick	B5@.067	SF	2.47	2.48	4.95
3" thick	B5@.068	SF	2.88	2.52	5.40
4" thick	B5@.069	SF	3.27	2.56	5.83
5" thick	B5@.070	SF	3.67	2.59	6.26
6" thick	B5@.071	SF	4.04	2.63	6.67
Slab base Aggregate base for slabs. No waste included. Labor costs are for spreading aggregate from piles only. Add for fine grading, using hand tools.					
Crushed stone base 1.4 tons equal 1 cubic yard					
Using crushed stone, per CY	—	CY	43.20	—	43.20
1" base (.309 CY per CSF)	BL@.001	SF	.13	.03	.16
2" base (.617 CY per CSF)	BL@.003	SF	.27	.09	.36
3" base (.926 CY per CSF)	BL@.004	SF	.40	.12	.52
4" base (1.23 CY per CSF)	BL@.006	SF	.53	.18	.71
5" base (1.54 CY per CSF)	BL@.007	SF	.66	.21	.87
6" base (1.85 CY per CSF)	BL@.008	SF	.80	.24	1.04
Sand fill base 1.40 tons equal 1 cubic yard					
Using sand, per CY	—	CY	20.10	—	20.10
1" fill (.309 CY per CSF)	BL@.001	SF	.06	.03	.09
2" fill (.617 CY per CSF)	BL@.002	SF	.12	.06	.18
3" fill (.926 CY per CSF)	BL@.003	SF	.19	.09	.28
4" fill (1.23 CY per CSF)	BL@.004	SF	.25	.12	.37
5" fill (1.54 CY per CSF)	BL@.006	SF	.31	.18	.49
6" fill (1.85 CY per CSF)	BL@.007	SF	.37	.21	.58
Add for fine grading for slab on grade	BL@.008	SF	—	.24	.24
Slab membrane Material costs are for 10' wide membrane with 6" laps. Labor costs are to lay membrane over a level slab base.					
4 mil polyethylene	BL@.002	SF	.07	.06	.13
6 mil polyethylene	BL@.002	SF	.08	.06	.14
Detaching membrane, Ditra, polyethylene laminate, SF costs include 5% waste					
Laid on a level slab	BL@.002	SF	1.73	.06	1.79
Add for adhesive cemented seams	BL@.001	SF	.07	.03	.10

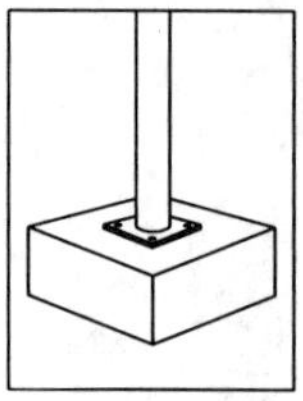

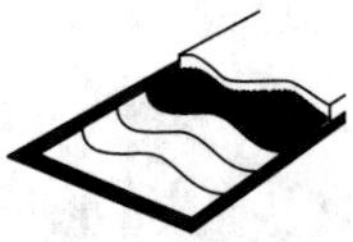

	Craft@Hrs	Unit	Material	Labor	Total
Curbs and gutters Small quantities. Material costs are for 2,000 PSI, 5.0 sack mix with 1" aggregate. No waste included. Labor cost is for placing and finishing concrete only. Add for excavation, wood forming, steel reinforcing.					
Per CY of concrete	B6@1.61	CY	125.00	53.00	178.00
Steps-on-grade Costs include layout, fabrication, and placing forms, setting and tying steel reinforcing, installation of steel nosing, placing 2,000 PSI concrete directly from the chute of a ready-mix truck, finishing, stripping forms, and curing. Costs assume excavation, back filling, and compacting have been completed. For scheduling purposes, estimate that a crew of 3 can set forms, place steel, and pour 4 to 5 CY of concrete cast-in-place steps in an 8 hour day. See also Cast-in-place Concrete Steps-on-Grade in the Industrial Section 3. Costs shown are for concrete steps with a 6" rise height and 12" tread depth supported by a 6" thick monolithic slab.					
Total cost of steps per CY of concrete	B1@5.43	CY	363.00	184.00	547.00
Concrete Finishing					
Slab finishes					
Broom finish	B6@.012	SF	—	.40	.40
Float finish	B6@.010	SF	—	.33	.33
Trowel finishing					
Steel, machine work	B6@.015	SF	—	.49	.49
Steel, hand work	B6@.018	SF	—	.59	.59
Finish treads and risers					
No abrasives, no plastering, per LF of tread	B6@.042	LF	—	1.38	1.38
With abrasives, plastered, per LF of tread	B6@.063	LF	.77	2.07	2.84
Scoring concrete surface, hand work	B6@.005	LF	—	.16	.16
Sweep, scrub and wash down	B6@.006	SF	.04	.20	.24
Liquid curing and sealing compound, water-based Acrylic Concrete Cure and Seal, spray-on, 500 SF at $110.00 per 5 gallon	B6@.003	SF	.25	.10	.35
Exposed aggregate (washed, including finishing), no disposal of slurry	B6@.017	SF	.16	.56	.72
Non-metallic color and hardener, troweled on, 2 applications, red, gray or black					
60 pounds per 100 SF	B6@.021	SF	.55	.69	1.24
100 pounds per 100 SF	B6@.025	SF	.91	.82	1.73
Add for other standard colors	—	%	50.0	—	—
Wall finishes					
Snap ties and patch	B6@.011	SF	.15	.36	.51
Remove fins	B6@.008	LF	.05	.26	.31
Grind smooth, typical	B6@.021	SF	.10	.69	.79
Burlap rub with cement grout	B6@.022	SF	.06	.72	.78
Bush hammer green concrete	B6@.061	SF	.05	2.01	2.06
Bush hammer cured concrete	B6@.091	SF	.11	3.00	3.11
Wash with acid and rinse	B6@.004	SF	.23	.13	.36
Break fins, patch voids, Carborundum dry rub	B6@.035	SF	.07	1.15	1.22
Carborundum wet rub	B6@.057	SF	.15	1.88	2.03
Specialty finishes					
Monolithic natural aggregate topping					
3/16"	B6@.020	SF	.34	.66	1.00
1/2"	B6@.022	SF	.39	.72	1.11

	Craft@Hrs	Unit	Material	Labor	Total
Integral colors					
Various colors, 10 oz. bottle	—	Ea	6.95	—	6.95
Colored release agent	—	Lb	2.58	—	2.58
Dry shake colored hardener	—	Lb	.57	—	.57
Stamped finish (embossed concrete) including touch-up of joints, if required					
Diamond, square, octagonal patterns	B6@.047	SF	—	1.55	1.55
Spanish paver pattern	B6@.053	SF	—	1.75	1.75
Add for grouting joints	B6@.023	SF	.38	.76	1.14

Countertops Custom-fabricated straight, "U"- or "L"-shaped tops. See also Tile for ceramic tile countertops.

Laminated plastic countertops (such as Formica, Textolite or Wilsonart) on a particleboard base. 22" to 25" wide. Cost per LF of longest edge (either back or front) in solid colors with 3-1/2" to 4" backsplash.

	Craft@Hrs	Unit	Material	Labor	Total
Square edge, separate backsplash	B1@.181	LF	16.40	6.13	22.53
Rolled drip edge (post formed)	B1@.181	LF	23.50	6.13	29.63
Full wrap (180 degree) front edge	B1@.181	LF	25.10	6.13	31.23
Accent color front edge	B1@.181	LF	31.90	6.13	38.03
Inlaid front and back edge	B1@.181	LF	37.60	6.13	43.73
Additional costs for laminated countertops					
Add for textures, patterns	—	%	20.0	—	—
Add for square end splash	—	Ea	19.90	—	19.90
Add for contour end splash	—	Ea	28.60	—	28.60
Add for mitered corners	—	Ea	23.70	—	23.70
Add for seamless tops	—	Ea	34.20	—	34.20
Add for sink, range or vanity cutout	—	Ea	9.23	—	9.23
Add for drilling 3 plumbing fixture holes	—	LS	11.80	—	11.80
Add for quarter round corner	—	Ea	23.80	—	23.80
Add for half round corner	—	Ea	34.00	—	34.00

Granite countertops, custom made to order from a template. 22" to 25" wide. Per square foot of top and backsplash, not including cutting, polishing, sink cut out, range cut out and a flat polish edge. Add the cost of edge polishing for undermount sink, faucet holes, angle cuts, radius ends, edge detail and jobsite delivery as itemized below. 7/8" granite weighs about 30 pounds per square foot. 1-1/4" granite weighs about 45 pounds per square foot. 7/8" tops should be set on 3/4" plywood and set in silicon adhesive every 2'. 1-1/4" granite tops can be set directly on base cabinets with silicon adhesive.

	Craft@Hrs	Unit	Material	Labor	Total
Most 3/4" (2cm) granite tops	B1@.128	SF	46.80	4.33	51.13
Most 1-1/4" (3cm) granite tops	B1@.128	SF	61.00	4.33	65.33
Add for radius or beveled edge	—	LF	8.38	—	8.38
Add for half bullnose edge	—	LF	12.10	—	12.10
Add for full bullnose edge	—	LF	24.00	—	24.00
Add for 1/2" beveled edge	—	LF	8.38	—	8.38
Add for backsplash seaming and edging	—	LF	15.40	—	15.40
Add for cooktop overmount cutout	—	Ea	155.00	—	155.00
Add for delivery (typical)	—	Ea	181.00	—	181.00
Add for eased edge	—	LF	5.99	—	5.99
Add for electrical outlet cutout	—	Ea	42.20	—	42.20
Add for faucet holes	—	Ea	31.50	—	31.50
Add for rounded corners	—	Ea	36.10	—	36.10
Add for undermount sink, polished	—	Ea	359.00	—	359.00

Engineered stone countertops, quartz particles with acrylic or epoxy binder. Trade names include Crystalite, Silestone and Cambria. Custom made from a template. Per square foot of top and backsplash surface measured one side.

	Craft@Hrs	Unit	Material	Labor	Total
Small light chips, 3/4" square edge	B1@.128	SF	57.40	4.33	61.73
Large dark chips, 3/4" square edge	B1@.128	SF	64.50	4.33	68.83

	Craft@Hrs	Unit	Material	Labor	Total
Add for 3/4" bullnose edge	—	LF	29.50	—	29.50
Add for 3/4" ogee edge	—	LF	38.60	—	38.60
Add for 1-1/2" bullnose edge	—	LF	56.20	—	56.20
Add for 1-1/2" ogee edge	—	LF	98.10	—	98.10
Add for sink cutout	—	Ea	294.00	—	294.00
Add for electrical outlet cutout	—	Ea	35.10	—	35.10
Add for radius corner or end	—	Ea	218.00	—	218.00
Add for delivery	—	Ea	176.00	—	176.00
Cultured stone vanity tops with integral back splash and sink, 22" deep					
Cultured marble					
24" long	B1@2.60	Ea	362.00	88.00	450.00
36" long	B1@2.60	Ea	467.00	88.00	555.00
48" long	B1@2.60	Ea	571.00	88.00	659.00
Cultured onyx					
24" long	B1@3.42	Ea	488.00	116.00	604.00
36" long	B1@3.42	Ea	625.00	116.00	741.00
48" long	B1@3.42	Ea	760.00	116.00	876.00
Corian vanity tops and integral sink, 1/2" thick, 22" deep. Series 100 includes matching integrated bowls. Series 300 has a solid bowl with different deck colors					
Series 100					
25" long	B1@.654	Ea	429.00	22.10	451.10
31" long	B1@.742	Ea	495.00	25.10	520.10
37" long	B1@.830	Ea	563.00	28.10	591.10
43" long	B1@.924	Ea	630.00	31.30	661.30
49" long	B1@1.02	Ea	710.00	34.50	744.50
Series 300					
25" long	B1@.654	Ea	576.00	22.10	598.10
31" long	B1@.742	Ea	601.00	25.10	626.10
37" long	B1@.830	Ea	710.00	28.10	738.10
43" long	B1@.924	Ea	778.00	31.30	809.30
49" long	B1@1.02	Ea	856.00	34.50	890.50
All side splashes, 22" L	B1@.314	Ea	34.50	10.60	45.10

Cupolas Add the cost of weather vanes below. Estimate the delivery cost at $75 to $100 per unit.

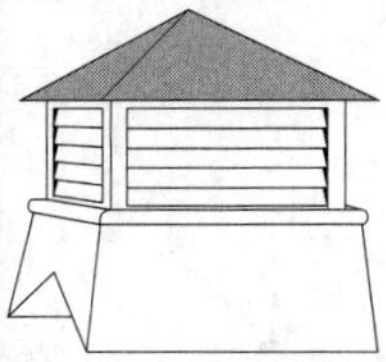

	Craft@Hrs	Unit	Material	Labor	Total
White vinyl with copper roof covering					
18" square base x 22-1/2" high	B1@.948	Ea	463.00	32.10	495.10
22" square base x 27-1/2" high	B1@.948	Ea	517.00	32.10	549.10
26" square base x 32-1/2" high	B1@1.43	Ea	642.00	48.40	690.40
32" square base x 40" high	B1@2.02	Ea	868.00	68.40	936.40
White pine with copper roof covering					
18" square base x 22-1/2" high	B1@.948	Ea	408.00	32.10	440.10
22" square base x 27-1/2" high	B1@.948	Ea	451.00	32.10	483.10
26" square base x 32-1/2" high	B1@1.43	Ea	549.00	48.40	597.40
30" square base x 37-1/2" high	B1@2.02	Ea	664.00	68.40	732.40
Weather vanes for cupolas					
Standard aluminum, baked black finish					
30" long	B1@.275	Ea	72.00	9.31	81.31
Deluxe model, gold-bronze finish aluminum					
46" long, ornamental	B1@.368	Ea	263.00	12.50	275.50

	Craft@Hrs	Unit	Material	Labor	Total

Decks These costs assume 5/4" x 6" southern yellow pine decking, 2" x 8" redwood decking, 5/4" x 6" recycled plastic lumber decking or 2" x 8" recycled composite lumber decking supported by #2 & better 2" x 8" pressure treated joists spaced 24" on center over 4" x 8" pressure treated beams. Beams are supported by 4" x 4" pressure treated posts set 6' on center in concrete. Post length is assumed to be 2' above grade. Fasteners are 16d galvanized nails, galvanized steel joist hangers and post anchors. Decking is spaced at 1/8" to permit drainage. Costs are based on a rectangular deck, with one side fastened to an existing structure. Larger decks will reduce labor costs per square foot. Where better support is required, add the cost of round concrete forms (Sonotubes) and additional framing fasteners. Deck 3' above ground level with joists, beams, posts and hardware as described above and with decking material as shown.

	Craft@Hrs	Unit	Material	Labor	Total
10' x 45'					
Pine, pressure treated decking	B1@.170	SF	6.46	5.75	12.21
Redwood, select heart decking	B1@.170	SF	8.61	5.75	14.36
5/4" x 6" recycled composite lumber decking	B1@.225	SF	10.30	7.62	17.92
2" x 8" recycled composite lumber decking	B1@.225	SF	16.80	7.62	24.42
15' x 45'					
Pine, pressure treated decking	B1@.170	SF	5.78	5.75	11.53
Redwood, select heart decking	B1@.170	SF	7.93	5.75	13.68
5/4" x 6" recycled composite lumber decking	B1@.225	SF	9.65	7.62	17.27
2" x 8" recycled composite lumber decking	B1@.225	SF	16.10	7.62	23.72
15' x 65'					
Pine, pressure treated decking	B1@.170	SF	5.80	5.75	11.55
Redwood, select heart decking	B1@.170	SF	7.95	5.75	13.70
5/4" x 6" recycled composite lumber decking	B1@.225	SF	9.67	7.62	17.29
2" x 8" recycled composite lumber decking	B1@.225	SF	16.10	7.62	23.72
20' x 35'					
Pine, pressure treated decking	B1@.170	SF	5.25	5.75	11.00
Redwood, select heart decking	B1@.170	SF	7.40	5.75	13.15
5/4" x 6" recycled composite lumber decking	B1@.225	SF	9.12	7.62	16.74
2" x 8" recycled composite lumber decking	B1@.225	SF	15.60	7.62	23.22
20' x 55'					
Pine, pressure treated decking	B1@.170	SF	5.04	5.75	10.79
Redwood, select heart decking	B1@.170	SF	7.19	5.75	12.94
5/4" x 6" recycled composite lumber decking	B1@.225	SF	8.91	7.62	16.53
2" x 8" recycled composite lumber decking	B1@.225	SF	15.40	7.62	23.02

Deck flooring only These costs assume 5/4" x 6" southern yellow pine decking, 2" x 8" redwood decking, 5/4" x 6" recycled plastic lumber decking or 2" x 8" recycled composite lumber decking, and 5% waste. No deck support system included. Costs shown are based on a 200 SF job.

	Craft@Hrs	Unit	Material	Labor	Total
Pine, pressure treated deck flooring	B1@.030	SF	1.87	1.02	2.89
Redwood, select heart deck flooring	B1@.030	SF	4.02	1.02	5.04
5/4" x 6" recycled composite lumber decking	B1@.077	SF	5.74	2.61	8.35
2" x 8" recycled composite lumber decking	B1@.077	SF	12.20	2.61	14.81
Add for stain and sealer finish	B1@.006	SF	.17	.20	.37
Add for diagonal pattern decking					
Pine decking, pressure treated	B1@.007	SF	.26	.24	.50
Redwood decking	B1@.007	SF	.56	.24	.80
5/4" x 6" recycled composite lumber decking	B1@.007	SF	.80	.24	1.04
2" x 8" recycled composite lumber decking	B1@.007	SF	1.71	.24	1.95

	Craft@Hrs	Unit	Material	Labor	Total
Deck cover framing Can also be referred to as a pergola. Conventionally framed wood cover joists. Per SF of area covered. Figures in parentheses indicate board feet per square foot of ceiling including end joists, header joists, and 5% waste. Costs shown are based on a job with 200 SF of area covered and include normal waste. Add the cost of posts and finish roof.					
2" x 4", Std & Btr grade					
16" centers (.59 BF per SF)	B1@.020	SF	.46	.68	1.14
24" centers (.42 BF per SF)	B1@.014	SF	.33	.47	.80
2" x 6", Std & Btr grade					
16" centers (.88 BF per SF)	B1@.020	SF	.67	.68	1.35
24" centers (.63 BF per SF)	B1@.015	SF	.48	.51	.99
Add for posts to support conventionally framed wood cover joists. Posts are usually required at each corner. Includes one sack of concrete but no excavation.					
4" x 4" pressure treated, 10' long	B1@.750	Ea	15.90	25.40	41.30
6" x 6" pressure treated, 10' long	B1@.750	Ea	36.50	25.40	61.90
Deck roof cover Cover over conventionally framed wood ceiling joists. Flat deck built-up roofing. Using 1/2" CDX roof sheathing with 3 ply asphalt surface consisting of 2 plies of 15 lb felt with and 3 hot mop coats of asphalt and 90 lb cap sheet. Add the deck cover framing cost from the previous section.					
Flat roof cover cost per SF	B1@.029	SF	2.47	.98	3.45
Deck railing 42" high handrail. 2" x 2" paling 5" OC run vertically, lag bolted to the edge of the deck, one 2" x 4" horizontal top rail and one 2" x 6" placed on edge directly below the top rail.					
Pine, pressure treated, per running foot	B1@.333	LF	5.09	11.30	16.39
Redwood, select heart, per running foot	B1@.333	LF	11.80	11.30	23.10
Recycled composite lumber, per running foot	B1@.333	LF	30.70	11.30	42.00
Deck stairs All stairs assume 12" tread (step) composed of two pieces of 2" x 6" framing lumber, a riser and supporting stringers. Add the cost of concrete supports below.					
One or two steps high, box construction. Cost per linear foot of step. A 4' wide stairway with 2 steps has 8 linear feet of step.					
Pine treads, open risers	B1@.270	LF	5.10	9.14	14.24
Pine treads, with pine risers	B1@.350	LF	9.56	11.80	21.36
Redwood treads, open risers	B1@.270	LF	4.98	9.14	14.12
Redwood treads, with redwood risers	B1@.350	LF	9.21	11.80	21.01
5/4" recycled composite lumber treads, open risers	B1@.270	LF	9.82	9.14	18.96
5/4" recycled composite lumber treads, with recycled composite lumber risers	B1@.350	LF	22.20	11.80	34.00
2" x 6" recycled composite lumber treads, open risers	B1@.270	LF	10.90	9.14	20.04
2" x 6" recycled composite lumber treads, with recycled composite lumber risers	B1@.350	LF	25.50	11.80	37.30
Three or more steps high, 36" wide. 3 stringers cut from 2" x 12" pressure treated lumber. Cost per riser.					
Pine treads, open risers	B1@.530	Ea	18.20	17.90	36.10
Pine treads, with pine risers	B1@.620	Ea	31.60	21.00	52.60
Redwood treads, open risers	B1@.530	Ea	17.80	17.90	35.70
Redwood treads, with redwood risers	B1@.620	Ea	30.50	21.00	51.50
5/4" recycled composite lumber treads, open risers	B1@.270	LF	33.10	9.14	42.24
5/4" recycled composite lumber treads, with recycled composite lumber risers	B1@.350	LF	70.20	11.80	82.00

	Craft@Hrs	Unit	Material	Labor	Total
2" x 6" recycled composite lumber treads, open risers	B1@.270	LF	36.50	9.14	45.64
2" x 6" recycled composite lumber treads, with recycled composite lumber risers	B1@.350	LF	80.20	11.80	92.00
Concrete footing to support deck stairway. Cost includes brackets and fasteners to attach stairway to the footing. Add the cost of excavation.					
18" x 18" x 12" footing	B1@.530	Ea	33.10	17.90	51.00

Demolition Itemized costs for demolition of building components when building is being remodeled, repaired or rehabilitated, not completely demolished. Costs include protecting adjacent areas and normal clean-up. Costs are to break out the items listed and pile debris on site only. No hauling, dump fees or salvage value included. Equipment cost includes one air compressor and a pneumatic breaker with jackhammer bits. (Figures in parentheses show the volume before and after demolition and weight of the materials after demolition.) Use $250.00 as a minimum charge.

	Craft@Hrs	Unit	Material	Labor	Equipment	Total
Brick walls and walks, cost per SF removed, measured on one face, using pneumatic breaker						
4" thick walls (60 SF per CY and 36 lbs. per SF)	BL@.061	SF	—	1.85	1.12	2.97
8" thick walls (30 SF per CY and 72 lbs. per SF)	BL@.110	SF	—	3.33	2.02	5.35
12" thick walls (20 SF per CY and 108 lbs. per SF)	BL@.133	SF	—	4.03	2.45	6.48
Brick sidewalks, cost per SF removed, 5 brick (3-3/4" x 2-1/2" x 8") per SF, salvage condition						
2-1/2" thick bricks on sand base, no mortar bed, removed using hand tools (100 SF per CY and 28 lbs. per SF)	BL@.020	SF	—	.61	—	.61
Brick pavers up to 4-1/2" thick with mortar bed, removed using a pneumatic breaker (55 SF per CY and 50 lbs. per SF)	BL@.050	SF	—	1.52	.92	2.44
Ceiling tile, cost per in-place SF removed using hand tools						
Stapled or glued 12" x 12" (250 SF per CY and .25 lbs. per SF)	BL@.015	SF	—	.45	—	.45
Suspended panels 2' x 4' (250 SF per CY and .25 lbs. per SF)	BL@.010	SF	—	.30	—	.30
Concrete masonry walls, cost per in-place SF removed, using a pneumatic breaker						
4" thick walls (60 SF per CY and 19 lbs. per SF)	BL@.066	SF	—	2.00	1.21	3.21
6" thick walls (40 SF per CY and 28 lbs. per SF)	BL@.075	SF	—	2.27	1.38	3.65
8" thick walls (30 SF per CY and 34 lbs. per SF)	BL@.098	SF	—	2.97	1.80	4.77
12" thick walls (20 SF per CY and 46 lbs. per SF)	BL@.140	SF	—	4.24	2.57	6.81
Reinforced or grouted walls add	—	%	—	50.0	50.0	—
Concrete foundations (footings), steel reinforced, removed using a pneumatic breaker. Concrete at 3,900 pounds per in place cubic yard.						
Cost per CY (.75 CY per CY)	BL@3.96	CY	—	120.00	72.80	192.80
Cost per LF with width and depth as shown						
6" W x 12" D (35 LF per CY)	BL@.075	LF	—	2.27	1.38	3.65
8" W x 12" D (30 LF per CY)	BL@.098	LF	—	2.97	1.80	4.77
8" W x 16" D (20 LF per CY)	BL@.133	LF	—	4.03	2.45	6.48
8" W x 18" D (18 LF per CY)	BL@.147	LF	—	4.46	2.70	7.16
10" W x 12" D (21 LF per CY)	BL@.121	LF	—	3.67	2.23	5.90
10" W x 16" D (16 LF per CY)	BL@.165	LF	—	5.00	3.03	8.03
10" W x 18" D (14 LF per CY)	BL@.185	LF	—	5.61	3.40	9.01

	Craft@Hrs	Unit	Material	Labor	Equipment	Total
12" W x 12" D (20 LF per CY)	BL@.147	LF	—	4.46	2.70	7.16
12" W x 16" D (13 LF per CY)	BL@.196	LF	—	5.94	3.60	9.54
12" W x 20" D (11 LF per CY)	BL@.245	LF	—	7.43	4.51	11.94
12" W x 24" D (9 LF per CY)	BL@.294	LF	—	8.91	5.41	14.32
Concrete sidewalks, to 4" thick, cost per SF removed. Concrete at 3,900 pounds per in place cubic yard.						
Non-reinforced, removed by hand						
(60 SF per CY)	BL@.050	SF	—	1.52	—	1.52
Reinforced, removed using pneumatic breaker						
(55 SF per CY)	BL@.033	SF	—	1.00	.61	1.61
Concrete slabs, non-reinforced, removed using pneumatic breaker. Concrete at 3,900 pounds per in-place cubic yard.						
Cost per CY (.80 CY per CY)	BL@3.17	CY	—	96.10	58.30	154.40
Cost per SF with thickness as shown						
3" slab thickness (90 SF per CY)	BL@.030	SF	—	.91	.55	1.46
4" slab thickness (60 SF per CY)	BL@.040	SF	—	1.21	.74	1.95
6" slab thickness (45 SF per CY)	BL@.056	SF	—	1.70	1.03	2.73
8" slab thickness (30 SF per CY)	BL@.092	SF	—	2.79	1.69	4.48
Concrete slabs, steel reinforced, removed using pneumatic breaker. Concrete at 3,900 pounds per in-place cubic yard.						
Cost per CY (1.33 CY per CY)	BL@3.96	CY	—	120.00	72.80	192.80
Cost per SF with thickness as shown						
3" slab thickness (80 SF per CY)	BL@.036	SF	—	1.09	.66	1.75
4" slab thickness (55 SF per CY)	BL@.050	SF	—	1.52	.92	2.44
6" slab thickness (40 SF per CY)	BL@.075	SF	—	2.27	1.38	3.65
8" slab thickness (30 SF per CY)	BL@.098	SF	—	2.97	1.80	4.77
Concrete walls, steel reinforced, removed using pneumatic breaker. Concrete at 3,900 pounds per in-place cubic yard.						
Cost per CY (1.33 CY per CY)	BL@4.76	CY	—	144.00	87.50	231.50
Cost per SF with thickness as shown (deduct openings over 25 SF)						
3" wall thickness (80 SF per CY)	BL@.045	SF	—	1.36	.83	2.19
4" wall thickness (55 SF per CY)	BL@.058	SF	—	1.76	1.07	2.83
5" wall thickness (45 SF per CY)	BL@.075	SF	—	2.27	1.38	3.65
6" wall thickness (40 SF per CY)	BL@.090	SF	—	2.73	1.66	4.39
8" wall thickness (30 SF per CY)	BL@.120	SF	—	3.64	2.21	5.85
10" wall thickness (25 SF per CY)	BL@.147	SF	—	4.46	2.70	7.16
12" wall thickness (20 SF per CY)	BL@.176	SF	—	5.33	3.24	8.57
Curbs and 18" gutter, concrete, removed using pneumatic breaker. Concrete at 3,900 pounds per in-place cubic yard.						
Cost per LF (8 LF per CY)	BL@.422	LF	—	12.80	7.76	20.56
Doors, typical cost to remove door, frame and hardware						
3' x 7' metal (2 doors per CY)	BL@1.00	Ea	—	30.30	—	30.30
3' x 7' wood (2 doors per CY)	BL@.497	Ea	—	15.10	—	15.10
Flooring, cost per in-place SY of floor area removed (1 square yard = 9 square feet)						
Ceramic tile						
(25 SY per CY and 34 lbs. per SY)	BL@.263	SY	—	7.97	—	7.97
Hardwood, nailed						
(25 SY per CY and 18 lbs. per SY)	BL@.290	SY	—	8.79	—	8.79
Hardwood, glued						
(25 SY per CY and 18 lbs. per SY)	BL@.503	SY	—	15.20	—	15.20
Laminated wood, floating, engineered, "Pergo"						
(30 SY per CY and 5 lbs. per SY)	BL@.013	SY	—	.39	—	.39

Demolition

	Craft@Hrs	Unit	Material	Labor	Equipment	Total
Linoleum, sheet						
(30 SY per CY and 3 lbs. per SY)	BL@.056	SY	—	1.70	—	1.70
Carpet						
(40 SY per CY and 5 lbs. per SY)	BL@.028	SY	—	.85	—	.85
Carpet pad						
(35 SY per CY and 1.7 lbs. per SY)	BL@.014	SY	—	.42	—	.42
Resilient tile						
(30 SY per CY and 3 lbs. per SY)	BL@.070	SY	—	2.12	—	2.12
Terrazzo						
(25 SY per CY and 34 lbs. per SY)	BL@.286	SY	—	8.67	—	8.67
Remove mastic, using power sander	BL@.125	SY	—	3.79	—	3.79
Insulation, fiberglass batts, cost per in-place SF removed						
R-11 to R-19						
(500 SF per CY and .3 lb per SF)	BL@.003	SF	—	.09	—	.09
Pavement, asphaltic concrete (bituminous) to 6" thick, removed using pneumatic breaker						
Cost per SY						
(4 SY per CY and 660 lbs. per SY)	BL@.250	SY	—	7.58	4.60	12.18
Plaster walls or ceilings, interior, cost per in-place SF removed by hand						
(300 SF per CY and 8 lbs. per SF)	BL@.015	SF	—	.45	—	.45
Roofing, cost per in-place square (100 SF), removed using hand tools, 1- or 2-story, easy access, pitch to 6 in 12. Add $20 per square when fall protection (rope & harness) is required. Add $15 per square for pitch over 6 in 12 (support planks required).						
Built-up, 5 ply or cap sheet						
(2.5 Sq per CY and 250 lbs per Sq)	BL@1.79	Sq	—	54.30	—	54.30
Built-up roofing with rock dress, solid mopped						
(2.5 Sq per CY and 240 lbs per Sq)	BL@2.02	Sq	—	61.20	—	61.20
Shingles, composition, single layer						
(2.5 Sq per CY and 240 lbs per Sq)	BL@1.85	Sq	—	56.10	—	56.10
Shingles, composition, double layer						
(1.2 Sq per CY and 480 lbs per Sq)	BL@3.05	Sq	—	92.40	—	92.40
Shingles, wood, single layer						
(1.7 Sq per CY and 400 lbs per Sq)	BL@2.02	Sq	—	61.20	—	61.20
Shingles, wood, double layer						
(0.8 Sq per CY and 800 lbs per Sq)	BL@3.05	Sq	—	92.40	—	92.40
Concrete "S" tile roofing						
(0.8 Sq per CY and 900 lbs per Sq)	BL@3.81	Sq	—	115.00	—	115.00
Clay tile roofing, 2-piece, pans and caps						
(0.8 Sq per CY and 900 lbs per Sq)	BL@4.80	Sq	—	145.00	—	145.00
Slate roofing						
(0.9 Sq per CY and 1000 lbs per Sq)	BL@3.81	Sq	—	115.00	—	115.00
Sheathing, up to 1" thick, cost per in-place SF, removed using hand tools						
Gypsum						
(250 SF per CY and 2.3 lbs. per SF)	BL@.017	SF	—	.52	—	.52
Plywood						
(200 SF per CY and 2 lbs. per SF)	BL@.017	SF	—	.52	—	.52
Siding, up to 1" thick, cost per in-place SF, removed using hand tools						
Metal						
(200 SF per CY and 2 lbs. per SF)	BL@.027	SF	—	.82	—	.82
Plywood						
(200 SF per CY and 2 lbs. per SF)	BL@.017	SF	—	.52	—	.52
Wood, boards						
(250 SF per CY and 2 lbs. per SF)	BL@.030	SF	—	.91	—	.91
Stucco walls or soffits, cost per in-place SF, removed using hand tools						
stripping stucco wall cover back to the sheathing						
(300 SF per CY and 8 lbs. per SF)	BL@.036	SF	—	1.09	—	1.09
Trees. See Excavation						
Wallboard up to 1" thick, cost per in-place SF, removed using hand tools						
Gypsum, walls or ceilings						
(250 SF per CY and 2.3 lbs. per SF)	BL@.018	SF	—	.55	—	.55
Plywood or insulation board						
(200 SF per CY and 2 lbs. per SF)	BL@.018	SF	—	.55	—	.55

	Craft@Hrs	Unit	Material	Labor	Equipment	Total
Windows, typical cost to remove window, frame and hardware, cost per SF of window						
Metal (36 SF per CY)	BL@.058	SF	—	1.76	—	1.76
Wood (36 SF per CY)	BL@.063	SF	—	1.91	—	1.91
Wood stairs, cost per in-place SF or LF						
Risers (with tread) (25 SF per CY)	BL@.116	SF	—	3.52	—	3.52
Landings (50 SF per CY)	BL@.021	SF	—	.64	—	.64
Handrails (100 LF per CY)	BL@.044	LF	—	1.33	—	1.33
Posts (200 LF per CY)	BL@.075	LF	—	2.27	—	2.27

Wood Framing Demolition Typical costs for demolition of wood frame structural components using hand tools. Normal center to center spacing (12" thru 24" OC) is assumed. Costs include removal of type NM non-metallic (Romex) cable as necessary, protecting adjacent areas, and normal clean-up. Costs do not include temporary shoring to support structural elements above or adjacent to the work area. (Add for demolition of flooring, roofing, sheathing, etc.) Figures in parentheses give the approximate "loose" volume and weight of the materials after being demolished.

	Craft@Hrs	Unit	Material	Labor	Total
Ceiling joists, per in-place SF of ceiling area removed					
2" x 4" (720 SF per CY and 1.18 lbs. per SF)	BL@.009	SF	—	.27	.27
2" x 6" (410 SF per CY and 1.76 lbs. per SF)	BL@.013	SF	—	.39	.39
2" x 8" (290 SF per CY and 2.34 lbs. per SF)	BL@.018	SF	—	.55	.55
2" x 10" (220 SF per CY and 2.94 lbs. per SF)	BL@.023	SF	—	.70	.70
2" x 12" (190 SF per CY and 3.52 lbs. per SF)	BL@.027	SF	—	.82	.82
Floor joists, per in-place SF of floor area removed					
2" x 6" (290 SF per CY and 2.04 lbs. per SF)	BL@.016	SF	—	.48	.48
2" x 8" (190 SF per CY and 2.72 lbs. per SF)	BL@.021	SF	—	.64	.64
2" x 10" (160 SF per CY and 3.42 lbs. per SF)	BL@.026	SF	—	.79	.79
2" x 12" (120 SF per CY and 4.10 lbs. per SF)	BL@.031	SF	—	.94	.94
Rafters, per in-place SF of actual roof area removed					
2" x 4" (610 SF per CY and 1.42 lbs. per SF)	BL@.011	SF	—	.33	.33
2" x 6" (360 SF per CY and 2.04 lbs. per SF)	BL@.016	SF	—	.48	.48
2" x 8" (270 SF per CY and 2.68 lbs. per SF)	BL@.020	SF	—	.61	.61
2" x 10" (210 SF per CY and 3.36 lbs. per SF)	BL@.026	SF	—	.79	.79
2" x 12" (180 SF per CY and 3.94 lbs. per SF)	BL@.030	SF	—	.91	.91
Stud walls, interior or exterior, includes allowance for plates and blocking, per in-place SF of wall area removed, measured on one face					
2" x 3" (430 SF per CY and 1.92 lbs. per SF)	BL@.013	SF	—	.39	.39
2" x 4" (310 SF per CY and 2.58 lbs. per SF)	BL@.017	SF	—	.52	.52
2" x 6" (190 SF per CY and 3.74 lbs. per SF)	BL@.025	SF	—	.76	.76

	Craft@Hrs	Unit	Material	Labor	Total

Wood Framed Assemblies Demolition Typical costs for demolition of wood framed structural assemblies using hand tools when a building is being remodeled, repaired or rehabilitated but not completely demolished. Costs include removal of type NM non-metallic (Romex) cable as necessary, protecting adjacent areas and normal clean-up. Costs do not include temporary shoring to support structural elements above or adjacent to the work area, loading, hauling, dump fees or salvage value. Costs shown are per in-place square foot (SF) of area being demolished. Normal center to center spacing (12" thru 24" OC) is assumed. Figures in parentheses give the approximate "loose" volume and weight of the materials (volume after being demolished and weight.)

	Craft@Hrs	Unit	Material	Labor	Total
Ceiling assemblies. Remove ceiling joists, fiberglass insulation and gypsum board up to 5/8" thick					
2" x 4" (135 SF per CY and 3.78 lbs. per SF)	BL@.030	SF	—	.91	.91
2" x 6" (118 SF per CY and 4.36 lbs. per SF)	BL@.034	SF	—	1.03	1.03
2" x 8" (106 SF per CY and 4.94 lbs. per SF)	BL@.039	SF	—	1.18	1.18
2" x 10" (95 SF per CY and 5.54 lbs. per SF)	BL@.043	SF	—	1.30	1.30
2" x 12" (89 SF per CY and 6.12 lbs. per SF)	BL@.048	SF	—	1.45	1.45
Floor assemblies. Remove floor joists and plywood subfloor up to 3/4" thick					
2" x 8" (97 SF per CY and 4.72 lbs. per SF)	BL@.035	SF	—	1.06	1.06
2" x 10" (88 SF per CY and 5.42 lbs. per SF)	BL@.040	SF	—	1.21	1.21
2" x 12" (75 SF per CY and 6.10 lbs. per SF)	BL@.043	SF	—	1.30	1.30
For gypsum board ceiling removed below floor joists, add to any of above (250 SF per CY and 2.3 lbs. per SF)	BL@.018	SF	—	.55	.55
Wall assemblies, interior. Remove studs, 2 top plates, 1 bottom plate and gypsum drywall up to 5/8" thick on both sides					
2" x 3" (97 SF per CY and 6.52 lbs. per SF)	BL@.048	SF	—	1.45	1.45
2" x 4" (89 SF per CY and 7.18 lbs. per SF)	BL@.052	SF	—	1.58	1.58
2" x 6" (75 SF per CY and 8.34 lbs. per SF)	BL@.059	SF	—	1.79	1.79
Wall assemblies, exterior. Remove studs, 2 top plates, 1 bottom plate, insulation, gypsum drywall up to 5/8" thick on one side, plywood siding up to 3/4" thick on other side					
2" x 4" (70 SF per CY and 7.18 lbs. per SF)	BL@.067	SF	—	2.03	2.03
2" x 6" (75 SF per CY and 8.34 lbs. per SF)	BL@.074	SF	—	2.24	2.24
For stucco in lieu of plywood, add to any of above (SF per CY is the same and add 6 lbs. per SF)	BL@.006	SF	—	.18	.18

Demolition, Subcontract Costs for demolishing and removing an entire building using a dozer and front-end loader. Costs shown include loading and hauling up to 5 miles, but no dump fees. Dump charges vary widely; see Disposal Fees in the Site Work Section of the Industrial and Commercial division of this book. Costs shown are for above ground structures only, per in-place SF of total floor area with ceilings up to 10' high. No salvage value assumed. Add the cost of foundation demolition. Figures in parentheses give the approximate "loose" volume of the materials (volume after being demolished

	Craft@Hrs	Unit	Material	Labor	Total
Light wood-frame structures, up to three stories in height. Based on 2,500 SF job. No basements included. Estimate each story separately. Cost per in-place SF floor area					
First story (8 SF per CY)	—	SF	—	—	2.47
Second story (8 SF per CY)	—	SF	—	—	3.24
Third story (8 SF per CY)	—	SF	—	—	4.18
Masonry building, cost per in-place SF floor area based on 5,000 SF job (50 SF per CY)	—	SF	—	—	4.07
Concrete building, cost per in-place SF floor area based on 5,000 SF job (30 SF per CY)	—	SF	—	—	5.59
Reinforced concrete building, cost per in-place SF floor area based on 5,000 SF job (20 SF per CY)	—	SF	—	—	6.00

	Craft@Hrs	Unit	Material	Labor	Total
Door Chimes Electric, typical installation, add transformer and wire below.					
Surface mounted, 2 notes					
Simple white plastic chime, 4" x 7"	BE@3.50	Ea	26.60	142.00	168.60
Modern oak grained finish, plastic, 8" x 5"	BE@3.50	Ea	48.90	142.00	190.90
White, with repeating tones	BE@3.50	Ea	72.60	142.00	214.60
Maple finish, plastic, 8" x 5"	BE@3.50	Ea	49.10	142.00	191.10
Designer, wood-look plastic strips across a cloth grille					
9" x 7"	BE@3.50	Ea	48.50	142.00	190.50
Modern real oak wood, with brass plated chimes					
9" x 7"	BE@3.50	Ea	88.50	142.00	230.50
Surface mounted, 4 to 8 notes, solid wood door chime					
Three 12" long tubes	BE@3.64	Ea	216.00	148.00	364.00
Four 55" long tubes	BE@3.64	Ea	276.00	148.00	424.00
Any of above					
Add for chime transformer	—	Ea	12.30	—	12.30
Add for bell wire, 65' per coil	—	Ea	5.02	—	5.02
Add for lighted push buttons	—	Ea	9.14	—	9.14
Non-electric, push button type, door mounted					
Modern design, 2-1/2" x 2-1/2"	BE@.497	Ea	27.10	20.20	47.30
With peep sight, 7" x 3-1/2"	BE@.497	Ea	16.30	20.20	36.50
Wireless door chimes, with push button transmitter, 3-year battery, 150' range, 2" speaker, 128 codes					
Oak housing with satin chime tubes	BE@.358	Ea	47.70	14.50	62.20
Door Closers					
Residential and light commercial door closers, doors to 140 lbs and 38" wide. 150 degree maximum swing, non-hold open, adjustable closing speed, ANSI A156.4					
Pneumatic, back door closer	BC@.750	Ea	11.00	28.00	39.00
Medium duty door closers, interior doors to 36" wide.					
Bronze, residential	BC@1.04	Ea	55.00	38.90	93.90
Aluminum, commercial	BC@1.04	Ea	90.00	38.90	128.90
Heavy duty door closers, doors to 170 lbs. and 36" wide. Schlage					
Aluminum	BC@1.04	Ea	65.00	38.90	103.90
Aluminum with cover	BC@1.04	Ea	72.00	38.90	110.90
Screen door closers, brass finish					
Pneumatic closer, light duty	BC@.546	Ea	17.50	20.40	37.90
Spring loaded, automatic, for doors up to 30 lbs, brass finish					
Brass finish	BC@.250	Ea	9.50	9.35	18.85
Sliding door closers, pneumatic, aluminum finish					
Screen	BC@.250	Ea	170.00	9.35	179.35
Glass	BC@.250	Ea	136.00	9.35	145.35

Doors, Exterior

	Craft@Hrs	Unit	Material	Labor	Total

Exterior Slab Doors Exterior doors are usually 1-3/4" thick and solid core – a thin veneer laid over a frame but with foam or composition board filling the door cavity. Flush doors are smooth and flat with no decorative treatment. Slab doors are the door alone, as distinguished from prehung doors which are sold with jamb, hinges, trim and threshold. Installation times for slab doors will be up to 50% faster when an experienced carpenter has the use of a router, door jig and pneumatic nailer.

Flush lauan exterior doors. Solid core. 1-3/4" thick. Unfinished wood grain. Lauan is a tropical hardwood like mahogany. Labor includes setting three hinges on the door and jamb and hanging the door in an existing cased opening.

	Craft@Hrs	Unit	Material	Labor	Total
30" x 80"	BC@1.45	Ea	61.00	54.20	115.20
32" x 80"	BC@1.45	Ea	68.20	54.20	122.40
36" x 80"	BC@1.45	Ea	70.30	54.20	124.50

Flush hardboard exterior doors. Particle board core, 1-3/4" thick, primed. Labor includes setting three hinges on the door and jamb and hanging the door in an existing cased opening.

	Craft@Hrs	Unit	Material	Labor	Total
30" x 80"	BC@1.45	Ea	86.80	54.20	141.00
32" x 80"	BC@1.45	Ea	81.70	54.20	135.90
34" x 80"	BC@1.45	Ea	81.70	54.20	135.90
36" x 80"	BC@1.45	Ea	81.70	54.20	135.90

Steel exterior panel doors. Insulating core. Primed. Six panels. 1-3/4" thick. Labor includes setting three hinges on the door and jamb and hanging the door in an existing cased opening.

	Craft@Hrs	Unit	Material	Labor	Total
30" x 80"	BC@1.45	Ea	123.00	54.20	177.20
32" x 80"	BC@1.45	Ea	123.00	54.20	177.20
36" x 80"	BC@1.45	Ea	123.00	54.20	177.20

1-lite exterior doors. Insulating core. Primed white wood. 1-3/4" thick. Insulated obscure tempered glass. Labor includes setting three hinges on the door and jamb and hanging the door in an existing cased opening.

	Craft@Hrs	Unit	Material	Labor	Total
28" x 80"	BC@1.45	Ea	361.00	54.20	415.20
30" x 80"	BC@1.45	Ea	361.00	54.20	415.20
32" x 80"	BC@1.45	Ea	361.00	54.20	415.20
36" x 80"	BC@1.45	Ea	361.00	54.20	415.20
42" x 80"	BC@1.45	Ea	516.00	54.20	570.20
Add for 84" or 96" height	—	Ea	46.50	—	46.50
Add for prehung door with matching jambs	—	Ea	257.00	—	257.00

Entry Slab Doors Any exterior door can be used at the front entry of a home. But entry doors usually include decorative elements, such as glass panels set in a border of brass caming. Slab doors are the door alone, as distinguished from prehung doors which are sold with jamb, hinges, trim and threshold attached. Installation times for entry doors will be up to 50% faster when an experienced carpenter has the use of a router, door jig and pneumatic nailer.

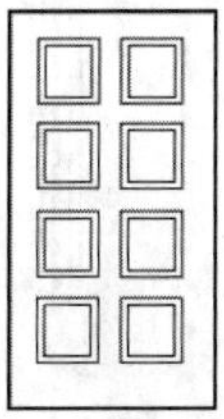

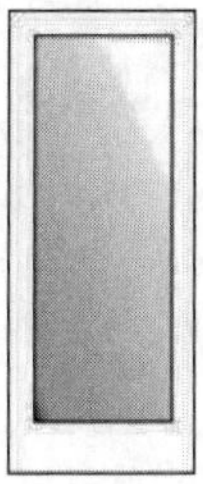

	Craft@Hrs	Unit	Material	Labor	Total
Hardwood panel entry doors. 1-3/4" thick. Unfinished solid wood. Ready to paint or stain. Labor includes setting three hinges on the door and jamb and hanging the door in an existing cased opening.					
30" x 80"	BC@1.45	Ea	671.00	54.20	725.20
32" x 80"	BC@1.45	Ea	671.00	54.20	725.20
36" x 80"	BC@1.45	Ea	671.00	54.20	725.20
42" x 80"	BC@1.45	Ea	877.00	54.20	931.20
Add for 96" height	—	Ea	51.70	—	51.70
Add for prehung door with matching jambs	—	Ea	257.00	—	257.00
Hardwood 1-lite entry doors. 1-3/4" thick. Dual glazed. Unfinished. Suitable for stain or paint. Labor includes setting three hinges on the door and jamb and hanging the door in an existing cased opening.					
28" x 80"	BC@1.70	Ea	309.00	63.50	372.50
30" x 80"	BC@1.70	Ea	330.00	63.50	393.50
32" x 80"	BC@1.70	Ea	340.00	63.50	403.50
36" x 80"	BC@1.70	Ea	361.00	63.50	424.50
42" x 80"	BC@1.70	Ea	516.00	63.50	579.50
Beveled glass entry doors. 1-3/4" thick. Triple-glazed. Unfinished hardwood. Labor includes setting three hinges on the door and jamb and hanging the door in an existing cased opening.					
28" x 80"	BC@1.70	Ea	722.00	63.50	785.50
30" x 80"	BC@1.70	Ea	722.00	63.50	785.50
32" x 80"	BC@1.70	Ea	722.00	63.50	785.50
36" x 80"	BC@1.70	Ea	722.00	63.50	785.50
Add for 12" W beveled glass sidelight	BC@1.00	Ea	516.00	37.40	553.40
Add for 14" H beveled glass transom	BC@1.00	Ea	981.00	37.40	1,018.40
Add for 96" height	—	Ea	103.00	—	103.00
Add for prehung door with matching jambs	—	Ea	257.00	—	257.00
Carved hardwood double doors. Hand carved hardwood. Unfinished. 1-3/4" thick. Labor includes setting six hinges on the door and jamb and hanging the doors in an existing cased opening.					
72" x 80"	BC@3.40	Set	1,130.00	127.00	1,257.00
72" x 96"	BC@3.40	Set	1,270.00	127.00	1,397.00
Add for prehung set with matching jambs	—	Set	386.00	—	386.00

	Craft@Hrs	Unit	Material	Labor	Total
Trim for Exterior Slab Doors Trim for an exterior slab door includes two side jambs, head jamb, threshold, stop molding, interior casing and exterior molding. Installation time for exterior door trim will be up to 33% faster when an experienced carpenter has the use of a pneumatic nailer					
Exterior door jamb. A door jamb set consists of two legs and one 3' head.					
4-5/8" x 1-1/4" x 7', composite	BC@.204	Ea	35.80	7.63	43.43
4-5/8" x 1-1/4" x 7' pine jamb set	BC@.500	Ea	56.30	18.70	75.00
5-1/4" wide, per set	BC@.500	Ea	63.90	18.70	82.60
6-9/16" x 1-1/4" x 7' PVC jamb set	BC@.500	Set	133.00	18.70	151.70
6-9/16" x 1-1/4" x 8', PVC jamb set	BC@.500	Set	197.00	18.70	215.70
Oak high boy threshold. Fits standard door sizes.					
5/8" x 3-1/2" x 36"	BC@.518	Ea	11.10	19.40	30.50
Stop molding. Nails to face of the door jamb to prevent door from swinging through the opening. Solid pine.					
3/8" x 1-1/4" x 96", pine	BC@.120	Ea	5.83	4.49	10.32
3/8" x 1-1/4"x 84", knotty adler	BC@.120	Ea	12.00	4.49	16.49
9/16" x 1-5/8" x 96", poly	BC@.120	LF	7.34	4.49	11.83
Door casing. Casing is the trim around each side and head of the interior side of an exterior door. Casing covers the joint between jamb and the wall.					
19/32" x 2-1/4" x 7', MDF	BC@.105	Ea	3.87	3.92	7.79
11/16" x 2-1/4" x 7', pine	BC@.105	Ea	6.24	3.92	10.16
11/16" x 2-1/2" x 7', pine, 5 pieces	BC@.525	Set	22.30	19.60	41.90
Brick mold. Brick mold and stucco mold are the casing around each side and head on the exterior side of an exterior door.					
1-1/4" x 2" x 7', pine, 3-piece set	BC@.255	Set	21.50	9.53	31.03
1-1/4" x 2" x 10', vinyl	BC@.150	Ea	18.70	5.61	24.31
1-1/4" x 2", PVC	BC@.015	LF	1.90	.56	2.46
1-5/8" x 11/16" x 8', vinyl	BC@.120	Ea	10.40	4.49	14.89
1-1/4" x 2", treated pine	BC@.015	LF	3.31	.56	3.87
Stucco molding. Finger joint					
1" x 1-3/8" pine	BC@.015	LF	1.20	.56	1.76
T-astragal molding. Covers the vertical joint where a pair of doors meet.					
1-1/4" x 2" x 7', pine	BC@.529	Ea	18.20	19.80	38.00

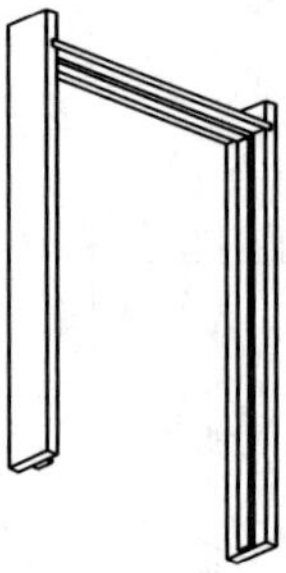

	Craft@Hrs	Unit	Material	Labor	Total

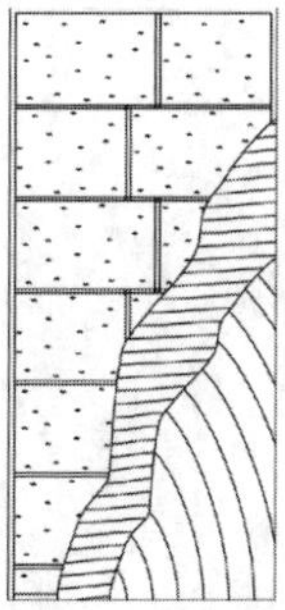

Fire-Rated Doors Fire-rated doors are designed to meet building code requirements for specialized occupancies, such as hotel rooms and dormitories. Most building codes require that 20-minute fire doors be used between a house and an attached garage.

6-panel prehung steel fire-rated exterior doors. 24-gauge galvanized steel. Foam core. Caming matches hinge and sill finishes. Jamb guard security plate. No brick mold. Fixed sill. 4-9/16" primed jamb. Triple sweep compression weatherstripping. Factory primed. Thermal-break threshold. 20-minute fire rating. 10-year limited warranty.

	Craft@Hrs	Unit	Material	Labor	Total
30" x 80"	BC@1.00	Ea	390.00	37.40	427.40
32" x 80"	BC@1.00	Ea	395.00	37.40	432.40
36" x 80"	BC@1.00	Ea	400.00	37.40	437.40

Prehung hardboard fire-rated interior doors. 20-minute fire rating. Labor includes hanging the door in an existing framed opening.

	Craft@Hrs	Unit	Material	Labor	Total
30" x 80"	BC@1.00	Ea	194.00	37.40	231.40
32" x 80"	BC@1.00	Ea	194.00	37.40	231.40
36" x 80"	BC@1.00	Ea	194.00	37.40	231.40

Flush fire-rated steel slab doors. 1-3/4" thick. 20-minute fire rating. Primed. Labor includes setting three hinges on the door and jamb and hanging the door in an existing cased opening.

	Craft@Hrs	Unit	Material	Labor	Total
30" x 80"	BC@1.45	Ea	149.00	54.20	203.20
32" x 80"	BC@1.45	Ea	149.00	54.20	203.20
36" x 80"	BC@1.45	Ea	149.00	54.20	203.20

Flush 90-minute fire-rated steel slab doors. 1-3/4" thick. Primed. With hardware. Labor includes assembling the door, frame and lockset and hanging the door in an existing cased opening.

	Craft@Hrs	Unit	Material	Labor	Total
36" x 80" door and knocked down frame	BC@1.85	Ea	419.00	69.20	488.20
36" x 84" door and knocked down frame	BC@1.85	Ea	429.00	69.20	498.20
36" x 80" door and assembled frame	BC@1.45	Ea	450.00	54.20	504.20
36" x 84" door and assembled frame	BC@1.45	Ea	460.00	54.20	514.20
Add for panic bar hardware	—	Ea	230.00	—	230.00
Add for deadbolt	—	Ea	30.00	—	30.00

Steel cellar doors. See Basement Doors.

Doors, Prehung Exterior

Prehung Wood Exterior Doors Prehung doors are sold as a package with the door, jamb, hinges, weatherstripping, threshold and trim already assembled.

Flush hardboard prehung exterior doors. 1-3/4" door. Solid core. Weatherstripped. Includes sill and threshold with vinyl insert. Finger joint 4-9/16" jamb and finger joint brick mold. 2-1/8" bore for lockset with 2-3/8" backset. Flush doors are smooth and flat with no decorative treatment. Labor includes hanging the door in an existing framed opening.

	Craft@Hrs	Unit	Material	Labor	Total
32" x 80"	BC@1.00	Ea	204.00	37.40	241.40
36" x 80"	BC@1.00	Ea	204.00	37.40	241.40

Rustic knotty adler prehung exterior doors. Two panel. Solid core. Weatherstripped. Unfinished. Includes sill and threshold. Labor includes hanging the door in an existing framed opening.

	Craft@Hrs	Unit	Material	Labor	Total
30" x 80"	BC@1.00	Ea	694.00	37.40	731.40
32" x 80"	BC@1.00	Ea	702.00	37.40	739.40
36" x 80"	BC@1.00	Ea	703.00	37.40	740.40
42" x 80"	BC@1.00	Ea	852.00	37.40	889.40
30" x 96"	BC@1.20	Ea	728.00	44.90	772.90
32" x 96"	BC@1.20	Ea	763.00	44.90	807.90
36" x 96"	BC@1.20	Ea	887.00	44.90	931.90
42" x 96"	BC@1.20	Ea	973.00	44.90	1,017.90
30" x 80" with two 14" wide sidelights	BC@2.80	Ea	1,720.00	105.00	1,825.00

9-lite engineered wood prehung exterior doors. Solid core. Weatherstripped. Includes sill and threshold. Unfinished. Finger joint 4-9/16" jamb and finger joint brick mold. 2-1/8" bore for lockset with 2-3/8" backset. Labor includes hanging the door in an existing framed opening.

	Craft@Hrs	Unit	Material	Labor	Total
32" x 80"	BC@1.00	Ea	807.00	37.40	844.40
36" x 80"	BC@1.00	Ea	807.00	37.40	844.40

Sidelites for wood prehung exterior doors, 1-3/4" thick, tempered clear insulated glass, assembled, unfinished hardwood. Per sidelight.

	Craft@Hrs	Unit	Material	Labor	Total
12" x 80", single lite	BC@1.36	Ea	283.00	50.80	333.80
12" x 80", triple lite	BC@1.36	Ea	361.00	50.80	411.80
14" x 96", rustic, low-E glass	BC@1.36	Ea	753.00	50.80	803.80

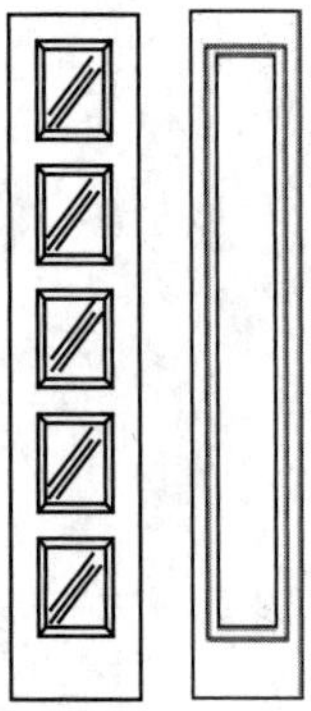

Prehung Steel Exterior Doors Prehung doors are sold as a package with the door, jamb, hinges, weatherstripping, threshold and trim already assembled. Add for the lockset. Flush doors have a smooth, flat face with no decorative treatment.

Utility flush prehung steel exterior doors. No brick mold. Primed 26-gauge galvanized steel. Foam core.

	Craft@Hrs	Unit	Material	Labor	Total
30" x 80"	BC@1.00	Ea	182.00	37.40	219.40
32" x 80"	BC@1.00	Ea	182.00	37.40	219.40
36" x 80"	BC@1.00	Ea	182.00	37.40	219.40

Premium flush prehung steel exterior doors. No brick mold. 24-gauge galvanized steel. Foam core. Compression weatherstrip. Triple fin sweep. Thermal threshold.

	Craft@Hrs	Unit	Material	Labor	Total
24" x 80"	BC@1.00	Ea	266.00	37.40	303.40
30" x 80"	BC@1.00	Ea	331.00	37.40	368.40
32" x 80"	BC@1.00	Ea	288.00	37.40	325.40
36" x 80"	BC@1.00	Ea	330.00	37.40	367.40

6-panel prehung steel exterior doors. With brick mold. Non-thermal threshold. Bored for lockset with 2-3/4" backset. Includes compression weatherstrip and thermal-break threshold. Panel doors have decorative raised panels in the colonial style. Six or nine panels are most common.

	Craft@Hrs	Unit	Material	Labor	Total
32" x 80"	BC@1.00	Ea	202.00	37.40	239.40
36" x 80"	BC@1.00	Ea	202.00	37.40	239.40

	Craft@Hrs	Unit	Material	Labor	Total
6-panel premium prehung exterior steel doors. 4-9/16" jamb. Adjustable thermal-break sill. 24-gauge galvanized steel. Bored for 2-3/8" lockset. 12" lock block. Polyurethane core. Triple sweep and compression weatherstripping. Factory primed.					
30" x 80"	BC@1.00	Ea	317.00	37.40	354.40
32" x 80"	BC@1.00	Ea	323.00	37.40	360.40
36" x 80"	BC@1.00	Ea	339.00	37.40	376.40
42" x 80"	BC@1.00	Ea	382.00	37.40	419.40
6-panel prehung steel entry door with two 16" wide sidelites. Primed. Each sidelites has 3 divided lites.					
72" x 80"	BC@2.00	Ea	1,090.00	74.80	1,164.80
Fan lite premium prehung steel exterior doors. No brick mold. 24-gauge galvanized steel. Foam core. Fixed sill. Compression weatherstripping. Factory primed. Thermal-break threshold.					
32" x 80"	BC@1.00	Ea	202.00	37.40	239.40
36" x 80"	BC@1.00	Ea	245.00	37.40	282.40
Half lite prehung steel exterior doors. Tempered low-E glass. Adjustable sill. 24-gauge galvanized steel. Poly core. 4-9/16" jamb. Pet door.					
30" x 80"	BC@1.00	Ea	548.00	37.40	585.40
32" x 80"	BC@1.00	Ea	549.00	37.40	586.40
36" x 80"	BC@1.00	Ea	567.00	37.40	604.40
Full lite prehung steel exterior doors. 22" x 64" light. 4-9/16" jamb. Adjustable sill. With brick mold. 24-gauge galvanized steel. Tempered insulated glass.					
32" x 80"	BC@1.00	Ea	490.00	37.40	527.40
36" x 80"	BC@1.00	Ea	490.00	37.40	527.40
6-lite, 2-panel prehung steel doors. 4-9/16" jamb. Adjustable sill. 24-gauge galvanized steel. Poly core. Primed. With brick mold.					
30" x 80"	BC@1.00	Ea	387.00	37.40	424.40
32" x 80"	BC@1.00	Ea	387.00	37.40	424.40
9-lite prehung steel exterior doors. Insulating glass with external 9-lite grille. Adjustable sill. 24-gauge galvanized steel. No brick mold.					
32" x 80"	BC@1.00	Ea	261.00	37.40	298.40
36" x 80"	BC@1.00	Ea	363.00	37.40	400.40
15-lite prehung steel exterior doors. Triple Low-E glazed with internal blinds and muttins, 4-9/16" jamb. 22" x 62" light. Adjustable sill. With brick mold.					
32" x 80"	BC@1.00	Ea	1,010.00	37.40	1,047.40
36" x 80"	BC@1.00	Ea	969.00	37.40	1,006.40

	Craft@Hrs	Unit	Material	Labor	Total

Decorative Prehung Steel Entry Doors Entry doors are decorative exterior doors, often with glass panels set in a border of brass caming. Prehung doors are sold as a package with the door, jamb, hinges, threshold and trim already assembled.

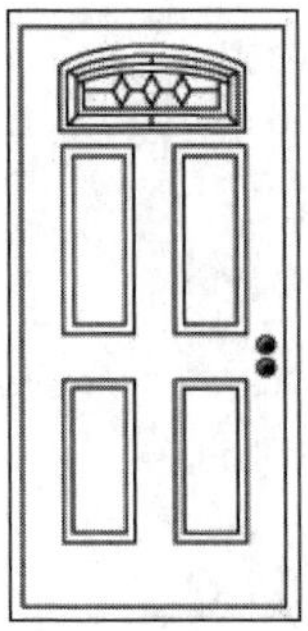

Center arch lite prehung steel entry doors. 24-gauge galvanized steel. High-performance light frames. Decorative impact-resistant glass. Insulated core. 4-9/16" jamb with adjustable sill. Includes brick mold.

	Craft@Hrs	Unit	Material	Labor	Total
36" x 80"	BC@1.00	Ea	473.00	37.40	510.40

Camber top glazed 4-panel prehung steel entry doors. 4-9/16" jamb. Primed. With brick mold.

	Craft@Hrs	Unit	Material	Labor	Total
32" x 80"	BC@1.00	Ea	448.00	37.40	485.40
36" x 80"	BC@1.00	Ea	469.00	37.40	506.40

Internal mini-blinds prehung steel entry doors. Internal white blinds are enclosed by clear tempered glass. 4-9/16" jamb. 24-gauge steel. Poly core. With brick mold.

	Craft@Hrs	Unit	Material	Labor	Total
36" x 80"	BC@1.00	Ea	710.00	37.40	747.40

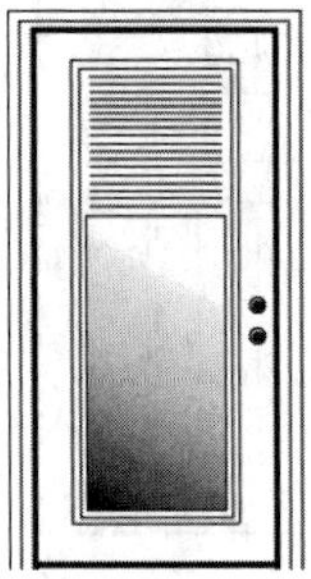

Oval lite prehung steel entry door. 40" x 18" decorative oval laminated glass with brass caming. 24-gauge galvanized steel. Poly core. 4-9/16" jamb. Compression weatherstripping. Primed.

	Craft@Hrs	Unit	Material	Labor	Total
36" x80"	BC@1.00	Ea	375.00	37.40	412.40

Fan lite prehung steel entry doors. Polyurethane core. 6-9/16" frame. Laminated insulating glass insert has 5-lite grille on the exterior. 24-gauge galvanized steel. Weatherstripped.

	Craft@Hrs	Unit	Material	Labor	Total
30" x 80"	BC@1.00	Ea	828.00	37.40	865.40
32" x 80"	BC@1.00	Ea	774.00	37.40	811.40
36" x 80"	BC@1.00	Ea	840.00	37.40	877.40

Vented half lite prehung steel entry doors. Poly core. 4-9/16" jamb. With screen. Tempered insulated glass.

	Craft@Hrs	Unit	Material	Labor	Total
32" x 80"	BC@1.00	Ea	693.00	37.40	730.40
36" x 80"	BC@1.00	Ea	661.00	37.40	698.40

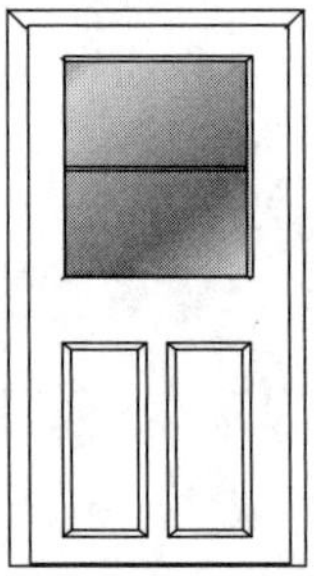

Fiberglass Prehung Entry Doors Fiberglass doors require very little maintenance and are available in simulated wood finish. Prehung doors include the door, jamb, hinges, threshold and trim already assembled.

6-panel fiberglass prehung exterior doors. Polyurethane core. PVC stiles and rails. Double bore. 4-9/16" prefinished jambs. Adjustable thermal-break brass threshold. Weatherstripped. With brick mold.

	Craft@Hrs	Unit	Material	Labor	Total
32" x 80"	BC@1.00	Ea	230.00	37.40	267.40
36" x 80"	BC@1.00	Ea	230.00	37.40	267.40

Fan lite prehung light oak fiberglass entry doors. With brick mold. Factory prefinished. Triple pane insulated glass with brass caming. Adjustable brass thermal-break threshold and fully weatherstripped. 4-9/16" jamb.

	Craft@Hrs	Unit	Material	Labor	Total
36" x 80"	BC@1.00	Ea	604.00	37.40	641.40

3/4 oval lite prehung fiberglass entry doors. With brick mold. Ready to finish.

	Craft@Hrs	Unit	Material	Labor	Total
36" x 80", 4-9/16" jamb	BC@1.00	Ea	691.00	37.40	728.40
36" x 80", 6-9/16" jamb	BC@1.00	Ea	821.00	37.40	858.40

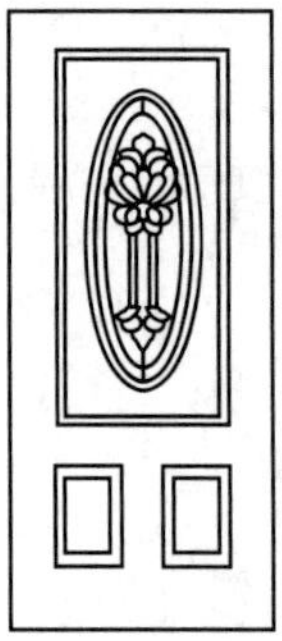

3/4 oval lite prehung light oak fiberglass doors. With brick mold. Prefinished. Polyurethane core. Triple pane insulated glass. Glue chip and clear 30" x 18" beveled glass surrounded by brass caming. Double bore. Extended wood lock block. 4-9/16" primed jamb. Thermal-break brass threshold with adjustable oak cap.

	Craft@Hrs	Unit	Material	Labor	Total
36" x 80", 4-9/16" jamb	BC@1.00	Ea	1,120.00	37.40	1,157.40
36" x 80", 6-9/16" jamb	BC@1.00	Ea	1,210.00	37.40	1,247.40

Full height oval lite prehung medium oak fiberglass entry doors.

	Craft@Hrs	Unit	Material	Labor	Total
36" x 80", 4-9/16" jamb	BC@1.00	Ea	1,010.00	37.40	1,047.40
36" x 80", 6-9/16" jamb	BC@1.00	Ea	1,620.00	37.40	1,657.40

	Craft@Hrs	Unit	Material	Labor	Total
Center arch lite medium oak prehung fiberglass doors. Factory prefinished. Triple pane insulated glass with brass caming. Adjustable brass thermal-break threshold and fully weatherstripped. 4-9/16" jamb except as noted. PVC stiles and rails.					
36" x 80", with brick mold	BC@1.00	Ea	1,080.00	37.40	1,117.40
36" x 80", with brick mold, 6-9/16" jamb	BC@1.00	Ea	1,610.00	37.40	1,647.40
Fan lite prehung fiberglass entry doors. With brick mold. Ready to finish. Insulated glass. Adjustable thermal-break brass threshold. 4-9/16" jamb except as noted.					
32" x 80"	BC@1.00	Ea	543.00	37.40	580.40
36" x 80"	BC@1.00	Ea	553.00	37.40	590.40
36" x 80", 6-9/16" jamb	BC@1.00	Ea	660.00	37.40	697.40
9-lite fiberglass prehung exterior doors. Inward swing. With brick mold. Smooth face.					
32" x 80"	BC@1.00	Ea	284.00	37.40	321.40
36" x 80"	BC@1.00	Ea	284.00	37.40	321.40
15-lite smooth prehung fiberglass entry doors. No brick mold. Factory prefinished. Left or right hinge. Triple pane, insulated glass with brass caming. Adjustable brass thermal-break threshold and fully weatherstripped. 4-9/16" jamb.					
32" x 80"	BC@1.00	Ea	695.00	37.40	732.40
36" x 80"	BC@1.00	Ea	673.00	37.40	710.40
Full lite prehung smooth fiberglass doors. With brick mold. Inward swing.					
36" x 80", 4-9/16" jamb	BC@1.00	Ea	1,050.00	37.40	1,087.40
36" x 80", 6-9/16" jamb	BC@1.00	Ea	1,680.00	37.40	1,717.40
Smooth prehung fiberglass ventlite exterior doors. Ready to finish. No brick mold.					
32" x 80"	BC@1.00	Ea	306.00	37.40	343.40
36" x 80"	BC@1.00	Ea	339.00	37.40	376.40

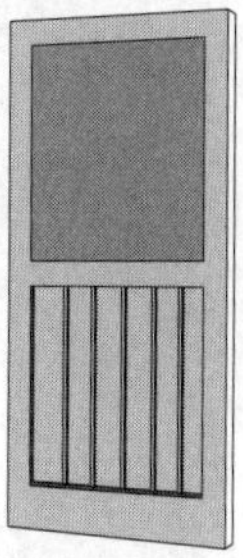

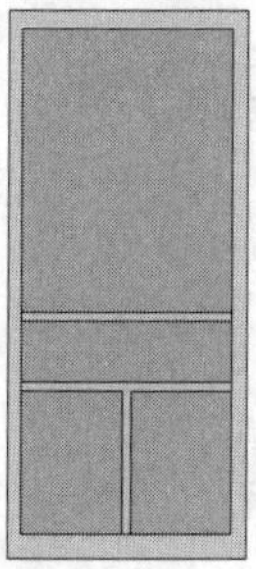

	Craft@Hrs	Unit	Material	Labor	Total
Screen Doors, Wood 3-3/4"-wide stile and rail with 7-1/4" bottom rail. Removable screen. Mortise and tenon construction. Wide center push bar. Ready to finish.					
32" x 80"	BC@2.17	Ea	49.30	81.10	130.40
36" x 80"	BC@2.17	Ea	49.30	81.10	130.40
T-style wood screen doors. 3-3/4"-wide stile and rail with 7-1/4" bottom rail. 1-1/8" thick pine. Removable screen. Mortise and dowel construction. All joints sealed with water-resistant adhesive. Wide center push bar.					
30" x 80"	BC@2.17	Ea	196.00	81.10	277.10
32" x 80"	BC@2.17	Ea	70.80	81.10	151.90
36" x 80"	BC@2.17	Ea	70.80	81.10	151.90
Screen doors, metal. Includes hardware and fiberglass screening. 1-piece steel frame. Heavy-duty pneumatic closer. 5" kickplate.					
32" x 80"	BC@1.35	Ea	96.40	50.50	146.90
36" x 80"	BC@1.35	Ea	96.40	50.50	146.90
Screen doors, vinyl. Right or left side installation. 32" to 36" wide. Hardware included.					
80" high, T-bar grid	BC@1.35	Ea	170.00	50.50	220.50
80" high, full panel grid	BC@1.35	Ea	170.00	50.50	220.50
80" high, decorative	BC@1.35	Ea	170.00	50.50	220.50
Five-bar solid vinyl screen doors. Accepts standard screen door hardware.					
32" x 80"	BC@1.35	Ea	141.00	50.50	191.50
36" x 80"	BC@1.35	Ea	150.00	50.50	200.50
Steel security screen door. Class I rated to withstand 300 pounds. All welded steel construction for strength and durability. Double lockbox with extension plate. Baked-on powder coating. Doors with specialty finishes and decorative or custom details will cost more.					
36" x 80"	BC@1.35	Ea	107.00	50.50	157.50

Doors, Storm

	Craft@Hrs	Unit	Material	Labor	Total
Storm Doors Self-storing aluminum storm and screen doors. Pneumatic closer and sweep. Tempered safety glass. Maintenance-free finish. Push-button hardware. 1" x 2-1/8" frame size. Bronze or white. Includes screen.					
30" x 80" x 1-1/4"	BC@1.45	Ea	105.00	54.20	159.20
32" x 80" x 1-1/4"	BC@1.45	Ea	123.00	54.20	177.20
36" x 80" x 1-1/4"	BC@1.45	Ea	123.00	54.20	177.20
Self-storing vinyl-covered wood storm doors. White vinyl-covered wood core. Push-button handle set. Self-storing window and screen. Single black closer.					
30" x 80"	BC@1.45	Ea	108.00	54.20	162.20
32" x 80"	BC@1.45	Ea	108.00	54.20	162.20
34" x 80"	BC@1.45	Ea	108.00	54.20	162.20
36" x 80"	BC@1.45	Ea	108.00	54.20	162.20
Store-in-Door™ storm doors. 1-1/2"-thick polypropylene frame. Reversible hinge. Slide window or screen, completely concealed when not in use. Brass-finished keylock hardware system with separate color-matched deadbolt. Triple-fin door sweep. 2 color-matched closers. Full-length piano hinge. Flexible weather seal. White.					
30" x 80", crossbuck style	BC@1.45	Ea	318.00	54.20	372.20
32" x 80", crossbuck style	BC@1.45	Ea	353.00	54.20	407.20
36" x 80", crossbuck style	BC@1.45	Ea	389.00	54.20	443.20
30" x 80", traditional style	BC@1.45	Ea	327.00	54.20	381.20
36" x 80", traditional style	BC@1.45	Ea	361.00	54.20	415.20
Aluminum and wood storm doors. Aluminum over wood core. Self-storing window and screen. Black lever handle set. Separate deadbolt. Single black closer. White finish. Traditional panel style.					
30" x 80"	BC@1.45	Ea	197.00	54.20	251.20
32" x 80"	BC@1.45	Ea	180.00	54.20	234.20
36" x 80"	BC@1.45	Ea	180.00	54.20	234.20
Triple-track storm doors. Low-maintenance aluminum over solid wood core. Ventilates from top, bottom or both. Solid brass exterior handle. Color-matched interior handle. Separate deadbolt. 80" high. White, almond or bronze.					
30" x 80"	BC@1.45	Ea	258.00	54.20	312.20
32" x 80"	BC@1.45	Ea	221.00	54.20	275.20
34" x 80"	BC@1.45	Ea	274.00	54.20	328.20
36" x 80"	BC@1.45	Ea	258.00	54.20	312.20
Colonial triple-track storm doors. 1-piece composite frame. 12-lite grille. Vents from top, bottom, or both. Solid-brass handle set with deadbolt security. Brass-finished sweep ensures tight seal across the entire threshold. Wood-grain finish. White, almond or sandstone.					
32" x 80"	BC@1.45	Ea	345.00	54.20	399.20
Full-view brass all-season storm doors. Water-diverting rain cap. Brass-finished, color-matched sweep. One closer. Window and insect screen snap in and out. Reversible. Opens 180 degrees when needed. Separate deadbolt for added security. Tempered glass. Heavy-gauge one-piece 1" aluminum construction with reinforced corners and foam insulation.					
36" x 80"	BC@1.45	Ea	354.00	54.20	408.20
Full-view aluminum storm doors. 1-1/2"-thick heavy-gauge aluminum frame with foam insulation. Extra perimeter weatherstripping and water-diverting rain cap. Solid brass handle set and double-throw deadbolt. Brass-finished sweep. Full-length, piano-style hinge. Reversible hinge for left- or right-side entry door handle. Two heavy-duty, color-matched closers. Solid brass perimeter locks. Insect screen. White, brown, green or almond.					
30" x 80"	BC@1.45	Ea	256.00	54.20	310.20
32" x 80"	BC@1.45	Ea	221.00	54.20	275.20
36" x 80"	BC@1.45	Ea	288.00	54.20	342.20

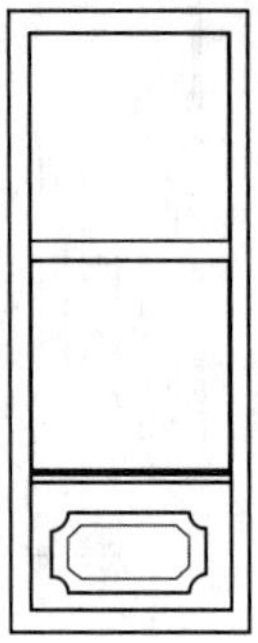

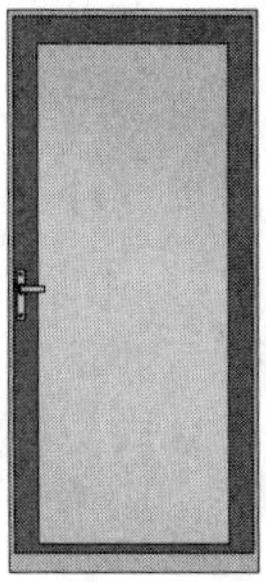

	Craft@Hrs	Unit	Material	Labor	Total
Full-view woodcore storm doors. Aluminum over solid wood core. Extra perimeter weatherstripping and water-diverting rain cap. Black push-button handle with night latch. Color-matched sweep. One heavy-duty closer. Snap-in, snap-out window and insect screen retainer system. White or bronze.					
32" x 84"	BC@1.45	Ea	146.00	54.20	200.20
36" x 84"	BC@1.45	Ea	148.00	54.20	202.20

Security Storm Doors 16-gauge steel. Brass deadbolt lock. Tempered safety glass. Interchangeable screen panel. Heavy-gauge all-welded steel frame with mitered top. Double weatherstripped jamb and sweep. Tamper-resistant hinges with concealed interior screws. Heavy-duty pneumatic closer and safety wind chain. Prehung with reversible hinge.

	Craft@Hrs	Unit	Material	Labor	Total
30" x 80"	BC@1.45	Ea	372.00	54.20	426.20
32" x 80"	BC@1.45	Ea	326.00	54.20	380.20
36" x 80"	BC@1.45	Ea	372.00	54.20	426.20
Class II security doors. Rated to withstand 400 pounds. Double lockbox with extension plate. Decorative geometric ornaments. All welded steel construction. Expanded, galvanized metal screen. 3/4" square frame design.					
32" x 80"	BC@1.45	Ea	115.00	54.20	169.20
36" x 80"	BC@1.45	Ea	118.00	54.20	172.20
Heavy-duty security door with screen. Right- or left-hand exterior mounting. All welded steel construction. Baked-on powder coating. Double lockbox with tamper-resistant extension plate. Uses standard 2-3/8" backset lock (not included). Galvanized perforated metal security screen. 1" x 1" door frame. 1" x 1-1/2" jambs, prehung on hinge side.					
32" x 80"	BC@1.45	Ea	159.00	54.20	213.20
36" x 80"	BC@1.45	Ea	162.00	54.20	216.20
Paradise style security door. Five semi-concealed hinges. Heavy-duty deadbolt. All steel frame.					
30" x 80"	BC@1.45	Ea	468.00	54.20	522.20
32" x 80"	BC@1.45	Ea	468.00	54.20	522.20
36" x 80"	BC@1.45	Ea	468.00	54.20	522.20
Folding security gates. Riveted 3/4" top and bottom channel. Gate pivots and folds flat to one side. Provides air circulation and positive visibility.					
48" max width, 79" high	BC@1.25	Ea	105.00	46.70	151.70

Interior Slab Doors Slab doors are the door alone, as distinguished from prehung doors which are sold with jamb, hinges and trim attached and bored for the door latch. Interior doors are usually 1-3/8" thick and have a "hollow" core. A wood frame made from stiles and rails is filled with a matrix of corrugated paper and covered with a thin wood veneer. Stiles are vertical and every door has two, a lock stile and the hinge stile. Rails run horizontally at the top and bottom of the door. Flush doors are smooth and flat, with no decorative treatment.

	Craft@Hrs	Unit	Material	Labor	Total
Flush hardboard interior doors. Hollow core. Not bored for lockset. Ready to paint or stain. 1-3/8" thick. Hardboard doors are made of composition wood veneer, usually the least expensive material available.					
24" x 80"	BC@1.15	Ea	41.20	43.00	84.20
28" x 80"	BC@1.15	Ea	46.20	43.00	89.20
30" x 80"	BC@1.15	Ea	45.30	43.00	88.30
32" x 80"	BC@1.15	Ea	48.40	43.00	91.40
36" x 80"	BC@1.15	Ea	49.90	43.00	92.90
Flush birch interior doors. Hollow core. 1-3/8" thick. Wood veneer. Stainable and paintable. All wood stile and rail. Bored for lockset.					
18" x 80"	BC@1.15	Ea	126.00	43.00	169.00
24" x 80"	BC@1.15	Ea	127.00	43.00	170.00
28" x 80"	BC@1.15	Ea	161.00	43.00	204.00
30" x 80"	BC@1.15	Ea	165.00	43.00	208.00
32" x 80"	BC@1.15	Ea	113.00	43.00	156.00
36" x 80"	BC@1.15	Ea	170.00	43.00	213.00

Doors, Interior Slab

	Craft@Hrs	Unit	Material	Labor	Total
Flush lauan interior doors. Hollow core. 1-3/8" thick. Wood veneer. Stainable and paintable. Lauan is a tropical hardwood like mahogany. All wood stile and rail.					
18" x 80"	BC@1.15	Ea	33.90	43.00	76.90
24" x 80"	BC@1.15	Ea	42.20	43.00	85.20
28" x 80"	BC@1.15	Ea	46.30	43.00	89.30
30" x 80"	BC@1.15	Ea	46.30	43.00	89.30
32" x 80"	BC@1.15	Ea	53.60	43.00	96.60
36" x 80"	BC@1.15	Ea	55.60	43.00	98.60
Flush oak interior doors. Hollow core. 1-3/8" thick. Wood veneer. Stainable and paintable. All wood stile and rail					
18" x 80"	BC@1.15	Ea	65.00	43.00	108.00
24" x 80"	BC@1.15	Ea	68.20	43.00	111.20
28" x 80"	BC@1.15	Ea	75.90	43.00	118.90
30" x 80"	BC@1.15	Ea	79.30	43.00	122.30
32" x 80"	BC@1.15	Ea	89.90	43.00	132.90
36" x 80"	BC@1.15	Ea	89.90	43.00	132.90
Flush hardboard solid core interior doors. Primed. 1-3/8" thick. Hardboard doors are made of composition wood veneer and are usually the least expensive.					
30" x 80"	BC@1.15	Ea	79.40	43.00	122.40
32" x 80"	BC@1.15	Ea	77.30	43.00	120.30
36" x 80"	BC@1.15	Ea	75.20	43.00	118.20
Flush lauan solid core interior doors. 1-3/8" thick. Stainable. Lauan doors are finished with a veneer of Philippine hardwood from the mahogany family.					
28" x 80"	BC@1.15	Ea	79.30	43.00	122.30
32" x 80"	BC@1.15	Ea	87.30	43.00	130.30
36" x 80"	BC@1.15	Ea	95.90	43.00	138.90
30" x 84"	BC@1.15	Ea	87.30	43.00	130.30
32" x 84"	BC@1.15	Ea	92.00	43.00	135.00
34" x 84"	BC@1.15	Ea	99.20	43.00	142.20
36" x 84"	BC@1.15	Ea	99.20	43.00	142.20
Flush birch solid core interior doors. 1-3/8" thick.					
24" x 80" (water heater closet door)	BC@1.15	Ea	169.00	43.00	212.00
32" x 80"	BC@1.15	Ea	127.00	43.00	170.00
36" x 80"	BC@1.15	Ea	139.00	43.00	182.00
Flush hardboard interior doors with lite. 1-3/8" thick.					
30" x 80" x 1-3/8"	BC@1.15	Ea	244.00	43.00	287.00
32" x 80" x 1-3/8"	BC@1.15	Ea	258.00	43.00	301.00
Flush hardboard walnut finish stile and rail hollow core doors. 1-3/8" thick.					
24" x 80"	BC@1.15	Ea	55.10	43.00	98.10
28" x 80"	BC@1.15	Ea	62.40	43.00	105.40
30" x 80"	BC@1.15	Ea	62.40	43.00	105.40
32" x 80"	BC@1.15	Ea	67.00	43.00	110.00
36" x 80"	BC@1.15	Ea	69.50	43.00	112.50

Interior Panel Doors Panel doors have decorative molding applied to the face.

	Craft@Hrs	Unit	Material	Labor	Total
Hardboard 6-panel molded face interior doors. 1-3/8" thick. Molded and primed hardboard. Embossed simulated woodgrain. Hollow core. Ready to paint. Bored for lockset.					
24" x 80"	BC@1.15	Ea	41.20	43.00	84.20
28" x 80"	BC@1.15	Ea	43.20	43.00	86.20
30" x 80"	BC@1.15	Ea	45.30	43.00	88.30
32" x 80"	BC@1.15	Ea	48.40	43.00	91.40
36" x 80"	BC@1.15	Ea	51.90	43.00	94.90

	Craft@Hrs	Unit	Material	Labor	Total
Lauan 6-panel molded face interior doors. Bored for latchset. 1-3/8" thick.					
24" x 80"	BC@1.15	Ea	49.70	43.00	92.70
28" x 80"	BC@1.15	Ea	54.30	43.00	97.30
30" x 80"	BC@1.15	Ea	56.20	43.00	99.20
32" x 80"	BC@1.15	Ea	57.00	43.00	100.00
36" x 80"	BC@1.15	Ea	59.20	43.00	102.20
Hardwood colonial 6-panel molded face interior doors. Primed. Solid core. 1-3/8" thick.					
24" x 80"	BC@1.15	Ea	149.00	43.00	192.00
28" x 80"	BC@1.15	Ea	152.00	43.00	195.00
30" x 80"	BC@1.15	Ea	154.00	43.00	197.00
32" x 80"	BC@1.15	Ea	156.00	43.00	199.00
36" x 80"	BC@1.15	Ea	158.00	43.00	201.00
Pine 6-panel stile and rail interior doors. Ready to paint or stain. 1-3/8" thick.					
24" x 80"	BC@1.15	Ea	115.00	43.00	158.00
28" x 80"	BC@1.15	Ea	120.00	43.00	163.00
30" x 80"	BC@1.15	Ea	126.00	43.00	169.00
32" x 80"	BC@1.15	Ea	131.00	43.00	174.00
36" x 80"	BC@1.15	Ea	137.00	43.00	180.00
Fir 1-panel stile and rail interior doors. 1-3/8" thick.					
28" x 80"	BC@1.15	Ea	270.00	43.00	313.00
30" x 80"	BC@1.15	Ea	273.00	43.00	316.00
32" x 80"	BC@1.15	Ea	275.00	43.00	318.00
Fir 3-panel stile and rail interior doors. 1-3/8" thick.					
28" x 80"	BC@1.15	Ea	331.00	43.00	374.00
30" x 80"	BC@1.15	Ea	331.00	43.00	374.00
32" x 80"	BC@1.15	Ea	332.00	43.00	375.00
Oak 6-panel stile and rail interior doors. Red oak. Double bevel hip raised panels. 1-3/8" thick.					
24" x 80"	BC@1.15	Ea	185.00	43.00	228.00
28" x 80"	BC@1.15	Ea	199.00	43.00	242.00
30" x 80"	BC@1.15	Ea	209.00	43.00	252.00
32" x 80"	BC@1.15	Ea	209.00	43.00	252.00
36" x 80"	BC@1.15	Ea	232.00	43.00	275.00
French stile and rail interior doors. Clear pine. Ready to paint or stain. 1-3/8" thick. Pre-masked tempered glass. French doors are mostly glass, with one, to as many as fifteen panes set in wood sash.					
24" x 80", 10 lite	BC@1.40	Ea	170.00	52.30	222.30
28" x 80", 10 lite	BC@1.40	Ea	161.00	52.30	213.30
30" x 80", 15 lite	BC@1.40	Ea	184.00	52.30	236.30
32" x 80", 15 lite	BC@1.40	Ea	190.00	52.30	242.30
36" x 80", 15 lite	BC@1.40	Ea	196.00	52.30	248.30
Half louver stile and rail interior doors. 1-3/8" thick. Louver doors include wood louvers that allow air to circulate but obscure vision, an advantage for enclosing a closet, pantry or water heater.					
24" x 80"	BC@1.15	Ea	347.00	43.00	390.00
28" x 80"	BC@1.15	Ea	354.00	43.00	397.00
30" x 80"	BC@1.15	Ea	360.00	43.00	403.00
32" x 80"	BC@1.15	Ea	371.00	43.00	414.00
36" x 80"	BC@1.15	Ea	374.00	43.00	417.00
Full louver doors. 1-3/8" thick, stile and rail interior doors.					
24" wide, 80" high	BC@1.15	Ea	183.00	43.00	226.00
30" wide, 80" high	BC@1.15	Ea	205.00	43.00	248.00
32" wide, 80" high	BC@1.15	Ea	313.00	43.00	356.00
36" wide, 80" high	BC@1.15	Ea	327.00	43.00	370.00

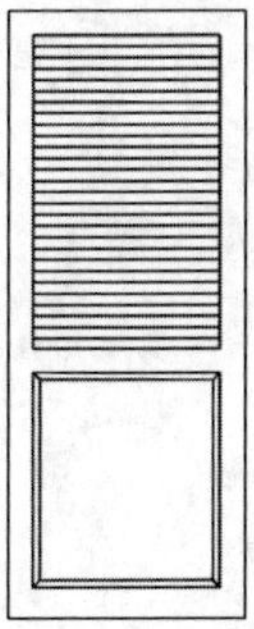

	Craft@Hrs	Unit	Material	Labor	Total
Stile and rail, louvered café doors, unfinished, per pair of doors. Add hardware from below.					
24" x 42"	BC@1.15	Pr	168.00	43.00	211.00
30" x 42"	BC@1.15	Pr	238.00	43.00	281.00
32" x 42"	BC@1.15	Pr	248.00	43.00	291.00
36" x 42"	BC@1.15	Pr	196.00	43.00	239.00
Satin brass café door pivot, 2-pak	—	Ea	7.92	—	7.92

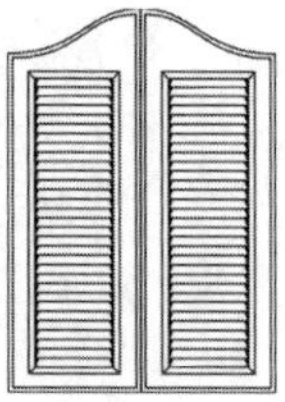

Interior Door Jambs Finger joint pine interior jamb set. Unfinished. Two 6'-8" legs and one 3' head.

	Craft@Hrs	Unit	Material	Labor	Total
4-9/16" x 11/16"	BC@.500	Ea	33.30	18.70	52.00
5-1/4" x 11/16"	BC@.500	Ea	69.80	18.70	88.50
Solid clear pine interior jamb. Varnish or stain. Jamb set includes two 6'-8" legs and one 3' head.					
11/16" x 4-9/16" x 7' leg	BC@.210	Ea	10.30	7.85	18.15
11/16" x 4-9/16" x 3' head	BC@.090	Ea	11.90	3.36	15.26
11/16" x 4-9/16" jamb set	BC@.500	Ea	46.10	18.70	64.80
Door jamb set with hinges.					
80" x 4-9/16", per set	BC@.500	Ea	52.60	18.70	71.30
80" x 6-9/16", per set	BC@.500	Ea	57.90	18.70	76.60

Prehung Interior Doors Prehung doors are sold as a package with the door, jamb, hinges, and trim already assembled and the door bored for a latchset. Flush doors are smooth and flat, with no decorative treatment.

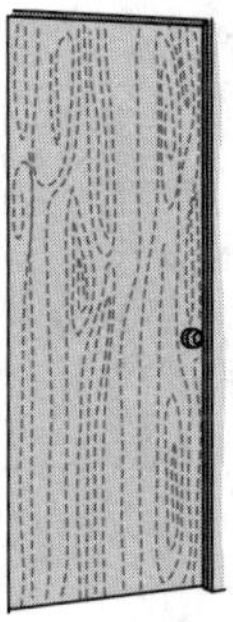

Flush prehung hardboard interior doors. Primed. 1-3/8" thick. Hollow core. Bored for lockset. Multi-finger jointed door jamb 11/16" x 4-9/16". 3 brass finish hinges 3-1/2" x 3-1/2".

	Craft@Hrs	Unit	Material	Labor	Total
24" x 80"	BC@.750	Ea	87.60	28.00	115.60
28" x 80"	BC@.750	Ea	87.60	28.00	115.60
30" x 80"	BC@.750	Ea	95.90	28.00	123.90
32" x 80"	BC@.750	Ea	100.00	28.00	128.00
36" x 80"	BC@.750	Ea	103.00	28.00	131.00
Flush prehung lauan interior doors. 1-3/8" thick. Hollow core. Bored for 2-1/8" lockset with 2-3/8" backset. Casing and lockset sold separately. Wood stile construction. Can be stained or finished naturally. Two brass hinges. Paint grade pine split jambs and 2-1/4" casings. 4" to 4-5/8" adjustable jamb.					
24" x 80"	BC@.750	Ea	132.00	28.00	160.00
28" x 80"	BC@.750	Ea	135.00	28.00	163.00
30" x 80"	BC@.750	Ea	139.00	28.00	167.00
32" x 80"	BC@.750	Ea	142.00	28.00	170.00
36" x 80"	BC@.750	Ea	147.00	28.00	175.00

6 PANEL

6 PANEL

	Craft@Hrs	Unit	Material	Labor	Total
Interior prehung lauan heater closet doors.					
24" x 60"	BC@.750	Ea	130.00	28.00	158.00
Composite prehung panel interior doors. Hollow core. Primed. 1-3/8" thick. Bored for lockset. Multi-finger jointed door jamb 11/16" x 4-9/16". 3 brass finish hinges 3-1/2" x 3-1/2". Panel doors have raised decorative wood panels that resemble doors popular in colonial America. Two, 5, 6 or 9 panels are most common.					
24" x 80"	BC@.750	Ea	194.00	28.00	222.00
28" x 80"	BC@.750	Ea	189.00	28.00	217.00
30" x 80"	BC@.750	Ea	189.00	28.00	217.00
32" x 80"	BC@.750	Ea	195.00	28.00	223.00
36" x 80"	BC@.750	Ea	203.00	28.00	231.00
Mahogany colonial panel prehung interior doors. 11/16" x 4-9/16" jamb. Stain grade. Bored for lockset. Hollow core. 1-3/8" thick.					
18" x 80"	BC@.750	Ea	343.00	28.00	371.00
24" x 80"	BC@.750	Ea	385.00	28.00	413.00
28" x 80"	BC@.750	Ea	417.00	28.00	445.00
30" x 80"	BC@.750	Ea	399.00	28.00	427.00
32" x 80"	BC@.750	Ea	406.00	28.00	434.00
36" x 80"	BC@.750	Ea	443.00	28.00	471.00
6-panel colonist prehung interior doors. 6-9/16" jamb. Hollow core. Prefinished.					
24" x 80"	BC@.750	Ea	159.00	28.00	187.00
30" x 80"	BC@.750	Ea	159.00	28.00	187.00
32" x 80"	BC@.750	Ea	159.00	28.00	187.00
36" x 80"	BC@.750	Ea	159.00	28.00	187.00
6-panel hardboard prehung interior doors. 4-9/16" adjustable split jambs. Hollow core. Paint grade casing applied. Pre-drilled for lockset. Ready to paint or gel stain.					
24" x 80"	BC@.750	Ea	114.00	28.00	142.00
28" x 80"	BC@.750	Ea	116.00	28.00	144.00
30" x 80"	BC@.750	Ea	119.00	28.00	147.00
32" x 80"	BC@.750	Ea	124.00	28.00	152.00
36" x 80"	BC@.750	Ea	128.00	28.00	156.00
6-panel hardboard prehung double interior doors. 1-3/8" thick. Flat jamb.					
48" x 80"	BC@1.25	Ea	281.00	46.70	327.70
60" x 80"	BC@1.25	Ea	301.00	46.70	347.70
6-panel oak prehung interior doors. Hollow core. 1-3/8" thick. 11/16" x 4-9/16" clear pine jamb.					
24" x 80"	BC@.750	Ea	164.00	28.00	192.00
28" x 80"	BC@.750	Ea	170.00	28.00	198.00
30" x 80"	BC@.750	Ea	174.00	28.00	202.00
32" x 80"	BC@.750	Ea	174.00	28.00	202.00
36" x 80"	BC@.750	Ea	185.00	28.00	213.00
6-panel prehung interior double doors. Bored for lockset. Ready to paint or stain. 1-3/8" thick. 4-9/16" jambs.					
4'0" x 6'8"	BC@1.50	Ea	158.00	56.10	214.10
6'0" x 6'8"	BC@1.50	Ea	162.00	56.10	218.10

	Craft@Hrs	Unit	Material	Labor	Total
6-panel hemlock prehung interior doors. Bored for lockset. Ready to paint or stain. 1-3/8" thick. 4-9/16" jambs.					
24" x 80"	BC@.750	Ea	289.00	28.00	317.00
28" x 80"	BC@.750	Ea	343.00	28.00	371.00
30" x 80"	BC@.750	Ea	303.00	28.00	331.00
32" x 80"	BC@.750	Ea	310.00	28.00	338.00
36" x 80"	BC@.750	Ea	316.00	28.00	344.00
2-panel knotty alder prehung interior doors. Bored for lockset. 1-3/8" thick.					
18" x 80"	BC@.750	Ea	466.00	28.00	494.00
24" x 80"	BC@.750	Ea	476.00	28.00	504.00
28" x 80"	BC@.750	Ea	476.00	28.00	504.00
30" x 80"	BC@.750	Ea	499.00	28.00	527.00
32" x 80"	BC@.750	Ea	499.00	28.00	527.00
36" x 80"	BC@.750	Ea	499.00	28.00	527.00
Add for 96" height	—	%	9.8	—	—
Pine full louver prehung interior doors. Ready to install. Provides ventilation while maintaining privacy. 11/16" x 4-9/16" clear face pine door jamb. 1-3/8" thick. Includes (3) 3-1/2" x 3-1/2" hinges with brass finish. Bored for lockset.					
24" x 80"	BC@.750	Ea	432.00	28.00	460.00
28" x 80"	BC@.750	Ea	435.00	28.00	463.00
30" x 80"	BC@.750	Ea	438.00	28.00	466.00
32" x 80"	BC@.750	Ea	438.00	28.00	466.00
36" x 80"	BC@.750	Ea	450.00	28.00	478.00
10-lite wood French prehung double interior doors. Pre-masked tempered glass for easy finishing. True divided light design. Ponderosa pine. 1-3/8" thick. French doors are mostly glass, with one, to as many as fifteen panes set in wood sash.					
60" x 80", unfinished	BC@1.25	Ea	2,450.00	46.70	2,496.70
64" x 80", unfinished	BC@1.25	Ea	2,280.00	46.70	2,326.70
72" x 80", unfinished	BC@1.25	Ea	2,140.00	46.70	2,186.70
60" x 80", stained	BC@1.25	Ea	3,070.00	46.70	3,116.70
64" x 80", stained	BC@1.25	Ea	2,900.00	46.70	2,946.70
78" x 80", stained	BC@1.25	Ea	2,760.00	46.70	2,806.70
Oak French prehung double interior doors. Bored for lockset. 1-3/8" thick.					
48" x 80"	BC@1.25	Ea	488.00	46.70	534.70
60" x 80"	BC@1.25	Ea	567.00	46.70	613.70
72" x 80"	BC@1.25	Ea	613.00	46.70	659.70
Patio Doors					
10-lite swinging patio double doors. White finish. Dual-glazed with clear tempered glass. Fully weatherstripped. Pre-drilled lock-bore.					
6'-0" wide x 6'-8" high	B1@3.58	Ea	511.00	121.00	632.00
Vinyl-clad hinged patio double doors, Frenchwood®, Andersen. White exterior. Perma-Shield® low-maintenance finish. Clear pine interior. 1-lite. 3-point locking system. Adjustable hinges with ball-bearing pivots. Low-E2 tempered insulating glass. Mortise and tenon joints.					
6'-0" x 6'-8"	B1@3.58	Ea	3,320.00	121.00	3,441.00
Center hinge 15-lite aluminum patio double doors. Sized for replacement. Unfinished clear pine interior. White extruded aluminum-clad exterior. Weatherstripped frame. Self-draining sill. Bored for lockset. 3/4" Low-E insulated safety glass.					
6'-0" x 6'-8"	B1@3.58	Ea	1,120.00	121.00	1,241.00
Aluminum inward swing 1-lite patio double doors. Low-E insulated safety glass. Clear wood interior ready to paint or stain.					
6'-0" x 6'-8"	B1@3.58	Ea	917.00	121.00	1,038.00
Aluminum inward swing 10-lite patio double doors. Unfinished interior. Low-E2 argon-filled insulated glass. Thermal-break sill. Bored for lockset. With head and foot bolts.					
6'-0" x 6'-8"	B1@3.58	Ea	974.00	121.00	1,095.00

	Craft@Hrs	Unit	Material	Labor	Total
200 series Narroline™ sliding wood patio doors, Andersen. Dual-pane Low-E glass. Anodized aluminum track with stainless steel cap. With hardware and screen. White.					
6'-0" x 6'-8"	B1@3.58	Ea	2,260.00	121.00	2,381.00
Vinyl-clad gliding patio doors, Andersen. White. Tempered 1" Low-E insulating glass. Anodized aluminum track.					
6'-0" x 6'-8"	B1@3.58	Ea	863.00	121.00	984.00
10-lite sliding patio doors. Solid pine core. Weatherstripped on 4 sides of operating panels. Butcher block 4-1/2"-wide stiles and 9-1/2" bottom rail. 4-9/16" jamb width. White. Actual dimensions: 71-1/4" wide x 79-1/2" high. Pre-drilled lock-bore.					
6'-0" wide x 6'-8" high	B1@3.58	Ea	377.00	121.00	498.00
Aluminum sliding patio doors. Unfinished interior. White aluminum-clad exterior. With lockset. Insulating Low-E2 glass.					
6'-0" x 6'-8", 1 lite	B1@3.58	Ea	879.00	121.00	1,000.00
6'-0" x 6'-8", 15 lites	B1@3.58	Ea	818.00	121.00	939.00
Aluminum sliding patio doors. Insulating glass. Reversible, self-aligning ball bearing rollers. Zinc finish lock. With screen. By nominal width x height. Actual height and width are 1/2" less.					
5' x 6'-8", bronze finish	B1@3.58	Ea	599.00	121.00	720.00
6' x 6'-8", bronze finish	B1@3.58	Ea	632.00	121.00	753.00
6' x 6'-8", mill finish	B1@3.58	Ea	466.00	121.00	587.00
Aluminum sliding patio doors. With screen. Insulated glass except as noted. Reversible, self-aligning ball bearing rollers. Zinc finish lock. By nominal width x height. Actual height and width are 1/2" less.					
5'-0" x 6'-8", mill finish, single glazed	B1@3.58	Ea	248.00	121.00	369.00
5'-0" x 6'-8", white finish	B1@3.58	Ea	351.00	121.00	472.00
5'-0" x 8'-0", white finish, with grids	B1@3.58	Ea	400.00	121.00	521.00
6'-0" x 6'-8", bronze finish, single glazed	B1@3.58	Ea	414.00	121.00	535.00
6'-0" x 6'-8", bronze finish, with grids	B1@3.58	Ea	400.00	121.00	521.00
6'-0" x 6'-8", white finish, single glazed	B1@3.58	Ea	355.00	121.00	476.00
8'-0" x 8'-0", white finish	B1@4.60	Ea	443.00	156.00	599.00
Screen for sliding or swinging patio doors. 72-1/2" wide x 6'8" high.					
Inswing/Outswing, French door, white	B1@.250	Ea	136.00	8.46	144.46
Traditional, aluminum frame, fiberglass screen	B1@.250	Ea	129.00	8.46	137.46
Retractable, for in-swing door, white 36" x 80"	B1@.250	Ea	118.00	8.46	126.46
Vinyl sliding patio doors. Includes screen. Low-E insulating glass.					
5'-0" x 6'-8"	B1@3.58	Ea	795.00	121.00	916.00
5'-0" x 6'-8", with internal mini-blinds	B1@3.58	Ea	1,090.00	121.00	1,211.00
6'-0" x 6'-8"	B1@3.58	Ea	809.00	121.00	930.00
6'-0" x 6'-8" with grid	B1@3.58	Ea	1,030.00	121.00	1,151.00
6'-0" x 6'-8" with internal mini-blinds	B1@3.58	Ea	1,100.00	121.00	1,221.00
1-lite swinging prehung steel patio double doors. Polyurethane core. High-performance weatherstrip. Adjustable thermal-break sill. Non-yellowing frame and grille. Inward swing.					
6'-0" x 6'-8"	B1@3.58	Ea	371.00	121.00	492.00

	Craft@Hrs	Unit	Material	Labor	Total
1-lite swinging steel patio double door with internal mini-blinds. Prehung. Double-pane insulated safety glass.					
6'-0" x 6'-8", outward swing	B1@3.58	Ea	605.00	121.00	726.00
6'-0" x 6'-8", inward swing, with brick mold	B1@3.58	Ea	680.00	121.00	801.00
6'-0" x 6'-8", outward swing, Dade County-approved (high wind)	B1@3.58	Ea	1,230.00	121.00	1,351.00
10-lite swinging steel patio double doors. Inward swing. Insulated Low-E glass.					
5'-0" x 6'-8"	B1@3.58	Ea	1,220.00	121.00	1,341.00
6'-0" x 6'-8"	B1@3.58	Ea	1,220.00	121.00	1,341.00
10-lite venting steel patio double doors. Inward swing. Insulated glass.					
6'-0" x 6'-8"	B1@3.58	Ea	748.00	121.00	869.00
8'-0" x 6'-8"	B1@3.58	Ea	843.00	121.00	964.00
15-lite swinging steel patio double doors. Inward swing					
5'-0" x 6'-8", insulated glass	B1@3.58	Ea	1,100.00	121.00	1,221.00
6'-0" x 6'-8", Low-E insulated glass	B1@3.58	Ea	1,100.00	121.00	1,221.00
6'-0" x 6'-8", single glazed	B1@3.58	Ea	1,010.00	121.00	1,131.00
15-lite prehung swinging fiberglass patio double doors. Outward swing. Insulated glass. Adjustable mill finish thermal-break threshold					
6'-0" x 6'-8"	B1@3.58	Ea	1,400.00	121.00	1,521.00

Accordion Folding Doors Vertical embossed surface. Includes hardware. Fully assembled. Hung in a cased opening.

	Craft@Hrs	Unit	Material	Labor	Total
32" x 80" vinyl, natural color, Horizon	BC@.750	Ea	34.70	28.00	62.70
32" x 80" vinyl, white, Horizon	BC@.750	Ea	26.30	28.00	54.30
32" x 80" vinyl, fruitwood color, Encore	BC@.750	Ea	72.20	28.00	100.20
32" x 80" vinyl, white, Horizon	BC@.750	Ea	71.40	28.00	99.40
32" x 80" vinyl, oak color, Horizon	BC@.750	Ea	81.60	28.00	109.60
32" x 80" vinyl, white, Capri	BC@.750	Ea	226.00	28.00	254.00
32" x 80" frosted Plexiglas, asstd colors	BC@.750	Ea	241.00	28.00	269.00
36" x 80" vinyl, oak color, Via	BC@.750	Ea	33.00	28.00	61.00
36" x 80" vinyl, white, Via	BC@.750	Ea	38.50	28.00	66.50
36" x 80" vinyl, white, Contempra	BC@.750	Ea	50.00	28.00	78.00
36" x 80" vinyl, white, Oakmont	BC@.750	Ea	65.10	28.00	93.10
36" x 96" vinyl, oak color, Express One	BC@.750	Ea	150.00	28.00	178.00
36" x 96" vinyl, white, Express One	BC@.750	Ea	148.00	28.00	176.00
48" x 96" vinyl, oak color, Express One	BC@.750	Ea	175.00	28.00	203.00
48" x 96" vinyl, white, Express One	BC@.750	Ea	179.00	28.00	207.00
Folding door lock.					
Door lock	BC@.250	Ea	9.59	9.35	18.94

Pet Doors Entrance doors, lockable, swinging, aluminum frame with security panel

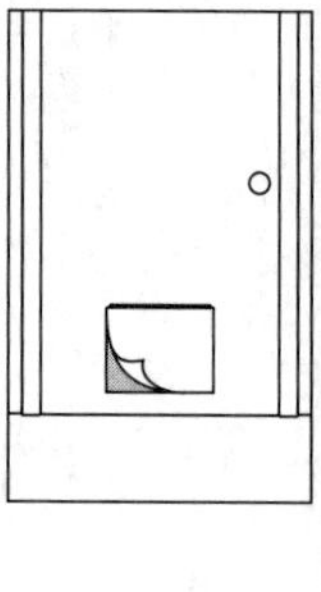

	Craft@Hrs	Unit	Material	Labor	Total
Small, 5" x 7" opening	BC@.800	Ea	36.50	29.90	66.40
Medium, 7" x 11-1/4" opening	BC@.800	Ea	36.00	29.90	65.90
Large, 10-1/2" x 15" opening	BC@.850	Ea	44.20	31.80	76.00
Super large, 15" x 20" opening	BC@.850	Ea	72.90	31.80	104.70
Entrance doors, lockable, swinging, aluminum frame with security panel, dual flap, insulated					
Small, 5" x 9-1/4" opening	BC@.800	Ea	103.00	29.90	132.90
Medium, 7-1/4" x 13" opening	BC@.800	Ea	103.00	29.90	132.90
Large, 9-3/4" x 17" opening	BC@.850	Ea	102.00	31.80	133.80
Super large, 15" x 23-1/2" opening	BC@.850	Ea	169.00	31.80	200.80

	Craft@Hrs	Unit	Material	Labor	Total
Entrance pet doors, lockable, with wall installation kit, swinging, aluminum frame with security panel, dual flap, insulated. Labor for creating wall opening not included					
Small, 5" x 9-1/4" opening	BC@.800	Ea	110.00	29.90	139.90
Medium, 7-1/4" x 13" opening	BC@.800	Ea	119.00	29.90	148.90
Large, 9-3/4" x 17" opening	BC@.850	Ea	131.00	31.80	162.80
Super large, 15" x 23-1/2" opening	BC@.850	Ea	201.00	31.80	232.80
Sliding screen or patio doors, adjustable full length 1/2" panel, 80" high, "Lexan" plastic above lockable, swinging PVC door, aluminum frame					
For cats and miniature dogs, panel is 11-1/2" wide with 5" x 7-1/2" door	BC@.500	Ea	74.40	18.70	93.10
For small dogs, panel is 15" wide with 8-1/2" x 12-1/2" door	BC@.500	Ea	111.00	18.70	129.70
For medium and large dogs, panel is 18" wide with 11-1/2" x 16-1/2" door	BC@.500	Ea	142.00	18.70	160.70
Pet screen, vinyl coated 48" x 84" Resists tears and punctures	BC@.500	Ea	20.50	18.70	39.20
Pet grill, steel, 36" x 31-3/8"	BC@.250	Ea	46.20	9.35	55.55

Bypass Closet Doors Bypass closet doors slide left or right on an overhead track, never revealing more than one-half of the interior.

White bypass closet doors. Prefinished white vinyl-covered hardboard panels instead of mirrors. White steel frame. Jump-proof bottom track. 1-1/2" dual race ball bearing wheels. Injection-molded top guides. Dimensions are width x height. Per pair of doors.

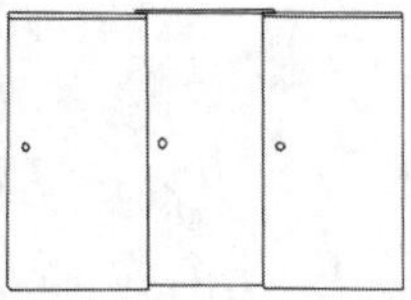

	Craft@Hrs	Unit	Material	Labor	Total
48" x 80"	BC@.750	Ea	73.70	28.00	101.70
60" x 80"	BC@1.00	Ea	90.10	37.40	127.50
72" x 80"	BC@1.00	Ea	100.00	37.40	137.40
48" x 96"	BC@.750	Ea	104.00	28.00	132.00
60" x 96"	BC@1.00	Ea	121.00	37.40	158.40
72" x 96"	BC@1.00	Ea	142.00	37.40	179.40
Economy mirrored bypass closet doors. Gold finished steel. Plate mirror with double strength glass. Bottom rail with jump-proof track. Dimensions are width x height. Per pair of doors.					
47" x 80"	BC@.750	Ea	93.20	28.00	121.20
59" x 80"	BC@1.00	Ea	120.00	37.40	157.40
71" x 80"	BC@1.00	Ea	132.00	37.40	169.40
95" x 80"	BC@1.25	Ea	209.00	46.70	255.70
Good quality mirrored bypass closet doors. White frame. Safety-backed mirror. Dimensions are width x height. Per pair of doors.					
48" x 80", silver nickel mirror	BC@.750	Ea	128.00	28.00	156.00
60" x 80", silver nickel mirror	BC@1.00	Ea	156.00	37.40	193.40
72" x 80", silver nickel mirror	BC@1.00	Ea	183.00	37.40	220.40
48" x 80", trimline bronze mirror door	BC@.750	Ea	240.00	28.00	268.00
60" x 80", trimline bronze mirror door	BC@1.00	Ea	265.00	37.40	302.40
72" x 80", trimline bronze mirror door	BC@1.00	Ea	293.00	37.40	330.40
48" x 80", satin mirror door	BC@.750	Ea	203.00	28.00	231.00
60" x 80", satin mirror door	BC@1.00	Ea	231.00	37.40	268.40
72" x 80", satin mirror door	BC@1.00	Ea	258.00	37.40	295.40
Beveled mirror bypass closet doors. 1/2" bevel on both sides of glass. Safety-backed mirror. Includes hardware. Dimensions are width x height. Per pair of doors.					
48" x 80"	BC@.750	Ea	141.00	28.00	169.00
60" x 80"	BC@1.00	Ea	161.00	37.40	198.40
72" x 80"	BC@1.00	Ea	217.00	37.40	254.40
96" x 80"	BC@1.25	Ea	270.00	46.70	316.70

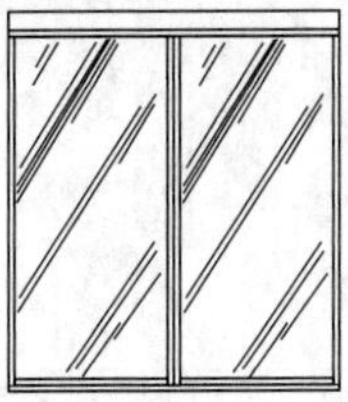

	Craft@Hrs	Unit	Material	Labor	Total
Premium mirrored bypass closet doors. Brushed nickel. Anodized aluminum finish with color-coordinated glazing vinyl. Color-matched mirror handles. "Select" quality 3mm plate mirror. Jump-proof bottom track and 1-1/2" dual race ball bearing wheels. Mitered frame corners. Dimensions are width x height. Per pair of doors.					
48" x 81"	BC@.750	Ea	244.00	28.00	272.00
60" x 81"	BC@1.00	Ea	272.00	37.40	309.40
72" x 81"	BC@1.00	Ea	300.00	37.40	337.40
96" x 81"	BC@1.25	Ea	341.00	46.70	387.70
Bypass door accessories					
Bumper	BC@.175	Ea	3.18	6.54	9.72
Carpet riser	BC@.175	Ea	2.76	6.54	9.30
Guide	BC@.175	Ea	2.91	6.54	9.45

Bi-Fold Closet Doors Bi-fold closet doors fold in half when open, revealing nearly the full interior.

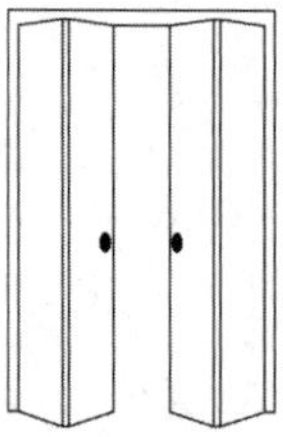

	Craft@Hrs	Unit	Material	Labor	Total
Lauan bi-fold flush closet doors. 1-3/8" thick. 2 prehinged panels. Ready to paint, stain, or varnish.					
24" x 80"	BC@.700	Ea	43.20	26.20	69.40
30" x 80"	BC@.700	Ea	49.00	26.20	75.20
32" x 80"	BC@.700	Ea	51.30	26.20	77.50
36" x 80"	BC@.700	Ea	54.80	26.20	81.00
Primed hardboard bi-fold flush closet doors. 1-3/8" thick. 2 prehinged panels.					
24" x 80"	BC@.700	Ea	108.00	26.20	134.20
30" x 80"	BC@.700	Ea	109.00	26.20	135.20
32" x 80"	BC@.700	Ea	117.00	26.20	143.20
36" x 80"	BC@.700	Ea	112.00	26.20	138.20
4-panel birch bi-fold flush closet doors. Wood stile and rail construction. 1-3/8" thick. Open left or right. Includes track and hardware.					
24" x 80"	BC@.700	Ea	42.90	26.20	69.10
30" x 80"	BC@.700	Ea	49.80	26.20	76.00
36" x 80"	BC@.700	Ea	56.80	26.20	83.00
48" x 80"	BC@.800	Ea	84.60	29.90	114.50
4-panel lauan flush bi-fold closet doors. Wood stile and rail construction. 1-3/8" thick. Open left or right. Includes track and hardware.					
48" x 80"	BC@.800	Ea	67.80	29.90	97.70
4-panel red oak flush bi-fold closet doors. Wood stile and rail construction. 1-3/8" thick. Open left or right. Includes track and hardware.					
24" x 80"	BC@.700	Ea	56.80	26.20	83.00
30" x 80"	BC@.700	Ea	63.90	26.20	90.10
36" x 80"	BC@.700	Ea	73.10	26.20	99.30
48" x 80"	BC@.800	Ea	106.00	29.90	135.90
Pine colonial panel bi-fold doors. Includes hardware and track. Can be painted or stained. Two hinged panels.					
24" x 80"	BC@.700	Ea	87.10	26.20	113.30
30" x 80"	BC@.700	Ea	94.70	26.20	120.90
36" x 80"	BC@.700	Ea	102.00	26.20	128.20
Clear pine 2-panel colonial bi-fold doors. Clear pine. Recessed rails. Unfinished. Open left or right. Includes all hardware and track. Two hinged panels.					
24" x 80"	BC@.700	Ea	153.00	26.20	179.20
30" x 80"	BC@.700	Ea	159.00	26.20	185.20
32" x 80"	BC@.700	Ea	165.00	26.20	191.20
36" x 80"	BC@.700	Ea	173.00	26.20	199.20

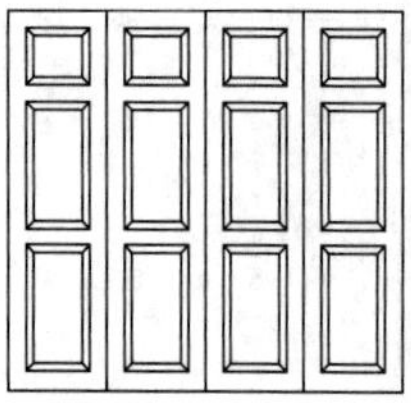

	Craft@Hrs	Unit	Material	Labor	Total
Oak panel bi-fold doors. Includes track and hardware. 1-3/8" thick. Ready to finish. Classic. Two hinged panels.					
24" x 80"	BC@.700	Ea	143.00	26.20	169.20
30" x 80"	BC@.700	Ea	155.00	26.20	181.20
36" x 80"	BC@.700	Ea	166.00	26.20	192.20
Pine louver over louver bi-fold doors. 1-1/8" thick ponderosa pine. 3-11/16" wide rails. 1-1/4" wide stiles. Two prehinged panels. Unfinished.					
24" x 80"	BC@.700	Ea	67.30	26.20	93.50
30" x 80"	BC@.700	Ea	73.50	26.20	99.70
32" x 80"	BC@.700	Ea	83.30	26.20	109.50
36" x 80"	BC@.700	Ea	88.10	26.20	114.30
Pine louver over panel bi-fold doors. Recessed rails. Open left or right. 1/2" swing space. Two prehinged panels. Includes track and hardware. Unfinished stain grade.					
24" x 80"	BC@.700	Ea	66.80	26.20	93.00
30" x 80"	BC@.700	Ea	104.00	26.20	130.20
36" x 80"	BC@.700	Ea	118.00	26.20	144.20
Bi-fold door hardware					
Bi-fold hinge	BC@.175	Ea	4.44	6.54	10.98
Carpet riser	BC@.175	Ea	2.64	6.54	9.18
Hardware set	BC@.175	Ea	9.73	6.54	16.27
48" track	—	Ea	30.10	—	30.10
60" track	—	Ea	30.90	—	30.90
72" track	—	Ea	32.80	—	32.80

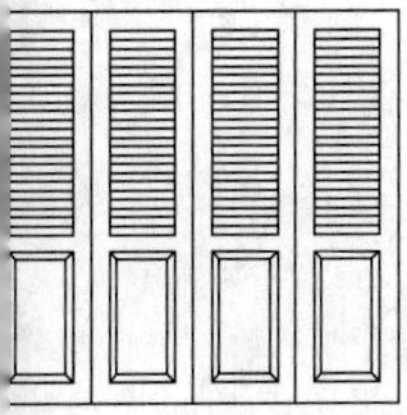

	Craft@Hrs	Unit	Material	Labor	Total
Mirrored Bi-Fold Closet Doors Framed bi-fold mirror doors. White frame. Top-hung with single wheel top hanger. Snap-in bottom guide and fascia. Low rise bottom track. Non-binding door operation. Reversible top and bottom track. 3 mm safety-backed mirror. Two hinged panels.					
24" x 80"	BC@.700	Ea	111.00	26.20	137.20
30" x 80"	BC@.700	Ea	126.00	26.20	152.20
36" x 80"	BC@.700	Ea	139.00	26.20	165.20
Bevel edge bi-fold mirror doors. 1/2" vertical bevel with bearing hinges. White finished steel frame with safety-backed mirror. Includes hardware. Full access to closet opening. Reversible high- and low-profile top and bottom tracks. Two hinged panels.					
24" x 80"	BC@.700	Ea	128.00	26.20	154.20
30" x 80"	BC@.700	Ea	141.00	26.20	167.20
Frameless bi-fold mirror doors. Frameless style maximizes the mirror surface. Beveled edge glass. All preassembled hinges. Safety-reinforced mirror backing. Two hinged panels. Includes hardware.					
36" x 80"	BC@.700	Ea	115.00	26.20	141.20
30" x 80"	BC@.700	Ea	139.00	26.20	165.20
36" x 80"	BC@.700	Ea	154.00	26.20	180.20
Chrome bi-fold mirror doors. Two hinged panels. Includes hardware.					
24" x 80"	BC@.700	Ea	200.00	26.20	226.20
30" x 80"	BC@.700	Ea	213.00	26.20	239.20
36" x 80"	BC@.700	Ea	228.00	26.20	254.20

	Craft@Hrs	Unit	Material	Labor	Total
Drafting Per SF of floor area, architectural only, not including engineering fees. See also Architectural Illustrations and Blueprinting. Typical prices.					
Apartments	—	SF	—	—	2.26
Warehouses and storage buildings	—	SF	—	—	2.00
Office buildings	—	SF	—	—	3.93
Residences					
Minimum quality tract work	—	SF	—	—	3.05
Typical work	—	SF	—	—	3.78
Detailed jobs, exposed woods, hillsides	—	SF	—	—	4.72
Drainage Piping Corrugated plastic drainage pipe, plain or perforated and snap-on fittings. Installed in trenches or at foundation footings. No excavation, gravel or backfill included.					
Polyethylene pipe					
3" pipe perforated	BL@.010	LF	.54	.30	.84
4" pipe solid	BL@.010	LF	.65	.30	.95
6" pipe slotted	BL@.012	LF	2.20	.36	2.56
Corrugated drain snap pipe fittings					
3" internal coupling	P1@.100	Ea	2.17	3.69	5.86
3" perforated end cap	P1@.055	Ea	2.35	2.03	4.38
3" snap adapter	P1@.100	Ea	5.07	3.69	8.76
3" corrugated x smooth adapter	P1@.100	Ea	2.58	3.69	6.27
4" internal coupling	P1@.100	Ea	3.62	3.69	7.31
4" universal adapter	P1@.100	Ea	4.69	3.69	8.38
4" x 3" reducer	P1@.100	Ea	3.68	3.69	7.37
4" snap adapter	P1@.100	Ea	3.96	3.69	7.65
6" snap adapter	P1@.110	Ea	13.00	4.06	17.06
6" x 4" reducer	P1@.110	Ea	8.30	4.06	12.36
6" snap coupling	P1@.110	Ea	4.43	4.06	8.49
6" wye	P1@.150	Ea	7.46	5.53	12.99
6" tee	P1@.150	Ea	19.50	5.53	25.03
6" blind tee	P1@.150	Ea	14.50	5.53	20.03
6" split end cap	P1@.060	Ea	6.07	2.21	8.28
Filter sock sieve. Keeps soil out of perforated pipe. Reduces need for aggregate filters. By pipe size. Per linear foot of sock.					
3", 10' length	P1@.006	LF	.56	.22	.78
4", 10' length	P1@.007	LF	.60	.26	.86
4", 100' length	P1@.007	LF	.22	.26	.48
Rock or sand fill for drainage systems. Labor cost is for spreading base and covering pipe. 3 mile haul, dumped on site and placed by wheelbarrow.					
Crushed stone (1.4 tons per CY)					
3/4" (Number 3)	BL@.700	CY	41.20	21.20	62.40
1-1/2" (Number 2)	BL@.700	CY	43.20	21.20	64.40
Crushed slag (1.86 tons per CY)					
3/4"	BL@.700	CY	27.70	21.20	48.90
Sand (1.35 tons per CY)	BL@.360	CY	20.10	10.90	31.00

	Craft@Hrs	Unit	Material	Labor	Total

Precast Residential Rain Drain System System includes 5 interlocking tongue and groove connection channels with galvanized steel slotted grate, one meter long each, 4" outlet and closing end caps, catch basin, and 4" PVC pipe outlet. Channel has 4" internal width. System withstands imposed loadings up to 3,500 lbs. Set in concrete, not including concrete or forming costs.

	Craft@Hrs	Unit	Material	Labor	Total
System components					
1 meter channel with grate	—	Ea	81.10	—	81.10
4" outlet cap	—	Ea	7.16	—	7.16
4" closed end cap	—	Ea	7.15	—	7.15
Catch basin with PVC trash bucket and steel grating	—	Ea	95.60	—	95.60
4" PVC pipe outlet	—	Ea	22.30	—	22.30
Typical 5 meter rain drain system	BL@4.0	Ea	538.00	121.00	659.00

Draperies, Custom, Subcontract Custom draperies include 4" double hems and headers, 1-1/2" side hems, and weighted corners. Finished sizes allow 4" above, 4" below (except for sliding glass openings), and 5" on each side of wall openings. Prices are figured at one width, 48" of fabric, pleated to 16". Costs listed include fabric, full liner, manufacturing, all hardware, and installation. Add 50% per LF of width for jobs outside working range of metropolitan centers. Use $300 as a minimum job charge.

	Craft@Hrs	Unit	Material	Labor	Total
Minimum quality, 200% fullness, average is 6 panels of fabric, limited choice of fabric styles, colors, and textures					
To 95" high	—	LF	—	—	49.90
To 68" high	—	LF	—	—	46.80
To 54" high	—	LF	—	—	45.30
Good quality, fully lined, 250% fullness, average is 5 panels of fabric, better selection of fabric styles, colors, and textures, weighted seams					
To 95" high	—	LF	—	—	119.00
To 84" high	—	LF	—	—	114.00
To 68" high	—	LF	—	—	106.00
To 54" high	—	LF	—	—	100.00
To 44" high	—	LF	—	—	96.30
Deduct for multi-unit jobs	—	%	—	—	-25.0
Add for insulated fabrics or liners					
Pleated shade liner	—	SY	—	—	32.80
Thermal liner	—	SY	—	—	35.40
Better quality, fully lined, choice of finest fabric styles, colors, and textures, does not include special treatments such as elaborate swags, or custom fabrics					
To 95" high	—	LF	—	—	147.00
To 84" high	—	LF	—	—	142.00
To 68" high	—	LF	—	—	126.00
To 54" high	—	LF	—	—	117.00
To 44" high	—	LF	—	—	110.00

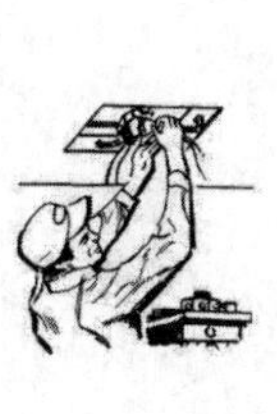

Electrical Work, Subcontract Costs listed below are for wiring new residential and light commercial buildings with Romex cable and assume circuit lengths averaging 40 feet. If flex cable is required, add $15.00 for 15 amp circuits and $35 for 20 amp circuits. No fixtures or appliances included except as noted. Work on second and higher floors may cost 25% more. Work performed by a qualified subcontractor.

Rule of thumb: Total cost for electrical work, performed by a qualified subcontractor, per SF of floor area. Includes service entrance, outlets, switches, basic lighting fixtures and connecting appliances only.

	Craft@Hrs	Unit	Material	Labor	Total
All wiring and fixtures	—	SF	—	—	6.05
Lighting fixtures only (no wiring)	—	SF	—	—	1.75

Electrical Work, Subcontract

	Craft@Hrs	Unit	Material	Labor	Total
Air conditioners (with thermostat)					
Central, 2 ton (220 volt)	—	LS	—	—	832.00
First floor room (115 volt)	—	LS	—	—	248.00
Second floor room (115 volt)	—	LS	—	—	501.00
Add for thermostat on second floor	—	LS	—	—	170.00
Alarms. See also Security Alarms					
Fire or smoke detector, wiring and outlet box only	—	LS	—	—	188.00
Add for detector unit	—	LS	—	—	95.50
Bathroom fixtures, wiring only, no fixtures or equipment included					
Mirror lighting (valance or side lighted mirrors)	—	LS	—	—	165.00
Sauna heater (40 amp branch circuit)	—	LS	—	—	502.00
Steam bath generator	—	LS	—	—	501.00
Heat lamp with timer wall switch	—	LS	—	—	248.00
Whirlpool bath system and wall switch	—	LS	—	—	417.00
Clock outlets (recessed)	—	LS	—	—	125.00
Closet lighting					
Ceramic "pull chain" ceiling fixture	—	LS	—	—	126.00
Switch-operated fixture with wall switch	—	LS	—	—	169.00
Clothes dryers					
Gas dryer, receptacle only	—	LS	—	—	170.00
Direct connection for up to 5,760 watt (30 amp) electric dryer, 220 volt	—	LS	—	—	248.00
Direct connection for over 5,760 watt (40 amp) electric dryer, 220 volt	—	LS	—	—	293.00
Clothes washers (115 volt)	—	LS	—	—	124.00
Dishwashers	—	LS	—	—	170.00
Door bells, rough wiring, front and rear with transformer					
Add the cost of two push-buttons and the chime	—	LS	—	—	247.00
Fans (exhaust)					
Attic fans (wiring only)	—	LS	—	—	168.00
Bathroom fans (includes 70 CFM fan)	—	LS	—	—	245.00
Garage fans (wiring only)	—	LS	—	—	171.00
Kitchen fans (includes 225 CFM fan)	—	LS	—	—	334.00
Furnace wiring and blower hookup only	—	LS	—	—	203.00
Garage door opener, wiring and hookup only	—	LS	—	—	172.00
Garbage disposers, wiring, switch and connection only					
No disposer included	—	LS	—	—	210.00
Grounding devices (see also Lightning protection systems below)					
Grounding entire electrical system	—	LS	—	—	241.00
Grounding single appliance	—	LS	—	—	103.00
Ground fault circuit interrupter (GFCI), rough and finish wiring					
Includes outlet box and GFCI	—	LS	—	—	210.00
Heaters					
Baseboard (115 volt) per branch circuit	—	LS	—	—	170.00
Bathroom (ceiling type) wiring, switch connection (with GFCI) only	—	LS	—	—	197.00
Ceiling heat system (radiant-resistance type) 1,000 watt, 120 volt, per branch circuit, including thermostat	—	LS	—	—	382.00
Space heating (flush in-wall type) up to 2,000 watt, 220 volt	—	LS	—	—	348.00
Humidifiers, central	—	LS	—	—	170.00

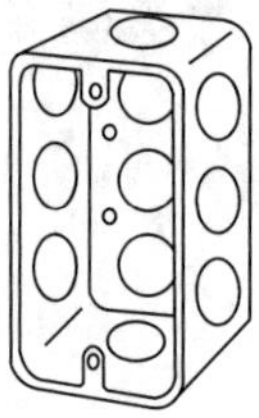

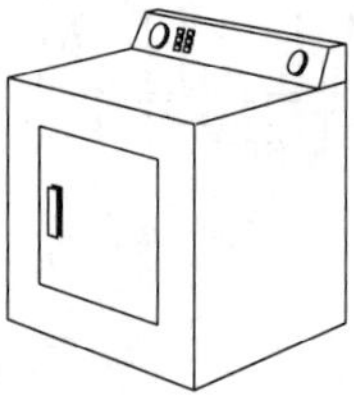

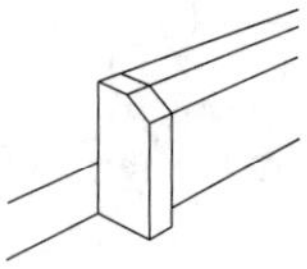

	Craft@Hrs	Unit	Material	Labor	Total
Exterior lamp posts, wiring and hookup only, to 25'					
Using buried wire and conduit	—	LS	—	—	996.00
Lighting fixture outlets (rough wiring and box only)					
Ceiling	—	Ea	—	—	82.50
Floor	—	Ea	—	—	125.00
Set in concrete	—	Ea	—	—	167.00
Set in masonry	—	Ea	—	—	167.00
Underground	—	Ea	—	—	218.00
Valance	—	Ea	—	—	99.30
Wall outlet	—	Ea	—	—	82.50
Lightning protection systems (static electric grounding system) Residential, ridge protection including one chimney and connected garage (houses with cut-up roofs will cost more)					
Typical home system	—	LS	—	—	3,550.00
Barns and light commercial buildings	—	LS	—	—	6,940.00
Ovens, wall type (up to 10' of wiring and hookup only), 220 volt					
To 4,800 watts (20 amp)	—	LS	—	—	203.00
4,800 to 7,200 watts (30 amp)	—	LS	—	—	236.00
7,200 to 9,600 watts (40 amp)	—	LS	—	—	308.00
Ranges, (up to 10' of wiring and hookup only), 220 volt					
Countertop type					
To 4,800 watts (20 amp)	—	LS	—	—	166.00
4,800 to 7,200 watts (30 amp)	—	LS	—	—	237.00
7,200 to 9,600 watts (40 amp)	—	LS	—	—	308.00
Freestanding type (50 amp)	—	LS	—	—	370.00
Receptacle outlets (rough wiring, box, receptacle and plate)					
Ceiling	—	Ea	—	—	68.20
Countertop wall	—	Ea	—	—	74.00
Floor outlet	—	Ea	—	—	102.00
Split-wired	—	Ea	—	—	127.00
Standard indoor, duplex wall outlet	—	Ea	—	—	68.20
Waterproof, with ground fault circuit	—	Ea	—	—	109.00
Refrigerator or freezer wall outlet	—	Ea	—	—	81.40
Service entrance connections, complete (panel box hookup but no wiring)					
100 amp service including meter socket, main switch, GFCI and 5 single pole breakers in 20 breaker space exterior panel box	—	LS	—	—	1,280.00
200 amp service including meter socket, main switch, 2 GFCI and 15 single pole breakers in 40 breaker space exterior panel box	—	LS	—	—	2,120.00
Sub-panel connections (panel box hookup but no wiring)					
40 amp circuit panel including 12 single pole breakers in 12 breaker indoor panel box	—	LS	—	—	478.00
50 amp circuit panel including 16 single pole breakers in 16 breaker indoor panel box	—	LS	—	—	510.00
Sump pump connection including 15' of underground conduit	—	Ea	—	—	244.00
Switches (includes rough wiring, box, switch and plate)					
Dimmer	—	Ea	—	—	71.60
Lighted	—	Ea	—	—	71.80
Quiet	—	Ea	—	—	57.40
Mercury	—	Ea	—	—	71.50
Standard indoor wall switch	—	Ea	—	—	56.20
Stair-wired (3 way)	—	Ea	—	—	151.00
Waterproof	—	Ea	—	—	122.00
Television outlet wiring (300 ohm wire)	—	Ea	—	—	57.40

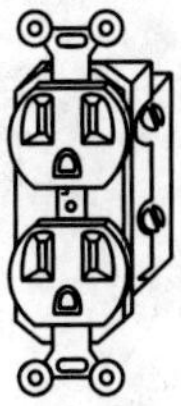

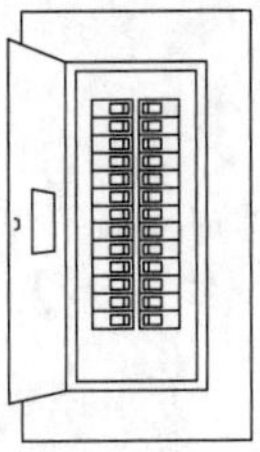

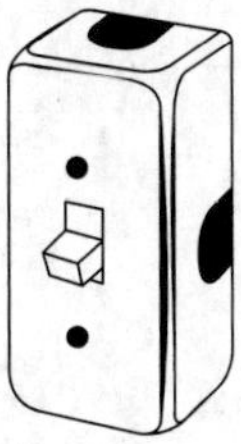

	Craft@Hrs	Unit	Material	Labor	Total
Trash compactor, 15" (includes compactor installed under counter and wiring)					
Standard	—	LS	—	—	640.00
Deluxe	—	LS	—	—	748.00
Vacuuming system, central					
Central unit hookup	—	LS	—	—	143.00
Remote vacuum outlets					
Receptacle wiring only	—	Ea	—	—	68.20
Water heaters					
(up to 10' of wiring and hookup only), 220 volt	—	LS	—	—	212.00
Water pumps, domestic potable water					
Connection only	—	LS	—	—	151.00

Residential computer wiring and network setup These costs are based on work done with wall cavities exposed. Labor costs in existing dwellings will be up to four times higher if cable has to be fished through enclosed walls. Single story homes use stranded wire. Multi story homes use solid wire on vertical runs. Includes normal (5%) waste. Costs assume cable runs terminate at the point of phone or cable service entry and that connections are made at a wall-mounted punch down block with RJ45 connectors. The local building code may require wire runs in conduit or use of plenum type cable.

	Craft@Hrs	Unit	Material	Labor	Total
Network cable, twisted pair category 5e, rated for 350 Mbps, material price based on 1,000' rolls. Add the cost of conduit, if required. Costs per linear foot of cable run.					
4 pair UTP PVC stranded wire	BE@.008	LF	.15	.33	.48
4 pair UTP PVC solid wire	BE@.008	LF	.15	.33	.48
Add for plenum grade wire	—	%	60.0	—	—
Termination to structured cable panel. Includes structured cable panel with telephone, data and video connectors for 6, 12 or 18 stations. Also includes RJ45 keystone jack and wall plate at the room/station end.					
12 station termination	BE@1.40	Ea	198.00	56.90	254.90
18 station termination	BE@2.10	Ea	222.00	85.30	307.30
24 station termination	BE@2.80	Ea	256.00	114.00	370.00
Cable testing using a dedicated cable tester					
Shielded/Unshielded twisted pair, per cable	E4@.125	Ea	—	6.35	6.35
Distribution of Internet connection to network switch or router. Includes 10/100 network switch/wireless router and patch cables					
6 station connection	BE@.166	Ea	99.80	6.74	106.54
12 station connection	BE@.333	Ea	103.00	13.50	116.50
18 station connection	BE@.500	Ea	152.00	20.30	172.30
Wireless access points. Preferred location is one foot below the ceiling on a small shelf. Each access point counts as one station termination and connection. Add the cost of network cable wiring to the access point and an electrical outlet at the access point.					
Wireless access point	BE@.100	Ea	59.20	4.06	63.26
Remote high gain antenna for a wireless network access point. (Extends the range of wireless connections beyond the usual 50 to 100 feet.) Add the cost of cable connection to the wireless router/access point.					
8 Dbi high gain panel antenna	—	Ea	62.80	—	62.80
Cable for high gain antennae, thin ethernet, 50 ohm, (RG58). Used to connect a high gain antenna to the wireless access points.					
PVC cable	BE@.008	LF	.16	.33	.49
Plenum cable	BE@.008	LF	.51	.33	.84

	Craft@Hrs	Unit	Material	Labor	Total
Connection of live internet feed to each computer. Includes physical connection of DSL or cable internet feed, internet setup per carriers' instruction, setup and testing of live feed at each outlet and wireless access point. Testing assumes the computers are installed and running.					
Connection and setup of Internet feed	BE@2.00	Ea	—	81.30	81.30
Testing of live feed at each computer	BE@1.00	Ea	—	40.60	40.60
Post installation of room/station computer setup. Assumes a peer to peer network with resources shared per the customers' preference, including browser and email setup.					
Cost per computer configuration	—	LS	—	—	50.70
Digital Networking Systems, Subcontract Modular and expandable electronic gateway for the in-home distribution of external services such as CATV, satellite TV, broadcast TV, telephone and high speed internet access. System also processes and redistributes in-home generated signals such as those from VCRs, DVD players, audio, security cameras and computers. Provides (6) computer local area network (LAN) outlets, (6) telephone jacks and (6) cable hookups where required. Costs include standalone console, 1,000' of each type of cable (phone, network, video), installation and connection.					
Basic networking system					
Six TV and eight voice locations	—	LS	—	—	617.00
Apartment type networking system					
Six video, six data and six voice locations	—	LS	—	—	675.00
Amplified networking system. Video and voice surge protection					
Six video, six data and 15 voice locations	—	LS	—	—	786.00
Large amplified networking system. Video and voice surge protection					
Six video, 8 data and 18 voice locations	—	LS	—	—	876.00
Electrical generators, residential Suitable for standby or extended primary power generation. Dual fuel (liquid propane or natural gas) two-stroke, V-twin cylinder, 60 Hz, single phase, UL and CSA listed. Emissions certified to EPA Tier 3 rating. 65 decibels sound output rating at 10 feet. Control package includes digital engine and generator control panel, ground fault interruption, lightning shield and combination voltage regulator and automatic transfer switch with automatic dual utility connection lockout. Includes fused main circuit breaker, electronic load-sharing module for generator ganging, electric starter motor, battery and trickle charger. Add the cost of connecting electrical loads and electrical controls. Add 4,000 lb. capacity rough-terrain fork lift, if required. Includes set in place only.					
7 KW, 120 volt	B8@1.00	Ea	4,600.00	36.50	4,636.50
10 KW, 120 volt	B8@1.00	Ea	5,620.00	36.50	5,656.50
12 KW, 120 volt	B8@1.00	Ea	9,130.00	36.50	9,166.50
15 KW, 120 volt	B8@1.00	Ea	11,800.00	36.50	11,836.50
20 KW, 120 volt	B8@1.00	Ea	18,100.00	36.50	18,136.50
65 KW, 400/480 volt	B8@1.00	Ea	76,200.00	36.50	76,236.50
100 KW, 400/480 volt	B8@1.00	Ea	118,000.00	36.50	118,036.50
150 KW, 400/480 volt	B8@1.00	Ea	175,000.00	36.50	175,036.50
200 KW, 400/480 volt	B8@1.00	Ea	235,000.00	36.50	235,036.50
250 KW, 400/480 volt	B8@1.00	Ea	293,000.00	36.50	293,036.50
Residential motor generator installation					
Form and pour slab foundation	B5@.069	SF	3.20	2.56	5.76
Tie-down and leveling	B1@1.00	Ea	26.60	33.90	60.50
Piping for twin fuel trains, lube oil cooling, and dedicated fire protection	B9@0.04	LF	2.93	1.32	4.25
Mount and wire automatic transfer switch to household main breaker box	BE@.184	LF	.44	7.48	7.92
Check and test wiring	BE@.250	LF	.36	10.20	10.56
RFI, lightning and ground fault wiring	BE@.184	LF	.39	7.48	7.87
350 gallon propane tank	B9@1.00	Ea	758.00	33.10	791.10
Fire protection CO2 extinguisher and piping	B9@2.00	Ea	184.00	66.10	250.10

Electrical Generators, Residential

	Craft@Hrs	Unit	Material	Labor	Total
Soundproof "doghouse" enclosure for reduction of noise level to 10 decibels at 10 feet distance. Includes vertical support studs, spacers, fasteners and trim. Complies with American Institute of Sound Engineering specifications. Per square foot of wall or ceiling covered.					
Sidewall coverage	D1@.040	SF	1.94	1.46	3.40
Ceiling coverage	D1@.060	SF	1.94	2.19	4.13
Utility shed generator enclosure, 5/8" plywood with 2 x 4 frame, prefabricated kit, weatherized, with mansard roof, double door, lock assembly, and dual galvanized metal screened lintel air inlet and exhaust vents					
Generator enclosure, per SF of floor	D1@.020	SF	9.30	.73	10.03
Combination digital load/voltage controller, usage meter with main breaker box and controls tie-in					
Controller	BE@.184	Ea	1,620.00	7.48	1,627.48
Zone control fused panel box to shield sensitive electronics and home medical electronics for handicapped					
Fused panel box	BE@.184	Ea	676.00	7.48	683.48
Uninterruptible power supply and trickle charger for sensitive electronic and medical appliances					
UPS	BE@.184	Ea	601.00	7.48	608.48
Automatic supervisory control and data acquisition (SCADA) notification circuit to local emergency services to prevent electrical shock of electrical utility repair technicians or fire department personnel					
Notification circuit	BE@.184	Ea	258.00	7.48	265.48
Generator-activated power failure lighting system. Self-diagnostic emergency lighting fixtures, microprocessor based, continuously monitored, with battery and lamps.					
Two-lamp emergency fixture	BE@.825	Ea	178.00	33.50	211.50

Wind turbine generators Vertical dual-use ventilator or conventional horizontal type, rated and certified to California Construction Code and American Wind Energy Association standards. Technospin, Rooftop Wind Power LLC, or equal. Rated wind speed 11 m/s (24.6 mph) start-up wind: 2.5 m/s (5.6 mph) survival wind: 60 m/s (134 mph) max. Permanent magnet generator. Generator voltage for battery charging: 12 to 48 V DC. Voltage for grid connection is adjusted to requirements of inverter. Overspeed protection, mechanical and electrical system. Maximum axis load: 150 Kg force (330 lb). Installation specifications are for rooftop mounting. For tax incentives, see https://smarterhouse.org/resources/federal-tax-incentives. Costs include weather-proof metal enclosure, wind rotor, generator, main wiring and breaker, overspeed protection, control modules and basic power meter. Add the cost of design work, regulatory fees and insurance inspection, electrical interconnection to the power grid and battery backup, if required.

	Craft@Hrs	Unit	Material	Labor	Total
Wind turbine electrical generator					
100 watts	R1@2.50	Ea	464.00	90.00	554.00
500 watts	R1@3.00	Ea	2,010.00	108.00	2,118.00
750 watts	R1@3.00	Ea	3,490.00	108.00	3,598.00
1.0 Kw	R1@3.50	Ea	4,640.00	126.00	4,766.00
1.5 Kw	R1@3.50	Ea	6,960.00	126.00	7,086.00
2.0 Kw	R1@4.00	Ea	9,300.00	144.00	9,444.00
Base plate for rooftop mount	BE@1.00	Ea	155.00	40.60	195.60
Tie-down for generator	R1@.250	Ea	316.00	9.00	325.00
Electric and control modules	BE@.350	Ea	29.60	14.20	43.80
Install electrical wiring (typical)	BE@.150	LF	2.16	6.09	8.25
Install controls	BE@.500	Ea	—	20.30	20.30
Commission and test	BE@4.00	Ea	—	163.00	163.00

	Craft@Hrs	Unit	Material	Labor	Total
Elevators and Lifts, Subcontract Elevators for apartments or commercial buildings, hydraulic vertical cab, meets code requirements for public buildings, 2,500 pound capacity, to 13 passengers. Includes side opening sliding door, illuminated controls, emergency light, alarm, code-approved fire service operation, motor control unit, wiring in hoistway, cab and door design options.					
Basic 2 stop, typical costs					
100 feet per minute	—	LS	—	—	47,200.00
125 feet per minute	—	LS	—	—	51,700.00
150 feet per minute	—	LS	—	—	55,600.00
Add per stop to 5 stops	—	LS	—	—	5,090.00
Add for infrared door protection	—	Ea	—	—	1,910.00
Add for hall position indicator	—	Ea	—	—	468.00
Add for car position indicator	—	Ea	—	—	468.00
Add for car direction light & tone	—	Ea	—	—	468.00
Add for hall lantern with audible tone	—	Ea	—	—	468.00
Elevators for private residences, electric cable, motor driven, 500 pound capacity, includes complete installation of elevator, controls and safety equipment. Meets code requirements for residences					
2 stops (up to 10' rise)	—	LS	—	—	24,600.00
3 stops (up to 20' rise)	—	LS	—	—	27,900.00
4 stops (up to 30' rise)	—	LS	—	—	31,300.00
5 stops (up to 40' rise)	—	LS	—	—	34,500.00
Add for additional gate	—	Ea	—	—	1,080.00
Dumbwaiters, electric					
75 pound, 2 stop, 24" x 24" x 30"	—	LS	—	—	9,530.00
75 pound, add for each extra stop	—	Ea	—	—	1,720.00
100 pound, 2 stop, 24" x 30" x 36"	—	LS	—	—	10,700.00
100 pound, add for each extra stop	—	Ea	—	—	1,930.00
100 pound, 2 stop, 24" x 24" x 36", tray type	—	LS	—	—	14,700.00
100 pound tray type, add for each extra stop	—	Ea	—	—	2,300.00
300 pound, 2 stop, 30" x 30" x 36", tray type	—	LS	—	—	21,600.00
300 pound, add for each extra stop	—	Ea	—	—	3,410.00
500 pound, 2 stop, 23" x 56" x 48"	—	LS	—	—	23,000.00
500 pound, add for each extra stop	—	Ea	—	—	3,410.00
Hydraulic elevators, private residence, 750 pound capacity. Includes controls and safety equipment with standard unfinished birch plywood cab and one gate.					
2 stops (up to 15' rise)	—	LS	—	—	26,600.00
3 stops (up to 22' rise)	—	LS	—	—	30,300.00
4 stops (up to 28' rise)	—	LS	—	—	33,400.00
5 stops (up to 34' rise)	—	LS	—	—	39,300.00
Add for adjacent opening	—	Ea	—	—	628.00
Add for additional gate	—	Ea	—	—	1,090.00
Add for plastic laminate cab	—	Ea	—	—	47.40
Add for oak raised panel cab	—	Ea	—	—	3,360.00
Stairlifts (incline lifts), single passenger, indoor. Lift to 18' measured diagonally. 300 pound capacity. Includes top and bottom call button, safety chair, track, power unit, installation by a licensed elevator contractor. Single family residential use					
Straight stairs	—	LS	—	—	4,340.00
Wheelchair lift (porch lift), screw driven, fully enclosed sides. Typical electrical connections and control included. Up to 5' rise					
Residential wheelchair lift	—	LS	—	—	9,800.00

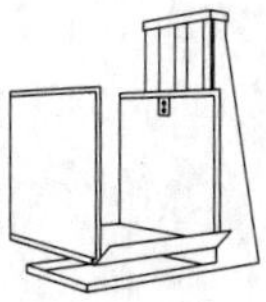

Engineering Fees

	Craft@Hrs	Unit	Material	Labor	Total
Engineering Fees Typical cost for consulting work.					
Acoustical engineering (Based on an hourly wage of $70.00 to $135.00)					
Environmental noise survey of a lot; includes technician with measuring equipment, data reduction and analysis, and written report with recommendations					
Written report with recommendations	—	LS	—	—	2,020.00
Exterior to interior noise analysis	—	LS	—	—	663.00
Measure "Impact Insulation Class" and "Sound Transmission Class" in existing buildings, (walls, floors, and ceilings)					
Minimum cost	—	LS	—	—	1,320.00
Priced by wall, floor, or ceiling sections					
Per section, approx. 100 SF	—	Ea	—	—	662.00
Analyze office, conference room, or examining room to assure acoustical privacy					
Per room analyzed	—	LS	—	—	582.00
Prepare acoustical design for church, auditorium, or lecture hall, (fees vary greatly with complexity of acoustics desired)					
Typical cost	—	LS	—	—	2,470.00
Evaluate noise problems from proposed building					
Impact on surrounding environment	—	LS	—	—	1,320.00
Evaluate noise problems from surrounding environment					
Impact on a proposed building	—	LS	—	—	1,080.00
Front end scheduling. Coordinate architectural, engineering and other consultant services, plan check times and other approval times					
For residential and commercial projects	—	LS	—	—	7,710.00
Project scheduling using CPM (Critical Path Method). Includes consultation, review of construction documents, development of construction logic, and graphic schedule. Comprehensive schedules to meet government or owner specifications will cost more.					
Wood frame buildings, 1 or 2 stories	—	LS	—	—	5,150.00
Structural engineering plan check, typical 2-story, 8 to 10 unit apartment building					
Typical price per apartment building	—	LS	—	—	1,350.00
Add for underground parking	—	LS	—	—	1,100.00

Entrances, Colonial An entrance consists of two pilasters (one at each side of the exterior opening) and a crosshead at the top of the door. A decorative pediment may rest on the crosshead. No crosshead is required if the pediment includes a breastboard. No door, frame or sill costs are included in the estimates below. Unpainted urethane.

	Craft@Hrs	Unit	Material	Labor	Total
Molded one-piece pilasters with plinth blocks, per set of two pilasters					
1-1/2" wide x 86" high	BC@.800	Ea	50.90	29.90	80.80
3-1/2" wide x 81" high	BC@.800	Ea	64.00	29.90	93.90
3-1/2" wide x 108" high	BC@.800	Ea	78.70	29.90	108.60
5" wide x 108" high	BC@.800	Ea	118.00	29.90	147.90
7" wide x 90" high	BC@.800	Ea	142.00	29.90	171.90
9" wide x 90" high	BC@.800	Ea	183.00	29.90	212.90
9" wide x 108" high	BC@.800	Ea	184.00	29.90	213.90
11" wide x 144" high	BC@.800	Ea	330.00	29.90	359.90
Molded entrance crosshead, without pediment					
40" wide by 6" high	BC@.400	Ea	52.40	15.00	67.40
48" wide by 6" high	BC@.400	Ea	62.90	15.00	77.90
78" wide by 6" high	BC@.400	Ea	102.00	15.00	117.00
40" wide by 10" high	BC@.400	Ea	89.10	15.00	104.10
48" wide by 10" high	BC@.400	Ea	105.00	15.00	120.00
78" wide by 10" high	BC@.400	Ea	166.00	15.00	181.00

	Craft@Hrs	Unit	Material	Labor	Total
40" wide by 14" high	BC@.400	Ea	156.00	15.00	171.00
48" wide by 14" high	BC@.400	Ea	192.00	15.00	207.00
78" wide by 14" high	BC@.400	Ea	233.00	15.00	248.00
96" wide by 14" high	BC@.400	Ea	295.00	15.00	310.00
Molded pediment without breastboard (crosshead required)					
38" wide, 10" high peaked cap	BC@.400	Ea	112.00	15.00	127.00
48" wide, 13" high peaked cap	BC@.400	Ea	203.00	15.00	218.00
78" wide, 21" high peaked cap	BC@.400	Ea	214.00	15.00	229.00
42" wide, 12" high decorative acorn	BC@.400	Ea	105.00	15.00	120.00
56" wide, 13" high decorative acorn	BC@.400	Ea	94.70	15.00	109.70
78" wide, 16" high decorative acorn	BC@.400	Ea	199.00	15.00	214.00
49" wide, 18" high ram's head	BC@.400	Ea	183.00	15.00	198.00
61" wide, 21" high ram's head	BC@.400	Ea	172.00	15.00	187.00
91" wide, 29" high ram's head	BC@.400	Ea	252.00	15.00	267.00
Molded pediment with breastboard (no crosshead required)					
40" wide, 17" high peaked cap	BC@.400	Ea	112.00	15.00	127.00
48" wide, 19" high peaked cap	BC@.400	Ea	136.00	15.00	151.00
80" wide, 29" high peaked cap	BC@.400	Ea	219.00	15.00	234.00
50" wide, 21" high decorative acorn	BC@.400	Ea	115.00	15.00	130.00
58" wide, 22" high decorative acorn	BC@.400	Ea	158.00	15.00	173.00
80" wide, 26" high decorative acorn	BC@.400	Ea	210.00	15.00	225.00
50" wide, 24" high ram's head	BC@.400	Ea	183.00	15.00	198.00
58" wide, 25" high ram's head	BC@.400	Ea	227.00	15.00	242.00
80" wide, 36" high ram's head	BC@.400	Ea	300.00	15.00	315.00

Excavation and Backfill by Hand Using hand tools.

	Craft@Hrs	Unit	Material	Labor	Total
General excavation, using a pick and shovel (loosening and one throw)					
Light soil	BL@1.10	CY	—	33.30	33.30
Average soil	BL@1.70	CY	—	51.50	51.50
Heavy soil or loose rock	BL@2.25	CY	—	68.20	68.20
Backfilling (one shovel throw from stockpile)					
Sand	BL@.367	CY	—	11.10	11.10
Average soil	BL@.467	CY	—	14.20	14.20
Rock or clay	BL@.625	CY	—	18.90	18.90
Add for compaction, average soil or sand	BL@.400	CY	—	12.10	12.10
Fine grading	BL@.008	SF	—	.24	.24
Footings, light soil, using a pick and shovel					
6" deep x 12" wide (1.85 CY per CLF)	BL@.034	LF	—	1.03	1.03
8" deep x 12" wide (2.47 CY per CLF)	BL@.050	LF	—	1.52	1.52
8" deep x 16" wide (3.29 CY per CLF)	BL@.055	LF	—	1.67	1.67
8" deep x 18" wide (3.70 CY per CLF)	BL@.060	LF	—	1.82	1.82
10" deep x 12" wide (3.09 CY per CLF)	BL@.050	LF	—	1.52	1.52
10" deep x 16" wide (4.12 CY per CLF)	BL@.067	LF	—	2.03	2.03
10" deep x 18" wide (4.63 CY per CLF)	BL@.075	LF	—	2.27	2.27
12" deep x 12" wide (3.70 CY per CLF)	BL@.060	LF	—	1.82	1.82
12" deep x 16" wide (4.94 CY per CLF)	BL@.081	LF	—	2.46	2.46
12" deep x 20" wide (6.17 CY per CLF)	BL@.100	LF	—	3.03	3.03
12" deep x 24" wide (7.41 CY per CLF)	BL@.125	LF	—	3.79	3.79
16" deep x 16" wide (6.59 CY per CLF)	BL@.110	LF	—	3.33	3.33
Add for average soil - loose rock or roots	—	%	—	50.0	—
Loading trucks (shoveling, one throw)					
Average soil	BL@1.45	CY	—	43.90	43.90
Rock or clay	BL@2.68	CY	—	81.20	81.20

	Craft@Hrs	Unit	Material	Labor	Total
Pits to 5' (pits over 5' require shoring)					
Light soil	BL@1.34	CY	—	40.60	40.60
Average soil	BL@2.00	CY	—	60.60	60.60
Heavy soil	BL@2.75	CY	—	83.40	83.40
Shaping trench bottom for pipe					
To 10" pipe	BL@.024	LF	—	.73	.73
12" to 20" pipe	BL@.076	LF	—	2.30	2.30
Shaping embankment slopes					
Up to 1 in 4 slope	BL@.060	SY	—	1.82	1.82
Over 1 in 4 slope	BL@.075	SY	—	2.27	2.27
Add for top crown or toe	—	%	—	50.0	—
Add for swales	—	%	—	90.0	—
Spreading material piled on site					
Average soil	BL@.367	CY	—	11.10	11.10
Stone or clay	BL@.468	CY	—	14.20	14.20
Strip and pile top soil, depths to 6"	BL@.024	SF	—	.73	.73
Tamping, hand tamp only	BL@.612	CY	—	18.50	18.50
Trenches to 5', soil piled beside trench					
Light soil	BL@1.13	CY	—	34.30	34.30
Average soil	BL@1.84	CY	—	55.80	55.80
Heavy soil or loose rock	BL@2.86	CY	—	86.70	86.70

Trenching and Backfill with Heavy Equipment These costs and productivity are based on utility line trenches and continuous footings where the spoil is piled adjacent to the trench. Linear feet (LF) and cubic yards (CY) per hour shown are based on a crew of two. Reduce productivity by 10% to 25% when spoil is loaded in trucks. Shoring, dewatering or unusual conditions are not included.

	Craft@Hrs	Unit	Material	Labor	Equipment	Total
Wheel loader 55 HP, with integral backhoe						
12" wide bucket, for 12" wide trench. Depths 3' to 5'						
Light soil (60 LF per hour)	B8@.033	LF	—	1.20	.74	1.94
Medium soil (55 LF per hour)	B8@.036	LF	—	1.31	.81	2.12
Heavy or wet soil (35 LF per hour)	B8@.057	LF	—	2.08	1.29	3.37
18" wide bucket, for 18" wide trench. Depths 3' to 5'						
Light soil (55 LF per hour)	B8@.036	LF	—	1.31	.81	2.12
Medium soil (50 LF per hour)	B8@.040	LF	—	1.46	.90	2.36
Heavy or wet soil (30 LF per hour)	B8@.067	LF	—	2.45	1.51	3.96
24" wide bucket, for 24" wide trench. Depths 3' to 5'						
Light soil (50 LF per hour)	B8@.040	LF	—	1.46	.90	2.36
Medium soil (45 LF per hour)	B8@.044	LF	—	1.61	.99	2.60
Heavy or wet soil (25 LF per hour)	B8@.080	LF	—	2.92	1.80	4.72
Backfill trenches from loose material piled adjacent to trench. No compaction included.						
Soil, previously excavated						
Front-end loader 60 HP (50 CY per hour)	B8@.040	CY	—	1.46	.80	2.26
D-3 crawler dozer (25 CY per hour)	B8@.080	CY	—	2.92	2.19	5.11
3/4 CY crawler loader (33 CY per hour)	B8@.061	CY	—	2.23	1.37	3.60
D-7 crawler dozer (130 CY per hour)	B8@.015	CY	—	.55	.90	1.45
Sand or gravel bedding						
3/4 CY wheel loader (80 CY per hour)	B8@.025	CY	—	.91	.41	1.32

	Craft@Hrs	Unit	Material	Labor	Equipment	Total
Compaction of soil in trenches in 8" layers						
Pneumatic tampers						
(40 CY per hour)	BL@.050	CY	—	1.52	1.34	2.86
Vibrating rammers, gasoline powered "Jumping Jack"						
(20 CY per hour)	BL@.100	CY	—	3.03	1.19	4.22

	Craft@Hrs	Unit	Material	Labor	Total

Excavation with Heavy Equipment These figures assume a crew of one operator unless noted otherwise. Only labor costs are included here. See equipment rental costs at the end of this section. Use the productivity rates listed here to determine the number of hours or days that the equipment will be needed. For larger jobs and commercial work, see excavation costs under Site Work in the Commercial and Industrial division of this book.

	Craft@Hrs	Unit	Material	Labor	Total
Excavation rule of thumb for small jobs	—	CY	—	2.85	2.85
Backhoe, operator and one laborer, 3/4 CY bucket					
Light soil (13.2 CY per hour)	B8@.152	CY	—	5.55	5.55
Average soil (12.5 CY per hour)	B8@.160	CY	—	5.84	5.84
Heavy soil (10.3 CY per hour)	B8@.194	CY	—	7.08	7.08
Sand (16 CY per hour)	B8@.125	CY	—	4.56	4.56
Add when using 1/2 CY bucket	—	%	—	25.0	—
Bulldozer, 65 HP unit					
Backfill (36 CY per hour)	OE@.027	CY	—	1.15	1.15
Clearing brush (900 SF per hour)	OE@.001	SF	—	.04	.04
Add for thick brush	—	%	—	300.0	—
Spread dumped soil (42 CY per hour)	OE@.024	CY	—	1.03	1.03
Strip topsoil (17 CY per hour)	OE@.059	CY	—	2.52	2.52
Bulldozer, 90 HP unit					
Backfill (40 CY per hour)	OE@.025	CY	—	1.07	1.07
Clearing brush (1,000 SF per hour)	OE@.001	SF	—	.04	.04
Add for thick brush	—	%	—	300.0	—
Spread dumped soil (45 CY per hour)	OE@.023	CY	—	.98	.98
Strip top soil (20 CY per hour)	OE@.050	CY	—	2.14	2.14
Bulldozer, 140 HP unit					
Backfill (53 CY per hour)	OE@.019	CY	—	.81	.81
Clearing brush (1,250 SF per hour)	OE@.001	SF	—	.04	.04
Add for thick brush	—	%	—	200.0	—
Spread dumped soil (63 CY per hour)	OE@.016	CY	—	.68	.68
Strip top soil (25 CY per hour)	OE@.040	CY	—	1.71	1.71
Dump truck, spot, load, unload, travel					
3 CY truck					
Short haul (9 CY per hour)	B7@.222	CY	—	6.82	6.82
2-3 mile haul (6 CY per hour)	B7@.333	CY	—	10.20	10.20
4 mile haul (4 CY per hour)	B7@.500	CY	—	15.40	15.40
5 mile haul (3 CY per hour)	B7@.666	CY	—	20.50	20.50
4 CY truck					
Short haul (11 CY per hour)	B7@.182	CY	—	5.59	5.59
2-3 mile haul (7 CY per hour)	B7@.286	CY	—	8.79	8.79
4 mile haul (5.5 CY per hour)	B7@.364	CY	—	11.20	11.20
5 mile haul (4.5 CY per hour)	B7@.444	CY	—	13.60	13.60
5 CY truck					
Short haul (14 CY per hour)	B7@.143	CY	—	4.39	4.39
2-3 mile haul (9.5 CY per hour)	B7@.211	CY	—	6.48	6.48
4 mile haul (6.5 CY per hour)	B7@.308	CY	—	9.46	9.46
5 mile haul (5.5 CY per hour)	B7@.364	CY	—	11.20	11.20

Excavation Equipment Rental

	Craft@Hrs	Unit	Material	Labor	Total
Jackhammer, one laborer (per CY of unloosened soil)					
Average soil (2-1/2 CY per hour)	BL@.400	CY	—	12.10	12.10
Heavy soil (2 CY per hour)	BL@.500	CY	—	15.20	15.20
Igneous or dense rock (.7 CY per hour)	BL@1.43	CY	—	43.30	43.30
Most weathered rock (1.2 CY per hour)	BL@.833	CY	—	25.20	25.20
Soft sedimentary rock (2 CY per hour)	BL@.500	CY	—	15.20	15.20
Air tamp (3 CY per hour)	BL@.333	CY	—	10.10	10.10
Loader (tractor shovel)					
Piling earth on premises, 1 CY bucket					
Light soil (43 CY per hour)	OE@.023	CY	—	.98	.98
Heavy soil (35 CY per hour)	OE@.029	CY	—	1.24	1.24
Loading trucks, 1 CY bucket					
Light soil (53 CY per hour)	OE@.019	CY	—	.81	.81
Average soil (43 CY per hour)	OE@.023	CY	—	.98	.98
Heavy soil (40 CY per hour)	OE@.025	CY	—	1.07	1.07
Deduct for 2-1/4 CY bucket	—	%	—	-43.0	—
Sheepsfoot roller (18.8 CSF per hour)	OE@.001	SF	—	.04	.04
Sprinkling with truck, (62.3 CSF per hour)	TR@.001	SF	—	.03	.03
Tree and brush removal, labor only (clear and grub, one operator and one laborer)					
Light brush	B8@34.8	Acre	—	1,270.00	1,270.00
Heavy brush	B8@45.2	Acre	—	1,650.00	1,650.00
Wooded	B8@48.7	Acre	—	1,780.00	1,780.00
Tree removal, cutting trees, removing branches, cutting into short lengths with chain saws and axes, by tree diameter, labor only					
8" to 12" (5 manhours per tree)	BL@5.00	Ea	—	152.00	152.00
13" to 18" (7 manhours per tree)	BL@7.00	Ea	—	212.00	212.00
19" to 24" (11 manhours per tree)	BL@11.0	Ea	—	333.00	333.00
25" to 36" (14 manhours per tree)	BL@14.0	Ea	—	424.00	424.00
Tree stump removal, using a small backhoe, by tree diameter, operator only					
6" to 10" (1.6 manhours per stump)	OE@1.60	Ea	—	68.30	68.30
11" to 14" (2.1 manhours per stump)	OE@2.10	Ea	—	89.70	89.70
15" to 18" (2.6 manhours per stump)	OE@2.60	Ea	—	111.00	111.00
19" to 24" (3.1 manhours per stump)	OE@3.10	Ea	—	132.00	132.00
25" to 30" (3.3 manhours per stump)	OE@3.30	Ea	—	141.00	141.00
Trenching machine, crawler-mounted					
Light soil (27 CY per hour)	OE@.037	CY	—	1.58	1.58
Heavy soil (21 CY per hour)	OE@.048	CY	—	2.05	2.05
Add for pneumatic-tired machine	—	%	—	15.0	—

Excavation Equipment Rental Costs Typical cost not including fuel, delivery or pickup charges. Add labor costs from the previous section. Half day minimums.

	1/2 day	Day	Week
Backhoe, wheeled mounted			
55 HP unit, 1/8 to 3/4 CY bucket	291.00	416.00	1,150.00
65 HP unit, 1/4 to 1 CY bucket	341.00	487.00	1,580.00
Add for each delivery or pickup	160.00	160.00	160.00
Bulldozer, crawler tractor			
65 HP	354.00	505.00	1,510.00
90 to 105 HP unit, D-4 or D-5	467.00	667.00	1,800.00
140 HP unit, D-6	638.00	912.00	2,600.00
Add for each delivery or pickup	160.00	160.00	160.00

	1/2 day	Day	Week
Dump truck, on-highway type			
3 CY	298.00	426.00	1,120.00
5 CY	315.00	450.00	1,180.00
10 CY	664.00	949.00	3,000.00
Wheel loaders, front-end load and dump, diesel			
3/4 CY bucket, 4WD, articulated	138.00	197.00	691.00
1 CY bucket, 4WD, articulated	280.00	400.00	1,050.00
2 CY bucket, 4WD, articulated	385.00	550.00	1,660.00
3-1/4 CY bucket, 4WD, articulated	606.00	866.00	2,490.00
5 CY bucket, 4WD, articulated	714.00	1,020.00	3,070.00
Add for each delivery or pickup	160.00	160.00	160.00
Sheepsfoot roller, towed type, 40" diameter, 48" wide, double drum	144.00	206.00	626.00
Trenching machine, to 5'6" depth, 6" to 16" width capacity, crawler-mounted type	166.00	237.00	778.00
Add for each delivery or pickup	160.00	160.00	160.00
Compactor, 32" plate width, manually guided, gasoline engine, vibratory plate type	239.00	342.00	861.00
Chain saw, 18" to 23" bar, gasoline engine	110.00	157.00	379.00
Breakers, pavement, medium duty, with blade Including 50' of 1" hose	67.00	96.00	276.00
Air compressors, trailer-mounted, gas powered, silenced			
100 CFM to 150 CFM	143.00	204.00	526.00
175 CFM	251.00	358.00	919.00

Fans

Economy ceiling and wall exhaust fan. For baths, utility, and recreation rooms. For baths up to 45 square feet, other rooms up to 60 square feet. Installs in ceiling or in wall. Plastic duct collar. White polymeric grille. UL listed for use in tub and shower enclosure with GFI branch circuit wiring. Housing dimensions: 8-1/16-inch length, 7-3/16-inch width, 3-7/8-inch depth. Grille size, 8-11/16-inch x 9-1/2-inch. 3-inch duct. 0.75 amp. CFM (cubic feet of air per minute). Labor includes setting and connecting only. Add the cost of wiring and ducting.

	Craft@Hrs	Unit	Material	Labor	Total
50 CFM, 2.5 sones	BE@1.00	Ea	14.80	40.60	55.40
70 CFM, 4.0 sones	BE@1.00	Ea	35.30	40.60	75.90

Vertical discharge bath fan. Galvanized steel housing, with built-in damper and spin-on white polymeric grille. Polymeric fan blade and duct connectors. Built-in double steel mounting ears with keyhole slots. Fits 8-inch ducts. UL listed. CFM (cubic feet of air per minute). Labor includes setting and connecting only. Add the cost of wiring and ducting.

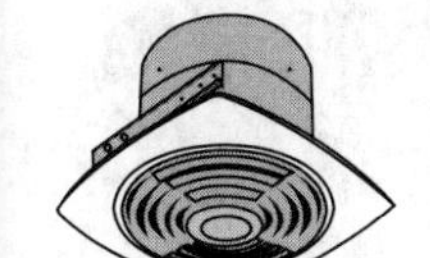

	Craft@Hrs	Unit	Material	Labor	Total
80 CFM, 1.0 sones	BE@1.00	Ea	99.00	40.60	139.60

Vertical discharge utility fan. Mounts in ceiling. Discharges through duct to roof or wall. Pre-wired motor with plug-in receptacle. Adjustable hanger bars for 16- or 24-inch on-center joists. Silver anodized aluminum grille. Fits 7-inch round ducts. Housing dimensions: 11-inch diameter x 5-5/8-inch deep. UL listed. CFM (cubic feet of air per minute). Labor includes setting and connecting only. Add the cost of wiring and ducting.

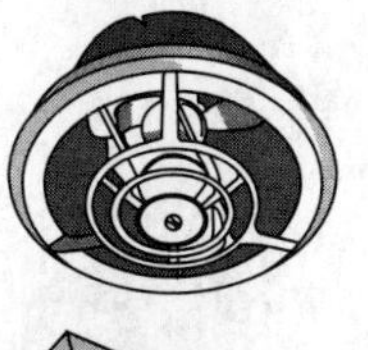

	Craft@Hrs	Unit	Material	Labor	Total
210 CFM, 6.5 sones	BE@1.00	Ea	67.70	40.60	108.30

Ceiling or wall bath exhaust fan. White polymeric grille. Torsion spring grille mounting requires no tools. Plug-in, permanently lubricated motor. Centrifugal blower wheel. Rugged, 26 gauge galvanized steel housing. Sturdy key holes mounting brackets for quick, accurate installation. Tapered, polymeric duct fitting with built-in backdraft damper. U.L. listed for use over bathtubs and showers when connected to a GFCI circuit. 120 volts, 0.5 amps, 2.5 sones, 80 CFM (HVI-2100 certified) and 4-inch round duct. Labor includes setting and connecting only. Add the cost of wiring and ducting.

	Craft@Hrs	Unit	Material	Labor	Total
80 CFM, 2.5 sones	BE@1.00	Ea	71.80	40.60	112.40

	Craft@Hrs	Unit	Material	Labor	Total

Bath exhaust fan. Pre-wired outlet box for plug-in receptacle, torsion spring-mounted low-profile grille. Steel housing, damper to eliminate back drafts. Labor includes setting and connecting only. Add the cost of wiring and ducting.

80 CFM, 2.5 sones, to 80 SF bath	BE@1.00	Ea	99.50	40.60	140.10

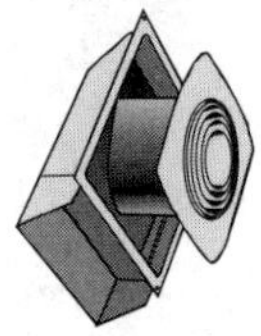

Thru-the-wall utility fan. Steel housing with built-in damper and white polymeric grille. Permanently lubricated motor. Rotary on and off switch. Housing dimensions: 14-1/4-inch length, 14-1/4-inch width, 4-1/2-inch depth. UL listed. CFM (cubic feet of air per minute). Labor includes setting and connecting only. Add the cost of wiring and exterior finish.

180 CFM, 5.0 sones	BE@1.00	Ea	67.60	40.60	108.20

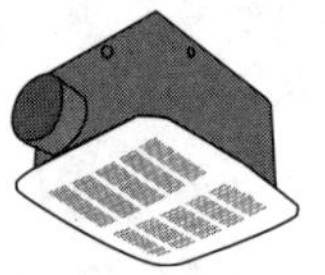

QuieTTest® low-sound bath fan. For 105 square foot bath. Pre-wired outlet box with plug-in receptacle. Adjustable hanger brackets. Fits 4-inch round ducts. Low-profile white polymeric grille, torsion-spring mounted. Housing dimensions: 9-3/8-inch length, 11-1/4-inch width, 7-7/8-inch depth. Grille size, 14-1/4-inch x 12-1/16-inch. UL listed for use in tub and shower when used with GFI branch circuit wiring. Not recommended for kitchen use. CFM (cubic feet of air per minute). Labor includes setting and connecting only. Add the cost of wiring and ducting.

110 CFM, 2.0 sones	BE@1.00	Ea	126.00	40.60	166.60

QuieTTest® low-sound ceiling blower. For 375 square foot room. Pre-wired outlet box with plug-in receptacle. Rounded, low-profile white polymeric grille with silver anodized trim at each end. Fits 3-1/4-inch x 10-inch ducts. Housing dimensions: 14-1/4-inch length, 10-inch width, 9-inch depth. Grille size, 16-1/2-inch x 12-3/32 inch. CFM (cubic feet of air per minute). Labor includes setting and connecting only. Add the cost of wiring and ducting.

300 CFM, 4.5 sones	BE@1.00	Ea	153.00	40.60	193.60

Lighted Bath Exhaust Fans

ValueTest™ economy bath fan and light, NuTone. Fan and light operate separately or together. Fits 4-inch ducts. White polymeric grille with break-resistant lens. Uses 100-watt lamp (not included). Housing dimensions: 9-inch length, 9-inch width, 5-1/2-inch depth. Grille size, 10-3/4-inch x 12-1/8-inch. UL listed for use in tub and shower when used with GFI branch circuit wiring. CFM (cubic feet of air per minute). Labor includes setting and connecting only. Add the cost of wiring and ducting.

50 CFM, 2.5 sones, 45 SF bath	BE@1.00	Ea	34.80	40.60	75.40
70 CFM, 4.5 sones, 65 SF bath	BE@1.00	Ea	75.70	40.60	116.30

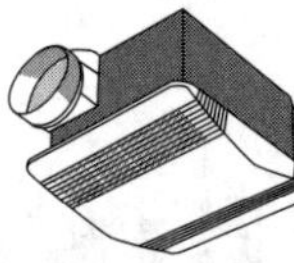

Decorative bath exhaust fan with light, Broan Manufacturing. Corrosion-resistant finish. Frosted melon glass globe. 60 watt max. CFM (cubic feet of air per minute). Labor includes setting and connecting only. Add the cost of wiring and ducting.

70 CFM, 3.5 sones	BE@1.00	Ea	78.20	40.60	118.80

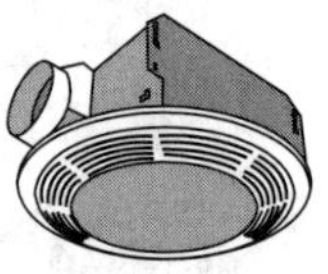

Exhaust Air deluxe bath fan with light, NuTone. Ventilation for baths up to 95 square feet, other rooms up to 125 square feet. 100 and 7 watt ceiling and night-light or energy-saving fluorescent light (lamps not included). Snap-on grille assembly. Housing dimensions: 9-inch length, 9-inch width, 6-inch depth. Polymeric white grille, 15-inch diameter. UL listed for use in tub and shower when used with GFI branch circuit wiring. CFM (cubic feet of air per minute). Labor includes setting and connecting only. Add the cost of wiring and ducting.

100 CFM, 3.5 sones	BE@1.00	Ea	97.60	40.60	138.20

Bath Exhaust Fan with Heater

Infrared bulb heater and fan. 4-point adjustable mounting brackets span up to 24-inches. Uses 250 watt, 120 volt R-40 infrared bulbs (not included). Heater and fan units include 70 CFM, 3.5 sones ventilator fan. Damper and duct connector included. Plastic matte-white molded grille and compact housings. CFM (cubic feet of air per minute). Labor includes setting and connecting only. Add the cost of wiring and ducting.

1-bulb, 70 CFM, 3.5 sones	BE@1.00	Ea	65.40	40.60	106.00
2-bulb heater, 7" duct	BE@1.10	Ea	79.90	44.70	124.60

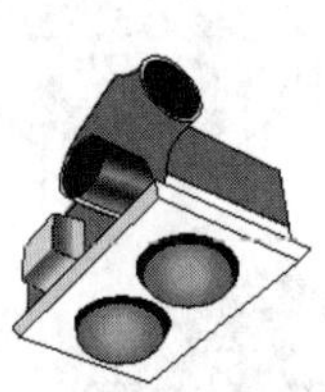

	Craft@Hrs	Unit	Material	Labor	Total
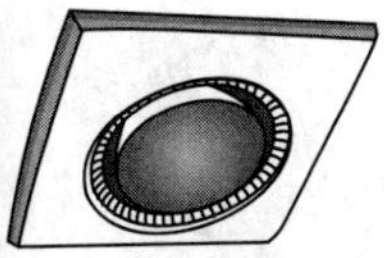 Heat-A-Lamp® bulb heater and fan, NuTone. Non-IC. Swivel-mount. Torsion spring holds plates firmly to ceiling. 250-watt radiant heat from one R-40 infrared heat lamp. Uses 4-inch duct. Adjustable socket for ceilings up to 1-inch thick. Adjustable hanger bars. Automatic reset for thermal protection. White polymeric finish. UL listed. Btu (British Thermal Unit). 6-7/8" high. Labor includes setting and connecting only. Add the cost of wiring and ducting.					
2.6 amp, 1 lamp, 12-1/2" x 10"	BE@1.50	Ea	58.30	60.90	119.20
5.0 amp, 2 lamp, 15-3/8" x 11"	BE@1.50	Ea	87.50	60.90	148.40
Surface-mount ceiling bath resistance heater and fan. 1250 watt. 4266 Btu (British Thermal Unit). 120 volt. Chrome alloy wire element for instant heat. Built-in fan. Automatic overheat protection. Low-profile housing. Permanently lubricated motor. Mounts to standard 3-1/4-inch round or 4-inch octagonal ceiling electrical box. Satin-finish aluminum grille extends 2-3/4-inch from ceiling. 11" diameter x 2-3/4" deep. Labor includes setting and connecting only. Add the cost of wiring and ducting.					
10.7 amp	BE@.750	Ea	68.60	30.50	99.10
Designer Series bath heater and exhaust fan, Broan Manufacturing. 1500-watt fan-forced heater. 120-watt light capacity, 7-watt night-light (bulbs not included). Permanently lubricated motor. Polymeric damper prevents cold back drafts. 4-point adjustable mounting brackets with keyhole slots. Torsion-spring grille mounting, no tools needed. Non-glare light diffusing glass lenses. Fits single gang opening. Suitable for use with insulation. Includes 4-function control unit. CFM (cubic feet of air per minute). 100 CFM, 1.2 sones. Labor includes setting and connecting only. Add the cost of wiring and ducting.					
4" duct, 100 watt lamp	BE@1.00	Ea	273.00	40.60	313.60
Exhaust Fan Accessories					
Timer switch					
60-minute timer, analog	BE@.250	Ea	24.90	10.20	35.10
60-minute timer, digital	BE@.250	Ea	21.70	10.20	31.90
Exhaust fan switch					
On/Off switch with humidity control, white	BE@.300	Ea	30.60	12.20	42.80
SensAire® 4-function wall control switch. Fits single gang opening. Top switch for on-auto-off. Other switches for light and night-light. For use with SensAire® fans and lights.					
White	BE@.250	Ea	23.50	10.20	33.70
Bath vent kit, thru-wall, UL listed, 5' of 4" duct, polymeric louvered wall cap, 3" to 4" increaser and 2 clamps. Fire resistant.					
Flexible duct	SW@.650	Ea	19.60	27.40	47.00
Roof vent kit. For venting kitchen or bath exhaust fan through slanted roof. Works with both 3-inch and 4-inch ducted units.					
8-foot length	SW@.650	Ea	26.20	27.40	53.60
Ventilators					
Roof turbine vent with base 					
12", galvanized	SW@1.00	Ea	28.30	42.20	70.50
12", weathered wood	SW@1.00	Ea	66.90	42.20	109.10
12", white aluminum	SW@1.00	Ea	66.90	42.20	109.10
Add for steep pitch base	SW@.440	Ea	10.30	18.60	28.90
Add for weather cap	—	Ea	12.00	—	12.00
Belt drive attic exhaust fan, 1/3 HP, with aluminum shutter and plenum boards					
24" diameter	SW@3.00	Ea	246.00	126.00	372.00
30" diameter	SW@3.00	Ea	338.00	126.00	464.00
36" diameter	SW@3.00	Ea	343.00	126.00	469.00
Add for wifi controls	—	Ea	220.00	—	220.00
Deduct for direct drive exhaust fans	—	%	−15.0	—	—
12-hour timer switch	BE@.950	Ea	42.70	38.60	81.30

Fans

	Craft@Hrs	Unit	Material	Labor	Total
Power attic gable vent					
1,280 CFM	SW@1.65	Ea	72.30	69.60	141.90
1,540 CFM	SW@1.65	Ea	91.00	69.60	160.60
1,600 CFM	SW@1.65	Ea	101.00	69.60	170.60
Shutter for gable vent	SW@.450	Ea	42.00	19.00	61.00
Humidistat control	BE@.550	Ea	30.10	22.30	52.40
Thermostat control	BE@.550	Ea	26.30	22.30	48.60
Roof-mount power ventilator					
1,250 CFM	SW@1.65	Ea	92.40	69.60	162.00
1,600 CFM	SW@1.65	Ea	149.00	69.60	218.60

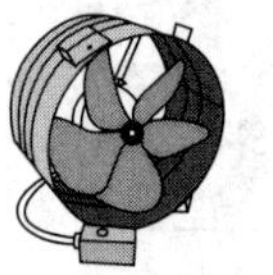

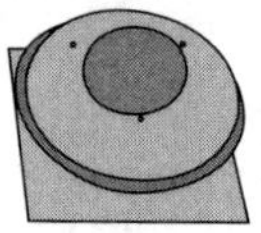

Ceiling Fans

Ceiling fans, decorative, 3-speed reversible motors, lighting kits optional (see below). Includes 10' of type NM cable, installation and connection.

	Craft@Hrs	Unit	Material	Labor	Total
42" four-blade fan, white finish	BE@1.50	Ea	87.20	60.90	148.10
44" five blade fan with 3 spotlights	BE@1.50	Ea	95.20	60.90	156.10
44" five-blade reversible fan	BE@1.50	Ea	117.00	60.90	177.90
48" five rattan blade fan	BE@1.50	Ea	173.00	60.90	233.90
56" five-blade leaf design premium fan	BE@1.50	Ea	269.00	60.90	329.90
Optional lighting fixtures for ceiling fans					
Vaulted ceiling mount	BE@.350	Ea	22.60	14.20	36.80
Schoolhouse or round globe, brass trim	BE@.283	Ea	20.30	11.50	31.80
Add for ball pull chain	BE@.017	Ea	5.81	.69	6.50
Add for pack of four ceiling fan light bulbs	BE@.017	Pack	10.20	.69	10.89

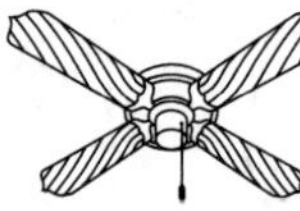

Garage exhaust fans For enclosed automotive garage space. U.S. Green Building Council, Underwriters Laboratories and CSA approved. Includes tamper-proof metal enclosure, sensor, fan actuator, weatherproof exhaust grille and cover, outlet duct and relay switch. Add for electrical connection.

	Craft@Hrs	Unit	Material	Labor	Total
Home garage exhaust fan, roof or upper sidewall mount, 110 volts.					
118 CFM	SW@2.00	Ea	533.00	84.30	617.30
235 CFM	SW@2.00	Ea	595.00	84.30	679.30
416 CFM	SW@2.50	Ea	625.00	105.00	730.00
Parking garage exhaust fan, 208 volts, remote sensor controlled					
400 CFM	SW@2.00	Ea	533.00	84.30	617.30
600 CFM	SW@2.00	Ea	595.00	84.30	679.30
800 CFM	SW@2.50	Ea	625.00	105.00	730.00
1,000 CFM	SW@2.75	Ea	678.00	116.00	794.00
1,500 CFM	SW@3.00	Ea	988.00	126.00	1,114.00
2,000 CFM	SW@3.50	Ea	1,250.00	148.00	1,398.00
Mount sensors	SW@.250	Ea	511.00	10.50	521.50
Apply fan frame sealant	SW@.150	LF	2.60	6.32	8.92
Install electrical wiring	BE@.150	LF	1.89	6.09	7.98
Install controls	BE@.500	Ea	—	20.30	20.30
Commission and test	P1@4.00	Ea	—	148.00	148.00

Fencing, Chain Link

Galvanized steel, 11.5 gauge 2" x 2" fence fabric, 2-3/8" terminal post with post caps, 1-5/8" line posts at 10' with loop line post caps, 1-3/8" top rail with rail ends, tension bands, tension bars and required bolts with nuts. Material includes 2/3 CF sack of concrete per post. Use 50 LF of fence as a minimum job cost.

	Craft@Hrs	Unit	Material	Labor	Total
36" high	BL@.125	LF	4.61	3.79	8.40
42" high	BL@.125	LF	4.88	3.79	8.67

	Craft@Hrs	Unit	Material	Labor	Total
48" high	BL@.125	LF	5.20	3.79	8.99
60" high	BL@.125	LF	5.93	3.79	9.72
72" high	BL@.125	LF	6.80	3.79	10.59
Add for redwood filler strips	BL@.024	LF	5.35	.73	6.08
Add for aluminum filler strips	BL@.018	LF	6.30	.55	6.85
Add for PVC filler strips	BL@.018	LF	8.71	.55	9.26
Gates, driveway or walkway. Same construction as fencing shown above, assembled units ready to install. Add for gate hardware from below.					
Driveway gates, costs per linear foot (LF)					
36" high	BL@.025	LF	25.60	.76	26.36
42" high	BL@.025	LF	26.40	.76	27.16
48" high	BL@.025	LF	27.30	.76	28.06
60" high	BL@.033	LF	28.60	1.00	29.60
72" high	BL@.033	LF	30.40	1.00	31.40
3'6" wide walkway gate, costs per gate					
36" high	BL@.500	Ea	102.00	15.20	117.20
42" high	BL@.500	Ea	105.00	15.20	120.20
48" high	BL@.500	Ea	108.00	15.20	123.20
60" high	BL@.666	Ea	114.00	20.20	134.20
72" high	BL@.666	Ea	118.00	20.20	138.20
Add for gate hardware, per gate. Labor is included with labor shown for gate above. Includes latch, hanger brackets, bolts and hinge.					
Driveway gate hardware					
36" or 42" high	—	Ea	35.70	—	35.70
48" or 60" high	—	Ea	35.70	—	35.70
72" high	—	Ea	35.70	—	35.70
Walkway gate hardware					
36" or 42" high	—	Ea	10.90	—	10.90
48" or 60" high	—	Ea	10.90	—	10.90
72" high	—	Ea	10.90	—	10.90
Pet enclosure fencing panels. Chain link fence, galvanized steel, 11 gauge, 2" x 2" mesh fence fabric, 1-3/8" tubular steel frame, does not include any foundation costs.					
5'H x 3'W, panel	BL@.750	Ea	103.00	22.70	125.70
5'H x 4'W, panel	BL@.750	Ea	107.00	22.70	129.70
5'H x 6'W, panel	BL@.850	Ea	116.00	25.80	141.80
6'H x 3'W, panel	BL@.750	Ea	108.00	22.70	130.70
6'H x 4'W, panel	BL@.750	Ea	113.00	22.70	135.70
6'H x 6'W, panel	BL@.850	Ea	122.00	25.80	147.80
8'H x 6'W, panel	BL@1.00	Ea	148.00	30.30	178.30
5'H x 4'W, panel w/ gate	BL@1.00	Ea	216.00	30.30	246.30
5'H x 8'W, panel w/ gate	BL@1.50	Ea	233.00	45.50	278.50
6'H x 4'W, panel w/ gate	BL@1.00	Ea	226.00	30.30	256.30
6'H x 8'W, panel w/ gate	BL@1.50	Ea	245.00	45.50	290.50
8'H x 6'W, panel w/ gate	BL@4.75	Ea	282.00	144.00	426.00

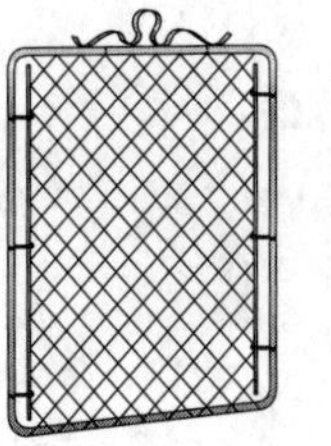

Fence, Galvanized Wire Mesh With 1-5/8" galvanized steel posts, set without concrete 10' OC.
12-1/2 gauge steel, 12" vertical wire spacing

	Craft@Hrs	Unit	Material	Labor	Total
36" high, 6 horizontal wires	BL@.127	LF	2.61	3.85	6.46
48" high, 8 horizontal wires	BL@.127	LF	2.82	3.85	6.67
60" high, 8 horizontal wires	BL@.127	LF	3.02	3.85	6.87
72" high, 8 horizontal wires	BL@.127	LF	3.25	3.85	7.10

	Craft@Hrs	Unit	Material	Labor	Total
11 gauge fence fabric, 9" vertical wire spacing					
42" high, 8 horizontal wires	BL@.127	LF	2.77	3.85	6.62
48" high, 9 horizontal wires	BL@.127	LF	3.04	3.85	6.89
14 gauge fence fabric, 6" vertical wire spacing					
36" high, 8 horizontal wires	BL@.127	LF	2.98	3.85	6.83
48" high, 9 horizontal wires	BL@.127	LF	2.62	3.85	6.47
60" high, 10 horizontal wires	BL@.127	LF	3.22	3.85	7.07
Add for components for electrified galvanized wire mesh fence					
15 gauge aluminum wire, single strand	BL@.050	LF	.26	1.52	1.78
12-1/2 gauge barbed wire, 4 barbs per LF	BL@.050	LF	.12	1.52	1.64
Charging unit for electric fence, Solar powered,					
10 mile range, built in 6V battery	BL@.500	Ea	199.00	15.20	214.20
Charging unit, Solar powered,					
3 mile range, indoors or out	BL@.500	Ea	137.00	15.20	152.20
Charging unit, 110V,					
15 mile range, indoors or out	BL@.500	Ea	52.80	15.20	68.00
Fence stays for barbed wire, 48" high	BL@.250	Ea	1.10	7.58	8.68
Add for electric fence warning sign					
Yellow with black lettering	BL@.125	Ea	1.00	3.79	4.79
Add for polyethylene insulators	BL@.250	Ea	.26	7.58	7.84
Add for non-conductive gate fastener	BL@.500	Ea	4.74	15.20	19.94
Add for lightning arrestor kit	BL@.500	Ea	11.30	15.20	26.50

Fence Post Holes

Based on holes 1' diameter and 2' deep with easy access on level terrain. Adjustments for other conditions are below. Per hole dug.

	Craft@Hrs	Unit	Material	Labor	Total
Excavate post hole by hand					
Light soil, sand or loam	BL@.400	Ea	—	12.10	12.10
Medium soil, gravel or light clay	BL@.600	Ea	—	18.20	18.20
Heavy soil, shale, sandstone, rocky	BL@1.00	Ea	—	30.30	30.30
Excavate post hole with power auger. Add the auger cost.					
Light soil, sand or loam	BL@.200	Ea	—	6.06	6.06
Medium soil, gravel or light clay	BL@.250	Ea	—	7.58	7.58
Heavy soil, shale, sandstone, rocky	BL@.300	Ea	—	9.09	9.09

Setting Fence Posts

Posts set with concrete, including temporary 1" x 6" bracing and stakes. Heights to 6'. Concrete assumes post hole is 1' x 1' x 2' deep. Per post set, using either wood or metal post.

	Craft@Hrs	Unit	Material	Labor	Total
Set and brace wood or metal fence post					
Lay in gravel for drainage	BL@.010	Ea	.02	.30	.32
Set 4" x 4" x 8' treated wood post	BL@.015	Ea	9.76	.45	10.21
Set 18 gauge 1-7/8" metal tube post with cap	BL@.015	Ea	18.60	.45	19.05
Check and adjust post alignment	BL@.010	Ea	—	.30	.30
Plumb and brace post (5 uses)	BL@.100	Ea	.50	3.03	3.53
Backfill with concrete or soil	BL@.030	Ea	—	.91	.91
Tamp soil or rod concrete	BL@.010	Ea	—	.30	.30
Trowel drainage crown	BL@.010	Ea	—	.30	.30
Strip bracing and inspect	BL@.020	Ea	—	.61	.61
Concrete for post base, 60 lb. sack, mixed	BL@.125	Ea	3.37	3.79	7.16
Total per fence post (wood)	BL@.330	Ea	13.65	9.99	23.64
Wood posts 10' OC, per LF of fence	BL@.033	LF	1.37	1.00	2.37
Total per fence post (metal)	BL@.330	Ea	22.49	9.99	32.48
Metal posts 10' OC, per LF of fence	BL@.033	LF	2.25	1.00	3.25

	Craft@Hrs	Unit	Material	Labor	Total
Setting Fence Rail on Wood Posts					
Stringing 2" x 4" wood rail between fence posts, including two 2" x 4" pressure treated rails at $.76 per linear foot.					
Measure opening between posts	BL@.010	Ea	—	.30	.30
Measure and cut two treated rails	BL@.015	Ea	13.00	.45	13.45
Measure rail position on post	BL@.010	Ea	—	.30	.30
Nail one end in place	BL@.010	Ea	.02	.30	.32
Position other end and check for level	BL@.020	Ea	—	.61	.61
Nail second end in place	BL@.010	Ea	.02	.30	.32
Recheck level and adjust as needed	BL@.015	Ea	—	.45	.45
Paint cut ends, post connections, rail side	BL@.100	Ea	—	3.03	3.03
Set two rails nailed in place, total	**BL@.190**	**Ea**	**13.04**	**5.74**	**18.78**
Set two rails, per LF of fence, 10' rails	**BL@.038**	**LF**	**1.30**	**.57**	**1.88**
Setting Fence Rail on Metal Posts					
Stringing 2" x 4" wood fence rail between metal posts, including 2" x 4" pressure treated rail at $.76 per linear foot and one 5" lag bolt connecting adjacent rail at each post.					
Measure opening between posts	BL@.010	Ea	—	.30	.30
Measure and cut two 10' rail	BL@.030	Ea	13.00	.91	13.91
Measure rail position on post	BL@.010	Ea	—	.30	.30
Drill 2 rail and metal tube post for lag bolt	BL@.167	Ea	—	5.06	5.06
Set two rail on tube post with lag bolt	BL@.133	Ea	1.54	4.03	5.57
Recheck level and adjust as needed	BL@.015	Ea	—	.45	.45
Paint cut ends, post connections, rail side	BL@.100	Ea	—	3.03	3.03
Set two rails, bolted in place, total	**BL@.465**	**Ea**	**14.54**	**14.08**	**28.62**
Set two rails, bolted in place, per LF of fence	**BL@.047**	**LF**	**1.45**	**1.41**	**2.86**
Installing Fence Face Board					
Hand nailing or stapling face board (pickets) to existing rail. Deduct 50% from labor costs for power nailing or power stapling. Includes measuring and cutting each picket, nailing or stapling to the top rail, plumbing with a level and nailing or stapling to the bottom rail. Two nails or staples at each rail. Cost per LF of fence. Based on 1" x 4" x 6', 1" x 6" x 6' and 1" x 8" x 6' face boards. Face board costs vary widely.					
Nailing 4" wide pressure treated southern pine fence face board (3.4 per LF of fence)					
French gothic, 1" x 4" x 3-1/2'	BL@.102	LF	2.78	3.09	5.87
French gothic, 5/8" x 4" x 4'	BL@.102	LF	4.42	3.09	7.51
Dog-eared, 7/16" x 4" x 6'	BL@.136	LF	3.91	4.12	8.03
Dog-eared, 1" x 4", 6'	BL@.136	LF	5.88	4.12	10.00
Nailing 5-1/2" wide pressure treated southern pine fence face board (2.4 per LF of fence)					
Dog-eared, 5/8" x 5-1/2" x 6'	BL@.120	LF	4.13	3.64	7.77
Nailing 6" wide pressure treated southern pine fence face board (2.2 per LF of fence)					
Dog-eared, 1" x 6" x 6'	BL@.110	LF	4.62	3.33	7.95
Dog-eared premium S4S, 1" x 6" x 6'	BL@.110	LF	5.27	3.33	8.60
Full cut premium, 1" x 6" x 6'	BL@.110	LF	4.96	3.33	8.29
Dog-eared, 5/8" x 5-1/2" x 8'	BL@.110	LF	6.12	3.33	9.45
Nailing 4" wide white wood fence face board (3.4 per LF of fence)					
Gothic, 3/4" x 4" x 6'	BL@.136	LF	6.51	4.12	10.63
Flat top, 1" x 4" x 6'	BL@.136	LF	6.64	4.12	10.76
Dog-eared, 1" x 4" x 6'	BL@.136	LF	7.09	4.12	11.21
Dog-eared, 1" x 4" x 8'	BL@.136	LF	6.70	4.12	10.82

Fencing, Wood

	Craft@Hrs	Unit	Material	Labor	Total
Nailing 4" wide cedar fence face board (3.4 per LF of fence)					
Dog-eared, No. 2, 3/4" x 4" x 8'	BL@.136	LF	10.10	4.12	14.22
Gothic, 3/4" x 4" x 6'	BL@.136	LF	6.70	4.12	10.82
Dog-eared, 9/16" x 4" x 6'	BL@.136	LF	6.70	4.12	10.82
Flat top, full-cut, 1" x 4" x 6'	BL@.136	LF	11.10	4.12	15.22
No. 1 flat top, full-cut, 1" x 4" x 8'	BL@.136	LF	13.50	4.12	17.62
Nailing 6" wide cedar fence face board (2.2 per LF of fence)					
Dog-eared, No. 2, 9/16" x 6" x 6'	BL@.110	LF	6.66	3.33	9.99
Dog-eared, No. 2, 9/16" x 6" x 8'	BL@.110	LF	11.60	3.33	14.93
Dog-eared, clear, 1" x 6" x 6'	BL@.110	LF	8.61	3.33	11.94
Flat top, full-cut, 1" x 6" x 6'	BL@.110	LF	8.68	3.33	12.01
Nailing 4" wide dog-eared common redwood fence face board (3.4 per LF of fence)					
3/4" x 4" x 6'	BL@.136	LF	6.70	4.12	10.82
Nailing 6" wide dog-eared common redwood fence face board (2.2 per LF of fence)					
3/4" x 6" x 5'	BL@.110	LF	4.59	3.33	7.92
3/4" x 6" x 6'	BL@.110	LF	7.19	3.33	10.52
3/4" x 6" x 6'	BL@.110	LF	8.86	3.33	12.19
Nailing 8" wide dog-eared common redwood fence face board (1.6 per LF of fence)					
3/4" x 8" x 6'	BL@.088	LF	7.63	2.67	10.30
3/4" x 8" x 6' Premium Const. Heart	BL@.088	LF	12.60	2.67	15.27
1" x 8" x 8'	BL@.088	LF	17.00	2.67	19.67
Nailing 10" wide dog-eared common redwood fence face board (1.3 per LF of fence)					
3/4" x 10" x 5'	BL@.072	LF	8.54	2.18	10.72
3/4" x 10" x 6'	BL@.072	LF	9.63	2.18	11.81
Nailing 12" wide dog-eared common redwood fence face board (1.05 per LF of fence)					
3/4" x 12" x 5' Rough	BL@.063	LF	9.42	1.91	11.33
3/4" x 12" x 6'	BL@.063	LF	10.50	1.91	12.41
Nailing 6" wide flat top redwood fence face board (2.2 per LF of fence)					
3/4" x 6" x 6' Const. Heart	BL@.110	LF	9.53	3.33	12.86
3/4" x 6" x 6' Merch. and Better	BL@.110	LF	9.27	3.33	12.60
3/4" x 6" x 6' Ridge Valley Redwood	BL@.110	LF	13.90	3.33	17.23
3/4" x 6" x 8' Ridge Valley Redwood	BL@.110	LF	23.40	3.33	26.73
Nailing 8" wide flat top redwood fence face board (1.6 per LF of fence)					
3/4" x 8" x 5'	BL@.088	LF	7.04	2.67	9.71
3/4" x 8" x 5' T&G	BL@.088	LF	9.89	2.67	12.56
3/4" x 8" x 6'	BL@.088	LF	8.06	2.67	10.73
3/4" x 8" x 6' Construction Heart	BL@.088	LF	13.90	2.67	16.57
1" x 8" x 8' Construction Heart	BL@.088	LF	17.00	2.67	19.67
Nailing 10" and 12" wide flat top redwood fence face board (1.3 per LF of fence for 10", 1.0 for 12")					
3/4" x 10" x 8' Redwood	BL@.072	LF	12.30	2.18	14.48
3/4" x 12" x 6' Dog-eared	BL@.072	LF	9.96	2.18	12.14
Deduct for power stapling or power nailing	—	%	—	-50.0	—

Building a Fence on a Hillside

Post hole excavation, post setting and fence erection will take longer when the site is obstructed or on a hillside. Adjust manhours as follows for sloping terrain.

Add for slope to 4 in 12	—	%	—	20.0	—
Add for slope over 4 in 12 to 8 in 12	—	%	—	50.0	—
Add for slope over 8 in 12 to 12 in 12	—	%	—	100.0	—

	Craft@Hrs	Unit	Material	Labor	Total
Build and Hang a Wood Fence Gate 5' high by 3' wide wood gate, 2" x 4" frame . Add the cost of fence posts from above. Add fence face boards from above. Units are for each gate.					
Measure, design and lay out gate	BL@.200	Ea	—	6.06	6.06
Measure and cut frame (11' x 2" x 4")	BL@.050	Ea	5.96	1.52	7.48
Nail frame together	BL@.100	Ea	.10	3.03	3.13
Square up and measure 4' diagonal brace	BL@.050	Ea	2.17	1.52	3.69
Cut cross brace and nail in place	BL@.083	Ea	.08	2.52	2.60
Square up and add metal corner brackets	BL@.333	Ea	1.25	10.10	11.35
Mark top pattern on face boards	BL@.133	Ea	—	4.03	4.03
Cut top pattern on face boards	BL@.089	Ea	—	2.70	2.70
Set hinges on gate and fence post	BL@.250	Ea	8.61	7.58	16.19
Set latch on gate and strike on fence post	BL@.100	Ea	7.60	3.03	10.63
Check and adjust as needed	BL@.125	Ea	—	3.79	3.79
Build and hang wood fence gate, total	BL@1.51	Ea	25.77	45.88	71.65

Fence Assemblies, Wood Costs shown include excavation of post holes, concrete and labor to set posts, attaching rails with nails or lag bolts, and hand nailing of face boards where applicable. See additional costs at the end of this section.

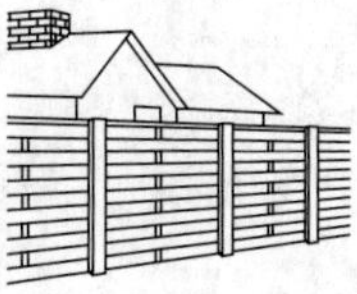

	Craft@Hrs	Unit	Material	Labor	Total
Basketweave fence, redwood, "B" grade, 1" x 6" boards, 2" x 4" stringers or spreaders, 4" x 4" posts					
Tight weave, 4' high, posts at 4' OC	B1@.332	LF	12.80	11.20	24.00
Tight weave, 6' high, posts at 4' OC	B1@.522	LF	15.50	17.70	33.20
Wide span, 4' high, posts at 8' OC	B1@.291	LF	7.22	9.85	17.07
Wide span, 8' high, posts at 8' OC	B1@.481	LF	9.78	16.30	26.08
4' high gate, tight weave	B1@.906	Ea	56.20	30.70	86.90
4' high gate, wide span	B1@.906	Ea	68.20	30.70	98.90
6' high gate, tight weave	B1@1.11	Ea	31.80	37.60	69.40
8' high gate, wide span	B1@1.26	Ea	43.00	42.70	85.70
Board fence, using 4" wide boards, hand nailed, posts at 10' OC					
Pressure treated Southern Pine, 1" x 4" boards					
6' high, 2 rail, wood posts	B1@.267	LF	6.42	9.04	15.46
6' high, 2 rail, metal posts	B1@.276	LF	7.07	9.34	16.41
Deduct for power stapling or power nailing	—	%	—	−22.0	—
Cedar, 1" x 4" boards					
6' high, 2 rail, wood posts	B1@.267	LF	12.70	9.04	21.74
8' high, 2 rail, wood posts	B1@.267	LF	14.90	9.04	23.94
6' high, 2 rail, metal posts	B1@.276	LF	13.40	9.34	22.74
8' high, 2 rail, metal posts	B1@.276	LF	15.40	9.34	24.74
Deduct for power stapling or power nailing	—	%	—	−22.0	—
Redwood, 3/4" x 4" boards					
6' high, 2 rail, wood posts	B1@.267	LF	8.88	9.04	17.92
6' high, 2 rail, metal posts	B1@.276	LF	9.53	9.34	18.87
Deduct for power stapling or power nailing	—	%	—	−22.0	—
Whitewoods, 1" x 4" boards					
6' high, 2 rail, wood posts	B1@.267	LF	8.83	9.04	17.87
8' high, 2 rail, wood posts	B1@.267	LF	8.88	9.04	17.92
6' high, 2 rail, metal posts	B1@.276	LF	9.48	9.34	18.82
8' high, 2 rail, metal posts	B1@.276	LF	9.53	9.34	18.87
Deduct for power stapling or power nailing	—	%	—	−22.0	—

Fencing, Wood

	Craft@Hrs	Unit	Material	Labor	Total
Board fence, using 6" wide boards, hand nailed, posts at 10' OC					
Pressure treated Southern Pine, 1" x 6" boards					
6' high, 2 rail, wood posts	B1@.241	LF	7.48	8.16	15.64
8' high, 2 rail, wood posts	B1@.241	LF	8.53	8.16	16.69
6' high, 2 rail, metal posts	B1@.250	LF	8.13	8.46	16.59
8' high, 2 rail, metal posts	B1@.250	LF	9.18	8.46	17.64
Deduct for power stapling or power nailing	—	%	—	-22.0	—
Cedar, 9/16" x 6" boards					
6' high, 2 rail, wood posts	B1@.241	LF	9.03	8.16	17.19
8' high, 2 rail, wood posts	B1@.241	LF	13.50	8.16	21.66
6' high, 2 rail, metal posts	B1@.250	LF	9.68	8.46	18.14
8' high, 2 rail, metal posts	B1@.250	LF	14.20	8.46	22.66
Deduct for power stapling or power nailing	—	%	—	-22.0	—
Redwood, 3/4" x 6" boards					
6' high, 2 rail, wood posts	B1@.241	LF	15.60	8.16	23.76
8' high, 2 rail, wood posts	B1@.241	LF	15.80	8.16	23.96
6' high, 2 rail, metal posts	B1@.250	LF	16.30	8.46	24.76
8' high, 2 rail, metal posts	B1@.250	LF	24.90	8.46	33.36
Deduct for power stapling or power nailing	—	%	—	-22.0	—
Split-rail fence, red cedar, 4" posts at 8' OC					
Split 2" x 4" rails, 3' high, 2 rail	B1@.095	LF	3.58	3.22	6.80
Split 2" x 4" rails, 4' high, 3 rail	B1@.102	LF	4.43	3.45	7.88
Rustic 4" round, 3' high, 2 rail	B1@.095	LF	4.31	3.22	7.53
Rustic 4" round, 4' high, 3 rail	B1@.102	LF	5.35	3.45	8.80
Picket fence, 1" x 2" pickets, 2" x 4" rails, 4" x 4" posts at 8' OC					
Pressure treated Southern Pine					
3' high, 2 rail	B1@.270	LF	2.16	9.14	11.30
5' high, 3 rail	B1@.385	LF	2.94	13.00	15.94
3' high gate	B1@.770	Ea	9.44	26.10	35.54
5' high gate	B1@.887	Ea	13.00	30.00	43.00
Red cedar, #3 & Better					
3' high, 2 rail	B1@.270	LF	4.71	9.14	13.85
5' high, 3 rail	B1@.385	LF	6.46	13.00	19.46
3' high gate	B1@.770	Ea	20.60	26.10	46.70
5' high gate	B1@.887	Ea	28.30	30.00	58.30
Redwood, B grade					
3' high, 2 rail	B1@.270	LF	5.04	9.14	14.18
5' high, 3 rail	B1@.385	LF	6.58	13.00	19.58
3' high gate	B1@.770	Ea	22.10	26.10	48.20
5' high gate	B1@.887	Ea	28.80	30.00	58.80
Picket fence gate hardware					
Latch, standard duty	B1@.281	Ea	4.38	9.51	13.89
Latch, heavy duty	B1@.281	Ea	14.00	9.51	23.51
Slide bolt	B1@.281	Ea	5.58	9.51	15.09
Hinges, standard, per pair	B1@.374	Pr	7.34	12.70	20.04
Hinges, heavy duty, per pair	B1@.374	Pr	9.94	12.70	22.64
No-sag cable kit	B1@.281	Ea	11.50	9.51	21.01
Self closing spring	B1@.281	Ea	13.00	9.51	22.51

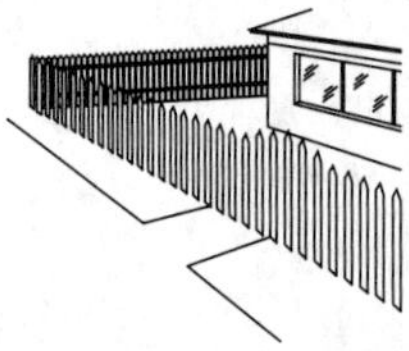

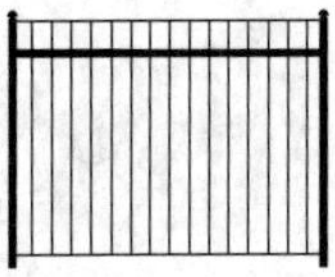

	Craft@Hrs	Unit	Material	Labor	Total
Fencing, Aluminum					
Decorative aluminum, 72-1/2" panel width, 2" x 2" posts, .060" wall thickness, 3-13/16" picket spacing, 1" x .055" top rail with 1-1/2" x .082" sides. Pre-routed holes in posts. Gates include hardware. Pool code compliant model has 48" space between horizontal rails					
48" high panel	BL@.170	Ea	70.40	5.15	75.55
54" pool code compliant panel	BL@.170	Ea	77.00	5.15	82.15
60" high panel	BL@.170	Ea	84.40	5.15	89.55
72" high panel	BL@.170	Ea	107.00	5.15	112.15
Fence posts					
48" high	BL@.830	Ea	24.50	25.20	49.70
54" high	BL@.830	Ea	26.20	25.20	51.40
60" high	BL@.830	Ea	26.20	25.20	51.40
72" high	BL@.830	Ea	35.20	25.20	60.40
Single swing gates, 5' wide					
48" high	BL@.175	Ea	402.00	5.30	407.30
54" high	BL@.175	Ea	328.00	5.30	333.30
60" high	BL@.175	Ea	327.00	5.30	332.30
72" high	BL@.175	Ea	352.00	5.30	357.30
Gate posts					
48" high	BL@.830	Ea	40.30	25.20	65.50
54" high	BL@.830	Ea	45.30	25.20	70.50
60" high	BL@.830	Ea	45.30	25.20	70.50
72" high	BL@.830	Ea	51.30	25.20	76.50
Add for setting post in concrete	BL@.330	Ea	3.60	10.00	13.60
Fencing, Vinyl					
Costs shown include concrete and labor to set posts.					
Vinyl picket fence, 1-1/2" pickets with 2" spacing, 2 rail, 2" x 4" rails, 4" x 4" posts at 8' OC, pre-assembled in 8' sections. Prices include post mounts, post top, screws and one post.					
4' high	B1@.110	LF	20.30	3.72	24.02
Gate with 4" posts	B1@1.00	Ea	397.00	33.90	430.90
Add for additional fence post with top	B1@.500	Ea	25.10	16.90	42.00
Vinyl picket fence, 3-1/2" pickets with 3" spacing, 2 rail, 2" x 4" rails, 4" x 4" posts at 6' OC, pre-assembled in 6' sections. Prices include post mounts, post top, screws and one post.					
4' high	B1@.110	LF	20.30	3.72	24.02
Gate with 4" posts	B1@1.00	Ea	397.00	33.90	430.90
Add for additional fence post with top	B1@.500	Ea	25.10	16.90	42.00
Vinyl shadowbox fence, 5-1/2" offset pickets, 3 rail, with galvanized steel support, posts at 71" OC. Prices include post mounts, post top, screws and one post.					
4' high	B1@.130	LF	26.90	4.40	31.30
5' high	B1@.140	LF	28.50	4.74	33.24
6' high	B1@.140	LF	30.40	4.74	35.14
Gate with 4" posts	B1@1.20	Ea	562.00	40.60	602.60
Add for additional fence post with top	B1@.500	Ea	31.40	16.90	48.30
Vinyl privacy fence, 6" boards, 3 rail, posts at 6' OC. Prices include post mounts, post top, screws and one post.					
6' high	B1@.140	LF	31.80	4.74	36.54
6' x 44" high gate	B1@1.20	Ea	579.00	40.60	619.60
Add for additional fence post with top	B1@.500	Ea	33.00	16.90	49.90
Vinyl post & rail fence, 2" x 6" x 96" notched rail, posts 8' OC. Includes post mounts, post top, and one post.					
42" high, 2 rail, 4" routed post	B1@.110	LF	5.36	3.72	9.08
48" high, 3 rail, 4" routed post	B1@.120	LF	6.64	4.06	10.70
54" high, 4 rail, 5" routed post	B1@.120	LF	8.37	4.06	12.43
48" gate with 4" posts	B1@1.00	Ea	228.00	33.90	261.90
54" gate with 5" posts	B1@1.00	Ea	270.00	33.90	303.90
Add for additional 4" fence post with top	B1@.500	Ea	17.90	16.90	34.80
Add for additional 5" fence post with top	B1@.500	Ea	22.50	16.90	39.40

	Craft@Hrs	Unit	Material	Labor	Total
Silt fence, black 6 mil poly with stakes 8' OC, staked and buried 9" deep					
3' high, 100 LF roll	BL@.030	LF	.53	.91	1.44

Fiberglass and Polycarbonate Panels Nailed or screwed onto wood frame.
Corrugated polycarbonate, 8', 10', 12' panels, 2-1/2" corrugations, standard colors. Costs include 10% loss for coverage and waste.

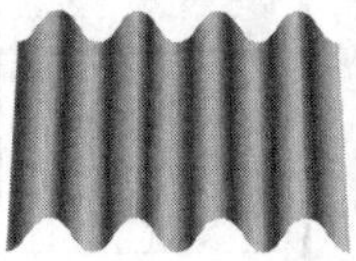

	Craft@Hrs	Unit	Material	Labor	Total
Polycarbonate, 26" wide, gray or white	BC@.012	SF	1.44	.45	1.89
Polycarbonate, 26" wide, clear	BC@.012	SF	1.44	.45	1.89
PVC, 26" wide panels	BC@.012	SF	.98	.45	1.43
Corrugated fiberglass, 8', 10', 12' panels, 2-1/2" corrugations, standard colors. Costs include 10% loss for coverage and waste.					
Fiberglass, 26" wide, gray or white	BC@.012	SF	2.53	.45	2.98
Fiberglass, 26" wide, clear	BC@.012	SF	2.53	.45	2.98
Flat panels, clear, green or white					
.06" flat sheets, 4' x 8', 10', 12'	BC@.012	SF	3.57	.45	4.02
.03" rolls, 24", 36", 48" x 50'	BC@.012	SF	3.04	.45	3.49
.037" rolls, 24", 36", 48" x 50'	BC@.012	SF	2.63	.45	3.08
Accessories					
Nails, ring shank with rubber washer, 1-3/4" (labor included with panels)					
100 per box (covers 130 SF)	—	CSF	3.79	—	3.79
Self-tapping screws, 1-1/4", rust-proof (labor included with panels)					
100 per box (covers 130 SF)	—	CSF	4.66	—	4.66
Horizontal closure strips, corrugated (labor included with panels)					
Molded plastic, 3/4" x 1-1/4"	—	LF	.52	—	.52
Wood, 3/4" x 13/16"	—	LF	.51	—	.51
Poly-foam, 15/16" x 3/4"	—	LF	.58	—	.58
Rubber, 1" x 1"	—	LF	.60	—	.60
Vertical crown molding					
Redwood, 1-1/2" x 1" or poly-foam, 1" x 1"	—	LF	.43	—	.43
Rubber, 1" x 1"	—	LF	1.12	—	1.12
Ridge cap, covers the joint where panels meet at the roof peak					
Polycarbonate, 48" long	—	LF	5.71	—	5.74

Ornamental Iron, Railings and Fence, Subcontract Typical prices, fabricated, delivered and installed.

	Craft@Hrs	Unit	Material	Labor	Total
Handrail, 1-1/2" x 1" rectangular top rail tubing, 1" square bottom rail tubing, 1/2" square pickets with 5-1/2" space between					
36" high railing for single family dwelling	—	LF	—	—	41.80
42" high apartment style railing	—	LF	—	—	33.30
Add for inclined runs	—	LF	—	—	7.67
Pool fence					
5' high, 4-1/2" centers	—	LF	—	—	41.80
Add for gate, with self-closer and latch	—	LS	—	—	197.00

Fire Sprinkler Systems, Subcontract Systems installed in new residences not over four stories high in accord with NFPA 13D and 13R. Includes hydraulic design, typical permits and tap fees ($350), connection to a domestic water line, exposed riser with shut-off and drain valves, flow switch, alarm, backflow preventer and inspection of the completed system. Using CPVC or PEX concealed pipe and residential sprinkler heads. Per SF of protected area, including closets, attached garage, attic and basement when required. For scheduling purposes, estimate that a crew of 2 can install the rough-in piping for 1,500 to 1,600 SF of protected area in an 8-hour day and about the same amount of finish work in another 8-hour day.

	Craft@Hrs	Unit	Material	Labor	Total
Fabricate, install, and test system					
Single residence, slab foundation	—	SF	—	—	1.64
Single residence, crawl space foundation	—	SF	—	—	1.88
Single residence with basement	—	SF	—	—	2.03
Tract work or multi-family residence	—	SF	—	—	1.73
Add if copper pipe is required	—	SF	—	—	2.03
Add if a booster pump is required (well water)	—	LS	—	—	3,500.00

	Craft@Hrs	Unit	Material	Labor	Total

Masonry Fireplaces

Fire box lined with refractory firebrick, backed with common brick and enclosed in a common brick wall. Includes fireplace throat and smoke chamber. Overall height of the fireplace and throat is 5'. Chimney (flue) is made from common brick and a flue liner. Including lintels, damper and 12" thick reinforced concrete foundation. For more on masonry fireplaces, see *National Concrete & Masonry Estimator,* http://CraftsmanSiteLicense.com.

	Craft@Hrs	Unit	Material	Labor	Total
30" wide x 29" high x 16" deep fire box	B9@39.7	LS	681.00	1,310.00	1,991.00
36" wide x 29" high x 16" deep fire box	B9@43.5	LS	718.00	1,440.00	2,158.00
42" wide x 32" high x 16" deep fire box	B9@48.3	LS	794.00	1,600.00	2,394.00
48" wide x 32" high x 18" deep fire box	B9@52.8	LS	873.00	1,750.00	2,623.00
12" x 12" chimney to 12' high	B9@9.50	LS	403.00	314.00	717.00
Add for higher chimney, per LF	B9@1.30	LF	55.00	43.00	98.00
Add for 8" x 10" ash cleanout door	B9@.500	SF	18.00	16.50	34.50
Add for combustion air inlet kit	B9@.750	SF	27.20	24.80	52.00
Add for common brick veneer interior face	B9@.451	SF	5.04	14.90	19.94
Add for rubble or cobble stone veneer face	B9@.480	SF	13.80	15.90	29.70
Add for limestone veneer face or hearth	B9@.451	SF	26.00	14.90	40.90
Add for 1-1/4" marble face or hearth	B9@.451	SF	39.20	14.90	54.10
Add for modern design 11" x 77" pine mantel	B1@3.81	Ea	772.00	129.00	901.00
Add for gas valve, log lighter and key	PM@.750	Ea	73.40	32.60	106.00

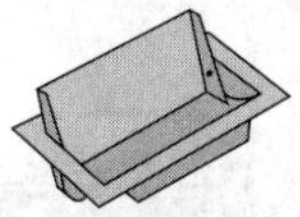

	Craft@Hrs	Unit	Material	Labor	Total
Angle iron (lintel support), lengths 25" to 96"					
3" x 3" x 3/16"	B9@.167	LF	5.21	5.52	10.73
Ash drops, cast iron top, galvanized container					
16-3/4" x 12-1/2" x 8"	B9@.750	Ea	85.30	24.80	110.10
Ash dumps, cast iron					
5-3/8" x 9-1/2" overall	B9@.500	Ea	16.90	16.50	33.40
5-3/8" x 9-1/2" overall, vented	B9@.500	Ea	33.80	16.50	50.30

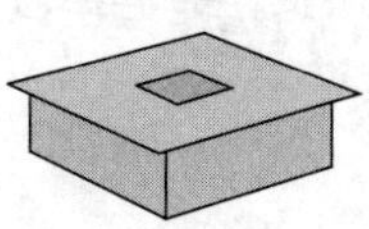

	Craft@Hrs	Unit	Material	Labor	Total
Chimney anchors, per pair					
48" x 1-1/2" x 3/16"	—	Pr	12.90	—	12.90
72" x 1-1/2" x 3/16"	—	Pr	17.20	—	17.20
Cleanout doors, cast iron, overall dimensions					
8" wide x 8" high	B9@.500	Ea	46.80	16.50	63.30
12" wide x 10" high	B9@.500	Ea	78.60	16.50	95.10
12" wide x 12" high	B9@.500	Ea	91.50	16.50	108.00

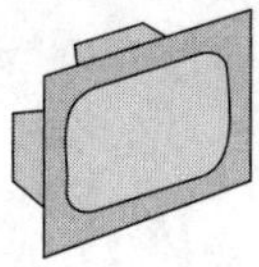

	Craft@Hrs	Unit	Material	Labor	Total
Dampers for single opening firebox, heavy steel with rockwool insulation					
14" high, 25" to 30" wide, 10" deep, 25 lbs	B9@1.33	Ea	59.60	44.00	103.60
14" high, 36" wide, 10" deep, 31 lbs	B9@1.33	Ea	64.50	44.00	108.50
14" high, 42" wide, 10" deep, 38 lbs	B9@1.33	Ea	78.90	44.00	122.90
14" high, 48" wide, 10" deep, 43 lbs	B9@1.75	Ea	102.00	57.90	159.90
16" high, 54" wide, 13" deep, 66 lbs	B9@2.50	Ea	175.00	82.70	257.70
16" high, 60" wide, 13" deep, 74 lbs	B9@2.50	Ea	211.00	82.70	293.70
16" high, 72" wide, 13" deep, 87 lbs	B9@2.50	Ea	253.00	82.70	335.70
Dampers for multiple opening or corner opening firebox, high capacity, steel downdraft shelf support					
35" wide	B9@1.33	Ea	208.00	44.00	252.00
41" wide	B9@1.33	Ea	297.00	44.00	341.00
47" wide	B9@1.75	Ea	357.00	57.90	414.90

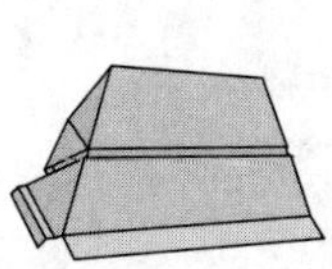

	Craft@Hrs	Unit	Material	Labor	Total
Chimney-top dampers, with cable to the firebox and handle mount, aluminum, by flue size					
8" x 8"	B9@1.33	Ea	208.00	44.00	252.00
8" x 13", with 3/4" mesh	B9@1.33	Ea	297.00	44.00	341.00
8" x 17"	B9@1.33	Ea	270.00	44.00	314.00
13" x 13"	B9@1.75	Ea	213.00	57.90	270.90
13" x 17"	B9@2.50	Ea	307.00	82.70	389.70
17" x 17"	B9@2.50	Ea	365.00	82.70	447.70

	Craft@Hrs	Unit	Material	Labor	Total
Fuel grates, steel bar fireplace grates					
27" with 5/8" bar	—	Ea	88.50	—	88.50
30" with 3/4" bar	—	Ea	138.00	—	138.00
36" with 3/4" bar	—	Ea	171.00	—	171.00

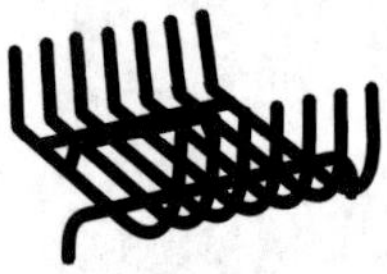

Factory-built wood-burning fireplaces Including refractory-lined firebox, fireplace front, combustion air kit and damper with control. By hearth opening width. 21" depth overall.

	Craft@Hrs	Unit	Material	Labor	Total
36" wide	B9@3.50	Ea	769.00	116.00	885.00
42" wide	B9@3.50	Ea	1,180.00	116.00	1,296.00
50" wide	B9@4.00	Ea	3,610.00	132.00	3,742.00
36" wide, 1 open end	B9@3.50	Ea	1,780.00	116.00	1,896.00
36" wide, 3 open sides	B9@4.00	Ea	2,590.00	132.00	2,722.00
42" wide, see-through	B9@4.00	Ea	3,080.00	132.00	3,212.00
25" wide, EPA Phase II compliant	B9@4.00	Ea	6,630.00	132.00	6,762.00
Add for 8" Class A vent, per vertical foot	B9@.250	LF	152.00	8.27	160.27

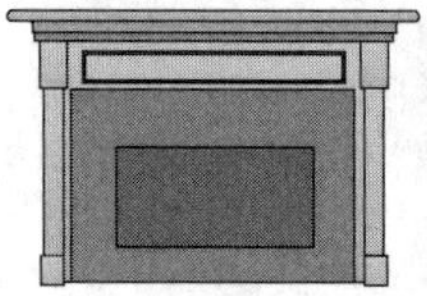

Gas-burning direct vent zero clearance fireplaces Vents directly through an exterior wall or the roof using sealed double chamber vent pipe. See vent pipe costs below. Waste gases exit through the vent inner chamber. Outside air enters the firebox through the vent outside chamber. Framing may be applied directly against the unit. Circulates heated air into the room. Includes brick firebox, fireplace front, bi-fold glass doors, temperature control, masonry logs and fuel grate. Electric ignition. Overall dimensions.

	Craft@Hrs	Unit	Material	Labor	Total
39" high x 36" wide x 21" deep	B9@3.50	Ea	1,820.00	116.00	1,936.00
39" high x 41" wide x 19" deep	B9@3.50	Ea	1,780.00	116.00	1,896.00
38" high x 36" wide x 18" deep	B9@3.50	Ea	2,570.00	116.00	2,686.00
33" high x 42" wide x 24" deep, 1 open end	B9@3.50	Ea	3,960.00	116.00	4,076.00
38" high x 40" wide x 24" deep, 2 open ends	B9@4.00	Ea	4,460.00	132.00	4,592.00
30" high x 38" wide x 24" deep, see-through	B9@4.00	Ea	3,520.00	132.00	3,652.00
Deduct for conventional B-vent units	—	Ea	–182.00	—	–182.00
Direct vent fireplace flue (chimney), double wall, typical cost for straight vertical installation					
4" inside diameter 6-5/8" outside diameter	B9@.167	LF	13.80	5.52	19.32
5" inside diameter, 8" outside diameter	B9@.167	LF	17.10	5.52	22.62
Flue spacers, for passing through ceiling					
1" or 2" clearance	B9@.167	Ea	15.00	5.52	20.52
Typical flue offset	B9@.250	Ea	95.50	8.27	103.77
Flashing and storm collar, one required per roof penetration					
Flat to 6/12 pitch roofs	B9@3.25	Ea	60.10	107.00	167.10
6/12 to 12/12 pitch roofs	B9@3.25	Ea	87.40	107.00	194.40
Spark arrestor top	B9@.500	Ea	122.00	16.50	138.50
Blower kit for heat-circulating fireplace, requires 110 volt electrical receptacle outlet (electrical wiring not included)					
Blower unit for connection to existing outlet	B9@.500	Ea	114.00	16.50	130.50
Add variable speed and thermostatic control	B9@.100	Ea	82.60	3.31	85.91

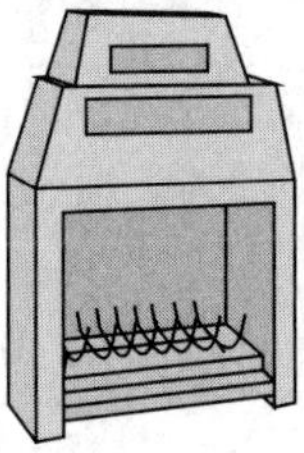

Electric fireplaces, built-in Prefabricated, 120 volt, including grate, ember bed, interior face, thermostat, brightness control and logs.

	Craft@Hrs	Unit	Material	Labor	Total
25" wide opening, 120 volt, 1,500 watts	B9@2.50	Ea	700.00	82.70	782.70
26" wide opening, 120 volt, 1,500 watts	B9@2.50	Ea	1,040.00	82.70	1,122.70

	Craft@Hrs	Unit	Material	Labor	Total
Sheet Vinyl Flooring					
Armstrong sheet vinyl flooring. By Performance Appearance Rating (PAR). Bonded with adhesive at perimeter and at seams. Including 10% waste and adhesive.					
Medley, urethane wear layer, 15 year	BF@.250	SY	22.50	8.57	31.07
Caspian, PAR 3.8, urethane wear layer, 15 year	BF@.250	SY	18.20	8.57	26.77
Themes, PAR 2.9, urethane wear layer, 10 year	BF@.250	SY	13.90	8.57	22.47
Sundial, urethane wear layer, .098", 10 year	BF@.250	SY	15.30	8.57	23.87
Metro, PAR 2.3, vinyl wear layer, 5 year	BF@.250	SY	7.97	8.57	16.54
Cambray FHA, PAR 1.7, vinyl wear layer, 5 year	BF@.250	SY	7.97	8.57	16.54
Memories, 12 year	BF@.250	SY	26.40	8.57	34.97
Successor, 10 year	BF@.250	SY	19.90	8.57	28.47
Enhancements, 6 year	BF@.250	SY	20.20	8.57	28.77
Initiator, 5 year	BF@.250	SY	13.70	8.57	22.27
Sentinel, 5 year	BF@.250	SY	11.10	8.57	19.67
Apartment One, 1 year	BF@.250	SY	10.90	8.57	19.47
Royelle, PAR 1.3, vinyl wear layer, 1 year	BF@.250	SY	5.54	8.57	14.11
Tarkett sheet vinyl, bonded with adhesive at perimeter and at seams. Including 10% waste and adhesive.					
Simply Brite	BF@.250	SY	32.80	8.57	41.37
Signature	BF@.250	SY	28.40	8.57	36.97
Naturelle	BF@.250	SY	27.70	8.57	36.27
Presence Felt	BF@.250	SY	21.70	8.57	30.27
Style Brite Flex	BF@.250	SY	18.70	8.57	27.27
Style Brite Felt	BF@.250	SY	18.60	8.57	27.17
Simply Brite Felt	BF@.250	SY	18.40	8.57	26.97
Fiber Floor	BF@.250	SY	10.90	8.57	19.47
Sierra	BF@.250	SY	9.86	8.57	18.43
Yosemite	BF@.250	SY	8.87	8.57	17.44
Preference	BF@.250	SY	7.76	8.57	16.33
Sandran	BF@.250	SY	5.16	8.57	13.73
Sheet vinyl, no wax, Mannington. Bonded with adhesive at perimeter and at seams. Including 10% waste and adhesive.					
Gold Series	BF@.250	SY	48.70	8.57	57.27
Silver Series	BF@.250	SY	34.60	8.57	43.17
Bronze Series	BF@.250	SY	34.60	8.57	43.17
Villa Series	BF@.250	SY	24.90	8.57	33.47
Ceramica	BF@.250	SY	31.00	8.57	39.57
Silverado	BF@.250	SY	28.20	8.57	36.77
Aurora	BF@.250	SY	25.10	8.57	33.67
Lumina	BF@.250	SY	20.70	8.57	29.27
Vega II, Omni	BF@.250	SY	16.20	8.57	24.77
Vinyl 12" x 12" Tile Flooring					
Armstrong vinyl tile, 12" x 12", including 10% waste and adhesive					
Solarian Stonegate, .094"	BF@.023	SF	3.52	.79	4.31
Natural Images, .094"	BF@.023	SF	3.52	.79	4.31
Chelsea (urethane), .08"	BF@.023	SF	2.81	.79	3.60
Chesapeake (urethane), .08"	BF@.023	SF	2.29	.79	3.08
Harbour, .08"	BF@.023	SF	2.17	.79	2.96
StoneTex, 1/8"	BF@.021	SF	1.96	.72	2.68
Stylistik, .065", self-adhesive	BF@.023	SF	1.56	.79	2.35
Themes, .08" (urethane)	BF@.023	SF	1.59	.79	2.38
Vernay, Metro, .045"	BF@.023	SF	1.33	.79	2.12
MultiColor, 1/8"	BF@.021	SF	1.12	.72	1.84
Excelon Civic Square, 1/8"	BF@.021	SF	.85	.72	1.57
Afton, .075"	BF@.023	SF	1.44	.79	2.23
Builder urethane, .080", self-adhesive	BF@.023	SF	2.40	.79	3.19
Builder urethane, .080", dry back	BF@.023	SF	2.29	.79	3.08

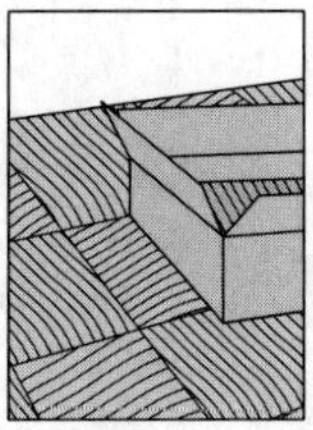

Flooring, Vinyl Tile

	Craft@Hrs	Unit	Material	Labor	Total
Elegant Images™ Series vinyl floor tile, Armstrong. 12" x 12". ToughGuard® durability. Resists stains, scratches, scuffs and indentations. 25-year warranty. Per square foot, including adhesive and 10% waste.					
Cornwall, Burnt Almond	BF@.023	SF	2.97	.79	3.76
Modern, Rose/Green Inset	BF@.023	SF	2.00	.79	2.79
Rubber studded tile. 12" x 12". Highly resilient to reduce fatigue. 10-year wear warranty. Slip-resistant. Sound absorbent. High abrasion resistance. For kitchens and utility rooms.					
All colors	BF@.025	SF	8.69	.86	9.55
Vinyl Flooring Accessories					
Resilient flooring adhesive					
Sheet vinyl adhesive, per gallon	—	Gal	22.20	—	22.20
Sheet vinyl adhesive, 71 SF per gallon	—	SF	.34	—	.34
Vinyl tile adhesive, per gallon	—	Gal	32.30	—	32.30
Vinyl tile adhesive, 190 SF per gallon	—	SF	.19	—	.19
Vinyl seam sealer kit (100 LF)	—	LF	.12	—	.12
Resilient flooring accessories					
Self-leveling compound					
1 pound per SF at .25" depth	BF@.016	SF	.63	.55	1.18
Latex masonry primer (used over dusting, porous or below grade concrete)					
100 SF per gallon	BF@.008	SF	.28	.27	.55
Liquid underlay (application over existing vinyl floor)					
Gallon covers 52 SF	BF@.010	SF	.78	.34	1.12
Lining felt, 15 Lb. asphalt felt (used over board subfloor)					
432 SF roll covers 350 SF	BF@.004	SF	.05	.14	.19
Tempered hardboard underlayment (levels uneven subfloor)					
1/8" x 4' x 8' sheet	BF@.016	SF	.29	.55	.84
Cove base, colors,					
2-1/2" high, .08" thick	BF@.025	LF	1.47	.86	2.33
4" high, .08" thick	BF@.025	LF	.77	.86	1.63
4" high, self-adhesive	BF@.016	LF	.96	.55	1.51
Cove base cement					
105 LF of 4" base per quart	—	LF	.09	—	.09
Accent strip, 1/8" x 24" long					
1/2" wide	BF@.025	LF	.38	.86	1.24
1" wide	BF@.025	LF	.49	.86	1.35
2" wide	BF@.025	LF	.91	.86	1.77
Vinyl edging strip, 1" wide					
1/16" thick	—	LF	.63	—	.63
1/8" thick	—	LF	.79	—	.79
Vinyl Plank Flooring (LVP). Luxury vinyl plank and tile consists of a clear wear layer, an embossed vinyl layer, a composite core and a cushion layer. Many colors and textures. Surface can look like wood, stone, travertine or marble. Planks are from 6" wide to 4' long and 8 mm to 12 mm thick. Floating plank is secured only at room edges with base molding. Includes 15% cutting waste.					
Economy, glue-down	BF@.051	SF	2.93	1.75	4.68
Most colors and textures, floating	BF@.051	SF	3.90	1.75	5.65
Premium -- high traffic, waterproof, deep colors	BF@.051	SF	4.30	1.75	6.05
Tread and riser, glue-down, with nosing, per stair	BF@.881	Ea	106.00	30.20	136.20
T mold strip (joins same level surface)	BF@.040	LF	5.23	1.37	6.60
Reducer strip (joins higher surface)	BF@.040	LF	3.98	1.37	5.35
End molding (joins lower surface)	BF@.040	LF	5.23	1.37	6.60
Wall base, to 4" high	BF@.040	LF	1.37	1.37	2.74
Scribe and seal around irregular surface (masonry)	BF@.554	LF	1.00	19.00	20.00
Add for floor prep, per room, typical	BF@1.50	Ea	2.00	51.40	53.40
Add for small or irregular rooms	BF@.011	SF	—	.38	.38
Add for diagonal patterns	BF@.004	SF	—	.14	.14

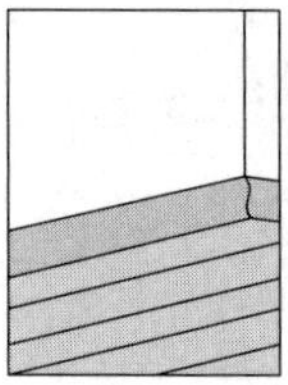

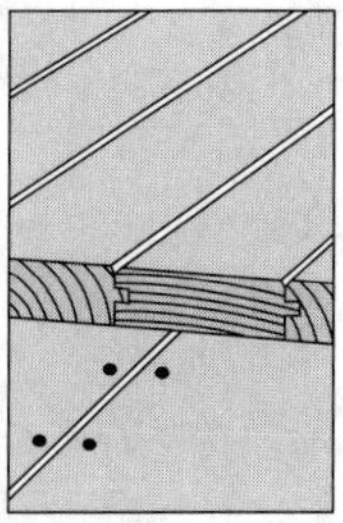

	Craft@Hrs	Unit	Material	Labor	Total
Wood Strip Flooring Unfinished tongue and groove 3/4" x 2-1/4" strip flooring. Bundle covers 19.5 square feet. See installation, sanding and finishing cost below.					
Select red oak, 19.5 SF per bundle	—	SF	4.07	—	4.07
Select white oak, 19.5 SF per bundle	—	SF	4.18	—	4.18
No. 1 common red oak, 19.5 SF per bundle	—	SF	3.20	—	3.20
No. 1 common white oak, 19.5 SF per bundle	—	SF	3.36	—	3.36
No. 2 common red oak, 19.5 SF per bundle	—	SF	1.87	—	1.87
Select ash, 19.5 SF per bundle	—	SF	3.74	—	3.74
Red oak stair nosing, 3/4"	—	LF	8.51	—	8.51
Red oak reducer strip, 3/4" x 2"	—	LF	3.70	—	3.70
Red oak quarter round, 3/4" x 3/4"	—	LF	1.44	—	1.44
Labor installing, sanding and finishing hardwood strip flooring on a prepared subfloor. Nailed in place.					
Install 1-1/2" width strips	BF@.066	SF	—	2.26	2.26
Install 2" or 2-1/4" width strips	BF@.062	SF	—	2.13	2.13
Install 3-1/4" width strips	BF@.060	SF	—	2.06	2.06
Install stair nose or reducer strip	BF@.040	LF	—	1.37	1.37
Sanding, 3 passes (60/80/100 grit)	BF@.023	SF	.08	.79	.87
2 coats of stain/sealer	BF@.010	SF	.12	.34	.46
2 coats of urethane	BF@.012	SF	.15	.41	.56
2 coats of lacquer	BF@.024	SF	.20	.82	1.02
Unfinished antique tongue and groove plank flooring 25/32" thick, random widths and lengths. Includes typical cutting waste. Installed over a prepared subfloor.					
Ash, select, 3" to 7" wide	BF@.057	SF	5.52	1.95	7.47
Chestnut, American, 3" to 7" wide	BF@.057	SF	11.50	1.95	13.45
Chestnut, distressed, 3" to 7" wide	BF@.057	SF	13.60	1.95	15.55
Chestnut, distressed, over 7" wide	BF@.057	SF	17.70	1.95	19.65
Cherry, #1, 3" to 7" wide	BF@.057	SF	12.90	1.95	14.85
Cherry, #1, 6" wide and up	BF@.057	SF	15.60	1.95	17.55
Hickory, #1, 3" to 7" wide	BF@.057	SF	5.35	1.95	7.30
Hemlock, 3" to 7" wide	BF@.057	SF	9.24	1.95	11.19
Hemlock, over 7" wide	BF@.057	SF	12.10	1.95	14.05
Oak, #1, red or white, 3" to 7" wide	BF@.057	SF	4.73	1.95	6.68
Oak, #1, red or white, over 7" wide	BF@.057	SF	7.47	1.95	9.42
Oak, 3" to 7" wide	BF@.057	SF	9.46	1.95	11.41
Oak, over 7" wide	BF@.057	SF	11.50	1.95	13.45
Oak, distressed, 3" to 7" wide	BF@.057	SF	10.90	1.95	12.85
Oak, distressed, over 7" wide	BF@.057	SF	13.70	1.95	15.65
Maple, FAS, 3" to 7" wide	BF@.057	SF	6.52	1.95	8.47
Poplar, 3" to 8" wide	BF@.057	SF	4.78	1.95	6.73
Poplar, over 8" wide	BF@.057	SF	6.44	1.95	8.39
Walnut, #3, 3" to 7" wide	BF@.057	SF	7.76	1.95	9.71
White pine, 3" to 7"	BF@.057	SF	7.25	1.95	9.20
White pine, distressed, 3" to 7"	BF@.057	SF	7.90	1.95	9.85
White pine, distressed, over 7" wide	BF@.057	SF	11.40	1.95	13.35
White pine, knotty grade, 12" and up wide	BF@.057	SF	11.70	1.95	13.65
Yellow pine, 3" to 5" wide	BF@.057	SF	8.45	1.95	10.40
Yellow pine, 6" to 10" wide	BF@.057	SF	11.50	1.95	13.45
Unfinished northern hard maple strip flooring					
25/32" x 2-1/4" (138.3 BF per 100 SF)					
1st grade	BF@.036	SF	6.70	1.23	7.93
2nd grade	BF@.036	SF	6.00	1.23	7.23
3rd grade	BF@.036	SF	5.54	1.23	6.77
25/32" x 1-1/2" (155 BF per 100 SF)					
1st grade	BF@.040	SF	7.99	1.37	9.36
2nd grade	BF@.040	SF	7.19	1.37	8.56
3rd grade	BF@.040	SF	6.63	1.37	8.00

	Craft@Hrs	Unit	Material	Labor	Total
33/32" x 1-1/2" (170 BF per 100 SF)					
1st grade	BF@.036	SF	7.45	1.23	8.68
2nd grade	BF@.036	SF	6.42	1.23	7.65
3rd grade	BF@.036	SF	6.04	1.23	7.27
Unfinished long plank flooring Random 3" to 5" widths, 1' to 16' lengths, 3/4" thick.					
Select grade, ash	BF@.062	SF	7.06	2.13	9.19
Common grade, cherry	BF@.062	SF	9.34	2.13	11.47
Select grade, cherry	BF@.062	SF	11.70	2.13	13.83
Select grade, rock maple	BF@.062	SF	8.43	2.13	10.56
Select grade, figured maple	BF@.062	SF	14.50	2.13	16.63
Select grade, red oak	BF@.062	SF	9.46	2.13	11.59
Select grade, white oak	BF@.062	SF	7.80	2.13	9.93
Unfinished wide plank flooring Random 6" to 8" widths, 1' to 16' lengths, 3/4" thick, including 8% waste, Specialty Wood Floors.					
Knotty grade, pine	BF@.074	SF	5.50	2.54	8.04
Select grade, cherry	BF@.074	SF	12.90	2.54	15.44
Select grade, maple	BF@.074	SF	11.40	2.54	13.94
Select grade, red oak	BF@.074	SF	10.60	2.54	13.14
Select grade, white oak	BF@.074	SF	9.54	2.54	12.08
Softwood flooring Material costs include typical waste and coverage loss. Estimates for sanding and finishing appear at the end of this section.					
Unfinished Douglas fir, C Grade and better, dry, vertical grain flooring. 1.25 board feet cover 1 square foot including end cutting and typical waste.					
1" x 2", square edge	BF@.037	SF	3.56	1.27	4.83
1" x 3", square edge	BF@.037	SF	3.59	1.27	4.86
1" x 4", tongue and groove	BF@.037	SF	2.92	1.27	4.19
Deduct for D Grade	—	SF	-.70	—	-.70
Add for B Grade and better	—	SF	.86	—	.86
Add for specific lengths	—	SF	.17	—	.17
Add for diagonal patterns	BF@.004	SF	—	.14	.14
Unfinished select kiln dried heart pine flooring, 97% dense heartwood, random lengths, including 5% waste. 1" to 1-1/4" thick.					
4" wide	BF@.042	SF	8.75	1.44	10.19
5" wide	BF@.042	SF	9.01	1.44	10.45
6" wide	BF@.042	SF	9.11	1.44	10.55
8" wide	BF@.046	SF	9.79	1.58	11.37
10" wide	BF@.046	SF	11.30	1.58	12.88
Add for diagonal patterns	BF@.004	SF	—	.14	.14
Unfinished plank flooring, 3/4" thick, 3" to 8" widths, 2' to 12' lengths.					
Antique white pine	BF@.100	SF	9.35	3.43	12.78
Antique yellow pine	BF@.100	SF	8.64	3.43	12.07
Milled heart pine	BF@.100	SF	10.20	3.43	13.63
Distressed oak	BF@.100	SF	11.10	3.43	14.53
Milled oak	BF@.100	SF	10.10	3.43	13.53
Distressed American chestnut	BF@.100	SF	10.30	3.43	13.73
Milled American chestnut	BF@.100	SF	11.10	3.43	14.53
Aged hemlock/fir	BF@.100	SF	10.30	3.43	13.73
Antique poplar	BF@.100	SF	4.71	3.43	8.14
Aged cypress	BF@.100	SF	5.61	3.43	9.04
Add for 9" to 15" widths	—	%	15.0	—	—
Add for sanding and finishing.					
Sanding, 3 passes (60/80/100 grit)	BF@.023	SF	.08	.79	.87
2 coats of stain/sealer	BF@.010	SF	.12	.34	.46
2 coats of urethane	BF@.012	SF	.15	.41	.56
2 coats of lacquer	BF@.024	SF	.20	.82	1.02

	Craft@Hrs	Unit	Material	Labor	Total
Prefinished strip flooring					
Tongue and groove, 25/32" thick, 2-1/4" wide. Includes typical cutting waste. Installed over a prepared subfloor					
Honey wheat oak, case covers 18.1 SF	BF@.062	SF	3.86	2.13	5.99
Marsh oak, case covers 20 SF	BF@.062	SF	4.07	2.13	6.20
Gunstock oak, case covers 20 SF	BF@.062	SF	4.07	2.13	6.20
Autumn wheat hickory, case covers 22 SF	BF@.062	SF	5.15	2.13	7.28
Natural hickory, case covers 22 SF	BF@.062	SF	5.90	2.13	8.03
Tawny oak, case covers 18.25 SF	BF@.062	SF	6.60	2.13	8.73
Fawn oak, case covers 24 SF	BF@.062	SF	6.76	2.13	8.89
Prefinished oak strip flooring trim					
7' 10" quarter round	BF@.320	Ea	21.50	11.00	32.50
6' 6" reducer	BF@.531	Ea	29.00	18.20	47.20
6' 6" stair nose	BF@.531	Ea	33.70	18.20	51.90
6' 6" T-molding	BF@.531	Ea	46.90	18.20	65.10
Floating hardwood flooring Tongue and groove. Install over concrete or other subfloor using an underfloor membrane. Edges and ends glued. Based on 3/8" gap at walls covered with 1/2" base or quarter round molding. The labor estimates below include laying the membrane, hardwood flooring and gluing.					
Poly foam membrane, 100 SF roll	—	SF	.30	—	.30
'Floor Muffler' poly foam, 100 SF roll	—	SF	.66	—	.66
Cork underlayment, 1/4", 200 SF roll	—	SF	.68	—	.68
Urethane adhesive, 150 SF per gallon	—	SF	.35	—	.35
1/2" tongue and groove hardwood flooring, various colors	FL@.051	SF	4.33	2.62	6.95
Laminate wood floor, Pergo Plastic laminate on pressed wood base, 7-7/8" x 47-1/4" x 3/8" (20 cm x 120 cm x 8 mm), loose lay with glued tongue and groove joints. Many wood finishes available. 20.67 SF (1.9 square meters) per pack. Includes 10% waste and joint glue (bottle covers 150 SF).					
Pergo Presto, on floors					
Most finishes	BF@.051	SF	2.87	1.75	4.62
Glued on stairs (treads and risers)	BF@.115	SF	3.73	3.94	7.67
Add for FloorMuffler underlay (100 SF per pack)	BF@.010	SF	.68	.34	1.02
Pergo sound block foam	BF@.002	SF	.42	.07	.49
Add for 8 mil poly vapor barrier (over concrete)	BF@.002	SF	.16	.07	.23
4-in1 molding; T-mold, reducer, end mold	BF@.040	LF	4.84	1.37	6.21
Wall base, 4" high	BF@.040	LF	2.62	1.37	3.99
Stair nosing	BF@.050	LF	5.68	1.71	7.39
Laminate wood floor, Dupont Plastic laminate on pressed wood base, 11-1/2" x 46-9/16" x .0462", foam back, tongue and groove joints. Pack covers 17 SF with 8% waste.					
Dupont Real Touch Elite on floors					
Most finishes	BF@.051	SF	5.26	1.75	7.01
Glued on stairs (treads and risers)	BF@.115	SF	6.72	3.94	10.66
6 mil vapor barrier (over concrete)	BF@.002	SF	.16	.07	.23
Bamboo flooring					
Laminated plank bamboo flooring, tongue and groove, 72" long panels. Treated and kiln dried. Installs over wood subfloor. Use 1/2" nail gun. Space fasteners 8" to 10" apart, with a minimum of two nails per board. Assorted shades and textures.					
5/8" x 3-3/4" prefinished	BF@.062	SF	4.81	2.13	6.94
1/2" x 3" unfinished	BF@.062	SF	4.81	2.13	6.94
Laminated bamboo baseboard					
3" beveled edge prefinished	BC@.040	LF	4.70	1.50	6.20

	Craft@Hrs	Unit	Material	Labor	Total
Laminated prefinished bamboo stair nose					
1/2" x 3-1/4"	BC@.040	LF	7.22	1.50	8.72
Laminated prefinished bamboo threshold					
9/16" x 3-5/8" flat grain	BC@.174	LF	5.53	6.50	12.03
9/16" x 3-5/8" edge grain	BC@.174	LF	5.60	6.50	12.10
5/8" x 2"	BC@.174	LF	7.22	6.50	13.72
Add for sanding and finishing					
Sanding, 3 passes (60/80/100 grit)	BF@.023	SF	.08	.79	.87
2 coats of stain/sealer	BF@.010	SF	.12	.34	.46
2 coats of urethane	BF@.012	SF	.15	.41	.56
2 coats of lacquer	BF@.024	SF	.20	.82	1.02

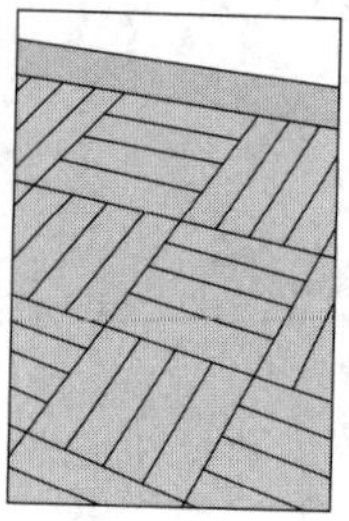

Parquet block flooring Includes typical waste and coverage loss, installed over a prepared subfloor.

Unfinished parquet block flooring, 3/4" thick, 10" x 10" to 39" x 39" blocks, includes 5% waste. Cost varies by pattern with larger blocks costing more. These are material costs only. Add labor cost below.

	Craft@Hrs	Unit	Material	Labor	Total
Ash or quartered oak, select	—	SF	20.60	—	20.60
Ash or quartered oak, natural	—	SF	15.00	—	15.00
Cherry or walnut select grade	—	SF	24.00	—	24.00
Cherry or walnut natural grade	—	SF	18.10	—	18.10
Oak, select plain	—	SF	16.70	—	16.70
Oak, natural plain	—	SF	14.40	—	14.40

Prefinished parquet block flooring, 5/16" thick, select grade, specified sizes, includes 5% waste. Cost varies by pattern and size, with larger blocks costing more. These are material costs only. Add labor cost below.

	Craft@Hrs	Unit	Material	Labor	Total
Cherry or walnut					
9" x 9"	—	SF	6.66	—	6.66
13" x 13"	—	SF	7.90	—	7.90
Oak					
12" x 12" chestnut	—	SF	4.51	—	4.51
12" x 12" desert	—	SF	4.51	—	4.51
Teak					
12" x 12"	—	SF	5.97	—	5.97
Prefinished natural hardwood, commodity grade					
12" x 12"	—	SF	3.85	—	3.85
Labor and mastic for installing parquet block flooring					
Parquet laid in mastic	BF@.055	SF	.32	1.89	2.21
Edge-glued over high density foam	BF@.052	SF	.53	1.78	2.31
Custom or irregular-shaped tiles, with adhesive	BF@.074	SF	.53	2.54	3.07
Add for installations under 1,000 SF	BF@.025	SF	.05	.86	.91
Add for sanding and finishing for unfinished parquet block flooring					
Sanding, 3 passes (60/80/100 grit)	BF@.023	SF	.08	.79	.87
2 coats of stain/sealer	BF@.010	SF	.12	.34	.46
2 coats of urethane	BF@.012	SF	.15	.41	.56
2 coats of lacquer	BF@.024	SF	.20	.82	1.02

Prefinished cross-band 3-ply birch parquet flooring, 6" to 12" wide by 12" to 48" blocks, Oregon Lumber. Costs include cutting, fitting and 5% waste, but no subfloor preparation.

	Craft@Hrs	Unit	Material	Labor	Total
"Saima", 9/16" thick, typical price	BF@.050	SF	5.23	1.71	6.94
Bonded blocks, 12" x 12", 1/8" thick, laid in mastic					
Vinyl bonded cork	BF@.050	SF	4.29	1.71	6.00
Vinyl bonded domestic woods	BF@.062	SF	8.56	2.13	10.69
Vinyl bonded exotic woods	BF@.062	SF	17.30	2.13	19.43

	Craft@Hrs	Unit	Material	Labor	Total
Acrylic (Permagrain) impregnated wood flooring. 12" x 12" x 5/16" thick block laid in mastic					
Oak block	BF@.057	SF	11.50	1.95	13.45
Ash block	BF@.057	SF	12.50	1.95	14.45
Cherry block	BF@.057	SF	13.00	1.95	14.95
Maple block	BF@.057	SF	12.80	1.95	14.75
Acrylic (Permagrain) impregnated 2-7/8" x random length plank laid in mastic					
Oak plank	BF@.057	SF	9.45	1.95	11.40
Maple plank	BF@.057	SF	12.60	1.95	14.55
Tupelo plank	BF@.057	SF	11.90	1.95	13.85
Lindenwood plank	BF@.057	SF	13.20	1.95	15.15
Cherry plank	BF@.057	SF	13.00	1.95	14.95
Wood flooring adhesive. For laminated wood plank and wood parquet flooring. Covers 150 square feet per gallon when applied with a 1/8" x 1/8" x 1/8" square-notch trowel for parquet or a 1/4" x 1/4" x 1/4" V-notch trowel for laminated plank.					
Quart	—	Ea	12.40	—	12.40
4 gallons	—	Ea	198.00	—	198.00
Foundation Bolts Galvanized, with nut and washer attached. Costs per bolt or bag.					
1/2" x 6", pack of 1	B1@.107	Ea	1.69	3.62	5.31
1/2" x 6", pack of 25	B1@5.35	Ea	28.00	181.00	209.00
1/2" x 8", pack of 1	B1@.107	Ea	2.00	3.62	5.62
1/2" x 8", pack of 25	B1@5.35	Ea	35.10	181.00	216.10
1/2" x 10", pack of 1	B1@.107	Ea	2.31	3.62	5.93
1/2" x 10", pack of 25	B1@5.35	Ea	41.30	181.00	222.30
1/2" x 12", pack of 1	B1@.107	Ea	2.84	3.62	6.46
1/2" x 12", pack of 25	B1@5.35	Ea	50.40	181.00	231.40
1/2" x 18", pack of 1	B1@.107	Ea	4.00	3.62	7.62
1/2" x 18", pack of 25	B1@5.35	Ea	71.50	181.00	252.50
5/8" x 8", pack of 1	B1@.107	Ea	3.93	3.62	7.55
5/8" x 8", pack of 10	B1@2.68	Ea	30.40	90.70	121.10
5/8" x 10", pack of 1	B1@.107	Ea	4.40	3.62	8.02
5/8" x 10", pack of 10	B1@2.68	Ea	32.90	90.70	123.60

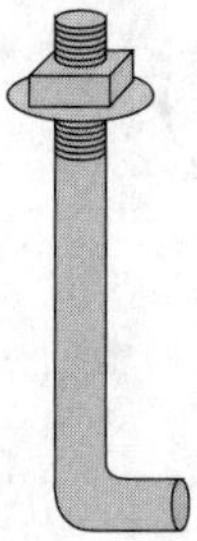

Framing Connectors All bolted connectors include nuts, bolts, and washers as needed. Costs are based on bulk purchases. Add 20% for smaller quantities.
Equivalent Simpson Strong-Tie Co. model numbers are shown in parentheses.

	Craft@Hrs	Unit	Material	Labor	Total
Angle clips (A34 and A35), 18 gauge, galvanized, no nails included					
3" x 5" connector (A35 or A35F)	BC@.030	Ea	.39	1.12	1.51
3" x 4" connector (A34)	BC@.030	Ea	.76	1.12	1.88
Angle clips ("L") for general utility use, 16 gauge, galvanized, no nails included					
3" (L30)	BC@.027	Ea	1.08	1.01	2.09
5" (L50)	BC@.027	Ea	1.28	1.01	2.29
7" (L70)	BC@.027	Ea	1.84	1.01	2.85
9" (L90)	BC@.027	Ea	2.29	1.01	3.30
Brick wall ties (BTR), 22 gauge, per 1,000					
7/8" x 6", corrugated	—	M	172.00	—	172.00
Bridging. See also Carpentry.					
Cross or Tension bridging for solid sawn lumber (NCA & TB), steel, per pair, no nails required					
12" joist spacing on center					
2" x 8" joists (NCA2X8-12)	BC@.022	Pr	2.58	.82	3.40
2" x 10" joists (NCA2X10-12)	BC@.022	Pr	1.84	.82	2.66
2" x 12" joists (NCA2X12-12)	BC@.022	Pr	1.84	.82	2.66
2" x 14" joists (NCA2X8-16)	BC@.022	Pr	2.00	.82	2.82
2" x 16" joists (NCA2X10-16)	BC@.022	Pr	2.00	.82	2.82

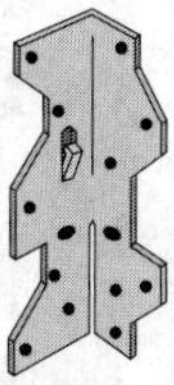

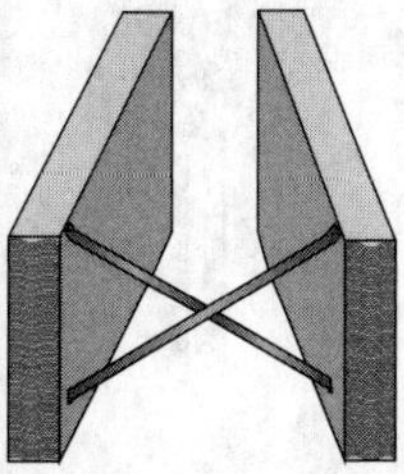

	Craft@Hrs	Unit	Material	Labor	Total
16" joist spacing on center					
2" x 8" joists (NCA2X8-16)	BC@.022	Pr	2.00	.82	2.82
2" x 10" joists (NCA2X10-16)	BC@.022	Pr	2.00	.82	2.82
2" x 12" joists (NCA2X12-16)	BC@.022	Pr	2.00	.82	2.82
2" x 14" to 2" x 16" joists (TB27)	BC@.022	Pr	5.01	.82	5.83
24" joist spacing on center					
2" x 10" to 2" x 16" joists (TB36)	BC@.022	Pr	2.70	.82	3.52
Cross or Tension bridging for I-Joists (TB), steel, per pair, no nails required					
12" joist spacing on center					
Joist heights 9-1/2" to 12" (TB20)	BC@.022	Pr	3.62	.82	4.44
Joist heights 14" to 18" (TB27)	BC@.022	Pr	4.05	.82	4.87
Joist heights 20" to 22" (TB30)	BC@.022	Pr	4.82	.82	5.64
Joist heights 24" to 30" (TB36)	BC@.022	Pr	4.97	.82	5.79
Joist height 32" (TB42)	BC@.022	Pr	9.23	.82	10.05
16" joist spacing on center					
Joist heights 9-1/2" to 16" (TB27)	BC@.022	Pr	4.05	.82	4.87
Joist heights 18" to 20" (TB30)	BC@.022	Pr	4.82	.82	5.64
Joist heights 22" to 28" (TB36)	BC@.022	Pr	4.97	.82	5.79
Joist heights 30" to 32" (TB42)	BC@.022	Pr	9.23	.82	10.05
24" joist spacing on center					
Joist heights 9-1/2" to 12" (TB30)	BC@.022	Pr	4.82	.82	5.64
Joist heights 14" to 22" (TB36)	BC@.022	Pr	4.97	.82	5.79
Joist heights 24" to 32" (TB42)	BC@.022	Pr	9.23	.82	10.05
Column bases, heavy duty (CB). Includes nuts and bolts. Labor shown is for placing column base before pouring concrete					
4" x 4" (CB44)	BC@.121	Ea	18.20	4.52	22.72
4" x 6" (CB46)	BC@.121	Ea	20.40	4.52	24.92
4" x 8" (CB48)	BC@.121	Ea	27.10	4.52	31.62
6" x 6" (CB66)	BC@.121	Ea	28.80	4.52	33.32
6" x 8" (CB68)	BC@.121	Ea	40.30	4.52	44.82
6" x 10" (CB610)	BC@.131	Ea	35.90	4.90	40.80
6" x 12" (CB612)	BC@.131	Ea	35.40	4.90	40.30
8" x 8" (CB88)	BC@.131	Ea	38.30	4.90	43.20
8" x 10" (CB810)	BC@.131	Ea	80.70	4.90	85.60
8" x 12" (CB812)	BC@.150	Ea	84.10	5.61	89.71
10" x 10" (CB1010)	BC@.150	Ea	100.00	5.61	105.61
10" x 12" (CB1012)	BC@.150	Ea	98.60	5.61	104.21
12" x 12" (CB1212)	BC@.150	Ea	110.00	5.61	115.61
Column caps or end column caps, heavy duty (CC) or (ECC). Includes nuts and bolts					
Column caps for solid lumber					
Beam size x post size					
4" x 4" (CC44)	BC@.260	Ea	42.80	9.72	52.52
4" x 6" (CC46)	BC@.300	Ea	69.50	11.20	80.70
6" x 4" (CC64)	BC@.300	Ea	93.10	11.20	104.30
6" x 6" (CC66)	BC@.400	Ea	74.00	15.00	89.00
6" x 8" (CC68)	BC@.600	Ea	93.10	22.40	115.50
8" x 6" (CC86)	BC@.600	Ea	103.00	22.40	125.40
8" x 8" (CC88)	BC@.750	Ea	103.00	28.00	131.00
10" x 6" (CC10X)	BC@.750	Ea	152.00	28.00	180.00
Column caps for glu-lam beams					
Beam size x post size					
3-1/4" x 4" (CC3-14-4)	BC@.260	Ea	85.70	9.72	95.42
3-1/4" x 6" (CC3-1/4-6)	BC@.300	Ea	82.90	11.20	94.10
5-1/4" x 6" (CC5-1/4-6)	BC@.400	Ea	108.00	15.00	123.00
5-1/4" x 8" (CC5-1/4-8)	BC@.600	Ea	104.00	22.40	126.40
7" x 6" (CC76)	BC@.600	Ea	105.00	22.40	127.40

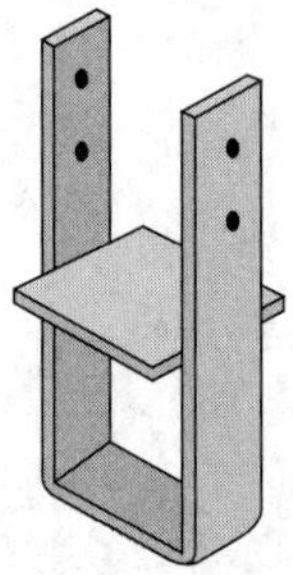

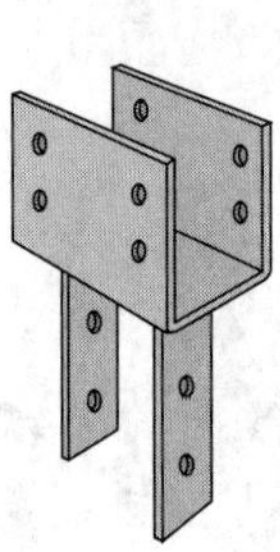

	Craft@Hrs	Unit	Material	Labor	Total
7" x 7" (CC77)	BC@.750	Ea	105.00	28.00	133.00
7" x 8" (CC78)	BC@.750	Ea	105.00	28.00	133.00
9" x 6" (CC96)	BC@.750	Ea	118.00	28.00	146.00
9" x 8" (CC98)	BC@.750	Ea	118.00	28.00	146.00
Floor tie anchors (FTA)					
2" x 38" (FTA2)	BC@.200	Ea	68.00	7.48	75.48
3-1/2" x 45" (FTA5)	BC@.200	Ea	93.50	7.48	100.98
3-1/2" x 56" (FTA7)	BC@.320	Ea	165.00	12.00	177.00
Header hangers (HH), 16 gauge, galvanized					
4" header (HH4)	BC@.046	Ea	6.74	1.72	8.46
6" header (HH6)	BC@.046	Ea	13.00	1.72	14.72
Hold downs (HD), including typical nuts, bolts and washers for studs. Add for foundation bolts					
HD2A	BC@.310	Ea	8.67	11.60	20.27
HD5A	BC@.310	Ea	22.70	11.60	34.30
HD8A	BC@.420	Ea	29.00	15.70	44.70
HD10A	BC@.500	Ea	31.30	18.70	50.00
HD20A	BC@.500	Ea	61.00	18.70	79.70
Threaded rod (ATR) 24" long. Labor includes drilling through 6" of wood					
1/2" rod, 12" length	BC@.185	LF	1.69	6.92	8.61
5/8" rod	BC@.185	LF	2.92	6.92	9.84
3/4" rod	BC@.200	LF	12.60	7.48	20.08
1" rod	BC@.220	LF	10.00	8.22	18.22
Hurricane and seismic ties (H)					
H1 tie	BC@.035	Ea	.70	1.31	2.01
H2 tie	BC@.027	Ea	1.44	1.01	2.45
H2.5 tie	BC@.027	Ea	.50	1.01	1.51
H3 tie	BC@.027	Ea	.43	1.01	1.44
H4 tie	BC@.027	Ea	.37	1.01	1.38
H5 tie	BC@.027	Ea	.56	1.01	1.57
H6 tie	BC@.045	Ea	4.12	1.68	5.80
H7Z tie	BC@.055	Ea	9.34	2.06	11.40
Mud sill anchors (MA)					
2" x 4" (MA4)	BC@.046	Ea	2.32	1.72	4.04
2" x 6" (MA6)	BC@.046	Ea	2.68	1.72	4.40
Panelized plywood roof hangers (F24N, F26N), for panelized plywood roof construction					
2" x 4" (F24N)	—	Ea	.93	—	.93
2" x 6" (F26N)	—	Ea	1.57	—	1.57
Purlin hangers (HU), without nails, 7 gauge					
4" x 4" (HU44)	BC@.052	Ea	7.33	1.94	9.27
4" x 6" (HU46)	BC@.052	Ea	8.54	1.94	10.48
4" x 8" (HU48)	BC@.052	Ea	14.50	1.94	16.44
4" x 10" (HU410)	BC@.070	Ea	9.74	2.62	12.36
4" x 12" (HU412)	BC@.070	Ea	9.78	2.62	12.40
4" x 14" (HU414)	BC@.087	Ea	18.10	3.25	21.35
4" x 16" (HU416)	BC@.087	Ea	20.90	3.25	24.15
6" x 6" (HU66)	BC@.052	Ea	12.80	1.94	14.74
6" x 8" (HU68)	BC@.070	Ea	12.70	2.62	15.32
6" x 10" (HU610)	BC@.087	Ea	15.80	3.25	19.05
6" x 12" (HU612)	BC@.087	Ea	28.00	3.25	31.25
6" x 16" (HU616)	BC@.117	Ea	40.80	4.37	45.17
8" x 10" (HU810)	BC@.087	Ea	23.10	3.25	26.35
8" x 12" (HU812)	BC@.117	Ea	26.20	4.37	30.57
8" x 14" (HU814)	BC@.117	Ea	35.00	4.37	39.37
8" x 16" (HU816)	BC@.117	Ea	42.50	4.37	46.87

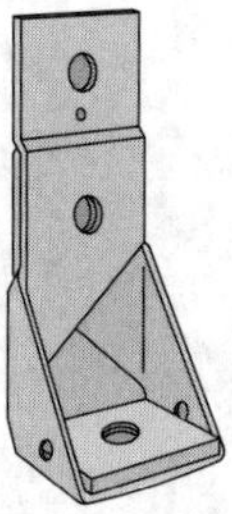

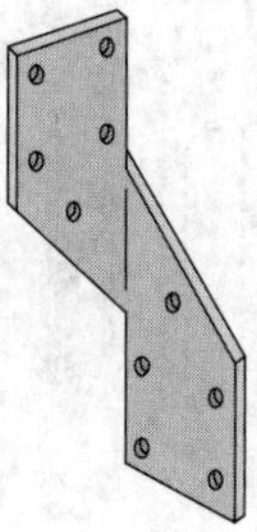

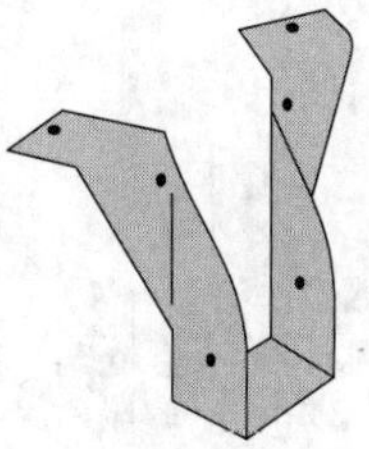

Framing Connectors

	Craft@Hrs	Unit	Material	Labor	Total
Top flange hangers (LB)					
2" x 6" (LB26)	BC@.046	Ea	3.37	1.72	5.09
2" x 8" (LB28)	BC@.046	Ea	3.66	1.72	5.38
2" x 10" (LB210)	BC@.046	Ea	5.08	1.72	6.80
2" x 12" (LB212)	BC@.046	Ea	13.00	1.72	14.72
2" x 14" (LB214)	BC@.052	Ea	9.00	1.94	10.94
Top flange hangers, heavy (HW)					
4" x 6" (HW46)	BC@.052	Ea	38.60	1.94	40.54
4" x 8" (HW48)	BC@.052	Ea	41.50	1.94	43.44
4" x 10" (HW410)	BC@.070	Ea	44.30	2.62	46.92
4" x 12" (HW412)	BC@.070	Ea	47.20	2.62	49.82
4" x 14" (HW414)	BC@.087	Ea	50.00	3.25	53.25
4" x 16" (HW416)	BC@.087	Ea	52.90	3.25	56.15
6" x 6" (HW66)	BC@.052	Ea	39.10	1.94	41.04
6" x 8" (HW68)	BC@.070	Ea	41.90	2.62	44.52
6" x 10" (HW610)	BC@.087	Ea	44.80	3.25	48.05
6" x 12" (HW612)	BC@.087	Ea	47.60	3.25	50.85
6" x 14" (HW614)	BC@.117	Ea	50.50	4.37	54.87
6" x 16" (HW616)	BC@.117	Ea	53.40	4.37	57.77
8" x 6" (HW86)	BC@.070	Ea	42.40	2.62	45.02
8" x 8" (HW88)	BC@.070	Ea	45.30	2.62	47.92
8" x 10" (HW810)	BC@.087	Ea	48.10	3.25	51.35
8" x 12" (HW812)	BC@.117	Ea	51.00	4.37	55.37
8" x 14" (HW814)	BC@.117	Ea	53.80	4.37	58.17
8" x 16" (HW816)	BC@.117	Ea	56.70	4.37	61.07
"U"-type or formed seat type hangers ("U"). Standard duty, 16 gauge, galvanized					
2" x 4" (U24)	BC@.040	Ea	1.33	1.50	2.83
2" x 6" (U26)	BC@.046	Ea	1.96	1.72	3.68
2" x 10" (U210)	BC@.046	Ea	2.68	1.72	4.40
2" x 14" (U214)	BC@.052	Ea	6.48	1.94	8.42
3" x 4" (U34)	BC@.046	Ea	4.07	1.72	5.79
3" x 6" (U36)	BC@.046	Ea	7.71	1.72	9.43
3" x 10" (U310)	BC@.052	Ea	4.42	1.94	6.36
3" x 14" (U314) or 3" x 16" (U316)	BC@.070	Ea	10.20	2.62	12.82
4" x 4" (U44)	BC@.046	Ea	2.82	1.72	4.54
4" x 6" (U46)	BC@.052	Ea	3.92	1.94	5.86
4" x 10" (U410)	BC@.070	Ea	4.76	2.62	7.38
4" x 14" (U414)	BC@.087	Ea	13.80	3.25	17.05
6" x 6" (U66)	BC@.052	Ea	13.40	1.94	15.34
6" x 10" (U610)	BC@.087	Ea	17.10	3.25	20.35
Plywood clips (PSCL, extruded aluminum, purchased in cartons of 500)					
3/8", 7/16", 1/2", or 5/8"	BC@.006	Ea	.12	.22	.34
Post base for decks (base with standoff, PBS), 12 gauge, galvanized					
4" x 4" (PBS44)	BC@.046	Ea	22.30	1.72	24.02
4" x 6" (PBS46)	BC@.046	Ea	15.20	1.72	16.92
6" x 6" (PBS66)	BC@.070	Ea	22.90	2.62	25.52
Add for rough lumber sizes	—	%	86.0	—	—
Post base (AB), adjustable, 16 gauge, galvanized					
4" x 4" (AB44B)	BC@.046	Ea	11.10	1.72	12.82
4" x 6" (AB46)	BC@.046	Ea	21.40	1.72	23.12
6" x 6" (AB66)	BC@.070	Ea	25.20	2.62	27.82
Add for rough lumber sizes	—	%	86.0	—	—
Post bases (PB), 12 gauge, galvanized					
4" x 4" (PB44)	BC@.046	Ea	7.41	1.72	9.13
4" x 6" (PB46)	BC@.046	Ea	10.60	1.72	12.32
6" x 6" (PB66)	BC@.070	Ea	14.70	2.62	17.32

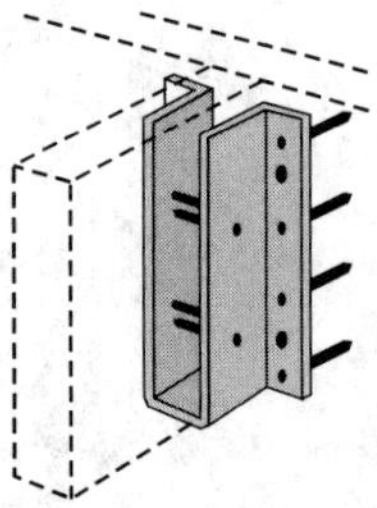

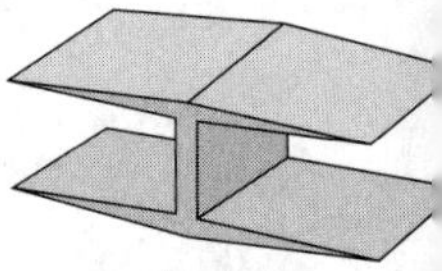

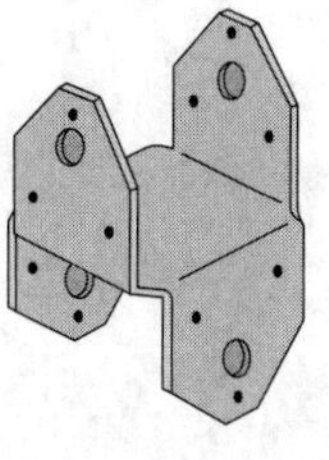

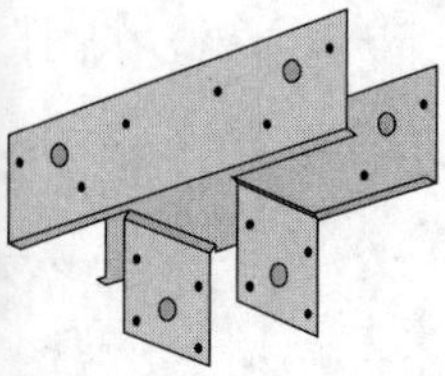

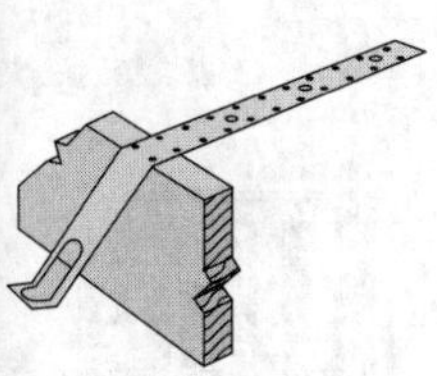

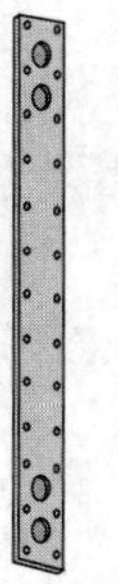

	Craft@Hrs	Unit	Material	Labor	Total
Post cap and base combination (BC), 18 gauge, galvanized					
4" x 4" (BC4)	BC@.037	Ea	4.54	1.38	5.92
4" x 6" (BC46)	BC@.037	Ea	5.80	1.38	7.18
6" x 6" (BC6)	BC@.054	Ea	13.10	2.02	15.12
8" x 8" (BC8)	BC@.054	Ea	47.70	2.02	49.72
Post caps and end post caps (PC), 12 gauge, galvanized. Beam size x post size					
4" x 4" (PC44)	BC@.052	Ea	14.00	1.94	15.94
4" x 6" (PC46)	BC@.052	Ea	13.60	1.94	15.54
4" x 8" (PC48)	BC@.052	Ea	25.20	1.94	27.14
6" x 4" (PC64)	BC@.052	Ea	22.10	1.94	24.04
6" x 6" (PC66)	BC@.077	Ea	22.10	2.88	24.98
6" x 8" (PC68)	BC@.077	Ea	22.80	2.88	25.68
8" x 8" (PC88)	BC@.077	Ea	36.40	2.88	39.28
Post top tie or anchor (AC), 18 gauge, galvanized					
4" x 4" (AC4)	BC@.040	Ea	4.55	1.50	6.05
6" x 6" (AC6)	BC@.040	Ea	6.06	1.50	7.56
Purlin anchors (PA), 12 gauge, 2" wide					
18" anchor (PA18)	BC@.165	Ea	6.74	6.17	12.91
23" anchor (PA23)	BC@.165	Ea	8.36	6.17	14.53
28" anchor (PA28)	BC@.185	Ea	8.25	6.92	15.17
35" anchor (PA35)	BC@.185	Ea	13.80	6.92	20.72
Split-ring connectors					
2-5/8" ring	BC@.047	Ea	3.03	1.76	4.79
4" ring	BC@.054	Ea	5.77	2.02	7.79
"L"-straps, 12 gauge (L)					
5" x 5", 1" wide (55L)	BC@.132	Ea	1.90	4.93	6.83
6" x 6", 1-1/2" wide (66L)	BC@.132	Ea	4.83	4.93	9.76
8" x 8", 2" wide (88L)	BC@.132	Ea	5.56	4.93	10.49
12" x 12", 2" wide (1212L)	BC@.165	Ea	8.15	6.17	14.32
Add for heavy duty straps, 7 gauge	—	%	330.0	—	—
Long straps (MST), 12 gauge					
27" (MST27)	BC@.165	Ea	9.64	6.17	15.81
37" (MST37)	BC@.165	Ea	7.09	6.17	13.26
48" (MST48)	BC@.265	Ea	9.39	9.91	19.30
60" (MST60)	BC@.265	Ea	18.90	9.91	28.81
72" (MST72)	BC@.285	Ea	23.80	10.70	34.50
Plate and stud straps (FHA), galvanized, 1-1/2" wide, 16 gauge					
6" (FHA6)	BC@.100	Ea	.35	3.74	4.09
9" (FHA9)	BC@.132	Ea	.43	4.93	5.36
12" (FHA12)	BC@.132	Ea	.59	4.93	5.52
18" (FHA18)	BC@.132	Ea	.73	4.93	5.66
24" (FHA24)	BC@.165	Ea	.98	6.17	7.15
32" (FHA30)	BC@.165	Ea	1.24	6.17	7.41
Tie straps (ST)					
2-1/16" x 9-5/16" 20 ga. (ST292)	BC@.132	Ea	.82	4.93	5.75
3/4" x 16-5/16" 20 ga. (ST2115)	BC@.046	Ea	1.04	1.72	2.76
2-1/16" x 16-5/16" 20 ga. (ST2215)	BC@.132	Ea	1.26	4.93	6.19
2-1/16" x 23-5/16" 16 ga. (ST6224)	BC@.165	Ea	3.36	6.17	9.53
2-1/16" x 33-13/16" 14 ga. (ST6236)	BC@.165	Ea	4.42	6.17	10.59
"T"-straps, 14 gauge (T)					
6" x 6", 1-1/2" wide (66T)	BC@.132	Ea	4.51	4.93	9.44
12" x 8", 2" wide (128T)	BC@.132	Ea	8.50	4.93	13.43
12" x 12", 2" wide (1212T)	BC@.132	Ea	10.10	4.93	15.03
Add for heavy duty straps, 7 gauge	—	%	330.0	—	—

	Craft@Hrs	Unit	Material	Labor	Total
Twist straps (TS), 16 gauge, galvanized, 1-1/4" wide					
9" (TS9)	BC@.132	Ea	2.62	4.93	7.55
11-5/8" (TS12)	BC@.132	Ea	1.88	4.93	6.81
17-3/4" (TS18)	BC@.132	Ea	5.34	4.93	10.27
21-5/8" (TS22)	BC@.165	Ea	3.34	6.17	9.51
Wall braces (WB), diagonal, 1-1/4" wide, 16 gauge					
10' long, corrugated or flat (WB106C or WB106)	BC@.101	Ea	12.30	3.78	16.08
12' long, flat (WB126)	BC@.101	Ea	10.90	3.78	14.68
14' long, flat (WB143C)	BC@.101	Ea	18.10	3.78	21.88
Wall braces (CWB), diagonal, 18 gauge, 1" wide					
10' long, L-shaped (CWB106)	BC@.125	Ea	11.70	4.67	16.37
12' long, L-shaped (CWB126)	BC@.125	Ea	13.60	4.67	18.27

Garage Door Openers Radio controlled, electric, single or double door, requires electrical outlet for plug-in connection, not included.

	Craft@Hrs	Unit	Material	Labor	Total
Security, chain drive, 1/2 HP	BC@3.90	Ea	128.00	146.00	274.00
Screw drive, 2 HP	BC@3.90	Ea	208.00	146.00	354.00
Security, belt drive, 3/4 HP	BC@3.90	Ea	198.00	146.00	344.00
Add for additional transmitter	—	Ea	30.00	—	30.00
Add for battery backup operator	—	Ea	128.00	—	128.00
Add for operator reinforcement kit	—	Ea	26.00	—	26.00
Add for low headroom kit	—	Ea	74.70	—	74.70
Add for emergency release	—	Ea	11.20	—	11.20
Belt rail extension kit	—	Ea	40.50	—	40.50
Chain glide extension kit	—	Ea	20.20	—	20.20
Chain rail extension kit	—	Ea	50.00	—	50.00
Screw drive extension kit	—	Ea	38.00	—	38.00

Garage Doors

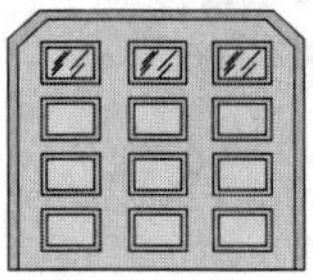

	Craft@Hrs	Unit	Material	Labor	Total
Corrugated panel steel rollup door. Economy model, 26 gauge construction, installation hardware, no insulation.					
8' x 7'	B1@6.46	Ea	401.00	219.00	620.00
9' x 7'	B1@6.46	Ea	430.00	219.00	649.00
10 x 7'	B1@8.33	Ea	490.00	282.00	772.00
Add for 8' height	—	%	10.5	—	—
Add for certified wind load	—	%	23.8	—	—
Corrugated panel steel rollup door. Heavy duty model, 26 gauge construction, installation hardware, no insulation.					
8' x 7'	B1@4.46	Ea	657.00	151.00	808.00
9' x 7'	B1@5.46	Ea	707.00	185.00	892.00
10' x 7'	B1@6.46	Ea	727.00	219.00	946.00
12' x 7'	B1@7.46	Ea	872.00	253.00	1,125.00
16' x 7'	B1@8.33	Ea	985.00	282.00	1,267.00
Add for certified wind load	—	%	46.7	—	—
Add for Miami-Dade County	—	%	93.3	—	—
Aluminum garage door. Uninsulated, 24 gauge woodgrain texture, side and bottom weatherstripping and hardware					
8' x 7'	B1@6.46	Ea	1,050.00	219.00	1,269.00
9' x 7'	B1@6.46	Ea	1,110.00	219.00	1,329.00
16' x 7'	B1@8.33	Ea	1,330.00	282.00	1,612.00
Add for 8' height, single wide	B1@0.86	Ea	83.10	29.10	112.20
Add for 8' height, double wide	B1@1.16	Ea	111.00	39.30	150.30
Add for pilot door	—	Ea	776.00	—	776.00
Raised steel panel garage door. Uninsulated, 24 gauge woodgrain texture, bottom weatherstripping and hardware					
8' x 7'	B1@6.46	Ea	1,440.00	219.00	1,659.00
9' x 7'	B1@6.46	Ea	1,550.00	219.00	1,769.00

	Craft@Hrs	Unit	Material	Labor	Total
16' x 7'	B1@8.33	Ea	1,770.00	282.00	2,052.00
Add for 8' height, single wide	B1@0.86	Ea	111.00	29.10	140.10
Add for 8' height, double wide	B1@1.16	Ea	139.00	39.30	178.30
Add for windows, single wide	—	Ea	222.00	—	222.00
Add for windows, double wide	—	Ea	305.00	—	305.00
Wood garage doors. 3/8" CDX paneling, unfinished, uninsulated, jamb hinges, and hardware.					
8' x 7'	B1@6.46	Ea	1,310.00	219.00	1,529.00
9' x 7'	B1@6.46	Ea	1,420.00	219.00	1,639.00
16' x 7'	B1@8.33	Ea	1,600.00	282.00	1,882.00
Add for 8' height, single wide	B1@0.86	Ea	109.00	29.10	138.10
Add for 8' height, double wide	B1@1.16	Ea	137.00	39.30	176.30
Add for 5/9" CDX paneling	—	%	10.8	—	—
Add for redwood or cedar 1" construction	—	%	287.0	—	—
Add for plant-on trim, pine, 1" x 6"	B1@.019	LF	5.42	.64	6.06
Add for plant-on trim, redwood or cedar, 1" x 6"	B1@.019	LF	9.03	.64	9.67
Add for windows, no grid	—	Ea	303.00	—	303.00
Add for windows, with grid	—	Ea	330.00	—	330.00
Sectional garage doors. Value series, 1-layer 25 gauge steel construction, bottom weatherstripping, and hardware.					
8' x 7'	B1@6.46	Ea	388.00	219.00	607.00
9' x 7'	B1@6.46	Ea	455.00	219.00	674.00
16' x 7'	B1@8.33	Ea	730.00	282.00	1,012.00
Add for plain windows	—	%	45.4	—	—
Sectional garage doors. Premium series, 3-layer 25 gauge steel construction, R-Value 18.4 insulation, bottom weatherstripping, and hardware.					
8' x 7'	B1@6.46	Ea	876.00	219.00	1,095.00
9' x 7'	B1@6.46	Ea	928.00	219.00	1,147.00
16' x 7'	B1@8.33	Ea	1,380.00	282.00	1,662.00
Add for plain windows	—	%	31.4	—	—
Sectional garage doors. Gallery series, 3-layer 25 gauge steel construction, R-Value 6.5 insulation, arch grill windows, stained wood-grained, bottom weatherstripping, and hardware.					
8' x 7'	B1@6.46	Ea	1,290.00	219.00	1,509.00
16' x 7'	B1@8.33	Ea	2,220.00	282.00	2,502.00
Garage door weather seal kit					
For 9' wide garage door	BC@.500	Ea	64.00	18.70	82.70
For garage door to 18' wide	BC@1.00	Ea	115.00	37.40	152.40
Garage door deadbolt lock with cylinder assembly					
Garage door lock	BC@.500	Ea	13.20	18.70	31.90
"T"-handle for rollup garage door bar lock					
Handle	BC@.250	Ea	8.92	9.35	18.27
Garage door hardware, jamb type, 7' height, with springs and slide bolt					
8' to 10' wide door	BC@4.36	Ea	159.00	163.00	322.00
10' to 16' wide door, with truss	BC@5.50	Ea	185.00	206.00	391.00
Truss assembly for 16' door	BC@.493	Ea	57.00	18.40	75.40
Garage door hardware, track type, 7' height, with springs and lock					
7' to 9' wide door	BC@4.36	Ea	317.00	163.00	480.00
10' to 16' double track	BC@5.50	Ea	548.00	206.00	754.00

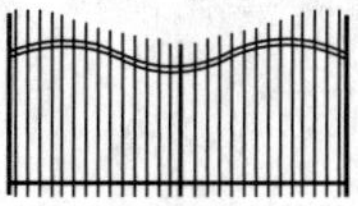

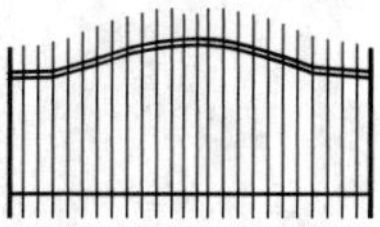

Gates, Ornamental Aluminum, Swing, Automatic

Welded aluminum, black driveway swing gates, double swing, arched up or down. Labor costs assume connection, but no wire runs. 2" square frame, 2" x 1-1/2" horizontal rails and 1" square pickets. Post and brackets not included. Hoover Fence (Jerith Estate style 202, 4' to 5' high)

	Craft@Hrs	Unit	Material	Labor	Total
12' wide opening	BL@1.00	Ea	2,560.00	30.30	2,590.30
16' wide opening	BL@1.20	Ea	3,240.00	36.40	3,276.40
20' wide opening	BL@1.40	Ea	4,000.00	42.40	4,042.40
Add for custom width gates	—	%	20.0	—	—

Glass

	Craft@Hrs	Unit	Material	Labor	Total
Gate posts					
4" x 9' post	BL@1.00	Ea	115.00	30.30	145.30
6" x 12' post	BL@1.00	Ea	279.00	30.30	309.30
Add for setting post in concrete	BL@.330	Ea	3.50	10.00	13.50
12 volt DC swing gate operator	BL@5.00	Ea	664.00	152.00	816.00
Dual gate unit	BL@5.00	Ea	779.00	152.00	931.00
Add for additional gate transmitters	—	Ea	43.20	—	43.20
Add for low voltage wire	—	LF	.31	—	.31
Glass Material only. See labor costs below.					
Cut window glass, clear DSB glass (double strength, B Grade)					
8" x 10"	—	Ea	2.06	—	2.06
10" x 12"	—	Ea	2.79	—	2.79
11" x 14"	—	Ea	3.30	—	3.30
12" x 16"	—	Ea	4.20	—	4.20
12" x 36"	—	Ea	7.51	—	7.51
16" x 20"	—	Ea	5.86	—	5.86
18" x 36"	—	Ea	11.20	—	11.20
24" x 30"	—	Ea	12.50	—	12.50
24" x 36"	—	Ea	14.70	—	14.70
30" x 36"	—	Ea	18.70	—	18.70
36" x 48"	—	Ea	34.20	—	34.20
SSB glass (single strength, B Grade)					
To 60" width plus length	—	SF	2.52	—	2.52
Over 60" to 70" width plus length	—	SF	3.13	—	3.13
Over 70" to 80" width plus length	—	SF	2.79	—	2.79
DSB glass (double strength, B Grade)					
To 60" width plus length	—	SF	3.52	—	3.52
Over 60" to 70" width plus length	—	SF	3.58	—	3.58
Over 70" to 80" width plus length	—	SF	3.65	—	3.65
Over 80" to 100" width plus length	—	SF	3.90	—	3.90
Non-glare glass	—	SF	6.02	—	6.02
Float glass, 1/4" thick					
To 25 SF	—	SF	3.95	—	3.95
25 to 35 SF	—	SF	4.25	—	4.25
35 to 50 SF	—	SF	4.61	—	4.61
Insulating glass, clear					
1/2" thick, 1/4" airspace, up to 25 SF	—	SF	8.53	—	8.53
5/8" thick, 1/4" airspace, up to 35 SF	—	SF	9.96	—	9.96
1" thick, 1/2" airspace, up to 50 SF	—	SF	11.60	—	11.60
Tempered glass, clear, 1/4" thick					
To 25 SF	—	SF	8.53	—	8.53
25 to 50 SF	—	SF	10.20	—	10.20
50 to 75 SF	—	SF	11.20	—	11.20
Tempered glass, clear, 3/16" thick					
To 25 SF	—	SF	8.39	—	8.39
25 to 50 SF	—	SF	9.60	—	9.60
50 to 75 SF	—	SF	10.60	—	10.60
Laminated safety glass, 1/4" thick, ASI safety rating					
Up to 25 SF	—	SF	10.90	—	10.90
25 to 35 SF	—	SF	11.40	—	11.40
Polycarbonate sheet, .093" thick, clear					
8" x 10"	—	Ea	4.98	—	4.98
12" x 24"	—	Ea	16.00	—	16.00
18" x 24"	—	Ea	21.90	—	21.90
36" x 48"	—	Ea	87.00	—	87.00
36" x 72"	—	Ea	108.00	—	108.00

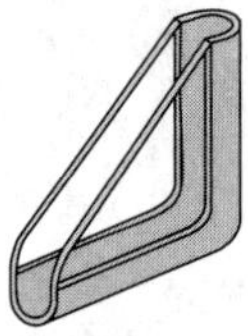

	Craft@Hrs	Unit	Material	Labor	Total
Acrylic plastic sheet (Plexiglas), clear					
11" x 14" .093" thick	—	Ea	6.67	—	6.67
12" x 24" .093" thick	—	Ea	8.00	—	8.00
18" x 24" .093" thick	—	Ea	13.50	—	13.50
18" x 24" .22" thick	—	Ea	29.80	—	29.80
30" x 36" .093" thick	—	Ea	32.80	—	32.80
30" x 36" .22" thick	—	Ea	73.30	—	73.30
36" x 48" .093" thick	—	Ea	48.00	—	48.00
36" x 72" .093" thick	—	Ea	70.00	—	70.00
36" x 72" .22" thick	—	Ea	156.00	—	156.00
48" x 96" 1/8" thick	—	Ea	130.00	—	130.00

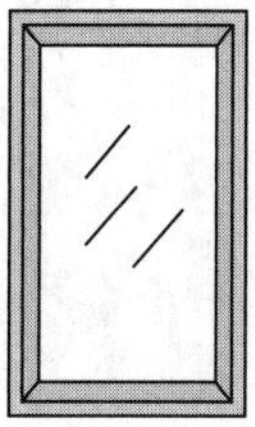

	Craft@Hrs	Unit	Material	Labor	Total
Beveled edge mirrors, no frame included	—	SF	9.14	—	9.14
Labor setting glass in wood or metal sash with vinyl bed					
To 15 SF, 1 hour charge	BG@1.77	LS	—	64.00	64.00
15 to 25 SF, 2 hour charge	BG@3.53	LS	—	128.00	128.00
25 to 35 SF, 3 hour charge	BG@5.30	LS	—	191.00	191.00
Labor to bevel edges, per linear inch					
1/2" beveled edge	BG@.013	Inch	—	.47	.47
1" beveled edge	BG@.063	Inch	—	2.28	2.28

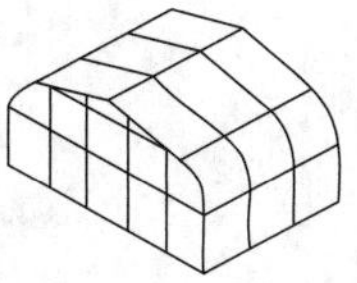

Greenhouses, Sun Porches, Spa Enclosures Freestanding or lean-to models. Anodized aluminum frame, acrylic glazed. Add the cost of excavation and concrete. Expect to see a wide variation in greenhouse costs for any given size.

	Craft@Hrs	Unit	Material	Labor	Total
Freestanding greenhouse enclosures, one door and four walls. 8' deep					
7' high, 6' wide	B1@21.0	Ea	5,270.00	711.00	5,981.00
7-1/2' high, 9' wide	B1@33.0	Ea	6,580.00	1,120.00	7,700.00
8' high, 12' wide	B1@47.0	Ea	7,650.00	1,590.00	9,240.00
8' high, 15' wide	B1@59.0	Ea	8,920.00	2,000.00	10,920.00
9' high, 18' wide	B1@80.0	Ea	10,100.00	2,710.00	12,810.00
Lean-to greenhouse enclosures attached on long dimension to an existing structure, one door and three walls. 8' deep					
7' high, 3' wide	B1@8.40	Ea	2,780.00	284.00	3,064.00
7' high, 6' wide	B1@16.8	Ea	4,170.00	569.00	4,739.00
7-1/2' high, 9' wide	B1@27.0	Ea	5,230.00	914.00	6,144.00
8' high, 12' wide	B1@38.4	Ea	6,340.00	1,300.00	7,640.00
8' high, 15' wide	B1@48.0	Ea	7,430.00	1,620.00	9,050.00
Add for additional outswing door	—	Ea	312.00	—	312.00
Add for additional sliding window	—	Ea	168.00	—	168.00

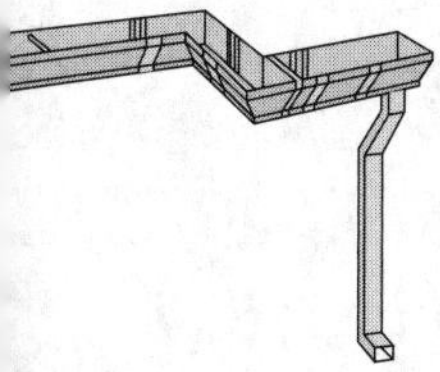

Gutters and Downspouts

	Craft@Hrs	Unit	Material	Labor	Total
Galvanized steel, 5" box type					
Gutter, 5", 10' lengths	SW@.070	LF	.80	2.95	3.75
Inside or outside miter corner	SW@.091	Ea	9.40	3.84	13.24
Fascia support brackets	—	Ea	3.02	—	3.02
Spike and ferrule support, 7"	—	Ea	.93	—	.93
Gutter slip-joint connector	—	Ea	3.42	—	3.42
End cap	—	Ea	2.07	—	2.07
Add per 2" x 3" downspout, with drop outlet, 3 ells, strainer, 2 bands and 15" extension					
10' downspout	SW@.540	Ea	47.00	22.80	69.80
20' downspout with coupling	SW@.810	Ea	61.30	34.10	95.40
Aluminum rain gutter, 5" box type, primed					
Gutter, 5", 10' lengths	SW@.070	LF	1.23	2.95	4.18
Inside or outside corner	SW@.091	Ea	6.33	3.84	10.17
Fascia support brackets	—	Ea	1.76	—	1.76
Gutter hanger and support	—	Ea	.45	—	.45
End cap	—	Ea	.70	—	.70

	Craft@Hrs	Unit	Material	Labor	Total
Add per 2" x 3" downspout, with drop outlet, 3 ells, strainer, 2 bands and 15" extension					
10' downspout	SW@.540	Ea	35.40	22.80	58.20
20' downspout with coupling	SW@.810	Ea	46.20	34.10	80.30

Gypsum Drywall and Accessories Labor costs are for good quality hanging and taping with smooth sanded joints (Level 4) and include 6% waste but no texturing. See texturing costs below. Installed costs include premixed joint compound, (5 gallons per 1,000 SF), 2" perforated joint tape (380 LF per 1,000 SF) and drywall screws (4-1/2 pounds per 1,000 SF) at the following material prices. Ea = 1 sheet

	Unit	4' x 8'	4' x 9'	4' x 10'	4' x 12'
Plain board					
1/4"	Ea	12.70	14.20	15.80	19.00
3/8"	Ea	11.30	12.70	14.10	16.90
1/2"	Ea	10.20	12.60	14.00	18.30
5/8" fire-rated	Ea	14.50	14.60	15.20	19.50
Lightweight board					
1/2"	Ea	12.10	14.90	13.70	18.30
5/8"fire-rated	Ea	14.40	15.70	16.20	21.60
Mold/moisture resistant board					
1/2"	Ea	16.90	18.20	19.80	23.60
5/8" fire-rated	Ea	17.30	18.30	19.60	23.80
Type 'C' & 'X' fire-rated					
1/2" Type 'C'	Ea	15.00	16.90	18.70	22.50
5/8" Type 'C'	Ea	15.70	17.70	19.60	23.60
5/8" Type 'X'	Ea	13.50	14.60	15.50	20.10

	Craft@Hrs	Unit	Material	Labor	Total
Drywall installation costs					
1/4" plain board					
Walls	D1@.016	SF	.40	.58	.98
3/8" plain board					
Walls	D1@.017	SF	.35	.62	.97
1/2" plain board					
Walls	D1@.018	SF	.42	.66	1.08
1/2" moisture-resistant green board					
Walls	D1@.018	SF	.50	.66	1.16
1/2" fire-rated mold-tough					
Walls	D1@.018	SF	.48	.66	1.14
5/8" fire-rated board					
Walls	D1@.020	SF	.41	.73	1.14
Add for 1/2" ceiling installation	—	%	—	33.3	—
Add for 5/8" ceiling installation	—	%	—	25.0	—
Add for level 5 drywall finishing, per 100 SF	D1@.060	CSF	.40	2.19	2.59
Deduct for no taping or joint finishing					
Walls	—	CSF	-.20	-72.80	-73.00
Ceilings	—	CSF	-.20	-96.80	-97.00
Drywall finishing. Per ASTM C840. Higher 'level' figures include prior 'levels'.					
Add for tape embedding only, no joint finishing	DT@.300	CSF	1.28	11.00	12.28
Level 1 – taping and finishing wall joints (firetape)	DT@.700	CSF	3.21	25.60	28.81
Level 2 – finishing wall joints	DT@1.20	CSF	4.37	43.90	48.27
Level 3 – finishing wall joints	DT@1.60	CSF	5.52	58.60	64.12
Level 4 – finishing wall joints	DT@2.00	CSF	5.85	73.20	79.05
Level 5 – finishing wall joints, skim entire surface	DT@2.60	CSF	7.70	95.20	102.90
Level 5 –only, skim entire surface	DT@.600	CSF	1.85	22.00	23.85
Add for taping and finishing ceiling joints	—	%	—	33.3	—

	Craft@Hrs	Unit	Material	Labor	Total
Drywall texture					
Light hand texture	DT@.500	CSF	.24	18.30	18.54
Medium hand texture	DT@.600	CSF	.34	22.00	22.34
Heavy hand texture	DT@.700	CSF	.56	25.60	26.16
Skim coat, smooth	DT@1.20	CSF	.21	43.90	44.11
Knockdown, spray applied and troweled	DT@.200	CSF	.29	7.32	7.61
Acoustic ceiling (popcorn), spray application					
Light coverage	DT@.800	CSF	1.67	29.30	30.97
Medium coverage	DT@1.10	CSF	2.34	40.30	42.64
Heavy coverage	DT@1.60	CSF	3.90	58.60	62.50
Glitter application to acoustic ceiling texture	DT@.200	CSF	1.34	7.32	8.66
Remove acoustic ceiling texture (no asbestos)	BL@1.13	CSF	—	34.30	34.30
Repair drywall "blow-out" patch					
Patch "blow-out"	D1@.333	Ea	2.34	12.20	14.54
Joint compounds					
All-purpose joint compound, premix, 4.5 gal	—	Ea	14.30	—	14.30
Lightweight joint finishing compound, 3.5 gal	—	Ea	12.00	—	12.00
Joint tapes					
Perforated joint tape, 500' roll	—	Ea	3.90	—	3.90
Self-adhesive fiberglass joint tape, 150' roll	—	Ea	6.93	—	6.93
Drywall screws, 5 pound box	—	Ea	18.60	—	18.60
Topping compounds, mix with water					
Wall and ceiling spray texture, 50 lb.	—	Ea	11.00	—	11.00
Wall and ceiling hand applied texture, 50 lb.	—	Ea	15.90	—	15.90
Drywall casing and channel trim.					
Stop or casing or jamb casing	D1@.020	LF	.29	.73	1.02
7/8" hat channel	D1@.011	LF	.42	.40	.82
Narrow soundproofing channel, metal	D1@.011	LF	.85	.40	1.25
Narrow soundproofing channel, PVC	D1@.011	LF	1.13	.40	1.53
Regular soundproofing channel, metal	D1@.011	LF	.85	.40	1.25
Regular soundproofing channel, w/ iso tape	D1@.011	LF	1.12	.40	1.52
RC-1 resilient hat channel	D1@.011	LF	.64	.40	1.04
RC-1 resilient hat channel, w/ iso tape	D1@.011	LF	.96	.40	1.36
RC-2 resilient hat channel (for ceilings)	D1@.011	LF	.83	.40	1.23
RC-2 resilient hat channel w/ iso tape	D1@.011	LF	1.08	.40	1.48
Drywall arch and corner trim, metal					
Corner bead, 1-1/4"	D1@.030	LF	.27	1.10	1.37
Corner bullnose, 3/4" radius	D1@.030	LF	.47	1.10	1.57
Type "J" bead, 1/2" or 5/8"	D1@.030	LF	.29	1.10	1.39
Drywall arch and corner trim, vinyl					
Corner bead, 1-1/4"	D1@.030	LF	.21	1.10	1.31
Corner bead, flexible (arch) 1-1/4"	D1@.030	LF	.34	1.10	1.44
Corner bullnose, 3/4" radius	D1@.030	LF	.18	1.10	1.28
Corner bullnose, 3/4" radius, flexible (arch)	D1@.030	LF	.76	1.10	1.86
Type "J" bead, 1/2" or 5/8"	D1@.030	LF	.18	1.10	1.28
Bullnose corner, 2-way	D1@.160	Ea	1.46	5.85	7.31
Bullnose corner, 3-way	D1@.160	Ea	1.23	5.85	7.08
Corner guard, nail on, 3/4"	D1@.030	LF	.36	1.10	1.46
Corner guard, stick on, 3/4"	D1@.030	LF	.41	1.10	1.51

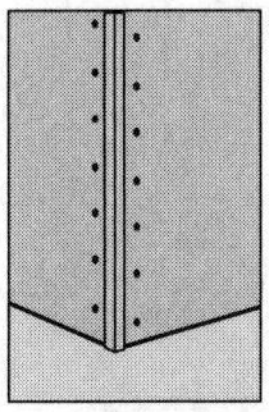

Hardware See also Bath Accessories, Door Chimes, Door Closers, Foundation Bolts, Garage Door Openers, Mailboxes, Nails, Screen Wire, Sheet Metal, Framing Connectors, and Weatherstripping. Rule of thumb: Cost of finish hardware (including door hardware, catches, stops, racks, brackets and pulls) per house.

Low to medium cost house (1,600 SF)	BC@16.0	LS	1,320.00	598.00	1,918.00
Better quality house (2,000 SF)	BC@20.0	LS	1,590.00	748.00	2,338.00

Hardware

	Craft@Hrs	Unit	Material	Labor	Total
Keyed entry locksets. Meets ANSI Grade 2 standards for residential security. One-piece knob. Triple option faceplate fits square, radius-round, and drive-in door preps.					
Antique brass	BC@.250	Ea	30.50	9.35	39.85
Antique pewter	BC@.250	Ea	33.60	9.35	42.95
Bright brass	BC@.250	Ea	28.50	9.35	37.85
Satin chrome	BC@.250	Ea	32.50	9.35	41.85
Lever locksets. Dual torque springs eliminate wobble.					
Antique brass	BC@.250	Ea	86.30	9.35	95.65
Polished brass	BC@.250	Ea	83.10	9.35	92.45
Egg knob entry locksets					
Satin nickel finish	BC@.250	Ea	38.60	9.35	47.95
Solid forged brass, polished brass finish	BC@.250	Ea	155.00	9.35	164.35
Colonial knob entry locksets					
Polished brass	BC@.250	Ea	146.00	9.35	155.35
Double cylinder high security lockset. Forged brass handle with thumb latch. Separate grade 1 security double cylinder deadbolt.					
Chrome finish	BC@.820	Ea	220.00	30.70	250.70
Construction keying system (minimum order of 20 keyed entry locks)					
Additional cost per lockset	—	Ea	7.73	—	7.73
Deadbolt and lockset combo. Includes keyed alike entry knob and grade 2 security deadbolt with 4 keys. Single cylinder.					
Polished brass finish	BC@.750	Ea	43.70	28.00	71.70
Mortise lockset and deadbolt. Steel reinforced cast 1" throw deadbolt. Solid brass latch. Rocker switch locks and unlocks exterior knob. Labor includes mortising of door.					
Left or right hand throw	BC@1.05	Ea	225.00	39.20	264.20
Deadbolts. All metal and brass. ANSI Grade 2 rating. 1" throw deadbolt. Includes 2 keys. Polished brass.					
Single cylinder	BC@.500	Ea	24.20	18.70	42.90
Double cylinder	BC@.500	Ea	45.80	18.70	64.50
Knob passage latch					
Dummy, brass	BC@.250	Ea	5.92	9.35	15.27
Dummy, satin nickel	BC@.250	Ea	7.53	9.35	16.88
Hall or closet, brass	BC@.250	Ea	8.37	9.35	17.72
Hall or closet, satin nickel	BC@.250	Ea	11.10	9.35	20.45
Egg knob privacy latchset					
Bright brass	BC@.250	Ea	24.50	9.35	33.85
Satin nickel	BC@.250	Ea	30.50	9.35	39.85
Privacy lever latchset. Both levers locked or unlocked by turn button. Outside lever can be unlocked by emergency key (included).					
Rubbed bronze	BC@.250	Ea	38.20	9.35	47.55
Polished brass	BC@.250	Ea	54.20	9.35	63.55
Satin nickel	BC@.250	Ea	32.50	9.35	41.85
Door knockers. Polished brass.					
Apartment type, brass, with viewer	BC@.250	Ea	7.38	9.35	16.73
4" x 8-1/2", ornate style	BC@.250	Ea	57.40	9.35	66.75
Door pull plates					
Brass finish, 4" x 16"	BC@.333	Ea	38.20	12.40	50.60
Door push plates					
Aluminum, 3" x 12"	BC@.333	Ea	10.20	12.40	22.60
Solid brass, 4" x 16"	BC@.333	Ea	11.90	12.40	24.30
Door kick plates					
6" x 30", brass	BC@.333	Ea	22.00	12.40	34.40
8" x 34", brass	BC@.333	Ea	20.30	12.40	32.70
8" x 34", magnetic, for metal door, brass	BC@.333	Ea	16.10	12.40	28.50
8" x 34", satin nickel	BC@.333	Ea	31.50	12.40	43.90
Floor mounted stop, satin nickel	BC@.333	Ea	5.07	12.40	17.47

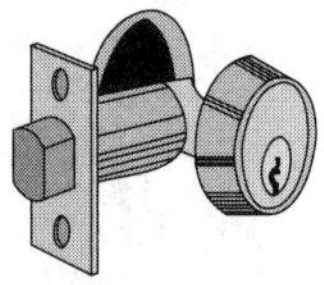

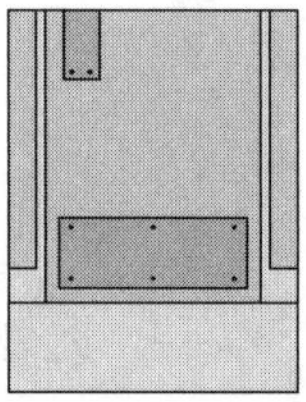

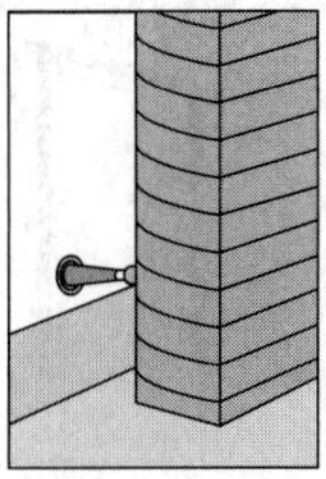

	Craft@Hrs	Unit	Material	Labor	Total
Door stops					
Spring type wall bumper, 3" long	BC@.116	Ea	2.52	4.34	6.86
Wall bumper, 3" long, brass	BC@.116	Ea	4.86	4.34	9.20
Floor mounted stop, satin nickel	BC@.333	Ea	5.07	12.40	17.47
Hinge pin door stop, brass	BC@.250	Ea	2.63	9.35	11.98
Kick down door holder, brass	BC@.250	Ea	11.00	9.35	20.35
Magnetic wall stop	BC@.333	Ea	6.59	12.40	18.99
Adhesive rubber cup knob strike	BC@.116	Ea	5.64	4.34	9.98
Door peep sights					
180-degree viewing angle	BC@.258	Ea	11.20	9.64	20.84

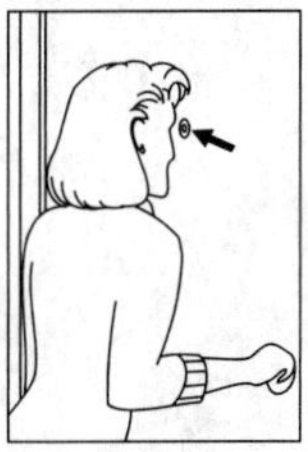

Pocket door frame and track. Fully assembled. Designed to hold 150-pound standard 80" door. Door sold separately.

	Craft@Hrs	Unit	Material	Labor	Total
24" x 80"	BC@1.00	Ea	221.00	37.40	258.40
28" x 80"	BC@1.00	Ea	237.00	37.40	274.40
30" x 80"	BC@1.00	Ea	222.00	37.40	259.40
32" x 80"	BC@1.00	Ea	218.00	37.40	255.40
36" x 80"	BC@1.00	Ea	219.00	37.40	256.40
Pocket door edge pulls					
Bronze passage pull, oil rubbed	BC@.300	Ea	28.80	11.20	40.00
Satin nickel privacy latch	BC@.300	Ea	19.80	11.20	31.00
Bronze privacy latch	BC@.300	Ea	16.30	11.20	27.50
Chrome privacy latch	BC@.300	Ea	14.70	11.20	25.90
Bronze passage pull	BC@.300	Ea	11.00	11.20	22.20
Oblong door pull	BC@.300	Ea	5.79	11.20	16.99
Ball bearing pocket door hangers					
Hanger	BC@.175	Ea	17.90	6.54	24.44
Converging pocket door hardware kit. For double pocket doors.					
Door kit	—	Ea	21.40	—	21.40
Pocket door hangers					
Pocket door hanger, 4-pack	BC@.175	Ea	9.34	6.54	15.88
1/16" offset, one wheel	BC@.175	Ea	10.50	6.54	17.04
7/8" offset, two wheel	BC@.175	Ea	9.55	6.54	16.09

Touch bar exit hardware. For use with 1-3/4"-thick hollow metal and wood doors. Extruded anodized aluminum with stainless steel spring. 3/4" throw stainless steel latch bolts. Strike for 5/8" stop; shim for 1/2" stop; 2-3/4" backset, 4-1/4" minimum stile. Includes standard mounting with sheet metal and machine screws. Recommended mounting height: 40-5/16" from ceiling to finished floor. 36" maximum width. Rim-type cylinders with Schlage "C" keyway. Includes measure and mark, drill holes, assemble, set strike plate.

	Craft@Hrs	Unit	Material	Labor	Total
Install, single door	BC@1.45	Ea	132.00	54.20	186.20
Install, per set of double doors	BC@2.97	Ea	264.00	111.00	375.00
Add for monitor switch for electrically operated locks					
Per lock	—	Ea	79.40	—	79.40

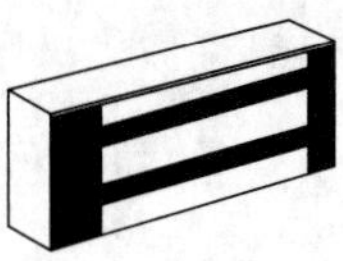

Electromagnetic security and life safety lock system. Surface mounted on door frame. Stainless steel finish. Includes magnet, strike plate, mounting fasteners and template. Costs include connection. Add for wire runs. Magnalock™.

	Craft@Hrs	Unit	Material	Labor	Total
600 lb holding force 12/24 VDC	E4@2.00	Ea	316.00	102.00	418.00
1,200 lb holding force 12/24 VDC	E4@2.00	Ea	379.00	102.00	481.00
1,800 lb holding force 12/24 VDC	E4@2.00	Ea	436.00	102.00	538.00
Digital timer, 12/24 AC/DC	E4@.500	Ea	153.00	25.40	178.40
Exit delay timer, regulated DC voltage	E4@2.50	Ea	107.00	127.10	234.10

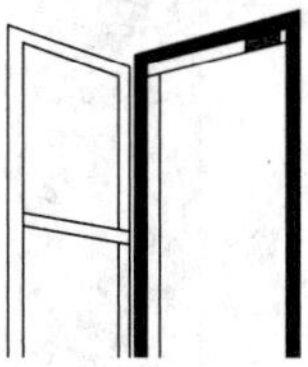

	Craft@Hrs	Unit	Material	Labor	Total
Exit delay system documentation and pressure sensitive vinyl door label					
for NFPA 101 requirements	—	Ea	14.70	—	14.70
Tamper-resistant plunger sex bolt	—	Ea	117.00	—	117.00
Energy absorbing sex bolt	—	Ea	224.00	—	224.00
Replacement strike plate and fasteners	—	Ea	103.00	—	103.00
Field mounted stainless steel housing. Includes cover, end caps,					
mounting plate and fasteners	BC@1.50	Ea	560.00	56.10	616.10
House street numbers, per number					
4" high, nail-on, aluminum	BC@.103	Ea	1.89	3.85	5.74
4" high, traditional brass	BC@.103	Ea	7.05	3.85	10.90
4" high, contemporary bronze	BC@.103	Ea	6.55	3.85	10.40
4" high, stainless steel	BC@.103	Ea	21.80	3.85	25.65
5" high, solid brass	BC@.103	Ea	11.60	3.85	15.45
Hinges					
Full mortise hinge, heavy duty, satin brass finish					
3-1/2" x 3-1/2", 6 screws, .123 gauge	BC@.333	Ea	9.14	12.40	21.54
4" x 4", 8 screws, .130 gauge	BC@.333	Ea	12.20	12.40	24.60
4" x 4", spring hinge	BC@.333	Ea	16.60	12.40	29.00
Full mortise hinge, light duty, satin brass finish					
3-1/2" x 3-1/2", loose pin	BC@.333	Ea	3.03	12.40	15.43
4" x 4", loose pin	BC@.333	Ea	3.85	12.40	16.25
Screen door hinge kit, 2 hinges, door pull and hook					
Bright zinc	BC@.750	Ea	16.80	28.00	44.80

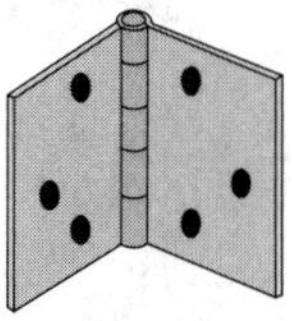

Hydronic Heating and Controls A complete system will consist of a hydronic boiler, cast iron radiators or hydronic radiation baseboard heaters, boiler controls and accessories. These systems are engineered to meet specific heating requirements. Once design requirements are known, use the figures that follow to estimate the cost of a complete installed system. For pipe, fittings, hangers and insulation costs, see the Commercial and Industrial section. For more detailed coverage, see the *National Plumbing & HVAC Estimator*, http://CraftsmanSiteLicense.com.

Hydronic boilers. U.S. Green Council and ASME "H" stamp certified to a rating of 95% AFUE (annual fuel usage efficiency) with EPA Tier II Nox emissions compliant burner, Kunkel safety valve, low-water cutoff, digital panel controls and automatic level controls. Weil-McClain UE-3 series or equal.

	Craft@Hrs	Unit	Material	Labor	Total
37,500 Btu with standard gas pilot	P1@3.00	Ea	1,980.00	111.00	2,091.00
62,000 Btu with standard gas pilot	P1@3.50	Ea	2,350.00	129.00	2,479.00
96,000 Btu with standard gas pilot	P1@3.50	Ea	2,590.00	129.00	2,719.00
130,000 Btu with standard gas pilot	P1@4.00	Ea	2,960.00	148.00	3,108.00
164,000 Btu with standard gas pilot	P1@4.00	Ea	3,400.00	148.00	3,548.00
198,000 Btu with standard gas pilot	P1@4.00	Ea	3,900.00	148.00	4,048.00
Add for electronic ignition	—	Ea	375.00	—	375.00
LEED certification for hydronic boilers. Requires 88% boiler efficiency, recording controls, compliance with SCAQMD 1146.2 emission standards and zone thermostats.					
Add for LEED certification, per project	—	Ea	—	—	2,000.00
Add for central performance monitor/recorder	—	Ea	1,190.00	—	1,190.00
Add for zone recording thermostat	—	Ea	168.00	—	168.00
Add for a LEED certified boiler with USGBC rating	—	%	15.0	—	—

	Craft@Hrs	Unit	Material	Labor	Total
Air eliminator-purger, threaded connections					
3/4", cast iron, steam & water, 150 PSI	P1@.250	Ea	469.00	9.22	478.22
3/4", cast iron, 150 PSI water	P1@.250	Ea	151.00	9.22	160.22
1", cast iron, 150 PSI water	P1@.250	Ea	175.00	9.22	184.22
3/8", brass, 125 PSI steam	P1@.250	Ea	122.00	9.22	131.22
1/2", cast iron, 250 PSI steam	P1@.250	Ea	256.00	9.22	265.22
3/4", cast iron, 250 PSI steam	P1@.250	Ea	323.00	9.22	332.22
Airtrol fitting, 3/4"	P1@.300	Ea	54.90	11.10	66.00
Air eliminator vents	P1@.150	Ea	18.60	5.53	24.13
Atmospheric (anti-siphon) vacuum breakers, rough brass, threaded					
1/2" vacuum breaker	P1@.210	Ea	29.00	7.75	36.75
3/4" vacuum breaker	P1@.250	Ea	31.00	9.22	40.22
1" vacuum breaker	P1@.300	Ea	49.10	11.10	60.20
1-1/4" vacuum breaker	P1@.400	Ea	81.50	14.80	96.30
1-1/2" vacuum breaker	P1@.450	Ea	96.20	16.60	112.80
2" vacuum breaker	P1@.500	Ea	143.00	18.40	161.40
Circuit balancing valves, bronze, threaded					
1/2" circuit balancing valve	P1@.210	Ea	81.40	7.75	89.15
3/4" circuit balancing valve	P1@.250	Ea	86.60	9.22	95.82
1" circuit balancing valve	P1@.300	Ea	100.00	11.10	111.10
1-1/2" circuit balancing valve	P1@.450	Ea	157.00	16.60	173.60
Baseboard fin tube radiation, per linear foot, copper tube with aluminum fins, wall mounted					
1/2" element and 8" cover	P1@.280	LF	12.20	10.30	22.50
3/4" element and 9"cover	P1@.280	LF	19.90	10.30	30.20
3/4" element, 10" cover, high capacity	P1@.320	LF	31.40	11.80	43.20
3/4" fin tube element only	P1@.140	LF	7.91	5.16	13.07
1" fin tube element only	P1@.150	LF	9.51	5.53	15.04
8" cover only	P1@.140	LF	7.38	5.16	12.54
9" cover only	P1@.140	LF	8.99	5.16	14.15
10" cover only	P1@.160	LF	9.81	5.90	15.71
Add for pipe connection and control valve	P1@2.15	Ea	195.00	79.30	274.30
Add for corners, fillers, caps, average per foot	—	%	10.0	—	—
Flow check valves, brass, threaded, horizontal type					
3/4" check valve	P1@.250	Ea	20.80	9.22	30.02
1" check valve	P1@.300	Ea	21.80	11.10	32.90
Thermostatic mixing valves					
1/2", soldered	P1@.240	Ea	51.30	8.85	60.15
3/4", threaded	P1@.250	Ea	66.30	9.22	75.52
3/4", soldered	P1@.300	Ea	56.50	11.10	67.60
1", threaded	P1@.300	Ea	258.00	11.10	269.10
Liquid level gauges					
1/2", 175 PSI bronze	P1@.210	Ea	88.70	7.75	96.45
Wye pattern strainers, threaded, Class 125, bronze body valves					
3/4" strainer	P1@.260	Ea	43.20	9.59	52.79
1" strainer	P1@.330	Ea	52.90	12.20	65.10
1-1/4" strainer	P1@.440	Ea	73.80	16.20	90.00
1-1/2" strainer	P1@.495	Ea	110.00	18.30	128.30
2" strainer	P1@.550	Ea	193.00	20.30	213.30
Boiler expansion tank					
2.1 gallon	P1@.300	Ea	39.60	11.10	50.70
4.5 gallon	P1@.300	Ea	65.80	11.10	76.90

Heating Systems, Hydronic Radiant Floor

	Craft@Hrs	Unit	Material	Labor	Total
Installation of packaged hydronic boilers. Add the cost of control wiring, supply lines (electric, feedwater and gas), drain line, circulating pump, vent stack, permits, final inspection and rental of an appliance dolly, come-a-long, a 1/2 ton chain hoist or a forklift, if required.					
Place 4' x 4' x 1/2" vibration pads	CF@.750	Ea	42.30	26.70	69.00
Bolt down boiler	P1@1.00	Ea	36.80	36.90	73.70
Connect gas and feedwater lines	P1@2.50	Ea	—	92.20	92.20
Mount interior boiler drain	P1@.500	Ea	8.22	18.40	26.62
Bore pipe hole in basement wall	P1@.250	Ea	—	9.22	9.22
Bore burner stack vent in exterior wall	P1@.250	Ea	—	9.22	9.22
Mount and edge-seal stack	P1@.500	Ea	42.30	18.40	60.70
Mount circulating pump	P1@.450	Ea	—	16.60	16.60

Hydronic radiant floor heating systems Includes PEX (cross-linked polyethylene) tube, the circulating pump, boiler, expansion tank, manifold, return piping, hangers, insulation, thermostatic controls, service fill and drain fittings, anti-crimp pipe support spacers, system commissioning and startup. Add the cost of control wiring, gas and electric connection, permit and post-installation inspection. By rated boiler capacity. Typically, 35,000 Btu per hour in boiler capacity will heat a 2,500 SF home.

	Craft@Hrs	Unit	Material	Labor	Total
Embedded system. 5/8" tube set 12" O.C. in a concrete slab. Includes 1" extruded polystyrene insulation under interior areas and 2" extruded polystyrene insulation at the building perimeter, forms, supports, mesh reinforcing and the concrete.					
35,000 Btu per hour (2,500 SF of floor)	P1@120.	Ea	6,400.00	4,430.00	10,830.00
70,000 Btu per hour (5,000 SF of floor)	P1@200.	Ea	10,100.00	7,380.00	17,480.00
105,000 Btu per hour (7,500 SF of floor)	P1@280.	Ea	15,600.00	10,300.00	25,900.00
Thin-slab system. 5/8" tube fastened 12" O.C. to the top of a wood-frame subfloor installed by others and then covered with 1-1/2" plasticized concrete.					
35,000 Btu per hour (2,500 SF of floor)	P1@160.	Ea	5,310.00	5,900.00	11,210.00
70,000 Btu per hour (5,000 SF of floor)	P1@300.	Ea	9,070.00	11,100.00	20,170.00
105,000 Btu per hour (7,500 SF of floor)	P1@400.	Ea	12,100.00	14,800.00	26,900.00
Add per SF of floor for a poured gypsum cover	—	SF	2.36	—	2.36
Add for installation in an existing structure	—	%	—	—	80.0
Plate-type system. 3/4" tube fastened 8" O.C. with aluminum heat transfer plates either above or below a wood-frame subfloor installed by others.					
35,000 Btu per hour (2,500 SF of floor)	P1@100.	Ea	4,580.00	3,690.00	8,270.00
70,000 Btu per hour (5,000 SF of floor)	P1@175.	Ea	7,830.00	6,460.00	14,290.00
105,000 Btu per hour (7,500 SF of floor)	P1@240.	Ea	11,400.00	8,850.00	20,250.00
Add for installation in an existing structure	—	%	—	—	50.0

Hybrid central heating and cooling High air velocity and narrow duct type. Attic or basement mounted modular system. Cooling is with a R410A refrigerant-charged A/C unit. Heating is with an electric hot water heating system. Rated at 13 SEER (Seasonal Energy Efficiency Rating). Provides precision zone control and low humidity for retrofit projects required to meet high energy-efficiency performance standards. Includes automatic mode switchover, individual zone digital thermostats, digital main controller module, transition-mounted duct fans and motor drive, hot water coils and a circulating pump mounted in the air handling unit. Designed for HVAC upgrades of historic buildings, condo conversions and for meeting stringent indoor air quality and occupant comfort standards. See central air filter systems in the section that follows. Add the cost of a hot water expansion tank. Add the cost of equipment rental, if required: an appliance dolly, a 3,000 lb. come-a-long and a 1-ton chain hoist.

	Craft@Hrs	Unit	Material	Labor	Total
Mount and bolt down hybrid A/C unit, hot water coils and air handler enclosure					
2.0-ton	P1@.750	Ea	7,010.00	27.70	7,037.70
3.0-ton	P1@.750	Ea	8,280.00	27.70	8,307.70
3.5-ton	P1@.750	Ea	8,520.00	27.70	8,547.70
4.0-ton	P1@.750	Ea	9,920.00	27.70	9,947.70
5.0-ton	P1@.750	Ea	11,100.00	27.70	11,127.70

	Craft@Hrs	Unit	Material	Labor	Total
Installation for hybrid central heating					
Reinforce joists in an attic	B1@3.00	LS	499.00	102.00	601.00
Place two vibration pads	CF@.750	LS	44.60	26.70	71.30
Core-drill and mount A/C drain	P1@.150	LF	3.27	5.53	8.80
Mount air mover in air handler duct	P1@.120	Ea	—	4.43	4.43
Connect ductwork mains to manifold	P1@4.50	Ea	165.00	166.00	331.00
Cut and braze copper A/C coil piping and run condensate drain	P1@4.00	Ea	9.91	148.00	157.91
Mount high-velocity ductwork and silencer tubing	P1@0.10	LF	20.20	3.69	23.89
Digital zone control thermostat, manual	BE@.750	Ea	137.00	30.50	167.50
Digital master heat/cool controller unit with auto change-over	BE@.750	Ea	327.00	30.50	357.50
Wiring of controls, typical	BE@3.00	Ea	1.80	122.00	123.80
Calibration and test	BE@2.00	Ea	—	81.30	81.30

Electric Heating Labor includes installation and connecting only. Add the cost of wiring from the Commercial and Industrial section of this manual.

Electric baseboard heaters, convection type, surface mounted, 20 gauge steel. Labor includes installation and connecting only. Add the cost of wiring. 7" high, 3-1/4" deep, 3.41 Btu/hr/watt, 240 volt. Low or medium density.

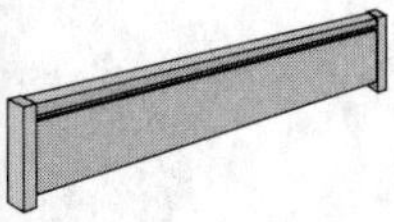

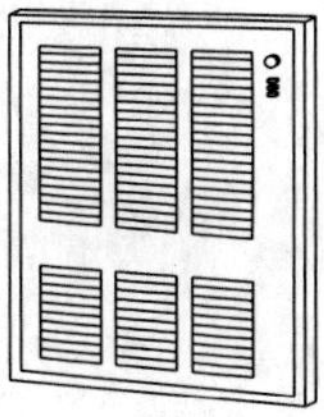

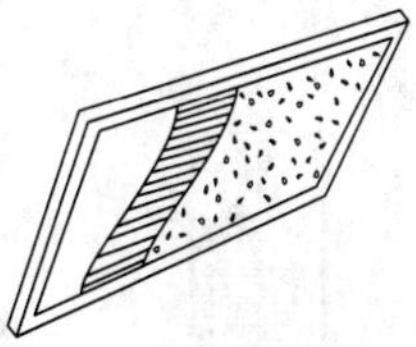

	Craft@Hrs	Unit	Material	Labor	Total
2'6" long, 500 watt (1,700 Btu)	BE@1.70	Ea	32.90	69.10	102.00
3'0" long, 750 watt (2,225 Btu)	BE@1.81	Ea	38.50	73.50	112.00
4'0" long, 1,000 watt (3,400 Btu)	BE@1.81	Ea	41.40	73.50	114.90
6'0" long, 1,500 watt (5,100 Btu)	BE@1.89	Ea	62.70	76.80	139.50
8'0" long, 2,000 watt (6,800 Btu)	BE@2.04	Ea	89.20	82.90	172.10
Add for integral thermostat	BE@.094	Ea	34.40	3.82	38.22
Add for wall mounted thermostat	BE@1.62	Ea	52.00	65.80	117.80
Fan-forced electric wall heaters, 12-3/4" x 6" rough opening. Add for 240 volt wiring and thermostat.					
700/900/1600 watt, 50 CFM	BE@.650	Ea	147.00	26.40	173.40
500 watt, 6.25 amp, 5118 Btu, 83 CFM	BE@.650	Ea	130.00	26.40	156.40
1,000 watt, 4.17 amp, 3412 Btu, 83 CFM	BE@.650	Ea	119.00	26.40	145.40
2,000 watt, 8.33 amp, 6824 Btu, 60 CFM	BE@.650	Ea	161.00	26.40	187.40
2,000 watt, 8.33 amp, 6824 Btu, 83 CFM	BE@.650	Ea	121.00	26.40	147.40
3,000 watt,12.5 amp, 12,236 Btu, 65 CFM	BE@.650	Ea	168.00	26.40	194.40
Double pole thermostat, 120 or 240 volt	BE@.440	Ea	44.10	17.90	62.00
Surface mounted 1" thick radiant ceiling panels. 120/208/240/277 volts AC.					
250 watts, 24" x 24"	BE@.850	Ea	175.00	34.50	209.50
310 watts, 24" x 24"	BE@.850	Ea	183.00	34.50	217.50
375 watts, 24" x 24"	BE@.850	Ea	209.00	34.50	243.50
625 watts, 24" x 48"	BE@1.11	Ea	317.00	45.10	362.10
750 watts, 24" x 48"	BE@1.31	Ea	313.00	53.20	366.20
Add for radiant line voltage wall thermostat	BE@.450	Ea	112.00	18.30	130.30
Add for motion sensing setback thermostat	BE@.450	Ea	128.00	18.30	146.30
Floor units, drop-in type, 14" long x 7-1/4" wide, includes fan motor assembly, housing and grille					
120 volts, 375 or 750 watts	BE@1.76	Ea	332.00	71.50	403.50
277 volts, 750 watts	BE@1.76	Ea	409.00	71.50	480.50
Add for wall thermostat kit	BE@1.62	Ea	125.00	65.80	190.80
Add for concrete accessory kit and housing	—	LS	24.30	—	24.30
Infrared quartz tube heaters, indoor or outdoor, chromed guard, polished aluminum reflector. Includes modulating control.					
3.2 KW, 24" long, 240 volts	BE@4.14	Ea	440.00	168.00	608.00
5 KW, 33" long, 240 volts	BE@4.14	Ea	580.00	168.00	748.00

	Craft@Hrs	Unit	Material	Labor	Total
7.3 KW, 46" long, 480 volts	BE@4.14	Ea	729.00	168.00	897.00
10.95 KW, 46" long, 480 volts	BE@4.14	Ea	1,220.00	168.00	1,388.00
Add for wall or ceiling brackets (pair)	—	LS	18.20	—	18.20
Deduct for indoor use only	—	%	-30.0	—	—
Suspension blower heaters, 208 or 240 volts, single phase, propeller type, direct drive					
1/4 HP	BE@4.80	Ea	414.00	195.00	609.00
1/3 HP	BE@4.80	Ea	482.00	195.00	677.00
1/2 HP	BE@4.80	Ea	672.00	195.00	867.00
Add for wall mounting bracket	—	LS	23.30	—	23.30
Add for line voltage wall thermostat					
Single pole	—	LS	49.70	—	49.70
Double pole	—	LS	74.60	—	74.60
Wall mounted fan-forced downflow insert heaters, heavy duty, built-in thermostat, 240 volts, 14" wide, 20" high, 4" deep rough-in, 3.41 Btu per hr per watt					
1,500 watts	BE@3.95	Ea	184.00	160.00	344.00
2,000 watts	BE@3.95	Ea	199.00	160.00	359.00
3,000 watts	BE@3.95	Ea	210.00	160.00	370.00
4,500 watts	BE@3.95	Ea	253.00	160.00	413.00
Add for surface mounting kit	—	LS	24.60	—	24.60

Central air filter for hybrid central heating system Drop-in module to fit in a high-velocity narrow duct air handling unit. Complies with Mil-STD 282 (certified removal of 99% of dust particles over .3 microns in size) as well as ASHRAE specifications. For residences requiring hypoallergenic air quality, medical clinics and pharmaceutical manufacturing/test facilities. DOP filter (di-octyl phthalate) is a non-woven denier nylon/cellulose acetate composite with an activated carbon final layer. Optional Dwyer-type pressure differential switch and relay provides automatic shutdown of the air handling unit and a warning light when filter elements are clogged. Pressure drop across the filter is 1" to 2" W.C. (water column). Sized by the nominal tonnage of associated cooling/heating equipment.

	Craft@Hrs	Unit	Material	Labor	Total
Central air filter					
2.5-ton unit, drop in filter	P1@.100	Ea	659.00	3.69	662.69
3.0-ton unit, drop in filter	P1@.100	Ea	696.00	3.69	699.69
3.5-ton unit, drop in filter	P1@.100	Ea	699.00	3.69	702.69
4.0-ton unit, drop in filter	P1@.100	Ea	725.00	3.69	728.69
5.0-ton unit, drop in filter	P1@.100	Ea	776.00	3.69	779.69
Mount Dwyer switch on the air handler	BE@.500	Ea	184.00	20.30	204.30
Wiring of Dwyer switch	BE@1.00	Ea	61.50	40.60	102.10
Calibration and test	BE@.500	Ea	—	20.30	20.30

Gas Furnaces Add the cost of piping, electrical connection and vent. See pipe costs in the Commercial and Industrial section of this manual. For more detailed coverage of gas heating, see the *National Plumbing & HVAC Estimator*, http://CraftsmanSiteLicense.com.

	Craft@Hrs	Unit	Material	Labor	Total
Gravity gas wall furnace. Natural gas or propane fired.					
8,000 Btu	PM@4.67	Ea	586.00	203.00	789.00
25,000 Btu	PM@4.67	Ea	588.00	203.00	791.00
25,000 Btu, high altitude	PM@4.67	Ea	1,120.00	203.00	1,323.00
35,000 Btu	PM@4.67	Ea	685.00	203.00	888.00
50,000 Btu	PM@4.67	Ea	858.00	203.00	1,061.00
Wall register kit for 2nd room	PM@1.00	Ea	61.10	43.50	104.60
Add for wall thermostat	PM@.972	Ea	60.90	42.30	103.20
Add for blower	PM@.500	Ea	175.00	21.70	196.70
Add for vent starter kit	PM@.254	LS	179.00	11.00	190.00
Add for gas valve for thermostat	PM@.250	Ea	179.00	10.90	189.90

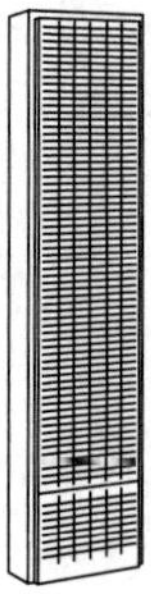

	Craft@Hrs	Unit	Material	Labor	Total
Direct vent gas wall furnace. Includes wall thermostat. No electricity required. Includes vent kit to outside wall. By input Btu rating. Natural gas or propane fired.					
14,000 Btu	PM@2.98	Ea	948.00	130.00	1,078.00
22,000 Btu	PM@2.98	Ea	1,000.00	130.00	1,130.00
30,000 Btu	PM@2.98	Ea	852.00	130.00	982.00
40,000 Btu	PM@2.98	Ea	1,360.00	130.00	1,490.00
Add for vent extension	PM@.500	Ea	78.50	21.70	100.20
Add for blower	PM@.500	Ea	148.00	21.70	169.70
Add for gas valve for thermostat	PM@.250	Ea	179.00	10.90	189.90
Gas floor furnace, including vent at $80, valve and wall thermostat					
30 MBtu input, 24 MBtu output	PM@7.13	Ea	1,220.00	310.00	1,530.00
50 MBtu input, 35 MBtu output	PM@8.01	Ea	1,390.00	348.00	1,738.00
Add for furnace serving two rooms	—	%	30.0	—	—
Add for spark ignition	—	LS	79.10	—	79.10
Forced air upflow gas furnace with electronic ignition. Includes vent at $100, typical piping, at $50, thermostat at $40 and distribution plenum at $100. No ducting included.					
50 MBtu input, 48 MBtu output	PM@7.13	Ea	3,970.00	310.00	4,280.00
75 MBtu input, 70 MBtu output	PM@7.13	Ea	4,180.00	310.00	4,490.00
100 MBtu input, 92 MBtu output	PM@7.80	Ea	4,420.00	339.00	4,759.00
125 MBtu input, 113 MBtu output	PM@7.80	Ea	4,720.00	339.00	5,059.00
Add for liquid propane models	—	LS	407.00	—	407.00
Add for time control thermostat	—	Ea	126.00	—	126.00
Ductwork for forced air furnace. Sheet metal, 6 duct and 2 air return residential system, with typical elbows and attaching boots.					
4" x 12" registers, and 2" R-5 insulation	SW@22.1	LS	1,220.00	932.00	2,152.00
Add for each additional duct run	SW@4.20	Ea	263.00	177.00	440.00
Fiberglass flex duct, insulated, 8" dia.	SW@.012	LF	5.28	.51	5.79
Suspended space heater, fan-forced, with tubular aluminum heat exchanger, mounting brackets and gas valve. Includes vent to 30' at $100, typical gas piping, at $50, and thermostat, at $40.					
30 MBtu input, 24 MBtu output	PM@2.75	Ea	1,020.00	120.00	1,140.00
45 MBtu input, 36 MBtu output	PM@2.75	Ea	1,120.00	120.00	1,240.00
60 MBtu input, 48 MBtu output	PM@2.75	Ea	1,200.00	120.00	1,320.00
75 MBtu input, 60 MBtu output	PM@2.75	Ea	1,330.00	120.00	1,450.00
Evaporative coolers, for roof installation. Add $110 for an electrical switch and connection and $90 for a recirculation pump and mounting hardware.					
3,000 CFM, down draft	PM@11.1	Ea	399.00	483.00	882.00
3,000 CFM, side draft	PM@11.1	Ea	399.00	483.00	882.00
4,000 CFM, side draft	PM@11.1	Ea	571.00	483.00	1,054.00
4,300 CFM, down draft	PM@11.1	Ea	500.00	483.00	983.00
5,500 CFM, down draft	PM@11.1	Ea	595.00	483.00	1,078.00
5,500 CFM, side draft	PM@11.1	Ea	399.00	483.00	882.00

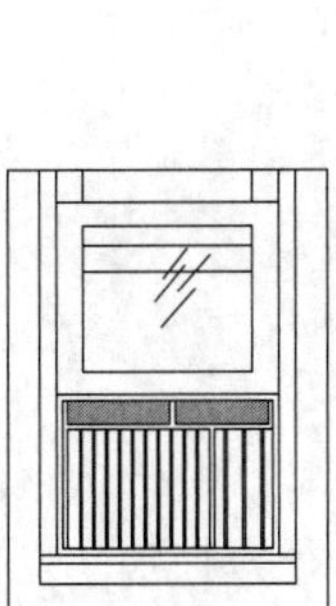

	Craft@Hrs	Unit	Material	Labor	Total
Window type air conditioners High-efficiency 115 volt units, adjustable thermostat, with remote. Labor is for installation in an existing wall opening, connected to an existing electric outlet.					
5,000 Btu, 150 SF room	PM@.751	Ea	163.00	32.60	195.60
8,000 Btu, 340 SF room	PM@.751	Ea	289.00	32.60	321.60
10,000 Btu, 450 SF room	PM@.751	Ea	361.00	32.60	393.60
15,000 Btu, 800 SF room	PM@.751	Ea	501.00	32.60	533.60
25,000 Btu, 1,500 SF room, 240 V	PM@.751	Ea	973.00	32.60	1,005.60

Heat Pumps

	Craft@Hrs	Unit	Material	Labor	Total
Packaged split system electric heat pumps Window-wall units with galvanized steel cabinet, 35' of tubing, two thermostats and control package. Installed on a concrete pad. Add for the electrical connection and concrete work.					
8 Mbtu cooling, 5 Mbtu heating	PM@10.9	Ea	1,380.00	474.00	1,854.00
15 Mbtu cooling, 13 Mbtu heating	PM@10.9	Ea	1,980.00	474.00	2,454.00
18 Mbtu cooling, 16 Mbtu heating	PM@12.9	Ea	2,220.00	561.00	2,781.00
Add for electrical connections, typical	PM@14.0	LS	288.00	609.00	897.00
Ductless mini-split heating and cooling units Includes pad-mounted compressor-condenser, 15' of insulated copper refrigerant lines, PVC condensate drain, control wiring, PVC wall chase, clamps, brackets, interior wall-mounted evaporator and wireless control. Add the cost of an exterior mounting slab, electrical connection and a NEC-approved safety switch.					
Single zone units					
9,000 BTU, ¾ ton, 230V	PM@3.59	Ea	831.00	156.00	987.00
9,000 BTU, ¾ ton, 115V	PM@3.59	Ea	1,250.00	156.00	1,406.00
12,000 BTU, 1 ton, 230V	PM@3.84	Ea	1,260.00	167.00	1,427.00
18,000 BTU, 1-1/2 ton, 230V	PM@3.84	Ea	1,430.00	167.00	1,597.00
24,000 BTU, 2 ton, 230V	PM@3.84	Ea	1,770.00	167.00	1,937.00
36,000 BTU, 3 ton, 230V	PM@4.09	Ea	2,290.00	178.00	2,468.00
42,000 BTU, 3-1/2 ton, 230V, ceiling mount	PM@7.18	Ea	3,100.00	312.00	3,412.00
Multi zone units					
24,000 BTU, 2 ton, 230V, 2 zones	PM@4.67	Ea	2,730.00	203.00	2,933.00
24,000 BTU, 2 ton, 230V, 3 zones	PM@5.60	Ea	3,160.00	243.00	3,403.00
36,000 BTU, 3 ton, 230V, 3 zones	PM@5.60	Ea	3,300.00	243.00	3,543.00
36,000 BTU, 3 ton, 230V, 4 zones	PM@7.00	Ea	4,180.00	304.00	4,484.00
42,000 BTU, 3-1/2 ton, 230V, 5 zones	PM@8.17	Ea	4,950.00	355.00	5,305.00
Add for 4" concrete slab, to 3' x 3'	B1@1.40	LS	33.40	47.40	80.80
Add for electrical connection and safety switch	BE@3.25	LS	98.00	132.00	230.00
Residential air-to-air heat pump Forced-air-aspirated heat pump, split system, slab mounted. Rated in nominal tonnage. Agency rating ARI and CSA. Installed in an existing air handling unit and with an optional filtration system. See the sections that follow. Trane or equal, rated at 13 SEER (Seasonal Energy Efficiency Rating), with automatic reversing valve for switching between heating and cooling modes, semiconductor thermocouple sensor for monitoring indoor/outdoor temperature differential, interior thermostat, controller relay, digital controller module, centrifugal compressor and motor drive. 208/230 V, 60 Hz, single phase. Requires two fan-aspirated pre-charged R410A refrigerant evaporator coils, one interior in the air handling unit and one outside in a weatherproof enclosure. See the air handler and evaporator coils that follow. Add, if required, for the cost of an appliance dolly, 3,000 lb. come-a-long and 1-ton chain hoist.					
Mount and bolt interior heat pump unit in air handler enclosure					
2.0-ton unit	P1@.750	Ea	2,610.00	27.70	2,637.70
3.0-ton unit	P1@.750	Ea	2,870.00	27.70	2,897.70
3.5-ton unit	P1@.750	Ea	3,480.00	27.70	3,507.70
4.0-ton unit	P1@.750	Ea	3,730.00	27.70	3,757.70
5.0-ton unit	P1@.750	Ea	4,350.00	27.70	4,377.70
Place 4' x 4' x 1/2" vibration pads	CF@.750	Ea	43.90	26.70	70.60
Mount interior evaporator drain	P1@.500	Ea	8.81	18.40	27.21
Bore piping hole through external coil	P1@.250	Ea	—	9.22	9.22
Mount and bolt down the external coil	P1@.450	Ea	32.80	16.60	49.40

	Craft@Hrs	Unit	Material	Labor	Total
Mount interior evaporator coil in air handler duct	P1@1.20	Ea	—	44.30	44.30
Tie-in of connecting ductwork to house air ductwork manifold and exhaust	P1@4.50	Ea	168.00	166.00	334.00
Cut and braze copper evaporator coil piping & drain	P1@4.00	Ea	9.33	148.00	157.33
Heat pump accessories					
Wiring of controls	BE@3.00	Ea	1.68	122.00	123.68
Calibration and test	BE@2.00	Ea	—	81.30	81.30
Fossil fuel kit	P1@2.50	Ea	279.00	92.20	371.20
High pressure cut-out kit	P1@.500	Ea	63.20	18.40	81.60
Outdoor stat/Low ambient sensors	BE@.500	Ea	68.40	20.30	88.70
Short cycle protection	BE@.500	Ea	85.20	20.30	105.50
Digital heat/cool thermostat, manual	BE@.750	Ea	146.00	30.50	176.50
Digital, programmable heat/cool thermostat with auto change-over	BE@.750	Ea	350.00	30.50	380.50
Heat pump supplemental electric heating coil					
5 KW, 208/230 Volt, 1-phase, 60 Hz	BE@1.50	Ea	174.00	60.90	234.90
7.5 KW, 208/230 Volt, 1-phase, 60 Hz	BE@1.75	Ea	199.00	71.10	270.10
10 KW, 208/230 Volt, 1-phase, 60 Hz	BE@2.00	Ea	216.00	81.30	297.30
12.5 KW, 208/230 Volt, 1-phase, 60 Hz	BE@2.25	Ea	310.00	91.40	401.40
15 KW, 208/230 Volt, 1-phase, 60 Hz	BE@2.75	Ea	435.00	112.00	547.00
20 KW, 208/230 Volt, 1-phase, 60 Hz	BE@3.50	Ea	584.00	142.00	726.00
25 KW, 208/230 Volt, 1-phase, 60 Hz	BE@4.25	Ea	651.00	173.00	824.00

Residential central air handling unit Two-piece 16-gauge steel sheet metal enclosure with main inlet and exhaust ductwork tie-ins and inlet dust filter mount. With 208/230 volt single-phase 60 Hz variable-speed fan, relay and control and breaker box. Designed to accommodate an optional evaporator coil, "drop-in" oil or gas heater to fit an existing integral air-to-air heat exchanger, electric heater coil or hot water/steam coil and filter (not included). See the sections that follow. Add for LEED certification if required.

	Craft@Hrs	Unit	Material	Labor	Total
Mount and bolt down air handler					
2.0-ton	P1@.750	Ea	1,390.00	27.70	1,417.70
3.0-ton	P1@.750	Ea	1,640.00	27.70	1,667.70
3.5-ton	P1@.750	Ea	1,900.00	27.70	1,927.70
4.0-ton	P1@.750	Ea	2,020.00	27.70	2,047.70
5.0-ton	P1@.750	Ea	2,270.00	27.70	2,297.70
Mount internal evaporator coil in an air handler	P1@1.20	Ea	63.20	44.30	107.50
Tie-in of connecting interior ductwork to house air ductwork manifold and exhaust	P1@4.50	Ea	121.00	166.00	287.00
Cut and braze copper evaporator coil piping and drain	P1@4.00	Ea	9.65	148.00	157.65
Wiring of controls	BE@3.00	Ea	1.82	122.00	123.82
Calibration and test	BE@2.00	Ea	—	81.30	81.30

Evaporator coils for a residential air handler Uncased, pre-charged with R410A refrigerant, with flanged mounting base plate, connector tubing, refrigerant fill valve and check valve, twin-finned radiator baffles. For use in conjunction with heat pump units, to be mounted indoors in air handler or air handler ductwork; cased units are to be used for outdoor mounting. Sized by the associated nominal tonnage of the heat pump. Add for LEED certification if required.

	Craft@Hrs	Unit	Material	Labor	Total
Place two 4' x 4' x 1/2" (vibration pads)	CF@.300	Ea	58.30	10.70	69.00
Mount interior evaporator drain	P1@.500	Ea	9.34	18.40	27.74
Bore piping hole through exterior wall	P1@.250	Ea	—	9.22	9.22

	Craft@Hrs	Unit	Material	Labor	Total
Mount external evaporator coil					
2.0-ton	P1@.750	Ea	510.00	27.70	537.70
3.0-ton	P1@.750	Ea	546.00	27.70	573.70
3.5-ton	P1@.750	Ea	589.00	27.70	616.70
4.0-ton	P1@.750	Ea	793.00	27.70	820.70
5.0-ton	P1@.750	Ea	908.00	27.70	935.70
Mount interior evaporator coil in air handler duct					
2.0-ton	P1@1.75	Ea	468.00	64.60	532.60
3.0-ton	P1@1.75	Ea	526.00	64.60	590.60
3.5-ton	P1@1.75	Ea	584.00	64.60	648.60
4.0-ton	P1@1.75	Ea	641.00	64.60	705.60
5.0-ton	P1@1.75	Ea	701.00	64.60	765.60
Tie-in of connecting interior ductwork manifold and exhaust	P1@4.50	Ea	116.00	166.00	282.00
Cutting and brazing of copper evaporator coil piping and drain	P1@4.00	Ea	9.15	148.00	157.15
Wiring of controls	BE@3.00	Ea	1.72	122.00	123.72
Calibration and test	BE@2.00	Ea	—	81.30	81.30

LEED Certified Heating and Cooling (Leadership in Energy & Environmental Design) offers an incentive to building owners to install energy-efficient and environmentally sensitive heating and cooling equipment. The HVAC system can earn a maximum of 17 points toward LEED certification by meeting ASHRAE 90 standards. A LEED certified air conditioning system must also meet ASHRAE 62.1-2016 standards for indoor air quality and include recording controls to measure system performance.

	Craft@Hrs	Unit	Material	Labor	Total
Add for LEED certification, registration and inspection, per project	—	Ea	2,490.00	—	2,490.00
Add for LEED central digital performance monitor/recorder, ComfortView 3 or equal	—	Ea	2,970.00	—	2,970.00
Add for LEED certified zone recording thermostat, USB remote-ready	—	Ea	443.00	—	443.00
Add for IAQ (Indoor Air Quality) CO2 sensor and duct-mounted aspirator box	—	Ea	539.00	—	539.00
Add for LEED certified residential systems with USGBC rating	—	%	20.0	—	—

Central air particulate removal filter system Residential or light commercial DOP (di-octyl phthalate) type. Provided as drop-in module to manually fit into an air handling units. Complies with Mil-STD 282 (certified removal of 99% of dust particles over .3 microns in size) as well as ASHRAE specifications. For homes, medical clinics and pharmaceutical manufacturing/test facilities. DOP filter type is non-woven denier nylon/cellulose acetate composite with activated carbon final layer. Optional Dwyer-type pressure differential switch and relay provides for automatic shutdown of air handling unit and triggering of signal light when filter elements are clogged with particulates and require cleaning or replacement. Pressure drop across filter is 1" W.C. (water column) to 2" W.C. Sized according to nominal tonnage of associated cooling/heating capacity.

	Craft@Hrs	Unit	Material	Labor	Total
Dropping in filter					
2.5-ton filter	P1@.100	Ea	846.00	3.69	849.69
3.0-ton filter	P1@.100	Ea	968.00	3.69	971.69
3.5-ton filter	P1@.100	Ea	1,030.00	3.69	1,033.69
4.0-ton filter	P1@.100	Ea	1,080.00	3.69	1,083.69
5.0-ton filter	P1@.100	Ea	1,140.00	3.69	1,143.69
Mount Dwyer switch on required air handler	BE@.500	Ea	181.00	20.30	201.30
Wiring of Dwyer switch	BE@1.00	Ea	60.40	40.60	101.00
Calibrate and test	BE@.500	Ea	20.30	20.30	40.60

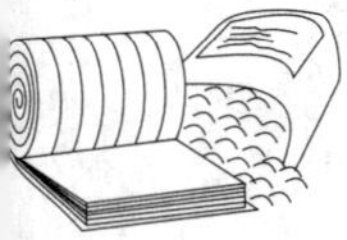

	Craft@Hrs	Unit	Material	Labor	Total
Insulation See also Building Paper and Polyethylene Film. Coverage allows for studs and joists.					
Fiberglass insulation, wall and ceiling application, coverage allows for framing					
Kraft-faced, 16" OC framing members					
3-1/2" (R-11)	BC@.007	SF	.45	.26	.71
3-1/2" (R-13)	BC@.007	SF	.53	.26	.79
3-1/2" (R-15)	BC@.007	SF	.80	.26	1.06
6-1/4" (R-19)	BC@.008	SF	.74	.30	1.04
5-1/2" (R-21)	BC@.008	SF	.94	.30	1.24
9-1/2" (R-30)	BC@.008	SF	1.12	.30	1.42
9-1/2" (R-30C) Cathedral ceiling	BC@.010	SF	.76	.37	1.13
12" (R-38)	BC@.009	SF	1.31	.34	1.65
Kraft-faced, 24" OC framing members					
3-1/2" (R-13)	BC@.005	SF	.52	.19	.71
3-1/2" (R-15)	BC@.005	SF	.52	.19	.71
6-1/4" (R-19)	BC@.006	SF	.71	.22	.93
5-1/2" (R-21)	BC@.006	SF	.92	.22	1.14
9-1/2" (R-30)	BC@.006	SF	1.06	.22	1.28
12" (R-38)	BC@.007	SF	1.34	.26	1.60
Unfaced, 16" OC framing members					
2" (R-6.7)	BC@.003	SF	1.11	.11	1.22
3-1/2" (R-13)	BC@.004	SF	.52	.15	.67
6-1/4" (R-19)	BC@.005	SF	.67	.19	.86
9-1/2" (R-30)	BC@.006	SF	1.10	.22	1.32
Unfaced, 24" OC framing members					
6-1/4" (R-19)	BC@.003	SF	.71	.11	.82
9-1/2" (R-30)	BC@.004	SF	1.08	.15	1.23
12" (R-38)	BC@.005	SF	.92	.19	1.11
Poly-faced insulation, vapor retarding twisted Miraflex fibers, ASTM C665, Type II, Class C, coverage allows for framing					
3-1/2" (R-13), 16" or 24" OC framing	BC@.005	SF	.63	.19	.82
8-3/4" (R-25), 16" or 24" OC framing	BC@.006	SF	.95	.22	1.17
Encapsulated fiberglass roll insulation, Johns Manville Comfort Therm™, coverage allows for framing					
3-1/2" (R-13) rolls, 16" OC framing	BC@.005	SF	.49	.19	.68
6-1/4" (R-19) batts, 16" or 24" OC framing	BC@.006	SF	.85	.22	1.07
8-1/4" (R-25) rolls, 16" or 24" OC framing	BC@.006	SF	1.17	.22	1.39
10-1/4" (R-30) batts, 16" or 24" OC framing	BC@.006	SF	1.28	.22	1.50
Insulation board, Owens Corning Foamular XAE rigid extruded polystyrene foam board, film-faced, stapled in place, including taped joints, 4' x 8' or 9' panels, tongue and groove or square edge, including 5% waste					
1/2" thick (R-2.5), 4' x 8' panel	BC@.010	SF	.44	.37	.81
3/4" thick (R-3.8), 4' x 8' panel	BC@.011	SF	.56	.41	.97
1" thick (R-5.0), 4' x 8' panel	BC@.011	SF	.65	.41	1.06
1-1/2" thick (R-7.5), 4' x 8' panel	BC@.015	SF	.82	.56	1.38
2" thick (R-10), 4' x 8' panel	BC@.015	SF	1.00	.56	1.56
Extruded polystyrene insulation panel, Dow Blue Board, water resistant. By thermal resistance value, (R-). Density of 1.6 lbs. per CF. Gray Board density is 1.3 lbs. per CF.					
3/4" x 2' x 8', tongue & groove, R-3.8	BC@.011	SF	1.24	.41	1.65
1" x 2' x 8', R-5.0	BC@.011	SF	.78	.41	1.19
1" x 2' x 8', tongue & groove, R-5.0	BC@.011	SF	.52	.41	.93
1" x 4' x 8', R-5.0	BC@.011	SF	.82	.41	1.23
1" x 4' x 8', tongue & groove, R-5.0	BC@.011	SF	.76	.41	1.17
1-1/2" x 2' x 8', R-7.5	BC@.015	SF	1.36	.56	1.92
1-1/2" x 2' x 8', tongue & groove, R-7.5	BC@.015	SF	1.30	.56	1.86

	Craft@Hrs	Unit	Material	Labor	Total
1-1/2" x 4' x 8', square edge, R-7.5	BC@.015	SF	1.36	.56	1.92
2" x 2' x 8', R-10	BC@.015	SF	1.50	.56	2.06
2" x 4' x 8', R-10	BC@.015	SF	1.41	.56	1.97
1" x 2' x 8' Gray Board (1.3 lbs. per CF)	BC@.015	SF	.77	.56	1.33
1-1/2" x 2' x 8' Gray Board	BC@.015	SF	1.09	.56	1.65
2" x 2' x 8' Gray Board	BC@.015	SF	1.39	.56	1.95
Rigid polyisocyanurate insulated sheathing, foil face on two sides, Dow/Celotex Tuff-R, 4' x 8' panels, including 5% waste.					
1/2" (R-3.3)	BC@.010	SF	.53	.37	.90
3/4" (R-5.6)	BC@.011	SF	.58	.41	.99
1" (R-5.9)	BC@.011	SF	.76	.41	1.17
1-1/2" (R-9.4)	BC@.011	SF	.95	.41	1.36
2" (R-13)	BC@.015	SF	1.17	.56	1.73
Fanfold extruded polystyrene insulation 4' x 50' panels, including 5% waste					
1/4" (R-1)	BC@.011	SF	.26	.41	.67
3/8" (R-1)	BC@.011	SF	.29	.41	.70
Add for nails, 25 lb cartons (large square heads)					
2-1/2", for 1-1/2" boards	—	LS	62.20	—	62.20
3", for 2" boards	—	LS	62.00	—	62.00
Foil-faced urethane sheathing, 4' x 8' panels, including 5% waste,					
1" (R-7.2)	BC@.011	SF	.64	.41	1.05
Asphalt impregnated sheathing board on walls, nailed, 4' x 8' panels					
1/2", standard	BC@.013	SF	.37	.49	.86
1/2", intermediate	BC@.013	SF	.46	.49	.95
1/2", nail base	BC@.013	SF	.65	.49	1.14
Dens Glass Gold insulating exterior sheathing. Glass mat embedded in a water-resistant treated gypsum core with bond-enhancing gold primer coating. Square edge.					
1/4" x 4' x 4' Dens-Shield	BC@.015	SF	.65	.56	1.21
1/2" x 32" x 4' Dens-Shield	BC@.015	SF	.53	.56	1.09
1/2" x 4' x 8'	BC@.016	SF	.73	.60	1.33
5/8" x 4' x 8'	BC@.016	SF	1.00	.60	1.60
Polystyrene foam underlay, polyethylene covered, R-Gard.					
3/8" x 4' x 24' fanfold	BC@.011	SF	.27	.41	.68
1/2" x 4' x 8'	BC@.011	SF	.26	.41	.67
3/8" x 4' x 8'	BC@.011	SF	.30	.41	.71
1" x 4' x 8'	BC@.011	SF	.37	.41	.78
1-1/2" x 2' x 8'	BC@.015	SF	.57	.56	1.13
2" x 2' x 8'	BC@.015	SF	.72	.56	1.28
Cant strips for insulated roof board, one piece wood, tapered					
2" strip	RR@.018	LF	.29	.75	1.04
3" strip	RR@.020	LF	.26	.83	1.09
4" strip	RR@.018	LF	.25	.75	1.00
Sill plate gasket. Fills gaps between the foundation and the plate. Also used for sealing around windows and doors.					
1/4" x 50', 3-1/2" wide	RR@.003	LF	.14	.12	.26
1/4" x 50', 5-1/2" wide	RR@.003	LF	.21	.12	.33
Perimeter foundation insulation, expanded polystyrene with polyethylene skinned surface. Low moisture retention. Minimum compressive strength of 1,440 lbs. per SF.					
3/4" x 4' x 8'	BC@.011	SF	.32	.41	.73
1-1/2" x 2' x 4'	BC@.015	SF	.71	.56	1.27
2" x 2' x 4'	BC@.015	SF	.89	.56	1.45
2" x 4' x 4'	BC@.015	SF	.73	.56	1.29

	Craft@Hrs	Unit	Material	Labor	Total
FBX 1240 industrial board insulation, rockwool, semi-rigid, no waste included, 24" OC framing members.					
2" (R-8)	BC@.004	SF	1.09	.15	1.24
3" (R-12)	BC@.004	SF	1.57	.15	1.72
3-1/2" (R-14)	BC@.004	SF	1.84	.15	1.99
Sound control insulation, fiberglass acoustically designed to absorb sound vibration, for use between interior walls, floors and ceilings, Quietzone™ batts, coverage allows for framing.					
3-1/2", 16" OC framing	BC@.006	SF	.43	.22	.65
3-1/2", 24" OC framing	BC@.006	SF	.43	.22	.65
Acoustic floor underlayment, 32 SF	BC@.003	SF	.66	.11	.77
Acoustic caulk, 28 oz. tube	—	Ea	8.39	—	8.39
Sound insulation board, 4' x 8' panels installed on walls					
1/2" Homasote	BC@.013	SF	1.46	.49	1.95
1/2" Soundstop	BC@.013	SF	.91	.49	1.40
1/2" Sound deadening board	BC@.013	SF	.53	.49	1.02
Add for installation on ceilings	BC@.004	SF	—	.15	.15
Sound Attenuation Fire Batt insulation (SAFB), rockwool, semi-rigid, no waste included, pressed between framing members					
16" OC framing members					
3-1/2" (R-15)	BC@.004	SF	.94	.15	1.09
5-1/2" (R-23)	BC@.004	SF	1.41	.15	1.56
7-1/2" (R-30)	BC@.005	SF	1.88	.19	2.07
24" OC framing members					
3-1/2" (R-15)	BC@.003	SF	1.16	.11	1.27
5-1/2" (R-23)	BC@.003	SF	1.68	.11	1.79
7-1/2" (R-30)	BC@.004	SF	2.23	.15	2.38
Housewrap building envelope, wrapped on exterior walls and stapled, including 10% waste					
9' x 150' roll	BC@.006	SF	.13	.22	.35
Tyvek tape, 2" x 165'	—	Roll	13.30	—	13.30
Stabilized cellulose insulation, for blown-in applications. Bag covers 40 SF of attic joists at 6" depth. Add the cost of blower rental.					
40 SF bag	BC@.010	SF	.31	.37	.68
Vermiculite insulation, poured over ceilings					
Vermiculite, 25 lb sack (2 CF)	—	Ea	20.60	—	20.60
At 3" depth (120 sacks per 1,000 SF)	BL@.007	SF	2.47	.21	2.68
At 4" depth (144 sacks per 1,000 SF)	BL@.007	SF	2.96	.21	3.17
Masonry batts, 1-1/2" x 15" x 48"	B9@.008	SF	.32	.26	.58
Masonry fill, poured in concrete block cores					
Using 2 CF bags of perlite, per bag	—	Ea	9.18	—	9.18
4" wall, 8.1 SF per CF	B9@.006	SF	1.13	.20	1.33
6" wall, 5.4 SF per CF	B9@.006	SF	1.70	.20	1.90
8" wall, 3.6 SF per CF	B9@.006	SF	2.55	.20	2.75
Natural fiber building insulation. EPA registered anti-microbial agent offers protection from mold, mildew, fungi and pests. Made from all natural cotton fibers. Friction fit. 94" long batting. Based on Ultra Touch.					
16" OC framing (R-13)	BC@.005	SF	.76	.19	.95
16" OC framing (R-19)	BC@.006	SF	.78	.22	1.00
16" OC framing (R-30)	BC@.007	SF	1.02	.26	1.28
24" OC framing (R-13)	BC@.006	SF	.97	.22	1.19
24" OC framing (R-19)	BC@.007	SF	1.83	.26	2.09
24" OC framing (R-30)	BC@.008	SF	1.78	.30	2.08

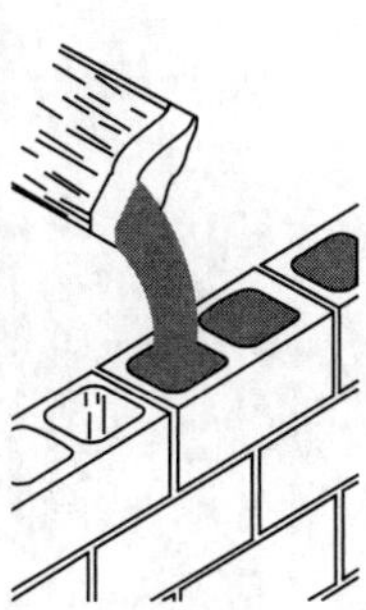

Insulation, Subcontract New construction, coverage includes framing.

	Craft@Hrs	Unit	Material	Labor	Total
Blown-in cellulose					
3-1/2" (R-12)	—	MSF	—	—	752.00
6" (R-21)	—	MSF	—	—	1,060.00

	Craft@Hrs	Unit	Material	Labor	Total
Sprayed-on polyurethane open cell foam (rigid). 2-part, R-Value 3.5 per inch, low density, vapor permable, cost per CSF. minimum job size 5,000sf, subcontract					
R-13, 3.7" thick	—	CSF	—	—	136.00
R-17, 4.9" thick	—	CSF	—	—	175.00
R-22, 6.3" thick	—	CSF	—	—	225.00
R-26, 7.4" thick	—	CSF	—	—	270.00
R-30, 8.6" thick	—	CSF	—	—	311.00
R-38, 10.9" thick	—	CSF	—	—	394.00
R-45, 12.9" thick	—	CSF	—	—	467.00
R-60, 17.1" thick	—	CSF	—	—	624.00
Sprayed-on polyurethane closed cell foam (rigid). 2-part, R-Value 6.5 per inch, high density, impervious to vapor, cost per CSF. minimum job size 5,000sf, subcontract					
R-13, 2.0" thick	—	CSF	—	—	181.00
R-17, 2.6" thick	—	CSF	—	—	175.00
R-22, 3.4" thick	—	CSF	—	—	294.00
R-26, 4.0" thick	—	CSF	—	—	351.00
R-30, 4.6" thick	—	CSF	—	—	403.00
R-38, 5.8" thick	—	CSF	—	—	505.00
R-45, 6.9" thick	—	CSF	—	—	594.00
R-60, 9.2" thick	—	CSF	—	—	785.00
Sprayed-on urethane foam (rigid)					
1" thick	—	MSF	—	—	1,930.00
Add for acrylic waterproofing	—	MSF	—	—	1,330.00
Add for urethane rubber waterproofing	—	MSF	—	—	2,250.00
Add for cleaning rock off existing roof	—	MSF	—	—	127.00
Insulation blown into walls in an existing structure, includes coring hole in exterior or interior of wall, filling cavity, sealing hole and paint to match existing surface. R-12 to R-14 rating depending on cavity thickness					
Stucco (exterior application)	—	MSF	—	—	2,190.00
Wallboard (interior application)	—	MSF	—	—	2,190.00
Wood siding (exterior application)	—	MSF	—	—	2,900.00
Thermal Analysis (Infrared thermography) Includes infrared video inspection of entire building, written report by qualified technician or engineer, and thermograms (infrared photographs) of all problem areas of building. Inspection is done using high-quality thermal sensitive instrumentation. Costs listed are for exterior facade shots or interior (room by room) shots. All travel expenses for inspector are extra.					
Residence, typically 4 hours required	—	Hr	—	—	279.00
Commercial structure ($800.00 minimum)	—	Hr	—	—	162.00
Add per day lost due to weather, lack of preparation by building occupants, etc., when inspector and equipment are at building site prepared to commence inspection					
Typical cost per day	—	LS	—	—	442.00
Add per night for accommodations when overnight stay is required. This is common when inspection must be performed at night to get accurate results					
Typical cost, per night	—	LS	—	—	152.00
Home Energy Rating System (HERS) Confirmed rating and index calculation by a certified Whole House Home Energy Rater. Some building departments require a HERS rating to verify building code compliance. Costs for rating a single-family home. Rating each unit of a multi-family dwelling will cost 25% to 50% less.					
Existing home HERS rating, repeated tests are the same price					
Duct pressure test, per system	—	Ea	—	—	228.00
Refrigerant charge verification	—	Ea	—	—	102.00
Maximum fan watt draw verification	—	Ea	—	—	51.00
Minimum airflow test, 3,500 CFM per ton	—	Ea	—	—	51.00
Add for data entry to calculate the HERS index	—	Ea	—	—	76.00

	Craft@Hrs	Unit	Material	Labor	Total
Typical duct test, refrigerant charge, airflow, fan watt draw with certificate processing	—	LS	—	—	508.00
Wait time to make adjustments for another test	—	Hr	—	—	91.00

New home energy rating, including plan review, software modeling, design specs, on-site inspections, performance testing, reports and certification, per home

Certification for code compliance	—	Ea	—	—	761.00

Insurance and Bonding Typical rates. Costs vary by state and class of construction.
Rule of thumb: Employer's cost for payroll taxes, and insurance.

Per $100 (C$) of payroll	—	C$	—	—	31.50

Rule of thumb: Complete insurance program (comprehensive general liability policy, truck, automobile, and equipment floaters and fidelity bond), contractor's typical cost

Per $100 of payroll	—	C$	—	—	7.35

Liability insurance Comprehensive contractor's liability insurance, including operations, completed operations, bodily injury and property damage, protective and contractual coverages, $1,000,000 policy limit. Minimum annual premium will be between $2,500 and $10,000. Rates vary by state and with the contractor's loss experience. Typical costs per $100 (C$) of payroll for each trade employed. (Calculate and add for each category separately.)

General contractors	—	C$	—	—	2.59
Carpentry	—	C$	—	—	4.10
Concrete, formed or flat	—	C$	—	—	5.25
Drywall hanging and finishing	—	C$	—	—	3.54
Electrical wiring	—	C$	—	—	3.57
Floor covering installation	—	C$	—	—	4.73
Glaziers	—	C$	—	—	3.54
Heating, ventilating, air conditioning	—	C$	—	—	4.94
Insulation	—	C$	—	—	4.10
Masonry, tile	—	C$	—	—	3.89
Painting	—	C$	—	—	5.36
Plastering and stucco	—	C$	—	—	3.78
Plumbing	—	C$	—	—	6.35

Workers' compensation coverage Rates vary from state to state and by a contractor's loss history. Coverage cost per $100 (C$) of base payroll excluding fringe benefits.

Bricklayer	—	C$	—	—	9.69
Carpenter					
1 and 2 family dwellings	—	C$	—	—	15.80
Multiple units and commercial	—	C$	—	—	5.50
Clerical (office worker)	—	C$	—	—	.99
Concrete					
1 and 2 family dwellings	—	C$	—	—	6.20
Other concrete	—	C$	—	—	6.68
Construction laborer	—	C$	—	—	15.80
Drywall taper	—	C$	—	—	8.25
Electrical wiring	—	C$	—	—	4.49
Elevator erectors	—	C$	—	—	2.37
Executive supervisors	—	C$	—	—	3.50
Excavation, grading	—	C$	—	—	9.27
Excavation, rock (no tunneling)	—	C$	—	—	12.10
Glazing	—	C$	—	—	10.50
Insulation work	—	C$	—	—	20.00
Iron or steel erection work	—	C$	—	—	11.70
Lathing	—	C$	—	—	5.43
Operating engineers	—	C$	—	—	9.27

	Craft@Hrs	Unit	Material	Labor	Total
Painting and paperhanging	—	C$	—	—	7.83
Pile driving	—	C$	—	—	7.71
Plastering and stucco	—	C$	—	—	13.00
Plumbing	—	C$	—	—	6.27
Reinforcing steel installation (concrete)	—	C$	—	—	11.70
Roofing	—	C$	—	—	27.20
Sewer construction	—	C$	—	—	9.10
Sheet metal work (on site)	—	C$	—	—	9.36
Steam and boiler work	—	C$	—	—	10.00
Tile, stone, and terrazzo work	—	C$	—	—	5.71
Truck driver	—	C$	—	—	9.27
Tunneling	—	C$	—	—	20.00

Payment and performance bonds Cost per $1,000 (M$) of final contract price. Rates depend on the experience, credit, and net worth of the applicant.

	Craft@Hrs	Unit	Material	Labor	Total
Preferred rates, contract coverage for:					
First $ 100,000	—	M$	—	—	14.40
Next $2,400,000	—	M$	—	—	8.68
Next $2,500,000	—	M$	—	—	6.88
Standard rates, contract coverage for:					
First $ 100,000	—	M$	—	—	29.90
Next $ 400,000	—	M$	—	—	18.00
Next $2,000,000	—	M$	—	—	12.00
Next $2,500,000	—	M$	—	—	8.98
Next $2,500,000	—	M$	—	—	8.38
Over $7,500,000	—	M$	—	—	7.78
Substandard rates, contract coverage for:					
First $100,000	—	M$	—	—	35.90
Balance of contract	—	M$	—	—	23.90

Ironing Centers, Built-In Wood frame with hinged door, can be recessed or surface mounted. Includes one 110 volt control panel where shown, receptacle outlet, timed shutoff switch, spotlight, storage shelf, and steel ironing board. No electrical work included. Iron-A-Way Products.

	Craft@Hrs	Unit	Material	Labor	Total
Type 1, no electric control panel, non-adjustable 42" board, 48" high, 15" wide, 6" deep	BC@.994	Ea	335.00	37.20	372.20
Type 2, with electric control panel, non-adjustable 42" board, 48" high, 15" wide, 6" deep	BC@.994	Ea	554.00	37.20	591.20
Type 3, with electric control panel, adjustable 46" board, 61" high, 15" wide, 6" deep	BC@.994	Ea	767.00	37.20	804.20
Added cost for any unit					
Add for sleeve board with holder	—	Ea	45.00	—	45.00
Add for door mirror	—	Ea	155.00	—	155.00
Add for oak paneled door front	—	Ea	135.00	—	135.00
Add for hot iron rest	—	Ea	37.60	—	37.60

Jackposts, Steel, Adjustable Building Columns Permanent or temporary adjustable steel posts, 3" diameter.

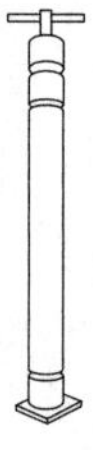

	Craft@Hrs	Unit	Material	Labor	Total
16" maximum extension	B1@.250	Ea	31.30	8.46	39.76
19" to 36" extension	B1@.250	Ea	36.50	8.46	44.96
34" to 55" extension	B1@.250	Ea	50.80	8.46	59.26
54" to 93" extension	B1@.250	Ea	59.10	8.46	67.56
58" to 100" extension	B1@.250	Ea	67.90	8.46	76.36
Heavy duty jack post	B1@.250	Ea	89.70	8.46	98.16
Jack post beam plate with 3-1/2" ring	B1@.130	Ea	26.00	4.40	30.40

	Craft@Hrs	Unit	Material	Labor	Total
Landscaping					
Seeding, level area					
Using tall fescue seed, per 20 lb bag	—	Ea	56.20	—	56.20
Seeding preparation, grade, rake, clean	BL@.003	SY	.12	.09	.21
Mechanical seeding (5 lbs per 1,000 SF)	BL@.002	MSF	14.00	.06	14.06
Hand seeding (10 lbs per 1,000 SF)	BL@.004	MSF	28.10	.12	28.22
Fertilizer, pre-planting,					
24-nitrogen, 24-phosphorus, 4-potassium					
(3.34 lb per 1,000 SF)	BL@.222	MSF	11.60	6.73	18.33
Liming, pelletized (10 lbs per 1,000 SF)	BL@.222	MSF	0.85	6.73	7.58
Placing topsoil, delivered to site, 1 CY covers 81 SF at 4" depth. Add cost for equipment, where needed, from Excavation Equipment Costs section. Labor shown below is for operation of equipment.					
With equipment, level site	BL@.092	CY	12.40	2.79	15.19
With equipment, sloped site	BL@.107	CY	12.40	3.24	15.64
By hand, level site	BL@.735	CY	12.40	22.30	34.70
By hand, sloped site	BL@.946	CY	12.40	28.70	41.10
Placing soil amendments, by hand spreading					
Natural wood chip mulch	BL@1.27	CY	22.60	38.50	61.10
Forest mulch	BL@1.27	CY	47.50	38.50	86.00
Peat loam	BL@1.27	CY	56.50	38.50	95.00
Organic compost	BL@1.27	CY	52.00	38.50	90.50
Bale of straw, 25 bales per ton	BL@.200	Ea	4.00	6.06	10.06
Landscape stepping stones, concrete					
12" round	BL@.133	Ea	3.48	4.03	7.51
14" round	BL@.133	Ea	4.67	4.03	8.70
18" round	BL@.153	Ea	8.09	4.64	12.73
24" round	BL@.153	Ea	13.70	4.64	18.34
Add for square shapes	—	%	20.0	—	—
18" or 24" diameter natural tree ring	BL@.133	Ea	2.92	4.03	6.95
Redwood benderboard, staked redwood					
1/8" x 3-3/8" x 8'	BL@.011	LF	.25	.33	.58
1/8" x 3-3/8" x 14'	BL@.016	LF	.36	.48	.84
1/4" x 4" x 12'	BL@.016	LF	.33	.48	.81
Roto-tilling light soil					
To 4" depth	BL@.584	CSY	—	17.70	17.70
Sodding, no soil preparation, nursery sod, Bermuda or Blue Rye mix					
Per SF (500 SF minimum charge)	BL@.013	SF	.77	.39	1.16
Hydroseeding subcontract (spray application of seed, binder and fertilizer slurry). Costs will vary based upon site conditions, quality/type of seed. For areas greater than 10,000 SF, see the hydroseeding cost in the commercial section.					
1,000 – 2,000 SF job	—	MSF	—	—	180.00
2,001 – 4,000 SF job	—	MSF	—	—	150.00
4,001 – 6,000 SF job	—	MSF	—	—	120.00
6,001 – 10,000 SF job	—	MSF	—	—	110.00
Lath					
Gypsum lath, perforated or plain, 1/2" x 2' x 8' sheets. Add the cost of gypsum base and finish plaster, includes 10% for waste and fasteners.					
On walls, nailed or stapled	BR@.090	SY	3.22	3.24	6.46
On walls, clipped	BR@.095	SY	3.35	3.42	6.77
On ceilings, nailed or stapled	BR@.125	SY	3.22	4.50	7.72
On ceilings, clipped	BR@.130	SY	3.35	4.68	8.03
Add soffits, arches	—	%	10.0	35.0	—

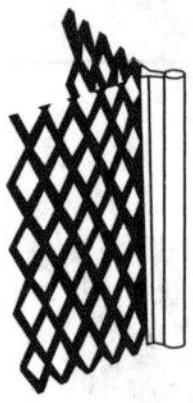

	Craft@Hrs	Unit	Material	Labor	Total
Steel lath, diamond pattern (junior mesh), 27" x 96" sheets, nailed to walls.					
1.75 pound	BR@.076	SY	3.58	2.73	6.31
2-1/2 pound, galvanized	BR@.076	SY	4.35	2.73	7.08
2-1/2 pounds, paper back, dimpled	BR@.076	SY	5.70	2.73	8.43
3.4 pounds, galvanized	BR@.076	SY	5.53	2.73	8.26
3.4 pounds, paper back	BR@.076	SY	5.16	2.73	7.89
3/8" hi rib, 29 gauge	BR@.076	SY	7.10	2.73	9.83
Add for ceiling applications	—	%	—	25.0	—
Galvanized stucco netting, 1-1/2" mesh, per roll, nailed to walls					
36" x 150', 20 gauge, roll	BR@2.80	Ea	71.60	101.00	172.60
36" x 150', 17-gauge, roll	BR@2.80	Ea	98.20	101.00	199.20
36" x 100', 17-gauge paper back	BR@2.80	Ea	92.60	101.00	193.60
6" x 50' stucco repair net	—	Ea	12.50	—	12.50
Corner bead, 26 gauge, 8' to 12' lengths.					
Expanded corner bead, 8' long	BR@.027	LF	.74	.97	1.71
Expanded corner bead, 10' long	BR@.027	LF	.91	.97	1.88
Cornerite corner bead, 3" x 3" x 8'	BR@.027	LF	.33	.97	1.30
Cornerite plaster corner, 2" x 2" x 4'	BR@.027	LF	.60	.97	1.57
Cornerite stucco corner, 3" x 3" 8' long	BR@.027	LF	.50	.97	1.47
Short flange corner bead, 8' long	BR@.027	LF	1.20	.97	2.17
Plaster J-trim, 1-3/8" wide x 10' long	BR@.027	LF	.76	.97	1.73
Casing beads					
Short flange, 1/2" x 10' long	BR@.025	LF	.58	.90	1.48
Short flange, 7/8" x 10' long	BR@.025	LF	.58	.90	1.48
Expanded flange, 3/4" x 10'	BR@.025	LF	.28	.90	1.18
Expansion joint, 26 gauge, 1/2" ground	BR@.050	LF	2.17	1.80	3.97

Lawn Sprinkler Systems

PVC Schedule 40 pipe laid in an open trench and connected. Add the cost of trenching, valves and sprinkler heads below.

	Craft@Hrs	Unit	Material	Labor	Total
1/2" Schedule 40 PVC pressure pipe and fittings					
1/2" pipe	BL@.010	LF	.19	.30	.49
1/2" 90 degree ell	BL@.100	Ea	.38	3.03	3.41
1/2" tee	BL@.130	Ea	.44	3.94	4.38
3/4" Schedule 40 PVC pressure pipe and fittings					
3/4" pipe	BL@.012	LF	.23	.36	.59
3/4" 90 degree ell	BL@.115	Ea	.48	3.49	3.97
3/4" tee	BL@.140	Ea	.59	4.24	4.83
1" Schedule 40 PVC pressure pipe and fittings					
1" pipe	BL@.015	LF	.34	.45	.79
1" 90 degree ell	BL@.120	Ea	1.01	3.64	4.65
1" tee	BL@.170	Ea	1.24	5.15	6.39
Deduct for Class 200 PVC pipe	—	%	-64.0	—	—
Trenching for sprinkler pipe installation, by hand, including backfill and tamp					
Light soil, 8" wide					
12" deep	BL@.027	LF	—	.82	.82
18" deep	BL@.040	LF	—	1.21	1.21
24" deep	BL@.053	LF	—	1.61	1.61
Average soil, 8" wide					
12" deep	BL@.043	LF	—	1.30	1.30
18" deep	BL@.065	LF	—	1.97	1.97
24" deep	BL@.087	LF	—	2.64	2.64

	Craft@Hrs	Unit	Material	Labor	Total
Heavy soil or loose rock, 8" wide					
12" deep	BL@.090	LF	—	2.73	2.73
18" deep	BL@.100	LF	—	3.03	3.03
24" deep	BL@.134	LF	—	4.06	4.06

	Craft@Hrs	Unit	Material	Labor	Total
Impact sprinkler heads, riser mounted, adjustable circle					
Brass	BL@.422	Ea	14.50	12.80	27.30
Plastic	BL@.422	Ea	7.15	12.80	19.95
Plastic, 3" pop-up	BL@.422	Ea	23.70	12.80	36.50
Gear drive rotor sprinkler, 3/4" inlet					
Adjustable, 30' radius	BL@.422	Ea	7.15	12.80	19.95
Spray head pop-up type, plastic					
2-1/2" height	BL@.056	Ea	2.22	1.70	3.92
4" height	BL@.056	Ea	5.09	1.70	6.79
6" height	BL@.056	Ea	7.70	1.70	9.40
Spray head, plastic with brass insert, for riser mounting					
Adjustable 0 to 330 degrees	BL@.056	Ea	3.97	1.70	5.67
Standard quarter, half or full pattern	BL@.056	Ea	1.71	1.70	3.41
Shrub spray, all patterns	BL@.056	Ea	2.97	1.70	4.67

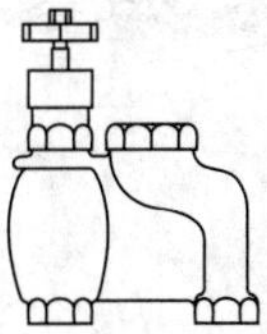

	Craft@Hrs	Unit	Material	Labor	Total
Sprinkler head and riser, 1/2" PVC riser connected to branch supply with three threaded fittings and plastic 4" pop-up head					
4" riser	BL@.056	Ea	9.44	1.70	11.14
6" riser	BL@.056	Ea	9.64	1.70	11.34
12" riser	BL@.056	Ea	10.20	1.70	11.90
18" riser	BL@.056	Ea	10.50	1.70	12.20
24" riser	BL@.056	Ea	11.10	1.70	12.80
Valves, non-siphon, manual, brass					
3/4" valve	BL@1.03	Ea	33.50	31.20	64.70
1" valve	BL@1.38	Ea	25.10	41.80	66.90
Valves, electric solenoid, plastic, with pressure-assisted flow control, hookup but no wire included					
3/4" valve	BL@1.26	Ea	15.40	38.20	53.60
1" valve	BL@1.26	Ea	17.90	38.20	56.10
Valve control wire, 16 gauge low voltage plastic jacket direct burial cable, laid with pipe. No trenching or end connections included.					
2 conductor	BL@.003	LF	.13	.09	.22
3 conductor	BL@.003	LF	.18	.09	.27
5 conductor	BL@.003	LF	.32	.09	.41
7 conductor	BL@.003	LF	.47	.09	.56
8 conductor	BL@.003	LF	.49	.09	.58

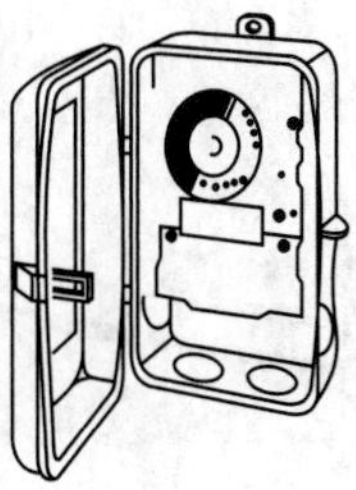

	Craft@Hrs	Unit	Material	Labor	Total
Programmable irrigation control stations, no valve or wiring included, add electrical connection if required.					
For up to 6 electric valves	BL@1.83	LS	50.80	55.50	106.30
For up to 8 electric valves	BL@1.83	LS	57.40	55.50	112.90
Add for 120 volt receptacle	—	LS	—	—	125.00
Residential sprinkler system, typical labor and material costs for irrigating 1,700 SF using 400 LF of 3/4" Schedule 40 PVC pipe, 35 LF of 1" Schedule 40 PVC pipe, four electric 3/4" valves, pop-up sprinkler heads on 6" risers spaced 10', 100 LF of 5-conductor control wire and 235 LF of trenching 12" deep in average soil.					
Large or regular area, 30 heads	BL@.023	SF	.27	.70	.97
Narrow or irregular area, 40 heads	BL@.025	SF	.32	.76	1.08
Add for freezing zones	—	SF	—	—	.12

Layout Foundation layout, medium to large size residence, 6 to 8 outside corners, includes shooting elevation from nearby reference, stakes and batterboards as required. No surveying or clearing included.

	Craft@Hrs	Unit	Material	Labor	Total
Typical cost per residence	B1@7.86	LS	88.00	266.00	354.00

Lighting Fixtures

Lighting Fixtures See also Electrical Work. Costs are to hang and connect fixtures only. Add the cost of wiring and fittings from the Commercial and Industrial section of this manual.

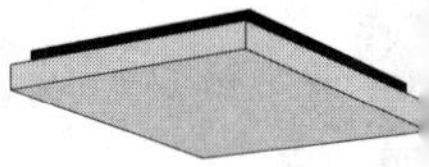

Fluorescent lighting fixtures

Surface mounted fluorescent fixtures, including ballasts but no lamps.

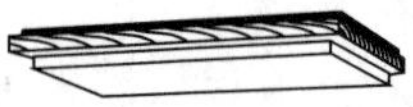

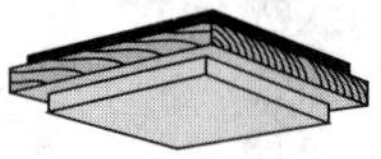

	Craft@Hrs	Unit	Material	Labor	Total
Wraparound acrylic diffuser					
24", two 20 watt tubes	BE@1.60	Ea	31.20	65.00	96.20
48", two 40 watt tubes	BE@1.60	Ea	47.80	65.00	112.80
48", four 40 watt tubes	BE@1.60	Ea	128.00	65.00	193.00
96" tandem, four 40 watt tubes	BE@1.60	Ea	130.00	65.00	195.00
Low profile wraparound model					
10" x 48" x 4", two 20 watt tubes	BE@1.60	Ea	81.50	65.00	146.50
15" x 48" x 4", four 40 watt tubes	BE@1.60	Ea	139.00	65.00	204.00
15" x 96" x 4", eight 40 watt tubes	BE@1.60	Ea	214.00	65.00	279.00
19" x 19" x 4", one 32/40 watt circline tube	BE@1.60	Ea	88.40	65.00	153.40
24" x 24" x 4", two 40 watt U/6 tubes	BE@1.60	Ea	114.00	65.00	179.00

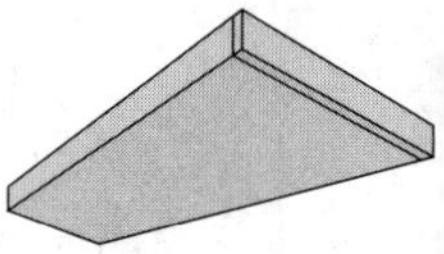

	Craft@Hrs	Unit	Material	Labor	Total
Basic wraparound acrylic diffusers, solid oak wood ends					
10" x 24" x 3", two 20 watt tubes	BE@1.60	Ea	52.50	65.00	117.50
10" x 48" x 3", two 40 watt tubes	BE@1.60	Ea	64.10	65.00	129.10
Economy, wraparound acrylic diffuser, basic metal ends					
14" x 48" x 2", four 40 watt tubes	BE@1.60	Ea	96.10	65.00	161.10
8" x 48" x 2", two 40 watt tubes	BE@1.60	Ea	52.50	65.00	117.50
Electronic ballast troffer fixture, for mounting in a suspended ceiling					
Four 32 watt T8 tubes	BE@.900	Ea	55.30	36.60	91.90
Four 32 watt T8 tubes, with flex connection	BE@.800	Ea	60.40	32.50	92.90

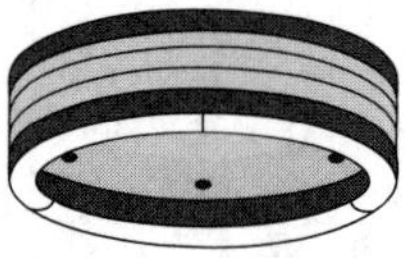

	Craft@Hrs	Unit	Material	Labor	Total
Basic circular fixtures for circline tubes					
Simulated glass crystal with antiqued metal band,					
11" round x 3" high, one 22 watt tube	BE@.696	Ea	20.30	28.30	48.60
Circular fixture					
12" round x 3" high, 22 and 32 watt tubes	BE@.696	Ea	27.90	28.30	56.20
Fixture with frosted glass diffuser					
19" round x 4" high, 32 and 40 watt tubes	BE@.696	Ea	86.20	28.30	114.50

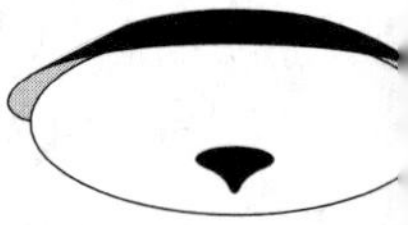

	Craft@Hrs	Unit	Material	Labor	Total
Low profile rectangular wall or ceiling mount fixture, metal housing, white acrylic diffuser					
9-5/8" x 1-7/8", two 9 watt energy saver bulbs	BE@.696	Ea	49.60	28.30	77.90
Rectangular indoor/outdoor model with discoloration resistant/impact resistant acrylic diffuser and cold weather ballast					
10" x 10" x 5" deep, one 22 watt tube	BE@.696	Ea	80.30	28.30	108.60
12" x 12" x 5" deep, one 34 watt tube	BE@.696	Ea	104.00	28.30	132.30
Hall lantern type, including tubes					
4-1/4" wide x 12-1/8" long x 4" deep	BE@.696	Ea	50.50	28.30	78.80

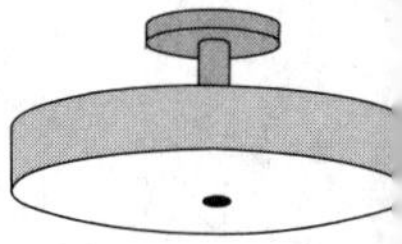

	Craft@Hrs	Unit	Material	Labor	Total
Decorative valance type, with solid oak frame and acrylic diffuser.					
12" x 25" x 4", two 20 watt tubes	BE@2.06	Ea	102.00	83.70	185.70
25" x 25" x 4", two 40 watt U/6 tubes	BE@1.59	Ea	128.00	64.60	192.60
12" x 49" x 4", two 40 watt tubes	BE@1.59	Ea	117.00	64.60	181.60

	Craft@Hrs	Unit	Material	Labor	Total
Economy valance type, with metal ends. Round or square models available					
All models are 2-5/8" wide x 4-1/4" deep					
24-3/4" L (requires one 15 watt tube)	BE@1.59	Ea	27.90	64.60	92.50
24-3/4" L (requires one 20 watt tube)	BE@1.59	Ea	30.20	64.60	94.80
36-3/4" L (requires one 30 watt tube)	BE@1.59	Ea	39.10	64.60	103.70
36-3/4" L (requires two 30 watt tubes)	BE@1.59	Ea	47.50	64.60	112.10
48-3/4" L (requires one 40 watt tube)	BE@1.59	Ea	53.50	64.60	118.10
48-3/4" L (requires two 40 watt tubes)	BE@1.59	Ea	60.30	64.60	124.90

	Craft@Hrs	Unit	Material	Labor	Total
Under shelf/cabinet type for wiring to wall switch					
18" x 5" x 2", one 15 watt tube	BE@.696	Ea	20.10	28.30	48.40
24" x 5" x 2", one 20 watt tube	BE@.696	Ea	26.90	28.30	55.20
36" x 5" x 2", one 30 watt tube	BE@.696	Ea	41.70	28.30	70.00
48" x 5" x 2", one 40 watt tube	BE@.696	Ea	58.70	28.30	87.00

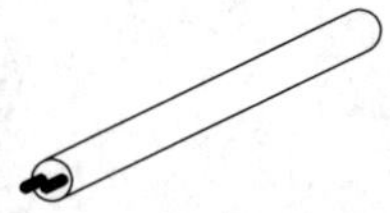

Fluorescent tubes, carton quantities

	Craft@Hrs	Unit	Material	Labor	Total
T8 (1" diameter) tubes, universal start except as noted					
15 watt, 18",preheat	BE@.035	Ea	3.31	1.42	4.73
17 watt, 24", #735	BE@.035	Ea	2.47	1.42	3.89
25 watt, 36", #835	BE@.035	Ea	4.82	1.42	6.24
28 watt, 40", #830	BE@.035	Ea	4.35	1.42	5.77
25 watt, 48", #ADV835	BE@.035	Ea	4.27	1.42	5.69
32 watt, 48", cool white	BE@.035	Ea	2.62	1.42	4.04
40 watt, 60", #865	BE@.035	Ea	6.64	1.42	8.06
58 watt, 60", #841	BE@.035	Ea	8.90	1.42	10.32
38 watt, 72", cool white	BE@.070	Ea	13.50	2.84	16.34
59 watt, 96", cool white	BE@.070	Ea	8.68	2.84	11.52
T12 (1-1/2" diameter) tubes, cool white					
20 watt, 24"	BE@.035	Ea	3.84	1.42	5.26
30 watt, 36"	BE@.035	Ea	3.32	1.42	4.74
39 watt, 48"	BE@.035	Ea	5.80	1.42	7.22
56 watt, 72"	BE@.070	Ea	4.76	2.84	7.60
70 watt, 84"	BE@.070	Ea	7.05	2.84	9.89
75 watt, 96"	BE@.070	Ea	12.10	2.84	14.94

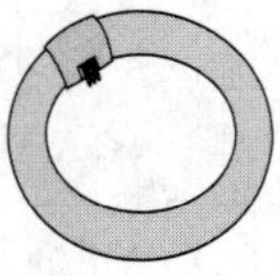

	Craft@Hrs	Unit	Material	Labor	Total
Circular (circline) tubes, T9 (1-1/8" diameter)					
22 watt, 8" diameter	BE@.035	Ea	3.67	1.42	5.09
32 watt, 12" diameter	BE@.035	Ea	4.06	1.42	5.48
40 watt, 16" diameter	BE@.035	Ea	4.38	1.42	5.80

	Craft@Hrs	Unit	Material	Labor	Total
U-shaped tubes					
31 watt, 22-1/2" long, 1-5/8" gap, T8	BE@.035	Ea	8.10	1.42	9.52
32 watt, 22-1/2" long, 6" gap, T8	BE@.035	Ea	7.30	1.42	8.72
40 watt, 22-1/2" long, 6" gap, T12	BE@.035	Ea	9.41	1.42	10.83
48 watt, 22-1/2" long, 6" gap, T12, high output (sign bulb)	BE@.070	Ea	48.30	2.84	51.14

Screw-base light fixtures

	Craft@Hrs	Unit	Material	Labor	Total
Outdoor post lantern fixtures, antique satin brass finish, no digging included					
Post lantern type fixture, cast aluminum	BE@2.00	Ea	78.20	81.30	159.50
Modern porch ceiling fixture					
7-1/2" x 7-1/2" x 3" drop, single light	BE@2.15	Ea	31.00	87.40	118.40
Flood light lampholders					
Cadmium steel plate	BE@2.15	Ea	36.70	87.40	124.10
1/2" male swivel 7-5/16" long, aluminum	BE@2.15	Ea	35.00	87.40	122.40
Path lighting, kits with cable and timer					
20 light low voltage	BE@2.63	LS	69.50	107.00	176.50
6 flood lights, 11 watt	BE@2.98	LS	73.90	121.00	194.90
12 tier lights, 7 watt, programmable	BE@2.63	LS	99.30	107.00	206.30
Recessed fixtures, including housing, screw base					
Integral thermally protected recessed (can) light housing					
4" recessed light housing, non-insulated	BE@1.00	Ea	21.70	40.60	62.30
5" recessed light housing, non-insulated	BE@1.00	Ea	27.50	40.60	68.10
6" recessed light housing, non-insulated	BE@1.00	Ea	13.90	40.60	54.50
Add for insulated housing	—	%	25.0	—	—
Add for low voltage	—	%	101.00	—	—

	Craft@Hrs	Unit	Material	Labor	Total
Recessed baffle light trim	BE@0.25	Ea	12.70	10.20	22.90
Recessed flat light trim	BE@0.25	Ea	12.60	10.20	22.80
Recessed eyeball light trim	BE@0.25	Ea	41.40	10.20	51.60
Recessed reflector light trim	BE@0.25	Ea	17.90	10.20	28.10
Recessed shower light trim	BE@0.25	Ea	16.70	10.20	26.90
Recessed open light trim	BE@0.25	Ea	5.51	10.20	15.71
Recessed adjustable light trim	BE@0.25	Ea	31.20	10.20	41.40
Recessed splay light trim	BE@0.25	Ea	13.80	10.20	24.00
Utility 12" x 10", diffusing glass lens	BE@1.00	Ea	61.30	40.60	101.90
Ceiling fixtures, 60 watt max bulb, pre-wired housing, white, canopy finish					
Cloud 9-3/4" x 5-1/4" (2 bulbs)	BE@1.59	Ea	32.60	64.60	97.20
Cloud 8-1/4" x 5-1/2" (1 bulb)	BE@1.59	Ea	41.40	64.60	106.00
Standard globe 8-3/4" x 5" (2 bulbs)	BE@1.59	Ea	28.40	64.60	93.00
Cloud globe, brass canopy 10" x 5"	BE@1.59	Ea	35.30	64.60	99.90

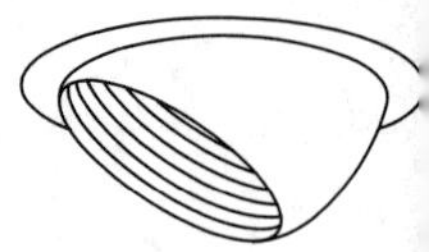

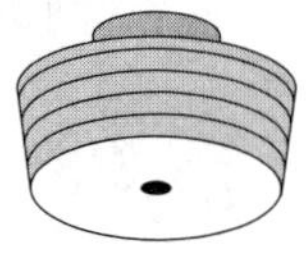

Screw-base light bulbs Case quantities.

	Craft@Hrs	Unit	Material	Labor	Total
Compact fluorescent (CFL)					
14 watt, 60-watt equivalent	BE@.035	Ea	1.99	1.42	3.41
23 watt, 100-watt equivalent	BE@.035	Ea	1.99	1.42	3.41
42 watt, 200-watt equivalent	BE@.035	Ea	8.38	1.42	9.80
65 watt, 300-watt equivalent	BE@.035	Ea	17.40	1.42	18.82
85 watt, 400-watt equivalent	BE@.035	Ea	26.40	1.42	27.82
105 watt, 500-watt equivalent	BE@.035	Ea	22.60	1.42	24.02
15 watt, 65 watt equivalent, dimmable flood	BE@.035	Ea	3.11	1.42	4.53
Light emitting diode bulbs (LED)					
9.5 watt A19 (60W) daylight	BE@.035	Ea	2.69	1.42	4.11
13 watt flood, PAR30 equivalent	BE@.035	Ea	9.96	1.42	11.38
20 watt flood, PAR38 equivalent	BE@.035	Ea	8.49	1.42	9.91
22 watt A21 (100W) soft white	BE@.035	Ea	7.67	1.42	9.09

Log Home Construction

Logs are cut from standing dead lodgepole pine or spruce. Add the foundation cost. Based on Authentic Log Homes.

Rule of thumb cost, including labor, material and hardware but no foundation, plumbing, HVAC, electrical work or interior finishing.

	Craft@Hrs	Unit	Material	Labor	Total
Total cost per square foot of wall (shell only)	—	SF	—	—	38.00
Lodgepole pine or spruce logs, including local delivery, per LF of log at 8" to 12" diameter					
8" machine peeled	—	LF	14.90	—	14.90
8" hand peeled	—	LF	15.90	—	15.90
10" machine peeled	—	LF	20.00	—	20.00
10" hand peeled	—	LF	22.10	—	22.10
12" machine peeled	—	LF	25.90	—	25.90
12" hand peeled	—	LF	28.20	—	28.20

Labor costs for log home construction. Using a crew experienced in log home construction. Add 10% to 50% for crews on their first log home project. Subfloor and porch joist hardware uses Type B Simpson Strong-Tie hangers. These labor estimates assume precut 8" x 6" log profiles. For 9" x 7" profiles, add 10%. For 10" x 8" profiles, add 20%. For random length logs, add 10%. The preferred crew is three carpenters and three helpers.

	Craft@Hrs	Unit	Material	Labor	Total
Subfloor					
CCA treated sill plate, anchor bolts.	B1@.057	LF	—	1.93	1.93
Built-up girders (using 2 x 8 lumber)	B1@.222	LF	—	7.51	7.51
Posts (8" log), with anchor	B1@.500	Ea	—	16.90	16.90
Rim joists and blocking (2 x 8)	B1@.065	LF	—	2.20	2.20
Floor joists (2 x 8), hangers, bridging/blocking	B1@.025	LF	—	.85	.85
Decking	B1@.014	SF	—	.47	.47

	Craft@Hrs	Unit	Material	Labor	Total
Porch					
Rim joists	B1@.017	LF	—	.58	.58
Posts (8" log), with anchor	B1@.500	Ea	—	16.90	16.90
Joists with hangers	B1@.025	SF	—	.85	.85
Decking (2 x 6 redwood)	B1@.025	SF	—	.85	.85
Balcony railing	B1@.125	LF	—	4.23	4.23
Sill log					
Flashing	B1@.010	LF	—	.34	.34
Sill log spiked onto subfloor	B1@.050	LF	—	1.69	1.69
Laying wall courses					
Courses 2 through 8	B1@.025	LF	—	.85	.85
Courses 9 through 16	B1@.033	LF	—	1.12	1.12
Course 17 (sill log)	B1@.040	LF	—	1.35	1.35
Courses 18 through 24	B1@.040	LF	—	1.35	1.35
Courses 25 through 32	B1@.050	LF	—	1.69	1.69
Doors and windows, per opening	B1@4.00	Ea	—	135.00	135.00
Interior trim	B1@2.00	Ea	—	67.70	67.70
Exterior trim	B1@2.00	Ea	—	67.70	67.70
Mantle (10 feet long)					
With bracing	B1@1.50	Ea	—	50.80	50.80
Log floor system					
Girder	B1@.050	LF	—	1.69	1.69
Support posts	B1@.500	Ea	—	16.90	16.90
Support wall (studs, top and bottom plates)	B1@.167	LF	—	5.65	5.65
Cutting wall notch to accept girder	B1@1.50	Ea	—	50.80	50.80
Floor joists	B1@.063	LF	—	2.13	2.13
Cutting wall notch to accept floor joist	B1@.500	Ea	—	16.90	16.90
T&G decking	B1@.025	SF	—	.85	.85
Log staircase					
Straight	B1@30.0	Ea	—	1,020.00	1,020.00
"L"- or "U"-shaped	B1@36.0	Ea	—	1,220.00	1,220.00
Wall stiffener					
6" x 6" or 8" x 8" beam channeled into wall	B1@2.00	Ea	—	67.70	67.70
Log rafter system, including dormers					
Ridge beam, main and secondary	B1@0.25	LF	—	8.46	8.46
Notching gable to accept ridge beam	B1@1.50	Ea	—	50.80	50.80
Built up truss pocket	B1@2.00	Ea	—	67.70	67.70
Valley beam layout and installation	B1@0.33	LF	—	11.20	11.20
Ridge beam support post	B1@0.50	Ea	—	16.90	16.90
Rafter 20' or less	B1@1.00	Ea	—	33.90	33.90
Rafter over 20'	B1@1.50	Ea	—	50.80	50.80
Valley rafter 16' or less	B1@1.50	Ea	—	50.80	50.80
Valley rafter between 16' and 20'	B1@2.00	Ea	—	67.70	67.70
Valley rafter over 20'	B1@2.50	Ea	—	84.60	84.60
Timber rafter 18' or less	B1@3.00	Ea	—	102.00	102.00
Timber rafter over 18'	B1@4.00	Ea	—	135.00	135.00
Rafter layout	B1@.250	Ea	—	8.46	8.46
Snow block	B1@1.00	Ea	—	33.90	33.90
Log trusses, 32' and less					
Hardware plate	B1@2.00	Ea	—	67.70	67.70
Collar ties	B1@1.00	Ea	—	33.90	33.90
Vertical or diagonal web	B1@3.00	Ea	—	102.00	102.00
Add for each 5' of truss over 32'	—	%	—	50.0	—

	Craft@Hrs	Unit	Material	Labor	Total
Cold roof construction					
Secondary rafters	B1@0.50	Ea	—	16.90	16.90
Jack rafters	B1@0.25	Ea	—	8.46	8.46
Fly rafters	B1@0.50	Ea	—	16.90	16.90
Blocking	B1@0.25	Ea	—	8.46	8.46
OSB roof sheathing					
Less than or equal to 6/12 pitch	B1@1.72	Sq	—	58.20	58.20
7/12 pitch to 9/12 pitch	B1@2.00	Sq	—	67.70	67.70
Less than or equal to 6/12 pitch	B1@2.50	Sq	—	84.60	84.60
Felt	B1@1.00	Sq	—	33.90	33.90
Asphalt shingles	B1@2.00	Sq	—	67.70	67.70
Metal roof, ridge cap and closure strips	B1@1.33	Sq	—	45.00	45.00
Ridge vents and soffit vents	B1@3.00	Ea	—	102.00	102.00
Fascia	B1@0.02	LF	—	.68	.68
Soffit	B1@0.03	SF	—	1.02	1.02
Caulking					
Exterior only	B1@0.02	SF	—	.68	.68
Preservative					
Exterior only	B1@.005	SF	—	.17	.17
Electrical chases					
Cut in log ends and down tops of rafters	B1@.083	LF	—	2.81	2.81
Holes drilled through ridge beams	B1@0.50	Ea	—	16.90	16.90

Framing Lumber

MBF means per 1,000 board feet. One board foot is the volume of lumber in a nominal 1" x 12" board one foot long. A 2" x 6" joist 10 feet long has 10 board feet. To determine the board feet of lumber in any piece, multiply the width in inches by the depth in inches by the length in feet. Then divide by 12.

	Unit	MBF	8' L	12' L	16' L
Douglas fir – #2 & Better					
2" x 4" – Green	Ea	837.00	4.46	6.69	8.92
2" x 6" – KD	Ea	917.00	7.34	11.00	14.70
2" x 8" – KD	Ea	767.00	8.18	12.30	16.40
2" x 10" – KD	Ea	950.00	12.70	19.00	25.30
2" x 12" – KD	Ea	910.00	14.60	21.80	29.10
Douglas fir – kiln dried Standard & Better					
2" x 4"	Ea	912.00	4.86	7.29	9.72
2" x 6"	Ea	924.00	7.39	11.10	14.80
2" x 8"	Ea	865.00	9.23	13.80	18.50
2" x 10"	Ea	942.00	12.60	18.80	25.10
2" x 12"	Ea	949.00	15.20	22.80	30.40
Douglas fir finish and clear – C & Better, vertical grain, S4S, dry. West Coast prices. Add 10% to 30% for transportation to other areas					
2" x 2"	Ea	3,440.00	8.58	13.00	17.30
2" x 3"	Ea	3,490.00	13.00	19.20	26.00
2" x 4"	Ea	3,870.00	19.20	29.20	39.00
2" x 6"	Ea	4,320.00	32.60	48.90	65.20
2" x 10"	Ea	6,060.00	76.60	116.00	153.00
2" x 12"	Ea	8,190.00	119.00	178.00	237.00
Douglas fir finish and clear – C & Better, flat grain, S4S, dry. West Coast prices. Add 10% to 30% for transportation to other areas					
2" x 2"	Ea	3,330.00	8.35	12.60	16.90
2" x 3"	Ea	3,330.00	12.60	18.80	25.00
2" x 4"	Ea	3,360.00	17.10	25.40	33.80

	Unit	MBF	8' L	12' L	16' L
2" x 6"	Ea	3,890.00	29.40	44.20	58.80
2" x 8"	Ea	3,890.00	39.40	58.80	78.30
2" x 10"	Ea	3,900.00	49.00	73.50	98.00
2" x 12"	Ea	5,170.00	78.20	118.00	155.00
Hemlock/fir, kiln dried					
2" x 4" – Standard & Better	Ea	610.00	3.25	4.87	6.50
2" x 6" – #2 & Better	Ea	596.00	4.77	7.15	9.54
2" x 8" – #2 & Better	Ea	645.00	6.88	10.30	13.80
2" x 10" – #2 & Better	Ea	736.00	9.80	14.70	19.60
2" x 12" – #2 & Better	Ea	737.00	11.80	17.70	23.60
Spruce pine fir (SPF), kiln dried					
2" x 4", #2 and Better	Ea	440.00	2.34	3.52	4.69
2" x 6", #2 and Better	Ea	577.00	4.62	6.93	9.23
2" x 8", #2 and Better	Ea	856.00	9.13	13.70	18.30
2" x 10", #2 and Better	Ea	751.00	10.00	15.00	20.00
2" x 12", #2 and Better	Ea	858.00	13.70	20.60	27.50
2" x 4", Standard and Better	Ea	912.00	4.86	7.29	9.71
4" x 4", Standard and Better	Ea	765.00	8.16	12.20	16.30
Red cedar – green S4S					
2" x 4"	Ea	1,860.00	9.95	14.90	19.90
2" x 6"	Ea	2,410.00	19.30	28.90	38.50
Red cedar – green – D and Better S4S					
2" x 2"	Ea	3,600.00	9.59	14.40	19.20
2" x 4"	Ea	4,450.00	23.80	35.70	47.50
2" x 6"	Ea	3,250.00	26.00	39.00	52.00
Red cedar – rough – Standard and Better					
2" x 2"	Ea	2,350.00	6.27	9.40	12.50
2" x 4"	Ea	2,030.00	10.80	16.20	21.70
2" x 6"	Ea	2,520.00	20.20	30.30	40.30
2" x 8"	Ea	3,050.00	32.50	48.70	65.00
Southern yellow pine – #1 S4S					
2" x 4"	Ea	1,120.00	5.97	8.95	11.90
2" x 6"	Ea	926.00	7.41	11.10	14.80
2" x 10"	Ea	852.00	11.40	17.00	22.70
2" x 12"	Ea	1,030.00	16.40	24.60	32.80
Southern yellow pine – #2 S4S					
2" x 4"	Ea	702.00	3.74	5.61	7.48
2" x 6"	Ea	741.00	5.93	8.90	11.90
2" x 8"	Ea	816.00	8.70	13.10	17.40
2" x 10"	Ea	680.00	9.06	13.60	18.10
2" x 12"	Ea	815.00	13.10	19.60	26.10
Southern yellow pine – Prime S4S					
2" x 4"	Ea	683.00	3.64	5.46	7.28
2" x 6"	Ea	629.00	5.03	7.55	10.10
2" x 8"	Ea	707.00	7.54	11.30	15.10
2" x 10"	Ea	647.00	8.62	12.90	17.30
2" x 12"	Ea	870.00	13.90	20.90	27.90
Redwood. West Coast prices. Add 10% to 30% for transportation to other areas.					
2" x 2" – B Grade S4S	Ea	2,940.00	7.84	11.80	15.70
2" x 2" – Green	Ea	2,070.00	5.51	8.27	11.00
2" x 3" – Green	Ea	1,710.00	6.84	10.30	13.70
2" x 4" – Construction Common	Ea	1,810.00	9.63	15.50	19.30
2" x 6" – Construction Common	Ea	1,630.00	13.00	19.50	26.00
2" x 4" – Construction Rough	Ea	2,400.00	12.80	19.20	25.60

	Unit	MBF	8' L	12' L	16' L
2" x 4" – Common S4S	Ea	2,110.00	11.30	16.90	22.50
2" x 6" – Common S4S	Ea	2,010.00	16.10	24.20	32.20
2" x 8" – Common S4S	Ea	2,220.00	23.60	35.50	42.30
2" x 12" – Common S4S	Ea	2,080.00	33.30	50.00	66.60
2" x 4" – Construction Heart, Rough	Ea	2,360.00	12.60	18.90	25.20
2" x 6" – Construction Heart, Rough	Ea	1,780.00	14.20	21.40	28.50
2" x 4" – Construction Heart, S4S	Ea	2,550.00	13.60	20.40	27.20
2" x 6" – Construction Heart, S4S	Ea	2,410.00	19.30	28.90	38.60
2" x 8" – Construction Heart, S4S	Ea	2,650.00	28.30	42.40	56.60
2" x 12" – Construction Heart, S4S	Ea	3,050.00	48.70	73.10	97.50

Studs Typical costs for pre-cut white wood studding material, stud grade. Nominal sizes. Actual width and depth are about 1/2" less when dry. White wood species includes Engelmann spruce, all true firs, hemlocks and pines (excluding Ponderosa pine).

	Craft@Hrs	Unit	Material	Labor	Total
2" x 3" x 84"	B1@.192	Ea	3.32	6.50	9.82
2" x 4" x 84"	B1@.196	Ea	3.20	6.63	9.83
2" x 4" x 88"	B1@.200	Ea	4.20	6.77	10.97
2" x 4" x 92-5/8"	B1@.216	Ea	3.94	7.31	11.25
2" x 4" x 96"	B1@.224	Ea	3.95	7.58	11.53
2" x 4" x 104-5/8"	B1@.230	Ea	4.42	7.79	12.21
2" x 6" x 92-5/8"	B1@.308	Ea	6.76	10.40	17.16

Boards

	Unit	MBF	8' L	12' L	16' L
Douglas fir finish and clear – C & Better (V/G) S4S, dry, vertical grain. West Coast prices. Add 10% to 30% for transportation to other areas.					
1" x 2"	Ea	6,670.00	8.87	13.30	17.90
1" x 3"	Ea	6,670.00	13.30	20.00	26.90
1" x 4"	Ea	6,500.00	17.90	26.90	35.90
1" x 6"	Ea	7,600.00	30.50	45.40	60.50
1" x 8"	Ea	9,270.00	49.60	73.80	98.70
1" x 10"	Ea	10,300.00	68.80	103.00	139.00
1" x 12"	Ea	11,000.00	88.20	132.00	175.00
Douglas fir finish and clear – C & Better (F/G) S4S, dry, flat grain. West Coast prices. Add 10% to 30% for transportation to other areas.					
1" x 2"	Ea	5,760.00	7.66	11.40	15.30
1" x 3"	Ea	5,760.00	11.60	17.30	22.90
1" x 4"	Ea	5,760.00	15.30	2.90	30.60
1" x 6"	Ea	6,020.00	24.10	36.20	48.10
1" x 8"	Ea	7,740.00	41.30	61.80	82.70
1" x 10"	Ea	10,800.00	71.70	108.00	143.00
1" x 12"	Ea	11,000.00	88.00	132.00	175.00
Southern pine boards – C & Better					
1" x 4"	Ea	3,130.00	8.33	12.50	16.70
1" x 6"	Ea	3,400.00	13.60	20.40	27.20
1" x 8"	Ea	3,870.00	20.60	30.90	41.20
1" x 12"	Ea	3,980.00	31.90	47.80	63.70
White pine boards, Select					
1" x 4"	Ea	4,110.00	10.90	16.40	21.90
1" x 6"	Ea	5,190.00	20.80	31.10	41.50
1" x 8"	Ea	4,650.00	24.80	37.20	49.60
1" x 10"	Ea	4,890.00	32.60	48.90	65.20
1" x 12"	Ea	5,340.00	42.70	64.10	85.50

	Unit	MBF	8' L	12' L	16' L
Eastern pine boards – Premium					
1" x 4"	Ea	2,320.00	6.18	9.27	12.40
1" x 6"	Ea	2,250.00	9.01	13.50	18.00
1" x 8"	Ea	1,760.00	9.35	14.00	18.70
1" x 10"	Ea	1,890.00	12.60	18.90	25.20
1" x 12"	Ea	2,500.00	20.00	30.00	40.00
Southern yellow pine flooring – D Grade					
1" x 4"	Ea	1,630.00	4.36	6.54	8.78
1" x 6"	Ea	1,850.00	7.34	11.10	14.60
1" x 8"	Ea	1,790.00	9.67	13.20	19.10
1" x 10"	Ea	1,640.00	11.10	14.60	21.80
1" x 12"	Ea	2,090.00	16.70	24.90	33.50
Fir flooring – C & Better tongue & groove					
1" x 3" vertical grain, C and Better	Ea	4,630.00	9.26	13.90	18.40
1" x 4" vertical grain, C and Better	Ea	4,630.00	12.40	18.40	24.80
1" x 3" flat grain, C and Better	Ea	2,780.00	5.56	8.32	11.20
1" x 4" flat grain, C and Better	Ea	2,780.00	7.40	11.20	14.80
1" x 3" vertical grain, D and Better	Ea	3,310.00	6.67	9.97	13.20
1" x 4" vertical grain, D and Better	Ea	3,310.00	8.88	13.20	17.20
1" x 3" flat grain, D and Better	Ea	2,220.00	4.35	6.58	8.72
1" x 4" flat grain, D and Better	Ea	2,170.00	5.84	8.72	11.70
Ponderosa pine boards – #4 & Better					
1" x 3"	Ea	2,920.00	5.85	8.77	11.70
1" x 4"	Ea	2,640.00	7.02	10.50	14.10
1" x 6"	Ea	2,710.00	10.80	16.30	21.70
1" x 8"	Ea	2,670.00	14.30	21.40	28.50
1" x 10"	Ea	2,760.00	18.40	27.60	36.70
White wood boards – Appearance Grade					
1" x 4"	Ea	2,480.00	6.60	9.91	13.20
1" x 6"	Ea	2,670.00	10.70	16.00	21.30
1" x 8"	Ea	2,710.00	14.50	21.70	28.90
1" x 12"	Ea	3,390.00	27.10	40.70	54.20
Cypress boards					
1" x 4"	Ea	2,340.00	6.22	9.33	12.40
1" x 6"	Ea	2,820.00	11.30	16.90	22.60
1" x 8"	Ea	3,160.00	16.80	25.30	33.70
1" x 10"	Ea	3,200.00	21.40	32.00	42.70
1" x 12"	Ea	3,700.00	29.60	44.40	59.20
Hemlock boards – C & Better					
1" x 2"	Ea	5,970.00	7.96	12.00	15.90
1" x 3"	Ea	6,200.00	12.40	18.60	24.80
1" x 4"	Ea	6,360.00	16.90	25.40	33.90
1" x 6"	Ea	8,020.00	32.10	48.10	64.20
Pine boards – Select					
1" x 2"	Ea	3,630.00	4.85	7.27	9.69
1" x 3"	Ea	4,520.00	9.05	13.60	18.10
Clear Douglas fir – S4S					
1" x 2"	Ea	5,160.00	6.88	10.30	13.80
1" x 3"	Ea	5,260.00	10.50	15.80	21.00
1" x 4"	Ea	6,040.00	16.10	24.10	32.20
1" x 6"	Ea	7,120.00	28.50	42.70	57.00
1" x 8"	Ea	6,110.00	32.60	48.90	65.10

Lumber, Boards

	Unit	MBF	8' L	12' L	16' L
Douglas fir / hemlock					
1" x 4"	Ea	2,020.00	5.39	8.09	10.80
1" x 6"	Ea	2,170.00	8.67	13.00	17.40
Southern yellow pine premium decking					
5/4" x 6"	Ea	3,400.00	17.00	25.50	34.00

	Unit	6' L	8' L	12' L	16' L
Red oak boards, S4S, East Coast and Midwest prices					
1" x 2"	Ea	5.71	7.60	9.83	11.70
1" x 3"	Ea	8.74	15.70	21.50	25.80
1" x 6"	Ea	18.00	24.00	31.80	37.90
1" x 8"	Ea	23.80	31.50	42.90	56.90
1" x 10"	Ea	35.10	47.50	58.60	70.30
1" x 12"	Ea	42.30	53.00	74.70	89.20

	Unit	MBF	8' L	12' L	16' L
Cedar boards – S1S2E (surfaced 1 side, 2 ends)					
3/4" x 2"	Ea	4,450.00	4.45	6.68	8.90
3/4" x 4"	Ea	3,440.00	6.88	10.30	13.80
3/4" x 6"	Ea	5,850.00	17.50	26.30	35.10
7/8" x 4"	Ea	4,610.00	10.80	16.10	21.50
7/8" x 6"	Ea	6,470.00	22.60	34.00	45.30
7/8" x 8"	Ea	5,280.00	24.60	37.00	49.30
7/8" x 10"	Ea	5,380.00	31.40	47.10	62.80
7/8" x 12"	Ea	5,780.00	40.50	60.70	80.90
1" x 4"	Ea	4,540.00	12.10	18.10	24.20
1" x 6"	Ea	5,620.00	22.50	33.70	44.90
Clear cedar trim boards					
1" x 2"	Ea	2,800.00	3.73	5.59	7.46
1" x 3"	Ea	4,080.00	8.17	12.30	16.30
1" x 4"	Ea	5,860.00	15.60	23.40	31.20
1" x 6"	Ea	8,800.00	35.20	52.80	70.40
1" x 8"	Ea	11,700.00	62.60	93.90	125.00
Red cedar boards, kiln dried					
1" x 4"	Ea	3,550.00	9.44	14.20	18.90
1" x 6"	Ea	3,950.00	15.80	23.70	31.60
1" x 8"	Ea	4,610.00	24.60	36.90	49.20
Redwood boards, West Coast prices.					
Add 10% to 30% for transportation to other areas.					
1" x 2" – B Grade S4S	Ea	4,500.00	6.00	9.00	12.00
1" x 3" – B Grade S4S	Ea	4,360.00	8.72	13.10	17.40
1" x 4" – B Grade S4S	Ea	4,900.00	13.10	19.60	26.10
1" x 6" – B Grade S4S	Ea	4,770.00	19.10	28.60	38.20
1" x 4" – Green	Ea	2,930.00	7.81	11.70	15.60
1" x 6" – Green	Ea	4,350.00	17.40	26.10	34.80
1" x 8" – Select S1S2E	Ea	2,960.00	15.80	23.70	31.60

	Craft@Hrs	Unit	Material	Labor	Total
Lath, Redwood "A" & Better, 50 per bundle, nailed to walls for architectural treatment.					
5/16" x 1-1/2" x 4'	BC@.500	Bdle	21.10	18.70	39.80
5/16" x 1-1/2" x 6'	BC@.625	Bdle	28.40	23.40	51.80
5/16" x 1-1/2" x 8'	BC@.750	Bdle	39.50	28.00	67.50

	Craft@Hrs	Unit	Material	Labor	Total
Board Siding					
Pine bevel siding, 1/2" thick by 6" wide. Each linear foot of 6" wide bevel siding covers .38 square feet of wall. Do not deduct for wall openings less than 10 square feet. Add 5% for typical waste and end cutting.					
8' lengths	B1@.038	SF	1.37	1.29	2.66
12' lengths	B1@.036	SF	1.35	1.22	2.57
16' lengths	B1@.033	SF	1.38	1.12	2.50
Western red cedar bevel siding. A Grade and Better, 1/2" thick by 6" wide. Each linear foot of 6" wide bevel siding covers .38 square feet of wall. Do not deduct for wall openings less than 10 square feet. Add 5% for typical waste and end cutting.					
8' lengths	B1@.038	SF	6.58	1.29	7.87
12' lengths	B1@.036	SF	6.38	1.22	7.60
16' lengths	B1@.033	SF	6.54	1.12	7.66
Clear cedar 1/2" bevel siding. Vertical grain, 1/2" thick by 6" wide, kiln dried. Each linear foot of 6" wide bevel siding covers .38 square feet of wall. Do not deduct for wall openings less than 10 square feet. Add 5% for typical waste and end cutting.					
8' lengths	B1@.038	SF	6.69	1.29	7.98
12' lengths	B1@.036	SF	6.75	1.22	7.97
16' lengths	B1@.033	SF	6.82	1.12	7.94
Cedar 3/4" bevel siding, 3/4" thick by 8" wide. Each linear foot of 8" wide bevel siding covers .54 square feet of wall. Do not deduct for wall openings less than 10 square feet. Add 5% for typical waste and end cutting.					
8' lengths	B1@.036	SF	3.48	1.22	4.70
12' lengths	B1@.034	SF	3.44	1.15	4.59
16' lengths	B1@.031	SF	3.50	1.05	4.55
Rustic cedar channel siding, 3/4" x 8". Each linear foot of 8" wide channel siding covers .54 square feet of wall. Do not deduct for wall openings less than 10 square feet. Add 5% for typical waste and end cutting.					
12' lengths	B1@.034	SF	5.19	1.15	6.34
Tongue and groove cedar siding, 1" x 6". Kiln dried, select. Each linear foot of 6" wide tongue and groove siding covers 0.43 square feet of wall. Do not deduct for wall openings less than 10 square feet. Add 5% for typical waste and end cutting.					
8' lengths	B1@.036	SF	5.54	1.22	6.76
10' lengths	B1@.035	SF	4.58	1.18	5.76
12' lengths	B1@.034	SF	4.96	1.15	6.11
Redwood 5/8" tongue and groove siding, 5/8" thick by 5-3/8" wide. Each linear foot of 5-3/8" wide tongue and groove siding covers 0.42 square feet of wall. Do not deduct for wall openings less than 10 square feet. Add 5% for typical waste and end cutting.					
8' lengths	B1@.042	SF	4.32	1.42	5.74
10' lengths	B1@.040	SF	5.19	1.35	6.54
12' lengths	B1@.038	SF	5.30	1.29	6.59
Redwood 5/8" shiplap siding, B Grade. 5/8" thick by 5-3/8" wide. Each linear foot of 5-3/8" wide shiplap siding covers 0.38 square feet of wall. Do not deduct for wall openings less than 10 square feet. Add 5% for typical waste and end cutting.					
8' lengths	B1@.038	SF	5.88	1.29	7.17
10' lengths	B1@.037	SF	5.87	1.25	7.12
12' lengths	B1@.036	SF	5.86	1.22	7.08
Southern yellow pine, 6" pattern 105 siding, 1" x 6". Select Grade except as noted. Each linear foot of 6" wide siding covers 0.38 square feet of wall. Do not deduct for wall openings less than 10 square feet. Add 5% for typical waste and end cutting.					
8' lengths	B1@.038	SF	4.74	1.29	6.03
10' lengths	B1@.037	SF	4.80	1.25	6.05
12' lengths, No. 2	B1@.036	SF	2.70	1.22	3.92
12' lengths	B1@.036	SF	4.76	1.22	5.98

	Craft@Hrs	Unit	Material	Labor	Total
Southern yellow pine, 8" pattern 105 siding, 1" x 8". Select Grade except as noted. Each linear foot of 8" wide siding covers 0.54 square feet of wall. Do not deduct for wall openings less than 10 square feet. Add 5% for typical waste and end cutting.					
8' lengths	B1@.036	SF	4.39	1.22	5.61
10' lengths	B1@.034	SF	4.24	1.15	5.39
12' lengths, No. 2	B1@.031	SF	2.16	1.05	3.21
12' lengths	B1@.031	SF	4.22	1.05	5.27
Southern yellow pine, 6" pattern 116 siding, 1" x 6". Select Grade except as noted. Each linear foot of 6" wide siding covers 0.38 square feet of wall. Do not deduct for wall openings less than 10 square feet. Add 5% for typical waste and end cutting.					
8' lengths	B1@.038	SF	4.78	1.29	6.07
10' lengths	B1@.037	SF	4.76	1.25	6.01
12' lengths	B1@.036	SF	4.82	1.22	6.04
Southern yellow pine, 6" pattern 117 siding, 1" x 6". Select Grade except as noted. Each linear foot of 6" wide siding covers 0.38 square feet of wall. Do not deduct for wall openings less than 10 square feet. Add 5% for typical waste and end cutting.					
8' lengths	B1@.038	SF	4.70	1.29	5.99
10' lengths	B1@.037	SF	4.81	1.25	6.06
12' lengths	B1@.036	SF	4.71	1.22	5.93
Southern yellow pine, 8" pattern 131 siding, 1" x 8". Select Grade except as noted. Each linear foot of 8" wide siding covers 0.54 square feet of wall. Do not deduct for wall openings less than 10 square feet. Add 5% for typical waste and end cutting.					
8' lengths	B1@.036	SF	4.27	1.22	5.49
10' lengths	B1@.034	SF	4.26	1.15	5.41
12' lengths	B1@.031	SF	4.25	1.05	5.30
Southern yellow pine, 8" pattern 122 siding, 1" x 8". "V"-joint. Select Grade except as noted. Each linear foot of 8" wide siding covers 0.54 square feet of wall. Do not deduct for wall openings less than 10 square feet. Add 5% for typical waste and end cutting.					
8' lengths	B1@.036	SF	4.22	1.22	5.44
10' lengths	B1@.034	SF	4.20	1.15	5.35
12' lengths	B1@.031	SF	4.18	1.05	5.23
Southern yellow pine, 6" pattern 122 siding, 1" x 6". Select Grade except as noted. Each linear foot of 6" wide siding covers 0.38 square feet of wall. Do not deduct for wall openings less than 10 square feet. Add 5% for typical waste and end cutting.					
8' lengths	B1@.038	SF	3.31	1.29	4.60
10' lengths	B1@.037	SF	3.30	1.25	4.55
12' lengths	B1@.036	SF	3.29	1.22	4.51
Southern yellow pine, 8" shiplap siding, 1" x 8". No. 2 Grade. Each linear foot of 8" wide siding covers 0.54 square feet of wall. Do not deduct for wall openings less than 10 square feet. Add 5% for typical waste and end cutting.					
8' lengths	B1@.036	SF	2.00	1.22	3.22
10' lengths	B1@.034	SF	1.80	1.15	2.95
12' lengths	B1@.031	SF	1.99	1.05	3.04
Rustic 8" pine siding, 1" x 8". "V"-grooved. Each linear foot of 8" wide siding covers 0.54 square feet of wall. Do not deduct for wall openings less than 10 square feet. Add 5% for typical waste and end cutting.					
16' lengths	B1@.031	SF	3.10	1.05	4.15
20' lengths	B1@.031	SF	3.16	1.05	4.21
Log cabin siding, 1-1/2" thick. Each linear foot of 6" wide siding covers 0.41 square feet of wall. Each linear foot of 8" wide siding covers .55 square feet of wall. Do not deduct for wall openings less than 10 square feet. Add 5% for typical waste and end cutting.					
6" x 8', T & G latia	B1@.038	SF	3.88	1.29	5.17
6" x 12', T & G latia	B1@.036	SF	3.95	1.22	5.17
8" x 12'	B1@.031	SF	4.28	1.05	5.33
8" x 16'	B1@.030	SF	4.26	1.02	5.28

	Craft@Hrs	Unit	Material	Labor	Total
Log lap spruce siding, 1-1/2" thick. Each linear foot of 6" wide siding covers 0.41 square feet of wall. Each linear foot of 8" wide siding covers .55 square feet of wall. Each linear foot of 10" wide siding covers 0.72 square feet of wall. Do not deduct for wall openings less than 10 square feet. Add 5% for typical waste and end cutting.					
6" width	B1@.038	SF	6.31	1.29	7.60
8" width	B1@.031	SF	6.23	1.05	7.28
10" width	B1@.030	SF	5.05	1.02	6.07

Timbers

	Unit	MBF	12' L	16' L	20' L
Green Douglas Fir timbers – #1 Grade					
4" x 8"	Ea	1,140.00	36.40	48.50	60.60
4" x 10"	Ea	1,110.00	44.50	59.40	74.20
4" x 12"	Ea	1,070.00	51.40	68.50	85.60
6" x 6"	Ea	1,680.00	60.40	80.60	101.00

	Unit	MBF	8' L	12' L	16' L
Green Douglas Fir timbers – #2 and Better					
4" x 4"	Ea	950.00	10.10	15.20	20.30
4" x 6"	Ea	918.00	14.70	22.00	29.40
4" x 8"	Ea	838.00	17.90	26.80	35.80
4" x 10"	Ea	965.00	25.70	38.60	51.50
4" x 12"	Ea	869.00	27.80	41.70	55.60

	Unit	MBF	12' L	16' L	20' L
Red Cedar timbers					
4" x 4" – Green S4S	Ea	3,930.00	62.90	83.80	105.00
4" x 4" – Rough	Ea	2,810.00	45.00	60.00	75.00
6" x 6" – Rough	Ea	4,530.00	163.00	217.00	272.00

	Unit	MBF	8' L	12' L	16' L
Redwood timbers West Coast prices. Add 10% to 30% for transportation to other areas.					
4" x 4" – Construction Common	Ea	1,880.00	20.10	30.10	40.10
4" x 4" – Construction Heart - Rough	Ea	2,270.00	24.20	36.30	48.30
4" x 4" – Construction Heart – S4S	Ea	2,520.00	26.90	40.40	53.80

Pressure-treated lumber, ACQ treatment

	Unit	MBF	8' L	12' L	16' L
Pressure-treated trim board S4S, .25 treatment, Appearance Grade					
1" x 4" – .25 appearance grade	Ea	2,090.00	5.56	8.34	11.10
1" x 6" – .25 appearance grade	Ea	1,530.00	6.11	9.16	12.20
1" x 8" – .25 appearance grade	Ea	1,540.00	8.22	12.30	16.40
Pressure-treated trim board S4S, .25 treatment, D Grade					
1" x 4", – .25 D grade	Ea	2,060.00	5.49	8.24	11.00
1" x 6", – .25 D grade	Ea	2,180.00	8.73	13.10	17.50
1" x 8", – .25 D grade	Ea	2,050.00	10.90	16.40	21.80
1" x 12", – .25 D grade	Ea	2,510.00	20.10	30.10	40.10
Pressure-treated lumber, .25 ACQ treatment					
2" x 3"	Ea	907.00	4.83	7.25	9.67
2" x 4"	Ea	1,160.00	6.20	9.30	12.40
2" x 6"	Ea	1,020.00	8.13	12.20	16.30
2" x 8"	Ea	974.00	10.40	15.60	20.80
2" x 10"	Ea	1,100.00	14.60	21.90	29.20
2" x 12"	Ea	1,230.00	19.70	29.50	39.40
4" x 4"	Ea	1,250.00	13.30	20.10	26.80
4" x 6"	Ea	1,330.00	21.20	31.80	42.50
4" x 8"	Ea	1,300.00	27.60	41.50	55.30

	Unit	MBF	8' L	12' L	16' L
4" x 10"	Ea	1,330.00	35.40	53.10	70.80
4" x 12"	Ea	1,390.00	44.50	66.70	89.00
6" x 6"	Ea	1,350.00	32.50	48.70	64.90
Pressure-treated southern yellow pine – .40 ACQ treatment, Prime					
1" x 4"	Ea	1,180.00	3.15	4.73	6.31
1" x 6"	Ea	1,050.00	4.20	6.30	8.41
2" x 4"	Ea	893.00	4.76	7.14	9.52
2" x 6"	Ea	821.00	6.57	9.85	13.10
2" x 8"	Ea	854.00	9.10	13.70	18.20
2" x 10"	Ea	811.00	10.80	16.20	21.60
2" x 12"	Ea	1,230.00	19.70	29.50	39.30
4" x 4"	Ea	2,000.00	21.30	31.90	42.60
4" x 6"	Ea	1,860.00	29.70	44.60	59.50
6" x 6"	Ea	2,110.00	50.60	75.90	101.00
Pressure-treated timbers .40 CCA pressure treatment. For uses with direct contact with water or the ground, or where moisture content exceeds 20%. Add 20% for .60 CCA treated southern yellow pine timber.					
4" x 4"	Ea	1,190.00	12.70	19.00	25.40
4" x 6"	Ea	1,260.00	20.10	30.20	40.20
6" x 6"	Ea	1,220.00	32.50	48.70	64.90

	Unit	8' L	10' L	12' L	16' L
Hibor treated Douglas fir (Hawaii)					
2" x 4", Standard and Better	Ea	5.94	7.61	8.98	12.10
2" x 6", No. 2 and Better	Ea	8.36	10.90	13.10	17.40
2" x 8", No. 2 and Better	Ea	12.80	15.50	18.60	24.90
2" x 10", No. 2 and Better	Ea	17.70	22.00	26.20	35.20
2" x 12", No. 2 and Better	Ea	20.90	26.20	31.40	42.90
4" x 4", No. 2 and Better	Ea	12.80	18.70	23.00	—
4" x 6", No. 2 and Better	Ea	21.50	27.60	34.50	48.80
4" x 8", No. 1 and Better, S4S	Ea	—	—	49.50	65.30
4" x 10", No. 1 and Better, S4S	Ea	—	—	61.10	81.70
4" x 12", No. 1 and Better, S4S	Ea	—	—	79.60	105.00

Identification Index: A set of two numbers separated by a slash that appears in the grade trademarks on standard sheathing, Structural I, Structural II and C-C Grades. Number on left indicates recommended maximum spacing in inches for supports when panel is used for roof decking. Number on right shows maximum recommended spacing in inches for supports when the panel is used for subflooring.

Plywood

	Unit	MSF	4' x 8'
Sanded Exterior Grade Western plywood – AC			
1/4" thick	Ea	1,340.00	42.80
3/8" thick	Ea	1,600.00	51.20
1/2" thick	Ea	1,730.00	55.50
5/8" thick	Ea	1,730.00	55.30
3/4" thick	Ea	1,840.00	58.80
Exterior Grade plywood – CDX			
3/8" thick	Ea	436.00	13.90
1/2" thick	Ea	621.00	19.90
1/2" thick, 4-ply	Ea	726.00	23.20
1/2" thick, 5-ply	Ea	974.00	31.20
5/8" thick, 4-ply	Ea	735.00	23.50
5/8" thick, 5-ply	Ea	1,130.00	36.10
3/4" thick	Ea	847.00	27.10
Sanded Exterior Grade Western plywood – BC			
1/4" thick	Ea	794.00	25.40
3/8" thick	Ea	776.00	24.80
1/2" thick	Ea	1,010.00	32.40
5/8" thick	Ea	957.00	30.60
3/4" thick	Ea	1,080.00	34.50

A-A EXT-DFPA

Designed for use in exposed applications where the appearance of both sides is important. Fences, wind screens, exterior cabinets and built-ins, signs, boats, commercial refrigerators, shipping containers, tanks, and ducts

A-A G-2 EXT-DFPA PS 1-66

Typical edge-mark

A-B EXT-DFPA

For uses similar to A-A EXT bu where the appearance of one side is a little less important th the face.

A-B G-3 EXT-DFPA PS 1-6

Typical edge-mark

	Craft@Hrs	Unit	Material	Labor	Total
Texture 1-11 (T-1-11) siding, rough sawn. Per 100 square feet installed including 10% cutting waste.					
3/8" x 4' x 8' Southern pine, grooved 4" OC	B1@2.18	Sq	95.20	73.80	169.00
3/8" x 4' x 8' Decorative southern pine	B1@2.18	Sq	87.40	73.80	161.20
3/8" x 4' x 8' Hibor treated, plain (Hawaii)	B1@2.18	Sq	152.00	73.80	225.80
5/8" x 4' x 8' Premium pine, grooved	B1@2.45	Sq	121.00	82.90	203.90
5/8" x 4' x 8' Treated pine, Decorative Grade	B1@2.45	Sq	203.00	82.90	285.90
5/8" x 4' x 9' Fir, grooved	B1@2.45	Sq	216.00	82.90	298.90
5/8" x 4' x 8' Hibor treated, grooved (Hawaii)	B1@2.45	Sq	203.00	82.90	285.90
5/8" x 4' x 9' Hibor treated, grooved (Hawaii)	B1@2.45	Sq	266.00	82.90	348.90

	Unit	MSF	4' x 8'
2-4-1 Sturdi-Floor subflooring. Tongue and groove attic decking			
5/8"	Ea	1,080.00	34.50
Concrete form (Plyform), square edged			
5/8", 4 ply	Ea	2,260.00	72.20
3/4", 4 ply	Ea	1,290.00	41.40
Structural I Grade plywood. Price per panel			
3/8"	Ea	671.00	21.40
1/2"	Ea	779.00	24.90
Medium-Density Overlay (MDO) plywood. Paintable paper surface bonded to plywood core.			
3/8"	Ea	2,110.00	67.50
1/2"	Ea	1,620.00	51.70
3/4"	Ea	2,100.00	67.30
Marine-Grade plywood			
1/2", AB Grade	Ea	1,910.00	61.00
3/4", AB Grade	Ea	2,520.00	80.70
OSB strand board – square edged, oriented grain			
1/4"	Ea	283.00	9.05
3/8"	Ea	411.00	13.20
7/16"	Ea	384.00	12.30
1/2"	Ea	530.00	16.90
3/4"	Ea	677.00	21.70
Underlayment "X"-Band, C Grade, tongue and groove			
5/8", 4 ply	Ea	1,170.00	37.50
3/4", 4 ply	Ea	1,270.00	40.60
Birch hardwood plywood			
1/8" thick	Ea	1,300.00	41.70
1/4" thick	Ea	902.00	28.90
1/2" thick	Ea	1,760.00	56.40
3/4" thick	Ea	1,760.00	56.20
Cedar hardwood plywood			
1/4" thick	Ea	1,820.00	58.10
3/8" thick	Ea	2,200.00	70.40
1/2" thick	Ea	3,060.00	97.90
5/8" thick	Ea	3,530.00	113.00
3/4" thick	Ea	4,110.00	131.00
Oak hardwood plywood			
1/8" thick	Ea	962.00	30.80
1/4" thick	Ea	1,160.00	37.10
1/2" thick	Ea	2,000.00	64.00
3/4" thick	Ea	1,820.00	58.40
Lauan plywood			
1/8" thick	Ea	401.00	12.80
1/4" thick	Ea	498.00	15.90
1/4" thick, moisture resistant	Ea	562.00	18.00

	Craft@Hrs	Unit	Material	Labor	Total
Hardboard, 4' x 8' panels					
1/8" tempered hardboard	BC@1.02	Ea	9.18	38.10	47.28
1/8" tempered pegboard	BC@1.02	Ea	15.00	38.10	53.10
1/8" backer board	BC@1.02	Ea	16.80	38.10	54.90
1/4" tempered hardboard	BC@1.02	Ea	14.50	38.10	52.60
3/16" white garage liner pegboard	BC@1.02	Ea	17.70	38.10	55.80
1/4" white vinyl coated	BC@1.02	Ea	25.80	38.10	63.90
1/4" tempered perforated pegboard	BC@1.02	Ea	15.60	38.10	53.70
Particleboard					
3/8" x 4' x 8'	—	Ea	10.60	—	10.60
1/2" x 4' x 8'	—	Ea	13.60	—	13.60
5/8" x 4' x 8'	—	Ea	16.40	—	16.40
3/4" x 4' x 8'	—	Ea	20.50	—	20.50
3/4" x 25" x 97" countertop	—	Ea	12.90	—	12.90
3/4" x 30" x 97", countertop	—	Ea	16.30	—	16.30
3/4" x 25" x 121", countertop	—	Ea	19.60	—	19.60
3/4" x 25" x 145", countertop	—	Ea	20.30	—	20.30
3/4" x 49" x 97", industrial grade	—	Ea	20.90	—	20.90

Recycled Plastic Lumber Produced from post-consumer plastics. Resistant to termites, rot, decay.

	Unit	MBF	8' L	12' L	16' L
2" x 4"	Ea	7,680.00	40.90	61.30	82.00
2" x 6"	Ea	7,820.00	62.20	93.90	124.00
2" x 8"	Ea	8,020.00	85.60	129.00	170.00
2" x 10"	Ea	7,260.00	96.60	146.00	193.00
2" x 12"	Ea	7,790.00	124.00	188.00	250.00
4" x 4"	Ea	8,090.00	86.30	130.00	174.00
4" x 6"	Ea	8,600.00	137.00	206.00	275.00
6" x 6"	Ea	7,510.00	181.00	269.00	360.00
1" x 6" siding, smooth edge	Ea	8,070.00	32.20	48.50	64.60
1" x 6" siding, tongue & groove	Ea	6,010.00	24.00	36.10	48.10

Poles Select Appearance Grade building poles. Poles have an average taper of 1" in diameter per 10' of length. Ponderosa pine treated with Penta-Dow or ACZA (.60 lbs/CF), meets AWPA-C 23-77. Costs based on quantity of 8 to 10 poles. For delivery of smaller quantities, add $50.00 to the total cost. See installation labor below. Costs are per linear foot.

	Unit	8" butt size	10" butt size	12" butt size
To 15' long pole	LF	12.90	16.80	22.00
To 20' long pole	LF	12.50	15.70	20.50
To 25' long pole	LF	12.10	13.20	18.80
Add for Douglas fir	LF	2.91	3.02	3.16
Add for delivery, typical per trip	Ea	87.70	87.70	87.70

	Unit	6' long	7' long	8' long	10' long
Posts Sawn posts, construction common, redwood					
4" x 4"	Ea	15.40	18.00	19.80	25.50
Yellow pine penta treated posts					
3" x 3"	Ea	7.88	9.53	11.00	13.00
3-1/2" x 3-1/2"	Ea	8.86	10.40	11.90	13.50
4" x 4"	Ea	10.90	13.00	13.90	15.70
4-1/2" x 4-1/2"	Ea	13.30	14.00	14.30	16.10
5" x 5"	Ea	13.00	15.70	16.60	19.60
6" x 6"	Ea	15.70	17.70	18.70	20.80

	Unit	8' long	10' long	12' long	16' long
Pressure-treated southern yellow pine posts No. 2, 0.40 CCA treatment					
4" x 4"	Ea	25.30	31.40	37.90	50.30
4" x 6"	Ea	35.10	43.70	52.60	70.10
6" x 6"	Ea	59.90	74.70	89.60	121.00

	Craft@Hrs	Unit	Material	Labor	Total
Labor to install poles and posts Costs shown are per post and include measuring, cutting one end, drilling two holes at the top and bottom and installation. Add for hardware and bolts as needed.					
3" x 3", 4" x 4" or 5" x 5" posts	B1@.333	Ea	—	11.30	11.30
6" x 6" or 7" x 7" posts	B1@.500	Ea	—	16.90	16.90
8" or 10" butt diameter poles	B1@.666	Ea	—	22.50	22.50
12" butt diameter poles	B1@.750	Ea	—	25.40	25.40

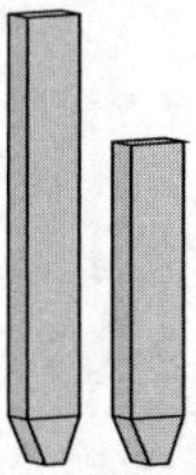

Stakes

	Craft@Hrs	Unit	Material	Labor	Total
Survey stakes, pine or fir, 1" x 2"					
18"	—	Ea	.29	—	.29
24"	—	Ea	.34	—	.34
36"	—	Ea	.71	—	.71
Ginnies, pine or fir, 1" x 1", per 1,000					
6"	—	M	110.00	—	110.00
8"	—	M	108.00	—	108.00
Pointed lath, pine or fir, per 1,000, 1/4" x 1-1/2", S4S					
18"	—	M	303.00	—	303.00
24"	—	M	328.00	—	328.00
36"	—	M	453.00	—	453.00
48"	—	M	619.00	—	619.00
Foundation stakes, 1" x 3", per 1,000, 20 bundles per 1000 except for 48" (40 bundles per 1000)					
12" or 14"	—	M	373.00	—	373.00
18"	—	M	479.00	—	479.00
24"	—	M	553.00	—	553.00
36"	—	M	781.00	—	781.00
48"	—	M	1,270.00	—	1,270.00
Hubs, pine or fir, 2" x 2", per 1,000					
8"	—	M	654.00	—	654.00
10"	—	M	728.00	—	728.00
12"	—	M	795.00	—	795.00
Form stakes (wedges), pine or fir, 5" point, per 1,000					
2" x 2" x 6"	—	M	255.00	—	255.00
2" x 2" x 8"	—	M	275.00	—	275.00
2" x 2" x 10"	—	M	301.00	—	301.00
2" x 4" x 6"	—	M	332.00	—	332.00
2" x 4" x 8"	—	M	391.00	—	391.00
2" x 4" x 10"	—	M	422.00	—	422.00
2" x 4" x 12"	—	M	479.00	—	479.00
Feather wedges	—	M	358.00	—	358.00

Lumber Grading Lumber grading services by West Coast Lumber Inspection Bureau.

	Craft@Hrs	Unit	Material	Labor	Total
Inspection per MBF	—	MBF	—	—	.42
Per month minimum – operating and shipping	—	Month	—	—	418.00
Per month min. – non-operating (No Shipments)	—	Month	—	—	130.00

	Craft@Hrs	Unit	Material	Labor	Total
Reinspection, certificate inspection and grade stamping service for WCLIB Members. Costs do not include travel and subsistence charges.					
On shipments west of the Rocky Mountains	—	Day	—	—	533.00
Overtime hours	—	Hour	—	—	101.00
Saturday, Sunday and holidays	—	Day	—	—	851.00
On shipments east of the Rocky Mountains	—	Day	—	—	543.00
Overtime hours	—	Hour	—	—	99.30
Saturday, Sunday and holidays	—	Day	—	—	851.00
Reinspection, certificate inspection and grade stamping service for WCLIB Non-Members. Costs do not include travel and subsistence charges.					
On shipments west of the Rocky Mountains	—	Day	—	—	737.00
Overtime hours	—	Hour	—	—	132.00
Saturday, Sunday and holidays	—	Day	—	—	1,060.00
On shipments east of the Rocky Mountains	—	Day	—	—	732.00
Overtime hours	—	Hour	—	—	132.00
Saturday, Sunday and holidays	—	Day	—	—	1,060.00
Certificate inspection service. Issuance of certificates to inspection subscribers employing WCLIB certified inspectors.					
Per thousand board feet, $30.00 minimum	—	MBF	—	—	0.37

Lumber Preservation Treatment See also Soil Treatments. Costs assume treatment at a treatment plant, not on the construction site. Treatments listed below are designed to protect wood and wood products from decay and destruction caused by moisture (fungi), wood-boring insects and organisms. All retention rates listed (in parentheses) are in pounds per cubic foot and are the minimum recommended by the Society of American Wood Preservers. Costs are for treatment only and assume treating of 10,000 board feet or more. No lumber or transportation included. Add $70.00 per MBF for kiln-drying after treatment.

	Craft@Hrs	Unit	Material	Labor	Total
Lumber submerged in or frequently exposed to salt water					
ACZA treatment (2.5)	—	MBF	—	—	978.00
ACZA treatment for structural lumber					
Piles and building poles (2.5)	—	CF	—	—	11.00
Board lumber and timbers (2.5)	—	MBF	—	—	972.00
Creosote treatment for structural lumber					
Piles and building poles (20.0)	—	CF	—	—	9.78
Board lumber and timbers (25.0)	—	MBF	—	—	581.00
Lumber in contact with fresh water or soil, ACZA treatment					
Building poles, structural (.60)	—	CF	—	—	6.12
Boards, timbers, structural (.60)	—	MBF	—	—	283.00
Boards, timbers, non-structural (.40)	—	MBF	—	—	247.00
Plywood, structural (.40), 1/2"	—	MSF	—	—	281.00
Posts, guardrail, signs (.60)	—	MBF	—	—	351.00
All weather foundation KD lumber (.60)	—	MBF	—	—	389.00
All weather foundation, 1/2" plywood (.60)	—	MSF	—	—	314.00
Lumber in contact with fresh water or soil, creosote treatment					
Piles, building poles, structural (12.0)	—	CF	—	—	6.95
Boards, timbers, structural (12.0)	—	MBF	—	—	422.00
Boards, timbers, non-structural (10.0)	—	MBF	—	—	389.00
Plywood, structural, 1/2" (10.0)	—	MSF	—	—	335.00
Posts (fence, guardrail, sign) (12.0)	—	MBF	—	—	422.00
Lumber used above ground, ACZA treatment					
Boards, timbers, structural (.25)	—	MBF	—	—	232.00
Boards, timbers, non-structural (.25)	—	MBF	—	—	227.00
Plywood, structural 1/2" (.25)	—	MSF	—	—	259.00

	Craft@Hrs	Unit	Material	Labor	Total
Lumber used above ground, creosote treatment					
Boards, timbers, structural (8.0)	—	MBF	—	—	351.00
Boards, timbers, non-structural (8.0)	—	MBF	—	—	351.00
Plywood, structural (8.0), 1/2"	—	MSF	—	—	313.00
Lumber used for decking, ACQ treatment					
Boards, structural (.41)	—	MBF	—	—	303.00
Boards, timbers, non-structural (.41)	—	MSF	—	—	303.00
Fire retardant treatments, structural use (interior only), "D-Blaze"					
Surfaced lumber	—	MBF	—	—	324.00
Rough lumber	—	MBF	—	—	324.00
Architectural use (interior and exterior), "NCX"					
Surfaced lumber	—	MBF	—	—	746.00
Rough lumber	—	MBF	—	—	746.00
Wolmanized treatment. Copper chromated arsenic preservative is not used for residential applications. The term "Wolmanized" is now being applied to ACQ and CA preservatives which do not contain arsenic.					
Lumber used above ground (.25)	—	MBF	—	—	119.00
Lumber in ground contact or fresh water (.40)	—	MBF	—	—	146.00
Lumber used as foundation (.60)	—	MBF	—	—	156.00

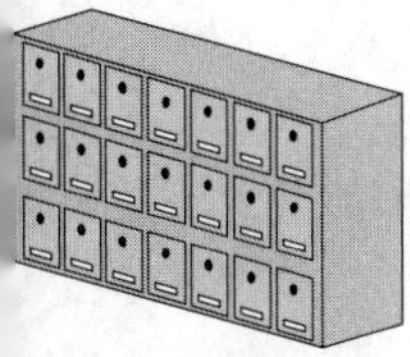

Mailboxes

	Craft@Hrs	Unit	Material	Labor	Total
Apartment type, vertical, meets current postal regulations, tumbler locks, aluminum or gold finish, price per unit, recessed					
3 box unit, 5-1/2" wide x 16" high	B1@1.88	Ea	214.00	63.60	277.60
4 box unit, 5-1/2" wide x 16" high	B1@1.88	Ea	275.00	63.60	338.60
5 box unit, 5-1/2" wide x 16" high	B1@1.88	Ea	336.00	63.60	399.60
6 box unit, 5-1/2" wide x 16" high	B1@1.88	Ea	397.00	63.60	460.60
7 box unit, 5-1/2" wide x 16" high	B1@1.88	Ea	458.00	63.60	521.60
Add for surface mounting collar	B1@.550	Ea	51.10	18.60	69.70
Office type, horizontal, meets postal regulations, tumbler locks, aluminum or brass finish					
For front or rear load, per box					
23" wide x 30" high x 12" deep	B1@1.02	Ea	916.00	34.50	950.50
Rural, aluminum finish, 19" long x 6-1/2" wide x 9" high, with flag					
Black, does not include mounting post	B1@.776	Ea	19.30	26.30	45.60
Rural heavy gauge steel mailboxes, aluminum finish, 19" long x 7" wide x 10" high, with flag					
Vandal-proof, does not include mounting post	B1@.776	Ea	84.90	26.30	111.20
Suburban style, finished, 16" long x 3" wide x 6" deep, with flag					
Post mount bracket, does not include post	B1@.776	Ea	30.30	26.30	56.60
Add for 5' high aluminum post	—	Ea	55.90	—	55.90
Cast aluminum mailbox and pedestal, 18" x 12" box, 4' pedestal,					
With base, lockable	B1@.776	Ea	182.00	26.30	208.30
Bronze mailbox and post, 18" x 12" box, 5' post,					
Steel anchor base	B1@.776	Ea	479.00	26.30	505.30
Plastic mailbox, mounting sleeve slides over 4' high post, lockable					
Size 1 box, add for post	B1@.776	Ea	63.70	26.30	90.00
Add for treated wood or aluminum post	—	Ea	32.50	—	32.50
Thru-the-wall type, 13" long x 3" high					
Gold or aluminum finish	B1@1.25	Ea	31.40	42.30	73.70
Wall- or post-mount security mailboxes, lockable, 15" wide x 13" high x 8" deep					
Black plastic and aluminum	B1@.450	Ea	94.10	15.20	109.30

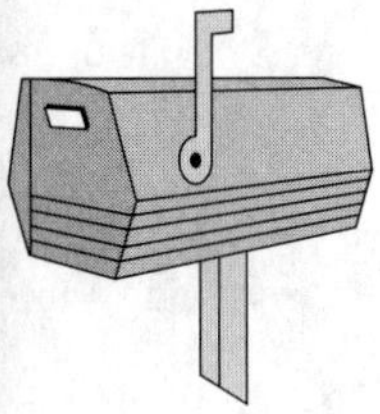

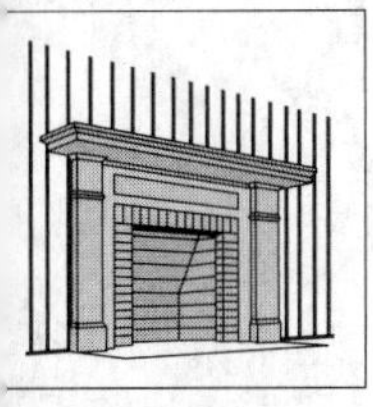

Mantels, Ponderosa Pine Unfinished.

	Craft@Hrs	Unit	Material	Labor	Total
Modern design, 50" x 37" opening, paint grade, 11" x 77" shelf	B1@3.81	Ea	1,200.00	129.00	1,329.00

	Craft@Hrs	Unit	Material	Labor	Total
Colonial design, 50" x 39" opening,					
stain grade, 7" x 72" shelf	B1@3.81	Ea	1,920.00	129.00	2,049.00
Ornate design, 51-1/2" x 39" opening,					
with detailing and scroll work, stain grade					
11" x 68" shelf	B1@3.81	Ea	3,560.00	129.00	3,689.00
Mantel molding (simple trim for masonry fireplace openings)					
15 LF, for opening 6'0" x 3'6" or less	B1@1.07	Set	424.00	36.20	460.20
Mantel shelf only, with iron or wood support brackets, prefinished					
4" x 8" x 8"	B1@.541	Ea	106.00	18.30	124.30
4" x 8" x 6"	B1@.541	Ea	83.90	18.30	102.20
4" x 10" x 10"	B1@.541	Ea	188.00	18.30	206.30

Marble Setting, Subcontract See also Tile section. Marble prices vary with quality, quantity, and availability of materials. Check prices with local suppliers. These prices are based on 200 SF quantities.

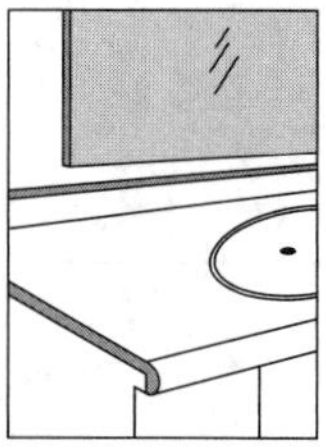

	Craft@Hrs	Unit	Material	Labor	Total
Marble tile flooring, tiles or slabs					
3/8" x 12" x 12", thin set over concrete slab.					
Typical cost per SF of area covered	—	SF	—	—	23.70
3/4" slabs set in mortar bed, cut to size.					
Typical cost per SF of area covered	—	SF	—	—	79.70
Marble bathroom vanity top, to 96" x 24" wide, with one sink cutout, bullnose or eased edge on 3 sides.					
Most colors and textures	—	Ea	—	—	1,220.00
Select colors and textures	—	Ea	—	—	1,490.00
Marble fireplace mantel and facing. 46" high to 67" wide overall. Including typical delivery. Custom-made mantels require several months for production and delivery.					
Minimum, plain design, white marble	—	Ea	—	—	1,290.00
Better quality, limestone	—	Ea	—	—	2,350.00
Ornet design, onyx	—	Ea	—	—	3,720.00

Markup Typical markup for light construction, percentage of gross contract price. No insurance or taxes included. See also Insurance and Taxes sections. Markup is the amount added to an estimate after all job costs have been accounted for: labor and materials, job fees, permits, bonds and insurance, job site supervision and similar job-related expenses. Profit is the return on money invested in the construction business.

	Craft@Hrs	Unit	Material	Labor	Total
Contingency (allowance for unknown and unforeseen conditions)					
Varies widely from job to job, typically	—	%	—	—	2.0
Overhead (office, administrative and general business expense)					
Typical overhead expense	—	%	—	—	10.0
Profit (return on the money invested in the business, varies with competitive conditions)					
Typical profit for residential construction	—	%	—	—	8.0
Total markup (add 25% to the total job cost to attain 20% of gross contract price)					
Total for Contingency, Overhead & Profit	—	%	—	—	20.0

Note that costs listed in this book do not include the general contractor's markup. However, sections identified as "subcontract" include the subcontractor's markup. Here's how to calculate markup:

Project Costs	
Material	$ 50,000
Labor (with taxes & insurance)	40,000
Subcontract	10,000
Total job costs	100,000
Markup (25% of $100,000)	**$ 25,000**
Contract price	$125,000

Markup is $25,000 which is 25% of the total job costs ($100,000) but only 20% of the contract price ($25,000 divided by $125,000 is .20).

Markup For General Contractors On larger commercial and industrial projects, a markup of 24.8% on the total job cost is suggested. See the paragraph General Contractor Markup at the beginning of the section General Requirements in the Industrial and Commercial Division of this manual. For example, note how markup is calculated on a project with these costs:

Material	$ 3,000,000
Labor (with taxes and insurance)	4,500,000
Equipment	1,000,000
Subcontracts	1,500,000
Total job cost	$10,000,000
Indirect overhead (8%)	**800,000**
Direct overhead (7.3%)	**730,000**
Contingency (2%)	**200,000**
Profit (7.5%)	**750,000**
Contract price	$12,480,000

Note that the total job cost includes both work done with the general contractor's crews and work done by subcontractor-specialists. Markup for the general contractor (overhead, including supervision expense, contingency and profit) is $2,480,000. This is 24.8% of the total job costs but only 19.87% of the contract price ($2,480,000 divided by $12,480,000 is 0.1987).

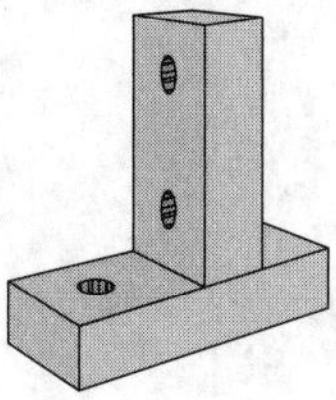

Masonry, Brick Wall Assemblies Typical costs for smooth red clay brick walls, laid in running bond with 3/8" concave joints. These costs include the bricks, mortar for bricks and cavities, typical ladder type reinforcing, wall ties and normal waste. Foundations are not included. Wall thickness shown is the nominal size based on using the type bricks described. "Wythe" means the quantity of bricks in the thickness of the wall. Costs shown are per square foot (SF) of wall measured on one face. Deduct for openings over 10 SF in size. The names and dimensions of bricks can be expected to vary, depending on the manufacturer. For more detailed coverage of brick and masonry see the *National Concrete & Masonry Estimator* at http://CraftsmanSiteLicense.com.

	Craft@Hrs	Unit	Material	Labor	Total
Standard brick, 3-3/4" wide x 2-1/4" high x 8" long					
Common brick, per thousand	—	M	780.00	—	780.00
4" thick wall, single wythe, veneer facing	B9@.211	SF	6.35	6.98	13.33
8" thick wall, double wythe, cavity filled	B9@.464	SF	12.50	15.30	27.80
12" thick wall, triple wythe, cavity filled	B9@.696	SF	18.70	23.00	41.70
Norman brick, 3-1/2" wide x 2-1/2" high x 11-1/2" long					
Norman brick, per thousand	—	M	1,330.00	—	1,330.00
4" thick wall, single wythe, veneer facing	B9@.211	SF	6.94	6.98	13.92
8" thick wall, double wythe, cavity filled	B9@.464	SF	13.70	15.30	29.00
12" thick wall, triple wythe, cavity filled	B9@.696	SF	20.50	23.00	43.50
Modular brick, 3" wide x 3-1/2" x 11-1/2" long					
Modular brick, per thousand	—	M	1,330.00	—	1,330.00
3-1/2" thick wall, single wythe, veneer face	B9@.156	SF	5.12	5.16	10.28
7-1/2" thick wall, double wythe, cavity filled	B9@.343	SF	10.10	11.30	21.40
11-1/2" thick wall, triple wythe, cavity filled	B9@.515	SF	15.10	17.00	32.10
Colonial brick, 3" wide x 3-1/2" x 10" long					
Colonial brick, per thousand	—	M	970.00	—	970.00
3-1/2" thick wall, single wythe, veneer face	B9@.177	SF	4.41	5.85	10.26
7-1/2" thick wall, double wythe, cavity filled	B9@.389	SF	8.65	12.90	21.55
11-1/2" thick wall, triple wythe, cavity filled	B9@.584	SF	12.90	19.30	32.20

Masonry, Face Brick

Masonry, Face Brick Laid in running bond with 3/8" concave joints. Mortar, wall ties and foundations (footings) not included. Includes normal waste and delivery up to 30 miles with a 5 ton minimum. Coverage (units per SF) includes 3/8" mortar joints but the SF cost does not include mortar cost. Add for mortar below.

	Craft@Hrs	Unit	Material	Labor	Total
Standard brick, 2-1/4" high x 3-3/4" deep x 8" long (6.45 units per SF)					
Brown, per square foot	B9@.211	SF	5.68	6.98	12.66
Brown, per thousand	B9@32.7	M	839.00	1,080.00	1,919.00
Burnt oak, per square foot	B9@.211	SF	6.34	6.98	13.32
Burnt oak, per thousand	B9@32.7	M	936.00	1,080.00	2,016.00
Flashed, per square foot	B9@.211	SF	7.44	6.98	14.42
Flashed, per thousand	B9@32.7	M	1,110.00	1,080.00	2,190.00
Red, per square foot	B9@.211	SF	5.28	6.98	12.26
Red, per thousand	B9@32.7	M	779.00	1,080.00	1,859.00
Norman brick, 2-1/2" high x 3-1/2" deep x 11-1/2" long (4.22 units per SF)					
Brown	B9@.211	SF	7.48	6.98	14.46
Burnt oak	B9@.211	SF	8.34	6.98	15.32
Flashed	B9@.211	SF	5.89	6.98	12.87
Red	B9@.211	SF	5.89	6.98	12.87
Modular, 3-1/2" high x 3" deep x 11-1/2" long (3.13 units per SF)					
Brown	B9@.156	SF	5.50	5.16	10.66
Burnt oak	B9@.156	SF	5.63	5.16	10.79
Flashed	B9@.156	SF	4.37	5.16	9.53
Red	B9@.156	SF	4.14	5.16	9.30
Jumbo (filler brick) 3-1/2" high x 3" deep x 11-1/2" long (3.13 units per SF)					
Fireplace, cored	B9@.156	SF	1.77	5.16	6.93
Fireplace, solid	B9@.156	SF	1.57	5.16	6.73
Mission, cored	B9@.156	SF	3.43	5.16	8.59
Mission, solid	B9@.156	SF	3.52	5.16	8.68
Padre brick, 4" high x 3" deep					
7-1/2" long cored, 4.2 per SF	B9@.156	SF	8.37	5.16	13.53
7-1/2" long solid, 4.2 per SF	B9@.156	SF	10.50	5.16	15.66
11-1/2" long cored, 2.8 per SF	B9@.177	SF	6.40	5.85	12.25
11-1/2" long solid, 2.8 per SF	B9@.177	SF	9.39	5.85	15.24
15-1/2" long cored, 2.1 per SF	B9@.211	SF	7.70	6.98	14.68
15-1/2" long solid, 2.1 per SF	B9@.211	SF	9.67	6.98	16.65
Commercial, 3-1/4" high x 3-1/4" deep x 10" long (3.6 per SF)					
Solid	B9@.156	SF	3.67	5.16	8.83
Cored	B9@.177	SF	3.67	5.85	9.52
Harlequin (manufactured "used" brick)	B9@.177	SF	3.89	5.85	9.74
Add for 6-11/16" 22 gauge galvanized wall ties					
50 ties per 100 SF	B9@.011	SF	.09	.36	.45
Add for header course every 6th course	B9@.009	SF	.88	.30	1.18
Add for Flemish bond					
With header course every 6th course	B9@.036	SF	.49	1.19	1.68
Add for raked joints, labor	—	%	—	3.0	—
Deduct for flush finished joints, labor	—	%	—	-4.0	—

Mortar for brick Based on an all-purpose Type S mortar mix used in single wythe walls laid with running bond. Includes normal waste. Type N mortar is used for severe conditions, such as chimneys. Costs are per CSF of wall face using the brick sizes (width x height x length) listed. Material costs published based upon purchasing mortar by ½ cubic foot bag. If purchasing by the CY, reduce material costs 36%. Mortar purchased by the CY and pumped in place will reduce mortar material costs by about 16%.

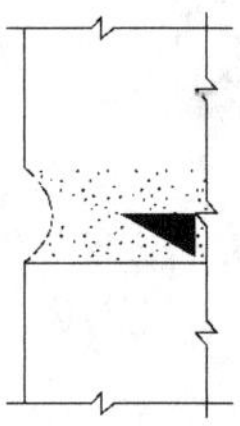

	Craft@Hrs	Unit	Material	Labor	Total
Type S mortar, per cubic foot	—	CF	11.30	—	11.30
Type S mortar, 60 lb. bag	—	Ea	5.65	—	5.65
Type S mortar, per cubic yard	—	%	-36.0	—	—
Type S mortar, per cubic yard, pumped	—	%	-16.0	—	—

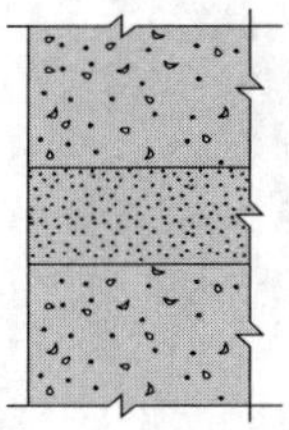

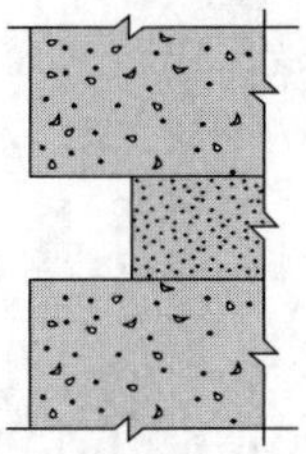

	Craft@Hrs	Unit	Material	Labor	Total
4" x 2-1/2" to 2-5/8" x 8" bricks					
3/8" joints (5.5 CF per CSF)	—	CSF	62.20	—	62.20
1/2" joints (7.0 CF per CSF)	—	CSF	79.20	—	79.20
4" x 3-1/2" to 3-5/8" x 8" bricks					
3/8" joints (4.8 CF per CSF)	—	CSF	54.30	—	54.30
1/2" joints (6.1 CF per CSF)	—	CSF	69.00	—	69.00
4" x 4" x 8" bricks					
3/8" joints (4.2 CF per CSF)	—	CSF	47.50	—	47.50
1/2" joints (5.3 CF per CSF)	—	CSF	59.90	—	59.90
4" x 5-1/2" to 5-5/8" x 8" bricks					
3/8" joints (3.5 CF per CSF)	—	CSF	39.60	—	39.60
1/2" joints (4.4 CF per CSF)	—	CSF	49.80	—	49.80
4" x 2" x 12" bricks					
3/8" joints (6.5 CF	—	CSF	73.50	—	73.50
1/2" joints (8.2 CF per CSF)	—	CSF	92.70	—	92.70
4" x 2-1/2" to 2-5/8" x 12" bricks					
3/8" joints (5.1 CF per CSF)	—	CSF	57.70	—	57.70
1/2" joints (6.5 CF per CSF)	—	CSF	73.50	—	73.50
4" x 3-1/2" to 3-5/8" x 12" bricks					
3/8" joints (4.4 CF per CSF)	—	CSF	49.80	—	49.80
1/2" joints (5.6 CF per CSF)	—	CSF	63.30	—	63.30
4" x 4" x 12" bricks					
3/8" joints (3.7 CF per CSF)	—	CSF	41.80	—	41.80
1/2" joints (4.8 CF per CSF)	—	CSF	54.30	—	54.30
4" x 5-1/2" to 5-5/8" x 12" bricks					
3/8" joints (3.0 CF per CSF)	—	CSF	33.90	—	33.90
1/2" joints (3.9 CF per CSF)	—	CSF	44.10	—	44.10
6" x 2-1/2" to 2-5/8" x 12" bricks					
3/8" joints (7.9 CF per CSF)	—	CSF	89.30	—	89.30
1/2" joints (10.2 CF per CSF)	—	CSF	115.00	—	115.00
6" x 3-1/2" to 3-5/8" x 12" bricks					
3/8" joints (6.8 CF per CSF)	—	CSF	76.90	—	76.90
1/2" joints (8.8 CF per CSF)	—	CSF	99.50	—	99.50
6" x 4" x 12" bricks					
3/8" joints (5.6 CF per CSF)	—	CSF	63.30	—	63.30
1/2" joints (7.4 CF per CSF)	—	CSF	83.70	—	83.70

Mini-brick veneer strips Wirecut texture. Figures in parentheses indicate coverage using 1/2" grouted joints. No waste included.

	Craft@Hrs	Unit	Material	Labor	Total
2-1/4" x 3/4" x 7-5/8" (6.7 units per SF)					
Unglazed, standard colors	B9@.300	SF	3.57	9.92	13.49
Unglazed, flashed	B9@.300	SF	4.56	9.92	14.48
Manufactured used	B9@.300	SF	3.78	9.92	13.70
3-5/8" x 1/2" x 7-5/8" (4.50 units per SF)					
Unglazed, standard colors	B9@.250	SF	3.51	8.27	11.78
Unglazed, flashed	B9@.250	SF	4.46	8.27	12.73
Manufactured used	B9@.250	SF	3.84	8.27	12.11
Mini-brick veneer strip corners					
Unglazed, standard colors	B9@.077	Ea	1.83	2.55	4.38
Unglazed, flashed	B9@.077	Ea	2.06	2.55	4.61
Manufactured used	B9@.077	Ea	1.97	2.55	4.52

	Craft@Hrs	Unit	Material	Labor	Total
Firebrick Used in chimneys and boilers, delivered to 30 miles, typical costs.					
Standard backs, 9" x 4-1/2" x 2-9/16"	B9@30.9	M	1,260.00	1,020.00	2,280.00
Split backs, 9" x 4-1/2" x 1-1/4"	B9@23.3	M	1,210.00	770.00	1,980.00
Fireclay, Dosch clay					
50 lb. sack	—	Ea	11.70	—	11.70
Brick paver Costs assume simple pattern with 1/2" mortar joints. Delivered to 30 miles, 10 ton minimum. Costs in material column include 8% for waste and breakage.					
Adobe pavers (Fresno)					
6" x 12" (2 units per SF)	B9@.193	SF	2.10	6.38	8.48
12" x 12" (1 unit per SF)	B9@.135	SF	2.10	4.46	6.56
California paver, 1-1/4" thick, brown					
3-5/8" x 7-5/8" (4.3 units per SF)	B9@.340	SF	4.51	11.20	15.71
Giant mission paver, 3" thick x 4" x 11-1/2"					
Red (2.67 units per SF)	B9@.193	SF	6.60	6.38	12.98
Redskin (2.67 units per SF)	B9@.193	SF	7.48	6.38	13.86
Mini-brick paver, 1/2" thick x 3-5/8" x 7-5/8"					
Sunset Red					
(4.5 units per SF)	B9@.340	SF	3.79	11.20	14.99
Red, flashed					
(4.5 units per SF)	B9@.340	SF	4.82	11.20	16.02
Manufactured					
(4.5 units per SF)	B9@.340	SF	4.15	11.20	15.35
Sunset Red, Dieskin texture					
(4.5 units per SF)	B9@.340	SF	2.98	11.20	14.18
Red, flashed, Dieskin texture					
(4.5 units per SF)	B9@.340	SF	3.69	11.20	14.89
Manufactured, Dieskin texture					
(4.5 units per SF)	B9@.340	SF	4.00	11.20	15.20
Re-roll texture, all colors					
(4.5 units per SF)	B9@.340	SF	3.59	11.20	14.79
Norman paver, 2-3/16" thick x 3-1/2" x 11-1/2" (3 units per SF)					
Sunset Red	B9@.222	SF	4.25	7.34	11.59
Red Flashed	B9@.222	SF	4.48	7.34	11.82
Split paver, 1-1/8" thick x 3-7/8" x 8-1/8" (4.5 units per SF)					
Red	B9@.209	SF	2.55	6.91	9.46
Manufactured, used	B9@.209	SF	3.07	6.91	9.98
Bullnose pavers, 2-3/16" thick x 3-1/2" x 11-1/2" (3 units per LF). Common applications include perimeter of brick patio, walkway and wall caps					
Single bullnose, Sunset Red	B9@.250	LF	7.50	8.27	15.77
Single bullnose, Brown Flashed	B9@.250	LF	8.86	8.27	17.13
Single bullnose, Iron Spot	B9@.250	LF	8.86	8.27	17.13
Double bullnose, Sunset Red	B9@.250	LF	11.20	8.27	19.47
Double bullnose, Brown Flashed	B9@.250	LF	11.90	8.27	20.17
Double bullnose, Iron Spot	B9@.250	LF	12.40	8.27	20.67
Bullnose corners, all colors	B9@.242	Ea	10.50	8.00	18.50
Mortar joints for pavers, 1/2" typical	B9@.010	SF	.22	.33	.55

	Craft@Hrs	Unit	Material	Labor	Total
Concrete block wall assemblies Typical costs for standard natural gray medium weight masonry block walls including blocks, mortar, typical reinforcing and normal waste. Foundations (footings) are not included. See also individual component material and labor costs for blocks, mortar and reinforcing on the pages that follow. For more detailed coverage of concrete block see the *National Concrete and Masonry Estimator* at http://CraftsmanSiteLicense.com.					
Walls constructed with 8" x 16" blocks laid in running bond					
4" thick wall	B9@.090	SF	2.89	2.98	5.87
6" thick wall	B9@.100	SF	3.57	3.31	6.88
8" thick wall	B9@.120	SF	4.26	3.97	8.23
12" thick wall	B9@.150	SF	6.00	4.96	10.96
Grouting concrete block wall cores Typical costs for filling concrete block wall cores by hand. For pumped concrete, subtract 7% from labor cost and add 14% to material cost. 10% waste included in cost.					
Using 2,000 psi (6.0 sack mix), per cubic yard	—	CY	148.00	—	148.00
Add for grouting cores poured by hand, all cores filled					
4" thick wall, (4.98 SF per CF)	B9@.022	SF	1.10	.73	1.83
6" thick wall, (4.56 SF per CF)	B9@.023	SF	1.20	.76	1.96
8" thick wall, (3.79 SF per CF)	B9@.026	SF	1.45	.86	2.31
10" thick wall, (3.08 SF per CF)	B9@.031	SF	1.79	1.02	2.81
12" thick wall, (2.46 SF per CF)	B9@.042	SF	2.24	1.39	3.63
Add for grouting cores at 16" intervals, poured by hand					
4" thick wall, (8.42 SF per CF)	B9@.012	SF	.65	.40	1.05
6" thick wall, (7.73 SF per CF)	B9@.013	SF	.71	.43	1.14
8" thick wall, (6.53 SF per CF)	B9@.016	SF	.84	.53	1.37
10" thick wall, (5.19 SF per CF)	B9@.019	SF	1.06	.63	1.69
12" thick wall, (4.21 SF per CF)	B9@.024	SF	1.31	.79	2.10
Add for grouting cores at 24" intervals, poured by hand					
4" thick wall, (10.24 SF per CF)	B9@.008	SF	.54	.26	.80
6" thick wall, (9.02 SF per CF)	B9@.010	SF	.61	.33	.94
8" thick wall, (8.61 SF per CF)	B9@.012	SF	.64	.40	1.04
10" thick wall, (6.76 SF per CF)	B9@.014	SF	.81	.46	1.27
12" thick wall, (5.57 SF per CF)	B9@.018	SF	.99	.60	1.59
Add for grouting cores at 32" intervals, poured by hand					
4" thick wall, (11.66 SF per CF)	B9@.007	SF	.47	.23	.70
6" thick wall, (10.24 SF per CF)	B9@.008	SF	.54	.26	.80
8" thick wall, (9.97 SF per CF)	B9@.011	SF	.55	.36	.91
10" thick wall, (8.06 SF per CF)	B9@.013	SF	.68	.43	1.11
12" thick wall, (6.65 SF per CF)	B9@.016	SF	.83	.53	1.36
Add for grouting cores per vertical linear foot (VLF) of core, poured by hand					
4" thick wall, (8.86 VLF per CF)	B9@.012	VLF	.93	.40	1.33
6" thick wall, (8.11 VLF per CF)	B9@.018	VLF	1.02	.60	1.62
8" thick wall, (6.73 VLF per CF)	B9@.025	VLF	1.22	.83	2.05
10" thick wall, (5.47 VLF per CF)	B9@.026	VLF	1.51	.86	2.37
12" thick wall, (4.37 VLF per CF)	B9@.029	VLF	1.89	.96	2.85
Add for pumped concrete, core grouting	—	%	11.0	-7.0	—
Add for 2" thick caps, natural gray concrete					
4" thick wall	B9@.027	LF	1.16	.89	2.05
6" thick wall	B9@.038	LF	1.39	1.26	2.65
8" thick wall	B9@.046	LF	1.60	1.52	3.12
12" thick wall	B9@.065	LF	2.34	2.15	4.49

Masonry, Block

	Craft@Hrs	Unit	Material	Labor	Total
Add for detailed block, 3/8" score					
Single score, one side	—	SF	.62	—	.62
Single score, two sides	—	SF	1.37	—	1.37
Multi-scores, one side	—	SF	.62	—	.62
Multi-scores, two sides	—	SF	1.37	—	1.37
Add for color block, any wall assembly					
Light colors	—	SF	.14	—	.14
Medium colors	—	SF	.21	—	.21
Dark colors	—	SF	.29	—	.29
Add for other than running bond	B9@.021	SF	—	.69	.69

Concrete block Foundations (footings) not included. Includes local delivery, mortar and 8% waste. Natural gray, medium weight, no reinforcing included. See also concrete block wall assemblies. Costs shown as Ea are for the block only, the mortar from the adjacent block will be sufficient for these blocks.

	Craft@Hrs	Unit	Material	Labor	Total
4" wide units					
8" x 16", 1.125 per SF	B9@.085	SF	2.08	2.81	4.89
8" x 8", 2.25 per SF	B9@.093	SF	3.58	3.07	6.65
4" x 16", 2.25 per SF	B9@.093	SF	3.09	3.07	6.16
4" x 12", corner	B9@.052	Ea	1.33	1.72	3.05
4" x 8", 4.5 per SF, (half block)	B9@.106	SF	5.58	3.50	9.08

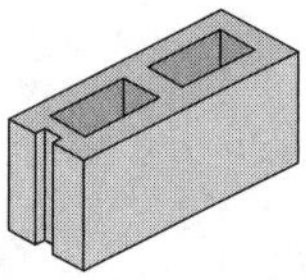

	Craft@Hrs	Unit	Material	Labor	Total
6" wide units					
8" x 16", 1.125 per SF	B9@.095	SF	2.59	3.14	5.73
8" x 16" corner	B9@.058	Ea	2.54	1.92	4.46
8" x 8", 2.25 per SF, (half block)	B9@.103	SF	4.62	3.41	8.03
4" x 16", 2.25 per SF	B9@.103	SF	3.85	3.41	7.26
4" x 14" corner	B9@.070	Ea	.88	2.31	3.19
4" x 8", 4.5 per SF, (half block)	B9@.114	SF	7.05	3.77	10.82
4" x 12" (3/4 block)	B9@.052	Ea	.83	1.72	2.55

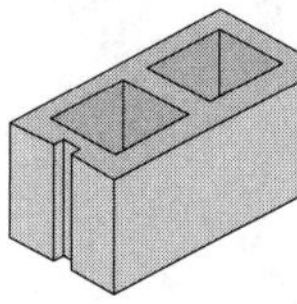

	Craft@Hrs	Unit	Material	Labor	Total
8" wide units					
4" x 16", 2.25 per SF	B9@.141	SF	4.65	4.66	9.31
8" x 16", 1.125 per SF	B9@.111	SF	3.07	3.67	6.74
6" x 8", 3 per SF	B9@.137	SF	7.90	4.53	12.43
8" x 12" (3/4 block)	B9@.074	Ea	2.18	2.45	4.63
8" x 8" (half)	B9@.052	Ea	2.08	1.72	3.80
8" x 8" (lintel)	B9@.052	Ea	2.44	1.72	4.16
6" x 16", 1.5 per SF	B9@.117	SF	4.37	3.87	8.24
4" x 8" (half block)	B9@.053	Ea	1.65	1.75	3.40
12" wide units					
8" x 16", 1.125 per SF	B9@.148	SF	4.50	4.89	9.39
8" x 8" (half)	B9@.082	Ea	3.23	2.71	5.94
8" x 8" (lintel)	B9@.082	Ea	3.60	2.71	6.31
Add for high strength units	—	%	27.0	—	—
Add for lightweight block, typical	—	%	25.0	—	—
Deduct for lightweight block, labor	—	%	—	-7.0	—
Add for ladder type reinforcement	B9@.004	SF	.38	.13	.51
Add for 1/2" rebars 24" OC	B9@.004	SF	.24	.13	.37
Add for other than running bond	—	%	—	20.0	—
Add for detailed block, 3/8" score, typical prices					
Single score, one side	—	SF	.64	—	.64
Single score, two sides	—	SF	1.42	—	1.42
Multi-scores, one side	—	SF	.64	—	.64
Multi-scores, two sides	—	SF	1.42	—	1.42

	Craft@Hrs	Unit	Material	Labor	Total
Add for color block					
Light colors	—	SF	.13	—	.13
Medium colors	—	SF	.20	—	.20
Dark colors	—	SF	.25	—	.25

Split-face concrete block Textured block, medium weight, split one side, structural. Includes 8% waste and local delivery.

	Craft@Hrs	Unit	Material	Labor	Total
8" wide, 4" x 16", 2.25 per SF	B9@.111	SF	7.36	3.67	11.03
8" wide, 8" x 16", 1.125 per SF	B9@.111	SF	3.85	3.67	7.52
12" wide, 8" x 8", 2.25 per SF	B9@.117	SF	10.60	3.87	14.47
12" wide, 8" x 16", 1.125 per SF	B9@.117	SF	5.48	3.87	9.35
Add for lightweight block	—	%	12.0	—	—
Add for color	—	SF	.40	—	.40
Add for mortar (at 7 cubic feet, per 100 square feet of wall)	—	SF	.79	—	.79

Concrete pavers Natural concrete 3/4" thick, including local delivery. Pavers installed in concrete bed but no concrete included.

	Craft@Hrs	Unit	Material	Labor	Total
6" x 6", 4 per SF	B9@.150	SF	18.80	4.96	23.76
6" x 12", 2 per SF	B9@.150	SF	9.60	4.96	14.56
12" x 12", 1 per SF	B9@.150	SF	4.48	4.96	9.44
12" x 18", .667 per SF	B9@.150	SF	3.15	4.96	8.11
18" x 18", .444 per SF	B9@.150	SF	2.16	4.96	7.12
Add for light colors	—	SF	.60	—	.60
Add for dark colors	—	SF	1.80	—	1.80
Add for pavers with beach pebble surface	—	SF	1.20	—	1.20
Euro-style concrete pavers, 45mm thick, including compacted 1" sand bed, cobble finish, various colors.					
Walk or drive (2.5 units per SF)	B9@.150	SF	1.83	4.96	6.79
Steps, per LF of width	B9@.750	LF	2.77	24.80	27.57
Pool coping, per LF of coping edge	B9@.750	LF	4.01	24.80	28.81

Concrete screen block Natural color. Foundations and supports not included. Material costs include 8% waste. (Quantity per SF is shown in parentheses)

	Craft@Hrs	Unit	Material	Labor	Total
Textured screen (no corebar defacements)					
4" x 12" x 12" (1 per SF)	B9@.211	SF	3.09	6.98	10.07
4" x 6" x 6" (3.68 per SF)	B9@.407	SF	3.65	13.50	17.15
4" x 8" x 8" (2.15 per SF)	B9@.285	SF	5.32	9.42	14.74
Four sided sculpture screens					
4" x 12" x 12" (1 per SF)	B9@.312	SF	3.07	10.30	13.37
Sculpture screens (patterned face, rug texture reverse)					
4" x 12" x 12" (1 per SF)	B9@.211	SF	4.12	6.98	11.10
4" x 16" x 16" (.57 per SF)	B9@.285	SF	4.09	9.42	13.51
4" x 16" x 12" (.75 per SF)	B9@.285	SF	4.35	9.42	13.77
Add for channel steel support (high rise)					
2" x 2" x 3/16"	—	LF	2.95	—	2.95
3" x 3" x 3/16"	—	LF	3.49	—	3.49
4" x 4" x 1/4"	—	LF	6.34	—	6.34
6" x 4" x 3/8"	—	LF	13.40	—	13.40

Masonry, Slump Block

Concrete slump block Natural concrete color, 4" widths are veneer, no foundation or reinforcing included. Costs in material column include 8% waste. Heights to 6'. (Quantity per SF is shown in parentheses.)

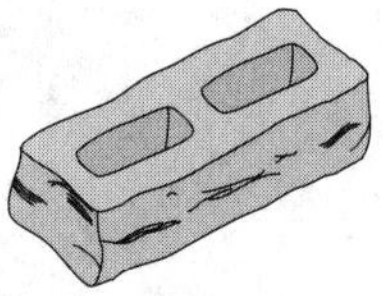

	Craft@Hrs	Unit	Material	Labor	Total
4" x 4" x 8" (4.5 per SF)	B9@.267	SF	6.18	8.83	15.01
4" x 4" x 12" (3 per SF)	B9@.178	SF	4.37	5.88	10.25
4" x 4" x 16" (2.25 per SF)	B9@.133	SF	3.27	4.40	7.67
6" x 4" x 16" (2.25 per SF)	B9@.146	SF	5.16	4.83	9.99
6" x 6" x 16" (1.5 per SF)	B9@.107	SF	2.81	3.54	6.35
8" x 4" x 16" (2.25 per SF)	B9@.161	SF	5.30	5.32	10.62
8" x 6" x 16" (1.5 per SF)	B9@.117	SF	3.96	3.87	7.83
12" x 4" x 16" (2.25 per SF)	B9@.193	SF	9.01	6.38	15.39
12" x 6" x 16" (1.5 per SF)	B9@.128	SF	6.52	4.23	10.75
Cap or slab block, 2" thick, 16" long, .75 units per LF. No waste included					
4" wide	B9@.160	LF	1.09	5.29	6.38
6" wide	B9@.160	LF	1.37	5.29	6.66
8" wide	B9@.160	LF	1.75	5.29	7.04
Add for curved slump block					
4" wide, 2' or 4' diameter circle	—	%	125.0	25.0	—
8" wide, 2' or 4' diameter circle	—	%	150.0	20.0	—
Add for slump one side block	—	SF	.05	—	.05
Add for light colors for slump block	—	%	13.0	—	—
Add for darker colors for slump block	—	%	25.0	—	—
Add for mortar for slump block. Cost includes normal waste					
Using mortar, per cubic foot	—	CF	11.30	—	11.30
4" x 4" x 8" (4 CF per CSF)	—	SF	.45	—	.45
6" x 6" x 16" (4 CF per CSF)	—	SF	.45	—	.45
8" x 6" x 16" (5 CF per CSF)	—	SF	.57	—	.57
12" x 6" x 16" (7.5 CF per CSF)	—	SF	.85	—	.85

Adobe block Walls to 8', not including reinforcement or foundations, plus delivery, 4" high, 16" long, 2.25 blocks per SF, including 10% waste.

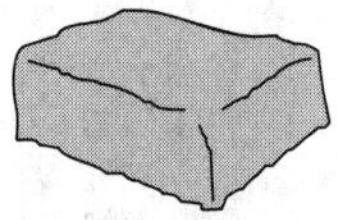

	Craft@Hrs	Unit	Material	Labor	Total
4" wide	B9@.206	SF	3.85	6.81	10.66
6" wide	B9@.233	SF	4.70	7.70	12.40
8" wide	B9@.238	SF	6.00	7.87	13.87
12" wide	B9@.267	SF	9.98	8.83	18.81
Add for reinforcement (24" OC both ways)	—	SF	.45	—	.45

Flagstone Including concrete bed.

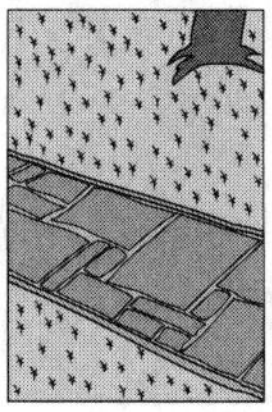

	Craft@Hrs	Unit	Material	Labor	Total
Veneer on walls, 3" thick	B9@.480	SF	6.29	15.90	22.19
Walks and porches, 2" thick	B9@.248	SF	3.10	8.20	11.30
Coping, 4" x 12"	B9@.272	SF	9.92	8.99	18.91
Steps, 6" risers	B9@.434	LF	3.56	14.30	17.86
Steps, 12" treads	B9@.455	LF	7.13	15.00	22.13

Flue lining Pumice, 1' lengths, delivered to 30 miles, including 8% waste.

	Craft@Hrs	Unit	Material	Labor	Total
8-1/2" round	B9@.148	Ea	7.33	4.89	12.22
8" x 13" oval	B9@.206	Ea	10.40	6.81	17.21
8" x 17" oval	B9@.228	Ea	11.70	7.54	19.24
10" x 17" oval	B9@.243	Ea	12.40	8.03	20.43
13" x 13" square	B9@.193	Ea	13.00	6.38	19.38
13" x 17" oval	B9@.193	Ea	13.00	6.38	19.38
13" x 21" oval	B9@.228	Ea	15.80	7.54	23.34

	Craft@Hrs	Unit	Material	Labor	Total
17" x 17" square	B9@.228	Ea	16.60	7.54	24.14
17" x 21" oval	B9@.254	Ea	20.40	8.40	28.80
21" x 21" square	B9@.265	Ea	31.10	8.76	39.86

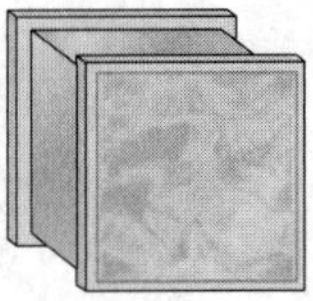

Glass block Costs include 6% for waste and local delivery. Add grout, spacer, sealant and reinforcing costs (accessories) and mortar from below. Labor cost includes laying the block, grouting and sealing. Costs assume a 100 SF job.

	Craft@Hrs	Unit	Material	Labor	Total
3-7/8" thick block, "cracked ice" faces					
4" x 8", 4.5 per SF	B9@.392	SF	33.90	13.00	46.90
6" x 6", 4 per SF	B9@.376	SF	28.60	12.40	41.00
6" x 8", 3 per SF	B9@.336	SF	23.10	11.10	34.20
8" x 8", 2.25 per SF	B9@.296	SF	20.30	9.79	30.09
12" x 12", 1 per SF	B9@.211	SF	26.50	6.98	33.48
End blocks	B9@.125	SF	21.40	4.13	25.53
Double end blocks	B9@.125	SF	41.80	4.13	45.93
Corner blocks	B9@.125	SF	25.60	4.13	29.73
Deduct for 'diamond pattern' block	—	%	-4.2	—	—
Add for 'wavy face' block	—	%	12.0	—	—
Add for clear face block	—	%	1.7	—	—
Add for frosted glass block	—	%	116.0	—	—
Add for colored glass blocks	—	%	74.0	—	—
3-1/8" thick Thinline® block, 'cracked ice' faces					
4" x 8" 4.5 per SF	B9@.391	SF	29.40	12.90	42.30
4" x 8" 4.5 per SF	B9@.391	SF	28.10	12.90	41.00
6" x 8" 3 per SF	B9@.376	SF	22.20	12.40	34.60
8" x 8" 2.25 per SF	B9@.296	SF	17.90	9.79	27.69
End units, most sizes and styles	B9@.125	Ea	48.70	4.13	52.83
Corner units, most sizes and styles	B9@.125	Ea	51.00	4.13	55.13
Deduct for 'diamond pattern' block	—	%	-5.9	—	—
Add for 'wavy face' block	—	%	1.5	—	—
Deduct for clear face block	—	%	-0.1	—	—
Add for frosted glass block	—	%	116.0	—	—
Add for colored glass blocks	—	%	74.0	—	—
Typical total cost of anchors, spacers, grout and sealer per SF					
4" x 8" block	—	SF	8.80	—	8.80
6" x 6" block	—	SF	7.82	—	7.82
6" x 8" block	—	SF	6.13	—	6.13
8" x 8" block	—	SF	4.79	—	4.79
12" x 12" block	—	Ea	2.48	—	2.48
Add for block with heat and glare reducing insert	—	%	75.0	—	—
Deduct for 100 SF to 500 SF job	—	%	-5.0	—	—
Deduct for over 500 SF job to 1,000 SF job	—	%	-10.0	—	—
Deduct for over 1,000 SF job	—	%	-12.0	—	—
Accessories for glass block					
Foam expansion strips	—	SF	1.46	—	1.46
Glass block anchors, package of 5	—	Ea	2.89	—	2.89
Panel anchors, 16" length	—	Ea	3.89	—	3.89
Reinforcing anchors, 36" length	—	Ea	4.80	—	4.80
Vertical spacers	—	Ea	1.83	—	1.83
Horizontal spacers, 40" length	—	Ea	8.04	—	8.04
Track spacers, 31" length	—	Ea	9.89	—	9.89
Perimeter channel, 48" length	—	Ea	13.90	—	13.90
Sealant, 10.3 oz	—	Ea	6.75	—	6.75
Block spacers	—	Ea	.59	—	.59

Masonry Accessories

	Craft@Hrs	Unit	Material	Labor	Total
Mortar for glass block. White cement mix (1 part white cement, 1/2 part hydrated lime, 2-1/4 to 3 parts #20 or #30 silica sand)					
White cement mix	—	CF	41.60	—	41.60
1/4" mortar joints, 3-7/8" thick block, white cement mix					
4" x 8" block	—	SF	1.94	—	1.94
6" x 6" block	—	SF	1.90	—	1.90
6" x 8" block	—	SF	1.77	—	1.77
8" x 8" block	—	SF	1.41	—	1.41
12" x 12" block	—	SF	.97	—	.97
1/4" mortar joints, 3" and 3-1/8" thick block, white cement mix					
4" x 8" block	—	SF	1.59	—	1.59
6" x 8" block	—	SF	1.54	—	1.54
8" x 8" block	—	SF	1.15	—	1.15
Masonry Accessories					
Non-fibered masonry waterproofing for below-grade application					
Gallon covers 80 SF	B9@.688	Gal	26.70	22.70	49.40
Glass reinforcing mesh	—	SF	.12	—	.12
Lime					
Hydrated (builders)					
25 lb sack	—	Sack	9.32	—	9.32
50 lb sack, Type S	—	Sack	15.30	—	15.30
50 lb sack, white lime	—	Sack	12.50	—	12.50
70 lb sack, portland lime	—	Sack	15.00	—	15.00
50 lb sack, athletic field marker	—	Sack	12.60	—	12.60
Silica sand, #30, 100 lb sack	—	Sack	9.02	—	9.02
Mortar colors					
Standard colors, 2 lb bag	—	Lb	4.51	—	4.51
Premium colors, 2 lb bag	—	Lb	7.64	—	7.64

	Craft@Hrs	Unit	Material	Labor	Total

Trowel-ready mortar (factory prepared, ready to use), 30 hour life. Deposit required on container, local delivery included. Type S mortar has high compressive strength (1,800 PSI) and high tensile bond strength. Type S is made from 2 parts portland cement, 1 part hydrated lime and 9 parts sand, and offers a longer board life. Type M mortar is made with 3 parts of Portland cement, 1 part lime and 12 parts sand. Type M has a high compressive strength (at least 2,500 PSI) and is recommended for masonry in structural walls and masonry below grade such as foundations, retaining walls, sidewalks and driveways. Type N is a medium compressive-strength (750 PSI) mortar made of 1 part Portland cement, 1 part lime and 6 parts sand. Type N is recommended for exterior above-grade walls exposed to severe weather, such as chimneys.

	Craft@Hrs	Unit	Material	Labor	Total
Type S natural mortar, 1/3 CY	—	Ea	145.00	—	145.00
Type M natural mortar, 1/3 CY	—	Ea	232.00	—	232.00
Add to natural mortar for colored, 1/3 CY	—	Ea	29.10	—	29.10
Type S white mortar, 1/3 CY	—	Ea	230.00	—	230.00
Trowel-ready mortar, cost per square foot of wall, 3/8" joint					
4" x 4" x 8" brick wall	—	SF	.66	—	.66
8" x 8" x 16" block wall	—	SF	.53	—	.53
Dry mortar mix					
Type S, 94 lb sack	—	Sack	6.93	—	6.93
Type N, 60 lb sack	—	Sack	5.96	—	5.96
Hi-rise channel reinforcing steel (hat channel)					
2" x 2" x 3/16"	—	LF	2.08	—	2.08
3" x 3" x 3/16"	—	LF	2.48	—	2.48
4" x 4" x 1/4"	—	LF	4.90	—	4.90
6" x 4" x 3/8"	—	LF	9.60	—	9.60
Welding	SW@.176	Ea	—	7.42	7.42
Cutting	SW@.088	Ea	—	3.71	3.71
Flanges, drill one hole, weld	SW@.272	Ea	—	11.50	11.50
Additional holes	SW@.028	Ea	—	1.18	1.18
Expansion joints					
1/2" x 3-1/2"	—	LF	.35	—	.35
1/4" x 3-1/2"	—	LF	.28	—	.28
1/2" x 4"	—	LF	.35	—	.35
Wall anchors, 1-3/4" x 24"	—	Ea	3.78	—	3.78
Dur-O-Wal reinforcing, Ladur or standard, 10' lengths					
3" wide or 4" wide wall	—	LF	.22	—	.22
6" wide wall	—	LF	.23	—	.23
8" wide wall	—	LF	.28	—	.28
10" wide wall	—	LF	.30	—	.30
12" wide wall	—	LF	.32	—	.32
Wired adobe blocks					
2" x 2"	—	Ea	.45	—	.45
3" x 3"	—	Ea	.55	—	.55
Tie wire, black, 16.5 gauge					
Roll, 400'	—	Ea	4.97	—	4.97
Wall ties, 22 gauge	—	M	174.00	—	174.00
Wall ties, 28 gauge	—	M	166.00	—	166.00
Angle iron					
3" x 3" x 3/16"	—	LF	6.34	—	6.34
4" x 4" x 1/4"	—	LF	11.60	—	11.60
6" x 4" x 3/8"	—	LF	17.00	—	17.00
Post anchors (straps)					
4" x 4" x 10"	—	Ea	11.10	—	11.10
4" x 4" x 16"	—	Ea	25.20	—	25.20

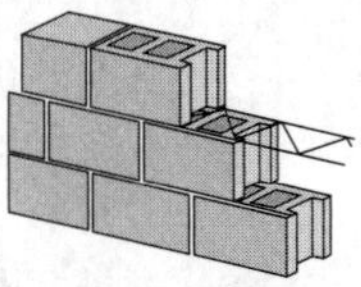

	Craft@Hrs	Unit	Material	Labor	Total
Masonry, Subcontract Typical prices.					
Fireplace chimneys, masonry only. Height above firebox shown.					
5' high chimney (3' opening)	—	Ea	—	—	2,830.00
13' high chimney (3' opening)	—	Ea	—	—	3,330.00
Floors					
Flagstone	—	SF	—	—	13.00
Patio tile	—	SF	—	—	10.20
Pavers	—	SF	—	—	11.10
Quarry tile, unglazed	—	SF	—	—	14.30
Mats, Runners and Treads Koffler Products.					
Mats					
Vinyl link mats, closed link, 1/2" thick, including nosing					
Solid colors incl. black 28" x 36"	B1@.167	Ea	189.00	5.65	194.65
For 9" to 12" letters add	—	Ea	27.90	—	27.90
Steel link mats, 3/8" deep, 1" mesh					
16" x 24"	B1@.501	Ea	19.50	17.00	36.50
22" x 36"	B1@.501	Ea	37.60	17.00	54.60
30" x 48"	B1@.501	Ea	65.30	17.00	82.30
36" x 54"	B1@.501	Ea	90.00	17.00	107.00
36" x 72"	B1@.501	Ea	119.00	17.00	136.00
Runners					
Corrugated rubber runner, cut lengths, 2', 3', 4' widths					
1/8" thick, black	B1@.060	SF	4.40	2.03	6.43
Corrugated or round ribbed vinyl runner, 1/8" thick, 2', 3', or 4' wide, cut lengths, flame resistant					
Black corrugated	B1@.060	SF	3.10	2.03	5.13
Black or brown, round ribbed	B1@.060	SF	2.97	2.03	5.00
Deduct for full rolls (100 LF)	—	%	-10.0	—	—
Safety strips, non-slip strips, press-on abrasive, black, 1/16" thick					
3/4" x 24", box of 50	B1@.080	Ea	1.32	2.71	4.03
6" x 24" cleats	B1@.080	Ea	8.92	2.71	11.63
Treads					
Stair treads, homogeneous rubber, 9/64" thick, 1-1/2" nosing, 12-1/4" deep					
Diamond design, marbleized, medium duty	B1@.080	LF	19.80	2.71	22.51
Plain, with abrasive strips	B1@.080	LF	18.30	2.71	21.01
Matching cove riser	B1@.080	LF	9.34	2.71	12.05
Medicine Cabinets					
Recessed or surface mount medicine cabinets, hinged door, no lighting					
Basic steel-frame mirror cabinet with polystyrene body, magnetic catch, three fixed shelves					
14" x 18"	BC@.850	Ea	15.30	31.80	47.10
Basic flat glass panel cabinet with enameled steel body, concealed brass hinges, one fixed shelf					
15" x 19"	BC@.850	Ea	30.60	31.80	62.40
Better quality etched and beveled mirror door cabinet, 2 adjustable shelves, polished brass knobs					
25" x 26"	BC@.850	Ea	122.00	31.80	153.80
Corner-mount frameless cabinet, one beveled mirror door, 2 adjustable shelves					
14" x 26"	BC@.850	Ea	134.00	31.80	165.80
Surface mount medicine cabinets, hinged door, no lighting					
Tri-view frame cabinet, flat glass panel, 2 adjustable shelves, brass exposed hinges					
24" x 24"	BC@.850	Ea	74.00	31.80	105.80
30" x 29"	BC@.941	Ea	99.00	35.20	134.20
36" x 29"	BC@.941	Ea	119.00	35.20	154.20

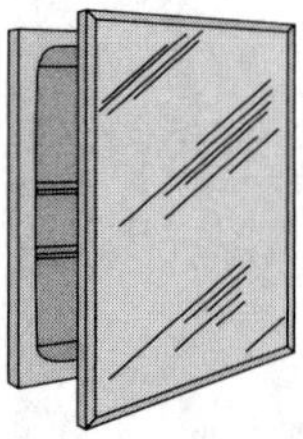

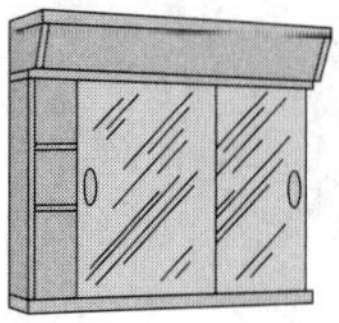

	Craft@Hrs	Unit	Material	Labor	Total
Beveled tri-view frame cabinet, flat glass panel, 2 adjustable shelves, concealed adjustable hinges					
24" x 26"	BC@.850	Ea	90.90	31.80	122.70
29" x 25"	BC@.941	Ea	101.00	35.20	136.20
36" x 30"	BC@.941	Ea	132.00	35.20	167.20
48" x 30"	BC@.941	Ea	152.00	35.20	187.20
Oval smoked bevel mirror, frameless swing door					
14" x 18"	BC@.850	Ea	103.00	31.80	134.80
All wood cabinets, 2 shelves, magnetic door latch, surface mount					
15" x 25", oak finish	BC@.850	Ea	35.70	31.80	67.50
15" x 25", white finish	BC@.850	Ea	35.00	31.80	66.80
Matching light bars for medicine cabinets, including electrical connection					
4 lights	BE@1.50	Ea	53.50	60.90	114.40
5 lights	BE@1.50	Ea	66.60	60.90	127.50
6 lights	BE@1.50	Ea	80.00	60.90	140.90
7 lights	BE@1.50	Ea	111.00	60.90	171.90
Meter Boxes Precast concrete, FOB manufacturer, inside dimension, approximately 100 to 190 lbs. each.					
13-1/4" x 19-1/8" x 11" deep					
With 1 piece concrete cover	BL@.334	Ea	27.70	10.10	37.80
With metal cover (cast iron)	BL@.334	Ea	39.00	10.10	49.10
14-5/8" x 19-3/4" x 11" deep					
With 1 piece concrete cover	BL@.334	Ea	22.50	10.10	32.60
With metal cover (cast iron)	BL@.334	Ea	39.80	10.10	49.90
15-3/4" x 22-3/4" x 11" deep					
With 1 piece concrete cover	BL@.334	Ea	40.80	10.10	50.90
With metal cover (cast iron)	BL@.334	Ea	72.10	10.10	82.20
Add hinged or reading lid, concrete cover	—	Ea	8.71	—	8.71
Plastic meter and valve boxes					
Standard 16" x 10-3/4" x 12" deep	BL@.167	Ea	20.00	5.06	25.06
Jumbo 20-1/4" x 14-1/2" x 12" deep	BL@.167	Ea	46.60	5.06	51.66
Round pit box, 10" diameter x 12" deep	BL@.167	Ea	13.00	5.06	18.06
Mirrors See also Bathroom Accessories.					
Door mirrors, polished edge					
12" wide x 48" high	BG@.251	Ea	19.00	9.07	28.07
16" wide x 60" high	BG@.301	Ea	29.40	10.90	40.30
18" wide x 68" high	BG@.331	Ea	35.30	12.00	47.30
Vanity mirrors, polished edge					
24" wide x 36" high	BG@.251	Ea	29.80	9.07	38.87
36" wide x 36" high	BG@.301	Ea	41.50	10.90	52.40
36" wide x 42" high	BG@.331	Ea	47.30	12.00	59.30
48" wide x 36" high	BG@.331	Ea	54.70	12.00	66.70
60" wide x 36" high	BG@.331	Ea	69.30	12.00	81.30
72" wide x 36" high	BG@.450	Ea	175.00	16.30	191.30
96" wide x 48" high	BG@.450	Ea	317.00	16.30	333.30
Frosted oval mirrors, floral design, polished edge					
23" x 29"	BG@.251	Ea	47.00	9.07	56.07
23" x 36"	BG@.251	Ea	70.30	9.07	79.37
27" x 30", decorative chrome frame	BG@.251	Ea	136.00	9.07	145.07
Mirror arches (radius, top edge)					
23" x 35" high, frosted pattern	BG@.251	Ea	57.30	9.07	66.37
Framed gallery mirrors					
30" x 36", sandalwood frame	BG@.450	Ea	127.00	16.30	143.30
30" x 32", metal frame	BG@.450	Ea	150.00	16.30	166.30
36" x 32", metal frame	BG@.450	Ea	163.00	16.30	179.30
42" x 34", antique black frame	BG@.450	Ea	187.00	16.30	203.30

Molding, Hardwood

Moldings Unfinished. Material costs include 5% waste. Labor costs are for typical installation only. (For installation costs of Hardwood Molding, see Softwood Moldings starting on next page under Moldings.)

	Unit	Oak	Poplar	Birch
Hardwood molding				
Base				
3/8" x 2-3/4"	LF	1.32	1.25	3.46
1/2" x 3-1/4"	LF	2.04	1.66	4.61
Base shoe, 1/2" x 3/4"	LF	.66	.45	1.15
Casing				
1/2" x 2-1/4"	LF	1.29	1.25	3.46
5/8" x 2-1/2"	LF	1.67	1.59	4.42
Cap, 3/4" x 1-1/4"	LF	1.65	.83	2.31
Crown, 9/16" x 3-5/8"	LF	2.76	1.66	4.61
Cove				
1/2" x 1/2"	LF	1.17	.53	1.25
3/4" x 3/4"	LF	.93	.42	1.12
Corner, outside				
3/4" x 3/4"	LF	1.13	.45	1.15
Round edge stop, 3/8" x 1-1/4"	LF	1.10	.83	2.31
Chair rail, 9/16" x 2-5/8"	LF	2.13	1.25	3.46
Quarter round				
1/2" x 1/2"	LF	.75	.41	1.15
3/4" x 3/4"	LF	.85	.45	1.15
Battens, 1/4" x 3/4"	LF	.86	.45	1.12
Door trim sets, 16'8" total length				
3/4" x 2-1/2" casing	Ea	23.20	17.60	34.50
3/4" x 3" casing	Ea	29.10	19.90	38.50
3/4" x 3-1/2" casing	Ea	36.40	24.10	42.60

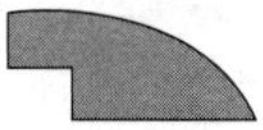
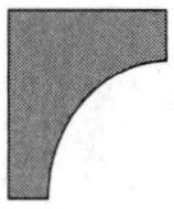

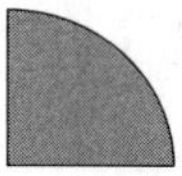

	Craft@Hrs	Unit	Material	Labor	Total
Oak threshold, LF of threshold					
5/8" x 3-1/2" or 3/4" x 3-1/2"	BC@.174	LF	3.90	6.50	10.40
5/8 x 5-5/8"	BC@.174	LF	7.44	6.50	13.94
5/8" x 4-5/8"	BC@.174	LF	5.66	6.50	12.16
Redwood molding					
Band molding, 3/4" x 5/16"	BC@.030	LF	1.52	1.12	2.64
Battens and lattice					
5/16" x 1-1/4"	BC@.026	LF	.87	.97	1.84
5/16" x 1-5/8"	BC@.026	LF	.88	.97	1.85
5/16" x 2-1/2"	BC@.026	LF	1.37	.97	2.34
5/16" x 3-1/2"	BC@.026	LF	1.38	.97	2.35
3/8" x 2-1/2"	BC@.026	LF	2.29	.97	3.26
Brick mold, 1-1/2" x 1-1/2"	BC@.026	LF	2.97	.97	3.94
Drip cap – water table					
1-5/8" x 2-1/2" (no lip)	BC@.060	LF	3.79	2.24	6.03
1-5/8" x 2-1/2"	BC@.060	LF	3.84	2.24	6.08

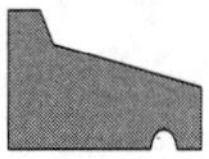

	Craft@Hrs	Unit	Material	Labor	Total
Quarter round, 3/4" x 3/4"	BC@.026	LF	1.80	.97	2.77
Rabbeted siding mold, 1-1/8" x 1-5/8"	BC@.026	LF	2.33	.97	3.30

	Craft@Hrs	Unit	Material	Labor	Total
S4S (rectangular)					
11/16" x 11/16"	BC@.026	LF	1.12	.97	2.09
1" x 2"	BC@.026	LF	1.69	.97	2.66
1" x 3"	BC@.026	LF	2.50	.97	3.47
1" x 4"	BC@.026	LF	3.19	.97	4.16

	Craft@Hrs	Unit	Material	Labor	Total
Stucco mold					
13/16" x 1-3/8"	BC@.026	LF	1.26	.97	2.23
13/16" x 1 1/2"	BC@.026	LF	1.27	.97	2.24
Window sill, 2" x 8"	BC@.043	LF	16.30	1.61	17.91

Softwood molding, pine (Labor costs here can also be used for hardwood moldings in the previous section.)

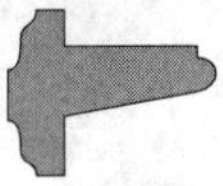

	Craft@Hrs	Unit	Material	Labor	Total
Astragal molding					
For 1-3/8" x 7' doors	BC@.032	LF	1.60	1.20	2.80
For 1-3/4" x 7' doors	BC@.032	LF	3.81	1.20	5.01

	Craft@Hrs	Unit	Material	Labor	Total
Base (all patterns)					
7/16" x 7/16"	BC@.016	LF	.76	.60	1.36
7/16" x 1-1/4"	BC@.016	LF	.87	.60	1.47
3/8" x 3"	BC@.016	LF	1.06	.60	1.66
1/2" x 2-1/4"	BC@.016	LF	1.26	.60	1.86
1/2" x 3-1/4"	BC@.016	LF	1.40	.60	2.00
17/32" x 3-7/32"	BC@.016	LF	1.44	.60	2.04

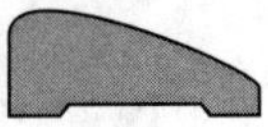

	Craft@Hrs	Unit	Material	Labor	Total
Base (combination or cove)					
11/16" x 1-1/8"	BC@.016	LF	1.09	.60	1.69
9/16" x 1-3/4"	BC@.016	LF	1.52	.60	2.12
1/2" x 3-1/4"	BC@.016	LF	1.72	.60	2.32
Base shoe					
1/2" x 3/4"	BC@.016	LF	.44	.60	1.04
Casing (all patterns)					
1/2" x 1-5/8"	BC@.023	LF	1.11	.86	1.97
11/16" x 2-1/4"	BC@.023	LF	3.52	.86	4.38
11/16" x 3-1/4"	BC@.023	LF	1.54	.86	2.40
11/16" x 3-1/2"	BC@.023	LF	2.37	.86	3.23

	Craft@Hrs	Unit	Material	Labor	Total
Chair rail					
1/2" x 1-1/2"	BC@.021	LF	1.06	.78	1.84
11/16" x 2-1/2"	BC@.021	LF	1.52	.78	2.30
Chamfer strip, 3/4" x 3/4"	BC@.016	LF	.24	.60	.84
Corner bead (outside corner molding)					
11/16" x 11/16"	BC@.016	LF	.78	.60	1.38
3/4" x 3/4"	BC@.016	LF	.79	.60	1.39
1-1/8" x 1-1/8"	BC@.016	LF	1.06	.60	1.66

Molding, Softwood

	Craft@Hrs	Unit	Material	Labor	Total	
Cove molding, solid						
3/8" x 3/8"	BC@.020	LF	.44	.75	1.19	
1/2" x 1/2"	BC@.020	LF	.67	.75	1.42	
11/16" x 11/16"	BC@.020	LF	.68	.75	1.43	
3/4" x 3/4"	BC@.020	LF	.85	.75	1.60	
1-1/2" x 1-1/2"	BC@.020	LF	1.20	.75	1.95	
Cove molding, sprung						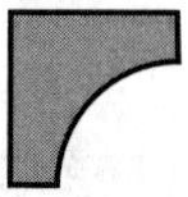
9/16" x 1-3/4"	BC@.020	LF	1.31	.75	2.06	
5/8" x 3/4"	BC@.020	LF	.99	.75	1.74	
Crown or bed molding						
9/16" x 1-5/8"	BC@.044	LF	.68	1.64	2.32	
9/16" x 2-3/4"	BC@.044	LF	1.26	1.64	2.90	
9/16" x 1-3/4"	BC@.044	LF	.82	1.64	2.46	
9/16" x 2-5/8"	BC@.044	LF	1.91	1.64	3.55	
9/16" x 3-5/8"	BC@.044	LF	1.64	1.64	3.28	
Add for special cutting, any crown molding shown:						
Inside corner, using coping saw	BC@.167	Ea	—	6.24	6.24	
Outside corners, using miter saw	BC@.083	Ea	—	3.10	3.10	
Drip cap (water table molding or bar nosing)						
1-1/16" x 1-5/8"	BC@.060	LF	2.46	2.24	4.70	
1-1/16" x 2"	BC@.060	LF	2.73	2.24	4.97	
Drip molding						
3/4" x 1-1/4"	BC@.030	LF	.75	1.12	1.87	
Glass bead						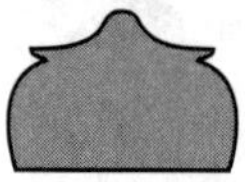
1/2" x 1-3/8"	BC@.016	LF	.63	.60	1.23	
Handrail, fir						
1-1/2" x 2-1/4"	BC@.060	LF	2.61	2.24	4.85	
1-7/16" x 1-3/4"	BC@.060	LF	2.60	2.24	4.84	
Lattice						
1/4" x 1-1/8"	BC@.016	LF	.47	.60	1.07	
1/4" x 1-1/2"	BC@.016	LF	.65	.60	1.25	
5/16" x 1-3/8"	BC@.016	LF	.99	.60	1.59	
5/16" x 1-3/4"	BC@.016	LF	1.15	.60	1.75	
Mullion casing						
3/8" x 2"	BC@.016	LF	1.64	.60	2.24	
Panel molding						
3/8" x 5/8"	BC@.030	LF	.84	1.12	1.96	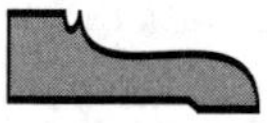
5/8" x 1-1/4"	BC@.030	LF	.90	1.12	2.02	
3/4" x 1"	BC@.030	LF	1.20	1.12	2.32	
11/16" x 1-5/8"	BC@.030	LF	.95	1.12	2.07	
3/4" x 2"	BC@.030	LF	1.34	1.12	2.46	
Parting bead						
3/8" x 3/4"	BC@.016	LF	.69	.60	1.29	
Picture frame mold						
3/4" x 3/4"	BC@.040	LF	.87	1.50	2.37	
7/8" x 1-1/2"	BC@.040	LF	1.18	1.50	2.68	
Plaster ground						
3/4" x 7/8"	BC@.010	LF	.66	.37	1.03	

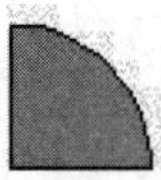
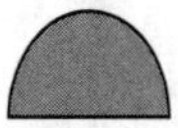

	Craft@Hrs	Unit	Material	Labor	Total
Quarter round					
1/4" x 1/4"	BC@.016	LF	.40	.60	1.00
1/2" x 1/2"	BC@.016	LF	.40	.60	1.00
21/32" x 21/32"	BC@.016	LF	.41	.60	1.01
11/16" x 11/16"	BC@.016	LF	.50	.60	1.10
3/4" x 3/4"	BC@.016	LF	1.13	.60	1.73
1" x 1-11/16"	BC@.016	LF	1.11	.60	1.71
Half round					
1/4" x 1/2" or 5/16" x 5/8"	BC@.016	LF	.89	.60	1.49
3/8" x 3/4" or 1/2" x 1"	BC@.016	LF	.70	.60	1.30
3/4" x 1-1/2"	BC@.016	LF	1.15	.60	1.75
Full round					
1/2" or 3/4" diameter	BC@.016	LF	.82	.60	1.42
1-1/4" or 1-3/8" diameter	BC@.016	LF	1.90	.60	2.50
1" diameter	BC@.016	LF	1.01	.60	1.61
1-1/2" diameter	BC@.016	LF	1.93	.60	2.53
2" diameter	BC@.016	LF	2.76	.60	3.36
S4S (rectangular)					
7/16" x 1-5/8", pine	BC@.020	Ea	1.10	.75	1.85
7/16" x 2-1/2", pine	BC@.020	Ea	1.48	.75	2.23
7/16" x 2-5/8", pine	BC@.020	Ea	1.76	.75	2.51
7/16" x 3-1/2", pine	BC@.020	Ea	2.53	.75	3.28
1/2" x 3/4", pine	BC@.016	Ea	.48	.60	1.08
1/2" x 2-1/2", pine	BC@.020	Ea	1.62	.75	2.37
1/2" x 3-1/2", pine	BC@.020	Ea	2.61	.75	3.36
11/16" x 11/16", pine	BC@.016	Ea	.89	.60	1.49
11/16" x 1-5/8", pine	BC@.016	Ea	1.30	.60	1.90
11/16" x 1-3/4", pine	BC@.016	Ea	1.33	.60	1.93
11/16" x 2-1/2", pine	BC@.020	Ea	2.47	.75	3.22
3/4" x 3/4", pine	BC@.016	Ea	.82	.60	1.42
1-1/16" x 1-3/4", pine	BC@.016	Ea	2.10	.60	2.70
Sash bar					
7/8" x 1-3/8"	BC@.016	LF	1.08	.60	1.68
Screen molding					
1/4" x 3/4" beaded	BC@.016	LF	.39	.60	.99
1/4" x 3/4" flat or insert	BC@.016	LF	.47	.60	1.07
3/8" x 3/4" clover leaf	BC@.016	LF	.53	.60	1.13
Square molding					
1/2" x 1/2"	BC@.016	LF	.58	.60	1.18
3/4" x 3/4"	BC@.016	LF	.97	.60	1.57
1" x 1"	BC@.016	LF	1.16	.60	1.76
2" x 2"	BC@.016	LF	2.20	.60	2.80
Stops, round edge					
3/8" x 7/8"	BC@.025	LF	.38	.93	1.31
3/8" x 1-1/4"	BC@.025	LF	.67	.93	1.60
3/8" x 1-3/8"	BC@.025	LF	.63	.93	1.56
3/8" x 1-5/8" or 1/2" x 3/4"	BC@.025	LF	.63	.93	1.56
7/16" x 3/4"	BC@.025	LF	.63	.93	1.56
7/16" x 1-1/4"	BC@.025	LF	.91	.93	1.84
7/16" x 1-5/8"	BC@.025	LF	1.05	.93	1.98
Wainscot cap					
5/8" x 1-1/4" or 1/2" x 1-1/2"	BC@.016	LF	1.24	.60	1.84

	Craft@Hrs	Unit	Material	Labor	Total
Window stool, beveled					
11/16" x 2-1/4"	BC@.037	LF	2.49	1.38	3.87
11/16" x 2-1/2"	BC@.037	LF	1.52	1.38	2.90
1" x 3-1/2"	BC@.037	LF	3.88	1.38	5.26
1" x 5-1/2"	BC@.037	LF	5.99	1.38	7.37
Window stool, flat					
11/16" x 4-5/8"	BC@.037	LF	2.42	1.38	3.80
1" x 5-1/2"	BC@.037	LF	5.47	1.38	6.85
Medium density fiberboard molding Primed, ready for painting.					
Base, 9/16" x 3-1/4"	BC@.012	LF	1.35	.45	1.80
Base, 1/2" x 4-1/4"	BC@.012	LF	1.43	.45	1.88
Casing, 5/8" x 2-1/2"	BC@.016	LF	.93	.60	1.53
Door casing set, fluted, 17' x 3/4" x 2-1/4"	BC@.272	Ea	29.70	10.20	39.90
Chair rail, 9/16" x 3"	BC@.015	LF	2.00	.56	2.56
Corner, bullnose, 2-1/4" x 2-1/4"	BC@.025	LF	.91	.93	1.84
Crown, 11/16" x 3-1/2"	BC@.025	LF	1.38	.93	2.31
Crown inside or outside corner block,					
3/4" x 6"	BC@.125	Ea	19.10	4.67	23.77
Plinth block, 1" x 3-3/4"	BC@.125	Ea	2.87	4.67	7.54
White vinyl molding Unfinished.					
Backband casing	BC@.016	LF	2.75	.60	3.35
Base cap, 11/16" x 1-1/8"	BC@.009	LF	.95	.34	1.29
Bead, 9/16" x 1-3/4"	BC@.016	LF	1.04	.60	1.64
Blind stop	BC@.016	LF	.95	.60	1.55
Casing, 5/8" x 2-1/2"	BC@.023	LF	1.05	.86	1.91
Crown, 1/2" x 3-1/4"	BC@.044	LF	2.46	1.64	4.10
Dentil, 27/32" x 5-7/8"	BC@.016	LF	5.01	.60	5.61
Dentil, 27/32" x 4-1/8"	BC@.016	LF	1.91	.60	2.51
Drip cap, 11/16" x 1-5/8"	BC@.016	LF	1.54	.60	2.14
Exterior bead 3/16" x 1/2"	BC@.016	LF	.52	.60	1.12
Flat utility trim	BC@.023	LF	2.25	.86	3.11
Quarter round, 3/4" x 3/4" x 12'	BC@.016	LF	.82	.60	1.42
Shingle molding, 11/16" x 1-3/4"	BC@.016	LF	1.73	.60	2.33
Extruded polymer molding Factory finished.					
Bead, Brite White	BC@.016	LF	.57	.60	1.17
Bead, Cherry/Mahogany	BC@.016	LF	.32	.60	.92
Bead, Cinnamon Chestnut	BC@.016	LF	.45	.60	1.05
Bed mold, Brite White	BC@.016	LF	.83	.60	1.43
Bed mold, Cherry/Mahogany	BC@.016	LF	.63	.60	1.23
Bed mold, Cinnamon Chestnut	BC@.016	LF	.85	.60	1.45
Casing and base, Brite White	BC@.023	LF	.88	.86	1.74
Casing and base, Cherry/Mahogany	BC@.023	LF	.86	.86	1.72
Casing and base, Cinnamon Chestnut	BC@.023	LF	.85	.86	1.71
Outside corner, Brite White	BC@.016	LF	.51	.60	1.11
Outside corner, Cherry/Mahogany	BC@.016	LF	.32	.60	.92
Outside corner, Cinnamon Chestnut	BC@.016	LF	.43	.60	1.03
Plywood cap, Brite White	BC@.016	LF	.73	.60	1.33
Shoe, Brite White	BC@.016	LF	.40	.60	1.00
Shoe, Cherry/Mahogany	BC@.016	LF	.32	.60	.92
Shoe, Cinnamon Chestnut	BC@.016	LF	.43	.60	1.03
Stop, Brite White	BC@.025	LF	.43	.93	1.36
Stop, Cinnamon Chestnut	BC@.025	LF	.43	.93	1.36

Nails and Fasteners

Nail sizes are usually identified by the "penny," abbreviated "d." Use the following figures to estimate nail quantities for framing:

Sills and plates – 8 pounds of 10d, 16d and 20d nails per MBF
Walls and partition studs – 10 pounds of 10d and 16d nails per MBF
2" x 6" or 2" x 8" joists and rafters – 9 pounds of 16d nails per MBF
2" x 10" or 2" x 12" joist and rafters – 7 pounds of 16d nails per MBF
Sheathing to 3/8" thick – 10 pounds of 6d nails per MSF
Sheathing over 3/8" thick – 20 pounds of 8d nails per MSF
Siding – 25 pounds of 8d nails per MSF

	Unit	Galvanized	Bright
Common nails Bright nails are tumbled to remove debris and have a polished appearance. Galvanized nails are zinc coated to protect against corrosion and have a dull sheen. Cost per box except as noted.			
3 penny, 1-1/4", 1-pound box, 568 nails	Box	5.37	4.38
4 penny, 1-1/2", 1-pound box, 316 nails	Box	5.36	4.19
4 penny, 1-1/2", 5-pound box, 2,840 nails	Box	18.80	15.40
5 penny, 1-3/4", 1-pound box, 271 nails	Box	—	4.69
6 penny, 2", 1-pound box, 181 nails	Box	5.36	—
6 penny, 2", 5-pound box, 905 nails	Box	18.80	14.70
6 penny, 2", 30-pound box, 5,430 nails	Box	61.60	46.10
6 penny, 2", 50-pound box, 9,050 nails	Box	71.50	—
7 penny, 2-1/2", 5-pound box, 805 nails	Box	20.00	—
7 penny, 2-1/2", 50-pound box, 8,050 nails	Box	81.60	—
8 penny, 2-1/2", 1-pound box, 106 nails	Box	5.28	4.24
8 penny, 2-1/2", 5-pound box, 530 nails	Box	18.80	14.70
8 penny, 2-1/2", 30-pound box, 3,180 nails	Box	67.30	50.80
8 penny, 2-1/2", 50-pound box, 5,300 nails	Box	—	61.60
10 penny, 3", 1-pound box, 69 nails	Box	5.36	4.24
10 penny, 3", 5-pound box, 345 nails	Box	18.80	14.70
10 penny, 3", 30-pound box, 2,070 nails	Box	67.30	49.90
10 penny, 3", 50-pound box, 3,450 nails	Box	80.30	59.30
12 penny, 3-1/4", 1-pound box, 64 nails	Box	5.23	—
12 penny, 3-1/4", 5-pound box, 320 nails	Box	18.80	14.60
12 penny, 3-1/4", 30-pound box, 1,920 nails	Box	66.90	51.60
12 penny, 3-1/4", 50-pound box, 3,200 nails	Box	—	63.50
16 penny, 3-1/2", 1-pound box, 49 nails	Box	5.30	4.27
16 penny, 3-1/2", 5-pound box, 245 nails	Box	19.00	15.00
16 penny, 3-1/2", 30-pound box, 1,470 nails	Box	78.80	51.60
16 penny, 3-1/2", 50-pound box, 2,450 nails	Box	67.70	62.50
20 penny, 4", 1-pound box, 31 nails	Box	5.36	4.24
20 penny, 4", 5-pound box, 155 nails	Box	18.80	14.80
40 penny, 5", per nail, 18 per pound	Ea	.07	.06
60 penny, 6", per nail, 11 per pound	Ea	.19	.09
60 penny, 6", 30-pound box, 330 nails	Box	—	52.30
Box nails Box nails are thinner and about 1/8" shorter than common nails of the same nominal size. Points are blunter to reduce wood splitting. Use box nails for molding and trim and when the lumber is dry or brittle. Cost per box.			
3 penny, 1-1/4", 1-pound box, 1,010 nails	Box	5.71	4.69
3 penny, 1-1/4", 5-pound box, 5,050 nails	Box	20.00	—
4 penny, 1-1/2", 1-pound box, 473 nails	Box	5.63	4.69
4 penny, 1-1/2", 5-pound box, 2,365 nails	Box	20.70	—

Nails

	Unit	Galvanized	Bright
5 penny, 1-3/4", 1-pound box, 406 nails	Box	5.71	—
5 penny, 1-3/4", 5-pound box, 2,030 nails	Box	20.10	—
6 penny, 2", 1-pound box, 236 nails	Box	5.66	4.69
6 penny, 2", 5-pound box, 1,180 nails	Box	19.80	16.10
7 penny, 2-1/4", 1-pound box, 210 nails	Box	5.71	—
8 penny, 2-1/2", 1-pound box, 145 nails	Box	5.66	4.72
8 penny, 2-1/2", 5-pound box, 725 nails	Box	19.80	16.10
8 penny, 2-1/2", 30-pound box, 4,350 nails	Box	68.90	—
10 penny, 3", 1-pound box, 132 nails	Box	5.70	4.69
10 penny, 3", 5-pound box, 660 nails	Box	20.00	16.20
12 penny, 3-1/4", 1-pound box, 94 nails	Box	5.54	4.72
12 penny, 3-1/4", 5-pound box, 470 nails	Box	19.80	—
16 penny, 3-1/2", 1-pound box, 71 nails	Box	5.68	4.69
16 penny, 3-1/2", 5-pound box, 355 nails	Box	19.80	16.20
16 penny, 3-1/2", 30-pound box, 2,130 nails	Box	72.60	65.90
20 penny, 4", 1-pound box, 62 nails	Box	5.71	4.70
20 penny, 4", 5-pound box, 310 nails	Box	20.00	—

	Unit	Screw shank	Ring shank
Deck nails For use with ACQ or CA pressure-treated lumber. Cost per box.			
6 penny, 2", 1-pound box	Box	5.86	6.05
6 penny, 2", 5-pound box	Box	20.30	21.00
8 penny, 2-1/2", 1-pound box	Box	5.92	6.05
8 penny, 2-1/2", 5-pound box	Box	20.60	20.30
10 penny, 3", 1-pound box	Box	5.88	6.05
12 penny, 3-1/4", 1-pound box	Box	5.88	6.05
12 penny, 3-1/4", 5-pound box	Box	20.80	20.00
16 penny, 3-1/2", 1-pound box	Box	5.92	6.05
16 penny, 3-1/2", 5-pound box	Box	20.60	21.00

	Craft@Hrs	Unit	Material	Labor	Total
Vinyl/cement-coated sinkers Vinyl coating lubricates the wood and holds fast when driven. Head sinks flush with surface.					
4 penny, 1-3/8", 1-pound box, 550 nails	—	Box	3.56	—	3.56
6 penny, 1-7/8", 1-pound box, 275 nails	—	Box	3.79	—	3.79
6 penny, 1-7/8", 5-pound box, 1,375 nails	—	Box	13.30	—	13.30
8 penny, 2-3/8", 1-pound box, 142 nails,	—	Box	3.79	—	3.79
8 penny, 2-3/8", 5-pound box, 710 nails	—	Box	13.30	—	13.30
8 penny, 2-3/8", 50-pound box, 7,100 nails	—	Box	58.80	—	58.80
10 penny, 2-7/8", 5-pound box, 104 nails	—	Box	13.40	—	13.40
12 penny, 3-1/8", 1-pound box, 77 nails	—	Box	3.79	—	3.79
12 penny, 3-1/8", 5-pound box, 385 nails	—	Box	13.30	—	13.30
12 penny, 3-1/8", 50-pound box, 3,850 nails	—	Box	57.80	—	57.80
16 penny, 3-3/8", 1-pound box, 61 nails	—	Box	3.79	—	3.79
16 penny, 3-3/8", 5-pound box, 305 nails	—	Box	13.30	—	13.30
16 penny, 3-3/8", 25-pound box, 1,525 nails	—	Box	39.50	—	39.50
16 penny, 3-3/8", 50-pound box, 3,050 nails	—	Box	58.70	—	58.70

	Craft@Hrs	Unit	Material	Labor	Total
Plain shank stick collated framing nails					
2" x 0.113", coated, box of 2,000	—	Box	40.50	—	40.50
2-1/2" x 0.120", coated, box of 2,000	—	Box	44.80	—	44.80
2-1/2" x 0.120", galvanized, box of 2,000	—	Box	72.50	—	72.50
3" x 0.120", coated, box of 2,000	—	Box	37.80	—	37.80
3" x 0.120", galvanized, box of 2,000	—	Box	86.00	—	86.00
3-1/4" x 0.120", coated, box of 2,000	—	Box	50.00	—	50.00
3-1/4" x 0.120", galvanized, box of 2,000	—	Box	87.60	—	87.60
3-1/2" x 0.131", coated, box of 2,000	—	Box	59.60	—	59.60
3 1/2" x 0.131", galvanized, box of 2,000	—	Box	83.60	—	83.60
Plain shank coil framing nails, galvanized and coated					
2" x 0.099", box of 3,600	—	Box	101.00	—	101.00
2-1/2" x 0.099", box of 3,600	—	Box	103.00	—	103.00
3" x 0.120", box of 2,700	—	Box	97.30	—	97.30
3-1/4" x 0.120", box of 2,700	—	Box	118.00	—	118.00
Screw shank coil framing nails, plastic coated					
1-5/8" x 0.099", box of 10,800, steel	—	Box	237.00	—	237.00
1-7/8" x 0.099", box of 9,000, aluminum	—	Box	251.00	—	251.00
1-3/4" x 0.086", box of 9,000, steel	—	Box	182.00	—	182.00
2" x 0.099", box of 9,000, steel	—	Box	144.00	—	144.00
2-1/4" x 0.099", box of 7,200, steel	—	Box	119.00	—	119.00
2-1/2" x 0.105", box of 4,000, steel	—	Box	87.40	—	87.40
2-7/8" x 0.105", box of 5,400, steel	—	Box	132.00	—	132.00
Brad nails for an impulse nailer, bright, 18-gauge					
1", box of 1,000	—	Box	5.74	—	5.74
1-1/4", box of 1,000	—	Box	5.45	—	5.45
2", box of 1,000	—	Box	6.61	—	6.61

Casing nails, galvanized. Used where the nail head must be hidden. Casing nails have small, conical heads. The nail diameter is smaller than a common nail but larger than a finishing nail. Casing nails are used to attach trim.

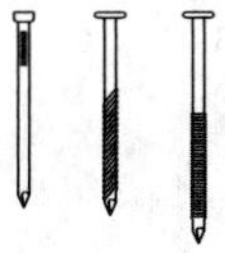

	Craft@Hrs	Unit	Material	Labor	Total
6 penny, 2", 1-pound box, 236 nails	—	Box	5.71	—	5.71
8 penny, 2-1/2", 1-pound box, 145 nails	—	Box	5.45	—	5.45
10 penny, 3", 1-pound box, 94 nails	—	Box	5.71	—	5.71
16 penny, 3-1/2", 1-pound box, 71 nails	—	Box	5.44	—	5.44

Drywall nails. Allow 6 pounds of nails (1,300 nails) per MSF of gypsum wallboard

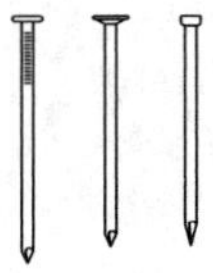

	Craft@Hrs	Unit	Material	Labor	Total
1-1/4", bright, ring shank, 5-pound box	—	Box	16.40	—	16.40
1-3/8", electro galvanized 5-pound box	—	Box	15.50	—	15.50
1-3/8", phosphate coated, 5-pound box	—	Box	16.60	—	16.60
1-3/8", blued, threaded, 5-pound box	—	Box	17.30	—	17.30
1-1/2", blued, threaded, 5-pound box	—	Box	17.30	—	17.30
1-5/8", blued, threaded, 5-pound box	—	Box	15.50	—	15.50
1-7/8", phosphate coated, 5-pound box	—	Box	17.30	—	17.30

Drywall screws. Black phosphate coating. For hanging drywall and plasterboard on wood or metal studs. Allow 1,300 screws per MSF of gypsum wallboard.

	Craft@Hrs	Unit	Material	Labor	Total
1-1/4", 5-pound box of 1,330	—	Box	26.10	—	26.10
1-5/8", 5-pound box of 1,300	—	Box	26.10	—	26.10
2", 5-pound box of 1,070	—	Box	26.10	—	26.10
2-1/2", 5-pound box of 480	—	Box	26.10	—	26.10
3", 5-pound box of 415	—	Box	26.10	—	26.10

Nails

	Craft@Hrs	Unit	Material	Labor	Total
Finishing nails, bright. Finishing nails have a barrel-shaped head with a small diameter and a dimple on the top. Cost per box.					
3 penny, 1-1/4", 1-pound box, 807 nails	—	Box	4.15	—	4.15
4 penny, 1-1/2", 1-pound box, 584 nails	—	Box	4.15	—	4.15
6 penny, 2", 1-pound box, 309 nails	—	Box	4.15	—	4.15
8 penny, 2-1/2", 1-pound box, 189 nails	—	Box	4.15	—	4.15
16 penny, 3-1/2", 1-pound box, 90 nails	—	Box	4.15	—	4.15
Finishing nail sticks for angled impulse nailer, 16 gauge, bright. Cost per box.					
1", box of 2,000	—	Box	11.90	—	11.90
1-1/4", box of 2,000	—	Box	14.10	—	14.10
1-1/2", box of 2,000	—	Box	17.00	—	17.00
1-3/4", box of 2,000	—	Box	17.40	—	17.40
2", box of 2,000	—	Box	19.00	—	19.00
2-1/2", box of 2,000	—	Box	24.20	—	24.20
Bright joist hanger nails, 9 gauge except as noted. Cost per box.					
1-1/4", 1-pound box	—	Box	4.96	—	4.96
1-1/2", 1-pound box	—	Box	4.96	—	4.96
1-1/2", 1-pound box, 10 gauge	—	Box	4.96	—	4.96
1-1/2", 5-pound box	—	Box	17.30	—	17.30
1-1/2", 5-pound box, 10 gauge	—	Box	17.30	—	17.30
1-1/2", 30-pound box	—	Box	68.70	—	68.70
Galvanized joist hanger nails. 9 gauge. Cost per box.					
1-1/4", 5-pound box	—	Box	20.90	—	20.90
1-1/4", 25-pound box	—	Box	66.20	—	66.20
1-1/2", 1-pound box	—	Box	5.71	—	5.71
1-1/2", 50-pound box	—	Box	91.60	—	91.60
Stainless steel joist hanger nails					
1-1/2", 9 gauge, 1-pound box, 126 nails	—	Box	12.70	—	12.70
1-1/2", 10 gauge, 5-pound box, 735 nails	—	Box	57.10	—	57.10
Masonry nails. Temper hardened, bright.					
1", fluted nail, 1-pound box	—	Box	6.99	—	6.99
1-1/2" fluted nail, 1-pound box	—	Box	6.86	—	6.86
2" fluted nail, 1-pound box	—	Box	6.83	—	6.83
2-1/2" cut nail, flat head, 1-pound box	—	Box	6.83	—	6.83
3", cut nail, flat head, 5-pound box	—	Box	25.20	—	25.20
4-1/2", cut nail, flat head, 1-pound box	—	Box	7.08	—	7.08
Plasterboard nails, 13 gauge, blued					
3/8" head, 1-1/8" (449) or 1-1/4" (405)	—	Lb	4.96	—	4.96
3/8" head, 1-5/8", 342 nails	—	Lb	4.42	—	4.42
Roofing nail coils, for pneumatic nailer					
2 penny, 1", 7,200 nails, galvanized	—	Box	79.40	—	79.40
3 penny, 1-1/4", 7,200 nails, galvanized	—	Box	44.10	—	44.10
5 penny, 2", 3,600 nails, bright	—	Box	62.70	—	62.70
Roofing nails, electro galvanized					
1/2", 1-pound box, 380 nails	—	Box	3.52	—	3.52
3/4", 1-pound box, 315 nails	—	Box	3.28	—	3.28
1-3/4" or 2", 5-pound box, 150 or 138 nails	—	Box	13.20	—	13.20
Roofing nails, galvanized. Ring shank.					
1-1/4", 30-pound box, 6,150 nails	—	Box	73.40	—	73.40
1-1/2", 30-pound box, 5,550 nails	—	Box	78.50	—	78.50
1-3/4", 5-pound box, 800 nails	—	Box	21.50	—	21.50
2-1/2", 50-pound box, 5,900 nails	—	Box	74.00	—	74.00

	Craft@Hrs	Unit	Material	Labor	Total
Roofing nails, plastic round cap. For securing felt on sandable roof decking or attaching foam board sheathing					
7/8", 11-1/2 gauge, box of 3,000	—	Box	44.60	—	44.60
2" x 0.113", galvanized, box of 5,000	—	Box	106.00	—	106.00
Galvanized roofing staples, wide crown. For shingles and polystyrene sheathing.					
7/8", box of 9,000	—	Box	59.60	—	59.60
1-1/4", box of 9,000	—	Box	77.30	—	77.30
Double head (duplex) nails for use on scaffolds, concrete forms and temporary construction					
6 penny, 2", 1-pound box, 143 nails	—	Box	5.37	—	5.37
6 penny, 2", 5-pound box, 715 nails	—	Box	18.80	—	18.80
8 penny, 2-1/4", 1-pound box, 88 nails	—	Box	5.35	—	5.35
8 penny, 2-1/4", 5-pound box, 440 nails	—	Box	18.20	—	18.20
8 penny, 2-1/4", 30-pound box, 2,640 nails	—	Box	60.70	—	60.70
16 penny, 3-1/4", 1-pound box, 44 nails	—	Box	5.28	—	5.28
16 penny, 3-1/4", 5-pound box, 220 nails,	—	Box	18.20	—	18.20
16 penny, 3-1/4", 30-pound box, 1,320 nails	—	Box	60.70	—	60.70
Siding nails					
1-1/2", aluminum, 1-pound box	—	Box	15.40	—	15.40
2", aluminum, 1-pound box	—	Box	14.80	—	14.80
1-3/4", galvanized, 5-pound box	—	Box	19.10	—	19.10
2-1/4", galvanized, 5-pound box	—	Box	20.80	—	20.80
2-1/2", galvanized, 5-pound box	—	Box	18.70	—	18.70
3", galvanized, 5-pound box	—	Box	18.20	—	18.20
3" double galvanized, 5-pound box	—	Box	22.80	—	22.80
Spikes, galvanized. For landscape timbers, railroad ties, log home construction.					
3/8" x 8", per spike	—	Ea	.60	—	.60
3/8" x 10", per spike	—	Ea	.73	—	.73
3/8" x 10", 5-pound box	—	Box	17.30	—	17.30
3/8" x 12", per spike	—	Ea	.89	—	.89
3/8" x 12", 5-pound box	—	Box	17.30	—	17.30
Powder-driven fastening nails, zinc plated					
3/4", per pack of 20	—	Ea	2.75	—	2.75
7/8", per pack of 20	—	Ea	4.98	—	4.98
1", per pack of 20	—	Ea	8.50	—	8.50
1-1/4", per pack of 20	—	Ea	8.62	—	8.62
1-1/2", per pack of 20	—	Ea	7.99	—	7.99
1-7/8", per pack of 20	—	Ea	8.83	—	8.83
2-1/2", per pack of 20	—	Ea	8.41	—	8.41
3", per pack of 20	—	Ea	8.85	—	8.85
Powder-driven 0.300 pins, with washers					
1-1/2", per pack of 100	—	Ea	16.90	—	16.90
2-1/2", per pack of 100	—	Ea	17.20	—	17.20
3", per pack of 100	—	Ea	18.70	—	18.70

Nuts, Bolts and Washers

	Length 4"	6"	8"	10"	12"
Nuts, Bolts and Washers Bolts, standard hex head, material cost per bolt.					
Heavy duty lag bolts, galvanized, deduct 25% for carton quantities					
1/2"	.61	.87	1.19	1.60	2.00
5/8"	1.52	2.23	2.90	3.54	3.90
3/4"	2.19	2.89	3.46	4.25	5.18
Machine bolts (hex bolts), galvanized, deduct 25% for carton quantities					
1/2", 13 threads per inch	.77	1.12	1.46	1.74	2.25
5/8", 11 threads per inch	1.36	1.97	2.57	2.95	3.38
3/4", 10 threads per inch	1.93	2.57	3.20	4.00	4.84
7/8", 9 threads per inch	4.30	5.43	6.98	8.62	9.40
1", 8 threads per inch	5.36	7.39	9.15	11.10	12.80
Carriage bolts (domed top and a square under the head), galvanized, deduct 25% for carton quantities					
1/2", 13 threads per inch	.55	.70	1.06	1.19	1.55
5/8", 11 threads per inch	.93	1.41	1.78	2.13	2.42
3/4", 10 threads per inch	1.59	2.10	2.67	3.20	3.55

	Craft@Hrs	Unit	Material	Labor	Total
Labor to install machine bolts or lag bolts. Includes installation of nuts and washers and drilling as needed.					
4" to 6" long	BC@.100	Ea	—	3.74	3.74
8" to 10" long	BC@.150	Ea	—	5.61	5.61
12" long	BC@.200	Ea	—	7.48	7.48
Nuts, standard hex, galvanized					
1/2"	—	Ea	.12	—	.12
5/8"	—	Ea	.18	—	.18
3/4"	—	Ea	.25	—	.25
7/8"	—	Ea	.51	—	.51
1"	—	Ea	.69	—	.69
Washers, standard cut steel, galvanized AKA Lock Washers					
1/2"	—	Ea	.14	—	.14
5/8"	—	Ea	.23	—	.23
3/4"	—	Ea	.37	—	.37
7/8"	—	Ea	.60	—	.60
1"	—	Ea	.92	—	.92
Washers, USS Flat steel, galvanized					
1/2"	—	Ea	.18	—	.18
5/8"	—	Ea	.30	—	.30
3/4"	—	Ea	.42	—	.42
7/8"	—	Ea	.57	—	.57
1"	—	Ea	.69	—	.69
Dock washers, larger OD than flat washers, galvanized, OD typically 3"					
1/2"	—	Ea	1.98	—	1.98
5/8"	—	Ea	1.98	—	1.98
3/4"	—	Ea	1.98	—	1.98
1"	—	Ea	1.98	—	1.98

Paint Removal Dustless removal of lead-based paints. The removal system is a mechanical process and no water, chemicals or abrasive grit are used. Containment or special ventilation is not required. Based on Pentek Inc. Costs shown are for a 5,000 SF or larger job. For estimating purposes figure one 55-gallon drum of contaminated waste per 2,500 square feet of coatings removed from surfaces with an average coating thickness of 12 mils. Waste disposal costs are not included. Use $5,000 as a minimum charge for work of this type. On pre-1978 homes, child care facilities and schools, rules adopted by the Environmental Protection Agency require that: (1) a trained supervisor be on site during paint removal, (2) those affected be given a copy of the EPA pamphlet on lead paint removal, (3) records be retained for three years and (4) steps be taken to prevent the spread of dust and debris. For more information, see http://www.epa.gov/lead/renovation-repair-and-painting-program.

Removing paint from ceilings, doors, door and window frames, roofs, siding Equipment includes three pneumatic needle scaler units attached to one air-powered vacuum-waste packing unit and one 150 CFM gas or diesel powered air compressor including all hoses and connectors. Add the one-time charge listed below for move-on, move-off and refurbishing of equipment.

	Craft@Hrs	Unit	Material	Labor	Equipment	Total
Ceilings						
Plaster, 70 SF per hour	PT@.042	SF	—	1.61	1.41	3.02
Doors, wood or metal. Remove and re-hang doors, no carpentry included						
To 3'0" x 6'8"	PT@1.00	Ea	—	38.20	—	38.20
Over 3'0" x 6'8" to 6'0" x 8'0"	PT@1.50	Ea	—	57.30	—	57.30
Over 6'0" x 8'0" to 12'0" x 20'0"	PT@2.00	Ea	—	76.40	—	76.40
Paint removal (assumes doors are laid flat on saw horses)						
80 SF per hour	PT@.038	SF	—	1.45	1.28	2.73
Door or window frames						
To 3'0" x 6'8"	PT@1.50	Ea	—	57.30	50.50	107.80
Over 3'0" x 6'8" to 6'0" x 8'0"	PT@2.00	Ea	—	76.40	67.30	143.70
Over 6'0" x 8'0" to 12'0" x 20'0"	PT@3.00	Ea	—	115.00	99.20	214.20
Lintels						
Per SF of surface area	PT@.033	SF	—	1.26	1.11	2.37
Roofs						
Metal roofs to 3 in 12 pitch						
75 SF of surface per hour	PT@.040	SF	—	1.53	1.35	2.88
Metal roofs over 3 in 12 pitch						
65 SF of surface per hour	PT@.046	SF	—	1.76	1.55	3.31
Wood roofs to 3 in 12 pitch						
80 SF of surface per hour	PT@.038	SF	—	1.45	1.28	2.73
Wood roofs over 3 in 12 pitch						
70 SF of surface per hour	PT@.042	SF	—	1.61	1.41	3.02
Siding						
Metal siding, 80 SF per hour	PT@.038	SF	—	1.45	1.28	2.73
Wood siding, 85 SF per hour	PT@.035	SF	—	1.34	1.18	2.52
Walls measured on one face of wall						
Concrete, 80 SF per hour	PT@.038	SF	—	1.45	1.28	2.73
Concrete block, 70 SF per hour	PT@.042	SF	—	1.61	1.41	3.02
Plaster, 85 SF per hour	PT@.035	SF	—	1.34	1.18	2.52
Add for mobilization and demobilization, per job						
Move-on & off and refurbish	—	LS	—	—	—	2,500.00

	Craft@Hrs	Unit	Material	Labor	Equipment	Total
Removing paint from concrete floor and slab surfaces. Equipment includes three pneumatic manually-operated wheel-mounted scabblers attached to one air-powered vacuum-waste packing unit to scarify concrete floors and slabs and one 150 CFM gas- or diesel-powered air compressor, including all hoses and connectors. Add the one-time charge listed below for move-on, move-off and refurbishing of equipment.						
Large unobstructed areas; floor slabs, driveways, sidewalks						
90 SF of surface per hour	PT@.033	SF	—	1.26	1.11	2.37
Obstructed areas; narrow aisles, areas around equipment						
60 SF of surface per hour	PT@.050	SF	—	1.91	1.68	3.59
Small areas; around decks						
40 SF of surface per hour	PT@.075	SF	—	2.87	2.52	5.39
Add for mobilization and demobilization, per job						
Move-on and off and refurbish	—	LS	—	—	—	2,500.00

Paints, Coatings, and Supplies Costs are for good to better quality coatings purchased in single-residence quantities. Add 30% for premium quality paints. Contractor prices may be discounted 10% to 15% on residential job quantities. Painting contractors receive discounts of 20% to 25% on steady volume accounts. Labor costs for painting are listed at the end of this section. For more complete coverage of painting costs, see the *National Painting Cost Estimator* at http://CraftsmanSiteLicense.com/

Primers

	Craft@Hrs	Unit	Material	Labor	Total
Oil-based exterior primer-sealer, universal undercoat for use on wood, hardboard, aluminum and wrought iron. Prevents extractive bleeding.					
Quart (100 SF per quart)	—	Qt	10.00	—	10.00
Gallon (400 SF per gallon)	—	Gal	25.40	—	25.40
5 gallon (2,000 SF per 5-gallon)	—	5-Gal	96.10	—	96.10
Acrylic (vinyl acrylic) thermoplastic rust-inhibiting metal primer					
(500 SF per gallon)	—	Gal	63.30	—	63.30
Acrylic latex interior primer and sealer, for drywall, plaster, masonry or wood					
Gallon (300-400 SF per gallon)	—	Gal	11.70	—	11.70
5 gallon (1,500-2,000 SF per 5-gallon)	—	Gal	50.10	—	50.10
Linseed (oil base) exterior/ interior primer					
Quart (75 SF per quart)	—	Gal	9.69	—	9.69
Gallon (300 SF per gallon)	—	Gal	26.50	—	26.50
Red oxide metal primer					
(500 SF per gallon)	—	Gal	71.50	—	71.50
Concrete bonding primer, clear					
(350 to 400 SF per gallon)	—	Gal	22.50	—	22.50
Zinc chromate primer					
Quart (100 SF per quart)	—	Qt	101.00	—	101.00
Gallon (400 SF per gallon)	—	Qt	160.00	—	160.00
KILZ® exterior sealer, primer, stainblocker. Mildew-resistant. Blocks tannin bleed on redwood and cedar.					
Kilz® Original, solvent-based,					
1 gallon (300 SF per gallon)	—	Gal	25.50	—	25.50
Kilz® Original, solvent-based,					
5 gallons (1,500 SF per 5 gallons)	—	5 Gal	86.90	—	86.90
Kilz® Complete, solvent-based, low VOC,					
1 gallon (300 SF per gallon)	—	Gal	19.70	—	19.70
Kilz® odorless,					
1 gallon (300 SF per gallon)	—	Gal	22.80	—	22.80
Kilz® 2, water-based,					
1 gallon (300 SF per gallon)	—	Gal	18.10	—	18.10
Kilz® 2, water-based,					
5 gallons (1,500 SF per 5 gallons)	—	5 Gal	82.00	—	82.00

	Craft@Hrs	Unit	Material	Labor	Total
Kilz® Premium, water-based, 1 gallon (300 SF per gallon)	—	Gal	23.80	—	23.80
Kilz® Premium, water-based, 5 gallons (1,500 SF per 5 gallons)	—	5 Gal	104.00	—	104.00
Kilz® Ceiling paint & primer, water-based, 5 gallons (1,500 SF per 5 gallons)	—	5 Gal	122.00	—	122.00

House paint

Exterior acrylic latex house paint. Mildew and fade resistant. For wood, masonry, brick, stucco, vinyl and aluminum siding and metal. Typical coverage is 400 square feet per gallon.

	Craft@Hrs	Unit	Material	Labor	Total
Flat, gallon	—	Gal	36.80	—	36.80
Flat, 5 gallons	—	5 Gal	150.00	—	150.00
Satin, gallon	—	Gal	43.00	—	43.00
Satin, 5 gallons	—	5 Gal	192.00	—	192.00
Semi-gloss, gallon	—	Gal	42.30	—	42.30
Semi-gloss, 5 gallons	—	5 Gal	191.00	—	191.00

Interior acrylic latex house paint. Typical coverage is 400 square feet per gallon.

	Craft@Hrs	Unit	Material	Labor	Total
Flat base, gallon	—	Gal	30.60	—	30.60
Flat base, 5 gallons	—	5 Gal	124.00	—	124.00
Flat white, gallon	—	Gal	20.90	—	20.90
Flat white, 5 gallons	—	5 Gal	92.00	—	92.00
Eggshell enamel, quart	—	Qt	19.00	—	19.00
Eggshell enamel, gallon	—	Gal	35.50	—	35.50
Eggshell enamel, 5 gallons	—	5 Gal	160.00	—	160.00
Satin enamel, quart	—	Qt	22.90	—	22.90
Satin enamel, gallon	—	Gal	38.10	—	38.10
Satin enamel, 5 gallons	—	5 Gal	151.00	—	151.00
Semi gloss enamel, quart	—	Qt	20.00	—	20.00
Semi gloss enamel, gallon	—	Gal	36.80	—	36.80
Semi gloss enamel, 5 gallons	—	5 Gal	160.00	—	160.00
High gloss enamel, quart	—	Qt	15.20	—	15.20
High gloss enamel, gallon	—	Gal	39.30	—	39.30
Ceiling paint, gallon	—	Gal	32.00	—	32.00
Ceiling paint, 5 gallons	—	5-Gal	128.00	—	128.00
Texture paint, fiber-reinforced, 2 gallons	—	2 Gal	38.90	—	38.90

Stucco, masonry and concrete paint

Masonry and stucco paint. Acrylic latex paint for interior or exterior. Smooth, rough or textured masonry surfaces

	Craft@Hrs	Unit	Material	Labor	Total
Gallon	—	Gal	25.00	—	25.00
5 gallons	—	5 Gal	110.00	—	110.00
Elastomeric waterproofing, gallon	—	Gal	29.60	—	29.60
Elastomeric waterproofing, 5 gallons	—	5 Gal	133.00	—	133.00
Penetrating sealer, gallon	—	Gal	22.20	—	22.20
Penetrating sealer, 5 gallons	—	5 Gal	91.30	—	91.30

Concrete stain. Forms a tough film on properly prepared concrete patios, basements, pool decks, pillars, brick and sidewalks. Natural slate color. 100 percent acrylic.

	Craft@Hrs	Unit	Material	Labor	Total
Gallon	—	Gal	38.60	—	38.60
5 gallons	—	5 Gal	183.00	—	183.00

Gloss porch and floor enamel. 100 percent acrylic. Mildew-resistant. Recoat in 24 to 48 hours. Full cure in 30 days

	Craft@Hrs	Unit	Material	Labor	Total
Gloss, gallon	—	Gal	31.70	—	31.70
Low luster, gallon	—	Gal	30.70	—	30.70
Low luster, 5 gallons	—	5 Gal	134.00	—	134.00

Masonry waterproofer, for concrete, stucco and masonry, white when applied, dries clear

	Craft@Hrs	Unit	Material	Labor	Total
150 SF per gallon	—	Gal	34.30	—	34.30
750 SF per 5 gallons	—	5 Gal	136.00	—	136.00

	Craft@Hrs	Unit	Material	Labor	Total
Metal coatings					
Clean metal primer. White. For use on bare, lightly rusted or previously painted surfaces. Creates a strong surface for better topcoat adhesion and weather resistance.					
Quart	—	Qt	9.69	—	9.69
Rust-converting metal primer. Non-toxic, USDA and FDA approved. Works on clean or rusty steel, zinc galvanized metal, aluminum, tin and previously painted surfaces					
Quart	—	Qt	9.69	—	9.69
Gallon	—	Gal	36.00	—	36.00
Oil-based enamel. Industrial grade. Prevents rust, resists cracking, peeling, chipping, and fading. Scuff-, abrasion- and moisture-resistant. Lead-free. Not low volatile organic compound compliant.					
Quart	—	Qt	9.18	—	9.18
Gallon	—	Gal	42.40	—	42.40
Wood finishes					
Exterior opaque stain. For wood siding, decks and fences. Water repellent and mildew-resistant. Gallon covers 400 square feet.					
Acrylic latex, tint or white, gallon	—	Gal	35.50	—	35.50
Acrylic latex, tint or white, 5 gallons	—	5 Gal	161.00	—	161.00
Oil and latex, accent tint, gallon	—	Gal	32.70	—	32.70
Oil and latex, accent tint, 5 gallons	—	5 Gal	138.00	—	138.00
Exterior semi-opaque stain. For wood siding, decks and fences. Water repellent and mildew-resistant. Gallon covers 400 square feet.					
Oil-based stain, gallon	—	Gal	35.30	—	35.30
Oil-based stain, 5 gallons	—	5 Gal	145.00	—	145.00
Water-based stain, gallon	—	Gal	36.80	—	36.80
Water-based stain, 5 gallons	—	5 Gal	172.00	—	172.00
Exterior clear wood finish. For exterior wood doors, windows, furniture and trim. Gallon covers 300 to 400 square feet.					
Tung oil spar varnish, pint	—	Pt	11.20	—	11.20
Tung oil spar varnish, quart	—	Qt	20.90	—	20.90
Marine varnish, gloss or satin, quart	—	Qt	24.50	—	24.50
Urethane clear finish, gloss or satin, quart	—	Qt	16.30	—	16.30
Urethane clear finish, gloss or satin, gallon	—	Gal	46.50	—	46.50
Varathane® gloss, semi or satin, quart	—	Qt	15.30	—	15.30
Varathane® gloss, semi or satin, gallon	—	Gal	53.10	—	53.10
Waterproofing wood finish. For wood siding, decks and fences. Water repellent and mildew resistant. Clear or tinted. Gallon covers 300 to 400 square feet.					
Premium wood weatherproofing, gallon	—	Gal	26.60	—	26.60
Premium wood weatherproofing, 5 gallons	—	5 Gal	114.00	—	114.00
UV-resistant wood finish, gallon	—	Gal	20.40	—	20.40
UV-resistant wood finish, 5 gallons	—	5 Gal	91.00	—	91.00
Penetrating wood finish, gallon	—	Gal	33.70	—	33.70
Penetrating wood finish, 5 gallons	—	5 Gal	152.00	—	152.00
Log home gloss finish, clear or tint, gallon	—	Gal	36.50	—	36.50
Wood water sealer. Clear. Helps maintain wood's natural color. Protects against damage from water and sun. Provides a mildew-resistant coating. Gallon covers 225 to 325 square feet of smooth wood or as little as 125 square feet for a first application on rough-sawn wood.					
Thompson's WaterSeal, gallon	—	Gal	12.30	—	12.30
Thompson's WaterSeal, 5 gallons	—	5 Gal	57.20	—	57.20
Waterproofing wood protector, gallon	—	Gal	21.10	—	21.10
Waterproofing wood protector, 5 gallons	—	5 Gal	103.00	—	103.00

	Craft@Hrs	Unit	Material	Labor	Total
Wood preservative. Helps maintain wood's natural color. Protects against wood rot, warping, swelling, termite damage, mildew and moisture. Gallon covers 100 to 300 square feet when applied by brush or roller.					
Seasonite® new wood treatment, liter	—	Liter	19.00	—	19.00
Seasonite® new wood treatment, 2.5 liter	—	2.5 Ltr	40.50	—	40.50
Below ground wood preservative, quart	—	Qt	16.20	—	16.20
Below ground wood preservative, gallon	—	Gal	19.30	—	19.30
Below ground wood preservative, 5 gallon	—	5-Gal	86.90	—	86.90
Copper-Green® preservative, 13.5 ounces	—	Can	12.20	—	12.20
Copper-Green® preservative, gallon	—	Gal	24.60	—	24.60
Interior oil stain. Penetrates into unfinished or stripped wood to highlight and seal the grain.					
Tinted wiping stain, half pint	—	Ea	6.11	—	6.11
Tinted wiping stain, quart	—	Qt	7.14	—	7.14
Tinted wiping stain, gallon	—	Gal	28.60	—	28.60
Danish oil, pint	—	Pt	9.59	—	9.59
Danish oil, quart	—	Qt	12.10	—	12.10
Danish oil, gallon	—	Gal	34.20	—	34.20
Gel stain, quart	—	Qt	17.40	—	17.40
Interior water-based stain. Fast-drying and easy clean-up.					
White wash pickling stain, quart	—	Qt	33.70	—	33.70
White wash pickling stain, gallon	—	Gal	61.30	—	61.30
Tinting stain, half-pint	—	Ea	7.96	—	7.96
Tinting stain, quart	—	Qt	14.30	—	14.30
Paint specialties					
Asphalt-fiber roof and foundation coating, 75 SF per gallon on roof or concrete.					
Solvent type, 900 SF per 4 gallons	—	4 Gal	31.20	—	31.20
Driveway coating					
Acrylic driveway revitalizer (500-700 SF per 4 Gal)	—	4 Gal	42.90	—	42.90
Latex block filler (1,000 SF per 5 Gal)	—	5 Gal	118.00	—	118.00
Traffic paint, acrylic, 450 SF per gallon					
Blue, white, yellow or red, 1 gallon	—	Gal	25.00	—	25.00
Blue, white, yellow or red, 5 gallon	—	5 Gal	87.10	—	87.10
Swimming pool enamel					
Insul-X, rubber-based pool paint (350 SF per Gal)	—	Gal	68.00	—	68.00
Insul-X, acrylic, waterborne pool paint (250 SF per Gal)	—	Gal	50.10	—	50.10
Multi-surface waterproofer. For wood, brick, concrete, stucco and masonry. Can be applied to new pressure-treated wood. Paintable. Allows wood to weather naturally. Goes on milky white, dries clear.					
Aerosol can, 11.5 ounces	—	Can	5.09	—	5.09
Gallon	—	Gal	12.30	—	12.30
5 gallon	—	5 Gal	81.40	—	81.40
Paint and varnish remover, 150 SF per gallon					
Quart	—	Qt	14.00	—	14.00
Gallon	—	Gal	42.80	—	42.80

	Craft@Hrs	Unit	Material	Labor	Total
Spackling compound (vinyl-paste)					
Interior, 8-ounce	—	Ea	5.70	—	5.70
Wood filler paste	—	Pint	8.21	—	8.21
Thinners					
Acetone	—	Gal	18.00	—	18.00
Industrial thinner	—	Qt	8.15	—	8.15
Denatured alcohol	—	Qt	7.44	—	7.44
Mineral spirits	—	Gal	15.30	—	15.30
Paint thinner	—	Gal	12.90	—	12.90
Shellac or lacquer thinner	—	Gal	19.70	—	19.70
Turpentine	—	Qt	7.48	—	7.48

Painting, Labor Single coat applications except as noted. Not including equipment rental costs. These figures are based on hand work (roller, and brush where required) on residential jobs. Where spray equipment can be used to good advantage, reduce these costs 30% to 40%. Spray painting will increase paint requirements by 30% to 60%. Protection of adjacent materials is included in these costs, but little or no surface preparation is assumed. Per SF of surface area to be painted. Figures in parentheses show how much work should be done in an hour. For more complete coverage of painting costs, see *National Painting Cost Estimator* at http://CraftsmanSiteLicense.com/

	Craft@Hrs	Unit	Material	Labor	Total
Exterior surfaces, per coat, paint grade					
Door and frame, 6 sides (2.5 doors/hour)	PT@.400	Ea	—	15.30	15.30
Siding, smooth, wood (250 SF/hour)	PT@.004	SF	—	.15	.15
Siding, rough or shingle (200 SF/hour)	PT@.005	SF	—	.19	.19
Shutters (50 SF/hour)	PT@.020	SF	—	.76	.76
Stucco (300 SF/hour)	PT@.003	SF	—	.11	.11
Trim, posts, rails (20 LF/hour)	PT@.050	LF	—	1.91	1.91
Windows, including mullions, per SF of opening,					
one side only (67 SF/hour)	PT@.015	SF	—	.57	.57
Add for light sanding (330 SF/hour)	PT@.003	SF	—	.11	.11
Interior surfaces, per coat					
Ceiling, flat latex (250 SF/hour)	PT@.004	SF	—	.15	.15
Ceiling, enamel (200 SF/hour)	PT@.005	SF	—	.19	.19
Walls, flat latex (500 SF/hour)	PT@.002	SF	—	.08	.08
Walls, enamel (400 SF/hour)	PT@.003	SF	—	.11	.11
Baseboard (120 LF/hour)	PT@.008	LF	—	.31	.31
Bookcases, cabinets (90 SF/hour)	PT@.011	SF	—	.42	.42
Floors, wood					
Filling	PT@.007	SF	—	.27	.27
Staining	PT@.006	SF	—	.23	.23
Shellacking	PT@.006	SF	—	.23	.23
Varnishing	PT@.006	SF	—	.23	.23
Waxing, machine	PT@.006	SF	—	.23	.23
Polishing, machine	PT@.008	SF	—	.31	.31
Sanding, hand	PT@.012	SF	—	.46	.46
Sanding, machine	PT@.007	SF	—	.27	.27

	Craft@Hrs	Unit	Material	Labor	Total
Walls, brick, concrete and masonry					
Oiling and sizing (140 SF/hour)	PT@.007	SF	—	.27	.27
Sealer coat (150 SF/hour)	PT@.007	SF	—	.27	.27
Brick or masonry (165 SF/hour)	PT@.006	SF	—	.23	.23
Concrete (200 SF/hour)	PT@.005	SF	—	.19	.19
Concrete steps, 3 coats (38 SF/hour)	PT@.026	SF	—	.99	.99
Window frames and sash, using primer to mask glass and prime sash, topcoats as shown					
1 topcoat (100 SF/hour)	PT@.010	SF	—	.38	.38
2 topcoats (67 SF/hour)	PT@.015	SF	—	.57	.57
Score and peel primer from glass (peels from glass only)					
Per lite	PT@.020	Ea	—	.76	.76

Paint Spraying Equipment Rental Complete spraying outfit including paint cup, hose, spray gun.

	Day	Week	Month
8 CFM electric compressor	107.00	317.00	645.00
44 CFM gas-driven compressor	201.00	522.00	1,100.00
Professional airless, complete outfit	192.00	642.00	1,790.00

Painting, Subcontract, Rule of Thumb Including material, labor, equipment and the subcontractor's overhead and profit.

	Craft@Hrs	Unit	Material	Labor	Total
Typical subcontract costs per square foot of floor area for painting the interior and exterior of residential buildings, including only minimum surface preparation					
Economy, 1 or 2 coats, little brushwork	—	SF	—	—	3.08
Good quality, 2 or 3 coats	—	SF	—	—	7.15

Painting, Subcontract, Cost Breakdown The costs that follow are based on the area of the surface being prepared or painted. Typical subcontract costs, including labor, material, equipment and the subcontractor's overhead and profit.

Surface preparation, subcontract Work performed by hand.

	Craft@Hrs	Unit	Material	Labor	Total
Water blasting (pressure washing), using wheel-mounted portable 2,200 PSI pressure washer					
Light blast (250 SF per hour)	—	SF	—	—	.23
Most work (150 SF per hour)	—	SF	—	—	.38
Rough surface, grime (75 SF per hour)	—	SF	—	—	.72
Light cleaning to remove surface dust and stains					
Concrete or masonry surfaces	—	SF	—	—	.38
Gypsum or plaster surfaces	—	SF	—	—	.38
Wood surfaces	—	SF	—	—	.36
Normal preparation including scraping, patching and puttying					
Concrete or masonry surface					
Painted	—	SF	—	—	.38
Unpainted	—	SF	—	—	.30
Gypsum or plaster surfaces					
Painted	—	SF	—	—	.38
Unpainted	—	SF	—	—	.19
Metal surfaces, light sanding	—	SF	—	—	.18
Wood surfaces, surface preparation, subcontract					
Painted	—	SF	—	—	.36
Unpainted	—	SF	—	—	.18
Puttying	—	LF	—	—	1.64

	Craft@Hrs	Unit	Material	Labor	Total
Exterior painting, subcontract The estimates below are for hand work (brush and roller). Costs will be 15% to 30% lower when spray equipment can be used to good advantage. These costs include only minimum surface preparation. Add additional surface preparation, if required, from the figures above. Typical subcontract costs.					
Brick or concrete, including acrylic latex masonry primer and latex paint					
1 coat latex	—	SF	—	—	.96
2 coats latex	—	SF	—	—	1.33
Concrete floors, etch and epoxy enamel	—	SF	—	—	.55
Columns and pilasters, per coat	—	SF	—	—	.77
Cornices, per coat	—	SF	—	—	1.97
Doors, including trim, exterior only					
3 coats	—	Ea	—	—	63.20
2 coats	—	Ea	—	—	45.50
Downspouts and gutters					
Per coat	—	LF	—	—	1.60
Eaves					
No rafters, per coat	—	SF	—	—	.77
With rafters, per coat, brush	—	SF	—	—	1.33
Fences (gross area)					
Plain, 2 coats (per side)	—	SF	—	—	1.85
Plain, 1 coat (per side)	—	SF	—	—	1.11
Picket, 2 coats (per side)	—	SF	—	—	1.72
Picket, 1 coat (per side)	—	SF	—	—	.99
Lattice work					
1 coat 1 side, gross area	—	SF	—	—	.85
Metal, typical					
1 coat	—	SF	—	—	.69
2 coats	—	SF	—	—	1.20
Porch rail and balusters, per coat					
Gross area	—	SF	—	—	1.69
Handrail only	—	LF	—	—	1.16
Roofs, wood shingle					
1 coat stain plus 1 coat sealer					
Flat roof	—	SF	—	—	.80
4 in 12 pitch	—	SF	—	—	1.03
8 in 12 pitch	—	SF	—	—	1.08
12 in 12 pitch	—	SF	—	—	1.28
1 coat stain plus 2 coats sealer					
Flat roof	—	SF	—	—	1.27
4 in 12 pitch	—	SF	—	—	1.53
8 in 12 pitch	—	SF	—	—	1.65
12 in 12 pitch	—	SF	—	—	1.77
Siding, plain					
Sanding and puttying, typical	—	SF	—	—	.52
Siding and trim, 3 coats	—	SF	—	—	1.61
Siding and trim, 2 coats	—	SF	—	—	1.20
Trim only, 2 coats	—	SF	—	—	1.27
Trim only, 3 coats	—	SF	—	—	1.72
Siding, shingle, including trim					
2 coats oil paint	—	SF	—	—	1.23
1 coat oil paint	—	SF	—	—	.76
2 coats stain	—	SF	—	—	1.16
1 coat stain	—	SF	—	—	.67

	Craft@Hrs	Unit	Material	Labor	Total
Steel sash					
3 coats (per side)	—	SF	—	—	1.55
Stucco					
1 coat, smooth surface	—	SF	—	—	.77
2 coats, smooth surface	—	SF	—	—	1.17
1 coat, rough surface	—	SF	—	—	.85
2 coats, rough surface	—	SF	—	—	1.40
Window frames and sash, 3 coats					
Per side, one lite	—	Ea	—	—	48.30
Per side, add for each additional lite	—	Ea	—	—	2.69

Interior painting, subcontract The estimates below are for hand work (roller with some brush cut-in). Costs will be 15% to 30% lower when spray equipment can be used to good advantage. These costs include only minimum surface preparation. Add for additional surface preparation, if required, from the preceding pages. Typical subcontract costs.

	Craft@Hrs	Unit	Material	Labor	Total
Cabinets, bookcases, cupboards, per SF of total surface area					
3 coats, paint	—	SF	—	—	3.88
Stain, shellac, varnish or plastic	—	SF	—	—	3.98
Concrete block or brick					
Primer and 1 coat latex	—	SF	—	—	.90
Doors, including trim					
3 coats (per side)	—	SF	—	—	2.39
2 coats (per side)	—	SF	—	—	1.66
Plaster or drywall walls, latex. Add for ceilings from below					
Prime coat or sealer	—	SF	—	—	.49
1 coat smooth surface	—	SF	—	—	.58
1 coat rough surface	—	SF	—	—	.65
1 coat sealer, 1 coat flat					
Smooth surface	—	SF	—	—	.80
Rough surface	—	SF	—	—	1.07
1 coat sealer, 2 coats flat					
Smooth surface	—	SF	—	—	1.08
Rough surface	—	SF	—	—	1.42
1 coat sealer, 2 coats gloss or semi-gloss					
Smooth surface	—	SF	—	—	1.02
Rough surface	—	SF	—	—	1.40
Add for ceilings	—	%	—	—	45.0
Stairs, including risers					
3 coats paint	—	SF	—	—	2.72
Stain, shellac, varnish	—	SF	—	—	2.80
Woodwork, painting					
Priming	—	SF	—	—	.65
2 coats	—	SF	—	—	1.01
2 coats, top workmanship	—	SF	—	—	1.27
3 coats	—	SF	—	—	1.66
3 coats, top workmanship	—	SF	—	—	2.20
Woodwork, staining					
Apply stain	—	SF	—	—	.53
Filling (paste wood filler)	—	SF	—	—	.85
Sanding	—	SF	—	—	.50
Apply wax and polish	—	SF	—	—	.51

Paneling

	Craft@Hrs	Unit	Material	Labor	Total
Paneling See also Hardwood under Lumber and Hardboard.					
Solid plank paneling, unfinished, "V"-joint or T&G, costs include nails and waste.					
Cherry, 3-1/8" wide	BC@.050	SF	2.88	1.87	4.75
Red oak, 3-1/8" wide	BC@.050	SF	6.16	1.87	8.03
Hickory, 3-1/8" wide	BC@.050	SF	5.26	1.87	7.13
Maple, beaded, 3-1/8" wide	BC@.050	SF	5.26	1.87	7.13
Knotty pine, beaded, 3-1/2" wide	BC@.050	SF	1.54	1.87	3.41
Knotty pine, wainscot, 3-1/2" wide	BC@.050	SF	1.09	1.87	2.96
Cape Cod, beaded, 7" wide	BC@.050	SF	1.68	1.87	3.55
Pine, V-edge, 3-1/2" wide	BC@.050	SF	1.54	1.87	3.41
Plywood and hardboard paneling Prefinished 4' x 8' x 1/8" panels with hardboard back. Costs include nails, adhesive and 5% waste.					
Harbor white	BC@.030	SF	1.35	1.12	2.47
Vintage maple	BC@.030	SF	1.32	1.12	2.44
Traditional oak	BC@.030	SF	1.30	1.12	2.42
Honey oak	BC@.030	SF	1.30	1.12	2.42
Cherry oak	BC@.030	SF	1.30	1.12	2.42
Beadboard, v-groove, white	BC@.030	SF	.74	1.12	1.86
Aquatile, water-resistant	BC@.030	SF	.82	1.12	1.94
Aquatile, water-resistant with mosaic insert	BC@.030	SF	.95	1.12	2.07
Hardwood plywood paneling Unfinished 4' x 8' panels. Costs include nails, adhesive and 5% waste					
Birch plywood paneling					
1/8" x 4' x 8'	BC@.032	SF	.76	1.20	1.96
1/4" x 4' x 8'	BC@.032	SF	.94	1.20	2.14
1/2" x 4' x 8'	BC@.040	SF	1.54	1.50	3.04
3/4" x 4' x 8'	BC@.042	SF	1.89	1.57	3.46
Oak plywood paneling					
1/4" x 4' x 8'	BC@.032	SF	2.06	1.20	3.26
1/2" x 4' x 8'	BC@.040	SF	1.70	1.50	3.20
3/4" x 4' x 8', red oak	BC@.042	SF	1.89	1.57	3.46
Cedar hardwood paneling, natural					
1/4" x 4' x 8'	BC@.032	SF	1.11	1.20	2.31
3/8" x 4' x 8'	BC@.040	SF	1.26	1.50	2.76
1/2" x 4' x 8'	BC@.040	SF	2.01	1.50	3.51
5/8" x 4' x 8'	BC@.042	SF	2.32	1.57	3.89
3/4" x 4' x 8'	BC@.042	SF	2.69	1.57	4.26
Golden Virola paneling					
1/4" x 2' x 2'	BC@.032	SF	1.24	1.20	2.44
1/4" x 2' x 4'	BC@.032	SF	1.24	1.20	2.44
1/4" x 4' x 4'	BC@.032	SF	.82	1.20	2.02
1/4" x 4' x 8'	BC@.032	SF	.88	1.20	2.08
3/8" x 4' x 8'	BC@.040	SF	1.20	1.50	2.70
1/2" x 2' x 2'	BC@.040	SF	1.89	1.50	3.39
5/8" x 4' x 8'	BC@.042	SF	1.68	1.57	3.25
3/4" x 2' x 2'	BC@.042	SF	2.65	1.57	4.22
Maple paneling					
1/2" x 4' x 8', C-2 grade	BC@.040	SF	1.92	1.50	3.42
3/4" x 4' x 8', B-3 grade	BC@.042	SF	3.19	1.57	4.76
3/4" x 4' x 8,' maple/birch	BC@.042	SF	1.89	1.57	3.46

	Craft@Hrs	Unit	Material	Labor	Total
Vinyl-clad hardboard paneling Vinyl-clad film over hardboard, 4' x 8' x 1/4" panels. Costs include nails, adhesive and 5% waste.					
White or Aegean Gold	BC@.032	SF	1.49	1.20	2.69
Blue marble	BC@.032	SF	.56	1.20	1.76
Harvest pattern	BC@.032	SF	1.15	1.20	2.35
FRP wall and ceiling paneling Fiberglass-reinforced plastic, textured, 0.09" thick, Class C flame spread, 24" x 48" panels. Includes fasteners, adhesive and 5% waste.					
White or almond	BC@.032	SF	1.12	1.20	2.32
Bamboo tambour paneling 4' x 8' panels. Costs include nails, adhesive and 5% waste.					
Unfinished natural	BC@.032	SF	4.26	1.20	5.46
Prefinished natural	BC@.032	SF	4.86	1.20	6.06
Unfinished amber	BC@.032	SF	4.26	1.20	5.46
Prefinished amber	BC@.032	SF	4.86	1.20	6.06
Raw amber	BC@.032	SF	4.26	1.20	5.46
Raw green	BC@.032	SF	4.26	1.20	5.46
Raw black	BC@.032	SF	4.26	1.20	5.46
Z-brick paneling Non-ceramic mineral brick-like veneer. Interior or exterior. Coverage per carton is 3-1/2 square feet, 5% added for waste. Include the cost for adhesive from below.					
Red classic brick, 2-1/4" x 8" x 7/16"	BC@.050	SF	6.15	1.87	8.02
Inca decorative brick, 2-1/4" x 8" x 7/16"	BC@.050	SF	5.46	1.87	7.33
Used brick (Inca), 2-1/4" x 8" x 5/16"	BC@.050	SF	5.46	1.87	7.33
Old Chicago brick, 2-3/8" x 8-1/8" x 5/16"	BC@.050	SF	5.46	1.87	7.33
Liberty grey brick, 2-1/4" x 8" x 7/16"	BC@.050	SF	6.15	1.87	8.02
Wheat brick, 2-1/4" x 8" x 7/16"	BC@.050	SF	5.46	1.87	7.33
Burnt sienna brick, 2-1/4" x 8" x 7/16"	BC@.050	SF	6.83	1.87	8.70
Mesa beige brick, 2-1/4" x 8" x 7/16"	BC@.050	SF	6.83	1.87	8.70
Z-Ment mortar adhesive	BC@.012	SF	1.74	.45	2.19
Z-Ment mortar adhesive, 16 to 20 SF per Gal	—	Gal	31.30	—	31.30
Paving, Subcontract Small areas such as walks and driveways around residential buildings. Typical costs including material, labor, equipment and subcontractor's overhead and profit. No substrate preparation included. Use $1,800 as a minimum job charge.					
Asphalt paving, including oil seal coat, small or irregular areas (driveways)					
2" asphalt wear course	—	SF	—	—	2.81
3" asphalt wear course	—	SF	—	—	3.16
4" asphalt wear course	—	SF	—	—	4.05
6" stone base, compacted and graded	—	SF	—	—	1.75
8" stone base, compacted and graded	—	SF	—	—	2.28
Asphalt seal coats					
Applied with broom or squeegee	—	SF	—	—	.47
Fog seal, thin layer of diluted SS1H oil	—	SF	—	—	.20
Seal and sand					
Thin layer of oil with sand finish	—	SF	—	—	.47
Simco "walk-top"					
or other quick-dry applications					
Creamy oil	—	SF	—	—	.46
Brick paving					
On concrete, grouted, laid flat, including concrete base	—	SF	—	—	17.10

	Craft@Hrs	Unit	Material	Labor	Total
On concrete, laid solid on edge, 8" x 2-1/4" exposure, no grouting,					
including concrete base	—	SF	—	—	18.60
On sand bed, laid flat	—	SF	—	—	13.20
On sand bed, 8" x 2-1/4" exposure	—	SF	—	—	14.90
Concrete (including fine grading) paving					
3" concrete, unreinforced	—	SF	—	—	3.88
4" concrete, unreinforced	—	SF	—	—	4.65
4" concrete, mesh reinforcing	—	SF	—	—	4.73
4" concrete, seeded aggregate finish	—	SF	—	—	8.16
Add for colored concrete, most colors	—	SF	—	—	.56
Excavate to 18" below final grade, remove spoil, set edge forms, import Class 2 base, fine grade, set and tie 1/2" rebar 18" o.c. each way, pump 3,250 p.s.i. 6" concrete, score and broom finish concrete	—	SF	—	—	12.20

Porous paving systems Thin-walled HDPE plastic rings connected by an interlocking geogrid structure, installed on a porous base course for residential applications. Rings transfer loads from the surface to the grid structure to an engineered course base. Installed on a prepared base. www.invisiblestructures.com

	Craft@Hrs	Unit	Material	Labor	Total
Porous paving system with grass filler. Grid rolled out over base course and seeded with grass mixture. Includes fertilizer and soil polymer mix for spreading over base.					
3.3' wide by 33' long rolls	BL@.003	SF	2.82	.09	2.91
Add for 1" sand fill	BL@.001	SF	.05	.03	.08
Porous paving system with gravel fill. Grid rolled out over base course and covered with decorative fill gravel.					
3.3' wide by 33' long rolls	BL@.004	SF	2.74	.12	2.86
Add for 1" gravel fill	BL@.001	SF	.11	.03	.14

Plastering, Subcontract See also Lathing. Typical costs including material, labor, equipment and subcontractor's overhead and profit.

	Craft@Hrs	Unit	Material	Labor	Total
Acoustical plaster					
Including brown coat, 1-1/4" total thickness	—	SY	—	—	40.20
Plaster on concrete or masonry, with bonding agent					
Gypsum plaster, 1/2" sanded	—	SY	—	—	21.00
Plaster on interior wood frame walls, no lath included					
Gypsum plaster, 7/8", 3 coats	—	SY	—	—	31.60
Keene's cement finish, 3 coats	—	SY	—	—	34.70
Cement plaster finish, 3 coats	—	SY	—	—	36.60
Gypsum plaster, 2 coats, tract work	—	SY	—	—	28.80
Add for ceiling work	—	%	—	—	15.0
Plaster for tile					
Scratch coat	—	SY	—	—	15.40
Brown coat and scratch coat	—	SY	—	—	23.30
Exterior plaster (stucco)					
Walls, 3 coats, 7/8", no lath included					
Textured finish	—	SY	—	—	21.50
Float finish	—	SY	—	—	25.40
Dash finish	—	SY	—	—	28.30
Add for soffits	—	%	—	—	15.0
Portland cement plaster, including metal lath, exterior, 3 coats, 7/8" on wood frame					
Walls	—	SY	—	—	36.40
Soffits	—	SY	—	—	41.90
Deduct for paper back lath	—	SY	—	—	-.15

Plumbing Fixtures and Equipment Costs are for good to better quality fixtures and trim installed with the accessories listed. All vitreous china, enameled steel, cast iron, and fiberglass fixtures are white except as noted. Colored acrylic fiberglass fixtures will cost about 6% more. Colored enameled steel, cast iron, or vitreous fixtures will cost about 25% more. No rough plumbing included. Rough plumbing is the drain, waste and vent (DWV) piping and water supply piping that isn't exposed when construction is complete. See costs for rough plumbing at the end of this section. Minimum quality fixtures and trim will cost 10% to 20% less. Deluxe fixtures will cost much more. Installation times assume standard quality work and uncomplicated layouts. For expanded coverage of plumbing cost estimates, see the *National Plumbing & HVAC Estimator* at http://CraftsmanSiteLicense.com/

Bathtubs

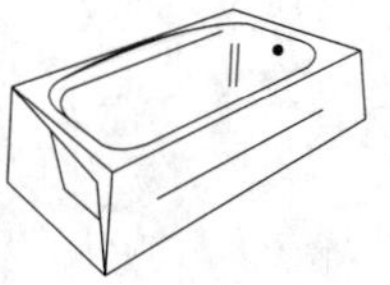

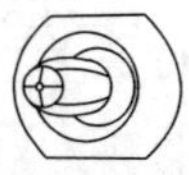

	Craft@Hrs	Unit	Material	Labor	Total
Acrylic fiberglass one-piece bathtub and shower, 5' L, 32" W, 72" H. Includes $300 allowance for polished chrome pop-up drain/overflow. Mixing valve, tub filler, and 2.5 GPM shower head					
Acrylic tub, shower and trim	P1@4.50	Ea	547.00	166.00	713.00
Enameled cast iron bathtub, 5' L, 32" W, 15" H for recessed installation. Includes $300 allowance for polished chrome pop-up drain/overflow, mixing valve, tub filler and 2.5 GPM shower head					
Cast iron tub and trim	P1@3.50	Ea	708.00	129.00	837.00
Enameled steel bathtub, 5' L, 30" W, 15" H for recessed installations. With full wall flange, and $300 allowance for pop-up drain/overflow, chrome mixing valve, tub filler, shower flange and 2.5 GPM shower head					
Enameled steel tub and trim	P1@1.40	Ea	502.00	51.60	553.60
Enameled steel bathtub with chrome grab rails, 5' L, 32" W, 16" H. Includes $160 allowance for polished chrome pop-up drain/overflow, mixing valve, tub filler, and 2.5 GPM shower head					
Enameled steel tub with handrail and trim	P1@5.25	Ea	931.00	194.00	1,125.00
Recessed whirlpool bathtub with built-in 1.25 HP 115-volt motor and pump, integral drain. With eight multidirectional and adjustable jets. Acrylic with fiberglass reinforcement. White. Includes $300 allowance for polished chrome pop-up drain/overflow, mixing valve, tub filler, and 2.5 GPM shower head					
Whirlpool tub and trim	P1@5.50	Ea	1,210.00	203.00	1,413.00
Add for electrical connection	—	Ea	—	—	240.00

Indoor whirlpool tub Acrylic fiberglass drop-in whirlpool bathtub, includes $400 allowance for chrome pop-up drain/overflow, mixing valve and tub filler, with pump and air actuator switch. Add for the electrical connection and tub-support system

	Craft@Hrs	Unit	Material	Labor	Total
6 jets, 1.25 HP, 60" x 36" x 20"	P1@4.00	Ea	1,610.00	148.00	1,758.00
6 jets, 1.25 HP, 60" x 36" x 20", corner	P1@4.00	Ea	1,590.00	148.00	1,738.00
8 jets, 2 HP, 72" x 42" x 22"	P1@5.00	Ea	2,270.00	184.00	2,454.00
8 jets, 2 HP, 72" x 42" x 22", corner	P1@5.00	Ea	2,790.00	184.00	2,974.00
Add for polished brass Roman tub filler	P1@1.50	Ea	300.00	55.30	355.30
Add for chrome Roman tub hand shower	P1@1.50	Ea	200.00	55.30	255.30
Add for auxiliary in-line water heater	P1@2.00	Ea	178.00	73.80	251.80
Add for non-load-bearing tub apron	P1@1.00	Ea	290.00	36.90	326.90
Add for electrical connection	—	Ea	—	—	237.00
Whirlpool tub support system, including 150 pounds per square foot pre-tested bracing joists, galvanized cross members, vertical structural 2" pipe bracing, vertical support plate and tub grout pad.					
1,500 pound capacity (60" x 36" x 20")	B1@8.00	Ea	510.00	271.00	781.00
2,500 pound capacity (72" x 42" x 22")	B1@8.00	Ea	616.00	271.00	887.00

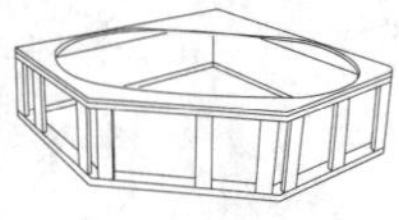

Hot tub Whirlpool type, illuminated, corner or central, 24" platform mounted, with water temperature regulating heater, whirlpool re-circulating pump, 2" diameter drain, filter and cleanout, custom plywood frame reinforcement, underfloor joist cross-bracing and joist support bracing, subfloor PEX piping to hot water and cold water lines, with valves, control wiring and ground fault protection. NSF, Underwriters Laboratories, and CSA rating.

	Craft@Hrs	Unit	Material	Labor	Total
56-gallon tub and trim	—	Ea	5,470.00	—	5,470.00
85-gallon tub and trim	—	Ea	6,560.00	—	6,560.00
110-gallon tub and trim	—	Ea	7,070.00	—	7,070.00

	Craft@Hrs	Unit	Material	Labor	Total
Prepping and sealing of floor pad	B9@8.00	Ea	—	264.00	264.00
Installation of drain	P1@2.00	Ea	330.00	73.80	403.80
Installation of PEX piping and valves	P1@2.00	Ea	209.00	73.80	282.80
Cutting and assembly of wood frame	B1@16.0	Ea	388.00	542.00	930.00
Final electrical connections to circulation pump and submerged tub lighting	CE@4.00	Ea	173.00	242.00	415.00

Walk-in Doored Bathtub, ADA-compliant, aerated hydrotherapy type, step-in with watertight sealing door, reinforced fiberglass, illuminated, corner or stand-alone, floor flush-mounted, with submersible seat, handrails and non-slip integral floor and seat surfaces, handheld flexible shower fixture with switchover valve, water temperature regulating 1,500 watt heater, whirlpool re-circulating pump, 2" diameter drain, filter and cleanout, under-floor joist cross-bracing and joist support vertical bracing, sub-floor PEX piping to hot water and cold water lines, with valves, control wiring and ground fault protection. NSF, Underwriters Laboratories, Americans with Disabilities Act, and CSA ratings.

	Craft@Hrs	Unit	Material	Labor	Total
55" long x 30" wide x 40" high (tub only)	—	Ea	2,000.00	—	2,000.00
Prepping and sealing of floor pad	B9@8.00	Ea	—	264.00	264.00
Installation of drain	P1@2.00	Ea	324.00	73.80	397.80
Installation of PEX piping, pump and valves	P1@2.00	Ea	209.00	73.80	282.80
Mounting of tub, cross-joists, vertical column support bracing, and leveling	B1@16.0	Ea	926.00	542.00	1,468.00
Final electrical connections to circulation pump, submerged tub lighting and grounding	CE@4.00	Ea	170.00	242.00	412.00

Acrylic shower stalls

Acrylic fiberglass shower stall, 36" W, 36" D, 72" H, includes mixing valve, shower head and door

	Craft@Hrs	Unit	Material	Labor	Total
Fiberglass 32" shower stall and trim	P1@4.15	Ea	1,120.00	153.00	1,273.00

Acrylic fiberglass shower stall, 48" W, 35" D, 72" H with integral soap dishes, grab bar and drain, mixing valve, shower head and door

	Craft@Hrs	Unit	Material	Labor	Total
Fiberglass 48" shower stall and trim	P1@4.65	Ea	1,240.00	172.00	1,412.00

Acrylic fiberglass shower stall, 60" W, 35" D, 72" H with integral soap dishes, grab bar, drain, mixing valve, shower head and door

	Craft@Hrs	Unit	Material	Labor	Total
Fiberglass 60" shower stall and trim	P1@4.80	Ea	1,340.00	177.00	1,517.00
Roll-in wheelchair stall and trim	P1@5.40	Ea	1,890.00	199.00	2,089.00
Add for shower cap (roof)	P1@.500	Ea	194.00	18.40	212.40

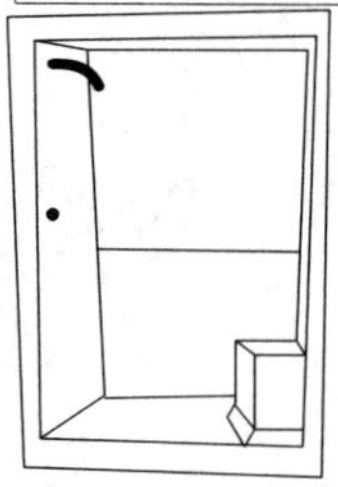

Tile shower stalls, subcontract

Framing, plumbing and hot mop for a tiled corner stall shower. Includes framing for L-access dam under door, corner niche and floor slope to center drain, hang and tape Dens Shield tile backer, connect valve, shower head and drain to existing rough-in piping, hot mop shower floor to 10" height. Subcontract. Add the cost of tile, glass enclosure, valve and shower head.

	Craft@Hrs	Unit	Material	Labor	Total
36" x 36" corner shower stall	—	Ea	—	—	2,720.00

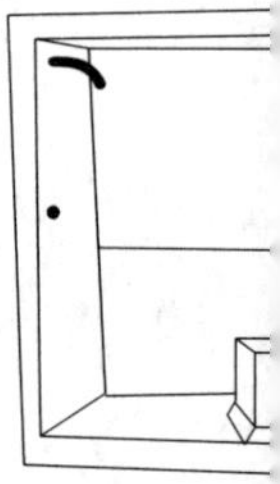

Tile for a corner stall shower. Includes 60 SF of 12" x 24" matte finish wall tile with bull nose edges, 14 SF of floor tile and corner shelf. Stacked joint pattern with 1/8" sealed grout joints. Subcontract

	Craft@Hrs	Unit	Material	Labor	Total
36" x 36" corner shower stall	—	Ea	—	—	2,700.00

Glass enclosure for a corner stall shower. Hinged door. Frameless 3/8" clear or rain glass. Subcontract

	Craft@Hrs	Unit	Material	Labor	Total
36" x 36" corner shower stall	—	Ea	—	—	1,400.00

Framing and plumbing for a tiled bathtub/shower. Includes alignment of framing and drain for the tub, frame a built-in wall niche, tub installation, hang and tape Dens Shield tile backer on three walls above the tub, connect valve, shower head and drain to existing rough-in piping, installation of valve, shower head and drain. Includes a 5' porcelain tub. Add the cost of tile, glass enclosure, valve and shower head.

	Craft@Hrs	Unit	Material	Labor	Total
5' bathtub/shower	—	Ea	—	—	2,510.00

Tile for three walls above a bathtub/shower. Includes 80 SF of 12" x 24" matte finish wall tile with 11' of accent border tile and a wall niche. Stacked joint pattern with 1/8" sealed grout joints.

	Craft@Hrs	Unit	Material	Labor	Total
5' bathtub/shower	—	Ea	—	—	2,240.00

Glass enclosure for a tiled bathtub/shower. Sliding, by-passing doors. Frameless 1/4" clear or rain glass.

	Craft@Hrs	Unit	Material	Labor	Total
5' bathtub/shower	—	Ea	—	—	465.00

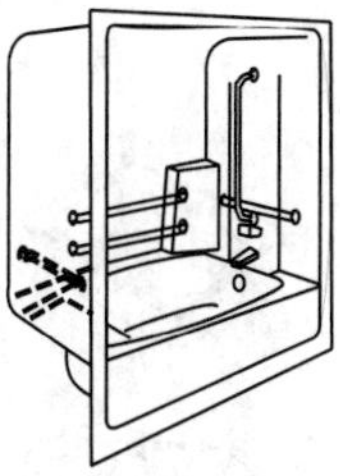

	Craft@Hrs	Unit	Material	Labor	Total
Handicapped tub and shower					
Handicapped and elderly access fiberglass tub and shower, 60" x 30" H with integral soap dishes, seat and four grab bars, body washer shower, polished chrome pop-up drain/overflow, mixing valve and tub filler					
Handicapped shower-tub and trim	P1@4.75	Ea	5,010.00	175.00	5,185.00
Add for shower curtain rod	P1@.572	Ea	26.50	21.10	47.60
Water closets					
Floor-mounted, residential tank type 1.6 gal. vitreous china toilet, valved closet supply, and toilet seat with cover					
Floor-mount tank type water closet and trim	P1@2.10	Ea	211.00	77.50	288.50
Floor-mounted, back outlet, residential tank type 1.6 gal. vitreous china toilet, valved closet supply, elongated bowl, and toilet seat with cover					
Floor-mount, back outlet tank type WC and trim	P1@2.35	Ea	331.00	86.70	417.70
Wall-mounted, tank type 1.6 gal. vitreous china toilet, toilet carrier, valved closet supply, elongated bowl, and toilet seat with cover					
Wall-mount, tank type WC, carrier and trim	P1@3.65	Ea	426.00	135.00	561.00
One piece, 1.6 gal. floor-mounted vitreous china toilet including toilet seat and valved closet supply					
One-piece water closet and trim	P1@2.35	Ea	341.00	86.70	427.70
Floor-mounted vitreous china 1.6 gal. pressure assist toilet, including toilet seat and valved closet supply					
Pressure assist water closet and trim	P1@2.25	Ea	228.00	83.00	311.00
Add for elongated bowl models	—	Ea	67.10	—	67.10
Bidets Standard vitreous china bidet with floor-mounted hardware, hot and cold valved supplies and polished chrome faucet					
Vitreous china bidet, vertical spray, and trim	P1@2.50	Ea	432.00	92.20	524.20
Vitreous china bidet, over the rim, and trim	P1@2.50	Ea	642.00	92.20	734.20
Lavatories					
Oval self-rimming enameled steel lavatory, hot and cold valved supplies, single lever faucet and pop-up drain fitting and trap assembly					
Oval self-rim steel lavatory and trim	P1@2.50	Ea	150.00	92.20	242.20
Oval, self-rimming vitreous china lavatory, hot and cold valved supplies, single lever faucet and pop-up drain fitting and trap assembly					
Oval self-rim china lavatory and trim	P1@2.00	Ea	215.00	73.80	288.80
Oval, pedestal-mounted vitreous china lavatory, hot and cold valved supplies, single lever faucet and pop-up drain fitting and trap					
Oval pedestal-mount china lavatory and trim	P1@2.50	Ea	301.00	92.20	393.20
Rectangular, pedestal-mount vitreous china lavatory, hot and cold valved supplies, single lever faucet and pop-up drain fitting and trap					
Rectangular pedestal china lavatory and trim	P1@2.50	Ea	517.00	92.20	609.20
Rectangular, self-rimming vitreous china lavatory, hot and cold valved supplies, single lever faucet and pop-up drain fitting and trap assembly					
Counter-type rectangular china lavatory & trim	P1@2.00	Ea	466.00	73.80	539.80
Rectangular, wall-hung vitreous china lavatory, hot and cold valved supplies, single lever faucet and pop-up drain fitting and trap assembly					
Wall-hung china lavatory and trim	P1@2.50	Ea	238.00	92.20	330.20
Wheelchair access lavatory, wall-hung vitreous china, with carrier insulated hot and cold valved supplies, gooseneck faucet with wrist handles and pop-up drain and insulated offset trap					
Wall-hung wheelchair lavatory and trim	P1@2.75	Ea	284.00	101.00	385.00
Bar sinks Includes $115 allowance for chrome faucet, hot and cold water valved supplies and P-trap assembly.					
Acrylic bar sink, 15" L, 15" W, 6" D, self-rimming.					
Acrylic bar sink and trim	P1@2.00	Ea	262.00	73.80	335.80
Enameled cast iron bar sink, 13" L, 15" W, 7" D, undermount					
Enameled cast iron bar sink and trim	P1@2.25	Ea	476.00	83.00	559.00
Stainless steel bar sink, 15" L, 15" W, 5", drop-in					
Stainless steel bar sink and trim	P1@2.00	Ea	184.00	73.80	257.80

Plumbing Fixtures and Equipment

	Craft@Hrs	Unit	Material	Labor	Total
Kitchen sinks Includes $160 allowance for chrome faucet and sprayer, P-trap assembly and valved supplies.					
Single bowl, enameled cast iron, self-rimming, 25" L, 22" W, 8" D					
Single bowl cast iron sink and trim	P1@1.75	Ea	368.00	64.60	432.60
Single bowl, stainless steel, self-rimming sink, 25" L, 22" W, 10" D					
Single bowl stainless sink and trim	P1@2.00	Ea	299.00	73.80	372.80
Double bowl, enameled cast iron, self-rimming sink, 33" L, 22" W, 8" D					
Double bowl cast iron sink and trim	P1@2.00	Ea	613.00	73.80	686.80
Double bowl, stainless steel, self-rimming sink, 32" L, 22" W, 8" D					
Double bowl stainless sink and trim	P1@2.25	Ea	283.00	83.00	366.00
Triple bowl, stainless steel, self-rimming sink, 43" L, 22" W					
Triple bowl stainless sink and trim	P1@2.75	Ea	732.00	101.00	833.00
Laundry sinks					
Enameled cast iron laundry sink, 48" L, 20" D, 14" D, wall-mounted faucet with integral stops and vacuum breaker, strainer and P-trap assembly					
Cast iron laundry sink and trim	P1@2.76	Ea	2,600.00	102.00	2,702.00
Acrylic laundry sink, 25" L, 22" D, 12" D, deck-mounted faucet valved supplies, and P-trap assembly					
Acrylic laundry sink and trim	P1@2.00	Ea	398.00	73.80	471.80
Service sinks					
Enameled cast iron service sink, 22" L, 18" D, wall mounted faucet with integral stops and vacuum breaker, strainer and cast iron P-trap					
Cast iron service sink and trim	P1@3.00	Ea	640.00	111.00	751.00
Garbage disposers					
Small, 1/3 HP kitchen disposer, including fittings, no waste pipe					
1/3 HP kitchen disposer	P1@2.00	Ea	164.00	73.80	237.80
Standard, 5/8 HP kitchen disposer, including fittings, no waste pipe					
5/8 HP kitchen disposer	P1@2.00	Ea	254.00	73.80	327.80
Standard, 3/4 HP kitchen disposer, including fittings, no waste pipe					
3/4 HP kitchen disposer	P1@2.00	Ea	209.00	73.80	282.80
Septic system, 3/4 HP kitchen disposer, including fittings, no waste pipe					
3/4 HP kitchen disposer	P1@2.00	Ea	313.00	73.80	386.80
Large capacity, 1 HP kitchen disposer, including fittings, no waste pipe					
1 HP kitchen disposer	P1@2.15	Ea	406.00	79.30	485.30
Add for electrical connection and switch	BE@1.00	Ea	35.90	40.60	76.50
Dishwashers Under-counter installation, connected to existing drain. Add the cost of electrical work, if required.					
Deluxe, stainless steel, steam pre wash	P1@2.40	Ea	1,640.00	88.50	1,728.50
Standard, 5-cycle	P1@2.40	Ea	749.00	88.50	837.50
Economy, 3 wash levels	P1@2.40	Ea	339.00	88.50	427.50
Add for electrical connection	BE@1.00	Ea	36.00	40.60	76.60
Water heaters See also Accessories, water heater for safety pans, earthquake strapping, stands and connections					
Gas water heaters. Includes labor to connect to existing water supply piping and gas line. 6 year warranty. Labor column includes cost of installing heater and making the gas and water connections, but not the cost of the supply lines.					
30 gallon tall, 30,000 BTU, 30.3 GPH	P1@1.90	Ea	499.00	70.10	569.10
40 gallon short, 34,000 BTU, 36.4 GPH	P1@2.00	Ea	419.00	73.80	492.80
40 gallon tall, 36,000 BTU, 38.4 GPH	P1@2.00	Ea	399.00	73.80	472.80
50 gallon tall, 40,000 BTU, 40.4 GPH	P1@2.15	Ea	599.00	79.30	768.30

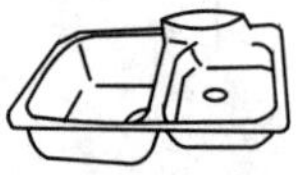

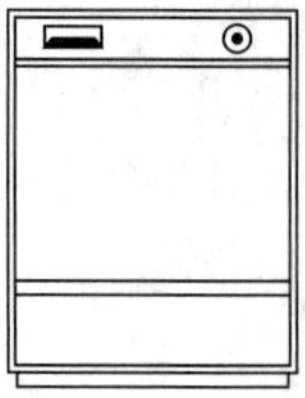

	Craft@Hrs	Unit	Material	Labor	Total
75 gallon tall, 75,100 BTU, 75.8 GPH	P1@3.50	Ea	965.00	129.00	1,094.00
40 gallon, 40 MBtu, power vent	P1@2.00	Ea	837.00	73.80	910.80
50 gallon, 42 MBtu, power vent	P1@2.15	Ea	966.00	79.30	1,045.30
Add for power vent electrical connection	BE@1.00	Ea	33.70	40.60	74.30
Tankless gas water heaters. Includes labor to connect to existing water supply piping and gas line. 6 year warranty. Labor column includes cost of installing the heater and making the gas and water connections but not the cost of the supply lines.					
6.4 GPM, 150 MBTU	P1@4.15	Ea	704.00	153.00	857.00
8.4 GPM, 180 MBTU	P1@4.15	Ea	799.00	153.00	952.00
9.5 GPM, 200 MBTU	P1@4.15	Ea	1,020.00	153.00	1,173.00
Add for Cat III stainless horizontal vent kit	P1@2.00	Ea	142.00	73.80	215.80
Add for remote temperature control	BE@1.00	Ea	33.70	40.60	74.30
Add for electrical connection	BE@1.00	Ea	36.00	40.60	76.60
Propane water heaters. Includes labor to connect to existing water supply piping. 6 year warranty. Flammable vapor ignition resistant. Labor column includes cost of installing heater and making the water connections, but not the cost of the supply lines.					
30 gallon, 30 MBtu	P1@2.00	Ea	639.00	73.80	712.80
40 gallon, 32 MBtu	P1@2.00	Ea	569.00	73.80	642.80
50 gallon, 36 MBtu	P1@2.15	Ea	749.00	79.30	828.30
40 gallon, 40 MBtu, power vent	P1@2.00	Ea	1,040.00	73.80	1,113.80
50 gallon, 36 MBtu, power vent	P1@2.15	Ea	1,090.00	79.30	1,169.30
Add for power vent electrical connection	BE@1.00	Ea	33.60	40.60	74.20
Electric water heaters. Includes labor to connect to existing water supply piping. Add for the cost of supply piping.					
30 gallon 30 GPH, 6 year	P1@2.15	Ea	348.00	79.30	427.30
40 gallon 53 GPH, 6 year	P1@2.15	Ea	449.00	79.30	528.30
50 gallon 63 GPH, 6 year	P1@2.25	Ea	379.00	83.00	462.00
50 gallon 55 GPH, 9 year	P1@2.15	Ea	528.00	79.30	607.30
50 gallon 63 GPH, 12 year	P1@2.25	Ea	609.00	83.00	692.00
85 gallon 87 GPH, 12 year	P1@3.50	Ea	1,310.00	129.00	1,439.00
105 gallon 108 GPH, 9 year	P1@3.50	Ea	1,550.00	129.00	1,679.00
40 gallon tall, heat pump technology, 12 year	P1@3.50	Ea	1,970.00	129.00	2,099.00
50 gallon tall, heat pump technology, 12 year	P1@4.00	Ea	2,500.00	148.00	2,648.00
Thermal expansion tank. Controls thermal expansion of water in domestic hot water systems					
2 gallon, polypropylene lined steel	P1@.300	Ea	50.60	11.10	61.70
4 gallon, polypropylene lined steel	P1@.300	Ea	87.70	11.10	98.80
Solar water heating system Water storage tanks compatible with most closed-loop solar water heating systems, heat transfer by insulated all-copper heat exchanger, collector feed and return fittings. With pressure-temperature relief valve and back-up 4,500 watt electric heating element. Rheem.					
80 gallon	P1@8.44	Ea	945.00	311.00	1,256.00
Passive thermosiphon domestic hot water system with integral 80 gallon water tank, retrofitted to an existing single story structure, with 5 year limited warranty					
Passive solar water heater system (retrofit)	P1@6.50	Ea	3,700.00	240.00	3,940.00
Active solar hot water system for 100 or 120 gallon water supply tank, fitted with automatic drain retrofitted to existing single story, single family unit, 5 year warranty					
Active solar water heater system (retrofit)	—	Ea	—	—	5,950.00
Add for strengthening existing roof structure under solar collectors					
Per SF of roof strengthened	—	SF	—	—	1.22

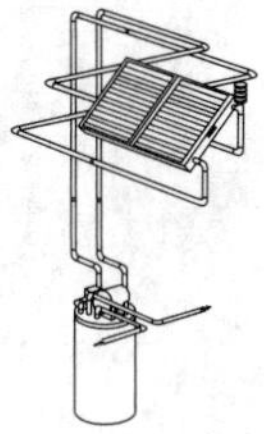

	Craft@Hrs	Unit	Material	Labor	Total
Active solar hot water system for new one-story home					
Including design and engineering (new work)	—	Ea	—	—	5,150.00
For designs requiring special cosmetic treatment					
Add for concealment of pipe, collectors, etc.	—	%	—	—	15.5
Solar pool heater, active heater for pools with freeze-tolerant collector, roof-mounted					
Per SF of collector area	—	SF	—	—	7.04

Water softening system 24 volt electronic controls, demand-driven regeneration, 5,200 grams per gallon efficiency, 200 pound salt capacity, with bypass valve and drain tubing, 2 hour regeneration time.

	Craft@Hrs	Unit	Material	Labor	Total
30,400 grain capacity, 95 grams/gallon max hardness removal, 5 grams/gallon max iron reduction, 23 to 30 gallon regeneration	P1@4.00	Ea	374.00	148.00	522.00
40,000 grain capacity, 100 grams/gallon max hardness removal, 7 grams/gallon max iron reduction, 40 to 50 gallon regeneration	P1@4.00	Ea	447.00	148.00	595.00

Water distillation unit Potable central household water system type, Polar Bear 200-L or equal. Underwriters Laboratories and CSA approved, Water Quality Association and certified performance tested to U.S. Environmental Protection Agency Water Quality Act testing standards. Permanent basement mounting, all-electric, 2 parts per million total dissolved solids warranted purity. 220/208/240 volts, 22 amps, 5,300 watts electrical rating. For residential single- and multi-family applications. Includes process condition and flow monitor and 75 gallon tank. Add $500.00 for optional auto-drain kit.

	Craft@Hrs	Unit	Material	Labor	Total
50 gal/day distilled water unit	—	Ea	8,040.00	—	8,040.00
Prepping and pouring of pad	P1@2.00	Ea	158.00	73.80	231.80
Mounting of unit	P1@4.00	Ea	—	148.00	148.00
Piping of unit	P1@3.00	Ea	210.00	111.00	321.00
Wiring of controls	CE@4.00	Ea	158.00	242.00	400.00
Piping of vents, pipe and drains	P1@1.00	Ea	158.00	36.90	194.90
Startup and inspection	P1@1.00	Ea	—	36.90	36.90

Plumbing System Components

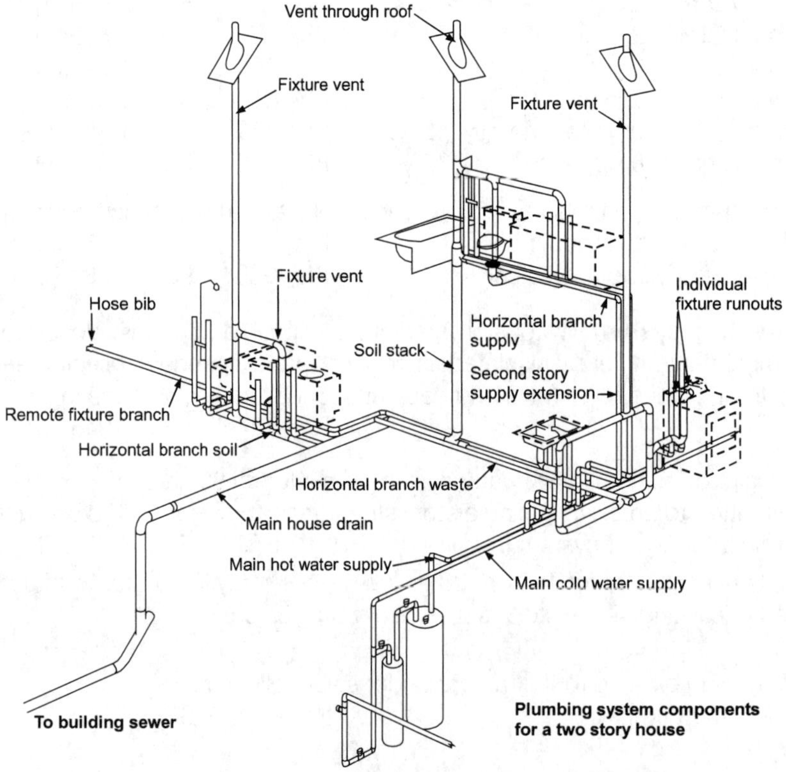

Plumbing system components for a two story house

	Craft@Hrs	Unit	Material	Labor	Total

Whole House Plumbing Rough-In

Rough plumbing is the drain, waste and vent (DWV) piping and water supply piping that isn't visible when construction is complete. Rough plumbing costs vary with the number of fixtures and length of the pipe runs. The figures in this section show rough plumbing costs for a typical single-family home using plastic drainage and copper water supply materials. No plumbing fixtures, equipment or their final connections are included in these costs. See Plumbing Fixtures and Equipment for fixture and fixture connection costs. These costs include the subcontractor's markup. Add the general contractor's markup when applicable. For more complete information on plumbing and piping costs, see *National Plumbing & HVAC Estimator* at http://CraftsmanSiteLicense.com/

	Craft@Hrs	Unit	Material	Labor	Total
Single story homes					
Hot and cold potable water rough-in	P1@15.0	Ea	917.00	553.00	1,470.00
Drainage and venting rough-in	P1@20.0	Ea	504.00	738.00	1,242.00
Single story, total plumbing rough-in	P1@35.0	Ea	1,421.00	1,291.00	2,712.00
Two story homes					
Hot and cold potable water rough-in	P1@20.0	Ea	1,350.00	738.00	2,088.00
Drainage and venting rough-in	P1@25.0	Ea	622.00	922.00	1,544.00
Two story, total plumbing rough-in	P1@45.0	Ea	1,972.00	1,660.00	3,632.00

Plumbing Fixture Rough-In Assemblies Includes labor and material costs for the installation of a typical water supply, drain and vent piping system on new residential construction projects. For renovation projects, add 20% to labor and 10% to material costs to allow for connection to existing service lines and working within existing spaces. Add the cost of any demolition or removal required before the new rough-in can be installed. No plumbing fixtures or fixture connections are included in these costs. See Plumbing Fixtures and Equipment on the following pages for fixture and fixture connection costs. These costs include the subcontractor's markup. Add the general contractor's mark-up.

3-piece washroom group rough-in assembly Includes the water supply, drain and vent piping to connect all three fixtures (tub, toilet and sink) in the group to one common waste, one vent, one hot and one cold water supply line that will be connected to each respective main service drain, vent or supply pipe. These figures are based on the main service piping being within 5' of the fixture group. Add the cost of main water supply, drain and vent lines to which the fixture group will connect.

Hot and cold water supply: 26' of 1/2" type M hard copper pipe (straight lengths), including associated soldered wrought copper fittings, solder, flux, and pipe clips.

Drains and vents: 5' of 3" drainage pipe on the water closet, 38' of 1-1/2" pipe serving all other drains and vents. 43' total plastic drain and vent pipe, with associated fittings, glue and strapping. Make additional allowances for final fixture connections. (See Plumbing Fixtures and Equipment for fixture and connection costs.)

	Craft@Hrs	Unit	Material	Labor	Total
Hot and cold water supply	P1@2.50	Ea	22.70	92.20	114.90
Drains and vents	P1@3.35	Ea	28.30	124.00	152.30
Total washroom group rough-in assembly	P1@5.85	Ea	51.00	216.20	267.20
Add for shower head rough-in	P1@.350	Ea	5.23	12.90	18.13

Kitchen sink rough-in assembly

Hot and cold water supply: 10' of 1/2" type M hard copper pipe, (straight lengths), including associated soldered wrought copper fittings, solder, flux, and pipe clips. Drains and vents: 15' of 1-1/2" plastic drain and vent pipe with associated fittings, glue and strapping. Make additional allowance for final fixture connection. (See Plumbing Fixtures and Equipment for fixture and connection costs.)

	Craft@Hrs	Unit	Material	Labor	Total
Hot and cold water supply	P1@.750	Ea	8.71	27.70	36.41
Drains and vents	P1@1.00	Ea	8.09	36.90	44.99
Total kitchen sink rough-in assembly	P1@1.75	Ea	16.80	64.60	81.40

Plumbing Rough-In Assemblies

	Craft@Hrs	Unit	Material	Labor	Total
Laundry tub and washing machine rough-in assembly					
Hot and cold water supply: 16' of 1/2" type M hard copper pipe (straight lengths), including associated fittings, solder, flux, and pipe clips. Drains and vents: 21' of 1-1/2" plastic drain and vent pipe with associated fittings, glue and strapping.					
Hot and cold water supply	P1@1.00	Ea	13.90	36.90	50.80
Drains and vents	P1@1.35	Ea	11.30	49.80	61.10
Total tub & washer rough-in assembly	P1@2.35	Ea	25.20	86.70	111.90
Hot water tank rough-in assembly					
Hot and cold water supply: 10' of 3/4" type M hard copper pipe (straight lengths), including associated soldered wrought copper fittings, solder, flux, and pipe clips					
Hot and cold water supply	P1@.500	Ea	14.90	18.40	33.30
Add for 3/4" isolation valve	P1@.250	Ea	23.00	9.22	32.22
Water softener rough-in assembly					
Hot and cold water supply: 10' of 3/4" type M hard copper pipe (straight lengths), including associated soldered wrought copper fittings, solder, flux, and pipe clips. Regeneration drain: 10' of Schedule 40 PVC, including associated fittings, glue and strapping					
Cold water supply and return	P1@.500	Ea	14.90	18.40	33.30
Regeneration drain	P1@.500	Ea	2.56	18.40	20.96
Natural gas appliance rough-in assembly					
Includes labor and material to install and test 12' of 3/4" Schedule 40 black steel piping, associated 150 lb malleable iron fittings and a plug valve to serve a typical residential gas fired appliance. Add for the natural gas main supply line running through the building, meter connection and final connection to the appliance. Assembly assumes the appliance is within 5' of the main supply line.					
Gas fired domestic hot water heater	P1@.650	Ea	27.10	24.00	51.10
Gas fired hot water heating boiler	P1@.650	Ea	27.10	24.00	51.10
Gas fired forced air furnace	P1@.650	Ea	27.10	24.00	51.10
Gas fired stove and oven	P1@.650	Ea	27.10	24.00	51.10
Gas fired clothes dryer	P1@.650	Ea	27.10	24.00	51.10
Gas main, 1" dia. with fittings and hangers	P1@.120	LF	11.70	4.43	16.13
Gas meter connection (house side only)	P1@.750	Ea	63.00	27.70	90.70
Natural gas appliance connections					
Includes labor and material to connect and test a typical residential natural gas fired appliance. Make additional allowances for the natural gas main supply line running through the building, the appliance gas supply rough-in and labor to set the appliance in place.					
1/2" FIP x 1/2" MIP coated stainless steel					
12" L	P1@.650	Ea	11.20	24.00	35.20
24" L	P1@.650	Ea	12.00	24.00	36.00
36" L	P1@.650	Ea	13.90	24.00	37.90
48" L	P1@.650	Ea	22.10	24.00	46.10
60" L	P1@.650	Ea	22.70	24.00	46.70
3/4" FIP x 3/4" MIP coated stainless steel					
24" L	P1@.650	Ea	26.60	24.00	50.60
36" L	P1@.650	Ea	22.90	24.00	46.90
48" L	P1@.650	Ea	37.20	24.00	61.20

	Craft@Hrs	Unit	Material	Labor	Total

Central hot water heating system

Includes 150' of 1-1/2" insulated supply and return mains, 150' of 3/4" insulated branch piping, 10 radiant baseboard convectors (50'), a 110 Mbh high efficiency gas fired hot water boiler, a circulation pump, electric controls, installed and tested. (Based on 1,200 SF of heated space)

	Craft@Hrs	Unit	Material	Labor	Total
Distribution system	P1@46.0	Ea	1,150.00	1,700.00	2,850.00
Distribution system (second floor)	P1@16.0	Ea	496.00	590.00	1,086.00
Boiler, pump and controls	P1@16.0	Ea	5,770.00	590.00	6,360.00
Radiant baseboard and valves	P1@16.0	Ea	3,520.00	590.00	4,110.00
Radiant baseboard and valves (2nd floor)	P1@12.0	Ea	2,360.00	443.00	2,803.00
Total hot water heating system, 1 story	P1@78.0	Ea	10,440.00	2,880.00	13,320.00
Total hot water heating system, 2 story	P1@106	Ea	13,296.00	3,913.00	17,209.00

Plumbing Access Doors for plumbing, primer coated steel 14 gauge door, 18 gauge frame, with cam lock, for masonry, drywall, tile, wall or ceiling. L&L Louvers

Standard, wall or ceiling

	Craft@Hrs	Unit	Material	Labor	Total
8" x 8"	SW@.500	Ea	18.61	21.10	39.71
12" x 12"	SW@.500	Ea	21.80	21.10	42.90
14" x 14"	SW@.500	Ea	31.60	21.10	52.70
16" x 16"	SW@.500	Ea	33.30	21.10	54.40
18" x 18"	SW@.500	Ea	36.50	21.10	57.60
22" x 22"	SW@.500	Ea	49.50	21.10	70.60
22" x 30"	SW@.500	Ea	60.20	21.10	81.30
24" x 24"	SW@.500	Ea	49.90	21.10	71.00
24" x 36"	SW@.500	Ea	72.20	21.10	93.30
30" x 30"	SW@.500	Ea	98.50	21.10	119.60
Add for cylinder lock	—	Ea	13.10	—	13.10
Add for louvers	—	%	150.0	—	—
Add for fire rating, non-insulated	—	%	400.0	—	—
Add for fire rating and insulated	—	%	500.0	—	—
Add for stainless steel, 304-2B	—	%	400.0	—	—

Polyethylene Film, Clear or Black Material costs include 5% for waste and 10% for laps.

Labor shown is for installation on grade.

	Craft@Hrs	Unit	Material	Labor	Total
4 mil (.004" thick)					
50 LF rolls, 3' to 20' wide	BL@.002	SF	.07	.06	.13
6 mil (.006" thick)					
50 LF rolls, 3' to 40' wide	BL@.002	SF	.08	.06	.14
Add for installation on walls, ceilings and roofs, tack stapled, typical	BL@.001	SF	—	.03	.03

Railings, Steel, Prefabricated See also Ornamental Iron. Porch or step rail, site fitted.

2'-10" high, 6" OC 1/2" solid twisted pickets, 4' or 6' sections.

	Craft@Hrs	Unit	Material	Labor	Total
1" x 1/2" rails	RI@.171	LF	4.81	6.73	11.54
1" x 1" rails	RI@.180	LF	6.64	7.08	13.72
Add for newel post 3' H with hardware	—	Ea	18.30	—	18.30
Add lamb's tongue for end post	—	Ea	6.66	—	6.66

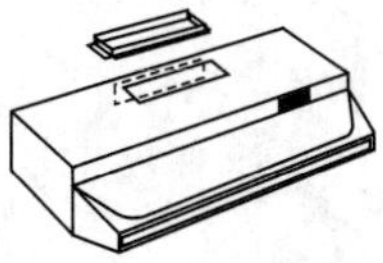

Range Hoods Material costs are for ducted or ductless range hood only, no electrical wiring included. Add for ducting and electrical connection. Labor costs are for installation of range hood only. No carpentry work included. All models are steel construction with baked enamel finish in various colors. Economy ducted range hood. Under-cabinet-mounted 190 CFM (cubic feet per minute) exhaust. 6.0 sones. 7" duct connector. 18" deep x 6" high. Washable charcoal filter with replaceable charcoal filter pad. Uses 75-watt lamp. Polymeric lens.

	Craft@Hrs	Unit	Material	Labor	Total
24" or 30" wide, enamel finish	SW@1.42	Ea	95.90	59.90	155.80
24" or 30" wide, stainless steel	SW@1.42	Ea	141.00	59.90	200.90

Range Hoods

	Craft@Hrs	Unit	Material	Labor	Total
36" wide, enamel finish	SW@1.42	Ea	95.90	59.90	155.80
36" wide, stainless steel	SW@1.42	Ea	141.00	59.90	200.90
42" wide, enamel finish	SW@1.42	Ea	99.00	59.90	158.90
42" wide, stainless steel	SW@1.42	Ea	144.00	59.90	203.90
Add for ducted hood with a duct damper	—	Ea	16.00	—	16.00

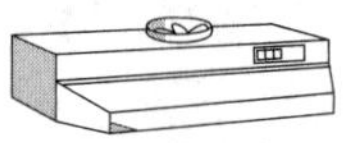

Standard quality ducted range hood. Under-cabinet-mounted 190 CFM (cubic feet per minute) 3-speed blower. 3.5 sones. Either vertical or horizontal 3-1/4" x 10" duct, 7" round duct. Powder-coated 22 gauge steel. 18" deep x 6" high. Uses one 40-watt incandescent lamp.

24" or 30" wide, ducted, black	SW@1.42	Ea	138.00	59.90	197.90
24" or 30" wide, ducted, stainless	SW@1.42	Ea	244.00	59.90	303.90
36" wide, ducted, black	SW@1.42	Ea	153.00	59.90	212.90
36" wide, ducted, stainless	SW@1.42	Ea	223.00	59.90	282.90
42" wide, ducted, black	SW@1.42	Ea	164.00	59.90	223.90
42" wide, ducted, stainless	SW@1.42	Ea	255.00	59.90	314.90
Add for ductless range hood	—	Ea	53.00	—	53.00

Better quality range hood, Allure III NuTone. Under-cabinet-mounted 400 CFM (cubic feet per minute). 0.4 sones at 100 CFM. Teflon-coated bottom pan. Dual halogen lamps. Sensor detects excessive heat and adjusts vent speed. 20" deep x 7-1/4" high. Four ducting options: 3 1/4" x 10" horizontal or vertical vent, 7" round vertical vent or non-ducted.

30" wide, polyester finish	SW@1.42	Ea	518.00	59.90	577.90
30" wide, stainless steel finish	SW@1.42	Ea	565.00	59.90	624.90
36" wide, polyester finish	SW@1.42	Ea	527.00	59.90	586.90
36" wide, stainless steel finish	SW@1.42	Ea	580.00	59.90	639.90
42" wide, polyester finish	SW@1.42	Ea	516.00	59.90	575.90
42" wide, stainless steel finish	SW@1.42	Ea	597.00	59.90	656.90
Add for filter for ducted application	—	Ea	52.00	—	52.00
Add for filter for non-ducted application	—	Ea	27.70	—	27.70

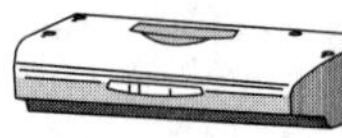

Wall-mount range hood, Ballista NuTone. Stainless steel finish with hood-mounted blower. Three-speed control. Dual 20-watt halogen bulbs. Adjusts to fit under 8' to 10' ceiling. Stainless steel grease filter. Built-in backdraft damper. 20" deep. 33" to 54" high.

30" wide, 450 CFM	SW@2.50	Ea	1,710.00	105.00	1,815.00
36" wide, 450 CFM	SW@2.50	Ea	1,730.00	105.00	1,835.00
48" wide, 900 CFM	SW@2.50	Ea	1,930.00	105.00	2,035.00
Deduct for exterior blower	—	Ea	– 456.00	—	– 456.00

Ceiling-hung range hood, Provisa NuTone. Stainless steel finish with hood-mounted blower. Three-speed control. Four 20-watt halogen bulbs. Telescopic flue adjusts to fit under 8' to 9' ceiling. Stainless steel grease filter. Built-in backdraft damper. 27" deep. 33" high.

40" wide, 900 CFM	SW@3.50	Ea	3,310.00	148.00	3,458.00
Deduct for exterior blower	—	Ea	– 320.00	—	– 320.00

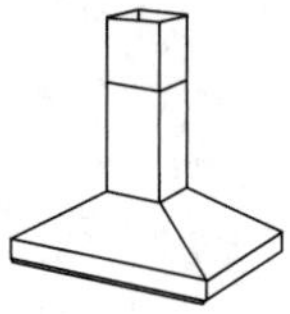

Custom range hood power package. Exhaust system components installed in a custom-built range hood 24" to 30" above the cooling surface. Stainless steel. With variable speed control, filters and halogen or incandescent lighting. Bulbs not included. No ductwork included. Add the cost of a decorative enclosure, ducting and electrical connection.

700 CFM, dual blowers, 7" duct, 1.5 to 4.6 sones

30" wide x 22" deep	SW@1.42	Ea	549.00	59.90	608.90
32" wide x 22" deep	SW@1.42	Ea	596.00	59.90	655.90
36" wide x 28" deep	SW@1.42	Ea	678.00	59.90	737.90
42" wide x 28" deep	SW@1.42	Ea	746.00	59.90	805.90
48" wide x 28" deep	SW@1.42	Ea	845.00	59.90	904.90

	Craft@Hrs	Unit	Material	Labor	Total
1,300 CFM, dual blowers, twin 7" ducts, 1.5 to 4.6 sones					
30" wide x 22" deep	SW@1.42	Ea	888.00	59.90	947.90
32" wide x 22" deep	SW@1.42	Ea	970.00	59.90	1,029.90
36" wide x 28" deep	SW@1.42	Ea	1,110.00	59.90	1,169.90
42" wide x 28" deep	SW@1.42	Ea	1,210.00	59.90	1,269.90
48" wide x 28" deep	SW@1.42	Ea	1,370.00	59.90	1,429.90
Range splash plate, Broan. Mounts behind range with screws.					
30" x 24", reversible white or almond	SW@.165	Ea	27.00	6.96	33.96
30" x 24", stainless steel	SW@.165	Ea	40.50	6.96	47.46
36" x 24", reversible white or almond	SW@.165	Ea	29.30	6.96	36.26
36" x 24", stainless steel	SW@.165	Ea	46.20	6.96	53.16

Ranges, Built-In Good to better quality counter-mounted cooktops. Labor costs are for carpentry installation only. Add for gas and electric runs and venting. Vented cooktops require exhaust venting. See Range Hoods above.

	Craft@Hrs	Unit	Material	Labor	Total
Gas, pilot-free ignition					
Four sealed burners, 30" wide x 21" deep					
Baked enamel top	P1@1.92	Ea	352.00	70.80	422.80
Stainless steel top	P1@1.92	Ea	394.00	70.80	464.80
Five sealed burners, 36" wide x 21" deep					
Stainless steel top	P1@1.92	Ea	765.00	70.80	835.80
Ceramic top	P1@1.92	Ea	1,180.00	70.80	1,250.80
Electric					
Conventional coil type cooktop					
Two coils, 21" wide	BE@.903	Ea	364.00	36.70	400.70
Four coils, 30" wide, black	BE@.903	Ea	412.00	36.70	448.70
Four coils, 30" wide, stainless	BE@.903	Ea	534.00	36.70	570.70
Four element smooth glass-ceramic cooktop, 30" wide					
6" and 9" elements	BE@.903	Ea	582.00	36.70	618.70
6"/9"/12" elements	BE@.903	Ea	881.00	36.70	917.70
6" and 12" elements, vented	BE@.903	Ea	1,310.00	36.70	1,346.70
Five element smooth glass-ceramic cooktop, 36" wide					
6"/9"/12" elements	BE@.903	Ea	879.00	36.70	915.70
6"/9"/12" elements, touch controls	BE@.903	Ea	1,350.00	36.70	1,386.70
Five element induction smooth glass-ceramic cooktop, 36" wide					
6"/7"/8"/11" elements, touch controls	BE@.903	Ea	1,960.00	36.70	1,996.70

Ovens, Built-In Material costs are for good to better quality 30" wide built-in self-cleaning ovens with stainless steel exterior and a clear window (except as noted). Labor costs are for setting the oven in a prepared opening and making the electrical connection. Add the cost of electric runs.

	Craft@Hrs	Unit	Material	Labor	Total
Single oven, black on black	BE@1.67	Ea	1,090.00	67.90	1,157.90
Single oven, stainless steel front	BE@1.67	Ea	1,280.00	67.90	1,347.90
Single thermal oven, stainless steel	BE@1.67	Ea	2,080.00	67.90	2,147.90
Double convection/microwave oven	BE@1.67	Ea	2,360.00	67.90	2,427.90
Double convection/thermal oven	BE@1.67	Ea	2,670.00	67.90	2,737.90
Double thermal oven, GE Monogram series	BE@1.67	Ea	4,740.00	67.90	4,807.90
30" warming drawer, stainless steel	BE@1.00	Ea	1,490.00	40.60	1,530.60

Roofing Rule of Thumb Typical subcontract prices per square (100 SF). Based on a 1,500 to 2,000 SF job not over two stories above ground level. Add the cost of flashing and deck preparation, if required. See detailed labor and material costs in the following sections. Many communities restrict use of wood roofing products.

	Craft@Hrs	Unit	Material	Labor	Total
Asphalt shingles (class A, 235 Lb.)	—	Sq	—	—	147.00
Composition shingles (class C, 310 Lb.)	—	Sq	—	—	392.00
Built-up roof, 3-ply and gravel	—	Sq	—	—	264.00

Roofing

	Craft@Hrs	Unit	Material	Labor	Total
Cedar shingles, 16", 5" exposure	—	Sq	—	—	771.00
Split cedar shakes, 24", fire treated	—	Sq	—	—	960.00
Clay mission tile	—	Sq	—	—	372.00
Concrete tile	—	Sq	—	—	404.00

Built-Up Roofing Installed over existing suitable substrate. Add the cost of equipment rental (the kettle) and consumable supplies (mops, brooms, gloves). Typical cost for equipment and consumable supplies is $15 per 100 square feet applied.

	Craft@Hrs	Unit	Material	Labor	Total
Type 1: 2-ply felt and 1-ply 90-pound cap sheet, including 2 plies of hot mop asphalt					
Base sheet, nailed down, per 100 SF	R1@.250	Sq	5.78	9.00	14.78
Hot mop asphalt, 30 lbs. per 100 SF	R1@.350	Sq	16.30	12.60	28.90
Asphalt felt, 15 lbs. per 100 SF	R1@.100	Sq	5.78	3.60	9.38
Hot mop asphalt, 30 lbs. per 100 SF	R1@.350	Sq	16.30	12.60	28.90
Mineral surface					
90 lb. cap sheet, per 100 SF	R1@.200	Sq	54.90	7.20	62.10
Type 1, total per 100 SF	**R1@1.25**	**Sq**	**99.06**	**45.00**	**144.06**
Type 2: 3-ply asphalt, 1-ply 30 lb felt, 2 plies 15 lb felt, 3 coats hot mop asphalt and gravel					
Asphalt felt, 30 lbs. nailed down	R1@.300	Sq	11.60	10.80	22.40
Hot mop asphalt,					
30 lbs. per 100 SF	R1@.350	Sq	16.30	12.60	28.90
Asphalt felt, 15 lbs. per 100 SF	R1@.100	Sq	5.78	3.60	9.38
Hot mop asphalt,					
30 lbs. per 100 SF	R1@.350	Sq	16.30	12.60	28.90
Asphalt felt, 15 lbs. per 100 SF	R1@.100	Sq	5.78	3.60	9.38
Hot mop asphalt,					
30 lbs. per 100 SF	R1@.350	Sq	16.30	12.60	28.90
Gravel, 400 lbs. per 100 SF	R1@.600	Sq	35.00	21.60	56.60
Type 2, total per 100 SF	**R1@2.15**	**Sq**	**107.06**	**77.40**	**184.46**
Type 3: 4-ply asphalt, 4 plies 15 lb felt including 4 coats hot mop and gravel					
Base sheet, nailed down, per 100 SF	R1@.250	Sq	5.78	9.00	14.78
Hot mop asphalt,					
30 lbs. per 100 SF	R1@.350	Sq	16.30	12.60	28.90
Asphalt felt, 15 pound, per 100 SF	R1@.100	Sq	5.78	3.60	9.38
Hot mop asphalt,					
30 lbs. per 100 SF	R1@.350	Sq	16.30	12.60	28.90
Asphalt felt, 15 pound, per 100 SF	R1@.100	Sq	5.78	3.60	9.38
Hot mop asphalt,					
30 lbs. per 100 SF	R1@.350	Sq	16.30	12.60	28.90
Asphalt felt, 15 lbs. per 100 SF	R1@.100	Sq	5.78	3.60	9.38
Hot mop asphalt,					
30 lbs. per 100 SF	R1@.350	Sq	16.30	12.60	28.90
Gravel, 400 lbs. per 100 SF	R1@.600	Sq	35.00	21.60	56.60
Type 3, total per 100 square feet	**R1@2.55**	**Sq**	**123.32**	**91.80**	**215.12**

Roof Coatings and Adhesives

	Craft@Hrs	Unit	Material	Labor	Total
Roofing asphalt, 100 lb carton					
145 to 165 degree and Type III (low melt)	—	Ea	49.40	—	49.40
185 degree, certified (high melt) — Type IV	—	Ea	39.80	—	39.80
Asphalt emulsion coating, (35 SF per gallon)					
4.75 gallons	—	Ea	40.30	—	40.30
Wet patch roof cement, Western Colloid #101, (12.5 SF per gallon at 1/8" thick)					
0.9 gallon	—	Ea	20.10	—	20.10
3.3 gallons	—	Ea	50.40	—	50.40
Roof patch elastomeric, seals vertical and horizontal seams (67 SF per gallon)					
0.9 gallon	—	Ea	40.30	—	40.30

Obtaining Roof Area from Plan Area

Rise	Factor	Rise	Factor
3"	1.031	8"	1.202
3½"	1.042	8½"	1.225
4"	1.054	9"	1.250
4½"	1.068	9½"	1.275
5"	1.083	10"	1.302
5½"	1.100	10½"	1.329
6"	1.118	11"	1.357
6½"	1.137	11½"	1.385
7"	1.158	12"	1.414
7½"	1.179		

When a roof has to be figured from a plan only, and the roof pitch is known, the roof area may be fairly accurately computed from the table above. The horizontal or plan area (including overhangs) should be multiplied by the factor shown in the table opposite the rise, which is given in inches per horizontal foot. The result will be the roof area.

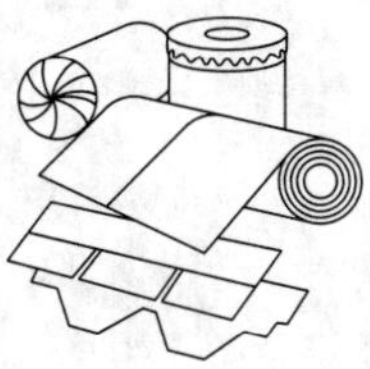

	Craft@Hrs	Unit	Material	Labor	Total
Elastomeric white roof coating, non-fibered, white acrylic (100 SF per gallon per coat)					
0.9 gallon	—	Ea	25.20	—	25.20
4.75 gallons	—	Ea	65.50	—	65.50
Fibered aluminum roof coating, non-asbestos fiber, (50 SF per gallon on built-up or smooth surface, 65 SF per gallon on metal surface)					
0.9 gallon	—	Ea	34.30	—	34.30
4.75 gallons	—	Ea	87.00	—	87.00
Silicon roof coating, Gaco, (50 SF per gallon using two coats)					
1 gallon	—	Ea	72.50	—	72.50
5 gallons	—	Ea	247.00	—	247.00
Flashing compound, Western Colloid #106, (12.5 SF per gallon at 1/8" thick)					
0.9 gallon	—	Ea	14.40	—	14.40
2.8 gallons	—	Ea	37.30	—	37.30
4.75 gallons	—	Ea	50.10	—	50.10
Lap cement, Henry #108, (280 LF at 2" lap per gallon)					
0.9 gallon	—	Ea	17.00	—	17.00
4.75 gallons	—	Ea	69.20	—	69.20
Plastic roof cement (12-1/2 SF at 1/8" thick per gallon)					
0.9 gallon	—	Ea	15.10	—	15.10
4.75 gallons	—	Ea	60.50	—	60.50
Non-fibered roof coating, (80 SF per gallon on masonry surfaces or roofing, 100 SF per gallon on metal surfaces)					
0.9 gallon	—	Ea	17.60	—	17.60
4.75 gallons	—	Ea	44.40	—	44.40
Reflective fibered aluminum-flake roof coating (50 SF per gallon on built-up roof or smooth surface, Henry 558 70 SF per gallon on metal surface)					
0.9 gallon	—	Ea	32.20	—	32.20
4.75 gallons	—	Ea	104.00	—	104.00
Wet-dry premium roof cement (12-1/2 SF per gallon at 1/8" thick)					
10.3 oz cartridge for caulking gun	—	Ea	2.79	—	2.79
0.9 gallon	—	Ea	12.80	—	12.80
4.75 gallons	—	Ea	44.40	—	44.40
Cotton mat reinforcing for roof coatings					
6" x 150' roll	—	Ea	25.80	—	25.80
Polyester fabric reinforcing for roof coatings, Henry					
3 oz per SY, 36" x 375'	—	Sq	26.60	—	26.60

Roofing Materials

	Craft@Hrs	Unit	Material	Labor	Total
Mineral surface roll roofing. Roll covers 1 square (100 square feet).					
90-pound fiberglass mat reinforced	R1@.200	Sq	47.50	7.20	54.70
GAF Mineral Guard	R1@.200	Sq	47.50	7.20	54.70
SBS-modified bitumen, Flintlastic	R1@.200	Sq	73.40	7.20	80.60
Add for mopping in 30-pound hot asphalt	R1@.350	Sq	16.30	12.60	28.90
Roofing felt. Asphalt saturated. Per square. 15-pound roll covers 400 square feet. 30-pound roll covers 200 square feet. Nailed down.					
15-pound, ASTM compliant	R1@.140	Sq	5.75	5.04	10.79
30-pound, ASTM-D226	R1@.150	Sq	11.50	5.40	16.90
Add for mopping in 30-pound hot asphalt	R1@.350	Sq	16.30	12.60	28.90
Fiberglass ply IV roll roofing. ASTM D-2178 Type IV. 500 square foot roll.					
Per 100 square feet	R1@.140	Sq	22.40	5.04	27.44
Add for mopping in 30-pound hot asphalt	R1@.350	Sq	16.30	12.60	28.90

	Craft@Hrs	Unit	Material	Labor	Total
Fiberglass base sheet ASTM D-4601. 300 square foot roll. Nailed down					
Per 100 square feet	R1@.300	Sq	17.70	10.80	28.50
Modified bitumen adhesive. Rubberized. Use to adhere SBS modified bitumen membranes and rolled roofing. Blind nailing cement. Brush grade.					
5 gallons	—	Ea	78.90	—	78.90
Cold process and lap cement. Bonds plies of built-up roofing and gravel to bare spots on existing gravel roof. Restores severely worn roof. Gallon covers 50 square feet.					
0.9 gallon	—	Ea	14.10	—	14.10
4.75 gallons	—	Ea	44.10	—	44.10
Cold-Ap® built-up roofing cement, Henry. Bonds layers of conventional built-up roofing or SBS base and cap sheets. Replaces hot asphalt in built-up roofing. For embedding polyester fabric, gravel and granules. Not recommended for saturated felt. ASTM D3019 Type III. Two gallons cover 100 square feet.					
0.9 gallon	—	Ea	18.20	—	18.20
4.75 gallons	—	Ea	70.90	—	70.90
Cold-process and lap cement. ASTM D3019 Type III. Two gallons cover 100 square feet.					
5 gallons	—	Ea	56.50	—	56.50

Composition Roofing Shingles Material costs include 5% waste. Labor costs include roof loading and typical cutting and fitting for roofs of average complexity. Class A shingles have the highest fire rating.

	Craft@Hrs	Unit	Material	Labor	Total
3-tab asphalt fiberglass® shingles, Three bundles per square (100 square feet). 5" exposure, Class A fire rating. 60 MPH wind resistance.					
20 year, no algae-resistance	R1@1.83	Sq	57.30	65.90	123.20
25-30 year, algae-resistant	R1@1.83	Sq	85.30	65.90	151.20
Architectural grade laminated shingles, Owens Corning, GAF and similar. Three bundles per square (100 square feet). Class A fire rating. 110 MPH to 130 MPH wind resistance. Limited lifetime warranty.					
No algae resistance	R1@1.83	Sq	107.00	65.90	172.90
Algae resistant, 110mph	R1@1.83	Sq	100.00	65.90	165.90
Algae resistant, 130mph	R1@1.83	Sq	107.00	65.90	172.90
Impact resistant, architectural grade laminated shingles, Class 4, limited lifetime warranty, incl algae-resistance, 130MPH wind resistance, Class A fire. Three bundles per square (100 square feet). Class A fire rating. 110 MPH to 130 MPH wind resistance.					
Class 4 impact rated, lifetime warranty, 130MPH	R1@1.83	Sq	119.00	65.90	184.90
Premium grade laminated shingles, Owens Corning, GAF and similar. Limited lifetime warranty, algae-resistant, Class A fire rating. 110 MPH to 130 MPH wind resistance. Three bundles per square (100 square feet).					
5-inch exposure, 110MPH	R1@1.83	Sq	181.00	65.90	246.90
5-inch exposure, cool roof Title 24, 130MPH	R1@1.83	Sq	216.00	65.90	281.90
Premium, to 8-inch exposure, 130mph	R1@1.83	Sq	304.00	65.90	369.90
Hip and ridge shingles with sealant, Per linear foot of hip or ridge.					
ProEdge hip and ridge	R1@.028	LF	1.67	1.01	2.68
StormMaster hip and ridge	R1@.028	LF	1.79	1.01	2.80
Decorative ridge	R1@.028	LF	2.54	1.01	3.55
Shingle starter strip, Peel 'n' stick SBS membrane. Rubberized to seal around nails and resist wind lift.					
9" x 33' roll	R1@.460	Ea	20.60	16.60	37.20
Per linear foot	R1@.014	LF	.62	.50	1.12
Allowance for felt, flashing, fasteners, and vents.					
Typical cost	—	Sq	22.00	—	22.00

Roofing Papers See also Building Paper. Labor laying paper on 3-in-12 pitch roof.

	Craft@Hrs	Unit	Material	Labor	Total
Asphalt roofing felt (115.5 SF covers 100 SF), labor to roll and mop					
15 lb (432 SF roll)	R1@.490	Sq	5.75	17.60	23.35
30 lb (216 SF roll)	R1@.500	Sq	11.50	18.00	29.50

	Craft@Hrs	Unit	Material	Labor	Total
Glass base sheet (40" x 98' roll covers 300 SF)					
Base for torch applied membranes	R1@.360	Sq	17.70	13.00	30.70
Roofing asphalt, 100 lbs/Sq	—	Sq	49.40	—	49.40
Mineral surfaced roll roofing, 36" x 36' roll covers 100 square feet (1 square)					
90 lb, black or white	R1@1.03	Sq	38.60	37.10	75.70
90 lb, tan	R1@1.03	Sq	47.60	37.10	84.70
Mineral surfaced selvage edge roll roofing, 39.4" x 32.6' roll covers 100 square feet (1 square) with 2" selvage edge overlap					
90 lb, white or colors	R1@1.03	Sq	47.50	37.10	84.60

Roofing Shakes and Shingles

Red cedar. No pressure treating. Labor includes typical flashing.

	Craft@Hrs	Unit	Material	Labor	Total
Taper split No. 1 medium cedar shakes, four bundles cover 100 square feet (1 square) at 10" exposure. Includes 10% for waste.					
No. 1 medium shakes	R1@3.52	Sq	364.00	127.00	491.00
Add for pressure treated shakes	—	%	30.0	—	—
Deduct in the Pacific Northwest	—	%	−20.0	—	—
Shake felt, 30 lb	R1@.500	Sq	11.90	18.00	29.90
Hip and ridge shakes, medium, 20 per bundle, covers 16.7 LF at 10" and 20 LF at 12" exposure					
Per bundle	R1@1.00	Ea	85.40	36.00	121.40
Per linear foot, 10" exposure	R1@.060	LF	5.12	2.16	7.28
Per linear foot, 12" exposure	R1@.058	LF	4.27	2.09	6.36
Sawn shakes, sawn 1 side, Class "C" fire retardant					
1/2" to 3/4" x 24" (4 bdle/sq at 10" exp.)	R1@3.52	Sq	469.00	127.00	596.00
3/4" to 5/4" x 24" (5 bdle/sq at 10" exp.)	R1@4.16	Sq	649.00	150.00	799.00
Cedar roofing shingles, No. 1 Grade. Four bundles of Perfection Grade 18" shingles cover 100 square feet (1 square) at 5-1/2" exposure. Five Perfections are 2-1/4" thick. Four bundles of 5X Perfect Grade shingles cover 100 square feet (1 square) at 5" exposure. Five Perfects are 2" thick.					
Perfections	R1@3.52	Sq	387.00	127.00	514.00
Perfects	R1@3.52	Sq	319.00	127.00	446.00
No. 2 Perfections	R1@3.52	Sq	319.00	127.00	446.00
Add for pitch over 6 in 12	—	%	—	40.0	—
No. 2 cedar ridge shingles, medium, bundle covers 16 linear feet					
Per bundle	R1@1.00	Ea	72.90	36.00	108.90
Per linear foot	R1@.062	LF	4.56	2.23	6.79
Fire treated cedar shingles, 18", 5-1/2" exposure, 5 shingles are 2-1/4" thick, (5/2-1/4)					
No. 1 (houses)	R1@3.52	Sq	553.00	127.00	680.00
No. 2, red label (houses or garages)	R1@3.52	Sq	461.00	127.00	588.00
No. 3 (garages)	R1@3.52	Sq	395.00	127.00	522.00
Eastern white cedar shingles, smooth butt edge, four bundles cover 100 square feet (1 square) at 5" exposure					
White extras	R1@3.52	Sq	305.00	127.00	432.00
White clears	R1@3.52	Sq	243.00	127.00	370.00
White No. 2 clears	R1@3.52	Sq	165.00	127.00	292.00
Cedar shim shingles, tapered Western red cedar					
Builder's 12-pack, per pack	—	Ea	5.16	—	5.16

	Craft@Hrs	Unit	Material	Labor	Total
Roofing Sheets See also Fiberglass Panels.					
Metal sheet roofing, utility gauge					
26" wide, 5-V crimp (includes 15% coverage loss)					
6' to 12' lengths	R1@.027	SF	1.74	.97	2.71
26" wide, corrugated (includes 15% coverage loss)					
6' to 12' lengths	R1@.027	SF	.99	.97	1.96
27-1/2" wide, corrugated (includes 20% coverage loss)					
6' to 12' lengths	R1@.027	SF	.96	.97	1.93
Ridge roll, plain					
10" wide	R1@.030	LF	3.30	1.08	4.38
Ridge cap, formed, plain, 12"					
12" x 10' roll	R1@.061	LF	1.57	2.20	3.77
Sidewall flashing, plain					
3" x 4" x 10'	R1@.035	LF	1.06	1.26	2.32
V-5 crimp closure strips					
24" long	R1@.035	Ea	1.61	1.26	2.87
Endwall flashing, 2-1/2" corrugated					
10" x 28"	R1@.035	LF	2.27	1.26	3.53
Wood filler strip, corrugated					
7/8" x 7/8" x 6'	R1@.035	LF	.37	1.26	1.63
Steel Panel Roofing Simulated tile, Met-Tile™. 15% waste included.					
Roofing panels, 2' to 20' long					
26 gauge .019" thick	R1@.027	SF	2.20	.97	3.17
End cap					
4-3/4"	R1@.030	Ea	4.28	1.08	5.36
5-3/4" round	R1@.030	Ea	4.28	1.08	5.36
9-1/2" oversized	R1@.030	Ea	5.69	1.08	6.77
Flashing, galvanized steel					
End wall	R1@.047	LF	2.20	1.69	3.89
Plain side wall	R1@.047	LF	2.20	1.69	3.89
Valley cover	R1@.047	LF	2.18	1.69	3.87
Valley pan	R1@.047	LF	2.89	1.69	4.58
Contoured end wall	R1@.047	LF	5.69	1.69	7.38
Ridge-hip-gables					
Spanish 18" x 14-1/2"	R1@.035	Ea	6.16	1.26	7.42
Standard 7-1/2" x 42"	R1@.030	Ea	12.50	1.08	13.58
Trim					
Standard eave trim	R1@.035	LF	1.75	1.26	3.01
Flat edge trim	R1@.035	LF	1.75	1.26	3.01
Shake eave trim	R1@.035	LF	2.28	1.26	3.54
Hood vents					
18" x 22"	R1@.448	Ea	2.15	16.10	18.25

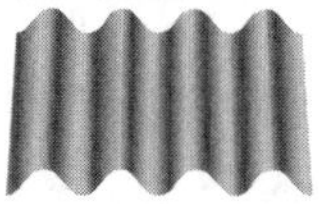

Roofing Slate Local delivery included. Costs will be higher where slate is not mined. Add freight cost at 800 to 1,000 pounds per 100 SF. Includes 20" long random width slate, 3/16" thick, 7-1/2" exposure. Meets Standard SS-S-451.

	Craft@Hrs	Unit	Material	Labor	Total
Semi-weathering green and gray	R1@11.3	Sq	518.00	407.00	925.00
Vermont black and gray black	R1@11.3	Sq	617.00	407.00	1,024.00
China black or gray	R1@11.3	Sq	699.00	407.00	1,106.00
Unfading and variegated purple	R1@11.3	Sq	699.00	407.00	1,106.00
Unfading mottled green and purple	R1@11.3	Sq	699.00	407.00	1,106.00
Unfading green	R1@11.3	Sq	572.00	407.00	979.00
Red slate	R1@13.6	Sq	1,790.00	489.00	2,279.00
Add for other specified widths and lengths	—	%	20.0	—	—

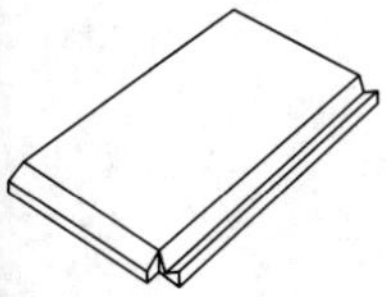

Fiber Cement Slate Roofing Eternit™, Stonit™, or Thrutone™, various colors. Non-asbestos formulation. Laid over 1/2" sheathing. Includes 30 lb. felt and one copper storm anchor per slate. Add for sheathing, flashing, hip, ridge and valley units.

	Craft@Hrs	Unit	Material	Labor	Total
23-5/8" x 11-7/8", English (420 lb, 30 year)					
2" head lap (113 pieces per Sq)	R1@5.50	Sq	559.00	198.00	757.00
3" head lap (119 pieces per Sq)	R1@5.75	Sq	587.00	207.00	794.00
4" head lap (124 pieces per Sq)	R1@6.00	Sq	608.00	216.00	824.00
Add for hip and ridge units, in mastic	R1@0.10	LF	11.40	3.60	15.00
15-3/4" x 10-5/8", Continental (420 lb, 30 year)					
2" head lap (197 pieces per Sq)	R1@6.50	Sq	577.00	234.00	811.00
3" head lap (214 pieces per Sq)	R1@6.75	Sq	628.00	243.00	871.00
4" head lap (231 pieces per Sq)	R1@7.00	Sq	681.00	252.00	933.00
Add for hip and ridge units, in mastic	R1@0.10	LF	10.50	3.60	14.10
Copper storm anchors, box of 1,000 ($44.00)	—	Ea	.04	—	.04
Stainless steel slate hooks	—	Ea	.45	—	.45
Add for extra felt under 5-in-12 pitch	R1@0.20	Sq	5.78	7.20	12.98

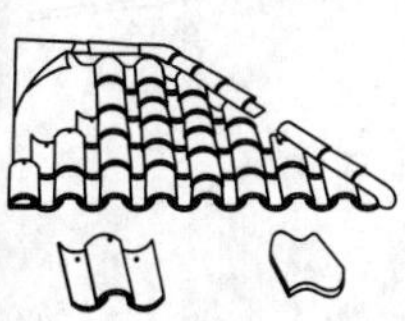

Roofing Tile, Clay Material costs include felt and flashing. No freight or waste included. Costs will be higher where clay tile is not manufactured locally. U.S. Tile Co.

	Craft@Hrs	Unit	Material	Labor	Total
Spanish tile, "S"-shaped, 88 pieces per square, (800 lbs per square at 11" centers and 15" exposure)					
Natural red clay tile	R1@4.50	Sq	321.00	162.00	483.00
Add for coloring ("flashed")	—	Sq	14.90	—	14.90
Red hip and ridge units	R1@.047	LF	1.13	1.69	2.82
Color hip and ridge units	R1@.047	LF	1.61	1.69	3.30
Red rake units	R1@.047	LF	2.15	1.69	3.84
Color rake units	R1@.047	LF	2.37	1.69	4.06
Red clay mission tile 2-piece, 86 pans and 86 tops per square, 7-1/2" x 18" x 8-1/2" tiles at 11" centers and 15" exposure					
Natural red clay tile	R1@5.84	Sq	374.00	210.00	584.00
Add for coloring (costs vary widely)	—	Sq	56.80	—	56.80
Red hip and ridge units	R1@.047	LF	1.18	1.69	2.87
Color hip and ridge units	R1@.047	LF	1.61	1.69	3.30
Red rake units	R1@.047	LF	2.15	1.69	3.84
Color rake units	R1@.047	LF	2.37	1.69	4.06

Concrete Roof Tile Material includes felt, nails and flashing. Approximately 90 pieces per square. Monier Lifetile

	Craft@Hrs	Unit	Material	Labor	Total
Shake, slurry color	R1@4.25	Sq	176.00	153.00	329.00
Slate, thru color	R1@4.25	Sq	214.00	153.00	367.00
Espana, slurry coated	R1@4.25	Sq	214.00	153.00	367.00
Monier 2000	R1@4.25	Sq	227.00	153.00	380.00
Vignette	R1@4.25	Sq	200.00	153.00	353.00
Collage	R1@4.25	Sq	200.00	153.00	353.00
Tapestry	R1@4.25	Sq	218.00	153.00	371.00
Split shake	R1@4.25	Sq	241.00	153.00	394.00
Villa, slurry coat	R1@4.25	Sq	199.00	153.00	352.00
Villa, Roma, thru color	R1@4.25	Sq	204.00	153.00	357.00
Trim tile					
Mansard "V"-ridge or rake, slurry coated	—	Ea	2.81	—	2.81
Mansard, ridge or rake, thru color	—	Ea	2.93	—	2.93
Hipstarters, slurry coated	—	Ea	24.10	—	24.10
Hipstarters, thru color	—	Ea	30.70	—	30.70

Safes

	Craft@Hrs	Unit	Material	Labor	Total
Accessories					
Eave closure or birdstop	R1@.030	LF	1.67	1.08	2.75
Hurricane or wind clips	R1@.030	Ea	.60	1.08	1.68
Underlayment or felt	R1@.050	Sq	11.50	1.80	13.30
Metal flashing and nails	R1@.306	Sq	12.60	11.00	23.60
Pre-formed plastic flashings					
Hip (13" long)	R1@.020	Ea	43.30	.72	44.02
Ridge (39" long)	R1@.030	Ea	44.40	1.08	45.48
Anti-ponding foam	R1@.030	LF	.38	1.08	1.46
Batten extenders	R1@.030	Ea	1.50	1.08	2.58
Roof loading					
Add to load tile and accessories on roof	R1@.822	Sq	—	29.60	29.60
Wall Safes, Residential UL approved combination lock, flush combination dial, 1/2" thick door. Fits between 16" on center studs. Installed during new construction.					
For 2 x 4 wall thickness, outside dimensions 13.5" x 14" x 3.75"					
Capacity 400 cu. inches	BC@.788	Ea	599.00	29.50	628.50
For 2 x 6 wall thickness, outside dimensions 13.5" x 14" x 5.75"					
Capacity 750 cu. inches	BC@.788	Ea	627.00	29.50	656.50
For 2 x 12 wall thickness, outside dimensions 13.5" x 14" x 10.25"					
Capacity 1,350 cu. inches	BC@.950	Ea	663.00	35.50	698.50
For 2 x 12 wall thickness, outside dimensions 14" x 14" x 10.25"					
Capacity 1,550 cu. inches	BC@.950	Ea	863.00	35.50	898.50
Optional equipment					
Jewelry interior	—	Ea	75.00	—	75.00
Installation kit	—	Ea	20.00	—	20.00
Floor Safes, Residential 1/2" thick spring counter-balanced square door (13" x 13"), UL approved Group Two combination lock, metal cover plate – creates flush floor surface. Installed during new construction.					
Outside dimensions 14.5" x 16" x 10.25"					
Capacity 1,100 cu. inches	BC@1.10	Ea	540.00	41.10	581.10
Outside dimensions 14.5" x 16" x 16.25"					
Capacity 2,325 cu. inches	BC@1.25	Ea	640.00	46.70	686.70
Outside dimensions 14.5" x 16" x 21.75"					
Capacity 3,545 cu. inches	BC@1.35	Ea	744.00	50.50	794.50
Outside dimensions 14.5" x 25" x 16.25"					
Capacity 3,970 cu. inches	BC@1.42	Ea	906.00	53.10	959.10
Outside dimensions 25" x 25" x 16.75"					
Capacity 7,050 cu. inches	BC@1.55	Ea	1,050.00	57.90	1,107.90
Outside dimensions 14.5" x 48" x 16.25"					
Capacity 7,775 cu. inches	BC@1.60	Ea	1,260.00	59.80	1,319.80
Upgrade to CB-Rating, 1" thick steel door, 1/4" body	—	%	15.0	—	—
Optional equipment					
Electronic push button lock	—	Ea	195.00	—	195.00
Dual key lock – in place of combination lock	—	Ea	35.00	—	35.00
Slotted doors (deposit slot)	—	Ea	75.00	—	75.00
Combination change kit	—	Ea	10.00	—	10.00

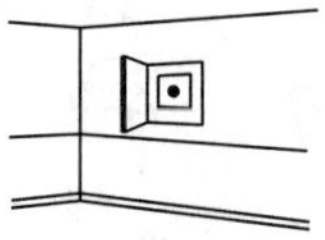

	Craft@Hrs	Unit	Material	Labor	Total
Man Safes, Residential Pry resistant door design, reinforced door jambs, 1" locking bolts, UL approved Group Two combination lock, basic drawer configuration. Installed during new construction.					
Outside dimensions 15" x 19" x 17"					
Capacity 2 cu. feet	BC@1.75	Ea	5,980.00	65.40	6,045.40
Outside dimensions 21" x 19" x 22"					
Capacity 4 cu. feet	BC@2.00	Ea	6,480.00	74.80	6,554.80
Outside dimensions 41" x 19" x 42"					
Capacity 7 cu. feet	BC@2.25	Ea	7,480.00	84.10	7,564.10

Sandblasting, Waterblasting, Subcontract The minimum charge for on-site (truck-mounted) sandblasting and waterblasting will usually be about $500.00. Add the cost of extra liability insurance and physical barriers to protect adjacent swimming pools, residences, process plants, etc. No scaffolding included. Based on sandblasting with 375 CFM, 125 PSI compressor. Portable hydroblast and sandblast equipment for worksites beyond 30 miles from base will incur a $50 transit time fee. Typical fuel surcharge is $100 per 8-hour shift.

	Craft@Hrs	Unit	Material	Labor	Total
Sandblasting most surfaces					
Water soluble paints	—	SF	—	—	2.75
Oil paints	—	SF	—	—	3.14
Heavy mastic	—	SF	—	—	3.47
Sandblasting masonry					
Brick	—	SF	—	—	4.05
Block walls, most work	—	SF	—	—	3.02
Remove heavy surface grime	—	SF	—	—	3.64
Heavy, exposing aggregate	—	SF	—	—	3.98
Sandblasting concrete tilt-up panels					
Light blast	—	SF	—	—	3.20
Medium, exposing aggregate	—	SF	—	—	4.08
Heavy, exposing aggregate	—	SF	—	—	4.59
Sandblasting steel					
New, uncoated (commercial grade)	—	SF	—	—	3.58
New, uncoated (near white grade)	—	SF	—	—	4.45
Epoxy coated (near white grade)	—	SF	—	—	5.14
Sandblasting wood					
Medium blast, clean and texture	—	SF	—	—	3.38
Waterblast (hydroblast) with mild detergent					
To 5,000 PSI blast (4 hour minimum)	—	Hr	—	—	402.00
5,000 to 10,000 PSI blast (8 hour min.)	—	Hr	—	—	416.00
Over 10,000 PSI blast (8 hour minimum)	—	Hr	—	—	664.00
Wet sandblasting					
(4 hour minimum)	—	Hr	—	—	559.00

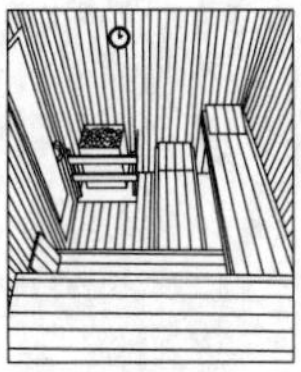

Sauna Rooms Costs listed are for labor and materials to install sauna rooms as described. Units are shipped as a disassembled kit complete with kiln dried softwood paneling boards, sauna heater, temperature and humidity controls and monitors, pre-assembled benches, prehung door, water bucket and dipper, and interior light. No electrical work included.

Western red cedar panel built sauna room package with heater, controls, duckboard floor and accessories. Glass front. Furniture grade interior. Ready for nailing to existing framed and insulated walls with exterior finish. Ceiling height 7'.

	Craft@Hrs	Unit	Material	Labor	Total
4' x 4' room	B1@6.68	Ea	5,990.00	226.00	6,216.00
4' x 6' room	B1@6.68	Ea	8,100.00	226.00	8,326.00
6' x 6' room	B1@8.00	Ea	8,670.00	271.00	8,941.00
6' x 8' room	B1@8.00	Ea	10,100.00	271.00	10,371.00
8' x 8' room	B1@10.7	Ea	13,400.00	362.00	13,762.00
8' x 10' room	B1@10.7	Ea	14,600.00	362.00	14,962.00
Add for electrical connection wiring	—	LS	—	—	335.00

Screen

	Craft@Hrs	Unit	Material	Labor	Total
Custom-cut 100% vertical grain redwood or clear western red cedar sauna room package with heater, controls and accessories (including non-skid removable rubberized flooring). Ready for nailing to existing framed and insulated walls, exterior 7' ceiling height.					
4' x 4' room	B1@8.00	Ea	4,580.00	271.00	4,851.00
4' x 6' room	B1@8.00	Ea	5,180.00	271.00	5,451.00
5' x 6' room	B1@8.00	Ea	5,470.00	271.00	5,741.00
6' x 6' room	B1@10.0	Ea	5,940.00	339.00	6,279.00
6' x 8' room	B1@12.0	Ea	6,830.00	406.00	7,236.00
8' x 8' room	B1@14.0	Ea	9,470.00	474.00	9,944.00
8' x 10' room	B1@15.0	Ea	10,200.00	508.00	10,708.00
10' x 10' room	B1@16.0	Ea	10,900.00	542.00	11,442.00
10' x 12' room	B1@16.0	Ea	11,800.00	542.00	12,342.00
Add for electrical connection wiring	—	LS	—	—	335.00

	7-foot roll	10-foot roll	25-foot roll	100-foot roll
Screen Wire Vinyl-coated fiberglass, noncombustible				
Charcoal or gray, cost per roll				
36" wide roll	7.48	—	16.30	49.00
48" wide roll	9.68	—	18.80	63.00
60" wide roll	—	10.30	32.60	135.00
72" wide roll	—	12.40	34.40	136.00
84" wide roll	—	14.50	27.80	205.00
96" wide roll	—	16.50	32.00	119.00

	7-foot roll	25-foot roll	50-foot roll	100-foot roll
Screen Wire, solar Blocks 90% of the sun's heat and glare. Protect interior surfaces from fading.				
Black, cost per roll				
36" wide roll	16.50	53.00	126.00	244.00
48" wide roll	22.00	66.00	173.00	307.00
60" wide roll	37.20	127.00	233.00	414.00
84" wide roll	—	—	357.00	541.00

	Craft@Hrs	Unit	Material	Labor	Total
Labor to install screen wire					
Includes measure, lay out, cut and attach screen wire to an existing metal or wood frame.					
Per linear foot of perimeter of frame	BC@.040	LF	—	1.50	1.50
Security Alarms, Subcontract Costs are for securing building perimeter and all accessible openings with electronic alarm system, including all labor and materials. Costs assume that no interior wall, floor, or ceiling finishes are in place. All equipment is good to better quality.					
Alarm control panel	—	Ea	—	—	550.00
Wiring, detectors per opening, with switch		Ea	—	—	95.40
Monthly monitoring charge	—	Mo	—	—	39.10
Alarm options (installed)					
Audio detectors	—	Ea	—	—	138.00
Communicator (central station service)	—	Ea	—	—	307.00
Digital touch pad control	—	Ea	—	—	169.00
Entry/exit delay	—	Ea	—	—	120.00
Fire/smoke detectors	—	Ea	—	—	204.00
Interior/exterior sirens	—	Ea	—	—	91.30
Motion detector	—	Ea	—	—	277.00
Panic button	—	Ea	—	—	67.90
Passive infrared detector	—	Ea	—	—	381.00
Pressure mat	—	LF	—	—	111.00
Security light control	—	Ea	—	—	668.00
Add for wiring detectors and controls in existing buildings					
With wall and ceiling finishes already in place	—	%	—	—	25.0

	Craft@Hrs	Unit	Material	Labor	Total
Security Guards, Subcontract Construction site security guards, unarmed, in uniform with two-way radio, backup patrol car, bond, and liability insurance. Per manhour.					
Short term (1 night to 1 week)	—	Hr	—	—	47.00
Medium duration (1 week to 1 month)	—	Hr	—	—	45.80
Long term (1 to 6 months)	—	Hr	—	—	31.00
Add for licensed armed guard	—	Hr	—	—	7.06
Add for holidays	—	%	—	—	55.0
Construction site guard dog service for sites with totally enclosed perimeter, 24 hour per day, 7 day per week service. Local business codes may restrict or prohibit unattended guard dogs. Includes dog handling training session, liability insurance, on-site kennel. Cost per month.					
Contractor feeding and tending dog	—	Mo	—	—	801.00
Daily delivery of guard dog at quitting time and pickup at starting time by guard dog service (special hours require advance notice)					
Service feeding and tending dog	—	Mo	—	—	838.00
Construction site man and dog guard team, includes two-way radio communication with guard service office, backup patrol car, and liability insurance. Guard service may require that a telephone and guard shack be provided by the contractor. Cost for man and dog per hour.					
Short term (1 week to 1 month)	—	Hr	—	—	50.90
Long term (1 to 6 months)	—	Hr	—	—	36.50

	Craft@Hrs	Unit	Material	Labor	Total
Septic Sewer Systems, Subcontract Soils testing (percolation test) by qualified engineer (required by some communities when applying for septic system permit). Does not include application fee.					
Minimum cost	—	Ea	—	—	2,410.00
Residential septic sewer tanks. Costs include excavation for tank with good site conditions, placing of tank, inlet and outlet fittings, and backfill after hookup.					
Steel reinforced concrete tanks					
1,250 gallons (3 or 4 bedroom house)	—	Ea	—	—	2,630.00
1,500 gallons (5 or 6 bedroom house)	—	Ea	—	—	2,790.00
Fiberglass tanks					
1,000 gallons (3 bedroom house)	—	Ea	—	—	2,410.00
1,250 gallons (4 bedroom house)	—	Ea	—	—	2,460.00
1,500 gallons (5 or 6 bedroom house)	—	Ea	—	—	2,660.00
Polyethylene tanks					
500 gallons	—	Ea	—	—	759.00
750 gallons	—	Ea	—	—	1,250.00
1,000 gallons	—	Ea	—	—	1,370.00
1,250 gallons	—	Ea	—	—	2,190.00
1,500 gallons	—	Ea	—	—	2,450.00
Residential septic sewer drain fields (leach lines). Costs include labor, unsaturated paper, piping, gravel, excavation with good site conditions, backfill, and disposal of excess soil. 4" PVC pipe (ASTM D2729) laid in 3' deep by 1' wide trench.					
With 12" gravel base	—	LF	—	—	9.71
With 24" gravel base	—	LF	—	—	11.40
With 36" gravel base	—	LF	—	—	12.50
Add for pipe laid 6' deep	—	LF	—	—	3.28
Add for piping from house to septic tank, and from septic tank to remote drain fields					
4" PVC Schedule 40	—	LF	—	—	6.90
Basic pumping systems for residential waste, including fiberglass basin, pump, installation from septic tank or sewer line, 40' pipe run, and automatic float switch (no electric work or pipe included).					
To 15' head	—	LS	—	—	3,440.00
To 25' head	—	LS	—	—	4,070.00

	Craft@Hrs	Unit	Material	Labor	Total
To 30' head	—	LS	—	—	5,290.00
Add for high water or pump failure alarm	—	LS	—	—	752.00
Better quality pump system with two alternating pumps, 700 to 800 gallon concrete or fiberglass basin, automatic float switch, indoor control panel, high water or pump failure alarm, explosion proof electrical system but no electric work or pipe.					
Per pump system	—	LS	—	—	10,000.00
Pipe locating service to detect sewage and water leaks, breaks, and stoppages in pipes with diameter of 2" or more. Equipment can't be used where pipe has 90 degree turns. Maximum depth is 18" for cast iron and 30" for vitreous clay.					
Residential 1/2 day rate	—	LS	—	—	485.00
Commercial 1/2 day rate	—	LS	—	—	647.00
Add for each additional pipe entered	—	LS	—	—	76.70
Plus per LF of pipe length	—	LF	—	—	2.79
Add for travel over 15 miles, per mile	—	Ea	—	—	1.05
Sewer Connections, Subcontract Including typical excavation and backfill.					
4" vitrified clay pipeline, house to property line					
Long runs	—	LF	—	—	26.20
Short runs	—	LF	—	—	27.80
6" vitrified clay pipeline					
Long runs	—	LF	—	—	29.20
Short runs	—	LF	—	—	34.30
Street work	—	LF	—	—	69.70
4" PVC sewer pipe, city installed, property line to main line					
Up to 40 feet (connect in street)	—	LS	—	—	2,240.00
Up to 40 feet (connect in alley)	—	LS	—	—	1,620.00
Each foot over 40 feet	—	LF	—	—	50.30
6" PVC sewer pipe, city installed, property line to main line					
Up to 40 feet (connect in street)	—	LS	—	—	3,590.00
Up to 40 feet (connect in alley)	—	LS	—	—	2,570.00
Each foot over 40 feet	—	LF	—	—	80.30
8" PVC sewer pipe, city installed, property line to main line					
Up to 40 feet (connect in street)	—	LS	—	—	5,000.00
Up to 40 feet (connect in alley)	—	LS	—	—	3,900.00
Each foot over 40 feet	—	LF	—	—	104.00
Access Doors					
Metal access doors, concealed metal hinge					
8" x 8"	SW@.363	Ea	24.20	15.30	39.50
14" x 14"	SW@.363	Ea	26.10	15.30	41.40
18" x 18"	SW@.363	Ea	37.50	15.30	52.80
24" x 24"	SW@.363	Ea	57.00	15.30	72.30
ABS access doors, paintable					
6" x 9"	SW@.363	Ea	10.80	15.30	26.10
14" x 14"	SW@.363	Ea	16.40	15.30	31.70
24" x 18"	SW@.363	Ea	65.20	15.30	80.50
24" x 24"	SW@.363	Ea	76.70	15.30	92.00
24" x 18", screen only	—	Ea	21.10	—	21.10
24" x 24", screen only	—	Ea	24.20	—	24.20
Tub access doors					
6" x 9", white ABS	SW@.363	Ea	10.80	15.30	26.10
14" x 14", white ABS	SW@.363	Ea	16.10	15.30	31.40
14" x 14", galvanized steel	SW@.363	Ea	18.00	15.30	33.30

	Craft@Hrs	Unit	Material	Labor	Total
Sheet Metal Area Walls Provides light well for basement windows, galvanized, corrugated. Add the cost of excavation and backfill.					
12" deep, 6" projection, 37" wide	SW@.410	Ea	36.30	17.30	53.60
18" deep, 6" projection, 37" wide	SW@.410	Ea	47.80	17.30	65.10
24" deep, 6" projection, 37" wide	SW@.410	Ea	62.30	17.30	79.60
30" deep, 6" projection, 37" wide	SW@.410	Ea	74.30	17.30	91.60
Add for steel grille cover	—	Ea	84.50	—	84.50

Sheet Metal Flashing

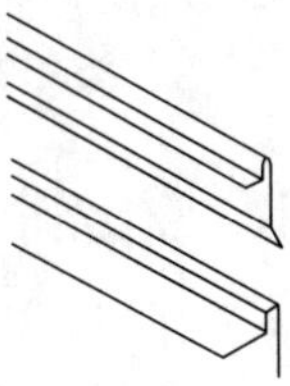

	Craft@Hrs	Unit	Material	Labor	Total
Aluminum flashing .0175" thickness is commercial grade. Mill finish except as noted.					
Chimney flash kit (base, cricket & step flash)	SW@.900	Ea	31.90	37.90	69.80
Drip cap, 1-5/8" x 10' x .0175", white	SW@.350	Ea	5.24	14.80	20.04
Drip edge, 2-1/2" x 1" x .0145", 10' long	SW@.350	Ea	3.67	14.80	18.47
Drip edge, 6-1/2" x 1", 10' long	SW@.350	Ea	11.80	14.80	26.60
Flex corner, 2" x 2" x 3-1/2" radius	SW@.050	Ea	3.23	2.11	5.34
Gravel stop, 10' x 5-1/2", "C"-shape	SW@.350	Ea	5.27	14.80	20.07
Roll 6" x 10' x .011"	SW@.400	Ea	5.46	16.90	22.36
Roll 6" x 25' x .0175"	SW@.400	Ea	12.70	16.90	29.60
Roll 8" x 10' x .011"	SW@.400	Ea	6.83	16.90	23.73
Roll 8" x 25' x .0175"	SW@.400	Ea	14.70	16.90	31.60
Roll 10" x 10' x .011"	SW@.400	Ea	8.26	16.90	25.16
Roll 10" x 10' x .0175"	SW@.400	Ea	13.40	16.90	30.30
Roll 14" x 10' x .011"	SW@.400	Ea	10.40	16.90	27.30
Roll 14" x 25' x .0175"	SW@.400	Ea	23.60	16.90	40.50
Roll 20" x 10' x .011"	SW@.400	Ea	13.10	16.90	30.00
Roll 20" x 25' x .0175"	SW@.400	Ea	33.70	16.90	50.60
Roof edge, 2-1/2" x 1-1/2" x 10'	SW@.350	Ea	4.96	14.80	19.76
Roof edge, 4-1/2" x 1-1/2" x 10'	SW@.350	Ea	13.10	14.80	27.90
Sheet, 1' x 1', black	SW@.250	Ea	9.88	10.50	20.38
Sheet, 1' x 1', mill finish	SW@.250	Ea	7.59	10.50	18.09
Sheet, 1' x 2', black	SW@.250	Ea	17.60	10.50	28.10
Sheet, 1' x 2' x .020", lincaine perforated	SW@.250	Ea	18.50	10.50	29.00
Sheet, 2' x 3', mill finish	SW@.500	Ea	11.80	21.10	32.90
Sheet, 3' x 3', mill finish	SW@.500	Ea	22.10	21.10	43.20
Sheet, 3' x 3', lincaine perforated	SW@.500	Ea	33.20	21.10	54.30
Step flashing bent, 2-1/2" x 2-1/2" x 7"	SW@.040	Ea	.51	1.69	2.20
Step flashing, bent, 4" x 4" x 8"	SW@.040	Ea	.56	1.69	2.25
Step flashing, bent, 5" x 7", pack of 10	SW@.400	Ea	2.61	16.90	19.51
Trim coil 24" x 50', white and black	SW@2.50	Ea	104.00	105.00	209.00
Trim coil nails, box of 800	—	Ea	8.28	—	8.28

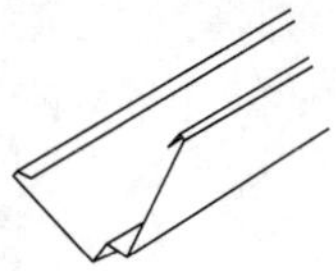

	Craft@Hrs	Unit	Material	Labor	Total
Copper flashing 16 ounce per square foot, .021 gauge, bright.					
Roll 8" x 20'	SW@.750	Ea	39.00	31.60	70.60
Roll 12" x 20'	SW@.500	Ea	56.80	21.10	77.90
Roll 12" x 20', 3 ounce	SW@1.00	Ea	65.60	42.20	107.80
Roof edging, 1-1/2" x 2" x 10'	SW@.350	Ea	83.00	14.80	97.80
Roof edging, 2" x 2" x 10'	SW@.350	Ea	94.90	14.80	109.70
Roof-to-wall flashing, 4" x 6" x 10'	SW@.350	Ea	227.00	14.80	241.80
Shingle flashing, 8" x 12"	SW@.040	Ea	26.50	1.69	28.19
Step flashing, 5" x 7"	SW@.040	Ea	13.60	1.69	15.29
W-valley flashing, 18" x 10'	SW@.500	Ea	334.00	21.10	355.10
Copper nails, 1-1/4", box of 100	—	Box	23.40	—	23.40

Sheet Metal, Flashing

	Craft@Hrs	Unit	Material	Labor	Total
Plastic/poly-backed copper flashing 3 ounce per square foot. Compatible with ACQ-treated lumber. Laminated to plastic/poly backing.					
Roll 8" x 20'	SW@.500	Ea	33.10	21.10	54.20
Roll 10" x 20'	SW@.500	Ea	38.00	21.10	59.10
Roll 12" x 20'	SW@.500	Ea	57.50	21.10	78.60
Galvanized steel flashing Galvanized mill (plain) finish except as noted. 26 gauge. Galvanized steel flashing has a zinc coating which resists corrosion. Bonderized steel flashing adds a colored phosphate coating which improves paint adhesion.					
ACQ-compatible flashing, 8" x 20'	SW@1.00	Ea	26.70	42.20	68.90
ACQ-compatible flashing, 10" x 20'	SW@1.00	Ea	37.20	42.20	79.40
Angle flashing, 3" x 5" x 10', 90-degree	SW@.500	Ea	7.40	21.10	28.50
Angle flashing, 4" x 4" x 10', 90-degree	SW@.500	Ea	6.30	21.10	27.40
Angle flashing, 6" x 6" x 10', 90-degree	SW@.500	Ea	9.06	21.10	30.16
Angle hem flashing, 4" x 3-1/2" x 10'	SW@.400	Ea	7.07	16.90	23.97
Chimney flash kit (base/cricket/step)	SW@.900	Ea	33.00	37.90	70.90
Counter flash, 1/2" x 6" x 10', bonderized	SW@.400	Ea	14.40	16.90	31.30
Deck ledger, 2" x 2" x 10', ACQ lumber	SW@.400	Ea	7.30	16.90	24.20
Deck ledger, 2" x 2" x 8', galvanized	SW@.350	Ea	5.40	14.80	20.20
Dormer flashing, 7", black	SW@.250	Ea	10.10	10.50	20.60
Dormer flashing, 7", mill finish	SW@.250	Ea	7.63	10.50	18.13
Drip cap, 1-1/2" x 10'	SW@.400	Ea	3.19	16.90	20.09
Drip edge, 2-1/2" x 1" x 10', white	SW@.400	Ea	4.22	16.90	21.12
Drip edge, 5" x 2' x 10', mill finish	SW@.400	Ea	6.03	16.90	22.93
Drip edge, 6" x 10', Beige,	SW@.400	Ea	8.25	16.90	25.15
Endwall flashing, 3" x 4" x 10'	SW@.400	Ea	9.23	16.90	26.13
Fascia cap, 2" x 10', bonderized	SW@.400	Ea	7.41	16.90	24.31
Fungus preventer, 2-1/2" x 50' zinc strip	SW@1.25	Ea	20.70	52.70	73.40
Girder shield flashing, 2" x 8" x 2" x 10'	SW@.400	Ea	9.93	16.90	26.83
Gravel guard, 6" x 10', type "E"	SW@.400	Ea	5.43	16.90	22.33
Gravel stop, 2" x 4" x 10', bonderized	SW@.400	Ea	8.80	16.90	25.70
Gravel stop, 2" x 4" x 10', galvanized	SW@.400	Ea	7.52	16.90	24.42
Gutter apron, 2' x 3' x 10', galvanized	SW@.400	Ea	9.08	16.90	25.98
Gutter apron, 2" x 3" x 10', bonderized	SW@.400	Ea	6.50	16.90	23.40
Half round square dormer, 12" x 12"	BC@.871	Ea	43.90	32.60	76.50
L-flashing, 2" x 2" x 10', bonderized	SW@.400	Ea	5.94	16.90	22.84
L-flashing, 2" x 2" x 10', galvanized	SW@.400	Ea	5.15	16.90	22.05
L-flashing, 4" x 6" x 10', bonderized	SW@.400	Ea	19.40	16.90	36.30
L-flashing, 4" x 6" x 10', galvanized	SW@.400	Ea	10.60	16.90	27.50
Moss preventer, 2-2/3" x 50', zinc	SW@1.25	Ea	32.30	52.70	85.00
Parapet coping, 2" x 8" x 2" x 10'	SW@.500	Ea	13.20	21.10	34.30
Vent pipe flash cone, 1/2" pipe	SW@.250	Ea	5.00	10.50	15.50
Vent pipe flash cone, 1" pipe	SW@.250	Ea	7.15	10.50	17.65
Vent pipe flash cone, 3" pipe	SW@.311	Ea	8.02	13.10	21.12
Vent pipe flash cone, 4" pipe	SW@.311	Ea	9.23	13.10	22.33
Vent pipe flash cone, 5" pipe	SW@.311	Ea	11.50	13.10	24.60
Rain diverter, 7-1/2" x 10'	SW@.400	Ea	7.62	16.90	24.52
Reglet, 3/4" x 10', snap top, bonderized	SW@.500	Ea	11.80	21.10	32.90
Reglet, 3/4" x 10', snap top, mill finish	SW@.500	Ea	6.55	21.10	27.65
Roll 6" x 10', galvanized	SW@.500	Ea	6.06	21.10	27.16
Roll 7" x 10', galvanized	SW@.500	Ea	7.17	21.10	28.27
Roll 8" x 10', bonderized	SW@.500	Ea	12.20	21.10	33.30
Roll 8" x 50', galvanized	SW@2.50	Ea	21.40	105.00	126.40

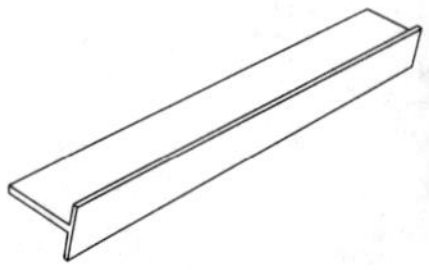

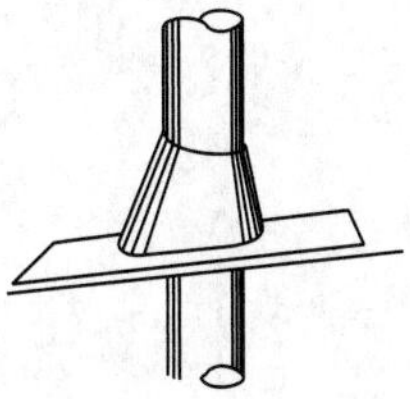

	Craft@Hrs	Unit	Material	Labor	Total
Roll 10" x 10', galvanized	SW@.500	Ea	10.60	21.10	31.70
Roll 14" x 10', galvanized	SW@.500	Ea	12.90	21.10	34.00
Roll 20" x 10', galvanized	SW@.500	Ea	21.20	21.10	42.30
Roll 20" x 50', galvanized	SW@.500	Ea	58.40	21.10	79.50
Roll valley, 20" x 50', gray	SW@2.50	Ea	64.80	105.00	169.80
Roll valley, 20" x 50', brown	SW@2.50	Ea	63.80	105.00	168.80
Roll valley, 30" x 25', galvanized	SW@1.75	Ea	31.40	73.80	105.20
Roll valley, 30" x 50', galvanized	SW@2.50	Ea	50.30	105.00	155.30
Roof apron, 5" x 10', bonderized	SW@.400	Ea	4.38	16.90	21.28
Roof edge, 1" x 2" x 10', brown	SW@.400	Ea	3.54	16.90	20.44
Roof edge, 1" x 2" x 10', gray	SW@.400	Ea	3.54	16.90	20.44
Roof edge, 3" x 3" x 10', brown	SW@.400	Ea	8.59	16.90	25.49
Roof edge, 2" x 2" x 10', weatherwood	SW@.400	Ea	3.65	16.90	20.55
Roof edge, 1-1/2" x 2" x 10', galvanized	SW@.400	Ea	5.43	16.90	22.33
Roof edge, 1-1/2" x 2" x 10', bonderized	SW@.500	Ea	5.43	21.10	26.53
Roof edge, 6" x 6" x 10', galvanized	SW@.400	Ea	14.80	16.90	31.70
Roof grip edge, 2" x 3" x 10', bonderized	SW@.400	Ea	7.52	16.90	24.42
Roof-to-wall flashing, 2" x 3" x 10'	SW@.400	Ea	7.03	16.90	23.93
Roof-to-wall flashing, 4" x 5" x 10'	SW@.400	Ea	14.20	16.90	31.10
Saddle stock, 4" x 14" x 10'	SW@.400	Ea	18.10	16.90	35.00
Sheet 3' x 4', 26-gauge	SW@.500	Ea	15.70	21.10	36.80
Shingle flashing, 5" x 7", box of 10	SW@.400	Box	2.68	16.90	19.58
Starter strip, 4-1/4" x 10', bonderized	SW@.500	Ea	4.77	21.10	25.87
Step flashing, bent 2" x 3" x 7", .031"	SW@.040	Ea	.39	1.69	2.08
Step flashing, bent, 4" x 12", bonderized	SW@.040	Ea	1.46	1.69	3.15
Step flashing, bent, 8" x 8", brown	SW@.040	Ea	.45	1.69	2.14
Trim coil, 24" x 50'	SW@2.50	Ea	83.90	105.00	188.90
Tile roof pan, bent 3-1/2" x 6" x 1/2" x 10'	SW@.400	Ea	16.40	16.90	33.30
Tin repair shingles, 5" x 7", galvanized	SW@.040	Ea	.59	1.69	2.28
Tin repair shingles, 8" x 12", bonderized	SW@.040	Ea	1.32	1.69	3.01
Water table, 1-1/2" x 10', bonderized	SW@.400	Ea	7.02	16.90	23.92
Water table, 1-1/2" x 10', galvanized	SW@.400	Ea	6.41	16.90	23.31
W-valley, 18" x 10', 28 gauge	SW@.500	Ea	21.10	21.10	42.20
W-valley, 20" x 10', 28 gauge, brown	SW@.500	Ea	19.60	21.10	40.70
W-valley, 24" x 10', bonderized	SW@.500	Ea	30.60	21.10	51.70
Z-bar flashing, 1/2" x 1-1/2" x 2" x 10'	SW@.400	Ea	2.73	16.90	19.63
Z-bar flashing, 2" x 5/8" x 1" x 10'	SW@.400	Ea	2.80	16.90	19.70
Z-bar flashing, 2" x 1" x 3" x 10'	SW@.400	Ea	8.88	16.90	25.78
Lead flashing					
Roll 8" wide, per linear foot	SW@.050	Ea	4.15	2.11	6.26
Roll 10" wide, per linear foot	SW@.066	Ea	5.44	2.78	8.22
Roll 12" wide, per linear foot	SW@.075	Ea	6.53	3.16	9.69
Vent pipe flash cone, 1-1/2" pipe	SW@.311	Ea	16.90	13.10	30.00
Vent pipe flash cone, 2" pipe	SW@.311	Ea	18.30	13.10	31.40
Vent pipe flash cone, 3" pipe	SW@.311	Ea	21.80	13.10	34.90
Vent pipe flash cone, 4" pipe	SW@.311	Ea	13.10	13.10	26.20

Sheet Metal, Hoods

	Craft@Hrs	Unit	Material	Labor	Total
Vinyl flashing For windows, fascia, soffits, siding and posts in contact with ACQ-treated lumber.					
Deck ledger, J-channel, 4" x 10' x .035"	SW@.350	Ea	13.30	14.80	28.10
Roll 20" x 50', tan	SW@3.50	Ea	53.60	148.00	201.60
Roll 10" x 50', white	SW@2.50	Ea	31.10	105.00	136.10
Roof edge, 1-7/8" x 10'	SW@.400	Ea	9.05	16.90	25.95
Vent pipe flash cone, 1" to 3" pipe	SW@.250	Ea	20.40	10.50	30.90
Vent pipe flash cone, 3" to 4" pipe	SW@.311	Ea	20.40	13.10	33.50
Sheet Metal Hoods					
Entrance hoods, galvanized					
48" x 22" x 12", double mold	SW@1.00	Ea	131.00	42.20	173.20
60" x 24" x 12", double mold	SW@1.00	Ea	125.00	42.20	167.20
48" x 22" x 12", scalloped edge	SW@1.00	Ea	165.00	42.20	207.20
60" x 24" x 12", scalloped edge	SW@1.00	Ea	172.00	42.20	214.20
Side hoods, galvanized, square					
4" x 4"	SW@.190	Ea	12.50	8.01	20.51
6" x 6"	SW@.216	Ea	21.20	9.11	30.31
7" x 7"	SW@.272	Ea	23.70	11.50	35.20

Shelving

Wood shelving, using 1" thick #3 & Btr paint grade board lumber. Costs shown include an allowance for ledger boards, nails and normal waste. Painting not included. Based on a six foot shelf. For other lengths up to ten feet, use the same labor cost but adjust for material.

	Craft@Hrs	Unit	Material	Labor	Total
Closet shelves, with 1" diameter clothes pole and pole support brackets each 3' OC					
10" wide shelf, 6'L	BC@.250	Ea	34.60	9.35	43.95
12" wide shelf, 6'L	BC@.250	Ea	37.50	9.35	46.85
18" wide shelf, 6'L	BC@.250	Ea	46.40	9.35	55.75
Linen cabinet shelves, cost of linen closet not included					
18" wide shelf, 6'L	BC@.250	Ea	39.20	9.35	48.55
24" wide shelf, 6'L	BC@.300	Ea	48.60	11.20	59.80
Utility shelves, laundry room walls, garage walls, etc.					
10" wide shelf, 6'L	BC@.250	Ea	26.00	9.35	35.35
12" wide shelf, 6'L	BC@.250	Ea	29.00	9.35	38.35
18" wide shelf, 6'L	BC@.250	Ea	39.20	9.35	48.55
24" wide shelf, 6'L	BC@.300	Ea	48.60	11.20	59.80
Wire shelving kits, vinyl coated steel wire 1" OC. Includes support braces and clamps.					
Heavy-duty garage shelf					
6' x 12"	BC@.800	Ea	21.00	29.90	50.90
6' x 16"	BC@.800	Ea	30.90	29.90	60.80
Linen shelf					
4' x 16"	BC@.600	Ea	28.80	22.40	51.20
Pantry shelf					
6' x 20"	BC@.600	Ea	51.70	22.40	74.10
Closet organizer. Wire shelf above and clothes hanging rack below					
5'-8' wide shelving	BC@1.00	Ea	63.10	37.40	100.50
5' wide, with free-slide clothes	BC@1.00	Ea	136.00	37.40	173.40
Glass shelving kits, includes wall support bracket(s)					
8" x 24" x 3/8", wall, silver support bracket	BC@.400	Ea	45.60	15.00	60.60
8" x 36" x 3/8", wall, silver support bracket	BC@.400	Ea	44.60	15.00	59.60
8" x 48" x 3/8", wall, silver support bracket	BC@.450	Ea	76.40	16.80	93.20
12" x 24" x 3/8", wall, silver support bracket	BC@.400	Ea	51.50	15.00	66.50
12" x 36" x 3/8", wall, silver support bracket	BC@.400	Ea	75.20	15.00	90.20
12" x 48" x 3/8", wall, silver support bracket	BC@.450	Ea	79.20	16.80	96.00
12" x 12", corner, silver support brackets	BC@.500	Ea	15.70	18.70	34.40
Add for opaque glass	—	%	11.1	—	—

	Craft@Hrs	Unit	Material	Labor	Total
Glass shelf, 3/8" glass. Add shelf supports below.					
24" x 8", clear	BC@.100	Ea	20.30	3.74	24.04
24" x 12", clear	BC@.100	Ea	21.80	3.74	25.54
36" x 8", clear	BC@.100	Ea	27.40	3.74	31.14
36" x 12", clear	BC@.100	Ea	32.40	3.74	36.14
48" x 8", clear	BC@.100	Ea	30.40	3.74	34.14
48" x 12", clear	BC@.100	Ea	44.60	3.74	48.34
Brackets for glass shelf, per bracket					
Pelican bracket, any color, min 2 per shelf	BC@.250	Ea	8.08	9.35	17.43
Decorator bracket, silver-ish finish	BC@.250	Ea	10.00	9.35	19.35

Shower and Tub Doors

	Craft@Hrs	Unit	Material	Labor	Total
Swinging shower doors, with hardware, tempered safety glass					
Minimum quality pivot shower door, 64" high, silver finish frame, obscure glass					
28" to 31" wide	BG@1.57	Ea	128.00	56.70	184.70
31" to 34" wide	BG@1.57	Ea	134.00	56.70	190.70
Better quality pivot shower door, 64" high, silver or gold tone frame, obscure glass					
24" to 26" wide	BG@1.57	Ea	154.00	56.70	210.70
26" to 28" wide	BG@1.57	Ea	168.00	56.70	224.70
30" to 32" wide	BG@1.57	Ea	175.00	56.70	231.70
32" to 34" wide	BG@1.57	Ea	190.00	56.70	246.70
48" wide	BG@1.57	Ea	250.00	56.70	306.70
Frameless swinging shower doors, to 60" wide by 70" high					
1/4" clear glass	BG@1.57	Ea	338.00	56.70	394.70
Silver solstice	BG@1.57	Ea	456.00	56.70	512.70
Nickel solstice	BG@1.57	Ea	497.00	56.70	553.70
Silver clear	BG@1.57	Ea	456.00	56.70	512.70
Sliding shower doors, 2 panels, 5/32" tempered glass, anodized aluminum frame, 70" high, outside towel bar					
Non-textured glass, 48" wide	BG@1.57	Ea	298.00	56.70	354.70
Non-textured glass, 56" wide	BG@1.57	Ea	311.00	56.70	367.70
Non-textured glass, 64" wide	BG@1.57	Ea	317.00	56.70	373.70
Texture, opaque, 48" wide	BG@1.57	Ea	340.00	56.70	396.70
Texture, opaque, 56" wide	BG@1.57	Ea	362.00	56.70	418.70
Texture, opaque, 64" wide	BG@1.57	Ea	372.00	56.70	428.70
One panel double mirrored, one bronze tinted	BG@1.57	Ea	384.00	56.70	440.70
Snap-on plastic trim kit, per set of doors	BG@.151	Ea	35.30	5.46	40.76
Sliding shower doors, 2 panels, 1/4" tempered glass, anodized aluminum frame, 70" high, outside towel bar					
Non-textured glass, 48" wide	BG@1.57	Ea	409.00	56.70	465.70
Non-textured glass, 56" wide	BG@1.57	Ea	404.00	56.70	460.70
Non-textured glass, 64" wide	BG@1.57	Ea	449.00	56.70	505.70
Frosted opaque design, 48" wide	BG@1.57	Ea	535.00	56.70	591.70
Frosted opaque design, 56" wide	BG@1.57	Ea	566.00	56.70	622.70
Frosted, opaque design, 64" wide	BG@1.57	Ea	596.00	56.70	652.70
Tub doors, two sliding panels, 54" high, to 60" wide opening, with towel bar					
Minimum quality, hammered glass	BG@1.77	Ea	128.00	64.00	192.00
Better quality, textured glass	BG@1.77	Ea	184.00	64.00	248.00
5/32-inch glass, silk screen design	BG@1.77	Ea	452.00	64.00	516.00
Frameless with 1/4" clear glass	BG@1.77	Ea	404.00	64.00	468.00
Frameless with 1/4" box lite glass	BG@1.77	Ea	376.00	64.00	440.00
Frameless with 1/4" delta frost glass	BG@1.77	Ea	443.00	64.00	507.00

	Craft@Hrs	Unit	Material	Labor	Total
Shower Stalls No plumbing, piping or valves included.					
Three-wall molded fiberglass shower stall with integrated soap shelf and textured bottom. White. 72" high. Add the cost of a shower door from the preceding section.					
32" x 32"	P1@3.90	Ea	367.00	144.00	511.00
36" x 36"	P1@3.90	Ea	368.00	144.00	512.00
48" x 34"	P1@3.90	Ea	483.00	144.00	627.00
48" x 34" with bench seats	P1@3.90	Ea	533.00	144.00	677.00
60" x 34" with bench seats	P1@3.90	Ea	536.00	144.00	680.00
Neo-angle 2-wall molded fiberglass shower stalls with integrated soap shelf and textured bottom but no door or glass walls. White. 72" high.					
38" x 38"	P1@2.50	Ea	507.00	92.20	599.20
Add for neo-angle glass walls and pivot door	P1@1.40	Ea	652.00	51.60	703.60
Neo-angle 4-wall molded fiberglass shower stalls with integrated soap shelf, textured bottom, glass walls and door. 72" high. Obscure glass in an aluminum frame.					
38" x 38", chrome frame	P1@3.90	Ea	557.00	144.00	701.00
38" x 38", chrome frame, French glass	P1@3.90	Ea	934.00	144.00	1,078.00
42" x 42", chrome frame	P1@3.90	Ea	888.00	144.00	1,032.00
42" x 42", nickel frame	P1@3.90	Ea	889.00	144.00	1,033.00
Corner entry shower stall, 2 molded polystyrene walls and a two-panel aluminum-framed sliding glass door. With integrated corner shelves, textured base and drain. White with chrome frame.					
32" x 32" x 74"	P1@3.250	Ea	578.00	120.00	698.00
Round shower stall, white aluminum frame and walls, polystyrene sliding door and panel. With soap dishes, 6" textured base, drain and drain cover.					
32" x 32" x 74"	P1@3.250	Ea	782.00	120.00	902.00
Fiberglass shower receptors One-piece molded fiberglass shower floor. Slip resistant with a starburst pattern. Drain molded-in with seal for 2" ABS, PVC, iron pipe and strainer. White. Single threshold 7" high.					
36", neo-angle	PM@.600	Ea	164.00	26.10	190.10
38", neo-angle	PM@.800	Ea	187.00	34.80	221.80
32" x 32", square	PM@.600	Ea	114.00	26.10	140.10
36" x 36", square	PM@.600	Ea	123.00	26.10	149.10
32" x 48", rectangular	PM@.800	Ea	140.00	34.80	174.80
34" x 48", rectangular	PM@.800	Ea	167.00	34.80	201.80
34" x 60", rectangular	PM@.800	Ea	179.00	34.80	213.80
Cultured marble receptor, 36" x 48"	PM@2.00	Ea	471.00	86.90	557.90
Shower bed, mortar Includes vapor barrier, lath, mortar and hand floating. Add adjustable floor drain and rough-in plumbing.					
Construct built-up mortar shower base	B6@.191	SF	4.08	6.29	10.37
Exterior shutters Louvered co-polymer. Price per pair. If needed, add hinges and anchors from the section below.					
15" x 39"	BC@.200	Pr	35.10	7.48	42.58
15" x 43"	BC@.200	Pr	39.30	7.48	46.78
15" x 48"	BC@.200	Pr	39.00	7.48	46.48
15" x 52"	BC@.320	Pr	43.10	12.00	55.10
15" x 55"	BC@.320	Pr	47.40	12.00	59.40
15" x 60"	BC@.320	Pr	48.40	12.00	60.40

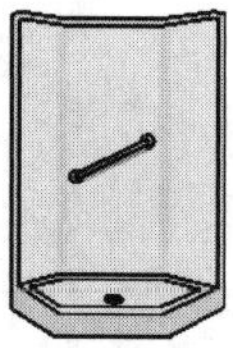

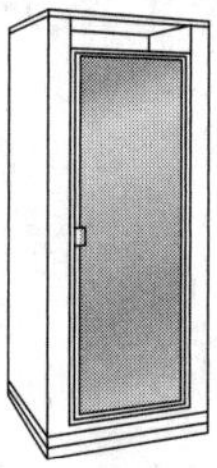

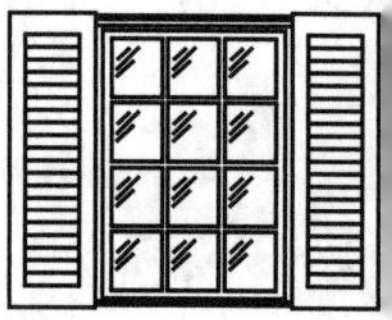

	Craft@Hrs	Unit	Material	Labor	Total
Installation of exterior shutters Figures in the material column show the cost of anchors and hinges.					
Installing shutters on hinges					
Wood frame construction, 1-3/8" throw					
25" to 51" high	BC@.400	Pr	34.60	15.00	49.60
52" to 80" high	BC@.634	Pr	52.00	23.70	75.70
Masonry construction, 4-1/4" throw					
25" to 51" high	BC@.598	Pr	55.50	22.40	77.90
52" to 80" high	BC@.827	Pr	74.00	30.90	104.90
Installing fixed shutters, any size	BC@.390	Pr	6.59	14.60	21.19

Shutters, hurricane protection Exterior shutters for residential and commercial applications. International Building Code Standard D-4355, Dade County Building Code standard E-1886. ASTM D-5621. Tested to ASTM specifications in excess of 150 MPH wind speed. Folding Shutter Corporation Armor Screen. Add for a 30-foot rolling scissor lift, if required, for installation.

Roll-up hurricane shutters, corrugated metal. Includes retractor reel, enclosure box, hand crank, guide rails, above-window aluminum support bar with lag bolt plate and mounting bolts. Electric drive module includes drive motor, switch and 12-volt rechargeable battery pack for power out operation.

	Craft@Hrs	Unit	Material	Labor	Total
Standard window and door sizes	B1@.015	SF	29.90	.51	30.41
Custom window and door sizes	B1@.015	SF	33.60	.51	34.11
Add for optional electric drive, battery & switch	—	Ea	1,310.00	—	1,310.00

CLOSED

OPEN

Accordion-type hurricane shutters, flat metal or reinforced vinyl panels. Includes above-window guide-rail mount with bottom rail bearing track, vertical retractor reel, enclosure box, bearing-mounted guide rails, supporting mount plates with lag bolts and hand crank. Electric drive module includes drive motor, switch and 12-volt rechargeable battery pack for power out operation.

	Craft@Hrs	Unit	Material	Labor	Total
Standard window and door sizes	B1@.010	SF	26.20	.34	26.54
Custom window and door sizes	B1@.010	SF	33.60	.34	33.94
Add for optional electric drive, battery & switch	—	Ea	1,020.00	—	1,020.00

Fixed corrugated panel hurricane shutters. Galvanized steel, ground anti-cut plastic-coated edges with F-shaped steel and paint-coated vertical mounting tracks. Includes studcons with wing nuts or lag bolt tie-downs and edge-seal water barrier stripping.

	Craft@Hrs	Unit	Material	Labor	Total
Standard window and door sizes	B1@.015	SF	14.20	.51	14.71
Custom window and door sizes	B1@.015	SF	15.40	.51	15.91

Bahama type coated metal, vinyl-coated wood or reinforced vinyl panels. Includes above-window single-panel swivel mount with bottom rail twin support outriggers. Not suitable for covering doors. Secured with either lag bolts or studcons with wing nuts.

	Craft@Hrs	Unit	Material	Labor	Total
Standard window sizes	B1@.012	SF	20.30	.41	20.71
Custom window sizes	B1@.012	SF	26.20	.41	26.61

Colonial type hurricane shutters. Coated metal, vinyl-coated wood, or reinforced vinyl panels. Includes side swivel-mounted twin-panel with hold-open lag bolts or studcons with wing nuts. Deployed mode uses supplied hold-closed barrier bar with tie-down lag bolts or studcons with wing nuts. Not suitable for covering doors.

	Craft@Hrs	Unit	Material	Labor	Total
Standard window sizes	B1@.015	SF	13.10	.51	13.61
Custom window sizes	B1@.015	SF	15.40	.51	15.91

Kevlar window and door hurricane protection. Padded flexible Kevlar or equal plastic fabric secured with lag bolts or studcons with wing nut tie-downs. Secured to wall studs or the window/door frame and removed.

	Craft@Hrs	Unit	Material	Labor	Total
Standard window sizes	B1@.010	SF	28.60	.34	28.94
Custom window sizes	B1@.010	SF	31.00	.34	31.34

	Craft@Hrs	Unit	Material	Labor	Total
Additional hurricane shutter costs, when applicable.					
Add for Lexan or equal ballistic plastic panels	—	%	15.0	—	—
Add for transparent flexible panels	—	%	10.0	—	—
Add for wind sensor module	—	%	10.0	—	—

Cover window or door with plywood panel Single use, minimum 5/8 inch thickness. Installed with lag bolts or studcons with wing nut tie-downs. Secured to wall studs or the window/door frame and removed.

	Craft@Hrs	Unit	Material	Labor	Total
Per SF or window or door covered	B1@.020	SF	1.04	.68	1.72

Siding See also Siding in the Lumber Section, Plywood and Hardboard.

Fiber cement lap siding, HardiPlank® 6-1/4" width requires 20 planks per 100 square feet of wall. 7-1/4" width requires 17 planks per 100 square feet of wall. 8-1/4" width requires 15 planks per 100 square feet of wall. 9-1/4" width requires 13 planks per 100 square feet of wall. 12" width requires 10 planks per 100 square feet of wall. Material price includes 10% for waste and fasteners.

	Craft@Hrs	Unit	Material	Labor	Total
6-1/4" x 12', cedarmill	B1@.058	SF	1.24	1.96	3.20
6-1/4" x 12', smooth	B1@.058	SF	1.59	1.96	3.55
7-1/4" x 12', cedarmill	B1@.052	SF	1.68	1.76	3.44
8-1/4" x 12', colonial roughsawn	B1@.048	SF	1.48	1.62	3.10
8-1/4" x 12', cedarmill	B1@.048	SF	1.32	1.62	2.94
8-1/4" x 12', beaded cedarmill	B1@.048	SF	1.60	1.62	3.22
8-1/4" x 12', beaded	B1@.048	SF	1.36	1.62	2.98
8-1/4" x 12', smooth	B1@.048	SF	1.55	1.62	3.17
9-1/4" x 12', cedarmill	B1@.046	SF	1.70	1.56	3.26
12" x 12', smooth	B1@.042	SF	1.54	1.42	2.96
12" x 12', cedarmill	B1@.042	SF	1.65	1.42	3.07

Fiber cement panel siding Primed, HardiPanel®, 4' x 8' panels. Includes 10% for waste and fasteners.

	Craft@Hrs	Unit	Material	Labor	Total
Sierra, Grooves 8" OC	BC@.042	SF	1.10	1.57	2.67
Stucco	BC@.042	SF	1.34	1.57	2.91

Fiber cement fiber trim Primed cement fiber trim, HardiTrim®, per linear foot

	Craft@Hrs	Unit	Material	Labor	Total
Rustic, 3/4" x 4", 12'	BC@.032	LF	1.42	1.20	2.62
Rustic, 3/4" x 6", 12'	BC@.032	LF	1.62	1.20	2.82
Smooth, 5/4" x 4", 10'	BC@.032	LF	1.56	1.20	2.76
Smooth, 5/4" x 6", 10'	BC@.032	LF	2.02	1.20	3.22

Fiber cement fiber soffit Primed cement fiber soffit, James Hardie

	Craft@Hrs	Unit	Material	Labor	Total
Solid, 1/4" x 4' x 8' panel	BC@.031	SF	1.30	1.16	2.46
Vented, 1/4" x 12" wide	BC@.031	LF	1.88	1.16	3.04

Hardboard panel siding Cost per square foot including 5% waste. 4' x 8' panels.

	Craft@Hrs	Unit	Material	Labor	Total
7/16" plain panel	B1@.022	SF	.96	.74	1.70
7/16" grooved 8" OC	B1@.022	SF	1.19	.74	1.93
7/16" Sturdi-Panel grooved 8" OC	B1@.022	SF	.71	.74	1.45
7/16" cedar, grooved 8" OC	B1@.022	SF	.94	.74	1.68
7/16" cedar, plain, textured	B1@.022	SF	1.11	.74	1.85
15/32" Duratemp, grooved 8" OC	B1@.022	SF	1.32	.74	2.06
5/16" SmartSide, grooved 8" OC	B1@.022	SF	1.11	.74	1.85
Add for 4' x 9' panels	—	SF	.19	—	.19

	Craft@Hrs	Unit	Material	Labor	Total
Hardboard lap siding Primed plank siding. With 8% waste, 6" x 16' covers 5.6 square feet, 8" x 16' covers 7.4 square feet, 9-1/2" x 16' covers 9.7 square feet.					
7/16" x 6" x 16', smooth lap	B1@.033	SF	1.08	1.12	2.20
7/16" x 6" x 16', textured cedar	B1@.033	SF	1.50	1.12	2.62
7/16" x 8" x 16', textured cedar	B1@.031	SF	1.14	1.05	2.19
7/16" x 8" x 16', smooth	B1@.031	SF	1.69	1.05	2.74
1/2" x 8" x 16', self-aligning	B1@.031	SF	1.70	1.05	2.75
1/2" x 8" x 16', old mill sure lock	B1@.031	SF	1.94	1.05	2.99
3/8" x 8" x 16', smartside lap siding	B1@.031	SF	1.74	1.05	2.79
7/16" x 6" joint cover	—	Ea	.60	—	.60
7/16" x 6" corner	—	Ea	.93	—	.93
7/16" x 8" joint cover	—	Ea	1.13	—	1.13
7/16" x 8" corner	—	Ea	1.15	—	1.15
7/16" x 9-1/2" joint cover	—	Ea	1.10	—	1.10
7/16" x 9-1/2" corner	—	Ea	1.19	—	1.19
OSB siding Oriented strand board. Includes 6% waste.					
Lap siding, smooth finish					
3/8" x 8" x 16' (190 LF per Sq)	B1@.033	SF	1.77	1.12	2.89
Lap siding, rough-sawn finish					
7/16" x 6" x 16' (250 LF per Sq)	B1@.033	SF	2.36	1.12	3.48
7/16" x 8" x 16' (190 LF per Sq)	B1@.031	SF	1.94	1.05	2.99
Smart Panel II siding					
3/8" x 4' x 8', smooth	B1@.022	SF	1.17	.74	1.91
3/8" x 4' x 9', 8" grooved	B1@.022	SF	1.27	.74	2.01
7/16" x 4' x 8', 4" grooved	B1@.022	SF	1.45	.74	2.19
7/16" x 4' x 8', 8" grooved	B1@.022	SF	1.48	.74	2.22
5/8" x 4' x 8', borate treated	B1@.022	SF	1.95	.74	2.69
Primed Smart Trim. Per linear foot of trim, including 10% waste.					
4/4" x 4" x 16'	B1@.012	LF	.68	.41	1.09
4/4" x 6" x 16'	B1@.017	LF	1.05	.58	1.63
4/4" x 8" x 16'	B1@.021	LF	1.41	.71	2.12
Pre-stained finish, Olympic machine coat, any of 85 colors, factory applied					
One-coat application, 5-year warranty	—	SF	.19	—	.19
Two-coat application, 10-year warranty	—	SF	.26	—	.26
Oriented strand board soffit panels. Textured Smart Soffit. Including 10% waste.					
3/8" x 4" x 8'	B1@.033	SF	1.40	1.12	2.52
Plywood siding 4' x 8' panels. Includes caulking, nails and 6% waste. For T1-11 siding, see Plywood in the Lumber section.					
11/32" satin bead	B1@.025	SF	1.05	.85	1.90
3/8" plybead, 16" grooved	B1@.025	SF	1.08	.85	1.93
3/8" southern pine	B1@.025	SF	1.08	.85	1.93
3/8" premium plain fir	B1@.025	SF	1.37	.85	2.22
15/32" primed, 8" grooved	B1@.025	SF	1.31	.85	2.16
15/32" fir, 8" grooved	B1@.025	SF	1.53	.85	2.38
19/32" primed, 8" grooved	B1@.025	SF	1.82	.85	2.67
5/8" rough sawn pine	B1@.025	SF	1.66	.85	2.51
5/8" premium fir	B1@.025	SF	2.21	.85	3.06
Yellow pine 4' x 8' plywood batten siding. Battens are 10" wide each 12" on center. Includes caulking, nails and 6% waste.					
19/32" thick	B1@.025	SF	1.38	.85	2.23
5/8" ACQ treated	B1@.025	SF	2.21	.85	3.06

Siding

	Craft@Hrs	Unit	Material	Labor	Total
Aluminum sheet siding					
Aluminum corrugated 4-V x 2-1/2", plain or embossed finish. Includes 15% waste and coverage loss.					
17 gauge, 26" x 6' to 24'	B1@.034	SF	2.69	1.15	3.84
19 gauge, 26" x 6' to 24'	B1@.034	SF	2.78	1.15	3.93
Rubber filler strip, 3/4" x 7/8" x 6'	—	LF	.41	—	.41
Flashing for corrugated aluminum siding, embossed					
End wall, 10" x 52"	B1@.048	Ea	4.81	1.62	6.43
Side wall, 7-1/2" x 10'	B1@.015	LF	2.07	.51	2.58
Aluminum smooth 24 gauge, horizontal patterns, non-insulated					
8" or double 4" widths, acrylic finish	B1@2.77	Sq	192.00	93.80	285.80
12" widths, bonded vinyl finish	B1@2.77	Sq	194.00	93.80	287.80
Add for foam backing	—	Sq	37.80	—	37.80
Starter strip	B1@.030	LF	.46	1.02	1.48
Inside and outside corners	B1@.033	LF	1.39	1.12	2.51
Casing and trim	B1@.033	LF	.46	1.12	1.58
Drip cap	B1@.044	LF	.47	1.49	1.96
Galvanized steel siding					
28 gauge, 27-1/2" wide (includes 20% coverage loss)					
6' to 12' standard lengths	B1@.034	SF	1.63	1.15	2.78
26 gauge, 26" wide (includes 15% coverage loss)					
6' to 12' standard lengths	B1@.034	SF	1.99	1.15	3.14
Shingle siding					
Cedar sidewall shingles, bundle covers 25 square feet, 16" long, 7-1/2" exposure, 5 shingles are 2" thick (5/2)					
#2 Western red cedar	B1@3.86	Sq	276.00	131.00	407.00
Bleached cedar, rebutted and re-jointed	B1@3.86	Sq	423.00	131.00	554.00
Sanded cedar	B1@3.86	Sq	506.00	131.00	637.00
Grooved cedar	B1@3.86	Sq	505.00	131.00	636.00
Primed smooth cedar	B1@3.86	Sq	536.00	131.00	667.00
Panelized shingle siding Shakertown, KD, regraded shingle on plywood backing, no waste included.					
8' long x 7" wide single course					
Colonial 1	B1@.033	SF	5.35	1.12	6.47
Cascade	B1@.033	SF	5.16	1.12	6.28
8' long x 14" wide, single course					
Colonial 1	B1@.033	SF	5.35	1.12	6.47
8' long x 14" wide, double course					
Colonial 2	B1@.033	SF	5.86	1.12	6.98
Cascade Classic	B1@.033	SF	5.16	1.12	6.28
Decorative shingles, 5" wide x 18" long, Shakertown, fancy cuts, 9 hand-shaped patterns					
7-1/2" exposure	B1@.035	SF	6.26	1.18	7.44
Deduct for 10" exposure	—	SF	-.68	—	-.68
Vinyl siding Solid vinyl. Embossed wood grain texture.					
Double 4" traditional lap profile, 12' 6" long panels, 8" exposure. Each panel covers 8.33 SF before cutting waste. Case of 24 panels covers 200 square feet. Cost per square (100 square feet).					
.040" thick, lighter colors	B1@3.34	Sq	66.60	113.00	179.60
.040" thick, darker colors and textures	B1@3.34	Sq	91.30	113.00	204.30
.042" thick, lighter colors	B1@3.34	Sq	84.80	113.00	197.80
.042" thick, darker colors and textures	B1@3.34	Sq	89.90	113.00	202.90
.044" thick, most colors and textures	B1@3.34	Sq	87.80	113.00	200.80

	Craft@Hrs	Unit	Material	Labor	Total
Double 4.5" traditional lap profile, 12' 1" long panels, 9" exposure. Each panel covers 9.09 SF. Case of 22 panels covers 200 square feet. Cost per square (100 square feet).					
.040" thick, most colors	B1@3.34	Sq	80.50	113.00	193.50
.040" thick, darker colors and textures	B1@3.34	Sq	80.50	113.00	193.50
Double 5" traditional lap profile, 12' long panels, 10" exposure. Each panel covers 10 SF. Case of 20 panels covers 200 square feet. Cost per square (100 square feet).					
.042" thick, lighter colors	B1@3.34	Sq	88.50	113.00	201.50
.042" thick, darker colors and textures	B1@3.34	Sq	88.50	113.00	201.50
Rigid PVC shingle panel lap siding. 3/4" thick. Cost per square (100 square feet).					
5" exposure, 6-1/2" x 5' panels	B1@3.34	Sq	328.00	113.00	441.00
7" exposure, 8-1/2" x 5' panels	B1@3.34	Sq	328.00	113.00	441.00
Trim for vinyl siding					
Starter strip, 2-1/4" x 12.6'	B1@.030	LF	.48	1.02	1.50
"J"-channel trim at wall openings, 12.5' long	B1@.033	LF	.51	1.12	1.63
Outside or inside corner, 10' long	B1@.033	LF	2.14	1.12	3.26
Casing and trim, 12.5' long	B1@.033	LF	.56	1.12	1.68
Mini mounting block, 4" x 6"	B1@.350	Ea	12.60	11.80	24.40
Vinyl "J"-block, 7" x 9"	B1@.350	Ea	13.50	11.80	25.30
Add for R-3 insulated vinyl siding	B1@.350	Sq	78.10	11.80	89.90
Thermoplastic resin siding Nailite™ 9/10" thick panels installed over sheathing. Add for trim board, corners, starter strips, "J"-channels and mortar fill. Based on five nails per piece. Includes 10% waste.					
Hand-split shake, 41-3/8" x 18-3/4"	B1@.043	SF	2.90	1.46	4.36
Hand-laid brick, 44-1/4" x 18-5/8"	B1@.043	SF	3.09	1.46	4.55
Hand-cut stone, 44-1/4" x 18-5/8"	B1@.043	SF	3.09	1.46	4.55
Rough sawn cedar, 59-1/4" x 15"	B1@.043	SF	3.21	1.46	4.67
Perfection plus cedar, 36-1/8" x 15"	B1@.043	SF	3.21	1.46	4.67
Ledge trim					
Brick ledge trim	B1@.033	LF	6.68	1.12	7.80
Stone ledge trim	B1@.033	LF	6.68	1.12	7.80
Corners					
Hand-split shake, 4" x 18"	B1@.030	LF	12.70	1.02	13.72
Rough sawn cedar 3" x 26"	B1@.030	LF	13.50	1.02	14.52
Hand-laid brick 4" x 18"	B1@.030	LF	13.50	1.02	14.52
Hand-cut stone 4" x 18"	B1@.030	LF	13.50	1.02	14.52
Perfection plus cedar 3" x 13"	B1@.030	LF	11.20	1.02	12.22
Starter strips					
12' universal	B1@.025	LF	.69	.85	1.54
"J"-channels					
Hand-split shake 3/4" opening	B1@.025	LF	1.01	.85	1.86
Hand-split shake 1-1/4" flexible opening	B1@.027	LF	2.03	.91	2.94
Rough sawn cedar 3/4" opening	B1@.025	LF	.76	.85	1.61
Rough sawn cedar 1-1/4" flexible opening	B1@.027	LF	2.03	.91	2.94
Hand-laid brick 3/4" opening	B1@.025	LF	.76	.85	1.61
Hand-cut stone 3/4" opening	B1@.025	LF	.76	.85	1.61
Perfection plus cedar 3/4" opening	B1@.025	LF	.76	.85	1.61
Thermoplastic siding accessories					
Mortar fill, 12 tubes and 200 LF per carton	—	Ea	40.10	—	40.10
Touch up paint, 6 oz. aerosol can	—	Ea	5.99	—	5.99
Skylights Polycarbonate dome, clear transparent or tinted, roof opening sizes, price each, Crestline Skylights, curb or flush mount, self-flashing. Comfort™					
Single dome, 2' x 2'	B1@2.58	Ea	90.70	87.30	178.00
Single dome, 2' x 4'	B1@2.58	Ea	141.00	87.30	228.30
Double dome, 4' x 4'	B1@2.84	Ea	262.00	96.10	358.10

Skylights

	Craft@Hrs	Unit	Material	Labor	Total
Tempered over laminated low-E argon gas filled doubled insulated fixed glass skylights. Includes costs for flashing. For installation on roofs with 15- to 85-degree slope. Labor costs are for installation of skylight and flashing. Roll shade costs are for factory attached shades. No carpentry or roofing included.					
Operable skylight, Velux®, VS® Comfort™ models. Prices include EDL® flashing.					
21-1/2" x 38-1/2", #104	B1@3.42	Ea	1,070.00	116.00	1,186.00
21-1/2" x 46-3/8", #106	B1@3.42	Ea	1,140.00	116.00	1,256.00
21-1/2" x 55", #108	B1@3.42	Ea	1,230.00	116.00	1,346.00
30-5/8" x 38-1/2", #304	B1@3.42	Ea	1,170.00	116.00	1,286.00
30-5/8" x 46-3/8", #306	B1@3.42	Ea	1,230.00	116.00	1,346.00
30-5/8" x 55", #308	B1@3.52	Ea	1,280.00	119.00	1,399.00
44-3/4" x 46-1/2", #606	B1@3.52	Ea	1,380.00	119.00	1,499.00
Add for electric operation	—	%	—	—	225.0
Add for ComfortPlus™ Laminated Low E	—	%	10.0	—	—
Add for roll shade, natural					
21-1/2" x 27-1/2" to 55" width	—	Ea	73.30	—	73.30
30-5/8" x 38-1/2" to 55" width	—	Ea	84.40	—	84.40
Fixed skylight, low-E laminated and tempered insulating glass. Wood frame. Aluminum exterior.					
5-5/16" x 46-3/8"	B1@3.42	Ea	264.00	116.00	380.00
21-1/2" x 27-1/2"	B1@3.42	Ea	213.00	116.00	329.00
21-1/2" x 38-1/2"	B1@3.42	Ea	272.00	116.00	388.00
21-1/2" x 46-3/8"	B1@3.42	Ea	304.00	116.00	420.00
30-5/8" x 38-1/2"	B1@3.42	Ea	321.00	116.00	437.00
30-5/8" x 46-3/8"	B1@3.42	Ea	364.00	116.00	480.00
30-5/8" x 55"	B1@3.52	Ea	411.00	119.00	530.00
Add for roll shade, natural					
21-1/2" x 27-1/2" to 70-7/8" width	—	Ea	78.10	—	78.10
30-5/8" x 38-1/2" to 55" width	—	Ea	82.50	—	82.50
Fixed ventilation skylight with removable filter on ventilation flap, Velux® model FSF® ComfortPlus™. Prices include EDL® flashing.					
21-1/2" x 27-1/2", #101	B1@3.14	Ea	295.00	106.00	401.00
21-1/2" x 38-1/2", #104	B1@3.14	Ea	344.00	106.00	450.00
21-1/2" x 46-1/2", #106	B1@3.14	Ea	392.00	106.00	498.00
21-1/2" x 70-7/8", #108	B1@3.42	Ea	427.00	116.00	543.00
30-5/8" x 38-1/2", #304	B1@3.14	Ea	422.00	106.00	528.00
30-5/8" x 46-3/8", #306	B1@3.14	Ea	480.00	106.00	586.00
30-5/8" x 55", #308	B1@3.39	Ea	522.00	115.00	637.00
44-3/4" x 27-1/2", #601	B1@3.36	Ea	459.00	114.00	573.00
44-3/4" x 46-1/2", #606	B1@3.39	Ea	605.00	115.00	720.00
Add for roll shade, natural					
21-1/2" x 27-1/2" to 70-7/8" width	—	Ea	88.00	—	88.00
30-5/8" x 38-1/2" to 55" width	—	Ea	99.60	—	99.60
Curb mounted fixed skylight, Velux model FCM™					
22-1/2" x 22-1/2", #2222	B1@3.14	Ea	163.00	106.00	269.00
22-1/2" x 34-1/2", #2234	B1@3.14	Ea	214.00	106.00	320.00
22-1/2" x 46-1/2", #2246	B1@3.14	Ea	233.00	106.00	339.00
30-1/2" x 30-1/2", #3030	B1@3.14	Ea	259.00	106.00	365.00
46-1/2" x 46-1/2", #4646	B1@3.14	Ea	396.00	106.00	502.00

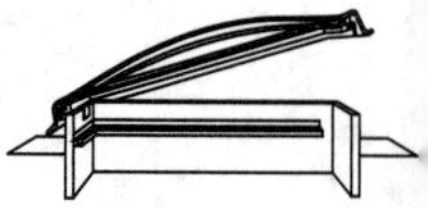

	Craft@Hrs	Unit	Material	Labor	Total
Top hinged roof windows Aluminum-clad wood frame, double insulated tempered over laminated low-E gas filled double insulated glass, including prefabricated flashing, exterior awning, interior roller blind and insect screen. Sash rotates 180 degrees. For installation on roofs with 20- to 55-degree slope. Labor costs are for installation of roof window, flashing and sun screening accessories. No carpentry or roofing work other than curb included. Add for interior trim. Listed by actual unit dimensions, top hung, Velux® model GPL™ Comfort™ Roof Window.					
30-5/8" wide x 55" high, #308	B1@3.42	Ea	940.00	116.00	1,056.00
44-3/4" wide x 46-3/8" high, #606	B1@3.52	Ea	1,050.00	119.00	1,169.00
Soffit Systems					
Baked enamel finish, 6" fascia, "J"-channel, 8" perforated or solid soffit, .019 gauge aluminum.					
12" soffit	B1@.047	LF	4.39	1.59	5.98
18" soffit	B1@.055	LF	5.10	1.86	6.96
24" soffit	B1@.060	LF	5.78	2.03	7.81
F-channel	B1@.019	LF	.62	.64	1.26
Vinyl soffit systems					
12" soffit	B1@.030	LF	3.94	1.02	4.96
18" soffit	B1@.030	LF	4.53	1.02	5.55
24" soffit	B1@.030	LF	5.11	1.02	6.13
F-channel	B1@.019	LF	.73	.64	1.37
Aluminum fascia alone					
4" fascia	B1@.030	LF	1.09	1.02	2.11
6" fascia	B1@.030	LF	1.33	1.02	2.35
8" fascia	B1@.030	LF	1.55	1.02	2.57
Soil Testing					
Field observation and testing					
Soil technician (average)	—	Hr	—	—	66.30
Soil testing, per test					
Moisture retention	—	Ea	—	—	37.80
Bulk density (loose or core)	—	Ea	—	—	28.50
Porosity	—	Ea	—	—	44.90
Organic matter	—	Ea	—	—	38.80
Plasticity (Liquid and Plastic Limit)	—	Ea	—	—	61.20
Water holding capacity	—	Ea	—	—	37.80
Herbicide detection	—	Ea	—	—	61.20
Complete mineral analysis	—	Ea	—	—	76.50
Foundation investigation (bearing capacity, lateral loads, piles, seismic, stability, settlement for design purposes) and preliminary soils investigation (depth of fill, classification and profile of soil, expansion, shrinkage, grading, drainage recommendations). Including drilling and sampling costs.					
Drill rig (driller and helper)	—	Hr	—	—	158.00
Staff engineer	—	Hr	—	—	76.50
Project engineer, RCE	—	Hr	—	—	91.90
Principal engineer	—	Hr	—	—	153.00
Transportation	—	Mile	—	—	1.33
Transportation	—	Hr	—	—	15.30
Laboratory testing (general)	—	Hr	—	—	76.50
Laboratory testing (varies on individual test basis)	—	Ea	—	—	56.10
Report preparation					
Analysis, conclusions, recommendations	—	Ea	—	—	2,280.00
Court preparation (Principal Engineer)	—	Hr	—	—	179.00
Expert witness court appearance	—	Hr	—	—	307.00
Add for hazardous studies	—	%	—	—	20.0

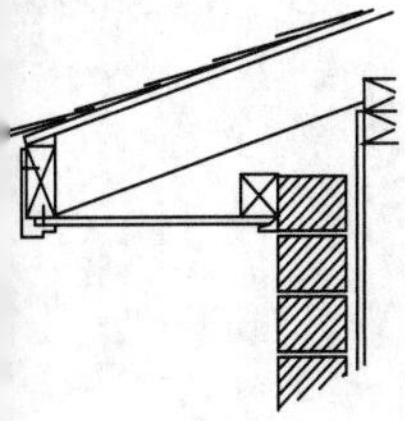

	Craft@Hrs	Unit	Material	Labor	Total
Soil Treatments, Subcontract Costs based on total square footage inside of, and including, foundation. Includes inside and outside perimeter of foundation, interior foundation walls, and underneath all slabs. Three-plus year re-application guarantee against existence of termites. Use $300 as a minimum job charge.					
Dursban T.C, Primus, or Equity. Mix applied per manufacturers' and state and federal specifications.					
Complete application	—	SF	—	—	.48
Solar Photovoltaic Electrical Systems, Subcontract Costs are for solar electric generating systems. These estimates include engineering, installation, application for permits and application for financial incentives, where available. Costs do not consider tax incentives or rebates. Production capacity figures assume 8 hours of sun time daily. Cost will be higher where less sun time is available.					
Small remote vacation home system (12 volt DC). 64 watt solar electric module (98 amp hours), digital voltage regulator, mounting rack and wiring.					
384 watt-hours per day	—	LS	—	—	1,150.00
Larger remote primary home system (120 volt AC). Includes eight storage batteries (1,050 amp hours), voltage regulator, mounting rack, 2,400 watt DC to AC inverter.					
2,880 watt-hours per day	—	LS	—	—	6,900.00
Basic two room solar power package. Includes three 48 watt PV panels, one 12 amp voltage regulator, one 220 Amp hour battery with hydrocaps, one 600 watt inverter, mounting frame, hardware and two receptacles					
12 amp regulator, with 600 watt inverter	—	LS	—	—	2,790.00
Small home solar power package. 90% solar powered system for 1,500 SF home. Includes six 60 watt PV panels, one 750 Amp hour battery, 20 amp voltage regulator and DC distribution box and one 2.2 kW inverter. Costs also include one solar hot water system, one water source heat pump, one 19 cubic foot refrigerator freezer, one ringer type washing machine, six 12 volt lights and three 12 volt ceiling fans					
20 amp regulator, 12 volt system	—	LS	—	—	14,500.00
Medium sized home solar power package. 80% solar powered system for 2,500 SF home. Includes ten 45 watt PV panels, one 750 Amp hour battery, one 30 amp voltage regulator and one 2 kW inverter with charger. Costs also include one solar domestic hot water system and 22 assorted 12 volt light fixtures					
30 amp regulator, 12 volt system	—	LS	—	—	8,730.00
Grid-connected solar power package. For use when the electric utility company buys excess power (meter spins backward). 102 poly panels (1,768 SF) with inverter and mounting rack. Peak power is 23.5 kW DC and 21.5 kW AC. Annual production is 35,350 kWh. Includes a 5-year warranty and one year of maintenance.					
Net-metered 21 kW system	—	LS	—	—	81,600.00
Photovoltaic roofing systems Photovoltaic panels and shingles. Converts sunlight into electric energy and distributes it directly to the building. The solar electric roofing products are configured in series or parallel on the roof deck to form an array. The array is then integrated into the roof following standard roofing specifications. Installation time does not include electrical connections.					
Architectural or structural standing photovoltaic seam panels					
70 watt panel, 58" x 14"	RR@.035	SF	170.00	1.46	171.46
100 watt panel, 45" x 27"	RR@.035	SF	233.00	1.46	234.46
205 watt panel, 60" x 40"	RR@.033	SF	293.00	1.37	294.37
285 watt panel, 65" x 39"	RR@.033	SF	334.00	1.37	335.37
Photovoltaic shingles, 12" x 86" panel					
62 watt shingle panel	RR@.230	Ea	319.00	9.58	328.58
144 watt shingle panel	RR@.260	Ea	381.00	10.80	391.80

	Craft@Hrs	Unit	Material	Labor	Total
Photovoltaic roofing system accessories					
Add for combiner box	—	Ea	556.00	—	556.00
Add for 2.8 kW inverter	—	Ea	1,680.00	—	1,680.00
Add for 3.6 kW inverter	—	Ea	1,890.00	—	1,890.00
Add for 6 volt DC 350 Ah storage batteries	—	Ea	166.00	—	166.00
Add for utility ground fault protection device	—	Ea	319.00	—	319.00
Solar pool heating system					
Pool system, eight panels, valves, and piping	—	LS	—	—	5,230.00
Spa system, one panel, valves and piping	—	LS	—	—	1,570.00
Spas, fiberglass, outdoor Includes pump and standard heater. Add the cost of a concrete slab base.					
63" x 79", 31 jets	P1@3.50	Ea	2,800.00	129.00	2,929.00
72" x 72", 14 jets	P1@4.00	Ea	2,600.00	148.00	2,748.00
76" x 76", 51 jets	P1@4.00	Ea	2,800.00	148.00	2,948.00
92" x 92", 104 jets	P1@4.00	Ea	4,800.00	148.00	4,948.00
Add for electrical connection	—	Ea	—	—	230.00

Stairs

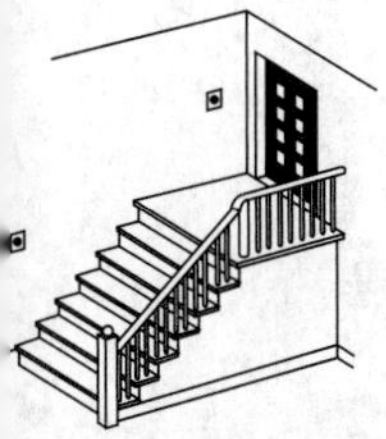

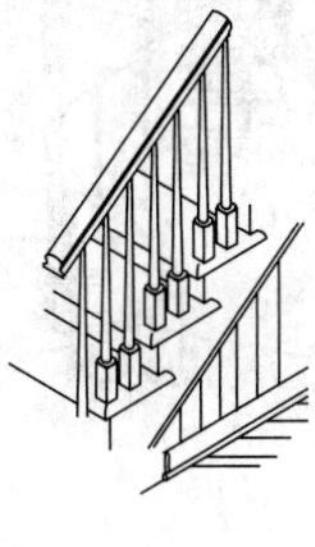

	Craft@Hrs	Unit	Material	Labor	Total
Factory-cut and assembled straight closed box stairs, unfinished, 36" width					
Oak treads with 7-1/2" risers, price per riser					
3'0" wide	B1@.324	Ea	121.00	11.00	132.00
3'6" wide	B1@.324	Ea	157.00	11.00	168.00
4'0" wide	B1@.357	Ea	168.00	12.10	180.10
Deduct for pine treads and plywood risers	—	%	-22.0	—	—
Add for prefinished assembled stair rail with balusters and newel, per riser	B1@.257	Ea	62.30	8.70	71.00
Add for prefinished handrail, with brackets and balusters	B1@.135	LF	21.70	4.57	26.27
Basement stairs, open riser, delivered to job site assembled, 12 treads, 2' 11-3/4" wide					
13 risers at 7-13/16" riser height	B1@4.00	Ea	270.00	135.00	405.00
13 risers at 8" riser height	B1@4.00	Ea	277.00	135.00	412.00
13 risers at 8-3/16" riser height	B1@4.00	Ea	284.00	135.00	419.00
Add for handrail	B1@.161	LF	11.30	5.45	16.75
Curved stair, clear oak, self-supporting, 8'6" radii, factory cut, unfinished, unassembled					
Open one side (1 side against wall)					
8'9" to 9'4" rise	B1@24.6	Ea	6,280.00	833.00	7,113.00
9'5" to 10'0" rise	B1@24.6	Ea	6,770.00	833.00	7,603.00
10'1" to 10'8" rise	B1@26.5	Ea	7,250.00	897.00	8,147.00
10'9" to 11'4" rise	B1@26.5	Ea	7,780.00	897.00	8,677.00
Open two sides					
8'9" to 9'4" rise	B1@30.0	Ea	11,300.00	1,020.00	12,320.00
9'5" to 10'0" rise	B1@30.0	Ea	12,100.00	1,020.00	13,120.00
10'1" to 10'8" rise	B1@31.9	Ea	12,800.00	1,080.00	13,880.00
10'9" to 11'4" rise	B1@31.9	Ea	13,600.00	1,080.00	14,680.00
Add for newel posts	B1@.334	Ea	78.30	11.30	89.60
Straight stairs, red oak, factory cut, unassembled, 36" tread, includes two 1-1/2" x 3-1/2" handrails and 7/8" round balusters.					
70" to 77" with 10 risers	B1@12.0	Ea	1,690.00	406.00	2,096.00
77" to 85" with 11 risers	B1@12.0	Ea	1,910.00	406.00	2,316.00
85" to 93" with 12 risers	B1@12.0	Ea	2,240.00	406.00	2,646.00
93" to 100" with 13 risers	B1@14.0	Ea	2,250.00	474.00	2,724.00
100" to 108" with 14 risers	B1@14.0	Ea	2,440.00	474.00	2,914.00

Stairs

	Craft@Hrs	Unit	Material	Labor	Total
108" to 116" with 15 risers	B1@14.0	Ea	2,570.00	474.00	3,044.00
116" to 124" with 16 risers	B1@16.0	Ea	2,790.00	542.00	3,332.00
124" to 131" with 17 risers	B1@16.0	Ea	2,880.00	542.00	3,422.00
131" to 139" with 18 risers	B1@16.0	Ea	3,220.00	542.00	3,762.00
Add for 44" tread, any of above	—	Ea	106.00	—	106.00
Add for straight rail, unbored	B1@.060	LF	12.60	2.03	14.63
Add for straight nosing	B1@.060	LF	7.83	2.03	9.86
Add for round balusters, 7/8" x 42"	B1@.334	Ea	4.92	11.30	16.22
Add for square balusters, 1-1/8" x 1-1/8" x 44"	B1@.334	Ea	10.10	11.30	21.40
Add for newel posts, 3" x 3" x 44"	B1@.334	Ea	44.40	11.30	55.70
Spiral stairs, red oak, FOB factory, double handrails, 5' diameter					
74" to 82" with 9 risers	B1@16.0	Ea	3,680.00	542.00	4,222.00
82" to 90" with 10 risers	B1@16.0	Ea	3,940.00	542.00	4,482.00
90" to 98" with 11 risers	B1@16.0	Ea	4,010.00	542.00	4,552.00
98" to 106" with 12 risers	B1@16.0	Ea	4,090.00	542.00	4,632.00
106" to 114" with 13 risers	B1@20.0	Ea	4,160.00	677.00	4,837.00
114" to 122" with 14 risers	B1@20.0	Ea	4,320.00	677.00	4,997.00
122" to 130" with 15 risers	B1@20.0	Ea	4,540.00	677.00	5,217.00
Add for 6' diameter	—	%	20.0	—	—
Add for 8'6" diameter	—	%	25.0	—	—
Add for mahogany, any of above	—	%	10.0	—	—
Add for straight rail, unbored	B1@.060	LF	16.70	2.03	18.73
Add for straight nosing, unbored	B1@.060	LF	8.01	2.03	10.04
Add for balusters, 7/8" x 42"	B1@.334	Ea	5.14	11.30	16.44
Add for newel posts 1-7/8" x 44"	B1@.334	Ea	30.90	11.30	42.20
Spiral stairs, aluminum, delivered to job site unassembled, 7-3/4" or 8-3/4" riser heights, 5' diameter					
85-1/4" to 96-1/4" with 10 treads	B1@9.98	Ea	2,610.00	338.00	2,948.00
93" to 105" with 11 treads	B1@10.7	Ea	2,830.00	362.00	3,192.00
100-3/4" to 113-3/4" with 12 treads	B1@11.3	Ea	3,090.00	383.00	3,473.00
108-1/2" to 122-1/2" with 13 treads	B1@12.0	Ea	3,320.00	406.00	3,726.00
116-1/4" to 131-1/4" with 14 risers	B1@12.6	Ea	3,520.00	427.00	3,947.00
124" to 140" with 15 risers	B1@12.8	Ea	3,810.00	433.00	4,243.00
131-3/4" to 148-3/4" with 16 risers	B1@13.5	Ea	4,000.00	457.00	4,457.00
138-1/2" to 157-1/2" with 17 risers	B1@14.2	Ea	4,200.00	481.00	4,681.00
147-1/4" to 166-1/4" with 18 risers	B1@14.8	Ea	4,490.00	501.00	4,991.00
Deduct for 4' diameter	—	%	−20.0	—	—
Deduct for 4'6" diameter	—	%	−10.0	—	—
Add for additional aluminum treads	—	Ea	240.00	—	240.00
Add for oak tread inserts	—	Ea	93.70	—	93.70
Spiral stairs, steel, tubular steel handrail, composition board treads, delivered unassembled, 5' diameter					
86" to 95" with 10 risers	B1@9.98	Ea	1,600.00	338.00	1,938.00
95" to 105" with 11 risers	B1@10.7	Ea	1,770.00	362.00	2,132.00
105" to 114" with 12 risers	B1@11.3	Ea	1,880.00	383.00	2,263.00
114" to 124" with 13 risers	B1@12.0	Ea	2,110.00	406.00	2,516.00
124" to 133" with 14 risers	B1@12.7	Ea	2,400.00	430.00	2,830.00
Deduct for 4' diameter	—	%	−20.0	—	—
Add for 6' diameter	—	%	24.0	—	—
Add for oak treads	—	%	25.0	—	—
Add for oak handrail	—	%	45.0	—	—

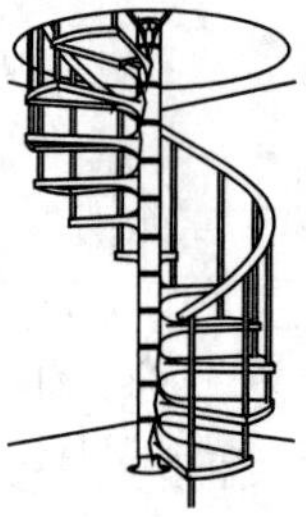

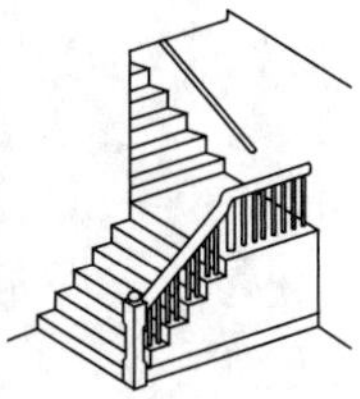

	Craft@Hrs	Unit	Material	Labor	Total
Job-built stairways 3 stringers cut from 2" x 12" Douglas fir material, treads and risers from 3/4" CDX plywood or OSB sheathing. Cost per 7-1/2" rise, 36" wide					
Using 2" Douglas fir, per MBF	—	MBF	949.00	—	949.00
Using 3/4" CDX plywood, per MSF	—	MSF	847.00	—	847.00
Using 3/4" OSB sheathing, per MSF	—	MSF	677.00	—	677.00
Using 1" x 6" white pine, per MBF	—	MBF	2,230.00	—	2,230.00
Straight run, 8'0" to 10'0" rise, plywood, per riser	B1@.530	Ea	15.70	17.90	33.60
Straight run, 8'0" to 10'0" rise, OSB, per riser	B1@.530	Ea	14.20	17.90	32.10
"L"- or "U"-shape, plywood, add for landings	B1@.625	Ea	17.70	21.20	38.90
"L"- or "U"-shape, per riser, OSB, add for landings	B1@.625	Ea	16.30	21.20	37.50
Semi-circular, repetitive work, plywood, per riser	B1@.795	Ea	17.70	26.90	44.60
Semi-circular, repetitive work, OSB, per riser	B1@.795	Ea	16.30	26.90	43.20
Landings, from 2" x 6" Douglas fir and 3/4" CDX plywood or 3/4" OSB, surfaced,					
per SF of landing surface, plywood	B1@.270	SF	3.66	9.14	12.80
per SF of landing surface, OSB	B1@.270	SF	3.36	9.14	12.50
Stair treads and risers Unfinished. Including layout, cutting, fitting, and installation of treads, risers and typical tread nosing. Includes a miter return on one side of each tread. 9' rise is usually 14 treads and 15 risers					
Yellow pine treads, 11-1/2" x 48"	—	Ea	10.80	—	10.80
Oak treads, 11-1/2" x 48"	—	Ea	38.50	—	38.50
Oak curved first (return) tread, 11-1/2" x 48"	—	Ea	30.40	—	30.40
Oak risers, 8" x 48"	—	Ea	21.90	—	21.90
Oak nosing	—	LF	8.03	—	8.03
Oak treads, risers and nosing for 9' rise stairway	BC@2.50	Ea	903.00	93.50	996.50
Skirt board with dadoes for treads and risers	BC@3.75	Ea	37.70	140.00	177.70
Skirt board on open side, mitered risers	BC@5.50	Ea	37.70	206.00	243.70
Oak shoe rail with fillet, 1-1/4" plowed,					
2-1/2" x 3/4"	BC@.030	LF	3.31	1.12	4.43
Oak landing tread, 1" x 5-1/2"	BC@.180	LF	6.39	6.73	13.12
False treads, 4-3/4" x 16-1/4" x 6"					
Right end	BC@.180	Ea	14.20	6.73	20.93
Left end	BC@.180	Ea	14.20	6.73	20.93
Wall tread, 4-3/4" x 13-1/4"	BC@.180	Ea	17.20	6.73	23.93
False stair tread cap and riser - Repair	BC@.250	Ea	39.20	9.35	48.55
Anti-skid adhesive strips. Peel and stick on wood, concrete or metal.					
2-3/4" x 14"	BC@.050	Ea	4.14	1.87	6.01
4" x 16"	BC@.050	Ea	6.51	1.87	8.38
Stair rails, posts and balusters Unfinished. Including layout, cutting, fitting and installation					
Newel posts, 3" x 3" x 48" high					
Half newel, ball top, hemlock	BC@2.50	Ea	29.40	93.50	122.90
Half newel, ball top, oak	BC@2.50	Ea	37.00	93.50	130.50
Starting newel, ball top, hemlock	BC@2.50	Ea	35.20	93.50	128.70
Starting newel, ball top, oak	BC@2.50	Ea	49.30	93.50	142.80
Starting newel, peg top, oak	BC@2.50	Ea	49.50	93.50	143.00
Landing newel, ball top, hemlock	BC@2.50	Ea	48.60	93.50	142.10
Landing newel, ball top, oak	BC@2.50	Ea	66.00	93.50	159.50
Starting newel, peg top, oak	BC@2.50	Ea	69.70	93.50	163.20
Starting newel, ball top, poplar	BC@2.50	Ea	41.70	93.50	135.20

	Craft@Hrs	Unit	Material	Labor	Total
Handrail, 2-3/8" D x 2-1/4" W, set between posts					
Oak, set over newel posts	BC@.150	LF	6.26	5.61	11.87
Oak, set between newel posts	BC@.250	LF	6.26	9.35	15.61
Oak with fillet, set over newel posts	BC@.250	LF	7.39	9.35	16.74
Hemlock, set between newel posts	BC@.150	LF	4.93	5.61	10.54
Poplar, set between newel posts	BC@.150	LF	4.89	5.61	10.50
Hemlock, set over newel posts	BC@.250	LF	4.89	9.35	14.24
Poplar, set over newel posts	BC@.250	LF	4.89	9.35	14.24
Flat bottom, set over newel posts	BC@.250	LF	3.06	9.35	12.41
Balusters, 1-1/4" D x 2-1/4" W, round top					
Oak, 34" high	BC@.330	Ea	7.21	12.30	19.51
Oak, 36" high	BC@.330	Ea	8.08	12.30	20.38
Poplar, 34" high	BC@.330	Ea	4.89	12.30	17.19
Poplar, 36" high	BC@.330	Ea	5.15	12.30	17.45
Hemlock, 31" high, square top	BC@.330	Ea	4.67	12.30	16.97
Hemlock, 34" high, tapered top	BC@.330	Ea	5.19	12.30	17.49
Hemlock, 36" high, tapered top	BC@.330	Ea	5.84	12.30	18.14
Hemlock, 36" high, square top	BC@.330	Ea	5.54	12.30	17.84
Hemlock, 41" high, tapered top	BC@.330	Ea	6.46	12.30	18.76
Hemlock, 41" high, square top	BC@.330	Ea	7.08	12.30	19.38
Handrail easings and transition fittings, oak					
Gooseneck riser	BC@1.75	LF	66.90	65.40	132.30
Upeasing	BC@1.75	Ea	21.30	65.40	86.70
Opening cap	BC@1.75	Ea	17.40	65.40	82.80
Quarter return	BC@1.75	Ea	16.50	65.40	81.90
Volute	BC@1.75	Ea	74.00	65.40	139.40
Turnout	BC@1.75	Ea	41.40	65.40	106.80
Starting easing	BC@1.75	Ea	29.40	65.40	94.80
Over easing	BC@1.75	Ea	20.90	65.40	86.30
Stairs, attic Economy folding stairway, tri-fold design, sanded plywood door, full width main hinge, fir door panel, 3/16" handrail, preassembled, 1" x 4" x 13" treads, 1" x 5" stringer, 22" x 54" opening size					
7' to 8'9" ceiling height, 64" landing	B1@5.00	Ea	110.00	169.00	279.00
8' 9" to 10' ceiling height, 67" landing	B1@5.00	Ea	125.00	169.00	294.00
Economy all-aluminum tri-fold stairway, sanded plywood door, full width main hinge, double-riveted treads, 3/16" handrail, preassembled, 25" x 54" opening size					
8'9" ceiling height, 64" landing	B1@5.00	Ea	209.00	169.00	378.00
10' ceiling height, 67" landing	B1@5.00	Ea	237.00	169.00	406.00
Good quality folding stairway, Bessler Stairways, full width main hinge, fir door panel, molded handrail, preassembled, 1" x 6" treads, 1" x 5" stringer and frame of select yellow pine, "space saver" for narrow openings, 22", 25-1/2", or 30" wide by 54" long					
8'9" or 10' height	B1@5.00	Ea	458.00	169.00	627.00
Superior quality, Bessler Stairways, solid one-piece stringer sliding stairway, stringer and treads of clear yellow pine, unassembled, full-width piano hinge at head of stairs, with springs.					
Compact model 26/26T, for a 22-1/2" x 54" to 22-1/2" x 74" opening, 7'7" to 9'3" height					
1" x 4" stringers and treads	B1@6.00	Ea	886.00	203.00	1,089.00
Standard unit, for openings from 25-1/2" x 5'6" to 2'6" x 6'0", 7'7" to 10'10" heights					
1" x 6" stringers and treads	B1@6.00	Ea	886.00	203.00	1,089.00
Heavy-duty unit, for openings from 2'6" x 5'10" to 2'6" x 8'0", 7'7" to 12'10" heights					
1" x 8" stringers and treads	B1@9.00	Ea	1,690.00	305.00	1,995.00

	Craft@Hrs	Unit	Material	Labor	Total
Steam Bath Generators Steam bath equipment, 240 volts AC, single phase, UL approved. Costs include steam generator and controls. Labor costs include installation of steam unit and connections to existing supply, steam and drain piping, no rough plumbing or electrical included. Installed in existing, adequately sealed, tub enclosure. Maximum enclosure size as shown. www.amerec.com					
4.5kW, 160 cubic feet max	P1@2.50	Ea	1,920.00	92.20	2,012.20
6kW, 180 cubic feet max	P1@2.50	Ea	2,060.00	92.20	2,152.20
7.5kW, 220 cubic feet max	P1@2.50	Ea	2,230.00	92.20	2,322.20
9kW, 260 cubic feet max	P1@2.50	Ea	2,060.00	92.20	2,152.20
10.5kW, 300 cubic feet max	P1@2.50	Ea	2,040.00	92.20	2,132.20
12kW, 360 cubic feet max	P1@2.50	Ea	2,500.00	92.20	2,592.20
20kW, 875 cubic feet max	P1@2.50	Ea	5,380.00	92.20	5,472.20
30kW, 1,275 cubic feet max	P1@2.50	Ea	5,960.00	92.20	6,052.20
Tarpaulins					
Polyethylene, heavy duty. Water repellant, with rustproof grommets, cut sizes					
6' x 8'	—	Ea	8.77	—	8.77
9' x 9'	—	Ea	14.10	—	14.10
8' x 10'	—	Ea	12.20	—	12.20
12' x 16'	—	Ea	28.80	—	28.80
16' x 20'	—	Ea	45.50	—	45.50
20' x 30'	—	Ea	77.30	—	77.30
40' x 60'	—	Ea	214.00	—	214.00
Canvas, 8 oz.					
8' x 10'	—	Ea	49.50	—	49.50
10' x 12'	—	Ea	72.90	—	72.90
10' x 16'	—	Ea	98.90	—	98.90
14' x 20'	—	Ea	180.00	—	180.00
20' x 20'	—	Ea	228.00	—	228.00
Taxes, Payroll					
Employer's cost for payroll taxes and insurance, expressed as a percent of total payroll. See also, Insurance for more detailed information.					
Rule of thumb: When actual payroll taxes and insurance are not known, estimate that for each $1 paid in wages the employer must pay an additional $.30					
Payroll taxes and insurance	—	%	—	—	30.0
Specific taxes, percent of total payroll					
Typical SUI, State unemployment insurance	—	%	—	—	3.40
Typical Disability Insurance (CA, HI, NJ, NY, RI)	—	%	—	—	.90
FICA Social Security 6.20%, Medicare 1.45%	—	%	—	—	7.65
FUTA, Federal Unemployment Insurance	—	%	—	—	.60
Thresholds					
Aluminum threshold with vinyl feet					
3-3/8" x 5/8" x 36", economy	BC@.515	Ea	10.00	19.30	29.30
3-3/4" x 1" x 36", bronze	BC@.515	Ea	10.90	19.30	30.20
3-3/4" x 1" x 36", silver	BC@.515	Ea	13.80	19.30	33.10
3-1/2" x 5/8" x 72", brown	BC@.730	Ea	28.50	27.30	55.80
3-1/2" x 5/8" x 72", silver	BC@.730	Ea	24.70	27.30	52.00
3-1/2" x 5/8" x 72", gold	BC@.730	Ea	30.20	27.30	57.50
Aluminum bumper threshold with replaceable vinyl insert and vinyl feet					
3-3/16" x 5/8" x 36", silver	BC@.515	Ea	14.20	19.30	33.50
3-3/8" x 1" x 36" silver	BC@.515	Ea	10.10	19.30	29.40
3-3/8" x 1" x 36", gold	BC@.515	Ea	22.90	19.30	42.20

Thresholds

	Craft@Hrs	Unit	Material	Labor	Total
3-1/2" x 3/4" x 36", silver	BC@.515	Ea	10.50	19.30	29.80
3-1/2" x 3/4" x 36", gold	BC@.515	Ea	25.60	19.30	44.90
3-3/8" x 1" x 72", silver	BC@.730	Ea	36.20	27.30	63.50
Aluminum saddle interior threshold, smooth flat top, covers floor seams					
1-3/4" x 1/8" x 36", silver	BC@.515	Ea	7.82	19.30	27.12
1-3/4" x 1/8" x 36", gold	BC@.515	Ea	12.00	19.30	31.30
2-1/2" x 1/4" x 36", gold	BC@.515	Ea	8.62	19.30	27.92
Aluminum commercial fluted saddle threshold, UL fire labeled					
5" x 1/2" x 36", mill finish	BC@.515	Ea	19.40	19.30	38.70
5" x 1/2" x 72", mill finish	BC@.730	Ea	48.00	27.30	75.30
Aluminum adjustable threshold, height adjusts from 7/8" to 1-5/16", vinyl top insert and vinyl feet					
3-1/2" x 36", silver	BC@.515	Ea	19.60	19.30	38.90
Aluminum saddle exterior threshold, 1" minimum door clearance, for under-door and drip cap door bottoms.					
3-1/2" x 1" x 36", silver	BC@.515	Ea	11.10	19.30	30.40
4" x 1" x 36", silver	BC@.515	Ea	15.30	19.30	34.60
Aluminum saddle exterior threshold, with vinyl bottom insert					
5" x 36", chrome	BC@.515	Ea	20.40	19.30	39.70
5" x 36", gold	BC@.515	Ea	19.10	19.30	38.40
Oak and aluminum adjustable threshold, height adjusts from 1-1/8" to 1-3/8"					
5-5/8" x 36", silver	BC@.515	Ea	25.10	19.30	44.40
Oak bumper threshold, clear vinyl insert					
3-1/2" x 1" x 36"	BC@.515	Ea	22.40	19.30	41.70
Oak low boy threshold					
3-1/2" x 3/4" x 36"	BC@.515	Ea	11.90	19.30	31.20
3-1/2" x 3/4" x 72"	BC@.730	Ea	37.30	27.30	64.60
Aluminum under-door threshold kit, with vinyl insert.					
1-1/4" x 36", silver	BC@.515	Ea	6.31	19.30	25.61
3-3/4" x 36", gold	BC@.515	Ea	22.00	19.30	41.30
Vinyl replacement threshold insert					
1-7/8" x 36", gray	BC@.100	Ea	2.59	3.74	6.33
1-1/2" x 36", brown	BC@.100	Ea	2.79	3.74	6.53
Oak sill, adjustable, commercial grade, adjusts to accommodate gaps					
1-1/8" x 4-9/16" x 36", in-swing	BC@.750	Ea	25.60	28.00	53.60
1-1/8" x 4-9/16" x 36", out-swing	BC@.750	Ea	53.90	28.00	81.90
Aluminum sill nosing					
1-1/2" x 2-3/4" x 36", silver	BC@.381	Ea	6.31	14.20	20.51
2-3/4" x 4-1/2" x 36", bronze	BC@.381	Ea	14.50	14.20	28.70
2-3/4" x 1-1/2" x 72", mill	BC@.540	Ea	25.80	20.20	46.00
Aluminum sill cover, for use over rough concrete sills					
2-3/4" x 1-1/2" x 36"	BC@.381	Ea	11.90	14.20	26.10
2-3/4" x 1-1/2" x 72"	BC@.540	Ea	13.60	20.20	33.80
Aluminum sill edging					
2-3/4" x 1-1/2" x 36"	BC@.381	Ea	10.00	14.20	24.20
Aluminum door shoe, with vinyl insert					
1-3/8" x 36", brown	BC@.381	Ea	9.53	14.20	23.73
1-3/4" x 36" brown, with drip cap	BC@.381	Ea	12.00	14.20	26.20
Aluminum "L"-shape door bottom, with drip cap and vinyl weather seal					
1-3/4" x 36", gold	BC@.381	Ea	11.20	14.20	25.40

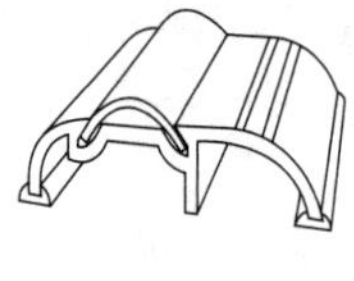

	Craft@Hrs	Unit	Material	Labor	Total
Aluminum "U"-shape door bottom, for exterior doors, with vinyl insert					
1-3/4" x 36"	BC@.381	Ea	13.30	14.20	27.50
1-3/4" x 36", with drip cap	BC@.381	Ea	22.90	14.20	37.10
Aluminum commercial door bottom, UL fire labeled					
36", mill finish	BC@.381	Ea	10.90	14.20	25.10
36", bronze anodized	BC@.381	Ea	9.41	14.20	23.61
Brush door bottom, with brush sweep					
1-3/4" x 36", vinyl	BC@.381	Ea	7.37	14.20	21.57
2-1/8" x 36", rubber	BC@.381	Ea	9.03	14.20	23.23
2" x 36", wood	BC@.381	Ea	12.10	14.20	26.30
Aluminum drip cap door bottom					
1-3/4" x 36", silver	BC@.381	Ea	8.83	14.20	23.03
1-1/2" x 36", heavy duty	BC@.381	Ea	13.40	14.20	27.60
Vinyl slide-on door bottom					
1-3/4" x 36"	BC@.381	Ea	9.53	14.20	23.73
Aluminum and vinyl door bottom					
36", aluminum	BC@.381	Ea	9.87	14.20	24.07
Aluminum door bottom and sweep, interior or exterior doors					
2" x 36", heavy duty	BC@.381	Ea	13.30	14.20	27.50
Oak door sweep, unfinished					
36" wide	BC@.381	Ea	12.30	14.20	26.50

Tile Typical materials costs for common sizes from 4" x 4" to 20" x 20". Subtract 20% for minimum or builder quality tile. Add 25% for better quality tile. Add the cost of mortar or adhesive, grout and labor to install tile from the section below. Costs assume a standard 'checkerboard' layout and 10% breakage and cutting waste. Allow an additional 5% to 10% for any other layout pattern. Tiles can vary greatly in cost. Decorative and imported tile will cost more. See also Shower Stalls.

	Craft@Hrs	Unit	Material	Labor	Total
Ceramic tile					
4-1/4" x 4-1/4", 8 tile cover 1 SF	—	SF	4.01	—	4.01
12" x 12", 1 tile covers 1 SF	—	SF	1.44	—	1.44
16" x 16", 1 tile covers 1.8 SF	—	SF	1.39	—	1.39
18" x 18", 1 tile covers 2.25 SF	—	SF	1.58	—	1.58
Porcelain tile					
6" x 6", 4 tile cover 1 SF	—	SF	4.87	—	4.87
12" x 12", 1 tile covers 1 SF	—	SF	1.94	—	1.94
18" x 18", 1 tile covers 2.25 SF	—	SF	2.35	—	2.35
20" x 20", 1 tile covers 2.8 SF	—	SF	2.00	—	2.00
Travertine tile					
4" x 4", 9 tile cover 1 SF	—	SF	6.56	—	6.56
6" x 6", 4 tile cover 1 SF	—	SF	10.50	—	10.50
12" x 12", 1 tile covers 1 SF	—	SF	3.28	—	3.28
16" x 16", 1 tile covers 1.8 SF	—	SF	2.19	—	2.19
18" x 18", 1 tile covers 2.25 SF	—	SF	3.41	—	3.41
Slate tile					
4" x 4", 9 tile cover 1 SF	—	SF	6.57	—	6.57
12" x 12", 1 tile covers 1 SF	—	SF	1.65	—	1.65
12" x 24", 1 tile covers 2 SF	—	SF	4.61	—	4.61
Marble tile					
6" x 6", 4 tile cover 1 SF	—	SF	9.21	—	9.21
12" x 12", 1 tile covers 1 SF	—	SF	6.72	—	6.72
18" x 18", 1 tile covers 2.25 SF	—	SF	6.59	—	6.59

	Craft@Hrs	Unit	Material	Labor	Total
Granite tile					
12" x 12", 1 tile covers 1 SF	—	SF	7.87	—	7.87
Glass tile					
2" x 2", 36 tile cover 1 SF	—	SF	35.20	—	35.20
3" x 6", 8 tile cover 1 SF	—	SF	14.80	—	14.80
4" x 4", 9 tile cover 1 SF	—	SF	36.00	—	36.00
Unglazed ceramic tile (pavers), costs do not include sealing					
Minimum quality 'Saltillo'	—	SF	1.09	—	1.09
Good quality 'Paver'	—	SF	1.31	—	1.31
Better quality 'kiln-dried'	—	SF	3.97	—	3.97
Handmade	—	SF	8.25	—	8.25
Handmade, medallion	—	SF	28.60	—	28.60
Mosaic tile, face-mounted or mesh-backed sheets, typically 12" x 12". Costs will vary widely					
Ceramic mosaic tile					
Good quality	—	SF	5.57	—	5.57
Glass mosaic tile					
Good quality	—	SF	15.10	—	15.10
Combination media (glass and stone) mosaic tile					
Good quality	—	SF	14.50	—	14.50
Natural stone mosaic tile					
Good quality	—	SF	18.60	—	18.60
Decorative tile, listellos, pencil liners, mosaic trim, bullnose and accent tiles, etc. Costs will vary widely.					
Bullnose or wall cap tiles					
Good quality, per SF	—	SF	13.40	—	13.40
Good quality, per LF	—	LF	3.06	—	3.06
Listellos, pencil liners					
Good quality	—	LF	4.57	—	4.57
Decorative trim and accent tile					
Typical cost	—	SF	27.10	—	27.10
Ceramic fixtures, glazed.					
Toothbrush/tumbler holder	TL@.250	Ea	7.65	8.92	16.57
Soap dish	TL@.250	Ea	11.20	8.92	20.12
Towel bar assembly, 24" long	TL@.550	Ea	18.30	19.60	37.90
Bath corner shelf, 8" x 8"	TL@.500	Ea	14.80	17.80	32.60
Toilet tissue holder, 4-1/4" x 6"	TL@.250	Ea	30.90	8.92	39.82
Towel ring	TL@.550	Ea	13.40	19.60	33.00
Robe hook	TL@.550	Ea	6.08	19.60	25.68

Tile installation The costs below are for setting and grouting tile only. Smaller and more complex jobs will cost more. Add the cost of preparing the surface for installation (tile backer) and the tile. See Ditra Slab Membrane for detachable membrane costs.

Ceramic tile adhesive. Premixed Type 1, Acryl-4000. 1 gallon covers 70 SF applied with #1 trowel (3/16" x 5/32" "V"-notch), 50 SF applied with #2 trowel (3-/16" x 1/4" "V"-notch) or 40 SF applied with #3 trowel (1/4" x 1/4" square-notch).

	Craft@Hrs	Unit	Material	Labor	Total
1 quart	—	Ea	7.25	—	7.25
1 gallon	—	Ea	12.30	—	12.30
3-1/2 gallons	—	Ea	38.50	—	38.50
Tile adhesive applied with #2 trowel	—	SF	.23	—	.23

	Craft@Hrs	Unit	Material	Labor	Total
Thin-set tile mortar. 50 pound bag covers 100 SF applied with #1 trowel (1/4" x 1/4" square-notch), 80 SF applied with #2 trowel (1/4" x 3/8" square-notch), 45 SF applied with #3 trowel (1/2" x 1/2" square notch). Cost per 50 pound bag.					
Standard, gray	—	Ea	5.97	—	5.97
Standard, white	—	Ea	7.77	—	7.77
VersaBond, gray	—	Ea	14.30	—	14.30
VersaBond, white	—	Ea	15.40	—	15.40
FlexiBond, gray	—	Ea	34.30	—	34.30
Marble and granite mix	—	Ea	31.00	—	31.00
VersaBond, gray applied with #3 trowel	—	SF	.32	—	.32
Tile grout. Polymer-modified dry grout for joints 1/16" to 1/2". Coverage varies with tile and joint size. Typically, a 25 lb. bag of sanded grout will cover 100 SF of 12" x 12" tile with a 1/8" spacing. CustomBuildingProducts.com offers a grout material calculator.					
Unsanded, 10 lb. bag	—	Ea	11.90	—	11.90
Sanded, all colors, 25 lb. bag	—	Ea	15.10	—	15.10
Saltillo grout, gray, 50 lb. bag	—	Ea	14.40	—	14.40
Installation of tile in adhesive Includes adhesive and grout. Adhesive installation not recommended for 'wet' areas. Add the cost of preparing the surface for installation (tile backer) and the cost of tile.					
Countertops and backsplashes					
Mosaic tile	TL@.203	SF	.29	7.24	7.53
4-1/4" x 4-1/4" to 6" x 6" glazed field tile	TL@.180	SF	.35	6.42	6.77
Countertop trim pieces and edge tile	TL@.180	LF	.07	6.42	6.49
Floors					
Mosaic tile	TL@.121	SF	.37	4.31	4.68
6" x 6" to 20" x 20" glazed field tile	TL@.110	SF	.38	3.92	4.30
Floor trim pieces and edge tile	TL@.110	LF	.07	3.92	3.99
Walls					
Mosaic tile	TL@.143	SF	.37	5.10	5.47
6" x 6" glazed field tile	TL@.131	SF	.38	4.67	5.05
Wall trim pieces and edge tile	TL@.131	LF	.07	4.67	4.74
Installation of tile in thin-set mortar Includes grout. Costs are for mortar and grout. Add the cost of surface preparation (backerboard) and tile.					
Countertops and backsplashes					
Mosaic tile	TL@.407	SF	.26	14.50	14.76
4-1/4" x 4-1/4" to 6" x 6" glazed field tile	TL@.352	SF	.26	12.60	12.86
Stone; granite, marble, travertine, 3/8" thick	TL@.455	SF	.51	16.20	16.71
Countertop trim pieces and edge tile	TL@.352	LF	.04	12.60	12.64
Floors					
Mosaic tile	TL@.238	SF	.33	8.49	8.82
4-1/4" x 4-1/4" to 6" x 6" glazed field tile	TL@.210	SF	.33	7.49	7.82
8" x 8" to 12" x 12" glazed field tile	TL@.200	SF	.33	7.13	7.46
16" x 16" to 20" x 20" glazed field tile	TL@.200	SF	.34	7.13	7.47
Floor trim pieces and edge tile	TL@.210	LF	.06	7.49	7.55
Quarry or paver tile	TL@.167	SF	.46	5.96	6.42
Stone; granite, marble, travertine, 3/8" thick	TL@.354	SF	.51	12.60	13.11
Walls					
Mosaic tile	TL@.315	SF	.54	11.20	11.74
4-1/4" x 4-1/4" to 6" x 6" glazed field tile	TL@.270	SF	.33	9.63	9.96
Stone; granite, marble, travertine, 3/8" thick	TL@.455	SF	.51	16.20	16.71
Wall trim pieces and edge tile	TL@.270	LF	.06	9.63	9.69

Tile Backerboard

	Craft@Hrs	Unit	Material	Labor	Total

Tile backerboard (Durock™ or Wonderboard™). Water-resistant underlayment for ceramic tile on floors, walls, countertops and other interior wet areas. Material cost for 100 square feet (CSF) of board includes waterproofing membrane, the backerboard (and 10% waste), 50 pounds of job mixed latex-fortified mortar for the joints and surface skim coat, 75 linear feet of fiberglass joint tape, 200 1-1/4" backerboard screws. For scheduling purposes, estimate that a crew of 2 can install, tape and apply the skim coat on the following quantity of backerboard in an 8-hour day: countertops 180 SF, floors 525 SF, and walls 350 SF. Use $250 as a minimum charge for this type work.

	Craft@Hrs	Unit	Material	Labor	Total
Using 15 Lb. felt waterproofing, per 400 SF roll	—	Roll	22.10	—	22.10
Using 1/4" backerboard, per 100 SF	—	CSF	61.70	—	61.70
Using 1/2" backerboard, per 100 SF	—	CSF	78.80	—	78.80
Using 50 Lb. of latex-fortified mortar each 100 SF, per 50 Lb. sack	—	Sack	14.30	—	14.30
Using 75 LF of backerboard tape each 100 SF, per 50 LF roll	—	Roll	4.60	—	4.60
Using 200 backerboard screws for each 100 SF, per pack of 200 screws	—	Pack	9.77	—	9.77
1/2" Backerboard with waterproofing, mortar, tape and screws					
Floors	T1@.030	SF	1.16	.99	2.15
Walls	T1@.045	SF	1.16	1.48	2.64
Countertops	T1@.090	SF	1.16	2.97	4.13
Subtract for 1/4" backerboard	—	SF	-0.17	—	-0.17

Vacuum Cleaning Systems, Central Subcontract. Costs listed are for better quality central vacuum power unit, piping to 4 remote outlets, hose and attachments (adequate for typical 2,000 SF home). Assumes that all vacuum tubes are installed before any interior finishes are applied.

	Craft@Hrs	Unit	Material	Labor	Total
Basic package with 23' hose	—	LS	—	—	1,670.00
Additional remote outlets	—	Ea	—	—	156.00
Add for electric or turbo power head	—	Ea	—	—	210.00

Vanity cabinets Sink base with no countertop, no lavatory bowl and no plumbing included. Prefinished. See also Countertops and Plumbing. 3/4" furniture-grade sides with veneer interior, overlay doors and drawers, and concealed hinges, 31-1/2" high.

	Craft@Hrs	Unit	Material	Labor	Total
Door only sink base vanity cabinets, white exterior finish. Maple interior finish, concealed hinges.					
18" x 16", 1 door	BC@.400	Ea	82.60	15.00	97.60
24" x 18", 2 doors	BC@.400	Ea	108.00	15.00	123.00
30" x 18", 2 doors	BC@.400	Ea	121.00	15.00	136.00
Standard quality vanity cabinets, veneer doors, drawer front(s) and face frame					
24" x 18", 1 door, 2 drawers	BC@.400	Ea	186.00	15.00	201.00
30" x 18", 1 door, 2 drawers	BC@.400	Ea	206.00	15.00	221.00
36" x 18", 2 doors, 2 drawers	BC@.400	Ea	235.00	15.00	250.00
Good quality vanity cabinets, white or hardwood exterior finish, ball bearing drawer glides					
24" x 21", 1 door, 1-drawer	BC@.400	Ea	321.00	15.00	336.00
30" x 21", 1 door, 4-drawers	BC@.400	Ea	331.00	15.00	346.00
36" x 21", 2 doors, 4 drawers	BC@.400	Ea	369.00	15.00	384.00
48" x 21", 2 doors, 7 drawers	BC@.500	Ea	437.00	18.70	455.70
Premium quality vanity cabinets, cinnamon oak doors and drawer fonts, adjustable hinges					
24" x 21", 1 door, 2 drawer	BC@.400	Ea	286.00	15.00	301.00
30" x 21", 1 door, 2 drawer	BC@.400	Ea	381.00	15.00	396.00
36" x 21", 1 door, 2 drawers	BC@.400	Ea	451.00	15.00	466.00
48" x 21", 1 door, 4 drawers	BC@.500	Ea	598.00	18.70	616.70
60" x 21", 2 doors, 4 drawers	BC@.500	Ea	654.00	18.70	672.70
Over the toilet vanity cabinet, 8" deep x 24" high					
24" wide, 2 doors, 1 shelf	B1@1.37	Ea	132.00	46.40	178.40
30" wide, 2 doors, 1 shelf	B1@1.37	Ea	178.00	46.40	224.40

	Craft@Hrs	Unit	Material	Labor	Total
Vents and Louvers					
Attic and gable louver vents, UV stabilized copolymer, screened, rough opening sizes					
12" x 12", 38 sq. inch vent area	SW@.448	Ea	34.30	18.90	53.20
12" x 18", 86 sq. inch vent area	SW@.448	Ea	40.80	18.90	59.70
18" x 24", 140 sq. inch vent area	SW@.871	Ea	50.10	36.70	86.80
21" x 27" oval	SW@.871	Ea	98.10	36.70	134.80
22" x 34", half round, 100 sq. inch vent area	SW@.871	Ea	75.90	36.70	112.60
16" round, 50 sq. inch vent area	SW@.448	Ea	80.50	18.90	99.40
12" x 18", round top 50 sq. inch vent area	SW@.448	Ea	59.90	18.90	78.80
22" octagon, 54 sq. inch vent area	SW@.871	Ea	62.70	36.70	99.40
Chimney caps					
9" x 9" rectangular	SW@.324	Ea	28.70	13.70	42.40
9" x 13" rectangular	SW@.324	Ea	31.30	13.70	45.00
13" x 13" rectangular	SW@.324	Ea	33.70	13.70	47.40
13" x 13" rectangular, stainless	SW@.324	Ea	53.90	13.70	67.60
8" x 8" to 13" x 13" adjustable	SW@.324	Ea	33.00	13.70	46.70
13" x 18" fixed, black	SW@.324	Ea	36.90	13.70	50.60
Clothes dryer vent set, aluminum, with hood, inside plate, 8' of flexible duct pipe, clamps and collar					
4" diameter vent kit	SW@.440	Ea	13.80	18.60	32.40
Flex hose, 4" diameter, 8' length	—	Ea	10.60	—	10.60
Flex hose clamps, 4" diameter	—	Ea	1.80	—	1.80
Code caps					
4" diameter, top only	SW@.324	Ea	24.70	13.70	38.40
6" diameter, top only	SW@.324	Ea	31.50	13.70	45.20
8" diameter, top only	SW@.324	Ea	38.40	13.70	52.10
6" diameter shake base	SW@.324	Ea	29.50	13.70	43.20
8" diameter shake base	SW@.324	Ea	30.80	13.70	44.50
Dormer louver vents, galvanized, 1/4" mesh screen					
19" x 3", low profile, rectangular	BC@.871	Ea	44.80	32.60	77.40
24" x 12", half round	BC@.871	Ea	46.20	32.60	78.80
Add for 1/8" mesh	—	%	3.0	—	—
Under-eave louver vents, rectangular, with 1/4" mesh screen, 16" wide					
16" x 4", mill finish	SW@.255	Ea	1.78	10.80	12.58
16" x 8", mill finish	SW@.255	Ea	2.22	10.80	13.02
16" x 8", brown finish	SW@.255	Ea	2.28	10.80	13.08
16" x 4", white finish	SW@.255	Ea	2.04	10.80	12.84
16" x 8", white finish	SW@.255	Ea	2.16	10.80	12.96
Foundation screen vents, galvanized, with screen, no louvers					
14" x 6"	SW@.255	Ea	3.59	10.80	14.39
16" x 4"	SW@.255	Ea	3.06	10.80	13.86
16" x 6"	SW@.255	Ea	3.31	10.80	14.11
16" x 8"	SW@.255	Ea	3.75	10.80	14.55
Automatic foundation vent, fits 8" x 16" concrete block opening, aluminum mesh on front and molded plastic screen on back. Opens at 72 degrees, closes at 38 degrees. 1" frame each side					
Automatic open and close	SW@.255	Ea	17.60	10.80	28.40
Foundation vent with manual damper, sheet metal					
4" x 16"	SW@.255	Ea	7.35	10.80	18.15
6" x 16"	SW@.255	Ea	8.06	10.80	18.86
8" x 16"	SW@.255	Ea	8.51	10.80	19.31
Foundation access door					
24" x 24"	BC@.363	Ea	32.00	13.60	45.60
32" x 24"	BC@.363	Ea	38.00	13.60	51.60

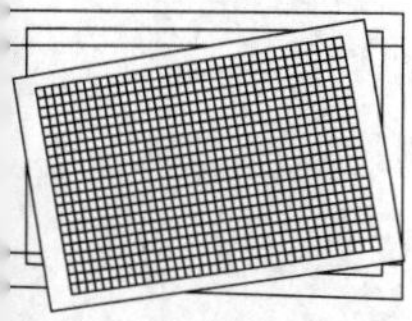

Vents and Louvers

	Craft@Hrs	Unit	Material	Labor	Total
Heater closet door vents, louver					
70 square inches, louvers only	SW@.220	Ea	6.52	9.28	15.80
70 square inches, louvers and screen	SW@.255	Ea	12.00	10.80	22.80
38 square inches, louvers only	SW@.190	Ea	6.34	8.01	14.35
38 square inches, louvers and screen	SW@.210	Ea	9.59	8.85	18.44
Circular louver vents, for moisture control in sidewalls, resin					
2" circular vent	SW@.255	Ea	1.57	10.80	12.37
3" circular vent	SW@.255	Ea	3.40	10.80	14.20
4" circular vent	SW@.255	Ea	3.18	10.80	13.98
Rafter eve vents, galvanized steel with nailing flange, 1/8" mesh, galvanized, louver					
14" x 5"	SW@.220	Ea	4.46	9.28	13.74
14" x 6"	SW@.220	Ea	5.51	9.28	14.79
22" x 3"	SW@.220	Ea	4.35	9.28	13.63
22" x 6"	SW@.220	Ea	5.73	9.28	15.01
22" x 7"	SW@.220	Ea	5.74	9.28	15.02
Rafter bay vent channel, keeps attic insulation away from vents, promotes circulation.					
Rafters 16" on center,					
14" wide, 15" net-free vent area	BC@.220	Ea	2.04	8.22	10.26
Rafters 24" on center,					
22" wide, 26" net-free vent area	BC@.220	Ea	2.72	8.22	10.94
Ridge ventilators, 1/8" louver opening, double baffle, aluminum					
10' long, black	BC@.650	Ea	19.70	24.30	44.00
10' long, brown	BC@.650	Ea	18.60	24.30	42.90
10' long, white	BC@.650	Ea	18.60	24.30	42.90
4' long, hinged for steep roof	BC@.255	Ea	11.90	9.53	21.43
Joint strap	BC@.010	LF	1.97	.37	2.34
End connector plug	BC@.010	Ea	2.40	.37	2.77
Roof vents, with mesh screen, for roof venting of kitchen and bath exhaust fans					
Square cap type, 26" L x 23" D x 5" H	SW@.448	Ea	57.50	18.90	76.40
Dormer type, 20" L x 10" D x 6" H	SW@.448	Ea	37.90	18.90	56.80
Rotary roof ventilators, with base, by turbine diameter					
12", galvanized	SW@.694	Ea	29.70	29.30	59.00
12", brown	SW@.694	Ea	38.20	29.30	67.50
14", galvanized	SW@.694	Ea	46.60	29.30	75.90
14", brown	SW@.694	Ea	72.10	29.30	101.40
16", galvanized	SW@.930	Ea	114.00	39.20	153.20
18", galvanized	SW@1.21	Ea	133.00	51.00	184.00
Round louver vents, 1/8" mesh, galvanized					
12" or 14" diameter	SW@.440	Ea	49.70	18.60	68.30
16" diameter	SW@.440	Ea	57.20	18.60	75.80
18" diameter	SW@.440	Ea	63.00	18.60	81.60
24" diameter	SW@.661	Ea	113.00	27.90	140.90
Soffit vents, aluminum louvers, 8' long, reversible					
2-5/8" wide, white finish	SW@.440	Ea	5.25	18.60	23.85
2-5/8" wide, mill finish	SW@.440	Ea	3.50	18.60	22.10
Under eave soffit vents, screen type					
4" or 8" x 16"	B1@.500	Ea	10.10	16.90	27.00
Continuous aluminum soffit vents					
2" x 8'	B1@.050	LF	.75	1.69	2.44

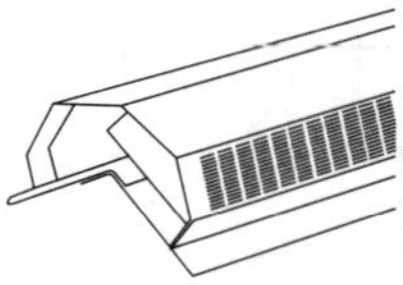

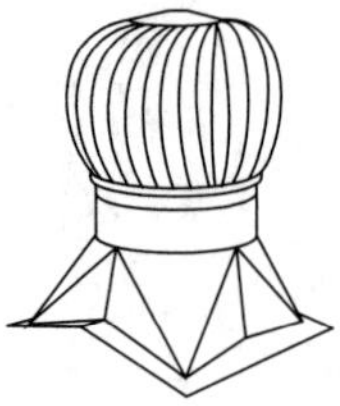

	Craft@Hrs	Unit	Material	Labor	Total
Wall louvers, reversible for flush or recessed mounting. White finish. Screened					
12" x 12", aluminum	SW@.440	Ea	10.90	18.60	29.50
12" x 18", aluminum	SW@.440	Ea	13.30	18.60	31.90
14" x 24", aluminum	SW@.440	Ea	20.50	18.60	39.10
18" x 24", aluminum	SW@.440	Ea	23.60	18.60	42.20
12" x 18", plastic	SW@.440	Ea	8.70	18.60	27.30
18" x 24", plastic	SW@.440	Ea	14.80	18.60	33.40

Wallboard Partitions, Subcontract Costs for interior partitions in one- and two-story buildings. 1/4" gypsum wallboard on 2 sides with "V"-grooved edges and plastic molding at corners fastened to 25 gauge metal framing at 24" OC, including framing, per LF of wall.

	Craft@Hrs	Unit	Material	Labor	Total
Vinyl covered 8' high	—	LF	—	—	44.00
Vinyl covered 10' high	—	LF	—	—	55.00
Paintable paper-covered 8' high	—	LF	—	—	32.00
Paintable paper-covered 10' high	—	LF	—	—	44.60
Add for glued vinyl base on two sides	—	LF	—	—	4.42

Wallcoverings Costs listed are for good to better quality materials installed on a clean, smooth surface and include adhesive, edge trimming, pattern matching, and normal cutting and fitting waste. Surface preparation such as patching and priming are extra. Typical roll is 8 yards long and 18" wide (approximately 36 square feet).

	Craft@Hrs	Unit	Material	Labor	Total
Scrape off old wallpaper, up to 2 layers	PP@.015	SF	—	.51	.51
Paper stripper (1,000 SF per gallon)	—	Gal	14.70	—	14.70
Patch holes, scrape marks	PP@.010	SF	.05	.34	.39
Blank stock (underliner)					
Bath, kitchen, and laundry room	PP@.668	Roll	10.00	22.90	32.90
Other rooms	PP@.558	Roll	10.00	19.10	29.10
Textured basket weave					
Bath, kitchen, and laundry rooms	PP@.995	Roll	24.40	34.10	58.50
Other rooms	PP@.830	Roll	24.40	28.40	52.80
Papers, vinyl-coated papers, trimmed, and pre-pasted					
Bath, kitchen, and laundry rooms	PP@.884	Roll	25.00	30.30	55.30
Other rooms	PP@.780	Roll	25.00	26.70	51.70
Misc. patterns					
Bath, kitchen, and laundry rooms	PP@1.12	Roll	13.70	38.40	52.10
Other rooms	PP@.844	Roll	13.70	28.90	42.60
Designer paper and hand-painted prints					
Bath, kitchen, and laundry rooms	PP@1.68	Roll	69.10	57.60	126.70
Other rooms	PP@1.41	Roll	69.10	48.30	117.40
Murals, no pattern					
Solid vinyl	PP@.844	Yd	24.00	28.90	52.90
Coordinating borders, vinyl coated					
roll is 4" to 6" x 12' to 15'	PP@.017	LF	.95	.58	1.53
Wallpaper adhesive					
Clear, strippable (300 SF per gallon)	—	Gal	20.70	—	20.70
Clear, strippable, per SF	—	SF	.07	—	.07
Mildew-resistant (250 SF per gallon)	—	Gal	15.80	—	15.80
Adhesive, per SF	—	SF	.06	—	.06

	Craft@Hrs	Unit	Material	Labor	Total
Waterproofing					
Below grade waterproofing, applied to concrete or masonry walls, no surface preparation, excavation, or backfill included, typical job					
Bentonite waterproofing					
One layer, nailed in place	BL@.079	SF	1.25	2.39	3.64
Cementitious waterproofing with protection board					
Spray or brush applied, 2 coats	BL@.077	SF	3.06	2.33	5.39
Crystalline waterproofing					
Spray or brush applied, 3 coats	BL@.110	SF	1.66	3.33	4.99
Elastomeric waterproofing 30 mm per coat					
Sprayed, troweled, or rolled, 2 coats	BL@.065	SF	2.21	1.97	4.18
Above grade waterproofing, applied to smooth concrete or plywood deck, no surface preparation included, typical job					
Between slabs membrane					
Sprayed, troweled or rolled, 2 coats	PT@.047	SF	1.51	1.80	3.31
Pedestrian walking surface, elastomeric membrane,					
Applied 4 coats thick with aggregate	PT@.086	SF	2.44	3.29	5.73
Chloroprene/Neoprene latex deck					
Surfacing	PT@.144	SF	4.16	5.50	9.66

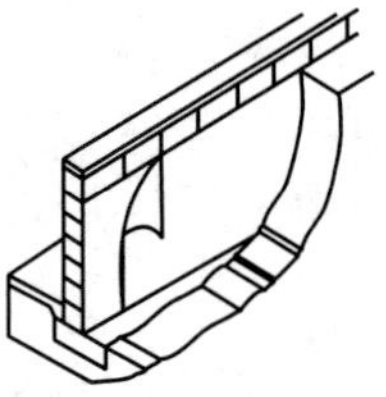

Waterproofing system for foundations Wrapped over concrete foundation footing. System should be tied into a perimeter drain system at or around the footing. Cover top of system with at least 6 inches of soil and backfill immediately after installation. No surface preparation, excavation, or backfill included.

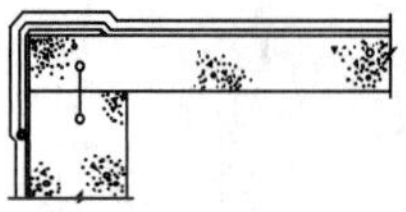

	Craft@Hrs	Unit	Material	Labor	Total
MiraDRI™ 860					
rubberized asphalt membrane	B1@.075	SF	.83	2.54	3.37
Latex-based primer (400 SF per gal)	B1@.075	SF	.21	2.54	2.75
LM-800 liquid membrane	B1@.034	SF	2.19	1.15	3.34
Carlisle 704 mastic,					
1/8" x 3/4", 130 LF per gallon	B1@.034	LF	.46	1.15	1.61
Mira Drain™ 6200 (200 SF Roll)	B1@.075	SF	1.09	2.54	3.63
Quick Drain™ (16" x 50' Roll)	B1@.075	SF	4.17	2.54	6.71

Weatherstripping Materials

	Craft@Hrs	Unit	Material	Labor	Total
Door bottom seals, brass					
Brass "U"-shaped door bottom with adjustment for gaps					
36" x 1-3/8"	BC@.250	Ea	18.60	9.35	27.95
36" x 1-3/4"	BC@.250	Ea	20.60	9.35	29.95
Door frame seal sets					
Spring bronze, nailed every 1-3/8 inch					
36" x 6'8" door	BC@.500	Ea	20.90	18.70	39.60
36" x 7'0" door	BC@.500	Ea	22.10	18.70	40.80
Rigid PVC frame, with silicon bulb / screws	BC@.008	Ea	14.70	.30	15.00
Header and jamb side stripping, adhesive (Peel N Stick®)					
36" x 6'8" door, brass stripping	BC@.500	Ea	29.00	18.70	47.70
Window seal sets, spring brass, adhesive (Peel N Stick®), linear feet per side					
Double hung window, head and sill	BC@.008	LF	1.71	.30	2.01
Add to remove & replace window sash	BC@.250	Ea	—	9.35	9.35
Casement window, head and sill	BC@.008	LF	.75	.30	1.05
Gray or black pile gasket	BC@.008	LF	.38	.30	.68
Gray or black pile gasket with adhesive	BC@.006	LF	.80	.22	1.02
Garage door top and side seal					
Vinyl garage door top and side seal					
9' x 7' door / screws	BC@.500	Ea	23.10	18.70	41.80
16' x 7' door / screws	BC@.600	Ea	30.14	22.40	52.54
Flexible EPDM in aluminum frame	BC@.050	LF	1.81	1.87	3.68

	Craft@Hrs	Unit	Material	Labor	Total
Garage door bottom seal. Set with adhesive					
'U' shape, vinyl, 2-2/4" wide	BC@.042	LF	.89	1.57	2.46
'U' shape, vinyl, with aluminum door bottom	BC@.064	LF	2.31	2.39	4.70
Blade style, vinyl, 2-1/4"	BC@.042	LF	.96	1.57	2.53
Rodent blocking kit, 1 car garage	BC@3.50	Ea	81.70	131.00	212.70
Rodent blocking kit, 2 car garage	BC@4.00	Ea	156.00	150.00	306.00

Well Drilling, Subcontract Typical costs shown, based on well depth including welded steel casing (or continuous PVC casing). Actual costs will depend on specific conditions, i.e. hard-rock, alluvial riverbed or a combination of conditions. The amount of casing needed depends on soil conditions. Some types of rock require casings at the well surface only. Your local health department can probably provide information on the average well depth and subsurface conditions in the community. Note that unforeseen subsurface conditions can increase drilling costs substantially. Most subcontractors will estimate costs on an hourly basis.

	Craft@Hrs	Unit	Material	Labor	Total
Well hole with 4" ID F480 PVC casing	—	LF	—	—	35.70
Well hole with 6" ID steel casing	—	LF	—	—	60.50
Well hole with 8" ID steel casing	—	LF	—	—	82.80
6" well hole in sturdy rock (no casing)	—	LF	—	—	22.30
Add per well for 6" diameter bottom filter screen, if needed due to site conditions					
Stainless steel	—	LS	—	—	194.00
Low carbon steel	—	LS	—	—	102.00
Add per well for drive shoe	—	LS	—	—	184.00
Add for 6" surface seal, if needed due to local code or site conditions					
20' sanitary seal – for individual well	—	LS	—	—	19.80
50' sanitary seal – for community well	—	LS	—	—	3,060.00
Add per well for well drilling permit. Costs varies per local area.					
Individual water well	—	LS	—	—	552.00
Community water well with Source Assessment	—	LS	—	—	1,470.00
Add for automatic electric pumping system with pressure tank(s) domestic use, no electrical work included.					
Individual (18 GPM @ 400 TDH), typical	—	LS	20,400.00	—	20,400.00
Community (60 GPM @ 400 TDH), typical	—	LS	20,400.00	—	20,400.00
Add for electrical service drop pole					
Typical cost 100 amp 230 volt 1 phase service	—	LS	—	—	1,540.00

Window and Door Mantels, Aluminum Includes hardware, aluminum crown mold and roof. Modern design, bright copper or primed aluminum finish.

	Craft@Hrs	Unit	Material	Labor	Total
Up to 24" width	SW@.500	Ea	141.00	21.10	162.10
25" to 36" width	SW@.500	Ea	189.00	21.10	210.10
37" to 48" width	SW@.500	Ea	235.00	21.10	256.10
49" to 60" width	SW@.600	Ea	281.00	25.30	306.30
61" to 72" width	SW@.600	Ea	328.00	25.30	353.30
73" to 84" width	SW@.600	Ea	377.00	25.30	402.30
85" to 96" width	SW@.700	Ea	426.00	29.50	455.50
97" to 108" width	SW@.700	Ea	427.00	29.50	456.50
109" to 120" width	SW@.700	Ea	520.00	29.50	549.50
Add for aged copper or brass aluminum finish	—	%	10.0	—	—
Add for units over 120"	—	LF	63.30	—	63.30

Window Sills

	Craft@Hrs	Unit	Material	Labor	Total
Window Sills, Cultured Stone					
Marble sill 40" or less	B1@.687	Ea	58.00	23.30	81.30
Marble sill 41" to 60"	B1@.730	Ea	79.00	24.70	103.70
Onyx sill 40" or less	B1@.687	Ea	79.00	23.30	102.30
Onyx sill 41" to 60"	B1@.730	Ea	110.00	24.70	134.70
Granite sill 40" or less	B1@.687	Ea	95.00	23.30	118.30
Granite sill 41" to 60"	B1@.730	Ea	142.00	24.70	166.70
Window Sills, Vinyl Solid vinyl. Set with latex or solvent base adhesive. Hard, scratch resistant surface. Ultraviolet protection to prevent yellowing. Gloss finish					
3-1/2" x 3'	BC@.129	Ea	17.70	4.82	22.52
3-1/2" x 4'	BC@.172	Ea	22.60	6.43	29.03
3-1/2" x 5'	BC@.215	Ea	27.50	8.04	35.54
3-1/2" x 6'	BC@.258	Ea	38.30	9.64	47.94
4-1/4" x 3'	BC@.129	Ea	22.20	4.82	27.02
4-1/4" x 4'	BC@.172	Ea	28.30	6.43	34.73
4-1/4" x 5'	BC@.215	Ea	33.50	8.04	41.54
4-1/4" x 6'	BC@.258	Ea	47.30	9.64	56.94
5-1/2" x 3'	BC@.129	Ea	25.50	4.82	30.32
5-1/2" x 4'	BC@.172	Ea	32.50	6.43	38.93
5-1/2" x 5'	BC@.215	Ea	42.20	8.04	50.24
5-1/2" x 6'	BC@.258	Ea	39.60	9.64	49.24
6-1/4" x 3'	BC@.129	Ea	38.30	4.82	43.12
6-1/4" x 4'	BC@.172	Ea	52.20	6.43	58.63
6-1/4" x 5'	BC@.215	Ea	60.60	8.04	68.64
6-1/4" x 6'	BC@.258	Ea	78.10	9.64	87.74
Window Treatments Blinds and shades. See also Draperies.					
Horizontal blinds. Per square foot of blind, width × height. Includes head rail and wand tilter. Standard colors and custom sizes.					
1" wide PVC	BC@.083	SF	1.55	3.10	4.65
1" wide aluminum	BC@.083	SF	1.63	3.10	4.73
1" wide basswood	BC@.083	SF	6.87	3.10	9.97
2" wide faux wood	BC@.083	SF	2.46	3.10	5.56
2" wide basswood	BC@.083	SF	5.78	3.10	8.88
2" wide American hardwood	BC@.083	SF	9.18	3.10	12.28
2-1/2" wide faux wood	BC@.083	SF	3.14	3.10	6.24
2-1/2" wide beveled basswood	BC@.083	SF	7.00	3.10	10.10
Roll-up blinds. Per square foot of blind, width × height. Includes aluminum head rail, valance and roller chain lift. Standard colors and custom sizes.					
Woven wood (rattan and jute)	BC@.083	SF	6.77	3.10	9.87
Bamboo	BC@.083	SF	6.74	3.10	9.84
Vinyl-fiberglass, translucent	BC@.083	SF	2.25	3.10	5.35
Room darkening fabric	BC@.083	SF	7.15	3.10	10.25
Denim fabric	BC@.083	SF	1.94	3.10	5.04
Decorative woven cotton fabric	BC@.083	SF	3.78	3.10	6.88
Sun control vinyl fiberglass sheer weave	BC@.083	SF	3.76	3.10	6.86
Vertical blinds. 3-1/2" vanes. Per square foot of blind, width × height. Includes aluminum head rail, tension pulley and dust cover valance. Standard colors and custom sizes. Left or right pull.					
Smooth surface PVC	BC@.083	SF	2.75	3.10	5.85
Textured surface PVC	BC@.083	SF	3.51	3.10	6.61
Premium textured surface PVC	BC@.083	SF	5.52	3.10	8.62
Faux wood	BC@.083	SF	3.47	3.10	6.57
Add for center pull, per blind	—	Ea	25.30	—	25.30
Add for tile or molding cutout, per blind	—	Ea	25.30	—	25.30
Add for motorized remote control, per blind	—	Ea	127.00	—	127.00

	Craft@Hrs	Unit	Material	Labor	Total
Cellular shades, polyester. With head rail and mounting hardware.					
3/8" double cell light filter	BC@.083	SF	4.59	3.10	7.69
3/8" single cell translucent	BC@.083	SF	6.42	3.10	9.52
3/8" double cell room darkening	BC@.083	SF	5.86	3.10	8.96
3/8" single cell blackout	BC@.083	SF	7.25	3.10	10.35
1/2" double cell light filter	BC@.083	SF	6.49	3.10	9.59
1/2" single cell light filter	BC@.083	SF	6.24	3.10	9.34
3/4" single cell extreme light	BC@.083	SF	6.78	3.10	9.88
3/4" single cell blackout	BC@.083	SF	9.57	3.10	12.67
Add for width over 8'	—	%	20.0	—	—
Add for continuous loop lift cord	—	%	25.0	—	—
Add for no lift cord (child safety), per blind	—	Ea	45.40	—	45.40
Add for tile or molding cutout, per blind	—	Ea	22.70	—	22.70

Windows See also Skylights.

Single-hung insulating glass vinyl windows. 5/8" insulating glass with grid between the lites. 4/4 grid means the upper lite is divided into four panes and the lower lite is divided into four panes. Tilt sash for easy cleaning. Includes half screen. Dimensions are rough opening sizes, width × height. White finish.

	Craft@Hrs	Unit	Material	Labor	Total
1'8" x 4'2", 4/4 grid	BC@.500	Ea	18.00	18.70	36.70
2'0" x 3'0", 4/4 grid	BC@.500	Ea	104.00	18.70	122.70
2'0" x 6'0", 6/4 grid	BC@.500	Ea	125.00	18.70	143.70
2'8" x 3'0", 6/6 grid	BC@.500	Ea	115.00	18.70	133.70
2'8" x 4'4", 6/6 grid	B1@1.00	Ea	133.00	33.90	166.90
2'8" x 5'0", 6/6 grid	B1@1.00	Ea	136.00	33.90	169.90
2'8" x 6'0", 6/6 grid	B1@1.00	Ea	142.00	33.90	175.90
3'0" x 3'0", 6/6 grid	BC@.500	Ea	120.00	18.70	138.70
3'0" x 4'0", 6/6 grid	B1@1.00	Ea	135.00	33.90	168.90
3'0" x 4'4", 6/6 grid	B1@1.00	Ea	135.00	33.90	168.90
3'0" x 5'0", 6/6 grid	B1@1.50	Ea	151.00	50.80	201.80
3'0" x 6'0", 9/6 grid	B1@1.50	Ea	166.00	50.80	216.80

Single-hung insulated low-E glass vinyl windows. Low-E (energy efficient) 5/8" insulating glass with grids between the glass. 4/4 grid means the upper light is divided into four panes and the lower light is divided into four panes. White finish. Tilt sash for easy cleaning. Includes half screen. Dimensions are rough opening sizes, width × height.

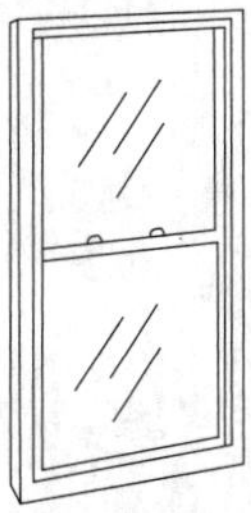

	Craft@Hrs	Unit	Material	Labor	Total
2'0" x 3'0", 4/4 grid	BC@.500	Ea	92.10	18.70	110.80
2'0" x 5'0", 4/4 grid	BC@.500	Ea	148.00	18.70	166.70
2'0" x 6'0", 6/4 grid	B1@1.00	Ea	167.00	33.90	200.90
2'8" x 3'0", 6/6 grid	BC@.500	Ea	123.00	18.70	141.70
2'8" x 4'4", 6/6 grid	B1@1.00	Ea	166.00	33.90	199.90
2'8" x 5'0", 6/6 grid	B1@1.00	Ea	150.00	33.90	183.90
2'8" x 6'0", 9/6 grid	B1@1.50	Ea	183.00	50.80	233.80
3'0" x 3'0", 6/6 grid	BC@.500	Ea	117.00	18.70	135.70
3'0" x 4'0", 6/6 grid	B1@1.00	Ea	154.00	33.90	187.90
3'0" x 4'4", 6/6 grid	B1@1.00	Ea	172.00	33.90	205.90
3'0" x 5'0", 6/6 grid	B1@1.50	Ea	174.00	50.80	224.80
3'0" x 6'0", 9/6 grid	B1@1.50	Ea	193.00	50.80	243.80

Double-hung insulating glass vinyl windows with low-E glass insulating glass. Upper and lower lites are divided into panes by a vinyl grid between the sheets of glass. Sash tilts for easy cleaning. With full screen. 4-9/16" white jamb. Built-in "J"-channel. Designed for new construction. Dimensions are rough opening sizes, width × height.

	Craft@Hrs	Unit	Material	Labor	Total
2'4" x 3'2"	BC@.500	Ea	166.00	18.70	184.70
2'4" x 3'10"	BC@.500	Ea	175.00	18.70	193.70
2'4" x 4'2"	BC@.500	Ea	191.00	18.70	209.70
2'4" x 4'6"	BC@.500	Ea	196.00	18.70	214.70

	Craft@Hrs	Unit	Material	Labor	Total
2'8" x 3'2"	BC@.500	Ea	172.00	18.70	190.70
2'8" x 3'10"	BC@.500	Ea	190.00	18.70	208.70
2'8" x 4'2"	BC@.500	Ea	196.00	18.70	214.70
2'8" x 4'6"	B1@1.00	Ea	200.00	33.90	233.90
3'0" x 4'2"	B1@1.50	Ea	202.00	50.80	252.80
3'0" x 4'6"	B1@1.00	Ea	217.00	33.90	250.90

Double-hung insulating glass vinyl windows. White, with full screen. Low-E (energy-efficient) insulating glass. By rough opening size, width × height. Actual size is 1/2" less. Upper and lower lites are divided into six panes by a vinyl grid between the sheets of glass. 4-9/16" wide jamb.

	Craft@Hrs	Unit	Material	Labor	Total
2'0" x 3'2"	BC@.500	Ea	162.00	18.70	180.70
2'4" x 2'10"	BC@.500	Ea	150.00	18.70	168.70
2'4" x 3'2"	BC@.500	Ea	160.00	18.70	178.70
2'4" x 3'10"	BC@.500	Ea	165.00	18.70	183.70
2'4" x 4'6"	B1@1.00	Ea	185.00	33.90	218.90
2'8" x 2'10"	BC@.500	Ea	165.00	18.70	183.70
2'8" x 3'2"	BC@.500	Ea	160.00	18.70	178.70
2'8" x 3'10"	BC@.500	Ea	170.00	18.70	188.70
2'8" x 4'2"	B1@1.00	Ea	167.00	33.90	200.90
2'8" x 4'6"	B1@1.00	Ea	181.00	33.90	214.90
3'0" x 3'10"	B1@1.00	Ea	205.00	33.90	238.90
3'0" x 4'6"	B1@1.00	Ea	216.00	33.90	249.90

Horizontal sliding single-glazed vinyl windows. By nominal size, width × height. Actual size is 1/2" less. With screen.

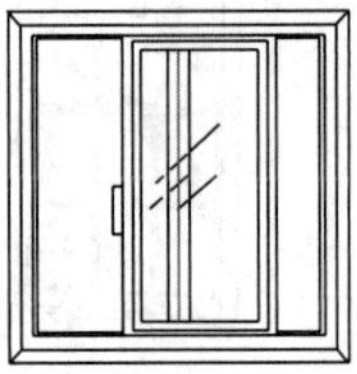

	Craft@Hrs	Unit	Material	Labor	Total
2'0" x 2'0"	BC@.500	Ea	80.20	18.70	98.90
3'0" x 2'0"	BC@.500	Ea	101.00	18.70	119.70
3'0" x 3'0"	BC@.500	Ea	120.00	18.70	138.70
4'0" x 3'0"	B1@1.00	Ea	137.00	33.90	170.90
4'0" x 4'0"	B1@1.50	Ea	161.00	50.80	211.80
5'0" x 4'0"	B1@1.50	Ea	177.00	50.80	227.80

Horizontal sliding insulated low-E glass vinyl windows. Argon filled. For new construction. By rough opening size, width × height. With screen.

	Craft@Hrs	Unit	Material	Labor	Total
2'0" x 2'0"	BC@.500	Ea	92.80	18.70	111.50
2'0" x 3'0"	BC@.500	Ea	101.00	18.70	119.70
2'4" x 4'6"	BC@.500	Ea	164.00	18.70	182.70
2'8" x 4'6"	B1@1.00	Ea	174.00	33.90	207.90
3'0" x 2'0"	BC@.500	Ea	118.00	18.70	136.70
3'0" x 3'0"	BC@.500	Ea	120.00	18.70	138.70
3'0" x 4'0"	B1@1.00	Ea	165.00	33.90	198.90
3'0" x 5'2"	B1@1.50	Ea	188.00	50.80	238.80
3'0" x 6'0"	B1@1.50	Ea	188.00	50.80	238.80
4'0" x 2'0"	BC@.500	Ea	167.00	18.70	185.70
4'0" x 3'0"	B1@1.00	Ea	163.00	33.90	196.90
4'0" x 4'0"	B1@1.50	Ea	164.00	50.80	214.80
5'0" x 4'0"	B1@1.50	Ea	226.00	50.80	276.80

Horizontal sliding replacement windows, white vinyl frame, insulated low-E glass. Argon filled. For existing construction. Set in an existing frame. Including on site measure, custom fabrication, delivery, breakout and disposal of the existing glass. By frame size, width × height. With screen.

	Craft@Hrs	Unit	Material	Labor	Total
2'0" x 2'0" (fixed)	BC@0.75	Ea	186.00	28.00	214.00
3'0" x 2'0" (fixed)	BC@0.85	Ea	201.00	31.80	232.80
3'9" x 2'0" (fixed)	BC@0.90	Ea	221.00	33.60	254.60
5'0" x 4'0" (two lites, half venting)	BC@2.00	Ea	328.00	74.80	402.80
6'0" x 3'6" (two lites, half venting)	BC@2.00	Ea	334.00	74.80	408.80
6'0" x 4'0" (two lites, half venting)	BC@2.00	Ea	358.00	74.80	432.80
6'0" x 4'0" (four lites, 22" x 22" venting)	BC@2.00	Ea	547.00	74.80	621.80
6'0" x 5'0" (two lites, half venting)	BC@2.25	Ea	408.00	84.10	492.10
10'0" x 6'8" door (three lites, one sliding)	BC@8.00	Ea	2,150.00	299.00	2,449.00
Add for color vinyl frame	—	%	10.0	—	—

Casement insulated low-E glass vinyl windows. Argon filled. By window size, width × height. With screen. Sash opening direction when viewed from the interior.

	Craft@Hrs	Unit	Material	Labor	Total
28" x 48", left opening	BC@.500	Ea	245.00	18.70	263.70
28" x 48", right opening	BC@.500	Ea	245.00	18.70	263.70
30" x 36", left opening	BC@.500	Ea	292.00	18.70	310.70
30" x 36", right opening	B1@1.00	Ea	292.00	33.90	325.90
30" x 48", right opening	B1@1.00	Ea	333.00	33.90	366.90
30" x 48", right opening	B1@1.00	Ea	333.00	33.90	366.90
36" x 42", right opening	B1@1.50	Ea	318.00	50.80	368.80
36" x 42", left opening	B1@1.50	Ea	318.00	50.80	368.80

Casement bay insulating glass vinyl windows. Fixed center lite and two casement flankers. White vinyl. Factory assembled. By nominal (opening) size, width × height. Actual size is 1/2" less in both width and height. Includes two screens.

	Craft@Hrs	Unit	Material	Labor	Total
69" x 50"	B1@4.00	Ea	1,260.00	135.00	1,395.00
74" x 50"	B1@4.00	Ea	1,270.00	135.00	1,405.00
93" x 50"	B1@4.50	Ea	1,470.00	152.00	1,622.00
98" x 50"	B1@4.50	Ea	1,550.00	152.00	1,702.00

Garden insulating glass vinyl windows. Single front awning vent. White vinyl construction with wood frame. Tempered glass shelf. 5/4" vinyl laminated head and seat board. With hardware and screen. By nominal (opening) size, width × height. Replacement window. Labor includes removing the old stops and sash and setting new "J"-trim as needed.

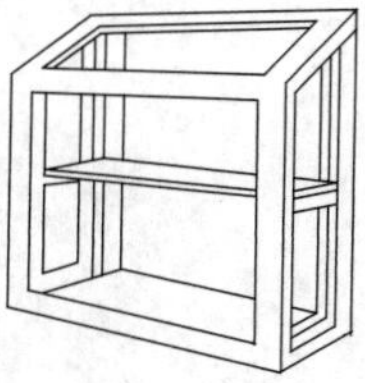

	Craft@Hrs	Unit	Material	Labor	Total
36" x 36"	B1@2.75	Ea	689.00	93.10	782.10
36" x 36", low-E glass	B1@2.75	Ea	731.00	93.10	824.10
36" x 48", low-E glass	B1@2.75	Ea	793.00	93.10	886.10

Fixed half circle (picture) insulating glass vinyl windows. White frame. Low-E (energy-efficient) glass. Stock units for new construction. By width × height.

	Craft@Hrs	Unit	Material	Labor	Total
20" x 10"	B1@2.75	Ea	576.00	93.10	669.10
30" x 16"	B1@2.75	Ea	576.00	93.10	669.10
40" x 20"	B1@2.75	Ea	769.00	93.10	862.10
50" x 26"	B1@2.75	Ea	909.00	93.10	1,002.10
60" x 30"	B1@2.75	Ea	1,030.00	93.10	1,123.10
80" x 40"	B1@2.75	Ea	1,500.00	93.10	1,593.10

Fixed (picture) low-E insulating glass vinyl windows. Argon filled. White frame. Dimensions are rough opening sizes, width × height.

	Craft@Hrs	Unit	Material	Labor	Total
24" x 36"	BC@.500	Ea	96.40	18.70	115.10
24" x 48"	BC@.500	Ea	124.00	18.70	142.70
24" x 60"	BC@.500	Ea	137.00	18.70	155.70
30" x 36"	BC@.500	Ea	132.00	18.70	150.70
30" x 48"	BC@.500	Ea	134.00	18.70	152.70
36" x 48"	B1@1.00	Ea	137.00	33.90	170.90
36" x 60"	B1@1.00	Ea	166.00	33.90	199.90
48" x 48"	B1@1.50	Ea	164.00	50.80	214.80
48" x 60"	B1@1.50	Ea	181.00	50.80	231.80
60" x 48"	B1@1.50	Ea	189.00	50.80	239.80

Jalousie (louver) vinyl windows. Positive locking handle for security. By opening size, width × height.

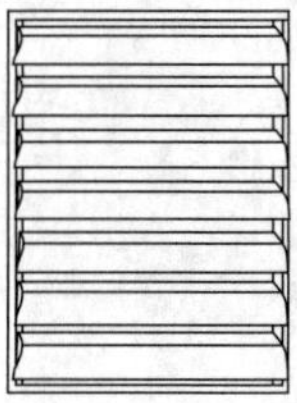

	Craft@Hrs	Unit	Material	Labor	Total
24" x 35-1/2", clear	BC@.500	Ea	326.00	18.70	344.70
24" x 35-1/2", obscure glass	BC@.500	Ea	370.00	18.70	388.70
30" x 35-1/2", clear	BC@.500	Ea	348.00	18.70	366.70
30" x 35-1/2", obscure glass	BC@.500	Ea	400.00	18.70	418.70
36" x 35-1/2", clear	BC@.500	Ea	360.00	18.70	378.70
36" x 35-1/2", obscure glass	BC@.500	Ea	425.00	18.70	443.70

Windows

	Craft@Hrs	Unit	Material	Labor	Total
Hopper insulating glass vinyl windows. Low-E (energy-efficient) insulating glass. Argon filled. Frame depth 3-5/16". By opening size, width × height.					
32" x 15"	BC@.500	Ea	102.00	18.70	120.70
32" x 17"	BC@.500	Ea	108.00	18.70	126.70
32" x 19"	BC@.500	Ea	112.00	18.70	130.70
32" x 23"	BC@.500	Ea	117.00	18.70	135.70
Vinyl-clad double-hung insulating glass wood windows. Pine interior. White vinyl exterior. Tilt sash. By nominal (opening) size, width × height. Actual width is 1-5/8" more. Actual height is 3-1/4" more. Add the cost of screens and colonial grilles.					
2'0" x 3'0"	BC@.500	Ea	200.00	18.70	218.70
2'4" x 3'6"	BC@.500	Ea	235.00	18.70	253.70
2'4" x 4'0"	BC@.500	Ea	257.00	18.70	275.70
2'4" x 4'6"	B1@1.00	Ea	274.00	33.90	307.90
2'4" x 4'9"	B1@1.00	Ea	286.00	33.90	319.90
2'8" x 3'0"	B1@1.00	Ea	228.00	33.90	261.90
2'8" x 3'6"	B1@1.00	Ea	250.00	33.90	283.90
2'8" x 4'0"	B1@1.00	Ea	265.00	33.90	298.90
2'8" x 4'6"	B1@1.00	Ea	289.00	33.90	322.90
2'8" x 4'9"	B1@1.00	Ea	300.00	33.90	333.90
3'0" x 3'6"	B1@1.00	Ea	264.00	33.90	297.90
3'0" x 4'0"	B1@1.00	Ea	285.00	33.90	318.90
3'0" x 4'9"	B1@1.00	Ea	312.00	33.90	345.90
Screens for vinyl-clad wood windows. By window nominal size.					
2'0" x 3'0"	BC@.050	Ea	26.60	1.87	28.47
2'4" x 3'0"	BC@.050	Ea	29.30	1.87	31.17
2'4" x 3'6"	BC@.050	Ea	32.40	1.87	34.27
2'4" x 4'0"	BC@.050	Ea	33.60	1.87	35.47
2'4" x 4'6"	BC@.050	Ea	36.60	1.87	38.47
2'4" x 4'9"	BC@.050	Ea	37.90	1.87	39.77
2'8" x 3'0"	BC@.050	Ea	28.90	1.87	30.77
2'8" x 3'6"	BC@.050	Ea	33.40	1.87	35.27
2'8" x 4'0"	BC@.050	Ea	36.70	1.87	38.57
2'8" x 4'6"	BC@.050	Ea	38.00	1.87	39.87
2'8" x 4'9"	BC@.050	Ea	39.10	1.87	40.97
3'0" x 3'6"	BC@.050	Ea	33.50	1.87	35.37
3'0" x 4'0"	BC@.050	Ea	38.10	1.87	39.97
3'0" x 4'6"	BC@.050	Ea	40.70	1.87	42.57
3'0" x 4'9"	BC@.050	Ea	40.80	1.87	42.67
Vinyl-clad insulating glass wood awning windows. Prefinished pine interior. White vinyl exterior. Add the cost of screens. By nominal (opening) size, width × height.					
2'1" x 2'0"	BC@.500	Ea	248.00	18.70	266.70
3'1" x 2'0"	BC@.500	Ea	298.00	18.70	316.70
4'1" x 2'0"	BC@.500	Ea	313.00	18.70	331.70
White vinyl-clad insulating glass wood casement windows, Andersen. Prefinished pine interior. White vinyl exterior. Tilt sash. With nailing flange for new construction. By nominal (opening) size, width × height. Add the cost of screens. Hinge operation as viewed from the exterior.					
2'1" x 3'0", right hinge	BC@.500	Ea	289.00	18.70	307.70
2'1" x 3'0", left hinge	BC@.500	Ea	289.00	18.70	307.70
2'1" x 3'6", right hinge	BC@.500	Ea	326.00	18.70	344.70
2'1" x 3'6", left hinge	BC@.500	Ea	331.00	18.70	349.70
2'1" x 4'0", right hinge	BC@.500	Ea	345.00	18.70	363.70
2'1" x 4'0", left hinge	BC@.500	Ea	338.00	18.70	356.70

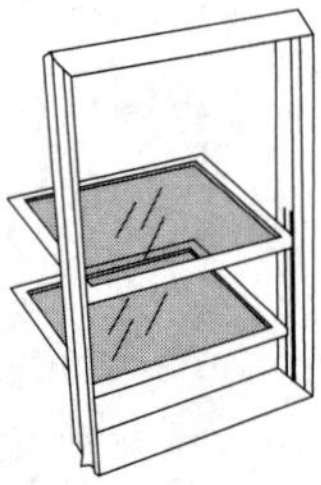

	Craft@Hrs	Unit	Material	Labor	Total
2'1" x 5'0", right hinge	B1@1.00	Ea	384.00	33.90	417.90
2'1" x 5'0", left hinge	B1@1.00	Ea	384.00	33.90	417.90
4'1" x 3'0", left and right hinge	B1@1.00	Ea	428.00	33.90	461.90
4'1" x 3'5", left and right hinge	B1@1.00	Ea	584.00	33.90	617.90
4'1" x 4'0", left and right hinge	B1@1.00	Ea	714.00	33.90	747.90
2'1" x 3'6", right hinge, egress	BC@.500	Ea	635.00	18.70	653.70
2'1" x 3'6", left hinge, egress	BC@.500	Ea	331.00	18.70	349.70
2'1" x 4'0", right hinge, egress	BC@.500	Ea	372.00	18.70	390.70
3'5" x 3'5", left hinge, egress	B1@1.00	Ea	646.00	33.90	679.90

Vinyl-clad insulating glass wood casement windows. Vinyl exterior. Unfinished wood interior. With hardware. Add the cost of grilles and screens. By nominal size, width × height.

	Craft@Hrs	Unit	Material	Labor	Total
2'1" x 3'6", single opening, egress	BC@.500	Ea	294.00	18.70	312.70
2'1" x 4'0", single opening, egress	BC@.500	Ea	374.00	18.70	392.70
3'5" x 3'5", single opening	BC@.500	Ea	522.00	18.70	540.70
4'1" x 3'0", double opening	B1@1.50	Ea	544.00	50.80	594.80
4'1" x 3'5", double opening	B1@1.50	Ea	584.00	50.80	634.80
4'1" x 4'0", double opening	B1@1.50	Ea	673.00	50.80	723.80

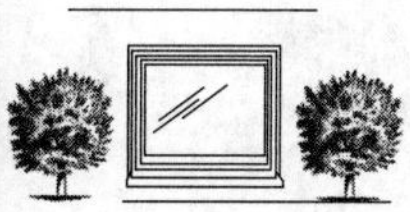

Vinyl-clad insulating glass wood basement windows. Prefinished pine interior. White vinyl exterior. Tilt sash. With nailing flange for new construction. By nominal (opening) size, width × height. With screen.

	Craft@Hrs	Unit	Material	Labor	Total
2'8" x 1'3"	BC@.500	Ea	110.00	18.70	128.70
2'8" x 1'7"	BC@.500	Ea	125.00	18.70	143.70
2'8" x 2'0"	BC@.500	Ea	139.00	18.70	157.70

Aluminum single-hung vertical sliding windows. Removable sash. Dual sash weatherstripping. Includes screen. By nominal (opening) size, width × height. With nailing flange for new construction.

	Craft@Hrs	Unit	Material	Labor	Total
Mill finish, single glazed					
2'0" x 3'0"	BC@.500	Ea	80.70	18.70	99.40
2'8" x 3'0"	BC@.500	Ea	91.00	18.70	109.70
2'8" x 4'4"	BC@.500	Ea	112.00	18.70	130.70
2'8" x 5'0"	BC@.500	Ea	124.00	18.70	142.70
3'0" x 3'0"	BC@.500	Ea	93.80	18.70	112.50
3'0" x 4'0"	BC@.500	Ea	111.00	18.70	129.70
3'0" x 4'4"	BC@.500	Ea	111.00	18.70	129.70
3'0" x 5'0"	BC@.500	Ea	128.00	18.70	146.70
White finish, insulated glass, with grid					
2'0" x 3'0"	BC@.500	Ea	98.20	18.70	116.90
2'8" x 3'0"	BC@.500	Ea	111.00	18.70	129.70
2'8" x 4'4"	BC@.500	Ea	137.00	18.70	155.70
2'8" x 5'0"	BC@.500	Ea	151.00	18.70	169.70
3'0" x 3'0"	BC@.500	Ea	101.00	18.70	119.70
3'0" x 4'0"	B1@1.00	Ea	137.00	33.90	170.90
3'0" x 4'4"	B1@1.00	Ea	145.00	33.90	178.90
3'0" x 5'0"	B1@1.50	Ea	154.00	50.80	204.80
3'0" x 6'0"	B1@1.50	Ea	177.00	50.80	227.80
Solar bronze insulating glass					
2'0" x 2'0"	BC@.500	Ea	116.00	18.70	134.70
2'0" x 3'0"	BC@.500	Ea	116.00	18.70	134.70
2'0" x 4'0"	BC@.500	Ea	138.00	18.70	156.70
3'0" x 3'0"	BC@.500	Ea	149.00	18.70	167.70
3'0" x 4'0"	B1@1.00	Ea	201.00	33.90	234.90

Impact-resistant aluminum single hung windows. Glass bonded with clear polyvinyl. With screen.

	Craft@Hrs	Unit	Material	Labor	Total
26" x 38", obscure	BC@.500	Ea	260.00	18.70	278.70
37" x 26"	BC@.500	Ea	290.00	18.70	308.70
37" x 50"	B1@1.00	Ea	378.00	33.90	411.90

	Craft@Hrs	Unit	Material	Labor	Total
37" x 63"	B1@1.50	Ea	452.00	50.80	502.80
53" x 38"	B1@1.50	Ea	427.00	50.80	477.80
53" x 50"	B1@1.50	Ea	532.00	50.80	582.80

Aluminum horizontal sliding windows. Right sash is operable when viewed from the interior. With screen, 7/8" nailing fin setback for 3-coat stucco or wood siding. By nominal (opening) size, width × height. Obscure glass is usually available in smaller (1' and 2') windows at no additional cost.

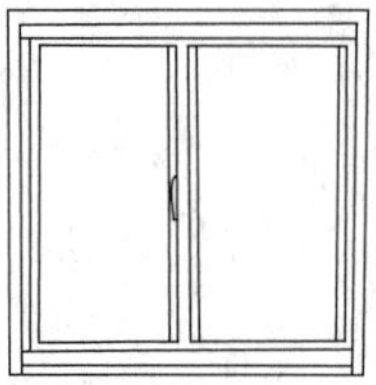

	Craft@Hrs	Unit	Material	Labor	Total
Mill finish windows, single glazed					
2'0" x 2'0"	BC@.500	Ea	44.40	18.70	63.10
3'0" x 2'0"	BC@.500	Ea	50.50	18.70	69.20
3'0" x 3'0"	BC@.500	Ea	63.20	18.70	81.90
3'0" x 4'0"	B1@1.00	Ea	76.50	33.90	110.40
4'0" x 3'0"	B1@1.00	Ea	76.50	33.90	110.40
4'0" x 4'0"	BC@1.50	Ea	89.40	56.10	145.50
6'0" x 3'0"	BC@1.50	Ea	102.00	56.10	158.10
6'0" x 4'0"	BC@1.50	Ea	116.00	56.10	172.10
White finish windows, insulating glass					
2'0" x 2'0"	BC@.500	Ea	63.20	18.70	81.90
3'0" x 1'0"	BC@.500	Ea	74.10	18.70	92.80
3'0" x 2'0"	BC@.500	Ea	82.10	18.70	100.80
3'0" x 3'0"	BC@.500	Ea	102.00	18.70	120.70
3'0" x 4'0"	B1@1.00	Ea	124.00	33.90	157.90
4'0" x 3'0"	B1@1.00	Ea	124.00	33.90	157.90
4'0" x 4'0"	BC@1.50	Ea	129.00	56.10	185.10
White finish windows, insulating glass, with grid					
3'0" x 3'0"	BC@.500	Ea	131.00	18.70	149.70
3'0" x 4'0"	B1@1.00	Ea	159.00	33.90	192.90
4'0" x 3'0"	B1@1.00	Ea	158.00	33.90	191.90
4'0" x 4'0"	B1@1.50	Ea	184.00	50.80	234.80
5'0" x 3'0"	B1@1.50	Ea	183.00	50.80	233.80
5'0" x 4'0"	B1@1.50	Ea	195.00	50.80	245.80
6'0" x 3'0"	B1@1.50	Ea	210.00	50.80	260.80
6'0" x 4'0"	B1@1.50	Ea	224.00	50.80	274.80
Solar bronze insulating glass windows					
2'0" x 2'0"	BC@.500	Ea	84.60	18.70	103.30
3'0" x 3'0"	BC@.500	Ea	135.00	18.70	153.70
3'0" x 4'0"	B1@1.00	Ea	142.00	33.90	175.90
4'0" x 3'0"	B1@1.00	Ea	142.00	33.90	175.90
4'0" x 4'0"	B1@1.50	Ea	168.00	50.80	218.80
5'0" x 4'0"	B1@1.50	Ea	187.00	50.80	237.80
6'0" x 4'0"	B1@1.50	Ea	218.00	50.80	268.80
White finish windows, insulating low-E glass					
3'0" x 3'0"	BC@.500	Ea	131.00	18.70	149.70
3'0" x 4'0"	B1@1.00	Ea	165.00	33.90	198.90
4'0" x 3'0"	B1@1.00	Ea	158.00	33.90	191.90
4'0" x 4'0"	B1@1.50	Ea	176.00	50.80	226.80
5'0" x 4'0"	B1@1.50	Ea	195.00	50.80	245.80
6'0" x 4'0"	BC@1.50	Ea	236.00	56.10	292.10

Aluminum single glazed awning windows. With hardware and screen. Painted powder polyurethane finish. Solar bronze glass. Opening (nominal) sizes, width × height.

	Craft@Hrs	Unit	Material	Labor	Total
24" x 20-1/8", one lite high	BC@.500	Ea	57.30	18.70	76.00
24" x 28-3/4", two lites high	BC@.500	Ea	82.10	18.70	100.80
24" x 37-3/8", three lites high	B1@1.00	Ea	85.90	33.90	119.80

	Craft@Hrs	Unit	Material	Labor	Total
24" x 46", four lites high	B1@1.00	Ea	85.90	33.90	119.80
24" x 54-5/8", five lites high	B1@1.50	Ea	110.00	50.80	160.80
24" x 63-1/4", six lites high	B1@1.50	Ea	116.00	50.80	166.80
30" x 20-1/8", one lite high	BC@.500	Ea	70.20	18.70	88.90
30" x 28-3/4", two lites high	BC@.500	Ea	80.40	18.70	99.10
30" x 37-3/8", three lites high	B1@1.00	Ea	93.70	33.90	127.60
30" x 46", four lites high	B1@1.00	Ea	104.00	33.90	137.90
30" x 54-5/8", five lites high	B1@1.50	Ea	123.00	50.80	173.80
30" x 63-1/4", six lites high	B1@1.50	Ea	142.00	50.80	192.80
36" x 20-1/8", one lite high	BC@.500	Ea	70.00	18.70	88.70
36" x 28-3/4", two lites high	BC@.500	Ea	89.90	18.70	108.60
36" x 37-3/8", three lites high	B1@1.00	Ea	95.30	33.90	129.20
36" x 46", four lites high	B1@1.00	Ea	110.00	33.90	143.90
36" x 54-5/8", five lites high	B1@1.50	Ea	133.00	50.80	183.80
36" x 63-1/4", six lites high	B1@1.50	Ea	192.00	50.80	242.80

Double-hung insulating glass wood windows. Treated western pine. Natural wood interior. 4-9/16" jamb width. 5/8" insulating glass. Weatherstripped. Tilt-in, removable sash. With hardware. Nominal sizes, width × height. With screen.

	Craft@Hrs	Unit	Material	Labor	Total
2'0" x 3'2"	BC@.500	Ea	189.00	18.70	207.70
2'4" x 3'2"	BC@.500	Ea	208.00	18.70	226.70
2'4" x 4'6"	BC@.500	Ea	237.00	18.70	255.70
2'8" x 3'2"	BC@.500	Ea	222.00	18.70	240.70
2'8" x 3'10"	BC@.500	Ea	229.00	18.70	247.70
2'8" x 4'6"	B1@1.00	Ea	248.00	33.90	281.90
2'8" x 5'2"	B1@1.00	Ea	260.00	33.90	293.90
2'8" x 6'2"	B1@1.00	Ea	288.00	33.90	321.90
3'0" x 3'2"	BC@.500	Ea	229.00	18.70	247.70
3'0" x 3'10"	B1@1.00	Ea	226.00	33.90	259.90
3'0" x 4'6"	B1@1.00	Ea	257.00	33.90	290.90
3'0" x 5'2"	B1@1.00	Ea	267.00	33.90	300.90
3'0" x 6'2"	B1@1.00	Ea	323.00	33.90	356.90
2'8" x 4'6", twin	B1@1.00	Ea	459.00	33.90	492.90
3'0" x 4'6", twin	B1@1.00	Ea	534.00	33.90	567.90

Fixed octagon wood windows. Stock units for new construction.

	Craft@Hrs	Unit	Material	Labor	Total
24", 9-lite beveled glass	BC@1.50	Ea	184.00	56.10	240.10
24", insulating glass	BC@1.50	Ea	160.00	56.10	216.10
24", beveled glass	BC@1.50	Ea	128.00	56.10	184.10
24", single glazed	BC@1.50	Ea	124.00	56.10	180.10
24", venting insulating glass	BC@1.50	Ea	213.00	56.10	269.10

Angle bay windows. Fixed center lite and two double-hung flankers. 30-degree angle. Pine with aluminum cladding insulating glass. With screen. White or bronze finish. 4-9/16" wall thickness. Opening (nominal) sizes, width × height. Add the cost of interior trim and installing or framing the bay window roof. See the figures that follow.

	Craft@Hrs	Unit	Material	Labor	Total
6'4" x 4'8"	B1@4.00	Ea	2,060.00	135.00	2,195.00
7'2" x 4'8"	B1@4.00	Ea	2,070.00	135.00	2,205.00
7'10" x 4'8"	B1@4.50	Ea	2,230.00	152.00	2,382.00
8'6" x 4'8"	B1@4.50	Ea	2,570.00	152.00	2,722.00
8'10" x 4'8"	B1@4.50	Ea	2,710.00	152.00	2,862.00
9'2" x 4'8"	B1@5.00	Ea	2,670.00	169.00	2,839.00
9'10" x 4'8"	B1@5.00	Ea	2,800.00	169.00	2,969.00
Add for 45 degree angle windows	—	Ea	105.00	—	105.00
Add for roof framing kit	—	Ea	224.00	—	224.00

	Craft@Hrs	Unit	Material	Labor	Total

Bay window roof cover. Architectural copper roof system for standard angle bay windows. Includes hardware. Stock units for new construction.

	Craft@Hrs	Unit	Material	Labor	Total
Up to 48" width	SW@.500	Ea	1,180.00	21.10	1,201.10
49" to 60" width	SW@.500	Ea	1,360.00	21.10	1,381.10
61" to 72" width	SW@.600	Ea	1,490.00	25.30	1,515.30
73" to 84" width	SW@.600	Ea	1,660.00	25.30	1,685.30
85" to 96" width	SW@.600	Ea	1,830.00	25.30	1,855.30
97" to 108" width	SW@.700	Ea	1,990.00	29.50	2,019.50
109" to 120" width	SW@.700	Ea	2,180.00	29.50	2,209.50
121" to 132" width	SW@.800	Ea	2,480.00	33.70	2,513.70
133" to 144" width	SW@.800	Ea	2,640.00	33.70	2,673.70
145" to 156" width	SW@1.00	Ea	2,820.00	42.20	2,862.20
157" to 168" width	SW@1.00	Ea	2,980.00	42.20	3,022.20
Add for aged copper, brass or aluminum finish	—	%	20.0	—	—
Add for 24" to 26" projection	—	%	10.0	—	—
Add for 26" to 28" projection	—	%	15.0	—	—
Add for 28" to 30" projection	—	%	20.0	—	—
Add for brick soffit kit	—	%	45.0	—	—
Add for 90-degree bays	—	Ea	87.60	—	87.60

Casement bow windows. Insulating glass, assembled, with screens, weatherstripped, unfinished pine, 16" projection, 22" x 56" lites, 4-7/16" jambs. Add the cost of interior trim and installing or framing the bow window roof. Stock units for new construction. Generally a roof kit is required for projections of 12" or more. See the figures that follow.

	Craft@Hrs	Unit	Material	Labor	Total
8'1" wide x 4'8" (4 lites, 2 venting)	B1@4.75	Ea	2,320.00	161.00	2,481.00
8'1" wide x 5'4" (4 lites, 2 venting)	B1@4.75	Ea	2,510.00	161.00	2,671.00
8'1" wide x 6'0" (4 lites, 2 venting)	B1@4.75	Ea	2,710.00	161.00	2,871.00
10' wide x 4'8" (5 lites, 2 venting)	B1@4.75	Ea	2,820.00	161.00	2,981.00
10' wide x 5'4" (5 lites, 2 venting)	B1@4.75	Ea	3,040.00	161.00	3,201.00
10' wide x 6'0" (5 lites, 2 venting)	B1@4.75	Ea	3,350.00	161.00	3,511.00
Add for roof framing kit, 5 lites	—	Ea	199.00	—	199.00
Add for interior and exterior trim					
3, 4 or 5 lites	B1@2.00	Set	62.50	67.70	130.20

Bow or bay window roof framed on site. 1/2" plywood sheathing, fiberglass batt insulation, fascia board, cove molding, roof flashing, 15-pound felt, 240-pound seal-tab asphalt shingles, and cleanup.

	Craft@Hrs	Unit	Material	Labor	Total
Up to 120" width	B1@3.50	Ea	91.90	118.00	209.90
Add per linear foot of width over 10'	B1@.350	LF	9.19	11.80	20.99

Basement storm windows. White aluminum frame with removable Plexiglass window. Clips on over aluminum or wood basement window. Screen included. Nominal window sizes, width x height.

	Craft@Hrs	Unit	Material	Labor	Total
32" x 14"	BC@.420	Ea	27.60	15.70	43.30
32" x 18"	BC@.420	Ea	27.60	15.70	43.30
32" x 22"	BC@.420	Ea	26.40	15.70	42.10

Aluminum storm windows. Removable glass inserts. Removable screen. Double track. Includes weatherstripping. Adaptable to aluminum single-hung windows.

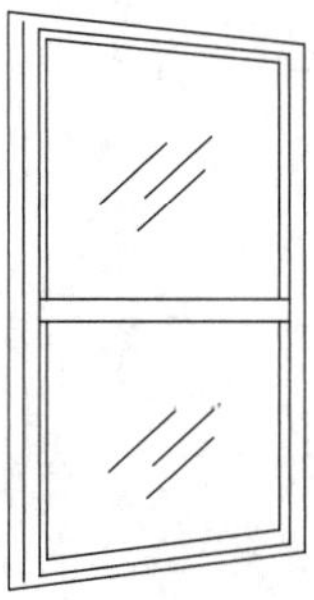

	Craft@Hrs	Unit	Material	Labor	Total
24" x 39", mill finish	BC@.420	Ea	39.90	15.70	55.60
24" x 39", white finish	BC@.420	Ea	44.60	15.70	60.30
24" x 55", mill finish	BC@.420	Ea	58.50	15.70	74.20
24" x 55", white finish	BC@.420	Ea	58.50	15.70	74.20
28" x 39", mill finish	BC@.420	Ea	45.40	15.70	61.10
28" x 39", white finish	BC@.420	Ea	48.00	15.70	63.70
28" x 47", white finish	BC@.420	Ea	54.60	15.70	70.30
28" x 55", mill finish	BC@.420	Ea	53.20	15.70	68.90
28" x 55", white finish	BC@.420	Ea	59.80	15.70	75.50
32" x 39", mill finish	BC@.420	Ea	46.10	15.70	61.80

	Craft@Hrs	Unit	Material	Labor	Total
32" x 39", white finish	BC@.420	Ea	51.70	15.70	67.40
32" x 47", white finish	BC@.420	Ea	62.80	15.70	78.50
32" x 55", mill finish	BC@.420	Ea	54.70	15.70	70.40
32" x 55", white finish	BC@.420	Ea	58.50	15.70	74.20
32" x 63", mill finish	BC@.420	Ea	65.20	15.70	80.90
32" x 63", white finish	BC@.420	Ea	65.20	15.70	80.90
32" x 75", white finish	BC@.420	Ea	78.50	15.70	94.20
36" x 39", mill finish	BC@.420	Ea	46.80	15.70	62.50
36" x 39", white finish	BC@.420	Ea	54.70	15.70	70.40
36" x 55", mill finish	BC@.420	Ea	55.90	15.70	71.60
36" x 55", white finish	BC@.420	Ea	62.30	15.70	78.00
36" x 63", mill finish	BC@.420	Ea	64.00	15.70	79.70
36" x 63", white finish	BC@.420	Ea	69.80	15.70	85.50

Window wells ScapeWel egress window, meets code requirements for basement escape window. Snaps into place on site. For new construction and remodeling, attaches directly to foundation. Bilco.

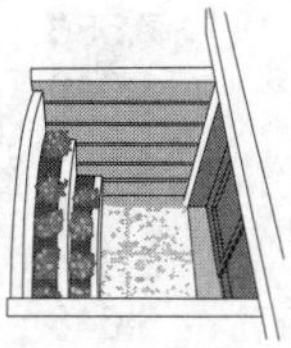

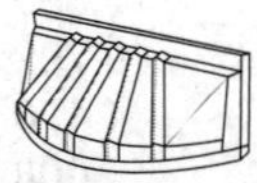

	Craft@Hrs	Unit	Material	Labor	Total
Model 4048-42, 42" x 48" two tier	B1@1.50	Ea	1,090.00	50.80	1,140.80
4042C polycarbonate window well cover					
Fits Model 4048-42	—	Ea	424.00	—	424.00
Model 4048-54, 54" x 48" two tier	B1@1.50	Ea	1,100.00	50.80	1,150.80
4054C polycarbonate window well cover					
Fits Model 4048-54	—	Ea	495.00	—	495.00
Model 4048-66, 66" x 48" two tier	B1@1.50	Ea	1,150.00	50.80	1,200.80
4066C polycarbonate window well cover					
Fits Model 4048-66	—	Ea	517.00	—	517.00
Model 4862-42, 42" x 62" three tier	B1@1.50	Ea	1,310.00	50.80	1,360.80
4842C polycarbonate window well cover					
Fits Model 4862-42	—	Ea	455.00	—	455.00
Model 4862-54, 54" x 62" three tier	B1@1.50	Ea	1,460.00	50.80	1,510.80
4854C polycarbonate window well cover					
Fits Model 4862-54	—	Ea	459.00	—	459.00
Model 4862-66, 66" x 62" three tier	B1@1.50	Ea	1,560.00	50.80	1,610.80
4866C polycarbonate window well cover					
Fits Model 4862-66	—	Ea	528.00	—	528.00

Single Family Home Costs

Use the costs below to check your estimates and to verify bids submitted by subcontractors. These costs are based on a 1,600 square foot home (as described on page 307) built during the third quarter of 2020 at a cost of $130.44 per square foot. Figures in the column "% of Total" are the same as those listed in the Residential Rule of Thumb Construction Costs on page 307. These are averages and will vary widely with the type and quality of construction.

Item	Total manpower required	% of Total	Unit	$ Material	$ Labor	$ Equipment	Total $ per SF	Total $ 1600 SF
Excavation	3 men 2 days	1.2%	SF	—	$1.18	$0.39	$1.57	$2,512
Foundation, slab, piers	3 men 4 days	3.7%	SF	$1.93	2.42	0.48	4.83	7,728
Flatwork (drive and walk)	3 men 3 days	2.4%	SF	1.25	1.57	0.31	3.13	5,008
Brick hearth & veneer	2 men 1 day	0.7%	SF	0.36	0.46	0.09	0.91	1,456
Rough hardware		0.6%	SF	0.31	0.39	0.08	0.78	1,248
Finish hardware		0.2%	SF	0.16	0.10	—	0.26	416
Rough lumber		6.4%	SF	8.35	—	—	8.35	13,360
Finish lumber		0.5%	SF	0.65	—	—	0.65	1,040
Rough carpentry labor	2 men 20 days	8.9%	SF	—	11.61	—	11.61	18,576
Finish carpentry labor	1 man 7 days	1.7%	SF	—	2.22	—	2.22	3,552
Countertops	1 man 2 days	1.5%	SF	1.18	0.78	—	1.96	3,136
Cabinets	2 men 2 days	3.7%	SF	3.86	0.97	—	4.83	7,728
Insulation (R19 ceiling)	1 man 3 days	2.3%	SF	1.95	1.05	—	3.00	4,800
Roofing	4 men 3 days	5.5%	SF	4.30	2.87	—	7.17	11,472
Painting	2 men 3 days	3.6%	SF	1.65	3.06	—	4.71	7,536
Shower & tub enclosure	1 man 1 day	0.5%	SF	0.39	0.26	—	0.65	1,040
Prefabricated fireplace	1 man 1 day	0.9%	SF	0.88	0.23	0.06	1.17	1,872
Bath accessories	1 man 1 day	0.7%	SF	0.61	0.30	—	0.91	1,456
Built-in appliances	1 man 1 day	1.6%	SF	1.88	0.21	—	2.09	3,344
Heating and ducting	2 men 5 days	2.9%	SF	1.51	2.27	—	3.78	6,048
Plmbg & sewer connections	3 men 5 days	7.3%	SF	3.81	4.76	0.95	9.52	15,232
Doors	2 men 2 days	1.9%	SF	1.61	0.87	—	2.48	3,968
Garage door	1 man 1 day	0.4%	SF	0.39	0.13	—	0.52	832
Alum windows/slidg drs	1 man 2 days	1.2%	SF	0.94	0.63	—	1.57	2,512
Exterior stucco	3 men 3 days	6.4%	SF	5.43	2.51	0.41	8.35	13,360
Gypsum wallboard	2 men 6 days	4.7%	SF	2.74	3.38	—	6.12	9,792
Resilient flooring	1 man 1 day	2.0%	SF	1.23	1.38	—	2.61	4,176
Carpeting	2 men 1 day	2.4%	SF	2.50	0.63	—	3.13	5,008
Wiring (Romex)	1 man 10 days	3.2%	SF	1.67	2.50	—	4.17	6,672
Lighting fixtures		1.2%	SF	1.26	0.31	—	1.57	2,512
Subtotal, DIRECT JOB COSTS		**80.2%**		**$52.80**	**$49.05**	**$2.77**	**$104.62**	**$167,392**
Amount above, as a percent of total direct costs				50.47%	46.88%	2.65%	100.00%	—

Indirect Costs	% of Total	Unit	$ Material	$ Labor	$ Equipment	Total $ per SF	Total $ 1600 SF
Insurance, payroll tax	4.8%	SF	$6.26	—	—	$6.26	$10,016
Plans & specs	0.4%	SF	0.52	—	—	0.52	832
Permits & utilities	1.7%	SF	2.22	—	—	2.22	3,552
Final cleanup	0.4%	SF	—	0.52	—	0.52	832
Subtotal, INDIRECT JOB COSTS	**7.3%**		**$9.00**	**$0.52**	—	**$9.52**	**15,232**
Overhead & profit	**12.5%**	**SF**	**$16.30**	**—**	**—**	**$16.30**	**$26,080**
Total all costs, rounded (based on 1600 SF)	**100.0%**	**SF**	**$78.10**	**$49.57**	**$2.77**	**$130.44**	**$208,704**
Amount above, as a percent of total direct costs =			59.87%	38.00%	2.12%	100.00%	—

The "Manpower" column assumes work is done in phases. Elapsed time, from breaking ground to final cleanup, will be about 10 weeks, plus delays due to weather, shortages and schedule conflicts.

Construction Economics Division

Construction Cost Index for New Single Family Homes

Period	% of 1967 Cost	$ per SF of Floor	Period	% of 1967 Cost	$ per SF of Floor	Period	% of 1967 Cost	$ per SF of Floor
2003			2009			2015		
1st quarter	539.22	75.45	1st quarter	707.78	99.03	1st quarter	814.22	113.92
2nd quarter	540.58	75.63	2nd quarter	704.72	98.60	2nd quarter	815.65	114.12
3rd quarter	541.11	75.71	3rd quarter	704.69	98.59	3rd quarter	820.60	114.82
4th quarter	554.32	77.56	4th quarter	704.85	98.62	4th quarter	823.08	115.16
2004			2010			2016		
1st quarter	557.54	78.01	1st quarter	712.93	99.75	1st quarter	833.78	116.66
2nd quarter	578.42	80.93	2nd quarter	726.72	101.68	2nd quarter	838.41	117.31
3rd quarter	587.05	82.10	3rd quarter	732.20	102.45	3rd quarter	837.71	117.98
4th quarter	611.14	85.51	4th quarter	735.44	102.90	4th quarter	840.98	118.44
2005			2011			2017		
1st quarter	608.70	85.17	1st quarter	744.17	104.12	1st quarter	848.78	119.54
2nd quarter	616.87	86.31	2nd quarter	751.04	104.94	2nd quarter	858.77	120.95
3rd quarter	621.21	87.18	3rd quarter	755.55	105.91	3rd quarter	865.06	121.83
4th quarter	631.35	88.34	4th quarter	757.83	106.66	4th quarter	868.41	122.30
2006			2012			2018		
1st quarter	641.63	89.77	1st quarter	762.28	106.66	1st quarter	876.46	123.44
2nd quarter	641.73	89.79	2nd quarter	767.30	107.37	2nd quarter	881.32	124.12
3rd quarter	644.78	89.87	3rd quarter	770.24	107.82	3rd quarter	894.46	125.97
4th quarter	655.91	91.77	4th quarter	773.50	108.23	4th quarter	901.95	127.03
2007			2013			2019		
1st quarter	656.08	91.80	1st quarter	778.13	108.87	1st quarter	904.05	127.32
2nd quarter	653.57	91.45	2nd quarter	781.69	109.37	2nd quarter	904.36	127.37
3rd quarter	655.00	91.67	3rd quarter	785.74	109.94	3rd quarter	907.56	127.82
4th quarter	658.00	92.07	4th quarter	788.05	110.26	4th quarter	913.09	128.60
2008			2014			2020		
1st quarter	665.00	93.04	1st quarter	792.90	110.94	1st quarter	919.74	129.53
2nd quarter	677.06	94.73	2nd quarter	796.73	111.48	2nd quarter	922.73	129.95
3rd quarter	699.06	95.17	3rd quarter	805.49	112.70	3rd quarter	926.19	130.44
4th quarter	720.45	100.80	4th quarter	813.67	113.85	4th quarter		

The figures under the column "$ per SF of Floor" show construction costs for building a good quality home in a suburban area under competitive conditions in each calendar quarter since 2003. This home is described below under the section "Residential Rule of Thumb." These costs include the builder's overhead and profit and a 450 square foot garage but no basement. The cost of a finished basement per square foot will be approximately 30% of the square foot cost of living area. If the garage area is more than 450 square feet, use 50% of the living area cost to adjust for the larger or smaller garage. To find the total construction cost of the home, multiply the living area (excluding the garage) by the cost in the column "$ per SF of Floor."

Deduct for rural areas	5.0%
Add for 1,800 SF house (better quality)	4.0
Add for 2,000 SF house (better quality)	3.0
Deduct for over 2,400 SF house	3.0
Add for split level house	3.0
Add for 3-story house	10.0
Add for masonry construction	9.0

Construction costs are higher in some cities and lower in others. Square foot costs listed in the table above are national averages. To modify these costs to your job site, apply the appropriate area modification factor from pages 12 through 15 of this manual. But note that area modifications on pages 12 through 15 are based on recent construction and may not apply to work that was completed many years ago.

Residential Rule of Thumb

Construction Costs

The following figures are percentages of total construction cost for a standard quality single family residence: 1,600 square foot single story, 3-bedroom, 1¾ bath home plus attached two car (450 SF) garage. Costs assume a conventional floor, stucco exterior, wallboard interior, shingle roof, single fireplace, forced air heat, PVC water supply and drain lines, range with double oven, disposer, dishwasher and 900 SF of concrete flatwork.

Item	Percent	Item	Percent	Item	Percent	Item	Percent	Item	Percent
Excavation	1.2	Finish lumber	.5	Painting	3.6	Doors	1.9	Wiring (Romex)	3.2
Flatwork (drive & walk)	2.4	Rough carpentry labor	8.9	Shower & tub enclosure	.5	Garage door	.4	Lighting fixtures	1.2
Foundation, slab, piers	3.7	Finish carpentry labor	1.7	Prefabricated fireplace	.9	Alum. windows, door	1.2	Insurance, tax	4.8
Brick hearth & veneer	.7	Countertops	1.5	Bath accessories	.7	Exterior stucco	6.4	Plans and specs	.4
Rough hardware	.6	Cabinets	3.7	Built-in appliances	1.6	Gypsum wallboard	4.7	Permits & utilities	1.7
Finish hardware	.2	Insulation (R19 ceiling)	2.3	Heating and ducting	2.9	Resilient flooring	2.0	Final cleanup	.4
Rough lumber	6.4	Roofing	5.5	Plumb. & sewer conn.	7.3	Carpeting	2.4	Overhead & profit	12.5

Industrial and Commercial Division Contents

A complete index begins on page 640

Industrial and Commercial Division

Hourly Labor Costs

The hourly labor costs shown in the column headed "Hourly Cost" have been used to compute the manhour costs for the crews on pages 8 and 9 and the costs in the "Labor" column on pages 310 to 639 of this book. All figures are in U.S. dollars per hour.

"Hourly Wage and Benefits" includes the wage, welfare, pension, vacation, apprentice and other mandatory contributions. The "Typical Employer's Burden" is the cost to the contractor for Unemployment Insurance (FUTA), Social Security (FICA) and Medicare, state unemployment insurance, workers' compensation insurance and liability insurance. Tax and insurance expense included in these labor-hour costs are itemized in the sections beginning on pages 185 and 285.

These hourly labor costs will apply within a few percent on many jobs. But wages may be much higher or lower on the job you are estimating. If the hourly cost on this page is not accurate for your jobs, use the labor cost adjustment procedure on page 11.

If your hourly labor cost is not known and can't be estimated, use both labor and material figures in this book without adjustment. When all material and labor costs have been compiled, multiply the total by the appropriate figure in the area modification table on pages 12 through 15.

Craft	Hourly Wage and Benefits ($)	Typical Employer Burden (%)	Employer's Burden Per Hour ($)	Hourly Cost ($)
Air Tool Operator	32.01	37.74%	12.08	44.09
Asbestos Worker	43.85	38.97%	17.09	60.94
Boilermaker	44.62	38.26%	17.07	61.69
Bricklayer	40.42	33.75%	13.64	54.06
Bricklayer Tender	30.97	33.71%	10.44	41.41
Building Laborer	30.80	33.93%	10.45	41.25
Carpenter	39.93	32.78%	13.09	53.02
Cement Mason	38.01	35.10%	13.34	51.35
Crane Operator	41.74	37.76%	15.76	57.50
Drywall Installer	39.95	30.89%	12.34	52.29
Electrician	46.48	29.97%	13.93	60.41
Elevator Constructor	44.47	28.63%	12.73	57.20
Floor Layer	37.98	35.31%	13.41	51.39
Glazier	41.88	32.59%	13.65	55.53
Iron Worker (Structural)	44.40	49.08%	21.79	66.19
Lather	36.15	32.70%	11.82	47.97
Marble Setter	40.81	32.76%	13.37	54.18
Millwright	40.61	32.65%	13.26	53.87
Mosaic & Terrazzo Worker	38.49	32.79%	12.62	51.11
Painter	40.14	32.66%	13.11	53.25
Pile Driver	41.49	37.31%	15.48	56.97
Pipefitter	46.94	33.08%	15.53	62.47
Plasterer	40.66	35.12%	14.28	54.94
Plasterer Helper	33.54	35.12%	11.78	45.32
Plumber	47.74	33.05%	15.78	63.52
Reinforcing Ironworker	46.52	40.18%	18.69	65.21
Roofer	35.67	38.83%	13.85	49.52
Sheet Metal Worker	45.94	32.06%	14.73	60.67
Sprinkler Fitter	49.21	31.72%	15.61	64.82
Tractor Operator	41.59	37.73%	15.69	57.28
Truck Driver	33.34	37.73%	12.58	45.92

01 General Requirements

General Contractor's Markup Costs in this manual do not include the general contractor's markup. Costs in sections identified as *subcontract* are representative of prices quoted by subcontractors and include the subcontractor's markup. See pages 3 through 5 for more on subcontracted work and markup. Typical markup for general contractors handling commercial and industrial projects is shown at the bottom of this page. The two sections that follow, Indirect Overhead and Direct Overhead, give a more detailed breakdown.

Indirect Overhead (home office overhead)
This cost, usually estimated as a percentage, is calculated by dividing average annual indirect overhead costs by average annual receipts. Temporary increases or decreases in revenue usually won't affect indirect overhead expense as much as direct overhead expense.

The figures below show typical indirect overhead costs per $1,000 of estimated project costs for a general contractor handling non-residential projects from $1 to $5 million. Indirect overhead costs vary widely but will be about 8% of gross for most profitable firms. Total indirect overhead cost ($20.00 per $1,000 for materials and $60.00 per $1,000 for labor) appears as 2.0% and 6.0% under Total General Contractor's Markup at the bottom of this page.

	Craft@Hrs	Unit	Material	Labor	Total
Rent, office supplies, utilities, equipment, advertising, etc.	—	M$	20.00	—	20.00
Office salaries and professional fees	—	M$	—	60.00	60.00
General Contractor's indirect overhead	—	M$	20.00	60.00	80.00

Direct Overhead (job site overhead)
The figures below show typical direct overhead costs per $1,000 of a project's total estimated costs for a general contractor handling non-residential projects from $1 to $5 million and require 6 to 12 months for completion. Use these figures for preliminary estimates and to check final bids. Add the cost of mobilization, watchmen, fencing, hoisting, permits, bonds, scaffolding and testing. Total direct overhead cost ($14.30 per $1,000 for materials and $58.70 per $1,000 for labor) appears as 1.4% and 5.9% under Total General Contractor's Markup at the bottom of this page. These costs can be expected to vary and will usually be lower on larger projects.

	Craft@Hrs	Unit	Material	Labor	Total
Job supervision	—	M$	—	44.00	44.00
Truck and fuel for superintendent ($450 per month)	—	M$	4.50	—	4.50
Temporary power, light and heat ($250 per month)	—	M$	2.50	—	2.50
Temporary water ($100 per month)	—	M$	1.00	—	1.00
Cellphone ($50 per month)	—	M$	.50	—	.50
Job site toilets ($100 per month)	—	M$	1.00	—	1.00
Job site office trailer 8' x 16' ($150 per month)	—	M$	1.50	—	1.50
Storage bin and tool shed 8' x 8' ($80 per month)	—	M$	.80	—	.80
Job site cleanup & debris removal ($300 per month)	—	M$	—	3.00	3.00
Job signs & first aid equipment ($50 per month)	—	M$	.50	—	.50
Small tools, supplies ($200 per month)	—	M$	2.00	—	2.00
Taxes and insurance on wages (typical)	—	M$	—	11.70	11.70
Total General Contractor's direct overhead	—	M$	14.30	58.70	73.00

Total General Contractor's Markup Typical costs for commercial and industrial projects.

	Craft@Hrs	Unit	Material	Labor	Total
Indirect overhead (home office overhead)	—	%	2.0	6.0	8.0
Direct overhead (job site overhead)	—	%	1.4	5.9	7.3
Contingency (allowance for unknown conditions)	—	%	—	—	2.0
Profit (varies widely, mid-range shown)	—	%	—	—	7.5
Total General Contractor's markup	—	%	—	—	24.8

	Craft@Hrs	Unit	Material	Labor	Total

Project Financing Construction loans are usually made for a term of up to 18 months. The maximum loan will be based on the value of the land and building when completed. Typically, this maximum is 75% for commercial, industrial and apartment buildings and 77.5% for tract housing.

The initial loan disbursement will be about 50% of the land cost. Periodic disbursements are based on the percentage of completion as verified by voucher or inspection. The last 20% of loan proceeds is disbursed when an occupancy permit is issued. Fund control fees cover the cost of monitoring disbursements. Typical loan fees, loan rates and fund control fees are listed below.

	Craft@Hrs	Unit	Material	Labor	Total
Loan origination fee, based on amount of loan					
Tracts	—	%	—	—	2.5
Apartments	—	%	—	—	2.0
Commercial, industrial buildings	—	%	—	—	3.0
Loan interest rate, prime rate plus					
Tracts, commercial, industrial	—	%	—	—	2.0
Apartments	—	%	—	—	1.5
Fund control fees (costs per $1,000 disbursed)					
To $100,000	—	LS	—	—	800.00
Over $100,000 to $300,000, $800 plus	—	M$	—	—	3.00
Over $300,000 to $500,000, $1,340 plus	—	M$	—	—	2.25
Over $500,000 to $1,000,000, $1,790 plus	—	M$	—	—	2.00
Over $1,000,000 to $7,000,000, $2,795 plus	—	M$	—	—	.90
Over $7,000,000, $8,195 plus	—	M$	—	—	.75

Project Scheduling by CPM (Critical Path Method). Includes consultation, review of construction documents, development of construction logic, and graphic schedule. Project scheduling software can be purchased for home use. Costs typically will be between $1,000.00 and $2,500.00

	Craft@Hrs	Unit	Material	Labor	Total
Wood frame buildings, one or two stories					
Simple schedule	—	LS	—	—	907.00
Complex schedule	—	LS	—	—	2,170.00
Tilt-up concrete buildings, 10,000 to 50,000 SF					
Simple schedule	—	LS	—	—	1,240.00
Complex schedule	—	LS	—	—	1,850.00
Two to five story buildings (mid rise)					
Simple schedule	—	LS	—	—	2,230.00
Complex schedule	—	LS	—	—	3,160.00
Five to ten story buildings (high rise)					
Simple schedule	—	LS	—	—	3,620.00
Complex schedule	—	LS	—	—	9,070.00
Manufacturing plants and specialized use low rise buildings					
Simple schedule	—	LS	—	—	1,610.00
Complex schedule	—	LS	—	—	2,220.00

Comprehensive schedules to meet government or owner specifications may cost 20% to 40% more. Daily schedule updates can increase costs by 40% to 50%.

Sewer Connection Fees Check with the local sanitation district for actual charges. These costs are typical for work done by city or county crews and include excavation, re-compaction and repairs to the street. Note that these costs are set by local government and will vary widely. These costs do not include capacity fees or other charges which are often levied on connection to new construction. The capacity fee per living unit may be $3,000 or more. For commercial buildings, figure 20 fixture units equal one living unit. A 6" sewer connection will be required for buildings that include more than 216 fixture units. (Bathtubs, showers and sinks are 2 fixture units, water closets are 4, clothes washers are 3 and lavatories are 1.) The costs shown assume that work will be done by sanitation district crews. Similar work done by a private contractor under a public improvement permit may cost 50% less.

	Craft@Hrs	Unit	Material	Labor	Total
Typical charges based on main up to 11' deep and lateral up to 5' deep.					
4" connection and 40' run to main in street	—	LS	—	—	1,820.00
4" pipe runs over 40' to street	—	LF	—	—	40.90
6" connection and 40' run to main in street	—	LS	—	—	2,950.00
6" pipe runs over 40' to street	—	LF	—	—	69.90
4" connection and 15' run to main in alley	—	LS	—	—	1,320.00
6" connection and 15' run to main in alley	—	LS	—	—	2,120.00
Manhole cut-in	—	Ea	—	—	359.00
Add for main depths over 5'					
Over 5' to 8'	—	%	—	—	30.0
Over 8' to 11'	—	%	—	—	60.0
Over 11'	—	%	—	—	100.0

Water Meters Check with the local water district for actual charges. These costs are typical for work done by city or county crews and include excavation and pipe to 40' from the main, meter, vault, re-compaction and repairs to the street. These costs do not include capacity fees or other charges which are often levied on connection to new construction. The capacity fee per living unit is typically $5,000. For commercial buildings, figure 20 fixture units equal one living unit. (Bathtubs, showers and sinks are 2 fixture units, water closets are 4, clothes washers are 3 and lavatories are 1.) The cost for discontinuing service will usually be about the same as the cost for starting new service, but no capacity fee will be charged. Add the backflow device and capacity fee, if required.

	Craft@Hrs	Unit	Material	Labor	Total
1" service, 3/4" meter	—	LS	—	—	3,130.00
1" service, 1" meter	—	LS	—	—	3,220.00
Add for 1" service per LF over 40'	—	LF	—	—	74.50
2" service, 1-1/2" meter	—	LS	—	—	3,600.00
2" service, 2" meter	—	LS	—	—	3,760.00
Add for 2" service per LF over 40'	—	LF	—	—	80.20
Two 2" service lines and meter manifold	—	LS	—	—	5,930.00
Add for two 2" lines per LF over 40'	—	LF	—	—	108.00
Hydrant meter, typical deposit is $1,000 to $2,000, typical water cost is $5 per 1,000 gallons					
Rental per day	—	Day	—	—	13.20
Installation of meter only. Connected to existing water service if correct size line exists from the water main to the meter box location					
3/4" meter	—	LS	—	—	138.00
1" x 3/4" meter	—	LS	—	—	131.00
1" meter	—	LS	—	—	156.00
1-1/2" meter	—	LS	—	—	505.00
2" meter	—	LS	—	—	735.00
2" meter (double line)	—	LS	—	—	1,300.00
Backflow preventer with single check valve. Includes pressure vacuum breaker (PVB), two ball valves, one air inlet and one check valve					
1" pipe	—	LS	—	—	311.00
2" pipe	—	LS	—	—	611.00
Backflow preventer with double check valves. Includes pressure vacuum breaker (PVB), two ball or gate valves, one air inlet and two check valves					
3/4" pipe	—	LS	—	—	406.00
1" pipe	—	LS	—	—	427.00
1-1/2" pipe	—	LS	—	—	498.00
2" pipe	—	LS	—	—	667.00
Reduced pressure backflow preventer. Includes pressure reducing vacuum breaker (PRVB), two ball or gate valves, one air inlet and two check valves and a relief valve					
1" pipe	—	LS	—	—	1,070.00
2" pipe	—	LS	—	—	1,310.00
Two 2" pipes (double installation)	—	LS	—	—	2,580.00

	Craft@Hrs	Unit	Material	Labor	Total
Surveying					
Surveying party, 2 or 3 technicians					
Typical cost	—	Day	—	—	1,340.00
Higher cost	—	Day	—	—	1,710.00
Data reduction and drafting	—	Hr	—	—	80.80
Surveys Including wood hubs or pipe markers as needed. These figures assume that recorded monuments are available adjacent to the site. See also Building Layout in the Earthwork section.					
Residential lot, tract work, 4 corners	—	LS	—	—	804.00
Residential lot, individual, 4 corners	—	LS	—	—	1,380.00
Commercial lot, based on 30,000 SF lot	—	LS	—	—	1,480.00
Over 30,000 SF, add per acre	—	Acre	—	—	234.00
Lots without recorded markers cost more, depending on distance to the nearest recorded monument.					
Add up to	—	%	—	—	100.0
Some states require that a corner record be prepared and filed with the county surveyor's office when new monuments are set. The cost of preparing and filing a corner record will be about $400.00.					
Aerial Mapping Typical costs based on a scale of 1" to 40'.					
Back up ground survey including flagging model	—	Ea	—	—	3,900.00
(Typical "model" is approximately 750' by 1,260' or 25 acres)					
Aerial photo flight, plane and crew, per local flight. One flight can cover several adjacent models					
Per local flight	—	Ea	—	—	478.00
Vertical photos (2 required per model)	—	Ea	—	—	52.00
Data reduction and drafting, per hour	—	Hr	—	—	72.70
Complete survey with finished drawing, per model, including both field work and flying					
Typical cost per model	—	Ea	—	—	4,000.00
Deduct if ground control is marked on the ground by others					
Per model	—	LS	—	—	–1,040.00
Typical mapping cost per acre including aerial control, flight and compilation					
Based on 25 acre coverage	—	Acre	—	—	187.00
Aerial photos, oblique (minimum 4 per job), one 8" x 10" print					
Black and white	—	Ea	—	—	52.00
Color	—	Ea	—	—	104.00
Quantitative studies for earthmoving operations to evaluate soil quantities moved					
Ground control and one flight	—	Ea	—	—	3,280.00
Each additional flight	—	Ea	—	—	2,230.00
Engineering Fees Typical billing rates.					
Registered engineers (calculations, design and drafting)					
Assistant engineer	—	Hr	—	—	99.30
Senior engineer	—	Hr	—	—	169.00
Principal engineers (cost control, project management, client contact)					
Assistant principal engineer	—	Hr	—	—	178.00
Senior principal engineer	—	Hr	—	—	239.00
Job site engineer (specification compliance)	—	Hr	—	—	99.40
Estimating Cost Compiling detailed labor and material cost estimate for commercial and industrial construction, in percent of job cost. Actual fees are based on time spent plus cost of support services.					
Most types of buildings, typical fees					
Under $100,000 (range of .75 to 1.5%)	—	%	—	—	1.1
Over $100,000 to $500,000 (range of .5 to 1.25%)	—	%	—	—	0.9
Over $500,000 to $1,000,000 (range of .5 to 1.0%)	—	%	—	—	0.8
Over $1,000,000 (range of .25 to .75%)	—	%	—	—	0.5

	Craft@Hrs	Unit	Material	Labor	Total
Complex, high-tech, research or manufacturing facilities or other buildings with many unique design features, typical fees					
Under $100,000 (range of 2.3 to 3%)	—	%	—	—	2.7
Over $100,000 to $500,000 (range of 1.5 to 2.5%)	—	%	—	—	2.0
Over $500,000 to $1,000,000 (range of 1.0 to 2.0%)	—	%	—	—	1.5
Over $1,000,000 (range of .5 to 1.0%)	—	%	—	—	0.8
Typical estimator's fee per hour	—	Hr	—	—	50.40

Specifications Fee Preparing detailed construction specifications to meet design requirements for commercial and industrial buildings, in percent of job cost. Actual fees are based on time spent plus cost of support services, if any.

	Craft@Hrs	Unit	Material	Labor	Total
Typical fees for most jobs	—	%	—	—	0.5
Small or complex jobs					
Typical cost	—	%	—	—	1.0
High cost	—	%	—	—	1.5
Large jobs or repetitive work					
Typical cost	—	%	—	—	0.2
High cost	—	%	—	—	0.5

Job Layout Setting layout stakes for the foundation from monuments identified on the plans and existing on site. Per square foot of building first floor area. Typical costs. Actual costs will be based on the time required.

	Craft@Hrs	Unit	Material	Labor	Total
Smaller or more complex jobs	—	SF	—	—	.94
Large job, easy work	—	SF	—	—	.60

General Non-Distributable Supervision and Expense

	Craft@Hrs	Unit	Material	Labor	Total
Project manager, typical	—	Mo	—	—	7,050.00
Job superintendent	—	Mo	—	—	5,470.00
Factory representative	—	Day	—	—	842.00
Timekeeper	—	Mo	—	—	2,260.00
Job site engineer for layout	—	Mo	—	—	4,210.00
Office manager	—	Mo	—	—	2,540.00
Office clerk	—	Mo	—	—	1,880.00

Mobilization Typical costs for mobilization and demobilization within a 50 mile radius as a percent of total contract price. Includes cost of moving general contractor-owned equipment and job office to the site, setting up a fenced material yard, and removing equipment, office and fencing at job completion.

	Craft@Hrs	Unit	Material	Labor	Total
Allow, as a percentage of total contract price	—	%	—	—	0.5

Aggregate Testing

	Craft@Hrs	Unit	Material	Labor	Total
Add for sample prep	—	Hr	—	—	52.70
Abrasion, L.A. Rattler, 100/500 cycles, ASTM C 131	—	Ea	—	—	130.00
Absorption, ASTM C 127, 128	—	Ea	—	—	63.90
Acid solubility	—	Ea	—	—	37.40
Aggregate test for mix design, including sieve analysis, specific gravity, number 200 wash, organic impurities	—	Ea	—	—	52.70
Clay lumps and friable particles, ASTM C 142	—	Ea	—	—	70.30
Coal and lignite, ASTM C 123	—	Ea	—	—	113.00
Material finer than #200 sieve, ASTM C 117	—	Ea	—	—	43.50
Organic impurities, ASTM C 40	—	Ea	—	—	55.40
Percent crushed particles, CAL 205	—	Ea	—	—	73.30
Percent flat or elongated particles, CRD C 119	—	Ea	—	—	118.00
Potential reactivity, chemical method, 3 determinations per series, ASTM C 289	—	Ea	—	—	370.00
Potential reactivity, mortar bar method, ASTM C 227	—	Ea	—	—	351.00

	Craft@Hrs	Unit	Material	Labor	Total
Sieve analysis, pit run aggregate	—	Ea	—	—	73.30
Lightweight aggregate ASTM C 123	—	Ea	—	—	82.00
Sand equivalent	—	Ea	—	—	93.60
Sieve analysis, processed (each size), ASTM C 136	—	Ea	—	—	85.20
Soft particles, ASTM C 235	—	Ea	—	—	73.30
Soundness, sodium or magnesium, 5 cycle, per series, ASTM C 88	—	Ea	—	—	159.00
Specific gravity, coarse, ASTM C 127	—	Ea	—	—	63.90
Specific gravity, fine, ASTM C 127	—	Ea	—	—	88.20
Unit weight per cubic foot, ASTM C 29	—	Ea	—	—	37.40
Asphaltic Concrete Testing Minimum fee is usually $40.00.					
Asphaltic concrete core drilling, field or laboratory					
Per linear inch	—	Ea	—	—	5.64
Add for equipment and technician for core drilling	—	Hr	—	—	74.40
Asphaltic core density	—	Ea	—	—	26.60
Extraction, percent asphalt (Method B), excluding ash correction, ASTM D 2172	—	Ea	—	—	63.80
Gradation on extracted sample (including wash), ASTM C 136	—	Ea	—	—	79.90
Maximum density, lab mixed, Marshall, 1559	—	Ea	—	—	187.00
Maximum density, premixed, Marshall, 1559	—	Ea	—	—	134.00
Maximum theoretical unit weight (Rice Gravity), ASTM 2041	—	Ea	—	—	79.90
Penetration, ASTM D 5	—	Ea	—	—	63.90
Stability, lab mixed, Marshall, ASTM D 1559	—	Ea	—	—	266.00
Stability, premixed, Marshall, ASTM D 1559	—	Ea	—	—	161.00
Concrete Testing Minimum fee is usually $40.00.					
Aggregate tests for concrete mix designs only, including sieve analysis, specific gravity, number 200 wash, organic impurities, weight per cubic foot					
Per aggregate size	—	Ea	—	—	76.60
Amend or re-type existing mix designs					
Not involving calculations	—	Ea	—	—	44.60
Compression test, 2", 4", or 6" cores (excludes sample preparation) ASTM C 42	—	Ea	—	—	39.30
Compression test, 6" x 12" cylinders, including mold ASTM C 39	—	Ea	—	—	13.90
Core cutting in laboratory	—	Ea	—	—	44.60
Cylinder pickup within 40 miles of laboratory					
Cost per cylinder (minimum of 3)	—	Ea	—	—	9.57
Flexure test, 6" x 6" beams, ASTM C 78	—	Ea	—	—	56.40
Laboratory trial, concrete batch, ASTM C 192	—	Ea	—	—	368.00
Length change (3 bars, 4 readings, up to 90 days)					
ASTM C 157 modified	—	LS	—	—	254.00
Additional readings, per set of 3 bars	—	LS	—	—	39.30
Storage over 90 days, per set of 3 bars, per month	—	Mo	—	—	39.50
Modulus of elasticity test, static, ASTM C 469	—	Ea	—	—	77.60
Mix design, determination of proportions	—	Ea	—	—	84.10
Pick up aggregate sample					
Within 40 mile radius of laboratory, per trip	—	Ea	—	—	50.00
Pickup or delivery of shrinkage molds, per trip	—	Ea	—	—	34.10
Prepare special strength documentation for mix design	—	Ea	—	—	94.60

	Craft@Hrs	Unit	Material	Labor	Total
Proportional analysis, cement factor and percent of aggregate					
Per analysis	—	Ea	—	—	243.00
Review mix design prepared by others	—	Ea	—	—	72.30
Splitting tensile, 6" x 12" cylinder, ASTM C 496	—	Ea	—	—	34.10
Weight per cubic foot determination of lightweight concrete cylinders	—	Ea	—	—	6.39
Masonry and Tile Testing					
Brick, ASTM C 67					
Modulus of rupture (flexure) or compressive strength	—	Ea	—	—	28.80
Absorption initial rate, 5 hour or 24 hour	—	Ea	—	—	23.30
Boil, 1, 2, or 5 hours	—	Ea	—	—	23.20
Efflorescence	—	Ea	—	—	28.70
Dimensions, overall, coring, shell and web	—	Ea	—	—	23.30
Compression of core	—	Ea	—	—	39.30
Cores, shear, 6" and 8" diameter, 2 faces, per core	—	Ea	—	—	50.00
Coefficient of friction (slip test)	—	Ea	—	—	89.30
Concrete block, ASTM C 140					
Moisture content as received	—	Ea	—	—	23.30
Absorption	—	Ea	—	—	28.70
Compression	—	Ea	—	—	34.10
Shrinkage, modified British, ASTM C 426	—	Ea	—	—	72.30
Compression, 4", 6", 8" cores	—	Ea	—	—	39.30
Fireproofing, oven dry density	—	Ea	—	—	34.10
Gunite					
Compression, 2", 4", 6" cores, ASTM C 42	—	Ea	—	—	39.50
Pickup gunite field sample (40 mile trip maximum)	—	Ea	—	—	56.40
Building stone					
Compression	—	Ea	—	—	34.10
Flex strength	—	Ea	—	—	34.10
Modules/rupture	—	Ea	—	—	34.10
Specific gravity	—	Ea	—	—	34.10
Water absorption	—	Ea	—	—	34.10
Masonry prisms, ASTM E 447					
Compression test, grouted prisms	—	Ea	—	—	145.00
Pickup prisms, within 40 miles of lab	—	Ea	—	—	39.30
Mortar and grout, UBC Standard 24-22 & 24-28					
Compression test, 2" x 4" mortar cylinder	—	Ea	—	—	19.20
Compression test, 3" x 6" grout prisms	—	Ea	—	—	25.40
Compression test, 2" cubes, ASTM C 109	—	Ea	—	—	50.00
Roof fill, lightweight ASTM C 495					
Compression test	—	Ea	—	—	23.30
Density	—	Ea	—	—	17.10
Roofing tile					
Roofing tile breaking strength, UBC	—	Ea	—	—	23.20
Roofing tile absorption	—	Ea	—	—	23.20
Reinforcement Testing					
Sampling at fabricator's plant (within 40 miles of lab), $50.00 minimum					
During normal business hours, per sample	—	Ea	—	—	19.20
Other than normal business hours, per sample	—	Ea	—	—	28.80
Tensile test, mechanically spliced bar	—	Ea	—	—	106.00
Tensile test, number 11 bar or smaller, ASTM 615	—	Ea	—	—	27.70

	Craft@Hrs	Unit	Material	Labor	Total
Tensile test, number 14 bar or smaller, ASTM 615	—	Ea	—	—	61.70
Tensile test, number 18 bar, ASTM 615	—	Ea	—	—	72.30
Tensile test, welded number 11 bar or smaller	—	Ea	—	—	39.50
Tensile test, welded number 14 bar	—	Ea	—	—	72.20
Tensile test, welded number 18 bar	—	Ea	—	—	89.30
Tensile and elongation test for pre-stress strands					
24" test, ASTM A 416	—	Ea	—	—	89.20
10" test, ASTM A 421	—	Ea	—	—	50.00
Soils and Aggregate Base Testing Minimum fee is usually $400.					
Bearing ratio (excluding moisture-density curve)	—	Ea	—	—	118.00
Consolidation test (single point)	—	Ea	—	—	79.80
Consolidation test (without rate data)	—	Ea	—	—	101.00
Direct shear test					
Unconsolidated, undrained	—	Ea	—	—	69.20
Consolidated, undrained	—	Ea	—	—	106.00
Consolidated, drained	—	Ea	—	—	134.00
Durability index – coarse and fine	—	Ea	—	—	149.00
Expansion index test, UBC 29-2	—	Ea	—	—	118.00
Liquid limit or plastic limit, Atterberg limits	—	Ea	—	—	106.00
Mechanical analysis – ASTM D1140 (wash 200 sieve)	—	Ea	—	—	43.50
Mechanical analysis – sand and gravel (wash sieve)	—	Ea	—	—	124.00
Moisture content	—	Ea	—	—	16.10
Moisture-density curve for compacted fill, ASTM 1557					
4-inch mold	—	Ea	—	—	139.00
6-inch mold	—	Ea	—	—	149.00
Permeability (falling head)	—	Ea	—	—	237.00
Permeability (constant head)	—	Ea	—	—	187.00
Resistance value	—	Ea	—	—	232.00
Sand equivalent	—	Ea	—	—	69.30
Specific gravity – fine-grained soils	—	Ea	—	—	63.90
Unconfined compression test (undisturbed sample)	—	Ea	—	—	74.40
Unit dry weight and moisture content (undisturbed sample)	—	Ea	—	—	22.30
Steel Testing $100.00 minimum for machine time.					
Charpy impact test, reduced temperature	—	Ea	—	—	27.70
Charpy impact test, room temperature	—	Ea	—	—	13.90
Electric extensometer	—	Ea	—	—	66.90
Hardness tests, Brinell or Rockwell	—	Ea	—	—	23.30
Photo micrographs					
20× to 2,000×	—	Ea	—	—	23.30
With negative	—	Ea	—	—	27.70
Tensile test, under 100,000 lbs	—	Ea	—	—	39.30
Welder Qualification Testing. Add $36 minimum per report					
Tensile test	—	Ea	—	—	39.30
Bend test	—	Ea	—	—	27.70
Macro etch	—	Ea	—	—	56.40
Fracture test	—	Ea	—	—	34.10
Machining for weld tests, 1/2" and less	—	Ea	—	—	39.50
Machining for weld tests, over 1/2"	—	Ea	—	—	56.40

	Craft@Hrs	Unit	Material	Labor	Total
Construction Photography Digital, professional quality work, hand printed, labeled, numbered and dated. High resolution photographs on a memory card or lower resolution delivered as an email attachment.					
Job progress photos, includes shots of all building corners, two 8" x 10" color prints of each shot, per visit					
Typical cost	—	LS	—	—	586.00
High cost	—	LS	—	—	668.00
Periodic survey visits to job site to figure angles (for shots of all building corners)					
Minimum two photos, per visit	—	Ea	—	—	380.00
Exterior completion photographs, two 8" x 10" prints (two angles)					
Black and white	—	Ea	—	—	580.00
Color	—	Ea	—	—	582.00
Interior completion photographs, with lighting setup, two 8" x 10" prints of each shot (minimum three shots)					
Black and white	—	Ea	—	—	663.00
Color	—	Ea	—	—	681.00
Reprints or enlargements from existing digital file. Hand (custom) prints					
8" x 10", black and white	—	Ea	—	—	26.20
11" x 14", black and white	—	Ea	—	—	36.80
8" x 10", color	—	Ea	—	—	28.90
11" x 14", color	—	Ea	—	—	39.70
Retouching services (taking out phone lines, power poles, autos, signs, etc.) will run about $100.00 per hour of computer time.					
Signs and Markers Pipe markers, self-stick vinyl, by overall outside diameter of pipe or covering, meets OSHA and ANSI requirements. Costs are based on standard wording and colors.					
3/4" to 1-3/8" diameter, 1/2" letters, 8" long	PA@.077	Ea	3.40	4.10	7.50
1-1/2" to 2 3/8" diameter, 3/4" letters, 8" long	PA@.077	Ea	3.40	4.10	7.50
2 1/2" to 7 7/8" diameter, 1-1/4" letters, 12" long	PA@.077	Ea	5.20	4.10	9.30
8" to 10" diameter, 2-1/2" letters, 24" long	PA@.095	Ea	7.40	5.06	12.46
Flow arrows, 2" wide tape x 108' roll, perforated every 8" (use $50.00 as minimum material cost)	PA@.095	Ea	3.40	5.06	8.46
Barrier tapes, 3" wide x 1,000' long. "Caution", "Danger", "Open Trench", and other stock wording (Use $35.00 as minimum material cost.) Labor shown is based on one man installing 500 LF in 1 hour.					
3 mil thick, short-term or indoor use	PA@.002	LF	.02	.11	.13
4 mil thick, long-term or outdoor use	PA@.002	LF	.05	.11	.16
Traffic control signage, "No Parking Between Signs", "Customer Parking", and other stock traffic control signs and graphics, reflective aluminum signs except as noted.					
12" x 18"	PA@.455	Ea	47.40	24.20	71.60
18" x 24"	PA@.455	Ea	82.70	24.20	106.90
24" x 8", Diamond grade (highly reflective)	PA@.455	Ea	87.90	24.20	112.10
24" x 12", Diamond grade (highly reflective)	PA@.455	Ea	100.00	24.20	124.20
24" x 18"	PA@.455	Ea	82.70	24.20	106.90
24" x 24"	PA@.455	Ea	92.40	24.20	116.60
30" x 30"	PA@.455	Ea	147.00	24.20	171.20
Add for 8' breakaway pole and mounting	CL@1.00	Ea	30.50	41.30	71.80
Add for aluminum signs	—	Ea	8.85	—	8.85
Temporary Utilities No permit fees included.					
Drop pole for electric service					
Power pole installation, wiring, 6 months rent and pickup					
100 amp meter pole	—	Ea	—	—	503.00
200 amp meter pole	—	Ea	—	—	662.00

	Craft@Hrs	Unit	Material	Labor	Total
Electric drop line and run to contractor's panel (assuming proper phase, voltage and service are available within 100' of site)					
Overhead run to contractor's "T" pole (including removal)					
Single phase, 100 amps	—	LS	—	—	404.00
Single phase, over 100 to 200 amps	—	LS	—	—	546.00
Three phase, to 200 amps	—	LS	—	—	628.00
Underground run in contractor's trench and conduit (including removal)					
Single phase, 100 amps, "USA" wire	—	LS	—	—	582.00
Single phase, 101-200 amps, "USA" wire	—	LS	—	—	753.00
Three phase, to 200 amps, "USA" wire	—	LS	—	—	835.00
Typical power cost					
Per kilowatt hour ($5.00 minimum)	—	Ea	—	—	.15
Per 1,000 SF of building per month of construction	—	MSF	—	—	2.37
Temporary water service, meter installed on fire hydrant. Add the cost of distribution hose or piping.					
Meter fee, 2" meter (excluding $400 deposit)	—	LS	—	—	83.20
Water cost, per 1,000 gallons	—	M	—	—	2.03
Job phone, typical costs including message unit charges					
Cellular phone and one year service	—	LS	—	—	597.00
Portable job site toilets, including delivery, weekly service, and pickup, per 28 day month, six month contract					
Good quality (polyethylene)	—	Mo	—	—	74.60
Deluxe quality, with sink, soap dispenser, towel dispenser, mirror	—	Mo	—	—	120.00
Trailer-mounted male and female compartment double, 2 stalls in each, sink, soap dispenser, mirror and towel dispenser in each compartment					
Rental per week	—	Wk	—	—	333.00

Construction Elevators and Hoists

	Craft@Hrs	Unit	Material	Labor	Total
Hoisting towers to 200', monthly rent					
Material hoist	CO@176.	Mo	5,730.00	10,100.00	15,830.00
Personnel hoist	CO@176.	Mo	12,600.00	10,100.00	22,700.00
Tower cranes, self-climbing (electric), monthly rent					
5 ton lift at 180' radius, one operator	CO@176.	Mo	32,300.00	10,100.00	42,400.00
With two operators	CO@352.	Mo	33,000.00	20,200.00	53,200.00
7 ton lift at 170' radius, one operator	CO@176.	Mo	42,700.00	10,100.00	52,800.00
With two operators	CO@352.	Mo	46,400.00	20,200.00	66,600.00
Mobilize, erect and dismantle self-climbing tower cranes					
Good access	—	LS	—	—	76,800.00
Average access	—	LS	—	—	93,400.00
Poor access	—	LS	—	—	152,400.00

Hydraulic Truck Cranes Includes equipment rental and operator. Four hour minimum. Time charge begins at the rental yard. By rated crane capacity.

	Craft@Hrs	Unit	Material	Labor	Total
12-1/2 ton	—	Hr	—	—	300.00
15 ton	—	Hr	—	—	315.00
25 ton	—	Hr	—	—	293.00
50 ton	—	Hr	—	—	388.00
70 ton	—	Hr	—	—	479.00
80 ton	—	Hr	—	—	477.00
100 ton	—	Hr	—	—	492.00

	Craft@Hrs	Unit	Material	Labor	Total
125 ton	—	Hr	—	—	553.00
150 ton	—	Hr	—	—	583.00
Add for clamshell or breaker ball work	—	Hr	—	—	61.00

Conventional Cable Cranes Including equipment rental and operator. Four hour minimum. Time charge begins at the rental yard. By rated crane capacity with 80' boom.

	Craft@Hrs	Unit	Material	Labor	Total
50 tons	—	Hr	—	—	445.00
70 tons	—	Hr	—	—	502.00
90 tons	—	Hr	—	—	564.00
125 tons	—	Hr	—	—	781.00
140 tons	—	Hr	—	—	606.00

Equipment Rental Rates Costs are for equipment in good condition but exclude accessories. Includes the costs of damage waiver (about 10% of the rental cost), insurance, fuel, and oil. Add the cost of an equipment operator, pickup, return to yard and repairs, if necessary. Delivery and pickup within 30 miles of the rental yard are usually offered at an additional cost of one day's rent. A rental "day" is assumed to be one 8-hour shift and begins when the equipment leaves the rental yard. A "week" is 40 hours in five consecutive days. A "month" is 176 hours in 30 consecutive days.

	Day	Week	Month
Air equipment rental			
Air compressors, wheel-mounted			
16 CFM, shop type, electric	79.00	184.00	549.00
30 CFM, shop type, electric	84.00	252.00	756.00
80 CFM, shop type, electric	98.00	299.00	893.00
100 CFM, gasoline unit	131.00	391.00	1,100.00
125 CFM, gasoline unit	162.00	488.00	1,460.00
Air compressors wheel-mounted diesel units			
to 159 CFM	122.00	365.00	1,100.00
160 - 249 CFM	162.00	488.00	1,460.00
250 - 449 CFM	245.00	732.00	2,190.00
450 - 749 CFM	325.00	974.00	2,920.00
750 - 1,200 CFM	649.00	1,950.00	5,850.00
1,400 CFM and over	812.00	2,440.00	8,280.00
Paving breakers (no bits included) hand-held, pneumatic			
to 40 lb	51.00	163.00	359.00
41 - 55 lb	81.00	288.00	612.00
56 - 70 lb	68.00	234.00	463.00
71 - 90 lb	117.00	276.00	593.00
Paving breakers jackhammer bits			
Moil points, 15" to 18"	10.00	22.00	41.00
Chisels, 3"	10.00	20.00	38.00
Clay spades, 5-1/2"	18.00	51.00	99.00
Asphalt cutters, 5"	13.00	26.00	61.00
Rock drills, jackhammers, hand-held, pneumatic			
to 29 lb	47.00	139.00	345.00
30 - 39 lb	73.00	303.00	613.00
40 - 49 lb	108.00	277.00	629.00
50 lb and over	63.00	217.00	743.00
Rock drill bits, hexagonal			
7/8", 2' long	14.00	33.00	62.00
1", 6' long	12.00	33.00	67.00

	Day	Week	Month
Pneumatic chippers, medium weight, 10 lb	105.00	239.00	445.00
Pneumatic tampers, medium weight, 30 lb	37.00	124.00	435.00
Pneumatic grinders, hand-held, 7 lb (no stone)	30.00	73.00	193.00
Air hose, 50 LF section			
5/8" air hose	9.00	18.00	45.00
3/4" air hose	11.00	24.00	57.00
1" air hose	14.00	33.00	69.00
1-1/2" air hose	22.00	66.00	169.00
Compaction equipment rental			
Vibro plate, 300 lb, 24" plate width, gas	161.00	514.00	1,090.00
Vibro plate, 600 lb, 32" plate width, gas	326.00	861.00	1,890.00
Rammer, 60 CPM, 200 lb, gas powered	113.00	344.00	730.00
Rollers, two axle steel drum, road type			
1 ton, gasoline	379.00	1,140.00	2,880.00
6 - 8 ton, gasoline	490.00	1,490.00	3,680.00
8 - 10 ton	604.00	1,920.00	4,910.00
Rollers, rubber tired, self propelled			
12 ton, 9 wheel, diesel	503.00	1,530.00	4,490.00
15 ton, 9 wheel, diesel	696.00	2,970.00	6,300.00
30 ton, 11 wheel, diesel	703.00	2,400.00	5,280.00
Rollers, towed, sheepsfoot type			
40" diameter, double drum, 28" wide	188.00	571.00	1,710.00
60" diameter, double drum, 54" wide	329.00	959.00	2,940.00
Rollers, self-propelled vibratory dual sheepsfoot drum, gas			
25 HP, 26" wide roll	554.00	1,870.00	5,640.00
100 HP, 36" wide roll	1,150.00	4,550.00	13,400.00
Rollers, vibrating steel drum, gas powered, walk behind			
7 HP, 1,000 lb, one drum, 2' wide	198.00	682.00	1,520.00
10 HP, 2,000 lb, two drum, 2'-6" wide	148.00	564.00	1,580.00
Rollers, self-propelled riding type, vibrating steel drum			
9,000 lb, gasoline, two drum	299.00	929.00	2,540.00
15,000 lb, diesel, two drum	513.00	2,550.00	4,510.00
25,000 lb, diesel, two drum	720.00	2,050.00	5,940.00
Concrete equipment rental			
Buggies, push type, 7 CF	91.00	638.00	940.00
Buggies, walking type, 12 CF	133.00	288.00	835.00
Buggies, riding type, 14 CF	181.00	508.00	834.00
Buggies, riding type, 18 CF	125.00	396.00	818.00
Vibrator, electric, 3 HP, flexible shaft	71.00	223.00	525.00
Vibrator, gasoline, 6 HP, flexible shaft	98.00	288.00	860.00
Troweling machine, 36", 4 paddle	75.00	243.00	672.00
Cement mixer, 6 CF	135.00	402.00	839.00
Towable mixer (10+ CF)	126.00	422.00	685.00
Power trowel 36", gas, with standard handle	75.00	243.00	672.00
Bull float	16.00	48.00	113.00
Concrete saws, gas powered, excluding blade cost			
10 HP, push type	142.00	350.00	773.00
20 HP, self propelled	195.00	567.00	1,150.00
37 HP, self propelled	283.00	852.00	1,910.00

	Day	Week	Month
Concrete bucket, bottom dump 1 CY	98.00	289.00	619.00
Plaster mixer, gas, portable, 5 CF	103.00	309.00	636.00
Concrete conveyor, belt type, portable, gas powered			
All sizes	154.00	559.00	1,620.00
Vibrating screed, 16', single beam	94.00	302.00	651.00
Column clamps, to 48", per set	—	—	10.00
Crane rental Add for clamshell, dragline, or pile driver attachments from below.			
Cable controlled crawler-mounted lifting cranes, diesel			
45 ton	—	3,660	10,000.00
60 ton	—	6,360.00	12,200.00
100 ton (125 ton)	2,060.00	6,230.00	20,000.00
150 ton	3,030.00	8,970.00	27,300.00
Cable controlled, truck-mounted lifting cranes, diesel			
50 ton	723.00	2,130.00	6,930.00
75 ton	920.00	2,740.00	8,310.00
100 ton	1,330.00	4,000.00	10,400.00
Hydraulic – rough terrain			
10 ton, gasoline	455.00	1,320.00	3,820.00
17 ton, diesel	568.00	1,610.00	4,500.00
35 ton, diesel	669.00	2,370.00	7,000.00
50 ton, diesel	1,550.00	4,700.00	13,200.00
Clamshell, dragline, and pile driver attachments Add to crane rental costs shown above.			
Clamshell buckets			
Rehandling type, 1 CY	—	373.00	1,100.00
General purpose, 2 CY	94.00	601.00	1,580.00
Dragline buckets			
1 CY bucket	51.00	128.00	358.00
2 CY bucket	99.00	358.00	744.00
Pile drivers, hammers			
25,000 - 49,999 ft-lb	573.00	2,560.00	4,600.00
75 - 99 tons vibratory	1,380.00	3,300.00	9,000.00
1,000 - 1,999 ft-lb extractor	—	819.00	2,170.00
Excavation equipment rental			
Backhoe/loaders, crawler mounted, diesel			
3/8 CY backhoe	344.00	1,220.00	3,340.00
3/4 CY backhoe	388.00	1,380.00	3,210.00
1-1/2 CY backhoe	423.00	1,330.00	3,970.00
2 CY backhoe	653.00	2,000.00	4,750.00
2-1/2 CY backhoe	963.00	2,980.00	8,160.00
Backhoe/loaders, wheel mounted, diesel or gasoline			
1/2 CY bucket capacity, 55 HP	259.00	796.00	1,840.00
1 CY bucket capacity, 65 HP	240.00	740.00	2,230.00
1-1/4 CY bucket capacity, 75 HP	234.00	787.00	2,180.00
1-1/2 CY bucket capacity, 100 HP	417.00	1,150.00	2,940.00
Mounted with 750-lb. breaker	546.00	1,900.00	5,680.00
Mounted with 2,000-lb. breaker	811.00	3,070.00	8,540.00

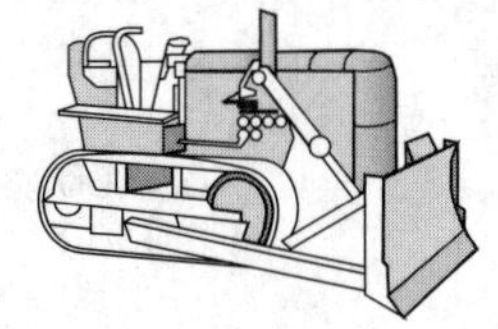

	Day	Week	Month
Crawler dozers, with angle dozer or bulldozer blade, diesel			
65 HP, D-3	477.00	1,440.00	4,030.00
90-105 HP, D-4 or D-5	668.00	1,810.00	5,010.00
140 HP, D-6	911.00	2,600.00	7,530.00
200 HP, D-7	1,340.00	3,830.00	11,100.00
335 HP, D-8	1,800.00	5,540.00	16,900.00
460 HP, D-9	3,880.00	9,120.00	27,300.00
Crawler loaders, diesel			
3/4 CY loader	380.00	1,380.00	3,210.00
1-1/2 CY loader	423.00	1,330.00	3,970.00
2 CY loader	653.00	2,000.00	4,750.00
Hydraulic excavators, crawler mounted with backhoe type arm, diesel			
.2 - .4 CY bucket	591.00	1,710.00	3,940.00
.4 - .6 CY bucket	556.00	1,660.00	3,780.00
.6 - .8 CY bucket	536.00	1,660.00	4,770.00
Gradall, truck mounted, diesel			
3/4 CY bucket	1,060.00	3,170.00	9,140.00
1 CY bucket	1,290.00	5,630.00	16,700.00
Front-end loader, diesel or gas (Skiploader)			
40-hp	167.00	568.00	1,490.00
60-hp	290.00	948.00	2,250.00
80-hp	326.00	951.00	2,280.00
Skid steer loaders			
Bobcat 643, 1,000-lb capacity	256.00	893.00	2,040.00
Bobcat 753, 1,350-lb capacity	251.00	807.00	1,780.00
Bobcat 763, 1,750-lb capacity	307.00	893.00	2,020.00
Bobcat 863, 1,900-lb capacity	298.00	901.00	2,120.00
Skid steer attachments			
Auger	156.00	495.00	898.00
Hydraulic breaker	193.00	567.00	1,640.00
Backhoe	127.00	289.00	1,160.00
Sweeper	158.00	381.00	920.00
Grapple bucket	62.00	172.00	503.00
Wheel loaders, front-end load and dump, diesel			
3/4 CY bucket, 4WD, articulated	201.00	685.00	2,070.00
1 CY bucket, 4WD, articulated	354.00	1,030.00	2,890.00
3-1/4 CY bucket, 4WD, articulated	858.00	1,450.00	6,680.00
5 CY bucket, 4WD, articulated	1,010.00	3,070.00	9,720.00
Motor scraper-hauler, 2 wheel tractor			
Under 18 CY capacity, single engine	2,120.00	5,810.00	16,200.00
18 CY and over, single engine	2,500.00	7,980.00	23,700.00
Under 18 CY capacity, Two engine	3,040.00	8,690.00	25,100.00
18 CY and over, Two engine	1,880.00	6,920.00	24,100.00
Graders, diesel, pneumatic tired, articulated			
100 HP	694.00	1,960.00	5,520.00
150 HP	939.00	2,840.00	9,800.00
200 HP	1,290.00	4,160.00	12,400.00
Trenchers, inclined chain boom type, pneumatic tired			
15 HP, 12" wide, 48" max. depth, walking	224.00	651.00	1,780.00
20 HP, 12" wide, 60" max. depth, riding	342.00	1,460.00	2,940.00
100 HP, 24" x 96" deep, crawler mount	1,710.00	5,020.00	13,400.00

	Day	Week	Month
Trenching shields, steel, 8' high x 12' long			
Single wall	148.00	382.00	1,130.00
Hydraulic trench braces, 8' long, to 42" wide	26.00	75.00	229.00
Truck-mounted wagon drills, self propelled, crawler mounted			
4" drifter, straight boom	655.00	1,730.00	4,720.00
4-1/2" drifter, hydraulic swing boom	1,000.00	3,840.00	8,830.00
Truck rental			
1-1/2 ton truck	110.00	327.00	983.00
Flatbed with boom	615.00	1,890.00	5,440.00
Dump trucks, rental rate plus mileage			
3 CY	426.00	1,200.00	2,160.00
5 CY	450.00	1,180.00	3,400.00
10 CY	949.00	3,000.00	3,830.00
25 CY off highway	—	4,690.00	13,500.00

Forklift rental

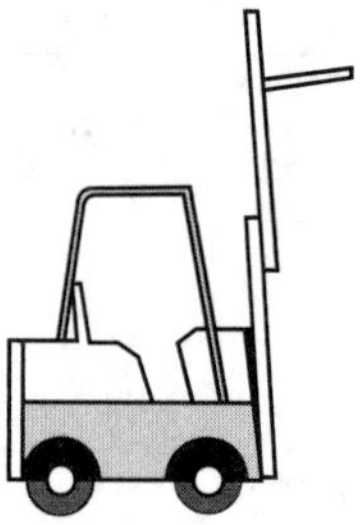

	Day	Week	Month
Rough terrain, towable, gas powered			
4,000 lb capacity	300.00	837.00	2,140.00
8,000 lb capacity	461.00	1,150.00	2,610.00
Extension boom, 2 wheel steering			
4,000 lb, 30' lift	546.00	1,160.00	2,480.00
6,000 lb, 35' lift	524.00	1,410.00	2,890.00
8,000 lb, 40' lift, 4 wheel steering	631.00	1,540.00	3,010.00

Aerial platform rental

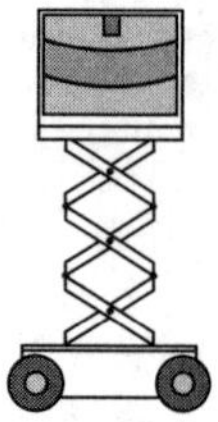

	Day	Week	Month
Rolling scissor lifts, 2' x 3' platform, 650 lb capacity, push around, electric powered			
30' high	339.00	633.00	1,080.00
40' high	388.00	978.00	1,850.00
50' high	566.00	1,430.00	2,850.00
Rolling scissor lifts, self-propelled, hydraulic, electric powered			
To 20'	162.00	333.00	647.00
21' - 30'	356.00	1,080.00	1,670.00
31' - 40'	223.00	466.00	954.00
Rolling scissor lifts, self-propelled, hydraulic, diesel powered			
To 20'	110.00	274.00	713.00
21' - 30'	305.00	650.00	1,320.00
31' - 40'	342.00	713.00	1,490.00
Boomlifts, telescoping and articulating booms, self-propelled, gas or diesel powered, 2-wheel drive			
21' - 30'	308.00	658.00	1,842.00
31' - 40'	418.00	1,040.00	2,050.00
41' - 50'	547.00	1,380.00	3,070.00
51' - 60'	610.00	1,490.00	3,220.00
Bucket truck, 38 ft insulated bucket on articulating arm, gas powered, 4-wheel drive			
Bucket truck w/ 3 story reach, articulating arm, 4x4	650.00	1,950.00	4,950.00

Pump rental Hoses not included.

	Day	Week	Month
Submersible pump rental			
1-1/2" to 2", electric	70.00	213.00	495.00
3" to 4", electric	117.00	257.00	604.00
All diameters, hydraulic	241.00	724.00	2,160.00
Trash pumps, self-priming, gas			
1-1/2" connection	78.00	239.00	617.00
4" connection	66.00	231.00	677.00
6" connection	142.00	411.00	1,030.00

	Day	Week	Month
Diaphragm pumps			
2", gas, single action	100.00	315.00	1,200.00
4", gas, double action	199.00	445.00	1,210.00
Hose, coupled, 25 LF sections			
2" suction line	16.00	38.00	103.00
1-1/2" discharge line	12.00	23.00	57.00
3" discharge line	15.00	36.00	108.00
Sandblasting equipment rental			
Compressor and hopper			
To 250 PSI	73.00	249.00	689.00
Over 250 to 300 PSI	102.00	327.00	944.00
Over 600 PSI to 1,000 PSI	147.00	474.00	1,220.00
Sandblasting accessories			
Hoses, 50', coupled			
3/4" sandblast hose or air hose	15.00	45.00	117.00
1" air hose	23.00	72.00	201.00
1-1/4" air hose or sandblast hose	13.00	34.00	88.00
Nozzles, all types	32.00	97.00	291.00
Valve, remote control (deadman), all sizes	46.00	56.00	167.00
Air-fed hood	28.00	79.00	128.00
Roadway equipment rental			
Boom mounted pavement breaker, hydraulic 1,500 lb	417.00	1,220.00	2,970.00
Paving breaker, backhoe mount, pneumatic, 1,000 lb	247.00	837.00	2,130.00
Asphalt curbing machine	131.00	400.00	1,210.00
Paving machine diesel, 10' width, self propelled	—	5,070.00	15,100.00
Distribution truck for asphalt prime coat, 3,000 gallon	1,410.00	4,310.00	13,900.00
Pavement striper, 1 line, walk behind,	93.00	192.00	481.00
Water blast truck for 1,000 PSI pavement cleaning	1,840.00	4,940.00	16,000.00
Router-groover for joint or crack sealing in pavement	277.00	941.00	2,830.00
Sealant pot for joint or crack sealing	332.00	998.00	3,290.00
Self-propelled street sweeper, vacuum (7 CY max.)	1,200.00	3,680.00	11,000.00
Water trucks/tanks			
1,800-gallon water truck	277.00	953.00	2,850.00
3,500-gallon water truck	479.00	1,920.00	5,480.00
Water tower	208.00	620.00	1,860.00
Tow behind trailer, 500 gal.	103.00	267.00	807.00
Off-road water tanker, 10,000 gal.	416.00	1,430.00	4,280.00
Steel road plate, 1" thick A-36 grade steel, with lifting eyes. Add the cost of delivery and pickup.			
4' x 4'	79.00	79.00	236.00
5' x 10'	23.00	65.00	260.00
7' x 10'	54.00	129.00	412.00
8' x 8'	81.00	170.00	505.00
8' x 20'	58.00	144.00	438.00

	Day	Week	Month
Traffic control equipment rental			
Trailer-mount solar powered LED message board	239.00	612.00	1,280.00
Arrow board – 25 lights	104.00	291.00	719.00
Barricades	10.00	27.00	78.00
Barricades with flashers	11.00	30.00	90.00
Delineators	11.00	17.00	26.00
Drill rental			
1/2" cordless drill, 18 volt	22.00	86.00	217.00
3/8" or 1/2", electric drill	33.00	11.00	172.00
3/4" electric drill	37.00	133.00	356.00
1/2" right angle electric drill	34.00	111.00	345.00
1/2" electric hammer drill	40.00	160.00	424.00
Electric generator rental			
2.5 kw, gasoline	68.00	272.00	710.00
5 kw, gasoline	91.00	367.00	1,320.00
15 kw, diesel	120.00	455.00	1,130.00
60 kw, diesel	435.00	1,190.00	3,140.00
Floor equipment rental			
Carpet blower	29.00	117.00	276.00
Carpet cleaner	32.00	128.00	365.00
Carpet kicker	18.00	72.00	200.00
Carpet power stretcher	35.00	140.00	382.00
Carpet stapler, electric	23.00	83.00	247.00
Carpet seamer, electric	19.00	76.00	200.00
Floor edger, 7", electric	47.00	188.00	473.00
Floor maintainer	58.00	232.00	658.00
Grinder 9"	37.00	147.00	385.00
Mini grinder, 4-1/2"	21.00	82.00	211.00
Pergo installation kit	43.00	130.00	351.00
Tile roller	23.00	92.00	242.00
Tile stripper, electric	61.00	244.00	650.00
Tile stripper, manual	13.00	40.00	118.00
Vacuum, 10 gallons, wet/dry	50.00	199.00	607.00
Hammer rental			
Electric brute breaker	65.00	260.00	814.00
Gas breaker	89.00	358.00	972.00
Demolition hammer, electric	58.00	323.00	650.00
Roto hammer, 7/8", electric	64.00	256.00	690.00
Roto hammer, 1-1/2", electric	62.00	248.00	600.00
Heater rental, fan forced			
Kerosene heater, to 200 MBtu	107.00	269.00	731.00
Kerosene heater, over 200 to 300 MBtu	66.00	243.00	624.00
Kerosene heater, over 500 to 1,000 MBtu	570.00	1,730.00	5,480.00
Salamanders, LP gas (no powered fan)	52.00	199.00	452.00
Ladder rental			
Step ladder, 6' or 8'	20.00	71.00	198.00
Step ladder, 10' or 14'	26.00	100.00	255.00
Extension ladder, 24'	46.00	182.00	470.00
Extension ladder, 28' or 32'	50.00	200.00	479.00
Extension ladder, 40'	59.00	214.00	528.00
Stairway step ladder	22.00	81.00	243.00

	Day	Week	Month
Landscape equipment rental			
Aerator, gas	89.00	354.00	1000.00
Auger, 2 man (gas)	118.00	472.00	1000.00
6" chipper, gas	292.00	856.00	2,130.00
Brush cutter, gas	48.00	192.00	509.00
Brush hog, 24"	66.00	259.00	762.00
Clamshovel, manual	15.00	41.00	119.00
Digging bar, 5'	15.00	48.00	142.00
Edger, lawn, gas	34.00	132.00	400.00
Fertilizer spreader	14.00	41.00	119.00
Hand auger, 6"	17.00	52.00	148.00
Hedge trimmer, 24", electric	20.00	73.00	217.00
Hedge trimmer, 30", electric	24.00	89.00	282.00
Hedge trimmer, 30", gas	41.00	164.00	485.00
Lawn roller	23.00	90.00	239.00
Leaf blower, backpack, gas	40.00	154.00	454.00
Log splitter, gas	100.00	400.00	1,240.00
Overseeder, gas	68.00	232.00	689.00
Power rake, gas	60.00	237.00	712.00
Sod cutter	105.00	422.00	1,200.00
Stump grinder, 9 HP	155.00	620.00	1,660.00
Tiller, light duty, gas	61.00	244.00	847.00
Tiller, medium duty, gas	71.00	284.00	808.00
Tiller, heavy duty, gas	97.00	388.00	1,120.00
Tree pruning shears	19.00	57.00	170.00
Weed eater, gas	44.00	176.00	468.00
Wheelbarrow	18.00	72.00	163.00
Level rental			
Laser level, small	29.00	87.00	328.00
Level kit	35.00	117.00	339.00
Transit level kit	49.00	190.00	575.00
Light tower rental			
Floodlight, 1,000 watt, on stand	39.00	110.00	266.00
To 7,000 watt trailer mounted light set, gas	147.00	351.00	811.00
Over 7,000 watt trailer mounted light set, gas	155.00	799.00	1,420.00
Extension cord, 50'	12.00	35.00	108.00
Nailer and stapler rental			
Drywall screwdriver	19.00	68.00	192.00
Finish nailer, pneumatic or cordless	39.00	156.00	383.00
Floor stapler, pneumatic	29.00	116.00	422.00
Framing nailer, cordless	29.00	116.00	354.00
Framing nailer, pneumatic, 1-1/2" to 3-1/4"	31.00	107.00	356.00
Hardwood floor nailer, 3/4"	26.00	102.00	303.00
Low velocity nail gun, single	21.00	74.00	226.00
Low velocity gun, multi	37.00	148.00	390.00
Roofing nailer, pneumatic, 1/2" to 2"	29.00	116.00	336.00
Screw gun	44.00	170.00	507.00
Underlay spot nailer	20.00	72.00	218.00

	Day	Week	Month
Painting equipment rental			
Airless paint sprayer – large	85.00	300.00	875.00
Mud mixing paddle	12.00	38.00	110.00
Pressure washer – cold, 1,500 PSI	66.00	237.00	813.00
Pressure washer – cold, 2,000 PSI	81.00	324.00	963.00
Pressure washer – cold, 3,500 PSI	98.00	392.00	1,270.00
Texture sprayer with compressor	69.00	415.00	1,200.00
Wallpaper steamer, electric	37.00	148.00	360.00
Plumbing and piping equipment rental			
Basin wrench, 3/8" to 1-1/4"	20.00	48.00	128.00
Chain wrench	17.00	46.00	127.00
Conduit & pipe cutter	23.00	65.00	187.00
Drain cleaner, corded drill, 3/8"	47.00	170.00	479.00
Laser pipe level	70.00	220.00	636.00
Pipe reamer, 1/2" to 2"	16.00	60.00	163.00
Pipe stand	20.00	64.00	184.00
Pipe wrench, 18" or 24"	22.00	65.00	183.00
Pipe wrench, 36"	22.00	65.00	183.00
Sewer snake, 100' x 5/8", electric	95.00	374.00	913.00
Sewer snake, 25' x 5/16", manual	50.00	198.00	339.00
Sewer snake, 50' x 1/2", electric	60.00	239.00	683.00
Sewer snake, 50' x 1/2", manual	39.00	148.00	440.00
Soil pipe cutter, ratchet, 6"	36.00	142.00	243.00
Toilet auger	17.00	64.00	171.00
Sanding equipment rental			
Belt sander, 3" x 21"	30.00	126.00	380.00
Belt sander, 4" x 24"	29.00	116.00	342.00
Drywall sander and vacuum	57.00	225.00	612.00
Floor sander, drum type	67.00	268.00	651.00
Floor sander, square	55.00	217.00	683.00
Orbit sander	25.00	89.00	255.00
Palm sander	15.00	60.00	163.00
Vibrator sander	24.00	83.00	249.00
Saw rental			
Band saw, electric	34.00	136.00	407.00
Bolt cutters, 24"	14.00	38.00	121.00
Bolt cutters, 36"	15.00	58.00	153.00
Chain saws, 18", gasoline	70.00	274.00	791.00
Chop saw, 14", electric	42.00	167.00	488.00
Circular saw, 8-1/4" (electric)	21.00	85.00	215.00
Compound miter saw	44.00	169.00	489.00
Jamb saw	33.00	121.00	354.00
Jig saw, electric	18.00	72.00	234.00
Masonry table saw, 2 HP	70.00	280.00	773.00
Reciprocating saw, electric	23.00	92.00	409.00
Router, 2 HP, fixed base	36.00	136.00	399.00
Sliding compound miter saw	47.00	173.00	536.00
Table saw, 10", electric	53.00	192.00	550.00
Tile cutter, manual	17.00	68.00	162.00
Tile saw and stand, wet cut	71.00	323.00	752.00

	Day	Week	Month
Scaffolding, mobile rental			
5' high, with casters	41.00	82.00	215.00
10' high, with casters	61.00	122.00	188.00
15' high, with casters	81.00	162.00	202.00
5' high, with leg jacks	39.00	78.00	181.00
10' high with leg jacks	59.00	118.00	222.00
15' high, with leg jacks	79.00	158.00	357.00
14' wide with base plates	46.00	87.00	245.00
21' wide with base plates	63.00	117.00	219.00
14' wide with leg jacks	50.00	117.00	219.00
21' wide with leg jacks	81.00	148.00	219.00
14' wide with casters	51.00	117.00	219.00
21' wide with casters	73.00	151.00	282.00
Drywall panel lift, 5 piece	38.00	153.00	247.00
Drywall scaffold	55.00	165.00	453.00
Scissor lift	382.00	652.00	1,160.00
Hook end scaffold plank, each	—	—	18.00
Plain end microlam scaffold plank 9 ft., each	—	—	4.70
Plain end microlam scaffold plank 12 ft., each	—	—	5.75
Welding equipment rental, with helmet			
To 200 amp	79.00	203.00	444.00
201 to 300 amp	119.00	263.00	598.00
Miscellaneous equipment rental			
Aluminum break, 10'	65.00	254.00	712.00
Appliance dolly	19.00	81.00	194.00
Chain hoist, 1 ton, 20' lift	28.00	101.00	305.00
Chain hoist, 5 ton, 20' lift	38.00	144.00	426.00
Come-a-long, 3,000 pounds	21.00	76.00	229.00
Dehumidifier, electric	70.00	282.00	433.00
Dolly, 4 wheel	13.00	45.00	137.00
Fan, low profile	78.00	168.00	427.00
Fan, 30", with pedestal	101.00	255.00	663.00
Fishtape, 200', 1/8"	17.00	55.00	169.00
Hydraulic jack, 12 ton	18.00	62.00	184.00
Loading ramps	14.00	54.00	112.00
Metal detector	20.00	72.00	221.00
Pavement line marker	20.00	73.00	221.00
Screwjack, 10 ton	15.00	50.00	148.00

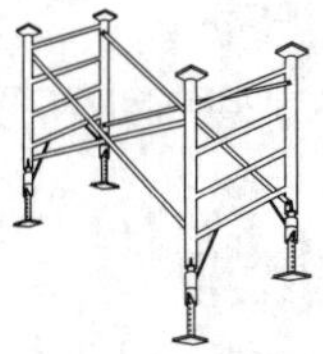

Scaffolding Rental Exterior scaffolding, tubular steel, 60" wide, with 6'4" open end frames set at 7', with cross braces, base plates, mud sills, adjustable legs, post-mounted guardrail, climbing ladders and landings, brackets, clamps and building ties. Including two 2" x 10" scaffold planks on all side brackets and six 2" x 10" scaffold planks on scaffold where indicated. Add local delivery and pickup. Minimum rental is one month.

	Craft@Hrs	Unit	Material	Labor	Total
Costs are per square foot of building wall covered, per month					
With plank on scaffold only	—	SF	1.07	—	1.07
With plank on side brackets and scaffold	—	SF	1.34	—	1.34
Add for erection and dismantling, level ground, truck accessible					
With plank on scaffold only	CL@.008	SF	—	.33	.33
With planks on side brackets and scaffold	CL@.012	SF	—	.50	.50

	Craft@Hrs	Unit	Material	Labor	Total
Caster-mounted interior scaffold, purchase. Light duty					
51" high x 4' long x 22" wide	—	Ea	184.00	—	184.00
72" high x 56" long x 25" wide	—	Ea	228.00	—	228.00
Aluminum extension scaffold plank, purchase. 250-pound load capacity. 2"-deep box section extrusions. Plank length extends in 12" increments. OSHA compliant					
8' to 13' long, 14" wide	—	Ea	250.00	—	250.00
Swinging stage, 10', complete, motor operated, purchase	CL@4.00	Ea	1,420.00	165.00	1,585.00

Heavy Duty Shoring Adjustable vertical tower type shoring. Rated capacity 5.5 tons per leg. Base frames are 4' wide x 6' high or 2' wide x 5' high. Extension frames are 4' wide x 5'4" high or 2' wide x 4'4" high. Frames are erected in pairs using cross-bracing to form a tower. Combinations of base frames and extension frames are used to reach the height required. Screw jacks with base plates are installed in the bottom of each leg. Similar screw jacks with "U"-bracket heads are installed in the top of each leg. Material costs shown are rental rates based on a 1-month minimum. Add the cost of delivery and pickup. For scheduling purposes, estimate that a crew of 2 can unload, handle and erect 8 to 10 frames (including typical jacks and heads) per hour. Dismantling, handling and moving or loading will require nearly the same time.

	Craft@Hrs	Unit	Material	Labor	Total
Frames (any size), including braces and assembly hardware					
Rental per frame per month	—	Mo	13.30	—	13.30
Screw jacks (four required per frame with base plate or "U"-head)					
Rental per jack per month	—	Mo	5.46	—	5.46
Add for erecting each frame	CL@.245	Ea	—	10.10	10.10
Add for dismantling each frame	CL@.197	Ea	—	8.13	8.13

Temporary Structures Portable job site office trailers with electric air conditioners and baseboard heat, built-in desks, plan tables, insulated and paneled walls, tiled floors, locking doors and windows with screens, closet, fluorescent lights, and electrical receptacles. Add $30 per month for units with toilet and lavatory. Monthly rental based on 6 month minimum. Dimensions are length, width and height overall and floor area (excluding hitch area).

	Craft@Hrs	Unit	Material	Labor	Total
16' x 8' x 7' high (108 SF)	—	Mo	—	—	155.00
20' x 8' x 7' high (160 SF)	—	Mo	—	—	173.00
24' x 8' x 7' high (192 SF)	—	Mo	—	—	181.00
28' x 8' x 7' high (240 SF)	—	Mo	—	—	192.00
28' x 10' x 10' high (360 SF)	—	Mo	—	—	237.00
40' x 10' x 10' high (440 SF)	—	Mo	—	—	280.00
48' x 10' x 10' high (500 SF)	—	Mo	—	—	319.00
40' x 12' x 10' high (552 SF)	—	Mo	—	—	322.00
60' x 12' x 10' high (720 SF)	—	Mo	—	—	411.00
60' x 14' x 10' high (840 SF)	—	Mo	—	—	423.00
Add for skirting, per LF of perimeter	—	LF	—	—	10.80
Deduct for unit without heating & cooling	—	Mo	—	—	–28.20
Add per set of steps	—	LS	—	—	29.20
Add for delivery, setup, blocking and dismantling of office trailers within 15 miles					
Delivery and setup	—	LS	—	—	274.00
Dismantle and pickup	—	LS	—	—	274.00
Electrical hookup	—	LS	—	—	164.00
Plumbing hookup	—	LS	—	—	222.00
Add for delivery or pickup over 15 miles, per mile					
8' wide units	—	Mile	—	—	3.75
10' wide units	—	Mile	—	—	4.05
12' wide units	—	Mile	—	—	4.36
14' wide units	—	Mile	—	—	4.88

	Craft@Hrs	Unit	Material	Labor	Total
Portable steel storage containers (lockable), suitable for job site storage of tools and materials. Rental per month, based on 6 month rental					
8' x 8' x 20'	—	Mo	—	—	79.00
8' x 8' x 24'	—	Mo	—	—	103.00
8' x 8' x 40'	—	Mo	—	—	165.00
Add for delivery and pickup, within 15 miles					
One time charge	—	LS	—	—	224.00
Portable job site shacks with lights, power receptacles, locking door and window. Rental per month, based on 6 month rental					
12' x 8' x 8'	—	Mo	—	—	81.60
8' x 8' x 8'	—	Mo	—	—	70.70
Add for typical delivery and pickup, within 15 miles					
One time charge	—	LS	—	—	76.90
Temporary Enclosures Rented chain link fence and accessories. Costs are a one-time charge for up to six months usage on a rental basis. Costs include installation and one trip for removal, and assume level site with truck access along pre-marked fence line. Add for gates and barbed wire as shown. Minimum charge is $350.					
Chain link fence, 6' high					
Less than 250 feet	—	LF	—	—	2.66
250 to 500 feet	—	LF	—	—	2.57
501 to 750 feet	—	LF	—	—	2.45
751 to 1,000 feet	—	LF	—	—	2.04
Over 1,000 feet	—	LF	—	—	1.77
Add for gates					
6' x 10' single	—	Ea	—	—	156.00
6' x 12' single	—	Ea	—	—	193.00
6' x 15' single	—	Ea	—	—	255.00
6' x 20' double	—	Ea	—	—	292.00
6' x 24' double	—	Ea	—	—	393.00
6' x 30' double	—	Ea	—	—	486.00
Add for barbed wire					
per strand, per linear foot	—	LF	—	—	.29
Contractor furnished items, installed and removed, based on single use and no salvage value					
Railing on stairway, two sides, 2" x 4"	CL@.121	LF	.72	4.99	5.71
Guardrail at second and higher floors					
toe rail, mid rail and top rail	CL@.124	LF	4.41	5.12	9.53
Plywood barricade fence					
Bolted to pavement, 8' high	CL@.430	LF	22.40	17.70	40.10
Post in ground, 8' high	CL@.202	LF	18.70	8.33	27.03
8' high with 4' wide sidewalk cover	CL@.643	LF	59.90	26.50	86.40
Cleanup					
Progressive "broom clean" cleanup, per 1,000 SF of floor per cleaning					
Typical cost	CL@.183	MSF	—	7.55	7.55
Final, total floor area (no glass cleaning)	CL@1.65	MSF	—	68.10	68.10
Glass cleaning, per 1,000 square feet of glass cleaned on one side. (Double these figures when both sides are cleaned.) Add the cost of staging or scaffolding when needed					
Cleaning glass with sponge and squeegee	CL@1.34	MSF	16.20	55.30	71.50
Cleaning glass and window trim					
with solvent, towel, sponge and squeegee	CL@5.55	MSF	20.40	229.00	249.40
Removing paint and concrete splatter from windows and trim					
by scraping and solvent	CL@15.9	MSF	50.90	656.00	706.90
Mop resilient floor by hand	CL@1.20	MSF	1.86	49.50	51.36

01 General Requirements

	Craft@Hrs	Unit	Material	Labor	Total
Waste Disposal					

Dump fees. Tippage charges for solid waste disposal at the dump or transfer station vary from $30 to $120 per ton. For planning purposes, estimate waste disposal at $75 per ton plus the hauling cost. Call the dump or trash disposal company for actual charges. Typical costs are shown below.

	Craft@Hrs	Unit	Material	Labor	Total
Dumpster, 3 CY trash bin, emptied weekly	—	Mo	—	—	385.00
Dumpster, 40 CY solid waste bin (lumber, drywall, roofing)					
Hauling cost, per load	—	Ea	—	—	272.00
Add to per load charge, per ton	—	Ton	—	—	66.70
Low-boy, 14 CY solid waste container (asphalt, dirt, masonry, concrete)					
Hauling cost, per load (use 7 CY as maximum load)	—	Ea	—	—	261.00
Add to per load charge, per ton	—	Ton	—	—	66.70

Recycler fees. Recycling construction waste materials can substantially reduce disposal costs. Recycling charges vary from $95 to $120 per load, depending on the type material and the size of the load. Call the recycling company for actual charges. Typical recycler fees are shown below. Add the cost for hauling.

	Craft@Hrs	Unit	Material	Labor	Total
Green waste	—	Ton	—	—	35.90
Asphalt, per load (7 CY)	—	Ea	—	—	113.00
Concrete, masonry or rock, per load (7 CY)	—	Ea	—	—	111.00
Dirt, per load (7 CY)	—	Ea	—	—	108.00
Mixed loads, per load (7 CY)	—	Ea	—	—	116.00

02 Existing Conditions

Paving and Curb Demolition

No salvage of materials. These costs include the cost of loading and hauling to a legal dump within 6 miles. Dump fees are not included. See Waste Disposal. Equipment cost includes one wheel-mounted air compressor, one paving breaker and jackhammer bits, one 55 HP wheel loader with integral backhoe and one 5 CY dump truck. The figures in parentheses give the approximate loose volume of the materials (volume after being demolished). Add the cost of saw cutting, if required. Use $500.00 as a minimum charge.

	Craft@Hrs	Unit	Material	Labor	Equipment	Total
Demolish bituminous paving, depths to 3" (10 SY per CY)						
Large area, with a wheel loader	C3@.048	SY	—	2.31	1.65	3.96
Strips 24" wide for utility lines	C3@.055	SY	—	2.65	1.89	4.54
Add for jobs under 50 SY	C3@.013	SY	—	.63	.45	1.08
Demolish bituminous curbs,						
to 12" width (65 LF per CY)	C3@.035	LF	—	1.69	1.20	2.89
Demolish concrete sidewalk or paving						
4" concrete with no reinforcing						
(1 CY of waste per 75 SF demolished)	C3@.045	SF	—	2.17	1.54	3.71
4" concrete with mesh but no rebars						
(1 CY of waste per 65 SF demolished)	C3@.050	SF	—	2.41	1.71	4.12
4" concrete with rebars						
(1 CY of waste per 55 SF demolished)	C3@.058	SF	—	2.79	1.99	4.78
5" concrete with mesh but no rebars						
(1 CY of waste per 55 SF demolished)	C3@.063	SF	—	3.03	2.16	5.19
5" concrete with rebars						
(1 CY of waste per 46 SF demolished)	C3@.073	SF	—	3.51	2.50	6.01
6" concrete with mesh but no rebars						
(1 CY of waste per 45 SF demolished)	C3@.078	SF	—	3.76	2.67	6.43

	Craft@Hrs	Unit	Material	Labor	Equipment	Total
6" concrete with rebars						
(1 CY of waste per 38 SF demolished)	C3@.089	SF	—	4.29	3.05	7.34
8" concrete with mesh but no rebars						
(1 CY of waste per 32 SF demolished)	C3@.109	SF	—	5.25	3.74	8.99
8" concrete with rebars						
(1 CY of waste per 27 SF demolished)	C3@.125	SF	—	6.02	4.29	10.31
Concrete over 8" to 12" thick						
Per CY without rebars						
(2 CY of waste per 1 CY demolished)	C3@4.60	CY	—	221.00	158.00	379.00
Per CY with rebars						
(2.4 CY of waste per 1 CY demolished)	C3@5.29	CY	—	255.00	181.00	436.00
Demolish concrete curb						
Curb and 24" monolithic gutter						
(7 LF per CY)	C3@.100	LF	—	4.82	3.43	8.25
Planter and batter type curbs, 6" wide						
(30 LF per CY)	C3@.043	LF	—	2.07	1.47	3.54
Remove pavement markings by water blasting. Use $100.00 as a minimum charge						
Water blaster, per hour	—	Hour	—	—	12.09	12.20
4" wide strips	CL@.032	LF	—	1.32	.39	1.71
Per square foot	CL@.098	SF	—	4.04	1.19	5.23

Fencing demolition Equipment includes one 5 CY dump truck. No salvage except as noted. These costs include loading and hauling to a legal dump within 6 miles. Dump fees are not included. See Waste Disposal. Use $250.00 as a minimum charge.

	Craft@Hrs	Unit	Material	Labor	Equipment	Total
Remove chain link fence,						
To 4' high	C4@.030	LF	—	1.28	.45	1.73
5' to 8' high	C4@.055	LF	—	2.35	.82	3.17
Remove and salvage chain link fence,						
To 8' high	C4@.073	LF	—	3.13	1.09	4.22
Remove and dispose wood fence						
Picket or board fence to 4' high	C4@.056	LF	—	2.40	.83	3.23
Picket or board fence 5' to 8' high	C4@.080	LF	—	3.42	1.19	4.61
Split rail fence, 2 or 3 rail	C4@.035	LF	—	1.50	.52	2.02
Remove and dispose wood or chain link fence gate						
To 8' high, including one gate post	C4@.333	LF	—	14.30	4.96	19.26

Highway-type guardrail demolition These costs include loading and hauling to a legal dump within 6 miles. Dump fees are not included. See Waste Disposal. No salvage except as noted. Equipment includes one wheel-mounted air compressor, one paving breaker and jackhammer bits, one 55 HP wheel loader with integral backhoe and one 5 CY dump truck. Use $500.00 as a minimum charge.

	Craft@Hrs	Unit	Material	Labor	Equipment	Total
Remove and dispose guardrail	C4@.043	LF	—	1.84	1.47	3.31
Remove guardrail in salvage condition	C4@.074	LF	—	3.17	2.54	5.71
Remove and dispose guardrail posts	C3@.245	Ea	—	11.80	8.40	20.20

Manhole, Piping and Underground Tank Demolition No salvage of materials except as noted. These costs include loading and hauling to a legal dump within 6 miles. Dump fees are not included. See Waste Disposal. Equipment includes one wheel-mounted air compressor, one paving breaker and jackhammer bits, one 55 HP wheel loader with integral backhoe and one 5 CY dump truck. Use $400.00 as a minimum charge.

	Craft@Hrs	Unit	Material	Labor	Equipment	Total
Manholes and catch basins, demolition, to 10' deep. Break below collar and plug						
Brick	C3@5.16	Ea	—	248.00	176.00	424.00
Masonry	C3@5.33	Ea	—	257.00	183.00	440.00

	Craft@Hrs	Unit	Material	Labor	Equipment	Total
Precast concrete	C3@6.64	Ea	—	320.00	228.00	548.00
Add for sand fill, any of above	C3@.125	CY	20.10	6.02	4.29	30.41
Frame and cover from manhole or catch basin						
Remove in salvage condition	C3@1.45	Ea	—	69.80	50.00	119.80
Remove and reset	C3@3.99	Ea	—	192.00	137.00	329.00
Fire hydrant demolition						
Remove and dispose	C3@5.57	Ea	—	268.00	191.00	459.00
Break out storm or sewer pipe, non-salvageable. Excavation or backfill not included						
Up to 12" diameter	C3@.114	LF	—	5.49	3.91	9.40
15" to 18"	C3@.134	LF	—	6.45	4.59	11.04
21" to 24"	C3@.154	LF	—	7.42	5.28	12.70
27" to 36"	C3@.202	LF	—	9.73	6.93	16.66
Remove welded steel pipe for salvage. Excavation or backfill not included						
4" diameter or smaller	C3@.111	LF	—	5.34	3.81	9.15
6" to 10" diameter	C3@.202	LF	—	9.73	6.93	16.66
Remove and haul away empty underground liquid storage tanks. (Draining and disposing of hazardous liquid in a tank may require special waste handling equipment.) Cost of draining not included. Includes excavation and backfill to 6' deep.						
50 to 250 gallon tank	C3@4.24	Ea	—	204.00	145.00	349.00
Over 250 to 600 gallon tank	C3@11.7	Ea	—	563.00	401.00	964.00
Over 600 to 1,000 gallon tank	C3@22.4	Ea	—	1,080.00	768.00	1,848.00
Add for sand fill, any of above	C3@.125	CY	20.10	6.02	4.29	30.41

Miscellaneous Sitework Demolition No salvage of materials except as noted. These costs include loading and hauling to a legal dump within 6 miles. Dump fees are not included. See Waste Disposal.

	Craft@Hrs	Unit	Material	Labor	Equipment	Total
Railroad demolition, siding quantities. Equipment includes one wheel-mounted air compressor, one paving breaker and jackhammer bits, one 55 HP wheel loader with integral backhoe and one 5 CY dump truck						
Remove track and ties for scrap	C5@.508	LF	—	23.60	13.10	36.70
Remove and dispose of ballast stone	C5@.111	CY	—	5.15	2.85	8.00
Remove wood ties alone	C5@.143	Ea	—	6.64	3.68	10.32
Remove light standards, flagpoles, playground poles, up to 30' high, including foundations. Equipment includes one wheel-mounted air compressor, one pneumatic breaker and jackhammer bits and one 5 CY dump truck. Use $400.00 as a minimum charge						
Remove item, in salvage condition	C4@6.24	Ea	—	267.00	143.00	410.00
Remove item, no salvage	C4@.746	Ea	—	31.90	17.10	49.00
Torch cutting steel plate. Equipment is an oxygen-acetylene manual welding and cutting torch with gases, regulator and goggles. Use $200.00 as a minimum charge						
To 3/8" thick	CL@.073	LF	—	3.01	.55	3.56

Building Demolition Costs for demolishing an entire building. Includes loading and hauling up to 6 miles but no dump fees. See Waste Disposal. Costs are by square foot of floor area based on 8' ceiling height. No salvage value assumed. Figures in parentheses give the approximate "loose" volume of the materials (volume after being demolished).

Light wood-frame structures Up to three stories in height. Based on 2,500 SF job. No basements included. Estimate each story separately. Equipment includes one 55 HP wheel loader with integral backhoe and one 5 CY dump truck. Use $3,200.00 as a minimum charge.

	Craft@Hrs	Unit	Material	Labor	Equipment	Total
First story (8 SF per CY)	C5@.038	SF	—	1.76	.75	2.51
Second story (8 SF per CY)	C5@.053	SF	—	2.46	1.04	3.50
Third story (8 SF per CY)	C5@.070	SF	—	3.25	1.38	4.63

Building demolition with pneumatic tools Equipment includes one wheel-mounted air compressor, three breakers and jackhammer bits, two 55 HP wheel loaders with integral backhoes and two 5 CY dump trucks. Use $10,000.00 as a minimum charge.

	Craft@Hrs	Unit	Material	Labor	Equipment	Total
Concrete building (30 SF per CY)	C6@.089	SF	—	4.04	1.73	5.77

	Craft@Hrs	Unit	Material	Labor	Equipment	Total
Reinforced concrete building						
(20 SF per CY)	C6@.101	SF	—	4.58	1.96	6.54
Masonry building (50 SF per CY)	C6@.074	SF	—	3.36	1.44	4.80

Building demolition with crane and headache ball Equipment includes one wheel-mounted air compressor, one pneumatic paving breaker and jackhammer bits, one 55 HP wheel loader with integral backhoe and backhoe mounted paving breaker, one 15-ton hydraulic crane with headache ball and three 5 CY dump trucks. Use $10,000.00 as a minimum charge.

	Craft@Hrs	Unit	Material	Labor	Equipment	Total
Concrete building (30 SF per CY)	C7@.031	SF	—	1.48	1.16	2.64
Reinforced concrete building						
(20 SF per CY)	C7@.037	SF	—	1.77	1.38	3.15
Masonry building (50 SF per CY)	C7@.026	SF	—	1.24	.97	2.21

Concrete foundation and footing demolition with D-6 crawler dozer and pneumatic tools. Equipment includes one wheel-mounted air compressor, one pneumatic paving breaker and jackhammer bits, one D-6 crawler dozer with attachments and one 5 CY dump truck. Use $5,000.00 as a minimum charge.

	Craft@Hrs	Unit	Material	Labor	Equipment	Total
Non-reinforced concrete						
(1 CY yields 1.33 loose CY)	C3@1.10	CY	—	53.00	55.90	108.90
Reinforced concrete						
(1 CY yields 1.66 loose CY)	C3@1.58	CY	—	76.10	80.30	156.40
Chip out concrete using paving breaker						
No dozer used, (.8 CF yields 1 loose CF)	CL@.203	CF	—	8.37	4.65	13.02

Gutting a building Interior finishes stripped back to the structural walls. Building structure to remain. No allowance for salvage value. These costs include loading and hauling up to 6 miles. Dump fees are not included. See Waste Disposal. Costs shown are per square foot of floor area based on 8' ceiling height. Costs will be about 50% less if a small tractor can be used and up to 25% higher if debris must be carried to ground level in an elevator. Equipment includes one air compressor, two pneumatic breakers with jackhammer bits and one 5 CY dump truck. Figures in parentheses give the approximate "loose" volume of the materials (volume after being demolished). Use $3,000.00 as a minimum charge.

	Craft@Hrs	Unit	Material	Labor	Equipment	Total
Residential buildings (125 SF per CY)	C4@.110	SF	—	4.71	2.52	7.23
Commercial buildings (140 SF per CY)	C4@.100	SF	—	4.28	2.29	6.57

Partition wall demolition Building structure to remain. No allowance for salvage value. Dump fees are not included. See Waste Disposal. Costs shown are per square foot of wall removed (as measured on one side). Knock down with pneumatic jackhammers and pile adjacent to site but no removal. Equipment includes one air compressor and two pneumatic breakers with jackhammer bits. Figures in parentheses give the approximate "loose" volume of the materials (volume after being demolished). Use $350.00 as a minimum charge.

	Craft@Hrs	Unit	Material	Labor	Equipment	Total
Brick or block partition demolition						
4" thick partition (60 SF per CY)	CL@.040	SF	—	1.65	1.22	2.87
8" thick partition (30 SF per CY)	CL@.057	SF	—	2.35	1.73	4.08
12" thick partition (20 SF per CY)	CL@.073	SF	—	3.01	2.22	5.23
Concrete partition demolition						
Non-reinforced (18 CF per CY)	CL@.273	CF	—	11.30	8.30	19.60
Reinforced (20 CF per CY)	CL@.363	CF	—	15.00	11.00	26.00
Knock down with hand tools and pile adjacent to site but no removal.						
Stud partition demolition (typically 75 to 100 SF per CY)						
Gypsum or terra cotta on metal lath	CL@.027	SF	—	1.11	—	1.11
Drywall on metal or wood studs	CL@.028	SF	—	1.16	—	1.16
Plaster on metal studs	CL@.026	SF	—	1.07	—	1.07

Ceiling demolition Building structure to remain. No allowance for salvage value. Dump fees are not included. See Waste Disposal. Costs shown are per square foot of ceiling (as measured on one side). Figures in parentheses give the approximate "loose" volume of the materials (volume after being demolished). Use $300.00 as a minimum charge. Knock down with hand tools to remove ceiling finish on framing at heights to 9'.

	Craft@Hrs	Unit	Material	Labor	Equipment	Total
Plaster ceiling (typically 175 to 200 SF per CY)						
Including lath and furring	CL@.025	SF	—	1.03	—	1.03
Including suspended grid	CL@.020	SF	—	.83	—	.83
Acoustic tile ceiling (typically 200 to 250 SF per CY)						
Including suspended grid	CL@.010	SF	—	.41	—	.41
Including grid in salvage condition	CL@.019	SF	—	.78	—	.78
Including strip furring	CL@.014	SF	—	.58	—	.58
Tile glued to ceiling	CL@.015	SF	—	.62	—	.62
Drywall ceiling (typically 250 to 300 SF per CY)						
Nailed or attached with screws to joists	CL@.012	SF	—	.50	—	.50
Including strip furring	CL@.023	SF	—	.95	—	.95

Roof demolition Building structure to remain. No allowance for salvage value. Add the cost of dump fees from the waste disposal section. Costs shown are per square foot of area removed (as measured on one side).

Roof surface removal, using hand tools. Figures in parentheses give the approximate "loose" volume of the materials (volume after being demolished). Use $900.00 as a minimum charge.

	Craft@Hrs	Unit	Material	Labor	Equipment	Total
Asphalt shingles (2.50 Sq per CY)	CL@.850	Sq	—	35.10	—	35.10
Built-up roofing, including sheathing and gravel (1.25 Sq per CY)	CL@2.91	Sq	—	120.00	—	120.00
Clay or concrete tile (.70 Sq per CY)	CL@1.03	Sq	—	42.50	—	42.50
Concrete plank, no covering (.80 Sq per CY)	CL@1.10	Sq	—	45.40	—	45.40
Gypsum plank, no covering (.70 Sq per CY)	CL@.820	Sq	—	33.80	—	33.80
Metal deck, no covering (.50 Sq per CY)	CL@2.27	Sq	—	93.60	—	93.60
Wood shingles or flashing (1.66 Sq per CY)	CL@.756	Sq	—	31.20	—	31.20
Remove gravel stop	CL@.070	LF	—	2.89	—	2.89

Floor slab demolition Using pneumatic jackhammers. Piled adjacent to site but no removal. Equipment includes one air compressor and two pneumatic breakers with jackhammer bits. Use $350.00 as a minimum charge.

	Craft@Hrs	Unit	Material	Labor	Equipment	Total
Slab on grade, 4" to 6" thick, reinforced						
With wire mesh (55 SF per CY)	CL@.057	SF	—	2.35	1.73	4.08
With number 4 bars (45 SF per CY)	CL@.063	SF	—	2.60	1.92	4.52
Slab, suspended, 6" to 8" thick, free fall (35 SF per CY)	CL@.092	SF	—	3.80	2.80	6.60
Slab fill, lightweight concrete fill						
On metal deck (45 SF per CY)	CL@.029	SF	—	1.20	.88	2.08
Topping, insulating (150 SF per CY)	CL@.023	SF	—	.95	.70	1.65

Floor covering demolition Using hand tools. Debris piled adjacent to site but no removal. Figures in parentheses give the approximate "loose" volume of the materials (volume after being demolished). Use $350.00 as a minimum charge.

	Craft@Hrs	Unit	Material	Labor	Equipment	Total
Ceramic or quarry tile, brick (200 SF per CY)	CL@.029	SF	—	1.20	—	1.20
Resilient materials only (270 SF per CY)	CL@.018	SF	—	.74	—	.74
Terrazzo tile (225 SF per CY)	CL@.032	SF	—	1.32	—	1.32

	Craft@Hrs	Unit	Material	Labor	Equipment	Total
Wood block floor, laid in mastic (200 SF per CY)	CL@.051	SF	—	2.10	—	2.10
Wood, residential strip floor (225 SF per CY)	CL@.032	SF	—	1.32	—	1.32

Cutting openings in frame walls Using hand tools. Cost per square foot of wall measured on one face.

	Craft@Hrs	Unit	Material	Labor	Equipment	Total
Metal stud wall with stucco or plaster	CL@.094	SF	—	3.88	—	3.88
Wood stud wall with drywall	CL@.051	SF	—	2.10	—	2.10
Dust control partitions, 6 mil plastic	C8@.011	SF	.08	.52	—	.60

Debris removal Break demolition debris into manageable size with hand tools, load into a 5 CF wheelbarrow, move to chute and dump. Costs shown are per cubic foot of material dumped.

	Craft@Hrs	Unit	Material	Labor	Equipment	Total
Wheelbarrow, 50' to trash chute and dump	CL@.018	CF	—	.74	—	.74
Wheelbarrow, 100' to trash chute and dump	CL@.022	CF	—	.91	—	.91
Wheelbarrow, 50' to elevator, descend 10 floors to trash chute and dump	CL@.024	CF	—	.99	—	.99
Trash chutes. Prefabricated steel chute installed and removed in a multi-story building. One-time charge for up to six-month's usage. Use 50 LF as minimum charge						
18" diameter	—	LS	—	—	—	1,160.00
36" diameter	—	LS	—	—	—	1,735.00

Load demolition debris on a truck and haul 6 miles to a dump site. Equipment includes one 5 CY dump truck and one 1 CY articulating wheel loader. Includes truck cost but dump fees are not included. See Waste Disposal. Per cubic yard of debris.

	Craft@Hrs	Unit	Material	Labor	Equipment	Total
Truck loaded by hand	C4@.828	CY	—	35.40	12.30	47.70
Truck loaded using a wheel loader	C5@.367	CY	—	17.00	7.87	24.87

Removal of interior items Using hand tools. Items removed in salvageable condition do not include an allowance for salvage value. Figures in parentheses give the approximate "loose" volume of the materials (volume after being demolished.) Removal in non-salvageable condition (demolished) except as noted.

	Craft@Hrs	Unit	Material	Labor	Equipment	Total
Hollow metal door and frame in a masonry wall. (2 doors per CY)						
Single door to 4' x 7'	CL@1.00	Ea	—	41.30	—	41.30
Two doors, per opening to 8' x 7'	CL@1.50	Ea	—	61.90	—	61.90
Wood door and frame in a wood-frame wall (2 doors per CY)						
Single door to 4' x 7'	CL@.500	Ea	—	20.60	—	20.60
Two doors, per opening to 8' x 7'	CL@.750	Ea	—	30.90	—	30.90
Remove door and frame in masonry wall, salvage condition						
Hollow metal door to 4' x 7'	C8@2.00	Ea	—	94.30	—	94.30
Wood door to 4' x 7'	C8@1.00	Ea	—	47.10	—	47.10
Frame for resilient mat, metal Per SF of mat area	C8@.054	SF	—	2.55	—	2.55
Lockers, metal 12" W, 60" H, 15" D	C8@.500	Ea	—	23.60	—	23.60
Sink and soap dispenser, wall-hung	C8@.500	Ea	—	23.60	—	23.60
Toilet partitions, wood or metal Per partition	C8@.750	Ea	—	35.40	—	35.40
Urinal screens, wood or metal Per partition	C8@.500	Ea	—	23.60	—	23.60
Window and frame, wood or metal	C8@.076	SF	—	3.58	—	3.58
Remove and reset airlock doors	C8@5.56	Ea	—	262.00	—	262.00

02 Existing Conditions

	Craft@Hrs	Unit	Material	Labor	Equipment	Total
Structure Moving Up to 5 mile haul, not including new foundation costs, utility hookup or finishing. These figures assume two stories maximum, no obstruction from trees or utility lines and that adequate right of way is available. Fees and charges imposed by government are not included. Costs shown are per SF of total floor area. Equipment cost includes one tow-truck equipped with dollies, jacks, support beams and hand tools. For estimating purpose, use 1,000 SF as a minimum job charge.						
Concrete or masonry structures, 12" maximum thick walls or floors						
1,000 to 2,000 SF	C1@.168	SF	—	7.09	12.90	19.99
2,000 to 4,000 SF	C1@.149	SF	—	6.28	11.50	17.78
Wood frame						
1,000 to 2,000 SF	C1@.142	SF	—	5.99	10.90	16.89
2,000 to 4,000 SF	C1@.131	SF	—	5.53	10.10	15.63
Steel frame						
1,000 to 2,000 SF	C1@.215	SF	—	9.07	16.60	25.67
2,000 to 4,000 SF	C1@.199	SF	—	8.39	15.30	23.69
Asbestos Hazard Surveys Building inspection, hazard identification, sampling and ranking of asbestos risk.						
Asbestos hazard survey and sample collection (10,000 SF per hour)						
4 hour minimum	—	Hour	—	—	—	90.90
Sample analysis (usually one sample per 1,000 SF)						
10 sample minimum	—	Ea	—	—	—	55.60
Report writing (per 1,000 SF of floor)						
$200 minimum	—	MSF	—	—	—	28.70
Asbestos Removal, Subcontract Typical costs including site preparation, monitoring, equipment, and removal of waste. Disposal of hazardous waste materials vary widely, consult your local waste disposal facility concerning prices and procedures.						
Ceiling insulation in containment structure						
500 to 5,000 SF job	—	SF	—	—	—	40.60
5,000 to 20,000 SF job	—	SF	—	—	—	28.70
Pipe insulation in containment structure						
100 to 1,000 LF of 6" pipe	—	LF	—	—	—	71.60
1,000 to 3,000 LF of 6" pipe	—	LF	—	—	—	45.90
Pipe insulation using glove bags						
100 to 1,000 LF of 6" pipe	—	LF	—	—	—	60.90
1,000 to 3,000 LF of 6" pipe	—	LF	—	—	—	45.90

03 Concrete

	Craft@Hrs	Unit	Material	Labor	Equipment	Total
Excavation for Concrete Work Add the cost of placing and removing shoring if required. Typical soil conditions.						
Batterboards, lay out for footings, per corner	C8@1.24	Ea	9.33	58.50	—	67.83
Trenching with a 1/2 CY utility backhoe/loader, small jobs, good soil conditions, no backfill included						
18" x 24" depth, .111 CY per LF (135 LF/Hr)	S1@.015	LF	—	.74	.33	1.07
24" x 36" depth, .222 CY per LF (68 LF/Hr)	S1@.029	LF	—	1.43	.64	2.07
36" x 48" depth, .444 CY per LF (34 LF/Hr)	S1@.059	LF	—	2.91	1.29	4.20
48" x 60" depth, .741 CY per LF (20 LF/Hr)	S1@.099	LF	—	4.88	2.17	7.05
Per cubic yard, 15 CY per hour	S1@.133	CY	—	6.55	2.92	9.47

	Craft@Hrs	Unit	Material	Labor	Equipment	Total
Hand labor						
Clearing trench shoulders						
of obstructions	CL@.017	LF	—	.69	—	.69
Hard pan or rock outcropping						
Breaking and stacking	CL@3.23	CY	—	133.00	—	133.00
Column pads and small piers,						
average soil	CL@1.32	CY	—	54.50	—	54.50
Backfilling against foundations, no import or export of materials						
Hand, including hand tamp	CL@.860	CY	—	35.50	—	35.50
Backfill with a 1/2 CY utility backhoe/loader						
Minimum compaction, wheel-rolled	S1@.055	CY	—	2.71	1.21	3.92
Backfill with 1/2 CY utility backhoe/loader, 150 CFM compressor & pneumatic tamper						
Spec grade compaction	S1@.141	CY	—	6.95	5.58	12.53
Disposal of excess backfill material with a 1/2 CY backhoe, no compaction						
Spot spread, 100' haul	S1@.034	CY	—	1.68	.75	2.43
Area spread, 4" deep						
(covers 81 SF per CY)	S1@.054	CY	—	2.66	1.18	3.84
Grading for slabs						
Using a D-4 crawler tractor with dozer blade						
(1000 SF per hour)	S1@.001	SF	—	.05	.03	.08
Fine grading, by hand, light to medium soil						
(165 to 170 SF per hour)	CL@.006	SF	—	.25	—	.25
Capillary fill, one CY covers 81 SF at 4" deep						
4", hand graded and rolled,						
small job	CL@.014	SF	.24	.58	—	.82
4", machine graded and rolled,						
larger job	S1@.006	SF	.25	.30	.19	.74
Add for each extra 1" hand graded	CL@.004	SF	.06	.17	—	.23
Add for each extra 1" machine graded	S1@.001	SF	.06	.05	.03	.14
Sand fill, 1 CY covers 162 SF at 2" deep						
2" sand cushion, hand spread, 1 throw	CL@.003	SF	.12	.12	—	.24
Add for each additional 1"	CL@.002	SF	.06	.08	—	.14
Waterproof membrane, polyethylene, over sand bed, including 15% lap and waste						
.004" (4 mil) clear or black	CL@.001	SF	.07	.04	—	.11
.006" (6 mil) clear or black	CL@.001	SF	.08	.04	—	.12

Formwork for Concrete Labor costs include the time needed to prepare formwork sketches at the job site, measure for the forms, fabricate, erect, align, brace, strip, clean and stack the forms. Costs for reinforcing and concrete are not included. Multiple use of forms shows the cost per use when a form is used several times on the same job without being totally disassembled or discarded. Normal cleaning and repairs are included in the labor cost on lines that show multiple use of forms. Costs will be higher if plans are not detailed enough to identify the work to be performed. No salvage value is assumed except as noted. Costs listed are per square foot of form in contact with the concrete (SFCA). These costs assume Standard and Better lumber price of $851 per MBF and $1,310 per MSF for 3/4" plyform before waste allowance. For more detailed coverage of concrete formwork, see *National Concrete & Masonry Estimator*, http://CraftsmanSiteLicense.com

Wall footing, grade beam or tie beam forms These figures assume nails, stakes and form oil costing $.25 per square foot and 2.5 board feet of lumber are used for each square foot of form in contact with the concrete (SFCA). To calculate the quantity of formwork required, multiply the depth of footing in feet by the length of footing in feet. Then double the results if two sides will be formed. For scheduling purposes, estimate that a crew of 5 can lay out, fabricate and erect 600 to 700 SF of footing, grade beam or tie beam forms in an 8-hour day.

	Craft@Hrs	Unit	Material	Labor	Total
1 use	F5@.070	SFCA	2.17	3.38	5.55
3 uses	F5@.050	SFCA	1.21	2.42	3.63
5 uses	F5@.040	SFCA	1.02	1.93	2.95
Add for stepped footings	F5@.028	SFCA	.51	1.35	1.86
Add for keyed joint, 1 use	F5@.020	LF	.92	.97	1.89

	Craft@Hrs	Unit	Material	Labor	Total
Reinforcing bar supports for footing, grade beam and tie beam forms. Bars suspended from 2" x 4" lumber, including stakes. Based on .86 BF of lumber per LF					
1 use	F5@.060	LF	.91	2.90	3.81
3 uses	F5@.050	LF	.58	2.42	3.00
5 uses	F5@.040	LF	.51	1.93	2.44
Integral starter wall forms (stem walls) formed monolithic with footings, heights up to 4'0", with 3 BF of lumber per SFCA plus an allowance of $0.25 for nails, stakes and form oil					
1 use	F5@.100	SFCA	2.55	4.83	7.38
3 uses	F5@.075	SFCA	1.40	3.62	5.02
5 uses	F5@.067	SFCA	1.17	3.24	4.41
Bulkheads or pour-stops. When integral starter walls are formed, forms will usually be required at the ends of each wall or footing. These are usually called bulkheads or pour-stops. These figures assume the use of 1.1 SF of 3/4" plyform per SFCA plus an allowance of $0.25 per SFCA for nails, stakes and bracing					
1 use	F5@.150	SFCA	1.67	7.25	8.92
3 uses	F5@.120	SFCA	.96	5.80	6.76
5 uses	F5@.100	SFCA	.82	4.83	5.65

Column footing or pile cap forms These figures include nails, stakes and form oil and 3.5 board feet of lumber for each square foot of form in contact with the concrete. For scheduling purposes, estimate that a crew of 5 can lay out, fabricate and erect 500 to 600 SF of square or rectangular footing forms in an 8-hour day or 350 to 450 SF of octagonal, hexagonal or triangular footing forms in an 8-hour day.

	Craft@Hrs	Unit	Material	Labor	Total
Square or rectangular column forms					
1 use	F5@.090	SFCA	2.94	4.35	7.29
3 uses	F5@.070	SFCA	1.59	3.38	4.97
5 uses	F5@.060	SFCA	1.32	2.90	4.22
Octagonal, hexagonal or triangular forms					
1 use	F5@.117	SFCA	2.94	5.65	8.59
3 uses	F5@.091	SFCA	1.59	4.40	5.99
5 uses	F5@.078	SFCA	1.32	3.77	5.09
Reinforcing bar supports for column forms. Bars suspended from 2" x 4" lumber, including stakes. Based on .86 BF of lumber per LF					
1 use	F5@.060	LF	.66	2.90	3.56
Anchor bolt templates or dowel supports for column forms. Includes cost of nails, stakes, bracing, and form oil and 1.1 SF of 3/4" plyform for each SF of column base or dowel support. No anchor bolts included					
1 use	F5@.150	SF	1.67	7.25	8.92
3 uses	F5@.100	SF	.96	4.83	5.79
5 uses	F5@.090	SF	.82	4.35	5.17

Slab-on-grade forms These costs assume nails, stakes, form oil, and accessories are used for each board foot of lumber. Note that costs listed below are per linear foot (LF) of form. Figures in parentheses show the average square feet of contact area (SFCA) per linear foot of form. Use this figure to convert costs and man hours per linear foot to costs and manhours per square foot. For scheduling purposes, estimate that a crew of 5 will lay out, fabricate and erect the following quantities of slab-on-grade edge forms in an 8-hour day:

Slabs to 6" high at 615 to 720 LF.
Slabs over 6" to 12" high at 450 to 500 LF
Slabs over 12" to 24" high at 320 to 350 LF.
Slabs over 24" to 36" high, 240 to 260 LF

	Craft@Hrs	Unit	Material	Labor	Total
Edge forms to 6" high, 1.5 BF per LF of form (.5 SFCA per LF)					
1 use	F5@.065	LF	1.40	3.14	4.54
3 uses	F5@.061	LF	.83	2.95	3.78
5 uses	F5@.055	LF	.71	2.66	3.37
Edge forms over 6" high to 12" high, 2.25 BF per LF of form (average .75 SFCA per LF)					
1 use	F5@.090	LF	1.98	4.35	6.33
3 uses	F5@.086	LF	1.11	4.15	5.26
5 uses	F5@.080	LF	.94	3.86	4.80

	Craft@Hrs	Unit	Material	Labor	Total
Edge forms over 12" high to 24" high, 4.5 BF per LF of form (average 1.5 SFCA per LF)					
1 use	F5@.124	LF	3.71	5.99	9.70
3 uses	F5@.119	LF	1.98	5.75	7.73
5 uses	F5@.115	LF	1.63	5.56	7.19
Edge forms over 24" high to 36" high, 7.5 BF per LF of forms (average 2.5 SFCA per LF)					
1 use	F5@.166	LF	6.01	8.02	14.03
3 uses	F5@.160	LF	3.13	7.73	10.86
5 uses	F5@.155	LF	2.55	7.49	10.04
Add for 2" x 2" tapered keyed joint, one-piece, .38 BF per LF					
1 use	F5@.044	LF	.29	2.13	2.42
3 uses	F5@.040	LF	.15	1.93	2.08
5 uses	F5@.035	LF	.12	1.69	1.81
Blockout and slab depression forms. Figure the linear feet required Use the linear foot costs for slab edge forms for the appropriate height and then add per linear foot					
Blockouts	F5@.030	LF	.79	1.45	2.24
Wall forms Formwork over 6' high includes an allowance for a work platform and handrail built on one side of the form for use by the concrete placing crew.					
Heights to 4', includes 1.1 SF of plyform, 1.5 BF of lumber and allowance for nails, ties and oil per SFCA					
1 use	F5@.119	SFCA	2.82	5.75	8.57
3 uses	F5@.080	SFCA	1.54	3.86	5.40
5 uses	F5@.069	SFCA	1.28	3.33	4.61
Add for 1 side battered	F5@.016	SFCA	.28	.77	1.05
Add for 2 sides battered	F5@.024	SFCA	.56	1.16	1.72
Heights over 4' to 6', includes 1.1 SF of plyform, 2.0 BF of lumber and allowance for nails, ties and oil.					
1 use	F5@.140	SFCA	3.21	6.76	9.97
3 uses	F5@.100	SFCA	1.73	4.83	6.56
5 uses	F5@.080	SFCA	1.43	3.86	5.29
Add for 1 side battered	F5@.016	SFCA	.32	.77	1.09
Add for 2 sides battered	F5@.024	SFCA	.64	1.16	1.80
Heights over 6' to 12', includes 1.2 SF of plyform, 2.5 BF of lumber and allowance for nails, ties and oil.					
1 use	F5@.160	SFCA	3.72	7.73	11.45
3 uses	F5@.110	SFCA	1.99	5.31	7.30
5 uses	F5@.100	SFCA	1.64	4.83	6.47
Add for 1 side battered	F5@.016	SFCA	.37	.77	1.14
Add for 2 sides battered	F5@.024	SFCA	.74	1.16	1.90
Heights over 12' to 16', includes 1.2 SF of plyform, 3.0 BF of lumber and allowance for nails, ties and oil.					
1 use	F5@.180	SFCA	4.11	8.70	12.81
3 uses	F5@.130	SFCA	2.18	6.28	8.46
5 uses	F5@.110	SFCA	1.79	5.31	7.10
Add for 1 side battered	F5@.016	SFCA	.41	.77	1.18
Add for 2 sides battered	F5@.024	SFCA	.82	1.16	1.98
Heights over 16', includes 1.3 SF of plyform, 3.5 BF of lumber and allowance for nails, ties and oil.					
1 use	F5@.199	SFCA	4.62	9.61	14.23
3 uses	F5@.140	SFCA	2.43	6.76	9.19
5 uses	F5@.119	SFCA	2.00	5.75	7.75
Add for 1 side battered	F5@.016	SFCA	.46	.77	1.23
Add for 2 sides battered	F5@.024	SFCA	.92	1.16	2.08
Architectural form liner for wall forms					
Low cost liners	F5@.020	SFCA	2.04	.97	3.01
Average cost liners	F5@.100	SFCA	3.14	4.83	7.97

	Craft@Hrs	Unit	Material	Labor	Total
Reveal strips 1" deep by 2" wide, one-piece, wood.					
1 use	F5@.069	LF	.15	3.33	3.48
3 uses	F5@.050	LF	.08	2.42	2.50
5 uses	F5@.020	LF	.07	.97	1.04
Blockouts for openings. Form area is the opening perimeter times the depth. These figures assume that nails and form oil costing $.25 per square foot, 1.2 SF of plyform and .5 board feet of lumber are used per SF of form. Blockouts usually can be used only once.					
1 use	F5@.250	SF	2.40	12.10	14.50
Bulkheads or pour-stops. These costs assume that nails, form oil and accessories, 1.1 SF of plyform and 1 board foot of lumber are used per SF of form.					
1 use	F5@.220	SF	2.44	10.60	13.04
3 uses	F5@.149	SF	1.35	7.20	8.55
5 uses	F5@.130	SF	1.13	6.28	7.41
Add for keyed wall joint, two-piece, tapered, 1.2 BF per SF.					
1 use	F5@.100	SF	1.17	4.83	6.00
3 uses	F5@.069	SF	.71	3.33	4.04
5 uses	F5@.061	SF	.62	2.95	3.57
Curved wall forms					
Smooth radius, add to straight wall cost	F5@.032	SFCA	.93	1.55	2.48
8' chord sections, add to straight wall cost	F5@.032	SFCA	.56	1.55	2.11
Haunches or ledges. Area is the width of the ledge times the length. These costs assume nails, form oil and accessories, 2 SF of plyform, and .5 board foot of lumber are used per SF of ledge.					
1 use	F5@.300	SF	3.22	14.50	17.72
3 uses	F5@.210	SF	1.74	10.10	11.84
5 uses	F5@.180	SF	1.44	8.70	10.14

Steel-framed plywood forms Rented steel-framed plywood forms can reduce forming costs on many jobs. Where rented forms are used 3 times in a month, use the wall-forming costs shown for 3 uses at the appropriate height but deduct 25% from the material cost and 50% from the labor manhours and labor costs. Savings will be smaller where layouts change from one use to the next, when form penetrations must be made and repaired before returning a form, where form delivery costs are high, and where non-standard form sizes are needed. For more detailed coverage of steel-framed plywood forms, see *National Concrete & Masonry Estimator*, http://CraftsmanSiteLicense.com

Column forms for square or rectangular columns Quantities in parentheses show the cross-section area of a square column. When estimating a rectangular column, use the costs for the square column with closest cross-section area. For scheduling purposes estimate that a crew of 5 can lay out, fabricate and erect about 550 to 600 SFCA of square or rectangular column forms in an 8-hour day.

	Craft@Hrs	Unit	Material	Labor	Total
Up to 12" x 12" (144 square inches), using nails, snap ties, oil and column clamps with 1.15 SF of plyform and 2 BF of lumber per SFCA					
1 use	F5@.130	SFCA	3.27	6.28	9.55
3 uses	F5@.090	SFCA	1.76	4.35	6.11
5 uses	F5@.080	SFCA	1.46	3.86	5.32
Over 12" x 12" to 16" x 16" (256 square inches), using nails, snap ties, oil and column clamps, with 1.125 SF of plyform and 2.1 BF of lumber per SFCA					
1 use	F5@.100	SFCA	3.32	4.83	8.15
3 uses	F5@.069	SFCA	1.78	3.33	5.11
5 uses	F5@.061	SFCA	1.48	2.95	4.43
Over 16" x 16" to 20" x 20" (400 square inches), using nails, snap ties, oil and column clamps, with 1.1 SF of plyform and 2.2 BF of lumber per SFCA					
1 use	F5@.080	SFCA	3.36	3.86	7.22
3 uses	F5@.061	SFCA	1.81	2.95	4.76
5 uses	F5@.050	SFCA	1.56	2.42	3.98

	Craft@Hrs	Unit	Material	Labor	Total
Over 20" x 20" to 24" x 24" (576 square inches), using nails, snap ties, oil and column clamps, with 1.1 SF of plyform and 2.4 BF of lumber per SFCA					
1 use	F5@.069	SFCA	3.52	3.33	6.85
3 uses	F5@.050	SFCA	1.88	2.42	4.30
5 uses	F5@.040	SFCA	1.56	1.93	3.49
Over 24" x 24" to 30" x 30" (900 square inches), using nails, snap ties, oil and column clamps, with 1.1 SF of plyform and 2.4 BF of lumber per SFCA					
1 use	F5@.061	SFCA	3.52	2.95	6.47
3 uses	F5@.040	SFCA	1.88	1.93	3.81
5 uses	F5@.031	SFCA	1.56	1.50	3.06
Over 30" x 30" to 36" x 36" (1,296 square inches), using nails, snap ties, oil and column clamps, with 1.1 SF of plyform and 2.4 BF of lumber per SFCA					
1 use	F5@.050	SFCA	3.52	2.42	5.94
3 uses	F5@.040	SFCA	1.88	1.93	3.81
5 uses	F5@.031	SFCA	1.56	1.50	3.06
Over 36" x 36" to 48" x 48" (2,304 square inches), using nails, snap ties, oil and column clamps, with 1.1 SF of plyform and 2.5 BF of lumber per SFCA					
1 use	F5@.040	SFCA	3.59	1.93	5.52
3 uses	F5@.031	SFCA	1.92	1.50	3.42
5 uses	F5@.020	SFCA	1.68	.97	2.65

Column capitals for square columns Capital forms for square columns usually have four symmetrical sides. Length and width at the top of the capital are usually twice the length and width at the bottom of the capital. Height is usually the same as the width at the capital base. These costs assume capitals installed not over 12' above floor level, use of nails, form oil, shores and accessories with 1.5 SF of plyform and 2 BF of lumber per SF of contact area (SFCA). Complexity of these forms usually makes more than 3 uses impractical.
For scheduling purposes estimate that a crew of 5 can lay out, fabricate and erect the following quantities of capital formwork in an 8-hour day:

70 to 80 SF for 12" to 16" columns — 90 to 100 SF for 20" to 24" columns
110 to 120 SF for 30" to 36" columns — 160 to 200 SF for 48" columns

	Craft@Hrs	Unit	Material	Labor	Total
Up to 12" x 12" column, 6.0 SFCA					
1 use of forms	F5@4.01	Ea	22.40	194.00	216.40
3 uses of forms	F5@3.00	Ea	11.20	145.00	156.20
Over 12" x 12" to 16" x 16" column, 10.7 SFCA					
1 use of forms	F5@6.00	Ea	39.90	290.00	329.90
3 uses of forms	F5@4.01	Ea	19.90	194.00	213.90
Over 16" x 16" to 20" x 20" column, 16.6 SFCA					
1 use of forms	F5@8.31	Ea	61.80	401.00	462.80
3 uses of forms	F5@6.00	Ea	30.90	290.00	320.90
Over 20" x 20" to 24" x 24" column, 24.0 SFCA					
1 use of forms	F5@12.0	Ea	89.40	580.00	669.40
3 uses of forms	F5@9.00	Ea	44.70	435.00	479.70
Over 24" x 24" to 30" x 30" column, 37.5 SFCA					
1 use of forms	F5@16.0	Ea	140.00	773.00	913.00
3 uses of forms	F5@12.0	Ea	69.90	580.00	649.90
Over 30" x 30" to 36" x 36" column, 54.0 SFCA					
1 use of forms	F5@20.0	Ea	201.00	966.00	1,167.00
3 uses of forms	F5@16.0	Ea	101.00	773.00	874.00
Over 36" x 36" to 48" x 48", 96.0 SFCA					
1 use of forms	F5@24.0	Ea	358.00	1,160.00	1,518.00
3 uses of forms	F5@18.0	Ea	179.00	870.00	1,049.00

	Craft@Hrs	Unit	Material	Labor	Total

Column forms for round columns Use the costs below to estimate round fiber tube forms (Sonotube is one manufacturer). Add the cost of column footings or foundations. These forms are peeled off when the concrete has cured. Costs shown include setting, aligning, bracing and stripping and assume that bracing and collars at top and bottom can be used 3 times. Column forms over 12'0" long will cost more per linear foot. Costs are per linear foot for standard weight column forms. Plastic lined forms have one vertical seam. For scheduling purposes, estimate that a crew of 5 can lay out, erect and brace the following quantities of 10' to 12' high round fiber tube forms in an 8-hour day: twenty 8" to 12" diameter columns; sixteen 14" to 20" columns and twelve 24" to 48" columns. For more detailed coverage of round column forms, see *National Concrete & Masonry Estimator*, http://CraftsmanSiteLicense.com

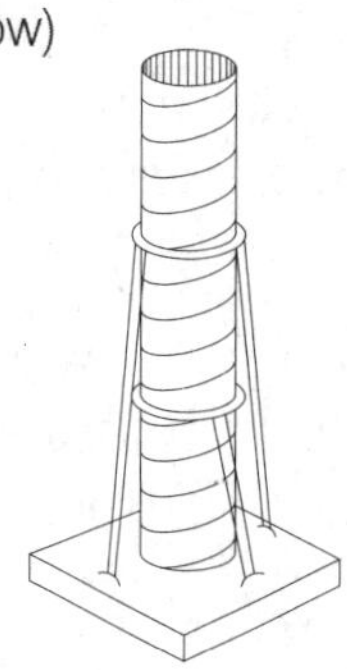

	Craft@Hrs	Unit	Material	Labor	Total
Bracing per LF (add to each cost below)	—	LF	.85	—	.85
8" spiral-type	F5@.166	LF	1.70	8.02	9.72
10" spiral-type	F5@.182	LF	2.06	8.79	10.85
12" spiral-type	F5@.207	LF	2.56	10.00	12.56
14" spiral-type	F5@.224	LF	3.41	10.80	14.21
16" spiral-type	F5@.232	LF	3.92	11.20	15.12
20" spiral-type	F5@.250	LF	4.78	12.10	16.88
24" spiral-type	F5@.275	LF	5.97	13.30	19.27
30" spiral-type	F5@.289	LF	7.76	14.00	21.76
36" spiral-type	F5@.308	LF	10.90	14.90	25.80
48" spiral-type	F5@.334	LF	13.60	16.10	29.70
8" heavy-duty, water resistant	F5@.166	LF	2.39	8.02	10.41
10" heavy-duty, water resistant	F5@.177	LF	2.84	8.55	11.39
12" heavy-duty, water resistant	F5@.207	LF	3.57	10.00	13.57
14" heavy-duty, water resistant	F5@.224	LF	5.19	10.80	15.99
16" heavy-duty, water resistant	F5@.232	LF	5.70	11.20	16.90
20" heavy-duty, water resistant	F5@.250	LF	8.45	12.10	20.55
24" heavy-duty, water resistant	F5@.275	LF	11.60	13.30	24.90
30" heavy-duty, water resistant	F5@.289	LF	16.50	14.00	30.50
36" heavy-duty, water resistant	F5@.308	LF	20.80	14.90	35.70
48" heavy-duty, water resistant	F5@.334	LF	39.50	16.10	55.60

Column capitals for round columns
Use these figures to estimate costs for rented prefabricated steel conical-shaped capital forms. Costs assume a minimum rental period of 1 month and include an allowance for nails and form oil. Labor shown assumes the capital will be supported from the deck formwork above the capital and includes laying out and cutting the hole in the deck to receive the capital. Capital bottom diameter is sized to fit into the column tube form. The column form size (diameter) does not significantly affect the capital form rental cost. Dimensions shown below are the top diameter. Form weights are shown in parentheses. Only 3 uses of these forms are usually possible in a 30-day period. Setting forms and installing reinforcing steel takes one day, concrete placing takes another day, curing requires 7 to 10 days, removing and cleaning forms takes another day. For scheduling purposes estimate that a crew of 5 can lay out, cut openings in floor deck formwork and install an average of 8 or 9 round column capital forms in an 8-hour day.

	Craft@Hrs	Unit	Material	Labor	Total
3'6" (100 pounds) 1 use	F5@4.01	Ea	273.00	194.00	467.00
3'6" (100 pounds) 3 uses	F5@4.01	Ea	90.90	194.00	284.90
4'0" (125 pounds) 1 use	F5@4.01	Ea	293.00	194.00	487.00
4'0" (125 pounds) 3 uses	F5@4.01	Ea	98.20	194.00	292.20
4'6" (150 pounds) 1 use	F5@4.30	Ea	304.00	208.00	512.00
4'6" (150 pounds) 3 uses	F5@4.30	Ea	101.00	208.00	309.00
5'0" (175 pounds) 1 use	F5@4.51	Ea	321.00	218.00	539.00
5'0" (175 pounds) 3 uses	F5@4.51	Ea	114.00	218.00	332.00
5'6" (200 pounds) 1 use	F5@4.51	Ea	369.00	218.00	587.00
5'6" (200 pounds) 3 uses	F5@4.51	Ea	123.00	218.00	341.00
6'0" (225 pounds) 1 use	F5@4.70	Ea	385.00	227.00	612.00
6'0" (225 pounds) 3 uses	F5@4.70	Ea	122.00	227.00	349.00

	Craft@Hrs	Unit	Material	Labor	Total

Beam and girder forms Using nails, snap ties and oil, 1.3 SF of 3/4" plyform and 2.1 BF of lumber per SFCA. For scheduling purposes, estimate that a crew of 5 can lay out, fabricate and erect 250 to 300 SF of beam and girder forms in an 8-hour day. For more detailed coverage of beam and girder forms, see *National Concrete & Masonry Estimator*, http://CraftsmanSiteLicense.com

1 use	F5@.149	SFCA	3.54	7.20	10.74
3 uses	F5@.141	SFCA	1.90	6.81	8.71
5 uses	F5@.120	SFCA	1.57	5.80	7.37

Shores for beams and girders Using 4" x 4" wooden posts. These figures assume an average shore height of 12'0" with a 2'0" long horizontal 4" x 4" head and 2" x 6" diagonal brace (30 BF of lumber per shore) and include nails, adjustable post clamps and accessories. For scheduling purposes estimate that a crew of 5 can lay out, fabricate and install 30 to 35 adjustable wood shores in an 8-hour day when shores have an average height of 12'0". Quantity and spacing of shores is dictated by the size of the beams and girders. Generally, allow one shore for each 6 LF of beam or girder. Costs for heavy-duty shoring are listed under General Requirements, Heavy-Duty Shoring.

1 use	F5@1.50	Ea	29.60	72.50	102.10
3 uses	F5@1.00	Ea	16.30	48.30	64.60
5 uses	F5@.748	Ea	13.60	36.10	49.70

Elevated slab forms These are costs for forms per square foot of finished slab area and include shoring and stripping at heights to 12'. Bays are assumed to be 20' x 20' bays.

Waffle slab-joist pans, monolithic Using rented forms (30-day rental period minimum). For scheduling purposes, estimate that a crew of 5 can lay out, fabricate and install 500 to 600 SF of waffle slab-joist pan forms and shoring in an 8-hour day. Two uses of the forms in a 30-day period is usually the maximum.

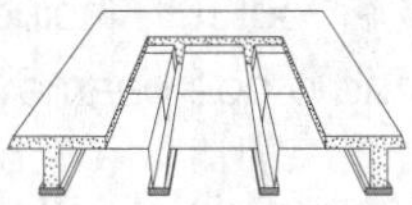

Metal pans, 10,000 to 20,000 SF					
1 use	F5@.100	SF	7.06	4.83	11.89
2 uses	F5@.066	SF	3.95	3.19	7.14
Fiberglass pans, 10,000 to 20,000 SF					
1 use	F5@.077	SF	8.26	3.72	11.98
2 uses	F5@.061	SF	4.71	2.95	7.66

Flat slab with beams, monolithic Including nails, braces, stiffeners and oil 1.2 SF of plyform and 3.2 BF of lumber per SFCA for one-way beam systems. Two-way beam systems require approximately 40% more forming materials than one-way beam systems. For scheduling purposes, estimate that a crew of 5 can lay out, fabricate and erect 350 to 400 SF of one-way beam systems and 250 to 300 SF of two-way beam systems in an 8-hour day, including shoring.

One-way beam 1 use	F5@.110	SFCA	4.26	5.31	9.57
One-way beam 2 uses	F5@.080	SFCA	3.15	3.86	7.01
Two-way beam 1 use	F5@.152	SFCA	5.86	7.34	13.20
Two-way beam 2 uses	F5@.100	SFCA	3.35	4.83	8.18

Structural flat-slab Using nails, braces, stiffeners and oil costing $.25, 1.2 SF of plyform and 2.25 BF of lumber per SFCA. For scheduling purposes, estimate that a crew of 5 can lay out, fabricate and erect 500 to 600 SFCA of structural flat-slab forms in an 8-hour day, including shoring.

Edge forms	F5@.072	LF	1.98	3.48	5.46
Slab forms 1 use	F5@.069	SFCA	3.53	3.33	6.86
Slab forms 3 uses	F5@.048	SFCA	1.89	2.32	4.21
Slab forms 5 uses	F5@.043	SFCA	1.56	2.08	3.64

Additional forming costs for elevated slabs, if required Based on single use of plyform and lumber. For scheduling purposes estimate that a 5 man crew can install 500 SFCA per 8-hour day.

Control joints	F5@.031	LF	2.12	1.50	3.62
Curbs and pads	F5@.083	SFCA	3.53	4.01	7.54
Depressions	F5@.083	SFCA	1.06	4.01	5.07
Keyed joints	F5@.031	LF	.89	1.50	2.39

	Craft@Hrs	Unit	Material	Labor	Total
Miscellaneous formwork Based on single use of plyform and lumber. For scheduling purposes, estimate that a crew of 5 can lay out, fabricate and erect 225 to 250 SFCA of these types of forms in an 8-hour day.					
Flat soffits & landings	F5@.166	SFCA	5.47	8.02	13.49
Sloping soffits	F5@.166	SFCA	5.65	8.02	13.67
Stair risers (steps)	F5@.120	SFCA	2.12	5.80	7.92
Reinforcing Steel Bars 20' lengths, material costs only. Add the cost of delivery, shop fabrication, cutting, bending, setting, lap and tying bars.					
ASTM-615 grade 60					
3/8" x 20'	—	Ea	6.23	—	6.23
1/2" x 20'	—	Ea	9.78	—	9.78
5/8" x 20'	—	Ea	15.30	—	15.30
3/4" x 20'	—	Ea	17.90	—	17.90
1" x 20'	—	Ea	42.30	—	42.30
ASTM-775 epoxy-coated					
1/2" x 20'	—	Ea	21.20	—	21.20
5/8" x 20'	—	Ea	30.40	—	30.40
3/4" x 20'	—	Ea	43.70	—	43.70
Reinforcing for Cast-in-Place Concrete Steel reinforcing bars (rebar), ASTM A615 Grade 60. Material costs are for deformed steel reinforcing rebar, including 10% lap allowance, cutting and bending. These costs also include detailed shop drawings and delivery to jobsite with identity tags per shop drawings. Add for epoxy or galvanized coating of rebar, chairs, splicing, spiral caissons and round column reinforcing, if required, from the sections following the data below. Costs per pound (Lb) and per linear foot (LF) including tie wire and tying.					
Reinforcing steel placed and tied in footings, foundations and grade beams					
1/4" diameter, #2 rebar	RB@.015	Lb	1.29	.98	2.27
1/4" diameter, #2 rebar (.17 lb per LF)	RB@.003	LF	.22	.20	.42
3/8" diameter, #3 rebar	RB@.011	Lb	.88	.72	1.60
3/8" diameter, #3 rebar (.38 lb per LF)	RB@.004	LF	.33	.26	.59
1/2" diameter, #4 rebar	RB@.010	Lb	.76	.65	1.41
1/2" diameter, #4 rebar (.67 lb per LF)	RB@.007	LF	.51	.46	.97
5/8" diameter, #5 rebar	RB@.009	Lb	.81	.59	1.40
5/8" diameter, #5 rebar (1.04 lb per LF)	RB@.009	LF	.84	.59	1.43
3/4" diameter, #6 rebar	RB@.008	Lb	.68	.52	1.20
3/4" diameter, #6 rebar (1.50 lb per LF)	RB@.012	LF	1.02	.78	1.80
7/8" diameter, #7 rebar	RB@.008	Lb	.83	.52	1.35
7/8" diameter, #7 rebar (2.04 lb per LF)	RB@.016	LF	1.69	1.04	2.73
1" diameter, #8 rebar	RB@.008	Lb	.70	.52	1.22
1" diameter, #8 rebar (2.67 lb per LF)	RB@.021	LF	1.88	1.37	3.25
1-1/8" diameter, #9 rebar	RB@.008	Lb	.89	.52	1.41
1-1/8" diameter, #9 rebar (3.40 lb per LF)	RB@.027	LF	3.01	1.76	4.77
1-1/4" diameter, #10 rebar	RB@.007	Lb	.89	.46	1.35
1-1/4" diameter, #10 rebar (4.30 lb per LF)	RB@.030	LF	3.81	1.96	5.77
1-3/8" diameter, #11 rebar	RB@.007	Lb	.89	.46	1.35
1-3/8" diameter, #11 rebar (5.31 lb per LF)	RB@.037	LF	4.70	2.41	7.11
Reinforcing steel placed and tied in structural slabs					
1/4" diameter, #2 rebar	RB@.014	Lb	1.29	.91	2.20
1/4" diameter, #2 rebar (.17 lb per LF)	RB@.002	LF	.22	.13	.35
3/8" diameter, #3 rebar	RB@.010	Lb	.88	.65	1.53
3/8" diameter, #3 rebar (.38 lb per LF)	RB@.004	LF	.33	.26	.59
1/2" diameter, #4 rebar	RB@.009	Lb	.76	.59	1.35
1/2" diameter, #4 rebar (.67 lb per LF)	RB@.006	LF	.51	.39	.90
5/8" diameter, #5 rebar	RB@.008	Lb	.81	.52	1.33

	Craft@Hrs	Unit	Material	Labor	Total
5/8" diameter, #5 rebar (1.04 lb per LF)	RB@.008	LF	.84	.52	1.36
3/4" diameter, #6 rebar	RB@.007	Lb	.68	.46	1.14
3/4" diameter, #6 rebar (1.50 lb per LF)	RB@.011	LF	1.02	.72	1.74
7/8" diameter, #7 rebar	RB@.007	Lb	.83	.46	1.29
7/8" diameter, #7 rebar (2.04 lb per LF)	RB@.014	LF	1.69	.91	2.60
1" diameter, #8 rebar	RB@.007	Lb	.70	.46	1.16
1" diameter, #8 rebar (2.67 lb per LF)	RB@.019	LF	1.88	1.24	3.12
1-1/8" diameter, #9 rebar	RB@.007	Lb	.89	.46	1.35
1-1/8" diameter, #9 rebar (3.40 lb per LF)	RB@.024	LF	3.01	1.57	4.58
1-1/4" diameter, #10 rebar	RB@.006	Lb	.89	.39	1.28
1-1/4" diameter, #10 rebar (4.30 lb per LF)	RB@.026	LF	3.81	1.70	5.51
1-3/8" diameter, #11 rebar	RB@.006	Lb	.89	.39	1.28
1-3/8" diameter, #11 rebar (5.31 lb per LF)	RB@.032	LF	4.70	2.09	6.79
Reinforcing steel placed and tied in columns, stairs and walls					
1/4" diameter, #2 rebar	RB@.017	Lb	1.29	1.11	2.40
1/4" diameter, #2 rebar (.17 lb per LF)	RB@.003	LF	.22	.20	.42
3/8" diameter, #3 rebar	RB@.012	Lb	.88	.78	1.66
3/8" diameter, #3 rebar (.38 lb per LF)	RB@.005	LF	.33	.33	.66
1/2" diameter, #4 rebar	RB@.011	Lb	.76	.72	1.48
1/2" diameter, #4 rebar (.67 lb per LF)	RB@.007	LF	.51	.46	.97
5/8" diameter, #5 rebar	RB@.010	Lb	.81	.65	1.46
5/8" diameter, #5 rebar (1.04 lb per LF)	RB@.010	LF	.84	.65	1.49
3/4" diameter, #6 rebar	RB@.009	Lb	.68	.59	1.27
3/4" diameter, #6 rebar (1.50 lb per LF)	RB@.014	LF	1.02	.91	1.93
7/8" diameter, #7 rebar	RB@.009	Lb	.83	.59	1.42
7/8" diameter, #7 rebar (2.04 lb per LF)	RB@.018	LF	1.69	1.17	2.86
1" diameter, #8 rebar	RB@.009	Lb	.70	.59	1.29
1" diameter, #8 rebar (2.67 lb per LF)	RB@.024	LF	1.88	1.57	3.45
1-1/8" diameter, #9 rebar	RB@.009	Lb	.89	.59	1.48
1-1/8" diameter, #9 rebar (3.40 lb per LF)	RB@.031	LF	3.01	2.01	5.28
1-1/4" diameter, #10 rebar	RB@.008	Lb	.89	.52	1.41
1-1/4" diameter, #10 rebar (4.30 lb per LF)	RB@.034	LF	3.81	2.22	6.03
1-3/8" diameter, #11 rebar	RB@.008	Lb	.89	.52	1.41
1-3/8" diameter, #11 rebar (5.31 lb per LF)	RB@.037	LF	4.70	2.41	7.11
Galvanized coating, add to uncoated bars, per pound					
Any #2 rebar, #3 rebar or #4 rebar, add	—	Lb	.51	—	.51
Any #5 rebar or #6 rebar, add	—	Lb	.48	—	.48
Any #7 rebar or #8 rebar, add	—	Lb	.45	—	.45
Any #9 rebar, #10 rebar or #11 rebar, add	—	Lb	.42	—	.42
Pre-bent rebar, 90 degree except as noted					
3/8" diameter, #3 rebar, 24" x 24"	RB@.014	Ea	2.16	.91	3.07
1/2" diameter, #4 rebar, 10" x 3'	RB@.021	Ea	4.69	1.37	6.06
1/2" diameter, #4 rebar, 2' x 3'	RB@.021	Ea	6.01	1.37	7.38
5/8" diameter, #5 rebar, 24" x 24"	RB@.014	Ea	6.76	.91	7.67
5/8" diameter, #5 rebar, 1' x 4'	RB@.035	Ea	8.59	2.28	10.87
5/8" diameter, #5 rebar, 3' x 3'	RB@.043	Ea	9.27	2.80	12.07
5/8" diameter, #5 rebar, 30" x 9" J-bar	RB@.028	Ea	3.65	1.83	5.48
3/4" diameter, #6 rebar, 24" x 24"	RB@.043	Ea	9.43	2.80	12.23
Rebar stirrups					
3/8" #3 bar, 6" x 12"	RB@.014	Ea	2.27	.91	3.18
3/8" #3 bar, 6" x 14"	RB@.014	Ea	2.61	.91	3.52
3/8" #3 bar, 6" x 18"	RB@.014	Ea	2.96	.91	3.87
3/8" #3 bar, 6" x 24"	RB@.014	Ea	2.96	.91	3.87
5/8" #8 bar, 6" x 48"	RB@.014	Ea	6.97	.91	7.88

	Craft@Hrs	Unit	Material	Labor	Total
Rebar rings					
Rectangular, 6" x 3-1/2"	RB@.014	Ea	1.77	.91	2.68
Rectangular, 9" x 5"	RB@.014	Ea	2.27	.91	3.18
Rectangular, 11" x 5"	RB@.014	Ea	2.11	.91	3.02
Rectangular, 12" x 3-1/2"	RB@.014	Ea	2.28	.91	3.19
Rectangular, 14" x 4"	RB@.014	Ea	2.28	.91	3.19
Rectangular, 14" x 5"	RB@.014	Ea	2.16	.91	3.07
Round, 6" diameter	RB@.014	Ea	1.97	.91	2.88
Round, 8" diameter	RB@.014	Ea	1.84	.91	2.75
Round, 10" diameter	RB@.014	Ea	2.29	.91	3.20
Square, 8"	RB@.014	Ea	2.22	.91	3.13
Reinforcing steel chairs. Labor for placing rebar shown above includes time for setting chairs.					
Chairs, individual type, cost each					
3" high					
Steel	—	Ea	.76	—	.76
Plastic	—	Ea	.30	—	.30
Galvanized steel	—	Ea	1.38	—	1.38
5" high					
Steel	—	Ea	1.16	—	1.16
Plastic	—	Ea	.78	—	.78
Galvanized steel	—	Ea	1.80	—	1.80
8" high					
Steel	—	Ea	2.45	—	2.45
Plastic	—	Ea	1.60	—	1.60
Galvanized steel	—	Ea	3.88	—	3.88
12" high					
Steel	—	Ea	4.90	—	4.90
Plastic	—	Ea	2.58	—	2.58
Galvanized steel	—	Ea	5.99	—	5.99
Chairs, continuous type, with legs 8" OC, cost per linear foot					
3" high					
Steel	—	LF	1.06	—	1.06
Plastic	—	LF	.65	—	.65
Galvanized steel	—	LF	1.60	—	1.60
6" high					
Steel	—	LF	1.45	—	1.45
Plastic	—	LF	.90	—	.90
Galvanized steel	—	LF	2.27	—	2.27
8" high					
Steel	—	LF	2.21	—	2.21
Plastic	—	LF	1.67	—	1.67
Galvanized steel	—	LF	3.19	—	3.19
12" high					
Steel	—	LF	4.80	—	4.80
Plastic	—	LF	2.64	—	2.64
Galvanized steel	—	LF	5.76	—	5.76
Reinforcing bar weld splicing. Cost per splice					
#8 bars, #9 bars or #10 bars	RB@.527	Ea	3.73	34.40	38.13
Reinforcing bar clip splicing, sleeve and wedge, with hand-held hydraulic ram. Cost per splice					
Number 4 bars, 1/2"	RB@.212	Ea	8.23	13.80	22.03
Number 5 bars, 5/8"	RB@.236	Ea	19.30	15.40	34.70
Number 6 bars, 3/4"	RB@.258	Ea	36.00	16.80	52.80

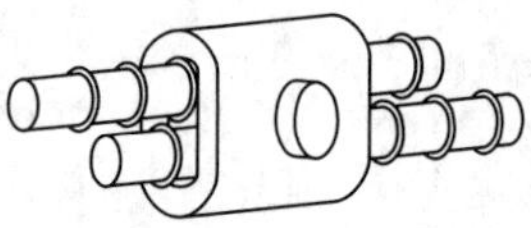

	Craft@Hrs	Unit	Material	Labor	Total
Waterstop, 3/8"					
Rubber, 6"	B2@.059	LF	1.57	2.07	3.64
Rubber, 9"	B2@.059	LF	3.39	2.07	5.46
Spiral caisson and round column reinforcing, 3/8" diameter hot rolled steel spirals with main vertical bars as shown. Costs include typical engineering and shop drawings. Shop fabricated spirals delivered, tagged, ready to install. Cost per vertical linear foot (VLF)					
16" diameter with 6 #6 bars, 16.8 lbs per VLF	RB@.041	VLF	44.80	2.67	47.47
24" diameter with 6 #6 bars, 28.5 lbs per VLF	RB@.085	VLF	76.60	5.54	82.14
36" diameter with 8 #10 bars, 51.2 lbs per VLF	RB@.216	VLF	140.00	14.10	154.10
Welded wire mesh steel, electric weld, including 15% waste and overlap					
2" x 2" W.9 x W.9 (#12 x #12), slabs	RB@.004	SF	1.20	.26	1.46
2" x 2" W.9 x W.9 (#12 x #12), beams and columns	RB@.020	SF	1.20	1.30	2.50
4" x 4" W1.4 x W1.4 (#10 x #10), slabs	RB@.003	SF	.58	.20	.78
4" x 4" W2.0 x W2.0 (#8 x #8), slabs	RB@.004	SF	.67	.26	.93
4" x 4" W2.9 x W2.9 (#6 x #6), slabs	RB@.005	SF	.75	.33	1.08
4" x 4" W4.0 x W4.0 (#4 x #4), slabs	RB@.006	SF	1.00	.39	1.39
6" x 6" W1.4 x W1.4 (#10 x #10), slabs	RB@.003	SF	.25	.20	.45
6" x 6" W2.0 x W2.0 (#8 x #8), slabs	RB@.004	SF	.44	.26	.70
6" x 6" W2.9 x W2.9 (#6 x #6), slabs	RB@.004	SF	.51	.26	.77
6" x 6" W4.0 x W4.0 (#4 x #4), slabs	RB@.005	SF	.70	.33	1.03
Add for lengthwise cut, LF of cut	RB@.002	LF	—	.13	.13
Welded wire mesh, galvanized steel, electric weld, including 15% waste and overlap					
2" x 2" W.9 x W.9 (#12 x #12), slabs	RB@.004	SF	2.43	.26	2.69
2" x 2" W.9 x W.9 (#12 x #12), beams and columns	RB@.020	SF	2.43	1.30	3.73
4" x 4" W1.4 x W1.4 (#10 x #10), slabs	RB@.003	SF	1.13	.20	1.33
4" x 4" W2.0 x W2.0 (#8 x #8), slabs	RB@.004	SF	1.36	.26	1.62
4" x 4" W2.9 x W2.9 (#6 x #6), slabs	RB@.005	SF	1.50	.33	1.83
4" x 4" W4.0 x W4.0 (#4 x #4), slabs	RB@.006	SF	1.96	.39	2.35
6" x 6" W1.4 x W1.4 (#10 x #10), slabs	RB@.003	SF	.64	.20	.84
6" x 6" W2.0 x W2.0 (#8 x #8), slabs	RB@.004	SF	.78	.26	1.04
6" x 6" W2.9 x W2.9 (#6 x #6), slabs	RB@.004	SF	1.00	.26	1.26
6" x 6" W4.0 x W4.0 (#4 x #4), slabs	RB@.005	SF	1.43	.33	1.76
Add for lengthwise cut, LF of cut	RB@.002	LF	—	.13	.13
Welded wire mesh, epoxy-coated steel, electric weld, including 15% waste and overlap					
2" x 2" W.9 x W.9 (#12 x #12), slabs	RB@.004	SF	4.99	.26	5.25
2" x 2" W.9 x W.9 (#12 x #12), beams and columns	RB@.020	SF	4.99	1.30	6.29
4" x 4" W1.4 x W1.4 (#10 x #10), slabs	RB@.003	SF	4.46	.20	4.66
4" x 4" W2.0 x W2.0 (#8 x #8), slabs	RB@.004	SF	4.43	.26	4.69
4" x 4" W2.9 x W2.9 (#6 x #6), slabs	RB@.005	SF	4.50	.33	4.83
4" x 4" W4.0 x W4.0 (#4 x #4), slabs	RB@.006	SF	4.73	.39	5.12
6" x 6" W1.4 x W1.4 (#10 x #10), slabs	RB@.003	SF	4.06	.20	4.26
6" x 6" W2.0 x W2.0 (#8 x #8), slabs	RB@.004	SF	4.15	.26	4.41
6" x 6" W2.9 x W2.9 (#6 x #6), slabs	RB@.004	SF	4.22	.26	4.48
6" x 6" W4.0 x W4.0 (#4 x #4), slabs	RB@.005	SF	4.46	.33	4.79
Add for lengthwise cut, LF of cut	RB@.002	LF	—	.13	.13
Reinforcing mesh mini-mats, electric weld, including 15% waste and overlap					
6" x 6" W1.4 x W1.4 (#10 x #10), 4' x 8'	RB@.004	SF	.25	.26	.51

	Craft@Hrs	Unit	Material	Labor	Total
Ready-Mix Concrete Ready-mix delivered by truck. Typical prices for most cities. Includes delivery up to 20 miles for 10 CY or more, 3" to 4" slump. Material cost only, no placing or pumping included. All concrete material costs in this manual are based on these figures.					
5.0 sack mix, 2,000 PSI	—	CY	125.00	—	125.00
6.0 sack mix, 3,000 PSI	—	CY	130.00	—	130.00
6.6 sack mix, 3,500 PSI	—	CY	132.00	—	132.00
7.1 sack mix, 4,000 PSI	—	CY	135.00	—	135.00
8.5 sack mix, 5,000 PSI	—	CY	154.00	—	154.00
Extra costs for ready-mix concrete					
Add for less than 10 CY per load	—	CY	54.50	—	54.50
Add for delivery over 20 miles	—	Mile	9.95	—	9.95
Add for standby charge in excess of 5 minutes per CY delivered, per minute of extra time	—	Ea	3.11	—	3.11
Add for super-plasticized mix, 7"-8" slump	—	%	8.0	—	—
Add for lightweight aggregate, typical	—	CY	57.20	—	57.20
Add for pump mix (pea-gravel aggregate)	—	CY	12.40	—	12.40
Add for granite aggregate, typical	—	CY	8.97	—	8.97
Add for white cement (architectural)	—	CY	74.00	—	74.00
Add for 1% calcium chloride	—	CY	2.08	—	2.08
Add for chemical compensated shrinkage	—	CY	27.30	—	27.30
Add for high early strength concrete					
5 sack mix	—	CY	16.20	—	16.20
6 sack mix	—	CY	21.50	—	21.50
Add for colored concrete, typical prices. The ready-mix supplier charges for cleanup of the ready-mix truck used for delivery of colored concrete. The usual practice is to provide one truck per day for delivery of all colored concrete for a particular job. Add the cost below to the cost per cubic yard for the design mix required. Also, add the cost for truck cleanup. Cost will be based on the quantity of pigment required. Pastels require one to two pounds of pigment per sack of cement. Greater color density may require up to five pounds of pigment per cubic yard. Cost per cubic yard based on a 5-sack mix and one pound of color per sack.					
Colored concrete, truck cleanup, per day	—	LS	100.00	—	100.00
Most colors (tan, brown, gray, beige)	—	CY	32.00	—	32.00
Green (requires white cement)	—	CY	58.10	—	58.10
Blue (requires white cement)	—	CY	176.00	—	176.00
White concrete pigment	—	CY	44.80	—	44.80
Concrete Pumping, Subcontract Small jobs, including trailer mounted pump and operator at 15 CY per hour. Based on 6 sack concrete mix designed for pumping. No concrete included. $125.00 minimum charge.					
3/8" aggregate mix (pea gravel), using hose to 200'					
Cost per cubic yard (pumping only)	—	CY	—	—	15.50
Add for hose over 200', per LF	—	LF	—	—	2.21
3/4" aggregate mix, using hose to 200'					
Cost per cubic yard (pumping only)	—	CY	—	—	16.10
Add for hose over 200', per LF	—	LF	—	—	1.94
Concrete Pumping with a Boom Truck, Subcontract Includes truck rent, operator, local travel but no concrete. Add costs equal to 1 hour for equipment setup and 1 hour for cleanup. Use 4 hours as the minimum cost for 23-, 28- and 32-meter boom trucks and 5 hours as the minimum cost for 36- through 52-meter boom trucks. Estimate the actual pour rate at 70% of the rated capacity on thicker slabs and 50% of the capacity on most other work. Costs include operator and oiler where necessary. Costs shown include subcontractor's markup.					
23-meter boom (75'), 70 CY per hour rating	—	Hr	—	—	140.00
Add per CY pumped with 23-meter boom	—	CY	—	—	3.19
28-meter boom (92'), 70 CY per hour rating	—	Hr	—	—	161.00
Add per CY pumped with 28-meter boom	—	CY	—	—	3.21
32-meter boom (105'), 90 CY per hour rating	—	Hr	—	—	189.00
Add per CY pumped with 32-meter boom	—	CY	—	—	3.27

	Craft@Hrs	Unit	Material	Labor	Total
36-meter boom (120'), 90 CY per hour rating	—	Hr	—	—	231.00
Add per CY pumped with 36-meter boom	—	CY	—	—	3.25
42-meter boom (138'), 100 CY per hour rating	—	Hr	—	—	305.00
Add per CY pumped with 42-meter boom	—	CY	—	—	3.87
52-meter boom (170'), 100 CY per hour rating	—	Hr	—	—	357.00
Add per CY pumped with 52-meter boom	—	CY	—	—	4.37

Ready-Mix Concrete and Placing No forms, finishing or reinforcing included. Material cost is based on 3,000 PSI concrete. Use $900 minimum charge for boom truck and $125 minimum for trailer-mounted pump.

	Craft@Hrs	Unit	Material	Labor	Equipment	Total
Columns						
By crane (60-ton crawler crane)	H3@.873	CY	130.00	40.80	23.60	194.40
By pump (28-meter boom truck and operator)	M2@.062	CY	141.00	2.80	6.15	149.95
Slabs-on-grade						
Direct from chute	CL@.430	CY	130.00	17.70	—	147.70
By crane (60-ton crawler crane)	H3@.594	CY	130.00	27.70	16.05	173.75
By pump (trailer-mounted, 20 CY/ hour)	M2@.188	CY	141.00	8.49	5.01	154.50
With buggy	CL@.543	CY	141.00	22.40	7.64	171.04
Elevated slabs						
By crane (60-ton crawler crane)	H3@.868	CY	130.00	40.50	23.50	194.00
By pump (28-meter boom truck and operator)	M2@.054	CY	141.00	2.44	5.62	149.06
Footings, pile caps, foundations						
Direct from chute	CL@.564	CY	130.00	23.30	—	23.30
By pump (trailer-mounted, 30 CY/ hour)	M2@.125	CY	141.00	5.65	2.13	148.78
With buggy	CL@.701	CY	141.00	28.90	9.86	179.76
Beams and girders						
By pump (28-meter boom truck and operator)	M2@.062	CY	141.00	2.80	6.15	149.95
By crane (60-ton crawler crane)	H3@.807	CY	141.00	37.70	21.80	200.50
Stairs						
Direct from chute	CL@.814	CY	130.00	33.60	—	155.20
By crane (60-ton crawler crane)	H3@1.05	CY	141.00	49.00	28.40	218.40
By pump (28-meter boom truck and operator)	M2@.108	CY	141.00	4.88	8.24	154.12
With buggy	CL@.948	CY	141.00	39.10	13.30	193.40
Walls and grade beams to 4' high						
Direct from chute	CL@.479	CY	130.00	19.80	—	19.80
By pump (trailer-mounted, 20 CY/ hour)	M2@.188	CY	141.00	8.49	1.67	151.16
With buggy	CL@.582	CY	141.00	24.00	8.19	173.19
Walls over 4' to 8' high						
By crane (60-ton crawler crane)	H3@.821	CY	130.00	38.30	22.20	190.50
By pump (28-meter boom truck and operator)	M2@.062	CY	141.00	2.80	4.15	147.95
Walls over 8' to 16' high						
By crane (60-ton crawler crane)	H3@.895	CY	130.00	41.80	24.20	196.00
By pump (28-meter boom truck and operator)	M2@.078	CY	141.00	3.52	7.23	151.75
Walls over 16' high						
By crane (60-ton crawler crane)	H3@.986	CY	130.00	46.00	26.64	202.64
By pump (28-meter boom truck and operator)	M2@.097	CY	141.00	4.38	8.50	153.88

	Craft@Hrs	Unit	Material	Labor	Equipment	Total
Concrete Slab-on-Grade Assemblies Typical costs including fine grading, edge forms, 3,000 PSI concrete, wire mesh, finishing and curing.						
4" thick 4' x 6' equipment pad						
Hand trimming and shaping, 24 SF	CL@.512	LS	—	21.10	—	21.10
Lay out, set and strip edge forms, 20 LF, 5 uses	C8@1.30	LS	14.20	61.30	—	75.50
Place .006" polyethylene vapor barrier 24 SF	CL@.048	LS	1.91	1.98	—	3.89
Place W2.9 x W2.9 x 6" x 6" mesh, 24 SF	RB@.097	LS	12.30	6.33	—	18.63
Place ready-mix concrete, from chute .3 CY	CL@.127	LS	39.00	5.24	—	44.24
Finish concrete, broom finish	CM@.591	LS	—	30.30	—	30.30
Cure concrete, curing paper	CL@.124	LS	5.17	5.12	—	10.29
Total job cost for 4" thick 24 SF pad	**—@2.80**	**LS**	**72.58**	**131.37**	**—**	**203.95**
Cost per SF for 4" thick 24 SF pad	—@.116	SF	3.02	5.47	—	8.80
Cost per CY of 4" thick concrete, .3 CY job	—@9.33	CY	242.00	477.00	—	719.00
8" thick 10' x 10' equipment pad						
Hand trimming and shaping, 100 SF	CL@2.79	LS	—	115.00	—	115.00
Lay out, set and strip edge forms, 40 LF, 5 uses	C8@3.28	LS	37.60	155.00	—	192.60
Place .006" polyethylene vapor barrier 100 SF	CL@.200	LS	7.96	8.25	—	16.21
Place W2.9 x W2.9 x 6" x 6" mesh, 100 SF	RB@.400	LS	51.10	26.10	—	77.20
Place ready-mix concrete, from chute 2.5 CY	CL@1.08	LS	325.00	44.60	—	369.60
Finish concrete, broom finish	CM@2.11	LS	—	108.00	—	108.00
Cure concrete, curing paper	CL@.515	LS	21.50	21.20	—	42.70
Total job cost for 8" thick 100 SF pad	**—@10.4**	**LS**	**443.16**	**478.15**	**—**	**921.31**
Cost per SF for 8" thick 100 SF job	—@.104	SF	4.43	4.78	—	9.21
Cost per CY of 8" thick concrete, 2.5 CY job	—@4.15	CY	177.00	212.00	—	389.00
Note: Ready-mix concrete used in both examples assumes a minimum of 10 cubic yards will be delivered (per load) with the excess used elsewhere on the same job.						
Add for each CY less than 10 delivered	—	CY	54.50	—	—	54.50
Floor Slab Assemblies Typical reinforced concrete slab-on-grade including excavation, gravel fill, forms, vapor barrier, wire mesh, 3,000 PSI concrete, finishing and curing.						
3,000 PSI concrete	—	CY	264.00	—	—	264.00
4" thick slab	—@.025	SF	3.27	1.28	.14	4.69
5" thick slab	—@.026	SF	3.67	1.33	.15	5.15
6" thick slab	—@.027	SF	4.07	1.38	.15	5.60
Detailed cost breakdown slab as described above:						
4" thick 100' x 75' slab						
Grade sandy loam site using a D-4 tractor, 140 CY, balanced job, (no import or export)	S1@2.66	LS	—	131.00	82.10	213.10
Buy and spread 6" crushed rock base using a D-4 tractor, 140 CY	S1@15.8	LS	6,040.00	778.00	487.00	7,305.00
Lay out, set and strip edge forms, 350 LF, 5 uses	C8@19.6	LS	249.00	924.00	—	1,173.00

	Craft@Hrs	Unit	Material	Labor	Equipment	Total
Place .006" polyethylene vapor barrier 7,500 SF	CL@8.84	LS	597.00	365.00	—	962.00
Place W2.9 x W2.9 x 6" x 6" mesh, 7,500 SF	RB@30.0	LS	3,830.00	1,960.00	—	5,790.00
Place and remove 2" x 4" keyway, 200 LF, 1 use	C8@8.80	LS	109.00	415.00	—	524.00
Place 4" concrete, 93 CY, from chute	CL@39.9	LS	12,100.00	1,650.00	—	13,750.00
Float finish 7,500 SF	CM@52.4	LS	—	2,690.00	488.00	3,178.00
Cure with slab curing paper	CM@5.58	LS	1,620.00	287.00	—	1,907.00
Total job cost 4" thick 100' x 75' floor slab	**—@184**	**LS**	**24,545.00**	**9,200.00**	**1,057.10**	**35,802.10**
Cost per SF for 4" thick 7,500 SF job	—@.025	SF	3.27	1.23	.14	4.64
Cost per CY for 4" thick 93 CY job	—@1.98	CY	264.00	101.00	11.40	376.40
Cost per each additional 1" of concrete	—@.001	SF	.40	.05	—	.45

Cast-in-Place Concrete, Subcontract Typical costs including forms, concrete, reinforcing, finishing and curing. These costs include the subcontractor's overhead and profit but no excavation, shoring or backfill. Use these figures only for preliminary estimates and on jobs that require a minimum of 1,000 CY of concrete.

	Craft@Hrs	Unit	Material	Labor	Equipment	Total
Foundations						
Institutional or office buildings	—	CY	—	—	—	629.00
Heavy engineered structures	—	CY	—	—	—	683.00
Structural concrete walls						
Single-story, 8" wall	—	CY	—	—	—	851.00
Single-story, 10" wall	—	CY	—	—	—	933.00
Multi-story, 8" wall	—	CY	—	—	—	1,080.00
Multi-story, 10"	—	CY	—	—	—	1,130.00
Slip-formed 8" wall	—	CY	—	—	—	958.00
Structural slabs, including shoring,						
6", 1 way beams, 100 pounds reinforcing	—	CY	—	—	—	995.00
6", 2 way beams, 225 pounds reinforcing	—	CY	—	—	—	918.00
8", flat, with double mat reinforcing over steel frame by others, 100 pounds reinforcing	—	CY	—	—	—	832.00
12" flat, 250 pounds reinforcing bars per CY	—	CY	—	—	—	752.00
7", post-tensioned, to 1 pound tempered bars	—	CY	—	—	—	933.00
6" to 8" including beam jacketing	—	CY	—	—	—	905.00
6" to 8" on permanent metal form	—	CY	—	—	—	820.00
8" concurrent with slipform construction	—	CY	—	—	—	870.00
Lift slab construction 6" to 8"	—	SF	—	—	—	19.40
Pan and joist slabs 3" thick, 30" pan, including shoring						
6" x 16" joist	—	CY	—	—	—	963.00
6" x 12" joist	—	CY	—	—	—	852.00
6" x 10" joist	—	CY	—	—	—	816.00
Pan and joist slabs 4-1/2" thick, 20" pan, including shoring						
6" x 20" joist	—	CY	—	—	—	815.00
6" x 16" joist	—	CY	—	—	—	797.00
6" x 12" joist	—	CY	—	—	—	789.00

	Craft@Hrs	Unit	Material	Labor	Equipment	Total
Parapet and fascia, 6" thick	—	CY	—	—	—	1,230.00
Loading docks,						
based on 8" walls and 8" slab	—	CY	—	—	—	566.00
Beams and girders, not slab integrated						
12" x 24", typical	—	CY	—	—	—	1,640.00
18" x 24", typical	—	CY	—	—	—	1,260.00
Columns, average reinforcing						
Square, wood formed, with chamfer						
12" column	—	CY	—	—	—	2,020.00
16" column	—	CY	—	—	—	1,870.00
18" column	—	CY	—	—	—	1,700.00
20" column	—	CY	—	—	—	1,570.00
24" column	—	CY	—	—	—	1,370.00
Round, fiber tube formed, 12" to 18"	—	CY	—	—	—	1,350.00

Cast-in-Place Concrete Steps-on-Grade Assemblies Typical in-place costs, including layout, fabrication and placing forms, setting and tying steel reinforcing, installation of steel nosing, placing 2,000 PSI concrete directly from the chute of a ready-mix truck, finishing, stripping forms and curing. Costs assume excavation, back filling and compaction have been completed by others. Crew is a carpenter, laborer and finisher. Formwork is based on using standard & better lumber and concrete and includes a 5% waste allowance. For scheduling purposes, estimate that a crew of 3 can set forms and place steel for and pour 4 to 5 CY of concrete cast-in-place steps in an 8-hour day. Costs shown are for concrete steps with a 6" riser height and 12" tread depth supported by a 6" thick monolithic slab. The "tricks of the trade" next page explains how to use these unit prices to estimate stairways of various widths and heights. Note: Total cost per CY has been rounded. For more detailed coverage of formed concrete stairs, see the *National Concrete & Masonry Estimator*, http://CraftsmanSiteLicense.com

	Craft@Hrs	Unit	Material	Labor	Total
Fabricate and erect forms, 2 uses of forms, includes stakes, braces, form oil and nails at $.13 per LF of forms					
Side forms, 1.7 BF per LF of tread	P9@.080	LF	.72	3.88	4.60
Riser forms, 1.5 BF per LF of tread	P9@.040	LF	.65	1.94	2.59
Rebar, #3, Grade 60, 1 pound per LF of tread	P9@.009	LF	.88	.44	1.32
Embedded steel step nosing, 2-1/2" x 2-1/2" x 1/4" black mild steel					
Angle iron, 4.5 pounds per LF of tread.	P9@.004	LF	4.74	.19	4.93
Concrete, .03 CY per LF of tread	P9@.030	LF	3.89	1.46	5.35
Total cost per LF of risers	P9@.163	LF	10.88	7.91	18.79
Total cost per CY of concrete	P9@5.43	CY	363.00	264.00	627.00

Tricks of the trade:

To quickly estimate the cost of cast-in-place concrete steps-on-grade, do this:

Multiply the width of the steps (in feet) times their height in feet and multiply the result times 2.

This will give the total linear feet (LF) of risers in the steps. Multiply the total LF by the costs per LF.

Sample estimates for cast-in-place concrete steps-on-grade using the procedure and costs from above:

2'6" wide by 3' high (6 steps) would be: 2.5' x 3' x 2 = 15 LF x $18.79 = $281.85

3' wide by 3' high (6 steps) would be: 3' x 3' x 2 = 18 LF x $18.79 = $338.22

4' wide by 4' high (8 steps) would be: 4' x 4' x 2 = 32 LF x $18.79 = $601.28

7' wide by 4'6" high (9 steps) would be: 7' x 4.5' x 2 = 63 LF x $18.79 = $1,183.77

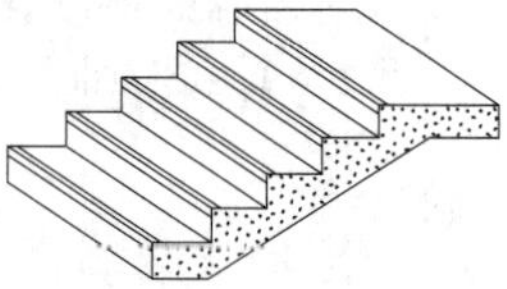

Tip for using these estimates with *The National Estimator* computer estimating program:

Calculate the linear feet of stair, copy and paste the line "Total cost per LF of risers" and type the quantity.

	Craft@Hrs	Unit	Material	Labor	Total
Concrete Accessories					
Bentonite					
50 pound bag, granules	—	Ea	80.00	—	80.00
3 gallon Volclay Bentoseal	—	Ea	198.00	—	198.00
4' x 15' Bentonite geotextile roll	—	Ea	150.00	—	150.00
Bond breaker and form release, SpecStrip					
Lumber & plywood form release, 1,000 SF/gal	CL@.006	SF	.01	.25	.26
Metal form release, 2,000 SF per gallon	CL@.003	SF	.01	.12	.13
Casting bed form breaker, 1,500 SF per gallon	CL@.005	SF	.01	.21	.22
Cure coat, 1,600 SF per gallon	CL@.005	SF	.01	.21	.22
Chamfer strip					
3/4" x 3/4" x 1", 10' lengths	CC@.015	LF	.34	.80	1.14
Chamfer corner forms					
3/4" corner forms	CC@.015	LF	15.20	.80	16.00
Column clamps single bar, per set, by column size,					
10" x 10" to 24" x 24", purchase	—	Set	164.00	—	164.00
24" x 24" to 36" x 36", purchase	—	Set	183.00	—	183.00
32" x 32" to 48" x 48", purchase	—	Set	253.00	—	253.00
Monthly rental cost as % of purchase price	—	%	10.0	—	—

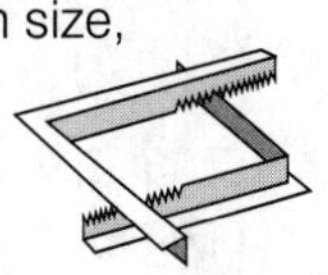

	Craft@Hrs	Unit	Material	Labor	Total
Scissor column clamps for lumber forms, per set, by column size					
10" x 10" to 24" x 24", purchase	—	Set	174.00	—	174.00
12" x 12" to 36" x 36", purchase	—	Set	209.00	—	209.00
24" x 24" to 48" x 48", purchase	—	Set	247.00	—	247.00
Monthly rental cost as % of purchase price	—	%	10.0	—	—

	Craft@Hrs	Unit	Material	Labor	Total
Concrete sleeves, circular polyethylene liner, any slab thickness					
1-1/2" to 3" diameter	—	Ea	2.82	—	2.82
4" to 6" diameter	—	Ea	5.31	—	5.31

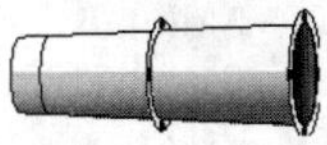

	Craft@Hrs	Unit	Material	Labor	Total
Embedded iron, installation only	C8@.045	Lb	—	2.12	2.12
Expansion joints, cane fiber, asphalt impregnated, pre-molded					
1/2" x 4", slabs	C8@.028	LF	1.51	1.32	2.83
1/2" x 6", in walls	C8@.035	LF	2.13	1.65	3.78
1/2" x 8", in walls	C8@.052	LF	2.69	2.45	5.14
Concrete footing form wedge ties					
6" wall thickness, pack of 250	—	Pack	111.00	—	111.00
8" wall thickness, pack of 250	—	Pack	116.00	—	116.00
Tie wedge, pack of 500	—	Pack	109.00	—	109.00
Form spreaders, 4" to 10"	—	Ea	.50	—	.50

	Craft@Hrs	Unit	Material	Labor	Total
Form oil, 800 to 1,200 SF per gallon	—	Gal	13.00	—	13.00
Grout for machine bases, mixed and placed. Add for edge forms, if required.					
Five Star epoxy					
per SF for each 1" of thickness	C8@.170	SF	17.60	8.01	25.61
Five Star NBEC non-shrink, non-metallic					
per SF for each 1" of thickness	C8@.170	SF	4.03	8.01	12.04
Embeco 636, metallic aggregate					
per SF for each 1" of thickness	C8@.163	SF	9.21	7.68	16.89
Forms for grout, based on using 2" x 4" lumber, 1 use	C8@.195	LF	2.98	9.19	12.17
Inserts, Unistrut, average	C8@.068	Ea	9.82	3.21	13.03
She bolt form clamps, with cathead and bolt, purchase					
17" rod	—	Ea	5.75	—	5.75
21" rod	—	Ea	9.55	—	9.55

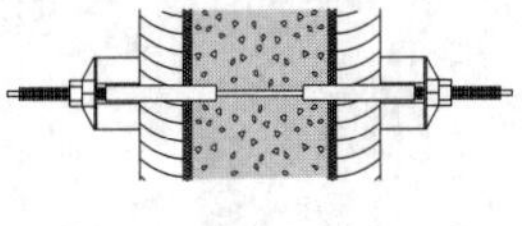

	Craft@Hrs	Unit	Material	Labor	Total
24" rod	—	Ea	10.30	—	10.30
Monthly rental as % of purchase price	—	%	15.0	—	—
Snap ties, average, 4,000 pound, 6" to 10"	—	Ea	.77	—	.77
Water stop, 3/8"					
Rubber, 6"	C8@.059	LF	.31	2.78	3.09
Rubber, 9"	C8@.059	LF	.19	2.78	2.97
Concrete waler brackets					
2" x 4"	—	Ea	12.30	—	12.30
2" x 6"	—	Ea	14.00	—	14.00
Waler jacks (scaffold support on form), purchase	—	Ea	54.60	—	54.60
Rental per month, each	—	Mo	6.60	—	6.60
Concrete Slab Finishes					
Float finish	CM@.009	SF	—	.46	.46
Trowel finishing					
Steel, machine work	CM@.014	SF	—	.72	.72
Steel, hand work	CM@.017	SF	—	.87	.87
Broom finish	CM@.012	SF	—	.62	.62
Scoring concrete surface, hand work	CM@.005	LF	—	.26	.26
Exposed aggregate (washed, including finishing), no disposal of slurry	CM@.015	SF	.37	.77	1.14
Color hardener, nonmetallic, trowel application					
Standard colors	—	Lb	1.22	—	1.22
Non standard colors	—	Lb	1.55	—	1.55
Light duty floors (40 pounds per 100 SF)	CM@.008	SF	—	.41	.41
Pastel shades (60 pounds per 100 SF)	CM@.012	SF	—	.62	.62
Heavy duty (90 pounds per 100 SF)	CM@.015	SF	—	.77	.77
Add for colored wax, 800 SF per gal	CM@.003	SF	.03	.15	.18
Sidewalk grits, abrasive, 25 pounds per 100 SF					
Aluminum oxide 100 pound bag	CM@.008	SF	.22	.41	.63
Silicon carbide, 100 pound bag	CM@.008	SF	.70	.41	1.11
Metallic surface hardener, dry shake, Masterplate 200					
Moderate duty, 1 pound per SF	CM@.008	SF	1.08	.41	1.49
Heavy duty, 1.5 pounds per SF	CM@.009	SF	1.69	.46	2.15
Concentrated traffic, 2 pounds per SF	CM@.010	SF	2.24	.51	2.75
Liquid curing and sealing compound, silicate based, 200 SF per gallon	CL@.004	SF	.25	.17	.42
Sweep, scrub and wash down	CL@.006	SF	.04	.25	.29
Finish treads and risers					
No abrasives, no plastering, per SF of tread	CM@.038	SF	—	1.95	1.95
With abrasives, plastered, per SF of tread	CM@.058	SF	.79	2.98	3.77
Wax coating	CL@.002	SF	.05	.08	.13
Concrete Wall Finishes					
Cut back ties and patch	CM@.010	SF	.15	.51	.66
Remove fins	CM@.007	LF	.05	.36	.41
Grind smooth	CM@.020	SF	.10	1.03	1.13
Sack, simple	CM@.012	SF	.06	.62	.68
Bush hammer light, green concrete	CM@.020	SF	.05	1.03	1.08
Bush hammer standard, cured concrete	CM@.029	SF	.07	1.49	1.56
Bush hammer, heavy, cured concrete	CM@.077	SF	.11	3.95	4.06

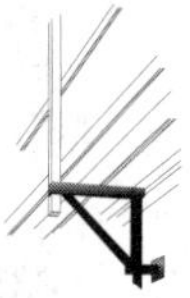

	Craft@Hrs	Unit	Material	Labor	Total
Needle gun treatment, large areas	CM@.058	SF	.15	2.98	3.13
Wire brush, green	CM@.014	SF	.06	.72	.78
Wash with acid and rinse	CM@.004	SF	.23	.21	.44
Break fins, patch voids, Carborundum rub	CM@.032	SF	.07	1.64	1.71
Break fins, patch voids, burlap grout rub	CM@.024	SF	.08	1.23	1.31
Sandblasting, Subcontract. No scaffolding included, flat vertical surfaces					
Light sandblast	—	SF	—	—	2.32
Medium, to expose aggregate	—	SF	—	—	2.66
Heavy, with dust control requirements	—	SF	—	—	3.74
Note: Minimum charge for sandblasting	—	LS	—	—	1,000.00
Miscellaneous Concrete Finishes					
Monolithic natural aggregate topping					
1/16" topping	P9@.006	SF	.26	.29	.55
3/16" topping	P9@.018	SF	.60	.87	1.47
1/2" topping	P9@.021	SF	1.52	1.02	2.54
Integral colors,					
Typically 8 pounds per sack of cement	—	Lb	2.91	—	2.91
Mono rock, 3/8" wear course only, typical cost	—	SF	1.79	—	1.79
Kalman 3/4", wear course only, typical cost	—	SF	2.74	—	2.74
Acid etching, 5% muriatic acid, typical cost	P9@.005	SF	.52	.24	.76
Felton sand, for use with white cement	—	CY	57.00	—	57.00
Specially Placed Concrete Typical subcontract prices.					
Gunite, no forms and no reinforcing included					
Flat plane, vertical areas, 1" thick	—	SF	—	—	4.60
Curved arch, barrel, per 1" thickness	—	SF	—	—	5.72
Pool or retaining walls, per 1" thickness	—	SF	—	—	4.40
Add for architectural finish	—	SF	—	—	1.75
Wire mesh for gunite 2" x 2", W.9 x W.9	—	SF	—	—	2.02
Pressure grouting, large quantity, 50/50 mix	—	CY	—	—	720.00

Precast Concrete Panel costs are based on 3,000 PSI natural gray concrete with a smooth or board finish on one side. Placing (lifting) costs include handling, hoisting, alignment, bracing and permanent connections. Erection costs vary with the type of crane. Heavier lifts over a longer radius (reach) require larger cranes. Equipment costs include the crane and a 300 amp gas powered welding machine. Add the cost of grouting or caulking joints. Costs will be higher on small jobs (less than 35,000 SF).

	Craft@Hrs	Unit	Material	Labor	Equipment	Total
Precast wall panels Costs include delivery to 40 miles, typical reinforcing steel and embedded items but no lifting. Use 2,500 SF as a minimum job charge. See placing costs below.						
4" thick wall panels (52 lbs per SF)	—	SF	15.80	—	—	15.80
5" thick wall panels (65 lbs per SF)	—	SF	17.30	—	—	17.30
6" thick wall panels (78 lbs per SF)	—	SF	18.80	—	—	18.80
8" thick wall panels (105 lbs per SF)	—	SF	19.90	—	—	19.90
Add for insulated sandwich wall panels						
2-1/2" of cladding and 2" of fiberboard	—	SF	6.59	—	—	6.59
Add for high strength concrete						
3,500 lb concrete mix	—	%	2.0	—	—	—
4,000 lb concrete mix	—	%	3.0	—	—	—
4,500 lb concrete mix	—	%	4.0	—	—	—
5,000 lb concrete mix	—	%	6.0	—	—	—
Add for white facing or integral white mix	—	%	20.0	—	—	—
Add for broken rib						
or fluted surface design	—	%	20.0	—	—	—
Add for exposed aggregate finish	—	%	17.0	—	—	—
Add for sandblasted surface finish	—	%	12.0	—	—	—

	Craft@Hrs	Unit	Material	Labor	Equipment	Total
Placing precast structural wall panels Figures in parentheses show the panels placed per day with a 100 ton crawler-mounted crane and welding machine. Use $9,000 as a minimum job charge.						
1 ton panels to 180' reach (23 per day)	H4@2.79	Ea	—	175.00	110.00	285.00
1 to 3 tons, to 121' reach (21 per day)	H4@3.05	Ea	—	191.00	123.00	314.00
3 to 5 tons, to 89' reach (18 per day)	H4@3.54	Ea	—	221.00	139.00	360.00
5 to 7 tons, to 75' reach (17 per day)	H4@3.76	Ea	—	235.00	148.00	383.00
7 to 9 tons, to 65' reach (16 per day)	H4@4.00	Ea	—	250.00	158.00	408.00
9 to 11 tons, to 55' reach (15 per day)	H4@4.28	Ea	—	268.00	169.00	437.00
11 to 13 tons, to 50' reach (14 per day)	H4@4.56	Ea	—	285.00	180.00	465.00
13 to 15 tons, to 43' reach (13 per day)	H4@4.93	Ea	—	308.00	194.00	502.00
15 to 20 tons, to 36' reach (11 per day)	H4@5.81	Ea	—	364.00	229.00	593.00
20 to 25 tons to 31' reach (10 per day)	H4@6.40	Ea	—	400.00	252.00	652.00
For placing panels with cladding, add	—	%	—	5.0	5.0	—
For placing sandwich wall panels, add	—	%	—	10.0	10.0	—
If a 45 ton crane can be used, deduct	—	%	—	—	-22.0	—
Placing precast partition wall panels Figures in parentheses show the panels placed per day with a 45 ton truck-mounted crane and welding machine. Use $6,000 as a minimum job charge.						
1 ton panels to 100' reach (23 per day)	H4@2.79	Ea	—	175.00	88.90	263.90
1 to 2 tons, to 82' reach (21 per day)	H4@3.05	Ea	—	191.00	97.10	288.10
2 to 3 tons, to 65' reach (18 per day)	H4@3.54	Ea	—	221.00	113.00	334.00
3 to 4 tons, to 57' reach (16 per day)	H4@4.00	Ea	—	250.00	127.10	377.10
4 to 5 tons, to 50' reach (15 per day)	H4@4.28	Ea	—	268.00	136.00	404.00
5 to 6 tons, to 44' reach (14 per day)	H4@4.56	Ea	—	285.00	145.00	430.00
6 to 7 tons, to 40' reach (13 per day)	H4@4.93	Ea	—	308.00	157.00	465.00
7 to 8 tons, to 36' reach (11 per day)	H4@5.81	Ea	—	364.00	185.00	549.00
8 to 10 tons, to 31' reach (10 per day)	H4@6.40	Ea	—	400.00	204.00	604.00
10 to 12 tons to 26' reach (9 per day)	H4@7.11	Ea	—	445.00	226.00	671.00
12 to 14 tons, to 25' reach (8 per day)	H4@8.02	Ea	—	502.00	255.00	757.00
14 to 16 tons, to 21' reach (7 per day)	H4@9.14	Ea	—	572.00	291.00	863.00
If a 35 ton crane can be used, deduct	—	%	—	—	-5.0	—
Precast flat floor slab or floor plank Costs include delivery to 40 miles, 3,000 PSI concrete, typical reinforcing steel and embedded items. Use $2,000 as a minimum job charge. See placing costs below.						
4" thick floor panels (52 lbs per SF)	—	SF	13.20	—	—	13.20
5" thick floor panels (65 lbs per SF)	—	SF	15.70	—	—	15.70
6" thick floor panels (78 lbs per SF)	—	SF	20.10	—	—	20.10
8" thick floor panels (105 lbs per SF)	—	SF	20.90	—	—	20.90
Placing panels with a 100 ton crawler-mounted crane and welding machine at $775 per day. Figures in parentheses show the number of panels placed per day. Use $8,500 as a minimum job charge						
2 ton panels to 150' reach (23 per day)	H4@2.79	Ea	—	175.00	67.70	242.70
2 to 3 tons, to 121' reach (21 per day)	H4@3.05	Ea	—	191.00	74.00	265.00
3 to 4 tons, to 105' reach (19 per day)	H4@3.37	Ea	—	211.00	81.70	292.70
4 to 5 tons, to 88' reach (18 per day)	H4@3.56	Ea	—	223.00	86.30	309.30
5 to 6 tons, to 82' reach (17 per day)	H4@3.76	Ea	—	235.00	91.20	326.20
6 to 7 tons, to 75' reach (16 per day)	H4@4.00	Ea	—	250.00	97.00	347.00
7 to 8 tons, to 70' reach (15 per day)	H4@4.28	Ea	—	268.00	104.00	372.00
8 to 9 tons, to 65' reach (14 per day)	H4@4.56	Ea	—	285.00	111.00	396.00
9 to 10 tons, to 60' reach (11 per day)	H4@5.82	Ea	—	364.00	141.00	505.00
20 to 25 tons, to 31' reach (10 per day)	H4@6.40	Ea	—	400.00	155.00	555.00

	Craft@Hrs	Unit	Material	Labor	Equipment	Total
Precast combination beam and slab units Beam and slab units with beam on edge of slab. Weight of beams and slabs will be about 4,120 lbs per CY. Use 40 CY as a minimum job charge. See placing costs below.						
Slabs with no intermediate beam	—	CY	1,060.00	—	—	1,060.00
Slabs with one intermediate beam	—	CY	1,130.00	—	—	1,130.00
Slabs with two intermediate beams	—	CY	1,230.00	—	—	1,230.00
Placing deck units with a 100 ton crawler-mounted crane and a welding machine. Figures in parentheses show the number of units placed per day. Use $8,500 as a minimum job charge.						
5 ton units to 88' reach (21 per day)	H4@3.05	Ea	—	191.00	74.00	265.00
5 to 10 tons, to 60' reach (19 per day)	H4@3.37	Ea	—	211.00	81.70	292.70
10 to 15 tons, to 43' reach (17 per day)	H4@3.76	Ea	—	235.00	91.20	326.20
15 to 20 tons, to 36' reach (15 per day)	H4@4.28	Ea	—	268.00	104.00	372.00
20 to 25 tons, to 31' reach (14 per day)	H4@4.57	Ea	—	286.00	111.00	397.00
If a 150 ton crane is required, add	—	%	—	—	16.0	—
Precast beams, girders and joists Beams, girders and joists, costs per linear foot of span, including 3,000 PSI concrete, reinforcing steel, embedded items and delivery to 40 miles. Use 400 LF as a minimum job charge. See placing costs below.						
1,000 lb load per foot, 15' span	—	LF	129.00	—	—	129.00
1,000 lb load per foot, 20' span	—	LF	143.00	—	—	143.00
1,000 lb load per foot, 30' span	—	LF	163.00	—	—	163.00
3,000 lb load per foot, 10' span	—	LF	129.00	—	—	129.00
3,000 lb load per foot, 20' span	—	LF	163.00	—	—	163.00
3,000 lb load per foot, 30' span	—	LF	197.00	—	—	197.00
5,000 lb load per foot, 10' span	—	LF	129.00	—	—	129.00
5,000 lb load per foot, 20' span	—	LF	179.00	—	—	179.00
5,000 lb load per foot, 30' span	—	LF	213.00	—	—	213.00
Placing beams, girders and joists with a 100 ton crawler-mounted crane and a welding machine. Figures in parentheses show the number of units placed per day. Use $8,500 as a minimum job charge.						
5 ton units to 88' reach (18 per day)	H4@3.56	Ea	—	223.00	86.30	309.30
5 to 10 tons, to 60' reach (17 per day)	H4@3.76	Ea	—	235.00	91.20	326.20
10 to 15 tons, to 43' reach (16 per day)	H4@4.00	Ea	—	250.00	97.00	347.00
15 to 20 tons, to 36' reach (15 per day)	H4@4.27	Ea	—	267.00	104.00	371.00
If a 150 ton crane is required, add	—	%	—	—	16.0	—
Precast concrete columns Precast concrete columns, 12" x 12" to 36" x 36" including concrete, reinforcing steel, embedded items and delivery to 40 miles. Use 40 CY as a minimum job charge. See placing costs below.						
Columns with 500 lbs of reinforcement per CY	—	CY	1,110.00	—	—	1,110.00
Columns with 350 lbs of reinforcement per CY	—	CY	1,090.00	—	—	1,090.00
Columns with 200 lbs of reinforcement per CY	—	CY	1,060.00	—	—	1,060.00
Placing concrete columns with a 100 ton crawler-mounted crane and a welding machine. Figures in parentheses show the number of units placed per day. Use $8,500 as a minimum job charge.						
3 ton columns to 121' reach (29 per day)	H4@2.21	Ea	—	138.00	53.60	191.60
3 to 5 tons, to 89' reach (27 per day)	H4@2.37	Ea	—	148.00	57.50	205.50
5 to 7 tons, to 75' reach (25 per day)	H4@2.55	Ea	—	160.00	61.80	221.80
7 to 9 tons, to 65' reach (23 per day)	H4@2.79	Ea	—	175.00	67.70	242.70
9 to 11 tons, to 55' reach (22 per day)	H4@2.92	Ea	—	183.00	70.80	253.80
11 to 13 tons, to 50' reach (20 per day)	H4@3.20	Ea	—	200.00	77.60	277.60
13 to 15 tons, to 43' reach (18 per day)	H4@3.56	Ea	—	223.00	86.30	309.30

	Craft@Hrs	Unit	Material	Labor	Equipment	Total
Precast concrete stairs Costs include concrete, reinforcing, embedded steel, nosing, and delivery to 40 miles. Use $500 as a minimum job charge. See placing costs below.						
Stairs, 44" to 48" wide, 10' to 12' rise, "U"- or "L"-shape, including typical landings,						
Cost per each step (7" rise)	—	Ea	63.40	—	—	63.40
Placing precast concrete stairs with a 45 ton truck-mounted crane and a welding machine. Figures in parentheses show the number of stair flights placed per day. Use $6,000 as a minimum job charge.						
2 ton stairs to 82' reach (21 per day)	H4@3.05	Ea	—	191.00	97.10	288.10
2 to 3 tons, to 65' reach (19 per day)	H4@3.37	Ea	—	211.00	107.00	318.00
3 to 4 tons, to 57' reach (18 per day)	H4@3.54	Ea	—	221.00	113.00	334.00
4 to 5 tons, to 50' reach (17 per day)	H4@3.76	Ea	—	235.00	120.00	355.00
5 to 6 tons, to 44' reach (16 per day)	H4@4.00	Ea	—	250.00	127.00	377.00
6 to 7 tons, to 40' reach (15 per day)	H4@4.28	Ea	—	268.00	136.00	404.00
7 to 8 tons, to 36' reach (14 per day)	H4@4.56	Ea	—	285.00	145.00	430.00
8 to 9 tons, to 33' reach (10 per day)	H4@6.40	Ea	—	400.00	204.00	604.00
If a 35 ton crane can be used, deduct	—	%	—	—	−10.0	—
Precast double tees 8' wide, 24" deep. Design load is shown in pounds per square foot (PSF). Costs include lifting and placing but no slab topping. Equipment cost is for a 45 ton truck crane and a welding machine. Use $6,000 as a minimum job charge.						
30' to 35' span, 115 PSF	H4@.019	SF	14.50	1.19	.61	16.30
30' to 35' span, 141 PSF	H4@.019	SF	15.90	1.19	.61	17.70
35' to 40' span, 78 PSF	H4@.018	SF	14.50	1.13	.57	16.20
35' to 40' span, 98 to 143 PSF	H4@.018	SF	15.90	1.13	.57	17.60
40' to 45' span, 53 PSF	H4@.017	SF	14.50	1.06	.54	16.10
40' to 45' span, 69 to 104 PSF	H4@.017	SF	15.90	1.06	.54	17.50
40' to 45' span, 134 PSF	H4@.017	SF	16.70	1.06	.54	18.30
45' to 50' span, 77 PSF	H4@.016	SF	15.90	1.00	.51	17.41
45' to 50' span, 101 PSF	H4@.016	SF	16.70	1.00	.51	18.21
Concrete topping, based on 350 CY job 3,000 PSI design mix with lightweight aggregate, no forms or finishing included.						
By crane	H3@.868	CY	130.00	40.50	23.50	194.00
By pump (28 meter boom truck and operator)	M2@.080	CY	141.00	3.61	7.36	151.97
Hollow core roof planks, not including topping, 35 PSF live load, 10' to 15' span						
4" thick	H4@.018	SF	7.58	1.13	.36	9.07
6" thick	H4@.018	SF	9.24	1.13	.36	10.73
8" thick	H4@.020	SF	10.90	1.25	.41	12.56
10" thick	H4@.026	SF	11.30	1.63	.53	13.46
Prestressed concrete support poles Costs shown are per linear foot for sizes and lengths shown. Equipment cost is for a 45 ton truck crane. These costs do not include base or excavation. Lengths other than as shown will cost more per foot. Use $6,000 as a minimum job charge.						
10" x 10" poles with four 7/16" 270 KSI ultimate tendon strand strength						
10', 14', 20', 25' or 30' long	H4@.028	LF	20.50	1.75	.86	23.11
12" x 12" poles with six 7/16" 270 KSI ultimate tendon strand strength						
10', 14' or 20' long	H4@.028	LF	24.80	1.75	.86	27.41
25' or 30' long	H4@.028	LF	27.60	1.75	.86	30.21

Tilt-up concrete construction Costs will be higher if access is not available from all sides or obstructions delay the work. Except as noted, no grading, compacting, engineering, design, permit or inspection fees are included.

	Craft@Hrs	Unit	Material	Labor	Equipment	Total
Foundations and footings for tilt-up Costs assume normal soil conditions with no forming or shoring required and are based on concrete poured directly from the chute of a ready-mix truck. Soil excavated and not needed for backfill can be stored on site and used by others. For scheduling purposes, estimate that a crew of 5 can set forms for and pour 40 to 50 CY of concrete footings and foundations in an 8-hour day.						
Lay out foundation from known point on site, set stakes and mark for excavation.						
Per SF of floor slab	C8@.001	SF	—	.05	—	.05
Excavation with a 1/2 CY utility backhoe						
27 CY per hour	S1@.075	CY	—	3.70	1.64	5.34
Set and tie grade A60 reinforcing bars, typical foundation has 50 to 60 pounds of reinforcing bar per CY of concrete	RB@.008	Lb	.69	.52	—	1.21
Place stringer supports for reinforcing bars (at 1.1 LF of support per LF of rebar), using 2" x 4" or 2" x 6" lumber. Includes typical stakes and hardware						
Based on 3 uses of supports	C8@.017	LF	.65	.80	—	1.45
(Inspection of reinforcing may be required before concrete is placed.)						
Make and place steel column anchor bolt templates (using 1.1 SF of plywood per SF of column base). Based on 3 uses of 3/4" plyform. If templates are furnished by the steel column fabricator, include only the labor cost to place the templates as shown						
Make and place templates	C8@.160	SF	.96	7.54	—	8.50
Place templates furnished by others	C8@.004	SF	—	.19	—	.19
Blockout form at foundation, step footings, columns, etc., per SF of contact area, using 2" x 6" lumber. Includes allowance for waste, typical stakes and hardware.						
Based on 3 uses of forms	C8@.018	SFCA	2.19	.85	—	3.04
Column anchor bolts, usually 4 per column. "J"-hook bolt includes flat washer and two nuts						
1/2" x 6"	C8@.037	Ea	1.69	1.74	—	3.43
3/4" x 12"	C8@.037	Ea	5.02	1.74	—	6.76
Concrete, 2,000 PSI design mix, including 3% allowance for waste,						
Placed directly from chute	CL@.552	CY	123.00	22.80	—	145.80
Remove, clean and stack						
reinforcing supports	CL@.020	LF	—	.83	—	.83
Dry pack non-shrink grout under column bases. Typical grout area is						
2' x 2' x 4" (1.33 CF of grout)	CM@.625	Ea	48.90	32.10	—	81.00
Panel support pads. (Supports panel when grout is placed.) One needed per panel. Based on						
3 CF of 2,000 PSI concrete per pad	C8@.141	Ea	13.60	6.65	—	20.25
Backfill at foundation with 1/2 CY utility backhoe.						
90 CY per hour	S1@.022	CY	—	1.08	.48	1.56
Dispose of excess soil on site,						
using backhoe	S1@.011	CY	—	.54	.24	.78
Concrete test cylinders, typically 5 required						
per 100 CY of concrete	—	CY	1.00	—	—	1.00

Floor slabs for tilt-up These costs assume that the site has been graded and compacted by others before slab work begins. The costs below include fine grading the site, placing a 2" layer of sand, a vapor barrier and a second 2" layer of sand over the barrier. Each layer of sand should be screeded level. Reinforcing may be either wire mesh or bars. When sand and vapor barrier are used, concrete may have to be pumped in place. If inspection of the reinforcing is required, the cost will usually be included in the building permit fee. Floor slabs are usually poured 6" deep in 14' to 18' wide strips with edge forms on both sides and ends. Edge forms are used as supports for the mechanical screed which consolidates the concrete with pneumatic vibrators as the surface is leveled. The screed is pulled forward by a winch and cable. Edge forms should have an offset edge to provide a groove which is filled by the adjacent slab. The slab perimeter should end 2' to 3' inside the finished building walls. This "pour strip" is filled in with concrete when the walls are up and braces have been removed. About 2 days after pouring, the slab should be saw-cut 1-1/2" to 2" deep and 1/4" wide each 20' both ways. This controls cracking as the slab cures. For scheduling purposes, estimate that a finishing crew of 10 workers can place and finish 10,000 to 12,000 square feet of slab in 8 hours.

	Craft@Hrs	Unit	Material	Labor	Equipment	Total
Fine grade the building pad with a utility tractor with blade and bucket						
2,500 SF per hour	S6@.001	SF	—	.05	.01	.06

	Craft@Hrs	Unit	Material	Labor	Equipment	Total
Spread sand 4" deep in 2" layers, (1.35 tons is 1 cubic yard and covers 81 SF at 4" depth), using a utility tractor						
Cost of sand	—	Ton	14.30	—	—	14.30
60 SF per hour	S6@.006	SF	.25	.28	.08	.61
Vapor barrier, 6 mil polyethylene	CL@.001	SF	.07	.04	—	.11
Welded wire mesh, 6" x 6", W1.4 x W1.4 including 10% for overlap and waste	RB@.004	SF	.24	.26	—	.50
Reinforcing bars, grade 60, typically #4 bars on 2' centers each way with 1.05 LF bars per SF	RB@.004	SF	.55	.26	—	.81
Dowel out for #4 bars at construction joints	RB@.004	LF	.34	.26	—	.60
Edge forms with keyed joint, rented	F5@.013	LF	—	.63	.09	.72
Ready-mix concrete for the slab (with 3% waste allowance)						
Placed from the chute of the ready-mix truck	CL@.421	CY	134.00	17.40	—	151.40
Pump mix, including pumping cost	M2@.188	CY	147.00	8.49	12.60	168.09
Finish the floor slab, using power trowels	CM@.003	SF	—	.15	.04	.19
Vibrating screed and accessories, (includes screeds, fuel, air compressor and hoses) rented						
Per SF of slab	—	SF	—	—	.13	.13
Curing compound, spray applied, 250 SF per gallon	CL@.001	SF	.20	.04	—	.24
Saw cut green concrete, 1-1/2" to 2" deep	C8@.010	LF	—	.47	.13	.60
Strip, clean and stack edge forms	CL@.011	LF	—	.45	—	.45
Ready-mix concrete for the pour strip including 3% waste						
Placed from the chute of the ready-mix truck	CL@.421	CY	134.00	17.40	—	151.40
Pump mix, including pumping cost	M2@.188	CY	147.00	8.49	12.60	168.09
Finish the pour strip	CM@.004	SF	—	.21	.04	.25
Special inspection of the concrete pour (if required) Based on 10,000 SF in 8 hours	—	SF	—	—	—	.04
Clean and caulk the saw joints, based on 50 LF per hour and caulk and 1,500 LF per gallon	CL@.020	LF	.06	.83	—	.89
Clean slab (broom clean)	CL@.001	SF	—	.04	—	.04

Tilt-up wall panels Wall thickness is usually a nominal 6" (5-1/2" actual) or a nominal 8" (7-1/2"). Panel heights over 40' are uncommon. Typical panel width is 20'. When the floor area isn't large enough to form all wall panels on the floor slab, stacking will be required. Construction period will be longer and the costs higher than the figures shown below when panels must be poured and cured in stacked multiple layers. When calculating the volume of concrete required, the usual practice is to multiply overall panel dimensions (width, length and thickness) and deduct only for panel openings that exceed 25 square feet. When pilasters (thickened wall sections) are formed as part of the panel, add the cost of extra formwork and the additional concrete. Use the production rates that follow for scheduling a job.

Production rates for tilt-up

Lay out and form panels, place reinforcing bars and install embedded lifting devices:
2,000 to 3,000 SF of panel face (measured one side) per 8-hour day for a crew of 5. Note that reinforcing may have to be inspected before concrete is poured.

Place and finish concrete: 4,000 to 5,000 SF of panel per 8-hour day for a crew of 5.

Continuous inspection of the concrete pour by a licensed inspector may be required.
The minimum charge will usually be 4 hours at $50 per hour plus travel cost.

Install ledgers with embedded anchor bolts on panels before the concrete hardens:
150 to 200 LF of ledger per 8-hour day for a crew of 2.

Sack and patch exposed panel face before panel is erected:
2,000 to 3,000 SF of panel face per 8-hour day for a crew of 2.

Install panel braces before lifting panels:
30 to 40 braces per 8-hour day for a crew of 2. Panels usually need 3 or 4 braces. Braces are usually rented for 30 days.

Tilt up and set panels 20 to 24 panels per 8-hour day for a crew of 11 (6 workers, the crane operator, oiler and 3 riggers). If the crew sets 22 panels averaging 400 SF each in an 8-hour day, the crew is setting 1,100 SF per hour. These figures include time for setting and aligning panels, drilling the floor slab for brace bolts, and securing the panel braces. Panel tilt-up will go slower if the crane can't work from the floor slab when lifting panels. Good planning of the panel lifting sequence and easy exit of the crane from the building interior will increase productivity. Size and weight of the panel has little influence on the setting time if the crane is capable of making the lift and is equipped with the right rigging equipment, spreader bars and strongbacks. Panels will usually have to cure for 14 days before lifting unless high early strength concrete is used.

Weld or bolt steel embedded in panels: 16 to 18 connections per 8-hour day for a crew of 2 working from ladders. Work more than 30 feet above the floor may take more time.

Sack and patch panel faces after erection: 400 SF of face per 8-hour day for a crew of 2.

	Craft@Hrs	Unit	Material	Labor	Equipment	Total
Tilt-up panel costs						
Engineering fee, per panel, typical	—	Ea	—	—	—	55.60
Fabricate and lay out forms for panel edges and blockouts, assumes 3 uses and includes typical hardware and chamfer						
2" x 6" per MBF	—	MBF	759.00	—	—	759.00
2" x 8" per MBF	—	MBF	776.00	—	—	776.00
2" x 6" per LF	F5@.040	LF	.52	1.93	—	2.45
2" x 8" per LF	F5@.040	LF	.68	1.93	—	2.61
Reveals (1" x 2" accent strips on exterior panel face)						
Based on 1 use of lumber						
Nailed to slab	C8@.018	LF	.17	.85	—	1.02
Clean and prepare the slab prior to placing the concrete for the panels,						
1,250 SF per hour	CL@.001	SF	—	.04	—	.04
Releasing agent (bond breaker), sprayed on,						
250 SF	CL@.001	SF	.01	.04	—	.05
Place and tie grade 60 reinforcing bars and supports. Based on using #3 and #4 bars, including waste and laps. A typical panel has 80 to 100 pounds of reinforcing steel per CY of concrete in the panel						
Reinforcing per CY of concrete	RB@.500	CY	53.20	32.60	—	85.80
Reinforcing per SF of 6" thick panel	RB@.009	SF	.99	.59	—	1.58
Reinforcing per SF of 8" thick panel	RB@.012	SF	1.31	.78	—	2.09
Ledger boards with anchor bolts. Based on 4" x 12" treated lumber and 3/4" x 12" bolts placed each 2 feet, installed prior to lifting panel						
Using 4" x 12" treated lumber	—	MBF	1,980.00	—	—	1,980.00
Typical ledgers and anchor bolts	C8@.353	LF	10.50	16.60	—	27.10

	Craft@Hrs	Unit	Material	Labor	Equipment	Total
Embedded steel for pickup and brace point hardware. Usually 10 to 12 points per panel, quantity and type depend on panel size						
Embedded pickup & brace hardware, typical	C8@.001	SF	.86	.05	—	.91
Note: Inspection of reinforcing may be required before concrete is placed.						
Concrete, 3,000 PSI, placed direct from chute						
Concrete only (before waste allowance)	—	CY	130.00	—	—	130.00
6" thick panels (54 SF per CY)	CL@.008	SF	2.48	.33	.09	2.90
8" thick panels (40.5 SF per CY)	CL@.010	SF	3.30	.41	.11	3.82
Concrete, 3,000 PSI, pumped in place						
Concrete only (before waste allowance)	—	CY	143.00	—	—	143.00
6" thick panels (54 SF per CY)	M2@.008	SF	2.72	.36	.03	3.11
8" thick panels (40.5 SF per CY)	M2@.011	SF	3.63	.50	.04	4.17
Finish concrete panels, one face before lifting	P8@.004	SF	—	.19	.02	.21
Continuous inspection of pour, if required, based on 5,000 to 6,000 SF being placed per 8-hour day						
Typical cost for continuous inspection of pour	—	SF	—	—	—	.08
Curing wall panels with spray-on curing compound, per SF of face, based on 250 SF per gallon	CL@.001	SF	.20	.04	—	.24
Strip, clean and stack 2" edge forms	CL@.030	LF	—	1.24	—	1.24
Braces for panels						
Install rented panel braces, based on an average of three braces per panel for panels averaging 400 to 500 SF each. See also, Remove panel braces						
Typical cost for braces, per SF of panel	F5@.005	SF	—	.24	.19	.43
Miscellaneous equipment rental, typical costs per SF of wall panel						
Rent power trowels and vibrators	—	SF	—	—	.12	.12
Rent compressors, hoses, rotohammers, fuel	—	SF	—	—	.12	.12
Lifting panels into place, with crane and riggers, using a 140 ton truck crane						
Move crane on and off site, typical	—	LS	—	—	3,560.00	3,560.00
Hourly cost (4 hr minimum applies), per hour	T2@11.0	Hr	—	585.00	606.00	1,191.00
Set, brace and align panels, per SF of panel measured on one face, Based on 1,100 SF per hour	T2@.010	SF	—	.53	.62	1.15
Allowance for shims, bolts for panel braces and miscellaneous hardware, labor cost is included with associated items						
Typical cost per SF of panel	—	SF	.49	—	—	.49
Weld or bolt panels together, typically 2 connections are required per panel, equipment is a welding machine.						
Typical cost per panel connection	T3@.667	Ea	109.00	35.50	3.47	147.97
Continuous inspection of welding, if required.						
Inspection of welds, per connection (3 per hour)	—	Ea	—	—	—	27.50
Set grout forms at exterior wall perimeter. Based on using 2" x 12" boards. Costs shown include stakes and assume 3 uses of the forms						
Using 2" x 12" boards (per MBF)	—	MBF	881.00	—	—	881.00
Cost of forms per linear foot (LF)	F5@.019	LF	.99	.92	—	1.91
Pour grout under panel bottoms. Place 2,000 PSI concrete (grout) directly from the chute of ready-mix truck.						
Typically 1.85 CY per 100 LF of wall	M2@.005	LF	.23	.23	—	.46

	Craft@Hrs	Unit	Material	Labor	Equipment	Total
Sack and patch wall, per SF of area (measure area to be sacked and patched, both inside and outside),						
per SF of wall face(s), before tilt-up	P8@.007	SF	.10	.32	—	.42
per SF of wall face(s), after tilt-up	P8@.040	SF	.10	1.85	—	1.95
Caulking and backing strip for panel joints. Cost per LF for caulking both inside & outside face of joint,						
per linear foot (LF) of joint	PA@.055	LF	.28	2.93	—	3.21
Remove panel braces,						
stack & load onto trucks	CL@.168	Ea	—	6.93	—	6.93
Final cleanup & patch floor,						
per SF of floor	P8@.003	SF	.01	.14	—	.15
Additional costs for tilt-up panels, if required						
Architectural form liner, minimum cost	F5@.001	SF	2.00	.05	—	2.05
Architectural form liner, typical cost	F5@.003	SF	2.50	.14	—	2.64
Sandblast, light and medium,						
subcontract	—	SF	—	—	—	2.49
Sandblast, heavy, subcontract	—	SF	—	—	—	3.74
Truck dock bumpers, installation only	C8@2.00	Ea	—	94.30	—	94.30
Dock levelers, installation only	C8@7.46	Ea	—	352.00	—	352.00
Angle iron guard around door opening,						
2" x 2" x 1/4", mild steel (4' lengths)	C8@.120	LF	3.06	5.66	—	8.72
Pipe guard at door opening,						
6" black steel, concrete filled	C8@.281	LF	38.90	13.20	—	52.10
Embedded reglet at parapet wall,						
aluminum	F5@.019	LF	1.35	.92	—	2.27
Integral color in concrete, light colors, add to concrete. Price per CY of						
concrete to be colored	—	CY	33.50	—	—	33.50
Backfill outside perimeter wall with a utility tractor.						
90 CY per hour	S1@.022	CY	—	1.08	.31	1.39

Cast-in-place columns for tilt-up Concrete columns are often designed as part of the entryway of a tilt-up building or to support lintel panels over a glass storefront. Both round and square freestanding columns are used. They must be formed and poured before the lintel panels are erected. Round columns are formed with plastic-treated fiber tubes (Sonotube is one manufacturer) that are peeled off when the concrete has cured. Square columns are usually formed with plywood and 2" x 4" wood braces or adjustable steel column clamps.

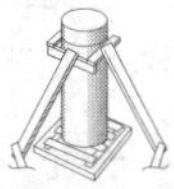

	Craft@Hrs	Unit	Material	Labor	Equipment	Total
Heavy wall water-resistant fiber tube forms, set and aligned, based on 12' long tubes. Longer tubes will cost more per LF						
12" diameter tubes	M2@.207	LF	3.57	9.35	—	12.92
20" diameter tubes	M2@.250	LF	8.45	11.30	—	19.75
24" diameter tubes	M2@.275	LF	11.60	12.40	—	24.00
Rectangular plywood forms, using 1.1 SF of 3/4" plyform and 2" x 4" bracing 3' OC						
Per SF of contact area						
based on 3 uses	F5@.083	SF	.80	4.01	—	4.81
Column braces, 2" x 4" at $768.00 per MBF, with 5 BF per LF of column height						
Per LF of column height						
based on 3 uses	F5@.005	LF	1.81	.24	1.77	3.82
Column clamps rented at $5.00 for 30 days, 1 per LF of column height, cost per LF of column height						
Per LF of column						
based on 2 uses a month	F5@.040	LF	—	1.93	5.00	6.93
Reinforcing bars, grade 60, placed and tied, typically 150 to 200 pounds per CY of concrete						
Cages, round or rectangular	RB@1.50	CY	95.00	97.80	—	192.80
Vertical bars						
attached to cages	RB@1.50	CY	95.00	97.80	—	192.80
Ready-mix concrete, 3,000 PSI pump mix						
Placed by pump (includes 3% waste)	M2@.094	CY	141.00	4.25	8.30	153.55

	Craft@Hrs	Unit	Material	Labor	Equipment	Total
Strip off fiber forms and dismantle bracing, per LF of height						
12" or 16" diameter	CL@.075	LF	—	3.09	—	3.09
24" diameter	CL@.095	LF	—	3.92	—	3.92
Strip wood forms and dismantle bracing						
Per SF of contact area, no salvage	CL@.011	SF	—	.45	—	.45
Clean and stack column clamps	CL@.098	Ea	—	4.04	3.84	7.88
Sack and patch concrete column face	P8@.011	SF	.17	.51	—	.68
Allowance for miscellaneous equipment rental (vibrators, compressors, hoses, etc.)						
Per CY of concrete in column	—	CY	—	—	2.50	2.50

Trash enclosures for tilt-up These usually consist of a 6" concrete slab measuring 5' x 10' and precast concrete tilt-up panels 6' high. A 6" ledger usually runs along the wall interior. Overall wall length is usually 20 feet. Cost for the trash enclosure foundation, floor slab and wall will be approximately the same as for the tilt-up foundation, floor slab and wall. The installed cost of a two-leaf steel gate measuring 6' high and 8' long overall will be about $460 including hardware.

Equipment Foundations Except as noted, no grading, compacting, engineering, design, permit or inspection fees are included. Costs assume normal soil conditions with no shoring or dewatering required and are based on concrete poured directly from the chute of a ready-mix truck. Costs will be higher if access is not available from all sides or if obstructions delay the work.

Labor costs include the time needed to prepare formwork sketches at the job site, measure for the forms, fabricate, erect, align and brace the forms, place and tie the reinforcing steel and embedded steel items, pour and finish the concrete and strip, clean and stack the forms.

Reinforcing steel costs assume an average of #3 and #4 bars at 12" on center each way. Weights shown include an allowance for waste and laps.

Form costs assume 3 uses of the forms and show the cost per use when a form is used on the same job without being totally disassembled. Normal cleaning and repairs are included. No salvage value is assumed. Costs listed are per square foot of form in contact with the concrete, assume using #2 & Btr lumber

For scheduling purposes, estimate that a crew of 5 can set the forms and place and tie the reinforcing steel for and pour 8 to 10 CY of concrete equipment foundations in an 8-hour day.

Rule-of-thumb estimates The costs below are based on the volume of concrete in the foundation. If plans for the foundation have not been prepared, estimate the quantity of concrete required from the weight of the equipment using the rule-of-thumb estimating data below. Design considerations may alter the actual quantities required. Based on the type foundation required, use the cost per CY given in the detailed cost breakdown section which follows the table on the next page.

Estimating concrete quantity from the weight of equipment:

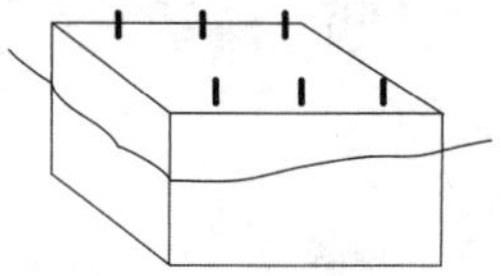

1. Rectangular pad type foundations —
   - Boilers and similar equipment mounted at grade:
     - Allow 1 CY per ton
   - Centrifugal pumps and compressors, including weight of motor:
     - Up to 2 HP, allow .5 CY per ton
     - Over 2 to 10 HP, allow 1 CY per ton
     - Over 10 to 30 HP, allow 2 CY per ton
     - Over 30 HP, allow 3 CY per ton
   - Reciprocating pumps and compressors, including weight of motor:
     - Up to 2 HP, allow .75 CY per ton
     - Over 2 to 10 HP, allow 1.5 CY per ton
     - Over 10 to 30 HP, allow 2.5 CY per ton
     - Over 30 HP, allow 4.5 CY per ton

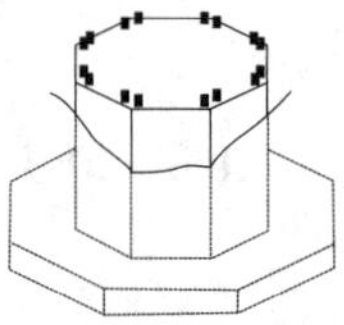

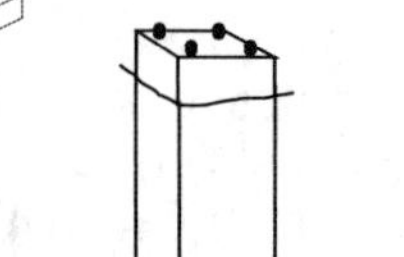

2. Rectangular pad and stem wall type foundations — Horizontal tanks or shell and tube heat exchangers, allow 6 CY per ton
3. Square pad and pedestal type foundations — Vertical tanks not over 3' in diameter, allow 6 CY per ton
4. Octagonal pad and pedestal type foundations — Vertical tanks over 3' in diameter, allow 4 CY per ton of empty weight

	Craft@Hrs	Unit	Material	Labor	Equipment	Total

Rectangular pad type foundations For pumps, compressors, boilers and similar equipment mounted at grade. Form costs assume nails, stakes and form oil costing $.50 per square foot and 1.1 SF of 3/4" plyform plus 2.2 BF of lumber per square foot of contact surface. Costs shown are per cubic yard (CY) of concrete within the foundation.

	Craft@Hrs	Unit	Material	Labor	Equipment	Total
Lay out foundation from known point on site, set stakes and mark for excavation, with 1 CY per CY of concrete	C8@.147	CY	.05	6.93	—	6.98
Excavation with utility backhoe, at 28 CY per hour, with 1.5 CY per CY of concrete	S1@.108	CY	—	5.32	4.74	10.06
Formwork, material (3 uses) and labor at .150 manhours per SF with 15 SF per CY of concrete	F5@2.25	CY	25.30	109.00	—	134.30
Place .006" polyethylene vapor barrier with 90 SF per CY of concrete	C8@.180	CY	7.17	8.49	—	15.66
Reinforcing bars, Grade 60, set and tied, material and labor .006 manhours per lb with 25 lb per CY of concrete	RB@.150	CY	22.00	9.78	—	31.78
Anchor bolts, sleeves, embedded steel, material and labor at .040 manhours per lb with 5 lb per CY of concrete	C8@.200	CY	8.42	9.43	—	17.85
Ready-mix concrete, 3,000 PSI mix after allowance for 10% waste with 1 CY per CY of concrete	C8@.385	CY	143.00	18.10	—	161.10
Concrete test cylinders including test reports, with 5 per 100 CY of concrete	—	CY	1.00	—	—	1.00
Finish, sack and patch concrete, material and labor at .010 manhours per SF with 15 SF per CY of concrete	P8@.150	CY	1.17	6.95	—	8.12
Backfill around foundation with utility backhoe at 40 CY per hour, with .5 CY per CY of concrete	S1@.025	CY	—	1.23	.55	1.78
Dispose of excess soil on site with utility backhoe at 80 CY per hour with 1 CY per CY of concrete	S1@.025	CY	—	1.23	.55	1.78
Rectangular pad type foundation Total cost per CY of concrete	—@3.62	CY	208.11	176.46	5.84	390.41

Rectangular pad and stem wall type foundations For horizontal cylindrical or shell and tube heat exchangers mounted above grade. Form costs assume nails, stakes and form oil costing $.50 per square foot and 1.1 SF of 3/4" plyform plus 4.5 BF of lumber per square foot of contact surface. Costs shown are per cubic yard (CY) of concrete within the foundations.

	Craft@Hrs	Unit	Material	Labor	Equipment	Total
Lay out foundation from known point on site, set stakes and mark for excavation, with 1 CY per CY of concrete	C8@.147	CY	.05	6.93	—	6.98
Excavation with utility backhoe, at $28 per hour, with 1 CY per CY of concrete	S1@.072	CY	—	3.55	1.58	5.13
Formwork, material (3 uses) per SF and labor at .200 manhours per SF with 60 SF per CY of concrete	F5@12.0	CY	182.00	580.00	—	762.00
Place .006" polyethylene vapor barrier with 90 SF per CY of concrete	C8@.180	CY	7.17	8.49	—	15.66
Reinforcing bars, Grade 60, set and tied, material per lb and labor at .006 manhours per lb with 45 lb per CY of concrete	RB@.270	CY	39.60	17.60	—	57.20
Anchor bolts, sleeves, embedded steel, material and labor at .040 manhours per lb with 5 lb per CY of concrete	C8@.200	CY	8.13	9.43	—	17.56
Ready-mix concrete, 3,000 PSI mix, after 10% waste allowance with 1 CY per CY	C8@.385	CY	143.00	18.10	—	161.10
Concrete test cylinders including test reports, with 5 per 100 CY	—	CY	1.00	—	—	1.00
Finish, sack and patch concrete, material per SF and labor at .010 manhours per SF with 60 SF per CY of concrete	P8@.600	CY	4.35	27.80	—	32.15

	Craft@Hrs	Unit	Material	Labor	Equipment	Total
Backfill around foundation with utility backhoe, at 40 CY per hour, with .5 CY per CY of concrete	S1@.025	CY	—	1.23	.55	1.78
Dispose of excess soil on site with utility backhoe, at 80 CY per hour, with .5 CY per CY of concrete	S1@.025	CY	—	1.23	.55	1.78
Rectangular pad and stem wall type foundation Total cost per CY of concrete	—@13.9	CY	385.30	674.36	2.68	1,062.34

Square pad and pedestal type foundations For vertical cylindrical tanks not over 3' in diameter. Form costs assume nails, stakes and form oil costing $.50 per square foot and 1.1 SF of 3/4" plyform plus 3 BF of lumber per square foot of contact surface. Costs shown are per cubic yard (CY) of concrete within the foundations.

	Craft@Hrs	Unit	Material	Labor	Equipment	Total
Lay out foundation from known point on site, set stakes and mark for excavation, with 1 CY per CY of concrete	C8@.147	CY	.05	6.93	—	6.98
Excavation with utility backhoe, at 28 CY per hour, with 1 CY per CY of concrete	S1@.072	CY	—	3.55	1.58	5.13
Formwork, material and labor at .192 manhours per SF with 13 SF per CY of concrete	F5@2.50	CY	30.70	121.00	—	151.70
Place .006" polyethylene vapor barrier with 90 SF per CY of concrete	C8@.180	CY	7.17	8.49	—	15.66
Reinforcing bars, Grade 60, set and tied, material and labor at .006 manhours per lb with 20 lb per CY of concrete	RB@.120	CY	39.60	7.83	—	47.43
Anchor bolts, sleeves, embedded steel, material and labor at .040 manhours per lb with 2 lb per CY of concrete	C8@.080	CY	3.36	3.77	—	7.13
Ready-mix concrete, 3,000 PSI mix, after 10% waste allowance with 1 CY per CY	C8@.385	CY	143.00	18.10	—	161.10
Concrete test cylinders including test reports, with 5 per 100 CY	—	CY	1.00	—	—	1.00
Finish, sack and patch concrete, material per SF and labor at .010 manhours per SF with 60 SF per CY of concrete	P8@.600	CY	5.54	27.80	—	33.34
Backfill around foundation with utility backhoe, at 40 CY per hour, with .5 CY per CY of concrete	S1@.025	CY	—	1.23	.55	1.78
Dispose of excess soil on site with utility backhoe, at 80 CY per hour, with .5 CY per CY of concrete	S1@.025	CY	—	1.23	.55	1.78
Square pad and pedestal type foundation Total cost per CY of concrete	—@4.13	CY	230.42	199.93	2.68	433.03

Octagonal pad and pedestal type foundations For vertical cylindrical tanks over 3' in diameter. Form costs assume nails, stakes and form oil costing $.50 per square foot and 1.1 SF of 3/4" plyform plus 4.5 BF of lumber per square foot of contact surface. Costs shown are per cubic yard (CY) of concrete within the foundation.

	Craft@Hrs	Unit	Material	Labor	Equipment	Total
Lay out foundation from known point on site, set stakes and mark for excavation, with 1 CY per CY of concrete	C8@.147	CY	.05	6.93	—	6.98
Excavation with utility backhoe, at $28 CY per hour, with 1 CY per CY of concrete	S1@.072	CY	—	3.55	1.58	5.13
Formwork, material SF and labor at .250 manhours per SF with 10 SF per CY of concrete	F5@2.50	CY	29.40	121.00	—	150.40
Place .006" polyethylene vapor barrier with 90 SF per CY of concrete	C8@.180	CY	7.17	8.49	—	15.66
Reinforcing bars, Grade 60, set and tied, material and labor at .006 manhours per lb with 20 lb per CY of concrete	RB@.120	CY	17.60	7.83	—	25.43
Anchor bolts, sleeves, embedded steel, material and labor at .040 manhours per lb with 2 lb per CY of concrete	C8@.080	CY	3.36	3.77	—	7.13
Ready-mix concrete, 3,000 PSI mix, after 10% waste allowance with 1 CY per CY of concrete	C8@.385	CY	143.00	18.10	—	161.10

	Craft@Hrs	Unit	Material	Labor	Equipment	Total
Concrete test cylinders including test reports,						
with 5 per 100 CY of concrete	—	CY	1.00	—	—	1.00
Finish, sack and patch concrete, material and labor at .010 manhours per SF						
with 60 SF per CY of concrete	P8@.600	CY	4.52	27.80	—	32.32
Backfill around foundation with utility backhoe, at 40 CY per hour,						
with .5 CY per CY of concrete	S1@.025	CY	—	1.23	.55	1.78
Dispose of excess soil on site with utility backhoe, at 80 CY per hour,						
with .5 CY per CY of concrete	S1@.025	CY	—	1.23	.55	1.78
Octagonal pad and pedestal type foundation						
Total cost per CY of concrete	—@4.13	CY	206.10	199.93	2.68	408.71

	Craft@Hrs	Unit	Material	Labor	Total
Cementitious Decks, Subcontract Typical costs including the subcontractor's overhead and profit.					
Insulating concrete deck, poured on existing substrate, 1-1/2" thick					
Under 3,000 SF	—	SF	—	—	2.70
Over 3,000 SF to 10,000 SF	—	SF	—	—	2.35
Over 10,000 SF	—	SF	—	—	1.96
Poured on existing metal deck, 2-5/8" thick, lightweight					
Concrete fill, trowel finish	—	SF	—	—	3.17
Gypsum decking, poured over form board, screed and float	—	SF	—	—	2.87
Vermiculite, screed and float, field mixed	—	SF	—	—	2.36
Exterior concrete deck for walking service, troweled					
Lightweight, 2-5/8", 110 lbs per CF	—	SF	—	—	4.10
Add for 4,000 PSI mix	—	SF	—	—	.65
Add for 5,000 PSI mix	—	SF	—	—	.49
Pool deck at pool side, 1/8" to 3/16" thick, colors, finished	—	SF	—	—	3.70
Fiber deck, tongue and groove, cementitious planks, complete					
2" thick	—	SF	—	—	3.12
2-1/2" thick	—	SF	—	—	3.79
3" thick	—	SF	—	—	4.14

Concrete Surfacing, Subcontract Load-bearing, architectural, three-part, acrylic polymer cementitious resurfacing system. 6,000 PSI compressive strength. Applied over existing concrete, aggregate, masonry, steel, asphalt, foam or wood surfaces. Installed on surfaces that do not require crack repair, brick or tile patterns or the removal of heavy grease contaminants. Includes stain sealer and colored texture coat. Based on a typical 1,000 square foot project. www.permacrete.com

	Craft@Hrs	Unit	Material	Labor	Total
Applied over new surface	—	SF	—	—	1.10
Applied over old concrete, includes cleaning	—	SF	—	—	1.98
Applied over pool interior, includes cleaning	—	SF	—	—	2.37
Applied over vertical surface	—	SF	—	—	2.72

Surface Imprinted Concrete Paving, Subcontract Patterned and colored to simulate slate, granite, limestone, sandstone, wood or cobblestone. 3 to 4 inch depth. Costs include imprinting and texturing, concrete placement and finish, color hardener, release agent and sealer application. Add the cost of grading, forms and form stripping. www.bomanite.com

	Craft@Hrs	Unit	Material	Labor	Total
Regular grade	—	SF	—	—	22.10
Heavy grade (for heavy road traffic and freeze areas)	—	SF	—	—	27.20

Troweled-on Cementitious Coating, Subcontract For direct use on interior flooring, accent areas or walls. Bonds to concrete, wood, metal, plastic or asphalt.

	Craft@Hrs	Unit	Material	Labor	Total
Cementitious coating	—	SF	—	—	16.40

	Unit	Brick or 200'	Concrete 1000'	Concrete 1000'

Wall Sawing, Subcontract Using an electric, hydraulic or air saw. Per LF of cut including overcuts at each corner equal to the depth of the cut. Costs shown assume electric power is available. Minimum cost will be $400.

	Unit	Brick or 200'	Concrete 1000'	Concrete 1000'
To 4" depth	LF	13.60	19.60	21.60
To 5" depth	LF	17.20	21.20	25.10
To 6" depth	LF	18.80	22.80	28.50
To 7" depth	LF	23.60	28.00	32.70
To 8" depth	LF	28.80	32.70	39.20
To 10" depth	LF	36.00	40.40	46.80
To 12" depth	LF	44.00	48.80	55.60
To 14" depth	LF	54.00	58.80	64.60
To 16" depth	LF	65.10	67.10	73.70
To 18" depth	LF	76.60	78.70	88.10

Concrete Core Drilling, Subcontract Using an electric, hydraulic or air drill. Costs shown are per LF of depth for diameter shown. Prices are based on one mat reinforcing with 3/8" to 5/8" bars and include cleanup. Difficult drill setups are higher. Prices assume availability of 110 volt electricity. Figure travel time at $110 per hour. Minimum cost will be $250.

	Craft@Hrs	Unit	Material	Labor	Total
1" or 1-1/2" diameter	—	LF	—	—	59.90
2" or 2-1/2" diameter	—	LF	—	—	61.90
3" or 3-1/2"diameter	—	LF	—	—	74.60
4" or 5" diameter	—	LF	—	—	90.80
6" or 8" diameter	—	LF	—	—	125.00
10" diameter	—	LF	—	—	172.00
12" diameter	—	LF	—	—	280.00
14" diameter	—	LF	—	—	321.00
16" diameter	—	LF	—	—	364.00
18" diameter	—	LF	—	—	405.00
20" diameter	—	LF	—	—	448.00
24" diameter	—	LF	—	—	535.00
30" diameter	—	LF	—	—	670.00
36" diameter	—	LF	—	—	790.00
Hourly rate, 2 hour minimum	—	Hr	—	—	132.00

Concrete Slab Sawing, Subcontract Using a gasoline powered saw. Costs per linear foot for cured concrete assuming a level surface with good access and saw cut lines laid out and pre-marked by others. Costs include local travel time. Minimum cost will be $250. Electric powered slab sawing will be approximately 40% higher for the same depth.

Depth	Unit	Under 200'	200'-1000'	Over 1000'
1" deep	LF	.72	.63	.53
1-1/2" deep	LF	1.08	.99	.81
2" deep	LF	1.41	1.25	1.08
2-1/2" deep	LF	1.79	1.61	1.33
3" deep	LF	2.14	1.87	1.61
3-1/2" deep	LF	2.48	2.23	1.87
4" deep	LF	2.84	2.48	2.14
5" deep	LF	3.83	3.12	2.66
6" deep	LF	4.27	3.75	3.21
7" deep	LF	5.16	4.42	3.83
8" deep	LF	5.87	5.16	4.42
9" deep	LF	6.68	5.87	5.09
10" deep	LF	7.56	6.68	5.79
11" deep	LF	8.44	7.46	6.47
12" deep	LF	9.35	8.28	7.21

03 Concrete

Green concrete (2 days old) sawing will usually cost 15 to 20% less. Work done on an hourly basis will cost $125 per hour for slabs up to 4" thick and $135 per hour for 5" or 6" thick slabs. A two hour minimum charge will apply on work done on an hourly basis.

Asphalt Sawing, Subcontract Using a gasoline powered saw. Minimum cost will be $200. Cost per linear foot of green or cured asphalt, assuming level surface with good access and saw cut lines laid out and pre-marked by others. Costs include local travel time. Work done on an hourly basis will cost $115 per hour for asphalt up to 4" thick and $125 per hour for 5" or 6" thick asphalt. A two hour minimum charge will apply on work done on an hourly basis.

Depth	Unit	Under 450'	450'-1000'	Over 1000'
1" or 1-1/2" deep	LF	.44	.35	.27
2" deep	LF	.72	.53	.44
2-1/2" deep	LF	.87	.72	.53
3" deep	LF	1.08	.81	.63
3-1/2" deep	LF	1.25	.99	.72
4" deep	LF	1.41	1.08	.81
5" deep	LF	1.79	1.33	.99
6" deep	LF	2.14	1.61	1.17

04 Masonry

Cleaning and Pointing Masonry These costs assume the masonry surface is in fair to good condition with no unusual damage. Add the cost of protecting adjacent surfaces such as trim or the base of the wall and the cost of scaffolding, if required. Labor required to presoak or saturate the area cleaned is included in the labor cost. Work more than 12' above floor level will increase costs.

	Craft@Hrs	Unit	Material	Labor	Total
Brushing (hand cleaning) masonry includes the cost of detergent or chemical solution.					
Light cleanup (100 SF per manhour)	M1@.010	SF	.04	.48	.52
Medium scrub (75 SF per manhour)	M1@.013	SF	.05	.62	.67
Heavy (50 SF per manhour)	M1@.020	SF	.07	.95	1.02

	Craft@Hrs	Unit	Material	Labor	Equipment	Total
Water blasting masonry, using rented 400 to 700 PSI power washer with 3 to 8 gallon per minute flow rate, includes blaster rental at $65 per day						
Smooth face (250 SF per manhour)	M1@.004	SF	—	.19	.03	.22
Rough face (200 SF per manhour)	M1@.005	SF	—	.24	.04	.28
Sandblasting masonry, using 150 PSI compressor (with accessories and sand) at $130.00 per day						
Smooth face (50 SF per manhour)	M1@.020	SF	.40	.95	.24	1.59
Rough face (40 SF per manhour)	M1@.025	SF	.46	1.19	.51	2.16
Steam cleaning masonry, using rented steam cleaning rig (with accessories) at $112.00 per day						
Smooth face (75 SF per manhour)	M1@.013	SF	—	.62	.14	.76
Rough face (55 SF per manhour)	M1@.018	SF	—	.86	.19	1.05

	Craft@Hrs	Unit	Material	Labor	Total
Repointing brick, cut out joint, mask (blend-in), and regrout (tuck pointing)					
30 SF per manhour	M1@.033	SF	.08	1.58	1.66
Add for masking adjacent surfaces	—	%	—	5.0	—
Add for difficult stain removal	—	%	50.0	50.0	—
Add for working from scaffold	—	%	—	20.0	—

	Craft@Hrs	Unit	Material	Labor	Total
Masonry Cleaning Costs to clean masonry surfaces using commercial cleaning agents, add for pressure washing and scaffolding equipment.					
Typical cleaning of surfaces					
Granite, sandstone, terra cotta, brick	CL@.015	SF	.31	.62	.93
Cleaning surfaces of heavily carbonated					
Limestone or cast stone	CL@.045	SF	.42	1.86	2.28
Typical wash with acid and rinse	CL@.004	SF	.48	.17	.65
Masonry Reinforcing and Flashing Reinforcing bars for concrete block, ASTM A615 grade 60 bars, cost per linear foot including 10% overlap and waste.					
#3 bars (3/8", 5,319 LF per ton), horizontal	M1@.005	LF	.37	.24	.61
#3 bars placed vertically	M1@.006	LF	.37	.29	.66
#3 galvanized bars, horizontal	M1@.005	LF	.74	.24	.98
#3 galvanized bars placed vertically	M1@.006	LF	.74	.29	1.03
#4 bars (1/2", 2,994 LF per ton), horizontal	M1@.008	LF	.55	.38	.93
#4 bars placed vertically	M1@.010	LF	.55	.48	1.03
#4 galvanized bars, horizontal	M1@.008	LF	.92	.38	1.30
#4 galvanized bars placed vertically	M1@.010	LF	.92	.48	1.40
#5 bars (5/8", 1,918 LF per ton), horizontal	M1@.009	LF	.74	.43	1.17
#5 bars placed vertically	M1@.012	LF	.74	.57	1.31
#5 galvanized bars, horizontal	M1@.009	LF	1.22	.43	1.65
#5 galvanized bars placed vertically	M1@.012	LF	1.22	.57	1.79
#6 bars (3/4", 1,332 LF per ton), horizontal	M1@.010	LF	1.02	.48	1.50
#6 bars placed vertically	M1@.013	LF	1.02	.62	1.64
#6 galvanized bars, horizontal	M1@.014	LF	1.48	.67	2.15
#6 galvanized bars placed vertically	M1@.014	LF	1.48	.67	2.15
Wall ties					
Rectangular, galvanized	M1@.005	Ea	.58	.24	.82
Rectangular, copper coated	M1@.005	Ea	.68	.24	.92
Cavity "Z"-type, galvanized	M1@.005	Ea	.55	.24	.79
Cavity "Z"-type, copper coated	M1@.005	Ea	.62	.24	.86
Masonry anchors, steel, including bolts					
3/16" x 18" long	M1@.173	Ea	4.93	8.26	13.19
3/16" x 24" long	M1@.192	Ea	6.18	9.17	15.35
1/4" x 18" long	M1@.216	Ea	6.34	10.30	16.64
1/4" x 24" long	M1@.249	Ea	7.74	11.90	19.64
Wall reinforcing					
Truss-type, plain					
4" wall	M1@.002	LF	.37	.10	.47
6" wall	M1@.002	LF	.44	.10	.54
8" wall	M1@.003	LF	.47	.14	.61
10" wall	M1@.003	LF	.52	.14	.66
12" wall	M1@.004	LF	.55	.19	.74
Truss-type, galvanized					
4" wall	M1@.002	LF	.45	.10	.55
6" wall	M1@.002	LF	.49	.10	.59
8" wall	M1@.003	LF	.60	.14	.74
10" wall	M1@.003	LF	.63	.14	.77
12" wall	M1@.004	LF	.71	.19	.90
Ladder-type, galvanized, Class 3					
2" wide, for 4" wall	M1@.003	LF	.25	.14	.39
4" wide	M1@.003	LF	.51	.14	.65
6" wide	M1@.003	LF	.51	.14	.65
8" wide	M1@.003	LF	.56	.14	.70

	Craft@Hrs	Unit	Material	Labor	Total
Control joints					
Cross-shaped PVC	M1@.024	LF	2.34	1.15	3.49
8" wide PVC	M1@.047	LF	3.13	2.24	5.37
Closed cell 1/2" joint filler	M1@.012	LF	.45	.57	1.02
Closed cell 3/4" joint filler	M1@.012	LF	.77	.57	1.34
Through-the-wall flashing					
5 ounce copper	M1@.023	SF	3.57	1.10	4.67
.030" elastomeric sheeting	M1@.038	SF	.68	1.81	2.49

Expansion Shields Masonry anchors set in block or concrete including drilling. With nut and washer. Length indicates drilled depth.

	Craft@Hrs	Unit	Material	Labor	Total
One wedge anchors, 1/4" diameter					
1-3/4" long	CL@.079	Ea	.90	3.26	4.16
2-1/4" long	CL@.114	Ea	1.07	4.70	5.77
3-1/4" long	CL@.171	Ea	1.42	7.05	8.47
One wedge anchors, 1/2" diameter					
4-1/4" long	CL@.227	Ea	2.25	9.36	11.61
5-1/2" long	CL@.295	Ea	2.99	12.20	15.19
7" long	CL@.409	Ea	3.66	16.90	20.56
One wedge anchors, 3/4" diameter					
5-1/2" long	CL@.286	Ea	6.14	11.80	17.94
8-1/2" long	CL@.497	Ea	8.77	20.50	29.27
10" long	CL@.692	Ea	10.30	28.50	38.80
One wedge anchors, 1" diameter					
6" long	CL@.295	Ea	15.00	12.20	27.20
9" long	CL@.515	Ea	18.60	21.20	39.80
12" long	CL@.689	Ea	21.70	28.40	50.10
Flush self-drilling anchors					
1/4" x 1-1/4"	CL@.094	Ea	.90	3.88	4.78
5/16" x 1-1/4"	CL@.108	Ea	1.07	4.46	5.53
3/8" x 1-1/2"	CL@.121	Ea	1.42	4.99	6.41
1/2" x 1-1/2"	CL@.159	Ea	2.12	6.56	8.68
5/8" x 2-3/8"	CL@.205	Ea	3.34	8.46	11.80
3/4" x 2-3/8"	CL@.257	Ea	5.54	10.60	16.14

Brick Wall Assemblies Typical costs for smooth red clay brick walls, laid in running bond with 3/8" concave joints. These costs include the bricks, mortar for bricks and cavities, typical ladder type reinforcing, wall ties and normal waste. Foundations are not included. Wall thickness shown is the nominal size based on using the type bricks described. "Wythe" means the quantity of bricks in the thickness of the wall. Costs shown are per square foot (SF) of wall measured on one face. Deduct for openings over 10 SF in size. The names and dimensions of bricks can be expected to vary, depending on the manufacturer. For more detailed coverage of brick wall assemblies, see *National Concrete & Masonry Estimator*, http://CraftsmanSiteLicense.com

	Craft@Hrs	Unit	Material	Labor	Total
Standard bricks, 3-3/4" wide x 2-1/4" high x 8" long					
4" thick wall, single wythe, veneer facing	M1@.211	SF	6.35	10.10	16.45
8" thick wall, double wythe, cavity filled	M1@.464	SF	12.50	22.20	34.70
12" thick wall, triple wythe, cavity filled	M1@.696	SF	18.70	33.20	51.90
Modular bricks, 3" wide x 3-1/2" x 11-1/2" long					
3-1/2" thick wall, single wythe, veneer facing	M1@.156	SF	5.12	7.45	12.57
7-1/2" thick wall, double wythe, cavity filled	M1@.343	SF	10.10	16.40	26.50
11-1/2" thick wall, triple wythe, cavity filled	M1@.515	SF	15.10	24.60	39.70
Colonial bricks, 3" wide x 3-1/2" x 10" long					
3-1/2" thick wall, single wythe, veneer facing	M1@.177	SF	4.41	8.45	12.86
7-1/2" thick wall, double wythe, cavity filled	M1@.389	SF	8.65	18.60	27.25
11-1/2" thick wall, triple wythe, cavity filled	M1@.584	SF	12.90	27.90	40.80

	Craft@Hrs	Unit	Material	Labor	Total
Add to any brick wall assembly above for:					
American bond or stacked bond	—	%	5.0	10.0	—
Basketweave bond or soldier bond	—	%	10.0	10.0	—
Flemish bond	—	%	10.0	15.0	—
Herringbone pattern	—	%	15.0	15.0	—
Institutional inspection	—	%	—	20.0	—
Short runs or cut-up work	—	%	5.0	15.0	—
Fireplaces Common brick, including the chimney foundation, damper, flue lining and stack to 15'					
30" box, brick to 5', large quantity	M1@30.3	Ea	1,690.00	1,450.00	3,140.00
36" box, brick to 5', custom	M1@33.7	Ea	2,050.00	1,610.00	3,660.00
42" box, brick to 8', custom	M1@48.1	Ea	2,400.00	2,300.00	4,700.00
48" box, brick to 8', custom	M1@53.1	Ea	2,760.00	2,530.00	5,290.00
Flue lining, 1' lengths					
8-1/2" round	M1@.148	LF	7.33	7.07	14.40
10" x 17" oval	M1@.206	LF	12.40	9.83	22.23
13" x 13" square	M1@.193	LF	13.00	9.21	22.21
Prefabricated cast concrete					
30" box and 15' chimney	M1@5.43	Ea	1,740.00	259.00	1,999.00
Face brick, mantle to ceiling	M1@.451	SF	5.28	21.50	26.78
Clay Backing Tile Load bearing, 12" x 12"					
4" thick	M1@.066	SF	5.10	3.15	8.25
6" thick	M1@.079	SF	5.75	3.77	9.52
8" thick	M1@.091	SF	6.75	4.34	11.09
Deduct for non-load bearing tile	—	%	−8.0	−10.0	—
Structural Glazed Tile Heavy-duty, fire-safe, structural glazed facing tile for interior surfaces. No foundations or reinforcing included.					
Glazed one side, all colors, 5-1/3" x 12"					
2" thick	M1@.125	SF	5.77	5.97	11.74
4" thick	M1@.136	SF	6.95	6.49	13.44
6" thick	M1@.141	SF	10.30	6.73	17.03
8" thick	M1@.172	SF	12.90	8.21	21.11
Glazed one side, all colors, 8" x 16" block					
2" thick	M1@.072	SF	6.47	3.44	9.91
4" thick	M1@.072	SF	6.95	3.44	10.39
6" thick	M1@.079	SF	9.60	3.77	13.37
8" thick	M1@.085	SF	11.20	4.06	15.26
Acoustical glazed facing tile, with small holes on a smooth ceramic glazed facing, and one mineral fiberglass sound batt located in the hollow core behind perforated face					
8" x 8" face size unit, 4" thick	M1@.136	SF	11.40	6.49	17.89
8" x 16" face size unit, 4" thick	M1@.141	SF	10.10	6.73	16.83
Reinforced glazed security tile, with vertical cores and knockouts for horizontal reinforcing, 8" x 16" block					
4" thick	M1@.092	SF	8.89	4.39	13.28
6" thick	M1@.095	SF	11.50	4.54	16.04
8" thick	M1@.101	SF	13.80	4.82	18.62
Add to 8" security tile for horizontal and vertical reinforcing and grout cores to meet high security standards	M1@.047	SF	3.78	2.24	5.98
Add for glazed 2 sides	—	%	55.0	10.0	—
Base, glazed 1 side	M1@.190	LF	8.60	9.07	17.67
Cap, glazed 2 sides	M1@.193	LF	14.40	9.21	23.61
Deduct for large areas	—	%	−5.0	−5.0	—
Add for institutional inspection	—	%	—	10.0	—

	Craft@Hrs	Unit	Material	Labor	Total

Chemical-Resistant Brick or Tile, Subcontract (also known as acid-proof brick).Typical prices for chemical-resistant brick or tile meeting ASTM C-279, types I, II, and III requirements. Installed with 1/8" thick bed and mortar joints over a membrane of either elastomeric bonded to the floors or walls, sheet membrane with a special seam treatment, squeegee hot-applied asphalt, cold-applied adhesive troweled on, or special spray-applied material. The setting bed and joint materials can be either 100% carbon-filled furan or phenolic, sodium or potassium silicates, silica-filled epoxy, polyester, vinyl ester or other special mortars. Expansion joints are required in floor construction, particularly where construction joints exist in the concrete. Additional expansion joints may be required, depending on the service conditions to which the floor will be subjected. Brick or tile will be either 3-3/4" x 8" face, 1-1/8" thick (splits); 3-3/4" x 8" face, 2-1/4" thick (singles); or 4" x 8" face, 1-3/8" thick (pavers). Costs are based on a 2,000 SF job. For smaller projects, increase the cost 5% for each 500 SF or portion of 500 SF less than 2,000 SF. For scheduling purposes estimate that a crew of 4 can install 75 to 100 SF of membrane and brick in an 8-hour day. These costs assume that the membrane is laid on a suitable surface prepared by others and include the subcontractor's overhead and profit.

	Craft@Hrs	Unit	Material	Labor	Total
Typical installed costs for chemical-resistant brick or tile (acid-proof brick), installed					
Less complex jobs	—	SF	—	—	34.90
More complex jobs	—	SF	—	—	42.20
Minimum job cost	—	LS	—	—	22,900.00

Concrete Block Retaining Walls Includes mortar, 8" x 8" x 16" regular block, U-block, inspection block (for walls six courses high or higher) grout, cavity caps and No. 5 reinforcing steel. Equipment is a trailer-mounted 15 CY per hour grout pump, locally rented. Add the cost of wall foundations from the section that follows. For more detailed coverage of concrete block retaining walls, see *National Concrete & Masonry Estimator*, http://CraftsmanSiteLicense.com

	Craft@Hrs	Unit	Material	Labor	Equipment	Total
Retaining wall with one lintel block course and grouted and reinforced vertical cells at 16" O.C.						
3' - 4" high wall	M1@.504	LF	16.70	24.10	.33	41.13
4' - 0" high wall	M1@.576	LF	20.20	27.50	.38	48.08
4' - 8" high wall	M1@.648	LF	23.10	30.90	.44	54.44
5' - 4" high wall	M1@.720	LF	25.90	34.40	.49	60.79
6' - 0" high wall	M1@.793	LF	28.90	37.90	.55	67.35
6' - 8" high wall	M1@.864	LF	31.70	41.20	.61	73.51
7' - 4" high wall	M1@.936	LF	34.60	44.70	.66	79.96
8' - 0" high wall	M1@1.01	LF	37.50	48.20	.72	86.42
Retaining wall with one lintel block course and grouted and reinforced vertical cells at 32" O.C.						
3' - 4" high wall	M1@.454	LF	14.20	21.70	.21	36.11
4' - 0" high wall	M1@.526	LF	16.90	25.10	.24	42.24
4' - 8" high wall	M1@.598	LF	19.20	28.50	.27	47.97
5' - 4" high wall	M1@.670	LF	21.60	32.00	.30	53.90
6' - 0" high wall	M1@.743	LF	24.00	35.50	.33	59.83
6' - 8" high wall	M1@.814	LF	26.40	38.90	.35	65.65
7' - 4" high wall	M1@.886	LF	28.70	42.30	.38	71.38
8' - 0" high wall	M1@.958	LF	31.20	45.70	.41	77.31
Retaining wall with one lintel block course and grouted and reinforced vertical cells at 48" O.C.						
3' - 4" high wall	M1@.436	LF	13.40	20.80	.18	34.38
4' - 0" high wall	M1@.508	LF	15.80	24.30	.20	40.30
4' - 8" high wall	M1@.580	LF	17.90	27.70	.21	45.81
5' - 4" high wall	M1@.652	LF	20.10	31.10	.23	51.43
6' - 0" high wall	M1@.725	LF	22.40	34.60	.25	57.25
6' - 8" high wall	M1@.797	LF	24.60	38.00	.27	62.87
7' - 4" high wall	M1@.869	LF	26.80	41.50	.29	68.59
8' - 0" high wall	M1@.941	LF	29.00	44.90	.31	74.21

	Craft@Hrs	Unit	Material	Labor	Equipment	Total
Retaining wall with two lintel block courses and grouted and reinforced vertical cells at 16" O.C.						
3' - 4" high wall	M1@.546	LF	18.30	26.10	.37	44.77
4' - 0" high wall	M1@.617	LF	21.80	29.50	.43	51.73
4' - 8" high wall	M1@.689	LF	24.70	32.90	.48	58.08
5' - 4" high wall	M1@.761	LF	27.50	36.30	.54	64.34
6' - 0" high wall	M1@.833	LF	30.50	39.80	.60	70.90
6' - 8" high wall	M1@.906	LF	33.40	43.30	.65	77.35
7' - 4" high wall	M1@.978	LF	36.20	46.70	.71	83.61
8' - 0" high wall	M1@1.05	LF	39.20	50.10	.76	90.06
Retaining wall with two lintel block courses and grouted and reinforced vertical cells at 32" O.C.						
3' - 4" high wall	M1@.495	LF	16.20	23.60	.29	40.09
4' - 0" high wall	M1@.567	LF	18.80	27.10	.32	46.22
4' - 8" high wall	M1@.639	LF	21.20	30.50	.34	52.04
5' - 4" high wall	M1@.711	LF	23.50	33.90	.37	57.77
6' - 0" high wall	M1@.783	LF	26.00	37.40	.40	63.80
6' - 8" high wall	M1@.856	LF	28.30	40.90	.43	69.63
7' - 4" high wall	M1@.928	LF	30.70	44.30	.46	75.46
8' - 0" high wall	M1@1.00	LF	33.10	47.70	.48	81.28
Retaining wall with two lintel block courses and grouted and reinforced vertical cells at 48" O.C.						
3' - 4" high wall	M1@.478	LF	15.50	22.80	.26	38.56
4' - 0" high wall	M1@.550	LF	17.90	26.30	.28	44.48
4' - 8" high wall	M1@.621	LF	20.00	29.60	.30	49.90
5' - 4" high wall	M1@.693	LF	22.20	33.10	.32	55.62
6' - 0" high wall	M1@.766	LF	24.50	36.60	.34	61.44
6' - 8" high wall	M1@.839	LF	26.70	40.10	.35	67.15
7' - 4" high wall	M1@.910	LF	28.90	43.40	.37	72.67
8' - 0" high wall	M1@.982	LF	31.10	46.90	.39	78.39
Retaining wall with three lintel block courses and grouted and reinforced vertical cells at 16" O.C.						
3' - 4" high wall	M1@.587	LF	20.00	28.00	.42	48.42
4' - 0" high wall	M1@.660	LF	23.40	31.50	.47	55.37
4' - 8" high wall	M1@.732	LF	26.30	34.90	.53	61.73
5' - 4" high wall	M1@.804	LF	29.20	38.40	.59	68.19
6' - 0" high wall	M1@.876	LF	32.10	41.80	.64	74.54
6' - 8" high wall	M1@.948	LF	35.00	45.30	.70	81.00
7' - 4" high wall	M1@1.02	LF	37.90	48.70	.75	87.35
8' - 0" high wall	M1@1.09	LF	40.80	52.00	.81	93.61
Retaining wall with three lintel block courses and grouted and reinforced vertical cells at 32" O.C.						
3' - 4" high wall	M1@.537	LF	18.20	25.60	.36	44.16
4' - 0" high wall	M1@.610	LF	20.80	29.10	.39	50.29
4' - 8" high wall	M1@.682	LF	23.20	32.60	.42	56.22
5' - 4" high wall	M1@.754	LF	25.50	36.00	.45	61.95
6' - 0" high wall	M1@.826	LF	28.00	39.40	.47	67.87
6' - 8" high wall	M1@.898	LF	30.30	42.90	.50	73.70
7' - 4" high wall	M1@.971	LF	32.70	46.40	.53	79.63
8' - 0" high wall	M1@1.04	LF	35.10	49.60	.56	85.26
Retaining wall with three lintel block course and grouted and reinforced vertical cells at 48" O.C.						
3' - 4" high wall	M1@.520	LF	17.60	24.80	.34	42.74
4' - 0" high wall	M1@.593	LF	20.00	28.30	.36	48.66
4' - 8" high wall	M1@.664	LF	22.20	31.70	.38	54.28
5' - 4" high wall	M1@.736	LF	24.30	35.10	.40	59.80
6' - 0" high wall	M1@.808	LF	26.60	38.60	.42	65.62
6' - 8" high wall	M1@.880	LF	28.80	42.00	.44	71.24
7' - 4" high wall	M1@.953	LF	31.00	45.50	.46	76.96
8' - 0" high wall	M1@1.03	LF	33.20	49.20	.47	82.87

	Craft@Hrs	Unit	Material	Labor	Total
Concrete Foundations for Retaining Walls Includes hand excavation in normal soil, backfilling, board or plywood forming as noted, grade 60 reinforcing steel and 3,000 P.S.I. concrete poured from the chute. Concrete waste when poured against earth is assumed to be 1" of concrete at the bottom of the footing and 2" along the walls. Concrete waste when poured against forms is assumed to be 1" at the bottom of the pad. When forms are used, estimate that excavation will be required 18" beyond the forms.					
36" wide x 12" deep foundation with 4 No. 5 bars, 2' deep					
Hand excavated, poured against earth					
Excavation	CL@.412	LF	—	17.00	17.00
Reinforcing steel	RB@.072	LF	3.55	4.70	8.25
Concrete	CL@.075	LF	16.90	3.09	19.99
Hand excavated, poured against forms					
Excavation	CL@.894	LF	—	36.90	36.90
Formwork	M2@.251	LF	1.98	11.30	13.28
Reinforcing steel	RB@.072	LF	3.55	4.70	8.25
Concrete	CL@.068	LF	16.00	2.81	18.81
36" wide x 12" deep with 4 No. 5 bars, 3' deep					
Hand excavated, poured against earth					
Excavation	CL@.635	LF	—	26.20	26.20
Reinforcing steel	RB@.072	LF	3.55	4.70	8.25
Concrete	CL@.075	LF	16.90	3.09	19.99
Hand excavated, poured against forms					
Excavation	CL@1.36	LF	—	56.10	56.10
Formwork	M2@.251	LF	1.98	11.30	13.28
Reinforcing steel	RB@.072	LF	3.55	4.70	8.25
Concrete	CL@.068	LF	16.00	2.81	18.81
36" wide x 12" deep with 6 No. 5 bars, 2' deep					
Hand excavated, poured against earth					
Excavation	CL@.412	LF	—	17.00	17.00
Reinforcing steel	RB@.108	LF	5.33	7.04	12.37
Concrete	CL@.075	LF	16.90	3.09	19.99
Hand excavated, poured against forms					
Excavation	CL@.894	LF	—	36.90	36.90
Formwork	M2@.251	LF	1.98	11.30	13.28
Reinforcing steel	RB@.108	LF	5.33	7.04	12.37
Concrete	CL@.068	LF	16.00	2.81	18.81
36" wide x 12" deep with 6 No. 5 bars, 3' deep					
Hand excavated, poured against earth					
Excavation	CL@.635	LF	—	26.20	26.20
Reinforcing steel	RB@.108	LF	5.33	7.04	12.37
Concrete	CL@.075	LF	16.90	3.09	19.99
Hand excavated, poured against forms					
Excavation	CL@1.36	LF	—	56.10	56.10
Formwork	M2@.251	LF	1.98	11.30	13.28
Reinforcing steel	RB@.108	LF	5.33	7.04	12.37
Concrete	CL@.068	LF	16.00	2.81	18.81
36" wide x 16" deep with 6 No. 5 bars, 2' deep, No. 4 transverse bars at 2' O.C.					
Hand excavated, poured against earth					
Excavation	CL@.400	LF	—	16.50	16.50
Reinforcing steel	RB@.108	LF	6.14	7.04	13.18
Concrete	CL@.096	LF	22.00	3.96	25.96

	Craft@Hrs	Unit	Material	Labor	Total
Hand excavated, poured against forms					
Excavation	CL@.882	LF	—	36.40	36.40
Formwork	M2@.337	LF	2.01	15.20	17.21
Reinforcing steel	RB@.108	LF	6.14	7.04	13.18
Concrete	CL@.089	LF	20.90	3.67	24.57
36" wide x 16" deep with 6 No. 5 bars, 3' deep, No. 4 transverse bars at 2' O.C.					
Hand excavated, poured against earth					
Excavation	CL@.624	LF	—	25.70	25.70
Reinforcing steel	RB@.108	LF	6.14	7.04	13.18
Concrete	CL@.096	LF	22.00	3.96	25.96
Hand excavated, poured against forms					
Excavation	CL@1.35	LF	—	55.70	55.70
Formwork	M2@.337	LF	2.01	15.20	17.21
Reinforcing steel	RB@.108	LF	6.14	7.04	13.18
Concrete	CL@.089	LF	20.90	3.67	24.57

Concrete Block Wall Assemblies Typical costs for standard natural gray medium weight masonry block walls including blocks, mortar, typical reinforcing and normal waste. Foundations are not included. For more detailed coverage of concrete block masonry, see *National Concrete & Masonry Estimator*, http://CraftsmanSiteLicense.com

	Craft@Hrs	Unit	Material	Labor	Total
Walls constructed with 8" x 16" blocks laid in running bond					
4" thick wall	M1@.090	SF	2.89	4.30	7.19
6" thick wall	M1@.100	SF	3.57	4.77	8.34
8" thick wall	M1@.120	SF	4.26	5.73	9.99
12" thick wall	M1@.150	SF	6.00	7.16	13.16

Grouting Concrete Block Wall Cores Typical costs for filling concrete block wall cores with pumped concrete and rodded. Costs shown are based on 2 cores per 16" block and include a 10% allowance for waste.

	Craft@Hrs	Unit	Material	Labor	Total
Using C476 grout, pumped	—	CY	166.00	—	166.00
Material pumped in place and rodded, all cores filled.					
4" thick wall, (4.98 SF per CF)	M1@.020	SF	1.23	.95	2.18
6" thick wall, (4.56 SF per CF)	M1@.022	SF	1.34	1.05	2.39
8" thick wall, (3.79 SF per CF)	M1@.024	SF	1.62	1.15	2.77
10" thick wall, (3.08 SF per CF)	M1@.031	SF	1.99	1.48	3.47
12" thick wall, (2.46 SF per CF)	M1@.040	SF	2.49	1.91	4.40
Add for grouting cores at 16" intervals, material pumped in place and rodded.					
4" thick wall, (8.42 SF per CF)	M1@.011	SF	.73	.53	1.26
6" thick wall, (7.73 SF per CF)	M1@.012	SF	.79	.57	1.36
8" thick wall, (6.53 SF per CF)	M1@.014	SF	.94	.67	1.61
10" thick wall, (5.19 SF per CF)	M1@.019	SF	1.18	.91	2.09
12" thick wall, (4.21 SF per CF)	M1@.023	SF	1.46	1.10	2.56
Add for grouting cores at 24" intervals, material pumped in place and rodded.					
4" thick wall, (10.24 SF per CF)	M1@.008	SF	.60	.38	.98
6" thick wall, (9.02 SF per CF)	M1@.009	SF	.68	.43	1.11
8" thick wall, (8.61 SF per CF)	M1@.011	SF	.71	.53	1.24
10" thick wall, (6.76 SF per CF)	M1@.014	SF	.91	.67	1.58
12" thick wall, (5.57 SF per CF)	M1@.017	SF	1.10	.81	1.91
Add for grouting cores at 32" intervals, material pumped in place and rodded.					
4" thick wall, (11.66 SF per CF)	M1@.007	SF	.53	.33	.86
6" thick wall, (10.24 SF per CF)	M1@.008	SF	.60	.38	.98
8" thick wall, (9.97 SF per CF)	M1@.010	SF	.61	.48	1.09
10" thick wall, (8.06 SF per CF)	M1@.013	SF	.76	.62	1.38
12" thick wall, (6.65 SF per CF)	M1@.014	SF	.92	.67	1.59

	Craft@Hrs	Unit	Material	Labor	Total
Add for grouting cores per vertical linear foot (VLF) of core, material pumped in place and rodded.					
4" thick wall, (8.86 VLF per CF)	M1@.011	VLF	1.04	.53	1.57
6" thick wall, (8.11 VLF per CF)	M1@.017	VLF	1.13	.81	1.94
8" thick wall, (6.73 VLF per CF)	M1@.024	VLF	1.37	1.15	2.52
10" thick wall, (5.47 VLF per CF)	M1@.026	VLF	1.68	1.24	2.92
12" thick wall, (4.37 VLF per CF)	M1@.028	VLF	2.10	1.34	3.44
Add for 2" thick caps, natural gray concrete					
4" thick wall	M1@.027	LF	1.06	1.29	2.35
6" thick wall	M1@.038	LF	1.26	1.81	3.07
8" thick wall	M1@.046	LF	1.45	2.20	3.65
12" thick wall	M1@.065	LF	2.12	3.10	5.22
Add for detailed block, 3/8" score					
Single score, one side	—	SF	.62	—	.62
Single score, two sides	—	SF	1.37	—	1.37
Multi-scores, one side	—	SF	.62	—	.62
Multi-scores, two sides	—	SF	1.37	—	1.37
Add for color block, any of above					
Light colors	—	%	12.0	—	—
Medium colors	—	%	18.0	—	—
Dark colors	—	%	25.0	—	—
Add for other than running bond	—	%	—	20.0	—

Glazed Concrete Block Prices are per square foot of wall and include allowance for mortar and waste but no foundation or excavation. 8" high x 16" long, 3/8" joints, no reinforcing or grout included. Based on 1.05 blocks per square foot (SF).

	Craft@Hrs	Unit	Material	Labor	Total
Glazed 1 side					
2" wide	M1@.102	SF	14.10	4.87	18.97
4" wide	M1@.107	SF	16.50	5.11	21.61
6" wide	M1@.111	SF	16.40	5.30	21.70
8" wide	M1@.118	SF	17.30	5.63	22.93
Glazed 2 sides					
4" wide	M1@.122	SF	24.80	5.82	30.62
6" wide	M1@.127	SF	26.30	6.06	32.36
8" wide	M1@.136	SF	26.60	6.49	33.09
Glazed cove base, glazed 1 side, 8" high					
4" length	M1@.127	LF	48.50	6.06	54.56
6" length	M1@.137	LF	36.60	6.54	43.14
8" length	M1@.147	LF	28.00	7.02	35.02

Decorative Concrete Block Prices are per square foot of wall and include allowance for mortar and waste but no foundation, reinforcing, grout or excavation. Regular weight units, 1.05 blocks per SF.

	Craft@Hrs	Unit	Material	Labor	Total
Split-face hollow block, 8" high x 16" long, 3/8" joints					
4" wide	M1@.110	SF	1.98	5.25	7.23
6" wide	M1@.121	SF	2.08	5.78	7.86
8" wide	M1@.133	SF	2.39	6.35	8.74
10" wide	M1@.140	SF	3.42	6.68	10.10
12" wide	M1@.153	SF	3.36	7.30	10.66
Split-rib (combed) hollow block, 8" high x 16" long, 3/8" joints					
4" wide	M1@.107	SF	2.90	5.11	8.01
6" wide	M1@.115	SF	3.01	5.49	8.50
8" wide	M1@.121	SF	3.32	5.78	9.10
10" wide	M1@.130	SF	4.36	6.21	10.57
12" wide	M1@.146	SF	4.31	6.97	11.28

	Craft@Hrs	Unit	Material	Labor	Total
Screen block, 3/8" joints					
6" x 6" x 4" wide	M1@.210	SF	3.93	10.00	13.93
8" x 8" x 4" wide (2.25 per SF)	M1@.140	SF	5.94	6.68	12.62
12" x 12" x 4" wide (1 per SF)	M1@.127	SF	3.01	6.06	9.07
8" x 16" x 8" wide (1.11 per SF)	M1@.115	SF	3.13	5.49	8.62
Acoustical slotted block, by rated Noise Reduction Coefficient (NRC)					
4" wide, with metal baffle, NRC, .45 to .55	M1@.121	SF	4.82	5.78	10.60
6" wide, with metal baffle, NRC, .45 to .55	M1@.130	SF	5.68	6.21	11.89
8" wide, with metal baffle, NRC, .45 to .55	M1@.121	SF	7.07	5.78	12.85
8" wide, with fiber filler, NRC, .65 to .75	M1@.143	SF	9.13	6.83	15.96

Concrete Block Bond Beams For door and window openings, no grout or reinforcing included.

	Craft@Hrs	Unit	Material	Labor	Total
Cost per linear foot of bond beam block					
6" wide, 8" high, 16" long	M1@.068	LF	3.00	3.25	6.25
8" wide, 8" high, 16" long	M1@.072	LF	3.43	3.44	6.87
10" wide, 8" high, 16" long	M1@.079	LF	4.71	3.77	8.48
12" wide, 8" high, 16" long	M1@.089	LF	4.71	4.25	8.96
12" wide, 8" high double bond beam, 16" long	M1@.102	LF	4.71	4.87	9.58
8" wide, 16" high, 16" long	M1@.127	LF	7.90	6.06	13.96
Grout for bond beams, 3,000 PSI concrete, by block size and linear foot of beam, no block or reinforcing included, based on block cavity at 50% of block volume					
8" high x 4" wide, .10 CF per LF	M1@.005	LF	.52	.24	.76
8" high x 6" wide, .15 CF per LF	M1@.010	LF	.79	.48	1.27
8" high x 8" wide, .22 CF per LF	M1@.017	LF	1.15	.81	1.96
8" high x 10" wide, .30 CF per LF	M1@.023	LF	1.57	1.10	2.67
8" high x 12" wide, .40 CF per LF	M1@.032	LF	2.09	1.53	3.62
16" high x 8" wide, .44 CF per LF	M1@.061	LF	2.30	2.91	5.21
16" high x 10" wide, .60 CF per LF	M1@.058	LF	3.14	2.77	5.91
16" high x 12" wide, .80 CF per LF	M1@.079	LF	4.19	3.77	7.96
Grout hollow metal door frame in a masonry wall					
Single door	M1@.668	Ea	12.90	31.90	44.80
Double door	M1@.851	Ea	17.20	40.60	57.80

Additional Costs for Concrete Block

	Craft@Hrs	Unit	Material	Labor	Total
Sill blocks	M1@.087	LF	1.85	4.15	6.00
Cutting blocks	M1@.137	LF	—	6.54	6.54
Stack bond	—	%	5.0	10.0	—
Add for cut-up jobs	—	%	5.0	5.0	—
Add for institutional grade work	—	%	5.0	15.0	—
Add for colored block	—	%	15.0	—	—

Glass Block Clear 3-7/8" thick block installed in walls to 8' high. Costs shown include 1/4" mortar joints, caulking, wall ties and 6% waste. Heights over 8' to 10' require additional scaffolding and handling and may increase labor costs up to 40%. Mortar is 1 part portland cement, 1/2 part lime, and 4 parts sand, plus integral waterproofer. Costs for continuous panel reinforcing in horizontal joints are listed below.

	Craft@Hrs	Unit	Material	Labor	Total
Flat glass block, under 1,000 SF job					
6" x 6", 4 per SF	M1@.323	SF	28.60	15.40	44.00
8" x 8", 2.25 per SF	M1@.245	SF	20.30	11.70	32.00
12" x 12", 1 per SF	M1@.202	SF	26.50	9.64	36.14
Deduct for jobs over 1,000 SF to 5,000 SF	—	%	−4.0	−4.0	—
Deduct for jobs over 5,000 SF	—	%	−10.0	−10.0	—
Deduct for Thinline interior glass block	—	%	−10.0	—	—
Add for thermal control fiberglass inserts	—	%	5.0	5.0	—

	Craft@Hrs	Unit	Material	Labor	Total
Replacing 8" x 8" x 4" clear glass block, 10 unit minimum					
Per block replaced, add for mortar	M1@.851	Ea	9.94	40.60	50.54
Additional costs for glass block					
Fiberglass or polymeric expansion joints	—	LF	1.46	—	1.46
Reinforcing steel mesh	—	LF	.54	—	.54
Wall anchors, 2' long					
Used where blocks aren't set into a wall	—	Ea	2.86	—	2.86
Asphalt emulsion, 600 LF per gallon	—	Gal	9.98	—	9.98
Waterproof sealant, 180 LF per gallon	—	Gal	16.70	—	16.70
Cleaning block after installation, using sponge and water only					
Per SF cleaned	CL@.023	SF	—	.95	.95

Stone Work The delivered price of stone can be expected to vary widely. These costs include mortar, based on 1/2" joints, but no scaffolding. Figures in parentheses show typical quantities installed per 8-hour day by a crew of two.

	Craft@Hrs	Unit	Material	Labor	Total
Rough stone veneer, 4", placed over stud wall					
Lava stone (79 SF)	M4@.202	SF	8.50	9.64	18.14
Rubble stone (40 SF)	M4@.400	SF	12.00	19.10	31.10
Most common veneer (60 SF)	M4@.267	SF	15.10	12.70	27.80
Cut stone					
Thinset granite tile, 1/2" thick (120 SF)	M4@.133	SF	17.80	6.35	24.15
Granite, 7/8" thick, interior (70 SF)	M4@.229	SF	29.00	10.90	39.90
Granite, 1-1/4" thick, exterior (60 SF)	M4@.267	SF	21.60	12.70	34.30
Limestone, 2" thick (70 SF)	M4@.229	SF	26.90	10.90	37.80
Limestone, 3" thick (60 SF)	M4@.267	SF	32.60	12.70	45.30
Marble, 7/8" thick, interior (70 SF)	M4@.229	SF	34.10	10.90	45.00
Marble, 1-1/4" thick, interior (70 SF)	M4@.229	SF	42.00	10.90	52.90
Sandstone, 2" thick (70 SF)	M4@.229	SF	24.00	10.90	34.90
Sandstone, 3" thick (60 SF)	M4@.267	SF	31.10	12.70	43.80
Add for honed finish	—	SF	2.80	—	2.80
Add for polished finish	—	SF	4.90	—	4.90
Marble specialties, typical prices					
Floors, 7/8" thick, exterior (70 SF)	M1@.229	SF	26.00	10.90	36.90
Thresholds, 1-1/4" thick (70 LF)	M1@.229	LF	13.70	10.90	24.60
Bases, 7/8" x 6" (51 LF)	M1@.314	LF	12.20	15.00	27.20
Columns, plain (15 CF)	M1@1.06	CF	144.00	50.60	194.60
Columns, fluted (13 CF)	M1@1.23	CF	199.00	58.70	257.70
Window stools, 5" x 1" (60 LF)	M1@.267	LF	15.10	12.70	27.80
Toilet partitions (1.5 Ea)	M1@10.6	Ea	796.00	506.00	1,302.00
Stair treads, 1-1/4" x 11" (50 LF)	M1@.320	LF	33.60	15.30	48.90
Limestone, rough cut large blocks (39 CF)	M1@.410	CF	41.50	19.60	61.10
Manufactured stone veneer, including mortar, Cultured Stone®					
Prefitted types (160 SF)	M1@.100	SF	8.60	4.77	13.37
Brick veneer type (120 SF)	M1@.133	SF	7.13	6.35	13.48
Random cast type (120 SF)	M1@.133	SF	7.88	6.35	14.23

Quarry Tile Unglazed natural red tile set in a portland cement bed with mortar joints.

	Craft@Hrs	Unit	Material	Labor	Total
Quarry floor tile					
4" x 4" x 1/2", 1/8" straight joints	M1@.112	SF	4.35	5.35	9.70
6" x 6" x 1/2", 1/4" straight joints	M1@.101	SF	4.08	4.82	8.90
6" x 6" x 3/4", 1/4" straight joints	M1@.105	SF	5.33	5.01	10.34
8" x 8" x 3/4", 3/8" straight joints	M1@.095	SF	5.05	4.54	9.59
8" x 8" x 1/2", 1/4" hexagon joints	M1@.112	SF	5.75	5.35	11.10
Quarry wall tile					
4" x 4" x 1/2", 1/8" straight joints	M1@.125	SF	4.32	5.97	10.29
6" x 6" x 3/4", 1/4" straight joints	M1@.122	SF	5.33	5.82	11.15

	Craft@Hrs	Unit	Material	Labor	Total
Quarry tile stair treads					
6" x 6" x 3/4", 12" wide tread	M1@.122	LF	5.87	5.82	11.69
Quarry tile window sill					
6" x 6" x 3/4" tile on 6" wide sill	M1@.078	LF	5.64	3.72	9.36
Quarry tile trim or cove base					
5" x 6" x 1/2" straight top	M1@.083	LF	4.32	3.96	8.28
6" x 6" x 3/4" round top	M1@.087	LF	5.05	4.15	9.20
Deduct for tile set in epoxy bed without grout joints	—	SF	—	−1.91	−1.91
Add for tile set in epoxy bed with grout joints	—	SF	1.53	—	1.53
Pavers and Floor Tile					
Brick, excluding platform cost					
Plate, glazed	M1@.114	SF	3.46	5.44	8.90
Laid in sand	M1@.089	SF	2.64	4.25	6.89
Pavers, on concrete, grouted	M1@.107	SF	4.65	5.11	9.76
Add for special patterns	—	%	25.0	35.0	—
Slate	M1@.099	SF	4.07	4.73	8.80
Terrazzo tiles, 1/4" thick					
Standard	M1@.078	SF	6.65	3.72	10.37
Granite	M1@.085	SF	10.70	4.06	14.76
Brick steps	M1@.186	SF	4.14	8.88	13.02
Interlocking Paving Stones These costs include fine sand to fill joints and machine vibration, but no excavation. No vapor(or other) barriers					
Interlocking pavers, rectangular, 60mm thick, Orion	M1@.083	SF	2.37	3.96	6.33
Interlocking pavers, hexagonal, 80mm thick, Omni	M1@.085	SF	2.88	4.06	6.94
Interlocking pavers, multi-angle, 80mm thick, Venus	M1@.081	SF	2.52	3.87	6.39
Concrete masonry grid pavers (erosion control)	M1@.061	SF	4.38	2.91	7.29
Add for a 1" sand cushion	M1@.001	SF	.06	.05	.11
Add for a 2" sand cushion	M1@.002	SF	.12	.10	.22
Deduct for over 5,000 SF	—	%	−3.0	−7.0	—
Masonry Lintels and Coping					
Reinforced precast concrete lintels					
4" wide x 8" high, to 6'6" long	M1@.073	LF	10.20	3.49	13.69
6" wide x 8" high, to 6'6" long	M1@.078	LF	18.20	3.72	21.92
8" wide x 8" high, to 6'6" long	M1@.081	LF	18.90	3.87	22.77
10" wide x 8" high, to 6'6" long	M1@.091	LF	24.30	4.34	28.64
4" wide x 8" high, over 6'6" to 10' long	M1@.073	LF	19.10	3.49	22.59
6" wide x 8" high, over 6'6" to 10' long	M1@.077	LF	22.40	3.68	26.08
8" wide x 8" high, over 6'6" to 10' long	M1@.081	LF	23.40	3.87	27.27
10" wide x 8" high, over 6'6" to 10' long	M1@.091	LF	32.20	4.34	36.54
Precast concrete coping, 5" average thickness, 4' to 8' long					
10" wide, gray concrete	M1@.190	LF	17.10	9.07	26.17
12" wide, gray concrete	M1@.200	LF	19.10	9.55	28.65
12" wide, white concrete	M1@.226	LF	47.20	10.80	58.00
Parging (Pargeting), Waterproofing and Dampproofing					
Parging, 2 coats, 1/2" thick	M3@.070	SF	.28	3.51	3.79
Parging, 2 coats, waterproof, 3/4" thick	M3@.085	SF	.40	4.26	4.66
Dampproofing, asphalt primer at 1 gallon per 100 SF, Dampproof coat at 30 pounds per 100 SF	CL@.029	SF	.14	1.20	1.34

	Craft@Hrs	Unit	Material	Labor	Equipment	Total

Structural Steel Costs shown below are for 60 to 100 ton jobs up to six stories high where the fabricated structural steel is purchased from a steel fabricator located within 50 miles of the job site. Material costs are for ASTM A36 steel, fabricated according to plans, specifications and AISC recommendations and delivered to the job site with connections attached, piece marked and ready for erection. Labor includes time to unload and handle the steel, erect and plumb, install permanent bolts, weld and all other work usually associated with erecting the steel, including field touch-up painting. Equipment includes a 60 ton crawler mounted crane, plus an electric powered welding machine, an oxygen/acetylene welding and cutting torch, a diesel powered 100 CFM air compressor with pneumatic grinders, ratchet wrenches, hoses, and other tools usually associated with work of this type. Structural steel is usually estimated by the tons of steel in the project. Labor for erection will vary with the weight of steel per linear foot. For example, a member weighing 25 pounds per foot will require more manhours per ton than one weighing 60 pounds per foot.

Structural shapes Estimate the total weight of "bare" fabricated structural shapes and then add 15% to allow for the weight of connections.

	Craft@Hrs	Unit	Material	Labor	Equipment	Total
Beams, purlins, and girts						
Under 20 pounds per LF	H8@14.0	Ton	4,560.00	859.00	465.00	5,884.00
From 20 to 50 lbs per LF	H8@11.0	Ton	2,900.00	675.00	365.00	3,940.00
Over 50 to 75 lbs per LF	H8@9.40	Ton	2,780.00	577.00	312.00	3,669.00
Over 75 to 100 lbs per LF	H8@8.00	Ton	2,700.00	491.00	265.00	3,456.00
Columns						
From 1 to 3 lbs per LF	H8@48.0	Ton	6,370.00	2,950.00	1,590.00	10,910.00
Over 3 to 6 lbs per LF	H8@34.8	Ton	5,960.00	2,140.00	1,160.00	9,260.00
Under 20 pounds per LF	H8@12.0	Ton	4,220.00	736.00	399.00	5,355.00
From 20 to 50 lbs per LF	H8@10.0	Ton	2,780.00	614.00	332.00	3,726.00
Over 50 to 75 lbs per LF	H8@9.00	Ton	2,630.00	552.00	299.00	3,481.00
Over 75 to 100 lbs per LF	H8@7.00	Ton	2,630.00	430.00	233.00	3,293.00
Sag rods and X-type bracing						
Under 1 pound per LF	H8@82.1	Ton	6,900.00	5,040.00	2,730.00	14,670.00
Over 6 to 10 lbs per LF	H8@28.0	Ton	5,430.00	1,720.00	930.00	8,080.00
Trusses and girders						
Under 20 pounds per LF	H8@10.0	Ton	4,200.00	614.00	332.00	5,146.00
From 20 to 50 lbs per LF	H8@7.50	Ton	2,780.00	460.00	249.00	3,489.00
Over 50 to 75 lbs per LF	H8@6.00	Ton	2,630.00	368.00	199.00	3,197.00
Over 75 to 100 lbs per LF	H8@5.00	Ton	2,540.00	307.00	166.00	3,013.00

Structural Steel, Subcontract, by Square Foot of Floor Use these figures for preliminary estimates on buildings with 20,000 to 80,000 SF per story, 100 PSF live load and 14' to 16' story height. A "bay" is the center-to-center distance between columns. Costs assume steel averaging $2,550 per ton including installation labor and material and the subcontractor's overhead and profit. Include all area under the roof when calculating the total square footage.

	Craft@Hrs	Unit	Material	Labor	Equipment	Total
Single story						
20' x 20' bays (8 to 9 lbs per SF)	—	SF	—	—	—	20.80
30' x 30' bays (10 to 11 lbs per SF)	—	SF	—	—	—	25.50
40' x 40' bays (12 to 13 lbs per SF)	—	SF	—	—	—	30.50
Two story to six story						
20' x 20' bays (9 to 10 lbs per SF)	—	SF	—	—	—	23.30
30' x 30' bays (11 to 12 lbs per SF)	—	SF	—	—	—	28.00
40' x 40' bays (13 to 14 lbs per SF)	—	SF	—	—	—	33.00

Tubular Columns Rectangular, round, and square structural columns. When estimating total weight of columns, figure the column weight and add 30% to allow for a shop attached "U"-bracket on the top, a square base plate on the bottom and four anchor bolts. This should be sufficient for columns 15' to 20' in length. Equipment cost includes a 10 ton hydraulic truck-mounted crane plus an electric powered welding machine, an oxygen/acetylene welding

	Craft@Hrs	Unit	Material	Labor	Equipment	Total
and cutting torch, a diesel powered 100 CFM air compressor with pneumatic grinders, ratchet wrenches, hoses, and other tools usually associated with work of this type.						
Rectangular tube columns, in pounds per LF						
3" x 2" to 12" x 4", to 20 lbs per LF	H7@9.00	Ton	3,340.00	561.00	268.00	4,169.00
6" x 4" to 16" x 8", 21 to 50 lbs per LF	H7@8.00	Ton	2,690.00	498.00	238.00	3,426.00
12 " x 6" to 20" x 12", 51 to 75 lbs per LF	H7@6.00	Ton	2,640.00	374.00	179.00	3,193.00
14" x 10" to 20" x 12", 76 to 100 lbs/LF	H7@5.00	Ton	2,550.00	311.00	149.00	3,010.00
Round columns, in pounds per LF						
3" to 6" diameter pipe, to 20 lbs per LF	H7@9.00	Ton	3,550.00	561.00	257.00	4,368.00
4" to 12" pipe, 20 to 50 lbs per LF	H7@8.00	Ton	2,870.00	498.00	229.00	3,597.00
6" to 12" pipe, 51 to 75 lbs per LF	H7@6.00	Ton	2,760.00	374.00	171.00	3,305.00
Square tube columns, in pounds per LF						
2" x 2" to 8" x 8", to 20 lbs per LF	H7@9.00	Ton	3,230.00	561.00	257.00	4,048.00
4" x 4" to 12" x 12", 21 to 50 lbs per LF	H7@8.00	Ton	2,640.00	498.00	228.00	3,366.00
8" x 8" to 16" x 16", 51 to 75 lbs per LF	H7@6.00	Ton	2,560.00	374.00	171.00	3,105.00
10" x 10" to 16" x 16", 76 to 100 lbs/LF	H7@5.00	Ton	2,540.00	311.00	143.00	2,994.00
Add for concrete fill in columns, 3,000 PSI design pump mix, placed by pump						
(including 10% waste)	M2@.738	CY	162.00	33.30	6.55	201.85
Space Frame System 10,000 SF or more. Equipment cost shown is for a 15 ton truck crane and a 2 ton truck equipped for work of this type.						
5' module 4.5 lb live load	H5@.146	SF	21.10	7.95	2.51	31.56
4' module, add	H5@.025	SF	3.08	1.36	.43	4.87
Open Web Steel Joists Estimate the total weight of "bare" joists and then add 10% to allow for connections and accessories						
"CS" Series, 8CS2 thru 28CS4						
Under 10 lbs per LF	H8@10.0	Ton	2,030.00	614.00	332.00	2,976.00
Over 10 lbs per LF	H8@8.00	Ton	2,010.00	491.00	266.00	2,767.00
"K" Series, 8K1 thru 18K5						
Under 5 lbs per LF	H8@8.00	Ton	1,870.00	491.00	266.00	2,627.00
Over 5 to 10 lbs per LF	H8@7.00	Ton	1,830.00	430.00	233.00	2,493.00
Over 10 lbs per LF	H8@6.00	Ton	1,720.00	368.00	199.00	2,287.00
Steel Floor and Roof Decking These costs assume a 40,000 SF job not over six stories high. Weight and cost include 10% for waste and connections. Equipment cost shown is for a 15 ton truck crane and a 2 ton truck equipped for work of this type.						
Floor and roof decking, 1-1/2" standard rib, simple non-composite section, non-cellular, shop prime painted finish						
22 gauge, 2.1 lbs per SF	H5@.013	SF	1.95	.71	.22	2.88
20 gauge, 2.5 lbs per SF	H5@.013	SF	2.03	.71	.22	2.96
18 gauge, 3.3 lbs per SF	H5@.013	SF	2.56	.71	.22	3.49
16 gauge, 4.1 lbs per SF	H5@.013	SF	2.83	.71	.22	3.76
Add for galvanized finish	—	SF	.36	—	—	.36
Steel floor deck system. Consists of 18 gauge, 1-1/2" standard rib, shop prime painted steel decking, installed over a structural steel beam and girder support system (cost of support structure not included) covered with 3" thick 6.0 sack mix, 3,000 PSI lightweight ready-mix concrete, placed by pump, reinforced with 6" x 6", W1.4 x W1.4 welded wire mesh. Costs shown assume shoring is not required and include curing and finishing the concrete.						
18 gauge decking	H5@.013	SF	2.03	.71	.22	2.96
Welded wire mesh	RB@.004	SF	.25	.26	—	.51
Lightweight concrete	M2@.006	SF	1.76	.27	.10	2.13
Cure and finish concrete	P8@.011	SF	.22	.51	—	.73
Total floor deck system	**—@.034**	**SF**	**4.26**	**1.75**	**.32**	**6.33**
Add for 16 gauge decking	—	SF	.36	—	—	.36

	Craft@Hrs	Unit	Material	Labor	Equipment	Total
Steel roof deck system. Consists of 18 gauge, 1-1/2" standard rib, shop prime painted steel decking, installed over open web steel joists 4' OC (costs of joists not included) covered with 1-1/4" R-11.1 polystyrene insulation board overlaid with .045" loose laid membrane EPDM (ethylene propylene diene monomer) elastomeric roofing. Joist pricing assumes "H" or "J" Series at 9.45 lbs per LF spanning 20'0", spaced 4' OC.						
18 gauge decking	H5@.013	SF	2.45	.71	.22	3.38
Insulation board	A1@.011	SF	.75	.56	—	1.31
EPDM roofing	R3@.006	SF	1.90	.28	—	2.18
Total roof deck system	—@.030	SF	5.10	1.55	.22	6.87
Add for 16 gauge decking	—	SF	.37	—	—	.37
Add for open web steel joists	H5@.005	SF	.30	.27	.09	.66

	Craft@Hrs	Unit	Material	Labor	Total
Checkered-Steel Plate Shop fabricated and primed or galvanized after fabrication.					
Checkered steel floor plate,					
1/4", 11-1/4 lbs per SF, painted	IW@.025	SF	15.50	1.65	17.15
3/8", 16-1/2 lbs per SF, painted	IW@.025	SF	22.00	1.65	23.65
1/4", 11-1/4 lbs per SF, galvanized	IW@.025	SF	16.80	1.65	18.45
3/8", 16-1/2 lbs per SF, galvanized	IW@.025	SF	24.90	1.65	26.55
Checkered-steel trench cover plate with frame					
1/4", 11-1/4 lbs per SF, primed	IW@.045	SF	20.30	2.98	23.28
1/4", 11-1/4 lbs per SF, galvanized	IW@.045	SF	23.40	2.98	26.38
3/8", 16-1/2 lbs per SF, primed	IW@.045	SF	29.30	2.98	32.28
3/8", 16-1/2 lbs per SF, galvanized	IW@.045	SF	35.50	2.98	38.48

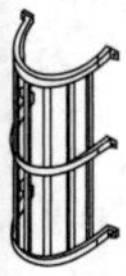

	Craft@Hrs	Unit	Material	Labor	Equipment	Total
Spiral Stairways Cost per riser based on a 6" diameter round tubular steel center column, 12 gauge steel pan type 10" treads with 7-1/2" open risers and 2" x 2" tubular steel handrail with 1" x 1" tubular steel posts at each riser. Shop fabricated and primed. Add for railings at top of stairways as required.						
4'0" diameter	H7@.551	Ea	423.00	34.30	4.31	461.61
6'0" diameter	H7@.551	Ea	577.00	34.30	4.31	615.61
8'0" diameter	H7@.551	Ea	732.00	34.30	4.31	770.61
Spiral stairs, 5' diameter. Steel, tubular handrail, composition board treads, prefabricated, shipped unassembled.						
86" to 95" with 10 risers	C8@9.98	Ea	1,580.00	470.00	—	2,050.00
95" to 105" with 11 risers	C8@10.7	Ea	1,760.00	504.00	—	2,264.00
105" to 114" with 12 risers	C8@11.3	Ea	1,870.00	533.00	—	2,403.00
114" to 124" with 13 risers	C8@12.0	Ea	2,090.00	566.00	—	2,656.00
124" to 133" with 14 risers	C8@12.7	Ea	2,370.00	599.00	—	2,969.00
Add for 6' diameter	—	%	24.0	—	—	—
Add for oak treads	—	%	25.0	—	—	—
Add for oak handrail	—	%	45.0	—	—	—
Straight Stairways Cost per LF based on sloping length. Rule of thumb: the sloping length of stairways is the vertical rise times 1.6. Costs assume standard "C"-shape structural steel channels for stringers, 12 gauge steel pan 10" treads with 7-1/2" closed risers. Posts are 2" diameter tubular steel, 5' OC. Handrails are 3'6" high, 1-1/2" diameter 2-rail type, on both sides of the stairs. Installation assumes stairs and landings are attached to an existing structure on two sides.						
3'0" wide	H7@.469	LF	230.00	29.20	13.40	272.60
4'0" wide	H7@.630	LF	307.00	39.20	18.00	361.20
5'0" wide	H7@.781	LF	386.00	48.60	22.30	456.90
Ladders, vertical type. 1'6" wide, shop fabricated,						
Without safety cage	H7@.300	LF	43.10	18.70	8.57	70.37
With steel safety cage	H7@.550	LF	66.10	34.30	15.72	116.12
Add for galvanized finish	—	LF	5.04	—	—	5.04
Landings. Costs assume standard "C"-shape structural steel channels for joists and frame, 10 gauge steel pan deck areas, shop prime painted. Add for support legs from Structural Steel Section.						
Cost per square foot	H7@.250	SF	122.00	15.60	7.14	144.74
Add for galvanized finish	—	SF	17.80	—	—	17.80

	Craft@Hrs	Unit	Material	Labor	Equipment	Total
Railings, Aluminum, Brass and Wrought Iron						
Aluminum railings. 3'6" high with two 1-1/2" square horizontal rails top and bottom, 5/8" square vertical bars at 4" OC, and 1-1/2" square posts spaced 4' OC. Welded construction with standard mill finish.						
Installed on balconies	H6@.184	LF	32.60	9.88	—	42.48
Installed on stairways	H6@.230	LF	36.60	12.40	—	49.00
Add for anodized finish, bronze or black	—	LF	16.40	—	—	16.40
Brass railings. Round tubular type, bright finish, .050" wall commercial quality with supports at 3' OC attached to existing structure using brass screws. Labor includes layout, measure, cut and end preparation						
1-1/2" tubing	H6@.058	LF	15.00	3.12	—	18.12
2" tubing	H6@.058	LF	19.00	3.12	—	22.12
Fittings, slip-on type, no soldering or brazing required						
1-1/2" elbows	H6@.092	Ea	27.10	4.94	—	32.04
1-1/2" bracket	H6@.166	Ea	18.40	8.92	—	27.32
2" elbows	H6@.115	Ea	33.10	6.18	—	39.28
2" bracket	H6@.166	Ea	20.00	8.92	—	28.92
Splices						
1-1/2" splice	H6@.092	Ea	9.02	4.94	—	13.96
2" splice	H6@.115	Ea	17.20	6.18	—	23.38
Wrought iron railings. Standard 3'6" high, welded steel construction, shop prime painted, attached to existing structure						
Stock patterns	H6@.171	LF	19.40	9.19	—	28.59
Custom patterns	H6@.287	LF	29.00	15.40	—	44.40
Stairway handrails	H6@.343	LF	32.20	18.40	—	50.60

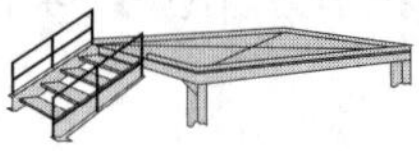

Steel Handrails, Kickplates, and Railings Material costs assume shop fabrication and assembly, prime painted and erection bolts. Equipment cost includes a 10-ton hydraulic truck-mounted crane, an electric powered welding machine, an oxygen/acetylene welding rig, a diesel powered 100 CFM air compressor and accessories.

	Craft@Hrs	Unit	Material	Labor	Equipment	Total
Handrails. Wall mounted, with brackets 5' OC, based on 12' lengths, welded steel, shop prime painted						
1-1/4" diameter rail	H7@.092	LF	11.30	5.73	2.63	19.66
1-1/2" diameter rail	H7@.102	LF	12.40	6.35	2.91	21.66
Add for galvanized finish	—	LF	1.82	—	—	1.82
Kickplates, 1/4" thick flat steel plate, shop prime painted, attached to steel railings, stairways or landings						
4" high	H7@.058	LF	7.00	3.61	1.66	12.27
6" high	H7@.069	LF	7.59	4.30	1.97	13.86
Add for galvanized finish	—	LF	1.36	—	—	1.36
Pipe and chain railings. Welded steel pipe posts with U-brackets attached to accept 1/4" chain, shop prime painted. Installed in existing embedded sleeves. Posts are 5'0" long (1'6" in the sleeve and 3'6" above grade). Usual spacing is 4' OC. Add chain per lineal foot						
1-1/4" diameter post	H7@.287	Ea	15.50	17.90	—	33.40
1-1/2" diameter post	H7@.287	Ea	19.20	17.90	—	37.10
2" diameter post	H7@.343	Ea	25.60	21.40	—	47.00
3" diameter post	H7@.343	Ea	50.60	21.40	—	72.00
Add for galvanized finish	—	Ea	6.46	—	—	6.46
Chain, 1/4" diameter galvanized	H7@.058	LF	5.15	3.61	—	8.76
Railings. Floor mounted, 3'6" high with posts 5' OC, based on 12' length, welded steel, shop prime painted						
1-1/4" diameter rails and posts						
2-rail type	H7@.115	LF	43.30	7.16	3.29	53.26
3-rail type	H7@.125	LF	64.90	7.79	3.57	76.26
1-1/2" diameter rails and posts						
2-rail type	H7@.125	LF	45.40	7.79	3.57	56.86
3-rail type	H7@.137	LF	68.90	8.53	3.91	81.34
Add for galvanized finish	—	LF	16.10	—	—	16.10

	Craft@Hrs	Unit	Material	Labor	Total
Fabricated metals					
Catch basin grating and frame					
24" x 24", standard duty	CL@8.68	Ea	407.00	358.00	765.00
Manhole rings with cover					
24", 330 lbs	CL@6.80	Ea	394.00	281.00	675.00
30", 400 lbs	CL@6.80	Ea	407.00	281.00	688.00
38", 730 lbs	CL@6.80	Ea	1,130.00	281.00	1,411.00
Welded steel grating Weight shown is approximate. Costs shown are per square foot of grating, shop prime painted or galvanized after fabrication as shown					
Grating bars as shown, 1/2" cross bars at 4" OC					
1-1/4" x 3/16" at 1-1/4" OC, 9 lbs per SF, painted	IW@.019	SF	8.92	1.26	10.18
1-1/4" x 3/16" at 1-1/4" OC, 9 lbs per SF, galvanized	IW@.019	SF	11.10	1.26	12.36
Add for banding on edges	—	LF	4.67	—	4.67
2" x 1/4" at 1-1/4" OC, 18.7 lbs per SF, painted	IW@.026	SF	21.00	1.72	22.72
2" x 1/4" at 1-1/4" OC, 18.7 lbs per SF, galvanized	IW@.026	SF	28.30	1.72	30.02
Add for banding on edges	—	LF	6.95	—	6.95
Add for toe-plates, steel, shop prime painted					
1/4" thick x 4" high attached after grating is in place	IW@.048	LF	8.97	3.18	12.15
Steel fabrications					
Canopy framing, steel	IW@.009	Lb	1.43	.60	2.03
Miscellaneous supports, steel	IW@.019	Lb	2.37	1.26	3.63
Miscellaneous supports, aluminum	IW@.061	Lb	15.30	4.04	19.34
Embedded steel (embedded in concrete)					
Light, to 20 lbs per LF	T3@.042	Lb	3.03	2.24	5.27
Medium, over 20 to 50 lbs per LF	T3@.035	Lb	2.61	1.86	4.47
Heavy, over 50 lbs per LF	T3@.025	Lb	2.20	1.33	3.53
Channel sill, 1/8" steel, 1-1/2" x 8" wide	T3@.131	LF	22.60	6.97	29.57
Angle sill, 1/8" steel, 1-1/2" x 1-1/2"	T3@.095	LF	7.16	5.06	12.22
Fire escapes, ladder and balcony, per floor	IW@16.5	Ea	2,690.00	1,090.00	3,780.00
Grey iron foundry items	T3@.014	Lb	1.32	.75	2.07
Stair nosing, 2-1/2" x 2-1/2", set in concrete	T3@.139	LF	11.30	7.40	18.70
Cast iron					
Lightweight sections	T3@.012	Lb	1.28	.64	1.92
Heavy section	T3@.010	Lb	1.03	.53	1.56
Cast column bases					
Iron, 16" x 16", custom	T3@.759	Ea	112.00	40.40	152.40
Iron, 32" x 32", custom	T3@1.54	Ea	468.00	82.00	550.00
Aluminum, 8" column, stock	T3@.245	Ea	25.60	13.00	38.60
Aluminum, 10" column, stock	T3@.245	Ea	32.20	13.00	45.20
Wheel type corner guards, per LF of height	T3@.502	LF	80.80	26.70	107.50
Angle corner guards, with anchors	T3@.018	Lb	2.40	.96	3.36
Channel door frames, with anchors	T3@.012	Lb	2.22	.64	2.86
Steel lintels, painted	T3@.013	Lb	1.35	.69	2.04
Steel lintels, galvanized	T3@.013	Lb	1.77	.69	2.46
Anodizing Add to cost of fabrication					
Aluminum	—	%	15.0	—	—
Bronze	—	%	30.0	—	—
Black	—	%	50.0	—	—
Galvanizing, add to cost of fabrication	—	Lb	.71	—	.71

	Craft@Hrs	Unit	Material	Labor	Total
Ornamental Metal					
Ornamental screens, aluminum	H6@.135	SF	43.20	7.25	50.45
Ornamental screens extruded metal	H6@.151	SF	36.20	8.11	44.31
Gates, wrought iron, 6' x 7', typical installed cost	—	Ea	—	—	1,640.00
Sun screens, aluminum stock design, manual	H6@.075	SF	46.50	4.03	50.53
Sun screens, aluminum stock design, motorized	H6@.102	SF	84.60	5.48	90.08
Aluminum work, general fabrication	H6@.160	Lb	23.10	8.60	31.70
Brass and bronze work, general fabrication	H6@.079	Lb	33.50	4.24	37.74
Stainless steel, general fabrication	H6@.152	Lb	27.10	8.17	35.27
Security Gratings					
Door grating, 1" tool steel vertical bars at 4" OC, 3/8" x 2-1/4" steel frame and horizontal bars at 18" OC,					
3' x 7' overall	H6@10.5	Ea	2,030.00	564.00	2,594.00
Add for butt hinges and locks, per door	H6@2.67	Ea	623.00	143.00	766.00
Add for field painting, per door	H6@1.15	Ea	9.46	61.80	71.26
Window grating, tool steel vertical bars at 4" OC, 3/8" x 2-1/4" steel frame, horizontal bars 6" OC,					
20" x 30" overall set with 1/2" bolts at 6" OC	H6@3.21	Ea	272.00	172.00	444.00
Louver vent grating, 1" x 3/16", "I" bearing bars 1-3/16" OC with 3/16" spaced bars 4" OC and banded ends,					
set with 1/2" bolts at 1" OC, prime painted	H6@.114	SF	33.30	6.12	39.42
Steel plate window covers, hinged, 3/8" plate steel, 32" W x 48" H overall, 10 lbs per SF,					
including hardware	H6@.150	SF	15.20	8.06	23.26

Steel fabrication on site These costs are for work at the job site and assume engineering and design, including detail drawings sufficient to do the work, have been prepared by others at no cost to the installing contractor. Costs are based on ASTM A36 all-purpose carbon steel, which is widely used in building construction. Equipment cost includes a 1-1/4-ton flatbed truck equipped with a diesel powered welding machine, an oxygen/acetylene welding and cutting torch, a diesel powered 100 CFM air compressor with pneumatic grinders, ratchet wrenches, hoses and hand tools appropriate for this type of work. Material cost for the steel is not included.

	Craft@Hrs	Unit	Material	Labor	Equipment	Total
Flat plate, cutting and drilling holes						
Flame cutting. Labor shown includes layout, marking, cutting and grinding of finished cut						
Square cut, thickness of plate as shown						
1/4", 5/16" or 3/8"	IW@.020	LF	—	1.32	1.10	2.42
1/2", 5/8" or 3/4"	IW@.025	LF	—	1.65	1.38	3.03
7/8", 1" or 1-1/4"	IW@.030	LF	—	1.99	1.66	3.65
Bevel cut 30 to 45 degrees, thickness of plate as shown						
1/4", 5/16" or 3/8"	IW@.030	LF	—	1.99	1.66	3.65
1/2", 5/8" or 3/4"	IW@.035	LF	—	2.32	1.93	4.25
7/8", 1" or 1-1/4"	IW@.043	LF	—	2.85	2.38	5.23
Drill holes. Using a hand-held drill motor. Labor shown includes layout, drill and ream holes with plate thickness and hole size as shown (note: hole size is usually 1/16" greater than bolt diameter)						
1/4", 5/16" or 3/8" plate thickness,						
5/16", 3/8" or 1/2" hole	IW@.084	Ea	—	5.56	4.64	10.20
1/2", 5/8" or 3/4" plate thickness,						
9/16", 3/4" or 13/16" hole	IW@.134	Ea	—	8.87	7.40	16.27
7/8", 1" or 1-1/4" plate thickness,						
1", 1-1/16" or 1-5/16" hole	IW@.200	Ea	—	13.20	11.10	24.30

05 Metals

	Craft@Hrs	Unit	Material	Labor	Equipment	Total
Welding Using manual inert gas shielded arc electric welding and coated electrodes (rods) of the appropriate size and type. Equipment is an electric welding machine with amperage suitable for the welding rod being used. Labor includes layout, fit-up and weld.						
Fillet welds for attaching base plates, clip angles, gussets. Welding in flat position						
Size of continuous fillet weld						
3/16"	IW@.300	LF	—	19.90	16.60	36.50
1/4"	IW@.400	LF	—	26.50	22.10	48.60
3/8"	IW@.585	LF	—	38.70	32.30	71.00
1/2"	IW@.810	LF	—	53.60	44.70	98.30
5/8"	IW@1.00	LF	—	66.20	55.20	121.40
3/4"	IW@1.20	LF	—	79.40	66.30	145.70
Buttweld joints, 100% penetration, flat plates						
Thickness at joint						
3/16"	IW@.200	LF	—	13.20	11.10	24.30
1/4"	IW@.250	LF	—	16.50	13.80	30.30
3/8"	IW@.440	LF	—	29.10	24.30	53.40
1/2"	IW@.660	LF	—	43.70	36.50	80.20
5/8"	IW@.825	LF	—	54.60	45.60	100.20
3/4"	IW@1.05	LF	—	69.50	58.00	127.50

06 Wood and Composites

	Craft@Hrs	Unit	Material	Labor	Total
Rough Carpentry Industrial and commercial work. Costs include 10% waste. Using standard and better dimension lumber at the following prices:					
2" x 4"	—	MBF	777.00	—	777.00
2" x 6"	—	MBF	759.00	—	759.00
2" x 8"	—	MBF	776.00	—	776.00
2" x 10"	—	MBF	794.00	—	794.00
2" x 12"	—	MBF	881.00	—	881.00
4" x 4"	—	MBF	950.00	—	950.00
4" x 6"	—	MBF	918.00	—	918.00
4" x 8"	—	MBF	838.00	—	838.00
4" x 10"	—	MBF	967.00	—	967.00
4" x 12"	—	MBF	869.00	—	869.00
6" x 6"	—	MBF	1,680.00	—	1,680.00
6" x 8"	—	MBF	1,700.00	—	1,700.00
6" x 10"	—	MBF	1,710.00	—	1,710.00
6" x 12"	—	MBF	1,730.00	—	1,730.00
Add for ACQ treatment	—	MBF	280.00	—	280.00
Stud walls, including plates, blocking, headers and diagonal bracing, per SF of wall, 16" OC					
2" x 4", 8' high, 1.1 BF per SF	C8@.021	SF	.94	.99	1.93
2" x 4", 10' high, 1.0 BF per SF	C8@.021	SF	.85	.99	1.84
2" x 6", 8' high, 1.6 BF per SF	C8@.031	SF	1.34	1.46	2.80
2" x 6", 10' high, 1.5 BF per SF	C8@.030	SF	1.25	1.41	2.66
12" OC, 2" x 6", 8' high, 2.0 BF per SF	C8@.037	SF	1.67	1.74	3.41
8" OC, 2" x 4", staggered on 2" x 6" plates, 1.8 BF per SF	C8@.034	SF	1.54	1.60	3.14
Pier caps, .60 ACQ treated					
2" x 6"	C8@.024	LF	1.03	1.13	2.16
Mud sills, treated material, add bolts or fastener					
Bolted, 2" x 4"	C8@.023	LF	1.05	1.08	2.13
Bolted, 2" x 6"	C8@.024	LF	1.03	1.13	2.16
Shot, 2" x 4"	C8@.018	LF	1.22	.85	2.07
Shot, 2" x 6"	C8@.020	LF	1.03	.94	1.97

	Craft@Hrs	Unit	Material	Labor	Total
Plates (add for .60 ACQ treatment if required)					
2" x 4"	C8@.013	LF	.57	.61	1.18
2" x 6"	C8@.016	LF	.83	.75	1.58
Posts, #1 structural					
4" x 4"	C8@.110	LF	1.39	5.19	6.58
6" x 6"	C8@.145	LF	5.54	6.84	12.38
Headers, 4" x 12"	C8@.067	LF	3.82	3.16	6.98
Blocking and nailers, 2" x 6"	C8@.034	LF	.83	1.60	2.43
Blocking, solid diagonal bracing, 2" x 4"	C8@.023	LF	.57	1.08	1.65
Beams and girders, #2 & better					
4" x 8" to 4" x 12"	C8@.094	LF	4.24	4.43	8.67
6" x 8" to 6" x 12"	C8@.115	LF	11.10	5.42	16.52
Ceiling joists and blocking, including rim joists, per LF of joist					
2" x 6"	C8@.028	LF	.83	1.32	2.15
2" x 8"	C8@.037	LF	1.14	1.74	2.88
2" x 10"	C8@.046	LF	1.45	2.17	3.62
2" x 12"	C8@.057	LF	1.94	2.69	4.63
Floor joists and blocking including rim joists and 6% waste, per LF of joist					
2" x 6", 1.06 BF per LF	C8@.017	LF	.83	.80	1.63
2" x 8", 1.41 BF per LF	C8@.018	LF	1.14	.85	1.99
2" x 10", 1.77 BF per LF	C8@.019	LF	1.45	.90	2.35
2" x 12", 2.12 BF per LF	C8@.021	LF	1.94	.99	2.93
Purlins, struts, ridge boards					
4" x 10"	C8@.050	LF	3.54	2.36	5.90
4" x 12"	C8@.055	LF	3.82	2.59	6.41
6" x 10"	C8@.066	LF	9.23	3.11	12.34
6" x 12"	C8@.066	LF	11.10	3.11	14.21
Rafters and outriggers, to 4 in 12 pitch					
2" x 4" to 2" x 8"	C8@.033	LF	1.14	1.56	2.70
2" x 10" to 2" x 12"	C8@.036	LF	1.94	1.70	3.64
Add for over 4 in 12 pitch roof	—	%	—	30.0	—

Sills and Ledgers Bolted to Concrete or Masonry Walls Costs are per linear foot of Standard and Better pressure treated sill or ledger with anchor bolt holes drilled each 2'6" center. Labor costs include handling, measuring, cutting to length and drilling holes at floor level and installation working on a scaffold 10' to 20' above floor level. Figures in parentheses show the board feet per linear foot of sill or ledger. Costs shown include 5% waste. For scheduling purposes, estimate that a crew of 2 can install 150 to 200 LF of sills with a single row of anchor bolts in an 8-hour day when working from scaffolds. Estimate that a crew of 2 can install 150 to 175 LF of ledgers with a single row of anchor bolt holes or 50 to 60 LF of ledgers with a double row of anchor bolt holes in an 8-hour day working from scaffolds. Add the cost of anchor bolts and scaffold, if required.

	Craft@Hrs	Unit	Material	Labor	Total
Sills with a single row of anchor bolt holes					
2" x 4" (0.70 BF per LF)	C8@.040	LF	.81	1.89	2.70
2" x 6" (1.05 BF per LF)	C8@.040	LF	1.07	1.89	2.96
2" x 8" (1.40 BF per LF)	C8@.040	LF	1.36	1.89	3.25
2" x 10" (1.75 BF per LF)	C8@.040	LF	1.92	1.89	3.81
2" x 12" (2.10 BF per LF)	C8@.040	LF	2.58	1.89	4.47
4" x 6" (2.10 BF per LF)	C8@.051	LF	2.79	2.40	5.19
4" x 8" (2.80 BF per LF)	C8@.051	LF	3.63	2.40	6.03
4" x 10" (3.33 BF per LF)	C8@.059	LF	4.42	2.78	7.20
4" x 12" (4.20 BF per LF)	C8@.059	LF	5.84	2.78	8.62

	Craft@Hrs	Unit	Material	Labor	Total
Ledgers with a single row of anchor bolt holes					
2" x 4" (0.70 BF per LF)	C8@.059	LF	.81	2.78	3.59
4" x 6" (2.10 BF per LF)	C8@.079	LF	2.79	3.72	6.51
4" x 8" (2.80 BF per LF)	C8@.079	LF	3.63	3.72	7.35
Ledgers with a double row of anchor bolt holes					
4" x 4" (1.40 BF per LF)	C8@.120	LF	1.76	5.66	7.42
4" x 6" (2.10 BF per LF)	C8@.160	LF	2.79	7.54	10.33
4" x 8" (2.80 BF per LF)	C8@.160	LF	3.63	7.54	11.17
4" x 12" (4.20 BF per LF)	C8@.250	LF	5.84	11.80	17.64
Sheathing Includes nails and normal waste					
Floors, hand nailed, underlayment C-D Grade plywood					
1/2"	C8@.012	SF	.76	.57	1.33
5/8"	C8@.012	SF	.77	.57	1.34
3/4"	C8@.013	SF	.89	.61	1.50
Floors, machine nailed OSB					
7/16" x 4' x 8'	C8@.009	SF	.40	.42	.82
7/16" x 4' x 9'	C8@.009	SF	.58	.42	1.00
7/16" x 4' x 10'	C8@.009	SF	.51	.42	.93
15/32" 4' x 8'	C8@.009	SF	.45	.42	.87
1/2" x 4' x 8'	C8@.009	SF	.45	.42	.87
5/8" x 4' x 8'	C8@.010	SF	.58	.47	1.05
5/8" x 4' x 8', tongue and groove	C8@.010	SF	.80	.47	1.27
23/32" x 4' x 8'	C8@.010	SF	.95	.47	1.42
23/32" 4' x 8' subfloor	C8@.010	SF	.84	.47	1.31
3/4" x 4' x 8', tongue and groove	C8@.011	SF	.71	.52	1.23
1-1/8" x 4' x 8', tongue and groove	C8@.015	SF	2.04	.71	2.75
15/32" x 4' x 8', hibor treated	C8@.011	SF	.85	.52	1.37
Walls, B-D sanded, standard, Interior Grade plywood					
1/4"	C8@.015	SF	.83	.71	1.54
3/8"	C8@.015	SF	.82	.71	1.53
1/2"	C8@.016	SF	1.06	.75	1.81
5/8"	C8@.018	SF	1.00	.85	1.85
3/4"	C8@.018	SF	1.13	.85	1.98
5/8" fire retardant, A-B, screwed to metal frame	C8@.026	SF	.80	1.23	2.03
Walls, Exterior Grade C-D plywood					
1/2"	C8@.016	SF	.76	.75	1.51
5/8"	C8@.018	SF	.77	.85	1.62
3/4"	C8@.020	SF	.89	.94	1.83
3/8" rough sawn T-1-11	C8@.018	SF	.91	.85	1.76
5/8" rough sawn T-1-11	C8@.018	SF	1.19	.85	2.04
5/8" rough sawn RBB	C8@.018	SF	1.19	.85	2.04
Walls, OSB					
11/32" or 3/8" x 4' x 8'	C8@.013	SF	.43	.61	1.04
7/16" x 4' x 8'	C8@.015	SF	.40	.71	1.11
7/16" x 4' x 9'	C8@.015	SF	.58	.71	1.29
7/16" x 4' x 10'	C8@.015	SF	.51	.71	1.22
15/32" 4' x 8'	C8@.015	SF	.45	.71	1.16
1/2" x 4' x 8'	C8@.018	SF	.45	.85	1.30
5/8" x 4' x 8'	C8@.018	SF	.58	.85	1.43
5/8" x 4' x 8', tongue and groove	C8@.018	SF	.80	.85	1.65
23/32" x 4' x 8'	C8@.020	SF	.95	.94	1.89
15/32" x 4' x 10', Structural 1	C8@.020	SF	.71	.94	1.65
Add for nailing shear walls	—	%	—	20.0	—

	Craft@Hrs	Unit	Material	Labor	Total
Roofs, C-D Exterior plywood, machine nailed					
3/8"	C8@.009	SF	.46	.42	.88
1/2"	C8@.009	SF	.76	.42	1.18
5/8"	C8@.009	SF	.77	.42	1.19
3/4"	C8@.011	SF	.89	.52	1.41
Roofs, OSB, machine nailed					
11/32" or 3/8" x 4' x 8'	C8@.009	SF	.43	.42	.85
7/16" x 4' x 8'	C8@.009	SF	.40	.42	.82
7/16" x 4' x 9'	C8@.009	SF	.58	.42	1.00
7/16" x 4' x 10'	C8@.009	SF	.51	.42	.93
15/32" 4' x 8'	C8@.009	SF	.45	.42	.87
1/2" x 4' x 8'	C8@.009	SF	.45	.42	.87
5/8" x 4' x 8'	C8@.010	SF	.58	.47	1.05
5/8" x 4' x 8', tongue and groove	C8@.010	SF	.80	.47	1.27
23/32" x 4' x 8'	C8@.010	SF	.95	.47	1.42
3/4" x 4' x 8', tongue and groove	C8@.011	SF	.71	.52	1.23
Blocking for panel joints,					
2" x 4"	C8@.010	LF	.57	.47	1.04
Lumber floor sheathing					
Diagonal, 1" x 6" Standard and Better					
1.14 BF per SF	C8@.018	SF	2.47	.85	3.32
Straight 2" x 6" Commercial Grade T&G fir					
2.28 BF per SF	C8@.032	SF	1.73	1.51	3.24
Straight 2" x 6" Commercial Grade T&G cedar					
2.28 BF per SF	C8@.032	SF	7.42	1.51	8.93
Timber deck, Southern Pine, 5/4" x 6", Premium Grade					
1.25 BF per SF	C8@.012	SF	4.25	.57	4.82
Lumber wall sheathing, diagonal, 1" x 6"					
Standard and Better, 1.14 BF per SF	C8@.024	SF	3.34	1.13	4.47
Lumber roof sheathing, diagonal, 1" x 6"					
Standard and Better, 1.14 BF per SF	C8@.018	SF	3.34	.85	4.19

Panelized Wood Roof Systems The costs shown will apply on 20,000 to 30,000 SF jobs where roof panels are fabricated near the point of installation and moved into place with a forklift. Costs will be higher on smaller jobs and jobs with poor access. 4' x 8' and 4' x 10' roof panels are made of plywood or OSB nailed to 2" x 4" or 2" x 6" stiffeners spaced 24" on centers and running the long dimension of the panel. Based on fabricated panels lifted by forklift (with metal hangers attached) and nailed to 4" x 12" or 4" x 14" roof purlins spaced 8' on center. Equipment cost is for a 4-ton forklift (40' lift), a truck with hand tools, a gas powered air compressor with air hoses and two pneumatic-operated nailing guns. Costs are per 1,000 square feet (MSF) of roof surface and do not include roof supports except as noted.

	Craft@Hrs	Unit	Material	Labor	Equipment	Total
For scheduling purposes, estimate that a crew of 5 can fabricate 6,000 to 6,400 SF of 4' x 8' or 4' x 10' panels in an 8-hour day. Estimate that the same crew of 5 can install and nail down 7,600 to 8,000 SF of panels in an 8-hour day. Based on the following material costs:						
2" x 4" stiffeners	—	MBF	777.00	—	—	777.00
2" x 6" stiffeners	—	MBF	759.00	—	—	759.00
Purlins	—	MBF	869.00	—	—	869.00
1/2" CDX plywood	—	MSF	726.00	—	—	726.00
1/2" OSB sheathing	—	MSF	530.00	—	—	530.00

	Craft@Hrs	Unit	Material	Labor	Equipment	Total
4' x 8' roof panels						
With 1/2" CDX structural #1 plywood attached to 2" x 4" Construction Grade fir stiffeners						
Panels fabricated, ready to install	F6@6.60	MSF	1,160.00	324.00	104.00	1,588.00
Equipment & labor						
to install and nail panels	F6@5.21	MSF	—	256.00	81.70	337.70
Total installed cost, 4' x 8' panels	**F6@11.8**	**MSF**	**1,160.00**	**580.00**	**185.70**	**1,925.70**
With 1/2" OSB structural sheathing attached to 2" x 4" Construction Grade fir stiffeners						
Panels fabricated, ready to install	F6@6.60	MSF	949.00	324.00	104.00	1,377.00
Equipment & labor						
to install and nail panels	F6@5.21	MSF	—	256.00	81.70	337.70
Total installed cost, 4' x 8' panels	**F6@11.8**	**MSF**	**949.00**	**580.00**	**185.70**	**1,714.70**
4' x 10' roof panels						
With 1/2" CDX structural #1 plywood attached to 2" x 6" Construction Grade fir stiffeners						
Panels fabricated, ready to install	F6@6.20	MSF	1,320.00	305.00	97.30	1,722.30
Equipment & labor						
to install and nail panels	F6@4.90	MSF	—	241.00	77.00	318.00
Total installed cost, 4' x 10' panels	**F6@11.1**	**MSF**	**1,320.00**	**546.00**	**174.30**	**2,040.30**
With 1/2" OSB structural sheathing attached to 2" x 6" Construction Grade fir stiffeners						
Panels fabricated, ready to install	F6@6.20	MSF	1,110.00	305.00	97.60	1,512.60
Equipment & labor						
to install and nail panels	F6@4.90	MSF	—	241.00	77.00	318.00
Total installed cost, 4' x 10' panels	**F6@11.1**	**MSF**	**1,110.00**	**546.00**	**174.60**	**1,830.60**

8' x 20' and 8' x 32' roof panels

These panels can be fabricated on site using the same crew and equipment as shown in the preceding section. However, the stiffeners run across the short dimension of the panel and one purlin is attached to the outside edge of the long dimension of each panel before lifting into place. Figures below include the cost of purlins but not supporting beams. For scheduling purposes, estimate that a crew of 5 can fabricate 6,400 to 7,000 SF of 8' x 20' or 8' x 32' panels in an 8-hour day. Estimate that the same crew of 5 can install and nail down 10,000 to 11,000 SF of panels in an 8-hour day.

	Craft@Hrs	Unit	Material	Labor	Equipment	Total
8' x 20' roof panels with purlins attached						
4' x 10' x 1/2" CDX structural #1 plywood attached to 2" x 4" Const. Grade fir stiffeners and 4" x 12" #1 Grade fir purlins						
Panels fabricated, ready to install	F6@6.23	MSF	2,060.00	306.00	97.60	2,463.60
Equipment & labor						
to install and nail panels	F6@3.96	MSF	—	195.00	62.10	257.10
Total installed cost, 8' x 20' panels	**F6@10.2**	**MSF**	**2,060.00**	**501.00**	**159.70**	**2,720.70**
8' x 20' x 1/2" OSB structural sheathing attached to 2" x 4" Const. Grade fir stiffeners and 4" x 12" #1 Grade fir purlins						
Panels fabricated, ready to install	F6@6.23	MSF	1,850.00	306.00	97.60	2,253.60
Equipment & labor						
to install and nail panels	F6@3.96	MSF	—	195.00	62.10	257.10
Total installed cost, 8' x 20' panels	**F6@10.2**	**MSF**	**1,850.00**	**501.00**	**157.70**	**2,508.70**
8' x 32' panel with purlins attached						
4' x 8' x 1/2" CDX structural #1 plywood attached to 2" x 4" Const. Grade fir stiffeners and 4" x 12" #1 Grade fir purlins						
Panels fabricated, ready to install	F6@5.82	MSF	2,250.00	286.00	91.10	2,627.10
Equipment & labor						
to install and nail panels	F6@3.54	MSF	—	174.00	55.70	229.70
Total installed cost, 8' x 32' panels	**F6@9.36**	**MSF**	**2,250.00**	**460.00**	**146.80**	**2,856.80**
4' x 8' x 1/2" OSB structural sheathing attached to 2" x 4" Const. Grade fir stiffeners and 4" x 12" #1 Grade fir purlins						
Panels fabricated, ready to install	F6@5.82	MSF	2,040.00	286.00	91.10	2,417.10
Equipment & labor						
to install and nail panels	F6@3.54	MSF	—	174.00	55.70	229.70
Total installed cost, 8' x 32' panels	**F6@9.36**	**MSF**	**2,040.00**	**460.00**	**146.80**	**2,646.80**

	Craft@Hrs	Unit	Material	Labor	Equipment	Total
Adjust to any of the panel costs for 5/8" CDX #1 structural plywood, instead of 1/2" attached before						
panels are erected	—	MSF	271.00	—	—	271.00
Adjust to any of the panel costs for 15/32" OSB Structural I sheathing, instead of 1/2" attached before						
panels are erected	—	MSF	-101.00	—	—	-101.00
Add for roof hatch opening, includes reinforced opening and curb. Does not include roof hatch, see below						
2" x 4" roof system	F6@.055	SF	5.16	2.70	—	7.86
2" x 6" roof system	F6@.060	SF	6.70	2.95	—	9.65

Panelized Wood Wall Panels These costs will apply on jobs with 20,000 to 30,000 SF of wall panels. Panel material costs are for prefabricated panels purchased from a modular plant located within 50 miles of the job site. Costs will be higher on smaller jobs and on jobs with poor access. Costs assume wall panels are fabricated according to job plans and specifications, delivered piece-marked, ready to install and finish. Labor costs for installation of panels are listed at the end of this section and include unloading and handling, sorting, moving the panels into position using a forklift, installing and nailing. Maximum panel height is usually 12'. Equipment cost includes a forklift, hand tools, a portable air compressor with air hoses and two pneumatic-operated nailing guns. Costs are per square foot of wall, measured on one face. For scheduling purposes, estimate that a crew of 4 can place and fasten 3,500 to 4,500 SF of panels in an 8-hour day.

	Craft@Hrs	Unit	Material	Labor	Equipment	Total
2" x 4" studs 16" OC with gypsum wallboard on both sides						
1/2" wallboard	—	SF	1.77	—	—	1.77
5/8" wallboard	—	SF	1.76	—	—	1.76
2" x 4" studs 16" OC with gypsum wallboard inside and plywood or OSB outside						
1/2" wallboard and 1/2" CDX plywood	—	SF	2.08	—	—	2.08
1/2" wallboard and 1/2" OSB sheathing	—	SF	1.89	—	—	1.89
1/2" wallboard and 5/8" CDX plywood	—	SF	2.48	—	—	2.48
1/2" wallboard and 5/8" OSB sheathing	—	SF	1.90	—	—	1.90
5/8" wallboard and 1/2" CDX plywood	—	SF	2.08	—	—	2.08
5/8" wallboard and 1/2" OSB sheathing	—	SF	1.88	—	—	1.88
5/8" wallboard and 5/8" CDX plywood	—	SF	2.48	—	—	2.48
5/8" wallboard and 5/8" OSB sheathing	—	SF	1.90	—	—	1.90
2" x 6" studs 12" OC with gypsum wallboard on both sides						
1/2" wallboard	—	SF	2.08	—	—	2.08
5/8" wallboard	—	SF	2.08	—	—	2.08
2" x 6" studs 12" OC with gypsum wallboard inside and plywood or OSB outside						
1/2" wallboard and 1/2" CDX plywood	—	SF	2.81	—	—	2.81
1/2" wallboard and 1/2" OSB sheathing	—	SF	2.61	—	—	2.61
1/2" wallboard and 5/8" CDX plywood	—	SF	3.21	—	—	3.21
1/2" wallboard and 5/8" OSB sheathing	—	SF	2.63	—	—	2.63
5/8" wallboard and 1/2" CDX plywood	—	SF	2.81	—	—	2.81
5/8" wallboard and 1/2" OSB sheathing	—	SF	2.61	—	—	2.61
5/8" wallboard and 5/8" CDX plywood	—	SF	3.21	—	—	3.21
5/8" wallboard and 5/8" OSB sheathing	—	SF	2.63	—	—	2.63
2" x 6" studs 16" OC with gypsum wallboard on both sides						
1/2" wallboard	—	SF	1.75	—	—	1.75
5/8" wallboard	—	SF	1.75	—	—	1.75
2" x 6" studs 16" OC with gypsum wallboard inside and plywood or OSB outside						
1/2" wallboard and 1/2" CDX plywood	—	SF	2.48	—	—	2.48
1/2" wallboard and 1/2" OSB sheathing	—	SF	2.28	—	—	2.28
1/2" wallboard and 5/8" CDX plywood	—	SF	2.88	—	—	2.88
1/2" wallboard and 5/8" OSB sheathing	—	SF	2.30	—	—	2.30
5/8" wallboard and 1/2" CDX plywood	—	SF	2.47	—	—	2.47
5/8" wallboard and 1/2" OSB sheathing	—	SF	2.28	—	—	2.28
5/8" wallboard and 5/8" CDX plywood	—	SF	2.87	—	—	2.87
5/8" wallboard and 5/8" OSB sheathing	—	SF	2.30	—	—	2.30

	Craft@Hrs	Unit	Material	Labor	Equipment	Total
Add to any of the above for the following, installed by panel fabricator:						
R-19 insulation	—	SF	1.47	—	—	1.47
R-13 insulation	—	SF	1.07	—	—	1.07
Vapor barrier	—	SF	.16	—	—	.16
Door or window openings to 16 SF each	—	SF	2.21	—	—	2.21
Door or window openings over 16 SF each	—	SF	2.01	—	—	2.01
Electrical receptacles	—	Ea	78.50	—	—	78.50
Electrical switches	—	Ea	81.20	—	—	81.20
Labor and equipment cost to install panels						
Up to 8' high	F7@.003	SF	—	.15	.04	.19
Over 8' to 12' high	F7@.004	SF	—	.20	.06	.26

	Craft@Hrs	Unit	Material	Labor	Total
Miscellaneous Rough Carpentry					
Furring, Utility Grade, unit costs incl. 5% allowance for waste and nails					
2" x 4" on masonry walls	C8@.024	LF	.54	1.13	1.67
1" x 4" machine nailed to ceiling	C8@.017	LF	.71	.80	1.51
1" x 4" nailed on concrete	C8@.016	LF	.71	.75	1.46
Skip sheathing, on roof rafters, machine nailed, #2 and Better, unit costs incl. 7% allowance for waste & nails					
1" x 6" at 9" centers (.67 BF per SF) Per SF of roof area	C8@.020	SF	1.55	.94	2.49
1" x 4" at 7" centers (.50 BF per SF) Per SF of roof area	C8@.030	SF	1.08	1.41	2.49
Particleboard, 4' x 8', used as underlayment, including 5% cutting waste.					
3/8" x 4' x 8' sheets	C8@.011	SF	.35	.52	.87
1/2" x 4' x 8' sheets	C8@.011	SF	.45	.52	.97
5/8" x 4' x 8' sheets	C8@.011	SF	.54	.52	1.06
3/4" x 4' x 8' sheets	C8@.011	SF	.66	.52	1.18
Add for attaching to metal frame	C8@.005	SF	—	.24	.24
15 pound felt on walls	C8@.003	SF	.06	.14	.20
Super Jumbo Tex asphalt saturated Kraft (162 SF roll)	C8@.004	SF	.11	.19	.30

Wood Trusses Material costs are for prefabricated wood trusses shipped to job site fully assembled ready for installation. Equipment is a 6,000 lb capacity fork lift. Labor includes unloading and handling and installing the trusses not over 20' above grade.

	Craft@Hrs	Unit	Material	Labor	Equipment	Total
Truss joists, TJI Type at 50 PSF load design, at 16" OC						
9-1/2" TJI/15	C8@.017	SF	3.11	.80	.43	4.34
11-7/8" TJI/15	C8@.017	SF	3.41	.80	.43	4.64
14" TJI/35	C8@.018	SF	4.80	.85	.46	6.11
16" TJI/35	C8@.018	SF	5.23	.85	.46	6.54
Add for job under 3,000 SF	C8@.004	SF	.83	.19	.10	1.12

Roof trusses, 24" OC, any slope from 3 in 12 to 12 in 12, total height not to exceed 12' high from bottom chord to highest point on truss. Prices for trusses over 12' high will be up to 100% higher. Square foot (SF) costs, where shown, are per square foot of roof area to be covered.

	Craft@Hrs	Unit	Material	Labor	Equipment	Total
Scissor truss, 2" x 4" top and bottom chords						
Up to 38' span	F5@.022	SF	3.81	1.06	.22	5.09
40' to 50' span	F5@.028	SF	4.78	1.35	.29	6.42
Fink truss "W" (conventional roof truss), 2" x 4" top and bottom chords						
Up to 38' span	F5@.017	SF	3.30	.82	.17	4.29
40' to 50' span	F5@.022	SF	3.92	1.06	.22	5.20

	Craft@Hrs	Unit	Material	Labor	Equipment	Total
Fink truss with 2" x 6" top and bottom chords						
Up to 38' span	F5@.020	SF	3.98	.97	.20	5.15
40' to 50' span	F5@.026	SF	4.80	1.26	.27	6.33
Fink truss with gable fill at 16" OC						
28' span, 5 in 12 slope	F5@.958	Ea	270.00	46.30	9.80	326.10
32' span, 5 in 12 slope	F5@1.26	Ea	334.00	60.90	12.90	407.80
40' span, 5 in 12 slope	F5@1.73	Ea	478.00	83.60	17.70	579.30

Laminated Glued Beams (Glu-lam beams) Typical costs for horizontal micro-lam beams. Figures in parentheses show the approximate weight per linear foot of beam. Equipment cost is based on using a 4,000 lb capacity forklift with 30' lift.

	Craft@Hrs	Unit	Material	Labor	Equipment	Total
Steel connectors and shoes for laminated beams, including bolts,						
Typical per end or splice connection	—	Ea	121.00	—	—	121.00
Drill holes in laminated beams and attach connectors at grade before installing beam, based on number of holes in the connector, with work performed at job site						
Labor per each hole	F6@.236	Ea	—	11.60	—	11.60
Install beams with connections attached	F6@.150	LF	—	7.37	1.03	8.40

West Coast Douglas fir, 24F-V4, H=240 PSI, exterior glue, camber is 3,500' R for beams. Industrial grade, without wrap. For other grades see the adjustments that follow.

	Craft@Hrs	Unit	Material	Labor	Equipment	Total
3-1/8" x 6" (4.4 pounds per LF)	—	LF	6.10	—	—	6.10
3-1/8" x 9" (6.6 pounds per LF)	—	LF	9.59	—	—	9.59
3-1/8" x 10-1/2" (7.5 pounds per LF)	—	LF	10.50	—	—	10.50
3-1/8" x 12" (8.9 pounds per LF)	—	LF	12.10	—	—	12.10
3-1/8" x 15" (11.1 pounds per LF)	—	LF	14.80	—	—	14.80
3-1/8" x 18" (13.2 pounds per LF)	—	LF	17.80	—	—	17.80
5-1/8" x 6" (7.3 pounds per LF)	—	LF	8.76	—	—	8.76
5-1/8" x 9" (10.7 pounds per LF)	—	LF	13.20	—	—	13.20
5-1/8" x 12" (14.5 pounds per LF)	—	LF	17.70	—	—	17.70
5-1/8" x 15" (18.1 pounds per LF)	—	LF	21.90	—	—	21.90
5-1/8" x 18" (21.7 pounds per LF)	—	LF	26.20	—	—	26.20
5-1/8" x 21" (25.4 pounds per LF)	—	LF	30.60	—	—	30.60
5-1/8" x 24" (29.0 pounds per LF)	—	LF	34.80	—	—	34.80
6-3/4" x 12" (19.1 pounds per LF)	—	LF	23.10	—	—	23.10
6-3/4" x 15" (23.8 pounds per LF)	—	LF	29.10	—	—	29.10
6-3/4" x 18" (28.6 pounds per LF)	—	LF	35.00	—	—	35.00
6-3/4" x 21" (33.3 pounds per LF)	—	LF	40.90	—	—	40.90
6-3/4" x 24" (38.1 pounds per LF)	—	LF	46.80	—	—	46.80
Add to any of the beam costs shown in this section for:						
Industrial grade, clean, wrapped, add	—	%	12.5	—	—	—
Architectural grade, wrapped, add	—	%	20.0	—	—	—
One-coat rez-latex stain, add	—	%	10.0	—	—	—
Transportation to job site, per delivery, maximum 50 miles one way, add	—	LS	326.00	—	—	326.00

LVL beams (laminated veneer lumber). 1.75" x depth of beam. Usually in used in pairs. Use installation costs for glu-lam beams above. For installation, use actual length of beam for a 2-ply. Use 1.15 x length of beam for 3-ply and 1.25 x length of beam for 4-ply.

	Craft@Hrs	Unit	Material	Labor	Equipment	Total
1.75" x 9.25" 1.8E	—	LF	4.17	—	—	4.17
1.75" x 11.25" 1.8E	—	LF	5.10	—	—	5.10
1.75" x 11.875" 1.8E	—	LF	5.10	—	—	5.10
1.75" x 14" 1.8E	—	LF	6.79	—	—	6.79
1.75" x 16" 1.8E	—	LF	8.00	—	—	8.00
1.75" x 18" 1.8E	—	LF	8.70	—	—	8.70
1.75" x 20" 1.8E	—	LF	9.79	—	—	9.79

06 Wood and Composites

	Craft@Hrs	Unit	Material	Labor	Total
Stairs Job-built stairways, 3 stringers cut from 2" x 12" material, treads and risers from either 3/4" CDX plywood or 3/4" OSB sheathing.					
Material costs based on:					
2" x 12"	—	MBF	949.00	—	949.00
3/4" CDX plywood	—	MSF	847.00	—	847.00
3/4" OSB sheathing	—	MSF	677.00	—	677.00
1" x 6"	—	MSF	2,230.00	—	2,230.00
Plywood sheathing cost per 7-1/2" rise, 36" wide					
Straight run, 8'0" to 10'0" rise, per riser	C8@.530	Ea	15.70	25.00	40.70
"L"- or "U"-shape, per riser, add for landings	C8@.625	Ea	17.70	29.50	47.20
OSB sheathing cost per 7-1/2" rise, 36" wide					
Straight run, 8'0" to 10'0" rise, per riser	C8@.530	Ea	14.20	25.00	39.20
"L"- or "U"-shape, per riser, add for landings	C8@.625	Ea	16.30	29.50	45.80
Landings, framed and 3/4" CDX plywood surface					
Per SF of landing surface	C8@.270	SF	3.66	12.70	16.36
Landings, framed and 3/4" OSB sheathing surface					
Per SF of landing surface	C8@.270	SF	3.36	12.70	16.06
Factory cut and assembled straight closed box stairs, unfinished, 36" width					
Oak treads with 7-1/2" risers, price per riser					
3'0" to 3'6" wide, per riser	C8@.324	Ea	152.00	15.30	167.30
4'0" wide, per riser	C8@.357	Ea	185.00	16.80	201.80
Add for prefinished assembled stair rail with balusters and newel, per riser	C8@.257	Ea	66.80	12.10	78.90
Add for prefinished handrail, brackets and balusters	C8@.135	LF	21.40	6.36	27.76

07 Thermal and Moisture Protection

	Craft@Hrs	Unit	Material	Labor	Total
Dampproofing					
Asphalt wall primer, per coat, gallon covers 250 SF	CL@.010	SF	.03	.41	.44
Asphalt emulsion, wall, per coat, gallon covers 33 SF, brush on	CL@.013	SF	.23	.54	.77
Hot mop concrete wall, 2 coats and glass fabric	CL@.033	SF	1.34	1.36	2.70
Hot mop deck, 3 ply, felt, typical subcontract price	—	Sq	—	—	267.00
Hot mop deck, 4 ply, felt, typical subcontract price	—	Sq	—	—	312.00
Add for 1/2" asphalt fiberboard, subcontract price	—	Sq	—	—	115.00
Bituthene waterproofing membrane, 60 mil plain surface	CL@.025	SF	.98	1.03	2.01
Waterproof baths in high rise	CL@.025	SF	2.40	1.03	3.43
Iron compound, internal coating, 2 coats	CL@.012	SF	2.29	.50	2.79
Roof vapor barrier, .004" polyethylene	CL@.002	SF	.07	.08	.15

	Craft@Hrs	Unit	Material	Labor	Total
Thermal Insulation					
Fiberglass batts, placed between or over framing members					
3-1/2" Kraft faced, R-11, between ceiling joists	A1@.006	SF	.45	.31	.76
3-1/2" Kraft faced, R-11, on suspended ceiling, working off ladders from below	A1@.018	SF	.45	.92	1.37
3-1/2" Kraft faced, R-11, in crawl space	A1@.020	SF	.45	1.02	1.47
3-1/2" Kraft faced, R-13, between ceiling joists	A1@.006	SF	.53	.31	.84
3-1/2" Kraft faced, R-13, on suspended ceiling, working off ladders from below	A1@.018	SF	.53	.92	1.45
3-1/2" Kraft faced, R-13, in crawl space	A1@.020	SF	.53	1.02	1.55
6-1/4" Kraft faced, R-19, between ceiling joists	A1@.006	SF	.74	.31	1.05
6-1/4" Kraft faced, R-19, on suspended ceiling, working off ladders from below	A1@.018	SF	.74	.92	1.66
6-1/4" Kraft faced, R-19, in crawl space	A1@.020	SF	.74	1.02	1.76
6-1/4" Kraft faced, R-19, between studs	A1@.006	SF	.74	.31	1.05
5-1/2" Kraft faced, R-21, between ceiling joists	A1@.006	SF	.94	.31	1.25
5-1/2" Kraft faced, R-21, on suspended ceiling, working off ladders from below	A1@.018	SF	.94	.92	1.86
5-1/2" Kraft faced, R-21, in crawl space	A1@.020	SF	.94	1.02	1.96
5-1/2" Kraft faced, R-21, between studs	A1@.006	SF	.94	.31	1.25
9-1/2" Kraft faced, R-30, between ceiling joists	A1@.006	SF	1.12	.31	1.43
9-1/2" Kraft faced, R-30, on suspended ceiling, working off ladders from below	A1@.018	SF	1.12	.92	2.04
9-1/2" Kraft faced, R-30, in crawl space	A1@.020	SF	1.12	1.02	2.14
9-1/2" Kraft faced, R-30, between studs	A1@.006	SF	1.12	.31	1.43
12-1/4" Kraft faced, R-38, between ceiling joists	A1@.006	SF	1.31	.31	1.62
12-1/4" Kraft faced, R-38, on suspended ceiling, working off ladders from below	A1@.018	SF	1.31	.92	2.23
12-1/4" Kraft faced, R-38, in crawl space	A1@.020	SF	1.31	1.02	2.33
12-1/4" Kraft faced, R-38, between studs	A1@.006	SF	1.31	.31	1.62
Add for supporting batts on wire rods, 1 per SF	A1@.001	SF	.04	.05	.09
Add for foil one side	—	SF	.06	—	.06
Add for foil two sides	—	SF	.10	—	.10
Deduct for unfaced one side	—	SF	–.03	—	–.03
Add for Kraft paper two sides	—	SF	.04	—	.04
Fasteners for batts placed under a ceiling deck, including flat washers					
2-1/2" long	A1@.025	Ea	.25	1.28	1.53
4-1/2" long	A1@.025	Ea	.31	1.28	1.59
6-1/2" long	A1@.025	Ea	.43	1.28	1.71
Domed self-locking washers	A1@.005	Ea	.20	.26	.46
Blown fiberglass or mineral wool, over ceiling joists. Add blowing equipment cost at $300 per day					
R-11, 5"	A1@.008	SF	.29	.41	.70
R-13, 6"	A1@.010	SF	.34	.51	.85
R-19, 9"	A1@.014	SF	.46	.72	1.18
Insulation board on walls, 4' x 8' Foamular® 150 polystyrene					
1/2" thick (R-2.5)	C8@.010	SF	.44	.47	.91
3/4" thick (R-3.8)	C8@.011	SF	.56	.52	1.08
1" thick (R-5.0)	C8@.011	SF	.65	.52	1.17
1-1/2" thick (R-7.5)	C8@.015	SF	.82	.71	1.53
2" thick (R-10)	C8@.015	SF	1.00	.71	1.71
Expanded polystyrene board installed on perimeter walls					
1/2", R-3.3	C8@.010	SF	.43	.47	.90
3/4", R-2.9	C8@.010	SF	.28	.47	.75

	Craft@Hrs	Unit	Material	Labor	Total
1", R-4.20	C8@.011	SF	.55	.52	1.07
1", R-5.9	C8@.011	SF	.51	.52	1.03
1-1/2", R-5.9	C8@.015	SF	.43	.71	1.14
1-3/8", R-8.3	C8@.015	SF	.95	.71	1.66
2", R-8	C8@.015	SF	.45	.71	1.16
2", R-13	C8@.015	SF	1.10	.71	1.81
Polyisocyanurate foam core sheathing, Super Tuff-R®, foil face, painted back, 4' x 8' panels on perimeter walls					
1/2", R-3.3	C8@.010	SF	.44	.47	.91
3/4", R-5.5	C8@.010	SF	.46	.47	.93
1", R-6.5	C8@.011	SF	.71	.52	1.23
1-3/8", R-9.1	C8@.015	SF	.98	.71	1.69
1-1/2", R-9.8	C8@.015	SF	.88	.71	1.59
2", R-13.0	C8@.015	SF	1.11	.71	1.82
Perlite or vermiculite, poured in concrete block cores					
Perlite only	—	CF	9.18	—	9.18
4" wall, 8.1 SF per CF	M1@.004	SF	1.13	.19	1.32
6" wall, 5.4 SF per CF	M1@.007	SF	1.70	.33	2.03
8" wall, 3.6 SF per CF	M1@.009	SF	2.55	.43	2.98
10" wall, 3.0 SF per CF	M1@.011	SF	3.06	.53	3.59
Poured vermiculite in wall cavities	M1@.032	CF	13.30	1.53	14.83
Sound board					
1/2", on walls	C8@.010	SF	1.02	.47	1.49
1/2", on floors	C8@.009	SF	1.02	.42	1.44
Cold box insulation					
2" polystyrene	A1@.012	SF	.49	.61	1.10
1" cork	A1@.013	SF	5.50	.66	6.16
Add for overhead work or poor access areas	—	SF	—	.10	.10
Add for enclosed areas	—	SF	—	.10	.10
Add for 1 hour fire rating	—	SF	.30	—	.30

	Craft@Hrs	Unit	Material	Labor	Equipment	Total
2-Part Spray Applied Foam Insulation						
Open cell, 2-part sprayed foam, 1" thick	A1@.020	CSF	14.70	1.02	1.10	16.82
Closed cell, 2-part spray foam, 1" thick	A1@.026	CSF	63.50	1.33	1.41	66.24

Roof Insulation Roof insulation. Local regulation can affect the cost and availability of urethanes, isocyanurates, phenolics and polystyrene roof insulation board.

	Craft@Hrs	Unit	Material	Labor	Total
Fiberglass board roof insulation					
3/4", R-2.80, C-0.36	R3@.570	Sq	113.00	26.70	139.70
1", R-4.20, C-0.24	R3@.636	Sq	133.00	29.70	162.70
1-3/8", R-5.30, C-0.19	R3@.684	Sq	172.00	32.00	204.00
1-5/8", R-6.70, C-0.15	R3@.706	Sq	195.00	33.00	228.00
2-1/4", R-8.30, C-0.12	R3@.797	Sq	239.00	37.30	276.30
Polystyrene rigid foam roof insulation. R-19 rating when used with batt insulation. Including 5% waste.					
1/2" 4' x 8' panels	R3@1.10	Sq	29.20	51.40	80.60
3/4" 4' x 8' panels	R3@1.10	Sq	32.40	51.40	83.80
1" 4' x 8' panels	R3@1.10	Sq	53.50	51.40	104.90
1-1/2" 4' x 8' panels	R3@1.10	Sq	71.00	51.40	122.40
2" 4' x 8' panels	R3@1.10	Sq	72.20	51.40	123.60
Expanded polystyrene board roof insulation					
3/4", R-5.30, C-0.19	R3@.478	Sq	32.40	22.40	54.80
1", R-6.70, C-0.15	R3@.478	Sq	32.90	22.40	55.30
1-1/2", R-11.1, C-0.09	R3@.570	Sq	71.00	26.70	97.70
2", R-14.3, C-0.07	R3@.684	Sq	72.20	32.00	104.20
2-1/4", R-16.7, C-0.06	R3@.684	Sq	95.40	32.00	127.40

	Craft@Hrs	Unit	Material	Labor	Total
Perlite board roof insulation					
1", R-2.80, C-0.36	R3@.639	Sq	120.00	29.90	149.90
1-1/2", R-4.20, C-0.24	R3@.728	Sq	176.00	34.00	210.00
2", R-5.30, C-0.19	R3@.820	Sq	217.00	38.30	255.30
2-1/2", R-6.70, C-0.15	R3@.956	Sq	271.00	44.70	315.70
3", R-8.30, C-0.12	R3@1.03	Sq	328.00	48.20	376.20
4", R-10.0, C-0.10	R3@1.23	Sq	434.00	57.50	491.50
5-1/4", R-14.3, C-0.07	R3@1.57	Sq	574.00	73.40	647.40
Cellular Foamglass (isocyanurates) board insulation, on roofs					
1-1/2"	R3@.775	Sq	437.00	36.20	473.20
Tapered 3/16" per foot	R3@.775	Sq	400.00	36.20	436.20
Polystyrene board roof insulation					
1", R-4.20, C-0.24, foil one side	R3@.545	Sq	41.80	25.50	67.30
1-1/2", R-5.9, C-0.16	R3@.639	Sq	41.70	29.90	71.60
2", R-8.30, C-0.12	R3@.797	Sq	46.50	37.30	83.80
Fasteners for board type insulation on roofs					
Typical 2-1/2" to 3-1/2" screws with 3" metal disks					
I-60	R3@.053	Sq	3.94	2.48	6.42
I-90	R3@.080	Sq	5.96	3.74	9.70
Add for plastic disks	—	Sq	.99	—	.99

Exterior Wall Insulation and Finish System (EIFS) Polymer based exterior non-structural wall finish applied to concrete, masonry, stucco or exterior grade gypsum sheathing (such as Dryvit). System consists of a plaster base coat approximately 1/4" thick, and a glass fiber mesh embedded in the adhesive base coat. The base coat is applied over polystyrene insulation boards bonded to an existing flat vertical wall surface with adhesive. Costs shown are per SF of finished wall surface. These costs do not include surface preparation or wall costs. Add the cost of scaffolding if required. Add 50% to the labor costs when work is done from scaffolding.
For scheduling purposes, estimate that a crew of three can field apply 250 SF of exterior wall insulation and finish systems in an 8-hour day.

	Craft@Hrs	Unit	Material	Labor	Total
Adhesive mixture, 2 coats					
2.1 SF per SF of wall area including waste	F8@.021	SF	1.05	1.09	2.14
Glass fiber mesh					
1.1 SF per SF of wall area including waste	F8@.010	SF	.39	.52	.91
Insulation board, 1" thick, R-5.0					
1.05 SF per SF of wall area including waste	F8@.021	SF	.65	1.09	1.74
Textured finish coat, with integral color					
1.05 SF per SF of wall area including waste	F8@.038	SF	.81	1.97	2.78
Total with 1" thick insulation	F8@.090	SF	2.90	4.67	7.57
Add for 2" thick insulation board, R-10	—	SF	.34	—	.34
Add for 3" thick insulation board, R-15	—	SF	1.34	—	1.34
Add for 4" thick insulation board, R-20	—	SF	1.68	—	1.68

Aluminum Wall Cladding System, Exterior These costs assume installation by a manufacturer-trained contractor on a framed and insulated exterior building surface, including track system, panels and trim. Alply, Inc.

	Craft@Hrs	Unit	Material	Labor	Total
Techwall solid aluminum panel, 1/8" thick, joints sealed with silicon sealer					
Kynar 500 paint finish	SM@.158	SF	21.20	9.59	30.79
Anodized aluminum finish	SM@.158	SF	21.30	9.59	30.89
Add for radius panels	SM@.032	SF	4.29	1.94	6.23

	Craft@Hrs	Unit	Material	Labor	Total
Cladding, Preformed Roofing and Siding Applied on metal framing.					
Architectural insulated metal panels with smooth .040 aluminum exterior face with Kynar 500 finish, 2" thick isocyanurate insulation, .040 mill finish aluminum interior sheet, shop applied extrusion and dry seal gasketed joint system, shop fabricated. Alply, Inc.					
Kynar 500 paint finish	SM@.136	SF	15.30	8.25	23.55
Add for radius panels	SM@.020	SF	2.19	1.21	3.40
Corrugated or ribbed roofing, colored galvanized steel, 9/16" deep, uninsulated					
18 gauge	SM@.026	SF	3.12	1.58	4.70
20 gauge	SM@.026	SF	2.72	1.58	4.30
22 gauge	SM@.026	SF	2.44	1.58	4.02
24 gauge	SM@.026	SF	2.07	1.58	3.65
Corrugated siding, colored galvanized steel, 9/16" deep, uninsulated					
18 gauge	SM@.034	SF	3.49	2.06	5.55
20 gauge	SM@.034	SF	3.03	2.06	5.09
22 gauge	SM@.034	SF	2.72	2.06	4.78
Ribbed siding, colored galvanized steel, 1-3/4" deep, box rib					
18 gauge	SM@.034	SF	3.66	2.06	5.72
20 gauge	SM@.034	SF	3.21	2.06	5.27
22 gauge	SM@.034	SF	2.82	2.06	4.88
Corrugated aluminum roofing, natural finish					
.020" aluminum	SM@.026	SF	1.72	1.58	3.30
.032" aluminum	SM@.026	SF	2.18	1.58	3.76
Add for factory painted finish	—	SF	.26	—	.26
Corrugated aluminum siding, natural finish					
.020" aluminum	SM@.034	SF	1.72	2.06	3.78
.032" aluminum	SM@.034	SF	2.12	2.06	4.18
Add for factory painted finish	—	SF	.26	—	.26
Vinyl siding					
Solid vinyl, .042", horizontal siding	SM@.026	SF	.87	1.58	2.45
Add for insulated siding backer panel	SM@.001	SF	.40	.06	.46
Vinyl window and door trim	SM@.040	LF	.49	2.43	2.92
Vinyl siding and fascia system	SM@.032	SF	1.14	1.94	3.08
Laminated sandwich panel siding, enameled 22 gauge aluminum face one side, polystyrene core					
1" core	SM@.069	SF	5.39	4.19	9.58
1-1/2" core	SM@.069	SF	6.02	4.19	10.21
Membrane Roofing (One square "Sq" = 100 square feet)					
Built-up roofing, asphalt felt					
3-ply, smooth surface top sheet	R3@1.61	Sq	99.00	75.30	174.30
4-ply, base sheet, 3-ply felt, smooth surface top sheet	R3@1.85	Sq	121.00	86.50	207.50
5-ply, 20 year	R3@2.09	Sq	143.00	97.70	240.70
Built-up fiberglass felt roof					
Base and 3-ply felt	R3@1.93	Sq	134.00	90.20	224.20
Add for each additional ply	R3@.188	Sq	38.70	8.79	47.49
Add for light rock dress off (250 lbs per Sq)	R3@.448	Sq	20.80	20.90	41.70
Add for heavy rock dress off (400 lbs per Sq)	R3@.718	Sq	33.30	33.60	66.90
Remove and replace rock (400 lbs per Sq) Including new flood coat	R3@1.32	Sq	49.60	61.70	111.30
Aluminized coating for built-up roofing	R3@.599	Sq	36.60	28.00	64.60
Fire rated type	R3@.609	Sq	37.70	28.50	66.20

	Craft@Hrs	Unit	Material	Labor	Total
Modified APP, SBS flashing membrane	R3@.033	SF	.73	1.54	2.27
Cap sheet	R3@.277	Sq	54.90	13.00	67.90
Modified asphalt, APP,					
SBS base sheet and membrane	R3@1.97	Sq	168.00	92.10	260.10
Roll roofing					
90 lb mineral surface	R3@.399	Sq	47.50	18.70	66.20
19" wide selvage edge mineral surface (110 lb)	R3@.622	Sq	189.00	29.10	218.10
Double coverage selvage edge roll (140 lb)	R3@.703	Sq	205.00	32.90	237.90
Asphalt impregnated walkway for built-up roofing					
1/2"	R3@.016	SF	5.00	.75	5.75
3/4"	R3@.017	SF	6.32	.79	7.11
1"	R3@.020	SF	7.66	.94	8.60
Strip off existing 4-ply roof, no disposal included	R3@1.32	Sq	—	61.70	61.70
Elastomeric Roofing					
Butyl, general purpose rubber					
1/16"	R3@1.93	Sq	156.00	90.20	246.20
3/32"	R3@1.93	Sq	239.00	90.20	329.20
Neoprene, commercial grade, 1/16"	R3@2.23	Sq	399.00	104.00	503.00
Neoprene, commercial grade, 1/8"	R3@2.23	Sq	746.00	104.00	850.00
w/ adhesive	—	%	55.0	—	—
Neoprene, high strength, 1/16"	R3@2.23	Sq	535.00	104.00	639.00
Neoprene, high strength, 1/8"	R3@2.23	Sq	1,000.00	104.00	1,104.00
w/ adhesive	—	%	15.0	—	—
Neoprene, Mil R 6855 E, 1/16"	R3@2.23	Sq	279.00	104.00	383.00
Neoprene, Mil R 6855 E, 1/8"	R3@2.23	Sq	550.00	104.00	654.00
Acrylic-urethane foam roof system					
Remove gravel and prepare existing built-up roof	R3@1.26	Sq	6.21	58.90	65.11
Apply base and top coats of acrylic (.030")	R3@.750	Sq	135.00	35.10	170.10
Urethane foam 1" thick (R-7)	R3@.280	Sq	125.00	13.10	138.10
Urethane foam 2" thick (R-14)	R3@.500	Sq	211.00	23.40	234.40
Spray-on mineral granules, 40 lbs per CSF	R3@.600	Sq	20.20	28.10	48.30
EPDM roofing system (Ethylene Propylene Diene Monomer)					
.045" loose laid membrane	R3@.743	Sq	83.00	34.70	117.70
.060" adhered membrane (excluding adhesive)	R3@1.05	Sq	154.00	49.10	203.10
.090" adhered membrane (excluding adhesive)	R3@1.30	Sq	196.00	60.80	256.80
Bonding adhesive	R3@.305	Sq	74.60	14.30	88.90
Lap splice cement, per 100 LF	R3@.223	CLF	31.10	10.40	41.50
Ballast rock, 3/4" to 1-1/2" gravel	R3@.520	Sq	13.40	24.30	37.70
Neoprene sheet flashing, .062"	R3@.021	SF	4.32	.98	5.30
Add for mechanical fasteners and washers					
6" long, 12" OC at laps	—	Ea	.93	—	.93
12" long, 12" OC at laps	—	Ea	1.83	—	1.83

Cementitious Roofing System Tectum™ roof deck systems for use on open beam ceilings with exposed joists. Provides a nailable top surface, a core of Styrofoam brand insulation and an exposed interior Tectum™ ceiling plank substrate. Tectum™ roof deck is highly moisture resistant and possesses high compressive strength, excellent sound absorption, insulative properties and a finished interior. Costs shown include nails, screws, and adhesive. Includes normal cutting waste.

Tectum I with T&G edges and square ends. Standard roof deck with foam insulation. Available in lengths up to 14' and widths to 3'

	Craft@Hrs	Unit	Material	Labor	Total
2" thick	C8@.017	SF	3.68	.80	4.48
2-1/2" thick	C8@.019	SF	4.34	.90	5.24
3" thick	C8@.021	SF	4.97	.99	5.96

	Craft@Hrs	Unit	Material	Labor	Total
Tectum III with T&G edges and square ends. Composite roof deck used where higher insulation values are required. Tectum III provides a finished interior surface, and foam insulation. Width is 47" and lengths are available from 4" to 16"					
3-1/2" thick	C8@.015	SF	8.36	.71	9.07
4" thick	C8@.021	SF	8.86	.99	9.85
5" thick	C8@.027	SF	9.91	1.27	11.18
6" thick	C8@.033	SF	11.10	1.56	12.66
7" thick	C8@.039	SF	13.50	1.84	15.34
8" thick	C8@.045	SF	14.50	2.12	16.62
9" thick	C8@.051	SF	15.00	2.40	17.40
10" thick	C8@.057	SF	17.20	2.69	19.89
Cant Strips					
3" fiber	R3@.017	LF	.19	.79	.98
6" fiber	R3@.017	LF	.40	.79	1.19
4" wood	R3@.017	LF	.99	.79	1.78
6" wood	R3@.017	LF	1.00	.79	1.79
Flashing and Sheet Metal					
Prefinished sheet metal fascia and mansards, standing beam and batten					
Straight or simple	SM@.054	SF	4.64	3.28	7.92
Curved or complex	SM@.082	SF	7.01	4.97	11.98
Coping, gravel stop and flashing	SM@.037	LF	3.38	2.24	5.62
Sheet metal wainscot, galvanized	SM@.017	SF	.94	1.03	1.97
Aluminum flashing .032",					
Coping and wall cap, 16" girth	SM@.069	LF	3.65	4.19	7.84
Counter flash, 8'	SM@.054	LF	3.24	3.28	6.52
Reglet flashing, 8"	SM@.058	LF	1.33	3.52	4.85
Neoprene gasket for flashing	SM@.015	LF	1.31	.91	2.22
Gravel stop and fascia, 10"	SM@.084	LF	3.83	5.10	8.93
Side wall flashing, 9"	SM@.027	LF	2.00	1.64	3.64
Gravel stop					
4"	SM@.058	LF	4.35	3.52	7.87
6"	SM@.063	LF	4.93	3.82	8.75
8"	SM@.068	LF	5.97	4.13	10.10
12"	SM@.075	LF	9.97	4.55	14.52
Valley, 24"	SM@.070	LF	2.55	4.25	6.80

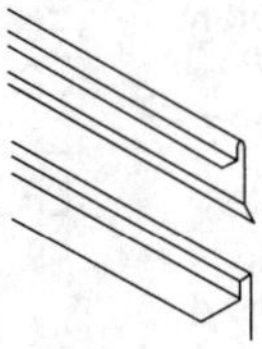

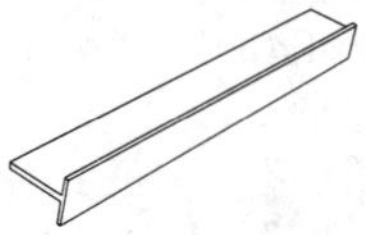

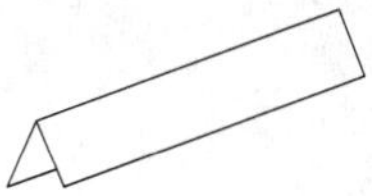

	Craft@Hrs	Unit	Material	Labor	Total
Copper flashing 16 oz,					
Roll 8" x 15'	SW@.750	Ea	200.00	31.60	231.60
Roof edging, 2" x 2" x 10'	SW@.350	Ea	110.00	14.80	124.80
Gravel stop					
4"	SM@.058	LF	22.70	3.52	26.22
6"	SM@.063	LF	26.20	3.82	30.02
8"	SM@.068	LF	30.60	4.13	34.73
10"	SM@.075	LF	37.50	4.55	42.05
Reglet flashing, 8"	SM@.054	LF	10.40	3.28	13.68
Neoprene gasket for flashing	SM@.015	LF	1.31	.91	2.22
Side wall flashing, 6"	SM@.027	LF	9.85	1.64	11.49
Base, 20 oz	SM@.072	LF	20.30	4.37	24.67
Valley, 24"	SM@.069	LF	18.40	4.19	22.59

	Craft@Hrs	Unit	Material	Labor	Total
Sheet lead flashing					
Plumbing vents, soil stacks, 4 lbs per square foot					
4" pipe size	P6@.709	Ea	37.60	37.10	74.70
6" pipe size	P6@.709	Ea	43.50	37.10	80.60
8" pipe size	P6@.709	Ea	53.10	37.10	90.20
Roof drains, flat pan type, 36" x 36"					
2.5 lbs/SF material	P6@1.49	Ea	45.70	78.10	123.80
4 lbs/SF material	P6@1.49	Ea	77.10	78.10	155.20
6 lbs/SF material	P6@1.49	Ea	110.00	78.10	188.10
Stainless steel flashing					
Fascia roof edge, .018"	SM@.054	LF	4.09	3.28	7.37
Base, .018"	SM@.054	LF	4.93	3.28	8.21
Counter flash, .015"	SM@.054	LF	3.86	3.28	7.14
Valley, .015", 24"	SM@.069	LF	3.85	4.19	8.04
Reglets, .020", 8"	SM@.035	LF	3.36	2.12	5.48
Galvanized sheet metal flashing					
Cap and counter flash, 8"	SM@.046	LF	1.59	2.79	4.38
Coping and wall cap, 16" girth	SM@.069	LF	2.04	4.19	6.23
Gravel stop, 6"	SM@.060	LF	.61	3.64	4.25
Neoprene gasket	SM@.005	LF	1.31	.30	1.61
Pitch pockets, 24 gauge, filled					
4" x 4"	SM@.584	Ea	23.60	35.40	59.00
6" x 6"	SM@.584	Ea	29.80	35.40	65.20
8" x 8"	SM@.584	Ea	34.70	35.40	70.10
8" x 10"	SM@.777	Ea	55.30	47.10	102.40
8" x 12"	SM@.777	Ea	48.70	47.10	95.80
Reglet flashing, 8"	SM@.054	LF	1.52	3.28	4.80
Shingles (chimney flash)	RF@.064	LF	1.18	3.17	4.35
Side wall flashing, 9"	SM@.027	LF	1.14	1.64	2.78
"W" valley, 24"	SM@.069	LF	2.33	4.19	6.52
Plumbers counter flash cone, 4" diameter	P8@.204	Ea	7.38	9.45	16.83
Roof safes and caps					
4" galvanized sheet metal	SM@.277	Ea	15.00	16.80	31.80
4" aluminum	SM@.277	Ea	14.80	16.80	31.60
Pitch pockets, 16 oz copper, filled					
4" x 4"	SM@.547	Ea	141.00	33.20	174.20
6" x 6"	SM@.547	Ea	178.00	33.20	211.20
8" x 8"	SM@.547	Ea	212.00	33.20	245.20
8" x 10"	SM@.679	Ea	247.00	41.20	288.20
8" x 12"	SM@.679	Ea	684.00	41.20	725.20
Galvanized corner guards, 4" x 4"	SM@.039	LF	14.80	2.37	17.17
Copper sheet metal roofing, 16 oz					
Batten seam	SM@.065	SF	15.40	3.94	19.34
Standing seam	SM@.056	SF	17.70	3.40	21.10
Gutters and Downspouts					
Aluminum, .032", including hangers					
Fascia gutter, 5"	SM@.050	LF	.85	3.03	3.88
Box gutter, 4"	SM@.050	LF	.78	3.03	3.81
Inside/Outside corner, for either of above	SM@.091	Ea	10.50	5.52	16.02
Dropouts, elbows, for either of above	SM@.101	Ea	10.60	6.13	16.73
Elbows, for either of above	SM@.101	Ea	3.40	6.13	9.53
Downspouts, to 24' height					
2" x 3"	SM@.037	LF	.91	2.24	3.15
3" x 4"	SM@.047	LF	.20	2.85	3.05

	Craft@Hrs	Unit	Material	Labor	Total
4" diameter, round, 12' to 24' high	SM@.047	LF	1.41	2.85	4.26
Add for height over 24'	SM@.017	LF	—	1.03	1.03
Copper, K-style (ogee), 16 oz, including hangers. Add 25% for 20 oz. material.					
Box gutter, 5"	SM@.054	LF	9.23	3.28	12.51
Box gutter, 6"	SM@.058	LF	11.80	3.52	15.32
Box gutter, 8"	SM@.062	LF	29.90	3.76	33.66
Copper, K-style, highback, 16 oz, including hangers, Add 25% for 20 oz. material.					
Box gutter, 5"	SM@.054	LF	17.70	3.28	20.98
Box gutter, 6"	SM@.058	LF	23.00	3.52	26.52
Box gutter, 8"	SM@.062	LF	24.00	3.76	27.76
Half round gutter, single bead, 16 oz, including hangers, Add 25% for 20 oz. material.					
5" gutter	SM@.039	LF	8.40	2.37	10.77
6" gutter	SM@.051	LF	11.30	3.09	14.39
8" gutter	SM@.056	LF	20.60	3.40	24.00
Half round gutter, highback, 16 oz, including hangers, Add 25% for 20 oz. material.					
5" gutter	SM@.039	LF	18.30	2.37	20.67
6" gutter	SM@.051	LF	22.40	3.09	25.49
8" gutter	SM@.056	LF	24.70	3.40	28.10
Miters					
K-style, 5"	SM@.154	Ea	19.40	9.34	28.74
K-style, 6"	SM@.160	Ea	30.50	9.71	40.21
K-style, 5", inside strip, 45 degrees	SM@.190	Ea	13.20	11.50	24.70
K-style, 5", inside strip, 90 degrees	SM@.190	Ea	9.22	11.50	20.72
K-style, 6", inside strip, 90 degrees	SM@.190	Ea	18.80	11.50	30.30
Highback, 5"	SM@.154	Ea	229.00	9.34	238.34
Highback, 6"	SM@.164	Ea	250.00	9.95	259.95
Highback, 8"	SM@.174	Ea	260.00	10.60	270.60
Half round, 5"	SM@.154	Ea	48.10	9.34	57.44
Half round, 6"	SM@.160	Ea	72.20	9.71	81.91
Half round, highback, 5"	SM@.174	Ea	210.00	10.60	220.60
Half round, highback, 6"	SM@.184	Ea	227.00	11.20	238.20
Half round, highback, 8"	SM@.194	Ea	237.00	11.80	248.80
Outlets					
K-style, rectangular	SM@.154	Ea	12.50	9.34	21.84
K-style, oval	SM@.160	Ea	5.88	9.71	15.59
Round, 3" dia	SM@.154	Ea	11.60	9.34	20.94
Round, 4" dia	SM@.174	Ea	13.80	10.60	24.40
Round, 5" dia	SM@.184	Ea	33.50	11.20	44.70
Round, 6" dia	SM@.194	Ea	42.70	11.80	54.50
Elbows					
Rectangular, 2" x 3"	SM@.154	Ea	12.00	9.34	21.34
Rectangular, 3" x 4"	SM@.160	Ea	17.20	9.71	26.91
Rectangular, 4" x 5"	SM@.180	Ea	44.90	10.90	55.80
Half round, "B" style, 3"	SM@.174	Ea	10.70	10.60	21.30
Half round, "B" style, 4"	SM@.184	Ea	15.80	11.20	27.00
Half round, "B" style, 5"	SM@.194	Ea	52.50	11.80	64.30
Half round, "B" style, 6"	SM@.204	Ea	84.90	12.40	97.30
Downspouts, to 24' height					
Rectangular, 2" x 3"	SM@.036	LF	10.40	2.18	12.58
Rectangular, 3" x 4"	SM@.047	LF	11.80	2.85	14.65
Rectangular, 4" x 5"	SM@.056	LF	25.40	3.40	28.80
Round, 3"	SM@.037	LF	9.37	2.24	11.61
Round, 4"	SM@.047	LF	12.90	2.85	15.75
Round, 5"	SM@.057	LF	18.30	3.46	21.76

	Craft@Hrs	Unit	Material	Labor	Total
Round, 6"	SM@.067	LF	24.20	4.06	28.26
Add for heights over 24'	SM@.017	LF	—	1.03	1.03
Scuppers, copper, 16 oz,					
8" x 8"	SM@.972	Ea	742.00	59.00	801.00
10" x 10"	SM@.972	Ea	901.00	59.00	960.00
Galvanized steel, 26 gauge, including hangers					
Box gutter 5"	SM@.054	LF	.93	3.28	4.21
Dropouts, elbows	SM@.082	Ea	1.42	4.97	6.39
Fascia gutter					
5" face	SM@.054	LF	1.10	3.28	4.38
7" face	SM@.062	LF	1.46	3.76	5.22
Dropouts, elbows, for either of above	SM@.088	Ea	2.16	5.34	7.50
Downspouts, with all fittings, height to 24'					
2" x 3"	SM@.036	LF	.78	2.18	2.96
3" x 4"	SM@.047	LF	1.19	2.85	4.04
3" round	SM@.037	LF	1.19	2.24	3.43
6" round	SM@.055	LF	1.12	3.34	4.46
Add for heights over 24'	SM@.017	LF	—	1.03	1.03
Roof sump, 18" x 18" x 5"	SM@.779	Ea	6.04	47.30	53.34
Scupper, 6" x 6" x 8"	SM@.591	Ea	18.20	35.90	54.10
Stainless steel, .015" thick, including hangers					
Box gutter, 5" wide, 4-1/2" high	SM@.054	LF	9.21	3.28	12.49
Dropouts, elbows	SM@.076	Ea	13.30	4.61	17.91
Downspout, 4" x 5", to 24' high	SM@.051	LF	8.19	3.09	11.28
Add for heights over 24'	SM@.017	LF	—	1.03	1.03

Vents, Louvers and Screens

	Craft@Hrs	Unit	Material	Labor	Total
Fixed louvers, with screen, typical	SM@.402	SF	13.70	24.40	38.10
Door louvers, typical	SM@.875	Ea	29.40	53.10	82.50
Manual operating louvers, typical	SM@.187	SF	21.60	11.30	32.90
Cooling tower screens	SM@.168	SF	12.10	10.20	22.30
Bird screens with frame	SM@.028	SF	1.82	1.70	3.52
Concrete block vents, aluminum	M1@.370	SF	16.10	17.70	33.80
Frieze vents, with screen, 14" x 4"	C8@.198	Ea	3.33	9.33	12.66
Foundation vents, 6" x 14", ornamental	C8@.317	Ea	9.03	14.90	23.93
Attic vents, with louvers, 14" x 24"	C8@.377	Ea	26.40	17.80	44.20
Architectural facade screen, aluminum	SM@.187	SF	25.20	11.30	36.50
Add for enamel or light anodized	—	SF	2.68	—	2.68
Add for porcelain or heavy anodized	—	SF	6.50	—	6.50

Rain Dispersing Gutters Rustproof aluminum, installed on mounting brackets. Disperses rain into a 4 foot area. No downspouts needed. Resists clogging by leaves and debris. Rainhandler™

	Craft@Hrs	Unit	Material	Labor	Total
Rain disperser	RF@.100	LF	5.59	4.95	10.54
Mounting brackets (use one each 18")	—	Ea	1.24	—	1.24
Horizontal adapter for roof edges that extend outward more than 2-1/2" from building (use one each 18")	RF@.020	Ea	2.50	.99	3.49
Vertical adapter for vertical fascias, under 3" from building (use one each 5')	RF@.020	Ea	2.50	.99	3.49
"Doorbrella" for installation above doors and windows	RF@.250	Ea	19.30	12.40	31.70
Drip edge extension for roof edges that extend less than 1-1/2" from vertical fascia (use one each 18")	RF@.020	Ea	5.03	.99	6.02
Roof valley rain diverter	RF@.050	Ea	7.60	2.48	10.08
Fascia adapter for angled fascia boards	RF@.050	Ea	2.50	2.48	4.98

	Craft@Hrs	Unit	Material	Labor	Total
Roof Accessories					
Roof hatches, steel, not including ladder					
30" x 30"	C8@3.09	Ea	535.00	146.00	681.00
30" x 72"	C8@4.69	Ea	1,290.00	221.00	1,511.00
36" x 36"	C8@3.09	Ea	610.00	146.00	756.00
36" x 72"	C8@4.69	Ea	1,370.00	221.00	1,591.00
Ceiling access hatches					
30" x 30"	C8@1.59	Ea	322.00	75.00	397.00
42" x 42"	C8@1.89	Ea	386.00	89.10	475.10
Smoke vents					
Aluminum, 48" x 48"	C8@3.09	Ea	1,390.00	146.00	1,536.00
Galvanized, 48" x 48"	C8@3.09	Ea	1,340.00	146.00	1,486.00
Fusible "shrink-out" heat and smoke vent (PVC dome in aluminum frame)					
4' x 8'	C8@5.15	Ea	1,220.00	243.00	1,463.00
Roof scuttle, aluminum, 2'6" x 3'0"	C8@3.50	Ea	547.00	165.00	712.00
Ventilators					
Rotary, wind driven					
6" diameter	SM@.913	Ea	80.40	55.40	135.80
12" diameter	SM@.913	Ea	98.20	55.40	153.60
24" diameter	SM@1.36	Ea	278.00	82.50	360.50
Ventilators, mushroom type, motorized, single speed, including damper and bird screen but no electrical work					
8", 180 CFM	SM@2.93	Ea	381.00	178.00	559.00
12", 1,360 CFM	SM@2.93	Ea	632.00	178.00	810.00
18", 2,000 CFM	SM@4.00	Ea	901.00	243.00	1,144.00
24", 4,000 CFM	SM@4.86	Ea	1,380.00	295.00	1,675.00
Add for two-speed motor	—	%	35.0	—	—
Add for explosive proof units	—	Ea	521.00	—	521.00

Windstorm Certified Roof Turbine Fans Complies with ASHRAE/American National Standards Institute specification 62.2-2007 and Air Conditioning Contractors of America standard ACCA 5QI-2007, "HVAC Indoor Air Quality Installation Specification 2007." U.S. Green Building Council and Underwriters Laboratory approved. Texas Department of Insurance report # RV-12. Air Vent, Empire, Lomanco or equal.

	Craft@Hrs	Unit	Material	Labor	Total
12" dia., galvanized steel	R1@2.50	Ea	279.00	90.00	369.00
14" dia., galvanized steel	R1@4.50	Ea	434.00	162.00	596.00
12" dia., high-impact polypropylene	R1@7.00	Ea	607.00	252.00	859.00
14" dia., high-impact polypropylene	R1@7.50	Ea	798.00	270.00	1,068.00
Add for duct hangers	R1@.250	Ea	3.90	9.00	12.90
Add for sheet metal duct	R1@.350	LF	6.17	12.60	18.77
Add for edge flashing sealant	R1@.150	LF	2.78	5.40	8.18

Cast-in-Place Concrete Fireproofing Costs per linear foot (LF) of steel beam, column or girder. Use these figures to estimate the cubic feet (CF) of concrete per linear foot and square feet (SF) of form required per linear foot for each type of beam, column or girder. Quantities include concrete required to fill the void between the web and flange and provide 2" protection at the flanges. A small change in concrete thickness at flanges has very little effect on cost. Use $7,500.00 as a minimum job cost for work of this type. Concrete thickness for fireproofing will usually be:

Members at least 6" x 6" but less than 8" x 8" — 3" for a 4 hour rating, 2" for a 3 hour rating, 1-1/2" for a 2 hour rating, and 1" for a 1 hour rating.

Members at least 8" x 8" but less than 12" x 12" — 2-1/2" for a 4 hour rating, 2" for a 3 hour rating, 1" for a 1 or 2 hour rating.

Members 12" x 12" or greater — 2" for a 4 hour rating and 1" for a 1, 2, or 3 hour rating.

Labor costs include the time needed to prepare formwork sketches at the job site, measure for the forms, fabricate, erect, align and brace the forms, cut, bend, place and tie the reinforcing steel, install embedded steel items, place and finish the concrete and strip, clean and stack the forms. Labor costs assume a concrete forming, placing and finishing crew of 1 carpenter, 1 laborer and 1 cement finisher. Concrete placing equipment assumes the use of a concrete pump.

	Craft@Hrs	Unit	Material	Labor	Equipment	Total

For scheduling purposes, estimate that a crew of 3 will fireproof the following quantities of steel in an 8-hour day:
15 LF of W21 through W36 members,
25 LF of W8 through W18 members, 22 LF of S12 through S24 members, and 42 LF of M4 through W6 or S6 through S8 members.

Material costs assume reinforcing steel is #3 and #4 bars at 12" on center each way and includes waste and laps. Form cost assumes 3 uses without completely disassembling the form. Normal cleaning and repairs are included. No salvage value is assumed. Cost for forms, before allowance for waste, is based on Standard & Better lumber and 3/4" plyform.

Concrete and accessories for fireproofing

	Craft@Hrs	Unit	Material	Labor	Equipment	Total
Concrete, 3,000 PSI pump mix with 5% allowance for waste including pump cost	P9@.600	CY	180.00	29.10	10.20	219.30
Grade A60 reinforcing bars, set and tied, with 50 lbs per CY of concrete	P9@.790	CY	31.60	38.30	—	69.90
Hangers, snap-ties, misc. embedded steel with 10 lb per CY of concrete	P9@.660	CY	63.10	32.00	—	95.10
Concrete test cylinders including test reports, with 5 per 100 CY	—	CY	1.00	—	—	1.00
Total for concrete and accessories	**P9@2.05**	**CY**	**275.70**	**99.40**	**10.20**	**385.30**

Forms for fireproofing These costs assume the following materials are used per square foot of contact area (SFCA): Nails, clamps and form oil costing $.25 per board foot of lumber, 1.2 SF of 3/4" plyform and 3.7 BF of lumber per SFCA.

	Craft@Hrs	Unit	Material	Labor	Equipment	Total
Make, erect, align and strip forms, 3 uses	P9@.150	SF	2.66	7.28	—	9.94
Sack and patch concrete SF	P9@.010	SF	.18	.49	—	.67
Total for forms and finishing, per use	**P9@.160**	**SF**	**2.84**	**7.77**	**—**	**10.61**

Sample fireproofing estimate for ten W24 x 55 beams 20' long. Note from the table below that this beam requires 2.7 cubic feet of concrete per linear foot and 6.9 square feet of form per linear foot. Using labor and material prices from above to estimate 200 linear feet of beam. (Total costs have been rounded)

	Craft@Hrs	Unit	Material	Labor	Equipment	Total
Concrete (200 × 2.7 = 540 CF or 20 CY)	P9@41.0	LS	5,510.00	1,990.00	697.00	8,197.00
Form and finish (200 × 6.9 = 1,380 SF)	P9@221	LS	3,920.00	10,700.00	—	14,620.00
Total job cost shown above	**P9@262**	**LS**	**9,430.00**	**12,690.00**	**697.00**	**22,827.00**
Cost per linear foot of beam	**P9@1.31**	**LF**	**47.10**	**63.50**	**3.49**	**114.09**

Cast-in-place concrete fireproofing Cost per LF, including concrete and forming.

	Craft@Hrs	Unit	Material	Labor	Equipment	Total
W36 x 135 to W36 x 300 5.13 CF and 10.07 SF per LF	P9@2.00	LF	80.90	97.10	1.94	179.94
W33 x 118 to W30 x 241 4.59 CF and 9.35 SF per LF	P9@1.84	LF	73.40	89.30	1.74	164.44
W30 x 99 to W30 x 211 3.78 CF and 8.4 SF per LF	P9@1.63	LF	62.40	79.10	1.43	142.93
W27 x 84 to W27 x 178 3.51 CF and 8.19 SF per LF	P9@1.57	LF	59.10	76.20	1.33	136.63
W24 x 55 to W24 x 162 2.7 CF and 6.9 SF per LF	P9@1.31	LF	47.10	63.60	1.02	111.72
W21 x 44 to W21 x 147 2.43 CF and 6.75 SF per LF	P9@1.26	LF	43.90	61.20	.92	106.02
W18 x 37 to W18 x 71 1.62 CF and 5.34 SF per LF	P9@.974	LF	31.70	47.30	.61	79.61
W16 x 26 to W16 x 100 1.62 CF and 5.4 SF per LF	P9@.987	LF	31.90	47.90	.61	80.41

	Craft@Hrs	Unit	Material	Labor	Equipment	Total
W14 x 90 to W14 x 730						
2.97 CF and 7.15 SF per LF	P9@1.37	LF	50.60	66.50	1.12	118.22
W14 x 22 to W14 x 82						
1.35 CF and 4.7 SF per LF	P9@.854	LF	27.10	41.50	.51	69.11
W12 x 65 to W12 x 336						
2.16 CF and 6.08 SF per LF	P9@1.13	LF	39.30	54.90	.82	95.02
W12 x 40 to W12 x 58						
1.62 CF and 5.4 SF per LF	P9@.987	LF	31.90	47.90	.61	80.41
W12 x 14 to W12 x 35						
1.08 CF and 4.44 SF per LF	P9@.790	LF	23.60	38.30	.41	62.31
W10 x 33 to W10 x 112						
1.35 CF and 4.75 SF per LF	P9@.862	LF	27.30	41.80	.51	69.61
W10 x 12 to W10 x 30						
1.08 CF and 4.56 SF per LF	P9@.808	LF	24.00	39.20	.41	63.61
W8 x 24 to W8 x 67						
1.08 CF and 4.4 SF per LF	P9@.784	LF	23.50	38.10	.41	62.01
W8 x 10 to W8 x 21						
0.81 CF and 3.87 SF per LF	P9@.678	LF	19.20	32.90	.31	52.41
W6 x 15 to W6 x 25						
0.81 CF and 3.84 SF per LF	P9@.672	LF	19.20	32.60	.31	52.11
W6 x 9 to W6 x 16						
0.54 CF and 2.92 SF per LF	P9@.507	LF	13.80	24.60	.20	38.60
W5 x 16 to W5 x 19						
0.54 CF and 2.86 SF per LF	P9@.499	LF	13.60	24.20	.20	38.00
W4 x 13						
0.54 CF and 3.2 SF per LF	P9@.552	LF	14.60	26.80	.20	41.60
M4 x 13 to M14 x 18						
0.54 CF and 2.9 SF per LF	P9@.504	LF	13.70	24.50	.20	38.40
S24 x 80 to S24 x 121						
2.43 CF and 7.11 SF per LF	P9@1.32	LF	45.00	64.10	.92	110.02
S20 x 66 to S20 x 96						
1.89 CF and 6.09 SF per LF	P9@1.12	LF	36.60	54.40	.71	91.71
S15 x 43 to S18 x 70						
1.62 CF and 5.82 SF per LF	P9@1.05	LF	33.00	51.00	.61	84.61
S12 x 35 to S12 x 50						
1.08 CF and 4.44 SF per LF	P9@.790	LF	23.60	38.30	.41	62.31
S8 x 23 to S10 x 35						
0.81 CF and 3.81 SF per LF	P9@.670	LF	19.10	32.50	.31	51.91
S6 x 13 to S7 x 20						
0.54 CF and 2.91 SF per LF	P9@.504	LF	13.80	24.50	.20	38.50

Spray-Applied Fireproofing, Subcontract Fire endurance coating made from inorganic vermiculite and Portland cement. Costs assume a 10,000 board foot job. (One BF is one square foot covered 1" thick.) For smaller jobs, increase the cost by 5% for each 500 BF less than 10,000 BF. Use $2,000 as a minimum subcontract price. For thickness other than 1", adjust these costs proportionately. For scheduling purposes, estimate that a crew of 2 plasterers and 1 helper can apply 200 to 250 board feet per hour.

	Craft@Hrs	Unit	Material	Labor	Total
Structural steel columns	—	BF	—	—	2.58
Structural steel beams	—	BF	—	—	2.30
Purlins, girts, and miscellaneous members	—	BF	—	—	2.12
Decks, ceilings or walls	—	BF	—	—	1.95
Add for 18 gauge 2" hex mesh reinforcing	—	BF	—	—	.45
Add for key coat bonded on primed surfaces	—	SF	—	—	.53

Beams and Columns

Rule-of-thumb method for estimating spray-applied fireproofing on bare structural steel by member size:

Beams and Columns	Beams	Cost LF	Columns	Cost LF
W36 x 135 to 300	10 BF/LF	23.00	11 BF/LF	28.30
W33 x 118 to 241	9 BF/LF	20.70	10 BF/LF	25.80
W30 x 99 to 211	8 BF/LF	18.40	9 BF/LF	23.20
W27 x 84 to 178	7 BF/LF	16.10	8 BF/LF	20.60
W24 x 55 to 182	6.5 BF/LF	14.90	7.5 BF/LF	19.30
W21 x 44 to 147	6 BF/LF	13.80	7 BF/LF	18.00
W18 x 35 to 118	5 BF/LF	11.50	6 BF/LF	15.50
W16 x 28 to 57	3.5 BF/LF	8.04	4.5 BF/LF	11.60
W14 x 61 to 132	5.5 BF/LF	12.60	6.5 BF/LF	16.80
W14 x 22 to 63	4 BF/LF	9.19	5 BF/LF	12.90
W12 x 65 to 190	5 BF/LF	11.50	6 BF/LF	15.50
W12 x 40 to 58	4 BF/LF	9.19	5 BF/LF	12.90
W12 x 14 to 35	3 BF/LF	6.89	4 BF/LF	10.30
W10 x 49 to 112	4 BF/LF	9.19	5 BF/LF	12.90
W10 x 22 to 45	3 BF/LF	6.89	4 BF/LF	10.30
W10 x 12 to 19	2 BF/LF	4.60	3 BF/LF	7.73
W8 x 24 to 67	3 BF/LF	6.89	4 BF/LF	10.30
W6 x 9 to 25	2 BF/LF	4.60	3 BF/LF	7.73
W5 x 16 to 19	2 BF/LF	4.60	2.5 BF/LF	6.44
W4 x 13	1 BF/LF	2.30	2 BF/LF	4.15

Purlins and Girts	Purlins or Girts	Cost LF
MC 18 members	4 BF/LF	8.47
MC 10 to MC 13 members	3 BF/LF	6.35
MC 8 members	2 BF/LF	4.23
C 10 to C 15 members	3 BF/LF	6.35
C 7 to C 9 members	2 BF/LF	4.23

Sealants and Caulking By joint size. Costs assume 10% waste. Twelve 10.5 ounce cartridges equal one gallon and yield 231 cubic inches of caulk or sealant. Productivity shown assumes one roofer using a bulk dispenser. Add the cost of joint cleaning, if required.

	Craft@Hrs	Unit	Material	Labor	Total
Silicone latex caulk					
1/4" x 1/4", 351 LF/gallon, 63 LF per hour	RF@.016	LF	.02	.79	.81
1/4" x 3/8", 234 LF/gallon, 60 LF per hour	RF@.017	LF	.03	.84	.87
1/4" x 1/2", 176 LF/gallon, 58 LF per hour	RF@.017	LF	.04	.84	.88
3/8" x 3/8", 156 LF/gallon, 58 LF per hour	RF@.017	LF	.05	.84	.89
3/8" x 1/2", 117 LF/gallon, 57 LF per hour	RF@.017	LF	.06	.84	.90
3/8" x 5/8", 94 LF/gallon, 56 LF per hour	RF@.018	LF	.08	.89	.97
3/8" x 3/4", 76 LF/gallon, 52 LF per hour	RF@.019	LF	.10	.94	1.04
1/2" x 1/2", 87 LF/gallon, 56 LF per hour	RF@.018	LF	.09	.89	.98
1/2" x 5/8", 70 LF/gallon, 50 LF per hour	RF@.020	LF	.11	.99	1.10
1/2" x 3/4", 58 LF/gallon, 48 LF per hour	RF@.021	LF	.13	1.04	1.17
1/2" x 7/8", 51 LF/gallon, 46 LF per hour	RF@.022	LF	.15	1.09	1.24
1/2" x 1", 44 LF/gallon, 45 LF per hour	RF@.022	LF	.17	1.09	1.26
3/4" x 3/4", 39 LF/gallon, 44 LF per hour	RF@.023	LF	.19	1.14	1.33
1" x 1", 22 LF/gallon, 30 LF per hour	RF@.033	LF	.34	1.63	1.97
Acrylic latex plus silicone caulk					
1/4" x 1/4", 351 LF/gallon, 63 LF per hour	RF@.016	LF	.10	.79	.89
1/4" x 3/8", 234 LF/gallon, 60 LF per hour	RF@.017	LF	.14	.84	.98
1/4" x 1/2", 176 LF/gallon, 58 LF per hour	RF@.017	LF	.19	.84	1.03

	Craft@Hrs	Unit	Material	Labor	Total
3/8" x 3/8", 156 LF/gallon, 58 LF per hour	RF@.017	LF	.22	.84	1.06
3/8" x 1/2", 117 LF/gallon, 57 LF per hour	RF@.017	LF	.29	.84	1.13
3/8" x 5/8", 94 LF/gallon, 56 LF per hour	RF@.018	LF	.36	.89	1.25
3/8" x 3/4", 76 LF/gallon, 52 LF per hour	RF@.019	LF	.44	.94	1.38
1/2" x 1/2", 87 LF/gallon, 56 LF per hour	RF@.018	LF	.39	.89	1.28
1/2" x 5/8", 70 LF/gallon, 50 LF per hour	RF@.020	LF	.48	.99	1.47
1/2" x 3/4", 58 LF/gallon, 48 LF per hour	RF@.021	LF	.58	1.04	1.62
1/2" x 7/8", 51 LF/gallon, 46 LF per hour	RF@.022	LF	.66	1.09	1.75
1/2" x 1", 44 LF/gallon, 45 LF per hour	RF@.022	LF	.76	1.09	1.85
3/4" x 3/4", 39 LF/gallon, 44 LF per hour	RF@.023	LF	.86	1.14	2.00
1" x 1", 22 LF/gallon, 30 LF per hour	RF@.033	LF	1.53	1.63	3.16
100 percent silicone caulk					
1/4" x 1/4", 351 LF/gallon, 63 LF per hour	RF@.016	LF	.33	.79	1.12
1/4" x 3/8", 234 LF/gallon, 60 LF per hour	RF@.017	LF	.50	.84	1.34
1/4" x 1/2", 176 LF/gallon, 58 LF per hour	RF@.017	LF	.67	.84	1.51
3/8" x 3/8", 156 LF/gallon, 58 LF per hour	RF@.017	LF	.75	.84	1.59
3/8" x 1/2", 117 LF/gallon, 57 LF per hour	RF@.017	LF	1.00	.84	1.84
3/8" x 5/8", 94 LF/gallon, 56 LF per hour	RF@.018	LF	1.25	.89	2.14
3/8" x 3/4", 76 LF/gallon, 52 LF per hour	RF@.019	LF	1.55	.94	2.49
1/2" x 1/2", 87 LF/gallon, 56 LF per hour	RF@.018	LF	1.35	.89	2.24
1/2" x 5/8", 70 LF/gallon, 50 LF per hour	RF@.020	LF	1.68	.99	2.67
1/2" x 3/4", 58 LF/gallon, 48 LF per hour	RF@.021	LF	2.03	1.04	3.07
1/2" x 7/8", 51 LF/gallon, 46 LF per hour	RF@.022	LF	2.30	1.09	3.39
1/2" x 1", 44 LF/gallon, 45 LF per hour	RF@.022	LF	2.67	1.09	3.76
3/4" x 3/4", 39 LF/gallon, 44 LF per hour	RF@.023	LF	3.01	1.14	4.15
1" x 1", 22 LF/gallon, 30 LF per hour	RF@.033	LF	5.34	1.63	6.97
Polyurethane sealant					
1/4" x 1/4", 351 LF/gallon, 63 LF per hour	RF@.016	LF	.24	.79	1.03
1/4" x 3/8", 234 LF/gallon, 60 LF per hour	RF@.017	LF	.37	.84	1.21
1/4" x 1/2", 176 LF/gallon, 58 LF per hour	RF@.017	LF	.49	.84	1.33
3/8" x 3/8", 156 LF/gallon, 58 LF per hour	RF@.017	LF	.55	.84	1.39
3/8" x 1/2", 117 LF/gallon, 57 LF per hour	RF@.017	LF	.73	.84	1.57
3/8" x 5/8", 94 LF/gallon, 56 LF per hour	RF@.018	LF	.91	.89	1.80
3/8" x 3/4", 76 LF/gallon, 52 LF per hour	RF@.019	LF	1.13	.94	2.07
1/2" x 1/2", 87 LF/gallon, 56 LF per hour	RF@.018	LF	.99	.89	1.88
1/2" x 5/8", 70 LF/gallon, 50 LF per hour	RF@.020	LF	1.23	.99	2.22
1/2" x 3/4", 58 LF/gallon, 48 LF per hour	RF@.021	LF	1.48	1.04	2.52
1/2" x 7/8", 51 LF/gallon, 46 LF per hour	RF@.022	LF	1.68	1.09	2.77
1/2" x 1", 44 LF/gallon, 45 LF per hour	RF@.022	LF	1.95	1.09	3.04
3/4" x 3/4", 39 LF/gallon, 44 LF per hour	RF@.023	LF	2.20	1.14	3.34
1" x 1", 22 LF/gallon, 30 LF per hour	RF@.033	LF	3.91	1.63	5.54
Backing rods for sealant					
Closed cell, 1/4" rod	RF@.010	LF	.04	.50	.54
Closed cell, 3/8" rod	RF@.011	LF	.10	.54	.64
Closed cell, 1/2" rod	RF@.011	LF	.14	.54	.68
Closed cell, 5/8" rod	RF@.012	LF	.13	.59	.72
Closed cell, 3/4" rod	RF@.012	LF	.19	.59	.78
Closed cell, 1" rod	RF@.013	LF	.49	.64	1.13
Closed cell, 1-1/4" rod	RF@.014	LF	.36	.69	1.05
Closed cell, 1-1/2" rod	RF@.015	LF	.34	.74	1.08
Closed cell, 2" rod	RF@.015	LF	1.09	.74	1.83
Closed cell, 3" rod	RF@.018	LF	1.86	.89	2.75

07 Thermal and Moisture Protection

	Craft@Hrs	Unit	Material	Labor	Total
Expansion Joints, Preformed					
Wall and ceiling, aluminum cover					
Drywall or panel type	CC@.067	LF	14.70	3.55	18.25
Plaster type	CC@.067	LF	14.70	3.55	18.25
Floor to wall, 3" x 3"	CC@.038	LF	8.00	2.01	10.01
Floor, 3"	CC@.038	LF	10.10	2.01	12.11
Neoprene joint with aluminum cover	CC@.079	LF	21.30	4.19	25.49
Wall to roof joint	CC@.094	LF	8.60	4.98	13.58
Bellows type expansion joints, butyl with neoprene backer					
16 oz copper, 4" wide	CC@.046	LF	16.40	2.44	18.84
28 gauge stainless steel, 4" wide	CC@.046	LF	14.20	2.44	16.64
26 gauge galvanized sheet metal, 4" wide	CC@.046	LF	9.38	2.44	11.82
16 oz copper, 6" wide	CC@.046	LF	18.60	2.44	21.04
28 gauge stainless steel, 6" wide	CC@.046	LF	16.60	2.44	19.04
26 gauge galvanized sheet metal, 6" wide	CC@.046	LF	11.30	2.44	13.74
Neoprene gaskets, closed cell					
1/8" x 2"	CC@.019	LF	.97	1.01	1.98
1/8" x 6"	CC@.023	LF	2.29	1.22	3.51
1/4" x 2"	CC@.022	LF	1.14	1.17	2.31
1/4" x 6"	CC@.024	LF	2.41	1.27	3.68
1/2" x 6"	CC@.025	LF	3.60	1.33	4.93
1/2" x 8"	CC@.028	LF	5.30	1.48	6.78
Acoustical caulking, drywall or plaster type	CC@.038	LF	.39	2.01	2.40
Polyisobutylene tapes, non-drying					
Polybutene	CC@.028	LF	.36	1.48	1.84
Polyisobutylene/butyl, preformed	CC@.020	LF	.19	1.06	1.25
Expansion Joint Covers					
Surface type, aluminum					
Floor, 1-1/2"	CC@.194	LF	27.60	10.30	37.90
Wall and ceiling, 1-1/2"	CC@.185	LF	15.50	9.81	25.31
Gymnasium base	CC@.099	LF	12.80	5.25	18.05
Roof, typical	CC@.145	LF	26.60	7.69	34.29

08 Openings

Complete Hollow Metal Door Assembly These figures show the costs normally associated with installing an exterior hollow core steel door.

Hollow metal exterior 3' x 7' flush door, with frame, hardware and trim, complete					
Stock hollow metal flush door,					
16 gauge, 3' x 7' x 1-3/4", non-rated	C8@.721	Ea	520.00	34.00	554.00
Closer plate reinforcing on door	—	Ea	20.40	—	20.40
Stock 18 gauge frame, 6" jamb, non-rated	C8@.944	Ea	158.00	44.50	202.50
Closer plate on frame	—	Ea	7.84	—	7.84
Three hinges, 4-1/2" x 4-1/2"	C8@.578	LS	131.00	27.20	158.20
Lockset, mortise type	C8@.949	Ea	346.00	44.70	390.70
Saddle type threshold, aluminum, 3'	C8@.276	Ea	25.40	13.00	38.40
Standard duty closer	C8@.787	Ea	150.00	37.10	187.10
Weatherstripping, bronze and neoprene	C8@2.58	LS	67.60	122.00	189.60
Paint with primer and 2 coats enamel	C8@.781	LS	15.20	36.80	52.00
Total cost door, frame and trim as described above	C8@7.62	Ea	1,441.44	359.30	1,800.74

	Craft@Hrs	Unit	Material	Labor	Total
Hollow Metal Exterior Doors Commercial quality doors.					
These costs do not include the frame, hinges, lockset, trim or finishing.					
6'8" high hollow flush doors, 1-3/8" thick, non-rated					
2'6" wide, 20 gauge	C8@.681	Ea	294.00	32.10	326.10
2'8" wide, 20 gauge	C8@.683	Ea	305.00	32.20	337.20
3'0" wide, 20 gauge	C8@.721	Ea	324.00	34.00	358.00
6'8" high hollow flush doors, 1-3/4" thick, non-rated					
2'6" wide, 20 gauge	C8@.681	Ea	358.00	32.10	390.10
2'8" wide, 20 gauge	C8@.697	Ea	366.00	32.90	398.90
2'8" wide, 18 gauge	C8@.697	Ea	428.00	32.90	460.90
2'8" wide, 16 gauge	C8@.697	Ea	497.00	32.90	529.90
3'0" wide, 20 gauge	C8@.721	Ea	387.00	34.00	421.00
3'0" wide, 18 gauge	C8@.721	Ea	446.00	34.00	480.00
3'0" wide, 16 gauge	C8@.721	Ea	520.00	34.00	554.00
7'0" high hollow flush doors, 1-3/4" thick, non-rated					
2'6" or 2'8" wide, 20 gauge	C8@.757	Ea	378.00	35.70	413.70
2'8" or 3'0" wide, 18 gauge	C8@.757	Ea	451.00	35.70	486.70
2'8" or 3'0" wide, 16 gauge	C8@.757	Ea	526.00	35.70	561.70
3'0" wide, 20 gauge	C8@.816	Ea	404.00	38.50	442.50
Additional costs for hollow metal doors, cost per door					
Add for steel astragal set on site	C8@.496	Ea	52.70	23.40	76.10
Add for factory applied steel astragal	—	Ea	52.70	—	52.70
Add for 90-minute "B" fire label rating	—	Ea	59.60	—	59.60
Add for R-7 polyurethane foam core	—	Ea	140.00	—	140.00
Add for 10" x 10" wired glass panel	—	Ea	103.00	—	103.00
Add for closer reinforcing plate	—	Ea	20.30	—	20.30
Add for chain or bolt reinforcing plate	—	Ea	152.00	—	152.00
Add for rim exit latch reinforcing	—	Ea	43.70	—	43.70
Add for vertical exit latch reinforcing	—	Ea	79.30	—	79.30
Add for pull plate reinforcing	—	Ea	31.90	—	31.90
Add for galvanizing 1-3/8" doors	—	Ea	39.60	—	39.60
Add for galvanizing 1-3/4" door	—	Ea	48.30	—	48.30
Add for cutouts to 4 SF	—	Ea	82.90	—	82.90
Add for cutouts over 4 SF	—	SF	17.40	—	17.40
Add for stainless steel doors	—	Ea	1,400.00	—	1,400.00
Add for baked enamel finish	—	Ea	106.00	—	106.00
Add for porcelain enamel finish	—	Ea	251.00	—	251.00
Add for larger sizes	—	SF	5.73	—	5.73
Add for special dapping	—	Ea	44.90	—	44.90

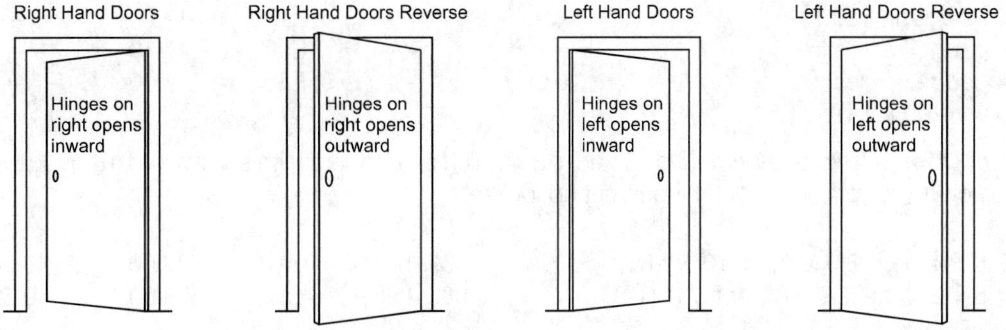

	Craft@Hrs	Unit	Material	Labor	Total
Hollow Metal Door Frames 18 gauge prefinished hollow metal door frames, non-rated, stock sizes, for 1-3/4" or 1-3/8" doors. These costs do not include the door, hinges, lockset, trim or finishing.					
6'8" high					
To 3'6" wide, to 4-1/2" jamb	C8@.944	Ea	139.00	44.50	183.50
To 3'6" wide, 4-3/4" to 6" jamb	C8@.944	Ea	145.00	44.50	189.50
To 3'6" wide, over 6" jamb	C8@.944	Ea	194.00	44.50	238.50
Over 4' wide, 4-1/2" jamb	C8@.944	Ea	165.00	44.50	209.50
Over 4' wide, 4-3/4" to 6" jamb	C8@.944	Ea	174.00	44.50	218.50
Over 4' wide, over 6" jamb	C8@.944	Ea	224.00	44.50	268.50
7' high					
To 3'6" wide, to 4-1/2" jamb	C8@.944	Ea	150.00	44.50	194.50
To 3'6" wide, 4-3/4" to 6" jamb	C8@.944	Ea	158.00	44.50	202.50
To 3'6" wide, over 6" jamb	C8@.944	Ea	205.00	44.50	249.50
Over 4' wide, 4-1/2" jamb	C8@.944	Ea	177.00	44.50	221.50
Over 4' wide, 4-3/4" to 6" jamb	C8@.944	Ea	185.00	44.50	229.50
Over 4' wide, over 6" jamb	C8@.944	Ea	236.00	44.50	280.50
8' high					
To 3'6" wide, to 4-1/2" jamb	C8@1.05	Ea	172.00	49.50	221.50
To 3'6" wide, 4-3/4" to 6" jamb	C8@1.05	Ea	183.00	49.50	232.50
To 3'6" wide, over 6" jamb	C8@1.05	Ea	235.00	49.50	284.50
Over 4' wide, 4-1/2" jamb	C8@1.05	Ea	199.00	49.50	248.50
Over 4' wide, 4-3/4" to 6" jamb	C8@1.05	Ea	204.00	49.50	253.50
Over 4' wide, over 6" jamb	C8@1.05	Ea	265.00	49.50	314.50
Cost additions or deductions for hollow metal door frames					
Add for concrete filled frames	C8@.382	Ea	10.80	18.00	28.80
Add for borrowed lite	C8@.086	SF	10.40	4.05	14.45
Add for fixed transom lite	C8@.099	SF	13.80	4.67	18.47
Add for movable transom lite	C8@.107	SF	15.70	5.04	20.74
Add for window frame sections	C8@.071	LF	8.39	3.35	11.74
Add for wall frame sections	C8@.071	LF	9.54	3.35	12.89
Add for 90-minute UL label	—	Ea	41.50	—	41.50
Add for aluminum casing	—	Ea	34.50	—	34.50
Add for communicator frame (back-to-back doors)	—	Ea	25.40	—	25.40
Add for lengthening, 7' to 8'10"	—	Ea	22.10	—	22.10
Add for extra hinge reinforcing	—	Ea	7.56	—	7.56
Add for stainless steel frames	—	Ea	725.00	—	725.00
Add for porcelain enamel finish	—	Ea	236.00	—	236.00
Add for reinforcing for chain and bolt	—	Ea	9.66	—	9.66
Add for closer plate reinforcing	—	Ea	8.56	—	8.56
Add for exit latch reinforcing	—	Ea	15.80	—	15.80
Deduct for 22 gauge frames	—	Ea	–17.00	—	–17.00
Add for 16 gauge frames	—	Ea	17.10	—	17.10
Add for 14 gauge frames	—	Ea	28.60	—	28.60
Add for galvanized finish	—	%	12.0	—	—
Prehung Steel Doors 18 gauge primed insulated 1-3/4" thick entry doors with sweep and 18 gauge steel frame. Costs shown include three 4" x 4" x 1/4" hinges but no lockset.					
Flush doors					
Jamb to 5-1/2" wide, 2'8" x 6'8", or 3'0" x 6'8"	C8@1.05	Ea	599.00	49.50	648.50
Jamb over 5-1/2" wide, 2'8" x 6'8", or 3'0" x 6'8"	C8@1.05	Ea	613.00	49.50	662.50
6 or 8 panel doors					
Jamb to 5-1/2" wide, 2'8" x 6'8", or 3'0" x 6'8"	C8@1.05	Ea	619.00	49.50	668.50
Jamb over 5-1/2" wide, 2'8" x 6'8", or 3'0" x 6'8"	C8@1.05	Ea	629.00	49.50	678.50

	Craft@Hrs	Unit	Material	Labor	Total
Additional costs for prehung steel doors					
90-minute Factory Mutual fire rating	—	Ea	30.80	—	30.80
60-minute Factory Mutual fire rating	—	Ea	23.70	—	23.70
Add for 16 gauge door and frame	—	Ea	18.70	—	18.70
Deduct for 22 gauge and door	—	Ea	-4.39	—	-4.39
Add for galvanized steel finish	—	Ea	16.30	—	16.30
Deduct for unfinished door	—	Ea	-17.00	—	-17.00
Add for installed weatherstripping	—	Ea	47.30	—	47.30
Add for aluminum threshold	—	Ea	47.00	—	47.00

Doors and Frames Commercial and institutional quality. Unfinished, no hardware included.

	Craft@Hrs	Unit	Material	Labor	Total
Hardwood, hollow core 1-3/8" thick prehung flush interior doors, 4-9/16 in. door frame.					
2'0" x 6'8"	C8@.936	Ea	210.00	44.10	254.10
2'4" x 6'8"	C8@.936	Ea	234.00	44.10	278.10
2'8" x 6'8"	C8@.936	Ea	188.00	44.10	232.10
3'0" x 6'8"	C8@.936	Ea	190.00	44.10	234.10
Steel 1-3/4" thick prehung flush exterior doors, welded steel 4-7/8" frame, 1-1/2 hour fire rating, with hardware.					
3'0" x 6'8", knocked down frame	C8@1.10	Ea	427.00	51.90	478.90
3'0" x 7'0", knocked down frame	C8@1.10	Ea	437.00	51.90	488.90
3'0" x 6'8", assembled frame	C8@.982	Ea	457.00	46.30	503.30
3'0" x 7'0", assembled frame	C8@.982	Ea	467.00	46.30	513.30
3'0" x 6'8", with panic bar hardware	C8@1.01	Ea	691.00	47.60	738.60
3'0" x 7'0", with panic bar hardware	C8@1.01	Ea	712.00	47.60	759.60
Fiberglass foam core 1-3/4" thick prehung exterior doors					
2'8" x 6'8", colonial panel face	C8@.982	Ea	231.00	46.30	277.30
3'0" x 6'8", colonial panel face	C8@1.01	Ea	231.00	47.60	278.60
2'8" x 6'8", French 15-lite	C8@.982	Ea	379.00	46.30	425.30
3'0" x 6'8", French 15-lite	C8@1.01	Ea	379.00	47.60	426.60

Special Doors Add the cost of electrical work. Equipment is a 4,000 lb. forklift.

	Craft@Hrs	Unit	Material	Labor	Equipment	Total
Sliding metal clad fire doors including electric motor						
Light duty, minimum	H5@.249	SF	48.70	13.60	1.71	64.01
Light duty, maximum	H5@.405	SF	85.00	22.10	2.78	109.88
Heavy duty, minimum	H5@.600	SF	97.20	32.70	4.13	134.03
Heavy duty, maximum	H5@.750	SF	167.00	40.90	5.16	213.06
Fire doors, overhead roll-up type, sectional steel, fusible link, UL label						
6' x 7', manual operation	F7@13.4	Ea	2,820.00	685.00	115.00	3,620.00
5' x 8', manual operation	F7@13.4	Ea	1,910.00	685.00	115.00	2,710.00
14' x 14', chain hoist operated	F7@26.2	Ea	5,550.00	1,340.00	225.00	7,115.00
18' x 14', chain hoist operated	F7@32.9	Ea	7,660.00	1,680.00	283.00	9,623.00

	Craft@Hrs	Unit	Material	Labor	Equipment	Total
Sliding metal fire doors. Motor operated, 3-hour rating, with fusible link. Add the cost of electrical hookup						
3' x 6'8"	H5@16.0	Ea	4,510.00	872.00	110.00	5,492.00
3'8" x 6'8"	H5@16.0	Ea	4,820.00	872.00	110.00	5,802.00
4' x 8'	H5@16.0	Ea	4,980.00	872.00	110.00	5,962.00
5' x 8'	H5@16.0	Ea	5,180.00	872.00	110.00	6,162.00
6' x 8'	H5@16.0	Ea	6,180.00	872.00	110.00	7,162.00
Refrigerator doors, manually operated, 4", with hardware and standard frame						
Galvanized, cooler, 3' x 7', hinged	F7@6.60	Ea	2,400.00	338.00	56.70	2,794.70
Stainless, cooler, 3' x 7', hinged	F7@6.60	Ea	2,740.00	338.00	56.70	3,134.70
Stainless, freezer, 3' x 7', hinged	F7@6.60	Ea	3,580.00	338.00	56.70	3,974.70
Stainless, cooler, 4' x 7', hinged	F7@6.60	Ea	3,100.00	338.00	56.70	3,494.70
Galvanized, cooler, 5' x 7', sliding	F7@7.93	Ea	4,080.00	406.00	68.20	4,554.20
Galvanized, freezer, 5' x 7' sliding	F7@7.93	Ea	4,080.00	406.00	68.20	4,554.20
Hangar doors, including hardware and motorized opener. Costs based on 150' wide doors, installed with a 25 ton hydraulic truck crane.						
To 20' high	H5@.213	SF	31.00	11.60	14.30	56.90
20' to 40' high	H5@.142	SF	40.10	7.74	9.50	57.34
40' to 60' high	H5@.085	SF	47.20	4.63	5.69	57.52
60' to 80' high	H5@.061	SF	56.20	3.32	4.08	63.60
More than 80' high	H5@.047	SF	92.90	2.56	3.14	98.60
Revolving doors, 6'6" to 7' diameter, manual controls						
Aluminum	F7@50.3	Ea	34,000.00	2,570.00	432.00	37,002.00
Stainless steel	F7@50.3	Ea	43,400.00	2,570.00	432.00	46,402.00
Bronze	F7@69.0	Ea	50,100.00	3,530.00	593.00	54,223.00
Add for automatic door controls	—	%	40.0	—	—	—
Security grilles, aluminum, overhead roll-up type, horizontal 5/16" rods at 2" OC, chain hoist operated						
8' x 8', clear anodized aluminum	F7@18.5	Ea	3,120.00	946.00	159.00	4,225.00
8' x 8', medium bronze aluminum	F7@18.5	Ea	4,400.00	946.00	159.00	5,505.00
10' x 10', anodized aluminum	F7@21.8	Ea	4,170.00	1,110.00	187.00	5,467.00
16' x 15', anodized, motor operated	F7@28.7	Ea	7,690.00	1,470.00	247.00	9,407.00
18' x 8', anodized aluminum	F7@26.3	Ea	6,390.00	1,340.00	226.00	7,956.00
18' x 8', anodized, motor operated	F7@28.7	Ea	7,460.00	1,470.00	247.00	9,177.00
Service doors, aluminum, overhead roll-up type						
4' x 4', manual counter shutter	F7@13.6	Ea	1,280.00	696.00	117.00	2,093.00
8' x 4', manual operation	F7@12.7	Ea	1,840.00	649.00	109.00	2,598.00
10' x 10', chain hoist operated	F7@12.7	Ea	2,820.00	649.00	109.00	3,578.00
Insulated overhead aluminum doors, roll-up, 22 gauge interior, 20 gauge exterior, 115 v. operator, with side seals, electric safety edge and button station. With two dock bumpers and electrical hookup only.						
6' x 10', R-7 insulation	F7@12.7	Ea	3,350.00	649.00	109.00	4,108.00
8' x 10', R-8 insulation	F7@13.6	Ea	4,780.00	696.00	117.00	5,593.00
Add for powder coat finish	—	%	25.0	—	—	—
Service doors, steel, overhead roll-up, chain hoist operated						
8' x 8'	F7@11.7	Ea	1,860.00	598.00	101.00	2,559.00
10' x 10'	F7@11.7	Ea	2,290.00	598.00	101.00	2,989.00
12' x 12'	F7@14.7	Ea	3,080.00	752.00	126.00	3,958.00
14' x 14'	F7@18.2	Ea	3,360.00	931.00	156.00	4,447.00
18' x 18'	F7@22.0	Ea	4,560.00	1,130.00	189.00	5,879.00
18' x 14', 240 volt motor operated	F7@25.0	Ea	5,930.00	1,280.00	215.00	7,425.00

	Craft@Hrs	Unit	Material	Labor	Equipment	Total
Sliding glass doors with 1/4" tempered float glass including frame, trim, and hardware						
6-0' wide economy grade	C8@2.75	Ea	1,200.00	130.00	—	1,330.00
6-0' wide premium grade	C8@3.00	Ea	1,390.00	141.00	—	1,531.00
12-0' wide economy grade	C8@4.80	Ea	1,900.00	226.00	—	2,126.00
12-0' wide premium grade	C8@5.00	Ea	2,790.00	236.00	—	3,026.00
Sliding glass doors with 5/8" insulating glass including frame, trim, and hardware						
6-0' wide economy grade	C8@2.75	Ea	1,700.00	130.00	—	1,830.00
6-0' wide premium grade	C8@3.00	Ea	2,050.00	141.00	—	2,191.00
12-0' wide economy grade	C8@4.80	Ea	2,330.00	226.00	—	2,556.00
12-0' wide premium grade	C8@5.00	Ea	3,330.00	236.00	—	3,566.00
Telescoping doors, with frame, enamel finish, electric operated						
10' high x 10' wide	H5@15.0	Ea	12,300.00	817.00	103.00	13,220.00
20' high x 10' wide	H5@19.3	Ea	19,400.00	1,050.00	133.00	20,583.00
20' high x 12' wide	H5@24.0	Ea	21,200.00	1,310.00	165.00	22,675.00
20' high x 16' wide	H5@26.4	Ea	25,400.00	1,440.00	182.00	27,022.00
Accordion folding doors, 4-1/2" wide, nylon wheels hung from straight track, with fittings, 6'8" to 12' high, manual operation, per SF of opening						
Vinyl surface	C8@.051	SF	25.60	2.40	—	28.00
Birch or oak veneer	C8@.051	SF	41.40	2.40	—	43.80
Clear or bronze acrylic	C8@.051	SF	48.50	2.40	—	50.90
Clear or bronze acrylic, with security	C8@.051	SF	58.20	2.40	—	60.60
Anodized aluminum, solid	C8@.051	SF	57.00	2.40	—	59.40
Anodized aluminum, perforated	C8@.051	SF	71.70	2.40	—	74.10
Add for curved track	C8@.102	LF	21.20	4.81	—	26.01
Add for hat channel (suspended ceiling) mount	C8@.102	LF	10.60	4.81	—	15.41
Add for sound rated folding doors	—	SF	7.96	—	—	7.96
Add for locking bolt, per side	—	Ea	46.60	—	—	46.60
Add for fire retardant accordion folding doors	—	%	40.0	—	—	—
Deduct for finished one side (closet) doors	—	%	-10.0	—	—	—
Air curtains. Add the cost of motor starters, transformers, door switches and temperature controls. Unheated, with minimal wind stoppage. Per linear foot of opening width.						
8-0' high, multiples of 3'-0" wide	C8@3.70	LF	331.00	174.00	—	505.00
10-0' high, multiples of 4'-0" wide	C8@3.80	LF	340.00	179.00	—	519.00
12-0' high, multiples of 3'-6" wide	C8@3.90	LF	357.00	184.00	—	541.00
16-0' high, multiples of 3'-6" wide	C8@4.00	LF	429.00	189.00	—	618.00
Add for high wind stoppage	—	%	20.0	—	—	—
Add for heated units	—	%	75.0	—	—	—
Door louvers. Non-vision design recommended for schools, Class "A" and institutional buildings. Suitable for both wood and metal doors. Manufactured from 18 gauge steel with a Jet Kote finish and supplied with #8-3/4" Phillips (pan head) L&L Louvers.						
12" x 12"	C8@.500	Ea	49.40	23.60	—	73.00
18" x 12"	C8@.500	Ea	61.60	23.60	—	85.20
18" x 18"	C8@.500	Ea	69.60	23.60	—	93.20
24" x 12"	C8@.500	Ea	72.00	23.60	—	95.60
24" x 18"	C8@.500	Ea	81.20	23.60	—	104.80
24" x 24"	C8@.500	Ea	104.00	23.60	—	127.60

	Craft@Hrs	Unit	Material	Labor	Equipment	Total
See-thru door frames. (Vision Lite). Recommended for applications where total visibility, light transmission and security are required. The beveled style frame provides a wider field of vision. Manufactured from 18 gauge Jetkote (steel). Installation screws are #8 x 2" Phillips flat head screws. Add the cost of glass below. L&L Louvers.						
6" x 27"	C8@.500	Ea	48.60	23.60	—	72.20
7" x 22"	C8@.500	Ea	45.60	23.60	—	69.20
12" x 12"	C8@.500	Ea	32.90	23.60	—	56.50
18" x 18"	C8@.500	Ea	54.60	23.60	—	78.20
24" x 24"	C8@.500	Ea	59.50	23.60	—	83.10
24" x 30"	C8@.500	Ea	64.70	23.60	—	88.30
24" x 36"	C8@.500	Ea	68.40	23.60	—	92.00
1/4" Wire glass for see-thru door frames						
6" x 27"	—	Ea	39.60	—	—	39.60
7" x 22"	—	Ea	39.80	—	—	39.80
12" x 12"	—	Ea	40.20	—	—	40.20
18" x 18"	—	Ea	54.70	—	—	54.70
24" x 24"	—	Ea	64.90	—	—	64.90
24" x 30"	—	Ea	69.70	—	—	69.70
24" x 36"	—	Ea	74.70	—	—	74.70

	Craft@Hrs	Unit	Material	Labor	Total
Steel access doors, 1" frame, concealed hinge, screwdriver access					
12" x 12", galvanized	CC@.250	Ea	33.40	13.30	46.70
14" x 14", galvanized	CC@.250	Ea	35.50	13.30	48.80
18" x 18"	CC@.275	Ea	48.80	14.60	63.40
14" x 14", vinyl	CC@.250	Ea	16.90	13.30	30.20

	Craft@Hrs	Unit	Material	Labor	Equipment	Total
Stock room doors, double-action .063" aluminum, with hardware and bumper strips both sides,7' high doors, plastic laminate finish, 12" high baseplate in each door						
2' wide opening, 1 door	F7@1.70	Ea	296.00	86.90	14.60	397.50
2'6" wide opening, 1 door	F7@1.70	Ea	330.00	86.90	14.60	431.50
3' wide opening, 1 door	F7@1.80	Ea	363.00	92.10	15.50	470.60
3'6" wide opening, 1 door	F7@1.90	Ea	405.00	97.20	16.30	518.50
4' wide opening, 2 doors, per pair	F7@3.36	Pr	590.00	172.00	28.90	790.90
5' wide opening, 2 doors, per pair	F7@3.36	Pr	662.00	172.00	28.90	862.90
6' wide opening, 2 doors, per pair	F7@3.98	Pr	727.00	204.00	34.20	965.20
7' wide opening, 2 doors, per pair	F7@3.98	Pr	789.00	204.00	34.20	1,027.20
Add for automatic openers, per pair	F7@8.00	Pr	2,280.00	409.00	—	2,689.00
Vault doors, minimum security						
3' x 7', 2 hour fire rating	F7@22.0	Ea	3,440.00	1,130.00	189.00	4,759.00
4' x 7', 2 hour fire rating	F7@23.4	Ea	4,940.00	1,200.00	201.00	6,341.00
3' x 7', 4 hour fire rating	F7@27.2	Ea	3,780.00	1,390.00	234.00	5,404.00
4' x 7', 4 hour fire rating	F7@28.7	Ea	5,140.00	1,470.00	247.00	6,857.00

Flexible strip doors Suitable for interior or exterior use. High strength USDA-approved clear transparent PVC plastic strips, with aluminum mounting hardware. Typical uses include truck dock door openings, railway car entrances, freezer doors and as positive draft protection to check the flow of unwanted air at +140 degrees to –40 degrees F. Costs shown per SF are per square foot of flexible strip area. To calculate the flexible strip area, add 2 linear feet to the opening width and height to allow for coverage at the sides and top. Costs shown per LF are per linear foot of mounting hardware. To calculate the length of the mounting hardware, add 2 LF to the opening width. Labor costs are based on work performed using ladders. Add the cost of scaffolding if required.

	Craft@Hrs	Unit	Material	Labor	Total
Openings to 8' in height, 8" wide strips x .080" thick					
With 1/2 strip overlap	C8@.058	SF	5.62	2.73	8.35
With 3/4 strip overlap	C8@.076	SF	6.22	3.58	9.80
With full strip overlap	C8@.096	SF	8.69	4.53	13.22
Openings over 8' to 14' in height, 12" wide strips x .120" thick					
With 2/3 strip overlap	C8@.100	SF	9.96	4.71	14.67
With full strip overlap	C8@.115	SF	11.90	5.42	17.32
Openings over 14' to 20' in height, 16" wide strips x .120" thick					
With 1/2 strip overlap	C8@.075	SF	10.70	3.54	14.24
With 3/4 strip overlap	C8@.100	SF	14.10	4.71	18.81
With full strip overlap	C8@.125	SF	16.00	5.89	21.89
Add for mounting hardware, aluminum, pre-drilled, complete with nuts, bolts, washers and flex strip mounting pins					
Ceiling- or header-mounted (1.5 lbs per LF)	C8@.400	LF	14.20	18.90	33.10
Wall-mounted (2.5 lbs per LF)	C8@.500	LF	51.80	23.60	75.40

Store front windows, subcontract

Typical subcontract prices including clear anodized thermally broken aluminum framing sections, including shop drawings and exterior caulking, add the cost of glass below. Per SF of wall opening.

	Craft@Hrs	Unit	Material	Labor	Total
2" x 4-1/2" sections	—	LF	—	—	33.90
1-3/4" x 4-1/2" sections	—	LF	—	—	32.30
Hinged entry door, 3' x 6'8", with closer and pulls	—	Ea	—	—	1,330.00
Stanley Dura-Glide bi-parting sliding automatic doors, per 14' x 7' 8" opening, with sensors and glass	—	Ea	—	—	7,310.00
Spandrel glass for aluminum storefront					
1" solar low-E insulated glass	—	SF	—	—	6.94
Tempered glass for automatic entry door, per door	—	Ea	—	—	814.00

Window tint film Applied on site. Full roll quantities. Partial rolls will cost more per square foot. Smaller windows will increase labor costs

	Craft@Hrs	Unit	Material	Labor	Total
Silver tint, 99% UV block, 20% to 50% light transmission	G1@.066	SF	1.15	3.19	4.34
Solar control, dual reflective, 45% to 70% light transmission	G1@.066	SF	1.57	3.19	4.76
Exterior safety film, 4 mil, clear, resists impact, 88% light transmission	G1@.085	SF	1.20	4.11	5.31
3M Prestige, sun control, safety or decorative, typical cost, with warranty	G1@.085	SF	6.92	4.11	11.03

Commercial and industrial grade steel windows, glazed. Per SF of wall opening.

	Craft@Hrs	Unit	Material	Labor	Total
Industrial grade, fixed 100%	G1@.086	SF	19.30	4.16	23.46
Industrial grade, vented 50%	G1@.086	SF	24.90	4.16	29.06
Projected, vented 50%	G1@.086	SF	27.80	4.16	31.96
Add for screen, SF of screen	—	SF	3.36	—	3.36

Custom wood windows. Architectural grade. Pine interior, vinyl-clad exterior, insulating. Argon-filled low-E insulating glass, with hardware and weatherstripping, stationary

	Craft@Hrs	Unit	Material	Labor	Total
20" x 53"	CG@.500	Ea	644.00	27.80	671.80
26" x 26"	CG@.500	Ea	504.00	27.80	531.80
36" x 36"	CG@.500	Ea	644.00	27.80	671.80
36" x 53"	CG@1.00	Ea	852.00	55.50	907.50
36" x 75"	CG@1.00	Ea	912.00	55.50	967.50
40" x 19"	CG@.500	Ea	456.00	27.80	483.80
72" x 75"	CG@1.00	Ea	1,820.00	55.50	1,875.50
Add for tempered insulating glass	—	SF	18.00	—	18.00

	Craft@Hrs	Unit	Material	Labor	Total
Hardware Commercial and industrial quality. Installation costs include drilling and routing of doors where required. Rule of thumb. Use these costs for preliminary estimates.					
Hardware for commercial buildings, per square foot of floor area					
Economy grade, for doors, cabinets, and toilet rooms	CC@.002	SF	.25	.11	.36
Standard grade, for doors, cabinets, and toilet rooms	CC@.004	SF	.53	.21	.74
Hospital, not including panic hardware, per door	CC@2.46	Ea	692.00	130.00	822.00
Office, not including panic hardware, per door	CC@1.57	Ea	332.00	83.20	415.20
School, not including panic hardware, per door	CC@1.94	Ea	463.00	103.00	566.00
Detail cost for individual hardware components					
Cabinet hardware, per LF of face, typical prices					
Commercial grade	CC@.145	LF	15.10	7.69	22.79
Institutional grade	CC@.181	LF	19.00	9.60	28.60
Closer, surface-mounted. Based on Schlage Lock					
Interior doors	CC@.616	Ea	151.00	32.70	183.70
Exterior doors	CC@.709	Ea	143.00	37.60	180.60
Exterior, heavy duty	CC@.894	Ea	167.00	47.40	214.40
Floor-mounted	CC@1.16	Ea	286.00	61.50	347.50
Deadbolts and deadlatches, chrome finish					
Standard deadbolt, single cylinder	CC@.745	Ea	43.80	39.50	83.30
Standard deadbolt, double cylinder	CC@.745	Ea	60.30	39.50	99.80
Standard turnbolt, no cylinder	CC@.745	Ea	33.70	39.50	73.20
Nightlatch, single cylinder	CC@.745	Ea	106.00	39.50	145.50
Nightlatch, double cylinder	CC@.745	Ea	118.00	39.50	157.50
Nightlatch, no cylinder, turnbolt	CC@.745	Ea	91.50	39.50	131.00
Heavy duty deadbolt, single cylinder	CC@.745	Ea	82.20	39.50	121.70
Heavy duty deadbolt, double cylinder	CC@.745	Ea	102.00	39.50	141.50
Heavy duty turnbolt, no cylinder	CC@.745	Ea	82.20	39.50	121.70
Extra heavy deadbolt, single cylinder	CC@.745	Ea	130.00	39.50	169.50
Extra heavy deadbolt, double cylinder	CC@.745	Ea	153.00	39.50	192.50
Add for brass or bronze finish	—	Ea	3.73	—	3.73
Door stops					
Rubber tip, screw base	CC@.060	Ea	5.80	3.18	8.98
Floor-mounted, with holder	CC@.279	Ea	24.00	14.80	38.80
Wall-mounted, with holder	CC@.279	Ea	23.40	14.80	38.20
Overhead-mounted	CC@.528	Ea	138.00	28.00	166.00
Hinges, butt type					
3-1/2" x 3-1/2"	CC@.357	Pr	13.40	18.90	32.30
5" x 5", hospital swing clear	CC@.547	Pr	178.00	29.00	207.00
4", spring, single acting	CC@.243	Pr	44.30	12.90	57.20
4-1/2", heavy duty	CC@.347	Pr	82.50	18.40	100.90
7", spring, double acting	CC@.491	Pr	108.00	26.00	134.00
Floor-mounted, interior, per door	CC@.665	Ea	362.00	35.30	397.30
Floor-mounted, exterior, per 3' door	CC@.665	Ea	389.00	35.30	424.30
Floor-mounted, exterior, over 3' wide door	CC@.799	Ea	824.00	42.40	866.40
Invisible, blind doors, interior, per door	CC@.574	Ea	43.00	30.40	73.40
Invisible, for blind doors, exterior	CC@.574	Pr	54.70	30.40	85.10
Kick plates (see also Plates below)					
10" x 34" 16 gauge, bronze	CC@.452	Ea	58.00	24.00	82.00
10" x 34" 18 gauge, stainless	CC@.452	Ea	47.90	24.00	71.90
Letter drop, for wood doors, brass plated	CC@.369	Ea	40.10	19.60	59.70

	Craft@Hrs	Unit	Material	Labor	Total
Locksets					
Heavy duty residential or light duty commercial locksets, chrome finish					
Classroom or storeroom, key lock	CC@.745	Ea	130.00	39.50	169.50
Dummy knob	CC@.247	Ea	24.40	13.10	37.50
Entrance lockset, key lock	CC@.745	Ea	119.00	39.50	158.50
Passage latch, no lock	CC@.689	Ea	56.10	36.50	92.60
Privacy latch, button lock	CC@.689	Ea	67.50	36.50	104.00
Add for lever handle (handicapped)	—	Ea	46.50	—	46.50
Add for brass or bronze finish	—	Ea	8.09	—	8.09
Heavy duty commercial, chrome finish					
Bored entrance lockset	CC@.745	Ea	298.00	39.50	337.50
Grip handle, with trim	CC@.855	Ea	329.00	45.30	374.30
Single deadbolt-lockset	CC@.745	Ea	145.00	39.50	184.50
Double deadbolt-lockset	CC@.745	Ea	191.00	39.50	230.50
Mortise deadbolt-lockset	CC@.855	Ea	329.00	45.30	374.30
No key lock, push-button pad entry	CC@.855	Ea	723.00	45.30	768.30
Add for lever handle (handicapped)	—	Ea	31.10	—	31.10
Add for brass or bronze finish	—	Ea	11.30	—	11.30
Panic type exit door hardware, with trim					
Mortise type, for aluminum, steel or wood doors					
Satin aluminum finish	CC@2.41	Ea	602.00	128.00	730.00
Dark bronze finish	CC@2.41	Ea	618.00	128.00	746.00
Polished chrome finish	CC@2.41	Ea	733.00	128.00	861.00
Add for external lockset	CC@.401	Ea	82.00	21.30	103.30
Rim lock type, for aluminum, steel or wood doors					
Satin aluminum finish	CC@1.50	Ea	440.00	79.50	519.50
Dark bronze finish	CC@1.50	Ea	464.00	79.50	543.50
Polished chrome finish	CC@1.50	Ea	567.00	79.50	646.50
Add for external lockset	CC@.401	Ea	61.80	21.30	83.10
Vertical rod type, satin aluminum finish, with trim					
Aluminum doors, concealed rod	CC@2.14	Ea	584.00	113.00	697.00
Metal or wood doors, external rod	CC@1.79	Ea	611.00	94.90	705.90
Wood doors, concealed rod	CC@2.14	Ea	718.00	113.00	831.00
Add for external lockset	CC@.401	Ea	79.60	21.30	100.90
Add for bronze or black finish	—	%	37.5	—	—
Add for chrome finish	—	%	70.0	—	—
Plates (see also Kick Plates above)					
Pull plates, bronze, 4" x 16"	CC@.190	Ea	47.80	10.10	57.90
Push plates bronze, 4" x 16"	CC@.190	Ea	37.10	10.10	47.20
Surface bolts					
4" bolt	CC@.308	Ea	7.39	16.30	23.69
6" bolt	CC@.310	Ea	10.10	16.40	26.50
Threshold					
Aluminum, 36"	CC@.241	Ea	23.70	12.80	36.50
Bronze, 36"	CC@.241	Ea	97.30	12.80	110.10

Weatherstripping

	Craft@Hrs	Unit	Material	Labor	Total
Bronze and neoprene, 3' x 7' door					
Wood door	CC@1.53	Ea	27.40	81.10	108.50
Steel door, adjustable	CC@2.32	Ea	66.10	123.00	189.10
Astragal, mortise-mounted, bronze, adjustable	CC@.064	LF	16.30	3.39	19.69
Glue-back foam for 3' x 7' door	CC@.006	LF	.47	.32	.79

	Craft@Hrs	Unit	Material	Labor	Total
Glazing					
Sheet (window) glass					
Single strength "B", 3/32"					
To 60" width plus length	G1@.057	SF	2.09	2.76	4.85
Over 60" to 70" width plus length	G1@.057	SF	2.16	2.76	4.92
Over 70" to 80" width plus length	G1@.057	SF	2.34	2.76	5.10
Over 80" width plus length	G1@.057	SF	2.38	2.76	5.14
Double strength window glass					
Double strength "B", 1/8"					
To 60" width plus length	G1@.057	SF	2.72	2.76	5.48
Over 60" to 70" width plus length	G1@.057	SF	2.83	2.76	5.59
Over 70" to 80" width plus length	G1@.057	SF	2.92	2.76	5.68
Over 80" width plus length	G1@.057	SF	3.02	2.76	5.78
Tempered "B"	G1@.057	SF	4.44	2.76	7.20
Obscure	G1@.057	SF	4.19	2.76	6.95
3/16" glass					
Crystal (clear)	G1@.068	SF	3.62	3.29	6.91
Tempered	G1@.068	SF	5.99	3.29	9.28
1/4" glass					
Float, clear, Quality 3	G1@.102	SF	3.45	4.94	8.39
Float, bronze or gray, Quality 3	G1@.102	SF	3.63	4.94	8.57
Float, obscure	G1@.102	SF	5.25	4.94	10.19
Float, heat absorbing	G1@.102	SF	5.74	4.94	10.68
Float, safety, laminated, clear	G1@.102	SF	6.35	4.94	11.29
Float, tempered	G1@.102	SF	5.74	4.94	10.68
Spandrel, plain	G1@.102	SF	7.74	4.94	12.68
Spandrel, tinted gray or bronze	G1@.102	SF	8.50	4.94	13.44
Tempered, reflective	G1@.102	SF	8.82	4.94	13.76
3/8" glass					
Float, clear	G1@.128	SF	5.91	6.19	12.10
Float, tinted	G1@.128	SF	8.26	6.19	14.45
Obscure, tempered	G1@.128	SF	8.82	6.19	15.01
Corrugated glass	G1@.128	SF	7.57	6.19	13.76
1/2" float, tempered	G1@.157	SF	21.80	7.60	29.40
1" bullet resistant, 12" x 12" panels	G1@1.32	SF	84.50	63.90	148.40
2" bullet resistant, 15 to 20 SF	G1@1.62	SF	50.60	78.40	129.00
Insulating glass, 2 layers of 1/8", 1/2" overall, 10 to 15 square foot lites					
"B" Quality sheet glass	G1@.131	SF	6.70	6.34	13.04
Float, polished bronze or gray	G1@.131	SF	9.34	6.34	15.68
Insulating glass, 2 layers of 1/4" float, 1" overall, 30 to 40 square foot lites					
Clear float glass	G1@.136	SF	10.30	6.58	16.88
Acrylic plastic sheet (Plexiglas), clear except as noted					
11" x 14" .093" thick	—	Ea	6.67	—	6.67
12" x 24" .093" thick	—	Ea	8.00	—	8.00
18" x 24" .093" thick	—	Ea	13.50	—	13.50
24" x 48" .093" thick	—	Ea	37.50	—	37.50
30" x 36" .093" thick	—	Ea	32.80	—	32.80
36" x 48" .093" thick	—	Ea	48.00	—	48.00
36" x 72" .093" thick	—	Ea	70.00	—	70.00
18" x 24" .236" thick	—	Ea	29.80	—	29.80
24" x 48" .236" thick	—	Ea	74.00	—	74.00
30" x 36" .236" thick	—	Ea	73.30	—	73.30
36" x 72" .236" thick	—	Ea	156.00	—	156.00
30" x 36" .093" thick, bronze	—	Ea	33.60	—	33.60

08 Openings

	Craft@Hrs	Unit	Material	Labor	Total
Wired glass, 1/4", Type 3					
Clear	G1@.103	SF	7.90	4.98	12.88
Hammered	G1@.103	SF	7.38	4.98	12.36
Obscure	G1@.103	SF	7.11	4.98	12.09
Mirrors, unframed					
Sheet glass, 3/16"	G1@.103	SF	5.83	4.98	10.81
Float glass, 1/4"	G1@.106	SF	9.02	5.13	14.15
Reflective, 1 way, in wood stops	G1@.118	SF	16.60	5.71	22.31
Small lites, adhesive mount	G1@.057	SF	3.80	2.76	6.56
Polycarbonate sheet glazing. 4' x 8' panels, Cyro					
Impact resistant, weather resistant sheets					
Clear 1/8"	G1@.027	SF	6.00	1.31	7.31
Clear 3/16"	G1@.027	SF	6.31	1.31	7.62
Clear 1/4"	G1@.027	SF	8.17	1.31	9.48
Clear 1/2"	G1@.035	SF	15.00	1.69	16.69
Add for tints	—	%	17.0	—	—
Chemical and abrasion resistant sheets					
Clear 1/8"	G1@.027	SF	9.21	1.31	10.52
Clear 3/16"	G1@.027	SF	10.50	1.31	11.81
Clear 1/4"	G1@.027	SF	15.40	1.31	16.71
Clear 1/2"	G1@.035	SF	23.40	1.69	25.09
Add for tints	—	%	17.0	—	—
Shock absorbent, high light transmission sheets (greenhouse applications)					
Clear 5/16"	G1@.027	SF	9.21	1.31	10.52
Clear 5/8"	G1@.035	SF	10.50	1.69	12.19

09 Finishes

Gypsum Wallboard Commercial grade work. Material costs include 6% for waste. Costs per square foot of area covered.

	Craft@Hrs	Unit	Material	Labor	Total
Gypsum wallboard nailed or screwed to wood framing or wood furring, no taping or finishing included					
3/8" on walls	CD@.007	SF	.33	.37	.70
3/8" on ceilings	CD@.009	SF	.33	.47	.80
3/8" on furred columns and beams	CD@.013	SF	.33	.68	1.01
1/2" on walls	CD@.007	SF	.40	.37	.77
1/2" on ceilings	CD@.009	SF	.40	.47	.87
1/2" on furred columns and beams	CD@.015	SF	.40	.78	1.18
5/8" on walls	CD@.007	SF	.39	.37	.76
5/8" on ceilings	CD@.010	SF	.39	.52	.91
5/8" on furred columns and beams	CD@.015	SF	.39	.78	1.17
Gypsum wallboard clipped to metal furring, no taping or finishing included. Add the cost of furring from the sections that follow.					
3/8" on wall furring	CD@.008	SF	.33	.42	.75
3/8" on ceiling furring	CD@.011	SF	.33	.58	.91
1/2" on wall furring	CD@.009	SF	.40	.47	.87
1/2" on ceiling furring	CD@.011	SF	.40	.58	.98
1/2" on column or beam furring	CD@.018	SF	.40	.94	1.34
5/8" on wall furring	CD@.009	SF	.39	.47	.86
5/8" on ceiling furring	CD@.011	SF	.39	.58	.97
5/8" on column or beam furring	CD@.018	SF	.39	.94	1.33
1/2", two layers on ceiling furring	CD@.022	SF	.79	1.15	1.94
1/2", two layers on furring	CD@.017	SF	.79	.89	1.68
1/4" sound board	CD@.008	SF	.38	.42	.80

	Craft@Hrs	Unit	Material	Labor	Total
Wallboard finishing. Per ASTM C840. Higher 'level' costs include prior 'levels'.					
Add for taping only, no joint finishing	CD@.300	CSF	1.28	15.70	16.98
Level 1 - taping and finishing wall joints (firetape)	CD@.700	CSF	3.21	36.60	39.81
Level 2 - finishing wall joints	CD@1.20	CSF	4.37	62.70	67.07
Level 3 - finishing wall joints	CD@1.60	CSF	5.52	83.70	89.22
Level 4 - finishing wall joints	CD@2.00	CSF	5.85	105.00	110.85
Level 5 - finishing wall joints, skim entire surface	CD@2.60	CSF	7.70	136.00	143.70
Add for taping and finishing ceiling joints	—	%	—	33.3	—
Additional costs for gypsum wallboard					
Add for foil-backed board	—	SF	.06	—	.06
Add for fire resistant board	—	SF	.05	—	.05
Add for water resistant board	—	SF	.15	—	.15
Add for 10' or 12' wall heights	CD@.001	SF	.02	.05	.07
Add for school jobs	CD@.002	SF	—	.10	.10
Add for trowel textured finish	CD@.009	SF	.43	.47	.90
Add for adhesive application, 1/4" bead					
Studs or joists 16" on center	CD@.056	CSF	4.24	2.93	7.17
Studs or joists 24" on center	CD@.042	CSF	2.83	2.20	5.03
Bead, casing and channels					
Corner bead, 1-1/4" x 1-1/4"	CD@.017	LF	.27	.89	1.16
Stop or casing	CD@.021	LF	.29	1.10	1.39
Jamb casing	CD@.023	LF	.29	1.20	1.49
RC-1 channel or 7/8" hat channel	CD@.011	LF	.64	.58	1.22
Vinyl clad gypsum board, adhesive or clip application on walls					
1/2", no moldings included	CD@.010	SF	.85	.52	1.37
5/8", no moldings included	CD@.011	SF	.88	.58	1.46
Drywall specialties Commercial grade work. Material costs include 6% for waste.					
Heat and sound reduction					
Noiseproofing adhesive, 28 oz covers 16 SF	CD@.005	SF	1.12	.26	1.38
1/8" sound membrane, applied over studs/joists	CD@.015	SF	5.32	.78	6.10
Hilti CP 777 top of wall 2" firestop and No. 673 joint spray					
New installation CP 777 firestop and spray	CD@.135	LF	3.10	7.06	10.16
Remove and replace CP 777 firestop and spray	CD@.150	LF	3.10	7.84	10.94
Hilti CP 777 top of wall 2" firestop and No. 606 1/2" fire caulk					
New installation CP 777 firestop and caulk	CD@.200	LF	2.21	10.50	12.71
Remove and replace CP 777 firestop and caulk	CD@.250	LF	2.21	13.10	15.31
Hilti CP 606 fire caulk					
Per penetration, CP 606 fire caulk	CD@.500	Ea	4.53	26.10	30.63
Per linear foot, CP 606 fire caulk	CD@.100	LF	1.81	5.23	7.04
Hilti CP 672 speed spray, per linear foot	CD@.068	LF	2.08	3.56	5.64
Wall and slab penetration firestop, intumescent sealant, 1/4" W x 1/2" D					
Average 1" wall penetration	CD@.125	Ea	.98	6.54	7.52
Opening to 1", wall penetration	CD@.125	Ea	1.03	6.54	7.57
Opening to 1", slab penetration	CD@.175	Ea	.16	9.15	9.31
Opening to 1-1/2" wall penetration	CD@.125	Ea	.15	6.54	6.69
Opening to 1-1/2" slab penetration	CD@.175	Ea	.21	9.15	9.36
Opening to 2-1/2" wall penetration	CD@.125	Ea	.26	6.54	6.80
Opening to 2-1/2" slab penetration	CD@.175	Ea	.30	9.15	9.45
Opening to 4" wall penetration	CD@.125	Ea	.41	6.54	6.95
Opening to 4" slab penetration	CD@.175	Ea	.42	9.15	9.57
Ductwork, per LF of sealant	CD@.125	LF	.37	6.54	6.91
Firestop ceiling bulkhead, furred-out gypsum board on resilient channels					
No existing ceiling	CD@1.10	LF	13.40	57.50	70.90
Light to medium obstructions	CD@1.33	LF	13.40	69.50	82.90
Heavily obstructed	CD@1.50	LF	13.40	78.40	91.80
Control joint reglet	CD@.050	LF	.62	2.61	3.23
Gypsum access panel, glass fiber reinforced, 12" to 36"	CD@2.25	Ea	227.00	118.00	345.00

	Craft@Hrs	Unit	Material	Labor	Total
Furring and Lathing For commercial applications. See plaster costs in the following section.					
Furring on walls, cold rolled, galvanized					
3/4", 12" on center	C8@.306	SY	4.45	14.40	18.85
3/4", 16" on center	C8@.270	SY	3.88	12.70	16.58
3/4", 24" on center	C8@.207	SY	2.94	9.76	12.70
1-1/2", 12" on center	C8@.342	SY	6.32	16.10	22.42
1-1/2", 16" on center	C8@.297	SY	5.40	14.00	19.40
1-1/2", 24" on center	C8@.234	SY	4.50	11.00	15.50
3-5/8", 12" on center, 25 gauge	C8@.360	SY	9.35	17.00	26.35
3-5/8", 16" on center, 25 gauge	C8@.315	SY	7.34	14.80	22.14
3-5/8", 24" on center, 25 gauge	C8@.261	SY	6.97	12.30	19.27
Furring on ceilings, cold rolled, galvanized					
3/4", 12" on center	C8@.413	SY	4.45	19.50	23.95
3/4", 16" on center	C8@.365	SY	3.88	17.20	21.08
3/4", 24" on center	C8@.280	SY	2.94	13.20	16.14
1-1/2", 12" on center	C8@.462	SY	6.32	21.80	28.12
1-1/2", 16" on center	C8@.400	SY	5.40	18.90	24.30
1-1/2", 24" on center	C8@.316	SY	4.50	14.90	19.40
1-1/2" x 3/4", coffered	C8@.887	SY	6.97	41.80	48.77
Furring on beams and columns, per linear foot of galvanized channel					
7/8" channel	C8@.059	LF	.50	2.78	3.28
1-5/8" channel	C8@.059	LF	.62	2.78	3.40
Resilient channel on beams and columns, per linear foot of channel					
Narrow soundproofing channel, metal	C8@.011	LF	.88	.52	1.40
Narrow soundproofing channel, PVC	C8@.011	LF	1.18	.52	1.70
Regular soundproofing channel, metal	C8@.011	LF	.88	.52	1.40
Regular soundproofing channel, with padding tape	C8@.011	LF	1.20	.52	1.72
RC-1 resilient hat channel	C8@.011	LF	.64	.52	1.16
RC-1 resilient hat channel, with padding tape	C8@.011	LF	.96	.52	1.48
RC-2 resilient hat channel (for ceilings)	C8@.011	LF	.83	.52	1.35
Ceiling suspension system for lath, installed 7' to 9' above floor level with rod hangers attached to structural steel or metal decking, 1-1/2" main at 24" OC. Add the cost of lath.					
With 3/4" cross at 12" OC	C8@.378	SY	6.25	17.80	24.05
With 3/4" cross at 24" OC	C8@.342	SY	5.57	16.10	21.67
With 1-1/2" cross at 16" OC	C8@.432	SY	6.84	20.40	27.24
With 2-1/2" cross at 24" OC	C8@.360	SY	5.98	17.00	22.98
Metal lath on walls and ceilings, nailed in place, includes 8% for fasteners and waste.					
2.5 lb., diamond lath	F8@.107	SY	4.02	5.54	9.56
2.5 lb., paper-backed	F8@.107	SY	5.23	5.54	10.77
3.4 lb., diamond lath	F8@.119	SY	5.01	6.16	11.17
3.4 lb., paper-backed	F8@.114	SY	6.22	5.90	12.12
3.4 lb., 3/8" high ribbed lath	F8@.121	SY	6.19	6.26	12.45
3.4 lb., 1/8" low ribbed lath	F8@.124	SY	6.50	6.41	12.91
Add for galvanized metal lath	—	%	10.0	—	—
Add for metal lath wired in place	—	%	—	15.0	—
Add for metal lath on columns and beams	—	%	—	100.0	—
Stucco mesh, reverse twist, self-furring, galvanized, includes 5% waste					
1" mesh, 18 gauge	F8@.079	SY	3.28	4.09	7.37
1-1/2" mesh, 17 gauge	F8@.079	SY	1.67	4.09	5.76
1-1/2" mesh, 17 gauge, paper back	F8@.079	SY	2.54	4.09	6.63
Gypsum lath, perforated or plain, clipped to metal studs					
3/8" regular	F8@.090	SY	3.26	4.66	7.92
3/8" firestop	F8@.090	SY	3.60	4.66	8.26

	Craft@Hrs	Unit	Material	Labor	Total
3/8" foil back	F8@.090	SY	3.76	4.66	8.42
1/2" regular	F8@.090	SY	3.39	4.66	8.05
1/2" firestop	F8@.090	SY	3.73	4.66	8.39
1/2" foil back	F8@.090	SY	3.90	4.66	8.56
Add for application to ceilings	—	%	—	50.0	—
Add for application to columns or beams	—	%	—	80.0	—
Deduct for gypsum lath screwed in place	—	%	-2.0	-5.0	—
Plaster bead, 1-3/4" perforated flange					
1" casing bead	F8@.025	LF	.46	1.29	1.75
1-1/4" casing bead	F8@.025	LF	.58	1.29	1.87
1-1/2" casing bead	F8@.025	LF	.71	1.29	2.00
3/4" casing bead, expanded wing	F8@.037	LF	1.45	1.91	3.36
2" casing bead	F8@.025	LF	.80	1.29	2.09
Square nose stop and casing	F8@.025	LF	.79	1.29	2.08
3/4" radius corner bead	F8@.025	LF	.86	1.29	2.15
Expanded nose corner bead	F8@.025	LF	1.62	1.29	2.91
Control joints, 4" perforated flange					
1/2" joint	F8@.035	LF	.97	1.81	2.78
5/8" joint	F8@.035	LF	1.04	1.81	2.85
3/4" joint	F8@.035	LF	1.08	1.81	2.89
3/4" joint, expanded wing	F8@.037	LF	3.45	1.91	5.36
7/8" joint	F8@.035	LF	1.33	1.81	3.14
Expansion joints, slip type					
3/4", 26 gauge, 1 piece	F8@.025	LF	1.62	1.29	2.91
1/4" to 5/8" adjustment, 1/2" to 3/4" deep	F8@.035	LF	2.45	1.81	4.26
1/4" to 5/8" adjustment, 7/8" deep	F8@.035	LF	2.68	1.81	4.49
5/8" to 1-1/8" adjustment, 1/2" to 3/4" deep	F8@.035	LF	2.59	1.81	4.40
5/8" to 1-1/8" adjustment, 7/8" deep	F8@.035	LF	2.68	1.81	4.49
1-1/8" to 1-5/8" adjustment, 1/2" to 3/4" deep	F8@.035	LF	2.59	1.81	4.40
1-1/8" to 1-5/8" adjustment, 7/8" deep	F8@.035	LF	2.69	1.81	4.50
Lathing accessories					
Base screed, 1/2", 26 gauge	F8@.032	LF	1.05	1.66	2.71
Vents, 1-1/2", galvanized	F8@.042	LF	2.94	2.17	5.11
Vents, 4", galvanized	F8@.061	LF	3.46	3.16	6.62
Archbead, plastic nose	F8@.028	LF	1.75	1.45	3.20
Stud clips for gypsum lath, field clip	F8@.004	Ea	.13	.21	.34
Joist clips for lath	F8@.005	Ea	.13	.26	.39
2-1/2" metal base, galvanized	F8@.042	LF	.80	2.17	2.97
Tie wire, 16.5 gauge, 400' roll	—	Ea	4.30	—	4.30

Plastering These costs do not include the furring or lath

	Craft@Hrs	Unit	Material	Labor	Total
Gypsum interior plaster, lime putty trowel finish					
Two coat application, on ceilings	F8@.381	SY	10.40	19.70	30.10
Two coat application, on walls	F8@.330	SY	10.40	17.10	27.50
Three coat application, on ceilings	F8@.448	SY	13.60	23.20	36.80
Three coat application, on walls	F8@.405	SY	13.60	21.00	34.60
Gypsum interior vermiculite plaster, trowel finish					
Two coat application, on ceilings	F8@.381	SY	10.90	19.70	30.60
Two coat application, on walls	F8@.330	SY	10.90	17.10	28.00
Three coat application, on ceilings	F8@.448	SY	14.20	23.20	37.40
Three coat application, on walls	F8@.405	SY	14.20	21.00	35.20
Keene's cement plaster, troweled lime putty, medium hard finish					
Two coat application, on ceilings	F8@.435	SY	17.20	22.50	39.70
Two coat application, on walls	F8@.381	SY	17.20	19.70	36.90

	Craft@Hrs	Unit	Material	Labor	Total
Three coat application, on ceilings	F8@.521	SY	22.40	27.00	49.40
Three coat application, on walls	F8@.459	SY	22.40	23.70	46.10
Portland cement stucco on exterior walls, scratch, brown and finish coats totaling 1" thick					
Natural gray, sand float finish	F8@.567	SY	9.90	29.30	39.20
Natural gray, trowel finish	F8@.640	SY	9.90	33.10	43.00
White cement, sand float finish	F8@.575	SY	13.00	29.70	42.70
White cement, trowel finish	F8@.650	SY	13.00	33.60	46.60
Deduct for spray pump application	—	%	—	-20.0	—
Add for a peristaltic stucco sprayer, per day	—	Ea	300.00	—	300.00
Portland cement stucco on soffits, scratch, brown and finish coats totaling 1" thick					
Natural gray, sand float finish	F8@.678	SY	9.90	35.10	45.00
Natural gray, trowel finish	F8@.829	SY	9.90	42.90	52.80
White cement, sand float finish	F8@.878	SY	13.00	45.40	58.40
White cement, trowel finish	F8@1.17	SY	13.00	60.50	73.50
Brown and scratch coat base for tile	F8@.308	SY	6.67	15.90	22.57
Scratch coat only for tile	F8@.152	SY	2.96	7.86	10.82
Thin coat plaster, 2 coats, with rock lath but not including studs					
3/8" rock lath (gypsum lath)	F8@.265	SY	13.70	13.70	27.40
Simulated acoustic texture, sometimes called "popcorn" or "cottage cheese"					
On ceilings	F8@.052	SY	2.02	2.69	4.71
Texture coat on exterior walls and soffits	F8@.045	SY	2.02	2.33	4.35
Patching gypsum plaster, including lath repair but no studding					
To 5 SF repairs	P5@.282	SF	2.26	12.80	15.06
Over 5 SF repairs	P5@.229	SF	2.26	10.40	12.66
Repair cracks only ($150 per job minimum)	P5@.055	LF	.39	2.50	2.89
Plaster moldings, ornate designs					
2"	CC@.090	LF	6.54	4.77	11.31
4"	CC@.115	LF	13.40	6.10	19.50
6"	CC@.132	LF	19.40	7.00	26.40

Metal-Framed Shaft Walls Shaft walls are used to enclose vertical shafts that surround plumbing and electrical chases, elevators and stairwells. A 2-hour wall can be made from 1" gypsum wallboard screwed to a 2-1/2" metal stud partition on the shaft side with two layers of 5/8" gypsum wallboard screwed to the partition exterior face. The wall cavity is filled with fiberglass batt insulation and the drywall is taped and finished on both sides. This wall will be 4-3/4" thick. Labor includes installing metal studs, installing the insulation, hanging, taping and finishing the drywall, and cleanup. Metal studs and insulation include a 10% allowance for waste. Wallboard costs include corner and edge trim and a 15% allowance for waste. Costs shown are per square foot of wall measured on one side. For scheduling purposes, estimate that a crew of 4 can install metal studs and insulation, hang, tape and finish 320 SF of shaft wall per 8-hour day.

	Craft@Hrs	Unit	Material	Labor	Total
Metal studs, "C" section, 2-1/2" wide, 20 gauge, 24" on center					
Complete with top runner and bottom plate	C8@.036	SF	.56	1.70	2.26
1" Type "X" gypsum shaftboard	CD@.029	SF	1.81	1.52	3.33
2 layers 5/8" Type "X" gypsum wallboard	CD@.027	SF	1.07	1.41	2.48
Fiberglass insulation, foil faced	A1@.006	SF	.81	.31	1.12
Total for metal framed shaft wall as described	**—@.098**	**SF**	**4.25**	**4.94**	**9.19**

Ceramic Tile Set in adhesive and grouted. Add the cost of adhesive below. No scratch or brown coat included. Based on standard U.S. grades and stock colors. Custom colors, designs and imported tile will cost more.

	Craft@Hrs	Unit	Material	Labor	Total
4" x 4" to 12" x 24" glazed wall tile					
Smooth gloss glaze, minimum quality	T4@.131	SF	2.17	6.05	8.22
Smooth gloss glaze, standard quality	T4@.131	SF	4.78	6.05	10.83
Matte finish, better quality	T4@.131	SF	6.30	6.05	12.35
High gloss finish	T4@.131	SF	8.39	6.05	14.44

	Craft@Hrs	Unit	Material	Labor	Total
Commercial quality					
Group 1 (matte glaze)	T4@.131	SF	3.83	6.05	9.88
Group 2 (bright glaze)	T4@.131	SF	4.69	6.05	10.74
Group 3 (crystal glaze)	T4@.131	SF	5.41	6.05	11.46
6" wall tile, smooth glaze					
6" x 6", gray or brown	T4@.131	SF	2.56	6.05	8.61
6" x 8", quilted look	T4@.131	SF	5.21	6.05	11.26
6" x 8", fume look	T4@.131	SF	4.60	6.05	10.65
Trim pieces for glazed wall tile					
Surface bullnose	T4@.077	LF	1.79	3.56	5.35
Surface bullnose corner	T4@.039	Ea	1.17	1.80	2.97
Sink rail or cap	T4@.077	LF	5.19	3.56	8.75
Radius bullnose	T4@.077	LF	2.35	3.56	5.91
Quarter round or bead	T4@.077	LF	2.80	3.56	6.36
Outside corner or bead	T4@.039	Ea	.91	1.80	2.71
Base	T4@.077	LF	6.36	3.56	9.92
Soap holder, soap dish	T4@.265	Ea	15.60	12.20	27.80
Tissue holder, towel bar	T4@.268	Ea	23.10	12.40	35.50
Glazed floor tile, 1/4" thick					
Minimum quality, standard colors	T4@.210	SF	2.91	9.70	12.61
Better quality, patterns	T4@.210	SF	3.48	9.70	13.18
Commercial quality, 6" x 6" to 12" x 12"					
Standard colors, reds and browns	T4@.210	SF	3.33	9.70	13.03
Blues and greens	T4@.210	SF	4.08	9.70	13.78
Add for abrasive surface	—	SF	.34	—	.34
1" x 1" mosaic tile, back-mounted, natural clays					
Group I colors (browns, reds)	T4@.143	SF	2.50	6.60	9.10
Group II colors (tans, grays)	T4@.143	SF	2.73	6.60	9.33
Group III colors (charcoal, blues)	T4@.143	SF	2.99	6.60	9.59
Ceramic tile adhesive, premixed Type 1, 1 gallon covers 70 SF applied with #1 trowel (3/16" x 5/32" "V"-notch), 50 SF applied with #2 trowel (3-/16" x 1/4" "V"-notch) or 40 SF applied with #3 trowel (1/4" x 1/4" square-notch).					
1 quart	—	Ea	7.25	—	7.25
1 gallon	—	Ea	12.30	—	12.30
3-1/2 gallons	—	Ea	38.50	—	38.50
Tile adhesive applied with #2 trowel	—	SF	.23	—	.23
Thin-set tile mortar. 50 pound bag covers 100 SF applied with #1 trowel (1/4" x 1/4" square-notch), 80 SF applied with #2 trowel (1/4" x 3/8" square-notch), 45 SF applied with #3 trowel (1/2" x 1/2" square notch). Cost per 50 pound bag.					
Standard, gray	—	Ea	5.97	—	5.97
Standard, white	—	Ea	7.77	—	7.77
VersaBond, gray	—	Ea	14.30	—	14.30
VersaBond, white	—	Ea	15.40	—	15.40
FlexiBond, gray	—	Ea	34.30	—	34.30
Marble and granite mix	—	Ea	31.00	—	31.00
VersaBond, gray applied with #3 trowel	—	SF	.32	—	.32
Polymer-modified dry grout for joints 1/16" to 1/2". Coverage varies with tile and joint size. Typically, a 25 lb. bag of sanded grout will cover 100 SF of 12" x 12" tile with a 1/8" spacing.					
Un-sanded, 10 lb. bag	—	Ea	11.90	—	11.90
Sanded, all colors, 25 lb. bag	—	Ea	15.10	—	15.10
Saltillo grout, gray, 50 lb. bag	—	Ea	14.40	—	14.40
Decorator tile panels, institutional quality, 6" x 9" x 3/4", typical costs					
Unglazed domestic	T4@.102	SF	5.94	4.71	10.65
Wash-glazed domestic	T4@.102	SF	9.86	4.71	14.57
Full glazed domestic	T4@.102	SF	10.40	4.71	15.11

	Craft@Hrs	Unit	Material	Labor	Total
Glazed imported, decorative	T4@.102	SF	24.80	4.71	29.51
Deduct for imported tile	—	%	−20.0	—	—
Plastic tile					
12" x 12"	T4@.010	Ea	3.62	.46	4.08
Ramp edges	T4@.010	Ea	1.34	.46	1.80
Aluminum tile, 12" x 12"	T4@.102	SF	40.30	4.71	45.01
Copper on aluminum, 4-1/4" x 4-1/4"	T4@.102	SF	80.50	4.71	85.21
Stainless steel tile, 4-1/4" x 4-1/4"	T4@.102	SF	80.50	4.71	85.21
Quarry tile set in Portland cement					
5" high base tile	T4@.109	LF	3.99	5.03	9.02
4" x 4" x 1/2" floor tile	T4@.096	SF	4.69	4.43	9.12
6" x 6" x 1/2" floor tile	T4@.080	SF	3.85	3.69	7.54
Quarry tile set in furan resin					
5" high base tile	T4@.096	LF	2.76	4.43	7.19
6" x 6" x 3/4" floor tile	T4@.093	SF	6.65	4.29	10.94
Add for abrasive finish	—	SF	.61	—	.61

Acoustical Treatment

Tile board and panels, no suspension grid included, applied to ceilings with staples, not including furring.

Decorative (non-acoustic) Armstrong ceiling tile,
12" x 12" x 1/2", T&G

	Craft@Hrs	Unit	Material	Labor	Total
Washable white	C8@.017	SF	1.41	.80	2.21
Grenoble	C8@.017	SF	2.01	.80	2.81
Tin design	C8@.017	SF	3.48	.80	4.28
Glenwood	C8@.017	SF	1.56	.80	2.36
Tundra Fire Guard, 2' x 2' x 5/8"	C8@.017	SF	3.58	.80	4.38

Wood fiber ceiling tile, Advantage Series, USG. Class C panels for non-acoustical and non fire-rated applications. Tongue-and-groove edging hides staples for a smooth, clean look. 12" x 12" x 1/2" with staple flange. Stapled or set with adhesive.

	Craft@Hrs	Unit	Material	Labor	Total
Lace	C8@.017	SF	1.64	.80	2.44
Tivoli	C8@.017	SF	1.91	.80	2.71
White wood fiber	C8@.017	SF	1.85	.80	2.65

Acoustical ceiling tile adhesive, 237, Henry. For use on 12" x 12" or 12" x 24" tile. Bonds to concrete, concrete block, drywall, plaster and brick. 30-minute working time. One gallon typically covers 60 square feet.

	Craft@Hrs	Unit	Material	Labor	Total
Per square foot	—	SF	.40	—	.40
Sound-absorbing fabric covered wall panels for attaching to structural walls					
AlphaSorb™, style 2100, 1" thick x 4' x 8'	C8@.038	SF	8.16	1.79	9.95
AlphaSorb™, style 2100, 2" thick x 4' x 8'	C8@.038	SF	10.50	1.79	12.29
Anchorage™, panels, 1" thick x 4' x 8'	C8@.038	SF	9.22	1.79	11.01
Anchorage™, panels, 2" thick x 4' x 8'	C8@.038	SF	11.10	1.79	12.89
Impaling clip fastener, per panel	—	Ea	5.91	—	5.91
Add for radius, mitered, or beveled edges, per panel	—	Ea	11.80	—	11.80
"Z"-Clip fasteners, per panel	—	Ea	23.60	—	23.60

Suspended Ceiling Grid Systems 5,000 SF job. Add for ceiling tile below.

	Craft@Hrs	Unit	Material	Labor	Total
"T"-bar suspension system, no tile included, suspended from ceiling joists with wires					
2' x 2' grid	C8@.011	SF	1.04	.52	1.56
2' x 4' grid	C8@.010	SF	.78	.47	1.25
4' x 4' grid	C8@.009	SF	.52	.42	.94
Add for jobs under 5,000 SF					
Less than 2,500 SF	C8@.007	SF	.61	.33	.94
2,500 SF to 4,500 SF	C8@.005	SF	.43	.24	.67

	Craft@Hrs	Unit	Material	Labor	Total
Ceiling Tile laid in suspended ceiling grid. No suspended ceiling grid system included. Labor column shows the cost of laying tile in a suspended ceiling grid.					
Acoustical rated suspended ceiling panels					
2' x 2', fissured, "A" fire rated	C8@.012	SF	1.14	.57	1.71
2' x 2', random texture, "A" fire rated	C8@.012	SF	1.82	.57	2.39
2' x 2' "A" fire rated, with Bioguard™	C8@.012	SF	2.58	.57	3.15
2' x 2', "A" fire rated, Armstrong "Sahara"	C8@.012	SF	2.68	.57	3.25
2' x 2', Armstrong "Classic"	C8@.012	SF	3.60	.57	4.17
2' x 2' x 3/4", foil back, USG "Cheyenne"	C8@.012	SF	2.26	.57	2.83
2' x 2' x 3/4", USG "Luna", fine textured	C8@.012	SF	3.24	.57	3.81
2' x 4' x 5/8", USG "5th Avenue"	C8@.007	SF	1.00	.33	1.33
2' x 4' x 5/8", fissured fire code	C8@.007	SF	1.47	.33	1.80
2' x 4', fiberglass Class "A" fire rated	C8@.007	SF	1.42	.33	1.75
2' x 4' x 5/8", "A" fire rated, USG "5th Ave"	C8@.007	SF	1.28	.33	1.61
Non-acoustical suspended ceiling panels					
2' x 4' x 1/2", Sheetrock® Gypsum Lay-In	C8@.012	SF	1.64	.57	2.21
2' x 2' x 5/8", USG "Ceramic ClimaPlus"	C8@.012	SF	2.37	.57	2.94
2' x 2' x 3/4", USG "Saville Row"	C8@.012	SF	2.89	.57	3.46
2' x 2', grid pattern, Armstrong "Prestige"	C8@.012	SF	.71	.57	1.28
2' x 4', mineral fiber, USG "Plateau"	C8@.007	SF	.58	.33	.91
2' x 4' x 9/16", mineral, USG "Stonehurst"	C8@.007	SF	.96	.33	1.29
2' x 4' random texture, "A" fire rated	C8@.007	SF	1.47	.33	1.80
2' x 4' clean room, non-perforated	C8@.007	SF	3.53	.33	3.86
Translucent panels, 2' x 4'					
Clear or frosted prismatic	C8@.004	SF	1.78	.19	1.97
Arctic opal or cracked ice	C8@.004	SF	3.17	.19	3.36
Clear acrylic	C8@.004	SF	1.73	.19	1.92
White acrylic	C8@.004	SF	1.75	.19	1.94
Wood Flooring					
Oak, 3/4" x 2-1/4", unfinished					
Select grade, white	F9@.062	SF	4.18	2.87	7.05
Select, grade, red	F9@.062	SF	4.07	2.87	6.94
Select, grade, ash	F9@.062	SF	3.74	2.87	6.61
Parquet, unfinished, 5/16"					
Ash or quartered oak, select	F9@.053	SF	22.30	2.45	24.75
Ash or quartered oak, natural	F9@.053	SF	16.20	2.45	18.65
Cherry or walnut select grade	F9@.053	SF	25.70	2.45	28.15
Cherry or walnut natural grade	F9@.053	SF	19.40	2.45	21.85
Oak, select plain	F9@.053	SF	18.00	2.45	20.45
Oak, natural plain	F9@.053	SF	15.60	2.45	18.05
Concrete moisture vapor barriers, liquid 1 or 2 part, roll, brush or squeegee applied					
RedGard, per coat, 2 coats typical for waterproofing	FL@.017	SF	.80	.87	1.67
Defender, per coat, 1 coat typical	FL@.017	SF	1.45	.87	2.32
PlaniSeal EMB, per coat, I coat typical	FL@.017	SF	2.05	.87	2.92
Gym floors, 3/4", maple, including finishing					
On sleepers and membrane	F9@.086	SF	7.75	3.98	11.73
On steel spring system	F9@.114	SF	9.21	5.28	14.49
Connected with steel channels	F9@.097	SF	8.09	4.49	12.58
Softwood floors, fir, unfinished					
1" x 2"	F9@.031	SF	3.57	1.44	5.01
1" x 3"	F9@.031	SF	3.60	1.44	5.04

	Craft@Hrs	Unit	Material	Labor	Total
Finishing wood flooring					
Fill and stain	F9@.010	SF	.11	.46	.57
Two coats urethane	F9@.047	SF	.15	2.18	2.33
Wax coating	F9@.001	SF	.03	.05	.08
Sand, scrape and edge hardwood floor					
Large room or hall, using 12" drum sander and 7" disc sander					
Three cuts	F9@.009	SF	.05	.42	.47
Four cuts	F9@.011	SF	.06	.51	.57
Closet or 4' x 10' area, using 7" disc sander					
Three cuts	F9@.010	SF	.04	.46	.50
Four cuts	F9@.012	SF	.04	.56	.60
Resilient Flooring					
Vinyl composition and vinyl tile, 12" x 12"					
No wax, self-stick, Metro, 5 year warranty	F9@.016	SF	1.33	.74	2.07
No wax, self-stick, Themes, 10 year warranty	F9@.016	SF	1.56	.74	2.30
Sheet vinyl flooring, Armstrong. Includes 10% waste and adhesive.					
Medley series, .08" thick, urethane no-wax wear layer. Includes 10% waste and adhesive.					
Chalk White	FL@.300	SY	22.40	15.40	37.80
Sage Stone	FL@.300	SY	23.10	15.40	38.50
White, Edinburgh	FL@.300	SY	22.90	15.40	38.30
Sentinel series, vinyl wear layer, .04" overall, ten year warranty. Includes 10% waste and adhesive.					
Most colors and textures	FL@.300	SY	11.10	15.40	26.50
Select designs	FL@.300	SY	11.70	15.40	27.10
Themes series, .08" thick, 2.9 Performance Appearance Rating					
Beige Cameo	FL@.300	SY	13.90	15.40	29.30
Everest White	FL@.300	SY	14.60	15.40	30.00
Green and Natural, Alexandria V	FL@.300	SY	13.70	15.40	29.10
Green, Florentino	FL@.300	SY	14.60	15.40	30.00
Light Shale, Leed's Landing	FL@.300	SY	14.60	15.40	30.00
Natural White, Prescott	FL@.300	SY	14.90	15.40	30.30
Sandstone	FL@.300	SY	13.90	15.40	29.30
White Crystal, Marble Wisp	FL@.300	SY	14.90	15.40	30.30
Sundial series, .098 thick. No adhesive needed					
Black/White, Florence 2	FL@.300	SY	15.20	15.40	30.60
Emerald and White, Florence 2	FL@.300	SY	15.30	15.40	30.70
Light Neutral, Antigua 2	FL@.300	SY	14.90	15.40	30.30
Light Oak, Myrtlewood	FL@.300	SY	14.60	15.40	30.00
Light Wood, Parquet de Luxe	FL@.300	SY	15.20	15.40	30.60
Limestone, Quinault Light	FL@.300	SY	14.50	15.40	29.90
Mushroom, Bologna 2	FL@.300	SY	15.30	15.40	30.70
Rust, Chestnut Corner	FL@.300	SY	14.50	15.40	29.90
Stone/White, Romanesque 2	FL@.300	SY	15.10	15.40	30.50
Metro series, .045" thick. vinyl no-wax wear layer. 2.3 Performance Appearance Rating					
Adobe Tan	FL@.300	SY	7.94	15.40	23.34
Blue Green, colorweave	FL@.300	SY	11.40	15.40	26.80
Bluelake	FL@.300	SY	8.48	15.40	23.88
Cocoa	FL@.300	SY	7.89	15.40	23.29
Jewel Flower, colorweave	FL@.300	SY	11.20	15.40	26.60
Media Heights, Sandstone	FL@.300	SY	9.01	15.40	24.41
Navy	FL@.300	SY	11.10	15.40	26.50
Sand	FL@.300	SY	8.42	15.40	23.82
Royelle series, .05" thick. 1.3 Performance Appearance Rating					
Black and White, Sheffley	FL@.300	SY	5.52	15.40	20.92
Dark Oak, Augusta	FL@.300	SY	5.96	15.40	21.36
Seashell, Kaley's Korner	FL@.300	SY	5.95	15.40	21.35

	Craft@Hrs	Unit	Material	Labor	Total
Vinyl Plank Flooring (LVP). Luxury vinyl plank and tile consists of a clear wear layer, an embossed vinyl layer, a composite core and a cushion layer. Many colors and textures available. Surface can look like wood, stone, travertine or marble. Planks are from 6" wide to 4' long and 8 mm to 12 mm thick. Floating plank is secured only at room edges with base molding. Includes 15% cutting waste.					
Most colors and textures, floating	FL@.051	SF	3.90	2.62	6.52
Premium – high traffic, waterproof, deep colors	FL@.051	SF	4.30	2.62	6.92
Armstrong Natural Creations, .125" thick	FL@.051	SF	6.34	2.62	8.96
Tread and riser, glue-down, with nosing, per stair	FL@.215	Ea	35.60	11.00	46.60
T mold strip (joins same level surface)	FL@.040	LF	5.23	2.06	7.29
Reducer strip (joins higher surface)	FL@.040	LF	3.98	2.06	6.04
End molding (joins lower surface)	FL@.040	LF	5.23	2.06	7.29
Wall base, to 4" high	FL@.040	LF	1.37	2.06	3.43
Add for floor prep, per room, typical	FL@1.50	Ea	2.02	77.10	79.12
Add for small or irregular rooms	FL@.011	SF	—	.57	.57
Add for diagonal patterns	FL@.004	SF	—	.21	.21
Plastic Interlocking Safety Floor Tiles Based on Duragrid for a 1,000 to 5,000 SF job.					
Firm, smooth tiles, for athletic courts, gym floors, industrial areas					
12" x 12" x 1/2"	F9@.003	SF	4.64	.14	4.78
2" x 12" x 1/2" line strips	F9@.003	LF	2.69	.14	2.83
Firm, non-slip (nippled) tile for tennis courts, wet-weather surface,					
12" x 12" x 1/2"	F9@.003	SF	4.10	.14	4.24
2" x 12" x 1/2" line strips	F9@.003	LF	2.69	.14	2.83
Soft tiles, for anti-fatigue matting, household or deck areas					
12" x 12" x 1/2"	F9@.003	SF	4.33	.14	4.47
2" x 12" x 1/2" line strips	F9@.003	LF	2.69	.14	2.83
Mitered edging strip, 2" x 12" x 1/2"	F9@.003	LF	2.84	.14	2.98
Monogramming/graphics pegs	F9@.085	C	4.54	3.94	8.48
Add for jobs under 1,000 SF	—	%	10.0	20.0	—
Deduct for jobs over 5,000 SF	—	%	–5.0	-5.0	—
Rubber Flooring and Accessories					
Rubber tile flooring					
17-13/16" x 17-13/16" x 1/8" circular pattern	F9@.021	SF	11.80	.97	12.77
Base, top set rubber, 1/8" thick					
2-1/2" high	F9@.018	LF	1.20	.83	2.03
4" high	F9@.018	LF	1.51	.83	2.34
6" high	F9@.018	LF	1.93	.83	2.76
Base corners, top set rubber, 1/8" thick					
2-1/2" or 4" high	F9@.028	Ea	1.93	1.30	3.23
6" high	F9@.028	Ea	2.44	1.30	3.74
Stair treads, molded rubber, 12-1/2" tread width, per LF of tread length					
1/4" circle design, colors	F9@.067	LF	18.20	3.10	21.30
Rib design, light duty	F9@.067	LF	19.50	3.10	22.60
Tread with abrasive strip, light duty	F9@.071	LF	21.90	3.29	25.19
Tread with abrasive strip, heavy duty	F9@.071	LF	28.30	3.29	31.59
Stair risers, molded rubber, 7" x 1/8"	F9@.038	LF	5.69	1.76	7.45
Stringer cover, 0.100", 10" high	F9@.106	LF	5.69	4.91	10.60
Add for project under 2,000 SF	F9@.010	LF	.33	.46	.79
Underlayment, plywood, 5/8"	C8@.009	SF	1.17	.42	1.59
Shock-absorbing resilient tile, rubber Installed over asphalt, concrete or compacted gravel base. Indoor or outdoor use, for playgrounds, factory floors, aerobic centers, recreational decks and docks. Unit costs below include single component polyurethane adhesive (also listed separately below). CSSI. www.carlsurf.com					
2-1/4" thickness, meets CPSC guidelines for 6' drop heights					
Full tile, 24" x 24"	F9@.014	SF	12.40	.65	13.05
Diagonal tile	F9@.014	Ea	29.10	.65	29.75

	Craft@Hrs	Unit	Material	Labor	Total
Transition ramp, 48" x 8"	F9@.056	Ea	35.50	2.59	38.09
Accessible ramp, 24" x 24"	F9@.056	Ea	55.10	2.59	57.69
90-degree molded outside corner 16" x 8"	F9@.112	Ea	27.00	5.19	32.19
90-degree molded inside corner 12" x 8"	F9@.110	Ea	26.60	5.10	31.70
45-degree molded outside corner 8" x 8"	F9@.110	Ea	26.30	5.10	31.40
45-degree molded inside corner 8" x 8"	F9@.109	Ea	23.90	5.05	28.95
3-3/4" thickness, meets CPSC guidelines for 11' drop heights					
Full tile, 24" x 24"	F9@.017	SF	21.40	.79	22.19
Ramp, 48" x 12"	F9@.056	Ea	83.30	2.59	85.89
Add for one part polyurethane adhesive (30 SF per gal)	—	Gal	62.10	—	62.10
Composition Flooring 1/4" thick					
Acrylic	F9@.075	SF	4.65	3.47	8.12
Epoxy terrazzo	F9@.105	SF	5.27	4.86	10.13
Conductive epoxy terrazzo	F9@.132	SF	7.31	6.11	13.42
Troweled neoprene	F9@.082	SF	5.96	3.80	9.76
Polyester	F9@.065	SF	3.98	3.01	6.99
Terrazzo					
Floors, 1/2" terrazzo topping on an underbed bonded to an existing concrete slab, over 2,000 SF job, #1 and #2 chips in gray Portland cement. Add divider strips below					
2" epoxy or polyester	T4@.128	SF	4.16	5.91	10.07
2" conductive	T4@.134	SF	5.42	6.19	11.61
2" with #3 and larger chips	T4@.134	SF	7.16	6.19	13.35
3" with 15 lb felt and sand cushion	T4@.137	SF	5.42	6.33	11.75
2-3/4" with mesh, felt and sand cushion	T4@.137	SF	5.26	6.33	11.59
Additional costs for terrazzo floors. Add for:					
White Portland cement	—	SF	.74	—	.74
Non-slip abrasive, light	—	SF	1.49	—	1.49
Non-slip abrasive, heavy	—	SF	2.27	—	2.27
Countertops, mud set	T4@.250	SF	12.10	11.50	23.60
Wainscot, precast, mud set	T4@.198	SF	11.50	9.14	20.64
Cove base, mud set	T4@.198	LF	2.78	9.14	11.92
Add for under 2,000 SF job	—	%	11.0	15.0	—
Add for under 1,000 SF job	—	%	44.0	60.0	—
Add for waterproof membrane	—	SF	1.69	—	1.69
Divider strips					
Brass, 12 gauge	T4@.009	LF	3.24	.42	3.66
White metal, 12 gauge	T4@.009	LF	1.49	.42	1.91
Brass 4' OC each way	T4@.004	SF	1.71	.18	1.89
Brass 2' OC each way	T4@.007	SF	3.30	.32	3.62
Carpeting Glue-down carpet installation includes sweeping the floor and applying adhesive. Carpet over pad installation includes laying the pad and stapling or spot adhesive.					
Nylon, cut pile, with 3/8" nova pad					
30 oz.	F9@.114	SY	18.10	5.28	23.38
36 oz.	F9@.114	SY	21.00	5.28	26.28
40 oz.	F9@.114	SY	23.80	5.28	29.08
Nylon, level loop, with 3/8" nova pad					
20 oz.	F9@.114	SY	18.10	5.28	23.38
24 oz.	F9@.114	SY	21.00	5.28	26.28
Base grade, level loop, with 50 oz. pad					
18 oz.	F9@.114	SY	9.36	5.28	14.64
20 oz.	F9@.114	SY	10.40	5.28	15.68
26 oz.	F9@.114	SY	10.40	5.28	15.68
Antron nylon, 20 oz., anti-static, no pad	F9@.068	SY	12.80	3.15	15.95
Lee's "Faculty IV" with unibond back, direct glue	F9@.114	SY	24.60	5.28	29.88

	Craft@Hrs	Unit	Material	Labor	Total
Carpet Tile					
Modular carpet tiles					
"Faculty II" tiles, 26 oz face weight	F9@.170	SY	19.30	7.87	27.17
"Surfaces" tiles, 38 oz face weight	F9@.170	SY	20.60	7.87	28.47
ESD 26 oz loop pile for computer floors	F9@.170	SY	22.60	7.87	30.47

Access Flooring Standard 24" x 24" steel flooring panels with 1/8" high pressure laminate surface. Costs shown include the floor panels and the supporting understructures listed. Add for accessories below. Raised Floor Installation, Inc.

	Craft@Hrs	Unit	Material	Labor	Total
Stringerless system, up to 10" finish floor height					
Under 1,000 SF job	D3@.058	SF	18.10	3.12	21.22
1,000 to 5,000 SF job	D3@.046	SF	15.40	2.47	17.87
Over 5,000 SF job	D3@.039	SF	13.60	2.10	15.70
Snap-on stringer system, up to 10" finish floor height					
Under 1,000 SF job	D3@.058	SF	19.70	3.12	22.82
1,000 to 5,000 SF job	D3@.046	SF	16.60	2.47	19.07
Over 5,000 SF job	D3@.039	SF	14.90	2.10	17.00
Rigid bolted stringer system, up to 18" finish floor height					
Under 1,000 SF job	D3@.058	SF	20.70	3.12	23.82
1,000 to 5,000 SF job	D3@.046	SF	17.60	2.47	20.07
Over 5,000 SF job	D3@.039	SF	15.90	2.10	18.00
Corner lock system, under 2,500 SF office areas, 6" to 10" finish floor height, blank panels	D3@.036	SF	9.52	1.94	11.46
Used flooring, most floor system types					
Unrefurbished, typical	D3@.058	SF	13.00	3.12	16.12
Refurbished, new panel surface and trim	D3@.058	SF	17.90	3.12	21.02
Extras for all floor systems, add to the costs above					
Carpeted panels	—	SF	1.79	—	1.79
Concrete-filled steel panels	—	SF	1.03	—	1.03
Ramps, per SF of actual ramp area	D3@.104	SF	11.30	5.59	16.89
Non-skid tape on ramp surface	D3@.033	SF	6.98	1.77	8.75
Portable ramp for temporary use	—	SF	77.00	—	77.00
Steps, per SF of actual tread area	D3@.208	SF	19.00	11.20	30.20
Fascia at steps and ramps, to 18" high	D3@.117	LF	13.10	6.29	19.39
Cove base, 4" high, black or brown	D3@.026	LF	2.15	1.40	3.55
Guardrail	D3@.573	LF	77.50	30.80	108.30
Handrail	D3@.573	LF	35.80	30.80	66.60
Cable cutouts					
Standard "L"-type trim	D3@.407	Ea	12.30	21.90	34.20
Type "F" trim, under floor plenum systems	D3@.407	Ea	14.30	21.90	36.20
Perforated air distribution panels	—	SF	4.97	—	4.97
Air distribution grilles, 6" x 18"					
With adjustable damper, including cutout	D3@.673	Ea	92.50	36.20	128.70
Fire extinguishing systems, smoke detectors, halon type, subcontract					
With halon gas suppression	—	SF	—	—	5.89
Automatic fire alarm	—	SF	—	—	.86

Wallcoverings Based on 2,000 SF job. These costs include 10% waste allowance. For estimating purposes, figure an average roll of wallpaper will cover 40 SF. The cost of wallpaper will vary greatly.

	Craft@Hrs	Unit	Material	Labor	Total
Paperhanging, average quality, labor only	PA@.013	SF	—	.69	.69
Paperhanging, good quality, labor only	PA@.016	SF	—	.85	.85
Vinyl wallcovering, typical costs					
7 oz, light grade	PA@.014	SF	.47	.75	1.22
14 oz, medium grade	PA@.015	SF	.79	.80	1.59
22 oz, heavy grade, premium quality	PA@.019	SF	1.23	1.01	2.24

	Craft@Hrs	Unit	Material	Labor	Total
Vinyl, 14 oz, on aluminum backer	PA@.035	SF	1.24	1.86	3.10
Flexwood, many veneers, typical job	PA@.053	SF	3.26	2.82	6.08
Cloth wallcovering					
Linen, acrylic backer, scotch guarded	PA@.021	SF	1.56	1.12	2.68
Grasscloth	PA@.021	SF	2.49	1.12	3.61
Felt	PA@.027	SF	3.14	1.44	4.58
Cork sheathing, 1/4", typical	PA@.027	SF	.68	1.44	2.12
Blank stock (underliner)	PA@.013	SF	1.24	.69	1.93
Laminated cork sheets, typical	PA@.015	SF	1.88	.80	2.68
Laminated cork sheets, colors	PA@.035	SF	2.72	1.86	4.58
Gypsum impregnated jute fabric Flexi-wall™, with #500 adhesive. Use 360 SF as minimum job size					
Medium weight plaster wall liner #605	PA@.014	SF	1.67	.75	2.42
Heavy duty plaster wall liner #609	PA@.014	SF	1.92	.75	2.67
Classics line	PA@.016	SF	1.98	.85	2.83
Images line	PA@.016	SF	2.47	.85	3.32
Trimmed paper, hand prints, foils	PA@.012	SF	1.50	.64	2.14
Add for job less than 200 SF (5 rolls)	—	%	—	20.0	—
Add for small rooms (kitchen, bath)	—	%	10.0	20.0	—
Add for patterns	—	%	—	15.0	—
Deduct for job over 2,000 SF (50 rolls)	—	%	—	-5.0	—
Vinyl Wallcovering and Borders Solid vinyl, prepasted, standard patterns and colors.					
Gold floral on green	PA@.028	SF	.73	1.49	2.22
Red, green and gold	PA@.028	SF	.69	1.49	2.18
Ivy and berries	PA@.035	SF	.69	1.86	2.55
Pastel shells on sand	PA@.017	SF	.56	.91	1.47
Coordinated border	PA@.028	SF	.45	1.49	1.94
Hardboard Wallcovering Vinyl clad, printed.					
3/16" pegboard	C8@.025	SF	.58	1.18	1.76
1/4" perforated white garage liner	C8@.025	SF	.85	1.18	2.03
Add for adhesive, 1/4" bead, 16" OC	—	SF	.11	—	.11
Add for metal trim	—	LF	.54	—	.54

Decontamination and Surface Preparation Dustless removal of undesirable surface contamination and paint from steel and concrete substrates. Applications include PCBs, radioactivity, toxic chemicals and lead-based paints. The removal system is a mechanical process and no water, chemicals or abrasive grit are used. Containment or special ventilation is not required. Based on Pentek Inc. For estimating purposes figure one 55-gallon drum of contaminated waste per 2,500 square feet of coatings removed from surfaces with an average coating thickness of 12 mils. Waste disposal costs are not included. Unit prices shown are based on a crew of three. Use $4,500 as a minimum charge for work of this type. Equipment is based on using three pneumatic needle scaler units attached to one air-powered vacuum-waste packing unit. Equipment cost includes one vacuum-waste packing unit, three needle scalers, and one 150 CFM gas or diesel powered air compressor including all hoses and connectors. Add the one-time charge for move-on, move-off and refurbishing of equipment as shown.

	Craft@Hrs	Unit	Material	Labor	Equipment	Total
Preparation of steel surfaces to bare metal. Steel Structures Painting Council Surface Preparation (SSPC-SP) specification codes are shown						
Steel surfaces, SSPC-SP-11 (coating mechanically removed, bare metal exposed)						
Overhead surfaces, box girders, obstructed areas						
30 SF of surface area per hour	PA@.100	SF	—	5.33	5.72	11.05
Large unobstructed structural steel members						
40 SF of surface area per hour	PA@.075	SF	—	3.99	4.29	8.28

	Craft@Hrs	Unit	Material	Labor	Equipment	Total
Above ground storage tanks						
50 SF of surface area per hour	PA@.060	SF	—	3.20	3.43	6.63
Steel surfaces, SSPC-SP-3 (coating mechanically removed, mill scale left in place)						
Overhead surfaces, box girders, obstructed areas						
50 SF of surface area per hour	PA@.060	SF	—	3.20	3.43	6.63
Large unobstructed structural steel members						
70 SF of surface area per hour	PA@.042	SF	—	2.24	2.40	4.64
Above ground storage tanks						
90 SF of surface area per hour	PA@.033	SF	—	1.76	1.89	3.65
Door or window frames						
To 3'0" x 6'8"	PA@1.50	Ea	—	79.90	85.80	165.70
Over 3'0" x 6'8" to 6'0" x 8'0"	PA@2.00	Ea	—	107.00	115.00	222.00
Over 6'0" x 8'0" to 12'0 x 20'0"	PA@3.00	Ea	—	160.00	172.00	332.00

Preparation of concrete walls and lintels

	Craft@Hrs	Unit	Material	Labor	Equipment	Total
Concrete lintels, per SF of area	PA@.033	SF	—	1.76	1.89	3.65
Concrete walls, measured on one face of wall						
80 SF of surface area per hour	PA@.038	SF	—	2.02	2.17	4.19
Concrete block walls, measured on one face of wall						
70 SF of surface area per hour	PA@.042	SF	—	2.24	2.40	4.64
Add for mobilization, demobilization and refurbish equipment, per job	—	LS	—	—	—	3,400.00

Preparation of concrete floors and slabs
Equipment is based on using three pneumatic manually-operated wheel-mounted scabblers attached to one air-powered vacuum-waste packing unit to scarify concrete floors and slabs. Equipment cost includes one vacuum-waste packing unit, three scabblers, and one 150 CFM gas or diesel powered air compressor including all hoses and connectors. Add the one-time charge for move-on, move-off and refurbishing of equipment as shown.

	Craft@Hrs	Unit	Material	Labor	Equipment	Total
Large unobstructed areas; warehouses and aircraft hanger floor slabs						
90 SF of surface area per hour	PA@.033	SF	—	1.76	2.07	3.83
Obstructed areas; narrow aisles, areas in pits						
60 SF of surface area per hour	PA@.050	SF	—	2.66	3.13	5.79
Small areas; around equipment, piping and conduit						
40 SF of surface area per hour	PA@.075	SF	—	3.99	4.70	8.69
Add for mobilization, demobilization and refurbish equipment	—	LS	—	—	—	4,450.00

Painting labor costs — commercial and industrial work Painting costs in this section assume work can be done from the floor or from ladders. Add the cost of scaffolding or staging when if required. Painting costs in this section include no surface preparation and no masking or protection of adjacent surfaces. Estimates for surface preparation and protection of adjacent surfaces are shown separately below. For more complete information on commercial and industrial painting costs, see *National Painting Cost Estimator* at http://CraftsmanSiteLicense.com/

	Craft@Hrs	Unit	Material	Labor	Total
Preparing metals for painting. SSPC is Steel Structures Painting Council.					
Brush, scrape, sand by hand					
(SSPC-2), 50 SF per hour	PA@.020	SF	—	1.07	1.07
Power tool cleaning (SSPC-3), 100 SF per hour	PA@.010	SF	—	.53	.53
Pressure washing (SSPC-12), 500 SF per hour	PA@.002	SF	—	.11	.11
Steam cleaning, 330 SF per hour	PA@.003	SF	—	.16	.16
Structural metals, machinery or equipment, paint one coat					
Brush work, light to medium coating	PA@.006	SF	—	.32	.32
Brush work, heavy coat	PA@.007	SF	—	.37	.37
Mitt, or glove, light to medium coating	PA@.007	SF	—	.37	.37

	Craft@Hrs	Unit	Material	Labor	Total
Roll, heavy coating	PA@.003	SF	—	.16	.16
Spray light or medium coat	PA@.002	SF	—	.11	.11
Spray heavy coat	PA@.003	SF	—	.16	.16
Spray machinery or equipment	PA@.003	SF	—	.16	.16
Exterior metals, paint one coat					
Brush metal siding	PA@.006	SF	—	.32	.32
Roll metal siding	PA@.003	SF	—	.16	.16
Spray metal siding	PA@.002	SF	—	.11	.11
Spray metal decking	PA@.003	SF	—	.16	.16
Brush metal trim	PA@.004	SF	—	.21	.21
Spray chain link fencing	PA@.003	SF	—	.16	.16
Pipe or HVAC duct, paint one coat. Consider each linear foot of conduit under 4" in diameter as having one square foot of surface regardless of the pipe diameter. Consider each valve as having 2 square feet of surface regardless of the size.					
Brush, no insulation	PA@.007	SF	—	.37	.37
Brush, with insulation	PA@.006	SF	—	.32	.32
Roll, mitt or glove, no insulation	PA@.005	SF	—	.27	.27
Roll, mitt or glove, with insulation	PA@.007	SF	—	.37	.37
Spray pipe or small ductwork	PA@.003	SF	—	.16	.16
Spray larger ductwork	PA@.003	SF	—	.16	.16
Conduit, hangers or fasteners, paint one coat					
Brush application	PA@.007	SF	—	.37	.37
Mitt or glove application	PA@.006	SF	—	.32	.32
Spray application	PA@.003	SF	—	.16	.16
Exterior metals coated with a single coat of epoxy or mastic, 8 to 10 mil film					
Brush epoxy coating	PA@.016	SF	—	.85	.85
Roll epoxy coating	PA@.006	SF	—	.32	.32
Spray epoxy coating	PA@.004	SF	—	.21	.21
Brush mastic coating	PA@.019	SF	—	1.01	1.01
Roll mastic coating	PA@.008	SF	—	.43	.43
Spray mastic coating	PA@.005	SF	—	.27	.27
Interior metals, paint one coat					
Spray joists and decking	PA@.003	SF	—	.16	.16
Brush hollow metal items	PA@.013	SF	—	.69	.69
Roll hollow metal items	PA@.006	SF	—	.32	.32
Spray hollow metal items	PA@.006	SF	—	.32	.32
Tanks or spheres, paint one coat					
Roll the exterior shell	PA@.004	SF	—	.21	.21
Roll the exterior roof	PA@.004	SF	—	.21	.21
Spray the exterior shell	PA@.003	SF	—	.16	.16
Spray the exterior roof	PA@.003	SF	—	.16	.16
Surface preparation for masonry or concrete					
Acid etching, 250 SF per hour	PA@.004	SF	—	.21	.21
Water blasting, 110 SF per hour	PA@.009	SF	—	.48	.48
Paint concrete, one coat					
Roll tilt up walls	PA@.004	SF	—	.21	.21
Spray tilt up walls	PA@.003	SF	—	.16	.16
Roll stucco walls	PA@.005	SF	—	.27	.27
Spray stucco walls	PA@.003	SF	—	.16	.16
Roll form-poured concrete walls	PA@.004	SF	—	.21	.21
Spray form-poured concrete walls	PA@.003	SF	—	.16	.16
Brush elastomeric or mastic, walls	PA@.019	SF	—	1.01	1.01

	Craft@Hrs	Unit	Material	Labor	Total
Roll elastomeric or mastic, walls	PA@.008	SF	—	.43	.43
Spray elastomeric or mastic, walls	PA@.005	SF	—	.27	.27
Brush epoxy coating on walls	PA@.014	SF	—	.75	.75
Roll epoxy coating on walls	PA@.007	SF	—	.37	.37
Spray epoxy coating on walls	PA@.005	SF	—	.27	.27
Roll ceiling	PA@.005	SF	—	.27	.27
Spray ceiling	PA@.003	SF	—	.16	.16
Spray concrete deck	PA@.003	SF	—	.16	.16
Brush concrete floor or steps	PA@.006	SF	—	.32	.32
Roll concrete floor or steps	PA@.005	SF	—	.27	.27
Masonry walls, paint one coat					
Brush concrete block	PA@.008	SF	—	.43	.43
Roll concrete block	PA@.004	SF	—	.21	.21
Spray concrete block	PA@.003	SF	—	.16	.16
Roll scored concrete block or brick	PA@.008	SF	—	.43	.43
Spray scored concrete block or brick	PA@.004	SF	—	.21	.21
Spray fluted masonry	PA@.006	SF	—	.32	.32
Brush block filler	PA@.019	SF	—	1.01	1.01
Roll block filler	PA@.008	SF	—	.43	.43
Spray block filler	PA@.005	SF	—	.27	.27
Swimming pool paint, elastomerics and mastics					
Brush application	PA@.008	SF	—	.43	.43
Roller application	PA@.005	SF	—	.27	.27
Spray application	PA@.003	SF	—	.16	.16
Polyurethane epoxy floor system					
Etch and neutralize concrete	PA@.006	SF	.03	.32	.35
Roll base coat	PA@.006	SF	.08	.32	.40
Roll first flood coat	PA@.006	SF	.11	.32	.43
Apply chip coat, by hand	PA@.003	SF	.06	.16	.22
Sanding and wiping, by machine	PA@.003	SF	.02	.16	.18
Roll second flood coat	PA@.002	SF	.11	.11	.22
Roll first finish glaze coat	PA@.002	SF	.11	.11	.22
Roll second finish glaze coat	PA@.002	SF	.08	.11	.19
Roll third finish glaze coat	PA@.002	SF	.08	.11	.19
Total cost poly-epoxy floor system	**PA@.032**	**SF**	**.68**	**1.72**	**2.40**
Wood floors and decks, paint one coat					
Brush porch floor	PA@.006	SF	—	.32	.32
Roll or spray porch floor	PA@.005	SF	—	.27	.27
Brush wood steps, risers and stringers	PA@.008	SF	—	.43	.43
Brush rail or baluster, per LF of rail or baluster	PA@.008	LF	—	.43	.43
Brush large post	PA@.010	SF	—	.53	.53
Shingles or siding, paint one coat					
Brush shingles or rough siding	PA@.010	SF	—	.53	.53
Roll shingles or rough siding	PA@.006	SF	—	.32	.32
Spray shingles or rough siding	PA@.003	SF	—	.16	.16
Brush mineral fiber shingles	PA@.010	SF	—	.53	.53
Roll mineral fiber shingles	PA@.008	SF	—	.43	.43
Spray mineral fiber shingles	PA@.003	SF	—	.16	.16
Brush shake siding	PA@.010	SF	—	.53	.53
Spray shake siding	PA@.006	SF	—	.32	.32
Brush rustic or lap siding	PA@.009	SF	—	.48	.48
Roll rustic or lap siding	PA@.007	SF	—	.37	.37
Spray rustic or lap siding	PA@.004	SF	—	.21	.21
Roll board and batten siding	PA@.006	SF	—	.32	.32

	Craft@Hrs	Unit	Material	Labor	Total
Spray board and batten siding	PA@.003	SF	—	.16	.16
Roll smooth siding	PA@.004	SF	—	.21	.21
Spray smooth siding	PA@.003	SF	—	.16	.16
Preparing interior surfaces for painting					
Lay and secure drop cloth, 1,300 SF per hour	PA@.078	CSF	.14	4.15	4.29
Masking with paper, 75 LF per hour	PA@.013	LF	.06	.69	.75
Cover up with plastic or paper, 3,200 SF per hour	PA@.031	CSF	.04	1.65	1.69
Light sanding of wood trim, 75 SF per hour	PA@.013	LF	.05	.69	.74
Wire brush surface, 100 SF per hour	PA@.010	SF	.05	.53	.58
Sand paneling, 110 SF per hour	PA@.009	SF	.05	.48	.53
Light hand wash, 250 SF per hour	PA@.004	SF	.03	.21	.24
Remove calcimine, 125 SF per hour	PA@.008	SF	.06	.43	.49
Interior walls, paint one coat					
Brush smooth plaster or drywall, 165 SF per hour	PA@.006	SF	—	.32	.32
Roll smooth plaster or drywall, 250 SF per hour	PA@.004	SF	—	.21	.21
Spray smooth plaster or drywall, 515 SF per hour	PA@.002	SF	—	.11	.11
Roll sand finish plaster or drywall, 250 SF per hour	PA@.004	SF	—	.21	.21
Spray sand finish plaster or drywall, 325 SF per hour	PA@.003	SF	—	.16	.16
Roll rough sand finish wall, 200 SF per hour	PA@.005	SF	—	.27	.27
Spray rough sand finish wall, 325 SF per hour	PA@.003	SF	—	.16	.16
Brush wood paneling, 165 SF per hour	PA@.006	SF	—	.32	.32
Spray wood paneling, 325 SF per hour	PA@.003	SF	—	.16	.16
Interior ceilings, paint one coat					
Roll acoustical ceiling, 140 SF per hour	PA@.007	SF	—	.37	.37
Spray acoustical ceiling, 250 SF per hour	PA@.004	SF	—	.21	.21
Roll acoustical metal pan ceiling, 250 SF per hour	PA@.004	SF	—	.21	.21
Spray acoustical metal pan ceiling, 525 SF per hour	PA@.002	SF	—	.11	.11
Roll smooth drywall ceiling, 250 SF per hour	PA@.004	SF	—	.21	.21
Spray smooth drywall ceiling, 325 SF per hour	PA@.003	SF	—	.16	.16
Spray open wood or ceiling, 325 SF per hour	PA@.003	SF	—	.16	.16
Roll tongue and groove ceiling, 200 SF per hour	PA@.005	SF	—	.27	.27
Spray tongue and groove ceiling, 325 SF per hour	PA@.003	SF	—	.16	.16
Cabinets or shelving, paint one coat					
Brush one coat, 125 SF per hour	PA@.008	SF	—	.43	.43
Spray one coat, 165 SF per hour	PA@.006	SF	—	.32	.32

Material cost for painting Cost per coat based on purchase in gallon quantities. Paint coverage per gallon is based on second and later coats applied by roller or brush. Add 10% for first coats. Add 20% when paint is applied with a sprayer.

	Craft@Hrs	Unit	Material	Labor	Total
Acrylic deck and siding stain					
350 SF per gallon	—	SF	.10	—	.10
Penetrating tinted natural stain					
250 SF per gallon	—	SF	.14	—	.14
Oil-based wiping stain					
225 SF per gallon	—	SF	.13	—	.13
Water-based urethane exterior clear finish					
400 SF per gallon	—	SF	.10	—	.10
Oil-based urethane interior clear finish					
400 SF per gallon	—	SF	.13	—	.13
Interior latex primer					
400 SF per gallon	—	SF	.06	—	.06
Interior flat latex					
400 SF per gallon	—	SF	.06	—	.06

09 Finishes

	Craft@Hrs	Unit	Material	Labor	Total
Interior latex gloss enamel					
400 SF per gallon	—	SF	.10	—	.10
Exterior oil-based primer-sealer					
350 SF per gallon	—	SF	.07	—	.07
Concrete and masonry bonding epoxy primer					
350 SF per gallon	—	SF	.06	—	.06
Exterior flat acrylic latex primer-sealer					
350 SF per gallon	—	SF	.11	—	.11
Exterior gloss acrylic latex primer-sealer					
350 SF per gallon	—	SF	.12	—	.12
Rust preventative metal primer, 3 mil dry film thickness					
300 SF per gallon	—	SF	.12	—	.12
Oil-based industrial enamel					
300 SF per gallon	—	SF	.14	—	.14
Chlorinated rubber swimming pool paint					
350 SF per gallon	—	SF	.19	—	.19
Waterborne epoxy architectural gloss coating					
350 SF per gallon	—	SF	.15	—	.15

10 Specialties

	Craft@Hrs	Unit	Material	Labor	Total
Chalkboards, Whiteboards, and Tackboards					
Chalkboard with aluminum frame, full-length chalk rail					
4' x 6' to 4' x 12'	CC@.034	SF	11.10	1.80	12.90
Chalkboard with oak frame, full-length chalk rail					
4' x 6' to 4' x 16'	CC@.034	SF	8.79	1.80	10.59
Melamine whiteboard with aluminum frame and tray					
4' x 3'	CC@.408	Ea	51.00	21.60	72.60
5' x 3'	CC@.510	Ea	109.00	27.00	136.00
5' x 4'	CC@.680	Ea	118.00	36.10	154.10
6' x 4'	CC@.816	Ea	134.00	43.30	177.30
8' x 4'	CC@1.22	Ea	159.00	64.70	223.70
10' x 4'	CC@1.36	Ea	258.00	72.10	330.10
12' x 4'	CC@1.63	Ea	264.00	86.40	350.40
Melamine whiteboard with wood frame and tray					
4' x 3'	CC@.408	Ea	58.00	21.60	79.60
5' x 3'	CC@.510	Ea	127.00	27.00	154.00
5' x 4'	CC@.680	Ea	143.00	36.10	179.10
6' x 4'	CC@.816	Ea	142.00	43.30	185.30
8' x 4'	CC@1.22	Ea	175.00	64.70	239.70
Porcelain on steel markerboard, aluminum frame and tray					
4' x 3'	CC@.408	Ea	178.00	21.60	199.60
5' x 3'	CC@.510	Ea	159.00	27.00	186.00
5' x 4'	CC@.680	Ea	249.00	36.10	285.10
6' x 4'	CC@.816	Ea	259.00	43.30	302.30
8' x 4'	CC@1.09	Ea	299.00	57.80	356.80
10' x 4'	CC@1.36	Ea	429.00	72.10	501.10
12' x 4'	CC@1.63	Ea	518.00	86.40	604.40
Porcelain on steel markerboard, wood frame and tray					
4' x 3'	CC@.408	Ea	189.00	21.60	210.60
5' x 3'	CC@.510	Ea	288.00	27.00	315.00
5' x 4'	CC@.680	Ea	327.00	36.10	363.10
8' x 4'	CC@.816	Ea	506.00	43.30	549.30

	Craft@Hrs	Unit	Material	Labor	Total
Natural corkboard with aluminum frame and tray					
5' x 3'	CC@.510	Ea	92.60	27.00	119.60
5' x 4'	CC@.680	Ea	101.00	36.10	137.10
6' x 4'	CC@.816	Ea	114.00	43.30	157.30
8' x 4'	CC@1.09	Ea	158.00	57.80	215.80
10' x 4'	CC@1.36	Ea	195.00	72.10	267.10
12' x 4'	CC@1.63	Ea	231.00	86.40	317.40
Identifying Devices					
Directory boards, felt-covered changeable letter boards, indoor mount					
Open faced, aluminum frame					
18" x 2', 1 door	C8@.635	Ea	181.00	29.90	210.90
2' x 3', 1 door	C8@1.31	Ea	260.00	61.80	321.80
4' x 3', 2 doors	C8@1.91	Ea	407.00	90.00	497.00
Open faced, wood frame					
18" x 2', 1 door	C8@.635	Ea	156.00	29.90	185.90
2' x 3', 1 door	C8@1.31	Ea	214.00	61.80	275.80
4' x 3', 2 doors	C8@1.91	Ea	318.00	90.00	408.00
Acrylic door, aluminum frame					
18" x 2', 1 door	C8@.635	Ea	407.00	29.90	436.90
2' x 3', 1 door	C8@1.31	Ea	571.00	61.80	632.80
4' x 3', 2 doors	C8@1.91	Ea	1,070.00	90.00	1,160.00
Hand-painted lettering, typical subcontract prices					
Standard, per square foot	—	SF	—	—	27.10
Gold leaf, per square foot	—	SF	—	—	53.30
Architectural signage, engraved, self-adhesive plastic signs with high contrast white lettering					
4" x 12", stock wording	PA@.191	Ea	37.70	10.20	47.90
4" x 12", custom wording	PA@.191	Ea	44.40	10.20	54.60
3" x 8", stock wording	PA@.191	Ea	33.10	10.20	43.30
3" x 8", custom wording	PA@.191	Ea	39.30	10.20	49.50
Add for aluminum mounting frame					
4" x 12"	PA@.096	Ea	28.10	5.11	33.21
3" x 8"	PA@.096	Ea	17.70	5.11	22.81
LED illuminated letters, porcelain enamel finish, stock letters, aluminum with Plexiglas face, add electrical work					
12" high x 2-1/2" wide, 1 tube per letter	C8@.849	Ea	196.00	40.00	236.00
24" high x 5" wide, 2 tubes per letter	C8@1.61	Ea	491.00	75.90	566.90
30" high x 5" wide, 2 tubes per letter	C8@3.28	Ea	975.00	155.00	1,130.00
Fabricated back-lighted letters, aluminum with LED illumination, baked enamel finish, script, add electrical work					
12" high x 3" deep, 1 tube	G1@.834	Ea	110.00	40.40	150.40
18" high x 6" deep, 2 tubes	G1@1.41	Ea	172.00	68.20	240.20
24" high x 8" deep, 2 tubes	G1@2.53	Ea	305.00	122.00	427.00
Cast aluminum letters, various styles, for use on building interior or exterior					
4" high	C8@.215	Ea	35.00	10.10	45.10
8" high	C8@.320	Ea	53.20	15.10	68.30
12" high	C8@.320	Ea	78.90	15.10	94.00
15" high	C8@.456	Ea	139.00	21.50	160.50
18" high	C8@.456	Ea	169.00	21.50	190.50
24" high	C8@.456	Ea	311.00	21.50	332.50
Deduct for injection molded plastic letters	—	%	–56.0	—	—
Add for cast bronze letters	—	%	80.0	—	—

	Craft@Hrs	Unit	Material	Labor	Total
Braille signage, meets ADA and CABO/ANSI A117.1 requirements, various colors, interior (See ADA section)					
8" x 8"	PA@.250	Ea	77.40	13.30	90.70
2" x 8"	PA@.250	Ea	44.70	13.30	58.00
Plaques, including standard lettering, expansion or toggle bolt applied					
Aluminum, cast 12" x 4"	G1@.900	Ea	146.00	43.60	189.60
Aluminum, cast 24" x 18"	G1@2.70	Ea	849.00	131.00	980.00
Aluminum, cast 24" x 36"	G1@2.91	Ea	1,320.00	141.00	1,461.00
Bronze, cast 12" x 4"	G1@.900	Ea	233.00	43.60	276.60
Bronze, cast 24" x 18"	G1@2.70	Ea	1,440.00	131.00	1,571.00
Bronze, cast 24" x 36"	G1@2.91	Ea	2,870.00	141.00	3,011.00
Safety and warning signs, stock signs ("High Voltage", "Fire Exit", etc.). Indoor, high performance plastic					
10" x 7"	PA@.099	Ea	22.00	5.27	27.27
14" x 10"	PA@.099	Ea	32.00	5.27	37.27
24" x 18"	PA@.099	Ea	121.00	5.27	126.27
Add for aluminum	—	%	45.6	—	—
Vandal-resistant 14" x 10"	PA@.099	Ea	38.60	5.27	43.87
Indoor, pressure sensitive vinyl signs					
10" x 7" or 14" x 10"	PA@.099	Ea	20.80	5.27	26.07
Compartments and Cubicles					
Toilet partitions, floor mounted. Standard sizes, include 1 panel, 1 door and all pilasters and hardware.					
Powder coated metal	T5@2.66	Ea	445.00	136.00	581.00
Solid plastic (polymer)	T5@4.00	Ea	875.00	204.00	1,079.00
Laminated plastic	T5@2.66	Ea	598.00	136.00	734.00
Stainless steel	T5@2.66	Ea	1,190.00	136.00	1,326.00
Add for wheel chair units	—	Ea	60.20	—	60.20
Add for ceiling hung units	T5@.500	Ea	25.10	25.50	50.60
Add for free-standing units (no adjacent wall)	T5@.900	Ea	148.00	45.90	193.90
Urinal screens, wall mounted with brackets, 18" wide by 48" high.					
Standard quality, powder coated	T5@1.95	Ea	104.00	99.40	203.40
Solid plastic (polymer)	T5@1.50	Ea	120.00	76.40	196.40
Laminated plastic	T5@1.03	Ea	95.90	52.50	148.40
Stainless steel	T5@1.03	Ea	260.00	52.50	312.50
Add for floor mounted, 24" wide	T5@.476	Ea	34.10	24.30	58.40
Accessories mounted on partitions					
Coat hooks and door stop, chrome	T5@.166	Ea	10.30	8.46	18.76
Purse shelf, chrome, 5" x 14"	T5@.166	Ea	102.00	8.46	110.46
Dressing cubicles, 80" high, with curtain, floor mounted, overhead braced					
Powder coated steel	T5@3.41	Ea	319.00	174.00	493.00
Solid plastic (polymer)	T5@4.52	Ea	555.00	230.00	785.00
Laminated plastic	T5@3.41	Ea	422.00	174.00	596.00
Stainless steel	T5@3.41	Ea	732.00	174.00	906.00
Shower compartments, industrial type, with receptor but no door or plumbing					
Powder coated steel	T5@2.68	Ea	824.00	137.00	961.00
Solid plastic (polymer)	T5@4.04	Ea	1,080.00	206.00	1,286.00
Laminated plastic	T5@2.68	Ea	1,020.00	137.00	1,157.00
Stainless steel	T5@2.68	Ea	1,820.00	137.00	1,957.00
Add for soap dish	T5@.166	Ea	10.60	8.46	19.06
Add for curtain rod	T5@.166	Ea	7.39	8.46	15.85
Doors for industrial shower compartments					
Wire or tempered glass, 24" x 72"	G1@1.03	Ea	114.00	49.80	163.80
Plastic, 24" x 72"	G1@1.03	Ea	76.20	49.80	126.00
Plastic, 1 panel door and 1 side panel	G1@1.03	Ea	155.00	49.80	204.80

	Craft@Hrs	Unit	Material	Labor	Total
Shower stalls, with receptor, 32" x 32", with door but no plumbing					
Fiberglass	P6@2.65	Ea	268.00	139.00	407.00
Painted metal	P6@2.65	Ea	297.00	139.00	436.00
Hospital cubicle curtain track, ceiling mount	MW@.060	LF	6.68	3.23	9.91

Movable Office Partitions Prefabricated units. Cost per SF of partition wall measured one side. Use 100 SF as minimum job size.

	Craft@Hrs	Unit	Material	Labor	Total
Gypsum board on 2-1/2" metal studs (includes finish on both sides)					
1/2" board, unpainted, STC 38	C8@.028	SF	7.66	1.32	8.98
5/8" board, unpainted, STC 40	C8@.028	SF	7.81	1.32	9.13
1/2" or 5/8", unpainted, STC 45	C8@.028	SF	8.60	1.32	9.92
1/2" vinyl-covered board, STC 38	C8@.028	SF	9.25	1.32	10.57
5/8" vinyl-covered board, STC 40	C8@.028	SF	9.72	1.32	11.04
Metal-covered, baked enamel finish	C8@.028	SF	20.20	1.32	21.52
Add for factory vinyl wrap, 15 to 22 oz	—	SF	.75	—	.75
Windows, including frame and glass, add to above, factory installed					
3'6" x 2'0"	—	Ea	94.80	—	94.80
3'6" x 4'0"	—	Ea	139.00	—	139.00
Wood doors, hollow core, prefinished, add to above, factory installed					
1-3/4", 3'0" x 7'0"	—	Ea	391.00	—	391.00
Additional costs for gypsum board partitions					
Metal door jambs, 3'6" x 7'0"	—	Ea	231.00	—	231.00
Metal door jambs, 6'0" x 7'0"	—	Ea	387.00	—	387.00
Passage hardware set	—	Ea	79.70	—	79.70
Lockset hardware	—	LS	110.00	—	110.00
Corner for gypsum partitions	—	Ea	116.00	—	116.00
Corner for metal-covered partitions	—	Ea	227.00	—	227.00
Starter, gypsum partitions	—	Ea	39.10	—	39.10
Starter, metal-covered partitions	—	Ea	82.40	—	82.40
Metal floor base	—	LF	2.33	—	2.33
Cubicles and welded booths, 5' x 5' x 5'	C8@.028	SF	13.20	1.32	14.52
Banker type divider partition, subcontract					
5'6" high including 18" glass top, 2" thick, vinyl finish, not including door or gates	—	SF	—	—	14.30

Demountable Partitions Prefinished units. Cost per SF of partition measured one side. Use 100 SF as minimum job size. Labor shown applies to installing or removing.

	Craft@Hrs	Unit	Material	Labor	Total
Modular panels, spring pressure, mounted to floor and ceiling with removable tracks					
Standard panel, non-rated	C8@.124	SF	26.90	5.85	32.75

Accordion Folding Partitions

Vinyl-covered particleboard core, top hung, including structural supports and track. STC = Sound Transmission Coefficient.

	Craft@Hrs	Unit	Material	Labor	Total
Economy, to 8' high, STC 36	—	SF	19.40	—	19.40
Economy, to 30' wide x 17' high, STC 41	—	SF	26.80	—	26.80
Good quality, to 30' W x 17' H, STC 43	—	SF	31.50	—	31.50
Better quality, to 30' W x 17' H, STC 44	—	SF	32.30	—	32.30
Better quality, large openings, STC 45	—	SF	30.20	—	30.20
Better quality, extra large openings, STC 47	—	SF	32.30	—	32.30
Installation of folding partitions, per LF of track	C8@.647	LF	—	30.50	30.50
Add for prefinished birch or ash wood slats accordion folding partitions					
With vinyl hinges, 15' W x 8' H maximum	—	SF	12.80	—	12.80

	Craft@Hrs	Unit	Material	Labor	Total
Folding fire partitions, accordion, with automatic closing system, baked enamel finish, with standard hardware and motor, cost per 5' x 7' module					
20 minute rating	C8@22.6	Ea	6,870.00	1,070.00	7,940.00
60 minute rating	C8@22.6	Ea	8,730.00	1,070.00	9,800.00
90 minute rating	C8@22.6	Ea	9,370.00	1,070.00	10,440.00
2 hour rating	C8@22.6	Ea	11,100.00	1,070.00	12,170.00
Folding leaf partitions, typical subcontract prices. Not including header or floor track recess, vinyl covered.					
Metal panels, 7.5 lbs per SF, top hung, hinged, (STC 52), 16' high x 60' wide maximum	—	SF	—	—	69.60
Metal panels, 7.5 lbs per SF, top hung, single panel pivot, (STC 48), 18' high x 60' wide maximum	—	SF	—	—	70.90
Wood panels, hinged, floor or ceiling hung, 6 lbs per SF, (STC 40), 12' high x 36' wide maximum	—	SF	—	—	57.60
Add for laminated plastic	—	SF	—	—	3.23
Add for unfinished wood veneer	—	SF	—	—	3.89
Add for chalkboard, large area	—	SF	—	—	3.13
Woven Wire Partitions 10 gauge painted, 1-1/2" steel mesh.					
Wall panels, 8' high, installed on a concrete slab					
1' wide	H6@.437	Ea	141.00	23.50	164.50
2' wide	H6@.491	Ea	166.00	26.40	192.40
3' wide	H6@.545	Ea	189.00	29.30	218.30
4' wide	H6@.545	Ea	216.00	29.30	245.30
5' wide	H6@.598	Ea	218.00	32.10	250.10
Add for galvanized mesh	—	SF	.92	—	.92
Corner posts for 8' high walls	H6@.270	Ea	49.00	14.50	63.50
Stiffener channel posts for 8' walls	H6@.277	Ea	96.50	14.90	111.40
Service window panel, 8' H x 5' W panel	H6@.836	Ea	465.00	44.90	509.90
Sliding doors, 8' high wall, 7' H door with 1' transom					
3' wide	H6@2.94	Ea	735.00	158.00	893.00
4' wide	H6@3.29	Ea	772.00	177.00	949.00
5' wide	H6@3.29	Ea	822.00	177.00	999.00
6' wide	H6@3.58	Ea	971.00	192.00	1,163.00
Hinged doors, 8' high wall, 7' H door with 1' transom					
3' wide	H6@2.85	Ea	572.00	153.00	725.00
4' wide	H6@3.14	Ea	653.00	169.00	822.00
Dutch doors, 8' high					
3' wide	H6@2.85	Ea	890.00	153.00	1,043.00
4' wide	H6@3.14	Ea	1,010.00	169.00	1,179.00
Complete wire partition installation including posts and typical doors, per SF of wall and ceiling panel					
Painted wall panels	H6@.029	SF	6.14	1.56	7.70
Galvanized wall panels	H6@.029	SF	7.05	1.56	8.61
Painted ceiling panels	H6@.059	SF	5.70	3.17	8.87
Galvanized ceiling panels	H6@.059	SF	6.44	3.17	9.61
Wall Protection Systems .063" extruded aluminum retainer with a .100" extruded plastic (Acrovyn) cover. Installed with adhesive or mechanical fasteners over existing drywall, doors or door frames. No substrate costs are included.					
Flush-mounted corner guards, 3" x 3" wide legs	CC@.194	LF	14.10	10.30	24.40
Surface-mounted corner guards, 3" x 3" wide legs	CC@.069	LF	7.95	3.66	11.61
Handrail	CC@.111	LF	15.70	5.89	21.59
Bumper guards, bed bumpers	CC@.138	LF	10.60	7.32	17.92
Door frame protectors	CC@.056	LF	15.90	2.97	18.87
Door protectors	CC@.083	SF	5.12	4.40	9.52
Protective wallcovering (vinyl only)	PA@.087	SF	4.01	4.63	8.64

	Unit	Commercial Industrial Grade	Institutional Grade
Toilet and Bath Accessories Material cost only. See labor following this section.			
Combination towel/waste units			
Recessed paper towel dispenser	Ea	202.00	252.00
Recessed roll towel dispenser	Ea	360.00	553.00
Surface paper towel dispenser	Ea	57.80	57.80
Surface mounted roll towel dispenser	Ea	220.00	334.00
Recessed roll towel dispenser with waste bin	Ea	580.00	677.00
Recessed paper towel dispenser with waste bin	Ea	160.00	478.00
Waste receptacles			
Recessed, 12 gallon	Ea	211.00	252.00
Surface mounted	Ea	81.30	199.00
Floor standing	Ea	169.00	274.00
Countertop chute	Ea	111.00	227.00
Wall urns			
Recessed	Ea	165.00	190.00
Surface mounted	Ea	107.00	147.00
Floor standing with waste	Ea	—	177.00
Sanitary napkin dispenser, recessed	Ea	269.00	543.00
Soap dispensers			
Liquid, 20 oz, lavatory mounted	Ea	42.20	46.70
Liquid, 34 oz, lavatory mounted	Ea	48.50	54.50
Powder	Ea	44.80	62.40
Under-counter reservoir system, with 3 stations	Ea	—	1,200.00
Add for additional stations	Ea	—	102.00
Liquid, surface mounted	Ea	19.70	42.20
Powdered, surface mounted	Ea	15.60	97.70
Toilet paper dispensers			
Multi roll, recessed	Ea	83.90	125.00
Multi roll, surface mounted	Ea	64.90	98.70
Toilet seat cover dispensers			
Recessed	Ea	73.20	130.00
Surfaced mounted	Ea	37.80	54.30
Soap dishes			
With grab bar, recessed	Ea	25.00	31.20
With grab bar, surface mounted	Ea	40.50	50.10
Grab bars, stainless steel, wall mounted			
1-1/2" x 12"	Ea	—	28.50
1-1/2" x 18"	Ea	—	27.20
1-1/2" x 24"	Ea	—	31.20
1-1/2" x 30"	Ea	—	32.70
1-1/2" x 36"	Ea	—	33.50
1-1/2" x 48"	Ea	—	36.70
1-1/4" x 18"	Ea	—	64.90
1-1/4" x 24"	Ea	—	70.40
1-1/4" x 36"	Ea	—	86.80
1", 90 degree angle, 30"	Ea	—	101.00
1-1/4", 90 degree angle, 30"	Ea	—	125.00
Towel bars			
18" chrome	Ea	—	44.80
24" chrome	Ea	—	46.30
18" stainless steel	Ea	—	47.30
24" stainless steel	Ea	—	50.20

	Unit	Commercial Industrial Grade	Institutional Grade
Medicine cabinets, with mirror			
Swing door, 16" x 22", wall hung	Ea	84.60	324.00
Swing door, 16" x 22", recessed	Ea	99.10	277.00
Mirrors, unframed, polished stainless steel back			
16" x 20"	Ea	47.70	—
16" x 24"	Ea	54.30	—
18" x 24"	Ea	57.70	—
18" x 30"	Ea	68.70	—
24" x 30"	Ea	88.60	—
24" x 36"	Ea	112.00	—
Mirrors, stainless steel frame, 1/4" glass			
16" x 24"	Ea	—	42.30
18" x 24"	Ea	—	44.80
18" x 30"	Ea	—	53.80
18" x 36"	Ea	—	70.40
24" x 30"	Ea	—	74.10
24" x 36"	Ea	—	86.90
24" x 48"	Ea	—	108.00
24" x 60"	Ea	—	151.00
72" x 36"	Ea	—	258.00
Shelves, stainless steel, 6" deep			
18" long	Ea	60.30	69.80
24" long	Ea	63.10	72.50
36" long	Ea	80.90	93.00
72" long	Ea	128.00	174.00
Shower rod, end flanges, vinyl curtain			
6' long, straight	Ea	63.50	79.10
Robe hooks			
Single	Ea	9.15	13.50
Double	Ea	11.10	15.00
Single with door stop	Ea	10.40	17.10
Straddle bar, stainless steel			
24" x 24" x 20"	Ea	135.00	157.00
Urinal bar, 24" long, stainless steel	Ea	109.00	131.00
Hot air hand dryer, 115 volt			
add electric connection	Ea	216.00	574.00

	Craft@Hrs	Unit	Material	Labor	Total
Labor to install toilet and bath accessories					
Toilet paper dispensers					
Surface mounted	CC@.182	Ea	—	9.65	9.65
Recessed	CC@.310	Ea	—	16.40	16.40
Toilet seat cover dispensers					
Surface mounted	CC@.413	Ea	—	21.90	21.90
Recessed	CC@.662	Ea	—	35.10	35.10
Feminine napkin dispenser, surface mounted	CC@.760	Ea	—	40.30	40.30
Feminine napkin disposer, recessed	CC@.882	Ea	—	46.80	46.80
Soap dishes	CC@.230	Ea	—	12.20	12.20
Soap dispensers, surface mounted	CC@.254	Ea	—	13.50	13.50
Soap dispensers, recessed	CC@.628	Ea	—	33.30	33.30
Soap dispenser system	CC@2.91	Ea	—	154.00	154.00
Paper towel dispensers and waste receptacles					
Semi-recessed	CC@1.96	Ea	—	104.00	104.00
Recessed	CC@2.57	Ea	—	136.00	136.00
Medicine cabinets with mirror, swing door					
Wall hung	CC@.943	Ea	—	50.00	50.00

	Craft@Hrs	Unit	Material	Labor	Total
Mirrors					
To 5 SF	CG@.566	Ea	—	31.40	31.40
5 to 10 SF	CG@.999	Ea	—	55.50	55.50
Over 10 SF	CG@.125	SF	—	6.94	6.94
Towel bars and grab bars	CC@.286	Ea	—	15.20	15.20
Shelves, stainless steel, to 72"	CC@.569	Ea	—	30.20	30.20
Robe hooks	CC@.182	Ea	—	9.65	9.65
Hot air hand dryer, add for electric circuit wiring	CE@.908	Ea	—	54.90	54.90

Baby Changing Stations Polyethylene or stainless steel with steel on steel hinges. Holds up to 350 lbs. Changing stations require 22" horizontal wall space. Costs include sanitary bed liner dispenser, safety straps, necessary hardware and metal door plaques.

	Craft@Hrs	Unit	Material	Labor	Total
Polyethylene					
Horizontal baby changing station, surface mount, 20" H x 35" W	CL@.750	Ea	208.00	30.90	238.90
Add for recess mount with stainless steel flange	CL@1.25	Ea	346.00	51.60	397.60
Vertical baby changing station, surface mount, 36" H x 22" W	CL@.750	Ea	208.00	30.90	238.90
Stainless Steel					
Horizontal baby changing station, surface mount, 20" H x 35" W	CL@.750	Ea	1,050.00	30.90	1,080.90
Horizontal baby changing station, recessed mount, 23" H x 37" W	CL@1.25	Ea	1,340.00	51.60	1,391.60
Add for sanitary bed liners, pack of 500	—	Ea	33.00	—	33.00
Add for changing stations replacement strap	—	Ea	15.20	—	15.20
Add for changing stations sign, plastic, 7" x 5"	—	Ea	11.00	—	11.00

Child Protection Seat Polyethylene with steel on steel hinges. Holds up to 150 lbs. Requires 19 square inches wall space. Costs include safety straps and necessary hardware.

	Craft@Hrs	Unit	Material	Labor	Total
Child protection seat, 19" H x 12" W	CL@.550	Ea	142.00	22.70	164.70
Add for replacement safety strap	—	Ea	15.20	—	15.20

Lockers, Metal Baked enamel finish, key lock 12" wide x 60" high x 15" deep overall dimensions

	Craft@Hrs	Unit	Material	Labor	Total
Single tier, cost per locker	D4@.571	Ea	93.60	27.20	120.80
Double tier, cost per 2 lockers	D4@.571	Ea	112.00	27.20	139.20
Five tier, cost per 5 lockers	D4@.571	Ea	126.00	27.20	153.20
Six tier, cost per 6 lockers	D4@.571	Ea	145.00	27.20	172.20
Add for 72" height	—	%	10.0	—	—
Add for 15" width	—	%	25.0	—	—
Subtract for unassembled	—	%	–20.0	—	—

Postal Specialties

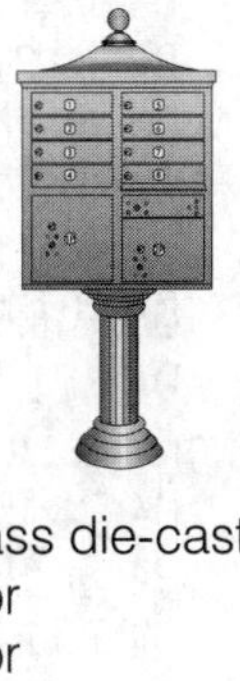

	Craft@Hrs	Unit	Material	Labor	Total
Letter boxes, cost per each, recessed mounted					
Aluminum					
15" x 19" private access	D4@1.10	Ea	255.00	52.30	307.30
15" x 19" USPS access	D4@1.10	Ea	225.00	52.30	277.30
Brass					
15" x 19" private access	D4@1.10	Ea	255.00	52.30	307.30
15" x 19" USPS access	D4@1.10	Ea	225.00	52.30	277.30
Brass indoor mailboxes for private use. Solid brass die-cast doors with lock, 1/4" glass window and name plate					
Rear loading 30 door unit, 3-1/2" W x 5" H door	C8@1.10	Ea	875.00	51.90	926.90
Rear loading 14 door unit, 3-1/2" W x 5" H door	C8@1.00	Ea	825.00	47.10	872.10
Add for front loading unit	—	%	20.0	—	—

Aluminum rack ladder system, private use, 1/4" extruded aluminum doors. 20 gauge cold rolled steel compartments, open back. Unit dimensions 23-1/4" W x 12-1/8" H x 15-1/2" D

	Craft@Hrs	Unit	Material	Labor	Total
Rear loading 12 door unit, 3-1/2" W x 5-1/2" H door	C8@1.50	Ea	270.00	70.70	340.70
Rear loading 8 door unit, 5-1/2" W x 5-1/2" H door	C8@1.50	Ea	260.00	70.70	330.70
Rear loading 4 door unit, 10-3/4" W x 5-1/2" H door	C8@1.50	Ea	250.00	70.70	320.70
Rack ladder, 61-7/8" H x 15-1/2" D	C8@.500	Ea	100.00	23.60	123.60
Steel rotary mail center, 30" W x 74" H x 24" D	C8@1.00	Ea	1,350.00	47.10	1,397.10

	Craft@Hrs	Unit	Material	Labor	Total
Vertical mailboxes, aluminum, USPS approved, surface mounted or recessed. Door size 5-1/2" W x 15-3/4" H, front loading					
7 door unit, 40-3/4" W x 19-1/2" H x 7-1/4" D	C8@1.00	Ea	420.00	47.10	467.10
5 door unit, 29-3/4" W x 19-1/2" H x 7-1/4" D	C8@1.00	Ea	300.00	47.10	347.10
3 door unit, 18-3/4" W x 19-1/2" H x 7-1/4" D	C8@1.00	Ea	180.00	47.10	227.10
Pedestal mailboxes, aluminum neighborhood delivery and collection box units with weather protection hood. USPS approved, rear access. Doors are 6-3/8" W x 5-1/4" H					
16 door unit, 26-1/2" W x 22-1/2" H x 22" D	C8@1.10	Ea	1,780.00	51.90	1,831.90
12 door unit, 20" W x 22-1/2" H x 22" D	C8@1.10	Ea	1,700.00	51.90	1,751.90
32" replacement pedestal	C8@1.00	Ea	150.00	47.10	197.10

Storage Shelving

	Craft@Hrs	Unit	Material	Labor	Total
Retail store gondolas (supermarket shelving units), material prices vary widely, check local source					
Install only	D4@.333	LF	—	15.80	15.80
Steel industrial shelving, enamel finish, 2 sides & back, 12" deep x 30" wide x 75" high					
5 shelves high	D4@.758	Ea	125.00	36.10	161.10
8 shelves high	D4@1.21	Ea	172.00	57.50	229.50
Steel industrial shelving, enamel finish, open on sides, 12" deep x 36" wide x 75" high					
5 shelves high	D4@.686	Ea	72.50	32.60	105.10
8 shelves high	D4@1.06	Ea	110.00	50.40	160.40
Stainless steel modular shelving, 20" deep x 36" wide x 63" high					
3 shelves, 16 gauge	D4@1.19	Ea	1,220.00	56.60	1,276.60
Stainless steel wall shelf, 12" deep, bracket mount	D4@.675	LF	55.70	32.10	87.80
Stainless steel work counters, with under-counter storage shelf, 16 gauge					
4' wide x 2' deep x 3' high	D4@1.36	Ea	1,310.00	64.70	1,374.70
6' wide x 2' deep x 3' high	D4@2.01	Ea	1,980.00	95.60	2,075.60
Library type metal shelving, 90" high, 8" deep, 5 shelves					
30" long units	D4@1.17	Ea	217.00	55.60	272.60
36" long units	D4@1.30	Ea	234.00	61.80	295.80

Flagpoles Including erection cost but no pre-mixed concrete. See foundation costs below. Costs also include all hardware required. By pole height above ground, except as noted. Buried dimension is usually 10% of pole height. Costs include typical shipping cost.

	Craft@Hrs	Unit	Material	Labor	Total
Fiberglass, tapered, external halyard, commercial grade, with hardware and ground sleeve, white					
25' high	D4@8.19	Ea	1,100.00	390.00	1,490.00
30' high	D4@9.21	Ea	1,240.00	438.00	1,678.00
35' high	D4@9.96	Ea	1,600.00	474.00	2,074.00
40' high	D4@10.2	Ea	1,890.00	485.00	2,375.00
50' high	D4@15.1	Ea	4,880.00	718.00	5,598.00
60' high	D4@18.5	Ea	5,100.00	880.00	5,980.00
70' high	D4@21.7	Ea	11,500.00	1,030.00	12,530.00
Aluminum, satin finish, tapered, external halyard, sectional, architectural grade					
20' high	D4@8.19	Ea	956.00	390.00	1,346.00
25' high	D4@8.19	Ea	1,180.00	390.00	1,570.00
30' high	D4@9.21	Ea	1,300.00	438.00	1,738.00
35' high	D4@9.96	Ea	1,750.00	474.00	2,224.00
40' high	D4@10.2	Ea	2,210.00	485.00	2,695.00
45' high	D4@10.5	Ea	2,560.00	499.00	3,059.00
50' high	D4@15.1	Ea	3,480.00	718.00	4,198.00
60' high	D4@18.5	Ea	6,710.00	880.00	7,590.00
70' high	D4@21.7	Ea	7,550.00	1,030.00	8,580.00
80' high	D4@25.2	Ea	9,500.00	1,200.00	10,700.00

10 Specialties

	Craft@Hrs	Unit	Material	Labor	Total
Additional costs for tapered aluminum flagpoles					
Add for nautical yardarm mast	—	%	20.0	—	—
Add for internal halyard (vandal resistant)	—	%	20.0	—	—
Add for clear finish	—	%	15.0	—	—
Add for bronze finish	—	%	20.0	—	—
Add for black finish	—	%	30.0	—	—
Wall-mounted aluminum poles, including wall mount on concrete or masonry structure					
8' high	D4@7.95	Ea	370.00	378.00	748.00
10' high	D4@9.69	Ea	385.00	461.00	846.00
17' with wall support, vertical	D4@11.1	Ea	374.00	528.00	902.00
20' with wall support, vertical	D4@14.4	Ea	381.00	685.00	1,066.00
Add for yardarm nautical mast					
6'6" aluminum yardarm	—	Ea	690.00	—	690.00
13'6" aluminum yardarm	—	Ea	670.00	—	670.00
Add for eagle mounted on spindle rod					
10" H gold finish, 24" wingspan	—	Ea	207.00	—	207.00
12" H gold finish, 11" wingspan	—	Ea	98.40	—	98.40
18" H gold finish, 15" wingspan	—	Ea	122.00	—	122.00
Poured concrete flagpole foundations with sand fill, including typical excavation. Metal collar, steel casing, base plate, sand fill and ground spike costs are included with the pole above. By pole height above ground.					
30' high or less	P9@10.5	Ea	69.00	510.00	579.00
35' high	P9@10.8	Ea	105.00	524.00	629.00
40' high	P9@12.5	Ea	117.00	607.00	724.00
45' high	P9@13.2	Ea	168.00	641.00	809.00
50' high	P9@15.8	Ea	286.00	767.00	1,053.00
60' high	P9@19.2	Ea	480.00	932.00	1,412.00
70' high	P9@22.5	Ea	547.00	1,090.00	1,637.00
80' high	P9@26.0	Ea	837.00	1,260.00	2,097.00
90' to 100' high	P9@30.1	Ea	881.00	1,460.00	2,341.00
Direct embedded pole base, augered in place, no concrete required, by pole height					
20' to 25' pole	D4@1.88	Ea	475.00	89.40	564.40
25' to 40' pole	D4@2.71	Ea	679.00	129.00	808.00
45' to 55' pole	D4@2.99	Ea	764.00	142.00	906.00
60' to 70' pole	D4@3.42	Ea	848.00	163.00	1,011.00

11 Equipment

Service Station Equipment These costs do not include excavation, concrete work, piping or electrical work

	Craft@Hrs	Unit	Material	Labor	Total
Air compressor, 1-1/2 HP with receiver	PF@5.54	Ea	2,400.00	346.00	2,746.00
Air compressor, 3 HP with receiver	PF@5.54	Ea	2,860.00	346.00	3,206.00
Hose reels with hose					
Air hose, 50', heavy duty	PF@8.99	Ea	1,220.00	562.00	1,782.00
Water hose, 50' and valve	PF@8.01	Ea	1,240.00	500.00	1,740.00
Lube rack, 3 hose, remote pump	PF@48.4	Ea	6,930.00	3,020.00	9,950.00
Lube rack, 5 hose, remote pump	PF@48.4	Ea	12,800.00	3,020.00	15,820.00
Air-operated pumps for hose reels, fit 55 gallon drum					
Motor oil or gear oil	PF@1.00	Ea	1,230.00	62.50	1,292.50
Lube oil	PF@1.00	Ea	2,570.00	62.50	2,632.50
Gasoline dispensers, commercial type, two-sided display, add the cost of hose and fill nozzles.					
Mechanical display, single product, one hose, low cabinet, standard suction pump	PF@9.94	Ea	5,340.00	621.00	5,961.00
Electronic display, two product, two hose, low cabinet, standard suction pump	PF@9.94	Ea	7,940.00	621.00	8,561.00

	Craft@Hrs	Unit	Material	Labor	Total
Electronic display, three product, four hose, high cabinet,					
PCI-compliant card payment terminal	PF@9.94	Ea	9,960.00	621.00	10,581.00
Remote control station, connects up to 16 dispensers to a point of sale					
terminal, add the cost of wire and conduit	PF@4.00	Ea	1,930.00	250.00	2,180.00
Vapor recovery fill nozzle, 8' hose with breakaway					
fitting, per hose and nozzle	PF@1.00	LS	40.20	62.50	102.70
Air and water service, post type with auto-inflator and retracting hoses,					
hoses included	PF@9.58	Ea	2,290.00	598.00	2,888.00
Add for electric thermal unit, factory installed	—	Ea	136.00	—	136.00
Auto hoist. Prices vary with the rating and capacity					
Hoist, single post frame contact					
8,000 lb semi hydraulic	D4@71.3	Ea	4,750.00	3,390.00	8,140.00
Hoist, single post frame contact					
8,000 lb fully hydraulic	D4@71.3	Ea	5,100.00	3,390.00	8,490.00
Hoist, two post, pneumatic, 11,000 lb	D4@114.	Ea	9,260.00	5,420.00	14,680.00
Hoist, two post, pneumatic, 24,000 lb	D4@188.	Ea	12,800.00	8,940.00	21,740.00
Two-post fully hydraulic hoists. Prices vary with the rating and capacity					
11,000 lb capacity	D4@188.	Ea	8,180.00	8,940.00	17,120.00
13,000 lb capacity	D4@188.	Ea	8,320.00	8,940.00	17,260.00
18,500 lb capacity	D4@188.	Ea	11,200.00	8,940.00	20,140.00
24,000 lb capacity	D4@188.	Ea	15,000.00	8,940.00	23,940.00
26,000 lb capacity	D4@188.	Ea	16,200.00	8,940.00	25,140.00
Cash box and pedestal stand	D4@2.55	Ea	378.00	121.00	499.00
Tire changer, 120 PSI pneumatic, auto tire	D4@10.6	Ea	3,690.00	504.00	4,194.00
Tire changer, hydraulic, truck tire	D4@21.4	Ea	11,400.00	1,020.00	12,420.00
Exhaust fume system, underground, complete					
Per station	D5@9.52	Ea	772.00	490.00	1,262.00

Parking Control Equipment Costs are for parking equipment only, no concrete work, paving, or electrical work included. Labor costs include installation and testing.

	Craft@Hrs	Unit	Material	Labor	Total
Parking gates, controllable by attendant, vehicle detector, ticket dispenser, card reader, or coin/token machine					
Barrier gate operator with 10' arm	D4@9.13	Ea	2,350.00	434.00	2,784.00
Barrier gate operator with 14' arm	D4@9.13	Ea	2,420.00	434.00	2,854.00
Barrier gate operator with counter-balanced arm	D4@9.13	Ea	4,300.00	434.00	4,734.00
Heavy-duty swing gate opener	D4@9.13	Ea	1,920.00	434.00	2,354.00
1/2 HP commercial slide gate opener	D4@9.13	Ea	3,780.00	434.00	4,214.00
Add for battery backup	—	Ea	571.00	—	571.00
Vehicle detector, for installation in approach lane,					
including cutting and grouting	D4@4.96	Ea	450.00	236.00	686.00
Ticket dispenser (spitter), with date/time imprinter					
actuated by vehicle detector or hand button	D4@9.13	Ea	6,890.00	434.00	7,324.00
Card readers					
Non-programmable, parking areas with long-term parking privileges					
Per station	D4@3.39	Ea	715.00	161.00	876.00
Programmable, parking areas for users paying a fee to renew parking privileges					
Per reader	D4@3.39	Ea	5,560.00	161.00	5,721.00
Access controls, keypad type					
Wall, post or gooseneck mounting, weatherproof	D4@1.00	Ea	182.00	47.60	229.60
Lane spikes, dragon teeth, installation includes cutting and grouting as needed					
6' wide, surface-mounted	D4@6.69	Ea	1,540.00	318.00	1,858.00
6' wide, flush-mounted	D4@9.69	Ea	1,440.00	461.00	1,901.00
Lighted warning sign for lane spikes	D4@5.71	Ea	721.00	272.00	993.00

	Craft@Hrs	Unit	Material	Labor	Equipment	Total
Loading Dock Equipment Costs shown assume that equipment is set in prepared locations. No excavation, concrete work or electrical work included. Equipment cost is for a 4,000 lb. forklift. Move equipment on or off job						
Allow, per move	—	LS	—	—	160.00	160.00
Dock levelers, Systems, Inc.						
Edge-of-dock leveler, manual	D6@2.25	Ea	3,580.00	124.00	25.80	3,729.80
Mechanical platform dock leveler, recessed, 25,000 lb. capacity						
6' wide x 6' long	D6@3.00	Ea	4,580.00	165.00	34.40	4,779.40
6' wide x 8' long	D6@3.00	Ea	4,910.00	165.00	34.40	5,109.40
6' wide x 10' long	D6@3.00	Ea	6,490.00	165.00	34.40	6,689.40
7' wide x 8' long	D6@3.00	Ea	5,660.00	165.00	34.40	5,859.40
Hydraulic, pit type						
6' wide x 6' long	D6@4.50	Ea	5,980.00	248.00	51.60	6,279.60
6' wide x 8' long	D6@4.50	Ea	6,310.00	248.00	51.60	6,609.60
Dock seals, foam pad type, 12" projection, with anchor brackets (bolts not included), door opening size as shown, Systems, Inc.						
8' wide x 8' high, standard duty	D6@3.75	Ea	834.00	206.00	43.00	1,083.00
8' wide x 10' high, heavy duty	D6@3.75	Ea	931.00	206.00	43.00	1,180.00
Dock lifts, portable, electro-hydraulic scissor lifts, Systems, Inc.						
4,000 lb. capacity, 6' x 6' dock	D6@2.25	Ea	12,800.00	124.00	25.80	12,949.80
Dock lifts, pit recessed, electro-hydraulic scissor lifts, Advance Lifts						
5,000 lb. capacity, 6' x 8' platform	D6@12.0	Ea	9,920.00	660.00	138.00	10,718.00
6,000 lb. capacity, 6' x 8' platform	D6@12.0	Ea	11,600.00	660.00	138.00	12,398.00
8,000 lb. capacity						
6' x 8' platform	D6@12.0	Ea	19,300.00	660.00	138.00	20,098.00
8' x 10' platform	D6@12.0	Ea	21,600.00	660.00	138.00	22,398.00
10,000 lb. capacity						
6' x 10' platform	D6@12.0	Ea	25,300.00	660.00	138.00	26,098.00
8' x 10' platform	D6@12.0	Ea	26,900.00	660.00	138.00	27,698.00
12,000 lb. capacity						
6' x 10' platform	D6@15.0	Ea	28,500.00	825.00	172.00	29,497.00
8' x 12' platform	D6@15.0	Ea	32,800.00	825.00	172.00	33,797.00
16,000 lb. capacity						
6' x 10' platform	D6@15.0	Ea	31,700.00	825.00	172.00	32,697.00
8' x 12' platform	D6@15.0	Ea	35,900.00	825.00	172.00	36,897.00
20,000 lb. capacity						
6' x 12' platform	D6@15.0	Ea	35,100.00	825.00	172.00	36,097.00
8' x 12' platform	D6@15.0	Ea	38,900.00	825.00	172.00	39,897.00
Combination dock lift and dock leveler, electro-hydraulic scissor lifts, pit recessed, 5,000 lb. capacity, Advance Lifts						
6' x 7'2" platform	D6@12.0	Ea	13,400.00	660.00	138.00	14,198.00
6' x 8' platform	D6@12.0	Ea	10,900.00	660.00	138.00	11,698.00
Dock bumpers, laminated rubber, add the cost of masonry anchors						
10" high x 18" wide x 4-1/2" thick	D4@.248	Ea	78.00	11.80	—	89.80
10" high x 24" wide x 4-1/2" thick	D4@.299	Ea	99.90	14.20	—	114.10
10" high x 36" wide x 4-1/2" thick	D4@.269	Ea	150.00	12.80	—	162.80
10" high x 24" wide x 6" thick	D4@.358	Ea	131.00	17.00	—	148.00
10" high x 36" wide x 6" thick	D4@.416	Ea	193.00	19.80	—	212.80

	Craft@Hrs	Unit	Material	Labor	Equipment	Total
20" high x 11" wide x 4-1/2" thick	D4@.499	Ea	93.40	23.70	—	117.10
20" high x 11" wide x 6" thick	D4@.259	Ea	131.00	12.30	—	143.30
12" high x 24" wide x 4-1/2" thick	D4@.328	Ea	123.00	15.60	—	138.60
12" high x 36" wide x 4-1/2" thick	D4@.432	Ea	184.00	20.50	—	204.50
Add for 4 masonry anchors	D4@1.19	LS	3.08	56.60	—	59.68
Barrier posts, 8' long concrete-filled steel posts set 4' underground in concrete						
3" diameter	P8@.498	Ea	115.00	23.10	—	138.10
4" diameter	P8@.498	Ea	162.00	23.10	—	185.10
6" diameter	P8@.752	Ea	206.00	34.80	—	240.80
8" diameter	P8@1.00	Ea	249.00	46.30	—	295.30
Loading dock shelter, fabric covered, steel frame,						
24" extension for 10' x 10' door	D4@9.91	Ea	1,140.00	471.00	—	1,611.00
Perimeter door seal,						
12" x 12", vinyl cover	D4@.400	LF	29.60	19.00	—	48.60

	Craft@Hrs	Unit	Material	Labor	Total

Truck Scales Fully electronic pit-type steel-deck scales. Add the cost of the concrete pit box, electrical service and excavation.

	Craft@Hrs	Unit	Material	Labor	Total
35 ton, 8' x 10' axle scale	D4@112.	Ea	8,690.00	5,330.00	14,020.00
50 ton, 10' x 90' truck scale	D4@167.	Ea	48,000.00	7,940.00	55,940.00

Turnstiles

	Craft@Hrs	Unit	Material	Labor	Total
Access control turnstiles, 3' high					
Non-register type, manual	D4@2.78	Ea	914.00	132.00	1,046.00
Register type, manual	D4@2.78	Ea	1,320.00	132.00	1,452.00
Add for coin, token, card or electronic control	—	Ea	327.00	—	327.00
Register type, portable	—	Ea	1,990.00	—	1,990.00
Security-type rotary turnstiles, 7'0" high, indoor or outdoor					
Free access, Type B (vertical bar outer cage)	D4@15.6	Ea	6,780.00	742.00	7,522.00
One way, Type B (vertical bar outer cage)	D4@15.6	Ea	7,340.00	742.00	8,082.00
Free access, Type AA (horizontal bar outer cage)	D4@18.4	Ea	8,760.00	875.00	9,635.00
One way, Type AA (horizontal bar outer cage)	D4@18.4	Ea	9,610.00	875.00	10,485.00
Add for electric control	—	Ea	755.00	—	755.00

Recessed Wall and Floor Safes Safes with 1" thick steel door, 1/4" hardplate protecting locking mechanism, welded deadbolts, key or combination lock and internal relock device.

	Craft@Hrs	Unit	Material	Labor	Total
In-floor safes					
15" L x 16" W x 11" D, floor safe	D4@2.33	Ea	652.00	111.00	763.00
15" L x 16" W x 22" D, floor safe	D4@2.33	Ea	868.00	111.00	979.00
25" L x 25" W x 17" D, floor safe	D4@2.33	Ea	1,190.00	111.00	1,301.00
14" L x 14" W x 4" D, wall safe	D4@2.00	Ea	590.00	95.10	685.10
14" L x 14" W x 11" D, wall safe	D4@2.00	Ea	863.00	95.10	958.10
Add for installation in existing building	D4@2.00	Ea	—	95.10	95.10

Bank Equipment

Fire-rated vault doors, 80" high. 18 bolt. 2300 degree. Installed with a 20-ton hydraulic crane. Add the cost of delivery.

	Craft@Hrs	Unit	Material	Labor	Equipment	Total
30" wide, 2 hour rating	D4@11.9	Ea	3,240.00	566.00	664.00	4,470.00
35" wide, 2 hour rating	D4@16.4	Ea	3,790.00	780.00	914.00	5,484.00
40" wide, 2 hour rating	D4@20.8	Ea	4,270.00	989.00	1,160.00	6,419.00
35" wide, 4 hour rating	D4@16.4	Ea	5,240.00	780.00	914.00	6,934.00
40" wide, 4 hour rating	D4@20.8	Ea	6,130.00	989.00	1,160.00	8,279.00

	Craft@Hrs	Unit	Material	Labor	Equipment	Total
Teller, transaction windows						
Drive-up, motorized drawer, projected	D4@26.8	Ea	7,270.00	1,270.00	—	8,540.00
Transaction window, 24" x 36"	D4@17.6	Ea	2,020.00	837.00	—	2,857.00
Transaction window, 36" x 36"	D4@17.6	Ea	2,230.00	837.00	—	3,067.00
Add for amplified speak-thru	—	Ea	920.00	—	—	920.00
After-hours depository doors.						
Envelope and bag, whole chest, complete	D4@37.1	Ea	6,090.00	1,760.00	—	7,850.00
Envelope only	D4@4.72	Ea	1,290.00	224.00	—	1,514.00
Flush-mounted, bag only	D4@5.44	Ea	1,980.00	259.00	—	2,239.00
Teller counter, modular components	C8@.532	LF	143.00	25.10	—	168.10
Square check desks, 48" x 48", 4 person	C8@2.00	Ea	1,710.00	94.30	—	1,804.30
Round check desks, 48" diameter, 4 person	C8@2.00	Ea	1,870.00	94.30	—	1,964.30
Rectangular check desks, 72" x 24", 4 person	C8@2.00	Ea	1,600.00	94.30	—	1,694.30
Rectangular check desks, 36" x 72", 8 person	C8@2.00	Ea	3,120.00	94.30	—	3,214.30
Bank partition, bullet resistant, 2.5" thick	C8@.093	SF	50.60	4.38	—	54.98
Safe deposit boxes, modular units.						
18 openings, 2" x 5"	D4@3.42	Ea	1,750.00	163.00	—	1,913.00
30 openings, 2" x 5"	D4@3.42	Ea	2,220.00	163.00	—	2,383.00
42 openings, 2" x 5"	D4@3.42	Ea	2,850.00	163.00	—	3,013.00
Base, 32" x 24" x 3"	D4@1.11	Ea	169.00	52.80	—	221.80
Canopy top	D4@.857	Ea	96.30	40.80	—	137.10
Cash dispensing automatic teller	CE@84.3	Ea	45,100.00	5,090.00	—	50,190.00
Video camera surveillance system, 3 cameras	CE@15.6	Ea	3,350.00	942.00	—	4,292.00
Perimeter alarm system, typical cost	CE@57.7	Ea	8,370.00	3,490.00	—	11,860.00

	Craft@Hrs	Unit	Material	Labor	Total
Checkroom Equipment					
Automatic electric checkroom conveyor, 350 coat capacity					
Conveyor and controls	D4@15.2	Ea	6,070.00	723.00	6,793.00
Add for 1 shelf	—	Ea	1,320.00	—	1,320.00
Add for electrical connection for checkroom conveyor, typical subcontract price					
40' wire run with conduit, circuit breaker, and junction box	—	LS	—	—	492.00

Coat and Hat Racks Assembly and installation of prefabricated coat and hat racks. Wall-mounted coat and hat rack with pilfer-resistant hangers, aluminum

	Craft@Hrs	Unit	Material	Labor	Total
24" length, 8 hangers	CC@.665	Ea	173.00	35.30	208.30
36" length, 12 hangers	CC@.748	Ea	203.00	39.70	242.70
48" length, 16 hangers	CC@.833	Ea	302.00	44.20	346.20
60" length, 20 hangers	CC@.916	Ea	330.00	48.60	378.60
72" length, 24 hangers	CC@.997	Ea	355.00	52.90	407.90

Food Service Equipment These costs do not include electrical work or plumbing. Add the cost of hookup when needed. (Figure in parentheses is equipment weight.)

Food stations, vinyl clad steel, with stainless steel work area and clear acrylic breath/sneeze guard, 24" D x 35" H, mounted on 4" casters

	Craft@Hrs	Unit	Material	Labor	Total
Hot food station, 60" long (182 lbs)	D4@1.00	Ea	3,270.00	47.60	3,317.60
Hot food station, 46" long (156 lbs)	D4@1.00	Ea	2,790.00	47.60	2,837.60
Cold food station, 60" long (166 lbs)	D4@1.00	Ea	2,630.00	47.60	2,677.60
Cold food station, 46" long (147 lbs)	D4@1.00	Ea	2,380.00	47.60	2,427.60
Plate rest with mounting kit (10 lbs)	D4@.250	Ea	509.00	11.90	520.90
Incandescent light assembly (20 lbs)	D4@.250	Ea	833.00	11.90	844.90

	Craft@Hrs	Unit	Material	Labor	Total
Food warmers, stainless steel top, hardwood cutting board, 12" x 20" openings, waterless					
58-1/2", gas, 4 openings (135 lbs)	P6@1.00	Ea	1,520.00	52.40	1,572.40
58-1/2", electric, 3,000 watt, 4 openings, (135 lbs)	E4@1.00	Ea	1,660.00	50.80	1,710.80
Convection countertop one-compartment steamer, stainless steel. Holds multiple pan inserts. Thermostatically controlled					
208 volt electric heater element. Holds 12" x 20" x 2-1/2" deep pans. Underwriters Laboratories and NSF listed. Add the cost of 3/4" water valve connection and 2" drain valve connection.					
3-pan inserts, 8.1 KW	P1@16.0	Ea	10,600.00	590.00	11,190.00
5-pan inserts, 11 KW	P1@20.0	Ea	15,000.00	738.00	15,738.00
Meat and deli case, self-contained with gravity cooling, stainless steel top, 54" high x 34" deep					
48-1/2" long (425 lbs)	D4@3.00	Ea	4,570.00	143.00	4,713.00
72-1/2" long (595 lbs)	D4@4.00	Ea	5,730.00	190.00	5,920.00
Freestanding bench type meat saw, 5/8" saw blade, belt-drive, toggle switch, 9.56" x 10.3" throat size. Includes a wheel and blade scraper, stainless steel carriage table with easy-slide moving height and a hose down cleanable epoxy enamel cabinet. 1.5 HP motor. Grade 304 stainless steel throughout. Underwriters Laboratories and NSF rated.					
14" x 14" table	D4@2.00	Ea	2,510.00	95.10	2,605.10
24" x 24" table	D4@2.00	Ea	4,410.00	95.10	4,505.10
Sandwich preparation units, free standing, stainless steel top, sides and back, 115 V AC, refrigerated 30" D x 43" H, full length 12" deep cutting board					
6.5 cubic feet, 27-1/2" long	D4@2.00	Ea	1,430.00	95.10	1,525.10
12 cubic feet, 48" long	D4@2.00	Ea	2,120.00	95.10	2,215.10
Pizza preparation units, free standing, stainless steel top, sides and back, 115 V AC, refrigerated 35-1/2" D x 41-1/2" H, full length 19-1/2" deep cutting board					
11.4 cubic feet, 44-1/2" long, one door	D4@2.00	Ea	3,420.00	95.10	3,515.10
20.6 cubic feet, 67" long, two doors	D4@2.00	Ea	4,870.00	95.10	4,965.10
30.9 cubic feet, 93-1/4" long, three doors	D4@2.00	Ea	6,600.00	95.10	6,695.10
Pan kit for prep tables	—	Ea	94.70	—	94.70
Sushi serving table, custom made with multiple sealed wells for wet or dry operation. Grade 304 stainless steel with understorage, 14 gauge base supports, individual drains and valves and adjustable legs. White polyethylene top, glass customer product screen and cutting board. Thermostatically controlled electric heater elements. Add for customer seating. Underwriters Laboratories and NSF rated.					
5-customer seating	T5@40.0	Ea	14,300.00	2,040.00	16,340.00
10-customer seating	T5@75.0	Ea	30,900.00	3,820.00	34,720.00
Four-station ice cream and shake serving and dispenser, heat-treatment freezer system type, multiple quart per station capacity, with syrup dispensers, product pumps, water valve connections, cleaning drain connections, thermostatic controls, product digital temperature and serve rate metering. Grade 304 stainless steel throughout. Underwriters Laboratories and NSF rated. Add the cost of forklift equipment rental if necessary.					
14 quart total capacity	D4@30.0	Ea	29,600.00	1,430.00	31,030.00
28 quart total capacity	D4@30.0	Ea	45,000.00	1,430.00	46,430.00
Shelving, aluminum, free-standing, 2,000 lb. capacity lower shelf, 400 lb capacity uppers					
18" x 36" x 68" high, 3 tier	C8@2.00	Ea	337.00	94.30	431.30
18" x 48" x 68" high, 3 tier	C8@2.00	Ea	371.00	94.30	465.30
18" x 36" x 76" high, 4 tier	C8@2.00	Ea	422.00	94.30	516.30
18" x 48" x 76" high, 4 tier	C8@2.00	Ea	458.00	94.30	552.30
Work tables, 16 gauge type 430 stainless steel, 30" high. Includes two 12" deep over-shelves, full depth under-shelf and pot and ladle rack.					
48" long (118 lbs.)	D4@1.00	Ea	1,160.00	47.60	1,207.60
60" long (135 lbs.)	D4@1.00	Ea	1,270.00	47.60	1,317.60
72" long (154 lbs.)	D4@1.00	Ea	1,330.00	47.60	1,377.60
Add to any work table above					
20" x 20" x 5" pull flange drawer (13 lbs.)	D4@.250	Ea	120.00	11.90	131.90
Stainless steel pot hooks	—	Ea	13.10	—	13.10

	Craft@Hrs	Unit	Material	Labor	Total
Exhaust hoods, 16 gauge grade 304 stainless steel with #3 polished finish. Conforms to NFPA code #96 and the National Sanitation Foundation requirements. Add for exhaust fans from the next section.					
48" deep angled front hood, 24" high with length as listed below					
6' long (205 lbs.)	T5@2.00	Ea	1,390.00	102.00	1,492.00
8' long (250 lbs.)	T5@3.00	Ea	1,820.00	153.00	1,973.00
10' long (285 lbs.)	T5@4.00	Ea	2,230.00	204.00	2,434.00
Additives to any hood above					
Installation kit	—	Ea	233.00	—	233.00
Grease filters, aluminum, cleanable, 2' deep	T5@.125	LF	50.30	6.37	56.67
Exhaust fans, 2,800 CFM, 1,265 RPM. Wall- or roof-mounted, for use with the exhaust hoods above. Heavy duty aluminum with 115 volt AC motor in a weathertight enclosure. These costs are based on installing the fan in an existing opening, add the cost of electrical hookup					
Fan for 6' long hood, 18-1/2" square curb size					
1/2 HP (75 lbs.)	T5@2.00	Ea	1,260.00	102.00	1,362.00
Fan for 8' or 10' long hood, 23-1/2" square curb size					
1/2 HP (100 lbs.)	T5@2.00	Ea	1,330.00	102.00	1,432.00
Additives to either fan above					
Roof curb	T5@1.00	Ea	363.00	51.00	414.00
Variable speed motor controller, 115 volt AC	—	Ea	168.00	—	168.00
Lights, incandescent, pre-wired, 115 volt AC	—	Ea	100.00	—	100.00
Ductwork, aluminized steel	T5@.100	LF	42.80	5.10	47.90
90-degree elbow for ductwork, aluminized steel	T5@.500	Ea	285.00	25.50	310.50
Electrostatic precipitators for restaurant exhaust air purification. Removes kitchen exhaust grease, smoke and odors. Meets EPA, state and most local air quality standards. Multi-stage, self-contained filtration unit with electrostatic precipitator ionizer module, 95% DOP (dioctyl phthalate) Mil-Std 282 media filter, and carbon modules for odor control. For applications in commercial and institutional kitchens such as restaurants, food courts, hospitals, and schools.					
1,200 CFM, 1.5 Amperes	P1@16.0	Ea	9,740.00	590.00	10,330.00
2,400 CFM, 5.0 Amperes	P1@20.0	Ea	13,800.00	738.00	14,538.00
Removable oven and stove exhaust hood filters with mounting flue enclosure. Seamless welded design, finished in marine-grade 316 stainless steel, 27" deep hood, with internal blower meeting Home Ventilating Institute certified performance standards. Fully enclosed with baffle filters, halogen lamps, marine grade controls to resist high moisture and heat in flue gases. With backsplash panel and soffit flue venting. Commercial and institutional grade. NSF and NFPA and Underwriters Laboratories approved.					
1,100 CFM	P6@20.0	Ea	5,340.00	1,050.00	6,390.00
1,200 CFM	P6@20.0	Ea	7,710.00	1,050.00	8,760.00
1,500 CFM	P6@20.0	Ea	8,310.00	1,050.00	9,360.00
Restaurant cooking area fire protection wet chemical system. Exceeds Underwriters Laboratories standards (UL-300, Fire Extinguishing Systems for Protection of Restaurant Cooking Areas) and complies with NFPA 17A (Wet Chemical Extinguishing Systems), NFPA 96 (Commercial Cooking Operations, Ventilation Control and Fire) and major insurance company guidelines.					
5' wide range hood	P6@16.0	Ea	2,280.00	838.00	3,118.00
12' wide range hood	P6@24.0	Ea	3,250.00	1,260.00	4,510.00
Charbroiler, radiant, countertop model, burner and control every 12", natural or LP gas					
80,000 Btu, 24" W (155 lbs.)	P6@2.00	Ea	2,990.00	105.00	3,095.00
120,000 Btu, 36" W (211 lbs.)	P6@2.00	Ea	4,260.00	105.00	4,365.00
160,000 Btu, 48" W (211 lbs.)	P6@2.00	Ea	5,220.00	105.00	5,325.00
Deep fat fryer, free standing floor model, electric, 45" height, stainless steel front and top					
40 lbs. capacity (200 lbs.)	P6@2.00	Ea	2,120.00	105.00	2,225.00
60 lbs. capacity (225 lbs.)	P6@2.00	Ea	2,750.00	105.00	2,855.00
Add for filter ready	—	Ea	378.00	—	378.00

	Craft@Hrs	Unit	Material	Labor	Total
Gas ranges, free standing, floor-mounted, 29-3/4" D x 59" H x 62-3/4" W, with twin ovens and 24" raised griddle/broiler					
6 burners, 35,000 Btu each (835 lbs.)	P6@4.00	Ea	6,170.00	210.00	6,380.00
Add for stainless steel shelf above range	—	Ea	133.00	—	133.00
Restaurant range, gas, 6 burners, 2 ovens, raised griddle/broiler, open burners with black porcelain top grates, stainless steel front, sides, back riser, high shelf and 6" legs. 3/4" rear gas connection with gas pressure regulator. NSF listed.					
50 MBtu/Hr	P6@8.00	Ea	8,650.00	419.00	9,069.00
75 MBtu/Hr	P6@8.00	Ea	10,100.00	419.00	10,519.00
100 MBtu/Hr	P6@8.00	Ea	15,100.00	419.00	15,519.00
Griddles, gas, 27,500 Btu, 1" thick x 24" deep griddle plate, countertop-mounted					
24" wide (295 lbs.)	P6@2.00	Ea	1,300.00	105.00	1,405.00
36" wide (385 lbs.)	P6@2.00	Ea	1,670.00	105.00	1,775.00
48" wide (520 lbs.)	P6@3.00	Ea	2,170.00	157.00	2,327.00
Ovens, free standing, floor-mounted					
Convection oven, natural gas, stainless steel, porcelain interior, 38" W x 36" D x 54-1/4" H					
60,000 Btu (550 lbs.)	D4@4.00	Ea	3,010.00	190.00	3,200.00
Conveyer oven, electric, stainless steel body, 18" H x 50" W x 31-3/8" D, 208 or 240 Volt AC					
16" W conveyor, 6 KW, UL listed (190 lbs.)	D4@4.00	Ea	5,360.00	190.00	5,550.00
Entry & exit shelves	—	Ea	244.00	—	244.00
Professional microwave oven, single shelf, permanent-mount, stainless steel throughout, with 6 minute dial timer, bottom energy feed, see-thru side hinged door, digital controls, cavity- or wall-mount, 120 Volt, 60 Hertz, single phase, Underwriters Laboratories and NSF listed.					
850 watt	E4@4.00	Ea	310.00	203.00	513.00
1,000 watt	E4@4.00	Ea	341.00	203.00	544.00
1,800 watt	E4@4.00	Ea	965.00	203.00	1,168.00
2,100 watt	E4@4.00	Ea	1,260.00	203.00	1,463.00
Pastry oven, gas, 6 burners, 2 ovens, raised griddle/broiler, open burners with black porcelain top grates. Stainless steel front, sides, back riser, high shelf and 6" legs. 3/4" rear gas connection with gas pressure regulator. NSF listed.					
50 MBtu/Hr	P6@8.00	Ea	8,260.00	419.00	8,679.00
75 MBtu/Hr	P6@8.00	Ea	10,300.00	419.00	10,719.00
100 MBtu/Hr	P6@8.00	Ea	15,200.00	419.00	15,619.00
Dough roller, production type, for bread, pastry, donut and bagel manufacture. Two-stage machine with stainless steel construction. Quick change handles, front infeed and front discharge. Rolls up to 18" diameter doughs. NSF 8 listed. 120 Volt, 60 Hertz, single phase, UL listed.					
450 pastry blanks per hour	E4@4.00	Ea	5,610.00	203.00	5,813.00
1,000 pastry blanks per hour	E4@4.00	Ea	8,480.00	203.00	8,683.00
2,000 pastry blanks per hour	E4@4.00	Ea	19,600.00	203.00	19,803.00
Bread slicer, hard or soft crusted breads. With stainless steel bagging trough. 3/8" (10 mm), 7/16" (11 mm), 1/2" (13 mm), or 3/4" (19 mm) pre-set slice thickness. Independently mounted heat-treated alloy carbon steel blades. Single phase 115 volt, 60 Hz AC power. ETL listed for safety.					
6.2 Amp/hr, 420 loaves per hour	E4@4.00	Ea	5,610.00	203.00	5,813.00
10 Amp/hr, 700 loaves per hour	E4@4.00	Ea	9,780.00	203.00	9,983.00
18 Amp/hr, 1,000 loaves per hour	E4@4.00	Ea	14,400.00	203.00	14,603.00
Toaster, conveyor type, stainless steel, fused quartz sheathing, countertop model					
350 slices per hour, 115 volt AC, 1,400 watts	D4@3.00	Ea	819.00	143.00	962.00
Pot and pan racks, galvanized steel, pot hooks placed 4 per linear foot					
Ceiling-mounted, 5'	C8@2.00	Ea	516.00	94.30	610.30
Wall-mounted, 5'	C8@2.00	Ea	343.00	94.30	437.30

	Craft@Hrs	Unit	Material	Labor	Total
Ice-maker, free standing, floor-mounted model					
147 lbs. per day capacity (165 lbs.)	P6@2.00	Ea	1,860.00	105.00	1,965.00
220 lbs. per day capacity (165 lbs.)	P6@2.00	Ea	2,180.00	105.00	2,285.00
290 lbs. per day capacity (215 lbs.)	P6@2.00	Ea	2,560.00	105.00	2,665.00
395 lbs. per day capacity (185 lbs.)	P6@2.00	Ea	3,710.00	105.00	3,815.00
Ice storage unit, self service for bagged ice, 40 cubic foot capacity, floor-mounted. Includes refrigeration unit.					
Indoor type	E4@3.00	Ea	2,650.00	152.00	2,802.00
Outdoor type, automatic defrost	E4@3.00	Ea	2,050.00	152.00	2,202.00
Refrigerators, CFC-free refrigeration system 115 volt AC					
Under counter, stainless steel front and top					
6.2 cubic foot (157 lbs.)	P6@3.00	Ea	1,870.00	157.00	2,027.00
11.8 cubic foot (230 lbs.)	P6@4.00	Ea	2,880.00	210.00	3,090.00
Beverage backbar refrigerator, 2 section glass doors, 34" high, condensing unit on right, galvanized top, stainless steel floors, galvanized interior walls, epoxy coated steel shelves. 208 volt, 1- or 3-phase, 60 Hz AC, Underwriters Laboratories and NSF rated.					
5 MBtu/Hr	E4@4.00	Ea	4,570.00	203.00	4,773.00
10 MBtu/Hr	E4@4.00	Ea	7,170.00	203.00	7,373.00
20 MBtu/Hr	E4@4.00	Ea	9,780.00	203.00	9,983.00
Freezers, under counter type, stainless steel front and top, CFC-free refrigeration system					
6.5 cubic foot (162 lbs.)	P6@.500	Ea	1,800.00	26.20	1,826.20
12.0 cubic foot (234 lb.)	P6@1.00	Ea	2,620.00	52.40	2,672.40
Reach-in refrigerator, bottom-mounted, stainless steel doors, anodized aluminum sides					
Single door, 23 cubic foot (276 lbs.)	P6@4.00	Ea	2,930.00	210.00	3,140.00
Double door, 49 cubic foot (410 lbs.)	P6@4.00	Ea	3,890.00	210.00	4,100.00
Triple door, 72 cubic foot (600 lbs.)	P6@4.00	Ea	5,250.00	210.00	5,460.00
Custom walk-in coolers and freezers, in an existing building. Including thermostatically controlled external remote condenser and temperature recorder. UL and NSF rated compound thermoplastic internal insulation, food-grade grouted tile floor. Fluorescent illumination. High-traffic stainless steel vault door with safety panic bar-style exit latch override. Shelving not included. Per square foot of floor.					
Cooler (to +35 degrees Fahrenheit)	—	SF	—	—	64.50
Freezer (to –35 degrees Fahrenheit)	—	SF	—	—	95.50
Sinks, stainless steel, free standing, floor-mounted, with 7" high backsplash and faucet holes drilled on 8" centers, no trim included					
Scullery sink, 16" x 20" tubs, 12" deep					
40" long, 1 tub, 1 drainboard (65 lbs.)	P6@2.00	Ea	446.00	105.00	551.00
58" long, 2 tubs, 1 drainboard (80 lbs.)	P6@2.00	Ea	678.00	105.00	783.00
103" long, 3 tubs, 2 drainboards (155 lbs.)	P6@2.00	Ea	1,340.00	105.00	1,445.00
126" long, 4 tubs, 2 drainboards (175 lbs.)	P6@2.00	Ea	1,450.00	105.00	1,555.00
Mop sink, faucet not included					
21" x 21" x 41", single compartment	P6@2.00	Ea	411.00	105.00	516.00
Dining facility maintenance and cleaning station, stainless steel throughout. Includes floor-mounted mop sink, hose and cleaning fluid dispenser and connections for mop and bucket fill, shelving and mop racks, shielded lighting fixture, grounded high-mount electrical outlet and floor drain. UL and NSF rated. Built into an existing structure. Add the cost of plumbing and electric rough-in. Per square foot of floor.					
Installed cost	—	SF	—	—	33.60
Planetary food mixing machines, floor-mounted					
20 quart, bench-mount (260 lbs.)	D4@2.00	Ea	2,180.00	95.10	2,275.10
30 quart (360 lbs.)	D4@3.00	Ea	15,000.00	143.00	15,143.00

	Craft@Hrs	Unit	Material	Labor	Total
Garbage disposers, includes control switch, solenoid valve, siphon breaker and flow control valve					
1/2 HP (56 lbs.)	P6@1.00	Ea	870.00	52.40	922.40
3/4 HP (57 lbs.)	P6@1.00	Ea	1,170.00	52.40	1,222.40
1 HP (60 lbs.)	P6@1.00	Ea	1,230.00	52.40	1,282.40
1-1/2 HP (76 lbs.)	P6@2.00	Ea	1,730.00	105.00	1,835.00
2 HP (81 lbs.)	P6@2.00	Ea	1,820.00	105.00	1,925.00
3 HP (129 lbs.)	P6@3.00	Ea	2,390.00	157.00	2,547.00
Dishwashers					
Under counter, 24 rack capacity per hour. Universal timer					
High temp 70° booster (245 lbs.)	P6@4.00	Ea	5,110.00	210.00	5,320.00
Low temp, chemical sanitizer (245 lbs.)	P6@4.00	Ea	4,440.00	210.00	4,650.00
Upright, heavy duty, semi-automatic, 58 racks per hour. Can be used for corner or straight-through applications					
With booster heater (420 lbs.)	P6@6.00	Ea	11,900.00	314.00	12,214.00
Without booster heater (420 lbs.)	P6@6.00	Ea	9,790.00	314.00	10,104.00
Cappuccino dispenser, for cappuccino, hot chocolate or other hot beverages, 1/4" water line required					
Two flavor, 42 servings	D4@1.00	Ea	1,670.00	47.60	1,717.60
Three flavor, 62 servings	D4@1.00	Ea	1,840.00	47.60	1,887.60
Multi-station decanter coffee brewer, stainless steel, with water feed tank valve connections, permanent countertop-mounted, 115/230 volt single phase 60 Hertz, with warmer plates. UL and NSF rated.					
Single brewer, three warmers	P6@4.00	Ea	788.00	210.00	998.00
Single brewer, five warmers	P6@4.00	Ea	894.00	210.00	1,104.00
Twin brewers, eight warmers	P6@8.00	Ea	1,750.00	419.00	2,169.00
Multi-station urn coffee percolator brewer, stainless steel, permanent countertop-mounted, with water feed tank valve connections, 115/230 volt single phase, 60 Hz, with warmer plates. UL and NSF rated.					
Single percolator urn, three warmers	P6@4.00	Ea	729.00	210.00	939.00
Twin percolator urn, five warmers	P6@8.00	Ea	969.00	419.00	1,388.00
Beverage dispenser, non-carbonated, refrigerated, countertop model					
5 gallon, 1 bowl	P6@2.00	Ea	900.00	105.00	1,005.00
5 gallon, 2 bowls	P6@2.00	Ea	1,210.00	105.00	1,315.00
2.4 gallon, 2 mini bowls	P6@2.00	Ea	1,090.00	105.00	1,195.00
2.4 gallon, 4 mini bowls	P6@2.00	Ea	1,730.00	105.00	1,835.00

Educational Equipment Labor includes unpacking, layout and complete installation of prefinished furniture and equipment.

	Craft@Hrs	Unit	Material	Labor	Total
Wardrobes, 40" x 78" x 26"					
Teacher type	C8@2.00	Ea	1,530.00	94.30	1,624.30
Student type	C8@2.00	Ea	774.00	94.30	868.30
Seating, per seat					
Lecture room, pedestal, with folding arm	C8@2.00	Ea	202.00	94.30	296.30
Horizontal sections	C8@2.00	Ea	96.50	94.30	190.80
Tables, fixed pedestal					
48" x 16"	C8@2.00	Ea	438.00	94.30	532.30
With chairs, 48" x 16"	C8@2.00	Ea	627.00	94.30	721.30
Projection screen					
Ceiling-mounted, pull down	D4@.019	SF	4.33	.90	5.23
Videotape recorder	CE@.500	Ea	125.00	30.20	155.20
T.V. camera	CE@.800	Ea	495.00	48.30	543.30
T.V. monitor, wall-mounted	CE@2.00	Ea	289.00	121.00	410.00

	Craft@Hrs	Unit	Material	Labor	Total
Language laboratory study carrels, plastic laminated wood					
Individual, 48" x 30" x 54"	C8@1.43	Ea	282.00	67.40	349.40
Two position, 73" x 30" x 47"	C8@1.93	Ea	750.00	91.00	841.00
Island, 4 position, 66" x 66" x 47"	C8@3.17	Ea	846.00	149.00	995.00

Library equipment, educational and institutional grade. Meets recommendations of the America Library Association. Complies with FEMA 356 standards and ANSI/NISO Z39.73-1994 seismic safety standards. Each 5-level shelf unit is 72" high by 36" wide by 21" deep. Floor-mounted units require four seismic assemblies. Wall-mounted units require two seismic assemblies.

	Craft@Hrs	Unit	Material	Labor	Total
Torch-cut or concrete-saw hole in steel or concrete structural frame for seismic mounts (floor or wall)	D4@1.50	Ea	—	71.30	71.30
Assemble, bolt down and level each seismic spring module	D4@0.25	Ea	153.00	11.90	164.90
Assemble and position bookshelf	D4@1.25	Ea	737.00	59.50	796.50
Bolt down and level completed assembly	D4@0.50	Ea	—	23.80	23.80
Load and vibration test	D4@1.00	Ea	—	47.60	47.60
Computer work station, 29" x 59" x 24", duplex unit, freestanding, Achieva or equal, including assembly and two seismic anchors	C8@1.00	Ea	452.00	47.10	499.10
Computer work center, hexagonal, 26" x 80" x 35", seats six, Paragon or equal, including assembly and three seismic anchors	C8@1.00	Ea	916.00	47.10	963.10
Double desk computer work station, 36" W x 30" D, MyOffice or equal, including assembly and two seismic anchors	C8@1.00	Ea	1,460.00	47.10	1,507.10

Rolling Ladders Rolling ladders for mercantile, library or industrial use.
Oak rolling ladder with top and bottom rolling fixtures, non-slip treads, pre-finished. By floor to track height. Painted aluminum hardware. See the cost of ladder track below.

	Craft@Hrs	Unit	Material	Labor	Total
Up to 9'6" high	D4@.819	Ea	1,270.00	39.00	1,309.00
9'6" to 10'6" high	D4@.819	Ea	1,330.00	39.00	1,369.00
10'6" to 11'6" high	D4@1.09	Ea	1,430.00	51.80	1,481.80
11'6" to 12'6" high	D4@1.09	Ea	1,510.00	51.80	1,561.80
12'6" to 13'6" high	D4@1.09	Ea	1,600.00	51.80	1,651.80
13' to 14'6" high	D4@1.09	Ea	1,660.00	51.80	1,711.80
Add for bend at ladder top or bottom	—	Ea	185.00	—	185.00
Add for brass or chrome hardware	—	Ea	210.00	—	210.00
Add for ladder work shelf	—	Ea	145.00	—	145.00
Add for handrail	—	Ea	98.70	—	98.70
Rolling ladder track, 7/8" slotted steel, per foot of length, 9' to 14' high					
Painted aluminum finish	D4@.089	LF	7.63	4.23	11.86
Painted black finish	D4@.089	LF	7.45	4.23	11.68
Brass or chrome plated finish	D4@.089	LF	17.60	4.23	21.83
Corner bend track, 90 degree, 30" radius					
Painted finish	D4@.363	Ea	63.10	17.30	80.40
Chrome or brass finish	D4@.363	Ea	101.00	17.30	118.30

Educational Computer Network Wiring
These estimates assume installation in steel frame interior walls and suspended ceilings before drywall and ceiling finish are installed. All cable runs terminate to either a telephone closet or a server room. All runs are to a punch block at both the distribution end and central interconnect. Underground cable runs assume communications duct has been installed by others. Central interconnect locations are usually a classroom located near or in a cluster of classroom buildings. One-hundred-pair cable is suitable for 12 network connections with 2 spares.
Campus network wiring pulled in underground communications duct from a central interconnection location to a distribution point. Based on a 1,000' cable run.

	Craft@Hrs	Unit	Material	Labor	Total
Category 5E cable					
25 pair cable	E4@.043	LF	1.31	2.19	3.50
100 pair cable	E4@.043	LF	4.75	2.19	6.94

	Craft@Hrs	Unit	Material	Labor	Total
Cable pulling come-along, 3,000 pound rating					
Rental per day	—	Day	21.00	—	21.00
Rental per week	—	Wk	76.00	—	76.00
Rental per month	—	Mo	229.00	—	229.00
Plywood backboard mount for a wall-mount rack supporting the patch panel and network switches. Set on a masonry wall.					
4' x 4' x 3/4"	E4@.938	Ea	13.60	47.70	61.30
4' x 8' x 3/4"	E4@1.10	Ea	27.10	55.90	83.00
Classroom punch down assembly, wall-mounted, includes frame and 12 port, 110 style punch down. Does not include labor to punch down cable connections.					
Wall mounting frame with 110 style punch down	E4@.250	Ea	139.00	12.70	151.70
Classroom network station wiring, category 5E twisted pair 350 mbps cable pulled in conduit from a classroom to a central interconnect point. Based on 1,000' cable run with conduit installed by others. Add the cost of cable testing below.					
4 pair UTP plenum-rated solid wire cable	E4@.008	LF	0.21	.41	.62
Network cable wall-mount rack with category 6 rack mount patch panels and 110 style punch down blocks. A wall-mount rack will hold eight 6" rack mount devices. Add the cost of cable punch down below.					
24 port patch panel	E4@.250	Ea	402.00	12.70	414.70
48 port patch panel	E4@.350	Ea	584.00	17.80	601.80
96 port patch panel	E4@.450	Ea	892.00	22.90	914.90
Cable punch down. Labor for punch down (connection) on a 110 style block mounted in a classroom, central interconnect point or at server room.					
Per four pair of cable connections	E4@.020	Ea	—	1.02	1.02
Network cable testing, using a dedicated cable tester, shielded or unshielded cable					
Per twisted pair	E4@.125	Ea	—	6.35	6.35
Distribution of patch panel connections to a network switch. Includes 10/100 network switch and patch cables					
24 station connection	CE@.330	Ea	397.00	19.90	416.90
48 station connection	CE@.500	Ea	1,060.00	30.20	1,090.20
96 station connection	CE@1.00	Ea	2,100.00	60.40	2,160.40
Wireless access point. Use the network wire pulling and termination costs above. Access points are commonly installed 12" below the finished ceiling on a small shelf. Add the cost of an electrical outlet at the access point. Count each access point as one station termination and connection.					
Wireless access point	CE@.100	Ea	72.20	6.04	78.24
High gain antenna for extended range on a wireless access point. Add the cost of a RG-6U cable run to the wireless access point.					
18Dbi high gain panel antenna	CE@.100	Ea	130.00	6.04	136.04

Ecclesiastical Equipment Labor includes unpacking, layout and complete installation of prefinished furniture and equipment.

	Craft@Hrs	Unit	Material	Labor	Total
Lecterns, 16" x 24"					
Plain	C8@4.48	Ea	769.00	211.00	980.00
Deluxe	C8@4.48	Ea	1,390.00	211.00	1,601.00
Premium	C8@4.48	Ea	2,700.00	211.00	2,911.00
Pulpits					
Plain	C8@4.77	Ea	869.00	225.00	1,094.00
Deluxe	C8@4.77	Ea	1,350.00	225.00	1,575.00
Premium	C8@4.77	Ea	3,370.00	225.00	3,595.00
Arks, with curtain					
Plain	C8@5.97	Ea	900.00	281.00	1,181.00
Deluxe	C8@5.97	Ea	1,180.00	281.00	1,461.00
Premium	C8@5.97	Ea	1,960.00	281.00	2,241.00

	Craft@Hrs	Unit	Material	Labor	Total
Arks, with door					
Plain	C8@8.95	Ea	1,020.00	422.00	1,442.00
Deluxe	C8@8.95	Ea	1,720.00	422.00	2,142.00
Premium	C8@8.95	Ea	2,700.00	422.00	3,122.00
Pews, bench type					
Plain	C8@.382	LF	56.50	18.00	74.50
Deluxe	C8@.382	LF	61.40	18.00	79.40
Premium	C8@.382	LF	73.60	18.00	91.60
Pews, seat type					
Plain	C8@.464	LF	70.90	21.90	92.80
Deluxe	C8@.491	LF	92.50	23.10	115.60
Premium	C8@.523	LF	110.00	24.70	134.70
Kneelers					
Plain	C8@.185	LF	13.70	8.72	22.42
Deluxe	C8@.185	LF	17.60	8.72	26.32
Premium	C8@.185	LF	27.80	8.72	36.52
Cathedral chairs, shaped wood					
Without accessories	C8@.235	Ea	183.00	11.10	194.10
With book rack	C8@.235	Ea	198.00	11.10	209.10
With book rack and kneeler	C8@.235	Ea	221.00	11.10	232.10
Cathedral chairs, upholstered					
Without accessories	C8@.285	Ea	190.00	13.40	203.40
With book rack	C8@.285	Ea	205.00	13.40	218.40
With book rack and kneeler	C8@.285	Ea	248.00	13.40	261.40
Adaptable fabric upholstered chair seating (Sauder)					
Hardwood laminated frame, interlocking legs, book rack, stackable, "Modlok"					
Standard	C8@.066	Ea	165.00	3.11	168.11
Deluxe	C8@.066	Ea	180.00	3.11	183.11
Solid oak frame, stackable, "Oaklok"	C8@.066	Ea	135.00	3.11	138.11
Laminated beech frame, stackable, "Plylok"	C8@.066	Ea	148.00	3.11	151.11
Laminated beech frame, stacks & folds, "Plyfold"	C8@.066	Ea	128.00	3.11	131.11
Confessionals, single, with curtain					
Plain	C8@9.11	Ea	3,240.00	429.00	3,669.00
Deluxe	C8@9.11	Ea	3,910.00	429.00	4,339.00
Premium	C8@9.11	Ea	4,460.00	429.00	4,889.00
Add for door in place of curtain	—	Ea	520.00	—	520.00
Confessionals, double, with curtain					
Plain	C8@13.7	Ea	5,160.00	646.00	5,806.00
Deluxe	C8@13.7	Ea	5,960.00	646.00	6,606.00
Premium	C8@13.7	Ea	7,350.00	646.00	7,996.00
Communion rail, hardwood, with standards					
Plain	C8@.315	LF	59.70	14.80	74.50
Deluxe	C8@.315	LF	74.90	14.80	89.70
Premium	C8@.315	LF	89.50	14.80	104.30
Communion rail, carved oak, with standards					
Embellished	C8@.315	LF	97.20	14.80	112.00
Ornate	C8@.315	LF	129.00	14.80	143.80
Premium	C8@.315	LF	215.00	14.80	229.80
Communion rail, bronze or stainless steel,					
With standards	H6@.285	LF	148.00	15.30	163.30

	Craft@Hrs	Unit	Material	Labor	Total
Altars, hardwood, sawn					
Plain	C8@5.97	Ea	1,060.00	281.00	1,341.00
Deluxe	C8@5.97	Ea	1,260.00	281.00	1,541.00
Premium	C8@5.97	Ea	1,680.00	281.00	1,961.00
Altars, carved hardwood					
Plain	C8@5.97	Ea	3,150.00	281.00	3,431.00
Deluxe	C8@6.73	Ea	7,310.00	317.00	7,627.00
Premium	C8@7.30	Ea	8,310.00	344.00	8,654.00
Altars, with Nimmerillium fonts, marble	D4@27.8	Ea	5,450.00	1,320.00	6,770.00
Altars, marble or granite					
Plain	D4@29.1	Ea	6,240.00	1,380.00	7,620.00
Deluxe	D4@29.1	Ea	9,060.00	1,380.00	10,440.00
Premium	D4@29.1	Ea	13,500.00	1,380.00	14,880.00
Altars, marble legs and base					
Deluxe	D4@29.1	Ea	3,730.00	1,380.00	5,110.00
Premium	D4@29.1	Ea	5,340.00	1,380.00	6,720.00

Theater & Stage Curtains

	Craft@Hrs	Unit	Material	Labor	Total
Straight track for manual curtains, see lifting and drawing equipment below					
Standard duty					
24' wide stage	D4@.511	LF	38.30	24.30	62.60
40' wide stage	D4@.330	LF	38.30	15.70	54.00
60' wide stage	D4@.246	LF	38.30	11.70	50.00
Medium duty					
24' wide stage	D4@.511	LF	55.30	24.30	79.60
40' wide stage	D4@.330	LF	55.30	15.70	71.00
60' wide stage	D4@.246	LF	55.30	11.70	67.00
Heavy duty					
24' wide stage	D4@.511	LF	53.10	24.30	77.40
40' wide stage	D4@.330	LF	53.10	15.70	68.80
60' wide stage	D4@.246	LF	53.10	11.70	64.80
Curved track, manual operation, see lifting and drawing equipment below					
Standard duty					
24' wide stage	D4@.511	LF	74.10	24.30	98.40
40' wide stage	D4@.392	LF	74.10	18.60	92.70
60' wide stage	D4@.330	LF	74.10	15.70	89.80
Heavy duty					
24' wide stage	D4@.644	LF	198.00	30.60	228.60
40' wide stage	D4@.469	LF	198.00	22.30	220.30
60' wide stage	D4@.378	LF	198.00	18.00	216.00
Cyclorama track, manual, see lifting and drawing equipment below					
24' wide stage	D4@.511	LF	51.50	24.30	75.80
40' wide stage	D4@.330	LF	51.50	15.70	67.20
60' wide stage	D4@.246	LF	51.50	11.70	63.20

Stage curtains, Subcontract Complete costs for custom fabricated, flameproof stage curtains including labor to hang. No track or curtain lifting or drawing equipment included. By percent of added fullness.

	Craft@Hrs	Unit	Material	Labor	Total
Heavyweight velour					
0% fullness	—	SF	—	—	6.80
50% fullness	—	SF	—	—	8.33
75% fullness	—	SF	—	—	8.58
100% fullness	—	SF	—	—	9.26

	Craft@Hrs	Unit	Material	Labor	Total
Lightweight velour					
0% fullness	—	SF	—	—	5.34
50% fullness	—	SF	—	—	6.02
75% fullness	—	SF	—	—	6.52
100% fullness	—	SF	—	—	8.13
Muslin, 0% fullness	—	SF	—	—	4.01
Repp cloth					
0% fullness	—	SF	—	—	4.32
50% fullness	—	SF	—	—	6.47
75% fullness	—	SF	—	—	6.42
100% fullness	—	SF	—	—	7.10

Stage curtain lifting and drawing equipment Labor is equipment installation, see electrical connection below

	Craft@Hrs	Unit	Material	Labor	Total
Lift curtain equipment					
3/4 HP	D4@8.35	Ea	7,870.00	397.00	8,267.00
1 HP	D4@8.35	Ea	78,500.00	397.00	78,897.00
Draw curtain equipment					
1/3 HP	D4@8.35	Ea	5,900.00	397.00	6,297.00
1/2 HP	D4@8.35	Ea	6,320.00	397.00	6,717.00
3/4 HP	D4@8.35	Ea	6,720.00	397.00	7,117.00
Add for electrical connection. Typical subcontract price for 40' wire run with conduit, circuit breaker, junction box and starter switch.					
Per electrical connection	—	Ea	—	—	2,100.00

Fresnel-type spotlights and general stage lighting for small to medium (1,500 seat) venues, specialty dimmer rheostats, and breaker panels. Cost includes fixed directional mounting pedestals, prewired electrical conduit, fusing, ground fault protection to *National Electrical Code* standards and main control panel. Equipment cost is a self-propelled electric accordion-style work platform. All electrical components are to Underwriters Laboratories standards.

	Craft@Hrs	Unit	Material	Labor	Total
1,000 watt Fresnel lens light, 6"	E4@5.00	Ea	322.00	254.00	576.00
5,000 watt Fresnel lens light, 10"	E4@5.00	Ea	1,320.00	254.00	1,574.00
Main breaker	E4@1.00	Ea	184.00	50.80	234.80
Dimmer rheostat	E4@1.50	Ea	91.70	76.20	167.90
Spotlight control panel	E4@3.00	Ea	430.00	152.00	582.00
Pre-wired conduit	E4@5.00	CLF	61.10	254.00	315.10
Calibration and test	E4@2.00	Ea	—	102.00	102.00

Stage entertainment sound system Appropriate for a small to medium (1,500 seat) venue. Includes prewired electrical conduit, 8-track digital 80 Gig sound recorder, high-definition 1080i-compliant digital motion picture camera and tripod, 64-channel sound mixing board, sound balancing system, 16-channel linear amplifier, filtered power supply, portable stage monitors, fixed acoustically tuned speaker system, fixed suspended stage microphones, ground fault protection to American Federation of Musicians safety standards and steel security cabinet with heavy-duty lockset for equipment storage. Not included, one day of self-propelled electric accordion-style work platform equipment rental, add as necessary.

	Craft@Hrs	Unit	Material	Labor	Total
Pre-wired conduit	E4@5.00	CLF	53.50	254.00	307.50
Power supply and amplifier	E4@.500	Ea	854.00	25.40	879.40
Fixed speakers	B1@.500	Ea	483.00	16.90	499.90
Ground fault protection	E4@1.00	Ea	321.00	50.80	371.80
Ceiling microphones	E4@1.00	Ea	267.00	50.80	317.80
Digital 1080i-compliant camcorder	—	Ea	6,280.00	—	6,280.00
Mixing and recording table	E4@2.50	Ea	2,670.00	127.00	2,797.00
Security cabinet for mixing and recording table	B1@1.50	Ea	1,290.00	50.80	1,340.80
Calibration and test	E4@4.00	Ea	—	203.00	203.00

	Craft@Hrs	Unit	Material	Labor	Total
Public address systems For small to medium (1,500 seat) venues such as school assembly halls or civic centers. Includes a linear amplifier, filtered power supply, stage-mounted cable fixtures with covers, pedestal stage microphones, ground fault protection to American Federation of Musicians safety standards, fixed wall-hung speakers, pre-wired permanent conduit runs, removable stage monitors, and security cabinet with lockset for equipment storage.					
Pre-wired conduit	E4@5.00	CLF	54.30	254.00	308.30
Stage cable fixtures	E4@2.00	Ea	11.00	102.00	113.00
Ground fault protection	E4@1.00	Ea	326.00	50.80	376.80
Fixed speakers	B1@.500	Ea	489.00	16.90	505.90
Amplifier and power supply	E4@.500	Ea	870.00	25.40	895.40
Security cabinet	B1@1.50	Ea	1,310.00	50.80	1,360.80
Calibration and test	E4@4.00	Ea	—	203.00	203.00
Acoustically engineered sound reduction paneling Cost includes vertical support studs, spacers, fasteners and trim. Complies with American Institute of Sound Engineering specifications. Per square foot of wall or ceiling covered.					
Sidewall coverage	D2@.040	SF	1.72	1.87	3.59
Ceiling coverage	D2@.060	SF	1.72	2.81	4.53
Specialty mobile HVAC for performing stage zone "spot" cooling to American Federation of Musicians and Screen Actors Guild safety standards. For below-stage mounting in live theaters and for shooting stages for cinema and television work. Includes integral ground fault protection. Material only. Directional ducting costs not included.					
250,000 Btu Unit	—	Ea	—	—	34,600.00
Specialty theater panic exit double doors Includes pre-hung frame, vertical center bar main brace, overhead illuminated light emitting diode "fire exit only" sign, fire alarm system interlocking switch and digital alarm horn, external-only safety lockset and panic bar. To National Fire Protection Association standards and specifications.					
Door frame and vertical bar	B1@8.00	Ea	903.00	271.00	1,174.00
Double doors, per pair	B1@.500	Ea	1,690.00	16.90	1,706.90
Wiring of interlock alarm and sign	E4@2.00	Ea	661.00	102.00	763.00
Calibration and test	E4@3.00	Ea	—	152.00	152.00
Gymnasium and Athletic Equipment					
Basketball backstops					
Fixed, wall-mounted	D4@8.00	Ea	806.00	380.00	1,186.00
Swing-up, wall-mounted	D4@10.0	Ea	1,060.00	476.00	1,536.00
Ceiling suspended, to 20', swing-up manual	D4@16.0	Ea	2,300.00	761.00	3,061.00
Add for glass backstop, fan shape	—	Ea	705.00	—	705.00
Add for glass backstop, rectangular	—	Ea	792.00	—	792.00
Add for power operation	—	Ea	—	—	660.00
Gym floors, typical subcontract prices, not including subfloor or base					
Synthetic gym floor, 3/16"	—	SF	—	—	6.52
Synthetic gym floor, 3/8"	—	SF	—	—	8.58
Built-up wood "spring system" maple floor	—	SF	—	—	12.20
Rubber cushioned maple floor	—	SF	—	—	10.80
Maple floor on sleepers and membrane					
Unfinished	—	SF	—	—	8.42
Apparatus inserts	—	Ea	—	—	45.30
Bleachers, telescoping, manual, per seat	D4@.187	Ea	51.40	8.89	60.29
Bleachers, hydraulic operated, per seat	D4@.235	Ea	70.20	11.20	81.40
Scoreboards, basketball, single face					
Economy	CE@7.01	Ea	1,540.00	423.00	1,963.00
Good	CE@13.0	Ea	2,090.00	785.00	2,875.00
Premium	CE@21.6	Ea	3,300.00	1,300.00	4,600.00

	Craft@Hrs	Unit	Material	Labor	Total
Weight and exercise equipment room, commercial and educational facility grade, on a 4" concrete slab supporting special composite low-impact padded exercise room flooring. Costs include labor for bolting of equipment to the floor but do not include the slab or flooring costs, electrical connections where required or cost of equipment assembly.					
Weight machine	B9@.500	Ea	2,880.00	16.50	2,896.50
Rowing machine	B9@.250	Ea	1,500.00	8.27	1,508.27
Treadmill	B9@.250	Ea	1,380.00	8.27	1,388.27
Stationary bicycle	B9@.250	Ea	950.00	8.27	958.27
Boxing ring	B9@4.00	Ea	3,000.00	132.00	3,132.00
Trampoline	B9@4.00	Ea	2,400.00	132.00	2,532.00
Parallel bars	B9@.500	Ea	1,930.00	16.50	1,946.50
Balance beam	B9@.250	Ea	1,580.00	8.27	1,588.27
Playing Fields Typical subcontract costs. Use 3,000 SF as a minimum job charge.					
Playing fields, synthetic surface					
Turf, including base and turf	—	SF	—	—	13.70
Turf, 3 layer, base foam, turf	—	SF	—	—	14.80
Uniturf, embossed running surface, 3/8"	—	SF	—	—	10.10
Running track					
Volcanic cinder, 7"	—	SF	—	—	3.39
Bituminous and cork, 2"	—	SF	—	—	4.59
Artificial grass turf, glue-down carpet installation includes cleaning application surface, adhesive, seam seal and rolling. Based on 100 SY job. Challenger Industries, www.challengerturf.com					
Economy grade non-directional turf	F9@.055	SY	5.77	2.55	8.32
Mid grade non-directional weather resistant turf	F9@.055	SY	6.91	2.55	9.46
High performance non-directional UV stabilized turf	F9@.055	SY	7.87	2.55	10.42
Miniature golf style weather resistant turf	F9@.055	SY	8.08	2.55	10.63
Premium spike-proof non-directional UV stabilized turf	F9@.065	SY	19.90	3.01	22.91
Padded spike-proof non-directional UV stabilized turf	F9@.065	SY	22.10	3.01	25.11
Carpet adhesive (25 SY per gallon)	—	Gal	13.90	—	13.90
Seam sealer (800 LF per gallon)	—	Gal	48.00	—	48.00
Spike-proof indoor carpeting					
Economy grade patterned carpet	F9@.060	SY	15.80	2.78	18.58
Mid grade patterned carpet	F9@.060	SY	17.40	2.78	20.18
Mid grade insignia carpet	F9@.060	SY	23.60	2.78	26.38
Premium patterned carpet	F9@.060	SY	27.60	2.78	30.38

	Craft@Hrs	Unit	Material	Labor	Equipment	Total
Athletic Equipment Installed with a 4,000 lb. capacity forklift. Football goals, costs shown are for two goals for one field. Galvanized steel pipe.						
4-1/2" center support post	S6@22.0	Pr	2,880.00	1,020.00	252.00	4,152.00
6-5/8" center support post	S6@24.0	Pr	5,680.00	1,120.00	275.00	7,075.00
Combination football/soccer goal, regulation size, galvanized steel pipe, dual uprights	S6@24.0	Pr	2,570.00	1,120.00	275.00	3,965.00
Soccer goals, regulation size, costs shown are for two goals for one field						
Aluminum frame with net	S6@24.0	Pr	2,920.00	1,120.00	275.00	4,315.00
Outdoor, playground style basketball goals, single support, adjustable, 6' backboard extension aluminum fan backboard, hoop and net						
Single goal	S6@12.0	Ea	997.00	559.00	138.00	1,694.00
Double goal, back to back	S6@15.0	Ea	1,400.00	699.00	172.00	2,271.00
Volleyball nets, with galvanized posts net, and ground sleeves						
Per net	S6@18.0	Ea	1,070.00	839.00	206.00	2,115.00

	Craft@Hrs	Unit	Material	Labor	Equipment	Total
Tennis Courts Typical costs for championship size single playing court installation including normal fine grading. These costs do not include site preparation, excavation, drainage, or retaining walls. Equipment, where shown, is a 4,000 lb. capacity forklift. Court is 60' x 120' with asphaltic concrete or Portland cement slab (4" thickness built up to 6" thickness at perimeter). Includes compacted base material and wire mesh reinforcing in concrete.						
Typical cost per court, slab-on-grade	—	LS	—	—	—	24,500.00
Court surface seal coat (7,200 SF)						
One color plus 2" wide boundary lines	—	LS	—	—	—	2,730.00
Fence, 10' high galvanized chain link (360 LF) at court perimeter						
Fencing including gates	—	LS	—	—	—	11,900.00
Lighting						
Typical installation	—	LS	—	—	—	12,500.00
Net posts, with tension reel						
Galvanized steel, 3-1/2" diameter	S6@6.00	Pr	579.00	280.00	68.80	927.80
Galvanized steel, 4-1/2" diameter	S6@6.00	Pr	640.00	280.00	68.80	988.80
Tennis nets						
Nylon	S6@1.50	Ea	517.00	69.90	17.20	604.10
Polypropylene	S6@1.50	Ea	398.00	69.90	17.20	485.10
Steel	S6@1.50	Ea	1,580.00	69.90	17.20	1,667.10
Ball wall, fiberglass, 8' x 12'						
Attached to existing wall	S6@3.00	Ea	1,520.00	140.00	17.20	1,677.20
Windbreak, 8' high, closed mesh polypropylene						
Lashed to existing chain link fence	S6@.003	SF	.61	.14	.03	.78

	Craft@Hrs	Unit	Material	Labor	Total
Athletic Benches Backed athletic benches, galvanized pipe frame, stationary					
Aluminum seat and back					
7' long	C8@.930	Ea	306.00	43.80	349.80
8' long	C8@1.16	Ea	356.00	54.70	410.70
15' long	C8@1.31	Ea	566.00	61.80	627.80
Fiberglass seat and back					
10' long	C8@.930	Ea	441.00	43.80	484.80
12' long	C8@1.16	Ea	508.00	54.70	562.70
16' long	C8@1.31	Ea	680.00	61.80	741.80
Galvanized steel seat and back					
15' long	C8@1.31	Ea	405.00	61.80	466.80
Backless athletic bench, galvanized pipe frame, stationary, 12" wide x 10' long					
Wood seat	C8@.776	Ea	217.00	36.60	253.60
Steel seat	C8@.776	Ea	236.00	36.60	272.60
Aluminum seat	C8@.776	Ea	273.00	36.60	309.60
Surface Preparation and Striping for Athletic Courts Use $150 as a minimum job charge.					
Surface preparation					
Acid etch concrete surface	PA@.013	SY	.31	.69	1.00
Primer on asphalt	PA@.006	SY	.46	.32	.78
Primer on concrete	PA@.006	SY	.64	.32	.96
Asphalt emulsion filler, 1 coat	PA@.008	SY	.88	.43	1.31
Acrylic filler, 1 coat	PA@.008	SY	1.13	.43	1.56
Rubber/acrylic compound, per coat	PA@.012	SY	2.84	.64	3.48
Acrylic emulsion texture, per coat					
Sand filled	PA@.006	SY	1.88	.32	2.20
Rubber filled	PA@.006	SY	1.96	.32	2.28
Acrylic emulsion color coat, per coat					
Tan, brown, or red	PA@.006	SY	.62	.32	.94
Greens	PA@.006	SY	.71	.32	1.03
Blue	PA@.006	SY	.77	.32	1.09

	Craft@Hrs	Unit	Material	Labor	Total
Rubber cushioned concrete pavers					
18" x 18", dry joints	FL@.039	SF	23.10	2.00	25.10
Striping for athletic courts					
Marked with white or yellow striping paint					
Lines 3" wide	PA@.005	LF	.08	.27	.35
Lines 4" wide	PA@.005	LF	.10	.27	.37
Lines 4" wide, reflectorized	PA@.002	LF	.25	.11	.36
Lines 8" wide, reflectorized	PA@.004	LF	.52	.21	.73
Marked with reflectorized thermoplastic tape					
Lines 4" wide	PA@.004	LF	1.86	.21	2.07
Lines 6" wide	PA@.006	LF	2.83	.32	3.15
Symbols, lettering					
Within 2'-0" x 8'-0" template	PA@2.50	Ea	72.90	133.00	205.90

Playground Equipment Equipment cost is for a 4,000 lb. capacity forklift. Use $2,500 as a minimum job charge.

	Craft@Hrs	Unit	Material	Labor	Equipment	Total
Balance beams. All are supported 12" above the ground by 2-3/8" OD galvanized pipe uprights.						
10' long "Z"-shaped beam	S6@6.00	Ea	438.00	280.00	68.80	786.80
10' long curved beam	S6@6.00	Ea	569.00	280.00	68.80	917.80
10' long straight beam	S6@6.00	Ea	429.00	280.00	68.80	777.80
15' long straight beam	S6@6.00	Ea	345.00	280.00	68.80	693.80
30' long "Z"-shaped beam	S6@9.00	Ea	672.00	419.00	103.00	1,194.00
Geodesic dome beehive climber, 1" galvanized pipe rungs						
8' diameter, 4' high	S6@24.0	Ea	594.00	1,120.00	275.00	1,989.00
13' diameter, 5' high	S6@36.0	Ea	1,780.00	1,680.00	413.00	3,873.00
18' diameter, 7' high	S6@48.0	Ea	2,230.00	2,240.00	550.00	5,020.00
Horizontal ladders, 20" wide with 1-1/16" OD galvanized pipe rungs 12" OC and 2-3/8" OD galvanized pipe headers and top rails						
12' long, 6' high	S6@6.00	Ea	760.00	280.00	68.80	1,108.80
18' long, 7' high	S6@9.00	Ea	934.00	419.00	103.00	1,456.00
Rope and pole climbs. Horizontal vertical end posts are 3-1/2" OD galvanized steel tubing.						
10' H x 10' W with three 1-5/8" diameter poles	S6@24.0	Ea	1,120.00	1,120.00	275.00	2,515.00
10' H x 10' W with three 1" diameter ropes	S6@24.0	Ea	1,210.00	1,120.00	275.00	2,605.00
16' H x 12' W with three 1-5/8" diameter poles	S6@24.0	Ea	1,520.00	1,120.00	275.00	2,915.00
16' H x 12' W with three 1-1/2" diameter ropes	S6@24.0	Ea	1,710.00	1,120.00	275.00	3,105.00
Sandboxes, prefabricated. Painted galvanized steel, 12" high, pine seats, sand not included						
6' x 6'	S6@9.00	Ea	474.00	419.00	103.00	996.00
12' x 12'	S6@12.0	Ea	673.00	559.00	138.00	1,370.00
Masonry sand	—	CY	44.90	—	—	44.90
Washed plaster sand	—	CY	57.30	—	—	57.30
Concrete sand	—	CY	74.50	—	—	74.50
White silica sand	—	CY	98.60	—	—	98.60
Sand scoopers, crane simulator. Heavy-duty metal construction. Two handles control crane arm height and sand scooper, set in concrete.						
3' high miniature scooper with seat	CL@2.15	Ea	518.00	88.70	73.90	680.60
4' high rotating stand up scooper	CL@2.75	Ea	532.00	113.00	94.50	739.50
Masonry sand	—	CY	44.90	—	—	44.90

	Craft@Hrs	Unit	Material	Labor	Equipment	Total
Seesaws, galvanized pipe beam with polyethylene saddle or animal seats. Seesaw beam pivots between two coil springs. Double units have seesaw beams spaced 90 degrees apart, set in concrete.						
Single unit, 7' metal base	S6@5.00	Ea	455.00	233.00	57.30	745.30
Double unit, 4 saddle seats	S6@9.00	Ea	1,540.00	419.00	103.00	2,062.00
Double unit, 2 animal & 2 saddle seats	S6@9.00	Ea	2,180.00	419.00	103.00	2,702.00
Double unit, 4 animal seats	S6@9.00	Ea	2,830.00	419.00	103.00	3,352.00
Spring saws, spring-mounted steel frame with aluminum seats, sets in concrete.						
2' x 12' with two saddle seats	S6@6.00	Ea	1,060.00	280.00	68.80	1,408.80
12' diameter with two animal seats	S6@6.00	Ea	715.00	280.00	68.80	1,063.80
12' diameter with four saddle seats	S6@8.50	Ea	2,160.00	396.00	97.40	2,653.40
12' diameter with four animal seats	S6@8.50	Ea	917.00	396.00	97.40	1,410.40
12' diameter with six saddle seats	S6@9.00	Ea	3,180.00	419.00	103.00	3,702.00
12' diameter with six animal seats	S6@9.00	Ea	1,250.00	419.00	103.00	1,772.00
Slides						
Traditional slide with 18" wide 16 gauge stainless steel slide and galvanized steel stairway.						
Chute 5'H x 10'L Overall length is 13'	S6@12.0	Ea	1,380.00	559.00	138.00	2,077.00
Chute 6'H x 12'L Overall length is 15'	S6@12.0	Ea	1,520.00	559.00	138.00	2,217.00
Chute 8'H x 16'L Overall length is 20'	S6@12.0	Ea	2,030.00	559.00	138.00	2,727.00
Swings, belt seats, galvanized pipe frame						
8' high two-leg ends						
2 seats wood framed	S6@8.00	Ea	1,560.00	373.00	91.70	2,024.70
2 seats	S6@12.0	Ea	661.00	559.00	138.00	1,358.00
4 seats	S6@18.0	Ea	1,130.00	839.00	206.00	2,175.00
6 seats	S6@24.0	Ea	1,590.00	1,120.00	275.00	2,985.00
10' high two-leg ends						
2 seats	S6@18.0	Ea	717.00	839.00	206.00	1,762.00
4 seats	S6@24.0	Ea	1,230.00	1,120.00	275.00	2,625.00
6 seats	S6@30.0	Ea	1,730.00	1,400.00	344.00	3,474.00
10' high three-leg ends						
4 seats	S6@24.0	Ea	1,560.00	1,120.00	275.00	2,955.00
6 seats	S6@30.0	Ea	1,890.00	1,400.00	344.00	3,634.00
8 seats	S6@36.0	Ea	2,710.00	1,680.00	413.00	4,803.00
12' high three-leg ends						
3 seats	S6@30.0	Ea	1,290.00	1,400.00	344.00	3,034.00
6 seats	S6@36.0	Ea	1,940.00	1,680.00	413.00	4,033.00
8 seats	S6@42.0	Ea	2,680.00	1,960.00	481.00	5,121.00
Add for platform for wheelchair						
Installed on any swing set	S6@12.0	Ea	746.00	559.00	138.00	1,443.00
Add for seat replacements						
Bucket seat for infant, exchange	—	Ea	45.90	—	—	45.90
Extra bucket seat for infant	—	Ea	106.00	—	—	106.00
Tetherball sets, galvanized pipe post, ground sleeve and chain, complete with nylon rope and ball	S6@3.00	Ea	190.00	140.00	34.40	364.40
Sand for pit (masonry sand)	—	CY	44.90	—	—	44.90

	Craft@Hrs	Unit	Material	Labor	Equipment	Total
Tower climber. Complete with 8' high fireman's slide pole, "loft" platform, cargo net, horizontal ladders and vertical ladders. Frame is 1-1/4" square steel tubing with painted finish, bracing, ladders and slide pole are 1" OD steel pipe with painted finish. The platform consists of two 30" x 96" fiberglass planks with integral color located 5'0" above the ground. Available in mixed or matched colors.						
8' L x 6' W x 8' H	S6@36.0	Ea	3,630.00	1,680.00	413.00	5,723.00
Arch climbers, 1.9" OD galvanized steel pipe, set in concrete						
2'2" x 10'7"	S6@6.75	Ea	673.00	314.00	31.50	1,018.50
2'2" x 13'11"	S6@7.00	Ea	743.00	326.00	80.20	1,149.20
2'2" x 15'1"	S6@7.00	Ea	856.00	326.00	80.20	1,262.20
15' x 20' four-way climber	S6@10.0	Ea	1,150.00	466.00	115.00	1,731.00
Funnel ball, 3-1/2" OD galvanized steel post with yellow polyethylene hopper						
10' high, set in concrete	S6@4.00	Ea	866.00	186.00	45.80	1,097.80
Chin-up bars, 1-1/2" OD galvanized steel post with 54" and 66" and 84" bar height levels						
12' width, set in concrete	S6@4.75	Ea	503.00	221.00	54.40	778.40
Parallel bars, 1-7/8" OD galvanized steel post, 2'9" high.						
2' x 9'2" set in concrete	S6@6.00	Ea	306.00	280.00	68.80	654.80
Add for motion beam attachment	S6@.250	Ea	210.00	11.60	2.86	224.46

	Craft@Hrs	Unit	Material	Labor	Total
Park Grills Steel grill, set in concrete. Add for cost of concrete.					
Rotating adjustable grill, 40" high with 300 sq. inch cooking area	CM@2.50	Ea	226.00	128.00	354.00
Large grill with two adjustable grates, 40" high with 1,008 sq. inch cooking area	CM@2.75	Ea	450.00	141.00	591.00
Hooded rotating grill, with hood vents, 40" high with 500 sq. inch cooking area	CM@3.00	Ea	567.00	154.00	721.00
Shelterhouse grill with shelves and two grates, 40" high with 1,368 sq. inch cooking area	CM@3.50	Ea	863.00	180.00	1,043.00
Campfire rings with 300 sq. inch cooking area and security brackets set in concrete					
Hinged grate	CM@2.25	Ea	196.00	116.00	312.00
Adjustable grate	CM@2.25	Ea	226.00	116.00	342.00
Medical Refrigeration Equipment Labor costs include unpacking, assembly and installation. Jewett Refrigerator.					
Blood bank refrigerators, upright enameled steel cabinets with locking glass doors, 7 day recording thermometer, LED temperature display, failure alarm, interior lights, and removable drawers. 2 to 4 degree C operating range.					
5 drawer, 240 bag, 16.9 CF, 29" wide x 30" deep x 74" high, #BBR17	D4@2.25	Ea	8,360.00	107.00	8,467.00
6 drawer, 360 bag, 24.8 CF, 29" wide x 36" deep x 83" high, #BBR25	D4@2.25	Ea	8,740.00	107.00	8,847.00
10 drawer, 480 bag, 37.4 CF, 59" wide x 30" deep x 74" high, #BBR37	D4@3.42	Ea	12,100.00	163.00	12,263.00
12 drawer, 720 bag, 55.0 CF, 59" wide x 36" deep x 83" high, #BBR55	D4@3.42	Ea	12,500.00	163.00	12,663.00
Blood plasma storage freezers, upright enameled steel cabinets with locking steel doors, 7 day recording thermometer, LED temperature display, failure alarm, and removable drawers. –30 degree C operating temperature.					
6 drawer, 265 pack, 13.2 CF, 34" wide x 30" deep x 74" high, #BPL13	D4@2.25	Ea	14,100.00	107.00	14,207.00
8 drawer, 560 pack, 24.8 CF, 29" wide x 36" deep x 83" high, #BPL25	D4@2.25	Ea	12,500.00	107.00	12,607.00
16 drawer, 1,120 pack, 55 CF, 59" wide x 36" deep x 83" high, #BPL55	D4@3.42	Ea	19,700.00	163.00	19,863.00

11 Equipment

	Craft@Hrs	Unit	Material	Labor	Total
Laboratory refrigerators, upright enameled steel cabinets with locking steel doors, enameled steel interior, and adjustable stainless steel shelves. 2 to 4 degree C operating temperature.					
4 shelf, 16.9 CF, 29" wide x 30" deep x 74" high #LR17B	D4@2.25	Ea	5,710.00	107.00	5,817.00
8 shelf, 37.4 CF, 59" wide x 30" deep x 74" high #LR37B	D4@3.42	Ea	8,740.00	163.00	8,903.00
Pharmacy refrigerators, upright enameled steel cabinets with locking steel doors, enameled steel interior, and adjustable stainless steel drawers and shelves. –2 degree C operating temperature.					
6 drawer, 1 shelf, 24.8 CF, 29" wide x 36" deep x 83" high, #PR25B	D4@2.25	Ea	6,390.00	107.00	6,497.00
9 drawer, 5 shelf, 55.0 CF, 59" wide x 36" deep x 83" high, #PR55B	D4@3.42	Ea	10,200.00	163.00	10,363.00
Hospital/Lab/Pharmacy undercounter refrigerators, stainless steel interior and exterior, locking door. 24" wide x 24" deep x 34-1/2" high. 2 degree C operating temperature.					
5.4 CF, with blower coil cooling system, stainless steel racks, and auto-defrost, #UC5B	D4@1.67	Ea	2,910.00	79.40	2,989.40
5.4 CF with cold wall cooling system, stainless steel racks, and auto-defrost, #UC5C	D4@1.69	Ea	3,770.00	80.40	3,850.40
Hospital/Lab/Pharmacy undercounter freezers, stainless steel interior and exterior, locking door. 24" wide x 24" deep x 34-1/2" high. –20 degree C operating temperature.					
4.6 CF, stainless steel racks, auto-defrost system, #UCF5B	D4@1.69	Ea	4,140.00	80.40	4,220.40
4.6 CF, stainless steel racks, manual hot gas defrost system, #UCF5C	D4@1.69	Ea	4,890.00	80.40	4,970.40
Morgue refrigerators					
1 or 2 body roll-in type, 39" wide x 96" deep x 76" high, with 1/2 HP, 4,380 Btu/hour condenser, #1SPEC	D4@15.8	Ea	13,200.00	751.00	13,951.00
2 body sliding tray type, 39" wide x 96" deep x 76" high, with 1/2 HP, 4,380 Btu/hour condenser, #2EC	D4@18.0	Ea	12,900.00	856.00	13,756.00
2 body side opening type, 96" wide x 39" deep x 76" high, with 1/2 HP, 4,380 Btu/hour condenser, #2SC	D4@18.0	Ea	14,500.00	856.00	15,356.00
4 or 6 body with roll-in type lower compartments, sliding tray type upper compartments, 73" wide x 96" deep x 102" high, 6,060 Btu/hr, 3/4 HP condenser, #4SPEC2W	D4@22.5	Ea	22,400.00	1,070.00	23,470.00

12 Furnishings

	Craft@Hrs	Unit	Material	Labor	Total
Church Glass Material cost includes fabrication of the lite. Labor cost includes setting in a prepared opening only. Minimum labor cost is usually $150 per job. Add the cost of scaffold or a hoist, if needed.					
Stained glass					
Simple artwork	G1@.184	SF	73.40	8.90	82.30
Moderate artwork	G1@.318	SF	185.00	15.40	200.40
Elaborate artwork	G1@.633	SF	590.00	30.60	620.60
Faceted glass					
Simple artwork	G1@.184	SF	65.10	8.90	74.00
Moderate artwork	G1@.318	SF	128.00	15.40	143.40
Elaborate artwork	G1@.633	SF	174.00	30.60	204.60
Colored glass, no artwork					
Single pane	G1@.056	SF	6.97	2.71	9.68
Patterned	G1@.184	SF	14.70	8.90	23.60
Small pieces	G1@.257	SF	37.70	12.40	50.10

	Craft@Hrs	Unit	Material	Labor	Total
Window Treatment					
Lead mesh fabrics, measure glass size only. Includes allowance for overlap, pleating and all hardware.					
Lead mesh (soundproofing)	—	SY	—	—	29.40
Lead mesh (x-ray) 2.5 lbs per SF	—	SY	—	—	33.60
Draperies, 8' height, fabric quality will cause major variation in prices, per LF of opening, typical installed prices					
Standard quality, window or sliding door	—	LF	—	—	25.40
Better quality, window	—	LF	—	—	84.10
Better quality, sliding door	—	LF	—	—	80.30
Drapery lining	—	LF	—	—	9.57
Fiberglass fabric	—	LF	—	—	81.80
Filter light control type	—	LF	—	—	73.20
Flameproofed	—	LF	—	—	79.40
Velour, grand	—	LF	—	—	106.00

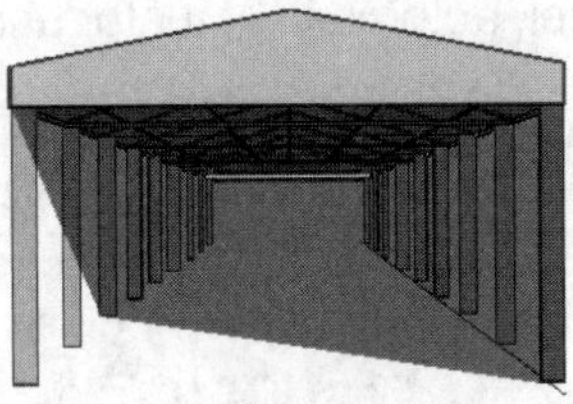
FREESTANDING

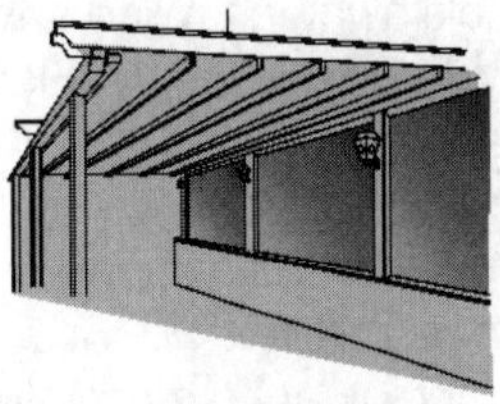
WALL BRACED

Commercial-grade awnings, for restaurant patios, cafés, office outdoor break areas and for solar thermal influx mitigation above glazing. These units meet Western Canvas Products Association standards. Standard fabric is weatherproofed woven, solution-dyed polyester. Complies with Professional Awning Manufacturers Association standards. Arquati Roma, Milano or equal. Add the cost of electric connection and backlighting, if required. Retractable wall-mounted fabric awnings. Lateral arm-type retractable units in lengths to 40 feet and projections to 17 feet. With pitch adjustment arm shoulders, aluminum frame and stainless-steel fasteners.

	Craft@Hrs	Unit	Material	Labor	Total
Reinforcing soffit/wall-mount support and attaching transverse-mount support to soffit or wall	H1@2.00	Ea	179.00	109.00	288.00
Lifting and mounting mechanical assembly	H1@2.00	Ea	99.30	109.00	208.30
Mounting and leveling frame, arm and fabric assembly, per SF of fabric	H1@.010	SF	24.10	.54	24.64
Adjusting fabric tautness, lateral arm tensioning and adjusting arm pulleys	H1@0.50	Ea	—	27.20	27.20

Retractable hood metal-frame lean-to-type awnings. With pre-assembled roller tube and hood assembly, vertical anodized aluminum support hood roller guide columns, curved lintel hood retractor roller guide and transverse wall- or soffit-mounting support plate assembly. Lengths to 42 feet and projections to 22 feet. Includes pitch adjustment arm shoulders, certified aluminum frame construction and stainless-steel fasteners.

	Craft@Hrs	Unit	Material	Labor	Total
Reinforcing soffit/wall-mount support and attaching transverse-mount support to soffit or wall	H1@2.00	Ea	198.00	109.00	307.00
Lifting and mounting mechanical assembly	H1@3.00	Ea	123.00	163.00	286.00
Mounting and leveling frame, vertical supports, reel, drive and fabric assembly, per SF of fabric	H1@.010	SF	25.60	.54	26.14
Adjusting fabric tautness, lateral arm tensioning and adjusting arm pulleys	H1@0.50	Ea	—	27.20	27.20

	Craft@Hrs	Unit	Material	Labor	Total
Freestanding or wall-braced canopy-type awning. With pre-assembled roller tube and hood assembly, vertical anodized aluminum support hood roller guide columns, transverse and parallel anodized aluminum girders with hood expander/retractor roller guide and mounting vertical support base-plate assemblies. Lengths to 42 feet and projections up to 22 feet. Aluminum frame construction, stainless-steel fasteners, motor and controls, rainproof hood, Kevlar pulley cord, roller-bearing pulley and hood guides.					
Reinforcing soffit/wall-mount support and attaching transverse-mount support to soffit or wall	H1@.010	Ea	299.00	.54	299.54
Lifting and mounting mechanical assembly	H1@1.45	Ea	199.00	78.90	277.90
Mounting and leveling frame, arm and fabric assembly, per SF of fabric	H1@.015	SF	30.80	.82	31.62
Adjusting fabric tautness and lateral arm tensioning and adjusting arm pulleys	H1@0.80	Ea	—	43.60	43.60
Additional costs for retractable awnings. Wind sensor, motorized reel, automatic actuator and safety interlock are mandatory for compliance with Dade County (Florida) construction code.					
Add for woven flame-retardant fiber	—	%	5.0	—	—
Add for expanded Teflon-coated glass fiber (PTFE)	—	%	8.0	—	—
Add for painted or laser-printed custom logo and lettering	—	%	3.0	—	—
Add for decal-mounted logo and text	—	%	2.0	—	—
Add for wind sensor, auto crank and safety interlock	—	%	5.0	—	—
Add for motorized crank	—	%	10.0	—	—
Add for calibrating and testing auto crank, wind sensor and automatic actuator	H1@0.80	Ea	—	43.60	43.60

Cabinets Cost per linear foot of the longer of either face or back dimension. Base cabinets are 34" high x 24" deep, wall cabinets are 42" high x 12" deep and full-height cabinets are 94" high x 24" deep. Labor shown is for installing shop-fabricated units. Add for countertops at the end of this section.

	Craft@Hrs	Unit	Material	Labor	Total
Metal cabinets, shop- and commercial-type, with hardware but no countertop					
Base cabinet, drawer, door and shelf	D4@.379	LF	130.00	18.00	148.00
Wall cabinet with door and 2 shelves	D4@.462	LF	119.00	22.00	141.00
Full-height cabinet, 5 shelves	D4@.595	LF	241.00	28.30	269.30
Library shelving, 48" high x 8" deep modules	D4@.336	LF	84.80	16.00	100.80
Wardrobe units, 72" high x 42" deep	D4@.398	LF	209.00	18.90	227.90
Custom-made wood cabinets, no hardware or countertops included, unfinished, 36" wide modules. For more complete coverage of custom-built cabinets, see *National Framing and Finish Carpentry Estimator* at http://CraftsmanSiteLicense.com					
Standard grade, inexpensive wood veneer or laminate face					
Base	C8@.256	LF	103.00	12.10	115.10
Wall	C8@.380	LF	79.00	17.90	96.90
Full-height	C8@.426	LF	181.00	20.10	201.10
Better grade, wenge wood					
Base, flat slab door panels	C8@.361	LF	199.00	17.00	216.00
Wall, with end panels, edge band, top trim	C8@.529	LF	183.00	24.90	207.90
Island base cabinets, matching back panel	C8@.629	LF	359.00	29.70	388.70
Additional costs for custom wood cabinets					
Prefinished exterior	—	LF	8.74	—	8.74
Prefinished interior	—	LF	15.00	—	15.00
Standard hardware, installed	—	LF	6.99	—	6.99
Institutional grade hardware, installed	—	LF	10.10	—	10.10
Drawer roller guides, per drawer	—	Ea	11.70	—	11.70
Drawer roller guides, suspension, per drawer	—	Ea	36.20	—	36.20

	Craft@Hrs	Unit	Material	Labor	Total
Extra drawers					
12" wide	—	Ea	75.30	—	75.30
18" wide	—	Ea	88.10	—	88.10
24" wide	—	Ea	96.40	—	96.40
Classroom-type wood cabinets, laminated plastic face, with hardware but no countertop					
Base cabinet, drawer, door and shelf	C8@.391	LF	241.00	18.40	259.40
Wall cabinet with door and 2 shelves	C8@.475	LF	210.00	22.40	232.40
Full height cabinet with doors	C8@.608	LF	343.00	28.70	371.70
Hospital-type wood cabinets, laminated plastic face, with hardware but no countertop					
Base cabinet, drawer, door and shelf	C8@.982	LF	238.00	46.30	284.30
Wall, with 2 shelves and door	C8@1.15	LF	220.00	54.20	274.20
Full height with doors	C8@1.35	LF	320.00	63.60	383.60
Laboratory-type metal cabinets, with hardware but no countertop					
Base cabinet with door	D4@.785	LF	197.00	37.30	234.30
Base cabinet with drawers	D4@.785	LF	247.00	37.30	284.30
Base cabinets, island base	D4@.785	LF	248.00	37.30	285.30
Wall cabinet with metal door	D4@.785	LF	185.00	37.30	222.30
Wall cabinet with framed glass door	D4@.785	LF	241.00	37.30	278.30
Wall cabinets with no doors	D4@.785	LF	158.00	37.30	195.30
Wardrobe or storage cabinet, 80" high, with door	D4@.939	LF	498.00	44.70	542.70
Storage cabinet, 80" high, no door	D4@.939	LF	300.00	44.70	344.70
Fume hoods, steel, without duct, typical cost	T5@3.88	Ea	996.00	198.00	1,194.00
Add for duct, without electric work, typical cost	T5@16.6	LF	1,440.00	846.00	2,286.00

Countertops, shop fabricated, delivered ready for installation.

	Craft@Hrs	Unit	Material	Labor	Total
Laminated plastic tops 2'0" wide over plywood base					
Custom work, square edge front, 4" splash	C8@.187	LF	35.10	8.82	43.92
Add for square edge 9" backsplash	—	LF	11.50	—	11.50
Add for solid colors	—	LF	3.39	—	3.39
Add for acid-proof tops	—	LF	26.10	—	26.10
Stainless steel, 2'0" wide with backsplash	C8@.366	LF	89.20	17.30	106.50

Cigarette Disposal Units

	Craft@Hrs	Unit	Material	Labor	Total
20 gauge stainless steel with grate. For cigarettes and cigars					
5-1/4" x 5-3/16" x 8-3/8" wall mounted	CM@.500	Ea	174.00	25.70	199.70
5-1/4" x 5-3/16" x 8-3/8" pole mounted	CM@.750	Ea	185.00	38.50	223.50
13" x 16" x 43" wall mounted	CM@.600	Ea	212.00	30.80	242.80
13" x 16" x 43" pole mounted	CM@.900	Ea	238.00	46.20	284.20
15" x 16" x 43" wall mounted with trash can	CM@.750	Ea	498.00	38.50	536.50
15" x 16" x 43" pole mounted with trash can	CM@1.25	Ea	521.00	64.20	585.20

Recessed Open Link Entry Mats These costs assume that mats are mounted in an aluminum frame recessed into a concrete walkway and do not include concrete work, special designs or lettering

	Craft@Hrs	Unit	Material	Labor	Total
Polypropylene, 3/8" thick	D4@.560	SF	7.69	26.60	34.29
Coconut husk fiber, 1/2" thick	D4@.560	SF	7.60	26.60	34.20
Recessed vinyl link	D4@.560	SF	22.00	26.60	48.60

	Craft@Hrs	Unit	Material	Labor	Total
Entrance Mats and Recessed Foot Grilles These costs assume installation of an extruded aluminum tread foot grille on a level surface or over a catch basin with or without a drain.					
Pedigrid/Pedimat extruded aluminum entrance mat					
Grid mat with carpet treads	D4@.150	SF	32.30	7.13	39.43
Grid mat with vinyl treads	D4@.150	SF	35.00	7.13	42.13
Grid mat with pool or shower vinyl treads	D4@.150	SF	39.00	7.13	46.13
Grid mat with abrasive serrated aluminum treads	D4@.150	SF	39.20	7.13	46.33
Recessed catch basin with 2" drain	D4@.302	SF	43.40	14.40	57.80
Recessed catch basin without drain	D4@.242	SF	40.80	11.50	52.30
Level base recessed mount	D4@.150	SF	38.90	7.13	46.03
Surface-mount frame, vinyl	—	LF	3.89	—	3.89
Recessed-mount frame, bronze aluminum	D4@.092	LF	8.87	4.38	13.25
Seating These costs do not include concrete work					
Theater style, economy	D4@.424	Ea	149.00	20.20	169.20
Theater style, lodge, rocking type	D4@.470	Ea	295.00	22.40	317.40
Bleachers, closed riser, extruded aluminum, cost per 18" wide seat					
Portable bleachers	D4@.090	Ea	64.60	4.28	68.88
Portable bleachers with guardrails	D4@.136	Ea	71.90	6.47	78.37
Team bleachers, stationary	D4@.090	Ea	55.50	4.28	59.78
Stadium seating, on concrete foundation by others, extruded aluminum, cost per 18" seat width					
10" flat bench seating, seatboard only	D4@.090	Ea	18.80	4.28	23.08
12" contour bench seating, seatboard only	D4@.090	Ea	19.90	4.28	24.18
Chair seating, molded plastic	D4@.310	Ea	107.00	14.70	121.70
Replacement bench seating, stadium or bleacher, extruded aluminum					
Cost per 18" seat width					
10" wide flat seatboard only	D4@.069	Ea	11.80	3.28	15.08
10" wide flat seatboard and footboard	D4@.136	Ea	25.40	6.47	31.87
12" contour seatboard only	D4@.069	Ea	13.90	3.28	17.18
Benches					
Floor-mounted wood locker room bench, metal pedestal bolted to a concrete floor.					
Hardwood top, 6' long, 12" wide	D4@.753	Ea	220.00	35.80	255.80
Park bench, for public and commercial use. Cast aluminum with treated 1-1/2" by 2-1/4" pine wood slats. Central Park or Victorian style.					
4' long	D4@.750	Ea	254.00	35.70	289.70
5' long	D4@.750	Ea	275.00	35.70	310.70
6' long	D4@.750	Ea	312.00	35.70	347.70
Bicycle, Moped and Motorcycle Security Racks Installation kit includes tamper proof bolts and quick setting cement. Locks supplied by users. Labor is to install units on concrete surface. Cost per bicycle or motorcycle of capacity. Add cost for drilling holes in concrete as needed. These costs are based on a minimum purchase of six racks.					
Basic bicycle rack					
5' long, looped steel, holds 8 bikes	C8@1.00	Ea	284.00	47.10	331.10
7' long, looped steel, holds 12 bikes	C8@1.25	Ea	349.00	58.90	407.90
10' long, single sided, holds 9 bikes	C8@.862	Ea	305.00	40.60	345.60
20' long, single sided, holds 18 bikes	C8@1.50	Ea	546.00	70.70	616.70
10' long, double sided, holds 18 bikes	C8@1.50	Ea	393.00	70.70	463.70
20' long, double sided, holds 36 bikes	C8@1.00	Ea	692.00	47.10	739.10

12 Furnishings

	Craft@Hrs	Unit	Material	Labor	Total
Moped or motorcycle rack					
With 24" security chain	C8@.575	Ea	142.00	27.10	169.10
Add for mounting track for use on asphalt or non-concrete surfaces. No foundation work included. Each 10' track section holds 6 bicycle racks or 4 moped or motorcycle racks.					
Per 10' track section, including drilling holes	C8@2.50	Ea	147.00	118.00	265.00
Add for purchasing less than six mounting racks	—	Ea	17.20	—	17.20
Add for drilling mounting holes in concrete, 2 required per rack, cost per rack	C8@.125	Ea	—	5.89	5.89
Bicycle racks, galvanized pipe rack, embedded or surface mounted to concrete, cost per rack					
Double entry					
5' long, 7 bikes	C8@3.31	Ea	320.00	156.00	476.00
10' long, 14 bikes	C8@3.31	Ea	461.00	156.00	617.00
20' long, 28 bikes	C8@4.88	Ea	838.00	230.00	1,068.00
30' long, 42 bikes	C8@6.46	Ea	1,210.00	305.00	1,515.00
Single side entry					
5' long, 4 bikes	C8@2.41	Ea	305.00	114.00	419.00
10' long, 8 bikes	C8@2.41	Ea	346.00	114.00	460.00
20' long, 16 bikes	C8@3.55	Ea	625.00	167.00	792.00
Wood and metal rack, embedded or surface mounted					
Double entry					
10' long, 14 bikes	C8@3.31	Ea	503.00	156.00	659.00
20' long, 28 bikes	C8@4.88	Ea	938.00	230.00	1,168.00
Single entry					
10' long, 8 bikes	C8@2.41	Ea	419.00	114.00	533.00
20' long, 10 bikes	C8@3.55	Ea	751.00	167.00	918.00
Bike post bollard, dimensional wood, concrete footing	C8@.223	Ea	228.00	10.50	238.50
Single tube galvanized steel, looped wave pattern, 30" high, surface mounted					
3' long, 5 bikes	C8@3.45	Ea	745.00	163.00	908.00
5' long, 7 bikes	C8@3.45	Ea	854.00	163.00	1,017.00
7' long, 9 bikes	C8@4.61	Ea	1,100.00	217.00	1,317.00
9' long, 11 bikes	C8@4.61	Ea	1,300.00	217.00	1,517.00
Bonded color, add	—	Ea	113.00	—	113.00
Add for embedded mounting	C8@1.77	Ea	28.40	83.40	111.80

13 Special Construction

Swimming Pools Complete in-ground pool including typical excavation, reinforcing, gunite, filter, pump, pop-up cleaning heads and circulation manifold, skimmer, PVC supply and backwash piping, float valve, ladder, electrical controls and one pool light. Add the cost of deck beyond the edge of coping, electrical supply, a pool equipment slab and enclosure, if required. Typical subcontract prices per SF of water surface.

	Craft@Hrs	Unit	Material	Labor	Total
Apartment building	—	SF	—	—	75.50
Community	—	SF	—	—	97.20
Hotel or resort	—	SF	—	—	91.40
School, training (42' x 75')	—	SF	—	—	102.00
School, Olympic (42' x 165')	—	SF	—	—	154.00

	Craft@Hrs	Unit	Material	Labor	Total
Swimming pool covers, retractable motor-operated, track mounted, including the motor, gearing, retracting reel, pulley system, electric controls and remote switch. For square or rectangular pools. Add the cost of concrete work for the winding reel enclosure, electric supply and the cover.					
3/4 HP drive motor and reel (to 600 SF water surface)	—	Ea	—	—	5,140.00
1-1/4 HP drive motor and reel (to 1,200 SF water surface)	—	Ea	—	—	6,420.00
Add for the vinyl cover, per SF of water surface	—	SF	—	—	4.21

Access for the Disabled

Use the following cost estimates when altering an existing building to meet requirements of the Americans with Disabilities Act (ADA). The ADA requires that existing public and private buildings be altered to accommodate the physically handicapped when that can be done without unreasonable difficulty or expense.

Ramps, flared aprons and landings Concrete access ramps, flared aprons and landings, 2,000 PSI concrete placed directly from the chute of a ready-mix truck, vibrated and finished. Costs include typical wire mesh reinforcing and an allowance for waste but no excavation, backfill or foundations.

	Craft@Hrs	Unit	Material	Labor	Equipment	Total
Access ramps, based on ramps with 1" rise per 1' of run, 4" thick walls and 4" thick slab. Includes pipe sleeves for railings, sand fill in cavity and non-slip surface finish						
24" vertical rise (4' wide x 25' long)	C8@40.0	Ea	1,400.00	1,890.00	—	3,290.00
36" vertical rise (4' wide x 38' long)	C8@60.0	Ea	2,680.00	2,830.00	—	5,510.00
48" vertical rise (4' wide x 50' long)	C8@96.0	Ea	3,920.00	4,530.00	—	8,450.00
Access aprons at curbs, flared and inclined, 2' long x 8' wide						
4" thick (80 SF per CY)	P9@.024	SF	3.40	1.16	—	4.56
6" thick (54 SF per CY)	P9@.032	SF	5.14	1.55	—	6.69
Landings, 4" thick walls on three sides and 4" thick top slab cast against an existing structure on one side. Costs include pipe sleeves for railings, sand fill in cavity and an allowance for waste.						
3'0" high with 6' x 6' square slab	C8@32.0	Ea	1,150.00	1,510.00	—	2,660.00
Add per vertical foot of height over 3'0"	—	VLF	219.00	—	—	219.00
Steel access ramps, 4140 carbon steel, 1" rise per foot of run, 8 gauge diamond pattern steel plate and 2" diameter handrail with electrostatic vinyl paint coating. Includes fabrication and assembly but no excavation. Add the cost of post foundations.						
Per square foot of ramp surface	T3@.150	SF	4.78	7.98	—	12.76
Redwood access ramps, S4S kiln-dried or better redwood, based on ramps with 1-inch rise per foot of run, 6" x 6" posts supporting 2" x 12" beams with steel cross-bracing 36" OC. 2" x 6" decking with 2" diameter railing. Includes fabrication and assembly but no excavation. Add the cost of post foundations.						
Per square foot of ramp surface	B9@.150	SF	2.94	4.96	—	7.90
Snow-melting cable for ramps and landings. Includes 208-277 volt AC self-regulating heater cable designed to be encased in concrete. Based on cable connected to an existing power source adjacent to the installation						
Heater cable (1.1 LF per SF of pavement)	CE@.015	SF	10.20	.91	—	11.11
Power connection kit	CE@.500	Ea	29.90	30.20	—	60.10
Thermostat	CE@.500	Ea	237.00	30.20	—	267.20
Railing for ramps and landings Welded steel. Equipment cost shown is for a flatbed truck and a welding machine. Wall-mounted handrails with brackets 5' OC, based on 12' lengths						
1-1/4" diameter rail, shop prime painted	H6@.092	LF	9.01	4.94	.48	14.43
1-1/2" diameter rail, shop prime painted	H6@.102	LF	10.50	5.48	.53	16.51
Add for galvanized finish	—	%	20.0	—	—	—

	Craft@Hrs	Unit	Material	Labor	Equipment	Total
Floor-mounted railings 3'6" high with posts 5' OC, based on 12' length						
1-1/4" diameter rails and posts, shop prime painted						
2-rail type	H6@.115	LF	37.00	6.18	.60	43.78
3-rail type	H6@.125	LF	48.00	6.72	.65	55.37
1-1/2" diameter rails and posts, shop prime painted						
2-rail type	H6@.125	LF	44.60	6.72	.65	51.97
3-rail type	H6@.137	LF	58.70	7.36	.71	66.77
Add for galvanized finish	—	%	20.0	—	—	—
Drinking fountains and water coolers for the disabled						
Remove an existing drinking fountain or water cooler and disconnect waste and water piping at the wall adjacent to the fixture for use with the new fixture. No salvage value assumed.						
Floor or wall-mounted fixture	P6@1.00	Ea	—	52.40	—	52.40
Install a wall-hung white vitreous china fountain with chrome plated spout, 14" wide, 13" high, non-electric, self-closing dispensing valve and automatic volume control						
Drinking fountain, trim and valves	P6@2.80	Ea	910.00	147.00	—	1,057.00
Wheelchair wall-hung water cooler, vitreous china, refrigerated, (no electrical work included)						
Wall-hung water cooler and trim (add rough-in)	P6@2.50	Ea	1,000.00	131.00	—	1,131.00
Install floor or wall-mounted electric water cooler, 8 gallons per hour, cold water only, connected to existing electrical outlet adjacent to the cooler (no electrical work included)						
Water cooler, trim and valves	P6@2.80	Ea	1,760.00	147.00	—	1,907.00
Parking stall marking for the disabled						
Remove existing pavement marking by water blasting						
4" wide stripes (allow 40 LF per stall)	CL@.032	LF	—	1.32	.45	1.77
Markings, per square foot (minimum 10 SF)	CL@.098	SF	—	4.04	1.38	5.42
Mark parking stall with handicapped symbol painted on, including layout						
Reflectorized stripes and symbol, one color. Add $75 per day for rental of a compressor, hose and spray gun.						
Per stall, no striping	PA@.425	Ea	15.70	22.60	—	38.30
Parking lot handicapped sign, 12" x 18" laminated aluminum, reflective lettering and handicapped symbol						
Sign on 2" galvanized steel pipe post 10' long, set 2' into the ground. Includes digging of hole						
Using a manual auger and backfill	CL@1.25	Ea	95.80	51.60	—	147.40
On walls with mechanical fasteners	PA@.455	Ea	34.10	24.20	—	58.30

Paving and curb removal These costs include breaking out the paving or curb for ADA improvements, loading and hauling debris to a legal dump within 6 miles but no dump fees. Equipment cost per hour is for one 90 CFM air compressor, one paving breaker with jackhammer bits, one 55 HP wheel loader with integral backhoe and one 5 CY dump truck. The figures in parentheses show the approximate "loose" volume of the materials (volume after being demolished). Use $250 as a minimum charge for this type work and add dump charges as a separate item.

	Craft@Hrs	Unit	Material	Labor	Equipment	Total
Asphalt paving, depths to 3" (27 SF per CY)	C3@.040	SF	—	1.93	1.28	3.21
Asphalt curbs, to 12" width (18 LF per CY)	C3@.028	LF	—	1.35	.90	2.25
Concrete paving and slabs on grade						
4" concrete without rebars (54 SF per CY)	C3@.060	SF	—	2.89	1.92	4.81
6" concrete without rebars (45 SF per CY)	C3@.110	SF	—	5.30	3.52	8.82
Add for removal of bar reinforced paving	C3@.200	SF	—	9.63	6.40	16.03

	Craft@Hrs	Unit	Material	Labor	Equipment	Total
Curb, gutter and paving for the disabled These costs assume 3 uses of forms and 2,000 PSI concrete placed directly from the chute of a ready-mix truck. Use $250 as a minimum charge for this type work.						
Concrete cast-in-place vertical curb, including 2% waste, forms and finishing. These costs include typical excavation and backfill with excess excavation spread on site.						
6" x 12" straight curb	P9@.136	LF	5.32	6.60	—	11.92
6" x 18" straight curb	P9@.149	LF	7.90	7.23	—	15.13
6" x 24" straight curb	P9@.154	LF	10.50	7.48	—	17.98
Add for curved sections	—	%	—	40.0	—	—
Curb and 24" monolithic gutter (7 LF per CY)	C3@.100	LF	11.10	4.82	—	15.92
Concrete paving and walkway, 4" thick	P8@.025	SF	3.27	1.16	—	4.43
Add for integral colors, most pastels	—	SF	.44	—	—	.44
Plumbing fixtures for the disabled						
Remove existing plumbing fixtures. Disconnect from existing waste and water piping at the wall adjacent to the fixture. Waste and water piping to remain in place for connection to a new fixture. No salvage value assumed.						
Lavatories	P6@1.00	Ea	—	52.40	—	52.40
Urinals	P6@1.00	Ea	—	52.40	—	52.40
Water closets, floor or wall mounted	P6@1.00	Ea	—	52.40	—	52.40
Install new fixtures. White vitreous china fixtures with typical fittings, hangers, trim and valves. Connected to waste and supply piping from lines adjacent to the fixture.						
Lavatories, wall hung	P6@1.86	Ea	733.00	97.40	—	830.40
Water closets, tank type, with elongated bowl, toilet seat, trim and valves						
Floor mounted, with bowl ring	P6@1.86	Ea	396.00	97.40	—	493.40
Wall hung, with carrier	P6@2.80	Ea	837.00	147.00	—	984.00
Plumbing partitions and grab bars for the disabled						
Remove a standard toilet partition, no salvage value included. Floor or ceiling mounted						
Remove one wall and one door	T5@1.00	Ea	—	51.00	—	51.00
Install toilet partition designed for wheelchair access. Floor or ceiling mounted. These costs include one wall and one door, mechanical fasteners and drilling of holes						
Powder coated metal	T5@2.66	Ea	530.00	136.00	—	666.00
Solid plastic (polymer)	T5@4.00	Ea	835.00	204.00	—	1,039.00
Laminated plastic	T5@2.66	Ea	628.00	136.00	—	764.00
Stainless steel	T5@2.66	Ea	1,200.00	136.00	—	1,336.00
Grab bars, stainless steel, wall mounted, commercial grade. Set of two required for each stall. Including mechanical fasteners and drilling of holes						
1-1/4" x 24" urinal bars	CC@1.00	Set	121.00	53.00	—	174.00
1-1/4" x 36" toilet partition bars	CC@1.00	Set	149.00	53.00	—	202.00

	Craft@Hrs	Unit	Material	Labor	Total
Signage in Braille Standard signs (Rest Room, Elevator, Telephone, Stairway, etc.) mounted with self-stick foam, velcro or in frame. Add the cost of frames, if required, from below.					
5/8" lettering raised 1/32". Grade 2 Braille raised 1/32"					
2" x 8" sign, raised letters and tactile Braille	PA@0.25	Ea	44.70	13.30	58.00
8" x 8" sign with words, graphic symbols and tactile Braille					
standard graphic symbols	PA@0.25	Ea	77.40	13.30	90.70
Sign frames. Signs snap into frames mounted with mechanical fasteners					
2" x 8" frames, black, almond or grey	PA@0.25	Ea	36.80	13.30	50.10
8" x 8" frames, black, almond or grey	PA@0.25	Ea	68.60	13.30	81.90

	Craft@Hrs	Unit	Material	Labor	Total
Elevator plates. Sign with graphic symbols and tactile Braille, standard colors					
Door jamb plates, 7" x 11", two per opening	PA@0.75	Set	87.60	39.90	127.50
Operation plates, Open Door, Close Door, Emergency Stop, Alarm, 1-1/4" x 1-1/4", set of four required per car	PA@1.00	Set	77.50	53.30	130.80
Operation plates, Floor Number, 1-1/4" x 1-1/4" One required for each floor per car	PA@0.25	Ea	19.10	13.30	32.40

Handicapped automatic remote door opener, 60 Hz, single phase, 110 volts, with manual override, electro-pneumatic actuator arm assembly, manual panic bar, door open-position locks, prehung twin metal doors, digital operation cycle setting module, actuator button panel, power/service panel. Americans With Disabilities Act compliant.

Twin door frame	C8@4.00	Ea	318.00	189.00	507.00
Twin doors, per pair	C8@.250	Ea	2,430.00	11.80	2,441.80
Actuator arms for twin doors	C8@0.50	Ea	372.00	23.60	395.60
Automatic remote door controls	C8@4.00	Ea	223.00	189.00	412.00
Actuator mechanism	—	Ea	2,760.00	—	2,760.00

Bus stop shelters Prefabricated structure systems, shipped knocked-down. Complete with all hardware and foundation anchors. Labor cost is for assembly on site. Add the cost of foundation and floor slab. Dimensions are approximate outside measurements. Based on Columbia Equipment Company.

Three-sided open front type. Clear satin silver anodized aluminum structure and fascia, 1/4" clear acrylic sheet glazing in panels and white baked enamel finish aluminum "V"-beam roof.

9'2" L x 5'3" W x 7'5" H					
Two rear panels, single panel each side	C8@8.00	Ea	4,930.00	377.00	5,307.00
Four rear panels, two panels each side	C8@12.0	Ea	5,170.00	566.00	5,736.00
11'3" L x 5'3" W x 7'5" H					
Four rear panels, two panels each side	C8@12.0	Ea	6,040.00	566.00	6,606.00
Add to three-sided open front shelters for the following:					
Wind break front entrance panel					
5'3" W x 7'5" H, with two glazed panels	C8@2.00	Ea	596.00	94.30	690.30

Bus stop enclosures, aluminum frame with Plexiglas sidewall elements, 12' wide by 30' long by 10' high, barrel roof with diamond pattern grille work, aluminum bench, solar lighting and bronze anodized finish.

Shelter assembly, bolted to the foundation	B5@8.00	Ea	20,900.00	296.00	21,196.00
Structure leveling	B5@2.00	Ea	100.00	74.10	174.10
Bus stop bench, all aluminum vandal-resistant seat and backrest					
8'0" long	C8@1.00	Ea	486.00	47.10	533.10
10'0" long	C8@1.50	Ea	631.00	70.70	701.70
Light fixture with unbreakable Lexan diffuser, wiring not included					
100 watt incandescent, photoelectric cell control	C8@2.00	Ea	275.00	94.30	369.30

Radiant heater, with vandal-resistant electric heating element in heavy duty enclosure and metal mesh guard over opening. Wiring not included.

2,500 watt unit (no controls)	C8@1.50	Ea	1,020.00	70.70	1,090.70
5,000 watt unit (no controls)	C8@1.50	Ea	1,200.00	70.70	1,270.70
Electronic timer control, add to above	C8@1.00	Ea	537.00	47.10	584.10

	Craft@Hrs	Unit	Material	Labor	Total
Integrated map/schedule display panel, anodized aluminum frame, tamper-proof fasteners and "spanner-head" tool for opening.					
Full panel width x 30" high					
3/16" clear Plexiglas	C8@1.00	Ea	186.00	47.10	233.10
3/16" polycarbonate with mar-resistant coating	C8@1.00	Ea	287.00	47.10	334.10
Graphics, words "Bus Stop" in white letters, on fascia					
First side	—	LS	116.00	—	116.00
Each additional side	—	Ea	40.40	—	40.40

Metal shelter structures Prefabricated structure systems, shipped knocked-down, complete with all necessary hardware. Labor cost is for assembly on site. Typical use is for picnic pavilions. These costs do not include foundation or floor slab. Dimensions are approximate outside measurements. Based on Americana Building Products. www.americana.com

	Craft@Hrs	Unit	Material	Labor	Total
Four-sided hip roof shelter. Steel structural rafters and columns, aluminum roof decking with stucco embossed, painted finish, 8' height at perimeter.					
12' L x 12' W	S4@32.0	Ea	6,310.00	1,320.00	7,630.00
16' L x 16' W	S4@32.0	Ea	7,750.00	1,320.00	9,070.00
16' L x 32' W	S4@36.0	Ea	10,500.00	1,490.00	11,990.00
20' L x 20' W	S4@36.0	Ea	9,700.00	1,490.00	11,190.00
20' L x 30' W	S4@36.0	Ea	12,500.00	1,490.00	13,990.00
20' L x 40' W	S4@36.0	Ea	15,400.00	1,490.00	16,890.00
24' L x 24' W	S4@36.0	Ea	12,500.00	1,490.00	13,990.00
24' L x 48' W	S4@40.0	Ea	18,100.00	1,650.00	19,750.00
Add for 48" x 48" cupola with tubular metal frame	S4@1.50	Ea	1,280.00	61.90	1,341.90
Add for 6' x 12' cupola with tubular metal frame	S4@3.50	Ea	5,220.00	144.00	5,364.00
Gable roof shelter. Steel structural rafters and columns, aluminum roof and trim. 8' height, 3 in 12 roof pitch.					
20' L x 20' W	S4@36.0	Ea	5,760.00	1,490.00	7,250.00
20' L x 24' W	S4@36.0	Ea	8,320.00	1,490.00	9,810.00
20' L x 30' W	S4@36.0	Ea	8,830.00	1,490.00	10,320.00
20' L x 50' W	S4@40.0	Ea	15,000.00	1,650.00	16,650.00
22' L x 20' W	S4@36.0	Ea	6,120.00	1,490.00	7,610.00
22' L x 30' W	S4@36.0	Ea	9,460.00	1,490.00	10,950.00
22' L x 40' W	S4@36.0	Ea	12,500.00	1,490.00	13,990.00
22' L x 50' W	S4@40.0	Ea	15,500.00	1,650.00	17,150.00

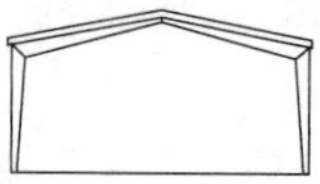

Modular Buildings (Manufactured housing)
Relocatable structures and institutional type housing for remote areas. Costs are per square foot under the roof. Based on 2" x 4" wood studs 16" OC, 1/2" gypsum wallboard inside and 1/2" CDX plywood outside, with minimum plumbing, heating, cooling and electrical systems for the intended use. Costs include factory assembly, delivery by truck to within 50 miles, setting on piers, on-site finishing ("button up"), skirting, steps and rails. Add the cost of utility hookups, permits, taxes and fees. Add 1.5% for each additional 50 miles of delivery. No site preparation or furnishings included. Cost for smaller, more complex structures will be higher. For more detailed coverage of manufactured housing costs, see Craftsman's National Appraisal Estimator.

	Craft@Hrs	Unit	Material	Labor	Total
Portable structures (temporary offices, school classrooms, etc.)					
Medium quality	—	SF	—	—	71.50
Better quality	—	SF	—	—	88.50
Institutional housing, four-plex modules					
Medium quality	—	SF	—	—	92.50
Better quality	—	SF	—	—	93.20
Construction or mining camp barracks, mess halls, kitchens, etc.					
Single story structures	—	SF	—	—	81.20

	Craft@Hrs	Unit	Material	Labor	Total
Air-Supported Structures Air-supported pool or tennis court enclosures, dual-layer polyester reinforced vinyl dome, with zippered entry air lock doors, cable tiedowns and air blower. Typical cost per square foot of area covered including foundation and indirect lighting. Add the cost of grading, drainage and electric service.					
Under 12,000 SF	D4@.030	SF	15.80	1.43	17.23
12,000 to 24,000 SF	D4@.030	SF	14.50	1.43	15.93
24,000 to 30,000 SF	D4@.030	SF	13.30	1.43	14.73
30,000 to 36,000 SF	D4@.030	SF	12.80	1.43	14.23
36,000 to 45,000 SF	D4@.030	SF	12.50	1.43	13.93
45,000 to 80,000 SF	D4@.030	SF	12.30	1.43	13.73
80,000 to 110,000 SF	D4@.030	SF	12.20	1.43	13.63
Add for standby blower motor	—	%	—	—	10.0
Add for revolving door	—	Ea	—	—	5,370.00
Add for emergency exit	—	Ea	—	—	1,820.00

Sunrooms, solariums and conservatories. Custom-designed three-wall building additions supplied in kit form for assembly on site. Aluminum frame mounted on an existing 6" concrete slab with 12" wide x 18" deep footing. Moving glass panels have two adjustable tandem nylon wheel assemblies. Size is limited to 20'-wide roof span, 100' length and 18' height. Meets Architectural Aluminum Manufacturers Association (AAMA), Insulating Glass Certification Council (IGCC) and National Sunroom Association (NSA) standards. Costs include supervision of installation by a manufacturer's representative. Sunrooms, solariums and conservatories have distinct definitions under most building codes. Smaller units in high wind or snow load climates will cost more than larger units built in moderate climates.

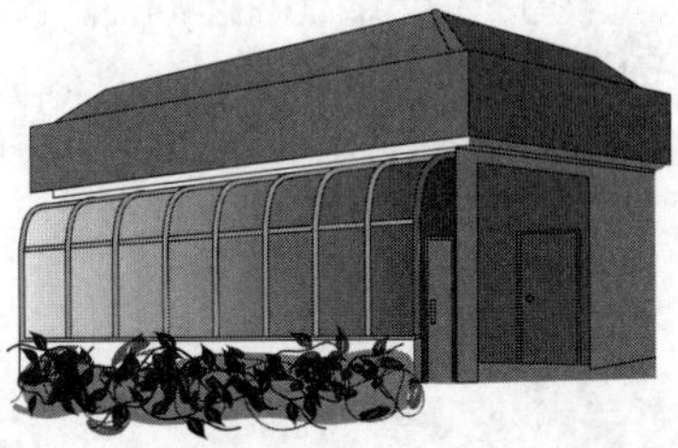

Three-season sunrooms and solariums have one twin-door single-pivot or double-hung external door and a movable sliding glass egress panel, fixed glass roof and sidewall panels and one movable screen panel. Structural main frame sections are 4-1/4" extruded 6060, 6063, 6061, 6005 or 6105 aluminum alloy with "teardrop" drip channels. Glazed with either Lexan, GE Plastics polycarbonate or equal bronze- or blue-tinted or clear glass.

Four-season sunrooms, solariums and conservatories have, in addition, minimum 3" thick compound foam sealing inside structural tubular elements and twin-pane tempered glass either gas-filled or DuPont Butacite-interlayered.

	Craft@Hrs	Unit	Material	Labor	Total
Sunrooms (residential lean-to patio enclosure), three-season, no engineering required. Costs will vary with the wind load and snow load. Cost per square foot of floor.					
Minimum cost, per SF	—	SF	—	—	154.00
Typical maximum cost per SF	—	SF	—	—	214.00
Add for four-season sunrooms	—	%	—	—	20.0
Residential three-season solarium. Custom-designed and engineered for the site. Cost per square foot of floor.					
Minimum cost per SF	—	SF	—	—	293.00
Typical maximum cost per SF	—	SF	—	—	368.00
Residential four-season solarium, with electric service, HVAC, fireproofing and abrasion-resistant protective coating. Meets code requirements for a room addition. Cost per square foot of floor.					
Minimum cost per SF	—	SF	—	—	490.00
Typical maximum cost per SF	—	SF	—	—	736.00
Residential conservatory (room addition). Four season. Stepped, bull-nose or gabled roof meets code requirements for glazed roof deflection and load. With electric service, HVAC, fireproofing, abrasion-resistant protective coating.					
Minimum cost per SF	—	SF	—	—	613.00
Typical maximum cost per SF	—	SF	—	—	1,110.00
Commercial solarium, four season, with electric service, HVAC, fireproofing, abrasion-resistant protective coating, store-type doors, locksets and closers. A sidewalk café or retail facility will usually require high-impact (falling object) glazing, fire sprinklers and alarms. Cost per square foot of floor.					
Typical cost per SF	—	SF	—	—	858.00
Sidewalk café or retail application, cost per SF	—	SF	—	—	1,860.00

	Craft@Hrs	Unit	Material	Labor	Total
Residential polycarbonate sheet glazing. 4' x 8' panels, Lexan, GE Plastics, or equal, for sunroom and 3-season service only.					
Clear 1/4"	G1@.027	SF	14.80	1.31	16.11
Clear 1/2"	G1@.035	SF	23.10	1.69	24.79
Add for tints	—	%	17.0	—	—
Add for hurricane and/or heavy snow load zones	—	%	25.0	—	—
Add for continuous-length custom glazing	—	%	20.0	—	—
Tempered glass, residential argon gas-filled twin-sheet Low-E glazing. PPG or equal, for 3-season and 4-season service.					
Clear, 5/8"	G1@.027	SF	19.50	1.31	20.81
Clear, 1"	G1@.035	SF	21.30	1.69	22.99
Add for tints	—	%	17.0	—	—
Add for hurricane and/or heavy snow load zones	—	%	25.0	—	—
Add for continuous-length custom glazing	—	%	20.0	—	—
High-impact sheet glazing, four-season, for conservatory and urban commercial service (tempered Low-E, PPG or equal) twin pane with DuPont Butacite interlayer. Certified for hurricane and heavy snow load.					
Clear, 5/8"	G1@.035	SF	27.30	1.69	28.99
Clear, 1"	G1@.045	SF	29.70	2.18	31.88
Add for tints	—	%	17.0	—	—
Add for curved eaves	—	%	5.0	—	—
Add for continuous-length custom glazing	—	%	20.0	—	—
Architectural aluminum structural elements					
Framing and joiner tube, 11 ga. x 1" x 3",	IW@.009	Lb	1.31	.60	1.91
Horizontal roof supports, 11 ga. x 4-1/4" x 4-1/4", with galvanized steel internal bracing	IW@.019	Lb	2.18	1.26	3.44
Vertical sidewall supports, 10 ga. x 4-1/4" x 4-1/4", with galvanized steel internal bracing	IW@.061	Lb	14.00	4.04	18.04
Add for 3" insulating foam (4-season units)	—	%	15.0	—	—
Concrete-embedded aluminum					
Light, to 20 lbs per LF	T3@.042	Lb	2.66	2.24	4.90
Medium, over 20 to 50 lbs per LF	T3@.035	Lb	2.38	1.86	4.24
Heavy, over 50 lbs per LF	T3@.025	Lb	2.03	1.33	3.36
Channel sill, 1/8" aluminum, 1-1/2" x 8" wide	T3@.131	LF	20.70	6.97	27.67
Angle sill, 1/8" aluminum, 1-1/2" x 1-1/2"	T3@.095	LF	6.53	5.06	11.59
Solariums or conservatory foundation, including forms, 3,000 p.s.i. concrete and finishing					
Footing 12" wide x 18" deep (0.058 CY per LF)	B4@.104	LF	9.90	3.89	13.79
Slab 6" thick, per SF or floor area	B5@.071	SF	4.07	2.63	6.70
Mount pre-fabricated aluminum frame	IW@.061	Lb	14.00	4.04	18.04
Allow for anchor bolts and leveling each 10' wall section	D4@4.00	Ea	204.00	190.00	394.00
Solarium or conservatory HVAC ducting					
Duct to the attached building, including plenums, crosses, tees, and air handler tie-in, per LF of duct	T6@0.03	LF	.92	1.63	2.55
Mount and connect electric service and lighting for a solarium or conservatory, including main breaker box tie-in					
Internal lighting, electric service, and wall switches, per LF of conduit	E2@.184	LF	.52	9.35	9.87
Fourth wall fabrication for a solarium or conservatory, including support frame fabrication and joist bolstering, with caulking and galvanized rain seal flashing					
Cut and fabricate wall opening	P9@.05	SF	1.14	2.43	3.57
Add for permitting and inspection	—	%	—	3.0	—

	Craft@Hrs	Unit	Material	Labor	Equipment	Total

Pre-Engineered Steel Buildings Vertical wall gable roof 26 gauge colored galvanized steel roof and siding with 4 in 12 (20 pound live load) roof. Cost per SF of floor area. These costs do not include foundation or floor slab. Add the cost of delivery to the site. Equipment is a 15 ton hydraulic crane and a 2-ton truck equipped for work of this type.

	Craft@Hrs	Unit	Material	Labor	Equipment	Total
40' x 100' (4,000 SF)						
14' eave height	H5@.081	SF	9.27	4.41	1.39	15.07
16' eave height	H5@.089	SF	10.40	4.85	1.53	16.78
20' eave height	H5@.102	SF	11.70	5.56	1.75	19.01
60' x 100' (6,000 SF)						
14' eave height	H5@.076	SF	8.96	4.14	1.31	14.41
16' eave height	H5@.078	SF	9.14	4.25	1.34	14.73
20' eave height	H5@.089	SF	10.60	4.85	1.53	16.98
80' x 100' (8,000 SF)						
14' eave height	H5@.076	SF	8.76	4.14	1.31	14.21
16' eave height	H5@.078	SF	9.13	4.25	1.34	14.72
20' eave height	H5@.088	SF	10.60	4.79	1.51	16.90
100' x 100' (10,000 SF)						
14' eave height	H5@.074	SF	8.71	4.03	1.27	14.01
16' eave height	H5@.078	SF	9.14	4.25	1.34	14.73
20' eave height	H5@.088	SF	10.20	4.79	1.51	16.50
100' x 150' (15,000 SF)						
14' eave height	H5@.072	SF	7.44	3.92	1.24	12.60
16' eave height	H5@.076	SF	7.94	4.14	1.31	13.39
20' eave height	H5@.081	SF	8.80	4.41	1.39	14.60
100' x 200' (20,000 SF)						
14' eave height	H5@.069	SF	7.25	3.76	1.19	12.20
16' eave height	H5@.073	SF	7.59	3.98	1.26	12.83
20' eave height	H5@.078	SF	8.22	4.25	1.34	13.81
140' x 150' (21,000 SF)						
14' eave height	H5@.064	SF	6.73	3.49	1.10	11.32
16' eave height	H5@.065	SF	6.96	3.54	1.12	11.62
20' eave height	H5@.073	SF	7.79	3.98	1.26	13.03
140' x 175' (24,500 SF)						
14' eave height	H5@.063	SF	6.50	3.43	1.08	11.01
16' eave height	H5@.064	SF	6.73	3.49	1.10	11.32
20' eave height	H5@.072	SF	7.44	3.92	1.24	12.60
160' x 200' (32,000 SF)						
14' eave height	H5@.061	SF	6.35	3.32	1.05	10.72
16' eave height	H5@.062	SF	6.50	3.38	1.07	10.95
20' eave height	H5@.067	SF	7.14	3.65	1.15	11.94
200' x 200' (40,000 SF)						
14' eave height	H5@.057	SF	6.13	3.11	.98	10.22
16' eave height	H5@.058	SF	6.27	3.16	1.00	10.43
20' eave height	H5@.064	SF	6.73	3.49	1.10	11.32
Deduct for arched roof:						
Quonset hut design	—	%	-25.0	-10.0	-10.0	—
Additional costs:						
Personnel door, 3'0" x 6'8"	H5@2.83	Ea	599.00	154.00	48.70	801.70
Overhead door, 8'0" x 8'0"	H5@8.02	Ea	1,860.00	437.00	138.00	2,435.00
Interior liner panel, 26 gauge						
Per SF of wall	H5@.012	SF	1.99	.65	.21	2.85

	Craft@Hrs	Unit	Material	Labor	Equipment	Total
Foam insulated sandwich panel roofing and siding						
Per SF of roof and sidewall	H5@.005	SF	5.39	.27	.09	5.75
Plastic skylight roof panel						
Per SF of panel	H5@.013	SF	5.92	.71	.22	6.85
R-11 blanket insulation,						
3-1/2", wall or floor	H5@.005	SF	.45	.27	.09	.81
Ridge ventilator, 9" throat	H5@.193	LF	50.70	10.50	3.32	64.52
24 gauge colored eave gutter	H5@.028	LF	7.12	1.53	.48	9.13
4" x 4" colored downspouts	H5@.014	LF	6.10	.76	.24	7.10
30 pound live load roof design	—	%	12.0	—	—	—

X-Ray Viewing Panels, Clear Lead-Plastic Based on SF of panel (rounded up to the next higher whole square foot). For panels 12 square feet or larger, add a crating charge. Panels larger than 72" x 96" are special order items. Weights shown are approximate.

	Craft@Hrs	Unit	Material	Labor	Total
7mm thick, 0.3mm lead equivalence, 2.3 lbs/SF	G1@.115	SF	128.00	5.56	133.56
12mm thick, 0.5mm lead equivalence, 3.9 lbs/SF	G1@.195	SF	172.00	9.44	181.44
18mm thick, 0.8mm lead equivalence, 5.9 lbs/SF	G1@.294	SF	186.00	14.20	200.20
22mm thick, 1.0mm lead equivalence, 7.2 lbs/SF	G1@.361	SF	197.00	17.50	214.50
35mm thick, 1.5mm lead equivalence, 11.5 lbs/SF	G1@.574	SF	214.00	27.80	241.80
46mm thick, 2.0mm lead equivalence, 15.0 lbs/SF	G1@.751	SF	290.00	36.30	326.30
70mm thick, 3.0mm lead equivalence, 18.0 lbs/SF	G1@1.00	SF	410.00	48.40	458.40
Crating charge	—	Ea	—	—	100.00

Mobile X-Ray Barriers Clear lead-plastic window panels on the upper portion and opaque panels on the lower portion, mounted within a framework with casters on the bottom. Labor shown is to uncrate factory assembled barrier and attach casters.

	Craft@Hrs	Unit	Material	Labor	Total
30" W x 75" H overall					
2.0mm lead equiv. window panel 10" x 12" and 2.0mm lead equiv. opaque panel	MW@.501	Ea	1,540.00	27.00	1,567.00
2.0mm lead equiv. window panel 30" x 24" and 2.0mm lead equiv. opaque panel 30" x 48"	MW@.501	Ea	2,700.00	27.00	2,727.00
2.0mm lead equiv. window panel 60" x 30" and 2.0mm lead equiv. opaque panel 12" x 30"	MW@.501	Ea	3,610.00	27.00	3,637.00
48" W x 72" H overall					
2.0mm lead equiv. window panel 48" x 36" and 2.0mm lead equiv. opaque panel 48" x 36"	MW@.501	Ea	5,000.00	27.00	5,027.00
72" W x 75" H, overall					
2.0mm lead equiv. window panel 72" x 36" and 2.0mm lead equiv. opaque panel 72" x 36"	MW@.751	Ea	6,290.00	40.50	6,330.50

Modular X-Ray Barriers Panels are mounted within a framework for attaching to floor, wall or ceiling. Shipped unassembled. Structural supports not included. Costs shown are based on typical 36" wide x 84" high panel sections. Clear lead-plastic window panels 48" high are the upper portion and opaque leaded panels 36" high are the bottom portion.

	Craft@Hrs	Unit	Material	Labor	Total
1-section barrier, 36" W x 84" H overall					
0.5mm lead equiv. panels	G1@2.78	Ea	2,930.00	135.00	3,065.00
0.8mm lead equiv. panels	G1@2.78	Ea	3,110.00	135.00	3,245.00
1.0mm lead equiv. panels	G1@3.34	Ea	3,180.00	162.00	3,342.00
1.5mm lead equiv. panels	G1@4.46	Ea	3,430.00	216.00	3,646.00

	Craft@Hrs	Unit	Material	Labor	Total
2-section barrier, 72" W x 84" H overall					
0.5mm lead equiv. panels	G1@5.56	Ea	6,240.00	269.00	6,509.00
0.8mm lead equiv. panels	G1@5.56	Ea	6,580.00	269.00	6,849.00
1.0mm lead equiv. panels	G1@6.68	Ea	6,720.00	323.00	7,043.00
1.5mm lead equiv. panels	G1@8.90	Ea	7,230.00	431.00	7,661.00
3-section barrier, 108" W x 84" H overall					
0.5mm lead equiv. panels	G1@8.34	Ea	9,550.00	404.00	9,954.00
0.8mm lead equiv. panels	G1@8.34	Ea	10,100.00	404.00	10,504.00
1.0mm lead equiv. panels	G1@10.0	Ea	10,400.00	484.00	10,884.00
1.5mm lead equiv. panels	G1@13.4	Ea	11,100.00	648.00	11,748.00
Larger than 3-section barriers, add to the cost of 1-section barriers for each section over 3					
Add per 18" W x 84" H section	—	%	50.0	—	—
Add per 36" W x 84" H section	—	%	100.0	—	—

Convenience Store Specialties

Convenience store display shelving, open glass with stainless steel frame, shell and shelves. Fluorescent indirect lighting on unit rear wall, 60 Hz, single phase, 110 Volt. Prehung slide-in label and pricing panels. Underwriters Laboratories and CSA approved.

	Craft@Hrs	Unit	Material	Labor	Total
38" wide 2-tower unit	C8@.250	Ea	1,130.00	11.80	1,141.80
72" wide 4-tower unit	C8@.350	Ea	1,550.00	16.50	1,566.50

Convenience store external signage, all-weather internally illuminated, freestanding, with internal fluorescent lighting fixtures, custom painted Lucite 48" x 72" twin-sided sign panel, structural aluminum welded frame and retainer moldings, 30 foot high by 16" diameter structural brushed and anodized aluminum vertical mounting post and reinforced base plate. Includes photocell-actuated night switch and in-store manual actuation override fused control panel. Add the cost of concrete pad, trenching, underground wiring from the electrical panel and crane rental.

	Craft@Hrs	Unit	Material	Labor	Total
Metal base plate	C8@1.50	Ea	697.00	70.70	767.70
Post and sign, installed	C8@3.00	Ea	6,720.00	141.00	6,861.00
Sign controls	C8@8.00	Ea	355.00	377.00	732.00

High-traffic convenience store aluminum twin-door portal, steel frame, pre-hung, with pneumatic adjustable closers, security deadbolt lockset, push bars both sides or "U"-section push/pull handgrips, swing-down swivel hold-open stanchions, clear glass single pane high impact tempered door glass.

	Craft@Hrs	Unit	Material	Labor	Total
Store glass double door, per pair of doors	SW@8.00	Ea	2,970.00	337.00	3,307.00

Convenience store display window security grillwork. After-hours anti-forced entry lockable grillwork, painted carbon steel horizontally-expanding accordion type, shop fabricated, 8' high by 20' long, with anchored tracking bars top and bottom.

	Craft@Hrs	Unit	Material	Labor	Total
Security grillwork, 8' x 20'	B9@8.00	Ea	1,100.00	264.00	1,364.00
Security grillwork, per SF	B9@0.05	SF	6.88	1.65	8.53

Convenience store bulletproof cashier booth (enclosure only, installed in an existing building), single panel, counter-mounted, with product/register transfer tray ("lazy Susan" type), glazed with ballistic Lucite, 5' high by 8' long.

	Craft@Hrs	Unit	Material	Labor	Total
Bulletproof cashier booth	B9@4.00	Ea	1,530.00	132.00	1,662.00

Modular prefabricated church steeple For houses of worship seating from 500 to 1,500 congregants. Includes 16' x 16' steeple base bolted and reinforced on a steel or wood frame, matched base plate steeple element, site-specific roof-mounted 1-1/2" diameter bolted joining plate with roof rafter and purlin support joists, lightning arrestor and #8 aluminum grounding cable with dielectric zinc grounding anchor. Labor cost includes laser leveling, vendor-supplied wind studies and roof-related load-bearing studies. Equipment cost is for a five-ton tracked spider crane and flatbed trailer truck with operator and truck driver. Add the cost of carillon speakers, special lighting, anti-bird/anti-bat nesting measures and internal access ladders, if required.

	Craft@Hrs	Unit	Material	Labor	Equipment	Total
Building of roof base plate and plate support	F5@40.0	Ea	5,010.00	1,930.00	—	6,940.00
Church steeple installation						
Steeple, bolted in and shimmed	S5@24.0	Ea	21,500.00	1,060.00	2,040.00	24,600.00
Roof flashing and roof edge seal	R3@16.0	Ea	1,110.00	748.00	—	1,858.00
Painting of steeple and trim	D7@40.0	Ea	423.00	1,890.00	—	2,313.00

Decorative ornamental fountains, interior (for shopping center and office complex atriums) and exterior (for public parks and large educational and industrial campuses). Costs are for nominal 1,300 gallon capacity 16' diameter by 1' deep precast concrete circular water reservoir pond with 6-foot diameter fountain centerpiece and spigot matrix. Costs include 110 volt, 3 phase 60 Hz 5 GPM pumps, integrated drains and recirculation piping with digital adjustable flow regulator. Add the cost of foundation and gravel sub-foundation, custom decorative bas relief fascia for reservoir pond sidewalls, fencing, associated decorative ironwork and circular walkway esplanade. Equipment cost is for a forklift for two days. No electrical service or foundation costs included.

	Craft@Hrs	Unit	Material	Labor	Equipment	Total
Positioning, anchoring and Gunite sealing of pond sidewalls	CM@40.0	Ea	18,400.00	2,050.00	275.00	20,725.00
Bolting and wiring of pump and controller	CE@8.00	Ea	1,840.00	483.00	—	2,323.00
Startup and adjustment of fountain pump	CE@2.00	Ea	—	121.00	—	121.00

Traffic signal 20-foot horizontal trombone mount, with controller, emergency default override, uninterruptible power system battery pack, LED low-voltage signal lighting elements. 15-foot vertical aluminum pole mount and cast aluminum base. Meets NHTSA standards. Add the cost of breaking out existing concrete and running electric power to the site. Equipment cost is for a backhoe and stinger truck crane. Per traffic signal installed. No electrical service or foundation costs included.

	Craft@Hrs	Unit	Material	Labor	Equipment	Total
Craning in, bolting and shimming						
Traffic light pole and base	B5@4.00	Ea	17,200.00	148.00	275.00	17,623.00
Electrical wiring and controls	CE@8.00	Ea	2,260.00	483.00	—	2,743.00
Calibration and test	CE@4.00	Ea	—	242.00	—	242.00

Pedestrian street crossing signal, right angle bi-directional, with LED low-wattage signal lamps, timing sequence box, SCADA or equal interconnect with central traffic controller module, with aluminum post and cast aluminum base, pedestrian high-impact manual button switches, to NHTSA standards. Add the cost of removing the existing concrete and bringing electric power to the site. Equipment is a backhoe and a stinger truck crane. Per signal installed. No electrical service or foundation costs included.

	Craft@Hrs	Unit	Material	Labor	Equipment	Total
Craning in, bolting and shimming of crosswalk light and base	B5@8.00	Ea	9,800.00	296.00	275.00	10,371.00
Fixtures plus assembly	CE@4.00	Ea	1,590.00	242.00	—	1,832.00
Wiring of main breaker and timer	CE@4.00	Ea	1,500.00	242.00	—	1,742.00
Calibration and test	CE@4.00	Ea	—	242.00	—	242.00

Street lighting, metal halide and high-pressure sodium twin luminaries mounted on twin 15-foot trombone horizontal extensions. Aluminum post with cast aluminum base and photocell switch actuator. Add the cost removing any existing concrete surface and excavation. Equipment is a backhoe and a stinger truck crane. Add the cost of the foundation, electrical wiring and conduit.

	Craft@Hrs	Unit	Material	Labor	Equipment	Total
Craning in and positioning of pole and base	B5@2.00	Ea	16,600.00	74.10	275.00	16,949.10
Wiring of controls and power	CE@8.00	Ea	1,880.00	483.00	—	2,363.00
Startup and adjustment	CE@4.00	Ea	—	242.00	—	242.00

Public park surveillance CCTV configuration, street lamp mounted, with 4-station DVD/CD recorder, 4-station low-light digital camera units, timed and dated image software, all-weather enclosure, power supply and control panel.

	Craft@Hrs	Unit	Material	Labor	Equipment	Total
Lamp-pole mount of camera	B5@4.00	Ea	604.00	148.00	—	752.00
Power supply positioning	CE@2.00	Ea	52.00	121.00	—	173.00
Wiring of controls and digital links	CE@2.00	Ea	434.00	121.00	—	555.00
Startup and adjustment	CE@1.00	Ea	—	60.40	—	60.40

	Craft@Hrs	Unit	Material	Labor	Equipment	Total
Subway platform egress barrier Pedestrian safety barrier, grade 304L stainless steel, with bolted mounting plates, electrical gate closure, master control switch relay and manual override. To American Railroad Association standards. Add the cost of removing any existing concrete surface, electrical service and foundation.						
Gate positioning and bolting	B5@2.00	Ea	4,630.00	74.10	—	4,704.10
Wiring of controls	CE@2.00	Ea	309.00	121.00	—	430.00
Startup and adjustment	CE@1.00	Ea	—	60.40	—	60.40
Pedestrian walkway bridge Over-street fully screened pedestrian walkway bridge. Pratt, Howe or Warren type double diagonal truss bridge span element, with open grid weathering steel metal walkway, 60-foot span with twin level staircases on both ends of bridge and galvanized mesh sidewall traffic protection screening. Complies with Federal Highway Association and National Steel Bridge Association design standards. Equipment includes a backhoe and a stinger truck crane. Add the foundation cost.						
Foundation plate/upright crane-in	B5@24.0	Ea	171,000.00	889.00	552.00	172,441.00
Craning in, bolt-up and weld of span	B5@16.0	Ea	551,000.00	593.00	827.00	552,420.00
Tensioning and adjustment of stressed diagonal brace elements	B5@24.0	Ea	1,950.00	889.00	—	2,839.00
Sandblast and paint structure	PT@16.0	Ea	18,500.00	612.00	662.00	19,774.00
Mounting of protective screening	B5@24.0	Ea	131,000.00	889.00	—	131,889.00
Inspection and test	MW@16.0	Ea	—	862.00	—	862.00

	Craft@Hrs	Unit	Material	Labor	Total
Decorative and ornamental lighting for convention centers, religious, educational and entertainment venues. Costs include vendor-supplied computer simulated lighting studies, concrete anchoring, trenching of electrical cable, main breaker, adjustable lighting array switch with digital timing actuation, calibration and aiming of installed fixtures. Add the cost of electrical service and the foundation.					
Bolting of fixtures	E4@0.50	Ea	368.00	25.40	393.40
Wiring of main breaker and timer	CE@4.00	Ea	253.00	242.00	495.00
Light aiming and calibration	E4@0.50	Ea	—	25.40	25.40
Subway and metro traffic control egress portals Includes swipe card reader, three-prong turnstile, twin 304 stainless steel stall median with maintenance doors, wiring to central controller module and lockset. Add the cost of electrical service and the foundation.					
Positioning of equipment	CE@2.00	Ea	5,510.00	121.00	5,631.00
Wiring of controls	CE@4.00	Ea	124.00	242.00	366.00
Startup and adjustment	CE@1.00	Ea	—	60.40	60.40
Magnetic metal detector for arch-type pedestrian traffic portals for schools, courthouses, airports and public safety facilities. Includes typical power supply wiring, permanent grouted and leveled cement foundation, trenched wiring, calibration, test, and operating personnel training and licensing. Installed to Department of Homeland Security and International Air Traffic Association specifications and standards. No electrical service or foundation costs included.					
Equipment and positioning	CE@2.00	Ea	16,000.00	121.00	16,121.00
Wiring of controls	CE@4.00	Ea	123.00	242.00	365.00
Startup and adjustment	CE@1.00	Ea	—	60.40	60.40
MRI parcel inspection station Magnetic resonance interference baggage inspection station for airports and public buildings. Includes foot-pedal-controlled baggage conveyor, inspection device with monitor screen, alarm matrix with emergency intercom, permanent grouted and leveled cement foundation, calibration, test and training of operation personnel. Installed to Department of Homeland Security and International Air Traffic Association specifications and standards. Add the cost of electrical service and the foundation.					
Equipment and positioning	CE@2.00	Ea	155,000.00	121.00	155,121.00
Wiring of controls	CE@2.00	Ea	305.00	121.00	426.00
Startup and adjustment	CE@1.00	Ea	—	60.40	60.40

13 Special Construction

	Craft@Hrs	Unit	Material	Labor	Total

Commercial high-definition digital cable-based FCC-licensed studio Facilities for production, post-production (editing) and broadcast. Includes architectural modifications to wall, floor and ceiling elements of a pre-existing office or warehouse structure to address standards-controlled sound mitigation and electronic spurious emissions limitation requirements. Add the cost of industry-specific television production equipment such as television cameras, mounts, lighting, microphones, recording equipment and esthetic trim such as paint and wall coverings in administration areas. Design parameters reflect compliance with standards specified by the Audio Engineering Society, Institute of Broadcast Sound, American Federation of TV and Recording Artists and the Society of Motion Picture and Television Engineers.

	Craft@Hrs	Unit	Material	Labor	Total
Wall modifications, soundproofing					
Staggered studs	C8@.021	SF	1.00	.99	1.99
Insulation	C8@.006	SF	0.77	.28	1.05
Specialty perfboard	C8@.007	SF	0.79	.33	1.12
Ceiling modifications, soundproofing					
Staggered joists	C8@.022	SF	1.00	1.04	2.04
Insulation	C8@.008	SF	0.77	.38	1.15
Specialty perfboard	C8@.009	SF	0.79	.42	1.21
Floor modifications (over existing slab)					
Prefab soundproof floor panels	FL@.020	SF	2.80	1.03	3.83
Acoustical mahogany parquet	FL@.020	SF	4.86	1.03	5.89
Prefab control room modules					
Harris Corporation or equal	CC@.030	SF	8.87	1.59	10.46
Scrim and lighting tracks, less scrims and lighting	E4@1.50	Ea	897.00	76.20	973.20
Electrical service					
Sunken outlet trays, 480 volt, three phase, 60 Hz	E4@1.00	Ea	355.00	50.80	405.80
Main electrical switchgear panel, 500 amp	E4@23.2	Ea	5,260.00	1,180.00	6,440.00
Ground fault and lightning protection	E4@16.0	Ea	1,430.00	813.00	2,243.00
Electronic control panel support framing and mounts					
Wood control panel supports, custom	C8@.256	LF	89.00	12.10	101.10
Prefab, custom, 20 gauge galvanized steel	D4@.785	LF	159.00	37.30	196.30
Control room soundproof glazing	G1@.086	SF	27.30	4.16	31.46
Uninterruptible power source					
Engine generator, 500 KW	E4@60.0	Ea	147,000.00	3,050.00	150,050.00
Radio frequency emissions screening					
Copper grounded	E4@1.16	Ea	36.60	59.00	95.60
Electrostatic discharge protective grounding	E4@1.13	Ea	33.60	57.40	91.00
Digital cable enclosure tray and connector panel	BE@0.50	Ea	132.00	20.30	152.30
Animation studio					
Multiple workstation cubicle gallery	C8@.028	SF	13.20	1.32	14.52

14 Conveying Equipment

Dumbwaiters These costs do not include allowance for constructing the hoistway walls or electrical work.

	Craft@Hrs	Unit	Material	Labor	Total
Manual, 2 stop, 25 feet per minute, no doors, by rated capacity, 24" x 24" x 36" high car					
25 pounds to 50 pounds	CV@39.8	Ea	3,180.00	2,280.00	5,460.00
75 pounds to 200 pounds	CV@42.7	Ea	4,340.00	2,440.00	6,780.00
Add for each additional stop	—	Ea	—	—	2,480.00

	Craft@Hrs	Unit	Material	Labor	Total
Electric, with machinery mounted above, floor loading, no security gates included					
50 lbs, 25 FPM, 2 stop, no doors	CV@42.2	Ea	2,830.00	2,410.00	5,240.00
50 lbs, 25 FPM, 2 stop, manual doors	CV@106.	Ea	7,030.00	6,060.00	13,090.00
50 lbs, 50 FPM, 2 stop, manual doors	CV@107.	Ea	7,070.00	6,120.00	13,190.00
75 lbs, 25 FPM, 2 stop, no doors	CV@42.2	Ea	2,830.00	2,410.00	5,240.00
75 lbs, 25 FPM, 2 stop, manual doors	CV@107.	Ea	8,500.00	6,120.00	14,620.00
75 lbs, 50 FPM, 2 stop, manual doors	CV@111.	Ea	8,520.00	6,350.00	14,870.00
100 lbs, 25 FPM, 2 stop, no doors	CV@50.6	Ea	4,120.00	2,890.00	7,010.00
100 lbs, 25 FPM, 2 stop, manual doors	CV@107.	Ea	8,730.00	6,120.00	14,850.00
100 lbs, 50 FPM, 2 stop, manual doors	CV@111.	Ea	8,920.00	6,350.00	15,270.00
100 lbs, 100 FPM, 5 stop, manual doors	CV@162.	Ea	9,360.00	9,270.00	18,630.00
200 lbs, 25 FPM, 2 stop, no doors	CV@52.3	Ea	4,230.00	2,990.00	7,220.00
200 lbs, 25 FPM, 2 stop, manual doors	CV@111.	Ea	9,040.00	6,350.00	15,390.00
200 lbs, 100 FPM, 5 stop, manual doors	CV@162.	Ea	11,000.00	9,270.00	20,270.00
300 lbs, 50 FPM, 2 stop, manual doors	CV@113.	Ea	18,600.00	6,460.00	25,060.00
300 lbs, 100 FPM, 5 stop, manual doors	CV@171.	Ea	24,700.00	9,780.00	34,480.00
400 lbs, 50 FPM, 2 stop, manual doors	CV@114.	Ea	18,800.00	6,520.00	25,320.00
400 lbs, 100 FPM, 5 stop, manual doors	CV@174.	Ea	27,300.00	9,950.00	37,250.00
500 lbs, 50 FPM, 2 stop, manual doors	CV@117.	Ea	19,400.00	6,690.00	26,090.00
500 lbs, 100 FPM, 5 stop, manual doors	CV@178.	Ea	28,700.00	10,200.00	38,900.00

Elevators, Passenger Typical subcontract costs excluding the shaft wall, supports, ladders, roof structure, pit and electric supply. Installation costs in an existing building will be higher. Automatic exit doors.

	Craft@Hrs	Unit	Material	Labor	Total
Hydraulic, office or apartment type					
100 FPM, automatic exit door, 2,000 lb. capacity					
2 stop	—	LS	—	—	69,200.00
3 stop	—	LS	—	—	78,100.00
Add for each additional stop	—	Ea	—	—	8,790.00
150 FPM, center opening doors, 2,500 lb. capacity					
2 stop	—	LS	—	—	75,800.00
3 stop	—	LS	—	—	84,000.00
Add for each additional stop	—	Ea	—	—	9,540.00
Geared passenger elevator, 200 FPM, 2,000 lb. capacity					
4 stop	—	LS	—	—	134,000.00
5 stop	—	LS	—	—	147,000.00
Add for each additional stop	—	LS	—	—	13,700.00
Gearless passenger elevator, 500 FPM, 3,500 lb. capacity					
5 stop	—	LS	—	—	190,000.00
10 stop	—	LS	—	—	264,000.00
Add for each additional stop	—	Ea	—	—	14,700.00
Gearless passenger elevator, 700 FPM, 4,500 lb. capacity					
10 stop	—	LS	—	—	269,000.00
15 stop	—	LS	—	—	348,000.00
Add for each additional stop	—	Ea	—	—	15,900.00
Gearless passenger elevator, 1000 FPM, 5,000 lb. capacity					
10 stop	—	LS	—	—	286,000.00
15 stop	—	LS	—	—	370,000.00
Add for each additional stop	—	Ea	—	—	16,900.00
Sidewalk elevators, 2 stops, 2,500 pounds	—	LS	—	—	52,000.00

	Craft@Hrs	Unit	Material	Labor	Total
Elevators, Freight Hydraulic, power doors, two stops. Typical subcontract costs excluding the shaft wall, roof structure and electric supply.					
3,000 lbs. 50 FPM	—	LS	—	—	71,400.00
4,000 lbs. 50 FPM	—	LS	—	—	78,000.00
6,000 lbs. 50 FPM	—	LS	—	—	91,400.00
3,000 lbs. 100 FPM	—	LS	—	—	80,500.00
4,000 lbs. 100 FPM	—	LS	—	—	85,300.00
6,000 lbs. 100 FPM	—	LS	—	—	101,000.00
3,000 lbs. 150 FPM	—	LS	—	—	88,700.00
4,000 lbs. 150 FPM	—	LS	—	—	92,600.00
6,000 lbs. 150 FPM	—	LS	—	—	109,000.00
Add for each additional stop	—	LS	—	—	8,140.00
Moving Stairs and Walks Typical subcontract prices.					
Escalators, 90 FPM, steel trim, 32" step width, glass balustrade					
13' rise	—	Ea	—	—	153,000.00
15' rise	—	Ea	—	—	152,000.00
17' rise	—	Ea	—	—	160,000.00
19' rise	—	Ea	—	—	165,000.00
21' rise	—	Ea	—	—	191,000.00
Add for 48" width	—	%	—	—	5.0
Add for stainless balustrade	—	%	—	—	8.0
Hoists and Cranes These costs do not include electrical work.					
Electric hoists, manual trolley, 20 FPM lift. Add cost of monorail below					
1/2 ton, swivel mount, 25' lift	D4@9.34	Ea	5,910.00	444.00	6,354.00
1/2 ton, swivel mount, 45' lift	D4@13.7	Ea	6,270.00	652.00	6,922.00
1/2 ton, swivel mount, 75' lift	D4@18.0	Ea	7,010.00	856.00	7,866.00
1 ton, geared trolley, 20' lift	D4@11.9	Ea	7,100.00	566.00	7,666.00
1 ton, geared trolley, 30' lift	D4@15.8	Ea	7,490.00	751.00	8,241.00
1 ton, geared trolley, 55' lift	D4@19.2	Ea	8,230.00	913.00	9,143.00
2 ton, geared trolley, 15' lift	D4@15.8	Ea	8,670.00	751.00	9,421.00
2 ton, geared trolley, 35' lift	D4@15.8	Ea	9,210.00	751.00	9,961.00
2 ton, geared trolley, 55' lift	D4@15.8	Ea	10,000.00	751.00	10,751.00
2 ton, geared trolley, 70' lift	D4@15.8	Ea	10,500.00	751.00	11,251.00
Electric hoists, power trolley, 20 FPM trolley speed. Add cost of monorail from below					
1/2 ton, 50 FPM lift to 25'	D4@8.94	Ea	7,010.00	425.00	7,435.00
1/2 ton, 100 FPM lift to 25'	D4@15.8	Ea	10,300.00	751.00	11,051.00
1/2 ton, 50 FPM lift to 45'	D4@8.94	Ea	7,370.00	425.00	7,795.00
1/2 ton, 100 FPM lift to 45'	D4@15.8	Ea	10,800.00	751.00	11,551.00
1/2 ton, 50 FPM lift to 75'	D4@11.9	Ea	8,080.00	566.00	8,646.00
1/2 ton, 100 FPM lift to 75'	D4@18.0	Ea	11,300.00	856.00	12,156.00
1 ton, 50 FPM lift to 20'	D4@15.8	Ea	7,140.00	751.00	7,891.00
1 ton, 50 FPM lift to 30'	D4@15.8	Ea	7,560.00	751.00	8,311.00
1 ton, 50 FPM lift to 55'	D4@18.0	Ea	8,380.00	856.00	9,236.00
2 ton, 50 FPM lift to 15'	D4@17.9	Ea	8,580.00	851.00	9,431.00
2 ton, 50 FPM lift to 35'	D4@19.9	Ea	9,430.00	946.00	10,376.00
2 ton, 50 FPM lift to 55'	D4@19.9	Ea	10,100.00	946.00	11,046.00
2 ton, 50 FPM lift to 70'	D4@19.9	Ea	10,200.00	946.00	11,146.00
Monorail for electric hoists, channel type					
100 pounds per LF	D4@.443	LF	13.80	21.10	34.90
200 pounds per LF	D4@.555	LF	21.50	26.40	47.90
300 pounds per LF	D4@.761	LF	32.20	36.20	68.40

14 Conveying Equipment

	Craft@Hrs	Unit	Material	Labor	Total
Jib cranes, self-supporting, swinging 8' boom, 220 degree rotation					
1,000 pounds	D4@7.90	Ea	2,170.00	376.00	2,546.00
2,000 pounds	D4@11.9	Ea	2,310.00	566.00	2,876.00
3,000 pounds	D4@13.5	Ea	2,570.00	642.00	3,212.00
4,000 pounds	D4@13.5	Ea	3,070.00	642.00	3,712.00
6,000 pounds	D4@15.8	Ea	3,250.00	751.00	4,001.00
10,000 pounds	D4@19.7	Ea	4,410.00	937.00	5,347.00
Jib cranes, wall mounted, swinging 8' boom, 180 degree rotation					
1,000 pounds	D4@8.19	Ea	1,150.00	390.00	1,540.00
2,000 pounds	D4@13.5	Ea	1,260.00	642.00	1,902.00
4,000 pounds	D4@13.5	Ea	1,890.00	642.00	2,532.00
6,000 pounds	D4@15.8	Ea	2,170.00	751.00	2,921.00
10,000 pounds	D4@19.7	Ea	3,930.00	937.00	4,867.00

Material Handling Systems

Conveyors, typical subcontract price. Foundations, support structures and electrical work not included

	Craft@Hrs	Unit	Material	Labor	Total
Belt type, 24" width	—	LF	—	—	267.00
Mail conveyors, automatic, electronic					
Horizontal	—	LF	—	—	2,290.00
Vertical, per 12' floor	—	Ea	—	—	29,200.00

Chutes, linen or solid waste handling, prefabricated unit including roof vent, 1-1/2 hour "B" rated doors, discharge and sprinkler system, gravity feed. Costs shown are for each floor based on 8' to 10' floor to floor height.

	Craft@Hrs	Unit	Material	Labor	Total
Light duty, aluminum, 20" diameter	D4@5.85	Ea	1,330.00	278.00	1,608.00
Standard, 18-gauge steel, 24" diameter	D4@5.85	Ea	1,480.00	278.00	1,758.00
Standard, 18-gauge steel, 30" diameter	D4@5.85	Ea	1,770.00	278.00	2,048.00
Heavy duty, 18-gauge stainless steel					
24" diameter	D4@5.85	Ea	2,210.00	278.00	2,488.00
30" diameter	D4@5.85	Ea	2,360.00	278.00	2,638.00
Manual door with stainless steel rim	D4@2.17	Ea	741.00	103.00	844.00
Disinfecting and sanitizing unit	D4@2.17	Ea	292.00	103.00	395.00
Discharge storage unit					
Aluminum	D4@1.00	Ea	1,330.00	47.60	1,377.60
Stainless steel	D4@1.00	Ea	2,010.00	47.60	2,057.60

Pneumatic Tube Systems Typical subcontract prices.

	Craft@Hrs	Unit	Material	Labor	Total
3" diameter, two station, single pipe, 100' between stations	—	LS	—	—	9,530.00
3" diameter, two station, twin pipe, 100' between stations	—	LS	—	—	11,900.00

21 Fire Suppression

Sprinkler systems Typical subcontract prices including the subcontractor's overhead and profit. These costs include design drawings, valves and connection to piping to within 5'0" outside the building. Costs will be higher where room sizes are smaller or where coverage per head averages less than 110 SF. Make additional allowances if a booster pump is required.

	Craft@Hrs	Unit	Material	Labor	Total
Exposed systems, wet, complete, cost per SF of floor protected					
5,000 SF	—	SF	—	—	4.73
Over 5,000 to 15,000 SF	—	SF	—	—	3.76
15,000 SF or more	—	SF	—	—	3.36

	Craft@Hrs	Unit	Material	Labor	Total
Concealed systems, wet, complete, cost per SF of floor protected					
5,000 SF	—	SF	—	—	4.40
Over 5,000 to 15,000 SF	—	SF	—	—	3.79
Ove 15,000 SF	—	SF	—	—	3.98
Add for dry systems	—	%	—	—	20.0
Fire sprinkler system components Add the cost of shutting down and draining the system if required					
Sprinkler heads only (remove and replace)					
Brass pendent or upright head, 155-200 degree	SP@.350	Ea	7.80	22.70	30.50
Brass pendent or upright head, 286 degree	SP@.350	Ea	7.80	22.70	30.50
Brass pendent or upright head, 360 degree	SP@.350	Ea	5.24	22.70	27.94
Brass pendent or upright head, 400-500 degree	SP@.350	Ea	23.30	22.70	46.00
Chrome pendent head, 155-286 degree	SP@.350	Ea	8.35	22.70	31.05
Chrome upright head, 155-286 degree	SP@.350	Ea	19.60	22.70	42.30
Dry pendent or upright head	SP@.350	Ea	21.60	22.70	44.30
Relocate wet sprinkler head and branch drop	SP@1.50	Ea	41.10	97.20	138.30
Add for heads more than 14' above floor	—	%	—	20.0	—
Wet system components (where freezing is not a hazard)					
Zone valves					
2-1/2" OS&Y gate valve, flanged or grooved	SP@1.75	Ea	380.00	113.00	493.00
3" OS&Y gate valve, flanged or grooved	SP@2.00	Ea	400.00	130.00	530.00
4" OS&Y gate valve, flanged or grooved	SP@2.25	Ea	462.00	146.00	608.00
6" OS&Y gate valve, flanged or grooved	SP@3.00	Ea	710.00	194.00	904.00
8" OS&Y gate valve, flanged or grooved	SP@3.50	Ea	1,130.00	227.00	1,357.00
4" alarm valve, flanged or grooved	SP@2.65	Ea	607.00	172.00	779.00
6" alarm valve, flanged or grooved	SP@3.50	Ea	747.00	227.00	974.00
8" alarm valve, flanged or grooved	SP@4.25	Ea	1,090.00	275.00	1,365.00
Alarm valve trim only (retard chamber and gauges)	SP@1.25	Ea	407.00	81.00	488.00
4" alarm valve package, complete	SP@4.00	Ea	1,910.00	259.00	2,169.00
6" alarm valve package, complete	SP@4.50	Ea	2,100.00	292.00	2,392.00
8" alarm valve package, complete	SP@5.25	Ea	2,570.00	340.00	2,910.00
Retard pressure switch	SP@1.75	Ea	380.00	113.00	493.00
Check valves					
3" swing check valve	SP@2.00	Ea	240.00	130.00	370.00
4" swing check valve	SP@2.25	Ea	214.00	146.00	360.00
6" swing check valve	SP@3.00	Ea	422.00	194.00	616.00
3" wafer check valve	SP@2.00	Ea	281.00	130.00	411.00
4" wafer check valve	SP@2.25	Ea	302.00	146.00	448.00
6" wafer check valve	SP@3.00	Ea	496.00	194.00	690.00
8" wafer check valve	SP@3.50	Ea	704.00	227.00	931.00
10" wafer check valve	SP@4.25	Ea	1,250.00	275.00	1,525.00
3" double check detector assembly	SP@3.75	Ea	2,960.00	243.00	3,203.00
4" double check detector assembly	SP@4.50	Ea	3,280.00	292.00	3,572.00
6" double check detector assembly	SP@5.75	Ea	5,150.00	373.00	5,523.00
8" double check detector assembly	SP@6.25	Ea	9,300.00	405.00	9,705.00
Dry system components (distribution piping holds no water)					
Dry valves (deluge)					
3" dry pipe valve	SP@2.25	Ea	1,130.00	146.00	1,276.00
4" dry pipe valve	SP@2.65	Ea	1,280.00	172.00	1,452.00
6" dry pipe valve	SP@3.50	Ea	1,620.00	227.00	1,847.00
Dry valve trim and gauges	SP@1.00	Ea	530.00	64.80	594.80

	Craft@Hrs	Unit	Material	Labor	Total
Wall hydrants for sprinkler systems, brass					
Single outlet, 2-1/2" x 2-1/2"	SP@2.00	Ea	398.00	130.00	528.00
2-way outlet, 2-1/2" x 2-1/2" x 4"	SP@2.50	Ea	641.00	162.00	803.00
3-way outlet, 2-1/2" x 2-1/2" x 3-1/3" x 4"	SP@2.75	Ea	1,170.00	178.00	1,348.00
Fire dept. connection, 4" (Siamese)	SP@2.50	Ea	622.00	162.00	784.00
Pumper connection, 6"	SP@3.00	Ea	1,260.00	194.00	1,454.00
Roof manifold, with valves	SP@3.90	Ea	749.00	253.00	1,002.00
Fire sprinkler system components					
Air maintenance device	SP@.781	Ea	230.00	50.60	280.60
Low air supervisory unit	SP@1.11	Ea	712.00	72.00	784.00
Low air pressure switch	SP@.784	Ea	230.00	50.80	280.80
Pressure switch (double circuit, open and close)	SP@1.92	Ea	223.00	124.00	347.00
1/2" ball drip at check valve and fire dept. connection	SP@.193	Ea	25.70	12.50	38.20
Water powered gong (local alarm)	SP@1.94	Ea	278.00	126.00	404.00
Cabinet with 6 spare heads and wrench	SP@.291	LS	107.00	18.90	125.90
Inspector's test connection	SP@.973	Ea	89.00	63.10	152.10
Escutcheon for sprinkler heads, chrome	SP@.071	Ea	1.51	4.60	6.11
Field testing and flushing, subcontract	—	LS	—	—	218.00
Disinfection of distribution system, subcontract	—	LS	—	—	218.00
Hydraulic design fee, subcontract					
Sprinklers in a high density or high risk area, typical	—	LS	—	—	3,010.00
Underground valve vault (if required), subcontract	—	LS	—	—	3,490.00
Fire hose cabinets, recessed, 24" x 30" x 5-1/2" with rack, full glass door, 1-1/2" hose, valve and nozzle. Standard.					
Painted steel, 75' hose, 24" x 30"	SP@1.95	Ea	539.00	126.00	665.00
Painted steel, 100' hose, 24" x 36"	SP@1.95	Ea	541.00	126.00	667.00
Aluminum, 75' hose	SP@1.95	Ea	741.00	126.00	867.00
Stainless steel, 75' hose	SP@1.95	Ea	965.00	126.00	1,091.00
Fire extinguishers Factory charged, complete with hose and horn and wall mounting bracket					
5 lb. carbon dioxide	C8@.488	Ea	176.00	23.00	199.00
10 lb. carbon dioxide	C8@.488	Ea	240.00	23.00	263.00
20 lb. carbon dioxide	C8@.488	Ea	351.00	23.00	374.00
5 lb. Halotron	C8@.488	Ea	220.00	23.00	243.00
11 lb. Halotron	C8@.488	Ea	453.00	23.00	476.00
15.5 lb. Halotron	C8@.488	Ea	715.00	23.00	738.00
Deduct for quantity purchase	—	%	-15.0	—	—
Extinguisher cabinets No extinguishers included, painted steel, recessed					
9" x 24" x 5" full glass door	C8@1.67	Ea	146.00	78.70	224.70
9" x 24" x 5" break glass door	C8@1.67	Ea	174.00	78.70	252.70
12" x 27" x 8" full glass door	C8@1.67	Ea	169.00	78.70	247.70
12" x 27" x 8" break glass door	C8@1.67	Ea	200.00	78.70	278.70
Add for semi-recessed or surface mount	—	%	10.0	—	—
Add for chrome cabinets	—	%	15.0	—	—
Add for stainless steel cabinets	—	Ea	211.00	—	211.00

	Craft@Hrs	Unit	Material	Labor	Total

Carbon Steel Pipe and Fittings (Black Steel) Pipe is ERW – A53 (electric resistance welded) with a factory-welded seam. Installation heights indicate the working height above the building floor. Assembly costs include hangers as required for the pipe diameter, a reducing tee and an elbow each 16 feet for 1/2" pipe, to each 50 feet for 12" pipe. For more detailed coverage, see *National Plumbing & HVAC Estimator*, http://CraftsmanSiteLicense.com

	Craft@Hrs	Unit	Material	Labor	Total
1/2" carbon steel (A53) threaded pipe and fittings					
Pipe, no fittings or supports included, 1/2", threaded ends					
Schedule 40 to 10' high	M5@.060	LF	1.39	3.11	4.50
Schedule 40 over 10' to 20'	M5@.070	LF	1.39	3.63	5.02
Schedule 80 to 10' high	M5@.070	LF	2.36	3.63	5.99
Schedule 80 over 10' to 20'	M5@.080	LF	2.36	4.15	6.51
Pipe assembly, Schedule 40, fittings, hangers and supports	M5@.130	LF	1.87	6.74	8.61
Add for seamless pipe (A106)	—	%	50.0	—	—
90-degree ells, 1/2", threaded					
150 lb, malleable iron	M5@.120	Ea	1.47	6.22	7.69
300 lb, malleable iron	M5@.132	Ea	8.11	6.85	14.96
45-degree ells, 1/2", threaded					
150 lb, malleable iron	M5@.120	Ea	1.98	6.22	8.20
300 lb, malleable iron	M5@.132	Ea	8.83	6.85	15.68
Tees, 1/2", threaded					
150 lb, malleable iron	M5@.180	Ea	1.92	9.33	11.25
300 lb, malleable iron	M5@.198	Ea	11.30	10.30	21.60
150 lb, reducing, malleable iron	M5@.170	Ea	3.35	8.82	12.17
300 lb, reducing, malleable iron	M5@.180	Ea	12.70	9.33	22.03
Caps, 1/2" threaded					
150 lb, malleable iron	M5@.090	Ea	1.44	4.67	6.11
300 lb, malleable iron	M5@.100	Ea	5.30	5.19	10.49
Couplings, 1/2" threaded					
150 lb, malleable iron	M5@.120	Ea	1.78	6.22	8.00
300 lb, malleable iron	M5@.132	Ea	5.49	6.85	12.34
Flanges, forged steel, 1/2"					
150 lb, threaded flange	M5@.489	Ea	16.30	25.40	41.70
300 lb, threaded flange	M5@.781	Ea	21.00	40.50	61.50
600 lb, threaded flange	M5@.859	Ea	73.40	44.50	117.90
Unions, 1/2"					
150 lb, malleable iron	M5@.140	Ea	6.40	7.26	13.66
300 lb, malleable iron	M5@.150	Ea	9.94	7.78	17.72
Add for galvanized 1/2" pipe	—	%	32.0	—	—
Add for galvanized 1/2" 150 lb. malleable fittings	—	%	15.0	—	—
Add for galvanized 1/2" 300 lb. malleable fittings	—	%	55.0	—	—
Add for galvanized 1/2" pipe assembly, Schedule 40	—	%	25.0	—	—
3/4" carbon steel (A53) threaded pipe and fittings					
Pipe, no fittings or supports included, 3/4", threaded					
Schedule 40 to 10' high	M5@.070	LF	1.70	3.63	5.33
Schedule 40 over 10' to 20'	M5@.080	LF	1.70	4.15	5.85
Schedule 80 to 10' high	M5@.080	LF	3.18	4.15	7.33
Schedule 80 over 10' to 20'	M5@.095	LF	3.18	4.93	8.11

	Craft@Hrs	Unit	Material	Labor	Total
Pipe assembly, Schedule 40, fittings, hangers and supports	M5@.140	LF	2.19	7.26	9.45
Add for seamless pipe (A106)	—	%	55.0	—	—
90-degree ells, 3/4" threaded					
150 lb, malleable iron	M5@.130	Ea	1.83	6.74	8.57
300 lb, malleable iron	M5@.143	Ea	9.48	7.42	16.90
45-degree ells, 3/4" threaded					
150 lb, malleable iron	M5@.130	Ea	2.56	6.74	9.30
300 lb, malleable iron	M5@.143	Ea	10.30	7.42	17.72
Tees, 3/4" threaded					
150 lb, malleable iron	M5@.190	Ea	2.66	9.85	12.51
300 lb, malleable iron	M5@.209	Ea	11.80	10.80	22.60
150 lb, reducing, malleable iron	M5@.180	Ea	3.81	9.33	13.14
300 lb, reducing, malleable iron	M5@.205	Ea	14.10	10.60	24.70
Caps, 3/4" threaded					
150 lb, malleable iron	M5@.100	Ea	1.89	5.19	7.08
300 lb, malleable iron	M5@.110	Ea	6.99	5.70	12.69
Couplings, 3/4" threaded					
150 lb, malleable iron	M5@.130	Ea	2.14	6.74	8.88
300 lb, malleable iron	M5@.143	Ea	6.50	7.42	13.92
Unions, 3/4"					
150 lb, malleable iron	M5@.150	Ea	7.48	7.78	15.26
300 lb, malleable iron	M5@.165	Ea	11.50	8.56	20.06
Flanges, forged steel, 3/4"					
150 lb, threaded flange	M5@.585	Ea	16.20	30.30	46.50
300 lb, threaded flange	M5@.781	Ea	21.10	40.50	61.60
600 lb, threaded flange	M5@.859	Ea	68.50	44.50	113.00
Add for galvanized 3/4" pipe	—	%	32.0	—	—
Add for galvanized 3/4" 150 lb. malleable fittings	—	%	25.0	—	—
Add for galvanized 3/4" 300 lb. malleable fittings	—	%	55.0	—	—
Add for galvanized 3/4" pipe assembly, Schedule 40	—	%	30.0	—	—
1" carbon steel (A53) threaded pipe and fittings					
Pipe, no fittings or supports included, 1", threaded					
Schedule 40 to 10' high	M5@.090	LF	2.05	4.67	6.72
Schedule 40 over 10' to 20'	M5@.110	LF	2.05	5.70	7.75
Schedule 80 to 10' high	M5@.100	LF	3.44	5.19	8.63
Schedule 80 over 10' to 20'	M5@.120	LF	3.44	6.22	9.66
Pipe assembly, Schedule 40, fittings, hangers and supports	M5@.160	LF	2.77	8.30	11.07
Add for seamless pipe (A106)	—	%	50.0	—	—
90-degree ells, 1" threaded					
150 lb, malleable iron	M5@.180	Ea	2.70	9.33	12.03
300 lb, malleable iron	M5@.198	Ea	10.50	10.30	20.80
45-degree ells, 1" threaded					
150 lb, malleable iron	M5@.180	Ea	3.26	9.33	12.59
300 lb, malleable iron	M5@.198	Ea	11.40	10.30	21.70
Tees, 1" threaded					
150 lb, malleable iron	M5@.230	Ea	3.91	11.90	15.81
300 lb, malleable iron	M5@.253	Ea	12.30	13.10	25.40
150 lb, reducing, malleable iron	M5@.205	Ea	5.36	10.60	15.96
300 lb, reducing, malleable iron	M5@.220	Ea	14.90	11.40	26.30

	Craft@Hrs	Unit	Material	Labor	Total
Caps, 1" threaded					
150 lb, malleable iron	M5@.140	Ea	2.32	7.26	9.58
300 lb, malleable iron	M5@.155	Ea	8.85	8.04	16.89
Couplings, 1" threaded					
150 lb, malleable iron	M5@.180	Ea	2.97	9.33	12.30
300 lb, malleable iron	M5@.198	Ea	7.03	10.30	17.33
Flanges, forged steel, 1"					
150 lb, threaded flange	M5@.731	Ea	14.50	37.90	52.40
300 lb, threaded flange	M5@1.05	Ea	24.10	54.50	78.60
600 lb, threaded flange	M5@1.15	Ea	69.90	59.60	129.50
Unions, 1"					
150 lb, malleable iron	M5@.210	Ea	9.30	10.90	20.20
300 lb, malleable iron	M5@.230	Ea	23.20	11.90	35.10
Add for galvanized 1" pipe	—	%	32.0	—	—
Add for galvanized 1" 150 lb. malleable fittings	—	%	20.0	—	—
Add for galvanized 1" 300 lb. malleable fittings	—	%	60.0	—	—
Add for galvanized 1" pipe assembly, Schedule 40	—	%	30.0	—	—
1-1/4" carbon steel (A53) threaded pipe and fittings					
Pipe, no fittings or supports included, 1-1/4", threaded					
Schedule 40 to 10' high	M5@.100	LF	2.56	5.19	7.75
Schedule 40 over 10' to 20'	M5@.120	LF	2.56	6.22	8.78
Schedule 80 to 10' high	M5@.110	LF	4.35	5.70	10.05
Schedule 80 over 10' to 20'	M5@.130	LF	4.35	6.74	11.09
Pipe assembly, Schedule 40, fittings, hangers and supports	M5@.200	LF	3.61	10.40	14.01
Add for seamless pipe (A106)	—	%	45.0	—	—
90-degree ells, 1-1/4" threaded					
150 lb, malleable iron	M5@.240	Ea	4.98	12.40	17.38
300 lb, malleable iron	M5@.264	Ea	16.40	13.70	30.10
45-degree ells, 1-1/4" threaded					
150 lb, malleable iron	M5@.240	Ea	6.69	12.40	19.09
300 lb, malleable iron	M5@.264	Ea	13.70	13.70	27.40
Tees, 1-1/4" threaded					
150 lb, malleable iron	M5@.310	Ea	6.75	16.10	22.85
300 lb, malleable iron	M5@.341	Ea	17.10	17.70	34.80
150 lb, reducing, malleable iron	M5@.290	Ea	11.30	15.00	26.30
300 lb, reducing, malleable iron	M5@.310	Ea	26.80	16.10	42.90
Caps, 1-1/4" threaded					
150 lb, malleable iron	M5@.180	Ea	3.29	9.33	12.62
300 lb, malleable iron	M5@.200	Ea	13.30	10.40	23.70
Couplings, 1-1/4" threaded					
150 lb, malleable iron	M5@.240	Ea	4.77	12.40	17.17
300 lb, malleable iron	M5@.264	Ea	10.60	13.70	24.30
Unions, 1-1/4"					
150 lb, malleable iron	M5@.280	Ea	14.60	14.50	29.10
300 lb, malleable iron	M5@.310	Ea	23.90	16.10	40.00
Flanges, forged steel, 1-1/4"					
150 lb, threaded flange	M5@.788	Ea	24.50	40.90	65.40
300 lb, threaded flange	M5@1.04	Ea	36.00	53.90	89.90
600 lb, threaded flange	M5@1.14	Ea	79.40	59.10	138.50

	Craft@Hrs	Unit	Material	Labor	Total
Add for galvanized 1-1/4" pipe	—	%	30.0	—	—
Add for galvanized 1-1/4" 150 lb. malleable fittings	—	%	20.0	—	—
Add for galvanized 1-1/4" 300 lb. malleable fittings	—	%	65.0	—	—
Add for galvanized 1-1/4" pipe assembly, Schedule 40	—	%	30.0	—	—
1-1/2" carbon steel (A53) threaded pipe and fittings					
Pipe, no fittings or supports included, 1-1/2", threaded					
Schedule 40 to 10' high	M5@.110	LF	4.20	5.70	9.90
Schedule 40 over 10' to 20'	M5@.130	LF	4.20	6.74	10.94
Schedule 80 to 10' high	M5@.120	LF	7.14	6.22	13.36
Schedule 80 over 10' to 20'	M5@.140	LF	7.14	7.26	14.40
Pipe assembly, Schedule 40, fittings, hangers and supports	M5@.230	LF	5.50	11.90	17.40
Add for seamless pipe (A106)	—	%	45.0	—	—
90-degree ells, 1-1/2" threaded					
150 lb, malleable iron	M5@.300	Ea	6.58	15.60	22.18
300 lb, malleable iron	M5@.333	Ea	19.80	17.30	37.10
45-degree ells, 1-1/2" threaded					
150 lb, malleable iron	M5@.390	Ea	6.65	20.20	26.85
300 lb, malleable iron	M5@.429	Ea	21.50	22.20	43.70
Tees, 1-1/2" threaded					
150 lb, malleable iron	M5@.390	Ea	9.14	20.20	29.34
300 lb, malleable iron	M5@.429	Ea	23.60	22.20	45.80
150 lb, reducing, malleable iron	M5@.360	Ea	17.30	18.70	36.00
300 lb, reducing, malleable iron	M5@.390	Ea	44.00	20.20	64.20
Caps, 1-1/2" threaded					
150 lb, malleable iron	M5@.230	Ea	4.66	11.90	16.56
300 lb, malleable iron	M5@.250	Ea	16.40	13.00	29.40
Couplings, 1-1/2" threaded					
150 lb, malleable iron	M5@.300	Ea	5.78	15.60	21.38
300 lb, malleable iron	M5@.330	Ea	14.40	17.10	31.50
Unions, 1-1/2"					
150 lb, malleable iron	M5@.360	Ea	16.30	18.70	35.00
300 lb, malleable iron	M5@.400	Ea	23.30	20.70	44.00
Flanges, forged steel, 1-1/2"					
150 lb, threaded flange	M5@.840	Ea	23.00	43.60	66.60
300 lb, threaded flange	M5@1.15	Ea	34.80	59.60	94.40
600 lb, threaded flange	M5@1.26	Ea	74.90	65.30	140.20
Add for galvanized 1-1/2" pipe	—	%	30.0	—	—
Add for galvanized 1-1/2" 150 lb. malleable fittings	—	%	20.0	—	—
Add for galvanized 1-1/2" 300 lb. malleable fittings	—	%	55.0	—	—
Add for galvanized 1-1/2" pipe assembly, Schedule 40	—	%	30.0	—	—
2" carbon steel (A53) threaded pipe and fittings					
Pipe, no fittings or supports included, 2", threaded					
Schedule 40 to 10' high	M5@.120	LF	4.67	6.22	10.89
Schedule 40 over 10' to 20'	M5@.140	LF	4.67	7.26	11.93
Schedule 80 to 10' high	M5@.130	LF	7.32	6.74	14.06
Schedule 80 over 10' to 20'	M5@.150	LF	7.32	7.78	15.10
Pipe assembly, Schedule 40, fittings, hangers and supports	M5@.250	LF	6.44	13.00	19.44
Add for seamless pipe (A106)	—	%	40.0	—	—

	Craft@Hrs	Unit	Material	Labor	Total
90-degree ells, 2" threaded					
150 lb, malleable iron	M5@.380	Ea	10.90	19.70	30.60
300 lb, malleable iron	M5@.418	Ea	27.00	21.70	48.70
45-degree ells, 2" threaded					
150 lb, malleable iron	M5@.380	Ea	9.40	19.70	29.10
300 lb, malleable iron	M5@.418	Ea	30.20	21.70	51.90
Tees, 2" threaded					
150 lb, malleable iron	M5@.490	Ea	13.30	25.40	38.70
300 lb, malleable iron	M5@.539	Ea	29.60	28.00	57.60
150 lb, reducing, malleable iron	M5@.460	Ea	13.70	23.90	37.60
300 lb, reducing, malleable iron	M5@.500	Ea	38.00	25.90	63.90
Caps, 2" threaded					
150 lb, malleable iron	M5@.290	Ea	5.90	15.00	20.90
300 lb, malleable iron	M5@.320	Ea	14.10	16.60	30.70
Couplings, 2" threaded					
150 lb, malleable iron	M5@.380	Ea	8.54	19.70	28.24
300 lb, malleable iron	M5@.418	Ea	20.20	21.70	41.90
Flanges, forged steel, 2"					
150 lb, threaded flange	M5@.290	Ea	29.10	15.00	44.10
300 lb, threaded flange	M5@.310	Ea	46.10	16.10	62.20
600 lb, threaded flange	M5@.320	Ea	119.00	16.60	135.60
Unions, 2"					
150 lb, malleable iron	M5@.450	Ea	19.90	23.30	43.20
300 lb, malleable iron	M5@.500	Ea	55.60	25.90	81.50
Add for galvanized 2" pipe, add	—	%	30.0	—	—
Add for galvanized 2" 50 lb. malleable fittings	—	%	20.0	—	—
Add for galvanized 2" 300 lb. malleable fittings	—	%	55.0	—	—
Add for galvanized 2" pipe assembly, Schedule 40	—	%	30.0	—	—
3" carbon steel pipe (A53) and welded fittings					
Pipe, no fittings or supports included, 3", plain end					
Schedule 40 to 10' high	MI@.190	LF	6.19	10.50	16.69
Schedule 40 over 10' to 20' high	MI@.230	LF	6.19	12.70	18.89
Schedule 80 to 10' high	MI@.280	LF	13.30	15.50	28.80
Schedule 80 over 10' to 20' high	MI@.335	LF	13.30	18.60	31.90
Pipe assembly, Schedule 40, fittings, hangers and supports	MI@.380	LF	9.47	21.10	30.57
Add for seamless pipe (A106)	—	%	40.0	—	—
Add for galvanized pipe assembly, Schedule 40	—	%	30.0	—	—
Butt welded joints, 3" pipe					
Schedule 40 pipe	MI@.930	Ea	—	51.50	51.50
Schedule 80 pipe	MI@1.11	Ea	—	61.50	61.50
90-degree ells, 3"					
Schedule 40 carbon steel, butt weld, long turn	MI@1.33	Ea	16.30	73.70	90.00
Schedule 80 carbon steel, butt weld, long turn	MI@1.77	Ea	23.10	98.10	121.20
45-degree ells, 3"					
Schedule 40, carbon steel, butt weld	MI@1.33	Ea	11.40	73.70	85.10
Schedule 80, carbon steel, butt weld	MI@1.77	Ea	16.10	98.10	114.20
Tees, 3"					
Schedule 40, carbon steel, butt weld	MI@2.00	Ea	33.00	111.00	144.00
Schedule 80, carbon steel, butt weld	MI@2.66	Ea	66.40	147.00	213.40
Reducing, Schedule 40, carbon steel, butt weld	MI@1.89	Ea	42.90	105.00	147.90

	Craft@Hrs	Unit	Material	Labor	Total
Caps, 3"					
Schedule 40, carbon steel, butt weld	MI@.930	Ea	20.10	51.50	71.60
Schedule 80, carbon steel, butt weld	MI@1.11	Ea	14.30	61.50	75.80
Reducing couplings					
Schedule 40, carbon steel, butt weld	MI@1.20	Ea	23.50	66.50	90.00
Weld-o-lets, 3"					
Schedule 40, carbon steel	MI@2.00	Ea	70.60	111.00	181.60
Welded pipe flanges, forged steel, 3" butt weld					
150 lb, slip-on flange	MI@.730	Ea	31.00	40.40	71.40
300 lb, slip-on flange	MI@.980	Ea	42.40	54.30	96.70
600 lb, slip-on flange	MI@1.03	Ea	84.70	57.10	141.80
150 lb, weld neck flange	MI@.730	Ea	38.60	40.40	79.00
300 lb, weld neck flange	MI@.980	Ea	48.00	54.30	102.30
600 lb, weld neck flange	MI@1.03	Ea	81.90	57.10	139.00
150 lb, threaded flange	MI@.460	Ea	56.00	25.50	81.50
300 lb, threaded flange	MI@.500	Ea	68.30	27.70	96.00
600 lb, threaded flange	MI@.510	Ea	112.00	28.30	140.30
Flange bolt & gasket kits, 3"					
Full face, red rubber gasket, 150 lb	MI@.750	Ea	9.17	41.60	50.77
Full face, red rubber gasket, 300 lb	MI@1.00	Ea	11.10	55.40	66.50
4" carbon steel pipe (A53) and welded fittings					
Pipe, no fittings or supports included, 4", plain end					
Schedule 40 to 10' high	MI@.260	LF	7.34	14.40	21.74
Schedule 40 over 10' to 20' high	MI@.360	LF	7.34	19.90	27.24
Schedule 80 to 10' high	MI@.340	LF	16.10	18.80	34.90
Schedule 80 over 10' to 20' high	MI@.400	LF	16.10	22.20	38.30
Pipe assembly, Schedule 40, fittings, hangers and supports	MI@.430	LF	11.90	23.80	35.70
Add for seamless pipe (A106)	—	%	35.0	—	—
Add for galvanized pipe assembly, Schedule 40	—	%	30.0	—	—
Butt welded joints, 4" pipe					
Schedule 40 pipe	MI@1.25	Ea	—	69.30	69.30
Schedule 80 pipe	MI@1.50	Ea	—	83.10	83.10
90-degree ells, 4"					
Schedule 40 carbon steel, butt weld, long turn	MI@1.33	Ea	26.30	73.70	100.00
Schedule 80 carbon steel, butt weld, long turn	MI@2.37	Ea	55.90	131.00	186.90
45-degree ells, 4"					
Schedule 40, carbon steel, butt weld	MI@1.33	Ea	17.30	73.70	91.00
Schedule 80, carbon steel, butt weld	MI@2.37	Ea	24.50	131.00	155.50
Tees, 4"					
Schedule 40, carbon steel, butt weld	MI@2.67	Ea	45.20	148.00	193.20
Schedule 80, carbon steel, butt weld	MI@3.55	Ea	70.50	197.00	267.50
Reducing, Schedule 40 carbon steel, butt weld	MI@2.44	Ea	46.40	135.00	181.40
Caps, 4"					
Schedule 40, carbon steel, butt weld	MI@1.25	Ea	26.30	69.30	95.60
Schedule 80, carbon steel, butt weld	MI@1.50	Ea	19.10	83.10	102.20
Reducing couplings, 4"					
Schedule 40, carbon steel, butt weld	MI@1.60	Ea	22.70	88.60	111.30
Weld-o-lets, 4"					
Schedule 40, carbon steel	MI@2.67	Ea	92.40	148.00	240.40

	Craft@Hrs	Unit	Material	Labor	Total
Welded flanges, forged steel, 4"					
150 lb, slip-on flange	MI@.980	Ea	42.00	54.30	96.30
300 lb, slip-on flange	MI@1.30	Ea	67.70	72.00	139.70
600 lb, slip-on flange	MI@1.80	Ea	166.00	99.70	265.70
150 lb, weld neck flange	MI@.980	Ea	52.10	54.30	106.40
300 lb, weld neck flange	MI@1.30	Ea	74.90	72.00	146.90
600 lb, weld neck flange	MI@1.80	Ea	150.00	99.70	249.70
150 lb, threaded flange	MI@.600	Ea	60.20	33.20	93.40
300 lb, threaded flange	MI@.640	Ea	76.50	35.50	112.00
600 lb, threaded flange	MI@.650	Ea	192.00	36.00	228.00
Flange bolt & gasket kits, 4"					
Full face, red rubber gasket, 150 lb	MI@1.00	Ea	11.10	55.40	66.50
Full face, red rubber gasket, 300 lb	MI@1.20	Ea	16.30	66.50	82.80
6" carbon steel pipe (A53) and welded fittings					
Pipe, no fittings or supports included, 6", plain end					
Schedule 40 to 10' high	M8@.420	LF	11.60	24.00	35.60
Schedule 40 over 10' to 20'	M8@.500	LF	11.60	28.60	40.20
Schedule 80 to 10' high	M8@.460	LF	22.00	26.30	48.30
Schedule 80 over 10' to 20'	M8@.550	LF	22.00	31.40	53.40
Pipe assembly, Schedule 40, fittings, hangers and supports	M8@.800	LF	21.10	45.70	66.80
Add for seamless pipe (A106)	—	%	40.0	—	—
Add for galvanized pipe assembly, Schedule 40	—	%	30.0	—	—
Butt welded joints, 6" pipe					
Schedule 40 pipe	M8@1.87	Ea	—	107.00	107.00
Schedule 80 pipe	M8@2.24	Ea	—	128.00	128.00
90-degree ells, 6"					
Schedule 40 carbon steel, butt weld, long turn	M8@2.67	Ea	75.10	153.00	228.10
Schedule 80 carbon steel, butt weld, long turn	M8@3.55	Ea	107.00	203.00	310.00
45-degree ells, 6"					
Schedule 40, carbon steel, butt weld	M8@2.67	Ea	44.50	153.00	197.50
Schedule 80, carbon steel, butt weld	M8@3.55	Ea	69.30	203.00	272.30
Tees, 6"					
Schedule 40, carbon steel, butt weld	M8@4.00	Ea	84.40	229.00	313.40
Schedule 80, carbon steel, butt weld	M8@5.32	Ea	114.00	304.00	418.00
Reducing, Schedule 40 carbon steel, butt weld	M8@3.78	Ea	106.00	216.00	322.00
Caps, 6"					
Schedule 40, carbon steel, butt weld	M8@1.87	Ea	31.10	107.00	138.10
Schedule 80, carbon steel, butt weld	M8@2.24	Ea	36.30	128.00	164.30
Reducing couplings, 6"					
Schedule 40, carbon steel, butt weld	M8@2.30	Ea	42.30	131.00	173.30
Weld-o-lets, 6"					
Schedule 40, carbon steel	M8@3.65	Ea	384.00	209.00	593.00
Welded flanges, forged steel, 6"					
150 lb, slip-on flange	M8@1.47	Ea	67.50	84.00	151.50
300 lb, slip-on flange	M8@1.95	Ea	128.00	111.00	239.00
150 lb, weld neck flange	M8@1.47	Ea	88.20	84.00	172.20
300 lb, weld neck flange	M8@1.95	Ea	136.00	111.00	247.00
Flange bolt & gasket kits, 6"					
Full face, red rubber gasket, 150 lb	M8@1.20	Ea	19.10	68.60	87.70
Full face, red rubber gasket, 300 lb	M8@1.65	Ea	30.60	94.30	124.90

	Craft@Hrs	Unit	Material	Labor	Total
8" carbon steel pipe (A53) and welded fittings					
Pipe, no fittings or supports included, 8" plain end					
Schedule 40 to 10' high	M8@.510	LF	26.00	29.20	55.20
Schedule 40 over 10' to 20'	M8@.600	LF	26.00	34.30	60.30
Schedule 80 to 10' high	M8@.560	LF	50.60	32.00	82.60
Schedule 80 over 10' to 20' high	M8@.670	LF	50.60	38.30	88.90
Add for seamless pipe (A106)	—	%	40.0	—	—
Butt welded joints, 8" pipe					
Schedule 40 pipe	M8@2.24	Ea	—	128.00	128.00
Schedule 80 pipe	M8@2.68	Ea	—	153.00	153.00
90-degree ells, 8"					
Schedule 40 carbon steel, butt weld, long turn	M8@3.20	Ea	150.00	183.00	333.00
Schedule 80 carbon steel, butt weld, long turn	M8@4.26	Ea	171.00	244.00	415.00
45-degree ells, 8"					
Schedule 40, carbon steel, butt weld	M8@3.20	Ea	91.60	183.00	274.60
Schedule 80, carbon steel, butt weld	M8@4.26	Ea	97.10	244.00	341.10
Tees, 8"					
Schedule 40, carbon steel, butt weld	M8@4.80	Ea	170.00	274.00	444.00
Schedule 80, carbon steel, butt weld	M8@6.38	Ea	200.00	365.00	565.00
Reducing, Schedule 40, carbon steel, butt weld	M8@4.40	Ea	227.00	252.00	479.00
Caps, 8"					
Schedule 40, carbon steel, butt weld	M8@2.24	Ea	48.30	128.00	176.30
Schedule 80, carbon steel, butt weld	M8@2.68	Ea	48.60	153.00	201.60
Reducing couplings, 8"					
Schedule 40, carbon steel, butt weld	M8@2.88	Ea	97.80	165.00	262.80
Weld-o-lets, 8"					
Schedule 40, carbon steel	M8@4.76	Ea	629.00	272.00	901.00
Welded flanges, forged steel, 8"					
150 lb, slip-on flange	M8@1.77	Ea	91.50	101.00	192.50
300 lb, slip-on flange	M8@2.35	Ea	174.00	134.00	308.00
150 lb, weld neck flange	M8@1.77	Ea	128.00	101.00	229.00
300 lb, weld neck flange	M8@2.35	Ea	186.00	134.00	320.00
Flange bolt & gasket kits, 8"					
Full face, red rubber gasket, 150 lb	M8@1.40	Ea	18.30	80.00	98.30
Full face, red rubber gasket, 300 lb	M8@1.85	Ea	28.60	106.00	134.60
10" carbon steel pipe (A53) and welded fittings					
Pipe, no fittings or supports included, 10", plain end					
Schedule 40 to 20' high	M8@.720	LF	37.30	41.20	78.50
Schedule 80 to 20' high	M8@.830	LF	87.70	47.50	135.20
Add for seamless pipe (A106)	—	%	40.0	—	—
Butt welded joints, 10" pipe					
Schedule 40 pipe	M8@2.70	Ea	—	154.00	154.00
Schedule 80 pipe	M8@3.22	Ea	—	184.00	184.00
90-degree ells, 10"					
Schedule 40 carbon steel, butt weld, long turn	M8@4.00	Ea	267.00	229.00	496.00
Schedule 80 carbon steel, butt weld, long turn	M8@5.75	Ea	313.00	329.00	642.00
45-degree ells, 10"					
Schedule 40, carbon steel, butt weld	M8@4.00	Ea	141.00	229.00	370.00
Schedule 80, carbon steel, butt weld	M8@5.75	Ea	156.00	329.00	485.00

	Craft@Hrs	Unit	Material	Labor	Total
Tees, 10"					
Schedule 40, carbon steel, butt weld	M8@6.00	Ea	383.00	343.00	726.00
Schedule 80, carbon steel, butt weld	M8@8.61	Ea	322.00	492.00	814.00
Reducing, Schedule 40, carbon steel, butt weld	M8@5.60	Ea	383.00	320.00	703.00
Caps, 10"					
Schedule 40, carbon steel, butt weld	M8@2.80	Ea	81.20	160.00	241.20
Schedule 80, carbon steel, butt weld	M8@3.62	Ea	72.00	207.00	279.00
Reducing couplings, 10"					
Schedule 40, carbon steel, butt weld	M8@3.60	Ea	86.90	206.00	292.90
Weld-o-lets, 10"					
Schedule 40, carbon steel	M8@6.35	Ea	863.00	363.00	1,226.00
Welded pipe flanges, forged steel, 10"					
150 lb, slip-on flange	M8@2.20	Ea	151.00	126.00	277.00
150 lb, weld neck flange	M8@2.20	Ea	207.00	126.00	333.00
300 lb, weld neck flange	M8@2.90	Ea	421.00	166.00	587.00
Flange bolt & gasket kits, 10"					
Full face, red rubber gasket, 150 lb	M8@1.80	Ea	36.10	103.00	139.10
Full face, red rubber gasket, 300 lb	M8@2.20	Ea	45.70	126.00	171.70
12" carbon steel pipe (A53) and welded fittings					
Pipe, no fittings or supports included, 12", plain end					
Schedule 40 to 20' high	M8@.910	LF	45.00	52.00	97.00
Schedule 80 to 20' high	M8@1.05	LF	101.00	60.00	161.00
Add for seamless pipe (A106)	—	%	40.0	—	—
Butt welded joints, 12" pipe					
Schedule 40 pipe	M8@3.25	Ea	—	186.00	186.00
Schedule 80 pipe	M8@3.88	Ea	—	222.00	222.00
90-degree ells, 12"					
Schedule 40 carbon steel, butt weld, long turn	M8@4.80	Ea	397.00	274.00	671.00
Schedule 80 carbon steel, butt weld, long turn	M8@7.76	Ea	437.00	444.00	881.00
45-degree ells, 12"					
Schedule 40, carbon steel, butt weld	M8@4.80	Ea	204.00	274.00	478.00
Schedule 80, carbon steel, butt weld	M8@7.76	Ea	234.00	444.00	678.00
Tees, 12"					
Schedule 40, carbon steel, butt weld	M8@7.20	Ea	440.00	412.00	852.00
Schedule 80, carbon steel, butt weld	M8@11.6	Ea	467.00	663.00	1,130.00
Reducing, Schedule 40, carbon steel, butt weld	M8@6.80	Ea	570.00	389.00	959.00
Caps, 12"					
Schedule 40, carbon steel, butt weld	M8@3.36	Ea	102.00	192.00	294.00
Schedule 80, carbon steel, butt weld	M8@4.88	Ea	95.50	279.00	374.50
Reducing couplings, 12"					
Schedule 40, carbon steel, butt weld	M8@4.30	Ea	255.00	246.00	501.00
Weld-o-lets, 12"					
Schedule 40, carbon steel	M8@8.48	Ea	1,060.00	485.00	1,545.00
Welded flanges, forged steel, 12"					
150 lb, slip-on flange	M8@2.64	Ea	306.00	151.00	457.00
300 lb, slip-on flange	M8@3.50	Ea	516.00	200.00	716.00
150 lb, weld neck flange	M8@2.64	Ea	392.00	151.00	543.00
300 lb, weld neck flange	M8@3.50	Ea	687.00	200.00	887.00

	Craft@Hrs	Unit	Material	Labor	Total
Flange bolt & gasket kits, 12"					
Full face, red rubber gasket, 150 lb	M8@2.20	Ea	47.40	126.00	173.40
Full face, red rubber gasket, 300 lb	M8@2.60	Ea	61.30	149.00	210.30

Copper Pressure Pipe and Soldered Copper Fittings Note that copper pipe and fitting prices can change very quickly as the price of copper changes. No hangers included. See pipe hangers in the sections that follow. Labor cost assumes pipe is installed either horizontally or vertically in a building and up to 10' above floor level. Add 25% to the labor cost for heights over 10' above floor level. For more detailed coverage of copper pressure pipe, see *National Plumbing & HVAC Estimator*, http://CraftsmanSiteLicense.com

Type M hard copper pipe Used for water supply pressure piping above ground inside residential buildings. Smaller quantities purchased from building material retailers may cost more. Larger quantities purchased from specialty suppliers will cost less. Add the cost of soldered wrought copper fittings and supports in the sections that follow.

	Craft@Hrs	Unit	Material	Labor	Total
1/2" pipe	P6@.032	LF	.79	1.68	2.47
3/4" pipe	P6@.035	LF	1.36	1.83	3.19
1" pipe	P6@.038	LF	2.57	1.99	4.56
1-1/4" pipe	P6@.042	LF	3.31	2.20	5.51
1-1/2" pipe	P6@.046	LF	4.77	2.41	7.18
2" pipe	P6@.053	LF	8.28	2.78	11.06
2-1/2" pipe	P6@.060	LF	9.99	3.14	13.13
3" pipe	P6@.066	LF	12.70	3.46	16.16
4" pipe	P6@.080	LF	22.00	4.19	26.19

Type L hard copper pipe is commonly used for water supply pressure piping in commercial buildings, either above or below ground. Larger quantities will cost less. Smaller quantities purchased from building material retailers will cost more. Add the cost of soldered wrought copper fittings and supports in the sections that follow.

	Craft@Hrs	Unit	Material	Labor	Total
1/2" pipe	P6@.032	LF	1.15	1.68	2.83
3/4" pipe	P6@.035	LF	1.91	1.83	3.74
1" pipe	P6@.038	LF	3.02	1.99	5.01
1-1/4" pipe	P6@.042	LF	4.11	2.20	6.31
1-1/2" pipe	P6@.046	LF	5.55	2.41	7.96
2" pipe	P6@.053	LF	8.19	2.78	10.97
2-1/2" pipe	P6@.060	LF	14.70	3.14	17.84
3" pipe	P6@.066	LF	19.90	3.46	23.36
4" pipe	P6@.080	LF	31.60	4.19	35.79

Type L soft copper tube Type L tube is commonly used for water supply pressure piping in commercial buildings, either above or below ground. Commercial quantities will cost less. Smaller quantities purchased from building material retailers will cost more. Add the cost of copper fittings and supports in the sections that follow.

	Craft@Hrs	Unit	Material	Labor	Total
1/4", 50' coil	P6@.020	LF	.95	1.05	2.00
3/8", per foot	P6@.020	LF	1.27	1.05	2.32
1/2", per foot	P6@.025	LF	2.61	1.31	3.92
1/2", 10' coil	P6@.025	LF	2.05	1.31	3.36
1/2", 20' coil	P6@.025	LF	1.98	1.31	3.29
1/2", 60' coil	P6@.025	LF	1.46	1.31	2.77
1/2", 100' coil	P6@.025	LF	1.46	1.31	2.77
5/8", 20' coil	P6@.030	LF	2.68	1.57	4.25
3/4", 60' coil	P6@.030	LF	2.68	1.57	4.25
3/4", 100' coil	P6@.030	LF	2.68	1.57	4.25
1", per foot	P6@.035	LF	4.36	1.83	6.19
1", 100' coil	P6@.035	LF	4.23	1.83	6.06
1-1/4", 60' coil	P6@.042	LF	6.04	2.20	8.24
1-1/2", 60' coil	P6@.046	LF	7.73	2.41	10.14

	Craft@Hrs	Unit	Material	Labor	Total
Type K hard copper pipe Installed in an open trench to 5' deep. No excavation or backfill included. Type K is acceptable for applications above and below ground, inside and outside of buildings. Use corporation (compression) fittings rather than soldered joints in underground applications. Based on commercial quantity purchases. Smaller quantities will cost up to 35% more. Add the cost of fittings and hangers when required.					
1/2" pipe	P6@.032	LF	1.80	1.68	3.48
3/4" pipe	P6@.035	LF	3.41	1.83	5.24
Type K soft copper tube Type K is acceptable for applications above and below ground, inside and outside of buildings. Use corporation (compression) fittings rather than soldered joints in underground applications. Commercial quantities will cost less. Smaller quantities purchased from building material retailers will cost more. Add the cost of copper fittings and supports in the sections that follow.					
1/2", 60' coil	P6@.025	LF	1.97	1.31	3.28
3/4", 60' coil	P6@.030	LF	3.00	1.57	4.57
3/4", 100' coil	P6@.030	LF	3.00	1.57	4.57
1", 100' coil	P6@.035	LF	6.56	1.83	8.39
Copper pressure fittings Soldered wrought copper fittings. Solder is 95% tin and 5% antimony (lead free). Installed either horizontally or vertically in a building up to 10' above floor level.					
1/2" copper pressure fittings					
1/2" 90-degree ell	P6@.107	Ea	.42	5.61	6.03
1/2" 45-degree ell	P6@.107	Ea	1.21	5.61	6.82
1/2" tee	P6@.129	Ea	.83	6.76	7.59
1/2" x 1/2" x 3/8" reducing tee	P6@.121	Ea	4.18	6.34	10.52
1/2" cap	P6@.069	Ea	.56	3.61	4.17
1/2" coupling	P6@.107	Ea	.44	5.61	6.05
1/2" copper x male pipe thread adapter	P6@.086	Ea	1.37	4.51	5.88
3/4" copper pressure fittings					
3/4" 90-degree ell	P6@.150	Ea	1.07	7.86	8.93
3/4" 45-degree ell	P6@.150	Ea	2.20	7.86	10.06
3/4" tee	P6@.181	Ea	2.59	9.48	12.07
3/4" x 3/4" x 1/2" reducing tee	P6@.170	Ea	3.88	8.91	12.79
3/4" cap	P6@.096	Ea	1.10	5.03	6.13
3/4" coupling	P6@.150	Ea	.73	7.86	8.59
3/4" copper x male pipe thread adapter	P6@.105	Ea	4.51	5.50	10.01
1" copper pressure fittings					
1" 90-degree ell	P6@.193	Ea	1.11	10.10	11.21
1" 45-degree ell	P6@.193	Ea	6.41	10.10	16.51
1" tee	P6@.233	Ea	9.83	12.20	22.03
1" x 1" x 3/4" reducing tee	P6@.219	Ea	10.60	11.50	22.10
1" cap	P6@.124	Ea	2.52	6.50	9.02
1" coupling	P6@.193	Ea	2.57	10.10	12.67
1" copper x male pipe thread adapter	P6@.134	Ea	7.05	7.02	14.07
1-1/4" copper pressure fittings					
1-1/4" 90-degree ell	P6@.236	Ea	6.06	12.40	18.46
1-1/4" 45-degree ell	P6@.236	Ea	8.70	12.40	21.10
1-1/4" tee	P6@.285	Ea	13.80	14.90	28.70
1-1/4" x 1-1/4" x 1" reducing tee	P6@.268	Ea	8.37	14.00	22.37
1-1/4" cap	P6@.151	Ea	3.62	7.91	11.53
1-1/4" coupling	P6@.236	Ea	4.26	12.40	16.66
1-1/4" copper x male pipe thread adapter	P6@.163	Ea	9.05	8.54	17.59

	Craft@Hrs	Unit	Material	Labor	Total
1-1/2" copper pressure fittings					
1-1/2" 90-degree ell	P6@.278	Ea	10.00	14.60	24.60
1-1/2" 45-degree ell	P6@.278	Ea	10.60	14.60	25.20
1-1/2" tee	P6@.337	Ea	19.20	17.70	36.90
1-1/2" x 1-1/2" x 1-1/4" reducing tee	P6@.302	Ea	10.90	15.80	26.70
1-1/2" cap	P6@.178	Ea	5.09	9.33	14.42
1-1/2" coupling	P6@.278	Ea	6.47	14.60	21.07
1-1/2" copper x male pipe thread adapter	P6@.194	Ea	12.40	10.20	22.60
2" copper pressure fittings					
2" 90-degree ell	P6@.371	Ea	19.10	19.40	38.50
2" 45-degree ell	P6@.371	Ea	17.90	19.40	37.30
2" tee	P6@.449	Ea	30.10	23.50	53.60
2" x 2" x 1-1/2" reducing tee	P6@.422	Ea	4.79	22.10	26.89
2" cap	P6@.238	Ea	9.11	12.50	21.61
2" coupling	P6@.371	Ea	12.10	19.40	31.50
2" copper x male pipe thread adapter	P6@.259	Ea	19.10	13.60	32.70
2-1/2" copper pressure fittings					
2-1/2" 90-degree ell	P6@.457	Ea	20.70	23.90	44.60
2-1/2" 45-degree ell	P6@.457	Ea	34.40	23.90	58.30
2-1/2" tee	P6@.552	Ea	62.40	28.90	91.30
2-1/2" x 2 1/2" x 2" reducing tee	P6@.519	Ea	72.60	27.20	99.80
2-1/2" cap	P6@.292	Ea	27.20	15.30	42.50
2-1/2" coupling	P6@.457	Ea	10.90	23.90	34.80
2-1/2" copper x male pipe thread adapter	P6@.319	Ea	64.80	16.70	81.50
3" copper pressure fittings					
3" 90-degree ell	P6@.543	Ea	47.40	28.40	75.80
3" 45-degree ell	P6@.543	Ea	50.00	28.40	78.40
3" tee	P6@.656	Ea	90.10	34.40	124.50
3" x 3" x 2" reducing tee	P6@.585	Ea	78.40	30.60	109.00
3" cap	P6@.347	Ea	36.80	18.20	55.00
3" coupling	P6@.543	Ea	27.90	28.40	56.30
3" copper x male pipe thread adapter	P6@.375	Ea	109.00	19.60	128.60
4" copper pressure fittings					
4" 90-degree ell	P6@.714	Ea	116.00	37.40	153.40
4" 45-degree ell	P6@.714	Ea	105.00	37.40	142.40
4" tee	P6@.863	Ea	223.00	45.20	268.20
4" x 4" x 3" reducing tee	P6@.811	Ea	157.00	42.50	199.50
4" cap	P6@.457	Ea	68.50	23.90	92.40
4" coupling	P6@.714	Ea	53.90	37.40	91.30
4" copper x male pipe thread adapter	P6@.485	Ea	232.00	25.40	257.40

Flexible PVC-Jacketed Copper Tubing For fuel oil, gas and propane transfer lines. Flame retardant and dielectric. Fungus, acid and moisture corrosion resistant. Acceptable for direct burial underground or under concrete. Installed in an open trench.

	Craft@Hrs	Unit	Material	Labor	Total
3/8" OD	PM@.010	LF	1.36	.43	1.79
1/2" OD	PM@.010	LF	1.64	.43	2.07
5/8" OD	PM@.010	LF	2.29	.43	2.72

Shrinkage kit for flexible PVC-jacketed copper tubing. Add for shrinkage tubing kit to allow for the coupling of sections with standard flare fittings. Per joint.

	Craft@Hrs	Unit	Material	Labor	Total
Kit for 3/8" flare fittings	—	Ea	14.00	—	14.00
Kit for 1/2" flare fittings	—	Ea	15.00	—	15.00
Kit for 5/8" flare fittings	—	Ea	17.20	—	17.20

	Craft@Hrs	Unit	Material	Labor	Total
Schedule 40 PVC Pressure Pipe and Socket-weld Fittings Installed in a building vertically or horizontally up to 10' above floor level.					
1/2" Schedule 40 PVC pressure pipe and fittings					
1/2" pipe	P6@.020	LF	.19	1.05	1.24
1/2" 90-degree ell	P6@.100	Ea	.38	5.24	5.62
1/2" tee	P6@.130	Ea	.44	6.81	7.25
3/4" Schedule 40 PVC pressure pipe and fittings					
3/4" pipe	P6@.025	LF	.23	1.31	1.54
3/4" 90-degree ell	P6@.115	Ea	.48	6.02	6.50
3/4" tee	P6@.140	Ea	.59	7.33	7.92
1" Schedule 40 PVC pressure pipe and fittings					
1" pipe	P6@.030	LF	.34	1.57	1.91
1" 90-degree ell	P6@.120	Ea	1.01	6.29	7.30
1" tee	P6@.170	Ea	1.24	8.91	10.15
1-1/4" Schedule 40 PVC pressure pipe and fittings					
1-1/4" pipe	P6@.035	LF	1.18	1.83	3.01
1-1/4" 90-degree ell	P6@.160	Ea	1.50	8.38	9.88
1-1/4" tee	P6@.220	Ea	2.14	11.50	13.64
1-1/2" Schedule 40 PVC pressure pipe and fittings					
1-1/2" pipe	P6@.040	LF	.60	2.10	2.70
1-1/2" 90-degree ell	P6@.180	Ea	1.70	9.43	11.13
1-1/2" tee	P6@.250	Ea	2.26	13.10	15.36
2" Schedule 40 PVC pressure pipe and fittings					
2" pipe	P6@.046	LF	.83	2.41	3.24
2" 90-degree ell	P6@.200	Ea	2.56	10.50	13.06
2" tee	P6@.280	Ea	3.03	14.70	17.73
2-1/2" Schedule 40 PVC pressure pipe and fittings					
2-1/2" pipe	P6@.053	LF	1.36	2.78	4.14
2-1/2" 90-degree ell	P6@.250	Ea	4.55	13.10	17.65
2-1/2" tee	P6@.350	Ea	5.38	18.30	23.68
3" Schedule 40 PVC pressure pipe and fittings					
3" pipe	P6@.055	LF	1.83	2.88	4.71
3" 90-degree ell	P6@.300	Ea	4.86	15.70	20.56
3" tee	P6@.420	Ea	7.14	22.00	29.14
4" Schedule 40 PVC pressure pipe and fittings					
4" pipe	P6@.070	LF	2.60	3.67	6.27
4" 90-degree ell	P6@.500	Ea	8.90	26.20	35.10
4" tee	P6@.560	Ea	12.90	29.30	42.20
Schedule 80 PVC Pressure Pipe and Socket-Weld Fittings Installed in a building vertically or horizontally up to 10' above floor level.					
1/2" Schedule 80 PVC pressure pipe and fittings					
1/2" pipe	P6@.021	LF	.38	1.10	1.48
1/2" 90-degree ell	P6@.105	Ea	.84	5.50	6.34
1/2" tee	P6@.135	Ea	2.36	7.07	9.43
3/4" Schedule 80 PVC pressure pipe and fittings					
3/4" pipe	P6@.026	LF	.50	1.36	1.86
3/4" 90-degree ell	P6@.120	Ea	1.06	6.29	7.35
3/4" tee	P6@.145	Ea	2.45	7.60	10.05
1" Schedule 80 PVC pressure pipe and fittings					
1" pipe	P6@.032	LF	.80	1.68	2.48
1" 90-degree ell	P6@.125	Ea	1.71	6.55	8.26
1" tee	P6@.180	Ea	3.11	9.43	12.54

	Craft@Hrs	Unit	Material	Labor	Total
1-1/4" Schedule 80 PVC pressure pipe and fittings					
1-1/4" pipe	P6@.037	LF	1.01	1.94	2.95
1-1/4" 90-degree ell	P6@.170	Ea	2.33	8.91	11.24
1-1/4" tee	P6@.230	Ea	8.49	12.00	20.49
1-1/2" Schedule 80 PVC pressure pipe and fittings					
1-1/2" pipe	P6@.042	LF	1.21	2.20	3.41
1-1/2" 90-degree ell	P6@.190	Ea	2.45	9.95	12.40
1-1/2" tee	P6@.265	Ea	8.75	13.90	22.65
2" Schedule 80 PVC pressure pipe and fittings					
2" pipe	P6@.047	LF	1.61	2.46	4.07
2" 90-degree ell	P6@.210	Ea	2.91	11.00	13.91
2" tee	P6@.295	Ea	11.10	15.50	26.60
2-1/2" Schedule 80 PVC pressure pipe and fittings					
2-1/2" pipe	P6@.052	LF	2.72	2.72	5.44
2-1/2" 90-degree ell	P6@.262	Ea	7.55	13.70	21.25
2-1/2" tee	P6@.368	Ea	12.50	19.30	31.80
3" Schedule 80 PVC pressure pipe and fittings					
3" pipe	P6@.057	LF	3.42	2.99	6.41
3" 90-degree ell	P6@.315	Ea	8.07	16.50	24.57
3" tee	P6@.440	Ea	14.50	23.10	37.60
4" Schedule 80 PVC pressure pipe and fittings					
4" pipe	P6@.074	LF	4.83	3.88	8.71
4" 90-degree ell	P6@.520	Ea	12.40	27.20	39.60
4" tee	P6@.585	Ea	17.50	30.60	48.10

CPVC Chlorinated Pressure Pipe and Socket-Weld Fittings Installed in a building vertically or horizontally up to 10' above floor level. CPVC pipe is the plastic alternative to traditional copper pipe. For hot and cold water distribution to 210 degrees F. Tan in color. Complies with ASTM D 2846 and has the same outside diameter as copper tubing. SDR 11 pressure pipe has the same pressure rating for all pipe diameters. FlowGuard Gold® pipe has a gold stripe.

	Craft@Hrs	Unit	Material	Labor	Total
1/2" CPVC chlorinated pressure pipe and fittings					
#4120 SDR 11 CPVC pipe	P6@.020	LF	.30	1.05	1.35
FlowGuard Gold pipe	P6@.020	LF	.35	1.05	1.40
90-degree elbow	P6@.100	Ea	.32	5.24	5.56
90-degree drop-ear elbow	P6@.100	Ea	1.11	5.24	6.35
FlowGuard drop-ear reducing elbow	P6@.100	Ea	.83	5.24	6.07
45-degree elbow	P6@.100	Ea	.38	5.24	5.62
Coupling	P6@.100	Ea	.30	5.24	5.54
90-degree street elbow	P6@.100	Ea	.30	5.24	5.54
Tee, 1/2" x 1/2" x 1/2"	P6@.130	Ea	.36	6.81	7.17
Tee, 1/2" x 3/4" x 3/4"	P6@.150	Ea	.87	7.86	8.73
Union	P6@.200	Ea	3.30	10.50	13.80
Compression coupling	P6@.200	Ea	2.91	10.50	13.41
Bushing, 1/2" x 1/8" bushing	P6@.080	Ea	3.02	4.19	7.21
Cap	P6@.060	Ea	.32	3.14	3.46
3/4" CPVC chlorinated pressure pipe and fittings					
#4120 SDR 11 CPVC pipe	P6@.025	LF	.53	1.31	1.84
FlowGuard Gold pipe	P6@.025	LF	.56	1.31	1.87
90-degree elbow	P6@.115	Ea	.50	6.02	6.52
45-degree elbow	P6@.115	Ea	.71	6.02	6.73
Coupling	P6@.115	Ea	.35	6.02	6.37
90-degree street elbow	P6@.115	Ea	.59	6.02	6.61
90-degree reducing elbow, 3/4" x 1/2"	P6@.115	Ea	.58	6.02	6.60

	Craft@Hrs	Unit	Material	Labor	Total
Tee, 3/4" x 3/4" x 3/4"	P6@.140	Ea	.74	7.33	8.07
Tee, 3/4" x 1/2" x 1/2"	P6@.140	Ea	.85	7.33	8.18
Tee, 3/4" x 1/2" x 3/4"	P6@.150	Ea	.91	7.86	8.77
Tee, 3/4" x 3/4" x 1/2"	P6@.150	Ea	.85	7.86	8.71
Tee, 3/4" x 1/2" x 1/2"	P6@.150	Ea	.85	7.86	8.71
Cap	P6@.070	Ea	.37	3.67	4.04
Bushing, 1" x 1/2"	P6@.080	Ea	1.95	4.19	6.14
Bushing, 3/4" x 1/2"	P6@.080	Ea	.40	4.19	4.59
Union	P6@.250	Ea	5.56	13.10	18.66
Reducing coupling, 3/4" x 1/2"	P6@.115	Ea	.39	6.02	6.41
Compression coupling	P6@.200	Ea	5.62	10.50	16.12
1" CPVC chlorinated pressure pipe and fittings					
FlowGuard Gold pipe	P6@.030	Ea	1.50	1.57	3.07
45-degree elbow	P6@.120	Ea	1.37	6.29	7.66
Coupling	P6@.120	Ea	1.33	6.29	7.62
Tee, 1" x 1" x 1"	P6@.170	Ea	3.20	8.91	12.11
Tee, 1" x 1" x 3/4"	P6@.170	Ea	10.80	8.91	19.71
Cap	P6@.070	Ea	1.02	3.67	4.69
Bushing, 1" x 3/4"	P6@.080	Ea	1.30	4.19	5.49
CPVC and brass transition fittings. FIPT means female iron pipe thread. MIPT means male iron pipe thread.					
1/2" union, slip x FIPT	P6@.150	Ea	8.90	7.86	16.76
1/2" drop ear 90-degree elbow, slip x FIPT	P6@.090	Ea	5.96	4.72	10.68
1/2" union, slip x MIPT	P6@.250	Ea	4.85	13.10	17.95
1/2" x 3/4" union, slip x MIPT	P6@.250	Ea	5.75	13.10	18.85
3/4" union, slip x FIPT	P6@.170	Ea	12.30	8.91	21.21
3/4" union, slip x MIPT	P6@.250	Ea	9.01	13.10	22.11
CPVC-to-copper-pipe transition fittings. One slip joint and one threaded joint. FIPT means female iron pipe thread. MIPT means male iron pipe thread.					
1/2" slip x FIPT	P6@.080	Ea	6.62	4.19	10.81
3/4" slip x FIPT	P6@.085	Ea	8.92	4.45	13.37
1/2" slip x MIPT	P6@.080	Ea	5.35	4.19	9.54
3/4" slip x MIPT	P6@.085	Ea	6.85	4.45	11.30
CPVC adapter fittings. One slip joint and one threaded joint. Joins CVPV pipe to threaded fittings or valves. FIPT means female iron pipe thread. MIPT means male iron pipe thread.					
1/2" slip x FIPT	P6@.090	Ea	1.18	4.72	5.90
1/2" slip x MIPT	P6@.090	Ea	.33	4.72	5.05
1/2" SPIG x compression	P6@.090	Ea	.84	4.72	5.56
3/4" slip x MIPT	P6@.100	Ea	.49	5.24	5.73
3/4" slip x FIPT	P6@.100	Ea	1.26	5.24	6.50
1" slip x FIPT	P6@.120	Ea	1.61	6.29	7.90
1" slip x MIPT	P6@.120	Ea	2.33	6.29	8.62
CPVC snap-on tubing strap. Secures CPVC pipe in a horizontal or vertical position. Polypropylene.					
1/2" pipe	P6@.110	Ea	.11	5.76	5.87
3/4" pipe	P6@.115	Ea	.15	6.02	6.17

Schedule 80 CPVC Chlorinated Pressure Pipe and Socket-weld Fittings Installed in a building vertically or horizontally up to 10' above floor level. Typical use is in fire protection systems.

	Craft@Hrs	Unit	Material	Labor	Total
3/4" Schedule 80 CPVC chlorinated pressure pipe and fittings					
3/4" pipe	SP@.055	LF	1.02	3.57	4.59
3/4" 90-degree ell	SP@.100	Ea	1.73	6.48	8.21
3/4" tee	SP@.150	Ea	3.24	9.72	12.96

	Craft@Hrs	Unit	Material	Labor	Total
1" Schedule 80 CPVC chlorinated pressure pipe and fittings					
1" pipe	SP@.055	LF	1.00	3.57	4.57
1" 90-degree ell	SP@.120	Ea	2.75	7.78	10.53
1" tee	SP@.170	Ea	3.97	11.00	14.97
1-1/4" Schedule 80 CPVC chlorinated pressure pipe and fittings					
1-1/4" pipe	SP@.065	LF	1.58	4.21	5.79
1-1/4" 90-degree ell	SP@.170	Ea	6.03	11.00	17.03
1-1/4" tee	SP@.230	Ea	9.33	14.90	24.23
1-1/2" Schedule 80 CPVC chlorinated pressure pipe and fittings					
1-1/2" pipe	SP@.075	LF	1.65	4.86	6.51
1-1/2" 90-degree ell	SP@.180	Ea	6.63	11.70	18.33
1-1/2" tee	SP@.250	Ea	9.57	16.20	25.77
2" Schedule 80 CPVC chlorinated pressure pipe and fittings					
2" pipe	SP@.085	LF	2.28	5.51	7.79
2" 90-degree ell	SP@.200	Ea	8.02	13.00	21.02
2" tee	SP@.280	Ea	10.60	18.10	28.70

PEX Tube and Fittings Cross-linked polyethylene tube installed in a building vertically or horizontally up to 10' above floor level. Using crimped connections. By copper tube size. Based on 100' rolls of color coded (red, blue or white) tube. For domestic water systems and in-floor hydronics heating systems. Oxygen-barrier PEX is required in heating systems.

	Craft@Hrs	Unit	Material	Labor	Total
3/8" PEX tube					
3/8" AQUAPEX	P6@.019	LF	.48	1.00	1.48
3/8" Oxygen Barrier PEX	P6@.019	LF	.38	1.00	1.38
3/8" ThermaPEX	P6@.019	LF	.50	1.00	1.50
3/8" hePEX	P6@.019	LF	.78	1.00	1.78
3/8" PEX fittings					
3/8" PEX brass elbow	P6@.160	Ea	.70	8.38	9.08
3/8" PEX brass coupler	P6@.160	Ea	.49	8.38	8.87
3/8" PEX crimp ring	P6@.008	Ea	.15	.42	.57
3/8" x 3/8" x 3/8" PEX brass tee	P6@.240	Ea	.52	12.60	13.12
3/8" PEX economy clamp	P6@.020	Ea	.10	1.05	1.15
1/2" PEX tube					
1/2" AQUAPEX, white	P6@.020	LF	.48	1.05	1.53
1/2" AQUAPEX, red or blue	P6@.020	LF	.48	1.05	1.53
1/2" PEX, red or blue	P6@.020	LF	.21	1.05	1.26
1/2" ViegaPEX, red or blue	P6@.020	LF	.44	1.05	1.49
1/2" Pre-Insulated AQUAPEX	P6@.020	LF	2.32	1.05	3.37
1/2" Oxygen Barrier PEX	P6@.020	LF	.24	1.05	1.29
1/2" ThermaPEX	P6@.020	LF	.56	1.05	1.61
1/2" hePEX	P6@.020	LF	.79	1.05	1.84
1/2" PEX fittings					
1/2" PEX brass elbow	P6@.160	Ea	.83	8.38	9.21
1/2" PEX brass coupler	P6@.160	Ea	.57	8.38	8.95
1/2" PEX ball valve	P6@.200	Ea	4.21	10.50	14.71
1/2" PEX crimp ring	P6@.008	Ea	.19	.42	.61
1/2" x 1/2" x 1/2" PEX brass tee	P6@.240	Ea	1.16	12.60	13.76
1/2" PEX x 1/2" copper pipe adapter	P6@.160	Ea	.71	8.38	9.09
1/2" PEX economy clamp	P6@.020	Ea	.17	1.05	1.22
1/2" PEX suspension clip	P6@.020	Ea	.22	1.05	1.27

	Craft@Hrs	Unit	Material	Labor	Total
5/8" PEX tube					
5/8" Oxygen Barrier PEX	P6@.021	LF	.37	1.10	1.47
5/8" ThermaPEX	P6@.021	LF	.76	1.10	1.86
5/8" hePEX	P6@.021	LF	1.03	1.10	2.13
5/8" PEX fittings					
5/8" PEX brass elbow	P6@.160	Ea	1.24	8.38	9.62
5/8" PEX brass coupler	P6@.160	Ea	.93	8.38	9.31
5/8" PEX crimp ring	P6@.009	Ea	.18	.47	.65
5/8" x 5/8" x 5/8" PEX brass tee	P6@.240	Ea	1.98	12.60	14.58
5/8" PEX x 1/2" copper pipe adapter	P6@.160	Ea	1.57	8.38	9.95
5/8" PEX x 3/4" copper pipe adapter	P6@.160	Ea	1.42	8.38	9.80
3/4" PEX tube					
3/4" AQUAPEX, white	P6@.021	LF	.78	1.10	1.88
3/4" AQUAPEX, red or blue	P6@.021	LF	.75	1.10	1.85
3/4" PEX, red or blue	P6@.021	LF	.37	1.10	1.47
3/4" ViegaPEX, red or blue	P6@.021	LF	.79	1.10	1.89
3/4" Pre-Insulated AQUAPEX	P6@.021	LF	3.09	1.10	4.19
3/4" Oxygen Barrier PEX	P6@.021	LF	.47	1.10	1.57
3/4" ThermaPEX	P6@.021	LF	.84	1.10	1.94
3/4" hePEX	P6@.021	LF	1.28	1.10	2.38
3/4" PEX fittings					
3/4" PEX brass elbow	P6@.160	Ea	1.30	8.38	9.68
3/4" PEX brass coupler	P6@.160	Ea	1.12	8.38	9.50
3/4" PEX ball valve	P6@.200	Ea	6.22	10.50	16.72
3/4" PEX crimp ring	P6@.009	Ea	.21	.47	.68
3/4" x 3/4" x 3/4" PEX brass tee	P6@.240	Ea	2.06	12.60	14.66
3/4" PEX x 3/4" copper pipe adapter	P6@.160	Ea	1.19	8.38	9.57
3/4" PEX economy clamp	P6@.160	Ea	.21	8.38	8.59
3/4" PEX suspension clip	P6@.020	Ea	.19	1.05	1.24
1" PEX tube					
1" AQUAPEX, white	P6@.025	LF	1.44	1.31	2.75
1" AQUAPEX, red or blue	P6@.025	LF	1.91	1.31	3.22
1" PEX, red or blue	P6@.025	LF	.56	1.31	1.87
1" ViegaPEX, red or blue	P6@.025	LF	1.79	1.31	3.10
1" Pre-Insulated AQUAPEX	P6@.025	LF	3.65	1.31	4.96
1" Oxygen Barrier PEX	P6@.025	LF	.74	1.31	2.05
1" ThermaPEX	P6@.025	LF	1.68	1.31	2.99
1" hePEX	P6@.025	LF	1.98	1.31	3.29
1" PEX fittings					
1" PEX brass elbow	P6@.200	Ea	2.10	10.50	12.60
1" PEX brass coupler	P6@.200	Ea	1.51	10.50	12.01
1" PEX x 1" copper pipe adapter	P6@.165	Ea	2.01	8.64	10.65
1" PEX ball valve	P6@.220	Ea	10.00	11.50	21.50
1" PEX crimp ring	P6@.010	Ea	.28	.52	.80
1" x 1" x 1" PEX brass tee	P6@.240	Ea	3.11	12.60	15.71
PEX manifolds					
1/2" 14 port manifold (6 hot, 8 cold)	P6@1.25	Ea	140.00	65.50	205.50
1/2" 18 port manifold (8 hot, 10 cold)	P6@1.50	Ea	163.00	78.60	241.60
1/2" 24 port manifold (9 hot, 15 cold)	P6@1.95	Ea	197.00	102.00	299.00
1/2" 36 port manifold (14 hot, 22 cold)	P6@2.90	Ea	289.00	152.00	441.00
1" copper manifold with 6 ports	P6@.600	Ea	17.60	31.40	49.00

	Craft@Hrs	Unit	Material	Labor	Total
1" copper manifold w/ 12 ports	P6@1.20	Ea	39.80	62.90	102.70
2-Loop radiant heat manifold	P6@1.00	Ea	197.00	52.40	249.40
4-Loop radiant heat manifold	P6@1.50	Ea	251.00	78.60	329.60
8-Loop radiant heat manifold	P6@1.00	Ea	407.00	52.40	459.40

PEX-AL Tube and Fittings Cross-linked polyethylene tube with aluminum middle layer, installed in a building vertically or horizontally up to 10' above floor level. Using crimped connections. By copper tube size. Based on 100' rolls of tube. For domestic water systems and in-floor hydronics heating systems.

	Craft@Hrs	Unit	Material	Labor	Total
1/2" PEX-AL tube and fittings					
1/2" PEX-AL tubing	P6@.020	LF	.43	1.05	1.48
1/2" PEX-AL press coupling	P6@.160	Ea	8.41	8.38	16.79
1/2" PEX-AL x 3/4" male adapter	P6@.160	Ea	15.80	8.38	24.18
1/2" PEX-AL x 3/4" copper pipe adapter	P6@.180	Ea	8.72	9.43	18.15
1/2" PEX crimp ring	P6@.008	Ea	.19	.42	.61
1/2" x 1/2" x 1/2" PEX brass tee	P6@.240	Ea	1.16	12.60	13.76
1/2" PEX economy clamp	P6@.020	Ea	.17	1.05	1.22
1/2" PEX suspension clip	P6@.020	Ea	.22	1.05	1.27
5/8" PEX-AL tube and fittings					
5/8" PEX-AL tubing	P6@.021	LF	.65	1.10	1.75
5/8" PEX-AL press coupling	P6@.160	Ea	10.90	8.38	19.28
5/8" PEX-AL press elbow	P6@.160	Ea	10.50	8.38	18.88
5/8" PEX-AL x 3/4" male adapter	P6@.160	Ea	17.00	8.38	25.38
5/8" PEX-AL x 3/4" copper pipe adapter	P6@.180	Ea	15.60	9.43	25.03
5/8" PEX crimp ring	P6@.008	Ea	.18	.42	.60
5/8" x 5/8" x 5/8" PEX brass tee	P6@.240	Ea	1.98	12.60	14.58
5/8" PEX economy clamp	P6@.020	Ea	.17	1.05	1.22
5/8" PEX suspension clip	P6@.020	Ea	.22	1.05	1.27
3/4" PEX-AL tube and fittings					
3/4" PEX-AL tubing	P6@.021	LF	.92	1.10	2.02
3/4" PEX-AL press coupling	P6@.160	Ea	12.30	8.38	20.68
3/4" PEX-AL press elbow	P6@.160	Ea	19.80	8.38	28.18
3/4" PEX-AL press tee	P6@.240	Ea	19.10	12.60	31.70
3/4" PEX-AL x 3/4" male adapter	P6@.160	Ea	19.90	8.38	28.28
3/4" PEX-AL x 3/4" copper pipe adapter	P6@.180	Ea	18.60	9.43	28.03
3/4" PEX crimp ring	P6@.008	Ea	.21	.42	.63
3/4" x 5/8" x 5/8" PEX brass tee	P6@.240	Ea	2.06	12.60	14.66
3/4" PEX economy clamp	P6@.020	Ea	.21	1.05	1.26
3/4" PEX suspension clip	P6@.020	Ea	.19	1.05	1.24
1" PEX-AL tube and fittings					
1" PEX-AL tubing	P6@.025	LF	1.33	1.31	2.64
1" PEX-AL press coupling	P6@.160	Ea	17.80	8.38	26.18
1" PEX-AL press elbow	P6@.160	Ea	42.20	8.38	50.58
1" PEX-AL press tee	P6@.240	Ea	26.20	12.60	38.80
1" PEX-AL x 3/4" male adapter	P6@.160	Ea	18.90	8.38	27.28
1" PEX-AL x 3/4" copper pipe adapter	P6@.180	Ea	36.10	9.43	45.53
1" PEX crimp ring	P6@.008	Ea	.28	.42	.70
1" x 5/8" x 5/8" PEX brass tee	P6@.240	Ea	3.11	12.60	15.71
1" PEX economy clamp	P6@.020	Ea	.21	1.05	1.26
1" PEX suspension clip	P6@.020	Ea	.19	1.05	1.24

	Craft@Hrs	Unit	Material	Labor	Total
Copper DWV Pipe and Fittings Straight rigid lengths. For commercial drain, waste and vent (DWV) systems. Labor assumes soldered joints with pipe installed vertically in a building up to 10' above floor level. Add the cost of supports.					
1-1/4" copper DWV pipe and fittings					
Cut pipe, per foot	P6@.042	LF	11.00	2.20	13.20
10' lengths	P6@.042	LF	3.80	2.20	6.00
Coupling	P6@.200	Ea	4.51	10.50	15.01
90-degree elbow	P6@.200	Ea	9.43	10.50	19.93
45-degree elbow	P6@.200	Ea	4.18	10.50	14.68
Tee	P6@.240	Ea	14.00	12.60	26.60
Trap adapter	P6@.145	Ea	15.50	7.60	23.10
1-1/2" copper DWV pipe and fittings					
Cut pipe, per foot	P6@.045	LF	10.80	2.36	13.16
10' lengths	P6@.045	LF	4.87	2.36	7.23
Coupling	P6@.200	Ea	5.45	10.50	15.95
90-degree elbow	P6@.350	Ea	12.50	18.30	30.80
45-degree elbow	P6@.200	Ea	7.19	10.50	17.69
Wye, cast brass	P6@.240	Ea	43.90	12.60	56.50
Tee	P6@.240	Ea	22.00	12.60	34.60
Test cap	P6@.075	Ea	1.65	3.93	5.58
Male adapter, C x MIP	P6@.150	Ea	13.50	7.86	21.36
Female adapter, FTG x C	P6@.200	Ea	10.80	10.50	21.30
Trap adapter	P6@.155	Ea	15.50	8.12	23.62
Trap adapter, with cleanout	P6@.235	Ea	45.20	12.30	57.50
2" copper DWV pipe and fittings					
Cut pipe, per foot	P6@.056	LF	15.60	2.93	18.53
10' lengths	P6@.056	LF	6.82	2.93	9.75
Coupling	P6@.270	Ea	7.29	14.10	21.39
90-degree elbow	P6@.270	Ea	22.10	14.10	36.20
45-degree elbow	P6@.270	Ea	16.40	14.10	30.50
Reducing bushing, 2" to 1-1/2"	P6@.140	Ea	10.10	7.33	17.43
Wye, cast brass	P6@.320	Ea	23.90	16.80	40.70
Tee, 2" x 2" x 2"	P6@.320	Ea	25.70	16.80	42.50
Tee, 2" x 2" x 1-1/2"	P6@.240	Ea	21.20	12.60	33.80
Male adapter C x MIP	P6@.185	Ea	17.20	9.69	26.89
Female adapter C x FIP	P6@.259	Ea	21.60	13.60	35.20
Trap adapter, with cleanout	P6@.325	Ea	50.70	17.00	67.70
PVC SDR 35 DWV Drainage Pipe Solvent weld, installed in an open trench inside a building (main building drain), including typical fittings (one wye and 45-degree elbow every 20'). SDR 35 is thin wall pipe suitable for below grade applications only. Add for excavation and backfill. Use these figures for preliminary estimates.					
3" pipe assembly below grade	P6@.160	LF	2.70	8.38	11.08
4" pipe assembly below grade	P6@.175	LF	4.14	9.17	13.31
6" pipe assembly below grade	P6@.220	LF	8.72	11.50	20.22
Add for interior excavation and backfill (shallow)	CL@.180	LF	—	7.43	7.43
ABS DWV Pipe and Fittings Acrylonitrile Butadiene Styrene (ASTM D 2661-73) pipe is made from rubber-based resins and used primarily for drain, waste and vent systems. The Uniform Plumbing Code limits ABS to residential buildings and below grade applications in commercial and public buildings. Solvent-weld ABS is easier to install than cast iron or copper drainage pipe. ABS does not rot, rust, corrode or collect waste and resists mechanical damage, even at low temperatures.					
1-1/2" pipe, 10' lengths	P6@.020	LF	.49	1.05	1.54
2" pipe, 10' lengths	P6@.025	LF	.68	1.31	1.99
3" pipe, 10' lengths	P6@.030	LF	1.41	1.57	2.98
4" pipe, 10' lengths	P6@.040	LF	1.77	2.10	3.87
Deduct for below grade applications	—	%	—	−15.0	—

	Craft@Hrs	Unit	Material	Labor	Total
ABS 90-degree elbow (1/4 bend), hub and hub except as noted. Street elbows are hub and spigot.					
1-1/2" ell	P6@.060	Ea	1.29	3.14	4.43
1-1/2" long sweep	P6@.200	Ea	2.16	10.50	12.66
1-1/2" street ell	P6@.120	Ea	1.99	6.29	8.28
1-1/2" venting	P6@.150	Ea	1.46	7.86	9.32
2" ell	P6@.125	Ea	1.62	6.55	8.17
2", long sweep	P6@.250	Ea	2.76	13.10	15.86
2", street ell	P6@.125	Ea	2.91	6.55	9.46
2", venting	P6@.150	Ea	3.03	7.86	10.89
3" ell	P6@.175	Ea	4.30	9.17	13.47
3", long sweep	P6@.500	Ea	5.47	26.20	31.67
3", street ell	P6@.150	Ea	4.93	7.86	12.79
3", venting	P6@.150	Ea	7.74	7.86	15.60
3" x 3" x 1-1/2", hub x hub x hub, side inlet	P6@.500	Ea	11.90	26.20	38.10
3" x 3" x 2", hub x hub x hub, side inlet	P6@.500	Ea	13.50	26.20	39.70
3" x 3" x 2" low heel elbow	P6@.500	Ea	6.23	26.20	32.43
3" x 3" x 1-1/2" low heel elbow	P6@.175	Ea	10.40	9.17	19.57
4" ell	P6@.175	Ea	6.90	9.17	16.07
4", long sweep	P6@.500	Ea	10.30	26.20	36.50
4", street ell	P6@.175	Ea	11.00	9.17	20.17
4" x 3" closet elbow, spigot x hub	P6@.150	Ea	10.60	7.86	18.46
4" x 3" closet elbow, hub x hub	P6@.260	Ea	7.64	13.60	21.24
ABS 60-degree elbow (1/6 bend), hub and hub					
1-1/2" bend	P6@.200	Ea	2.19	10.50	12.69
2" bend	P6@.250	Ea	2.83	13.10	15.93
3" bend	P6@.500	Ea	9.91	26.20	36.11
4" bend	P6@.500	Ea	14.30	26.20	40.50
ABS 45-degree elbow (1/8 bend). Regular bends are hub x hub. Street bends are hub and spigot.					
1-1/2" bend	P6@.120	Ea	1.46	6.29	7.75
1-1/2" street bend	P6@.120	Ea	1.32	6.29	7.61
2" bend	P6@.125	Ea	1.55	6.55	8.10
2" street bend	P6@.125	Ea	1.46	6.55	8.01
3" bend	P6@.175	Ea	3.55	9.17	12.72
3" street bend	P6@.150	Ea	3.18	7.86	11.04
4" bend	P6@.175	Ea	7.95	9.17	17.12
4" street bend	P6@.175	Ea	7.25	9.17	16.42
ABS 22-1/2 degree elbow (1/16 bend). Regular bends are hub x hub. Street bends are hub and spigot.					
1-1/2" bend	P6@.120	Ea	1.46	6.29	7.75
1-1/2", street bend	P6@.120	Ea	4.70	6.29	10.99
2" bend	P6@.125	Ea	1.55	6.55	8.10
2", street bend	P6@.125	Ea	4.70	6.55	11.25
3" bend	P6@.170	Ea	6.32	8.91	15.23
3" street bend	P6@.150	Ea	9.45	7.86	17.31
4" bend	P6@.175	Ea	6.97	9.17	16.14
4" street bend	P6@.175	Ea	13.00	9.17	22.17
ABS coupling, hub x hub					
1-1/2"	P6@.120	Ea	.73	6.29	7.02
2"	P6@.125	Ea	.97	6.55	7.52
2" x 1-1/2", reducing	P6@.125	Ea	2.27	6.55	8.82
3"	P6@.175	Ea	1.94	9.17	11.11
3" x 2", reducing	P6@.175	Ea	3.82	9.17	12.99
4"	P6@.250	Ea	3.81	13.10	16.91
4" x 3", reducing	P6@.250	Ea	7.01	13.10	20.11

	Craft@Hrs	Unit	Material	Labor	Total
ABS wye, connects two branch lines to a main horizontal drain line. Hub x hub x hub.					
1-1/2"	P6@.150	Ea	2.49	7.86	10.35
2"	P6@.190	Ea	2.87	9.95	12.82
2" x 1-1/2"	P6@.190	Ea	4.97	9.95	14.92
3"	P6@.260	Ea	5.81	13.60	19.41
3" x 1-1/2"	P6@.240	Ea	6.23	12.60	18.83
3" x 2"	P6@.260	Ea	6.23	13.60	19.83
4"	P6@.350	Ea	12.50	18.30	30.80
4" x 2"	P6@.350	Ea	9.13	18.30	27.43
4" x 3"	P6@.360	Ea	11.40	18.90	30.30
ABS double wye, joins three ABS branch lines to a main horizontal drain line. Hub x hub x hub x hub.					
1-1/2"	P6@.260	Ea	5.61	13.60	19.21
2"	P6@.290	Ea	7.08	15.20	22.28
3"	P6@.325	Ea	15.70	17.00	32.70
4" x 3"	P6@.350	Ea	24.70	18.30	43.00
ABS sanitary tee (TY), connects a branch line to a vertical ABS drain line. Regular sanitary tees are hub x hub x hub. Street sanitary tees are spigot x hub x hub.					
1-1/2"	P6@.150	Ea	1.80	7.86	9.66
1-1/2", long sweep	P6@.150	Ea	5.20	7.86	13.06
1-1/2", street tee	P6@.150	Ea	4.70	7.86	12.56
2" x 1-1/2"	P6@.160	Ea	1.58	8.38	9.96
2" x 1-1/2" x 1-1/2"	P6@.160	Ea	2.62	8.38	11.00
2" x 1-1/2" x 2"	P6@.160	Ea	2.60	8.38	10.98
2"	P6@.190	Ea	2.77	9.95	12.72
2", long sweep	P6@.190	Ea	6.21	9.95	16.16
2" x 1-1/2", long sweep	P6@.190	Ea	5.64	9.95	15.59
2" street tee	P6@.190	Ea	5.69	9.95	15.64
2" x 1-1/2" x 1-1/2" street tee	P6@.190	Ea	6.23	9.95	16.18
3"	P6@.260	Ea	6.48	13.60	20.08
3", long sweep	P6@.260	Ea	7.78	13.60	21.38
3" x 1-1/2"	P6@.210	Ea	4.70	11.00	15.70
3" x 1-1/2", long sweep	P6@.200	Ea	8.64	10.50	19.14
3" x 2"	P6@.235	Ea	5.37	12.30	17.67
3" x 2", long sweep	P6@.260	Ea	6.82	13.60	20.42
4"	P6@.350	Ea	11.60	18.30	29.90
4", long sweep	P6@.350	Ea	15.60	18.30	33.90
4" x 2"	P6@.275	Ea	10.80	14.40	25.20
4" x 2", long sweep	P6@.350	Ea	15.70	18.30	34.00
4" x 3"	P6@.325	Ea	12.50	17.00	29.50
4" x 3", long sweep	P6@.360	Ea	18.10	18.90	37.00
ABS bungalow fitting (Wisconsin tee). Connects vent (3" top inlet) and horizontal water closet discharge (3" branch) and bathtub discharge (1-1/2" branch) to a vertical soil stack. One fitting connects discharge and venting for a set of washroom fixtures.					
3", 1-1/2" left inlet	P6@.325	Ea	16.90	17.00	33.90
3", 2" right inlet	P6@.325	Ea	14.70	17.00	31.70
ABS double sanitary tee (double TY/cross), brings two ABS-DWV branch lines into a vertical waste or soil stack. All hub except as noted.					
1-1/2"	P6@.250	Ea	4.88	13.10	17.98
2" x 1-1/2"	P6@.260	Ea	5.20	13.60	18.80
2"	P6@.290	Ea	5.28	15.20	20.48
2" double fixture tee	P6@.290	Ea	10.70	15.20	25.90
2" x 1-1/2" x 1-1/2" x 1-1/2"	P6@.260	Ea	5.65	13.60	19.25

	Craft@Hrs	Unit	Material	Labor	Total
3"	P6@.325	Ea	16.60	17.00	33.60
3" double fixture tee, spigot x hub	P6@.450	Ea	23.00	23.60	46.60
3" x 1-1/2"	P6@.310	Ea	6.16	16.20	22.36
3" x 2"	P6@.335	Ea	9.26	17.60	26.86
4"	P6@.350	Ea	32.10	18.30	50.40
ABS cleanout tee, two-way					
3", hub x hub x hub	P6@.175	Ea	14.80	9.17	23.97
4", hub x hub x hub	P6@.250	Ea	29.00	13.10	42.10
ABS test tee, provides a cleanout opening flush with a finished wall. Includes a cleanout plug. FIPT means female iron pipe thread.					
1-1/2", hub x hub x cleanout	P6@.130	Ea	5.25	6.81	12.06
2", hub x hub x cleanout	P6@.170	Ea	8.29	8.91	17.20
3", hub x hub x cleanout	P6@.220	Ea	14.00	11.50	25.50
4", hub x hub x cleanout	P6@.240	Ea	27.20	12.60	39.80
1-1/2", hub x hub x FIPT	P6@.150	Ea	4.29	7.86	12.15
2", hub x hub x FIPT	P6@.190	Ea	5.20	9.95	15.15
3", hub x hub x FIPT	P6@.260	Ea	11.30	13.60	24.90
4", hub x hub x FIPT	P6@.350	Ea	15.60	18.30	33.90
Inset test cap with knockout					
1-1/2"	P6@.100	Ea	.43	5.24	5.67
2"	P6@.100	Ea	.40	5.24	5.64
3"	P6@.100	Ea	.47	5.24	5.71
4"	P6@.100	Ea	.50	5.24	5.74
Mechanical plastic test plug with galvanized wing nut, natural rubber O-ring. Max air pressure of 5 psi.					
1-1/2"	P6@.030	Ea	3.46	1.57	5.03
2"	P6@.030	Ea	4.58	1.57	6.15
3"	P6@.030	Ea	5.75	1.57	7.32
4"	P6@.030	Ea	6.98	1.57	8.55
ABS closet flange. Closet flanges are used for mounting water closets.					
4" x 3", fast set with test cap	P6@.225	Ea	12.90	11.80	24.70
4" x 3", closet flange x hub	P6@.225	Ea	3.69	11.80	15.49
4" x 3", closet adjustable flange x hub	P6@.225	Ea	12.30	11.80	24.10
4" x 3", offset, adjustabe	P6@.225	Ea	12.20	11.80	24.00
4", closet flange x hub	P6@.225	Ea	6.29	11.80	18.09
4", fast set with test cap	P6@.225	Ea	9.17	11.80	20.97
4", closet adjustable flange x hub	P6@.225	Ea	12.30	11.80	24.10
ABS female adapter, joins ABS pipe to standard male threaded pipe. FIPT means female iron pipe thread.					
1-1/2", hub x FIPT	P6@.080	Ea	1.41	4.19	5.60
1-1/2", spigot x FIPT	P6@.080	Ea	1.36	4.19	5.55
2", hub x FIPT	P6@.085	Ea	2.27	4.45	6.72
2", spigot x FIPT	P6@.085	Ea	1.66	4.45	6.11
3", hub x FIPT	P6@.155	Ea	4.23	8.12	12.35
3", spigot x FIPT	P6@.155	Ea	4.06	8.12	12.18
4", hub x FIPT	P6@.220	Ea	6.36	11.50	17.86
4", spigot x FIPT	P6@.220	Ea	6.64	11.50	18.14
ABS male adapter, joins ABS pipe to standard female threaded pipe. MIPT means male iron pipe thread.					
1-1/2", hub x MIPT	P6@.080	Ea	1.13	4.19	5.32
2", hub x MIPT	P6@.085	Ea	1.66	4.45	6.11
3", hub x MIPT	P6@.155	Ea	3.60	8.12	11.72
4", hub x MIPT	P6@.220	Ea	7.38	11.50	18.88

	Craft@Hrs	Unit	Material	Labor	Total
ABS trap adapter, joins ABS pipe to sink or bath waste outlet.					
1-1/2", hub x slip jam nut	P6@.200	Ea	1.46	10.50	11.96
1-1/2", spigot x slip jam nut	P6@.200	Ea	1.54	10.50	12.04
1-1/2" x 1-1/4", spigot x slip jam nut	P6@.200	Ea	1.58	10.50	12.08
1-1/2" x 1-1/4", hub x slip jam nut	P6@.200	Ea	1.65	10.50	12.15
ABS cleanout adapter, fits inside pipe, flush finish.					
2", insert	P6@.100	Ea	4.10	5.24	9.34
3", insert	P6@.150	Ea	4.63	7.86	12.49
4", insert	P6@.320	Ea	6.36	16.80	23.16
ABS-DWV cleanout plug, male pipe threads.					
1-1/2"	P6@.090	Ea	1.07	4.72	5.79
2"	P6@.120	Ea	1.14	6.29	7.43
3"	P6@.240	Ea	1.54	12.60	14.14
4"	P6@.320	Ea	2.86	16.80	19.66
2", countersunk	P6@.120	Ea	1.37	6.29	7.66
3", countersunk	P6@.240	Ea	1.63	12.60	14.23
ABS soil pipe adapter, joins ABS DWV to cast iron pipe soil pipe.					
3" ABS hub x cast iron spigot	P6@.155	Ea	6.84	8.12	14.96
4" ABS hub to cast iron spigot	P6@.250	Ea	9.84	13.10	22.94
4" cast iron spigot to 3" DWV hub	P6@.220	Ea	8.76	11.50	20.26
ABS P-trap, used at fixture waste outlets to prevent sewer gas from entering living space via the fixture drain.					
1-1/2", all hub	P6@.220	Ea	3.49	11.50	14.99
1-1/2", hub x hub, with union	P6@.280	Ea	4.76	14.70	19.46
1-1/2", hub, with cleanout	P6@.155	Ea	9.64	8.12	17.76
1-1/2", hub x spigot, with union	P6@.220	Ea	5.69	11.50	17.19
2", all hub	P6@.280	Ea	5.29	14.70	19.99
2", hub x hub, with union	P6@.280	Ea	8.72	14.70	23.42
2", hub, with cleanout	P6@.195	Ea	9.88	10.20	20.08
ABS return bend, bottom portion of P-trap, no cleanout.					
1-1/2", all hub	P6@.120	Ea	4.20	6.29	10.49
2", all hub	P6@.125	Ea	4.42	6.55	10.97
ABS cap, permanently caps ABS-DWV piping.					
1-1/2"	P6@.030	Ea	2.73	1.57	4.30
2"	P6@.040	Ea	4.13	2.10	6.23
3"	P6@.050	Ea	6.56	2.62	9.18
4"	P6@.090	Ea	7.86	4.72	12.58
ABS flush bushing, inserts into ABS fitting hub to reduce to a smaller pipe size.					
2" x 1-1/2"	P6@.062	Ea	1.13	3.25	4.38
3" x 1-1/2"	P6@.088	Ea	2.91	4.61	7.52
3" x 2"	P6@.088	Ea	2.57	4.61	7.18
4" x 2"	P6@.125	Ea	7.39	6.55	13.94
4" x 3"	P6@.125	Ea	6.10	6.55	12.65
ABS heavy-duty floor drain					
3", less sediment bucket	P6@.280	Ea	40.10	14.70	54.80
4", less sediment bucket	P6@.300	Ea	40.60	15.70	56.30

Hangers and Supports

	Craft@Hrs	Unit	Material	Labor	Total
Angle bracket hangers, steel, by rod size					
3/8" angle bracket hanger	M5@.070	Ea	2.31	3.63	5.94
1/2" angle bracket hanger	M5@.070	Ea	2.62	3.63	6.25
5/8" angle bracket hanger	M5@.070	Ea	5.73	3.63	9.36
3/4" angle bracket hanger	M5@.070	Ea	8.86	3.63	12.49
7/8" angle bracket hanger	M5@.070	Ea	15.90	3.63	19.53

	Craft@Hrs	Unit	Material	Labor	Total
Angle supports, wall mounted, welded steel					
12" x 18", medium weight	M5@.950	Ea	99.30	49.30	148.60
18" x 24", medium weight	M5@1.10	Ea	124.00	57.00	181.00
24" x 30", medium weight	M5@1.60	Ea	158.00	83.00	241.00
12" x 30", heavy weight	M5@1.10	Ea	142.00	57.00	199.00
18" x 24", heavy weight	M5@1.10	Ea	200.00	57.00	257.00
24" x 30", heavy weight	M5@1.60	Ea	222.00	83.00	305.00
C-clamps with lock nut, steel, by rod size					
3/8" C-clamp	M5@.070	Ea	2.36	3.63	5.99
1/2" C-clamp	M5@.070	Ea	2.90	3.63	6.53
5/8" C-clamp	M5@.070	Ea	5.87	3.63	9.50
3/4" C-clamp	M5@.070	Ea	8.43	3.63	12.06
7/8" C-clamp	M5@.070	Ea	22.60	3.63	26.23
Top beam clamps, steel, by rod size					
3/8" top beam clamp	M5@.070	Ea	2.81	3.63	6.44
1/2" top beam clamp	M5@.070	Ea	4.55	3.63	8.18
5/8" top beam clamp	M5@.070	Ea	5.59	3.63	9.22
3/4" top beam clamp	M5@.070	Ea	8.16	3.63	11.79
7/8" top beam clamp	M5@.070	Ea	10.80	3.63	14.43
Clevis hangers, standard duty, by intended pipe size, no threaded rod or beam clamp included					
1/2" clevis hanger	M5@.156	Ea	2.20	8.09	10.29
3/4" clevis hanger	M5@.156	Ea	2.20	8.09	10.29
1" clevis hanger	M5@.156	Ea	2.32	8.09	10.41
1-1/4" clevis hanger	M5@.173	Ea	2.68	8.97	11.65
1-1/2" clevis hanger	M5@.173	Ea	2.92	8.97	11.89
2" clevis hanger	M5@.173	Ea	3.25	8.97	12.22
2-1/2" clevis hanger	M5@.189	Ea	3.45	9.80	13.25
3" clevis hanger	M5@.189	Ea	4.55	9.80	14.35
4" clevis hanger	M5@.189	Ea	5.63	9.80	15.43
6" clevis hanger	M5@.202	Ea	9.51	10.50	20.01
8" clevis hanger	M5@.202	Ea	13.90	10.50	24.40
Add for epoxy coated	—	%	25.0	—	—
Add for copper plated	—	%	35.0	—	—
Deduct for light duty	—	%	-20.0	—	—
Swivel ring hangers, light duty, by intended pipe size, band hanger, galvanized steel, no hanger rod, beam clamp or insert included					
1/2" swivel ring hanger	M5@.125	Ea	.57	6.48	7.05
3/4" swivel ring hanger	M5@.125	Ea	.57	6.48	7.05
1" swivel ring hanger	M5@.125	Ea	.57	6.48	7.05
1-1/4" swivel ring hanger	M5@.125	Ea	.64	6.48	7.12
1-1/2" swivel ring hanger	M5@.125	Ea	.74	6.48	7.22
2" swivel ring hanger	M5@.125	Ea	.89	6.48	7.37
2-1/2" swivel ring hanger	M5@.135	Ea	1.20	7.00	8.20
3" swivel ring hanger	M5@.135	Ea	1.44	7.00	8.44
4" swivel ring hanger	M5@.135	Ea	2.00	7.00	9.00
6" swivel ring hanger	M5@.145	Ea	3.75	7.52	11.27
8" swivel ring hanger	M5@.145	Ea	4.48	7.52	12.00
Add for epoxy coating	—	%	45.0	—	—
Add for copper plated	—	%	55.0	—	—
Riser clamps, carbon steel, by intended pipe size					
1/2" riser clamp	M5@.100	Ea	1.89	5.19	7.08
3/4" riser clamp	M5@.100	Ea	2.78	5.19	7.97
1" riser clamp	M5@.100	Ea	2.84	5.19	8.03

	Craft@Hrs	Unit	Material	Labor	Total
1-1/4" riser clamp	M5@.115	Ea	3.37	5.96	9.33
1-1/2" riser clamp	M5@.115	Ea	3.60	5.96	9.56
2" riser clamp	M5@.125	Ea	3.77	6.48	10.25
2-1/2" riser clamp	M5@.135	Ea	3.96	7.00	10.96
3" riser clamp	M5@.140	Ea	4.35	7.26	11.61
4" riser clamp	M5@.145	Ea	5.48	7.52	13.00
6" riser clamp	M5@.155	Ea	9.51	8.04	17.55
8" riser clamp	M5@.165	Ea	15.50	8.56	24.06
Add for epoxy coating	—	%	25.0	—	—
Add for copper plated	—	%	35.0	—	—
Pipe clamps, medium duty, by intended pipe size					
3" pipe clamp	M5@.189	Ea	5.72	9.80	15.52
4" pipe clamp	M5@.189	Ea	8.16	9.80	17.96
6" pipe clamp	M5@.202	Ea	20.00	10.50	30.50
Pipe rolls					
3" pipe roll, complete	M5@.403	Ea	17.80	20.90	38.70
4" pipe roll, complete	M5@.518	Ea	18.70	26.90	45.60
6" pipe roll, complete	M5@.518	Ea	18.70	26.90	45.60
8" pipe roll, complete	M5@.578	Ea	32.90	30.00	62.90
3" pipe roll stand, complete	M5@.323	Ea	47.60	16.80	64.40
4" pipe roll stand, complete	M5@.604	Ea	71.00	31.30	102.30
6" pipe roll stand, complete	M5@.775	Ea	71.00	40.20	111.20
8" pipe roll stand, complete	M5@.775	Ea	124.00	40.20	164.20
Pipe straps, galvanized, two hole, lightweight					
2-1/2" pipe strap	M5@.119	Ea	2.26	6.17	8.43
3" pipe strap	M5@.128	Ea	2.92	6.64	9.56
3-1/2" pipe strap	M5@.135	Ea	3.72	7.00	10.72
4" pipe strap	M5@.144	Ea	4.14	7.47	11.61
Plumber's tape, galvanized, 3/4" x 10' roll					
26 gauge	—	LF	2.01	—	2.01
22 gauge	—	LF	2.65	—	2.65
Sliding pipe guides, welded					
3" pipe guide	M5@.354	Ea	20.50	18.40	38.90
4" pipe guide	M5@.354	Ea	27.50	18.40	45.90
6" pipe guide	M5@.354	Ea	39.60	18.40	58.00
8" pipe guide	M5@.471	Ea	59.50	24.40	83.90
Wall sleeves, cast iron					
4" sleeve	M5@.241	Ea	8.81	12.50	21.31
6" sleeve	M5@.284	Ea	11.00	14.70	25.70
8" sleeve	M5@.377	Ea	14.40	19.60	34.00
Threaded hanger rod, by rod size, in 6' to 10' lengths, per LF					
3/8" rod	—	LF	.48	—	.48
1/2" rod	—	LF	.74	—	.74
5/8" rod	—	LF	.99	—	.99
3/4" rod	—	LF	1.67	—	1.67
U-bolts, with hex nuts, light duty					
4" U-bolt	M5@.089	Ea	6.40	4.62	11.02
6" U-bolt	M5@.135	Ea	11.80	7.00	18.80

Gate Valves, for water, gas and steam applications; complies with American Society of Mechanical Engineers Standard B16, Manufacturers Standardization Society, Instrumentation Society of America standards.

	Craft@Hrs	Unit	Material	Labor	Total
1/2" bronze gate valves					
125 lb, threaded	P6@.210	Ea	14.20	11.00	25.20
125 lb, soldered	P6@.200	Ea	13.80	10.50	24.30
150 lb, threaded	P6@.210	Ea	24.50	11.00	35.50
200 lb, threaded	P6@.210	Ea	32.10	11.00	43.10
3/4" bronze gate valves					
125 lb, threaded	P6@.250	Ea	17.20	13.10	30.30
125 lb, soldered	P6@.240	Ea	16.10	12.60	28.70
150 lb, threaded	P6@.250	Ea	33.70	13.10	46.80
200 lb, threaded	P6@.250	Ea	41.80	13.10	54.90
1" bronze gate valves					
125 lb, threaded	P6@.300	Ea	24.40	15.70	40.10
125 lb, soldered	P6@.290	Ea	24.00	15.20	39.20
150 lb, threaded	P6@.300	Ea	39.50	15.70	55.20
200 lb, threaded	P6@.300	Ea	51.50	15.70	67.20
1-1/2" bronze gate valves					
125 lb, threaded	P6@.450	Ea	40.50	23.60	64.10
125 lb, soldered	P6@.440	Ea	39.20	23.10	62.30
150 lb, threaded	P6@.450	Ea	71.20	23.60	94.80
200 lb, threaded	P6@.450	Ea	86.80	23.60	110.40
2" bronze gate valves					
125 lb, threaded	P6@.500	Ea	67.70	26.20	93.90
125 lb, soldered	P6@.480	Ea	65.70	25.10	90.80
150 lb, threaded	P6@.500	Ea	112.00	26.20	138.20
200 lb, threaded	P6@.500	Ea	128.00	26.20	154.20
Cast iron, bronze trim, non-rising stem					
2-1/2" 125 lb, cast iron, flanged	MI@.600	Ea	285.00	33.20	318.20
2-1/2" 250 lb, cast iron, flanged	MI@.600	Ea	559.00	33.20	592.20
3" 125 lb, cast iron, flanged	MI@.750	Ea	309.00	41.60	350.60
4" 125 lb, cast iron, flanged	MI@1.35	Ea	454.00	74.80	528.80
4" 250 lb, cast iron, flanged	MI@1.35	Ea	1,150.00	74.80	1,224.80

Steel Gate, Globe and Check Valves

	Craft@Hrs	Unit	Material	Labor	Total
Cast steel Class 150 gate valves, OS&Y, flanged ends					
2-1/2" valve	MI@.600	Ea	1,130.00	33.20	1,163.20
3" valve	MI@.750	Ea	1,130.00	41.60	1,171.60
4" valve	MI@1.35	Ea	1,390.00	74.80	1,464.80
Cast steel Class 300 gate valves, OS&Y, flanged ends					
2-1/2" valve	MI@.600	Ea	1,500.00	33.20	1,533.20
3" valve	MI@.750	Ea	1,500.00	41.60	1,541.60
4" valve	MI@1.35	Ea	2,050.00	74.80	2,124.80

OS&Y Gate Valves Forged steel class 800 bolted bonnet outside stem and yoke valves for water, gas and steam applications, complies with American Society of Mechanical Engineers Standard B16, Manufacturers Standardization Society, Instrumentation Society of America standards.

	Craft@Hrs	Unit	Material	Labor	Total
Threaded ends OS&Y gate valves					
1/2" valve	P6@.210	Ea	119.00	11.00	130.00
3/4" valve	P6@.250	Ea	162.00	13.10	175.10
1" valve	P6@.300	Ea	294.00	15.70	309.70
1-1/2" valve	P6@.450	Ea	371.00	23.60	394.60
2" valve	P6@.500	Ea	568.00	26.20	594.20

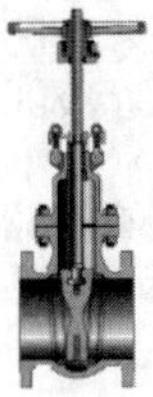

	Craft@Hrs	Unit	Material	Labor	Total
2-1/2" flanged iron OS&Y gate valves					
125 lb	MI@.600	Ea	393.00	33.20	426.20
250 lb	MI@.600	Ea	887.00	33.20	920.20
3" flanged iron OS&Y gate valves					
125 lb	MI@.750	Ea	418.00	41.60	459.60
250 lb	MI@.750	Ea	1,020.00	41.60	1,061.60
4" flanged iron OS&Y gate valves					
125 lb	MI@1.35	Ea	579.00	74.80	653.80
250 lb	MI@1.35	Ea	1,500.00	74.80	1,574.80
6" flanged iron OS&Y gate valves					
125 lb	MI@2.50	Ea	988.00	139.00	1,127.00
250 lb	MI@2.50	Ea	2,450.00	139.00	2,589.00

Butterfly Valves, Ductile Iron
Wafer body, flanged, with lever lock, 150 lb valves have aluminum bronze disk, stainless steel stem and EPDM seals. 200 lb nickel plated ductile iron disk and Buna-N seals.

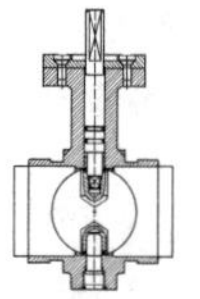

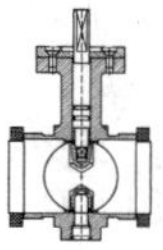

	Craft@Hrs	Unit	Material	Labor	Total
2-1/2" butterfly valve					
150 lb	MI@.300	Ea	129.00	16.60	145.60
200 lb	MI@.400	Ea	185.00	22.20	207.20
3" butterfly valve					
150 lb	MI@.400	Ea	142.00	22.20	164.20
200 lb	MI@.450	Ea	196.00	24.90	220.90
4" butterfly valve					
150 lb	MI@.500	Ea	176.00	27.70	203.70
200 lb	MI@.550	Ea	243.00	30.50	273.50
6" butterfly valve					
150 lb	MI@.750	Ea	277.00	41.60	318.60
200 lb	MI@.750	Ea	390.00	41.60	431.60
8" butterfly valve, with gear operator					
150 lb	MI@.950	Ea	391.00	52.60	443.60
200 lb	MI@.950	Ea	718.00	52.60	770.60
10" butterfly valve, with gear operator					
150 lb	MI@1.40	Ea	549.00	77.60	626.60
200 lb	MI@1.40	Ea	920.00	77.60	997.60

Bronze Globe Valves 125 lb and 150 lb ratings are saturated steam pressure. 200 lb rating is working steam pressure, union bonnet. 125 lb valves have bronze disks. 150 lb valves have composition disks. 300 lb valves have regrinding disks. For gas and steam applications, complies with American Society of Mechanical Engineers Standard B16, Manufacturers Standardization Society, Instrumentation Society of America and American Petroleum Institute standards.

	Craft@Hrs	Unit	Material	Labor	Total
1/2" threaded bronze globe valves					
125 lb	P6@.210	Ea	18.70	11.00	29.70
150 lb	P6@.210	Ea	33.20	11.00	44.20
300 lb	P6@.210	Ea	50.00	11.00	61.00
3/4" threaded bronze globe valves					
125 lb	P6@.250	Ea	25.20	13.10	38.30
150 lb	P6@.250	Ea	45.30	13.10	58.40
300 lb	P6@.250	Ea	63.50	13.10	76.60
1" threaded bronze globe valves					
125 lb	P6@.300	Ea	36.30	15.70	52.00
150 lb	P6@.300	Ea	70.40	15.70	86.10
300 lb	P6@.300	Ea	91.40	15.70	107.10
1-1/2" threaded bronze globe valves					
125 lb	P6@.450	Ea	68.40	23.60	92.00
150 lb	P6@.450	Ea	133.00	23.60	156.60
300 lb	P6@.450	Ea	176.00	23.60	199.60

	Craft@Hrs	Unit	Material	Labor	Total
2" threaded bronze globe valves					
125 lb	P6@.500	Ea	111.00	26.20	137.20
150 lb	P6@.500	Ea	200.00	26.20	226.20
300 lb	P6@.500	Ea	242.00	26.20	268.20

Iron Body Globe Valves Flanged, iron body, OS&Y (outside stem & yoke) 125 psi steam pressure and 200 psi cold water pressure rated.

	Craft@Hrs	Unit	Material	Labor	Total
3" flanged OS&Y, globe valve	MI@.750	Ea	515.00	41.60	556.60
3" 250 lb	MI@.750	Ea	997.00	41.60	1,038.60
4" flanged OS&Y, globe valve	MI@1.35	Ea	729.00	74.80	803.80
4" 250 lb	MI@1.35	Ea	944.00	74.80	1,018.80
6" flanged OS&Y, globe valve	MI@2.50	Ea	1,360.00	139.00	1,499.00
6" 250 lb	MI@2.50	Ea	2,450.00	139.00	2,589.00
8" flanged OS&Y, globe valve	MI@3.00	Ea	2,390.00	166.00	2,556.00
8" 250 lb	MI@3.00	Ea	4,210.00	166.00	4,376.00

Swing Check Valves for water and steam applications, complies with American Society of Mechanical Engineers Standard B16, Manufacturers Standardization Society, Instrumentation Society of America standards.

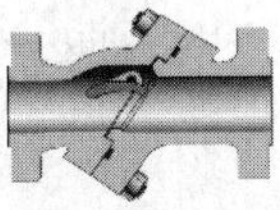

	Craft@Hrs	Unit	Material	Labor	Total
1/2" bronze check valves					
125 lb, threaded, swing	P6@.210	Ea	15.50	11.00	26.50
125 lb, soldered, swing	P6@.200	Ea	15.20	10.50	25.70
125 lb, threaded, vertical lift check	P6@.210	Ea	76.80	11.00	87.80
150 lb, threaded, swing, bronze disk	P6@.210	Ea	51.50	11.00	62.50
200 lb, threaded, swing, bronze disk	P6@.210	Ea	101.00	11.00	112.00
3/4" bronze check valves					
125 lb, threaded, swing	P6@.250	Ea	22.20	13.10	35.30
125 lb, soldered, swing	P6@.240	Ea	21.20	12.60	33.80
125 lb, threaded, swing, vertical check	P6@.250	Ea	105.00	13.10	118.10
150 lb, threaded, swing, bronze disk	P6@.250	Ea	64.30	13.10	77.40
200 lb, threaded, swing, bronze disk	P6@.250	Ea	120.00	13.10	133.10

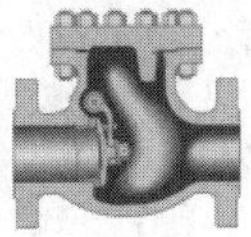

	Craft@Hrs	Unit	Material	Labor	Total
1" bronze check valves					
125 lb, threaded, swing	P6@.300	Ea	29.40	15.70	45.10
125 lb, soldered, swing	P6@.290	Ea	28.30	15.20	43.50
125 lb, threaded, swing, vertical check	P6@.300	Ea	133.00	15.70	148.70
150 lb, threaded, swing, bronze disk	P6@.300	Ea	87.20	15.70	102.90
200 lb, threaded, swing, bronze disk	P6@.300	Ea	186.00	15.70	201.70
1-1/2" bronze check valves					
125 lb, threaded, swing	P6@.450	Ea	57.60	23.60	81.20
125 lb, soldered, swing	P6@.440	Ea	56.30	23.10	79.40
125 lb, threaded, swing, vertical check	P6@.450	Ea	222.00	23.60	245.60
150 lb, threaded, swing, swing, bronze disk	P6@.450	Ea	152.00	23.60	175.60
200 lb, threaded, swing, bronze disk	P6@.450	Ea	299.00	23.60	322.60
2" bronze check valves					
125 lb, threaded, swing	P6@.500	Ea	96.40	26.20	122.60
125 lb, soldered, swing	P6@.480	Ea	94.40	25.10	119.50
125 lb, threaded, vertical check	P6@.500	Ea	329.00	26.20	355.20
150 lb, threaded, swing, bronze disk	P6@.500	Ea	221.00	26.20	247.20
200 lb, threaded, swing, bronze disk	P6@.500	Ea	421.00	26.20	447.20
2-1/2" flanged iron body check valve					
Swing check, bronze trim, 125 psi steam	MI@.600	Ea	191.00	33.20	224.20
Swing check, iron trim, 125 psi steam	MI@.600	Ea	268.00	33.20	301.20
Swing check, bronze trim, 250 psi steam	MI@.750	Ea	583.00	41.60	624.60
3" flanged iron body check valve					
Swing check, bronze trim, 125 psi steam	MI@.750	Ea	232.00	41.60	273.60
Swing check, iron trim, 125 psi steam	MI@.750	Ea	369.00	41.60	410.60
Swing check, bronze trim, 250 psi steam	MI@1.25	Ea	724.00	69.30	793.30

	Craft@Hrs	Unit	Material	Labor	Total
4" flanged iron body check valve					
Swing check, bronze trim, 125 psi steam	MI@1.35	Ea	373.00	74.80	447.80
Swing check, iron trim, 125 psi steam	MI@1.35	Ea	610.00	74.80	684.80
Swing check, bronze trim, 250 psi steam	MI@1.85	Ea	921.00	102.00	1,023.00
6" flanged iron body check valve					
Swing check, bronze trim, 125 psi steam	MI@2.50	Ea	606.00	139.00	745.00
Swing check, iron trim, 125 psi steam	MI@2.50	Ea	969.00	139.00	1,108.00
Swing check, bronze trim, 250 psi steam	MI@3.00	Ea	1,720.00	166.00	1,886.00
8" flanged iron body check valve					
Swing check, bronze trim, 125 psi steam	MI@3.00	Ea	1,120.00	166.00	1,286.00
Swing check, iron trim, 125 psi steam	MI@3.00	Ea	1,760.00	166.00	1,926.00
10" flanged iron body check valve					
Swing check, bronze trim, 125 psi steam	MI@4.00	Ea	2,280.00	222.00	2,502.00
Swing check, iron trim, 125 psi steam	MI@4.00	Ea	3,670.00	222.00	3,892.00
12" flanged iron body check valve					
Swing check, bronze trim, 125 psi steam	MI@4.50	Ea	3,010.00	249.00	3,259.00
Swing check, iron trim, 125 psi steam	MI@4.50	Ea	4,780.00	249.00	5,029.00

Miscellaneous Valves and Regulators For water and steam applications, complies with American Society of Mechanicals Engineers Standard B16, Manufacturers Standardization Society, Instrumentation Society of America standards.

	Craft@Hrs	Unit	Material	Labor	Total
Angle valves, bronze, 150 lb, threaded, Teflon disk					
1/2" valve	P6@.210	Ea	75.20	11.00	86.20
3/4" valve	P6@.250	Ea	103.00	13.10	116.10
1" valve	P6@.300	Ea	148.00	15.70	163.70
1-1/4" valve	P6@.400	Ea	191.00	21.00	212.00
1-1/2" valve	P6@.450	Ea	373.00	23.60	396.60
Lavatory supply valve with hand wheel shutoff, flexible compression connection tube with length as 1/2" angle or straight stops					
12" tube	P6@.294	Ea	27.80	15.40	43.20
15" tube	P6@.294	Ea	29.50	15.40	44.90
20" tube	P6@.473	Ea	35.00	24.80	59.80
Gas stops, lever handle					
1/2" stop	P6@.210	Ea	12.70	11.00	23.70
3/4" stop	P6@.250	Ea	16.80	13.10	29.90
1" stop	P6@.300	Ea	26.10	15.70	41.80
1-1/4" stop	P6@.450	Ea	39.20	23.60	62.80
1-1/2" stop	P6@.500	Ea	68.10	26.20	94.30
2" stop	P6@.750	Ea	106.00	39.30	145.30
Hose bibbs, threaded					
3/4", brass	P6@.350	Ea	6.26	18.30	24.56
Backflow preventers reduced pressure					
3/4", threaded, bronze, with 2 gate valves	P6@1.00	Ea	292.00	52.40	344.40
1", threaded, bronze, with 2 gate valves	P6@1.25	Ea	352.00	65.50	417.50
2", threaded, with 2 gate valves	P6@2.13	Ea	519.00	112.00	631.00
2-1/2", with 2 gate valves, flanged, iron body	MI@2.00	Ea	2,650.00	111.00	2,761.00
3", with 2 gate valves, flanged, iron body	MI@3.00	Ea	3,340.00	166.00	3,506.00
4", with 2 gate valves, flanged, iron body	MI@4.50	Ea	3,990.00	249.00	4,239.00
6", without gate valves, flanged, iron body	MI@8.00	Ea	6,530.00	443.00	6,973.00
6", with 2 gate valves, flanged, iron body	MI@9.00	Ea	7,570.00	499.00	8,069.00
8", without gate valves, flanged, iron body	MI@11.5	Ea	11,300.00	637.00	11,937.00
8", with 2 gate valves, flanged, iron body	MI@12.5	Ea	16,500.00	693.00	17,193.00
Ball valves, bronze, 150 lb, threaded, Teflon seat					
1/2" valve	P6@.210	Ea	11.40	11.00	22.40
3/4" valve	P6@.250	Ea	16.80	13.10	29.90
1" valve	P6@.300	Ea	23.80	15.70	39.50

	Craft@Hrs	Unit	Material	Labor	Total
1-1/4" valve	P6@.400	Ea	41.10	21.00	62.10
1-1/2" valve	P6@.450	Ea	50.00	23.60	73.60
2" valve	P6@.500	Ea	67.50	26.20	93.70
2-1/2" valve	MI@.750	Ea	127.00	41.60	168.60
3" valve	MI@.950	Ea	176.00	52.60	228.60
Hose gate valves, with cap, 200 lb					
2-1/2", non-rising stem	P6@1.00	Ea	111.00	52.40	163.40
Pressure regulator valves, bronze, 300 lb threaded, 25 to 75 PSI, with "Y" strainer					
3/4" valve	P6@.250	Ea	153.00	13.10	166.10
1" valve	P6@.300	Ea	203.00	15.70	218.70
1-1/4" valve	P6@.400	Ea	314.00	21.00	335.00
1-1/2" valve	P6@.450	Ea	482.00	23.60	505.60
2" valve	P6@.500	Ea	611.00	26.20	637.20
2-1/2" valve	P6@.750	Ea	1,190.00	39.30	1,229.30
3" valve	P6@.950	Ea	1,390.00	49.80	1,439.80
Water control valves, threaded, 3-way with actuator					
2-1/2", CV 54	MI@.750	Ea	2,240.00	41.60	2,281.60
3", CV 80	MI@.950	Ea	2,670.00	52.60	2,722.60
4", CV 157	MI@1.30	Ea	5,120.00	72.00	5,192.00

Closed Cell Elastomeric Pipe Insulation Semi-split, non-self-sealing, thickness as shown, by nominal pipe diameter. R factor equals 3.58 at 220 degrees F. Make additional allowances for scaffolding if required. Also see fittings, flanges and valves at the end of this section. For more detailed coverage of pipe insulation, see *National Plumbing & HVAC Estimator*, http://CraftsmanSiteLicense.com

	Craft@Hrs	Unit	Material	Labor	Total
1/4" pipe	P6@.039	LF	.23	2.04	2.27
3/8" pipe	P6@.039	LF	.24	2.04	2.28
1/2" pipe	P6@.039	LF	.17	2.04	2.21
3/4" pipe	P6@.039	LF	.21	2.04	2.25
1" pipe	P6@.042	LF	.35	2.20	2.55
1-1/4" pipe	P6@.042	LF	.40	2.20	2.60
1-1/2" pipe	P6@.042	LF	.58	2.20	2.78
2" pipe	P6@.046	LF	.81	2.41	3.22
2-1/2", 3/8" thick	P6@.056	LF	1.58	2.93	4.51
2-1/2", 1/2" thick	P6@.056	LF	2.13	2.93	5.06
2-1/2", 3/4" thick	P6@.056	LF	2.76	2.93	5.69
3", 3/8" thick	P6@.062	LF	1.65	3.25	4.90
3", 1/2" thick	P6@.062	LF	2.40	3.25	5.65
3", 3/4" thick	P6@.062	LF	3.12	3.25	6.37
4", 3/8" thick	P6@.068	LF	2.25	3.56	5.81
4", 1/2" thick	P6@.068	LF	2.82	3.56	6.38
4", 3/4" thick	P6@.068	LF	3.66	3.56	7.22
Add for self-sealing	—	%	75.0	—	—

Additional cost for insulating pipe fittings and flanges:

For each fitting or flange, add the cost of insulating 3 LF of pipe of the same size.

Additional cost for insulating valves: Valve body only. Add the cost of insulating 5 LF of pipe of the same size.

Body and bonnet or yoke valves. Add the cost of insulating 10 LF of pipe of the same size.

Fiberglass pipe insulation with AP-T Plus (all purpose self-sealing) jacket By nominal pipe diameter. R factor equals 2.56 at 300 degrees F. Add the cost of scaffolding, if required. Also see fittings, flanges and valves at the end of the previous section. Available in 3-foot lengths, price is per linear foot.

	Craft@Hrs	Unit	Material	Labor	Total
1/2" diameter pipe					
1/2" thick insulation	P6@.038	LF	2.46	1.99	4.45
1" thick insulation	P6@.038	LF	2.93	1.99	4.92
1-1/2" thick insulation	P6@.040	LF	5.87	2.10	7.97

	Craft@Hrs	Unit	Material	Labor	Total
3/4" diameter pipe					
1/2" thick insulation	P6@.038	LF	2.72	1.99	4.71
1" thick insulation	P6@.038	LF	3.35	1.99	5.34
1-1/2" thick insulation	P6@.040	LF	6.19	2.10	8.29
1" diameter pipe					
1/2" thick insulation	P6@.040	LF	2.86	2.10	4.96
1" thick insulation	P6@.040	LF	2.93	2.10	5.03
1-1/2" thick insulation	P6@.042	LF	6.50	2.20	8.70
1-1/4" diameter pipe					
1/2" thick insulation	P6@.040	LF	3.87	2.10	5.97
1" thick insulation	P6@.040	LF	3.91	2.10	6.01
1-1/2" thick insulation	P6@.042	LF	6.98	2.20	9.18
1-1/2" diameter pipe					
1/2" thick insulation	P6@.042	LF	3.38	2.20	5.58
1" thick insulation	P6@.042	LF	4.40	2.20	6.60
1-1/2" thick insulation	P6@.044	LF	7.53	2.31	9.84
2" diameter pipe					
1/2" thick insulation	P6@.044	LF	3.64	2.31	5.95
1" thick insulation	P6@.044	LF	5.01	2.31	7.32
1-1/2" thick insulation	P6@.046	LF	8.07	2.41	10.48

Meters, Gauges and Indicators

	Craft@Hrs	Unit	Material	Labor	Total
Water meters					
Disc type, 1-1/2"	P6@1.00	Ea	215.00	52.40	267.40
Turbine type, 1-1/2"	P6@1.00	Ea	325.00	52.40	377.40
Displacement type, AWWA C7000, 1"	P6@.941	Ea	331.00	49.30	380.30
Displacement type, AWWA C7000, 1-1/2"	P6@1.23	Ea	1,150.00	64.40	1,214.40
Displacement type, AWWA C7000, 2"	P6@1.57	Ea	1,720.00	82.30	1,802.30
Curb stop and waste valve, 1"	P6@1.00	Ea	121.00	52.40	173.40
Thermoflow indicators, soldered					
1-1/4" indicator	M5@2.01	Ea	443.00	104.00	547.00
2" indicator	M5@2.01	Ea	538.00	104.00	642.00
2-1/2" indicator	MI@1.91	Ea	786.00	106.00	892.00
Cast steel steam meters, in-line, flanged, 300 PSI					
1" pipe, threaded	M5@1.20	Ea	4,480.00	62.20	4,542.20
2" pipe	MI@1.14	Ea	5,090.00	63.20	5,153.20
3" pipe	MI@2.31	Ea	5,660.00	128.00	5,788.00
4" pipe	MI@2.71	Ea	6,280.00	150.00	6,430.00
Cast steel by-pass steam meters, 2", by line pipe size					
6" line	MI@16.7	Ea	10,800.00	925.00	11,725.00
8" line	MI@17.7	Ea	11,200.00	981.00	12,181.00
10" line	MI@18.5	Ea	11,800.00	1,020.00	12,820.00
12" line	MI@19.7	Ea	12,100.00	1,090.00	13,190.00
14" line	MI@21.4	Ea	12,800.00	1,190.00	13,990.00
16" line	MI@22.2	Ea	13,300.00	1,230.00	14,530.00
Add for steam meter pressure-compensated counter	—	Ea	1,850.00	—	1,850.00
Add for contactor used with dial counter	—	Ea	859.00	—	859.00
Add for wall or panel-mounted remote totalizer with contactor	—	Ea	1,420.00	—	1,420.00
Add for direct reading pressure gauge	M5@.250	Ea	104.00	13.00	117.00
Add for direct reading thermometer, stainless steel case, with trim, 2% accuracy					
3" dial	M5@.250	Ea	80.30	13.00	93.30

	Craft@Hrs	Unit	Material	Labor	Total
Plumbing Specialties					
Access doors for plumbing, primer coated steel 14 gauge door, 18 gauge frame, with cam lock, for masonry, drywall, tile, wall or ceiling. L&L Louvers					
Standard, wall or ceiling					
8" x 8"	SM@.500	Ea	29.80	30.30	60.10
12" x 12"	SM@.500	Ea	32.00	30.30	62.30
14" x 14"	SM@.500	Ea	37.70	30.30	68.00
16" x 16"	SM@.500	Ea	41.00	30.30	71.30
18" x 18"	SM@.500	Ea	46.90	30.30	77.20
22" x 22"	SM@.500	Ea	62.80	30.30	93.10
22" x 30"	SM@.500	Ea	80.20	30.30	110.50
24" x 24"	SM@.500	Ea	66.20	30.30	96.50
24" x 36"	SM@.500	Ea	96.10	30.30	126.40
30" x 30"	SM@.500	Ea	130.00	30.30	160.30
Add for cylinder lock	—	Ea	17.20	—	17.20
Add for louvers	—	%	150.0	—	—
Add for fire rating, non-insulated	—	%	400.0	—	—
Add for fire rating and insulated	—	%	500.0	—	—
Add for stainless steel, 304-2B	—	%	300.0	—	—
Cleanouts For drainage piping. A cleanout may be required: at the end of each waste line, or where a main building drain exits the building, or at regular 100' intervals for straight runs longer than 100', or at the base of soil or waste stacks, or where a 90-degree change in direction of a main building drain takes place. Consult your plumbing code for the regulations that apply to your area.					
Finished grade end cleanouts (Malcolm) with Neo-Loc & Dura-Coated cast iron body					
2" pipe, 4-1/8" round top	P6@.500	Ea	107.00	26.20	133.20
3" pipe, 5-1/8" round top	P6@.500	Ea	144.00	26.20	170.20
4" pipe, 6-1/8" round top	P6@.500	Ea	153.00	26.20	179.20
Cast iron in-line cleanouts (Barrett). Make additional allowances for access doors					
2" pipe	P6@.350	Ea	40.00	18.30	58.30
4" pipe	P6@.400	Ea	75.10	21.00	96.10
6" pipe	P6@.400	Ea	265.00	21.00	286.00
Cleanout access cover accessories					
Round polished bronze cover	—	Ea	22.20	—	22.20
Square chrome plated cover	—	Ea	201.00	—	201.00
Square bronze hinged cover box	—	Ea	144.00	—	144.00
Floor drains, body and grate only, add rough-in					
3" x 2" plastic grate and body	P6@.250	Ea	17.20	13.10	30.30
5" x 3" plastic grate and body	P6@.250	Ea	24.30	13.10	37.40
3" x 2" cast iron body, nickel-bronze grate	P6@.500	Ea	67.10	26.20	93.30
5" x 3" cast iron body, nickel-bronze grate	P6@.500	Ea	77.00	26.20	103.20
6" x 4" cast iron body, nickel-bronze grate	P6@.500	Ea	89.40	26.20	115.60
Add for a sediment bucket	—	Ea	12.90	—	12.90
Add for plastic backwater valve	—	Ea	44.80	—	44.80
Add for cast iron backwater valve	—	Ea	376.00	—	376.00
Add for trap seal primer fitting	—	Ea	9.10	—	9.10
Drain, general use, medium duty, PVC plastic, 3" or 4" pipe					
3" x 4", stainless steel strainer	P6@1.16	Ea	12.50	60.80	73.30
3" x 4", brass strainer	P6@1.32	Ea	30.80	69.20	100.00
4" with 5" brass strainer & spigot outlet	P6@1.55	Ea	57.70	81.20	138.90
Roof drains, cast iron mushroom strainer, bottom outlet					
2" to 4" drain	P6@1.75	Ea	282.00	91.70	373.70
5" or 6" drain	P6@1.98	Ea	394.00	104.00	498.00
8" drain	P6@2.36	Ea	519.00	124.00	643.00

	Craft@Hrs	Unit	Material	Labor	Total
Roof (jack) flashing, round					
4" jack	SM@.311	Ea	10.60	18.90	29.50
6" jack	SM@.416	Ea	11.50	25.20	36.70
8" jack	SM@.516	Ea	16.00	31.30	47.30

Plumbing Equipment Valves, supports, vents, gas or electric hookup and related equipment are not included except as noted.

Water heaters, commercial, gas fired 3-year limited warranty. Set in place only. Make additional allowances for pipe, circulating pump, gas and flue connections.

	Craft@Hrs	Unit	Material	Labor	Total
Medium duty					
75 gallon, 75 MBtu, low NOx	P6@2.00	Ea	1,990.00	105.00	2,095.00
75 gallon, 75 MBtu, ultra low NOx	P6@2.25	Ea	2,110.00	118.00	2,228.00
98 gallon, 75 MBtu, ultra low NOx	P6@2.50	Ea	2,620.00	131.00	2,751.00
100 gallon, 80 MBtu,	P6@2.50	Ea	2,560.00	131.00	2,691.00
Heavy duty					
37 gallon, 200 MBtu, low NOx	P6@2.00	Ea	7,330.00	105.00	7,435.00
65 gallon, 360 MBtu	P6@2.00	Ea	6,790.00	105.00	6,895.00
65 gallon, 400 MBtu	P6@2.00	Ea	7,570.00	105.00	7,675.00
72 gallon, 300 MBtu	P6@2.25	Ea	6,130.00	118.00	6,248.00
80 gallon, 130 MBtu, ultra-low NOx	P6@2.25	Ea	6,280.00	118.00	6,398.00
80 gallon, 160 MBtu, ultra-low NOx	P6@2.25	Ea	7,300.00	118.00	7,418.00
80 gallon, 200 MBtu, ultra-low NOx	P6@2.25	Ea	6,960.00	118.00	7,078.00
80 gallon, 300 MBtu, ultra-low NOx	P6@2.25	Ea	8,950.00	118.00	9,068.00
82 gallon, 156 MBtu, ultra-low NOx	P6@2.25	Ea	5,550.00	118.00	5,668.00
85 gallon, 300 MBtu	P6@2.25	Ea	6,500.00	118.00	6,618.00
100 gallon, 200 MBtu, ultra-low NOx	P6@2.50	Ea	4,450.00	131.00	4,581.00
100 gallon, 250 MBtu	P6@2.50	Ea	5,770.00	131.00	5,901.00
100 gallon, 270 MBtu	P6@2.50	Ea	5,940.00	131.00	6,071.00
100 gallon, 400 MBtu	P6@2.50	Ea	8,290.00	131.00	8,421.00
100 gallon, 400 MBtu, low NOx	P6@2.50	Ea	8,600.00	131.00	8,731.00
Add for ASME rating	—	%	10.0	—	—
Add for power vent kit	P6@2.00	Ea	818.00	105.00	923.00
Add for duplex equal flow manifold kit	—	Ea	561.00	—	561.00
Add for triplex equal flow manifold kit	—	Ea	1,110.00	—	1,110.00
Add for propane fired units, any of above	—	Ea	144.00	—	144.00
Commercial tankless condensing water heater, 9.5 GPM					
Indoor	P6@2.50	Ea	1,570.00	131.00	1,701.00
Outdoor	P6@4.15	Ea	1,590.00	217.00	1,807.00

Water heaters, commercial, electric 208/240 volts, with surface-mounted thermostat, Rheem. Set in place only. Make additional allowances for pipe, circulating pump, and electrical connections.

	Craft@Hrs	Unit	Material	Labor	Total
85 gallons, 12 kW, light duty, non-metallic	P6@1.75	Ea	2,550.00	91.70	2,641.70
105 gallons, 12 kW, light duty, non-metallic	P6@2.00	Ea	3,470.00	105.00	3,575.00
85 gallons, 18 kW, 3-ph, heavy duty, immersion stat	P6@1.75	Ea	4,580.00	91.70	4,671.70
120 gallons, 24 kW, 3-ph, heavy duty	P6@3.00	Ea	5,230.00	157.00	5,387.00
120 gallons, 24 kW, 3-ph, heavy duty, immersion stat	P6@3.00	Ea	6,170.00	157.00	6,327.00

Water heater stands Installed at same time as water heater. Raises flame elements 18" off floor. Secures to wall with seismic clips.

	Craft@Hrs	Unit	Material	Labor	Total
80 gallon capacity	P6@.250	Ea	41.60	13.10	54.70
100 gallon capacity	P6@.250	Ea	88.50	13.10	101.60
Fully enclosed, 80 gallon capacity	P6@.500	Ea	123.00	26.20	149.20

Water heater safety pans

	Craft@Hrs	Unit	Material	Labor	Total
1" side outlet drain, aluminum, installed at same time as water heater					
22" diameter	—	Ea	19.20	—	19.20
26" diameter	—	Ea	23.30	—	23.30
30" diameter	—	Ea	30.70	—	30.70
Tankless water heater drain pan	—	Ea	59.10	—	64.80
Subtract for polyethylene pan	—	%	–50.0	—	—

	Craft@Hrs	Unit	Material	Labor	Total
1" bottom outlet drain, 16 gauge steel, installed at same time as water heater. Piping not included.					
16" diameter	—	Ea	17.70	—	17.70
19" diameter	—	Ea	22.50	—	22.50
22" diameter	—	Ea	26.90	—	26.90
24" diameter	—	Ea	29.80	—	29.80
26-1/2" diameter	—	Ea	32.60	—	32.60
Water heater earthquake restraints State approved, installed at the same time as water heater					
Up to 52 gal heater, double strap	P6@.250	Ea	18.20	13.10	31.30
Up to 100 gal heater, double strap	P6@.250	Ea	20.30	13.10	33.40
Freestanding restraint system – 75 gal capacity	P6@.250	Ea	202.00	13.10	215.10
Freestanding restraint system – 100 gal capacity	P6@.250	Ea	218.00	13.10	231.10
Wall-mount platform with restraints – 75 gal capacity	P6@.500	Ea	194.00	26.20	220.20
Wall-mount platform with restraints – 100 gal capacity	P6@.500	Ea	215.00	26.20	241.20
Water heater leak detection system Auto shutoff when leak detected. Manual override. 110VAC with battery backup					
FloodStop leak detection system	P6@.250	Ea	257.00	13.10	270.10
Water heater connection assembly Includes typical pipe, fittings, valves, gages, and hangers					
Copper pipe connection, 3/4" supply	P6@2.25	Ea	187.00	118.00	305.00
Copper pipe connection, 1" supply	P6@2.75	Ea	332.00	144.00	476.00
Copper pipe connection, 1-1/4" supply	P6@3.50	Ea	408.00	183.00	591.00
Copper pipe connection, 1-1/2" supply	P6@3.75	Ea	421.00	196.00	617.00
Copper pipe connection, 2" supply	P6@4.50	Ea	451.00	236.00	687.00
Copper pipe connection, 2-1/2" supply	P6@5.75	Ea	940.00	301.00	1,241.00
Copper pipe connection, 3" supply	P6@6.50	Ea	1,450.00	341.00	1,791.00
Carbon steel gas pipe connection, 3/4"	P6@1.40	Ea	96.50	73.30	169.80
Carbon steel gas pipe connection, 1"	P6@1.50	Ea	125.00	78.60	203.60
Carbon steel gas pipe connection, 1-1/2"	P6@2.00	Ea	184.00	105.00	289.00
Double wall vent pipe connection, 4"	P6@1.40	Ea	127.00	73.30	200.30
Instantaneous water heaters, electric Maximum operating pressure of 150 PSI. Includes plumbing hookup only. Add for electrical work. 1/2" compression fittings used except where noted.					
120/208/240 volt single point for point-of-use handwashing. 33-degree F temperature rise at 1/2 GPM. Includes 3/8" compression fittings.					
2.4/3.0 kW unit	P6@1.00	Ea	618.00	52.40	670.40
208/240 volt flow controlled for kitchen, bar sink and dual lavatory sinks. 38-degree F temperature rise at 1.0 GPM.					
8.3 kW unit	P6@1.00	Ea	430.00	52.40	482.40
240/277 volt thermostatic for applications where accurate temperature control is required. May be used in combination with other water heating units. 41-degree F temperature rise at 1.0 GPM.					
6.0 kW unit	P6@1.00	Ea	551.00	52.40	603.40
240 volt twin heating module for residential showers, mop sinks, industrial processes, campgrounds and resort cabins. May be used in combination with other water heating units. 51-degree F temperature rise at 2.0 GPM.					
15.0 kW unit	P6@1.00	Ea	802.00	52.40	854.40
277 volt high capacity instantaneous water heater. May be used in combination with other water heating units. 35-degree F temperature rise at 3.5 GPM.					
18.0 kW unit	P6@1.00	Ea	1,770.00	52.40	1,822.40
240 volt high purity for microchip manufacturing, pharmaceutical production, ultrasonic cleaning and batch chemical mixing. Maintains water purity up to 18 MEG OHM quality. 38-degree F temperature rise at 1.0 GPM.					
5.5 kW unit	P6@1.00	Ea	1,050.00	52.40	1,102.40

	Craft@Hrs	Unit	Material	Labor	Total
Solar Water Heating Systems					
Solar collector panels, no piping included					
Typical 24 SF panel	P6@.747	Ea	426.00	39.10	465.10
Supports for solar panels, per panel	P6@2.25	Ea	45.60	118.00	163.60
Control panel for solar heating system	P6@1.56	Ea	158.00	81.70	239.70
Solar collector system pumps, no wiring or piping included					
5.4 GPM, 7.9' head	P6@1.89	Ea	279.00	99.00	378.00
10.5 GPM, 11.6' head or 21.6 GPM, 8.5' head	P6@2.25	Ea	506.00	118.00	624.00
12.6 GPM, 20.5' head or 22.5 GPM, 13.3' head	P6@3.26	Ea	777.00	171.00	948.00
46.5 GPM, 13.7' head	P6@4.59	Ea	117.00	240.00	357.00
60.9 GPM, 21.0' head	P6@5.25	Ea	1,320.00	275.00	1,595.00
Solar hot water storage tanks, no piping and no pad included					
40 gallon, horizontal	P6@1.12	Ea	319.00	58.70	377.70
110 gallon, horizontal	P6@3.54	Ea	1,290.00	185.00	1,475.00
180 gallon, vertical	P6@5.43	Ea	2,030.00	284.00	2,314.00
650 gallon, horizontal	P6@5.84	Ea	3,110.00	306.00	3,416.00
1,250 gallon, horizontal	P6@5.84	Ea	4,590.00	306.00	4,896.00
1,500 gallon, vertical	P6@11.4	Ea	7,300.00	597.00	7,897.00
2,200 gallon, horizontal	P6@17.1	Ea	6,630.00	896.00	7,526.00
2,700 gallon, vertical	P6@14.9	Ea	7,530.00	781.00	8,311.00
Grease interceptors					
2" cast iron, 4 GPM, 8 lb capacity	P6@4.00	Ea	734.00	210.00	944.00
2" cast iron, 10 GPM, 20 lb capacity	P6@5.00	Ea	1,190.00	262.00	1,452.00
2" steel, 15 GPM, 30 lb capacity	P6@7.00	Ea	1,770.00	367.00	2,137.00
3" steel, 20 GPM, 40 lb capacity	P6@8.00	Ea	2,180.00	419.00	2,599.00
4" steel, 750 lb capacity, 48" x 84" x 60"	P6@16.0	Ea	6,620.00	838.00	7,458.00
4" steel, 1,250 lb capacity, 60" x 102" x 60	P6@16.0	Ea	7,760.00	838.00	8,598.00
Hair interceptors					
1-1/2" cast iron	P6@.650	Ea	248.00	34.10	282.10
1-1/2" nickel bronze	P6@.750	Ea	349.00	39.30	388.30

Sewage ejector packaged systems with vertical pumps, float switch controls, poly tank, cover and fittings, no electrical work or pipe connections included.

	Craft@Hrs	Unit	Material	Labor	Total
Simplex sewage ejector systems (single pump)					
1/2 HP, 2" line, 20" x 30" tank	P6@4.75	Ea	717.00	249.00	966.00
3/4 HP, 2" line, 24" x 36" tank	P6@4.75	Ea	1,810.00	249.00	2,059.00
1 HP, 3" line, 24" x 36" tank	P6@6.00	Ea	2,110.00	314.00	2,424.00
Duplex sewage ejector systems (two pumps), alternator not included					
1/2 HP, 2" line, 30" x 36" tank	P6@6.50	Ea	2,780.00	341.00	3,121.00
3/4 HP, 2" line, 30" x 36" tank	P6@6.50	Ea	3,610.00	341.00	3,951.00
1 HP, 3" line, 30" x 36" tank	P6@8.00	Ea	4,050.00	419.00	4,469.00
Duplex pump controls (alternator)	—	Ea	1,480.00	—	1,480.00
Sump pumps With float switch, no electrical work included					
Submersible type					
1/4 HP, 1-1/2" outlet, ABS plastic	P6@2.00	Ea	145.00	105.00	250.00
1/3 HP, 1-1/4" outlet, cast iron	P6@2.00	Ea	213.00	105.00	318.00
1/3 HP, 1-1/4" outlet, ABS plastic	P6@2.00	Ea	176.00	105.00	281.00
Upright type					
1/3 HP, 1-1/4" outlet, cast iron	P6@2.00	Ea	170.00	105.00	275.00
1/3 HP, 1-1/2" outlet, ABS plastic	P6@2.00	Ea	125.00	105.00	230.00

	Craft@Hrs	Unit	Material	Labor	Total
Hot water storage tanks Insulated, floor mounted, includes pipe connection					
80 gallons	P6@4.00	Ea	685.00	210.00	895.00
120 gallons	P6@4.50	Ea	1,050.00	236.00	1,286.00
200 gallons	P6@5.25	Ea	2,820.00	275.00	3,095.00
980 gallons	P6@20.0	Ea	9,700.00	1,050.00	10,750.00
1,230 gallons	P6@22.0	Ea	11,500.00	1,150.00	12,650.00
1,615 gallons	P6@26.0	Ea	16,000.00	1,360.00	17,360.00
Septic tanks Includes typical excavation and piping					
500 gallons, polyethylene	U2@15.2	Ea	857.00	740.00	1,597.00
1,000 gallons, fiberglass	U2@16.1	Ea	1,230.00	784.00	2,014.00
2,000 gallons, concrete	U2@17.0	Ea	1,630.00	827.00	2,457.00
5,000 gallons, concrete	U2@22.3	Ea	6,050.00	1,090.00	7,140.00
Water softeners Automatic two tank unit, 3/4" valve					
1.0 CF, 30,000 grain capacity	P6@3.59	Ea	398.00	188.00	586.00
2.0 CF, 60,000 grain capacity	P6@3.59	Ea	520.00	188.00	708.00
Water filters In-line, filters for taste, odor, chlorine and sediment to 20 microns, with by-pass assembly. Includes pipe connection.					
Housing, by-pass and carbon filter, complete	P6@2.50	Ea	205.00	131.00	336.00
Water filter housing only	P6@1.00	Ea	51.40	52.40	103.80
By-pass assembly only, 3/4" copper	P6@1.25	Ea	111.00	65.50	176.50
Carbon core cartridge, 20 microns	P6@.250	Ea	25.50	13.10	38.60
Ceramic disinfection and carbon cartridge	P6@.250	Ea	68.40	13.10	81.50
Lead, chlorine, taste and odor cartridge	P6@.250	Ea	51.40	13.10	64.50
Water sterilizers Ultraviolet, point-of-use water. Add the cost of electrical and pipe connections. In gallons per minute (GPM) of rated capacity. 2 GPM and larger units include light-emitting diode (LED).					
1/2 GPM point of use filter, 1/2" connection	P6@2.00	Ea	284.00	105.00	389.00
3/4 GPM point of use filter, 1/2" connection	P6@2.00	Ea	303.00	105.00	408.00
2 GPM, 1/2" connection	P6@2.50	Ea	336.00	131.00	467.00
2 GPM, with alarm, 1/2" connection	P6@2.50	Ea	436.00	131.00	567.00
2 GPM, with alarm and monitor, 1/2" connection	P6@3.00	Ea	647.00	157.00	804.00
5 GPM, 3/4" connection	P6@2.50	Ea	614.00	131.00	745.00
5 GPM, with alarm, 3/4" connection	P6@2.50	Ea	700.00	131.00	831.00
5 GPM, with alarm and monitor, 3/4" connection	P6@3.00	Ea	796.00	157.00	953.00
8 GPM, with alarm, 3/4" connection	P6@2.50	Ea	647.00	131.00	778.00
8 GPM, with alarm and monitor, 3/4" connection	P6@3.00	Ea	865.00	157.00	1,022.00
12 GPM, with alarm, 3/4" connection	P6@2.50	Ea	825.00	131.00	956.00
12 GPM, with alarm and monitor, 3/4" connection	P6@3.00	Ea	1,000.00	157.00	1,157.00
Reverse osmosis water filters Economy system. Add the cost of electrical and pipe connections. In gallons per day of rated capacity.					
12 gallons per day	P6@3.50	Ea	314.00	183.00	497.00
16 gallons per day	P6@3.50	Ea	336.00	183.00	519.00
30 gallons per day	P6@3.50	Ea	473.00	183.00	656.00
60 gallons per day	P6@3.50	Ea	524.00	183.00	707.00
100 gallons per day	P6@3.50	Ea	797.00	183.00	980.00

	Craft@Hrs	Unit	Material	Labor	Total

Rough-in Plumbing Assemblies Includes rough-ins for commercial, industrial and residential buildings. This section shows costs for typical rough-ins of drain, waste and vent (DWV) and water supply piping using either plastic or metal pipe and fittings. Plastic ABS or PVC DWV pipe can be combined with plastic "poly b" supply pipe for a complete residential rough-in assembly. Cast iron or copper drainage DWV pipe can be combined with copper supply pipe for a complete commercial rough-in assembly. (Check local plumbing and building codes to determine acceptable materials for above and below grade installations in your area.) Detailed estimates of the piping requirements for each type plumbing fixture rough-in were made using the Uniform Plumbing Code as a guideline. For scheduling purposes, estimate that a plumber and an apprentice can install rough-in piping for 3 to 4 plumbing fixtures in an 8-hour day. The same plumber and apprentice will install, connect and test 3 to 4 fixtures a day. When roughing-in less than 4 fixtures in a building, increase the rough-in cost 25% for each fixture less than 4. Add the cost of the fixture and final connection assembly (as shown in Fixtures and Final Connection Assemblies) to the rough-in assembly cost. Rule of Thumb: Use plastic drainage and supply pipe in economy residential applications. Use plastic drainage and copper supply in quality residential applications. Use cast iron or copper DWV drainage and copper supply pipe in quality commercial applications. In some jurisdictions, plastic drainage pipe is allowed below grade for commercial applications only. In residential applications, plastic drainage pipe may be allowed in above and below grade applications. The difference is the liability of the owner to the patrons of a public building vs. the liability of the owner of a private residence in case of fire. ABS pipe releases toxic gases when it burns.

Water closet rough-in

	Craft@Hrs	Unit	Material	Labor	Total
Floor mounted, tank type, rough-in includes 7' of 3", 8' of 1-1/2" DWV pipe and 8' of 1/2" supply pipe with typical fittings, hangers, and strapping					
Plastic DWV and PEX supply rough-in	P6@1.90	Ea	19.40	99.50	118.90
Plastic DWV and copper supply rough-in	P6@2.00	Ea	22.20	105.00	127.20
Cast iron and copper supply rough-in	P6@2.25	Ea	106.00	118.00	224.00
Copper DWV and copper supply rough-in	P6@2.25	Ea	162.00	118.00	280.00
Floor mounted flush valve type, rough-in includes 7' of 3", 8' of 1-1/2" DWV pipe and 8' of 1" supply pipe with typical fittings, hangers, and strapping					
Plastic DWV and PVC schedule 40 supply rough-in	P6@1.90	Ea	18.20	99.50	117.70
Plastic DWV and copper supply rough-in	P6@2.00	Ea	37.80	105.00	142.80
Cast iron and copper supply rough-in	P6@2.25	Ea	121.00	118.00	239.00
Copper DWV and copper supply rough-in	P6@2.25	Ea	162.00	118.00	280.00
Wall hung, tank type, rough-in includes 5' of 4", 8' of 1-1/2" DWV pipe and 8' of 1/2" supply pipe with typical fittings, hangers, and strapping					
Plastic DWV and PEX supply rough-in	P6@1.80	Ea	18.30	94.30	112.60
Plastic DWV and copper supply rough-in	P6@1.90	Ea	21.00	99.50	120.50
Cast iron and copper supply rough-in	P6@2.35	Ea	102.00	123.00	225.00
Copper DWV and copper supply rough-in	P6@2.35	Ea	183.00	123.00	306.00
Add for fixture carrier	P6@.750	Ea	320.00	39.30	359.30
Wall hung flush valve type, rough-in includes 5' of 4", 6' of 1-1/2" DWV pipe and 8' of 1" supply pipe with typical fittings, hangers, and strapping					
Plastic DWV and PVC schedule 40 supply rough-in	P6@1.70	Ea	16.00	89.10	105.10
Plastic DWV and copper supply rough-in	P6@1.00	Ea	35.50	52.40	87.90
Cast iron and copper supply rough-in	P6@1.95	Ea	106.00	102.00	208.00
Copper DWV and copper supply rough-in	P6@1.95	Ea	170.00	102.00	272.00
Add for fixture carrier	P6@.750	Ea	290.00	39.30	329.30

Urinal rough-in

	Craft@Hrs	Unit	Material	Labor	Total
Wall-hung urinal, rough-in includes 15' of DWV pipe and 8' of supply pipe with typical fittings, hangers and strapping					
Plastic DWV and supply rough-in	P6@2.00	Ea	10.10	105.00	115.10
Plastic DWV and copper supply rough-in	P6@2.10	Ea	20.00	110.00	130.00
Copper DWV and copper supply rough-in	P6@2.35	Ea	108.00	123.00	231.00
Add for fixture carrier	P6@.850	Ea	230.00	44.50	274.50

	Craft@Hrs	Unit	Material	Labor	Total
Floor-mounted urinal, rough-in includes 15' of DWV pipe and 8' of supply pipe with typical fittings, hangers and strapping					
Plastic DWV and supply rough-in	P6@2.15	Ea	10.10	113.00	123.10
Plastic DWV and copper supply rough-in	P6@2.25	Ea	20.00	118.00	138.00
Copper DWV and copper supply rough-in	P6@2.50	Ea	108.00	131.00	239.00
Lavatory rough-in					
Lavatory, rough-in includes 15' of 1-1/2" DWV pipe and 15' of 1/2" supply pipe with typical fittings, hangers and strapping					
Plastic DWV and PEX supply rough-in	P6@1.70	Ea	16.00	89.10	105.10
Plastic DWV and copper supply rough-in	P6@1.75	Ea	21.20	91.70	112.90
Copper DWV and copper supply rough-in	P6@1.90	Ea	109.00	99.50	208.50
Add for carrier	P6@.750	Ea	229.00	39.30	268.30
Bathtub and shower Rough-in includes 15' of 1-1/2" DWV pipe and 15' of 1/2" supply pipe with typical fittings, hangers, and strapping					
Plastic DWV and PEX supply rough-in	P6@1.95	Ea	16.00	102.00	118.00
Plastic DWV and copper supply rough-in	P6@2.10	Ea	21.20	110.00	131.20
Copper DWV and copper supply rough-in	P6@2.35	Ea	109.00	123.00	232.00
Kitchen sink Rough-in includes 15' of 1-1/2" DWV pipe and 15' of 1/2" supply pipe with typical, fittings, hangers and strapping					
Plastic DWV and PEX supply rough-in	P6@1.70	Ea	16.00	89.10	105.10
Plastic DWV and copper supply rough-in	P6@1.75	Ea	21.20	91.70	112.90
Copper DWV and copper supply rough-in	P6@1.90	Ea	109.00	99.50	208.50
Drinking fountain and water cooler Rough-in includes 15' of 1-1/2" DWV pipe and 10' of 1/2" supply pipe with typical, fittings, strapping and hangers					
Plastic DWV and PEX supply rough-in	P6@1.80	Ea	13.40	94.30	107.70
Plastic DWV and copper supply rough-in	P6@2.00	Ea	16.80	105.00	121.80
Copper DWV and copper supply rough-in	P6@2.20	Ea	105.00	115.00	220.00
Wash fountain Rough-in includes 20' of 1-1/2" DWV pipe and 20' of 1/2" supply pipe with typical fittings, hangers and strapping					
Plastic DWV and supply rough-in	P6@1.90	Ea	21.40	99.50	120.90
Plastic DWV and copper supply rough-in	P6@2.00	Ea	28.20	105.00	133.20
Copper DWV and copper supply rough-in	P6@2.10	Ea	146.00	110.00	256.00
Service sink Rough-in includes 15' of DWV pipe and 15' of supply pipe with typical fittings, hangers, and strapping					
Wall-hung slop sink					
Plastic DWV and supply rough-in	P6@2.25	Ea	16.00	118.00	134.00
Plastic DWV and copper supply rough-in	P6@2.35	Ea	21.20	123.00	144.20
Cast iron DWV and copper supply rough-in	P6@2.45	Ea	109.00	128.00	237.00
Floor-mounted mop sink					
Plastic DWV and supply rough-in	P6@2.35	Ea	16.00	123.00	139.00
Plastic DWV and copper supply rough-in	P6@2.45	Ea	21.20	128.00	149.20
Cast iron DWV and copper supply rough-in	P6@2.60	Ea	109.00	136.00	245.00
Emergency drench shower and eye wash station Rough-in includes a valved water supply with 15' of supply pipe, typical fittings and hangers. Add the cost of a floor drain if required. See section below.					
3/4" PVC schedule 40	P6@1.25	Ea	26.80	65.50	92.30
3/4" Copper pipe	P6@1.50	Ea	45.40	78.60	124.00
Surgeons' scrub sink Rough-in includes 7' of 2" and 8' of 1-1/2" DWV pipe and 15' of 3/4" supply pipe with typical fittings and hangers					
Plastic DWV and supply rough-in	P6@2.25	Ea	13.40	118.00	131.40
Plastic DWV and copper supply rough-in	P6@2.35	Ea	31.90	123.00	154.90
Cast iron DWV and copper supply rough-in	P6@2.75	Ea	113.00	144.00	257.00

	Craft@Hrs	Unit	Material	Labor	Total
Floor sink, floor drain Rough-in includes 15' of drain and 15' of vent pipe, P-trap, typical fittings and hangers. Does not include the actual floor drain unit.					
2" plastic DWV rough-in	P6@1.50	Ea	28.40	78.60	107.00
3" plastic DWV rough-in	P6@1.75	Ea	66.80	91.70	158.50
2" cast iron DWV rough-in	P6@2.00	Ea	194.00	105.00	299.00
3" cast iron DWV rough-in	P6@2.50	Ea	256.00	131.00	387.00
4" cast iron DWV rough-in	P6@2.50	Ea	331.00	131.00	462.00
Fixtures and final connection assemblies					
Fixture costs are based on good to better quality white fixtures of standard dimensions and include all trim and valves required by code. Add 30% for colored fixtures.					
Water closets					
Floor-mounted, tank type, elongated vitreous china bowl					
Water closet, trim and valves (add rough-in)	P6@2.10	Ea	272.00	110.00	382.00
Deduct for round bowl	—	Ea	−46.60	—	−46.60
Floor-mounted flush valve type, elongated vitreous china bowl					
Water closet, trim and valves (add rough-in)	P6@2.60	Ea	352.00	136.00	488.00
Floor-mounted flush valve type, elongated vitreous china bowl, meets ADA requirements (18" high)					
Water closet, trim and valves (add rough-in)	P6@2.60	Ea	417.00	136.00	553.00
Wall-hung, tank type, elongated vitreous china bowl, cast iron carrier					
Water closet, trim and valves (add rough-in)	P6@3.00	Ea	794.00	157.00	951.00
Deduct for round bowl	—	Ea	−91.80	—	−91.80
Wall-hung flush valve type elongated vitreous china bowl, cast iron carrier					
Water closet, trim and valves (add rough-in)	P6@3.55	Ea	562.00	186.00	748.00
Add for bed pan cleanser (flush valve and rim lugs)	P6@1.50	Ea	244.00	78.60	322.60
Urinals					
Wall-hung urinal, vitreous china, washout flush action, 3/4" top spud with hand operated flush valve/vacuum breaker					
Urinal, trim and valves (add rough-in)	P6@2.35	Ea	456.00	123.00	579.00
Add for fixture carrier	P6@1.25	Ea	130.00	65.50	195.50
Floor-mounted urinal, 18" wide, sloping front vitreous china, washout flush action, 3/4" top spud with hand operated flush valve/vacuum breaker					
Urinal, trim and valves (add rough-in)	P6@5.25	Ea	1,090.00	275.00	1,365.00
Water-conserving urinals, faucets and flush valves					
Wall-mounted urinal, ABS-structural plastic. Fit between studs framed at 16" on center.					
Add the cost of wall finishing and rough-in plumbing					
10 oz water per flush	P6@1.50	Ea	344.00	78.60	422.60
Battery-powered sensor faucet, 6 volt DC. Continuous discharge up to 10 seconds. Less than one quart per cycle.					
Standard spout	P6@1.50	Ea	458.00	78.60	536.60
Gooseneck spout	P6@1.50	Ea	502.00	78.60	580.60
AC-powered sensor faucet, 12 volt. Continuous discharge up to 10 seconds. Less than one quart per cycle					
Standard spout	P6@1.50	Ea	458.00	78.60	536.60
Gooseneck spout	P6@1.50	Ea	502.00	78.60	580.60
Battery-powered sensor flush valves, 6 volt DC, exposed. Light flushing after brief use and full flushing after extended use. Includes rough fittings					
Urinal flush valve	P6@2.00	Ea	412.00	105.00	517.00
Toilet flush valve, 1.6 or 3.5 gallons	P6@2.00	Ea	451.00	105.00	556.00

	Craft@Hrs	Unit	Material	Labor	Total
AC-powered sensor flush valves, 24 volt. Light flushing after brief use and full flushing after extended use. Includes rough fittings					
Urinal flush valve, exposed	P6@2.00	Ea	525.00	105.00	630.00
Urinal flush valve, concealed	P6@2.00	Ea	536.00	105.00	641.00
Toilet flush valve	P6@2.00	Ea	568.00	105.00	673.00
Lavatories					
Wall-hung vitreous china lavatory with single handle faucet and pop-up waste					
Lavatory, trim and valves (add rough-in)	P6@2.50	Ea	464.00	131.00	595.00
Add for wheelchair type (ADA standards)	—	Ea	213.00	—	213.00
Countertop-mounted vitreous china lavatory with single handle water and pop-up waste					
Lavatory, trim and valves (add rough-in)	P6@2.00	Ea	347.00	105.00	452.00
Countertop-mounted enameled steel lavatory with single handle water faucet and pop-up waste					
Lavatory, trim and valves (add rough-in)	P6@2.00	Ea	292.00	105.00	397.00
Bathtubs and Showers					
Recessed enameled steel tub with shower					
Tub, trim and valves (add rough-in)	P6@2.50	Ea	357.00	131.00	488.00
Recessed enameled cast iron tub with shower					
Tub, trim and valves (add rough-in)	P6@4.50	Ea	609.00	236.00	845.00
Acrylic one-piece tub and shower enclosure					
Enclosure, trim and valves (add rough-in)	P6@4.75	Ea	408.00	249.00	657.00
Acrylic three-piece tub and shower enclosure (renovation)					
Enclosure, trim and valves (add rough-in)	P6@5.75	Ea	1,190.00	301.00	1,491.00
Fiberglass one-piece tub and shower enclosure					
Enclosure, trim and valves (add rough-in)	P6@4.75	Ea	655.00	249.00	904.00
Fiberglass three-piece tub and shower enclosure					
Enclosure, trim and valves (add rough-in)	P6@5.75	Ea	1,060.00	301.00	1,361.00
Acrylic one-piece shower stall					
Shower stall, trim and valves (add rough-in)	P6@3.50	Ea	925.00	183.00	1,108.00
Add for larger stall	—	Ea	179.00	—	179.00
Acrylic three-piece shower stall (renovation)					
Shower stall, trim and valves (add rough-in)	P6@4.25	Ea	1,300.00	223.00	1,523.00
Add for larger stall	—	Ea	179.00	—	179.00
Fiberglass one-piece shower stall					
Shower stall, trim and valves (add rough-in)	P6@3.50	Ea	607.00	183.00	790.00
Add for larger stall	—	Ea	140.00	—	140.00
Add for corner entry	—	Ea	105.00	—	105.00
Fiberglass three-piece shower stall (renovation)					
Shower stall, trim and valves (add rough-in)	P6@4.25	Ea	779.00	223.00	1,002.00
Add for larger stall	—	Ea	193.00	—	193.00
Add for corner entry	—	Ea	142.00	—	142.00
Acrylic shower base					
Base, trim and valves (add rough-in)	P6@2.50	Ea	381.00	131.00	512.00
Add for larger base	—	Ea	20.10	—	20.10
Add for corner entry	—	Ea	20.10	—	20.10
Fiberglass shower base					
Base, trim and valves (add rough-in)	P6@2.50	Ea	428.00	131.00	559.00
Add for larger base	—	Ea	20.10	—	20.10
Add for corner entry	—	Ea	20.10	—	20.10

	Craft@Hrs	Unit	Material	Labor	Total
Tub and shower doors					
Three panel sliding tub doors	P6@.500	Ea	364.00	26.20	390.20
Three panel sliding shower doors	P6@.500	Ea	318.00	26.20	344.20
Two panel sliding shower doors	P6@.500	Ea	269.00	26.20	295.20
One panel swinging shower door	P6@.500	Ea	129.00	26.20	155.20
Kitchen sinks					
Single compartment kitchen sink, 20" long, 21" wide, 8" deep, self rimming, countertop mounted, stainless steel with single handle faucet and deck spray					
Sink, trim and valves (add rough-in)	P6@2.00	Ea	358.00	105.00	463.00
Double compartment kitchen sink, 32" long, 21" wide, 8" deep, self rimming, countertop mounted, stainless steel with single handle faucet and deck spray					
Sink, trim and valves (add rough-in)	P6@2.15	Ea	268.00	113.00	381.00
Drinking fountains and water coolers					
Wall hung drinking fountains, 10" wide, 10" high, non-electric, white vitreous china					
Wall hung fountain, and trim (add rough-in)	P6@2.00	Ea	463.00	105.00	568.00
Recessed drinking fountains, 14" wide, 26" high, non-electric, white vitreous china					
Recessed fountain, and trim (add rough-in)	P6@2.50	Ea	821.00	131.00	952.00
Semi-recessed water cooler, vitreous china, refrigerated (no electrical work included)					
Semi-recessed cooler, and trim (add rough-in)	P6@2.50	Ea	144.00	131.00	275.00
Add for fully recessed	P6@.750	Ea	106.00	39.30	145.30
Free-standing water cooler, refrigerated (no electrical work included)					
Wall hung water cooler, and trim (add rough-in)	P6@2.50	Ea	941.00	131.00	1,072.00
Wash fountains					
54" circular wash fountain, precast stone (terrazzo), with foot operated water spray control					
Wash fountain, trim and valves (add rough-in)	P6@3.65	Ea	3,040.00	191.00	3,231.00
Add for stainless steel in lieu of precast stone	—	Ea	703.00	—	703.00
54" semi-circular wash fountain, precast stone (terrazzo), with foot operated water spray control					
Wash fountain, trim and valves (add rough-in)	P6@3.65	Ea	2,760.00	191.00	2,951.00
Add for stainless steel in lieu of precast stone	—	Ea	495.00	—	495.00
36" circular wash fountain, precast stone (terrazzo), with foot operated water spray control					
Wash fountain, trim and valves (add rough-in)	P6@3.50	Ea	2,440.00	183.00	2,623.00
Add for stainless steel in lieu of precast stone	—	Ea	422.00	—	422.00
36" semi-circular wash fountain, precast stone, (terrazzo), with foot operated water spray control					
Wash fountain, trim and valves (add rough-in)	P6@3.50	Ea	2,230.00	183.00	2,413.00
Add for stainless steel in lieu of precast stone	—	Ea	279.00	—	279.00
Service sinks					
Wall hung enameled cast iron slop sink, with wall-mounted faucet, hose and P-trap standard					
Slop sink, trim and valves (add rough-in)	P6@3.30	Ea	876.00	173.00	1,049.00
Floor mounted mop sink, precast molded stone (terrazzo), with wall mounted faucet and hose					
Mop sink, 24" x 24", 6" curbs (add rough-in)	P6@2.60	Ea	487.00	136.00	623.00
Mop sink, 32" x 32", 6" curbs (add rough-in)	P6@2.60	Ea	524.00	136.00	660.00
Mop sink, 36" x 36", 6" curbs (add rough-in)	P6@2.60	Ea	572.00	136.00	708.00
Add for 12" curbs, 6" drop front & stainless steel caps	—	Ea	278.00	—	278.00
Drench shower and emergency eye wash stations					
Drench shower, plastic pipe and head, wall mounted	P6@2.00	Ea	195.00	105.00	300.00
Drench shower galvanized pipe, free standing	P6@2.50	Ea	421.00	131.00	552.00
Drench shower, emergency eyewash combination	P6@2.75	Ea	1,140.00	144.00	1,284.00
Emergency eyewash station	P6@2.00	Ea	456.00	105.00	561.00
Walk-thru station, 18 heads	P6@12.5	Ea	2,940.00	655.00	3,595.00

22 Plumbing

	Craft@Hrs	Unit	Material	Labor	Total
Surgeons' scrub sink					
Wall-hung wash sink, white enameled cast iron, 48" long, 18" deep, trough-type with 2 twin-handled faucets and two soap dishes					
Wash sink, trim and valves (add rough-in)	P6@2.50	Ea	1,230.00	131.00	1,361.00
Add for foot or knee pedal operation	P6@.500	Ea	144.00	26.20	170.20
Add for electronic infrared hands free operation	P6@.500	Ea	177.00	26.20	203.20
Add for stainless steel in lieu of enameled cast iron	—	Ea	214.00	—	214.00
Floor sinks					
12" square sink, cast iron top and body (add rough-in)	P6@1.00	Ea	217.00	52.40	269.40
Add for an acid-resistant finish to the sink	—	Ea	36.40	—	36.40
Sauna Room Commercial dry type, with insulated prefabricated 6' wide by 12' long by 8' high enclosure, with premounted cedar inner walls and ceiling and three-tier benches, roof vent, electric stone floor-mounted heater module with thermostat regulator, grouted stone floor, sanitary floor drain with cleanout, adjoining three-stall fiberglass shower stall with fixtures and drain.					
Commercial sauna enclosure module	—	Ea	7,060.00	—	7,060.00
Prep & sealing of floor	B9@8.00	Ea	434.00	264.00	698.00
Pouring of floor	B9@8.00	Ea	—	264.00	264.00
Tiling of floor	B1@8.00	Ea	868.00	271.00	1,139.00
Ceiling fabrication	B1@8.00	Ea	—	271.00	271.00
Running of vents	SW@8.00	Ea	217.00	337.00	554.00
Running of drain	P6@4.00	Ea	109.00	210.00	319.00
Electrical for heat and lighting	CE@4.00	Ea	163.00	242.00	405.00
Mounting of benches	B1@4.00	Ea	—	135.00	135.00
Installation of sealed portal	B1@4.00	Ea	271.00	135.00	406.00
Running of CW/HW piping and valves	P6@8.00	Ea	353.00	419.00	772.00
3-stall shower module installation and piping	P6@16.0	Ea	814.00	838.00	1,652.00
Subtotal	—	Ea	3,229.00	3,369.00	6,598.00
Grand Total (with Sauna Module)	—	Ea	10,289.00	3,369.00	13,658.00

23 HVAC

Gas-fired heating equipment No gas pipe or electric runs included

Unit heaters, gas fired, ceiling suspended, with flue and gas valve, propeller fan with aluminized heat exchanger, Modine PAE series

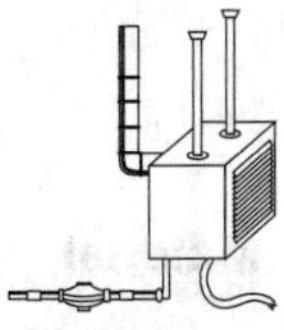

	Craft@Hrs	Unit	Material	Labor	Total
50 MBtu input	M5@4.75	Ea	1,050.00	246.00	1,296.00
75 MBtu input	M5@4.75	Ea	1,150.00	246.00	1,396.00
125 MBtu input	M5@5.25	Ea	1,440.00	272.00	1,712.00
175 MBtu input	M5@5.50	Ea	1,610.00	285.00	1,895.00
225 MBtu input	MI@6.75	Ea	1,840.00	374.00	2,214.00
300 MBtu input	MI@7.50	Ea	2,260.00	416.00	2,676.00
400 MBtu input	MI@8.75	Ea	3,010.00	485.00	3,495.00
Add for single stage intermittent ignition pilot	—	LS	238.00	—	238.00
Add for high efficiency units (PV series)	—	%	35.0	—	—
Add for stainless steel burner	—	%	20.0	—	—
Add for air blower style fan	—	%	10.0	—	—
Add for switch and thermostat	CE@1.00	Ea	64.50	60.40	124.90
Add for gas supply pipe connection	M5@1.75	Ea	102.00	90.80	192.80
Add for typical electric run, BX	E4@2.50	Ea	130.00	127.00	257.00

	Craft@Hrs	Unit	Material	Labor	Total
Furnaces, wall type, upflow, gas fired with gas valve, flue vent and electronic ignition					
35 MBtu input	M5@4.25	Ea	1,110.00	220.00	1,330.00
50 MBtu input	M5@4.25	Ea	1,240.00	220.00	1,460.00
65 MBtu input	M5@4.25	Ea	1,250.00	220.00	1,470.00
Add for gas supply pipe connection	M5@1.75	Ea	101.00	90.80	191.80
Add for power vent kit (direct sidewall vent)	M5@2.50	Ea	142.00	130.00	272.00
Add for thermostat	CE@1.00	Ea	57.00	60.40	117.40
Furnaces, non-condensing gas fired, multi-positional, mid-efficiency with gas valve, flue vent and electronic ignition					
40 MBtu input, 80% AFUE	M5@4.25	Ea	1,250.00	220.00	1,470.00
60 MBtu input, 80% AFUE	M5@4.25	Ea	1,390.00	220.00	1,610.00
80 MBtu input, 80% AFUE	M5@4.25	Ea	1,490.00	220.00	1,710.00
100 MBtu input, 80% AFUE	M5@4.50	Ea	1,460.00	233.00	1,693.00
120 MBtu input, 80% AFUE	M5@4.50	Ea	1,570.00	233.00	1,803.00
140 MBtu input, 80% AFUE	M5@4.50	Ea	1,740.00	233.00	1,973.00
Add for gas supply pipe connection	M5@1.75	Ea	101.00	90.80	191.80
Add for power vent kit (direct sidewall vent)	M5@2.50	Ea	137.00	130.00	267.00
Add for thermostat	CE@1.00	Ea	57.00	60.40	117.40
Furnaces, condensing gas fired, upflow, high-efficiency with gas valve, flue vent and electronic ignition					
50 MBtu input, 90% AFUE	M5@4.25	Ea	2,230.00	220.00	2,450.00
70 MBtu input, 90% AFUE	M5@4.25	Ea	2,510.00	220.00	2,730.00
90 MBtu input, 90% AFUE	M5@4.25	Ea	2,520.00	220.00	2,740.00
110 MBtu input, 90% AFUE	M5@4.50	Ea	2,720.00	233.00	2,953.00
130 MBtu input, 90% AFUE	M5@4.50	Ea	2,730.00	233.00	2,963.00
Add for gas supply pipe connection	M5@1.75	Ea	101.00	90.80	191.80
Add for power vent kit (direct sidewall vent)	M5@2.50	Ea	142.00	130.00	272.00
Air curtain, gas fired, ceiling suspended, includes flue, vent, and electrical ignition					
256 MBtu, 2,840 CFM	MI@7.50	Ea	2,500.00	416.00	2,916.00
290 MBtu, 4,740 CFM	MI@8.25	Ea	2,720.00	457.00	3,177.00
400 MBtu, 5,660 CFM	MI@9.75	Ea	3,010.00	540.00	3,550.00
525 MBtu, 7,580 CFM	MI@11.0	Ea	3,150.00	609.00	3,759.00
630 MBtu, 9,480 CFM	MI@12.5	Ea	3,520.00	693.00	4,213.00
850 MBtu, 11,400 CFM	MI@16.0	Ea	5,020.00	886.00	5,906.00
Add for gas supply pipe connection	M5@1.75	Ea	101.00	90.80	191.80
Electric Heat					
Air curtain electric heaters, wall mounted, includes electrical connection only					
37" long, 9.5 kW	H9@6.33	Ea	1,020.00	383.00	1,403.00
49" long, 12.5 kW	H9@8.05	Ea	1,460.00	487.00	1,947.00
61" long, 16.0 kW	H9@11.2	Ea	1,730.00	678.00	2,408.00
Baseboard electric heaters, with remote thermostat					
185 watts per LF	CE@.175	LF	34.30	10.60	44.90

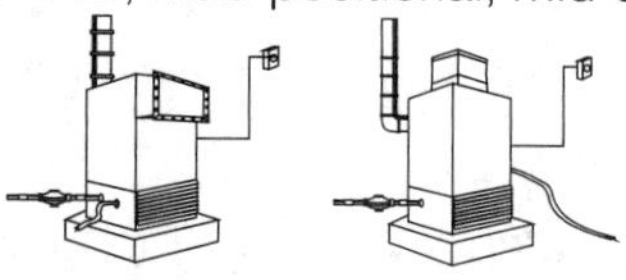

Hydronic hot water generators. U.S. Green Council and ASME "H" stamp certified to a rating of 95% AFUE (annual fuel usage efficiency) with EPA Tier II Nox emissions compliant burner, Kunkel safety valve, low-water cutoff, digital panel controls and automatic level controls, Parker Boiler 210-L series or equal. For commercial and light industrial applications. Equipment cost is for a 2-ton capacity forklift.

	Craft@Hrs	Unit	Material	Labor	Equipment	Total
4 BHP, 133 MBtu/Hr	M5@4.00	Ea	3,340.00	207.00	68.80	3,615.80
8 BHP, 263 MBtu/Hr	M5@4.00	Ea	4,450.00	207.00	68.80	4,725.80
12 BHP, 404 MBtu/Hr	M5@4.00	Ea	5,760.00	207.00	68.80	6,035.80
15 BHP, 514 MBtu/Hr	M5@5.00	Ea	8,710.00	259.00	85.90	9,054.90
19 BHP, 624 MBtu/Hr	M5@5.00	Ea	11,500.00	259.00	85.90	11,844.90
22 BHP, 724 MBtu/Hr	M5@6.00	Ea	11,900.00	311.00	103.00	12,314.00
29 BHP, 962 MBtu/Hr	M5@6.00	Ea	14,500.00	311.00	103.00	14,914.00
34 BHP, 1,125 MBtu/Hr	MI@8.00	Ea	16,100.00	443.00	91.70	16,634.70

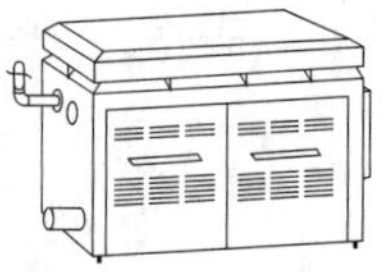

	Craft@Hrs	Unit	Material	Labor	Equipment	Total
40 BHP, 1,336 MBtu/Hr	MI@8.00	Ea	18,500.00	443.00	91.70	19,034.70
47 BHP, 1,571 MBtu/Hr	MI@9.00	Ea	19,100.00	499.00	103.00	19,702.00
53 BHP, 1,758 MBtu/Hr	MI@10.0	Ea	20,700.00	554.00	115.00	21,369.00
63 BHP, 2,100 MBtu/Hr	MI@12.0	Ea	21,500.00	665.00	138.00	22,303.00
89 BHP, 3,001 MBtu/Hr	MI@18.0	Ea	27,500.00	997.00	206.00	28,703.00
118 BHP, 4,001 MBtu/Hr	MI@22.0	Ea	28,500.00	1,220.00	252.00	29,972.00
LEED certification (Leadership in Energy and Environmental Design) requires 88% boiler efficiency, recording controls, compliance with SCAQMD (S. Calif. Air Quality Management District) 1146.2 emission standards and zone thermostats.						
Add for LEED registration and inspection	—	Ea	—	—	—	2,000.00
Add for LEED central performance monitor/recorder	—	Ea	2,740.00	—	—	2,740.00
Add for LEED-certified zone recording thermostats	—	Ea	409.00	—	—	409.00
Add for LEED-certified boiler with USGBC rating	—	Ea	%	10.0	—	—
Installation of packaged hydronic boilers. Add the cost of control wiring, supply lines (electric, feedwater and gas), drain line, circulating pump, expansion tank, vent stack, permits, final inspection and rental of an appliance doll, come-a-long and a 1/2-ton chain hoist if required.						
Place 4' x 4' vibration pads	CF@.750	Ea	44.80	26.70	—	71.50
Connect gas and feedwater lines	P1@2.50	Ea	—	92.20	—	92.20
Mount interior boiler drain	P1@.500	Ea	8.95	18.40	—	27.35
Bore pipe hole through basement wall	P1@.250	Ea	—	9.22	—	9.22
Bore stack vent through exterior wall	P1@.250	Ea	—	9.22	—	9.22
Mount and edge-seal stack	P1@.500	Ea	46.00	18.40	—	64.40
Mount piping for circulating pump	P1@.450	Ea	—	16.60	—	16.60
Install expansion tank						
2.1 gallon	P1@.300	Ea	38.00	11.10	—	49.10
4.5 gallon	P1@.300	Ea	63.30	11.10	—	74.40

	Craft@Hrs	Unit	Material	Labor	Total
Hydronic Heating					
Hot water baseboard fin tube radiation, copper tube and aluminum fin element, commercial quality, 18 gauge enclosure. Add for control wiring.					
9-7/8" enclosure and 1-1/4" element	P6@.280	LF	36.20	14.70	50.90
13-7/8" enclosure and 1-1/4" element, 2 rows	P6@.320	LF	62.70	16.80	79.50
9-7/8" enclosure only	P6@.130	LF	11.40	6.81	18.21
13-7/8" enclosure only	P6@.150	LF	17.40	7.86	25.26
1-1/4" element only	P6@.150	LF	25.70	7.86	33.56
1" element only	P6@.150	LF	12.80	7.86	20.66
3/4" element only	P6@.140	LF	10.30	7.33	17.63
Add for pipe connection and control valve	P6@2.25	Ea	239.00	118.00	357.00
Add for corners, fillers and caps, average per foot	—	%	10.0	—	—
End cap, 4"	P6@.090	Ea	7.82	4.72	12.54
End cap, 2"	P6@.090	Ea	3.95	4.72	8.67
Valve access door	P6@.250	Ea	19.60	13.10	32.70
Inside corner	P6@.120	Ea	7.78	6.29	14.07
Outside corner	P6@.120	Ea	11.10	6.29	17.39
Filler sleeve	P6@.090	Ea	4.95	4.72	9.67
Hot water baseboard fin tube radiation, steel element, commercial quality, 16 gauge, sloping top cover. Make additional allowances for control wiring.					
9-7/8" enclosure and 1-1/4" steel element	P6@.330	LF	42.50	17.30	59.80
1-1/4" steel element only	P6@.160	LF	29.70	8.38	38.08
Add for pipe connection and control valve	P6@2.25	Ea	242.00	118.00	360.00

	Craft@Hrs	Unit	Material	Labor	Total
Add for corners, fillers and caps, average per foot	—	%	10.0	—	—
End cap, 4"	P6@.090	Ea	15.20	4.72	19.92
End cap, 2"	P6@.090	Ea	7.29	4.72	12.01
Valve access door	P6@.250	Ea	20.10	13.10	33.20
Inside corner	P6@.120	Ea	13.60	6.29	19.89
Outside corner	P6@.120	Ea	18.00	6.29	24.29
Filler sleeve	P6@.090	Ea	9.73	4.72	14.45
Unit heaters, hot water, horizontal, fan driven					
12.5 MBtu, 200 CFM	M5@2.00	Ea	522.00	104.00	626.00
17 MBtu, 300 CFM	M5@2.00	Ea	577.00	104.00	681.00
25 MBtu, 500 CFM	M5@2.50	Ea	660.00	130.00	790.00
30 MBtu, 700 CFM	M5@3.00	Ea	695.00	156.00	851.00
50 MBtu, 1,000 CFM	M5@3.50	Ea	806.00	182.00	988.00
60 MBtu, 1,300 CFM	M5@4.00	Ea	959.00	207.00	1,166.00
Unit heaters, hot water, vertical, fan driven					
12.5 MBtu, 200 CFM	M5@2.00	Ea	589.00	104.00	693.00
17 MBtu, 300 CFM	M5@2.00	Ea	597.00	104.00	701.00
25 MBtu, 500 CFM	M5@2.50	Ea	775.00	130.00	905.00
30 MBtu, 700 CFM	M5@3.00	Ea	807.00	156.00	963.00
50 MBtu, 1,000 CFM	M5@3.50	Ea	976.00	182.00	1,158.00
60 MBtu, 1,300 CFM	M5@4.00	Ea	1,070.00	207.00	1,277.00
Steam Heating					
Steam baseboard radiation, per linear foot, wall mounted					
1/2" tube and cover	P6@.456	LF	13.50	23.90	37.40
3/4" tube and cover	P6@.493	LF	14.30	25.80	40.10
3/4" tube and cover, high capacity	P6@.493	LF	16.80	25.80	42.60
1/2" tube alone	P6@.350	LF	7.24	18.30	25.54
3/4" tube alone	P6@.377	LF	8.26	19.80	28.06
Unit heater, steam, horizontal, fan driven					
18 MBtu, 300 CFM	M5@2.00	Ea	487.00	104.00	591.00
45 MBtu, 500 CFM	M5@2.50	Ea	807.00	130.00	937.00
60 MBtu, 700 CFM	M5@3.00	Ea	911.00	156.00	1,067.00
85 MBtu, 1,000 CFM	M5@3.50	Ea	961.00	182.00	1,143.00
Unit heater, steam, vertical, fan driven					
12.5 MBtu, 200 CFM	M5@2.00	Ea	442.00	104.00	546.00
17 MBtu, 300 CFM	M5@2.00	Ea	451.00	104.00	555.00
40 MBtu, 500 CFM	M5@2.50	Ea	874.00	130.00	1,004.00
60 MBtu, 700 CFM	M5@3.00	Ea	1,010.00	156.00	1,166.00
70 MBtu, 1,000 CFM	M5@3.50	Ea	1,300.00	182.00	1,482.00
Hydronic Heating Specialties					
Air eliminator-purger, screwed connections					
3/4", cast iron, steam & water, 150 PSI	PF@.250	Ea	618.00	15.60	633.60
3/4", cast iron, 150 PSI water	PF@.250	Ea	199.00	15.60	214.60
1", cast iron, 150 PSI water	PF@.250	Ea	224.00	15.60	239.60
3/8", brass, 125 PSI steam	PF@.250	Ea	162.00	15.60	177.60
1/2", cast iron, 250 PSI steam	PF@.250	Ea	337.00	15.60	352.60
3/4", cast iron, 250 PSI steam	PF@.250	Ea	421.00	15.60	436.60
Airtrol fitting, 3/4"	PF@.300	Ea	71.60	18.70	90.30
Air eliminator vents, 1/4"	P1@.150	Ea	24.10	5.53	29.63
Atmospheric vacuum breakers, screwed					
1/2" vacuum breaker	PF@.210	Ea	34.80	13.10	47.90
3/4" vacuum breaker	PF@.250	Ea	36.90	15.60	52.50

	Craft@Hrs	Unit	Material	Labor	Total
1" vacuum breaker	PF@.300	Ea	58.70	18.70	77.40
1-1/4" vacuum breaker	PF@.400	Ea	97.80	25.00	122.80
1-1/2" vacuum breaker	PF@.450	Ea	115.00	28.10	143.10
2" vacuum breaker	PF@.500	Ea	171.00	31.20	202.20
Circuit balancing valves, for hot water applications, certified low-lead compliance.					
1/2" circuit balancing valve	PF@.210	Ea	77.80	13.10	90.90
3/4" circuit balancing valve	PF@.250	Ea	93.20	15.60	108.80
1" circuit balancing valve	PF@.300	Ea	101.00	18.70	119.70
1-1/2" circuit balancing valve	PF@.450	Ea	160.00	28.10	188.10
Flow check valves, brass, threaded, horizontal type					
3/4" check valve	PF@.250	Ea	36.00	15.60	51.60
1" check valve	PF@.300	Ea	51.70	18.70	70.40
1-1/2" valve	PF@.350	Ea	113.00	21.90	134.90
2" valve	PF@.400	Ea	142.00	25.00	167.00
Pressure-reducing valves, bronze body, for water, gas and steam applications, lead free, threaded.					
1/2", 25-75 PSI	PF@.210	Ea	150.00	13.10	163.10
1/2", 10-35 PSI	PF@.210	Ea	170.00	13.10	183.10
3/4", 25-75 PSI	PF@.250	Ea	174.00	15.60	189.60
3/4", 10-35 PSI	PF@.250	Ea	199.00	15.60	214.60
1", 25-75 PSI	PF@.300	Ea	278.00	18.70	296.70
1", 10-35 PSI	PF@.300	Ea	304.00	18.70	322.70
1-1/4", 25-75 PSI	PF@.350	Ea	559.00	21.90	580.90
1-1/4", 10-35 PSI	PF@.350	Ea	609.00	21.90	630.90
1-1/2", 25-75 PSI	PF@.250	Ea	600.00	15.60	615.60
1-1/2", 10-35 PSI	PF@.250	Ea	685.00	15.60	700.60
2", 25-75 PSI	PF@.250	Ea	895.00	15.60	910.60
2", 10-35 PSI	PF@.250	Ea	946.00	15.60	961.60
Pressure regulators, feed water 25-75 PSI, cast iron, screwed connections					
3/4" regulator	PF@.250	Ea	107.00	15.60	122.60
1" regulator	PF@.300	Ea	163.00	18.70	181.70
1-1/4" regulator	PF@.400	Ea	222.00	25.00	247.00
1-1/2" regulator	PF@.450	Ea	320.00	28.10	348.10
2" regulator	PF@.600	Ea	515.00	37.50	552.50
2-1/2" regulator	PF@.700	Ea	772.00	43.70	815.70
Combination pressure relief and reducing valves					
1/2", brass body	PF@.210	Ea	134.00	13.10	147.10
3/4", cast iron body	PF@.250	Ea	206.00	15.60	221.60
Wye pattern bronze strainers, for water, gas and steam applications, complies with American Society of Mechanical Engineers Standard B16, Manufacturers Standardization Society, Instrumentation Society of America standards.					
Wye pattern strainers, screwed connections, 250 PSI, cast iron body					
3/4" strainer	PF@.260	Ea	14.60	16.20	30.80
1" strainer	PF@.330	Ea	18.50	20.60	39.10
1-1/4" strainer	PF@.440	Ea	26.70	27.50	54.20
1-1/2" strainer	PF@.495	Ea	30.90	30.90	61.80
2" strainer	PF@.550	Ea	48.70	34.40	83.10
Wye pattern strainers, screwed connections, 250 PSI, cast bronze body					
1/2" strainer	PF@.210	Ea	32.80	13.10	45.90
3/4" strainer	PF@.250	Ea	44.30	15.60	59.90
1" strainer	PF@.300	Ea	56.60	18.70	75.30
1-1/4" strainer	PF@.400	Ea	80.00	25.00	105.00
1-1/2" strainer	PF@.450	Ea	104.00	28.10	132.10
2" strainer	PF@.500	Ea	179.00	31.20	210.20

	Craft@Hrs	Unit	Material	Labor	Total
Wye pattern strainers, screwed connections, 600 PSI, stainless steel body					
3/4" strainer	PF@.260	Ea	349.00	16.20	365.20
1" strainer	PF@.330	Ea	480.00	20.60	500.60
1-1/4" strainer	PF@.440	Ea	582.00	27.50	609.50
1-1/2" strainer	PF@.495	Ea	802.00	30.90	832.90
2" strainer	PF@.550	Ea	1,110.00	34.40	1,144.40
Wye pattern strainers, flanged connections, 125 PSI, cast iron body					
2" strainer	PF@.500	Ea	135.00	31.20	166.20
2-1/2" strainer	PF@.600	Ea	151.00	37.50	188.50
3" strainer	PF@.750	Ea	174.00	46.90	220.90
4" strainer	PF@1.35	Ea	297.00	84.30	381.30
6" strainer	PF@2.50	Ea	598.00	156.00	754.00
8" strainer	PF@3.00	Ea	1,010.00	187.00	1,197.00
Tempering valves, screwed connections, high temperature for hot water applications, complies with American Society of Mechanical Engineers Standard B16, Manufacturers Standardization Society, Instrumentation Society of America standards.					
3/4", screwed	PF@.250	Ea	596.00	15.60	611.60
1", screwed	PF@.300	Ea	853.00	18.70	871.70
1-1/4", screwed	PF@.400	Ea	1,220.00	25.00	1,245.00
1-1/2", screwed	PF@.450	Ea	1,490.00	28.10	1,518.10
2", screwed	PF@.500	Ea	1,870.00	31.20	1,901.20
Thermostatic mixing valves, 110 to 150 degrees F					
1/2", soldered	PF@.240	Ea	76.20	15.00	91.20
3/4", threaded	PF@.250	Ea	99.50	15.60	115.10
3/4", soldered	PF@.300	Ea	83.70	18.70	102.40
1", threaded	PF@.300	Ea	114.00	18.70	132.70
Float and thermostatic traps, cast iron body, parallel connection					
3/4" (15 to 75 PSI)	PF@.250	Ea	185.00	15.60	200.60
1" (15 to 30 PSI)	PF@.300	Ea	220.00	18.70	238.70
3/4"-1" (125 PSI)	PF@.250	Ea	284.00	15.60	299.60
3/4"-1" (175 PSI)	PF@.300	Ea	621.00	18.70	639.70
1-1/4" (15 to 30 PSI)	PF@.450	Ea	308.00	28.10	336.10
1-1/4"-1-1/2" (75 PSI)	PF@.450	Ea	523.00	28.10	551.10
1-1/4"-1-1/2" (125 PSI)	PF@.500	Ea	525.00	31.20	556.20
1-1/4"-1-1/2" (175 PSI)	PF@.500	Ea	754.00	31.20	785.20
1-1/2" (15 to 30 PSI)	PF@.450	Ea	463.00	28.10	491.10
2" (15 to 30 PSI)	PF@.450	Ea	1,580.00	28.10	1,608.10
2" (75 PSI)	PF@.550	Ea	1,590.00	34.40	1,624.40
2" (125 PSI)	PF@.600	Ea	1,600.00	37.50	1,637.50
2-1/2" (15 to 250 PSI)	PF@.800	Ea	4,060.00	50.00	4,110.00
Liquid level gauges					
3/4", aluminum	PF@.250	Ea	317.00	15.60	332.60
3/4", 125 PSI PVC	PF@.250	Ea	332.00	15.60	347.60
1/2", 175 PSI bronze	PF@.210	Ea	62.30	13.10	75.40
3/4", 150 PSI stainless steel	PF@.250	Ea	306.00	15.60	321.60
1", 150 PSI stainless steel	PF@.300	Ea	345.00	18.70	363.70

Tanks Double wall except as noted. Includes fittings and lift lugs. Add the cost of excavation, dewatering, shoring, supports, piping, backfill, paving and concrete.

	Craft@Hrs	Unit	Material	Labor	Total
Underground steel oil storage tanks					
600 gallon	MI@4.86	Ea	8,400.00	269.00	8,669.00
2,500 gallon	M8@18.5	Ea	17,200.00	1,060.00	18,260.00
5,000 gallon	M8@24.0	Ea	21,600.00	1,370.00	22,970.00
10,000 gallon	M8@37.3	Ea	31,800.00	2,130.00	33,930.00
Add for standard hold down straps	—	%	5.0	—	—

23 HVAC

	Craft@Hrs	Unit	Material	Labor	Total
Above-ground horizontal steel oil storage tanks, with electric fuel pump, meter, shutoff nozzle and vents.					
300 gallon	MI@2.98	Ea	4,110.00	165.00	4,275.00
500 gallon	MI@3.80	Ea	5,260.00	211.00	5,471.00
1,000 gallon	M8@7.64	Ea	7,320.00	437.00	7,757.00
1,500 gallon	M8@8.29	Ea	11,000.00	474.00	11,474.00
2,000 gallon	M8@10.5	Ea	14,000.00	600.00	14,600.00
5,000 gallon	M8@29.6	Ea	20,900.00	1,690.00	22,590.00
Add for two-product tanks	—	%	35.0	—	—
Add for skid mount	—	%	10.0	—	—
Deduct for single-wall tanks	—	%	-50.0	—	—
Propane tanks with valves, underground					
1,000 gallon	M8@10.0	Ea	3,400.00	572.00	3,972.00
Underground double-wall fiberglass oil storage tanks. Add the cost of excavation, testing and permit.					
550 gallon	MI@8.36	Ea	5,910.00	463.00	6,373.00
1,000 gallon	M8@16.8	Ea	10,700.00	960.00	11,660.00
2,000 gallon	M8@16.8	Ea	12,100.00	960.00	13,060.00
4,000 gallon	M8@25.9	Ea	15,900.00	1,480.00	17,380.00
6,000 gallon	M8@33.5	Ea	19,800.00	1,920.00	21,720.00
8,000 gallon	M8@33.5	Ea	23,100.00	1,920.00	25,020.00
10,000 gallon	M8@33.5	Ea	27,900.00	1,920.00	29,820.00
12,000 gallon	M8@84.4	Ea	32,700.00	4,830.00	37,530.00
15,000 gallon	M8@89.0	Ea	40,500.00	5,090.00	45,590.00
20,000 gallon	M8@89.0	Ea	48,600.00	5,090.00	53,690.00

26 Electrical

Typical In-Place Costs Preliminary estimates per square foot of floor area for all electrical work, including service entrance, distribution and lighting fixtures, by building type. These costs include the subcontractor's overhead and profit.

Commercial stores	—	SF	—	—	11.80
Market buildings	—	SF	—	—	12.10
Recreation facilities	—	SF	—	—	14.30
Schools	—	SF	—	—	16.40
Colleges	—	SF	—	—	23.50
Hospitals	—	SF	—	—	38.50
Office buildings	—	SF	—	—	14.50
Warehouses	—	SF	—	—	6.52
Parking lots	—	SF	—	—	2.47
Garages	—	SF	—	—	11.10

Underground Power and Communication Duct Type BE LTMC8 (encased burial) PVC duct in 20' lengths. Add for excavation, shoring, dewatering, spacers, concrete envelope around duct, backfill, compaction, wire, pavement removal and re-paving as required. Direct burial (DB) power and communication duct will cost about 25% more.

Single duct run					
2" duct	E1@.053	LF	.50	2.76	3.26
3" duct	E1@.055	LF	.97	2.87	3.84
4" duct	E1@.070	LF	1.75	3.65	5.40

Concrete Envelope for Duct No wire, duct, excavation, pavement removal or replacement included. Based on ready-mix concrete. Includes allowance for waste.

9" x 9" (.56 CF per linear foot)	E2@.020	LF	2.69	1.02	3.71
12" x 12" (1.00 CF per linear foot)	E2@.036	LF	4.81	1.83	6.64
12" x 24" (2.00 CF per linear foot)	E2@.072	LF	9.62	3.66	13.28
Per CY	E2@1.21	CY	130.00	61.50	191.50

	Craft@Hrs	Unit	Material	Labor	Total
Precast Concrete Pull and Junction Box Reinforced concrete with appropriate inserts, cast iron frame, cover and pulling hooks. Overall dimensions as shown.					
Precast handholes, 4' deep					
2' wide, 3' long	E1@4.24	Ea	1,330.00	221.00	1,551.00
3' wide, 3' long	E1@5.17	Ea	1,980.00	269.00	2,249.00
4' wide, 4' long	E1@13.2	Ea	2,740.00	688.00	3,428.00
Precast power manholes, 7' deep					
4' wide, 6' long	E1@24.6	Ea	4,010.00	1,280.00	5,290.00
6' wide, 8' long	E1@26.6	Ea	4,470.00	1,390.00	5,860.00
8' wide, 10' long	E1@26.6	Ea	4,700.00	1,390.00	6,090.00
Light and Power Circuits Costs per circuit including stranded THHN copper wire (except where noted), conduit, handy box, cover, straps, fasteners and connectors, but without fixture, receptacle or switch, except as noted.					
Circuits for an exit light, fire alarm bell or suspended ceiling lighting system, 20 amp, with 4" junction box and 30' of 1/2" EMT conduit and copper THHN wire					
3 #12 solid wire	E4@2.68	Ea	28.20	136.00	164.20
4 #12 solid wire	E4@2.90	Ea	32.70	147.00	179.70
5 #12 solid wire	E4@3.14	Ea	37.10	160.00	197.10
Under-slab circuit, with 4" square junction box, 10' of 1/2" RSC and 20' of 1/2" PVC conduit					
3 #12 wire, 20 amp	E4@1.75	Ea	40.30	89.00	129.30
4 #12 wire, 20 amp	E4@1.97	Ea	44.80	100.00	144.80
5 #12 wire, 20 amp	E4@2.21	Ea	49.30	112.00	161.30
3 #10 wire, 30 amp	E4@2.00	Ea	41.80	102.00	143.80
4 #10 wire, 30 amp	E4@2.31	Ea	46.80	117.00	163.80
Under-slab circuit, with 4" square junction box, 10' of 1/2" RSC conduit, 20' of 1/2" PVC conduit and 6' of liquid-tight flexible conduit					
3 #12 wire, 20 amp	E4@2.41	Ea	50.90	123.00	173.90
4 #12 wire, 20 amp	E4@2.69	Ea	53.40	137.00	190.40
3 #10 wire, 30 amp	E4@2.75	Ea	52.40	140.00	192.40
4 #10 wire, 30 amp	E4@3.81	Ea	57.40	194.00	251.40
20 amp switch circuit, 277 volt, with 30' of 1/2" EMT conduit, switch, cover and 2 indenter connectors					
One gang box					
2 #12 wire, Single pole switch	E4@2.82	Ea	34.60	143.00	177.60
3 #12 wire, Three-way switch	E4@2.93	Ea	41.00	149.00	190.00
3 #12 wire, Four-way switch	E4@3.14	Ea	48.20	160.00	208.20
Two gang box					
2 #12 wire, Single pole switch	E4@2.95	Ea	41.80	150.00	191.80
3 #12 wire, Three-way switch	E4@3.08	Ea	50.20	157.00	207.20
3 #12 wire, Four-way switch	E4@3.24	Ea	64.60	165.00	229.60
15 amp switch circuit, 125 volt, with 30' of #14 two conductor Romex non-metallic cable (NM) with ground, switch, cover and switch connection					
One gang box					
Single pole switch	E4@1.05	Ea	20.30	53.40	73.70
Three-way switch	E4@1.18	Ea	22.30	60.00	82.30
Two gang box					
Single pole switch	E4@1.17	Ea	27.50	59.50	87.00
Single pole & receptacle	E4@1.43	Ea	28.80	72.70	101.50
Single pole & 3-way switch	E4@1.43	Ea	32.50	72.70	105.20
One two pole & 3-way switch	E4@1.66	Ea	32.50	84.40	116.90
20 amp 2 pole duplex receptacle outlet circuit, 125 volt, 30' of 1/2" EMT conduit, wire and specification grade receptacle, connectors and box					
3 #12 wire	E4@2.80	Ea	29.60	142.00	171.60
4 #12 wire	E4@3.06	Ea	34.10	156.00	190.10
5 #12 wire	E4@3.26	Ea	38.50	166.00	204.50

	Craft@Hrs	Unit	Material	Labor	Total
Duplex receptacle outlet circuit with 30' of Romex non-metallic cable (NM) with ground, receptacle, cover and connection					
15 amp, 125 volt, #14/2 wire	E4@1.11	Ea	11.70	56.40	68.10
15 amp, 125 volt, #14/2 wire with ground fault circuit interrupter (GFCI)	E4@1.30	Ea	26.30	66.10	92.40
20 amp, 125 volt, #12/2 wire	E4@1.36	Ea	16.50	69.10	85.60
30 amp, 250 volt, #10/3 wire, dryer circuit	E4@1.77	Ea	33.40	90.00	123.40
50 amp, 250 volt, #8/3 wire, range circuit	E4@2.06	Ea	52.20	105.00	157.20
Rigid Galvanized Steel Conduit, standard wall. Installed exposed in a building either vertically or horizontally up to 10' above floor level. No wire, fittings or supports included. Each 10' length comes with one coupling. Add the cost of fittings, boxes, supports and wire.					
1/2" conduit	E4@.043	LF	2.04	2.19	4.23
3/4" conduit	E4@.054	LF	2.12	2.74	4.86
1" conduit	E4@.066	LF	3.33	3.35	6.68
1-1/4" conduit	E4@.077	LF	3.46	3.91	7.37
1-1/2" conduit	E4@.100	LF	5.60	5.08	10.68
2" conduit	E4@.116	LF	6.74	5.90	12.64
2-1/2" conduit	E4@.143	LF	13.40	7.27	20.67
3" conduit	E4@.164	LF	14.80	8.34	23.14
4" conduit	E4@.221	LF	20.50	11.20	31.70
Add for red plastic coating	—	%	80.0	—	—
Deduct for rigid steel conduit installed in a concrete slab or open trench	—	%	—	-40.0	—
90- or 45-degree ells, standard weight rigid galvanized steel, threaded both ends					
1/2" elbow	E4@.170	Ea	5.36	8.64	14.00
3/4" elbow	E4@.190	Ea	6.01	9.66	15.67
1" elbow	E4@.210	Ea	9.20	10.70	19.90
1-1/4" elbow	E4@.311	Ea	13.10	15.80	28.90
1-1/2" elbow	E4@.378	Ea	16.50	19.20	35.70
2" elbow	E4@.448	Ea	23.00	22.80	45.80
2-1/2" elbow	E4@.756	Ea	37.30	38.40	75.70
3" elbow	E4@1.10	Ea	57.90	55.90	113.80
4" elbow	E4@1.73	Ea	96.70	87.90	184.60
Add for 45 degree ells	—	%	7.0	—	—
Add for PVC coated ells	—	%	45.0	—	—
Rigid steel threaded couplings					
1/2"	E4@.062	Ea	1.52	3.15	4.67
3/4"	E4@.080	Ea	1.76	4.07	5.83
1"	E4@.092	Ea	2.79	4.68	7.47
1-1/4"	E4@.102	Ea	4.20	5.18	9.38
1-1/2"	E4@.140	Ea	5.06	7.12	12.18
2"	E4@.170	Ea	6.38	8.64	15.02
2-1/2"	E4@.202	Ea	16.20	10.30	26.50
3"	E4@.230	Ea	20.50	11.70	32.20
4"	E4@.425	Ea	28.10	21.60	49.70
Three-piece "Erickson" unions, by pipe size					
1"	E4@.394	Ea	7.96	20.00	27.96
Insulated grounding bushing					
1/2"	E4@.062	Ea	2.31	3.15	5.46
3/4"	E4@.080	Ea	3.26	4.07	7.33
1"	E4@.092	Ea	4.43	4.68	9.11
1-1/4"	E4@.102	Ea	6.49	5.18	11.67
1-1/2"	E4@.140	Ea	7.33	7.12	14.45
2"	E4@.170	Ea	7.80	8.64	16.44
3"	E4@.230	Ea	9.01	11.70	20.71
4"	E4@.425	Ea	13.80	21.60	35.40

	Craft@Hrs	Unit	Material	Labor	Total
Insulated thermoplastic bushing					
1/2"	E4@.020	Ea	.13	1.02	1.15
3/4"	E4@.025	Ea	.22	1.27	1.49
1"	E4@.030	Ea	.60	1.52	2.12
1-1/4"	E4@.040	Ea	.76	2.03	2.79
1-1/2"	E4@.045	Ea	1.03	2.29	3.32
2"	E4@.050	Ea	1.53	2.54	4.07
2-1/2"	E4@.050	Ea	2.29	2.54	4.83
3"	E4@.070	Ea	2.93	3.56	6.49
Type A, C, LB, E, LL or LR threaded conduit body with cover and gasket					
1/2"	E4@.191	Ea	4.18	9.71	13.89
3/4"	E4@.238	Ea	5.74	12.10	17.84
1"	E4@.285	Ea	8.45	14.50	22.95
1-1/4"	E4@.358	Ea	10.40	18.20	28.60
1-1/2"	E4@.456	Ea	13.80	23.20	37.00
2"	E4@.598	Ea	21.00	30.40	51.40
2-1/2"	E4@1.43	Ea	50.10	72.70	122.80
3"	E4@1.77	Ea	55.20	90.00	145.20
4"	E4@2.80	Ea	93.60	142.00	235.60

	Craft@Hrs	Unit	Material	Labor	Total
Type T threaded conduit body, with cover and gasket					
1/2"	E4@.285	Ea	4.91	14.50	19.41
3/4"	E4@.358	Ea	6.84	18.20	25.04
1"	E4@.433	Ea	9.87	22.00	31.87
1-1/4"	E4@.534	Ea	19.20	27.10	46.30
1-1/2"	E4@.679	Ea	18.10	34.50	52.60
2"	E4@.889	Ea	21.20	45.20	66.40
2-1/2"	E4@2.15	Ea	49.40	109.00	158.40
3"	E4@2.72	Ea	70.70	138.00	208.70
4"	E4@4.22	Ea	149.00	215.00	364.00
Service entrance cap, threaded					
1/2"	E4@.319	Ea	4.18	16.20	20.38
3/4"	E4@.373	Ea	4.67	19.00	23.67
1"	E4@.376	Ea	6.53	19.10	25.63
1-1/4"	E4@.482	Ea	7.45	24.50	31.95
1-1/2"	E4@.536	Ea	9.52	27.20	36.72
2"	E4@.591	Ea	13.40	30.00	43.40
2-1/2"	E4@.671	Ea	32.20	34.10	66.30
3"	E4@.749	Ea	59.10	38.10	97.20
4"	E4@.912	Ea	88.20	46.40	134.60
Add for heights over 10' to 20'	—	%	—	20.0	—

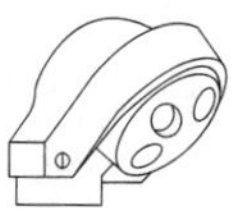

Electric Metallic Tubing (EMT) Installed exposed in a building either vertically or horizontally up to 10' above floor level. No wire, fittings or supports included except as noted.

	Craft@Hrs	Unit	Material	Labor	Total
1/2" conduit	E4@.036	LF	.41	1.83	2.24
3/4" conduit	E4@.043	LF	.72	2.19	2.91
1" conduit	E4@.055	LF	1.22	2.80	4.02
1-1/4" conduit	E4@.067	LF	2.02	3.41	5.43
1-1/2" conduit	E4@.070	LF	2.43	3.56	5.99
2" conduit	E4@.086	LF	2.87	4.37	7.24
2-1/2" conduit	E4@.106	LF	5.39	5.39	10.78
3" conduit	E4@.127	LF	6.81	6.46	13.27
4" conduit	E4@.170	LF	9.22	8.64	17.86

	Craft@Hrs	Unit	Material	Labor	Total
EMT 90-degree elbow					
1/2"	E4@.143	Ea	3.12	7.27	10.39
3/4"	E4@.170	Ea	4.10	8.64	12.74
1"	E4@.190	Ea	5.83	9.66	15.49
1-1/4"	E4@.216	Ea	7.13	11.00	18.13
1-1/2"	E4@.288	Ea	8.88	14.60	23.48
2"	E4@.358	Ea	13.00	18.20	31.20
2-1/2"	E4@.648	Ea	21.50	32.90	54.40
3"	E4@.858	Ea	25.00	43.60	68.60
4"	E4@1.33	Ea	45.80	67.60	113.40
EMT 90-degree pull elbow					
1/2" pull elbow	E4@.143	Ea	3.40	7.27	10.67
3/4" pull elbow	E4@.170	Ea	4.93	8.64	13.57
1" pull elbow	E4@.190	Ea	13.00	9.66	22.66
1-1/4" pull elbow	E4@.216	Ea	16.20	11.00	27.20
1-1/2" pull elbow	E4@.288	Ea	15.10	14.60	29.70
2" pull elbow	E4@.358	Ea	22.00	18.20	40.20
2-1/2" pull elbow	E4@.648	Ea	36.50	32.90	69.40
3" pull elbow	E4@.858	Ea	42.40	43.60	86.00
4" pull elbow	E4@1.33	Ea	77.70	67.60	145.30
EMT set screw connector, die cast					
1/2" EMT connector	E4@.085	Ea	.43	4.32	4.75
3/4" EMT connector	E4@.096	Ea	.61	4.88	5.49
1" EMT connector	E4@.124	Ea	1.20	6.30	7.50
1-1/4" EMT connector	E4@.143	Ea	2.03	7.27	9.30
1-1/2" EMT connector	E4@.162	Ea	3.20	8.23	11.43
2" EMT connector	E4@.237	Ea	3.93	12.00	15.93
2-1/2" EMT connector	E4@.363	Ea	11.50	18.50	30.00
3" EMT connector	E4@.479	Ea	11.50	24.30	35.80
4" EMT connector	E4@.655	Ea	14.30	33.30	47.60
Add for insulated set-screw connector	—	%	41.0	—	—
EMT compression connector, die cast					
1/2" EMT connector	E4@.085	Ea	.49	4.32	4.81
3/4" EMT connector	E4@.096	Ea	.95	4.88	5.83
1" EMT connector	E4@.124	Ea	1.24	6.30	7.54
1-1/4" EMT connector	E4@.143	Ea	2.18	7.27	9.45
1-1/2" EMT connector	E4@.162	Ea	3.15	8.23	11.38
2" EMT connector	E4@.237	Ea	5.52	12.00	17.52
2-1/2" EMT connector	E4@.363	Ea	9.36	18.50	27.86
3" EMT connector	E4@.479	Ea	12.40	24.30	36.70
4" EMT connector	E4@.655	Ea	17.70	33.30	51.00
Add for insulated compression connector	—	%	130.0	—	—
Add for raintight compression connector	—	%	121.0	—	—
EMT set screw coupling, steel					
1/2" EMT coupling	E4@.085	Ea	.26	4.32	4.58
3/4" EMT coupling	E4@.096	Ea	.43	4.88	5.31
1" EMT coupling	E4@.124	Ea	.84	6.30	7.14
1-1/4" EMT coupling	E4@.143	Ea	1.62	7.27	8.89
1-1/2" EMT coupling	E4@.162	Ea	1.94	8.23	10.17
2" EMT coupling	E4@.237	Ea	2.55	12.00	14.55
2-1/2" EMT coupling	E4@.363	Ea	3.83	18.50	22.33
3" EMT coupling	E4@.479	Ea	5.33	24.30	29.63
4" EMT coupling	E4@.655	Ea	5.82	33.30	39.12
Add for insulated set-screw connector	—	%	130.0	—	—

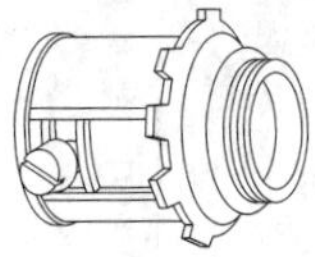

	Craft@Hrs	Unit	Material	Labor	Total
EMT compression coupling, die cast, rain tight					
1/2" EMT coupling	E4@.085	Ea	1.57	4.32	5.89
3/4" EMT coupling	E4@.096	Ea	2.25	4.88	7.13
1" EMT coupling	E4@.124	Ea	3.59	6.30	9.89
1-1/4" EMT coupling	E4@.143	Ea	6.40	7.27	13.67
1-1/2" EMT coupling	E4@.162	Ea	9.27	8.23	17.50
2" EMT coupling	E4@.237	Ea	13.00	12.00	25.00
2-1/2" EMT coupling	E4@.363	Ea	42.10	18.50	60.60
3" EMT coupling	E4@.479	Ea	53.80	24.30	78.10
4" EMT coupling	E4@.655	Ea	115.00	33.30	148.30
Add for heights over 10' to 20'	—	%	—	20.0	—

EMT Conduit with Wire THHN wire pulled in EMT conduit bent each 10', with one tap-on coupling each 10', one set screw connector each 50' and a strap and lag screw each 6'. Installed exposed on walls or ceilings. Add 15% to the labor cost for heights over 10' to 20'. Use these figures for preliminary estimates.

	Craft@Hrs	Unit	Material	Labor	Total
1-1/2" EMT conduit and wire as shown below					
2 #1 aluminum, 1 #8 copper	E4@.140	LF	5.05	7.12	12.17
3 #1 aluminum, 1 #8 copper	E4@.156	LF	6.06	7.93	13.99
4 #1 aluminum, 1 #8 copper	E4@.173	LF	7.07	8.79	15.86
4 #4 copper, 1 #8 copper	E4@.162	LF	5.44	8.23	13.67
2 #3 copper, 1 #8 copper	E4@.140	LF	4.69	7.12	11.81
3 #3 copper, 1 #8 copper	E4@.155	LF	5.52	7.88	13.40
4 #3 copper, 1 #8 copper	E4@.170	LF	6.34	8.64	14.98
2 #1 copper, 1 #8 copper	E4@.146	LF	6.34	7.42	13.76
3 #1 copper, 1 #8 copper	E4@.164	LF	8.00	8.34	16.34
4 #1 copper, 1 #8 copper	E4@.183	LF	9.66	9.30	18.96
2" EMT conduit and wire as shown below					
2 #2/0 aluminum, 1 #6 copper	E4@.170	LF	6.64	8.64	15.28
3 #2/0 aluminum, 1 #6 copper	E4@.190	LF	8.10	9.66	17.76
4 #2/0 aluminum, 1 #6 copper	E4@.210	LF	9.56	10.70	20.26
2 #3/0 aluminum, 1 #6 copper	E4@.174	LF	7.36	8.84	16.20
3 #3/0 aluminum, 1 #6 copper	E4@.195	LF	9.18	9.91	19.09
4 #3/0 aluminum, 1 #6 copper	E4@.218	LF	11.00	11.10	22.10
2 #1/0 copper, 1 #6 copper	E4@.171	LF	8.38	8.69	17.07
3 #1/0 copper, 1 #6 copper	E4@.193	LF	10.70	9.81	20.51
4 #1/0 copper, 1 #6 copper	E4@.213	LF	13.10	10.80	23.90
2 #3/0 copper, 1 #4 copper	E4@.175	LF	8.56	8.90	17.46
3 #3/0 copper, 1 #4 copper	E4@.197	LF	10.90	10.00	20.90
2-1/2" EMT conduit and wire as shown below					
2 250 MCM alum, 1 #4 copper	E4@.210	LF	12.10	10.70	22.80
3 250 MCM alum, 1 #4 copper	E4@.237	LF	14.50	12.00	26.50
4 #3 copper, 1 #4 copper	E4@.216	LF	10.50	11.00	21.50
2 #4 copper, 1 #2 copper	E4@.186	LF	8.68	9.45	18.13
3 #4 copper, 1 #2 copper	E4@.198	LF	9.29	10.10	19.39
4 #4 copper, 1 #2 copper	E4@.210	LF	9.89	10.70	20.59
3 250 MCM copper, 1 #2 copper	E4@.253	LF	18.60	12.90	31.50
3" EMT conduit and wire as shown below					
4 250 MCM alum, 1 #4 copper	E4@.288	LF	18.40	14.60	33.00
4 250 MCM copper, 1 #2 copper	E4@.290	LF	23.70	14.70	38.40
5 250 MCM copper, 1 #2 copper	E4@.319	LF	27.40	16.20	43.60

	Craft@Hrs	Unit	Material	Labor	Total
EMT Conduit Circuits Cost per circuit based on 30' run from the panel. Includes THHN copper wire pulled in conduit, 2 compression connectors, 2 couplings, conduit bending, straps, bolts and washers. Three-wire circuits are 120, 240 or 277 volt 1 phase, with 2 conductors and ground. Four-wire circuits are 120/208 or 480 volt 3 phase, with 3 conductors and ground. Five-wire circuits are 120/208 or 480 volt 3 phase, with 3 conductors, neutral and ground. Installed exposed in vertical or horizontal runs to 10' above floor level in a building. Add 15% to the manhours and labor costs for heights over 10' to 20'. Use these figures for preliminary estimates. Based on commercial quantity discounts.					
15 amp circuits					
3 #14 wire, 1/2" conduit	E4@2.39	Ea	22.60	121.00	143.60
4 #14 wire, 1/2" conduit	E4@2.58	Ea	25.60	131.00	156.60
20 amp circuits					
3 #12 wire, 1/2" conduit	E4@2.49	Ea	38.00	127.00	165.00
4 #12 wire, 1/2" conduit	E4@2.72	Ea	32.70	138.00	170.70
5 #12 wire, 1/2" conduit	E4@2.95	Ea	37.50	150.00	187.50
30 amp circuits					
3 #10 wire, 1/2" conduit	E4@2.75	Ea	30.10	140.00	170.10
4 #10 wire, 1/2" conduit	E4@3.08	Ea	35.60	157.00	192.60
5 #10 wire, 3/4" conduit	E4@3.58	Ea	50.90	182.00	232.90
50 amp circuits					
3 #8 wire, 3/4" conduit	E4@2.98	Ea	48.70	151.00	199.70
4 #8 wire, 3/4" conduit	E4@3.32	Ea	57.20	169.00	226.20
5 #8 wire, 1" conduit	E4@4.02	Ea	82.50	204.00	286.50
65 amp circuits					
2 #6, 1 #8 wire, 1" conduit	E4@3.42	Ea	76.60	174.00	250.60
3 #6, 1 #8 wire, 1" conduit	E4@3.76	Ea	90.50	191.00	281.50
4 #6, 1 #8 wire, 1-1/4" conduit	E4@4.48	Ea	131.00	228.00	359.00
85 amp circuits in 1-1/4" conduit					
2 #4, 1 #8 wire	E4@3.89	Ea	111.00	198.00	309.00
3 #4, 1 #8 wire	E4@4.25	Ea	129.00	216.00	345.00
4 #4, 1 #8 wire	E4@4.48	Ea	148.00	228.00	376.00
100 amp circuits in 1-1/2" conduit					
2 #3, 1 #8 wire	E4@4.20	Ea	141.00	213.00	354.00
3 #3, 1 #8 wire	E4@4.66	Ea	165.00	237.00	402.00
4 #3, 1 #8 wire	E4@5.10	Ea	190.00	259.00	449.00
125 amp circuits in 1-1/2" conduit					
2 #1, 1 #8 wire	E4@4.40	Ea	190.00	224.00	414.00
3 #1, 1 #8 wire	E4@4.92	Ea	240.00	250.00	490.00
4 #1, 1 #8 wire	E4@5.47	Ea	290.00	278.00	568.00
150 amp circuits in 2" conduit					
2 #1/0, 1 #6 wire	E4@5.16	Ea	252.00	262.00	514.00
3 #1/0, 1 #6 wire	E4@5.78	Ea	321.00	294.00	615.00
4 #1/0, 1 #6 wire	E4@6.43	Ea	391.00	327.00	718.00
200 amp circuits in 2" conduit					
2 #3/0, 1 #4 wire	E4@5.49	Ea	257.00	279.00	536.00
3 #3/0, 1 #4 wire	E4@6.27	Ea	327.00	319.00	646.00
4 #3/0, 1 #4 wire	E4@7.80	Ea	398.00	396.00	794.00
225 amp circuits in 2-1/2" conduit					
2 #4/0, 1 #2 wire	E4@6.48	Ea	401.00	329.00	730.00
3 #4/0, 1 #2 wire	E4@7.33	Ea	489.00	373.00	862.00
4 #4/0, 1 #2 wire	E4@8.19	Ea	578.00	416.00	994.00
250 amp circuits in 2-1/2" conduit					
2 250 MCM, 1 #2 wire	E4@6.63	Ea	446.00	337.00	783.00
3 250 MCM, 1 #2 wire	E4@8.24	Ea	557.00	419.00	976.00
4 250 MCM, 1 #2 wire	E4@9.56	Ea	667.00	486.00	1,153.00

	Craft@Hrs	Unit	Material	Labor	Total
Intermediate Metal Conduit (IMC) Installed exposed in a building either vertically or horizontally up to 10' above floor level. No wire, fittings or supports included.					
1/2" conduit	E4@.038	LF	1.29	1.93	3.22
3/4" conduit	E4@.048	LF	1.49	2.44	3.93
1" conduit	E4@.056	LF	2.19	2.85	5.04
1-1/4" conduit	E4@.073	LF	2.64	3.71	6.35
1-1/2" conduit	E4@.086	LF	3.47	4.37	7.84
2" conduit	E4@.101	LF	4.54	5.13	9.67
2-1/2" conduit	E4@.127	LF	9.25	6.46	15.71
3" conduit	E4@.146	LF	9.91	7.42	17.33
PVC Schedule 40 Conduit Installed in or under a building slab. No wire, fittings or supports included.					
1/2"	E4@.030	LF	.25	1.52	1.77
3/4"	E4@.036	LF	.30	1.83	2.13
1"	E4@.046	LF	.47	2.34	2.81
1-1/4"	E4@.056	LF	.65	2.85	3.50
1-1/2"	E4@.061	LF	.74	3.10	3.84
2"	E4@.072	LF	.91	3.66	4.57
2-1/2"	E4@.089	LF	1.57	4.52	6.09
3"	E4@.105	LF	1.95	5.34	7.29
3-12"	E4@.130	LF	2.42	6.61	9.03
4"	E4@.151	LF	2.12	7.68	9.80
5"	E4@.176	LF	3.92	8.95	12.87
PVC Schedule 80 Conduit Installed in or under a building slab. No wire, fittings or supports included.					
1/2"	E4@.030	LF	.43	1.52	1.95
3/4"	E4@.036	LF	.62	1.83	2.45
1"	E4@.046	LF	.78	2.34	3.12
1-1/4"	E4@.056	LF	1.04	2.85	3.89
1-1/2"	E4@.061	LF	1.30	3.10	4.40
2"	E4@.072	LF	1.60	3.66	5.26
2-1/2"	E4@.089	LF	2.32	4.52	6.84
3"	E4@.105	LF	2.97	5.34	8.31
Schedule 40 PVC conduit coupling					
1/2" coupling	E4@.020	Ea	.19	1.02	1.21
3/4" coupling	E4@.051	Ea	.21	2.59	2.80
1" coupling	E4@.062	Ea	.41	3.15	3.56
1-1/4" coupling	E4@.078	Ea	.51	3.96	4.47
1-1/2" coupling	E4@.084	Ea	.67	4.27	4.94
2" coupling	E4@.102	Ea	.82	5.18	6.00
2-1/2" coupling	E4@.113	Ea	1.86	5.74	7.60
3" coupling	E4@.129	Ea	2.31	6.56	8.87
4" coupling	E4@.156	Ea	3.81	7.93	11.74
90-degree Schedule 40 non-metallic elbow					
1/2" ell	E4@.082	Ea	.82	4.17	4.99
3/4" ell	E4@.102	Ea	.98	5.18	6.16
1" ell	E4@.124	Ea	1.89	6.30	8.19
1-1/4" ell	E4@.154	Ea	2.37	7.83	10.20
1-1/2" ell	E4@.195	Ea	3.29	9.91	13.20
2" ell	E4@.205	Ea	4.14	10.40	14.54
2-1/2" ell	E4@.226	Ea	7.40	11.50	18.90
3" ell	E4@.259	Ea	11.40	13.20	24.60
4" ell	E4@.313	Ea	18.00	15.90	33.90
1/2" access pull ell	E4@.082	Ea	3.87	4.17	8.04
3/4" access pull ell	E4@.102	Ea	3.91	5.18	9.09
1-1/4" ell, 24" radius	E4@.154	Ea	22.50	7.83	30.33

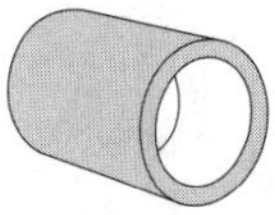

	Craft@Hrs	Unit	Material	Labor	Total
1-1/2" ell, 24" radius	E4@.195	Ea	10.80	9.91	20.71
2" ell, 24" radius	E4@.205	Ea	9.80	10.40	20.20
2" ell, 36" radius	E4@.205	Ea	16.20	10.40	26.60
2-1/2" ell, 24" radius	E4@.226	Ea	20.10	11.50	31.60
2-1/2" ell, 36" radius	E4@.226	Ea	20.30	11.50	31.80
3" ell, 24" radius	E4@.259	Ea	23.20	13.20	36.40
Increase for 45 or 30 degree ells	—	%	40.0	—	—
90-degree Schedule 80 non-metallic elbow					
1" ell	E4@.124	Ea	5.01	6.30	11.31
1-1/4" ell	E4@.154	Ea	5.22	7.83	13.05
1-1/2" ell	E4@.195	Ea	5.15	9.91	15.06
2" ell	E4@.205	Ea	12.00	10.40	22.40
2-1/2" ell	E4@.226	Ea	15.10	11.50	26.60
1-1/4" ell, 24" radius	E4@.124	Ea	31.90	6.30	38.20
1-1/2" ell, 24" radius	E4@.168	Ea	12.90	8.54	21.44
2" ell, 24" radius	E4@.205	Ea	22.40	10.40	32.80
2" ell, 36" radius	E4@.205	Ea	37.10	10.40	47.50
2-1/2" ell, 24" radius	E4@.226	Ea	36.00	11.50	47.50
3" ell, 36" radius	E4@.226	Ea	73.40	11.50	84.90
PVC conduit end bell					
1" bell end	E4@.105	Ea	2.81	5.34	8.15
1-1/4" bell end	E4@.115	Ea	3.90	5.85	9.75
1-1/2" bell end	E4@.124	Ea	3.79	6.30	10.09
2" bell end	E4@.143	Ea	5.60	7.27	12.87
2-1/2" bell end	E4@.221	Ea	5.87	11.20	17.07
3" bell end	E4@.285	Ea	8.37	14.50	22.87
PVC bell end reducer					
3" to 2-1/2"	E4@.200	Ea	21.50	10.20	31.70
4" to 3"	E4@.250	Ea	27.20	12.70	39.90
Thermoplastic insulating bushing					
1/2" bushing	E4@.025	Ea	.12	1.27	1.39
3/4" bushing	E4@.025	Ea	.17	1.27	1.44
1" bushing	E4@.030	Ea	.63	1.52	2.15
1-1/4" bushing	E4@.040	Ea	.80	2.03	2.83
1-1/2" bushing	E4@.040	Ea	.57	2.03	2.60
2" bushing	E4@.050	Ea	1.56	2.54	4.10
2-1/2" bushing	E4@.050	Ea	2.28	2.54	4.82
3" bushing	E4@.070	Ea	2.93	3.56	6.49
PVC reducer bushing, Schedule 40, socket ends					
3/4" x 1/2" bushing	E4@.030	Ea	1.10	1.52	2.62
1" x 1/2" bushing	E4@.030	Ea	2.08	1.52	3.60
1" x 3/4" bushing	E4@.040	Ea	2.53	2.03	4.56
1-1/4" x 1" bushing	E4@.050	Ea	3.29	2.54	5.83
1-1/2" x 1" bushing	E4@.050	Ea	2.91	2.54	5.45
1-1/2" x 1-1/4" bushing	E4@.050	Ea	3.38	2.54	5.92
2" x 1-1/4" bushing	E4@.050	Ea	4.08	2.54	6.62
2" x 1-1/2" bushing	E4@.070	Ea	3.64	3.56	7.20
3" x 2" bushing	E4@.100	Ea	16.40	5.08	21.48
PVC conduit box adapter					
1/2" adapter	E4@.050	Ea	.51	2.54	3.05
3/4" adapter	E4@.060	Ea	.58	3.05	3.63
1" adapter	E4@.080	Ea	.63	4.07	4.70
1-1/4" adapter	E4@.100	Ea	.93	5.08	6.01
1-1/2" adapter	E4@.100	Ea	1.05	5.08	6.13
2" adapter	E4@.150	Ea	1.30	7.62	8.92

	Craft@Hrs	Unit	Material	Labor	Total
PVC female conduit adapter, for joining conduit to threaded fittings					
1/2" adapter	E4@.050	Ea	.23	2.54	2.77
3/4" adapter	E4@.060	Ea	.38	3.05	3.43
1" adapter	E4@.080	Ea	.44	4.07	4.51
1-1/4" adapter	E4@.100	Ea	.69	5.08	5.77
1-1/2" adapter	E4@.100	Ea	.60	5.08	5.68
2" adapter	E4@.150	Ea	.37	7.62	7.99
2-1/2" adapter	E4@.178	Ea	2.00	9.05	11.05
4" adapter	E4@.244	Ea	4.10	12.40	16.50
PVC male conduit adapter, for joining conduit to threaded fittings					
1/2" adapter	E4@.050	Ea	.22	2.54	2.76
3/4" adapter	E4@.060	Ea	.37	3.05	3.42
1" adapter	E4@.080	Ea	.44	4.07	4.51
1-1/4" adapter	E4@.100	Ea	.79	5.08	5.87
1-1/2" adapter	E4@.100	Ea	.72	5.08	5.80
2" adapter	E4@.150	Ea	1.18	7.62	8.80
2-1/2" adapter	E4@.178	Ea	2.12	9.05	11.17
3" adapter	E4@.244	Ea	1.92	12.40	14.32
Type T PVC conduit body (access fitting)					
1/2" conduit body	E4@.150	Ea	2.70	7.62	10.32
3/4" conduit body	E4@.184	Ea	3.33	9.35	12.68
1" conduit body	E4@.225	Ea	3.36	11.40	14.76
1-1/4" conduit body	E4@.300	Ea	4.87	15.20	20.07
1-1/2" conduit body	E4@.350	Ea	6.76	17.80	24.56
2" conduit body	E4@.400	Ea	10.70	20.30	31.00
Type C PVC conduit body (access fitting)					
1/2" conduit body	E4@.100	Ea	2.76	5.08	7.84
3/4" conduit body	E4@.132	Ea	3.82	6.71	10.53
1" conduit body	E4@.164	Ea	4.23	8.34	12.57
1-1/4" conduit body	E4@.197	Ea	6.52	10.00	16.52
1-1/2" conduit body	E4@.234	Ea	6.11	11.90	18.01
2" conduit body	E4@.263	Ea	12.70	13.40	26.10
Type LB PVC conduit body (access fitting)					
1/2" conduit body	E4@.100	Ea	2.32	5.08	7.40
3/4" conduit body	E4@.132	Ea	3.18	6.71	9.89
1" conduit body	E4@.164	Ea	3.29	8.34	11.63
1-1/4" conduit body	E4@.197	Ea	5.01	10.00	15.01
1-1/2" conduit body	E4@.234	Ea	5.34	11.90	17.24
2" conduit body	E4@.263	Ea	9.60	13.40	23.00
3" conduit body	E4@.300	Ea	31.50	15.20	46.70
4" conduit body	E4@.350	Ea	34.40	17.80	52.20
Type LL PVC conduit body (access fitting)					
1/2" conduit body	E4@.100	Ea	2.14	5.08	7.22
3/4" conduit body	E4@.132	Ea	2.80	6.71	9.51
1" conduit body	E4@.164	Ea	2.74	8.34	11.08
1-1/4" conduit body	E4@.197	Ea	4.22	10.00	14.22
1-1/2" conduit body	E4@.234	Ea	4.75	11.90	16.65
2" conduit body	E4@.263	Ea	8.74	13.40	22.14
Type LR PVC conduit body (access fitting)					
1/2" conduit body	E4@.100	Ea	1.94	5.08	7.02
3/4" conduit body	E4@.132	Ea	2.68	6.71	9.39
1" conduit body	E4@.164	Ea	2.74	8.34	11.08
1-1/4" conduit body	E4@.197	Ea	4.81	10.00	14.81
1-1/2" conduit body	E4@.234	Ea	4.97	11.90	16.87
2" conduit body	E4@.263	Ea	8.74	13.40	22.14

	Craft@Hrs	Unit	Material	Labor	Total
Two-hole PVC clamp					
1/2" clamp	E4@.100	Ea	.20	5.08	5.28
3/4" clamp	E4@.100	Ea	.28	5.08	5.36
1" clamp	E4@.125	Ea	.35	6.35	6.70
1-1/4" clamp	E4@.150	Ea	.44	7.62	8.06
1-1/2" clamp	E4@.150	Ea	.47	7.62	8.09
2" clamp	E4@.175	Ea	.52	8.90	9.42
3" clamp	E4@.175	Ea	1.72	8.90	10.62

PVC Conduit with Wire Includes THHN wire pulled in Type 40 rigid PVC heavy wall conduit placed in a slab. Use these figures for preliminary estimates. Includes one rigid coupling every 10'. Add for fittings as required. Based on commercial quantity discounts.

	Craft@Hrs	Unit	Material	Labor	Total
1/2" PVC conduit with wire					
3 #12 solid copper	E4@.054	LF	.71	2.74	3.45
4 #12 solid copper	E4@.061	LF	.86	3.10	3.96
5 #12 solid copper	E4@.069	LF	1.01	3.51	4.52
3 #10 solid copper	E4@.062	LF	.76	3.15	3.91
4 #10 solid copper	E4@.073	LF	.93	3.71	4.64
3/4" PVC conduit with wire					
5 #10 solid copper	E4@.089	LF	1.15	4.52	5.67
3 #8 copper	E4@.069	LF	1.16	3.51	4.67
4 #8 copper	E4@.080	LF	1.45	4.07	5.52
1" PVC conduit with wire					
2 #6 copper, 1 #8 copper	E4@.081	LF	1.72	4.12	5.84
3 #6 copper, 1 #8 copper	E4@.092	LF	2.18	4.68	6.86
5 #8 copper	E4@.100	LF	1.91	5.08	6.99
1-1/2" PVC conduit with wire					
4 #6 copper, 1 #8 copper	E4@.117	LF	2.96	5.95	8.91
2 #4 copper, 1 #8 copper	E4@.097	LF	2.32	4.93	7.25
2 #1 alum, 1 #8 copper	E4@.102	LF	3.13	5.18	8.31
3 #1 alum, 1 #8 copper	E4@.119	LF	4.14	6.05	10.19
4 #4 copper, 1 #8 copper	E4@.124	LF	3.52	6.30	9.82
3 #3 copper, 1 #8 copper	E4@.116	LF	3.59	5.90	9.49
4 #3 copper, 1 #8 copper	E4@.132	LF	4.42	6.71	11.13
2 #1 copper, 1 #8 copper	E4@.108	LF	4.42	5.49	9.91
3 #1 copper, 1 #8 copper	E4@.125	LF	6.08	6.35	12.43
4 #1 copper, 1 #8 copper	E4@.143	LF	7.74	7.27	15.01
2" PVC conduit with wire					
4 #1 alum, 1 #8 copper	E4@.154	LF	5.41	7.83	13.24
2 2/0 alum, 1 #6 copper	E4@.123	LF	4.48	6.25	10.73
3 2/0 alum, 1 #6 copper	E4@.143	LF	5.94	7.27	13.21
4 2/0 alum, 1 #6 copper	E4@.163	LF	7.40	8.29	15.69
2 3/0 alum, 1 #6 copper	E4@.127	LF	5.20	6.46	11.66
3 3/0 alum, 1 #6 copper	E4@.148	LF	7.02	7.52	14.54
4 3/0 alum, 1 #6 copper	E4@.171	LF	8.84	8.69	17.53
2 1/0 & 1 #6 copper	E4@.124	LF	4.04	6.30	10.34
3 1/0 & 1 #6 copper	E4@.146	LF	5.28	7.42	12.70
4 1/0 & 1 #6 copper	E4@.167	LF	6.52	8.49	15.01
2 3/0 & 1 #4 copper	E4@.136	LF	5.34	6.91	12.25
3 3/0 & 1 #4 copper	E4@.162	LF	7.16	8.23	15.39

	Craft@Hrs	Unit	Material	Labor	Total
2-1/2" PVC conduit with wire					
2 250 MCM alum, 1 #4 copper	E4@.156	LF	7.33	7.93	15.26
3 250 MCM alum, 1 #4 copper	E4@.183	LF	9.79	9.30	19.09
4 3/0 alum, 1 #4 copper	E4@.206	LF	7.87	10.50	18.37
2 4/0 alum, 1 #2 copper	E4@.164	LF	6.78	8.34	15.12
3 4/0 alum, 1 #2 copper	E4@.193	LF	8.80	9.81	18.61
4 4/0 alum, 1 #2 copper	E4@.221	LF	10.80	11.20	22.00
2 250 MCM copper, 1 #2 copper	E4@.170	LF	10.10	8.64	18.74
3" PVC conduit with wire					
4 250 MCM alum, 1 #4 copper	E4@.226	LF	12.80	11.50	24.30
2 350 MCM alum, 1 #2 copper	E4@.186	LF	10.20	9.45	19.65
3 350 MCM alum, 1 #2 copper	E4@.217	LF	13.60	11.00	24.60
3 250 MCM alum, 1 #2 copper	E4@.217	LF	10.60	11.00	21.60
4 250 MCM alum, 1 #2 copper	E4@.248	LF	13.10	12.60	25.70
3-1/2" PVC conduit with wire					
4 350 MCM alum, 1 #2 copper	E4@.264	LF	17.50	13.40	30.90
4" PVC conduit with wire					
6 350 MCM alum, 1 #2 copper	E4@.293	LF	27.60	14.90	42.50
7 350 MCM alum, 1 #2 copper	E4@.391	LF	31.10	19.90	51.00
3 500 MCM alum, 1 1/0 copper	E4@.311	LF	21.70	15.80	37.50
4 500 MCM alum, 1 1/0 copper	E4@.355	LF	26.20	18.00	44.20

Flexible Aluminum Conduit Type RWA installed in a building to 10' above floor level. No wire, fittings or supports included.

	Craft@Hrs	Unit	Material	Labor	Total
3/8" conduit	E4@.025	LF	.60	1.27	1.87
1/2" conduit	E4@.028	LF	.62	1.42	2.04
3/4" conduit	E4@.030	LF	.58	1.52	2.10
1" conduit	E4@.033	LF	1.44	1.68	3.12
1-1/4" conduit	E4@.035	LF	2.05	1.78	3.83
1-1/2" conduit	E4@.038	LF	3.05	1.93	4.98
2" conduit	E4@.040	LF	4.03	2.03	6.06

Flexible Steel Conduit installed in a building to 10' above floor level. No wire, fittings or supports included.

	Craft@Hrs	Unit	Material	Labor	Total
3/8" conduit	E4@.025	LF	.57	1.27	1.84
1/2" conduit	E4@.028	LF	.57	1.42	1.99
3/4" conduit	E4@.030	LF	.78	1.52	2.30
1" conduit	E4@.033	LF	1.75	1.68	3.43
1-1/4" conduit	E4@.035	LF	1.89	1.78	3.67
1-1/2" conduit, 25' coil	E4@.038	LF	3.23	1.93	5.16
2" conduit	E4@.040	LF	3.88	2.03	5.91
90-degree flex screw-in connector					
3/8" connector	E4@.070	Ea	3.55	3.56	7.11
1/2" connector	E4@.086	Ea	5.06	4.37	9.43
3/4" connector	E4@.100	Ea	3.95	5.08	9.03
1" connector	E4@.113	Ea	13.10	5.74	18.84
1-1/4" connector	E4@.148	Ea	19.50	7.52	27.02
1-1/2" connector	E4@.191	Ea	48.70	9.71	58.41
2" connector	E4@.260	Ea	55.80	13.20	69.00
2-1/2" connector	E4@.326	Ea	258.00	16.60	274.60
3" connector	E4@.435	Ea	462.00	22.10	484.10
Add for insulated set-screw connector	—	%	100.0	—	—

	Craft@Hrs	Unit	Material	Labor	Total
Flex screw-in coupling					
1/2" coupling	E4@.086	Ea	1.23	4.37	5.60
3/4" coupling	E4@.100	Ea	2.04	5.08	7.12
1" coupling	E4@.113	Ea	3.20	5.74	8.94
1-1/4" coupling	E4@.148	Ea	5.93	7.52	13.45
1-1/2" coupling	E4@.191	Ea	7.37	9.71	17.08
2" coupling	E4@.260	Ea	11.30	13.20	24.50
Add for height over 10' to 20'	—	%	—	20.0	—
Flexible Non-metallic Conduit, (ENT) blue conduit installed in a building to 10' above floor level. NER-290. No wire, fittings or supports included.					
1/2" conduit	E4@.021	LF	.78	1.07	1.85
3/4" conduit	E4@.022	LF	.70	1.12	1.82
1" conduit	E4@.030	LF	1.08	1.52	2.60
Liquid-Tight Flexible Metal Conduit, construction grade installed exposed in a building either vertically or horizontally up to 10' above floor level. No wire, fittings or supports included.					
3/8" conduit	E4@.045	LF	.78	2.29	3.07
1/2" conduit	E4@.045	LF	1.24	2.29	3.53
3/4" conduit	E4@.047	LF	1.76	2.39	4.15
1" conduit	E4@.050	LF	2.67	2.54	5.21
1-1/4" conduit	E4@.055	LF	3.79	2.80	6.59
1-1/2" conduit	E4@.065	LF	4.37	3.30	7.67
2" conduit	E4@.070	LF	5.34	3.56	8.90
Liquid-Tight Flexible Metal Conduit, Type LT installed exposed in a building either vertically or horizontally up to 10' above floor level. No wire, fittings or supports included.					
3/8" conduit	E4@.045	LF	.91	2.29	3.20
1/2" conduit	E4@.045	LF	1.09	2.29	3.38
3/4" conduit	E4@.047	LF	1.45	2.39	3.84
1" conduit	E4@.050	LF	2.21	2.54	4.75
1-1/4" conduit	E4@.055	LF	3.02	2.80	5.82
1-1/2" conduit	E4@.065	LF	4.09	3.30	7.39
2" conduit	E4@.070	LF	5.13	3.56	8.69
Liquid-tight straight flex connector, die cast					
1/2" connector	E4@.129	Ea	3.30	6.56	9.86
3/4" connector	E4@.140	Ea	4.61	7.12	11.73
1" connector	E4@.221	Ea	6.59	11.20	17.79
1-1/4" connector	E4@.244	Ea	7.84	12.40	20.24
1-1/2" connector	E4@.293	Ea	11.80	14.90	26.70
2" connector	E4@.492	Ea	18.80	25.00	43.80
90-degree liquid-tight flex connector, die cast					
1/2" connector	E4@.129	Ea	5.93	6.56	12.49
3/4" connector	E4@.140	Ea	8.34	7.12	15.46
1" connector	E4@.221	Ea	17.00	11.20	28.20
1-1/4" connector	E4@.244	Ea	26.70	12.40	39.10
1-1/2" connector	E4@.293	Ea	40.80	14.90	55.70
2" connector	E4@.492	Ea	45.00	25.00	70.00
Non-Metallic Liquid-Tight Flexible Conduit installed exposed in a building either vertically or horizontally up to 10' above floor level. No wire, fittings or supports included.					
3/8" conduit, 100-foot rolls	E4@.051	LF	.55	2.59	3.14
1/2" conduit, 100-foot rolls	E4@.051	LF	.51	2.59	3.10
3/4" conduit, 100-foot rolls	E4@.067	LF	.67	3.41	4.08
1" conduit, 100-foot rolls	E4@.067	LF	1.90	3.41	5.31
1-1/4" conduit, 100-foot rolls	E4@.085	LF	2.47	4.32	6.79
1-1/2" conduit, 50-foot rolls	E4@.085	LF	3.30	4.32	7.62
2" conduit, 50-foot rolls	E4@.105	LF	4.30	5.34	9.64

	Craft@Hrs	Unit	Material	Labor	Total
Non-metallic liquid-tight flex connector					
1/2" zero to 90 degree connector	E4@.060	Ea	7.23	3.05	10.28
3/4" zero to 90 degree connector	E4@.070	Ea	7.28	3.56	10.84
1" zero to 90 degree connector	E4@.080	Ea	6.82	4.07	10.89
1-1/4" zero to 90 degree connector	E4@.100	Ea	14.60	5.08	19.68
1-1/2" zero to 90 degree connector	E4@.100	Ea	19.40	5.08	24.48
2" zero to 90 degree connector	E4@.140	Ea	33.20	7.12	40.32
1/2" 90 degree connector	E4@.060	Ea	6.51	3.05	9.56
3/4" 90 degree connector	E4@.070	Ea	9.12	3.56	12.68
1" 90 degree connector	E4@.080	Ea	20.20	4.07	24.27
1-1/4" 90 degree connector	E4@.100	Ea	25.20	5.08	30.28
1-1/2" 90 degree connector	E4@.100	Ea	32.30	5.08	37.38
2" 90 degree connector	E4@.140	Ea	46.50	7.12	53.62
Add for height over 10' to 20'	—	%	—	20.0	—

Conduit Supports and Hangers By conduit size. Installed exposed in a building to 10' above floor level. Hangers and supports installed at heights over 10' will add about 20% to the labor cost.

	Craft@Hrs	Unit	Material	Labor	Total
Right angle conduit supports					
3/8" support	E4@.030	Ea	.44	1.52	1.96
1/2" support or 3/4" support	E4@.040	Ea	.44	2.03	2.47
1" support	E4@.050	Ea	.67	2.54	3.21
1-1/4" support	E4@.060	Ea	.74	3.05	3.79
1-1/2" support	E4@.060	Ea	.80	3.05	3.85
2" support	E4@.100	Ea	1.08	5.08	6.16
2-1/2" support	E4@.100	Ea	1.28	5.08	6.36
3" support	E4@.150	Ea	1.59	7.62	9.21
3-1/2" support	E4@.150	Ea	2.12	7.62	9.74
4" support	E4@.150	Ea	4.43	7.62	12.05
Add for parallel conduit supports	—	%	50.0	—	—
Add for edge conduit supports	—	%	120.0	—	—

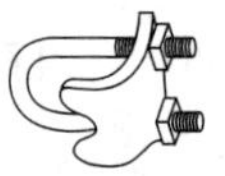

Conduit hangers, rigid with bolt, labor includes the cost of cutting threaded rod to length and attaching the rod. Add the material cost of the threaded rod from below.

	Craft@Hrs	Unit	Material	Labor	Total
1/2" hanger	E4@.097	Ea	.77	4.93	5.70
3/4" hanger	E4@.097	Ea	.79	4.93	5.72
1" hanger	E4@.108	Ea	1.29	5.49	6.78
1-1/4" hanger	E4@.108	Ea	1.80	5.49	7.29
1-1/2" hanger	E4@.108	Ea	2.18	5.49	7.67
2" hanger	E4@.119	Ea	2.38	6.05	8.43
2-1/2" hanger	E4@.119	Ea	3.07	6.05	9.12
3" hanger	E4@.119	Ea	3.67	6.05	9.72
3-1/2" hanger	E4@.129	Ea	5.22	6.56	11.78
4" hanger	E4@.129	Ea	12.30	6.56	18.86

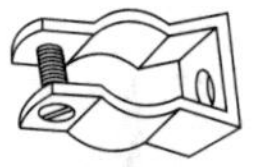

	Craft@Hrs	Unit	Material	Labor	Total
All threaded rod, plated steel, per linear foot of rod					
1/4", 20 thread	—	LF	.63	—	.63
5/16", 18 thread	—	LF	.70	—	.70
3/8", 16 thread	—	LF	.80	—	.80
1/2", 13 thread	—	LF	1.02	—	1.02
5/8", 11 thread	—	LF	1.67	—	1.67
Deduct for plain steel rod	—	%	−10.0	—	—
Rod beam clamps, for 1/4" or 3/8" threaded rod					
1" x 1" base, 15/16" jaw, 450 lb rating	E4@.200	Ea	2.44	10.20	12.64
2" x 2" base, 1" jaw, 1,300 lb rating	E4@.200	Ea	4.47	10.20	14.67
2-5/8" x 2-1/2" base, 1" jaw, 1,300 lb rating	E4@.234	Ea	6.24	11.90	18.14

	Craft@Hrs	Unit	Material	Labor	Total
Conduit clamps for EMT conduit					
1/2" or 3/4" clamp	E4@.062	Ea	.24	3.15	3.39
1" clamp	E4@.069	Ea	.32	3.51	3.83
1-1/4" clamp	E4@.069	Ea	.48	3.51	3.99
1-1/2" clamp	E4@.069	Ea	.50	3.51	4.01
2" clamp	E4@.075	Ea	.58	3.81	4.39
One hole heavy-duty stamped steel conduit straps					
1/2" strap	E4@.039	Ea	.17	1.98	2.15
3/4" strap	E4@.039	Ea	.22	1.98	2.20
1" strap	E4@.039	Ea	.38	1.98	2.36
1-1/4" strap	E4@.039	Ea	.58	1.98	2.56
1-1/2" strap	E4@.039	Ea	.77	1.98	2.75
2" strap	E4@.039	Ea	.99	1.98	2.97
2-1/2" strap	E4@.053	Ea	3.42	2.69	6.11
3" strap	E4@.053	Ea	4.78	2.69	7.47
3-1/2" strap	E4@.059	Ea	7.18	3.00	10.18
4" strap	E4@.059	Ea	7.43	3.00	10.43
Add for malleable iron one hole straps	—	%	30.0	—	—
Deduct for nail drive straps	—	%	−20.0	−30.0	—
Deduct for two hole stamped steel EMT straps	—	%	−70.0	—	—
Hanger channel, 1-5/8" x 1-5/8", based on 12" length					
No holes, solid back, 12 gauge steel	E4@.119	Ea	4.17	6.05	10.22
Holes 1-1/2" on center, 12 gauge aluminum	E4@.119	Ea	4.78	6.05	10.83
Channel strap for rigid steel conduit or EMT conduit, by conduit size, with bolts					
1/2" strap	E4@.020	Ea	1.20	1.02	2.22
3/4" strap	E4@.020	Ea	1.34	1.02	2.36
1" strap	E4@.023	Ea	1.44	1.17	2.61
1-1/4" strap	E4@.023	Ea	1.68	1.17	2.85
1-1/2" strap	E4@.023	Ea	1.89	1.17	3.06
2" strap	E4@.023	Ea	2.15	1.17	3.32
2-1/2" strap	E4@.039	Ea	2.35	1.98	4.33
3" strap	E4@.039	Ea	2.58	1.98	4.56
3-1/2" strap	E4@.039	Ea	3.15	1.98	5.13
4" strap	E4@.062	Ea	3.50	3.15	6.65
5" strap	E4@.062	Ea	4.31	3.15	7.46
6" strap	E4@.062	Ea	5.80	3.15	8.95
Lag screws, zinc plated, flattened end with stove bolt					
1/4" x 3"	E4@.092	Ea	.43	4.68	5.11
1/4" x 4"	E4@.092	Ea	.53	4.68	5.21
5/16" x 3-1/2"	E4@.092	Ea	.58	4.68	5.26
3/8" x 4"	E4@.119	Ea	.69	6.05	6.74
1/2" x 5"	E4@.129	Ea	1.36	6.56	7.92
Add for galvanized screws	—	%	100.0	—	—
Lag screw short expansion shields, without screws. Labor is for drilling hole					
1/4" or 5/16" x 1" shield	E4@.175	Ea	.61	8.90	9.51
3/8" x 1-3/4" shield	E4@.272	Ea	1.06	13.80	14.86
1/2" x 2" shield	E4@.321	Ea	1.42	16.30	17.72
5/8" x 2" shield	E4@.321	Ea	3.76	16.30	20.06
5/8" x 3-1/2" shield	E4@.345	Ea	5.67	17.50	23.17

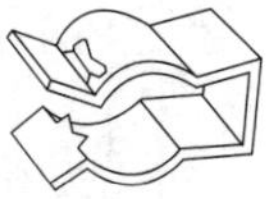
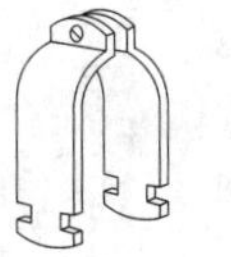
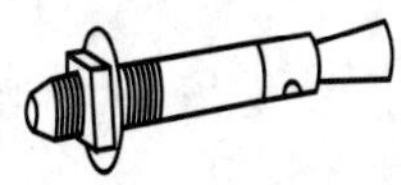

	Craft@Hrs	Unit	Material	Labor	Total
Self drilling masonry anchors					
1/4" anchor	E4@.127	Ea	.72	6.46	7.18
5/16" anchor	E4@.127	Ea	.98	6.46	7.44
3/8" anchor	E4@.191	Ea	1.13	9.71	10.84
1/2" anchor	E4@.191	Ea	1.77	9.71	11.48
5/8" anchor	E4@.259	Ea	2.94	13.20	16.14
3/4" anchor	E4@.259	Ea	4.86	13.20	18.06

Wiremold Raceway Steel, one-piece, installed on a finished wall in a building.Raceway including one coupling each 10 feet

	Craft@Hrs	Unit	Material	Labor	Total
V500 2 wire surface mounted raceway	E4@.059	LF	1.00	3.00	4.00
V700 2 wire surface mounted raceway	E4@.067	LF	1.80	3.41	5.21
Wiremold fittings					
V700 90-degree flat elbow	E4@.050	Ea	3.97	2.54	6.51
V700 90-degree twist elbow	E4@.050	Ea	7.68	2.54	10.22
V700 90-degree inside elbow	E4@.050	Ea	3.86	2.54	6.40
V700 90-degree outside elbow	E4@.050	Ea	4.40	2.54	6.94
V700 90-degree internal pull elbow	E4@.050	Ea	11.90	2.54	14.44
V700 90-degree internal twist elbow	E4@.150	Ea	4.24	7.62	11.86
V500 45-degree flat elbow	E4@.150	Ea	4.35	7.62	11.97
V500 90-degree flat elbow	E4@.150	Ea	2.18	7.62	9.80
V500/700 adjustable offset connector	E4@.150	Ea	8.73	7.62	16.35
V500 conduit connector	E4@.150	Ea	3.82	7.62	11.44
V700 connection cover	E4@.200	Ea	.43	10.20	10.63
V700 3-way branch "T"-fitting	E4@.100	Ea	5.42	5.08	10.50
V700 to 1/2" conduit transition fitting	E4@.050	Ea	6.38	2.54	8.92
V500/700 flexible section, 18"	E4@.350	Ea	17.00	17.80	34.80
V500/700 galvanized box connector	E4@.200	Ea	5.93	10.20	16.13
V500/700 coupling	E4@.200	Ea	.37	10.20	10.57
V500/700 support clip	—	Ea	.42	—	.42
Wiremold device box, V500/700 surface raceway					
1 gang, 1-3/8" diameter, 1 KO	E4@.250	Ea	6.87	12.70	19.57
1 gang, 2-1/4" diameter, 1 KO	E4@.250	Ea	15.00	12.70	27.70
1 gang, 4-5/8" x 2-7/8"	E4@.200	Ea	6.48	10.20	16.68
2 gang, 4-3/4" x 4-3/4"	E4@.300	Ea	12.00	15.20	27.20
2 gang, 15/16" diameter, 1 KO	E4@.300	Ea	5.35	15.20	20.55
2 gang, 1-3/4" diameter, 2 KO	E4@.300	Ea	14.20	15.20	29.40
2 gang, 2-1/4" diameter, 1 KO	E4@.300	Ea	18.80	15.20	34.00
Corner box, 2-1/2" diameter	E4@.250	Ea	15.00	12.70	27.70
Duplex receptacle box, 4-1/8" x 2" x 1-3/8"	E4@.360	Ea	13.20	18.30	31.50
Fixture box, 4-3/4" diameter	E4@.250	Ea	11.20	12.70	23.90
Fixture box, 6-3/8" diameter	E4@.250	Ea	13.20	12.70	25.90
Fixture box, 5-1/2" diameter	E4@.250	Ea	10.80	12.70	23.50
Junction and pull box, 1" x 5-1/2" diameter	E4@.250	Ea	11.00	12.70	23.70
Extension box, 4-3/4" diameter	E4@.250	Ea	10.60	12.70	23.30
Wiremold outlet box, V700 surface raceway					
Regular outlet box	E4@.250	Ea	6.97	12.70	19.67
Deep outlet box	E4@.250	Ea	8.39	12.70	21.09
Extra deep outlet box	E4@.250	Ea	8.48	12.70	21.18
Fan box	E4@.250	Ea	13.00	12.70	25.70
Starter box	E4@.250	Ea	6.98	12.70	19.68
Utility box, 2" x 4-1/8" x 1-3/8"	E4@.360	Ea	8.15	18.30	26.45

	Craft@Hrs	Unit	Material	Labor	Total
Plugmould® V2000 multi-outlet raceway					
Entrance end fitting	E4@.100	Ea	5.61	5.08	10.69
6 outlets, 36" long	E4@.450	Ea	31.10	22.90	54.00
6 outlets, 40" long, w/ circuit breaker	E4@.450	Ea	43.10	22.90	66.00
8 outlets, 52" long	E4@.550	Ea	42.00	28.00	70.00
10 outlets, 60" long	E4@.650	Ea	36.20	33.00	69.20

Cable Tray and Duct

Cable tray, zinc-plated steel wire basket type. Mounted on walls or posts or suspended from the ceiling.

	Craft@Hrs	Unit	Material	Labor	Total
6" or 8" wide, 2" deep, straight tray	E4@.144	LF	5.04	7.32	12.36
12" wide, 2" deep, straight tray	E4@.187	LF	5.23	9.51	14.74
18" wide, 2" deep, straight tray	E4@.187	LF	5.87	9.51	15.38
24" wide, 2" deep, straight tray	E4@.238	LF	6.60	12.10	18.70
6" or 8" wide, 4" deep, straight tray	E4@.144	LF	5.54	7.32	12.86
12" wide, 4" deep, straight tray	E4@.187	LF	6.25	9.51	15.76
18" wide, 4" deep, straight tray	E4@.187	LF	7.23	9.51	16.74
24" wide, 4" deep, straight tray	E4@.238	LF	8.11	12.10	20.21
Add for each L or reducer section	E4@.476	Ea	38.10	24.20	62.30
Add for each T or X junction section	E4@.476	Ea	76.20	24.20	100.40
Steel underfloor duct, including typical supports, fittings and accessories					
3-1/4" wide, 1 cell	E4@.097	LF	8.55	4.93	13.48
3-1/4" wide, 2 cell	E4@.104	LF	17.40	5.29	22.69
7-1/4" wide, 1 cell	E4@.148	LF	20.20	7.52	27.72
7-1/4" wide, 2 cell	E4@.148	LF	30.80	7.52	38.32

Wire and Cable

Copper wire and cable prices can change very quickly. Quarterly price updates for *National Estimator* are free and automatic during the year of issue. You'll be prompted when it's time to collect the next update. A Web connection is required.

Service Entrance Cable 600 volt stranded service entrance. Full spool prices.

SEU copper service entrance cable. Pulled in conduit. No excavation or conduit included. Type XHHW wire wound in a concentrically applied neutral and jacketed with gray sunlight-resistant PVC.

	Craft@Hrs	Unit	Material	Labor	Total
10-10-10	E4@.012	LF	.94	.61	1.55
8-8-8	E4@.012	LF	1.13	.61	1.74
6-6-8	E4@.012	LF	1.77	.61	2.38
6-6-6	E4@.012	LF	2.19	.61	2.80
4-4-6	E4@.014	LF	3.44	.71	4.15
4-4-4	E4@.014	LF	3.77	.71	4.48
3-3-5	E4@.014	LF	4.17	.71	4.88
3-3-3	E4@.015	LF	4.50	.76	5.26
2-2-4	E4@.016	LF	4.90	.81	5.71
2-2-2	E4@.016	LF	4.69	.81	5.50
1-1-1	E4@.018	LF	7.20	.91	8.11
1/0-1/0-1/0	E4@.020	LF	8.91	1.02	9.93
2/0-2/0-2/0	E4@.022	LF	11.30	1.12	12.42
3/0-3/0-3/0	E4@.024	LF	14.00	1.22	15.22
4/0-4/0-4/0	E4@.026	LF	15.70	1.32	17.02

SER aluminum service entrance cable. Three stranded aluminum conductors with color-coded cross-linked polyethylene (XLPE) insulation, bare ground wire and PVC jacket. For above ground service entrance, panel feeder and branch circuits.

	Craft@Hrs	Unit	Material	Labor	Total
6 gauge, 3 conductors, 6 gauge ground, 60 amps	E4@.012	LF	.76	.61	1.37
4 gauge, 3 conductors, 6 gauge ground, 75 amps	E4@.014	LF	.85	.71	1.56
2 gauge, 3 conductors, 4 gauge ground, 100 amps	E4@.016	LF	1.27	.81	2.08
1 gauge, 3 conductors, 2 gauge ground, 110 amps	E4@.018	LF	1.55	.91	2.46
1/0, 3 conductors, 2 gauge ground, 125 amps	E4@.020	LF	1.83	1.02	2.85
2/0, 3 conductors, 1 gauge ground, 150 amps	E4@.022	LF	2.20	1.12	3.32
3/0, 3 conductors, 1/0 ground, 175 amps	E4@.024	LF	2.76	1.22	3.98
4/0, 3 conductors, 2/0 ground, 200 amps	E4@.026	LF	3.13	1.32	4.45

	Craft@Hrs	Unit	Material	Labor	Total
USE underground service entrance wire. Stranded conductor insulated with abrasion, heat, moisture, and sunlight-resistant cross-linked polyethylene (XLP). General purpose wire, including conduit, direct burial and overhead.					
8 gauge, copper	E4@.009	LF	.48	.46	.94
6 gauge, copper	E4@.010	LF	.69	.51	1.20
2 gauge, copper	E4@.016	LF	1.54	.81	2.35
1/0 gauge, copper	E4@.017	LF	2.66	.86	3.52
2/0 gauge, copper	E4@.018	LF	3.33	.91	4.24
4/0 gauge, copper	E4@.018	LF	5.31	.91	6.22
250 MCM, copper	E4@.020	LF	5.75	1.02	6.77
500 MCM, copper	E4@.022	LF	9.29	1.12	10.41
Deduct for aluminum USE service entrance wire	—	%	-60.0	—	—
URD triplex aluminum service entrance cable. For direct burial or installation in ducts, in either wet or dry locations.					
6 gauge, Erskine	E4@.011	LF	.68	.56	1.24
4 gauge, Vassar	E4@.012	LF	.78	.61	1.39
2 gauge, Ramapo	E4@.013	LF	1.01	.66	1.67
2/0 gauge, Converse	E4@.017	LF	1.45	.86	2.31
4/0 gauge, Monmouth	E4@.020	LF	2.04	1.02	3.06
Bare Copper Ground Wire Pulled in conduit with conductor wires. No excavation or duct included. By American Wire Gauge. Cost based upon 1,000' reels. For cut-to-length prices, add 100% to the material cost.					
12 gauge, solid, 1,000' reel	E4@.004	LF	.15	.20	.35
10 gauge, solid, 1,000' reel	E4@.005	LF	.23	.25	.48
8 gauge, solid, 1,000' reel	E4@.005	LF	.34	.25	.59
6 gauge, solid, 1,000' reel	E4@.005	LF	.48	.25	.73
4 gauge, solid, 1,000' reel	E4@.006	LF	.71	.30	1.01
4 gauge, stranded, 1,000' reel	E4@.006	LF	.73	.30	1.03
2 gauge, solid, 1,000' reel	E4@.008	LF	1.20	.41	1.61
2 gauge, stranded, 1,000' reel	E4@.008	LF	1.25	.41	1.66
THHN/THWN-2 Copper Building Wire Pulled in conduit for feeder and branch circuits. No conduit included. THHN has a heat-resistant thermoplastic cover approved for working temperatures up to 90 degrees Celsius in dry locations. THWN resists moisture, oil and gasoline and is approved for temperatures to 75 degrees Celsius in dry, wet or oil locations. THHN/THWN is made from soft annealed copper and insulated with heat- and moisture-resistant PVC and covered with nylon (polyamide). Available in colors to simplify identification of conductors after wire is pulled in conduit. By American Wire Gauge (AWG). Stranded wire has 19 strands. Cost based on 1,000' reels. For cut-to-length prices, add 100% to the material cost. Copper wire prices are highly volatile.					
14 gauge, solid, 1,000' reel	E4@.006	LF	.09	.30	.39
14 gauge, stranded, 1,000' reel	E4@.006	LF	.09	.30	.39
12 gauge, solid, 1,000' reel	E4@.007	LF	.10	.36	.46
12 gauge, stranded, 1,000' reel	E4@.007	LF	.16	.36	.52
10 gauge, solid, 1,000' reel	E4@.008	LF	.18	.41	.59
10 gauge, stranded, 1,000' reel	E4@.008	LF	.26	.41	.67
8 gauge, stranded, 1,000' reel	E4@.009	LF	.33	.46	.79
6 gauge, stranded, 1,000' reel	E4@.010	LF	.53	.51	1.04
4 gauge, stranded, 1,000' reel	E4@.012	LF	.77	.61	1.38
3 gauge, stranded, 1,000' reel	E4@.013	LF	.96	.66	1.62
2 gauge, stranded, 1,000' reel	E4@.013	LF	1.24	.66	1.90
1 gauge, stranded, 1,000' reel	E4@.014	LF	1.52	.71	2.23
1/0 gauge, stranded, 1,000' reel	E4@.015	LF	1.73	.76	2.49
2/0 gauge, stranded, 1,000' reel	E4@.016	LF	1.95	.81	2.76
3/0 gauge, stranded, 1,000' reel	E4@.017	LF	2.48	.86	3.34
4/0 gauge, stranded, 1,000' reel	E4@.018	LF	3.06	.91	3.97
250 MCM, stranded, 1,000' reel	E4@.020	LF	3.66	1.02	4.68
350 MCM, stranded, 1,000' reel	E4@.038	LF	5.22	1.93	7.15
500 MCM, stranded, 1,000' reel	E4@.046	LF	7.04	2.34	9.38

	Craft@Hrs	Unit	Material	Labor	Total

XHHW Copper Building Wire Pulled in conduit for feeder and branch circuits. No conduit included. Abrasion-, moisture- and heat-resistant thermoplastic intended for harsh environments. Maximum operating temperature is 90 degrees Celsius in dry locations and 75 degrees Celsius in wet locations. Flame-retardant cross-linked synthetic polymer insulation. XHHW has no outer jacket or covering. Available in colors to simplify identification of conductors after wire is pulled in conduit. By American Wire Gauge (AWG). Stranded wire has 19 strands. Cost based on 1,000' reels. For cut-to-length prices, add 100% to the material cost. Copper wire prices are highly volatile.

	Craft@Hrs	Unit	Material	Labor	Total
14 gauge, stranded	E4@.006	LF	.12	.30	.42
12 gauge, stranded	E4@.007	LF	.19	.36	.55
10 gauge, solid	E4@.008	LF	.21	.41	.62
8 gauge, stranded	E4@.009	LF	.40	.46	.86
6 gauge, stranded	E4@.010	LF	.56	.51	1.07
4 gauge, stranded	E4@.012	LF	.77	.61	1.38
3 gauge, stranded	E4@.013	LF	.96	.66	1.62
2 gauge, stranded	E4@.014	LF	1.17	.71	1.88
1 gauge, stranded	E4@.015	LF	1.61	.76	2.37
1/0 gauge, stranded	E4@.016	LF	2.04	.81	2.85
2/0 gauge, stranded	E4@.017	LF	2.57	.86	3.43
4/0 gauge, stranded	E4@.018	LF	3.74	.91	4.65
250 MCM, stranded	E4@.020	LF	4.53	1.02	5.55

Type UF-B Direct Burial Sheathed Cable Installed in an open trench. No excavation or backfill included. UF-B is designed for burial in a trench but may also be used to wire interior branch circuits in residential and agricultural buildings. The cable jacket is sunlight-, fungus- and moisture-resistant gray PVC. Full-size ground wire. Full coil quantities. Copper wire prices are highly volatile.

	Craft@Hrs	Unit	Material	Labor	Total
14 gauge, 2 conductor	E4@.005	LF	.25	.25	.50
14 gauge, 3 conductor	E4@.005	LF	.39	.25	.64
12 gauge, 2 conductor	E4@.005	LF	.39	.25	.64
12 gauge, 3 conductor	E4@.005	LF	.57	.25	.82
10 gauge, 2 conductor	E4@.005	LF	.65	.25	.90
10 gauge, 3 conductor	E4@.006	LF	.94	.30	1.24
8 gauge, 2 conductor	E4@.007	LF	.98	.36	1.34
8 gauge, 3 conductor	E4@.007	LF	1.48	.36	1.84
6 gauge, 2 conductor	E4@.008	LF	1.32	.41	1.73
6 gauge, 3 conductor	E4@.008	LF	2.13	.41	2.54
Add for cut length quantities	—	%	20.0	—	—

Type NM-B (Romex) Sheathed Cable Installed in wood frame walls for outlets and switched fixtures, including boring out and pulling cable. NM-B cable can also be run through voids in masonry block or tile walls if little moisture is expected. Conductor insulation is color-coded PVC. 14 AWG (American Wire Gauge) is white, 12 AWG is yellow, 10 AWG is orange, and 8 and 6 AWG are black. Rated at 15 amps. With full-size ground wire. Full coil prices.

	Craft@Hrs	Unit	Material	Labor	Total
14 gauge, 2 conductor	E4@.027	LF	.23	1.37	1.60
14 gauge, 3 conductor	E4@.030	LF	.33	1.52	1.85
12 gauge, 2 conductor	E4@.030	LF	.35	1.52	1.87
12 gauge, 3 conductor	E4@.031	LF	.49	1.58	2.07
10 gauge, 2 conductor	E4@.031	LF	.54	1.58	2.12
10 gauge, 3 conductor	E4@.035	LF	.78	1.78	2.56
8 gauge, 2 conductor	E4@.040	LF	.85	2.03	2.88
8 gauge, 3 conductor	E4@.043	LF	1.27	2.19	3.46
6 gauge, 2 conductor	E4@.043	LF	1.20	2.19	3.39
6 gauge, 3 conductor	E4@.047	LF	1.90	2.39	4.29
4 gauge, 3 conductor	E4@.051	LF	4.29	2.59	6.88
2 gauge, 3 conductor	E4@.056	LF	6.60	2.85	9.45
Add for cut coil quantities	—	%	20.0	—	—
Deduct for no ground wire, #14 and #12 cable	—	%	−5.0	−5.0	—
Deduct for no ground wire, #10, #8 and #6 wire	—	%	−15.0	−5.0	—

	Craft@Hrs	Unit	Material	Labor	Total
MC Aluminum-Clad Copper Cable For use in dry sites. Exposed, concealed, or in approved raceway. Open or messenger-supported aerial runs. For powering lighting, control and signal circuits. Includes neutral, ground and one or two phase conductors. Installed with clamps or staples in a frame building or embedded in masonry, including approved bushings at terminations. Full coil prices.					
14 gauge, 2 conductor	E4@.009	LF	.44	.46	.90
14 gauge, 3 conductor	E4@.010	LF	.70	.51	1.21
14 gauge, 4 conductor	E4@.011	LF	.97	.56	1.53
12 gauge, 2 conductor	E4@.010	LF	.45	.51	.96
12 gauge, 3 conductor	E4@.011	LF	.77	.56	1.33
12 gauge, 4 conductor	E4@.012	LF	1.04	.61	1.65
10 gauge, 2 conductor	E4@.011	LF	.95	.56	1.51
10 gauge, 3 conductor	E4@.012	LF	1.33	.61	1.94
10 gauge, 4 conductor	E4@.013	LF	2.10	.66	2.76
Flexible Armored AC Cable, galvanized steel, 16 gauge integral bond wire to armor grounding path. Paper wrap conductor insulation covering. By American Wire Gauge and number of conductors. Installed exposed in a building either vertically or horizontally up to 10' above floor level. Sometimes referred to as "BX" cable.					
#14 wire, 2 conductor	E4@.030	LF	.61	1.52	2.13
#14 wire, 3 conductor	E4@.030	LF	.96	1.52	2.48
#12 wire, 2 conductor	E4@.030	LF	.46	1.52	1.98
#12 wire, 3 conductor	E4@.035	LF	.70	1.78	2.48
#12 wire, 4 conductor	E4@.038	LF	1.17	1.93	3.10
#10 wire, 2 conductor	E4@.031	LF	1.06	1.58	2.64
#10 wire, 3 conductor	E4@.039	LF	1.25	1.98	3.23
# 6 wire, 3 conductor	E4@.047	LF	3.36	2.39	5.75
# 4 wire, 3 conductor	E4@.051	LF	5.40	2.59	7.99
# 2 wire, 3 conductor	E4@.056	LF	7.68	2.85	10.53
Power Cable Single conductor medium voltage ozone-resistant stranded copper cable pulled in conduit. No conduit included. Labor cost assumes three bundled conductors are pulled at one time on runs up to 100 feet. Labor cost will be higher on longer cable pulls and about 50% lower when cable is laid in an open trench. No splicing included. Listed by American Wire Gauge. Note that wire prices can change very quickly. Check with supplier.					
5,000 volt, tape shielded, crosslinked polyethylene (XLP) insulated, with PVC jacket					
#6 gauge	E4@.014	LF	5.14	.71	5.85
#4 gauge	E4@.016	LF	5.36	.81	6.17
#2 gauge	E4@.021	LF	5.58	1.07	6.65
#1/0 gauge	E4@.026	LF	9.70	1.32	11.02
#2/0 gauge	E4@.028	LF	13.90	1.42	15.32
#4/0 gauge	E4@.038	LF	16.40	1.93	18.33
350 MCM	E4@.047	LF	24.30	2.39	26.69
500 MCM	E4@.053	LF	32.40	2.69	35.09
15,000 volt, tape shielded, ethylene propylene rubber (EPR) insulated, with PVC jacket					
#2 gauge	E4@.024	LF	11.30	1.22	12.52
#1/0	E4@.030	LF	14.40	1.52	15.92
#2/0	E4@.032	LF	16.90	1.63	18.53
350 MCM	E4@.055	LF	33.80	2.80	36.60
500 MCM	E4@.062	LF	34.10	3.15	37.25

	Craft@Hrs	Unit	Material	Labor	Total

Snow-Melting Cable For concrete pavement. Self-regulating heater cable 208-277 volt AC, encased in concrete pavement for walkways, steps, loading ramps or parking garages. Based on Raychem ElectroMelt™ System for concrete pavement. Cable is cut to length at the site and laid in a serpentine pattern using 12-inch center-to-center spacing. Use nylon cable ties to fasten cable to the top of reinforcing before concrete is placed. For scheduling purposes estimate that a crew of one can lay out, cut to length, install and tie 600 LF of cable in an 8-hour day. Based on 1.1 LF of cable per SF of pavement, including ties, "return bends" and waste, this yields 545 SF of pavement. These costs do not include reinforcing, concrete or concrete placing. A rule of thumb for sizing circuit breakers: For startup at 0 degrees F with 220 volts AC, allow 0.20 amps per LF of cable.

	Craft@Hrs	Unit	Material	Labor	Total
Heater cable (1.1 LF per SF of pavement)	CE@.015	SF	9.80	.91	10.71
Power connection kit, including end seals	CE@.500	Ea	34.40	30.20	64.60
Cable expansion joint kit	CE@.250	Ea	23.30	15.10	38.40
ElectroMelt™ junction box	CE@.500	Ea	131.00	30.20	161.20
System controller, automatic	CE@1.50	Ea	2,750.00	90.60	2,840.60
Thermostat, line sensing	CE@.500	Ea	281.00	30.20	311.20
Ground fault protection device	CE@.969	Ea	417.00	58.50	475.50

Ice-Melting Cable For roofs, gutters and downspouts. Self-regulating heater cable 120 or 208-277 volts AC, run exposed on the surface of the roof or within gutters. Based on Raychem IceStop™ System for roofs and gutters. Cable is cut to length on site and laid in a serpentine pattern using 24-inch center-to-center spacing and 32-inch loop height. Fasten to the roof with Raychem clips. For scheduling purposes estimate that a crew of one can cut to length and install 400 LF of cable in an 8-hour day. Based on 1.2 LF of cable per SF of protected roof area, including clips, "return bends" and waste, this yields 330 SF of protected area. Figure each LF of gutter as equal to one SF of roof. Figure each downspout as equal to 15 SF of roof. These costs do not include the roofing, gutters, or downspouts. A rule of thumb for sizing circuit breakers: For startup at 0 degrees F with 120 volts AC, allow 0.17 amps per LF of cable. For startup at 0 degrees F with 208-277 volts AC, allow 0.11 amps per LF of cable.

	Craft@Hrs	Unit	Material	Labor	Total
Heater cable (1.2 LF per SF of protected area)	CE@.033	LF	5.89	1.99	7.88
Power connection kit	CE@.500	Ea	34.40	30.20	64.60
Cable splice kit	CE@.374	Ea	15.70	22.60	38.30
End seal kit	CE@.374	Ea	14.80	22.60	37.40
Downspout hanger	CE@.374	Ea	28.70	22.60	51.30
Metal roof mounting kit	CE@.500	Ea	28.60	30.20	58.80

Electrical Outlet Boxes Steel boxes installed on an exposed wall or ceiling. The material cost for phenolic, PVC and fiberglass boxes will be 50% to 70% less. These costs include fasteners but no switch or receptacle

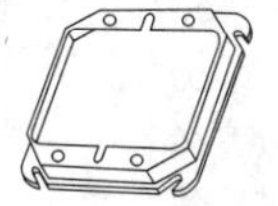

	Craft@Hrs	Unit	Material	Labor	Total
Square outlet boxes					
4" x 4" x 1-1/2" deep with					
1/2" and 3/4" knockouts	E4@.187	Ea	2.06	9.51	11.57
Side mounting bracket	E4@.187	Ea	3.03	9.51	12.54
4" x 4" x 2-1/8" deep with					
1/2" and 3/4" knockouts	E4@.245	Ea	2.84	12.50	15.34
Side mounting bracket	E4@.245	Ea	1.28	12.50	13.78
Add for					
1-1/2" deep extension rings	E4@.120	Ea	2.11	6.10	8.21
Romex or BX clamps	—	Ea	.99	—	.99
Steel flush cover blanks	E4@.039	Ea	.62	1.98	2.60
Plaster rings to 3/4" deep	E4@.080	Ea	1.84	4.07	5.91

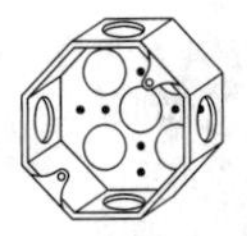

	Craft@Hrs	Unit	Material	Labor	Total
Octagon outlet boxes					
4" x 1-1/2" deep with					
1/2" knockouts	E4@.187	Ea	1.23	9.51	10.74
Mounting bracket, horizontal	E4@.187	Ea	2.27	9.51	11.78
4" x 2-1/8" deep with					
1/2" and 3/4" knockouts	E4@.245	Ea	4.96	12.50	17.46

	Craft@Hrs	Unit	Material	Labor	Total
Add for					
1-1/2" deep extension rings	E4@.120	Ea	2.48	6.10	8.58
1-1/2" with 18.5" adjustable bar set	E4@.282	Ea	2.92	14.30	17.22
3" deep concrete ring	E4@.516	Ea	2.12	26.20	28.32
4" steel flush cover blanks	E4@.039	Ea	.99	1.98	2.97
Plaster ring to 3/4" deep	E4@.080	Ea	1.91	4.07	5.98
Handy boxes, 4" x 2-1/8"					
1-1/2" deep, 1/2" knockouts	E4@.187	Ea	2.27	9.51	11.78
1-7/8" deep, 3/4" knockouts	E4@.187	Ea	.99	9.51	10.50
2-1/2" deep, 3/4" knockouts	E4@.245	Ea	2.84	12.50	15.34
2-1/8" deep, with side mounting bracket	E4@.245	Ea	2.82	12.50	15.32
1-1/2" deep extension rings	E4@.120	Ea	3.61	6.10	9.71
Blank or switch cover	E4@.039	Ea	.97	1.98	2.95
Weatherproof box and cover	E4@.059	Ea	4.14	3.00	7.14
Switch boxes, 3" x 2", square corner gangable boxes with mounting ears					
2" deep, 1/2" knockouts	E4@.245	Ea	1.86	12.50	14.36
2-1/2" deep, 1/2" knockouts	E4@.245	Ea	7.61	12.50	20.11
3-1/2" deep, 3/4" knockouts	E4@.324	Ea	5.11	16.50	21.61
Gang switch boxes, 2" x 3" x 1-5/8"					
2 gang	E4@.242	Ea	6.03	12.30	18.33
3 gang	E4@.342	Ea	9.46	17.40	26.86
4 gang	E4@.342	Ea	12.20	17.40	29.60
5 gang	E4@.482	Ea	20.70	24.50	45.20
6 gang	E4@.482	Ea	14.50	24.50	39.00
Floor boxes, watertight, cast iron, round					
4-3/16" x 3-3/4" deep, non-adjustable	E4@1.54	Ea	66.00	78.30	144.30
3-3/4" x 2" deep, semi-adjustable	E4@1.54	Ea	76.90	78.30	155.20
4-3/16" x 3-3/4" deep, adjustable	E4@1.54	Ea	91.50	78.30	169.80
2-1/8" single, round floor cover plates	E4@.156	Ea	43.00	7.93	50.93
Galvanized or gray enamel NEMA Class 1 (indoor) pull boxes, with screw cover, 4" deep					
4" x 4"	E4@.373	Ea	12.80	19.00	31.80
4" x 6"	E4@.373	Ea	15.30	19.00	34.30
6" x 6"	E4@.373	Ea	19.30	19.00	38.30
6" x 8"	E4@.391	Ea	21.10	19.90	41.00
8" x 8"	E4@.391	Ea	23.10	19.90	43.00
8" x 10"	E4@.444	Ea	28.40	22.60	51.00
8" x 12"	E4@.483	Ea	27.40	24.60	52.00
10" x 10"	E4@.492	Ea	25.90	25.00	50.90
10" x 12"	E4@.539	Ea	48.40	27.40	75.80
12" x 12"	E4@.593	Ea	54.60	30.10	84.70
12" x 16"	E4@.663	Ea	76.40	33.70	110.10
12" x 18"	E4@.785	Ea	79.50	39.90	119.40
Galvanized or gray enamel NEMA Class 1 (indoor) pull boxes, with screw cover, 6" deep					
6" x 6"	E4@.373	Ea	18.10	19.00	37.10
8" x 8"	E4@.391	Ea	25.00	19.90	44.90
8" x 10"	E4@.444	Ea	28.00	22.60	50.60
10" x 10"	E4@.492	Ea	33.20	25.00	58.20
10" x 12"	E4@.539	Ea	38.00	27.40	65.40
12" x 12"	E4@.593	Ea	47.50	30.10	77.60
12" x 16"	E4@.663	Ea	56.10	33.70	89.80

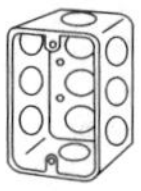

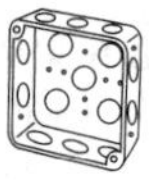

	Craft@Hrs	Unit	Material	Labor	Total
12" x 18"	E4@.785	Ea	60.60	39.90	100.50
16" x 16"	E4@.929	Ea	68.60	47.20	115.80
18" x 18"	E4@1.10	Ea	74.40	55.90	130.30
18" x 24"	E4@1.30	Ea	136.00	66.10	202.10
24" x 24"	E4@1.54	Ea	170.00	78.30	248.30
Cast aluminum NEMA Class 3R (weatherproof) screw cover junction boxes, recessed, flush mounted, with cover					
6" x 6" x 4" deep	E4@.930	Ea	339.00	47.30	386.30
6" x 8" x 4" deep	E4@.930	Ea	418.00	47.30	465.30
6" x 6" x 6" deep	E4@.930	Ea	418.00	47.30	465.30
6" x 12" x 6" deep	E4@1.42	Ea	621.00	72.20	693.20
8" x 8" x 4" deep	E4@.982	Ea	476.00	49.90	525.90
8" x 8" x 6" deep	E4@1.14	Ea	512.00	57.90	569.90
8" x 12" x 6" deep	E4@1.30	Ea	774.00	66.10	840.10
10" x 10" x 6" deep	E4@1.33	Ea	438.00	67.60	505.60
12" x 12" x 6" deep	E4@1.35	Ea	918.00	68.60	986.60
12" x 12" x 8" deep	E4@1.73	Ea	1,080.00	87.90	1,167.90
12" x 24" x 6" deep	E4@1.97	Ea	2,050.00	100.00	2,150.00
18" x 36" x 8" deep	E4@2.56	Ea	4,750.00	130.00	4,880.00
Hinged cover panel enclosures, NEMA 1, enamel, with cover					
16" x 12" x 7" deep	E4@1.30	Ea	183.00	66.10	249.10
20" x 20" x 7" deep	E4@1.30	Ea	251.00	66.10	317.10
30" x 20" x 7" deep	E4@1.77	Ea	267.00	90.00	357.00
24" x 20" x 9" deep	E4@1.30	Ea	311.00	66.10	377.10
30" x 24" x 9" deep	E4@1.77	Ea	354.00	90.00	444.00
36" x 30" x 9" deep	E4@1.77	Ea	442.00	90.00	532.00

Electrical Receptacles

Standard commercial grade except where noted. Ivory or brown receptacles. White or gray receptacles will cost about 10% more. Labor includes connecting wire and securing the device in the box. Add the cost of the box and the cover plate.

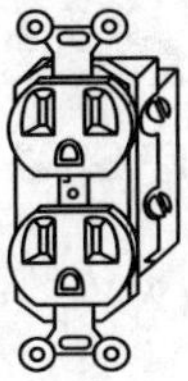

	Craft@Hrs	Unit	Material	Labor	Total
15 amp, 125 volt self-grounding, 2 pole, 3 wire duplex receptacles					
Residential grade, grounded duplex	CE@.162	Ea	.50	9.79	10.29
Screwless, not self-grounding	CE@.162	Ea	2.68	9.79	12.47
Side terminals	CE@.162	Ea	2.68	9.79	12.47
Back and side terminals	CE@.162	Ea	2.67	9.79	12.46
Feed thru wiring, back and side terminals	CE@.162	Ea	6.16	9.79	15.95
Safety ground, side terminals	CE@.162	Ea	9.86	9.79	19.65
Ground fault circuit interrupter receptacle	CE@.324	Ea	15.90	19.60	35.50
Add for NEMA 5 single receptacles	—	%	15.0	—	—
20 amp, 125 volt self-grounding, 2 pole, 3 wire duplex receptacles					
Side terminals	CE@.162	Ea	7.05	9.79	16.84
Back and side terminals	CE@.162	Ea	10.00	9.79	19.79
Feed thru wiring, back and side terminals	CE@.162	Ea	10.50	9.79	20.29
Hospital grade	CE@.162	Ea	10.90	9.79	20.69
Ground fault circuit interrupter receptacle	CE@.324	Ea	18.00	19.60	37.60
Add for NEMA 5 single receptacles	—	%	15.0	—	—
15 amp, 125 volt self-grounding, 2 pole, 3 wire receptacles with USB ports					
1 receptacle, 2 USB ports	CE@.162	Ea	9.92	9.79	19.71
2 receptacles, 2 USB ports	CE@.162	Ea	20.20	9.79	29.99
2 receptacles, 2 USB ports, 20 amp	CE@.162	Ea	25.90	9.79	35.69
4.2 amp, 4 USB ports only	CE@.162	Ea	26.00	9.79	35.79
250 volt receptacles, self-grounding, 2 pole, 3 wire, back & side terminals					
15 amp, duplex	CE@.187	Ea	12.20	11.30	23.50
15 amp, single	CE@.187	Ea	8.43	11.30	19.73
20 amp, duplex	CE@.187	Ea	9.48	11.30	20.78
20 amp, duplex, feed thru wiring	CE@.187	Ea	14.90	11.30	26.20
20 amp, single	CE@.187	Ea	10.10	11.30	21.40

	Craft@Hrs	Unit	Material	Labor	Total
Clock receptacle, 2 pole, 15 amp, 125 volt	CE@.329	Ea	7.14	19.90	27.04
120/208 volt 20 amp 4 pole, duplex receptacle	CE@.795	Ea	33.00	48.00	81.00
125/250 volt 3 pole receptacles, flush mount					
15 amp/10 amp	CE@.714	Ea	16.30	43.10	59.40
20 amp	CE@.820	Ea	39.00	49.50	88.50
30 amp	CE@.820	Ea	89.50	49.50	139.00
277 volt 30 amp 2 pole receptacle	CE@.268	Ea	52.40	16.20	68.60
Dryer receptacles, 250 volt, 30/50 amp, 3 wire	CE@.536	Ea	8.98	32.40	41.38
Accessories for 50 amp dryer receptacles					
Flush mounted plug	CE@.288	Ea	52.30	17.40	69.70
Surface mounted plug	CE@.288	Ea	35.80	17.40	53.20
Cord sets for dryer receptacles					
36 inch, three #10 wires	CE@.288	Ea	21.90	17.40	39.30
48 inch, three #10 wires	CE@.288	Ea	24.80	17.40	42.20
60 inch, three #10 wires	CE@.288	Ea	28.70	17.40	46.10

Electrical Switches Commercial grade, 120 to 277 volt rating except where noted. Ivory or brown. Add 10% for white or gray. Labor includes connecting wire to the switch and securing the switch in the box. Add the cost of the box and cover plate.

	Craft@Hrs	Unit	Material	Labor	Total
15 amp switches, back and side wired					
One pole quiet switch, residential (side wired only)	CE@.112	Ea	.68	6.77	7.45
One pole switch, commercial, minimum quality	CE@.112	Ea	1.29	6.77	8.06
Two pole switch	CE@.309	Ea	12.00	18.70	30.70
Three-way switch	CE@.309	Ea	7.59	18.70	26.29
Four-way switch	CE@.309	Ea	10.00	18.70	28.70
20 amp switches, back and side wired					
One pole switch	CE@.187	Ea	3.00	11.30	14.30
Two pole switch	CE@.433	Ea	6.00	26.20	32.20
Three-way switch	CE@.291	Ea	5.00	17.60	22.60
Four-way switch	CE@.435	Ea	12.20	26.30	38.50
30 amp switches, side wired					
One pole switch	CE@.246	Ea	13.50	14.90	28.40
Two pole switch	CE@.475	Ea	20.10	28.70	48.80
Three-way switch	CE@.372	Ea	19.70	22.50	42.20
Four-way switch	CE@.475	Ea	29.20	28.70	57.90
20 amp weatherproof switches, lever handle, with cover					
One pole switch	CE@.187	Ea	9.80	11.30	21.10
Two pole switch	CE@.433	Ea	18.80	26.20	45.00
Three-way switch	CE@.291	Ea	13.00	17.60	30.60
Single pole, two gang, 10 amp	CE@.358	Ea	22.20	21.60	43.80
Dimmer switches, push for off					
Incandescent, 600 watt, one pole	CE@.417	Ea	11.00	25.20	36.20
LED or incandescent, single or three-way	CE@.626	Ea	33.00	37.80	70.80
Smart lighting, LED/CFL or incandescent/halogen	CE@.626	Ea	55.20	37.80	93.00
Fluorescent dimmer, 10 lamp load	CE@.626	Ea	57.00	37.80	94.80
Astro dial time switch, 40 amp, with box	CE@3.00	Ea	118.00	181.00	299.00
15 minute timer switch, wall box mounted	CE@.426	Ea	52.30	25.70	78.00
Single pole, 1 throw time switch, 277 volt	CE@.890	Ea	55.10	53.80	108.90
Float switches for sump pumps, automatic 10A, 125/250/480 VAC	CE@1.03	Ea	37.10	62.20	99.30

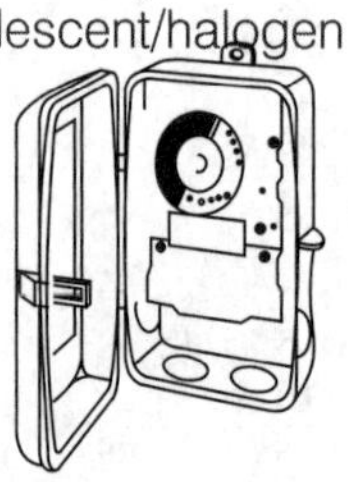

	Craft@Hrs	Unit	Material	Labor	Total
One-way 15 amp toggle switch with neon pilot	CE@.327	Ea	8.00	19.80	27.80
Three-way 15 amp toggle switch with neon pilot	CE@.372	Ea	12.00	22.50	34.50
Photoelectric switches, flush, with wall plate					
120 volt, 1,000 watt	CE@.426	Ea	8.27	25.70	33.97
208 volt, 1,800 watt	CE@.626	Ea	9.73	37.80	47.53
480 volt, 3,000 watt	CE@.795	Ea	13.60	48.00	61.60
Button control stations, surface mounted, NEMA Class 1, standard duty, 120/240 volt, with enclosure 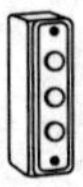					
Start-stop switch, 2 button	CE@.624	Ea	25.80	37.70	63.50
Start-stop switch with lockout, 2 button	CE@.624	Ea	38.60	37.70	76.30
Forward, reverse and stop buttons, 3 button	CE@.624	Ea	52.20	37.70	89.90
Forward, reverse, stop and lockout, 3 button	CE@.624	Ea	52.50	37.70	90.20
Manual toggle starter switches, surface mounted, NEMA Class 1, 120/240 volt, non-reversing, with enclosure					
Size 0 motors, 2 pole	CE@.613	Ea	105.00	37.00	142.00
Size 1 motors, 3 pole	CE@.698	Ea	135.00	42.20	177.20
Size 1-1/2 motors, 2 pole	CE@.901	Ea	155.00	54.40	209.40
Manual button starter switches, surface mounted, NEMA Class 1, 110 to 240 volt, 2 pole, 1 phase, with enclosure, start, stop, reset, with relay 					
Size 00 motors	CE@.712	Ea	140.00	43.00	183.00
Size 0 motors	CE@.712	Ea	151.00	43.00	194.00
Size 1 motors	CE@.820	Ea	170.00	49.50	219.50
Size 1-1/2 motors	CE@.975	Ea	204.00	58.90	262.90

Electrical Box Cover Plates Includes the cover plate and screws. Add the cost of the box and switch or receptacle. Labor includes attaching the cover plate to the box. Almond or ivory plastic except as noted.

	Craft@Hrs	Unit	Material	Labor	Total
Residential grade electrical box cover plates					
1 gang plate, duplex receptacle	CE@.050	Ea	.38	3.02	3.40
1 gang plate, toggle switch	CE@.050	Ea	.38	3.02	3.40
2 gang plate, 2 duplex receptacles	CE@.100	Ea	1.10	6.04	7.14
2 gang plate, two toggle switches	CE@.100	Ea	1.10	6.04	7.14
2 gang plate, oversize, toggle or receptacle	CE@.100	Ea	1.18	6.04	7.22
3 gang plate, toggle or receptacle	CE@.150	Ea	2.42	9.06	11.48
Decora multi-gang sectional plate, end or center	CE@.050	Ea	1.97	3.02	4.99
Stainless steel electrical box cover plates					
1 gang plate, blank, duplex or toggle	CE@.050	Ea	1.69	3.02	4.71
1 gang plate, power outlet	CE@.050	Ea	1.98	3.02	5.00
2 gang plate, blank, duplex or toggle	CE@.100	Ea	2.99	6.04	9.03
3 gang plate, blank, duplex or toggle	CE@.150	Ea	3.77	9.06	12.83
Specification grade electrical box cover plates					
1 gang plate, single receptacle or toggle switch	CE@.050	Ea	5.61	3.02	8.63
1 gang plate, duplex receptacle or toggle switch	CE@.050	Ea	8.36	3.02	11.38
1 gang plate, GFIC and rocker switch	CE@.050	Ea	8.36	3.02	11.38
2 gang plate, double duplex or toggle switches	CE@.100	Ea	7.16	6.04	13.20
2 gang plate, double GFIC and rocker switches	CE@.100	Ea	7.16	6.04	13.20
3 gang plate, duplex receptacles or switches	CE@.150	Ea	11.10	9.06	20.16

Grounding Devices No excavation or concrete included.

	Craft@Hrs	Unit	Material	Labor	Total
Copper-clad grounding rods, driven					
1/2" x 8'	E4@.365	Ea	11.80	18.60	30.40
5/8" x 8'	E4@.365	Ea	12.80	18.60	31.40
5/8" x 10'	E4@.420	Ea	18.80	21.30	40.10
3/4" x 8'	E4@.365	Ea	28.00	18.60	46.60
3/4" x 10'	E4@.420	Ea	29.30	21.30	50.60

	Craft@Hrs	Unit	Material	Labor	Total
Grounding locknuts					
1/2" locknuts	E4@.050	Ea	1.73	2.54	4.27
3/4" locknuts	E4@.060	Ea	2.20	3.05	5.25
1" locknuts	E4@.080	Ea	2.97	4.07	7.04
1-1/4" locknuts	E4@.100	Ea	3.97	5.08	9.05
1-1/2" locknuts	E4@.100	Ea	5.36	5.08	10.44
2" locknuts	E4@.150	Ea	7.29	7.62	14.91
2-1/2" locknuts	E4@.200	Ea	14.70	10.20	24.90
3" locknuts	E4@.200	Ea	18.50	10.20	28.70
4" locknuts	E4@.300	Ea	38.70	15.20	53.90
Ground rod clamps					
1/2" clamp	E4@.249	Ea	2.05	12.70	14.75
5/8" clamp	E4@.249	Ea	2.41	12.70	15.11
3/4" clamp	E4@.249	Ea	3.45	12.70	16.15
Coupling for threaded ground rod					
5/8" clamp	E4@.249	Ea	14.30	12.70	27.00
3/4" clamp	E4@.249	Ea	19.80	12.70	32.50
Copper bonding connector straps, 3/4" x .050"					
1" strap	E4@.286	Ea	12.40	14.50	26.90
2" strap	E4@.300	Ea	16.00	15.20	31.20
3" strap	E4@.315	Ea	21.40	16.00	37.40
4" strap	E4@.330	Ea	25.40	16.80	42.20
Brazed connections for wire					
#6 wire	E4@.194	Ea	1.45	9.86	11.31
#2 wire	E4@.194	Ea	1.70	9.86	11.56
#1/0 wire	E4@.295	Ea	4.58	15.00	19.58
#4/0 wire	E4@.391	Ea	11.60	19.90	31.50
Grounding using a 5/8" x 8' copper clad ground rod, includes 10' grounding conductor, clamps, connectors, locknut, and rod.					
100 amp service, #8 copper wire	E4@1.13	Ea	33.10	57.40	90.50
150 amp service, #6 copper wire	E4@1.16	Ea	34.50	59.00	93.50

Electric Motors General purpose, 3 phase, open drip-proof, industrial duty, 1,700-1,780 RPM, 208-230/460 volt, rigid welded or solid base, furnished and placed, no hookup included. Based on Dayton motors.

	Craft@Hrs	Unit	Material	Labor	Total
1/2 HP	E4@1.99	Ea	231.00	101.00	332.00
3/4 HP	E4@1.99	Ea	259.00	101.00	360.00
1 HP	E4@1.99	Ea	274.00	101.00	375.00
1-1/2 HP	E4@1.99	Ea	285.00	101.00	386.00
2 HP	E4@1.99	Ea	292.00	101.00	393.00
3 HP	E4@1.99	Ea	316.00	101.00	417.00
5 HP	E4@2.22	Ea	369.00	113.00	482.00
7-1/2 HP	E4@2.40	Ea	544.00	122.00	666.00
10 HP	E4@2.51	Ea	630.00	128.00	758.00

Electric Motor Connection Includes a NEMA-1 fusible heavy duty safety switch, connectors, fittings, ells, adapters, supports, anchors and conduit with wire appropriate for the load connected but no starter or motor.

Single phase, using 10' RSC, 20' PVC and 6' flex conduit, NEMA Class 1 (indoor) general duty switch, 240 V

	Craft@Hrs	Unit	Material	Labor	Total
For motor to 2 HP, 20 amps	E4@6.35	Ea	144.00	323.00	467.00
For 2.5 to 3 HP motor, 30 amps	E4@6.63	Ea	147.00	337.00	484.00
For 3 HP motor, 45 amps	E4@6.68	Ea	297.00	340.00	637.00
For 8 to 15 HP motor, 90 amps	E4@13.4	Ea	457.00	681.00	1,138.00

	Craft@Hrs	Unit	Material	Labor	Total
Three phase wiring using 10' RSC, 20' PVC and 6' flex conduit, NEMA Class 1 (indoor) switch, 600 V					
For motor to 2 HP, 20 amps	E4@7.18	Ea	296.00	365.00	661.00
For 3 to 5 HP motor, 30 amps	E4@7.90	Ea	299.00	402.00	701.00
For 7 to 10 HP motor, 45 amps	E4@8.30	Ea	351.00	422.00	773.00
For 25 to 50 HP motor, 90 amps	E4@9.30	Ea	729.00	473.00	1,202.00
For 50 to 100 HP motor, 135 amps	E4@14.1	Ea	1,200.00	717.00	1,917.00
For 100 to 200 HP motor, 270 amps	E4@21.9	Ea	3,050.00	1,110.00	4,160.00
Single phase, using 10' RSC, 20' PVC and 6' flex conduit, NEMA Class 3R (weatherproof) switch, 240 V					
For motor to 2 HP, 20 amps	E4@6.63	Ea	169.00	337.00	506.00
For 2 to 5 HP motor, 30 amps	E4@6.97	Ea	172.00	354.00	526.00
For 5 to 7.5 HP motor, 45 amps	E4@6.94	Ea	236.00	353.00	589.00
Three phase using 10' RSC, 20' PVC and 6' flex conduit, NEMA Class 3R (weatherproof) switch, 600 V					
For motor to 5 HP motor, 20 amps	E4@7.10	Ea	401.00	361.00	762.00
For 1 to 10 HP motor, 30 amps	E4@7.25	Ea	404.00	369.00	773.00
For 10 to 25 HP motor, 45 amps	E4@9.51	Ea	482.00	483.00	965.00
For 25 to 50 HP motor, 90 amps	E4@9.51	Ea	853.00	483.00	1,336.00
For 60 to 100 HP motor, 135 amps	E4@12.1	Ea	1,340.00	615.00	1,955.00
For 125 to 200 HP motor, 270 amps	E4@21.6	Ea	3,360.00	1,100.00	4,460.00

Electric Motor Connection Complete installation, including magnetic motor starter, overload relay, all wiring, a heavy duty fusible safety switch, junction box and cover, connectors, fittings, adapters, supports, anchors and conduit appropriate for the load connected. No motor included.

	Craft@Hrs	Unit	Material	Labor	Total
Single phase, using 10' RSC, 20' PVC and 6' flex conduit, NEMA Class 1 (indoor) starter, 230 V					
For motor to 2 HP, 20 amps	E4@8.11	Ea	346.00	412.00	758.00
For 2 to 3 HP motor, 30 amps	E4@8.32	Ea	388.00	423.00	811.00
For 3 to 8 HP motor, 45 amps	E4@8.45	Ea	557.00	430.00	987.00
For 8 to 15 HP motor, 90 amps	E4@15.5	Ea	952.00	788.00	1,740.00
Three phase wiring using 10' RSC, 20' PVC and 6' flex conduit, NEMA Class 1 (indoor) starter, 480 V					
For motor to 2 HP, 20 amps	E4@9.90	Ea	923.00	503.00	1,426.00
For 2 to 5 HP motor, 30 amps	E4@10.6	Ea	972.00	539.00	1,511.00
For 7 to 25 HP motor, 45 amps	E4@20.5	Ea	1,500.00	1,040.00	2,540.00
For 25 to 50 HP motor, 90 amps	E4@23.1	Ea	2,580.00	1,170.00	3,750.00
Single phase, using 10' RSC, 20' PVC and 6' flex conduit, NEMA Type 3R (weatherproof) starter, 230 V					
For motor to 2 HP, 20 amps	E4@8.91	Ea	475.00	453.00	928.00
For 2 to 5 HP motor, 30 amps	E4@9.15	Ea	538.00	465.00	1,003.00
For 5 to 7.5 HP motor, 45 amps	E4@9.25	Ea	764.00	470.00	1,234.00
Three phase using 10' RSC, 20' PVC and 6' flex conduit, NEMA Type 3R (weatherproof) starter, 480 V					
For motor to 5 HP, 20 amps	E4@10.9	Ea	1,330.00	554.00	1,884.00
For 5 to 10 HP motor, 30 amps	E4@11.7	Ea	1,390.00	595.00	1,985.00
For 10 to 25 HP motor, 45 amps	E4@22.5	Ea	2,170.00	1,140.00	3,310.00
For 25 to 50 HP motor, 90 amps	E4@25.4	Ea	3,680.00	1,290.00	4,970.00

Motor Starters Magnetic operated full voltage non-reversing motor controllers with thermal overload relays and enclosure.

	Craft@Hrs	Unit	Material	Labor	Total
Two pole, 1 phase contactors, NEMA Class 1 (indoor), electrically held with holding interlock, one reset					
Size 00, 1/3 HP, 9 amp	E4@1.47	Ea	273.00	74.70	347.70
Size 0, 1 HP, 18 amp	E4@1.62	Ea	316.00	82.30	398.30
Size 1, 2 HP, 27 amp	E4@1.73	Ea	359.00	87.90	446.90
Size 2, 3 HP, 45 amp	E4@1.73	Ea	461.00	87.90	548.90
Size 3, 7-1/2 HP, 90 amp	E4@2.02	Ea	657.00	103.00	760.00

	Craft@Hrs	Unit	Material	Labor	Total
Three pole polyphase NEMA Class 1 (indoor) AC magnetic combination starters with fusible disconnect and overload relays but no heaters, 208 to 240 volts					
Size 0, 3 HP, 30 amps	E4@2.75	Ea	865.00	140.00	1,005.00
Size 1, 7.5 HP, 30 amps	E4@3.89	Ea	910.00	198.00	1,108.00
Size 1, 10 HP, 60 amps	E4@3.89	Ea	910.00	198.00	1,108.00
Size 2, 10 HP, 60 amps	E4@5.34	Ea	1,450.00	271.00	1,721.00
Size 2, 25 HP, 100 amps	E4@5.34	Ea	1,450.00	271.00	1,721.00
Size 3, 25 HP, 100 amps	E4@6.76	Ea	2,380.00	344.00	2,724.00
Size 3, 50 HP, 200 amps	E4@6.76	Ea	2,380.00	344.00	2,724.00
Size 4, 40 HP, 200 amps	E4@12.0	Ea	4,610.00	610.00	5,220.00
Size 4, 75 HP, 400 amps	E4@12.0	Ea	4,610.00	610.00	5,220.00
On and off switches for starter enclosures, any motor starter above					
Switch kit without pilot light	E4@.744	Ea	90.40	37.80	128.20
Switch kit with pilot light	E4@.744	Ea	137.00	37.80	174.80
Accessories for any motor starter					
Add for 440 to 600 volt starters	—	%	2.0	—	—
Add for NEMA Type 3R (rainproof) enclosure	—	%	40.0	10.0	—
Add for NEMA Type 4 (waterproof) enclosure	—	%	40.0	20.0	—
Add for NEMA Type 12 (dust-tight) enclosure	—	%	15.0	15.0	—
Add for starters in an oversize enclosure	—	%	21.0	—	—
Deduct for starters with circuit breakers	—	%	-4.0	—	—

Safety Switches Wall mounted switches with enclosures as noted. No fuses or hubs included.

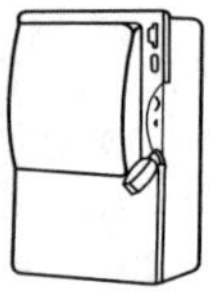

	Craft@Hrs	Unit	Material	Labor	Total
Heavy-duty (NEMA-1) 600 volt 2, 3 or 4 pole fusible safety switches					
30 amp	E4@3.06	Ea	198.00	156.00	354.00
60 amp	E4@3.89	Ea	229.00	198.00	427.00
100 amp	E4@4.20	Ea	428.00	213.00	641.00
200 amp	E4@6.92	Ea	616.00	352.00	968.00
400 amp	E4@11.4	Ea	1,520.00	579.00	2,099.00
600 amp	E4@14.3	Ea	2,260.00	727.00	2,987.00
800 amp	E4@19.6	Ea	3,140.00	996.00	4,136.00
1,200 amp	E4@22.7	Ea	5,300.00	1,150.00	6,450.00
Heavy-duty rainproof (NEMA-3R) 600 volt 2, 3 or 4 pole fusible safety switches					
30 amp	E4@3.32	Ea	294.00	169.00	463.00
60 amp	E4@4.61	Ea	348.00	234.00	582.00
100 amp	E4@4.77	Ea	541.00	242.00	783.00
200 amp	E4@7.51	Ea	744.00	382.00	1,126.00
400 amp	E4@12.4	Ea	1,800.00	630.00	2,430.00
600 amp	E4@15.6	Ea	3,600.00	793.00	4,393.00
800 amp	E4@21.4	Ea	5,410.00	1,090.00	6,500.00
1,200 amp	E4@25.8	Ea	5,930.00	1,310.00	7,240.00
Heavy-duty watertight (NEMA-4) 600 volt 3 pole, 4 wire fusible safety switches					
30 amp	E4@3.76	Ea	644.00	191.00	835.00
60 amp	E4@5.21	Ea	1,050.00	265.00	1,315.00
100 amp	E4@5.34	Ea	1,650.00	271.00	1,921.00
200 amp	E4@8.52	Ea	2,320.00	433.00	2,753.00
400 amp	E4@13.7	Ea	4,590.00	696.00	5,286.00
600 amp	E4@17.0	Ea	6,500.00	864.00	7,364.00
Heavy-duty dust-tight (NEMA-12) 600 volt 3 pole or 4 pole solid neutral fusible safety switches					
30 amp	E4@3.32	Ea	258.00	169.00	427.00
60 amp	E4@4.20	Ea	253.00	213.00	466.00
100 amp	E4@4.48	Ea	405.00	228.00	633.00
200 amp	E4@7.51	Ea	630.00	382.00	1,012.00
400 amp	E4@12.7	Ea	1,450.00	646.00	2,096.00
600 amp	E4@15.9	Ea	2,430.00	808.00	3,238.00

	Craft@Hrs	Unit	Material	Labor	Total
General duty (NEMA-1) 240 volt 3 pole, 4 wire non-fusible safety switches					
30 amp	E4@2.58	Ea	59.70	131.00	190.70
100 amp	E4@3.60	Ea	181.00	183.00	364.00
200 amp	E4@6.50	Ea	381.00	330.00	711.00
400 amp	E4@10.8	Ea	992.00	549.00	1,541.00
600 amp	E4@12.7	Ea	1,860.00	646.00	2,506.00
General duty rainproof (NEMA-3R) 240 volt 3 pole, 4 wire non-fusible safety switches					
30 amp	E4@2.88	Ea	80.50	146.00	226.50
60 amp	E4@3.76	Ea	124.00	191.00	315.00
100 amp	E4@3.89	Ea	230.00	198.00	428.00
200 amp	E4@7.23	Ea	411.00	368.00	779.00
400 amp	E4@11.8	Ea	1,030.00	600.00	1,630.00
600 amp	E4@14.0	Ea	2,220.00	712.00	2,932.00
Heavy duty watertight (NEMA-4) 240 volt 3 pole, 4 wire fusible safety switches					
30 amp	E4@3.19	Ea	475.00	162.00	637.00
60 amp	E4@3.76	Ea	557.00	191.00	748.00
100 amp	E4@4.33	Ea	1,140.00	220.00	1,360.00
200 amp	E4@7.80	Ea	1,550.00	396.00	1,946.00
400 amp	E4@13.0	Ea	3,390.00	661.00	4,051.00
600 amp	E4@15.4	Ea	4,750.00	783.00	5,533.00
Heavy duty dust-tight (NEMA-12) 240 volt 3 pole, 4 wire fusible safety switches					
30 amp	E4@2.88	Ea	267.00	146.00	413.00
60 amp	E4@3.76	Ea	343.00	191.00	534.00
100 amp	E4@4.04	Ea	493.00	205.00	698.00
200 amp	E4@7.23	Ea	659.00	368.00	1,027.00
400 amp	E4@11.8	Ea	1,650.00	600.00	2,250.00
600 amp	E4@14.0	Ea	2,770.00	712.00	3,482.00
Add for conduit hubs					
3/4" to 1-1/2", to 100 amp	—	Ea	11.90	—	11.90
2", 200 amp	—	Ea	20.80	—	20.80
2-1/2", 200 amp	—	Ea	35.10	—	35.10

Service Entrance and Distribution Switchboards MA Class 1 indoor, 600 volt, 3 phase, 4 wire, for 240/480 volt insulated case main breakers. Basic structure is 90" high by 21" deep. Width varies with equipment capacity. Labor cost includes setting and leveling on a prepared pad but excludes the pad cost. Add breaker, instrumentation and accessory costs for a complete installation. Based on Westinghouse Pow-R-Gear. These switchboards are custom designed for each installation. Costs can vary widely. Multiple units ordered at the same time may reduce costs per unit by 25% or more.

	Craft@Hrs	Unit	Material	Labor	Total
600 amp bus	E4@22.9	Ea	4,940.00	1,160.00	6,100.00
1,000 amp bus	E4@22.9	Ea	5,100.00	1,160.00	6,260.00
1,200 amp bus	E4@22.9	Ea	6,190.00	1,160.00	7,350.00
1,600 amp bus	E4@22.9	Ea	7,130.00	1,160.00	8,290.00
2,000 amp bus	E4@22.9	Ea	7,810.00	1,160.00	8,970.00
2,500 amp bus	E4@22.9	Ea	9,530.00	1,160.00	10,690.00
3,000 amp bus	E4@22.9	Ea	11,100.00	1,160.00	12,260.00
4,000 amp bus	E4@22.9	Ea	14,100.00	1,160.00	15,260.00
240/480 volt draw-out main breakers, 100K amp interrupt capacity. Includes connecting and testing breakers only. Based on Pow-R-Trip					
100 to 800 amp, manual operation	E4@10.2	Ea	14,300.00	518.00	14,818.00
1,000 to 1,600 amp, manual operation	E4@17.5	Ea	30,200.00	890.00	31,090.00
2,000 amp, manual operation	E4@23.2	Ea	36,700.00	1,180.00	37,880.00
2,500 amp, manual operation	E4@23.2	Ea	62,900.00	1,180.00	64,080.00
3,000 amp, manual operation	E4@23.2	Ea	70,000.00	1,180.00	71,180.00
4,000 amp, manual operation	E4@23.2	Ea	84,100.00	1,180.00	85,280.00

	Craft@Hrs	Unit	Material	Labor	Total
100 to 800 amp electric operation	E4@10.2	Ea	19,300.00	518.00	19,818.00
1,000 to 1,600 amp electric operation	E4@17.5	Ea	33,100.00	890.00	33,990.00
2,000 amp electric operation	E4@23.2	Ea	43,800.00	1,180.00	44,980.00
2,500 amp electric operation	E4@23.2	Ea	75,000.00	1,180.00	76,180.00
3,000 amp electric operation	E4@23.2	Ea	81,700.00	1,180.00	82,880.00
Additional space for future draw-out breakers					
100 to 800 amp	—	Ea	3,900.00	—	3,900.00
1,000 to 1,600 amp	—	Ea	5,670.00	—	5,670.00
2,000 amp	—	Ea	6,400.00	—	6,400.00
2,500 amp	—	Ea	6,840.00	—	6,840.00
3,000 amp	—	Ea	12,400.00	—	12,400.00

Service Entrance and Distribution Switchboards, Weatherproof

600 volt, 3 phase, 4 wire, for 480 volt insulated case main breakers. Basic structure is 90" high by 21" deep. Width varies with equipment capacity. Labor cost includes setting and leveling on a prepared pad but excludes the pad cost. Add breaker, instrumentation and accessory costs from below for a complete installation. These switchboards are custom designed for each installation. Costs can vary widely. Multiple units ordered at the same time can reduce costs per unit by 25% or more.

	Craft@Hrs	Unit	Material	Labor	Total
600 amp bus	E4@23.2	Ea	5,830.00	1,180.00	7,010.00
1,000 amp bus	E4@23.2	Ea	6,850.00	1,180.00	8,030.00
1,200 amp bus	E4@23.2	Ea	8,790.00	1,180.00	9,970.00
1,600 amp bus	E4@23.2	Ea	8,410.00	1,180.00	9,590.00
2,000 amp bus	E4@23.2	Ea	9,310.00	1,180.00	10,490.00
2,500 amp bus	E4@23.2	Ea	11,300.00	1,180.00	12,480.00
3,000 amp bus	E4@23.2	Ea	11,500.00	1,180.00	12,680.00
4,000 amp bus	E4@23.2	Ea	16,600.00	1,180.00	17,780.00

480 volt manual operated draw-out breakers. By amp interrupt capacity (AIC) as noted. Includes connecting and testing factory installed breakers only.

	Craft@Hrs	Unit	Material	Labor	Total
50 to 800 amp, 30K AIC	E4@10.2	Ea	19,500.00	518.00	20,018.00
50 to 1,600 amp, 50K AIC	E4@17.5	Ea	40,700.00	890.00	41,590.00
2,000 amp	E4@23.2	Ea	52,600.00	1,180.00	53,780.00
1,200 to 3,200 amp	E4@23.2	Ea	92,700.00	1,180.00	93,880.00
4,000 amp	E4@23.2	Ea	147,000.00	1,180.00	148,180.00

480 volt manual operated draw-out breakers. 200K amp interrupt capacity (AIC) as noted. Includes connecting and testing factory installed breakers only.

	Craft@Hrs	Unit	Material	Labor	Total
50 to 800 amp	E4@10.2	Ea	30,300.00	518.00	30,818.00
50 to 1,600 amp	E4@17.5	Ea	53,900.00	890.00	54,790.00
1,200 to 3,200 amp	E4@23.2	Ea	138,000.00	1,180.00	139,180.00
4,000 amp	E4@23.2	Ea	223,000.00	1,180.00	224,180.00

480 volt electrically operated draw-out breakers. By amp interrupt capacity (AIC) as noted. Includes connecting and testing factory installed breakers only.

	Craft@Hrs	Unit	Material	Labor	Total
50 to 800 amp, 30K AIC	E4@10.2	Ea	26,800.00	518.00	27,318.00
50 to 1,600 amp, 50K AIC	E4@17.5	Ea	55,600.00	890.00	56,490.00
2,000 amp	E4@23.2	Ea	70,700.00	1,180.00	71,880.00
1,200 to 3,200 amp	E4@23.2	Ea	107,000.00	1,180.00	108,180.00
4,000 amp	E4@23.2	Ea	165,000.00	1,180.00	166,180.00

480 volt electrically operated draw-out breakers. 200K amp interrupt capacity (AIC) as noted. Includes connecting and testing factory installed breakers only.

	Craft@Hrs	Unit	Material	Labor	Total
50 to 800 amp	E4@10.2	Ea	36,900.00	518.00	37,418.00
50 to 1,600 amp	E4@17.5	Ea	74,500.00	890.00	75,390.00
1,200 to 3,200 amp	E4@23.2	Ea	152,000.00	1,180.00	153,180.00
4,000 amp	E4@23.2	Ea	224,000.00	1,180.00	225,180.00

	Craft@Hrs	Unit	Material	Labor	Total
Additional space for future draw-out breakers					
50 to 800 amp	—	Ea	4,560.00	—	4,560.00
50 to 1,600 amp	—	Ea	7,410.00	—	7,410.00
2,000 amp	—	Ea	10,100.00	—	10,100.00
1,200 to 3,200 amp	—	Ea	15,700.00	—	15,700.00
4,000 amp	—	Ea	29,100.00	—	29,100.00

Switchboard Instrumentation and Accessories Add these costs to the cost of the basic enclosure and breakers to find the complete switchboard cost. These figures are for factory-installed instrumentation and accessories and include the cost of connecting and testing only.

	Craft@Hrs	Unit	Material	Labor	Total
Bus duct connection, 3 phase, 4 wire					
225 amp	CE@.516	Ea	883.00	31.20	914.20
400 amp	CE@.516	Ea	1,020.00	31.20	1,051.20
600 amp	CE@.516	Ea	1,240.00	31.20	1,271.20
800 amp	CE@.516	Ea	1,960.00	31.20	1,991.20
1,000 amp	CE@.516	Ea	2,270.00	31.20	2,301.20
1,350 amp	CE@1.01	Ea	2,960.00	61.00	3,021.00
1,600 amp	CE@1.01	Ea	3,420.00	61.00	3,481.00
2,000 amp	CE@1.01	Ea	4,180.00	61.00	4,241.00
2,500 amp	CE@1.01	Ea	4,970.00	61.00	5,031.00
3,000 amp	CE@1.01	Ea	5,660.00	61.00	5,721.00
4,000 amp	CE@1.01	Ea	6,270.00	61.00	6,331.00
Recording meters					
Voltmeter	CE@1.01	Ea	12,700.00	61.00	12,761.00
Ammeter	CE@1.01	Ea	13,000.00	61.00	13,061.00
Wattmeter	CE@1.01	Ea	15,900.00	61.00	15,961.00
Varmeter	CE@1.01	Ea	16,900.00	61.00	16,961.00
Power factor meter	CE@1.01	Ea	16,700.00	61.00	16,761.00
Frequency meter	CE@1.01	Ea	16,700.00	61.00	16,761.00
Watt-hour meter, 3 element	CE@1.01	Ea	21,600.00	61.00	21,661.00
Non-recording meters					
Voltmeter	CE@.516	Ea	2,100.00	31.20	2,131.20
Ammeter for incoming line	CE@.516	Ea	2,160.00	31.20	2,191.20
Ammeter for feeder circuits	CE@.516	Ea	901.00	31.20	932.20
Wattmeter	CE@1.01	Ea	7,000.00	61.00	7,061.00
Varmeter	CE@1.01	Ea	6,330.00	61.00	6,391.00
Power factor meter	CE@1.01	Ea	5,100.00	61.00	5,161.00
Frequency meter	CE@1.01	Ea	6,050.00	61.00	6,111.00
Watt-hour meter, 3 element	CE@1.01	Ea	6,330.00	61.00	6,391.00
Instrument phase select switch	CE@.516	Ea	1,100.00	31.20	1,131.20
Adjustable short time pickup and delay	CE@.516	Ea	1,640.00	31.20	1,671.20
Ground fault trip pickup and delay, 4 wire	CE@.525	Ea	1,760.00	31.70	1,791.70
Ground fault test panel	CE@.516	Ea	1,890.00	31.20	1,921.20
Shunt trip for breakers	CE@.516	Ea	1,280.00	31.20	1,311.20
Key interlock for breakers	CE@.516	Ea	1,280.00	31.20	1,311.20
Breaker lifting and transport truck	—	Ea	8,320.00	—	8,320.00
Breaker lifting device	—	Ea	7,250.00	—	7,250.00
Current transformers, by primary capacity					
800 amps and less	CE@1.01	Ea	1,570.00	61.00	1,631.00
1,000 to 1,500 amps	CE@1.01	Ea	2,320.00	61.00	2,381.00
2,000 to 6,000 amps	CE@1.01	Ea	2,740.00	61.00	2,801.00
Current transformer mount	—	Ea	742.00	—	742.00
Potential transformer	CE@1.01	Ea	2,030.00	61.00	2,091.00
Potential transformer mount	—	Ea	468.00	—	468.00

	Craft@Hrs	Unit	Material	Labor	Total
Feeder Section Breaker Panels					
Flush or surface mounted 277/480 volt, 3 phase, 4 wire, FA frame panels.					
225 amp, with 22K amp interrupt capacity breaker	E4@6.76	Ea	2,090.00	344.00	2,434.00
225 amp, with 25K amp interrupt capacity breaker	E4@6.76	Ea	3,900.00	344.00	4,244.00
400 amp, with 30K amp interrupt capacity breaker	E4@10.8	Ea	4,670.00	549.00	5,219.00
400 amp, with 35K amp interrupt capacity breaker	E4@10.8	Ea	5,590.00	549.00	6,139.00
225 amp, with main lugs only	E4@6.76	Ea	705.00	344.00	1,049.00
400 amp, with main lugs only	E4@10.8	Ea	994.00	549.00	1,543.00
600 amp, with main lugs only	E4@19.3	Ea	1,340.00	981.00	2,321.00
Transformers Indoor dry-type transformer, floor mounted, including connections.					
Single phase light and power circuit transformer, 240/480 volt primary, 120/240 secondary, no taps for voltage change					
1 KVA	E4@3.76	Ea	320.00	191.00	511.00
2 KVA	E4@4.20	Ea	479.00	213.00	692.00
3 KVA	E4@4.33	Ea	608.00	220.00	828.00
5 KVA	E4@5.47	Ea	790.00	278.00	1,068.00
7.5 KVA	E4@8.34	Ea	981.00	424.00	1,405.00
10 KVA	E4@9.38	Ea	1,210.00	477.00	1,687.00
15 KVA	E4@12.6	Ea	1,400.00	640.00	2,040.00
25 KVA	E4@12.6	Ea	1,920.00	640.00	2,560.00
Three phase light and power circuit transformers, 480 volt primary, 120/208 volt secondary, with 6 taps for voltage change					
30 KVA	E4@10.5	Ea	3,590.00	534.00	4,124.00
45 KVA	E4@12.6	Ea	4,290.00	640.00	4,930.00
50 KVA	E4@12.6	Ea	5,700.00	640.00	6,340.00
75 KVA	E4@14.8	Ea	6,470.00	752.00	7,222.00
112.5 KVA	E4@15.7	Ea	8,590.00	798.00	9,388.00
150 KVA	E4@16.7	Ea	11,100.00	849.00	11,949.00
225 KVA	E4@18.9	Ea	15,100.00	961.00	16,061.00
300 KVA	E4@21.2	Ea	19,500.00	1,080.00	20,580.00
Three phase 5,000 volt load center transformers, 4,160 volt primary, 480/277 volt secondary, with voltage change taps, insulation class H, 80 degree system					
225 KVA	E4@29.5	Ea	18,700.00	1,500.00	20,200.00
300 KVA	E4@33.7	Ea	22,000.00	1,710.00	23,710.00
500 KVA	E4@42.5	Ea	33,200.00	2,160.00	35,360.00
750 KVA	E4@53.1	Ea	43,400.00	2,700.00	46,100.00
1,000 KVA	E4@63.2	Ea	56,800.00	3,210.00	60,010.00
Panelboards Surface mounted lighting and appliance distribution panelboards for bolt-on circuit breakers. No breakers included.					
3 wire 120/240 volt, 250 amp, single phase AC panelboards with main lugs only for bolt-on breakers					
18 circuits	E4@10.7	Ea	326.00	544.00	870.00
30 circuits	E4@15.3	Ea	332.00	778.00	1,110.00
42 circuits	E4@20.9	Ea	437.00	1,060.00	1,497.00
Deduct for 3 wire 120/240 panelboards					
With main lugs only	—	%	−10.0	−15.0	—
4 wire 120/208 volt, 250 amp, 3 phase AC panelboards for bolt-on breakers, with main circuit breaker only					
18 circuits	E4@12.9	Ea	265.00	656.00	921.00
30 circuits	E4@21.5	Ea	376.00	1,090.00	1,466.00
42 circuits	E4@30.1	Ea	488.00	1,530.00	2,018.00
Deduct for 3 wire panelboards					
With circuit breaker mains only	—	%	−10.0	−15.0	—

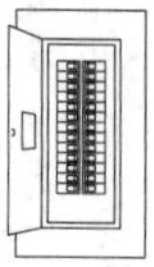

	Craft@Hrs	Unit	Material	Labor	Total
Combination Service Entrance Device Meter socket, service disconnect and loadcenter.					
Surface mount NEMA Type 3R enclosure with ring type utility meter socket, service disconnect, and integral HOM loadcenter. Single phase 3-wire. 120/240 Volt AC, 22,000 amp short circuit current rating. Overhead or underground service feed. Add the cost of distribution breakers and conduit hubs.					
100 amp, 16 spaces, 24 circuits	E4@1.20	Ea	83.20	61.00	144.20
125 amp, 16 spaces, 24 circuits	E4@1.20	Ea	109.00	61.00	170.00
200 amp, 20 spaces, 40 circuits	E4@1.20	Ea	149.00	61.00	210.00
200 amp, 20 spaces, 40 circuits	E4@2.60	Ea	143.00	132.00	275.00
200 amp, 30 spaces, 40 circuits	E4@2.60	Ea	313.00	132.00	445.00
200 amp, 40 spaces, 40 circuits	E4@2.60	Ea	155.00	132.00	287.00
320 amp, 30 spaces, 40 circuits, no bypass	E4@3.10	Ea	697.00	158.00	855.00
320 amp, 30 spaces, 40 circuits, test block bypass	E4@3.10	Ea	759.00	158.00	917.00
Surface mount NEMA Type 3R class 4120 enclosure with ring type utility meter socket, dual main breakers and HO load center. Single phase, 3-wire, 120/240 Volts AC, 25,000 amp short circuit current rating. Underground service feed. With 100 percent branch neutrals, horn by-pass and 5th jaw factory installed. Add the cost of distribution breakers and conduit hubs.					
400 amp, 30 spaces, 40 circuits, test block bypass	E4@3.50	Ea	794.00	178.00	972.00
400 amp, 30 spaces, 40 circuits, no test block	E4@3.50	Ea	794.00	178.00	972.00
Surface or semi-flush mount NEMA Type 1 (indoor) enclosure with multiple meter positions, main breaker and loadcenter. Line and load at top or bottom. 1 phase, 3-wire 120/240 Volt AC. 65,000 amp short circuit rating. Add the cost of distribution breakers and conduit hubs.					
125 amp, 200 amp bus, 2 meter positions	E4@1.20	Ea	222.00	61.00	283.00
125 amp, 300 amp bus, 3 meter positions	E4@1.20	Ea	291.00	61.00	352.00
125 amp, 400 amp bus, 4 meter position	E4@1.20	Ea	339.00	61.00	400.00
125 amp, 400 amp bus, 6 meter positions	E4@1.20	Ea	812.00	61.00	873.00
Loadcenters For plug-in branch breakers. Surface or recess mount. Add the cost of distribution breakers and conduit hubs.					
Indoor (NEMA 1) single phase 3-wire 120/240 volt loadcenter. Class 1170. 22,000 RMS amps short circuit rating. With factory installed main breaker only.					
100 amps, 8 spaces, 16 circuits	E4@1.20	Ea	57.70	61.00	118.70
100 amps, 12 spaces, 12 circuits	E4@1.20	Ea	85.20	61.00	146.20
100 amps, 20 spaces, 20 circuits	E4@1.20	Ea	75.30	61.00	136.30
100 amps, 24 spaces, 24 circuits	E4@1.20	Ea	101.00	61.00	162.00
100 amps, 30 spaces, 30 circuits	E4@1.20	Ea	111.00	61.00	172.00
125 amps, 12 spaces, 24 circuits	E4@1.52	Ea	46.20	77.30	123.50
125 amps, 24 spaces, 24 circuits	E4@1.52	Ea	131.00	77.30	208.30
150 amps, 30 spaces, 30 circuits	E4@2.30	Ea	168.00	117.00	285.00
200 amps, 20 spaces, 40 circuits	E4@2.60	Ea	107.00	132.00	239.00
200 amps, 30 spaces, 30 circuits	E4@2.60	Ea	118.00	132.00	250.00
200 amps, 40 spaces, 40 circuits	E4@2.60	Ea	162.00	132.00	294.00
Outdoor (NEMA 4) single phase 3-wire 120/240 volt loadcenter, Class 1170, 22,000 amps short circuit rating. With factory installed main breaker only.					
100 amps, 8 spaces, 16 circuits	E4@1.20	Ea	64.70	61.00	125.70
100 amps, 12 spaces, 12 circuits	E4@1.20	Ea	111.00	61.00	172.00
100 amps, 20 spaces, 20 circuits	E4@1.20	Ea	136.00	61.00	197.00
125 amps, 24 spaces, 24 circuits	E4@1.52	Ea	110.00	77.30	187.30
150 amps, 30 spaces, 30 circuits	E4@2.30	Ea	273.00	117.00	390.00
200 amps, 20 spaces, 40 circuits	E4@2.60	Ea	192.00	132.00	324.00
200 amps, 30 spaces, 30 circuits	E4@2.60	Ea	256.00	132.00	388.00
200 amps, 40 spaces, 40 circuits	E4@2.60	Ea	178.00	132.00	310.00

	Craft@Hrs	Unit	Material	Labor	Total
Indoor (NEMA 1) three phase 4 wire 120/208 volt loadcenter with factory-installed main circuit breaker only.					
100 amps, 12 circuits	E4@1.21	Ea	161.00	61.50	222.50
100 amps, 18 circuits	E4@1.60	Ea	216.00	81.30	297.30
125 amps, 30 circuits	E4@1.91	Ea	432.00	97.10	529.10
150 amps, 24 circuits	E4@2.18	Ea	415.00	111.00	526.00
150 amps, 42 circuits	E4@2.82	Ea	496.00	143.00	639.00
200 amps, 42 circuits	E4@3.63	Ea	496.00	185.00	681.00
225 amps, 42 circuits	E4@3.78	Ea	519.00	192.00	711.00
400 amps, 24 circuits	E4@3.91	Ea	1,050.00	199.00	1,249.00
400 amps, 42 circuits	E4@4.51	Ea	1,200.00	229.00	1,429.00
Three phase 4 wire 120/208 volt loadcenters with main lugs only.					
125 amps, 12 circuits	E4@1.19	Ea	95.50	60.50	156.00
150 amps, 18 circuits	E4@1.47	Ea	144.00	74.70	218.70
200 amps, 30 circuits	E4@1.90	Ea	194.00	96.60	290.60
200 amps, 40 circuits	E4@2.18	Ea	259.00	111.00	370.00
225 amps, 42 circuits	E4@2.75	Ea	272.00	140.00	412.00
400 amps, 24 circuits	E4@3.63	Ea	498.00	185.00	683.00
400 amps, 42 circuits	E4@3.78	Ea	553.00	192.00	745.00
600 amps, 24 circuits	E4@3.91	Ea	606.00	199.00	805.00
600 amps, 42 circuits	E4@6.53	Ea	742.00	332.00	1,074.00
Circuit Breakers No enclosures included. 10,000 amp interrupt capacity except as noted.					
Plug-in molded case 120/240 volt, 100 amp frame circuit breakers, 1" or 1/2" module					
15 to 50 amps, single pole	CE@.270	Ea	8.43	16.30	24.73
15 to 60 amps, two pole	CE@.374	Ea	10.30	22.60	32.90
70 amps, two pole	CE@.563	Ea	32.70	34.00	66.70
80 to 100 amps, two pole	CE@.680	Ea	36.40	41.10	77.50
Plug-in molded case 120/240 volt, 100 amp frame circuit breakers, GFCI					
GFCI, 15 amp, single pole	CE@.300	Ea	41.60	18.10	59.70
GFCI, 15 amp, two pole	CE@.400	Ea	90.70	24.20	114.90
GFCI, 20 amp, single pole	CE@.300	Ea	53.30	18.10	71.40
GFCI, 20 amp, two pole	CE@.400	Ea	115.00	24.20	139.20
Plug-in molded case 120/240 volt, 100 amp frame circuit breakers, AFCI					
AFCI, 15 amp, single pole	CE@.300	Ea	40.60	18.10	58.70
AFCI, 15 amp, two pole	CE@.400	Ea	84.80	24.20	109.00
AFCI, 20 amp, single pole	CE@.300	Ea	38.70	18.10	56.80
AFCI, 20 amp, two pole	CE@.400	Ea	84.80	24.20	109.00
Plug-in molded case 120/240 volt, 100 amp frame circuit breakers, combination AFCI/GFCI					
Combination GF/AF, 15 amp, single pole	CE@.300	Ea	55.80	18.10	73.90
Combination GF/AF, 15 amp, two pole	CE@.400	Ea	86.90	24.20	111.10
Combination GF/AF, 20 amp, single pole	CE@.300	Ea	54.60	18.10	72.70
Combination GF/AF, 20 amp, two pole	CE@.400	Ea	87.90	24.20	112.10
Plug-in molded case 240 volt, 100 amp frame circuit breakers					
15 thru 60 amps, three pole	CE@.863	Ea	29.90	52.10	82.00
60 thru 100 amps, two pole	CE@.577	Ea	32.70	34.90	67.60
60 thru 100 amps, three pole	CE@.897	Ea	55.20	54.20	109.40
Plug-in molded case 480 volt, 100 amp frame circuit breakers					
70 thru 100 amps, two pole	CE@1.22	Ea	333.00	73.70	406.70
70 thru 100 amps, three pole	CE@1.71	Ea	417.00	103.00	520.00
Plug-in molded case 600 volt, 100 amp frame circuit breakers					
15 thru 60 amps, two pole	CE@.577	Ea	279.00	34.90	313.90
15 thru 60 amps, three pole	CE@.897	Ea	358.00	54.20	412.20
70 thru 100 amps, two pole	CE@1.22	Ea	374.00	73.70	447.70
70 thru 100 amps, three pole	CE@1.71	Ea	469.00	103.00	572.00
Plug-in molded case 250/600 volt, 225 amp frame circuit breakers					
125 thru 225 amps, two pole	CE@2.06	Ea	870.00	124.00	994.00
125 thru 225 amps, three pole	CE@2.57	Ea	1,100.00	155.00	1,255.00

	Craft@Hrs	Unit	Material	Labor	Total
Plug-in molded case 250/600 volt, 400 amp frame circuit breakers					
250 thru 400 amps, two pole	CE@2.88	Ea	1,480.00	174.00	1,654.00
250 thru 400 amps, three pole	CE@4.33	Ea	1,730.00	262.00	1,992.00
Plug-in molded case 250/600 volt, 800 amp frame circuit breakers					
400 thru 600 amps, three pole	CE@6.04	Ea	2,190.00	365.00	2,555.00
700 thru 800 amps, two pole	CE@4.73	Ea	3,050.00	286.00	3,336.00
700 thru 800 amps, three pole	CE@6.71	Ea	3,920.00	405.00	4,325.00
Plug-in molded case 600 volt, 1,200 amp frame circuit breakers					
600 thru 1,200 amps, two pole	CE@9.60	Ea	5,030.00	580.00	5,610.00
600 thru 1,200 amps, three pole	CE@11.9	Ea	6,430.00	719.00	7,149.00
Space only for factory assembled panels					
Single pole space	—	Ea	22.60	—	22.60
Two pole space	—	Ea	20.90	—	20.90
Three pole space	—	Ea	28.00	—	28.00
Bolt-on molded case 120/240 volt circuit breakers					
15 thru 60 amps, one pole	CE@.320	Ea	18.90	19.30	38.20
15 thru 60 amps, two pole	CE@.484	Ea	24.70	29.20	53.90
15 thru 60 amps, three pole	CE@.638	Ea	76.80	38.50	115.30
70 thru 100 amps, two pole	CE@.712	Ea	71.10	43.00	114.10
70 thru 100 amps, three pole	CE@.946	Ea	131.00	57.10	188.10
Bolt-on molded case 480 volt circuit breakers, 65,000 amp interrupt capacity					
15 thru 60 amps, two pole	CE@.484	Ea	137.00	29.20	166.20
15 thru 60 amps, three pole	CE@.712	Ea	245.00	43.00	288.00
70 thru 100 amps, three pole	CE@.804	Ea	463.00	48.60	511.60

Circuit Breaker Panels 4 wire 3 phase 240 volts, flush-mounted, with main breaker, assembled

	Craft@Hrs	Unit	Material	Labor	Total
100 amp service, 12 circuits	E4@4.60	Ea	593.00	234.00	827.00
100 amp service, 18 circuits	E4@6.90	Ea	629.00	351.00	980.00
100 amp service, 24 circuits	E4@8.10	Ea	682.00	412.00	1,094.00
100 amp service, 30 circuits	E4@8.20	Ea	732.00	417.00	1,149.00
100 amp service, 36 circuits	E4@8.30	Ea	781.00	422.00	1,203.00
100 amp service, 42 circuits	E4@8.40	Ea	833.00	427.00	1,260.00
225 amp service, 12 circuits	E4@8.50	Ea	1,300.00	432.00	1,732.00
225 amp service, 18 circuits	E4@8.60	Ea	1,320.00	437.00	1,757.00
225 amp service, 24 circuits	E4@8.70	Ea	1,370.00	442.00	1,812.00
225 amp service, 30 circuits	E4@10.0	Ea	1,410.00	508.00	1,918.00
225 amp service, 36 circuits	E4@12.8	Ea	1,460.00	651.00	2,111.00
225 amp service, 42 circuits	E4@15.1	Ea	1,510.00	768.00	2,278.00

Fuses No enclosures included.

	Craft@Hrs	Unit	Material	Labor	Total
250 volt cartridge fuses, one time non-renewable					
To 30 amps	CE@.077	Ea	1.29	4.65	5.94
35 to 60 amps	CE@.077	Ea	2.98	4.65	7.63
70 to 100 amps	CE@.077	Ea	8.95	4.65	13.60
110 to 200 amps	CE@.077	Ea	15.90	4.65	20.55
225 to 400 amps	CE@.077	Ea	33.60	4.65	38.25
450 to 600 amps	CE@.077	Ea	76.30	4.65	80.95
600 volt cartridge fuses, one time non-renewable					
To 30 amps	CE@.077	Ea	12.20	4.65	16.85
35 to 60 amps	CE@.077	Ea	21.10	4.65	25.75
70 to 100 amps	CE@.077	Ea	55.90	4.65	60.55
110 to 200 amps	CE@.077	Ea	83.00	4.65	87.65
225 to 400 amps	CE@.087	Ea	166.00	5.26	171.26
450 to 600 amps	CE@.124	Ea	359.00	7.49	366.49

	Craft@Hrs	Unit	Material	Labor	Total
250 volt Class H renewable fuses					
To 10 amps	CE@.077	Ea	13.40	4.65	18.05
12 to 30 amps	CE@.077	Ea	14.20	4.65	18.85
35 to 60 amps	CE@.077	Ea	15.10	4.65	19.75
70 to 100 amps	CE@.077	Ea	52.90	4.65	57.55
110 to 200 amps	CE@.077	Ea	121.00	4.65	125.65
225 to 400 amps	CE@.080	Ea	249.00	4.83	253.83
450 to 600 amps	CE@.122	Ea	358.00	7.37	365.37
600 volt Class H renewable fuses					
To 10 amps	CE@.077	Ea	35.50	4.65	40.15
12 to 30 amps	CE@.077	Ea	28.50	4.65	33.15
35 to 60 amps	CE@.077	Ea	38.30	4.65	42.95
70 to 100 amps	CE@.077	Ea	105.00	4.65	109.65
110 to 200 amps	CE@.077	Ea	209.00	4.65	213.65
225 to 400 amps	CE@.153	Ea	480.00	9.24	489.24
450 to 600 amps	CE@.223	Ea	576.00	13.50	589.50
250 volt Class RK5 non-renewable cartridge fuses					
10 to 30 amps	CE@.077	Ea	2.78	4.65	7.43
35 to 60 amps	CE@.077	Ea	6.99	4.65	11.64
70 to 100 amps	CE@.077	Ea	9.75	4.65	14.40
110 to 200 amps	CE@.077	Ea	17.60	4.65	22.25
225 to 400 amps	CE@.230	Ea	70.30	13.90	84.20
450 to 600 amps	CE@.297	Ea	99.10	17.90	117.00
650 to 1,200 amps	CE@.372	Ea	122.00	22.50	144.50
1,400 to 1,600 amps	CE@.804	Ea	165.00	48.60	213.60
1,800 to 2,000 amps	CE@1.00	Ea	212.00	60.40	272.40
600 volt Class RK5 non-renewable cartridge fuses					
10 to 30 amps	CE@.077	Ea	7.27	4.65	11.92
35 to 60 amps	CE@.077	Ea	12.60	4.65	17.25
70 to 100 amps	CE@.077	Ea	25.70	4.65	30.35
110 to 200 amps	CE@.129	Ea	51.20	7.79	58.99
225 to 400 amps	CE@.257	Ea	102.00	15.50	117.50
450 to 600 amps	CE@.354	Ea	146.00	21.40	167.40
650 to 1,200 amps	CE@.372	Ea	234.00	22.50	256.50
600 volt Class L fuses, bolt-on					
600 to 1,200 amps	CE@.333	Ea	358.00	20.10	378.10
1,500 to 1,600 amps	CE@.615	Ea	402.00	37.20	439.20
1,400 to 2,000 amps	CE@.809	Ea	446.00	48.90	494.90
2,500 amps	CE@1.10	Ea	715.00	66.50	781.50
3,000 amps	CE@1.25	Ea	727.00	75.50	802.50
3,500 to 4,000 amps	CE@1.74	Ea	1,200.00	105.00	1,305.00
5,000 amps	CE@2.33	Ea	1,560.00	141.00	1,701.00

	Craft@Hrs	Unit	Material	Labor	Equipment	Total
Overhead Electrical Distribution						
Poles, pressure-treated wood, Class 4, Type C, set with crane or boom, including augured holes. Equipment is a flatbed truck with a boom and an auger						
25' high	E1@7.62	Ea	365.00	397.00	119.00	881.00
30' high	E1@7.62	Ea	469.00	397.00	119.00	985.00
35' high	E1@9.72	Ea	610.00	507.00	152.00	1,269.00
40' high	E1@11.5	Ea	724.00	599.00	180.00	1,503.00
Cross arms, wood, with typical hardware						
4' long	E1@2.86	Ea	91.40	149.00	44.80	285.20
5' long	E1@2.86	Ea	115.00	149.00	44.80	308.80
6' long	E1@4.19	Ea	164.00	218.00	65.60	447.60
8' long	E1@4.91	Ea	219.00	256.00	76.90	551.90
Transformers, pole-mounted, single phase 7620/13200 Y primary, 120/240 secondary, with two 2-1/2% taps above and below						
10 KVA	E1@4.14	Ea	1,400.00	216.00	64.80	1,680.80
15 KVA	E1@4.14	Ea	1,620.00	216.00	64.80	1,900.80
25 KVA	E1@4.14	Ea	1,990.00	216.00	64.80	2,270.80
36.5 KVA	E1@4.14	Ea	2,660.00	216.00	64.80	2,940.80
50 KVA	E1@4.14	Ea	3,020.00	216.00	64.80	3,300.80
75 KVA	E1@6.16	Ea	4,480.00	321.00	96.40	4,897.40
100 KVA	E1@6.16	Ea	5,120.00	321.00	96.40	5,537.40
167 KVA	E1@6.16	Ea	7,840.00	321.00	96.40	8,257.40
250 KVA	E1@6.16	Ea	8,040.00	321.00	96.40	8,457.40
333 KVA	E1@6.16	Ea	8,690.00	321.00	96.40	9,107.40
500 KVA	E1@6.16	Ea	12,100.00	321.00	96.40	12,517.40
Fused cutouts, pole mounted, 5 KV						
50 amp	E1@2.56	Ea	146.00	133.00	40.10	319.10
100 amp	E1@2.56	Ea	149.00	133.00	40.10	322.10
250 amp	E1@2.56	Ea	165.00	133.00	40.10	338.10
Switches, disconnect, pole mounted, pole arm throw, 5 KV, set of 3 with throw and lock						
400 amp	E1@45.8	Ea	2,820.00	2,390.00	717.00	5,927.00
600 amp	E1@45.8	Ea	5,310.00	2,390.00	717.00	8,417.00
1,200 amp	E1@51.4	Ea	10,300.00	2,680.00	805.00	13,785.00

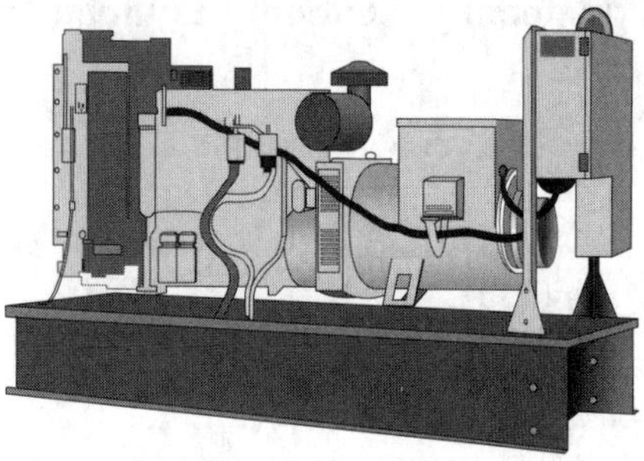

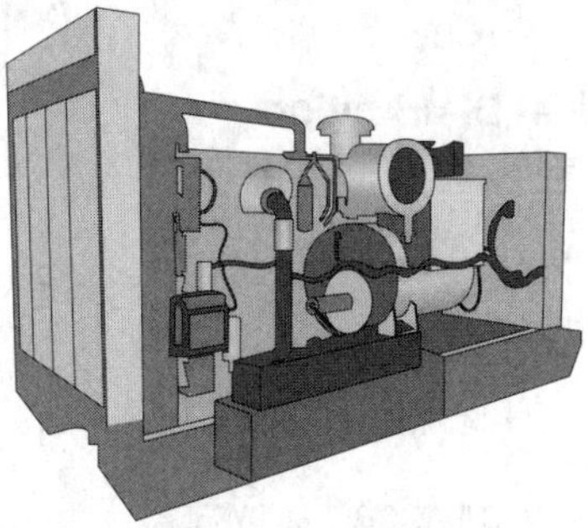

Motor generator sets Dual fuel (oil or gas) four-stroke, turbocharged eight-cylinder, 60 Hz, 480 volts, 3 phase, 1,800 RPM, UL 2200 listed, emissions certified to EPA Tier 2 rating, with *National Electrical Code*-compliant 3- or 4-pole generator and UL 1446 insulation. Control package includes digital engine and generator monitoring, metering, ground fault interruption and lightning shielding, R448 voltage regulator, RFI filter. Includes paralleling and synchronizing automatic transfer switch or (for standby emergencies) automatic dual lockout automatic transfer switch, fused main circuit breaker, electronic load-sharing module for generator ganging, electric starter motor, battery, and trickle charger, lube oil cooling system with radiator and fan, oil pump and sump, water cooling system with water pump, radiator and fan, mounting skid, sound- and weather-proof enclosure, stainless steel exhaust silencer and stack, natural gas fuel train with diaphragm regulator valve, modulating metering valve, pressure gauge and flowmeter, diesel fuel train with fuel pump, fuel pre-heater, day tank with level gauge, main dual-fuel engine inlet regulating valve, remote annunciation panel with alarms and warning lights, and NFPA-rated CO_2 fire extinguishing system. Add the cost of connecting electrical loads and electrical controls, a concrete pad for mounting on the ground or structural steel supports for mounting on a roof, approval of prints by an inspection bureau and post-construction inspection by insurance and fire inspectors. These figures assume exhaust heat is released into the atmosphere. Suitable for standby or primary power generation in commercial, light industrial, government and institutional buildings, schools and hospitals. Equipment cost assumes use of a 2-ton capacity crane.

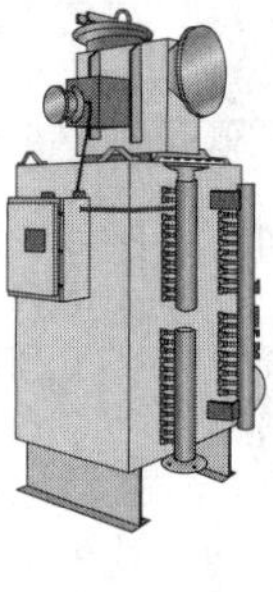

	Craft@Hrs	Unit	Material	Labor	Equipment	Total
13 KW net electrical output	D6@24.0	Ea	6,690.00	1,320.00	1,150.00	9,160.00
17 KW net electrical output	D6@24.0	Ea	8,870.00	1,320.00	1,150.00	11,340.00
30 KW net electrical output	D6@24.0	Ea	15,500.00	1,320.00	1,150.00	17,970.00
50 KW net electrical output	D6@32.0	Ea	25,900.00	1,760.00	1,160.00	28,820.00
80 KW net electrical output	D6@32.0	Ea	41,300.00	1,760.00	1,160.00	44,220.00
100 KW net electrical output	D6@32.0	Ea	51,500.00	1,760.00	1,160.00	54,420.00
150 KW net electrical output	D6@40.0	Ea	77,500.00	2,200.00	1,700.00	81,400.00
200 KW net electrical output	D6@40.0	Ea	103,000.00	2,200.00	1,700.00	106,900.00
300 KW net electrical output	D6@40.0	Ea	155,000.00	2,200.00	1,700.00	158,900.00
400 KW net electrical output	D6@80.0	Ea	207,000.00	4,400.00	1,890.00	213,290.00
545 KW net electrical output	D6@80.0	Ea	281,000.00	4,400.00	1,890.00	287,290.00

Add-on boiler modules for motor generators. Add these costs to the appropriate costs above when exhaust heat from the motor generator will be captured to power an ebullient hot water or steam boiler which is part of the building HVAC system. Based on 60 PSI hot water or 15 PSI steam. Includes boiler, temperature, pressure and level gauges, boiler feed pump, condensate return or circulating pump loop, main valve, pressure regulating valve with vent, drain line and enclosure extension. In pounds for per hour (PPH) rating, hot water or steam.

	Craft@Hrs	Unit	Material	Labor	Equipment	Total
3,500 PPH (200 KW generator)	D5@40.0	Ea	32,500.00	2,060.00	—	34,560.00
5,000 PPH (300 KW generator)	D5@40.0	Ea	48,700.00	2,060.00	—	50,760.00
6,750 PPH (400 KW generator)	D5@40.0	Ea	65,100.00	2,060.00	—	67,160.00
8,000 PPH (545 KW generator)	D5@40.0	Ea	88,100.00	2,060.00	—	90,160.00

Pollution control modules for motor generator sets NOx, SOx and VM (volatile materials) emissions reduction wet free-standing module for motor driven prime power and standby dual-fuel (natural gas or oil) electrical generator sets. Conforms to 2010 California Code, EPA Tier IV and European ISO standards. Verantis, Croll-Reynolds or equal. Either vertical counter-flow or packed bed wet type. For commercial and light industrial applications, schools, hospitals and governmental/institutional applications. Oil-fired turbine generators will add about 15% to the total cost, including a second stage, a second stage pump, venturi particulate separator and sludge tank. Add the cost of a permit. To calculate the annual lease rate for a complete installation, divide the total installed cost by five. Then add 2% per year to cover vendor-supplied maintenance.

	Craft@Hrs	Unit	Material	Labor	Equipment	Total
13 KW electrical output, net	U1@69.0	Ea	6,780.00	3,510.00	191.00	10,481.00
17 KW electrical output, net	U1@69.0	Ea	9,200.00	3,510.00	191.00	12,901.00
30 KW electrical output, net	U1@69.0	Ea	14,700.00	3,510.00	191.00	18,401.00
50 KW electrical output, net	U1@69.0	Ea	24,000.00	3,510.00	191.00	27,701.00
80 KW electrical output, net	U1@69.0	Ea	38,000.00	3,510.00	191.00	41,701.00
100 KW electrical output, net	U1@69.0	Ea	47,400.00	3,510.00	191.00	51,101.00
150 KW electrical output, net	U1@69.0	Ea	70,700.00	3,510.00	191.00	74,401.00
200 KW electrical output, net	U1@69.0	Ea	44,600.00	3,510.00	191.00	48,301.00
300 KW electrical output, net	U1@69.0	Ea	46,800.00	3,510.00	191.00	50,501.00
400 KW electrical output, net	U1@69.0	Ea	55,600.00	3,510.00	191.00	59,301.00
545 KW electrical output, net	U1@69.0	Ea	83,100.00	3,510.00	191.00	86,801.00

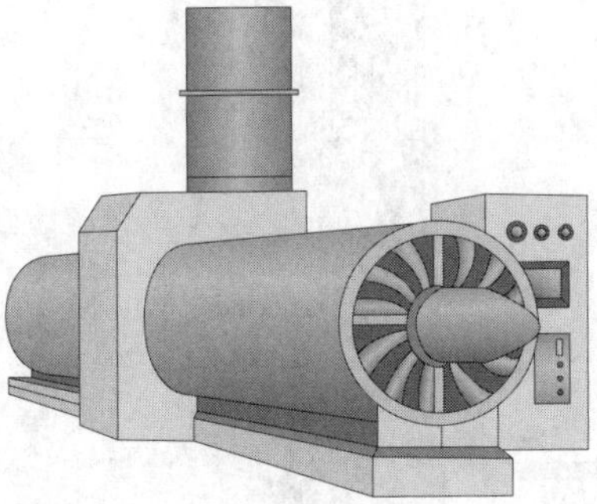

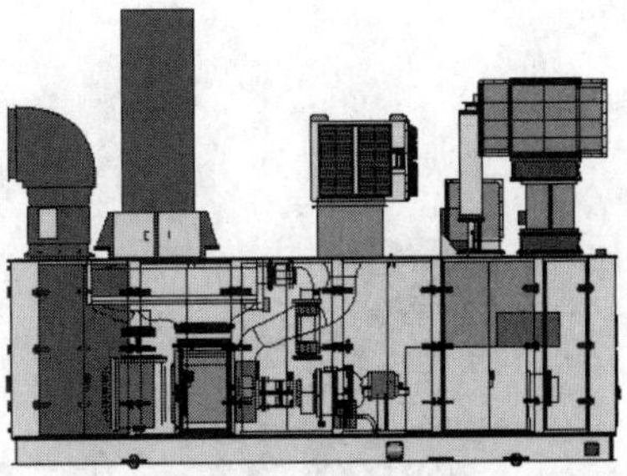

FRONT VIEW

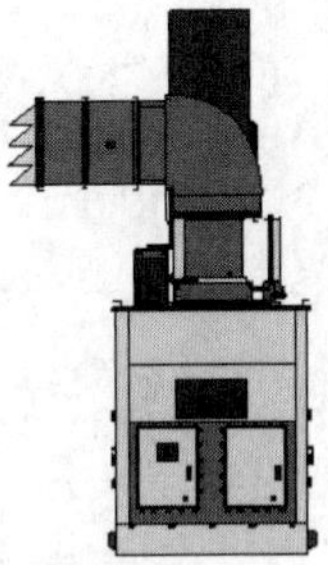

SIDE VIEW

Gas turbine generator sets Dual fuel (oil or gas) single shaft turbine with 11 stage compression, 2 stage hot section and single stage power turbine, 60 Hz, 480 volts, 3 phase, 1,800 RPM, UL 2200 listed, emissions compliance certified to California B.A.C.T. rating. Includes a *National Electrical Code*-compliant 3- or 4-pole generator with UL 1446 insulation, digital engine and generator monitoring, metering and protection with ground fault interruption and lightning shielding, R448 voltage regulator, RFI filter, Woodward API 611 governor and overspeed valve relay, paralleling and synchronizing automatic transfer switch or (for standby emergencies) automatic dual lockout automatic transfer switch, fused main circuit breaker, electronic load-sharing module for generator ganging, electric starter motor, battery, and trickle charger, lube oil cooling system with radiator and fan, oil pump and sump, water cooling system with water pump, radiator and fan, mounting skid, sound- and weather-proof enclosure, turbine inlet air filter, stainless steel exhaust silencer and stack, natural gas fuel train with diaphragm regulator valve, modulating metering valve, pressure gauge and flowmeter, liquid fuel train with fuel pump, fuel preheater, day tank with level gauge, main dual-fuel engine inlet regulating valve, remote annunciation panel with alarms and warning lights, and NFPA-rated CO_2 fire extinguishing system. Add the cost of approval of prints by an inspection bureau, connecting electrical loads and electrical controls, a concrete pad for mounting on the ground or structural steel supports for mounting on a roof, grouting, precision leveling, startup, commissioning, and post-construction inspection by insurance and fire inspectors. These figures assume turbine exhaust heat is released into the atmosphere. Suitable for standby or primary power generation for commercial and light to heavy industrial applications, schools, hospitals, government and institutional use and utility peak-shaving service. Equipment cost is for a 2-ton capacity crane.

1,000 KW electrical output	D6@80.0	Ea	1,080,000.00	4,400.00	2,250.00	1,086,650.00
3,500 KW electrical output	D6@80.0	Ea	3,800,000.00	4,400.00	2,330.00	3,806,730.00
5,000 KW electrical output	D6@120	Ea	5,400,000.00	6,600.00	3,490.00	5,410,090.00
6,000 KW electrical output	D6@120	Ea	6,520,000.00	6,600.00	3,490.00	6,530,090.00
7,500 KW electrical output	D6@160	Ea	10,300,000.00	8,800.00	4,760.00	10,313,560.00

Add-on heat recovery system for gas turbine generators. Add these costs to the appropriate gas turbine generator costs above when exhaust heat will be used to drive a 60 PSI hot water to 600 PSI steam boiler which is part of the building HVAC system. Includes a D- or A-Type watertube bundle, superheater and mud drums, primary stack, secondary stack with service exhaust gas sealed damper bypass plenum, temperature, pressure and level gauges, duplex boiler feed pump, auxiliary dual-fuel continuously-modulating burner, digital burner control and ignition annunciator panel with alarms, condensate return or circulating pump loop, main valve, twin pressure relief valves with vent, drain line, thermally and acoustically insulated enclosure extension, chemical feedwater treatment tank, pump with bladed mixer and relay valve. By pounds for per hour (PPH) rating, hot water or steam. Equipment cost is for a 2-ton capacity crane.

	Craft@Hrs	Unit	Material	Labor	Equipment	Total
3,000 PPH (1,000 KW turbine generator)	D6@80.0	Ea	219,000.00	4,400.00	2,250.00	225,650.00
10,500 PPH (3,500 KW turbine generator)	D6@80.0	Ea	749,000.00	4,400.00	2,250.00	755,650.00
15,000 PPH (5,000 KW turbine generator)	D6@120	Ea	1,110,000.00	6,600.00	3,390.00	1,119,990.00
18,000 PPH (6,000 KW turbine generator)	D6@120	Ea	1,280,000.00	6,600.00	3,390.00	1,289,990.00
22,500 PPH (7,500 KW turbine generator)	D6@160	Ea	2,040,000.00	8,800.00	5,130.00	2,053,930.00
34,500 PPH (11,500 KW turbine generator)	D6@160	Ea	2,900,000.00	8,800.00	5,130.00	2,913,930.00

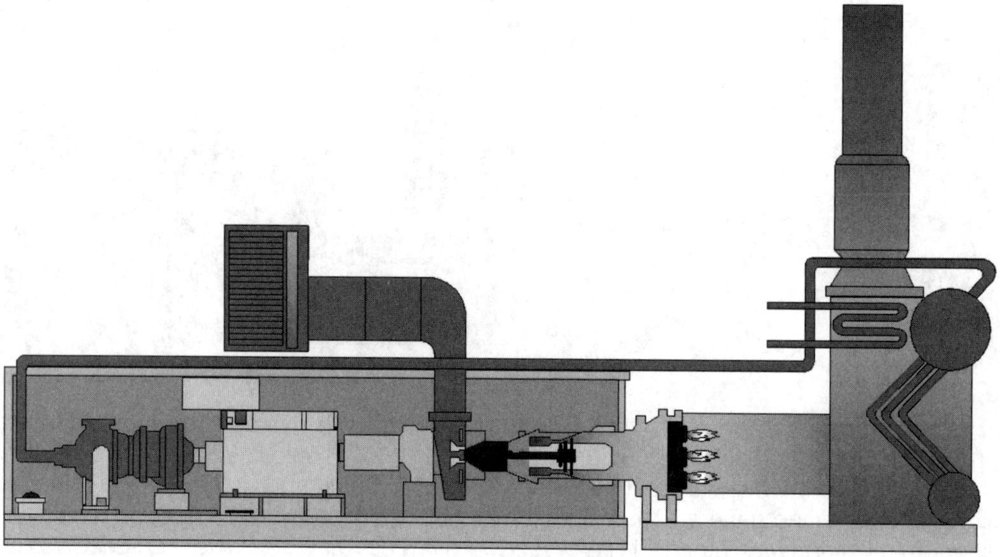

COMBINED CYCLE GAS TURBINE

Add for combined cycle gas turbine heat recovery generator sets. These costs assume exhaust heat drives a turbo generator for electric power cogeneration. Combined cycle operations increase generating capacity by approximately 20% over simple cycle gas turbine generators. Includes the steam turbo generator, backpressure single stage with Woodward API 611 governor and overspeed cutoff valve, main inlet throttling valve, *National Electrical Code*-compliant 4-pole 480 volt, 60 HZ, 3-phase electrical generator with paralleling and synchronizing automatic transfer switch, main breaker with ground fault interruption and lightning protection, ambient forced and air-cooled fintube coil and fan condenser array with condensate pump and return line, bypass drain, emergency vent to atmosphere, digital and thermostatically controlled annunciator panel with pressure/temp/flow rate metering, alarms and emergency cutoff capabilities in a NEMA 10 (wet environment) enclosure. Add the cost of electrical connection and control tie-in, grouting, precision equipment leveling, concrete pad or structural steel roof mount support, vibration isolation mounts, permitting, approvals or inspection. For a combined cycle gas turbine heat recovery generator, add the following percentages to the combined cost of the appropriate gas turbine generator set and matching heat recovery system.

	Craft@Hrs	Unit	Material	Labor	Equipment	Total
Add for power generation driven by exhaust heat	—	%	30.0	50.0	100.00	—

	Craft@Hrs	Unit	Material	Labor	Equipment	Total

Power generator exhaust stack Plate steel exhaust stack for high mass flow rate power generators. Mill-rolled, seam-welded and shop fabricated for field erection. Stack has ionically-bonded internal silicon lining with external aluminized coating, external spiral windbreaker banding, two gasketed and bolted flanges per stack section, buttressed base support sleeve, inlet and service bypass. T-plenum includes a soundproofing enclosure and structural steel support frame. Mounting includes a vibration-isolating spring-loaded circular base plus concrete-anchored guy wiring, eyelets and adjustable guy wire extension tensioners. Add the cost of a reinforced 3000 P.S.I. laser-leveled concrete pad. Equipment cost is for rental of a 3-ton 200-foot extensible truck mounted cable-drive spider gantry crane. Cost per stack section. Each exhaust assembly includes one T-plenum and enough stack sections to meet code requirements and manufacturer specifications. Typical stack height is 75' to 200'. Labor costs assume half of the stack is erected in place upright. The balance is assembled on the ground and lifted into place with a spider crane.

	Craft@Hrs	Unit	Material	Labor	Equipment	Total
10" diameter stack T-plenum with frame	D5@36.0	Ea	18,200.00	1,850.00	—	20,050.00
16" diameter stack T-plenum with frame	D5@36.0	Ea	24,000.00	1,850.00	—	25,850.00
20" diameter stack T-plenum with frame	D5@40.0	Ea	31,300.00	2,060.00	—	33,360.00
24" diameter stack T-plenum with frame	D5@48.0	Ea	37,400.00	2,470.00	—	39,870.00
30" diameter stack T-plenum with frame	D5@60.0	Ea	42,100.00	3,090.00	—	45,190.00
48" diameter stack T-plenum with frame	D5@72.0	Ea	50,800.00	3,710.00	—	54,510.00
60" diameter stack T-plenum with frame	D5@96.0	Ea	60,300.00	4,940.00	—	65,240.00
72" diameter stack T-plenum with frame	D5@120	Ea	94,100.00	6,180.00	—	100,280.00
96" diameter stack T-plenum with frame	D5@160	Ea	130,000.00	8,240.00	—	138,240.00
132" diameter stack T-plenum with frame	D5@180	Ea	266,000.00	9,260.00	—	275,260.00
10" diameter stack, 10' high section	D6@24.0	Ea	906.00	1,320.00	4,650.00	6,876.00
16" diameter stack, 10' high section	D6@24.0	Ea	1,070.00	1,320.00	4,650.00	7,040.00
20" diameter stack, 10' high section	D6@24.0	Ea	1,460.00	1,320.00	4,650.00	7,430.00
24" diameter stack, 10' high section	D6@32.0	Ea	1,930.00	1,760.00	4,650.00	8,340.00
30" diameter stack, 10' high section	D6@32.0	Ea	2,300.00	1,760.00	4,650.00	8,710.00
48" diameter stack, 10' high section	D6@32.0	Ea	2,660.00	1,760.00	4,650.00	9,070.00
60" diameter stack, 20' high section	D6@40.0	Ea	3,630.00	2,200.00	6,880.00	12,710.00
72" diameter stack, 20' high section	D6@40.0	Ea	4,340.00	2,200.00	6,880.00	13,420.00
96" diameter stack, 20' high section	D6@40.0	Ea	4,580.00	2,200.00	6,880.00	13,660.00
132" diameter stack, 20' high section	D6@80.0	Ea	5,430.00	4,400.00	6,880.00	16,710.00

Pollution control modules for gas turbine generators. N0x, S0x, VM (volatile materials) and particle emissions reduction wet module, free-standing, simple cycle. For natural gas fired prime (baseload) power and standby emergency electrical generators. Verantis, Croll-Reynolds, or equal. Complies with 2010 California Code, Tier IV, EPA and European ISO standards. Either vertical counter-flow or packed-bed wet type. For commercial and light to heavy industrial applications, schools, hospitals, and governmental/institutional applications and utility peak-shaving about 15% to the total cost, including a second stage, a second stage pump, venturi particulate separator and sludge tank. To calculate the annual lease rate for a complete installation, divide the total installed cost by five. Then add 2% per year to cover vendor-supplied maintenance.

	Craft@Hrs	Unit	Material	Labor	Equipment	Total
1,000 KW electrical	U1@69.0	Ea	80,100.00	3,510.00	—	83,610.00
3,500 KW electrical	U1@69.0	Ea	132,000.00	3,510.00	—	135,510.00
5,000 KW electrical	U1@69.0	Ea	160,000.00	3,510.00	—	163,510.00
6,000 KW electrical	U1@69.0	Ea	171,000.00	3,510.00	—	174,510.00
7,500 KW electrical	U1@69.0	Ea	188,000.00	3,510.00	—	191,510.00
11,500 KW electrical	U1@69.0	Ea	266,000.00	3,510.00	—	269,510.00

Installation costs for pollution control modules for gas turbine generators.

	Craft@Hrs	Unit	Material	Labor	Equipment	Total
Position main housing, fans and pumps	U1@4.00	Ea	—	203.00	—	203.00
Tie-down and leveling	U1@4.00	Ea	523.00	203.00	—	726.00
Mount piping system frame supports	U1@6.00	LF	1.57	305.00	—	306.57

	Craft@Hrs	Unit	Material	Labor	Equipment	Total
Rig and mount plenum and ducts	SM@5.00	Ea	—	303.00	—	303.00
Rig and mount tank for emission reduction fluid and housing inlet metering valve	U1@4.00	Ea	—	203.00	—	203.00
Weld systems piping	U1@8.00	LF	2.20	407.00	—	409.20
Wire electrical system	BE@8.00	LF	1.89	325.00	—	326.89
Wire controls system	BE@16.0	LF	2.00	650.00	—	652.00
Rotating equipment system level & balance	P1@8.00	Ea	210.00	295.00	—	505.00
Calibration & test	U1@2.00	Ea	—	102.00	—	102.00
Witnessed run trials (add the permit fee)	P1@4.00	Ea	—	148.00	—	148.00

Integrated Photovoltaic Systems For light commercial, government and institutional applications. In arrays of from 50 to 200 KW-hour capacity. Façade, skylight or vertically mounted (integrated into glazing). Includes photovoltaic modules (thin-film or polycrystalline/crystalline ribbon, or amorphous silicon), a charge controller to regulate the power into and out of the battery storage bank (in stand-alone systems), a power storage system or utility grid integration, an inverter to convert DC output to AC, appropriate support and mounting hardware, wiring, and safety disconnects. Thin film single crystal cells are laser-etched and vapor deposited into 2-pane 5/8" to 1" glazing. Polycrystalline or crystalline ribbon solar cells and amorphous silicon solar cells are opaque and are used most commonly for retrofit roof, pergola and canopy mounting. A 6 SF solar unit has 36 cells in an 18" x 4' panel with a 4" x 4" junction box. Add the cost of the permit, roof load resistance and façade deflection reinforcement and standby power generator, if required. Complies with Federal Spec 48 14 00.

	Craft@Hrs	Unit	Material	Labor	Total
Vertical framing mullions, 11 ga. x 1" x 3", aluminum	IW@.009	Lb	1.26	.60	1.86
Horizontal framing mullions, 11 ga. x 2" x 3", aluminum with galvanized steel internal bracing	IW@.019	Lb	2.10	1.26	3.36
Thin film single crystal solar cells	G1@.045	SF	97.40	2.18	99.58
Polycrystalline or crystalline ribbon solar cells	G1@.035	SF	88.70	1.69	90.39
Amorphous solar cells	G1@.035	SF	35.00	1.69	36.69
Add for thermally reflective or retentive coatings	—	%	15.0	—	—
Charge controller with fusing and emergency interrupts, 2.25 watt-hour	E4@4.0	Ea	195.00	203.00	398.00
Power storage system, utility grid paralleling switchgear and service bypass, 2.20 watt-hour	E4@8.0	Ea	389.00	407.00	796.00
Battery pack and fault protection, 6.00 watt-hour	E4@2.0	Ea	325.00	102.00	427.00
DC to AC inverter with power quality system filters, 1.85 watt-hour	E4@16.0	Ea	779.00	813.00	1,592.00
Electrical wiring for integrated PV system	E4@.007	LF	.37	.36	.73
Inspection and test of integrated PV system	E4@8.0	Ea	—	407.00	407.00
Typical installed cost per SF of cell (1.5 watts), including poly cells, supports, charge controller, power storage, grid interconnect, inverter, wiring, inspection and test, 50 to 200 KW array	—	LS	—	—	105.30
Add for architectural services and approvals	—	%	—	—	10.0

Fluorescent Lighting Commercial, industrial and architectural grade. Rapid start. With ballasts but no lamps, wire or conduit. Includes setting and connecting prewired fixtures only.

	Craft@Hrs	Unit	Material	Labor	Total
Surface mounted fluorescent fixtures, better quality, baked enamel finish, with hinged wraparound acrylic prismatic lens suitable for office or classroom use, 4' long, Lithonia LB series					
Two 40 watt lamp fixture (#240-A)	CE@.773	Ea	84.30	46.70	131.00
Four 40 watt lamp fixture (#440-A)	CE@.773	Ea	158.00	46.70	204.70
Eight 40 watt lamp fixture, 8' long (#8T440-A)	CE@.960	Ea	240.00	58.00	298.00
Surface mounted fluorescent fixtures, baked enamel finish, with wraparound acrylic prismatic lens suitable for industrial use, 4' long, Lithonia series					
One 40 watt lamp fixture (CB140A)	CE@.806	Ea	75.20	48.70	123.90
Two 40 watt lamp fixture (LB240A)	CE@.858	Ea	64.60	51.80	116.40
Four 40 watt lamp fixture (LB440A)	CE@1.07	Ea	110.00	64.60	174.60
Add for 40 watt lamps	—	Ea	4.40	—	4.40

	Craft@Hrs	Unit	Material	Labor	Total
Surface mounted steel sided fluorescent fixtures with acrylic prismatic diffuser, 7-1/16" x 4-1/2"					
Two 40 watt lamps	CE@.955	Ea	92.00	57.70	149.70
Four 40 watt lamps	CE@1.05	Ea	129.00	63.40	192.40
Add for 40 watt straight lamps	—	Ea	4.41	—	4.41
Wall surface mounted fluorescent fixtures, baked enamel finish, 2 lamps, 8" wide 5" high, hinged acrylic prismatic lens, Lightolier					
26" long fixture	CE@.737	Ea	193.00	44.50	237.50
38" long fixture	CE@.795	Ea	224.00	48.00	272.00
50" long fixture	CE@.858	Ea	217.00	51.80	268.80
Add for 24" 20 watt lamps	—	Ea	4.01	—	4.01
Add for 36" 30 watt lamps	—	Ea	6.24	—	6.24
Add for 48" 40 watt lamps	—	Ea	2.85	—	2.85
Industrial pendent or surface mounted open striplights, baked enamel finish, Lithonia C series					
One or two 40 watt lamps, 4' long (C240)	CE@.865	Ea	43.60	52.30	95.90
One or two 75 watt lamps, 8' long (C296)	CE@1.02	Ea	64.60	61.60	126.20
One or two 55 watt lamps, 6' long (C272)	CE@1.02	Ea	64.60	61.60	126.20
Add for 40 watt lamps	—	Ea	3.07	—	3.07
Add for 75 or 55 watt lamps	—	Ea	7.27	—	7.27
Add for 24" stem and canopy set, per fixture	—	Ea	7.11	—	7.11
Industrial pendent or surface mounted fluorescent fixtures, 12" wide baked enamel, steel reflector-shield, Lithonia L/LA series					
Two 40 watt lamps, 4' long (L-240-120)	CE@.903	Ea	46.90	54.60	101.50
Two 75 watt lamps, 8' long (L-296-120)	CE@1.21	Ea	92.00	73.10	165.10
Add for 40 watt lamps	—	Ea	3.07	—	3.07
Add for 75 watt lamps	—	Ea	7.33	—	7.33

	Craft@Hrs	Unit	Material	Labor	Total
Ceiling grid mounted fluorescent troffer fixtures, baked enamel finish, with hinged acrylic prismatic lens with energy saving ballast, Day-Brite					
Two 40 watt "U" lamp fixture, 2' x 2'	CE@.908	Ea	67.90	54.90	122.80
Two 40 watt lamp fixture, 2' x 4'	CE@.998	Ea	77.10	60.30	137.40
Four 40 watt lamp fixture, 2' x 4'	CE@1.05	Ea	83.30	63.40	146.70
Add for plaster frames, per fixture	—	Ea	9.93	—	9.93

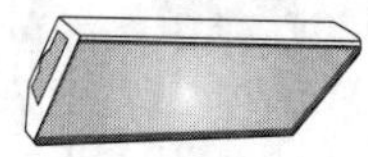

	Craft@Hrs	Unit	Material	Labor	Total
Air-handling grid mounted floating door, heat transfer troffer fixtures with acrylic lens, no ductwork included					
1' x 4', two 40 watt lamps	CE@.908	Ea	129.00	54.90	183.90
2' x 2', one U-shape 40 watt lamp	CE@.809	Ea	137.00	48.90	185.90
2' x 4', two 40 watt lamps	CE@1.00	Ea	170.00	60.40	230.40
2' x 4', three 40 watt lamps	CE@1.05	Ea	212.00	63.40	275.40
2' x 4', four 40 watt lamps	CE@1.05	Ea	214.00	63.40	277.40
Add for 40 watt 4' lamps	—	Ea	3.07	—	3.07
Add for 40 watt "U" lamps	—	Ea	12.90	—	12.90
Surface mounted vandal-resistant luminaire with tamper-resistant screw-type latching, Sylvania					
1 lamp	CE@.761	Ea	142.00	46.00	188.00
2 lamps	CE@.761	Ea	144.00	46.00	190.00
4 lamps	CE@.761	Ea	242.00	46.00	288.00

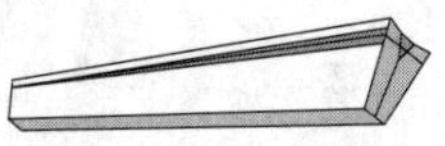

	Craft@Hrs	Unit	Material	Labor	Total
Parabolic fluorescent luminaire, 6" x 24" x 24" with semi-specular anodized aluminum reflector and parabolic louvers, I.C.E. AR series					
Two 40 watt lamp, bracket or pendent mount	CE@.955	Ea	89.30	57.70	147.00
Four 40 watt lamps, bracket or pendent mount	CE@.955	Ea	143.00	57.70	200.70
Round surface mounted fluorescent fixtures, aluminum housing, matte black finish, polycarbonate or acrylic opal globe, Circleline					
22 to 32 watt, 14" diameter	CE@.478	Ea	56.20	28.90	85.10
32 to 40 watt, 18" diameter	CE@.478	Ea	77.80	28.90	106.70
Add for circline tubes	—	Ea	9.11	—	9.11

Outdoor sign fluorescent fixtures, anodized aluminum housing with parabolic specular reflector and acrylic lens, with high output lamps and remote ballast

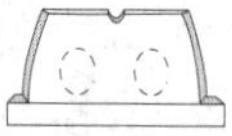

	Craft@Hrs	Unit	Material	Labor	Total
One 60 watt lamp. 48" long fixture	CE@2.39	Ea	266.00	144.00	410.00
One 85 watt lamp, 72" long fixture	CE@2.39	Ea	281.00	144.00	425.00
One 110 watt lamp, 96" long fixture	CE@2.39	Ea	310.00	144.00	454.00
Two 85 watt lamps, 144" long fixture	CE@2.39	Ea	420.00	144.00	564.00
Add for high output T12 800 MA lamps, sign white					
60 watt	—	Ea	8.45	—	8.45
85 watt	—	Ea	8.50	—	8.50
115 watt	—	Ea	23.70	—	23.70
Cost per linear foot of fixture	CE@.179	LF	70.70	10.80	81.50
Add for 90-degree elbows	CE@.475	Ea	185.00	28.70	213.70
Add for in-line connectors	CE@.475	Ea	92.90	28.70	121.60
Wet or damp location surface mounted fluorescent fixtures, hinge mounted acrylic diffuse lens, fiberglass or plastic housing with gaskets, Hubbell					
Two 40 watt lamps, 4' long fixture	CE@1.21	Ea	154.00	73.10	227.10
Two 40 watt lamps, 8' long fixture	CE@1.86	Ea	335.00	112.00	447.00
Add for 40 watt lamps	—	Ea	3.00	—	3.00

Commercial and industrial LED light fixtures

With lamps but no wire or conduit. Labor includes setting and connecting prewired fixtures only.

Recessed-LED 12 volt accent lights, aluminum reflector, 2-1/2" glass lens and pigtail connection, dimmable

	Craft@Hrs	Unit	Material	Labor	Total
1 watt	CE@1.15	Ea	18.50	69.50	88.00
5 watt	CE@1.15	Ea	27.90	69.50	97.40
6 watt, waterproof	CE@1.15	Ea	55.80	69.50	125.30

Recessed LED downlight, 100 to 240 volt, frosted dome lens, white baffle trim, dimmable

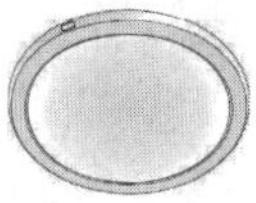

	Craft@Hrs	Unit	Material	Labor	Total
5" dia. 9 W, 60 W equivalent	CE@1.21	Ea	24.80	73.10	97.90
6" dia. 15 W, 75 W equivalent	CE@1.21	Ea	27.90	73.10	101.00
8" dia. 24 W, 190 W equivalent	CE@1.21	Ea	22.10	73.10	95.20
6" square, 9 W, 60 W equivalent	CE@1.21	Ea	16.70	73.10	89.80

Flush mount-LED ceiling lights, frosted dome lens, white aluminum trim, dimmable

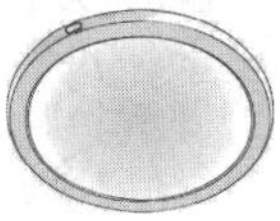

	Craft@Hrs	Unit	Material	Labor	Total
5-1/2" dia. 10 W, 60 W equivalent	CE@1.21	Ea	18.50	73.10	91.60
7" dia. 12 W, 75 W equivalent	CE@1.21	Ea	18.50	73.10	91.60
9" dia. 18 W, 100 W equivalent	CE@1.21	Ea	22.10	73.10	95.20
13" dia. 25 W, 100 W equivalent	CE@1.21	Ea	22.10	73.10	95.20
16" dia. 23 W, 100 W, bronze trim	CE@1.21	Ea	55.30	73.10	128.40
14" square, 10 W, 60 W equivalent	CE@1.21	Ea	22.10	73.10	95.20

LED panel lights, frosted dome lens, white aluminum trim, dimmable

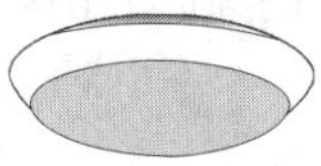

	Craft@Hrs	Unit	Material	Labor	Total
5-1/2" dia. 10 W, 60 W equivalent	CE@1.21	Ea	18.50	73.10	91.60
7" dia. 12 W, 75 W equivalent	CE@1.21	Ea	18.50	73.10	91.60
9" dia. 18 W, 100 W equivalent	CE@1.21	Ea	22.10	73.10	95.20
13" dia. 25 W, 100 W equivalent	CE@1.21	Ea	22.10	73.10	95.20
16" dia. 23 W, 100 W, bronze trim	CE@1.21	Ea	55.30	73.10	128.40
14" square, 10 W, 60 W equivalent	CE@1.21	Ea	22.10	73.10	95.20

	Craft@Hrs	Unit	Material	Labor	Total
Industrial LED wall packs, aluminum housing, bronze finish, polycarbonate lens, weatherproof, with lamps. 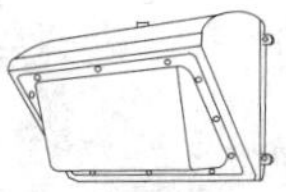					
20 watt, 70 W halide equivalent	CE@.955	Ea	35.70	57.70	93.40
28 watt, 70 W halide equivalent	CE@.955	Ea	47.40	57.70	105.10
40 watt, 250 W halide equivalent	CE@.955	Ea	91.80	57.70	149.50
80 watt, 400 W halide equivalent	CE@.955	Ea	102.00	57.70	159.70
80 watt, 400 W halide equivalent, rotatable	CE@.955	Ea	143.00	57.70	200.70
120 watt, 400 W halide equivalent	CE@.955	Ea	133.00	57.70	190.70
Add for photo cell control, factory-installed	—	Ea	14.80	—	14.80
High-bay LED industrial fixture, cast aluminum housing, 10" diameter tempered glass lens, suspended or surface mounted, with lamp, U-bracket, eye hook, and safety cable. 					
100 watt, 250 W halide equivalent	CE@1.30	Ea	153.00	78.50	231.50
150 watt, 400 W halide equivalent	CE@1.30	Ea	184.00	78.50	262.50
200 watt, 750 W halide equivalent	CE@1.30	Ea	214.00	78.50	292.50
300 watt, 1000 W halide equivalent	CE@1.30	Ea	316.00	78.50	394.50
400 watt, 1500 W halide equivalent	CE@1.30	Ea	520.00	78.50	598.50
500 watt, 1500 W halide equivalent	CE@1.30	Ea	622.00	78.50	700.50
Add for wire guard on lens	CE@.250	Ea	77.50	15.10	92.60
High-bay LED linear fixtures, white aluminum frame, frosted poly lens, suspension mount, by metal halide lamp equivalent 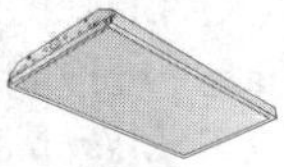					
80 watt, 3 lamps, 24" x 12", 250 W halide	CE@1.39	Ea	91.80	84.00	175.80
100 watt, 4 lamps, 48" x 12", 250 W halide	CE@1.39	Ea	81.50	84.00	165.50
110 watt, 3 lamp, 24" x 12", 320 W halide	CE@1.39	Ea	102.00	84.00	186.00
150 watt, 4 lamps, 48" x 12", 250 W halide	CE@1.39	Ea	102.00	84.00	186.00
165 watt, 4 lamps, 24" x 12", 400 W halide	CE@1.39	Ea	158.00	84.00	242.00
225 watt, 6 lamp, 48" x 12", 400 W halide	CE@1.39	Ea	179.00	84.00	263.00
250 watt, 8 lamps, 48" x 20", 400 W halide	CE@1.39	Ea	242.00	84.00	326.00
300 watt, 10 lamp, 48" x 20", 1000 W halide	CE@1.39	Ea	281.00	84.00	365.00
Add for conduit mounting	CE@.250	Ea	7.02	15.10	22.12
Add for emergency driver, 25 W backup power for 90 minutes, with test switch	CE@1.71	Ea	143.00	103.00	246.00
LED area flood light fixtures, U-bracket mount, aluminum frame, poly lens, weatherproof 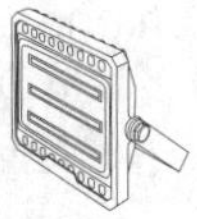					
30 watt, 150 W halide equivalent, 4" x 6"	CE@1.07	Ea	35.70	64.60	100.30
50 watt, 175 W halide equivalent	CE@1.07	Ea	51.00	64.60	115.60
100 watt, 250 W halide equivalent	CE@1.07	Ea	122.00	64.60	186.60
150 watt, 400 W halide equivalent	CE@1.07	Ea	173.00	64.60	237.60
200 watt, 600 W halide equivalent, 18" x 14"	CE@1.07	Ea	204.00	64.60	268.60
Vapor tight LED light fixtures, weatherproof aluminum housing and impact-resistant frosted polycarbonate lens. For use in harsh environments: gas stations, car washes, industrial kitchens, loading docks. 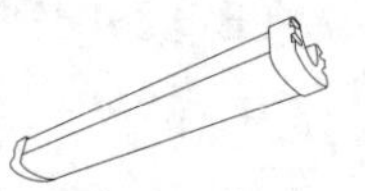					
30 watt, 2' long	CE@1.07	Ea	71.40	64.60	136.00
50 watt, 4' long	CE@1.21	Ea	112.00	73.10	185.10
60 watt, 4' long	CE@1.21	Ea	133.00	73.10	206.10
20 watt caged jelly jar fixture	CE@1.07	Ea	81.60	64.60	146.20

Incandescent Lighting Commercial and architectural grade. No wire, conduit or concrete included. Includes setting and connecting prewired fixtures only.

	Craft@Hrs	Unit	Material	Labor	Total
Step illumination light fixtures, 16 gauge steel housing with white enamel finish, 5" high, 4" deep, 11" long					
Polycarbonate or tempered glass lens fixture 	CE@1.07	Ea	226.00	64.60	290.60
Louvered sheet metal front fixture 	CE@1.07	Ea	185.00	64.60	249.60
Add for brushed aluminum trim, 2 lamps	—	Ea	51.50	—	51.50
Wall surface mounted fluorescent fixtures, baked enamel finish, 2 lamps, 8" wide 5" high, hinged acrylic prismatic lens, Lightolier					
26" long fixture	CE@.737	Ea	189.00	44.50	233.50
38" long fixture	CE@.795	Ea	219.00	48.00	267.00
50" long fixture	CE@.858	Ea	212.00	51.80	263.80

	Craft@Hrs	Unit	Material	Labor	Total
Add for 24" 20 watt lamps	—	Ea	4.08	—	4.08
Add for 36" 30 watt lamps	—	Ea	6.32	—	6.32
Add for 48" 40 watt lamps	—	Ea	2.87	—	2.87
Recessed round eyelid wall wash, 6" milligroove baffle, Prescolite					
150 watt fixture	CE@1.07	Ea	183.00	64.60	247.60
Exterior wall fixtures, cast anodized aluminum with white polycarbonate globe, gaskets between globe and housing and between housing and base, Prescolite					
Cylinder globe fixture	CE@.320	Ea	98.00	19.30	117.30
Round globe fixture	CE@.430	Ea	32.00	26.00	58.00
Add for 100 watt lamp	—	Ea	5.61	—	5.61
Add for 150 watt lamp	—	Ea	5.71	—	5.71
Obstruction light, meets Federal Aviation Administration Specification L-810, cast aluminum housing, two one-piece red, heat-resistant fresnel globes, with photoelectric control, mounted on 1" rigid steel conduit, including junction box and mounting plate					
Two 100 watt lamp fixture	CE@4.91	Ea	161.00	297.00	458.00

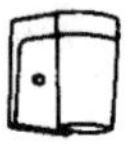

Vandal-Resistant Lighting Commercial and architectural grade. Includes setting and connecting prewired fixtures but no wire, conduit or lamps.

	Craft@Hrs	Unit	Material	Labor	Total
Ceiling mounted 12" x 12" x 6" fixture, polycarbonate prismatic lens					
Two 100 watt incandescent lamps	CE@.764	Ea	105.00	46.20	151.20
22 watt fluorescent circline lamp	CE@.955	Ea	76.60	57.70	134.30
Wall mounted 6" wide, 9" high, 7" deep fixture, polycarbonate prismatic diffuser					
One 100 watt incandescent lamp	CE@.572	Ea	75.70	34.60	110.30
13 watt fluorescent lamp	CE@.764	Ea	120.00	46.20	166.20
Lamps for vandal-resistant fixtures					
100 watt incandescent lamp	—	Ea	5.71	—	5.71
13 watt fluorescent lamp	—	Ea	11.80	—	11.80
35 to 70 watt high pressure sodium lamp	—	Ea	85.00	—	85.00

Lighted Exit Signs Includes setting and connecting prewired fixtures but no wire or conduit.

	Craft@Hrs	Unit	Material	Labor	Total
Universal mount (wall or ceiling), Thinline series, 6" letters on one side, stencil face					
Single	CE@.764	Ea	33.70	46.20	79.90
Twin	CE@.764	Ea	33.70	46.20	79.90
Universal mount, 6" letters on two sides of polycarbonate housing, two 15 watt lamps	CE@.764	Ea	52.60	46.20	98.80
Add for two circuit supply	—	Ea	10.90	—	10.90
Add for 24" stem hanger	—	Ea	15.00	—	15.00
Add for battery backup for exit signs	CE@.381	Ea	24.50	23.00	47.50

Explosion-Proof Lighting

No wire, conduit or concrete included. Includes setting and connecting prewired fixtures only.

	Craft@Hrs	Unit	Material	Labor	Total
Explosion proof LED light fixtures, rated for Class 1 Division 2 hazards (granaries, mills, mines, gas stations, airplane hangars, auto shops) cast aluminum housing, U-bracket mount, tempered glass lens					
100 watt, 175 W halide equivalent	CE@2.57	Ea	612.00	155.00	767.00
200 watt, 400 W halide equivalent	CE@2.57	Ea	918.00	155.00	1,073.00
Explosion proof LED light fixtures, rated for Class 1 Division 1 hazards (vapors and gases are constantly present, i.e. paint spray booth) cast aluminum housing, U-bracket mount, tempered glass lens					
150 watt, 175 W halide equivalent	CE@2.57	Ea	1,720.00	155.00	1,875.00

	Craft@Hrs	Unit	Material	Labor	Total

Emergency Lighting Includes setting and connecting prewired fixtures but no wire or conduit.
Shelf or wall mounted solid state battery pack with charger, lead-acid battery, baked enamel finish, with 2 halogen lamps, 90 minute operation, indoor use only

	Craft@Hrs	Unit	Material	Labor	Total
6 volt, 15 watt	CE@1.74	Ea	123.00	105.00	228.00
6 volt, 30 watt	CE@1.74	Ea	190.00	105.00	295.00
6 volt, 50 watt	CE@1.74	Ea	223.00	105.00	328.00
6 volt, 100 watt	CE@1.74	Ea	299.00	105.00	404.00
12 volt, 100 watt	CE@1.74	Ea	302.00	105.00	407.00

Self diagnostic emergency lighting fixtures, microprocessor based, continuously monitors battery/lamps

	Craft@Hrs	Unit	Material	Labor	Total
Emergency fixture, two lamps, wall mount	CE@.825	Ea	228.00	49.80	277.80
LED exit sign with emergency fixture, wall mount	CE@.825	Ea	401.00	49.80	450.80
LED exit sign only, wall mount	CE@.825	Ea	343.00	49.80	392.80

Yard and Street Lighting Includes setting and connecting prewired fixtures with ballast but no pole, concrete work, excavation, wire, lamps or conduit. See pole costs below. Equipment is a flatbed truck with a boom & auger
Rectangular LED floodlights, die-cast aluminum housing, tempered glass lens, photoelectric cell, add the cost of mounting pole or bracket

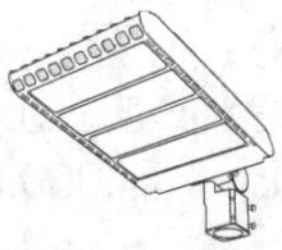

	Craft@Hrs	Unit	Material	Labor	Equipment	Total
100 watt, 250 W halide equivalent	E1@1.55	Ea	179.00	80.80	24.30	284.10
150 watt, 400 W halide equivalent	E1@1.55	Ea	194.00	80.80	24.30	299.10
200 watt, 750 W halide equivalent	E1@1.55	Ea	240.00	80.80	24.30	345.10
300 watt, 1,000 W halide equivalent	E1@1.55	Ea	332.00	80.80	24.30	437.10
Add for pole mount kit	E1@.547	Ea	15.30	28.50	8.56	52.36
Add for wall mount bracket	E1@.547	Ea	30.60	28.50	8.56	67.66

Canopy-mounted LED floodlights, die-cast anodized aluminum housing with shatterproof polycarbonate lens, flush or surface mount. Security lighting for parking garages, gas stations, drive-thrus and covered walkways.

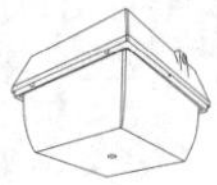

	Craft@Hrs	Unit	Material	Labor	Equipment	Total
60 watt, 100 W halide equivalent	E1@2.71	Ea	71.40	141.00	42.40	254.80
100 watt, 250 W halide equivalent	E1@2.71	Ea	86.70	141.00	42.40	270.10
150 watt, 400 W halide equivalent	E1@2.71	Ea	111.00	141.00	42.40	294.40

Yard and Street Lighting Poles

Hole for a pole foundation dug with a truck-mounted auger, no soil disposal included

	Craft@Hrs	Unit	Material	Labor	Equipment	Total
Per CF of undisturbed soil	E1@.064	CF	—	3.34	1.00	4.34

Concrete pole foundations, formed, poured and finished, with anchor bolts. Material costs shown include concrete, forms and anchor bolts

	Craft@Hrs	Unit	Material	Labor	Equipment	Total
12" diameter, 36" deep, for 12' pole	E1@.746	Ea	35.80	38.90	11.70	86.40
24" diameter, 72" deep, for 30' pole	E1@1.14	Ea	143.00	59.40	17.80	220.20
30" diameter, 76" deep, for 40' pole	E1@1.54	Ea	185.00	80.30	24.10	289.40

Yard and street light poles, including base plate but no top brackets. See labor costs below.

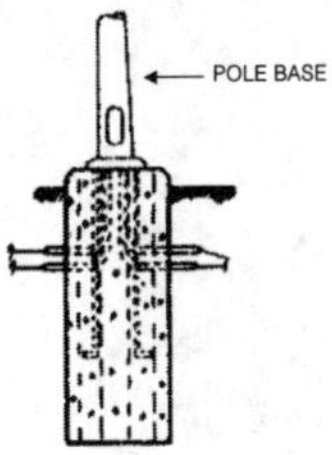

	Unit	Round steel	Square steel	Aluminum
12' high	Ea	808.00	526.00	280.00
16' high	Ea	947.00	615.00	350.00
20' high, 6" wide	Ea	1,280.00	776.00	496.00
25' high, 6" wide	Ea	1,550.00	947.00	1,100.00
30' high, 8" wide	Ea	1,790.00	1,440.00	1,240.00
35' high, 8" wide	Ea	2,300.00	1,810.00	1,920.00
40' high, 9" wide	Ea	2,680.00	2,030.00	2,200.00
50' high, 10" wide	Ea	3,000.00	2,960.00	—

	Craft@Hrs	Unit	Material	Labor	Equipment	Total
Labor setting metal light poles Equipment is a flatbed truck with a boom & auger						
To 20' high	E1@2.89	Ea	—	151.00	45.20	196.20
25' to 30' high	E1@4.35	Ea	—	227.00	68.10	295.10
35' to 40' high	E1@5.73	Ea	—	299.00	89.70	388.70
50' high	E1@8.57	Ea	—	447.00	134.00	581.00
Deduct for aluminum poles	—	%	—	-20.0	-20.0	—
Top brackets for steel and aluminum light poles, installed prior to setting pole						
Single arm	CE@.500	Ea	100.00	30.20	7.83	138.03
Two arm	CE@.500	Ea	119.00	30.20	7.83	157.03
Three arm	CE@.991	Ea	152.00	59.90	15.50	227.40
Four arm	CE@.991	Ea	190.00	59.90	15.50	265.40

Area Lighting, Installed on Poles

These costs include excavation for pole, pole foundation (2' x 2' x 3' deep), 150' of 2" PVC conduit run with 40' of RSC, 600' of #8 copper wire and terminations, 35' x 8" square steel pole and one arm and a 300 watt LED (1,000 watt metal halide equivalent) lamp for each fixture. Equipment is a flatbed truck with a boom and auger.

Cost per pole including fixtures as shown

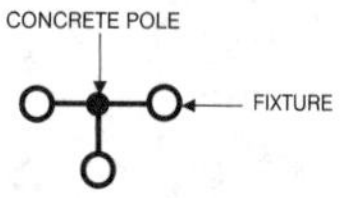

TOP VIEW

	Craft@Hrs	Unit	Material	Labor	Equipment	Total
1 fixture per pole	E1@30.4	Ea	3,110.00	1,580.00	476.00	5,166.00
2 fixtures per pole	E1@32.5	Ea	3,550.00	1,690.00	509.00	5,749.00
3 fixtures per pole	E1@34.8	Ea	4,000.00	1,810.00	545.00	6,355.00
4 fixtures per pole	E1@36.8	Ea	4,440.00	1,920.00	576.00	6,936.00

	Craft@Hrs	Unit	Material	Labor	Total
Security and Alarm Systems Sensor costs include connection but no wire runs.					
Monitor panels, including accessory section and connection to signal and power supply wiring, cost per panel					
1 zone wall-mounted cabinet with 1 monitor panel, tone, standard line supervision, and 115 volt power supply	E4@2.02	Ea	1,060.00	103.00	1,163.00
5 zone wall-mounted cabinet with 5 monitor panels, 10 zone monitor rack, 5 monitor panel blanks, tone, standard line supervision and 115 volt power supply	E4@8.21	Ea	6,010.00	417.00	6,427.00
10 zone wall-mounted cabinet with 10 monitor panels, 10 zone monitor rack, tone, standard line supervision and 115 volt power supply	E4@12.1	Ea	6,910.00	615.00	7,525.00
10 zone monitor rack and 10 monitor panels with tone and standard line supervision but no power supply and no cabinet	E4@11.1	Ea	5,710.00	564.00	6,274.00
1 zone wall-mounted cabinet with 1 monitor panel, tone, high security line supervision and 115 volt power supply	E4@2.02	Ea	1,420.00	103.00	1,523.00
high security line supervision but no power supply	E4@7.82	Ea	7,490.00	397.00	7,887.00
10 zone wall-mounted cabinet with 10 monitor panels, 10 zone monitor rack, tone, high security line supervision and 115 volt power supply	E4@12.0	Ea	8,780.00	610.00	9,390.00
Emergency power indicator for monitor panel	E4@1.14	Ea	281.00	57.90	338.90
Monitor panels					
Panel with accessory section, tone and standard line supervision	E4@.990	Ea	463.00	50.30	513.30
Panel with accessory section, tone and high security line supervision	E4@.904	Ea	697.00	46.00	743.00
Monitor racks					
1 zone with 115 volt power supply	E4@.904	Ea	382.00	46.00	428.00
10 zone with 115 volt power supply	E4@.904	Ea	1,960.00	46.00	2,006.00
10 zone with no power supply	E4@.904	Ea	1,530.00	46.00	1,576.00
Monitor cabinets					
1 zone monitor for wall mounted cabinet	E4@.990	Ea	598.00	50.30	648.30
5 zone monitor for wall mounted cabinet	E4@.990	Ea	765.00	50.30	815.30
10 zone monitor for wall mounted cabinet	E4@.990	Ea	934.00	50.30	984.30
20 zone monitor for wall mounted cabinet	E4@.990	Ea	1,280.00	50.30	1,330.30
50 zone monitor for wall mounted cabinet	E4@.990	Ea	2,840.00	50.30	2,890.30
50 zone monitor for floor mounted cabinet	E4@1.04	Ea	3,080.00	52.90	3,132.90
Balanced magnetic door switches					
Surface mounted	E4@2.02	Ea	117.00	103.00	220.00
Surface mounted with remote test	E4@2.02	Ea	164.00	103.00	267.00
Flush mounted	E4@2.02	Ea	113.00	103.00	216.00
Mounted bracket or spacer	E4@.249	Ea	6.77	12.70	19.47
Photoelectric sensors					
500' range, 12 volt DC	E4@2.02	Ea	320.00	103.00	423.00
800' range, 12 volt DC	E4@2.02	Ea	361.00	103.00	464.00
Fence type, 6 beam, without wire or trench	E4@3.89	Ea	11,700.00	198.00	11,898.00
Fence type, 9 beam, without wire or trench	E4@3.89	Ea	14,600.00	198.00	14,798.00
Capacitance wire grid systems					
Surface type	E4@.990	Ea	81.90	50.30	132.20
Duct type	E4@.990	Ea	66.90	50.30	117.20
Tube grid kit	E4@.990	Ea	123.00	50.30	173.30
Vibration sensors, to 30 per zone	E4@2.02	Ea	138.00	103.00	241.00
Audio sensors, to 30 per zone	E4@2.02	Ea	170.00	103.00	273.00
Inertia sensors, outdoor, without trenching	E4@2.02	Ea	113.00	103.00	216.00
Inertia sensors, indoor	E4@2.02	Ea	75.20	103.00	178.20
Electric sensor cable, 300 meters, no trenching	E4@3.89	Ea	1,710.00	198.00	1,908.00

	Craft@Hrs	Unit	Material	Labor	Total
Ultrasonic transmitters, to 20 per zone					
Omni-directional	E4@2.02	Ea	73.20	103.00	176.20
Directional	E4@2.02	Ea	81.90	103.00	184.90
Ultrasonic transceivers, to 20 per zone					
Omni-directional	E4@2.02	Ea	81.90	103.00	184.90
Directional	E4@2.02	Ea	87.80	103.00	190.80
High security	E4@2.02	Ea	298.00	103.00	401.00
Standard security	E4@2.02	Ea	123.00	103.00	226.00
Microwave perimeter sensor, to 4 per zone	E4@3.89	Ea	4,790.00	198.00	4,988.00
Passive interior infrared sensors, to 20 per zone					
Wide pattern	E4@2.02	Ea	665.00	103.00	768.00
Narrow pattern	E4@2.02	Ea	628.00	103.00	731.00
Access and secure control units					
For balanced magnetic door switches	E4@3.06	Ea	364.00	156.00	520.00
For photoelectric sensors	E4@3.06	Ea	665.00	156.00	821.00
For capacitance sensors	E4@3.06	Ea	674.00	156.00	830.00
For audio and vibration sensors	E4@3.06	Ea	777.00	156.00	933.00
For inertia sensors	E4@3.06	Ea	697.00	156.00	853.00
For nimmer (m.b.) detector	E4@3.06	Ea	579.00	156.00	735.00
For electric cable sensors	E4@3.06	Ea	3,510.00	156.00	3,666.00
For ultrasonic sensors	E4@3.06	Ea	1,060.00	156.00	1,216.00
For microwave sensors	E4@3.06	Ea	658.00	156.00	814.00
Accessories					
Tamper assembly for monitor cabinet	E4@.990	Ea	73.20	50.30	123.50
Monitor panel blank	E4@.249	Ea	8.17	12.70	20.87
Audible alarm	E4@.990	Ea	85.80	50.30	136.10
Audible alarm control	E4@.990	Ea	340.00	50.30	390.30
Termination screw terminal cabinet, 25 pair	E4@.990	Ea	246.00	50.30	296.30
Termination screw terminal cabinet, 50 pair	E4@1.36	Ea	400.00	69.10	469.10
Termination screw terminal cabinet, 150 pair	E4@3.45	Ea	651.00	175.00	826.00
Universal termination with remote test for cabinets and control panels	E4@1.47	Ea	60.20	74.70	134.90
Universal termination without remote test	E4@.990	Ea	35.30	50.30	85.60
High security line supervision termination					
With remote test and tone	E4@1.47	Ea	305.00	74.70	379.70
With tone only	E4@1.47	Ea	281.00	74.70	355.70
12" door cord for capacitance sensor	E4@.249	Ea	9.38	12.70	22.08
Insulation block kit for capacitance sensor	E4@.990	Ea	46.80	50.30	97.10
Termination block for capacitance sensor	E4@.249	Ea	9.94	12.70	22.64
200 zone graphic display	E4@3.06	Ea	4,680.00	156.00	4,836.00
210 zone multiplexer event recorder unit	E4@3.89	Ea	4,450.00	198.00	4,648.00
Guard alert display	E4@3.06	Ea	1,040.00	156.00	1,196.00
Uninterruptable power supply (battery)	E4@2.02	Ea	2,130.00	103.00	2,233.00
12 volt, 40VA plug-in transformer	E4@.495	Ea	40.30	25.20	65.50
18 volt, 40VA plug-in transformer	E4@.495	Ea	27.50	25.20	52.70
24 volt, 40VA plug-in transformer	E4@.495	Ea	20.00	25.20	45.20
Test relay	E4@.332	Ea	62.00	16.90	78.90
Sensor test control (average for sensors)	E4@.990	Ea	81.20	50.30	131.50
Cable, 2 pair 22 gauge, twisted, 1 pair shielded, run in exposed walls or per LF per pull, pulled in raceway and connected	E4@.008	LF	1.67	.41	2.08

Security access digital outdoor keypad/reader, modular single-unit type. Up to sixty users. Accepts cards, keyed-in passwords or both, non-volatile memory. Accepts any magnetic strip card format. Add the cost of the door actuator mechanism and the door. Cost includes control wiring.

Digital access outdoor keypad/reader	CE@4.0	Ea	339.00	242.00	581.00

	Craft@Hrs	Unit	Material	Labor	Total
Fire Alarm and Detection Systems No wiring included except as noted.					
Pedestal mounted master fire alarm box	E4@3.89	Ea	1,450.00	198.00	1,648.00
Automatic coded signal transmitter	E4@3.89	Ea	760.00	198.00	958.00
Fire alarm control panel, simplex	E4@3.89	Ea	713.00	198.00	911.00
Fire detection annunciator panel					
8 zone drop	E4@3.89	Ea	472.00	198.00	670.00
12 zone drop	E4@5.03	Ea	620.00	256.00	876.00
16 zone drop	E4@5.93	Ea	962.00	301.00	1,263.00
8 zone lamp panel only	E4@4.33	Ea	157.00	220.00	377.00
12 zone lamp panel only	E4@5.93	Ea	230.00	301.00	531.00
16 zone lamp panel only	E4@7.23	Ea	306.00	368.00	674.00
Battery charger and cabinet, simplex	E4@6.19	Ea	410.00	315.00	725.00
Add for nickel cadmium batteries	E4@3.89	Ea	445.00	198.00	643.00
Fire alarm pull stations, manual operation	E4@.497	Ea	23.00	25.30	48.30
Fire alarm 10" bell with outlet box	E4@.497	Ea	74.90	25.30	100.20
Magnetic door holder	E4@1.33	Ea	70.30	67.60	137.90
Combination door holder and closer	E4@2.48	Ea	285.00	126.00	411.00
Detex door lock	E4@2.72	Ea	33.80	138.00	171.80
Thermodetector	E4@.497	Ea	10.10	25.30	35.40
Ionization AC smoke detector, with wiring	E4@.710	Ea	174.00	36.10	210.10
Fixed temp. and rate of rise smoke detector	E4@.746	Ea	15.70	37.90	53.60
Carbon dioxide pressure switch	E4@.746	Ea	5.36	37.90	43.26
Telephone Wiring					
Plywood backboard mount for circuit wiring, set on masonry wall					
4' x 4' x 3/4"	E4@.938	Ea	13.60	47.70	61.30
4' x 8' x 3/4"	E4@1.10	Ea	27.10	55.90	83.00
Cable tap in a manhole or junction box					
25 to 50 pair cable	E4@7.80	Ea	134.00	396.00	530.00
100 to 200 pair cable	E4@10.1	Ea	156.00	513.00	669.00
300 pair cable	E4@12.0	Ea	157.00	610.00	767.00
400 pair cable	E4@13.0	Ea	169.00	661.00	830.00
Cable terminations in a manhole or junction box					
25 pair cable	E4@1.36	Ea	12.10	69.10	81.20
50 pair cable	E4@1.36	Ea	13.90	69.10	83.00
100 pair cable	E4@2.72	Ea	27.90	138.00	165.90
150 pair cable	E4@3.45	Ea	42.10	175.00	217.10
200 pair cable	E4@4.61	Ea	63.10	234.00	297.10
300 pair cable	E4@5.03	Ea	83.80	256.00	339.80
400 pair cable	E4@5.34	Ea	111.00	271.00	382.00
Communications cable, pulled in conduit or walls and connected					
2 pair cable	E4@.008	LF	.14	.41	.55
25 pair cable	E4@.030	LF	1.67	1.52	3.19
50 pair cable	E4@.043	LF	3.55	2.19	5.74
75 pair cable	E4@.043	LF	4.42	2.19	6.61
100 pair cable	E4@.043	LF	5.15	2.19	7.34
150 pair cable	E4@.045	LF	7.17	2.29	9.46
200 pair cable	E4@.051	LF	9.35	2.59	11.94
300 pair cable	E4@.051	LF	13.80	2.59	16.39
Telephone outlets (no junction box included)					
Wall outlet	E4@.396	Ea	7.32	20.10	27.42
Floor outlet, flush mounted	E4@.495	Ea	9.08	25.20	34.28

27 Communications

	Craft@Hrs	Unit	Material	Labor	Total
Closed Circuit Television Systems					
Outdoor television camera in weatherproof housing, cable preinstalled.					
Wall or roof mount, professional grade	E4@.500	Ea	1,560.00	25.40	1,585.40
Wall or roof mount, economy	E4@.500	Ea	218.00	25.40	243.40
Self-terminating outlet box, cover plate	E4@.245	Ea	4.90	12.50	17.40
Coaxial cable (RG59/J), 75 ohms, no raceway included	E4@.006	LF	.32	.30	.62
In-line cable taps (PTU) for 36" TV system	E4@.689	Ea	7.13	35.00	42.13
Cable blocks for in-line taps	—	Ea	3.71	—	3.71
Desk-type TV monitor, 19" diagonal screen, 75 ohms, labor includes hookup only					
4 camera inputs	E4@.500	Ea	334.00	25.40	359.40
Security CCTV digital video recorder central control station, modular single-unit type. Allows up to 16 discrete channels and simultaneous real-time monitoring of all 16 channels. Digital video recorder saves pictures every 3 seconds per channel. Password control access to DVD data only. Cost includes monitor, PC, software, cable connectors for sixteen stations, keyboard, mouse, software training and installation. Add the cost of wiring to digital CCTV's.					
Security CCTV recorder control station	CE@4.0	Ea	5,450.00	242.00	5,692.00
Public Address Paging Systems					
Signal cable, #22 solid copper polyethylene insulated, PVC jacketed wire					
Pulled in conduit, no conduit included	E4@.008	LF	.14	.41	.55
Microphone, desk type, push to talk, with					
7' of three conductor cable	E4@.250	Ea	113.00	12.70	125.70
Wall mounted enameled steel amplifier cabinet (18" high, 24" wide, 6" deep) with electrical receptacle					
and lockable door	E4@1.67	Ea	348.00	84.90	432.90
Amplifier, 100 watts, 4 inputs, installation includes hookup only, no wire pull					
Complete unit	E4@.500	Ea	373.00	25.40	398.40
Wall mounted paging horns, transformer type, 250 to 13,000 Hertz, 8 ohms, 30 Watts, 10" diameter, 12" deep, gray baked enamel, labor includes hookup only 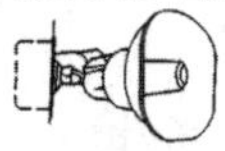					
Interior/exterior 15/30 Watts	E4@.250	Ea	70.20	12.70	82.90
Ceiling mounted 8" speaker with 12" grill, labor includes installation and hookup only, no wire pull					
8" ceiling speaker	E4@.330	Ea	30.20	16.80	47.00
8" ceiling speaker with volume	E4@.330	Ea	32.50	16.80	49.30
Outdoor weather resistant speakers					
Landscape weather resistant	E4@.330	Ea	237.00	16.80	253.80
Rock landscape (high end)	E4@.330	Ea	469.00	16.80	485.80
Computer Network Cable Pulled in conduit or walls. Add for connectors and cable testing. Prices are for cable purchased in bulk on 1,000' spools.					
Coaxial cable					
Thin Ethernet, 50 ohm, 10BASE2 (RG58). Used in modern networks for Wireless Network high gain antennae					
PVC cable	E4@.008	LF	.14	.41	.55
Plenum cable	E4@.008	LF	.37	.41	.78
Fiber optic cable					
Singlemode fiber optic cable, duplex is 4 strand, simplex is 1 strand					
Singlemode duplex fiber optic cables (8.3/125)	E4@.012	LF	.22	.61	.83
Singlemode simplex fiber optic cables (8.3/125)	E4@.012	LF	.21	.61	.82
Multimode fiber optic cable, duplex is a zip type					
Multimode duplex fiber optic cables (50/125)	E4@.012	LF	.25	.61	.86
Multimode duplex fiber optic cables (62.5/125)	E4@.012	LF	.25	.61	.86
Multimode simplex fiber optic cables (50/125)	E4@.012	LF	.25	.61	.86
Multimode simplex fiber optic cables (62.5/125)	E4@.012	LF	.25	.61	.86

	Craft@Hrs	Unit	Material	Labor	Total
Twisted pair Category 5, 100 Mbps, material price based on purchase of 1000' rolls. Use solid able for horizontal runs. STP is shielded					
4 pair UTP PVC stranded cable	E4@.008	LF	.12	.41	.53
4 pair UTP PVC solid cable	E4@.008	LF	.12	.41	.53
4 pair UTP plenum solid cable	E4@.008	LF	.24	.41	.65
4 pair STP PVC stranded cable	E4@.008	LF	.21	.41	.62
4 pair STP PVC solid cable	E4@.008	LF	.21	.41	.62
4 pair STP plenum solid cable	E4@.008	LF	.24	.41	.65
Twisted pair Category 5e, 350 Mbps, material price based on purchase of 1,000' rolls, use solid for horizontal runs. STP is shielded.					
4 pair UTP PVC solid	E4@.008	LF	.20	.41	.61
4 pair UTP PVC stranded	E4@.008	LF	.20	.41	.61
4 pair UTP plenum solid	E4@.008	LF	.29	.41	.70
4 pair STP PVC stranded	E4@.008	LF	.21	.41	.62
4 pair STP PVC solid	E4@.008	LF	.21	.41	.62
4 pair STP plenum solid	E4@.008	LF	.30	.41	.71
Twisted pair Category 6, 1 Gbps, material price based on purchase of 1,000' rolls, use solid for horizontal runs					
4 pair UTP PVC stranded	E4@.008	LF	.21	.41	.62
4 pair UTP PVC solid	E4@.008	LF	.22	.41	.63
4 pair UTP plenum solid	E4@.008	LF	.34	.41	.75
Add for multiple cable pulls of thin Ethernet or unshielded twisted pair cables when cables are pulled simultaneously in plenum or PVC, based on quantity of cables pulled					
Add for each cable pulled simultaneously, over one	E4@.250	Ea	—	12.70	12.70
Punch-down blocks					
Plywood backboard mount for patch panel or punch-down blocks, set on a masonry wall					
4' x 4' x 3/4"	E4@.938	Ea	13.60	47.70	61.30
4' x 8' x 3/4"	E4@1.10	Ea	27.10	55.90	83.00
Distribution frame for punch-down blocks					
Holds 5 punch-down blocks	E4@.250	Ea	34.00	12.70	46.70
Holds 10 punch-down blocks	E4@.250	Ea	40.40	12.70	53.10
Punch-down blocks, labor is to install block in distribution frame only, add labor to punch-down wire pairs as shown below					
50 pair	E4@.250	Ea	18.40	12.70	31.10
100 pair	E4@.250	Ea	26.80	12.70	39.50
Punch-down wire pairs, labor only, per pair	E4@.020	Ea	—	1.02	1.02
Computer network cable connectors					
Coax					
Thin Ethernet					
BNC type, crimp on, female	E4@.100	Ea	4.32	5.08	9.40
Fiber optic cable, terminated, 10' length					
ST-ST singlemode duplex riser	E4@.100	Ea	65.90	5.08	70.98
ST-SC singlemode duplex riser	E4@.100	Ea	65.90	5.08	70.98
SC-SC singlemode duplex riser	E4@.100	Ea	65.90	5.08	70.98
FC-SC singlemode duplex riser	E4@.100	Ea	65.90	5.08	70.98
ST-ST singlemode simplex riser	E4@.100	Ea	36.10	5.08	41.18
ST-SC singlemode simplex riser	E4@.100	Ea	36.10	5.08	41.18
SC-SC singlemode simplex riser	E4@.100	Ea	36.10	5.08	41.18
FC-SC singlemode simplex riser	E4@.100	Ea	36.10	5.08	41.18
ST-ST multimode duplex riser	E4@.100	Ea	30.00	5.08	35.08

27 Communications

	Craft@Hrs	Unit	Material	Labor	Total
ST-SC multimode duplex riser	E4@.100	Ea	30.00	5.08	35.08
SC-SC multimode duplex riser	E4@.100	Ea	30.00	5.08	35.08
FC-SC multimode duplex riser	E4@.100	Ea	89.90	5.08	94.98
FDDI-FDDI multimode duplex riser	E4@.100	Ea	114.00	5.08	119.08
FDDI OFNP plenum	E4@.100	Ea	107.00	5.08	112.08
Fiber optic cable connectors, special tools required					
SC multimode connector	E4@.150	Ea	9.63	7.62	17.25
SC singlemode connector	E4@.150	Ea	10.70	7.62	18.32
FC multimode connector	E4@.150	Ea	10.70	7.62	18.32
FC singlemode connector	E4@.150	Ea	10.70	7.62	18.32
ST multimode connector	E4@.150	Ea	9.63	7.62	17.25
ST singlemode connector	E4@.150	Ea	10.70	7.62	18.32
FDDI for round cable	E4@.150	Ea	18.20	7.62	25.82
FDDI for Zip cable	E4@.150	Ea	18.20	7.62	25.82
Shielded twisted pair (STP)					
IBM Type 2, 6 pair data connector	E4@.100	Ea	2.53	5.08	7.61
IBM Type 6, 2 pair data connector	E4@.150	Ea	3.54	7.62	11.16
IBM Type 9, 2 pair data connector	E4@.150	Ea	3.54	7.62	11.16
Twisted pair connectors (UTP) and (STP), modular hand tool required, material prices based on package of 50					
RJ11	E4@.100	Ea	.63	5.08	5.71
Cat5-rated RJ45 connectors for solid wire	E4@.100	Ea	.86	5.08	5.94
Cat5-rated RJ45 connectors for stranded wire	E4@.100	Ea	.86	5.08	5.94
Cat6-rated RJ45 connectors for stranded wire	E4@.100	Ea	.86	5.08	5.94
Shielded RJ45 connectors for solid or stranded wire	E4@.100	Ea	2.44	5.08	7.52
Cable testing, with dedicated cable tester					
Coax cable, per conductor	E4@.125	Ea	—	6.35	6.35
Fiber optic cable, per segment	E4@.160	Ea	—	8.13	8.13
Shielded twisted pair (STP), per pair	E4@.125	Ea	—	6.35	6.35
Unshielded twisted pair (UTP), per pair	E4@.125	Ea	—	6.35	6.35
Wall plates					
Coax wall plates with jacks (no junction box included)					
One or two jacks, including termination	E4@.396	Ea	.56	20.10	20.66
Modular wall plates with jacks for UTP (no junction box included), including termination					
One 4 or 6 wire jack (RJ11)	E4@.396	Ea	2.80	20.10	22.90
One 8 wire jack (RJ45)	E4@.396	Ea	2.80	20.10	22.90
Two 8 wire jacks (RJ45)	E4@.450	Ea	3.90	22.90	26.80

31 Earthwork

Site Clearing Using a dozer as described below, a 3/4 CY wheel loader and two 10 CY dump trucks. Clearing costs will be higher on smaller jobs and where the terrain limits production. These costs include hauling 6 miles to a legal dump. Dump fees are not included. See Waste Disposal. Figures in parentheses show the approximate "loose" volume of the material to be loaded and hauled to the dump. For estimating purposes, assume that the cost of moving equipment on and off the job site will be equal to the cost of clearing one acre. For more detailed coverage, see *National Earthwork and Heavy Equipment Estimator,* http://CraftsmanSiteLicense.com.

	Craft@Hrs	Unit	Material	Labor	Equipment	Total
Clear light brush and grub roots						
Using a 105 HP D-5 dozer (350 CY)	C2@34.8	Acre	—	1,720.00	2,300.00	4,020.00

	Craft@Hrs	Unit	Material	Labor	Equipment	Total
Clear medium brush and small trees, grub roots						
Using a 130 HP D-6 dozer (420 CY)	C2@41.8	Acre	—	2,070.00	2,550.00	4,620.00
Clear brush and trees to 6" trunk diameter						
Using a 335 HP D-8 dozer (455 CY)	C2@45.2	Acre	—	2,240.00	2,860.00	5,100.00
Clear wooded area, pull stumps						
Using a 460 HP D-9 dozer (490 CY)	C2@48.7	Acre	—	2,410.00	4,830.00	7,240.00
Strip, stockpile on site and then replace topsoil						
Using a 100 HP D-4 tractor	S1@.069	CY	—	3.40	6.85	10.25

Building Layout Typical cost for a survey crew to lay out site improvements for a 100,000 SF single-story commercial building and associated walks, drainage and parking. Includes preparation of a project control map, setting benchmarks, marking site disturbance limits at 50' intervals, aligning roadways and parking areas and setting lath or stakes as required for rough grading. Based on ten visits to the site by the survey crew.

	Craft@Hrs	Unit	Material	Labor	Equipment	Total
Initial boundary control survey	—	LS	—	—	—	1,040.00
Site rough grading, set lath	—	LS	—	—	—	1,500.00
Sanitary sewer, alignment and grade	—	LS	—	—	—	720.00
Storm drainage, alignment and grade	—	LS	—	—	—	2,250.00
Water main, hydrants, alignment and grade	—	LS	—	—	—	2,250.00
Curb, set stakes at 25' stations (3 visits)	—	LS	—	—	—	4,170.00
Building corners, location and grade	—	LS	—	—	—	1,150.00
Run-off detention pond, position and grade	—	LS	—	—	—	900.00
Retaining walls, alignment and grade	—	LS	—	—	—	1,050.00
Walkways, alignment and grade	—	LS	—	—	—	1,020.00
Light pole bases, location and grade	—	LS	—	—	—	750.00
Building I.D. sign, location and grade	—	LS	—	—	—	350.00

Rock Excavation Rock drilling costs. Based on using a pneumatic truck-mounted wagon drill. Equipment includes one wheel-mounted air compressor and one 4-1/2" pneumatic wagon drill with hydraulic swing boom and drill bits. Costs shown are per linear foot of hole drilled. Add blasting costs below. Use $2,500 as a minimum job charge. LF per hour shown is for a 2-man crew.

	Craft@Hrs	Unit	Material	Labor	Equipment	Total
Easy work, 38 LF per hour	S1@.052	LF	—	2.56	3.35	5.91
Moderate work, 30 LF per hour	S1@.067	LF	—	3.30	4.31	7.61
Most work, 25 LF per hour	S1@.080	LF	—	3.94	5.15	9.09
Hard work, 20 LF per hour	S1@.100	LF	—	4.93	6.44	11.37
Dense rock, 15 LF per hour	S1@.132	LF	—	6.50	8.50	15.00
Drilling 2-1/2" hole for						
rock bolts, 24 LF/hour	S1@.086	LF	—	4.24	5.54	9.78

Blasting costs Based on two cycles per hour and 20 linear foot lifts. These costs assume 75% fill of holes with explosives. Equipment includes one flatbed truck. Costs shown are per cubic yard of area blasted. Loading or hauling of blasted material not included. Use $3,500 as a minimum job charge. Load explosives in holes and detonate, by pattern spacing. CY per hour shown is for a 5-man crew.

	Craft@Hrs	Unit	Material	Labor	Equipment	Total
Using explosives, per pound	—	Lb	5.82	—	—	5.82
6' x 6' pattern (26 CY per hour)	C1@.192	CY	17.50	8.10	.82	26.42
7' x 7' pattern (35 CY per hour)	C1@.144	CY	13.10	6.07	.61	19.78
7' x 8' pattern (47 CY per hour)	C1@.106	CY	10.20	4.47	.45	15.12
9' x 9' pattern (60 CY per hour)	C1@.084	CY	8.73	3.54	.36	12.63
10' x 10' pattern (72 CY per hour)	C1@.069	CY	7.27	2.91	.29	10.47
12' x 12' pattern (108 CY per hour)	C1@.046	CY	4.95	1.94	.20	7.09
14' x 14' pattern (147 CY per hour)	C1@.034	CY	3.49	1.43	.14	5.06

	Craft@Hrs	Unit	Material	Labor	Equipment	Total
Site Grading Layout, staking, flagmen, lights, watering, ripping, rock breaking, loading or hauling not included. Site preparation grading based on using one crawler tractor. Use $3,000.00 as a minimum job charge. (One acre is 43,560 SF or 4,840 SY.)						
General area rough grading with 100 HP D-4 tractor (.5 acres per hour)	S1@4.00	Acre	—	197.00	138.00	335.00
General area rough grading with 335 HP D-8 tractor (1 acre per hour)	S1@2.00	Acre	—	98.50	186.00	284.50
Site grading based on using one 100 HP (10,000 lb) motor grader						
General area grading (.7 acres per hour)	S1@2.86	Acre	—	141.00	106.00	247.00
Fine grading subgrade to 1/10' (.45 acres per hour)	S1@4.44	Acre	—	219.00	164.00	383.00
Cut slope or shape embankment to 2' high (.25 acres per hour)	S1@8.00	Acre	—	394.00	295.00	689.00
Rough grade sub-base course on roadway (.2 acres per hour)	S1@10.0	Acre	—	493.00	369.00	862.00
Finish grade base or leveling course on roadway (.17 acres per hour)	S1@11.8	Acre	—	581.00	436.00	1,017.00
Finish grading for building slab, windrow excess (1,000 SF per hour)	S1@.002	SF	—	.10	.07	.17
Ripping rock Based on using a tractor-mounted ripper. Equipment includes a D-8 dozer and a D-9 dozer. Costs shown are per CY of area ripped. Loading or hauling of material not included. Use $2,000 as a minimum job charge.						
Clay or glacial tills, D-9 cat tractor with 2-shank ripper (500 CY per hour)	T0@.002	CY	—	.11	.60	.71
Clay or glacial tills, D-8 cat tractor with 1-shank ripper (335 CY per hour)	T0@.003	CY	—	.17	.56	.73
Shale, sandstone, or limestone, D-9 cat tractor with 2-shank ripper (125 CY per hour)	T0@.008	CY	—	.46	2.39	2.85
Shale, sandstone, or limestone, D-8 cat tractor with 1-shank ripper (95 CY per hour)	T0@.011	CY	—	.63	2.05	2.68
Slate, metamorphic rock, D-9 cat tractor with 2-shank ripper (95 CY per hour)	T0@.011	CY	—	.63	3.29	3.92
Slate, metamorphic rock, D-8 cat tractor with 1-shank ripper (63 CY per hour)	T0@.016	CY	—	.92	2.98	3.90
Granite or basalt, D-9 cat tractor with 2-shank ripper (78 CY per hour)	T0@.013	CY	—	.74	3.89	4.63
Granite or basalt, D-8 cat tractor with 1-shank ripper (38 CY per hour)	T0@.027	CY	—	1.55	5.03	6.58
Rock loosening Based on using pneumatic jackhammers. Equipment includes one compressor and two jackhammers with chisel points. Costs shown are per CY of area loosened. Loading and hauling not included. CY per hour shown is for a 2-man crew. Use $800 as a minimum job charge.						
Igneous or dense rock (1.4 CY per hour)	CL@1.43	CY	—	59.00	54.20	113.20
Most weathered rock (2.4 CY per hour)	CL@.835	CY	—	34.40	31.60	66.00
Soft sedimentary rock (4 CY per hour)	CL@.500	CY	—	20.60	18.90	39.50

	Craft@Hrs	Unit	Material	Labor	Equipment	Total
Embankment Grading Earth embankment spreading, shaping, compacting and watering, and finish shaping. Use $15,000 as a minimum job charge, loading or hauling of earth fill not included.						
Spreading and shaping. Spread and shape earth from loose piles, based on using a D-8 tractor.						
6" to 10" lifts (164 CY per hour)	TO@.006	CY	—	.34	1.11	1.45
Compacting and watering. (Add for cost of water from below.) CY per hour shown is for a 3-man crew. Based on using a self-propelled 100 HP vibrating roller and a 3,500 gallon truck. Productivity assumes 3 passes at 7' wide.						
6" lifts (500 CY per hour)	C3@.006	CY	—	.29	.29	.58
Compacting with a sheepsfoot roller towed behind a D-7 tractor and a 3,500 gallon truck. Productivity assumes 3 passes at 5' wide						
6" lifts (185 CY per hour)	C3@.016	CY	—	.77	1.28	2.05
8" lifts (245 CY per hour)	C3@.012	CY	—	.58	.96	1.54
Cost of water for compacted earth embankments. Based on water at $2.50 per 1,000 gallons and 66 gallons per cubic yard of compacted material. Assumes optimum moisture at 10%, natural moisture of 2% and evaporation of 2%. Placed in conjunction with compaction shown above.						
Cost per CY of compacted embankment	—	CY	.26	—	—	.26
Finish shaping of embankments. Earth embankment slopes and swales up to 1 in 4 incline. Based on using a 150 HP grader and a 15-ton self-propelled rubber tired roller. SY per hour shown is for a 3-man crew. (200 SY per hour)						
(200 SY per hour)	SS@.016	SY	—	.83	1.10	1.93
Finish shaping of embankments with a D-8 tractor						
(150 SY per hour)	TO@.007	SY	—	.40	1.29	1.69
Finish shaping of embankment slopes and swales by hand. SY per hour shown is for 1 man.						
Slopes up to 1 in 4 (16 SY per hour)	CL@.063	SY	—	2.60	—	2.60
Slopes over 1 in 4 (12.5 SY per hour)	CL@.080	SY	—	3.30	—	3.30
Trench Excavation and Backfill (200 SY per hour) These costs and productivity are based on utility line trenches and continuous footings where the spoil is piled adjacent to the trench. Linear feet (LF), cubic yards (CY), square feet (SF), or square yards (SY) per hour shown are based on a 2-man crew. Increase costs by 10% to 25% when spoil is loaded in trucks. Hauling, shoring, dewatering or unusual conditions are not included.						
12" wide bucket, for 12" wide trench. Depths 3' to 5'. Equipment is a wheel loader with 1 CY bucket and integral backhoe. Use $400 as a minimum job charge.						
Light soil (60 LF per hour)	S1@.033	LF	—	1.63	.54	2.17
Medium soil (55 LF per hour)	S1@.036	LF	—	1.77	.59	2.36
Heavy or wet soil (35 LF per hour)	S1@.057	LF	—	2.81	.93	3.74
18" wide bucket, for 18" wide trench. Depths 3' to 5'. Equipment is a wheel loader with 1 CY bucket and integral backhoe. Use $400 as a minimum job charge.						
Light soil (55 LF per hour)	S1@.036	LF	—	1.77	.59	2.36
Medium soil (50 LF per hour)	S1@.040	LF	—	1.97	.65	2.62
Heavy or wet soil (30 LF per hour)	S1@.067	LF	—	3.30	1.09	4.39
24" wide bucket, for 24" wide trench. Depths 3' to 5'. Equipment is a wheel loader with 1 CY bucket and integral backhoe. Use $400 as a minimum job charge.						
Light soil (50 LF per hour)	S1@.040	LF	—	1.97	.65	2.62
Medium soil (45 LF per hour)	S1@.044	LF	—	2.17	.72	2.89
Heavy or wet soil (25 LF per hour)	S1@.080	LF	—	3.94	1.30	5.24
Truck-mounted Gradall with 1 CY bucket. Use $700 as a minimum job charge.						
Light soil (40 CY per hour)	S1@.050	CY	—	2.46	4.18	6.64
Medium soil (34 CY per hour)	S1@.059	CY	—	2.91	4.93	7.84
Heavy or wet soil (27 CY per hour)	S1@.074	CY	—	3.65	6.18	9.83
Loose rock (23 CY per hour)	S1@.087	CY	—	4.29	7.27	11.56
Crawler-mounted hydraulic backhoe with 3/4 CY bucket. Use $500 as a minimum job charge.						
Light soil (33 CY per hour)	S1@.061	CY	—	3.01	3.03	6.04
Medium soil (27 CY per hour)	S1@.074	CY	—	3.65	3.68	7.33
Heavy or wet soil (22 CY per hour)	S1@.091	CY	—	4.48	4.52	9.00
Loose rock (18 CY per hour)	S1@.112	CY	—	5.52	5.57	11.09

	Craft@Hrs	Unit	Material	Labor	Equipment	Total
Crawler-mounted hydraulic backhoe with 1 CY bucket. Use $500 as a minimum job charge.						
Light soil (65 CY per hour)	S1@.031	CY	—	1.53	1.23	2.76
Medium soil (53 CY per hour)	S1@.038	CY	—	1.87	1.51	3.38
Heavy or wet soil (43 CY per hour)	S1@.047	CY	—	2.32	1.86	4.18
Loose rock (37 CY per hour)	S1@.055	CY	—	2.71	2.18	4.89
Blasted rock (34 CY per hour)	S1@.058	CY	—	2.86	2.30	5.16
Crawler-mounted hydraulic backhoe with 1-1/2 CY bucket. Use $500 as a minimum job charge.						
Light soil (83 CY per hour)	S1@.024	CY	—	1.18	1.07	2.25
Medium soil (70 CY per hour)	S1@.029	CY	—	1.43	1.29	2.72
Heavy or wet soil (57 CY per hour)	S1@.035	CY	—	1.72	1.56	3.28
Loose rock (48 CY per hour)	S1@.042	CY	—	2.07	1.87	3.94
Blasted rock (43 CY per hour)	S1@.047	CY	—	2.32	2.09	4.41
Crawler-mounted hydraulic backhoe with 2 CY bucket. Use $700 as a minimum job charge.						
Light soil (97 CY per hour)	S1@.021	CY	—	1.03	1.22	2.25
Heavy or wet soil (65 CY per hour)	S1@.031	CY	—	1.53	1.51	3.04
Loose rock (55 CY per hour)	S1@.036	CY	—	1.77	1.76	3.53
Blasted rock (50 CY per hour)	S1@.040	CY	—	1.97	1.95	3.92
Crawler-mounted hydraulic backhoe with 2-1/2 CY bucket. Use $750 as a minimum job charge.						
Light soil (122 CY per hour)	S1@.016	CY	—	.79	1.23	2.02
Medium soil (100 CY per hour)	S1@.020	CY	—	.99	1.54	2.53
Heavy or wet soil (82 CY per hour)	S1@.024	CY	—	1.18	1.84	3.02
Loose rock (68 CY per hour)	S1@.029	CY	—	1.43	2.23	3.66
Blasted rock (62 CY per hour)	S1@.032	CY	—	1.58	2.46	4.04
Chain-boom Ditch Witch digging trench to 12" wide and 5' deep. Use $400 as a minimum job charge.						
Light soil (10 CY per hour)	S1@.200	CY	—	9.85	3.12	12.97
Most soils (8.5 CY per hour)	S1@.235	CY	—	11.60	3.67	15.27
Heavy soil (7 CY per hour)	S1@.286	CY	—	14.10	4.47	18.57
Trenchers, chain boom, 55 HP, digging trench to 18" wide and 8' deep. Use $500 as a minimum job charge.						
Light soil (62 CY per hour)	S1@.032	CY	—	1.58	.69	2.27
Most soils (49 CY per hour)	S1@.041	CY	—	2.02	.89	2.91
Heavy soil (40 CY per hour)	S1@.050	CY	—	2.46	1.08	3.54
Trenchers, chain boom, 100 HP, digging trench to 24" wide and 8' deep. Use $500 as a minimum job charge.						
Light soil (155 CY per hour)	S1@.013	CY	—	.64	.92	1.56
Most soils (125 CY per hour)	S1@.016	CY	—	.79	1.13	1.92
Heavy soil (100 CY per hour)	S1@.020	CY	—	.99	1.41	2.40
Trim trench bottom to 1/10'						
By hand (200 SF per hour)	CL@.010	SF	—	.41	—	.41
Backfill trenches from loose material piled adjacent to a trench. No compaction included. Soil previously excavated. (200 SY per hour)						
Backfill trenches by hand						
(8 CY per hour)	CL@.250	CY	—	10.30	—	10.30
Wheel loader 55 HP. Use $400 as a minimum job charge						
Typical soils (50 CY per hour)	S1@.040	CY	—	1.97	.68	2.65
D-3 crawler dozer. Use $475 as a minimum job charge						
Typical soils (25 CY per hour)	S1@.080	CY	—	3.94	2.15	6.09
3/4 CY crawler loader. Use $450 as a minimum job charge						
Typical soils (33 CY per hr)	S1@.061	CY	—	3.01	1.33	4.34
D-7 crawler dozer. Use $700 as a minimum job charge						
Typical soils (130 CY per hour)	S1@.015	CY	—	.74	.91	1.65

	Craft@Hrs	Unit	Material	Labor	Equipment	Total
Wheel loader 55 HP. Sand or gravel bedding. Use $400 as a minimum job charge						
Typical soils (80 CY per hour)	S1@.025	CY	—	1.23	.43	1.66
Fine grade bedding by hand						
(22 SY per hr)	CL@.090	SY	—	3.71	—	3.71
Compaction of soil in trenches in 8" layers. Use $200 as a minimum job charge						
Pneumatic tampers						
(20 CY per hour)	CL@.050	CY	—	2.06	1.75	3.81
Vibrating rammers						
(10 CY per hour)	CL@.100	CY	—	4.13	1.26	5.39

Dragline Excavation For mass excavation, footings or foundations. Costs shown include casting the excavated soil adjacent to the excavation or loading it into trucks. Hauling costs are not included. Cubic yards (CY) per hour are as measured in an undisturbed condition (bank measure) and are based on a 2-man crew. Use $3,000 as a minimum job charge.

	Craft@Hrs	Unit	Material	Labor	Equipment	Total
1-1/2 CY dragline with a 45-ton crawler crane						
Loam or light clay (73 CY per hour)	H2@.027	CY	—	1.40	1.60	3.00
Sand or gravel (67 CY per hour)	H2@.030	CY	—	1.55	1.78	3.33
Heavy clay (37 CY per hour)	H2@.054	CY	—	2.79	3.20	5.99
Unclassified soil (28 CY per hour)	H2@.071	CY	—	3.67	4.21	7.88
2 CY dragline with a 60-ton crawler crane						
Loam or light clay (88 CY per hour)	H2@.023	CY	—	1.19	1.93	3.12
Sand or gravel (85 CY per hour)	H2@.024	CY	—	1.24	2.01	3.25
Heavy clay (48 CY per hour)	H2@.042	CY	—	2.17	3.52	5.69
Unclassified soil (36 CY per hour)	H2@.056	CY	—	2.90	4.70	7.60
2-1/2 CY dragline with a 100-ton crawler crane						
Loam or light clay (102 CY per hour)	H2@.019	CY	—	.98	1.82	2.80
Sand or gravel (98 CY per hour)	H2@.021	CY	—	1.09	2.01	3.10
Heavy clay (58 CY per hour)	H2@.035	CY	—	1.81	3.34	5.15
Unclassified soil (44 CY per hour)	H2@.045	CY	—	2.33	4.30	6.63
3 CY dragline with a 150-ton crawler crane						
Loam or light clay (116 CY per hour)	H2@.017	CY	—	.88	2.30	3.18
Sand or gravel (113 CY per hour)	H2@.018	CY	—	.93	2.43	3.36
Heavy clay (70 CY per hour)	H2@.029	CY	—	1.50	3.92	5.42
Unclassified soil (53 CY per hour)	H2@.038	CY	—	1.96	5.13	7.09

Backhoe Excavation For mass excavation, footing or foundation costs shown include casting the excavated soil adjacent to the excavation or loading it into trucks. Hauling costs are not included. Cubic yards (CY) per hour are as measured in an undisturbed condition (bank measure) and are based on a 2-man crew. Equipment costs are based on using a crawler-mounted hydraulic backhoe. Use $2,500 as a minimum job charge

	Craft@Hrs	Unit	Material	Labor	Equipment	Total
1 CY backhoe						
Light soil (69 CY per hour)	S1@.029	CY	—	1.43	.81	2.24
Most soils (57 CY per hour)	S1@.035	CY	—	1.72	.97	2.69
Wet soil, loose rock (46 CY per hour)	S1@.043	CY	—	2.12	1.20	3.32
1-1/2 CY backhoe						
Light soil (90 CY per hour)	S1@.022	CY	—	1.08	.60	1.68
Most soils (77 CY per hour)	S1@.026	CY	—	1.28	.71	1.99
Wet soil, loose rock (60 CY per hour)	S1@.033	CY	—	1.63	.91	2.54
Blasted rock (54 CY per hour)	S1@.044	CY	—	2.17	1.21	3.38
2 CY backhoe						
Light soil (100 CY per hour)	S1@.020	CY	—	.99	.94	1.93
Most soils (85 CY per hour)	S1@.023	CY	—	1.13	1.08	2.21
Wet soil, loose rock (70 CY per hour)	S1@.029	CY	—	1.43	1.37	2.80

	Craft@Hrs	Unit	Material	Labor	Equipment	Total
Moving and Loading Excavated Materials Costs shown include moving the material 50' and dumping it into piles or loading it into trucks. Add 25% for each 50' of travel beyond the first 50'. Hauling costs are not included. Cubic yards (CY) per hour are for material in a loose condition (previously excavated) and are based on a 2-man crew performing the work. Equipment costs are based on using a wheel-mounted front-end loader. Use $2,000 as a minimum job charge.						
3/4 CY loader (32 CY per hour)	S1@.062	CY	—	3.05	.97	4.02
1 CY loader (55 CY per hour)	S1@.036	CY	—	1.77	.74	2.51
2 CY loader (90 CY per hour)	S1@.022	CY	—	1.08	.64	1.72
3-1/4 CY loader (125 CY per hour)	S1@.016	CY	—	.79	.65	1.44
5 CY loader (218 CY per hour)	S1@.009	CY	—	.44	.43	.87
Hauling excavated material Using trucks. Costs shown include 4 minutes for loading, 3 minutes for dumping and travel time based on the one-way distance, speed and cycles per hour as noted. Costs for equipment to excavate and load the material are not included. Truck capacity is based on cubic yards of loose material. Use the following percentages to calculate swell (from bank measure) and shrinkage (when dumped at the fill site): clay (33%), common earth (25%), granite (65%), mud (21%), sand or gravel (12%).						
3 CY dump truck. Use $550 as a minimum job charge.						
1 mile haul at 20 MPH (4.62 cycles and 13.85 CY per hour)	TD@.072	CY	—	3.31	3.10	6.41
3 mile haul at 30 MPH (3.16 cycles and 9.47 CY per hour)	TD@.106	CY	—	4.87	4.56	9.43
6 mile haul at 40 MPH (2.4 cycles and 7.2 CY per hour)	TD@.139	CY	—	6.38	5.98	12.36
5 CY dump truck. Use $600 as a minimum job charge.						
1 mile haul at 20 MPH (4.62 cycles and 23.08 CY per hour)	TD@.043	CY	—	1.97	1.92	3.89
3 mile haul at 30 MPH (3.16 cycles and 15.79 CY per hour)	TD@.063	CY	—	2.89	2.82	5.71
6 mile haul at 40 MPH (2.4 cycles and 12 CY per hour)	TD@.083	CY	—	3.81	3.71	7.52
10 CY dump truck. Use $800 as a minimum job charge.						
1 mile haul at 20 MPH (4.62 cycles and 46.15 CY per hour)	TD@.022	CY	—	1.01	2.08	3.09
3 mile haul at 30 MPH (3.16 cycles and 31.58 CY per hour)	TD@.032	CY	—	1.47	3.03	4.50
6 mile haul at 40 MPH (2.4 cycles and 24 CY per hour)	TD@.042	CY	—	1.93	3.98	5.91
25 CY off-highway dump truck. Use $2,000 as a minimum job charge.						
1 mile haul at 20 MPH (4.62 cycles and 115.38 CY per hour)	TD@.009	CY	—	.41	1.27	1.68
3 mile haul at 30 MPH (3.16 cycles and 78.95 CY per hour)	TD@.013	CY	—	.60	1.84	2.44
6 mile haul at 40 MPH (2.4 cycles and 60 CY per hour)	TD@.017	CY	—	.78	2.40	3.18

	Craft@Hrs	Unit	Material	Labor	Equipment	Total

Dozer Excavation Mass excavation using a crawler tractor with a dozing blade. Costs shown include excavation and pushing soil 150' to a stockpile. Based on good access and a maximum of 5% grade. Increase or reduce costs 20% for each 50' of push more or less than 150'. Cubic yards (CY) per hour shown are undisturbed bank measure and are based on a 1-man crew. Use the following as minimum job charges: $850 if using a D-4 or a D-6 dozer; $1,350 if using a D-7 or D-8 dozer; or $2,000 if using a D-9 dozer.

	Craft@Hrs	Unit	Material	Labor	Equipment	Total
Gravel or loose sand						
100 HP D-4 dozer with "S"-blade (29 CY per hour)	T0@.034	CY	—	1.95	2.10	4.05
140 HP D-6 dozer with "S"-blade (56 CY per hour)	T0@.018	CY	—	1.03	1.51	2.54
200 HP D-7 dozer with "S"-blade (78 CY per hour)	T0@.013	CY	—	.74	1.57	2.31
335 HP D-8 dozer with "U"-blade (140 CY per hour)	T0@.007	CY	—	.40	1.15	1.55
460 HP D-9 dozer with "U"-blade (205 CY per hour)	T0@.005	CY	—	.29	1.32	1.61
Loam or soft clay						
100 HP D-4 dozer with "S"-blade (26 CY per hour)	T0@.038	CY	—	2.18	2.35	4.53
140 HP D-6 dozer with "S"-blade (50 CY per hour)	T0@.020	CY	—	1.15	1.67	2.82
200 HP D-7 dozer with "S"-blade (70 CY per hour)	T0@.014	CY	—	.80	1.69	2.49
335 HP D-8 dozer with "U"-blade (125 CY per hour)	T0@.008	CY	—	.46	1.32	1.78
460 HP D-9 dozer with "U" blade (185 CY per hour)	T0@.005	CY	—	.29	1.32	1.61
Shale, sandstone or blasted rock						
100 HP D-4 dozer with "S"-blade (20 CY per hour)	T0@.051	CY	—	2.92	3.15	6.07
140 HP D-6 dozer with "S"-blade (38 CY per hour)	T0@.026	CY	—	1.49	2.18	3.67
200 HP D-7 dozer with "S"-blade (53 CY per hour)	T0@.019	CY	—	1.09	2.30	3.39
335 HP D-8 dozer with "U"- blade (95 CY per hour)	T0@.011	CY	—	.63	1.81	2.44
460 HP D-9 dozer with "U"- blade (140 CY per hour)	T0@.007	CY	—	.40	1.84	2.24

Scraper-Hauler Excavation Mass excavation using a self-propelled scraper-hauler. Equipment costs include the scraper-hauler and a crawler tractor with a dozer blade attached pushing for 10 minutes each hour. Cubic yards (CY) per hour shown are undisturbed bank measure. Work done in clay, shale or soft rock will cost 10% to 25% more.

15 CY self-propelled 200 HP scraper-hauler and a D-8 335 HP tractor pushing. Use $6,000 as a minimum job charge.

	Craft@Hrs	Unit	Material	Labor	Equipment	Total
1,000' haul (9 cycles and 135 CY per hr)	SS@.016	CY	—	.83	1.55	2.38
2,500' haul (6 cycles and 90 CY per hr)	SS@.024	CY	—	1.25	2.32	3.57
4,000' haul (4.5 cycles and 68 CY per hr)	SS@.032	CY	—	1.66	3.10	4.76

24 CY self-propelled 350 HP scraper-hauler and a D-9 460 HP tractor pushing. Use $8,000 as a minimum job charge.

	Craft@Hrs	Unit	Material	Labor	Equipment	Total
1,000' haul (9 cycles and 225 CY per hr)	SS@.010	CY	—	.52	1.41	1.93
2,500' haul (6 cycles and 150 CY per hr)	SS@.014	CY	—	.73	1.97	2.70

	Craft@Hrs	Unit	Material	Labor	Equipment	Total
4,000' haul						
(4.5 cycles and 113 CY per hr)	SS@.019	CY	—	.99	2.68	3.67
32 CY self-propelled 550 HP scraper-hauler and a D-9 460 HP tractor pushing. Use $10,000 as a minimum job charge.						
1,000' haul						
(9 cycles and 315 CY per hr)	SS@.007	CY	—	.36	.83	1.19
2,500' haul						
(6 cycles and 219 CY per hr)	SS@.010	CY	—	.52	1.18	1.70
4,000' haul						
(4.5 cycles and 158 CY per hr)	SS@.014	CY	—	.73	1.66	2.39
Manual Excavation Based on one throw (except where noted) of shoveled earth from a trench or pit. Shoring or dewatering is not included.						
Trench or pit in light soil (silty sand or loess, etc.)						
Up to 4' deep (.82 CY per hour)	CL@1.22	CY	—	50.30	—	50.30
Over 4' to 6' deep (.68 CY per hour)	CL@1.46	CY	—	60.20	—	60.20
Over 6' deep, two throws						
(.32 CY per hour)	CL@3.16	CY	—	130.00	—	130.00
Trench or pit in medium soil (sandy clay, for example)						
Up to 4' deep (.68 CY per hour)	CL@1.46	CY	—	60.20	—	60.20
Over 4' to 6' deep (.54 CY per hour)	CL@1.86	CY	—	76.70	—	76.70
Over 6' deep, two throws						
(.27 CY per hour)	CL@3.66	CY	—	151.00	—	151.00
Trench or pit in heavy soil (clayey materials, shales, caliche, etc.)						
Up to 4' deep (.54 CY per hour)	CL@1.86	CY	—	76.70	—	76.70
Over 4' to 6' deep (.46 CY per hour)	CL@2.16	CY	—	89.10	—	89.10
Over 6' deep, 2 throws						
(.25 CY per hour)	CL@3.90	CY	—	161.00	—	161.00
Wheelbarrow (5 CF) on firm ground, load by shovel from pile, wheel 300 feet and dump						
Light soil (.74 CY per hour)	CL@1.35	CY	—	55.70	—	55.70
Medium soil (.65 CY per hour)	CL@1.54	CY	—	63.50	—	63.50
Heavy soil (.56 CY per hour)	CL@1.79	CY	—	73.80	—	73.80
Loose rock (.37 CY per hour)	CL@2.70	CY	—	111.00	—	111.00
Hand trim and shape						
Around utility lines (15 CF hour)	CL@.065	CF	—	2.68	—	2.68
For slab on grade (63 SY per hour)	CL@.016	SY	—	.66	—	.66
Trench bottom (100 SF per hour)	CL@.010	SF	—	.41	—	.41

Wellpoint Dewatering Based on header pipe connecting 2" diameter jetted wellpoints 5' on center. Includes header pipe, wellpoints, filter sand, pumps and swing joints. The header pipe length is usually equal to the perimeter of the area excavated.

Typical cost for installation and removal of wellpoint system with wellpoints 14' deep and placed 5' on center along 6" header pipe. Based on equipment rented for 1 month. Use 100 LF as a minimum job charge. Add the cost of an operator/attendant if required. Also add (if required) for additional months of rental, fuel for the pumps, a standby pump, water truck for jetting, outflow pipe, permits and consultant costs.

	Craft@Hrs	Unit	Material	Labor	Equipment	Total
6" header pipe and accessories, system per LF installed, rented 1 month and removed						
100 LF system	C5@.535	LF	1.72	24.80	25.80	52.32
200 LF system	C5@.535	LF	1.72	24.80	25.80	52.32
500 LF system	C5@.535	LF	1.72	24.80	25.80	52.32
1,000 LF system	C5@.535	LF	1.72	24.80	25.80	52.32
Add for 8" header pipe	C5@.010	LF	.05	.46	1.98	2.49
Add for 18' wellpoint depth	C5@.096	LF	.13	4.46	6.07	10.66
Add for second month	—	LF	—	—	19.00	14.30
Add for each additional month	—	LF	—	—	11.40	8.52
Add for operator, per hour	T0@1.00	Hr	—	57.30	—	57.30

	Craft@Hrs	Unit	Material	Labor	Equipment	Total
Roadway and Embankment Earthwork Cut & Fill Mass excavating, hauling, placing and compacting (cut & fill) using a 200 HP, 15 CY capacity self-propelled scraper-hauler with attachments. Productivity is based on a 1,500' haul with 6" lifts compacted to 95% per AASHO requirements. Cubic yards (CY) or square yards (SY) per hour shown are bank measurement. Use $3,000 as a minimum job charge.						
Cut, fill and compact, clearing or finishing not included						
Most soil types (45 CY per hour)	T0@.022	CY	—	1.26	3.76	5.02
Rock and earth mixed (40 CY per hour)	T0@.025	CY	—	1.43	4.27	5.70
Rippable rock (25 CY per hour)	T0@.040	CY	—	2.29	6.83	9.12
Earth banks and levees, clearing or finishing not included						
Cut, fill and compact (85 CY per hour)	T0@.012	CY	—	.69	2.05	2.74
Channelize compacted fill (55 CY per hour)	T0@.018	CY	—	1.03	3.07	4.10
Roadway subgrade preparation						
Scarify and compact (91 CY per hour)	T0@.011	CY	—	.63	1.88	2.51
Roll and compact base course (83 CY per hour)	T0@.012	CY	—	.69	2.05	2.74
Excavation, open ditches (38 CY per hour)	T0@.026	CY	—	1.49	4.44	5.93
Trimming and finishing						
Banks, swales or ditches (140 CY per hour)	T0@.007	CY	—	.40	1.20	1.60
Scarify asphalt pavement (48 SY per hour)	T0@.021	SY	—	1.20	3.59	4.79
Soil Covers						
Using staked straw erosion control blanket	CL@.019	SY	.73	.78	—	1.51
Staked 8" straw wattle	CL@0.23	LF	1.32	9.49	—	10.81
Using copolymer-base sprayed-on liquid soil sealant						
On slopes for erosion control	CL@.012	SY	1.50	.50	—	2.00
On level ground for dust abatement	CL@.012	SY	3.00	.50	—	3.50
Soil Stabilization See also Slope Protection. Lime slurry injection treatment. Equipment is a 100 HP grader, a 1-ton self-propelled steel roller and a 10-ton 100 HP vibratory steel roller. Use $3,000 as a minimum job charge. Cost per CY of soil treated.						
(25 CY per hour)	S7@.240	CY	17.30	11.80	9.12	38.22
Vibroflotation treatment Equipment includes a 50-ton hydraulic crane, a 1 CY wheel loader for 15 minutes of each hour, and a vibroflotation machine with pumps. Use $3,500 as a minimum job charge. Typical cost per CY of soil treated.						
Low cost (92 CY per hour)	S7@.065	CY	—	3.20	3.54	6.74
High cost (46 CY per hour)	S7@.130	CY	—	6.41	7.08	13.49
Soil cement treatment Includes materials and placement for 7% cement mix. Equipment is a cross shaft mixer, a 2-ton 3- wheel steel roller and a vibratory roller. Costs shown are per CY of soil treated. Use $3,000 as a minimum job charge.						
On level ground (5 CY per hour)	S7@1.20	CY	14.60	59.10	30.40	104.10
On slopes under 3 in 1 (4.3 CY per hour)	S7@1.40	CY	14.60	69.00	35.52	119.12
On slopes over 3 in 1 (4 CY per hour)	S7@1.50	CY	14.60	73.90	38.10	126.60
Construction fabrics (geotextiles) Mirafi products. Costs shown include 10% for lapover. Drainage fabric (Mirafi 140NC), used to line trenches, allows water passage but prevents soil migration into drains.						
Per SY of fabric placed by hand	CL@.016	SY	1.07	.66	—	1.73
Stabilization fabric (Mirafi 500X), used to prevent mixing of unstable soils with road base aggregate						
Per SY of fabric placed by hand	CL@.008	SY	.94	.33	—	1.27
Prefabricated drainage fabric (Miradrain), used to drain subsurface water from structural walls						
Per SY of fabric placed by hand	CL@.006	SY	1.04	.25	—	1.29
Erosion control mat (Miramat TM8), used to reduce surface soil erosion on slopes or in ditches while promoting seed growth						
Per SY of mat placed by hand	CL@.020	SY	.70	.83	—	1.53

	Craft@Hrs	Unit	Material	Labor	Equipment	Total
Slope Protection See also Soil Stabilization. Gabions as manufactured by Maccaferri Inc. Typical prices for gabions as described, placed by hand. Prices can be expected to vary based on quantity. Cost for stone is not included. Add for stone as required. Costs shown are per each gabion.						
Galvanized mesh						
6' x 3' x 3'	CL@2.70	Ea	186.00	111.00	—	297.00
9' x 3' x 3'	CL@2.90	Ea	109.00	120.00	—	229.00
12' x 3' x 3'	CL@3.10	Ea	230.00	128.00	—	358.00
Erosion and drainage control polypropylene geotextile fabric (Mirafi FW700)						
For use under riprap, hand placed	CL@.011	SY	2.76	.45	—	3.21
Riprap Dumped from trucks and placed using a 15-ton hydraulic crane and a 10 CY dump truck. Riprap costs will vary widely. Add $1.00 per CY per mile for trucking to the site. Cubic yards (CY) per hour shown in parentheses are based on a 7-man crew. Use $2,500 as a minimum job charge.						
Typical riprap cost, per CY	—	CY	89.20	—	—	59.20
5 to 7 CF pieces (9.4 CY per hour)	S5@.745	CY	89.20	33.00	16.10	138.30
5 to 7 CF pieces, sacked and placed, excluding bag cost (3 CY per hour)	S5@2.33	CY	89.20	103.00	50.40	242.60
Loose small riprap stone, under 30 lbs each, hand placed (2 CY per hour)	CL@.500	CY	89.20	20.60	—	109.80
Ornamental large rock Rock prices include local delivery of 10 CY minimum. Cubic yards (CY) per hour shown in parentheses are based on a 7-man crew. Equipment is a 15-ton hydraulic crane and a 10 CY dump truck. Use $2,500 as a minimum job charge. Expect wide variation in costs of ornamental rock.						
Volcanic cinder, 1,200 lbs per CY (8 CY per hour)	S5@.875	CY	436.00	38.70	18.90	493.60
Featherock, 1,000 lbs per CY (12 CY per hour)	S5@.583	CY	479.00	25.80	12.60	517.40
Rock fill Dumped from trucks and placed with a 100 HP D-4 tractor. Rock prices include local delivery of 10 CY minimum. Cubic yards (CY) per hour shown in parentheses are based on a 3-man crew. Use $1,350 as a minimum job charge.						
Drain rock, 3/4" to 1-1/2" (12 CY per hour)	S6@.250	CY	34.50	11.60	5.15	51.25
Bank run gravel (12 CY per hour)	S6@.250	CY	38.30	11.60	5.15	55.05
Pea gravel (12 CY per hour)	S6@.250	CY	38.30	11.60	5.15	55.05
Straw bales secured to ground with driven reinforcing bars, bale is 3'6" long, 2' wide, 1'6" high.						
Per bale of straw, placed by hand	CL@.166	Ea	13.00	6.85	—	19.85
Sedimentation control fence, installed vertically at bottom of slope, with stakes attached,						
36" high woven fabric (Mirafi 100X)	CL@.003	LF	.37	.12	—	.49
Stone tracking pad Washed 3" to 6" stone placed and removed at the site entrance to clean sediment from the tires of vehicles exiting the site. Typical size is 24' wide x 50' long x 12" deep (45 CY) Equipment is a wheel-mounted front end loader. Add the cost of excavation, bedding material and backfill if required.						
Per cubic yard, placed and removed	S6@.250	CY	38.90	11.60	6.96	57.46
Per pad 24' W x 50' L x 12" D (45 CY)	S6@.250	Ea	1,750.00	11.60	313.00	2,074.60
Per pad 24' W x 50' L x 6" D (23 CY)	S6@.250	Ea	896.00	11.60	158.00	1,065.60
Add for geotextile liner (muddy site)	CL@.020	SY	.68	.83	—	1.51
Drain inlet protection Sediment control for drains and curb inlets to meet National Pollutant Discharge Elimination System (NPDES) and state permit requirements.						
Poly 14" x 21" sandbags	—	Ea	.42	—	—	.42
Sandbag filled with 40 lb. of gravel, placed and removed, no salvage	CL@.083	Ea	.71	3.42	—	4.13
Sandbag barrier for a 5' curb inlet, 25 bags, placed and removed, no salvage	CL@2.08	Ea	17.70	85.80	—	103.50
Mulch-filled erosion control 8" diameter fiber sock, staked per liner foot of sock, no salvage	CL@.040	LF	1.32	1.65	—	2.97

	Craft@Hrs	Unit	Material	Labor	Equipment	Total
One-piece curb inlet and magnetic drain grate filter, 2' wide, 4' long inlet	CL@.340	LF	89.00	14.00	—	103.00
Curb inlet filter sock						
Opening to 6' long	CL@.400	Ea	152.00	16.50	—	168.50
Opening over 6' to 8' long	CL@.400	Ea	170.00	16.50	—	186.50
Opening over 8' to 10' long	CL@.400	Ea	202.00	16.50	—	218.50

Shoring, Bulkheads and Underpinning Hot-rolled steel sheet piling, driven and pulled, based on good driving conditions and using sheets 30' to 50' in length with 32 lbs of 38.5 KSI steel per SF. Material cost assumes the piling is salvaged. Per cubic yard, placed and removedUse $16,000 as a minimum job charge.

	Craft@Hrs	Unit	Material	Labor	Equipment	Total
Using steel at, per ton	—	Ton	955.00	—	—	955.00
Assumed steel salvage value, per ton	—	Ton	709.00	—	—	709.00
Typical driving and pulling cost, per ton	—	Ton	—	—	275.00	262.00
Up to 20' deep	S8@.096	SF	3.82	4.90	5.72	14.44
Over 20' to 35' deep	S8@.088	SF	3.82	4.49	5.28	13.59
Over 35' to 50' deep	S8@.087	SF	3.82	4.44	5.20	13.46
Over 50' deep	S8@.085	SF	3.82	4.34	5.08	13.24
Extra costs for sheet steel piling						
Add for:						
50' to 65' lengths	—	SF	.09	—	—	.09
65' to 100' lengths	—	SF	.21	—	—	.21
Epoxy coal tar 16 mil factory finish	—	SF	1.48	—	—	1.48
32 lb per SF piling material left in place	—	SF	4.09	—	—	4.09
38 lbs per SF (MZ 38) steel	—	SF	.87	—	—	.87
50 KSI high-strength steel	—	SF	.54	—	—	.54
Marine grade 50 KSI high strength steel	—	SF	.94	—	—	.94
Deductive costs for sheet steel piling						
Deduct for:						
28 lbs per SF (PS 28) steel	—	SF	–.81	—	—	–.81
23 lbs per SF (PS 23) steel	—	SF	–1.14	—	—	–1.14
Deduct labor & equipment cost when piling is left in place	—	SF	—	–1.50	–.59	–2.08

Timber trench sheeting and bracing per square foot of trench wall measured on one side of trench. Costs include pulling and salvage, depths to 12'. Equipment includes a 10-ton hydraulic crane and a 1-ton flat-bed truck. Use $4,000 as a minimum job charge.

	Craft@Hrs	Unit	Material	Labor	Equipment	Total
Less than 6' wide, open bracing	S5@.053	SF	2.11	2.34	.58	5.03
6' to 10' wide, open bracing	S5@.064	SF	2.21	2.83	.64	5.68
11' to 16' wide, open bracing	S5@.079	SF	2.61	3.49	.79	6.89
Over 16' wide, open bracing	S5@.091	SF	2.85	4.03	.91	7.79
Less than 6' wide, closed sheeting	S5@.114	SF	2.42	5.04	1.14	8.60
6' to 10' wide, closed sheeting	S5@.143	SF	2.16	6.33	1.43	9.92
11' to 16' wide, closed sheeting	S5@.163	SF	2.56	7.21	1.62	11.39
Over 16' wide, closed sheeting	S5@.199	SF	3.25	8.80	1.98	14.03
Additional costs for bracing on trenches over 12' deep						
Normal bracing, to 15' deep	S5@.050	SF	.40	2.21	.50	3.11
One line of bracing, over 15' to 22' deep	S5@.053	SF	.49	2.34	.53	3.36
Two lines of bracing, over 22' to 35' deep	S5@.061	SF	.83	2.70	.61	4.14
Three lines of bracing, over 35' to 45' deep	S5@.064	SF	.94	2.83	.64	4.41

	Craft@Hrs	Unit	Material	Labor	Equipment	Total
Pile Foundations These costs assume solid ground for support of the pile driving equipment with all site work performed by others at no cost prior to pile driving being performed. Costs shown per linear foot (LF) are per vertical foot of pile depth. Standby or idle time, access roads, rig mats, test piles or special engineering required by unusual conditions are not included.						
Pile testing Testing costs will vary with the soil type, method of testing, and seismic requirements for any given job site. Use the following as guideline costs for estimating purposes. Typical costs including cost for moving test equipment on and off job site. Add cost below for various types of piling.						
50- to 100-ton range	S8@224.	Ea	—	11,400.00	9,320.00	20,720.00
Over 100-ton to 200-ton range	S8@280.	Ea	—	14,300.00	11,700.00	26,000.00
Over 200-ton to 300-ton range	S8@336.	Ea	—	17,100.00	14,000.00	31,100.00
Prestressed concrete piles Equipment includes a 60-ton crawler mounted crane equipped with pile driving attachments, a 4-ton forklift, a truck with hand tools, a portable air compressor complete with hoses and pneumatic operated tools, a welding machine and an oxygen-acetylene cutting torch. Use $28,000 as minimum job charge, including 1,000 LF of piling and the cost for moving the pile driving equipment on and off the job site.						
Minimum job charge	—	LS	—	—	—	30,000.00
For jobs requiring over 1,000 LF of piling, add to minimum charge as follows. (Figures in parentheses show approximate production per day based on a 7-man crew.)						
12" square						
30' or 40' long piles (550 LF per day)	S8@.102	LF	20.20	5.20	5.49	30.89
50' or 60' long piles (690 LF per day)	S8@.082	LF	20.20	4.18	4.41	28.79
14" square						
30' or 40' long piles (500 LF per day)	S8@.113	LF	24.70	5.77	6.08	36.55
50' or 60' long piles (645 LF per day)	S8@.087	LF	24.70	4.44	4.68	33.82
16" square						
30' or 40' long piles (420 LF per day)	S8@.134	LF	35.20	6.84	7.21	49.25
50' or 60' long piles (550 LF per day)	S8@.102	LF	35.20	5.20	5.49	45.89
18" square						
30' or 40' long piles (400 LF per day)	S8@.143	LF	44.00	7.30	7.69	58.99
50' or 60' long piles (525 LF per day)	S8@.107	LF	44.00	5.46	5.75	55.21
Additional costs for prestressed concrete piles Pre-drilling holes for piles. Equipment includes a flatbed truck with a boom and a power-operated auger. Use $2,200 as a minimum job charge, including drilling 100 LF of holes and the cost to move the drilling equipment on and off the job site.						
Minimum job charge	—	LS	—	—	—	2,200.00
For jobs requiring more than 100 LF of holes drilled, add to minimum cost as shown below						
Pre-drilling first 10 LF, per hole	C9@1.50	LS	—	73.70	60.70	134.40
Add per LF of drilling, after first 10 LF	C9@.177	LF	—	8.70	7.16	15.86
Steel "HP" shape piles Equipment includes a 60-ton crawler-mounted crane equipped with pile driving attachments, a 4-ton forklift, a truck with hand tools, a portable air compressor complete with hoses and pneumatic operated tools, a welding machine and an oxygen-acetylene cutting torch. Use $25,000 as minimum job charge, including 1,000 LF of piling and cost for moving pile driving equipment on and off the job site.						
Minimum job charge	—	LS	—	—	—	20,000.00
For jobs requiring over 1,000 LF of piling add to minimum charge as follows. (Figures in parentheses show approximate production per day based on a 7-man crew.)						
HP8 8" x 8", 36 lbs per LF						
30' or 40' long piles (800 LF per day)	S8@.070	LF	16.00	3.57	3.76	23.33
50' or 60' long piles (880 LF per day)	S8@.064	LF	16.00	3.27	3.44	22.71
HP10 10" x 10", 42 lbs per LF						
30' or 40' long piles (760 LF per day)	S8@.074	LF	18.70	3.78	3.98	26.46
50' or 60' long piles (800 LF per day)	S8@.070	LF	18.70	3.57	3.76	26.03

	Craft@Hrs	Unit	Material	Labor	Equipment	Total
HP10 10" x 10", 48 lbs per LF						
30' or 40' long piles (760 LF per day)	S8@.074	LF	21.30	3.78	3.98	29.06
50' or 60' long piles (800 LF per day)	S8@.070	LF	21.30	3.57	3.76	28.63
HP12 12" x 12", 53 lbs per LF						
30' or 40' long piles (730 LF per day)	S8@.077	LF	23.60	3.93	4.14	31.67
50' or 60' long piles (760 LF per day)	S8@.074	LF	23.60	3.78	3.98	31.36
HP12 12" x 12", 74 lbs per LF						
30' or 40' long piles (730 LF per day)	S8@.077	LF	32.90	3.93	4.14	40.97
50' or 60' long piles (760 LF per day)	S8@.074	LF	32.90	3.78	3.98	40.66
HP14 14" x 14", 73 lbs per LF						
30' or 40' long piles (690 LF per day)	S8@.081	LF	32.40	4.13	4.36	40.89
50' or 60' long piles (730 LF per day)	S8@.077	LF	32.40	3.93	4.14	40.47
HP14 14" x 14", 89 lbs per LF						
30' or 40' long piles (630 LF per day)	S8@.089	LF	39.50	4.54	4.79	48.83
50' or 60' long piles (690 LF per day)	S8@.081	LF	39.50	4.13	4.36	47.99
HP14 14" x 14", 102 lbs per LF						
30' or 40' long piles (630 LF per day)	S8@.089	LF	45.30	4.54	4.79	54.63
50' or 60' long piles (690 LF per day)	S8@.081	LF	45.30	4.13	4.36	53.79
HP14 14" x 14", 117 lbs per LF						
30' or 40' long piles (630 LF per day)	S8@.089	LF	52.00	4.54	4.79	61.33
50' or 60' long piles (690 LF per day)	S8@.081	LF	52.00	4.13	4.36	60.49
Additional costs related to any of above						
Standard driving points or splices						
HP8	S8@1.50	Ea	51.30	76.50	28.20	156.00
HP10	S8@1.75	Ea	55.70	89.30	32.90	177.90
HP12	S8@2.00	Ea	70.20	102.00	37.60	209.80
HP14	S8@2.50	Ea	80.80	128.00	47.00	255.80
Cutting pile off to required elevation						
HP8 or HP10	S8@1.00	Ea	5.57	51.00	18.80	75.37
HP12 or HP14	S8@1.50	Ea	8.38	76.50	28.20	113.08

Steel pipe piles Equipment includes a 45-ton crawler-mounted crane equipped with pile driving attachments, a 2-ton forklift, a truck with hand tools, a portable air compressor complete with hoses and pneumatic operated tools, a welding machine and an oxygen-acetylene cutting torch. Use $20,000 as minimum job charge, including 500 LF of piling and cost for moving pile driving equipment on and off the job site.

	Craft@Hrs	Unit	Material	Labor	Equipment	Total
Minimum job charge	—	LS	—	—	—	20,000.00

For jobs requiring over 500 LF of piling add to minimum charge as follows. (Figures in parentheses show approximate production per day based on a 7-man crew.)

	Craft@Hrs	Unit	Material	Labor	Equipment	Total
Steel pipe piles, non-filled						
8" (660 LF per day)	S8@.085	LF	11.60	4.34	3.69	19.63
10" (635 LF per day)	S8@.088	LF	16.30	4.49	3.82	24.61
12" (580 LF per day)	S8@.096	LF	20.20	4.90	4.17	29.27
14" (500 LF per day)	S8@.112	LF	22.50	5.71	4.87	33.08
16" (465 LF per day)	S8@.120	LF	25.70	6.12	5.22	37.04
18" (440 LF per day)	S8@.128	LF	29.50	6.53	5.56	41.59
Steel pipe piles, concrete filled						
8" (560 LF per day)	S8@.100	LF	13.90	5.10	4.35	23.35
10" (550 LF per day)	S8@.101	LF	17.30	5.15	4.39	26.84
12" (500 LF per day)	S8@.112	LF	22.70	5.71	4.87	33.28
14" (425 LF per day)	S8@.131	LF	24.30	6.68	5.69	36.67
16" (400 LF per day)	S8@.139	LF	29.00	7.09	6.04	42.13
18" (375 LF per day)	S8@.149	LF	33.20	7.60	6.48	47.28

	Craft@Hrs	Unit	Material	Labor	Equipment	Total
Splices for steel pipe piles						
8" pile	S8@1.12	Ea	53.70	57.10	17.40	128.20
10" pile	S8@1.55	Ea	60.40	79.10	24.10	163.60
12" pile	S8@2.13	Ea	65.20	109.00	33.10	207.30
14" pile	S8@2.25	Ea	85.90	115.00	34.90	235.80
16" pile	S8@2.39	Ea	136.00	122.00	37.10	295.10
18" pile	S8@2.52	Ea	163.00	129.00	39.10	331.10
Standard points for steel pipe piles						
8" point	S8@1.49	Ea	82.30	76.00	23.10	181.40
10" point	S8@1.68	Ea	111.00	85.70	26.10	222.80
12" point	S8@1.84	Ea	149.00	93.90	28.60	271.50
14" point	S8@2.03	Ea	186.00	104.00	31.50	321.50
16" point	S8@2.23	Ea	277.00	114.00	34.60	425.60
18" point	S8@2.52	Ea	364.00	129.00	39.10	532.10

Wood piles End bearing Douglas fir, treated with 12 lb creosote. Piles up to 40' long are 8" minimum tip diameter. Over 45' long, 7" is the minimum tip diameter. Equipment includes a 45-ton crawler-mounted crane equipped with pile driving attachments, a 2-ton forklift, a truck with hand tools, a portable air compressor complete with hoses and pneumatic operated tools. Use $20,000 as minimum job charge, including 1,000 LF of piling and cost for moving pile driving equipment on and off the job site.

	Craft@Hrs	Unit	Material	Labor	Equipment	Total
Minimum job charge	—	LS	—	—	—	25,000.00

For jobs requiring over 1,000 LF of piling, add to minimum charge as follows. (Figures in parentheses show approximate production per day based on a 7-man crew.)

	Craft@Hrs	Unit	Material	Labor	Equipment	Total
To 30' long (725 LF per day)	S8@.077	LF	6.40	3.93	3.11	13.44
Over 30' to 40' (800 LF per day)	S8@.069	LF	6.51	3.52	2.79	12.82
Over 40' to 50' (840 LF per day)	S8@.067	LF	7.17	3.42	2.71	13.30
Add for drive shoe, per pile	—	Ea	29.30	—	—	29.30

Caisson Foundations Drilled in stable soil, no shoring required, filled with reinforced concrete. Add for belled bottoms, if required, from the following section. Equipment includes a truck-mounted A-frame hoist and a power operated auger and a concrete pump. Concrete is based on using 3,000 PSI pump mix delivered to the job site in ready-mix trucks and includes a 5% allowance for waste. Spiral caisson reinforcing is based on using 3/8" diameter hot rolled steel spirals with main vertical bars as shown, shop fabricated, delivered ready to install, with typical engineering and drawings. Costs for waste disposal are not included. Refer to Construction Materials Disposal section and add for same. Use $15,000 as a minimum charge, including 200 LF of reinforced concrete filled caissons and cost for moving the equipment on and off the job.

	Craft@Hrs	Unit	Material	Labor	Equipment	Total
Minimum job charge	—	LS	—	—	—	15,000.00

For jobs requiring over 200 LF of reinforced concrete-filled caissons, add to minimum charge as follows. (Figures in parentheses show approximate production per day based on a 3-man crew.)

	Craft@Hrs	Unit	Material	Labor	Equipment	Total
16" diameter, drilled caisson filled with reinforced concrete						
Drilling						
(680 VLF per day)	S6@.035	VLF	—	1.63	3.14	4.77
Spiral reinforcing plus 6 #6 bars						
(590 VLF per day)	S6@.041	VLF	34.70	1.91	3.68	40.29
Concrete filling						
(615 VLF per day)	S6@.039	VLF	7.19	1.82	3.50	12.51
Total for 16" caisson	**S6@.115**	**VLF**	**41.89**	**5.36**	**10.32**	**57.57**

31 Earthwork

	Craft@Hrs	Unit	Material	Labor	Equipment	Total
24" diameter, drilled caisson filled with reinforced concrete						
Drilling						
(570 VLF per day)	S6@.042	VLF	—	1.96	3.62	5.58
Spiral reinforcing plus 6 #6 bars						
(280 VLF per day)	S6@.085	VLF	59.60	3.96	7.62	71.18
Concrete filling						
(280 VLF per day)	S6@.086	VLF	16.00	4.01	7.71	27.72
Total for 24" caisson	**S6@.213**	**VLF**	**75.60**	**9.93**	**18.95**	**104.48**
36" diameter, drilled caisson filled with reinforced concrete						
Drilling						
(440 LF per day)	S6@.055	VLF	—	2.56	4.93	7.49
Spiral reinforcing plus 8 #10 bars						
(135 VLF per day)	S6@.176	VLF	108.00	8.20	15.80	132.00
Concrete filling						
(125 VLF per day)	S6@.194	VLF	36.20	9.04	17.40	62.64
Total for 36" caisson	**S6@.425**	**VLF**	**144.20**	**19.80**	**38.13**	**202.13**

Bell-bottom footings, concrete filled, for pre-drilled caissons. Add to the cost of any of the caissons above. (Figures in parentheses show approximate production per day based on a 3-man crew.)

	Craft@Hrs	Unit	Material	Labor	Equipment	Total
6' diameter bell bottom						
concrete filled (8 per day)	S6@3.00	Ea	416.00	140.00	269.00	825.00
8' diameter bell bottom						
concrete filled (4 per day	S6@6.00	Ea	984.00	280.00	538.00	1,802.00

32 Exterior Improvements

Asphalt Paving To arrive at the total cost for new asphalt paving jobs, add the cost of the subbase preparation and aggregate to the costs for the asphalt binder course, the rubberized interliner and the wear course. Cost for site preparation is not included. Based on roadway and parking lot jobs of 5,000 SY or more. For more detailed coverage, see *National Earthwork and Heavy Equipment Estimator*, http://CraftsmanSiteLicense.com.

Subbase and aggregate Equipment includes a pneumatic-tired articulated 10,000 pound motor grader, a 4-ton two axle steel drum roller and a 3,500 gallon water truck.

	Craft@Hrs	Unit	Material	Labor	Equipment	Total
Fine grading and compacting existing subbase						
To within plus or minus 1/10'	P5@.066	SY	.01	3.00	2.68	5.69
Stone aggregate base, Class 2. Includes grading and compacting of base material.						
Class 2 stone aggregate base, per CY	—	CY	43.20	—	—	43.20
Class 2 stone aggregate base, per ton	—	Ton	30.80	—	—	30.80
1" thick base (36 SY per CY)	P5@.008	SY	1.20	.36	.32	1.88
4" thick base (9 SY per CY)	P5@.020	SY	4.80	.91	.81	6.52
6" thick base (6 SY per CY)	P5@.033	SY	7.20	1.50	1.34	10.04
8" thick base (4.5 SY per CY)	P5@.039	SY	9.59	1.77	1.58	12.94
10" thick base (3.6 SY per CY)	P5@.042	SY	12.00	1.91	1.71	15.62
12" thick base (3 SY per CY)	P5@.048	SY	14.40	2.18	1.95	18.53

Asphalt materials Equipment includes a 10' wide self-propelled paving machine and a 4-ton two axle steel drum roller

	Craft@Hrs	Unit	Material	Labor	Equipment	Total
Binder course, spread and rolled						
Binder course, per ton	—	Ton	79.10	—	—	79.10
1" thick (18 SY per ton)	P5@.028	SY	4.39	1.27	1.02	6.68
1-1/2" thick (12 SY per ton)	P5@.036	SY	6.59	1.63	1.48	9.70

	Craft@Hrs	Unit	Material	Labor	Equipment	Total
2" thick (9 SY per ton)	P5@.039	SY	8.79	1.77	1.60	12.16
3" thick (6 SY per ton)	P5@.050	SY	13.20	2.27	2.05	17.52
Paving fabric interlayer with tack coat. Based on using 10' wide rolls by 378' long and one coat of mopped-on bituminous tack coat, MC70 (0.15 gallon per SY) before allowance for waste.						
Paving fabric interlayer, per 3,780 SF roll	—	Roll	625.00	—	—	625.00
Bituminous tack coat, per gallon	—	Gal	14.80	—	—	14.80
Laid, cut, mopped and rolled	P5@.005	SY	1.74	.23	.20	2.17
Asphaltic concrete curb, straight, placed during paving. Equipment includes an asphalt curbing machine						
8" x 6", placed by hand	P5@.141	LF	1.98	6.40	—	8.38
8" x 6", machine extruded	P5@.067	LF	1.80	3.04	.66	5.50
8" x 8", placed by hand	P5@.141	LF	3.16	6.40	—	9.56
8" x 8", machine extruded	P5@.068	LF	2.39	3.09	.32	5.80
Add for curved sections	P5@.034	LF	—	1.54	.16	1.70
Asphaltic concrete speed bumps, 3" high, 24" wide (135 LF and 2 tons per CY), placed on parking lot surface and rolled						
100 LF job	P5@.198	LF	1.27	8.99	2.58	12.84
Painting speed bumps, 24" wide, white	P5@.022	LF	.33	1.00	—	1.33

See also the section on Speed Bumps and Parking Blocks following Pavement Striping and Marking.

Asphalt Paving for Roadways, Assembly Costs On-site roadway, with 4" thick aggregate base, 2" thick asphalt binder course, rubberized asphalt interlayer, and 2" thick wear course. This is often called 4" paving over 4" aggregate base. Based on 5,000 SY job.

	Craft@Hrs	Unit	Material	Labor	Equipment	Total
Fine grading and compact existing subbase	P5@.066	SY	.01	3.00	2.70	5.71
Stone aggregate base, Class 2, 4" thick	P5@.020	SY	4.64	.91	.82	6.37
Binder course 2" thick (9 SY per ton)	P5@.039	SY	8.79	1.77	1.60	12.16
Rubberized asphalt interlayer	P5@.005	SY	1.37	.23	.20	1.80
Wear course 2" thick (9 SY per ton)	P5@.039	SY	9.76	1.77	1.60	13.13
Tar emulsion protective seal coat	P5@.034	SY	2.12	1.54	1.39	5.05
Total estimated cost for typical 10' wide roadway, 4" paving over 4" aggregate base						
Cost per SY of roadway	**P5@.203**	**SY**	**26.69**	**9.22**	**8.31**	**44.22**
Cost per SF roadway	**P5@.023**	**SF**	**2.97**	**1.02**	**.92**	**4.91**
Cost per LF, 10' wide roadway	**P5@.230**	**LF**	**29.66**	**10.24**	**9.23**	**49.13**

Asphalt Paving for Parking Areas, Assembly Costs Equipment includes a 10' wide self-propelled paving machine and a 4-ton two axle steel drum roller. On-site parking lot with 6" thick aggregate base, 3" thick asphalt binder course, rubberized asphalt interliner, and 3" thick wear course. This is often called 6" paving over 6" aggregate base.

	Craft@Hrs	Unit	Material	Labor	Equipment	Total
Fine grading and compact existing subbase	P5@.066	SY	.01	3.00	2.70	5.71
Stone aggregate base, Class 2, 6" thick	P5@.033	SY	6.99	1.50	1.35	9.84
Binder course 3" thick	P5@.050	SY	13.20	2.27	2.05	17.52
Rubberized asphalt interlayer	P5@.005	SY	1.37	.23	.20	1.80
Wear course 3" thick	P5@.050	SY	14.60	2.27	2.05	18.92
Tar emulsion protective seal coat	P5@.034	SY	2.12	1.54	1.39	5.05
Total estimated cost of typical 1,000 SY parking lot, 6" paving over 6" aggregate base						
Cost per SY of parking lot	**P5@.238**	**SY**	**38.29**	**10.81**	**9.74**	**58.84**
Cost per SF of parking lot	**P5@.026**	**SF**	**4.25**	**1.20**	**1.08**	**6.53**

	Craft@Hrs	Unit	Material	Labor	Equipment	Total

Cold Milling of Asphalt Surface to 1" Depth Equipment includes a motorized street broom, a 20" pavement miller, two 5 CY dump trucks and a pickup truck. Hauling and disposal not included. Use $3,000 as a minimum charge.

	Craft@Hrs	Unit	Material	Labor	Equipment	Total
Milling asphalt to 1" depth	C6@.017	SY	—	.77	.42	1.19

Asphalt Pavement Repairs to conform to existing street, strips of 100 to 500 SF. Equipment includes one wheel-mounted 150 CFM air compressor, paving breaker, jackhammer bits, one 55 HP wheel loader with integral backhoe, one medium weight pneumatic tamper, one 1-ton two axle steel roller and one 5 CY dump truck These costs include the cost of loading and hauling to a legal dump within 6 miles. Dump fees are not included. See Waste Disposal.

Asphalt pavement repairs, assembly costs. Use $3,600 as a minimum job charge.

	Craft@Hrs	Unit	Material	Labor	Equipment	Total
Cut and remove 2" asphalt and 36" subbase	P5@.250	SY	—	11.30	7.75	19.05
Place 30" fill compacted to 90%, 6" aggregate base, 2" thick asphalt and tack coat						
30" fill (30 SY per CY at $11.10 CY)	P5@.099	SY	.42	4.49	3.07	7.98
6" thick base (6 SY per CY)	P5@.033	SY	6.99	1.50	1.02	9.51
2" thick asphalt (9 SY per ton)	P5@.039	SY	9.76	1.77	1.21	12.74
Tar emulsion protective seal coat	P5@.034	SY	2.12	1.54	1.05	4.71
Total per SY	**P5@.455**	**SY**	**19.29**	**20.60**	**14.10**	**53.99**

Asphalt overlay on existing asphalt pavement. Equipment includes a 10' wide self-propelled paving machine and a 4-ton two axle steel drum roller. Costs shown assume unobstructed access to the area receiving overlay. Use $6,000 as a minimum job charge.

Paving fabric interlayer with tack coat. Based on using 10' wide rolls x 378' long and one coat of mopped-on bituminous tack coat, MC70 (with .15 gallon per SY) before allowance for waste.

	Craft@Hrs	Unit	Material	Labor	Equipment	Total
Paving fabric interlayer, per 3,870 SF roll	—	Roll	622.00	—	—	622.00
Bituminous tack coat, per gallon	—	Gal	14.10	—	—	14.10
Laid, cut, mopped and rolled	P5@.005	SY	2.60	.23	.20	3.03
Wear course						
Bituminous wear course, per ton	—	Ton	87.80	—	—	87.80
1" thick (18 SY per ton)	P5@.028	SY	4.88	1.27	1.15	7.30
1-1/2" thick (12 SY per ton)	P5@.036	SY	7.32	1.63	1.48	10.43
2" thick (9 SY per ton)	P5@.039	SY	9.76	1.77	1.60	13.13
Add to overlaid paving as described above, if required						
Bituminous prime coat, MC70	P5@.001	SY	.35	.05	.04	.44
Tar emulsion protective seal coat	P5@.034	SY	1.97	1.54	1.39	4.90
Asphalt slurry seal	P5@.043	SY	.70	1.95	1.76	4.41

Concrete Paving No grading or base preparation included.

	Craft@Hrs	Unit	Material	Labor	Equipment	Total
Steel edge forms to 15", rented	C8@.028	LF	—	1.32	.94	2.26

2,000 PSI concrete placed directly from the chute of a ready-mix truck, vibrated and broom finished. Costs include 4% allowance for waste but no forms, reinforcing, or joints.

	Craft@Hrs	Unit	Material	Labor	Equipment	Total
4" thick (80 SF per CY)	P8@.013	SF	1.57	.60	.03	2.20
6" thick (54 SF per CY)	P8@.016	SF	2.36	.74	.03	3.13
8" thick (40 SF per CY)	P8@.019	SF	3.14	.88	.04	4.06
10" thick (32 SF per CY)	P8@.021	SF	3.94	.97	.04	4.95
12" thick (27 SF per CY)	P8@.024	SF	4.73	1.11	.05	5.89
15" thick (21 SF per CY)	P8@.028	SF	6.00	1.30	.06	7.36

	Craft@Hrs	Unit	Material	Labor	Equipment	Total
Clean and Sweep Pavement Equipment cost is $53.00 per hour for a self-propelled vacuum street sweeper, 7 CY maximum capacity. Use $300 as a minimum charge for sweeping using this equipment.						
Pavement sweeping, using equipment	TO@.200	MSF	—	11.50	22.70	34.20
Clean and sweep pavement, by hand	CL@1.44	MSF	—	59.40	—	59.40
Joint Treatment for Concrete Pavement Seal joint in concrete pavement with ASTM D5893 and FAA P-605 low modulus silicone joint sealer, including 5% waste. Cost per linear foot (LF), by joint size.						
One part silicone joint sealant	—	Gal	113.00	—	—	113.00
3/8" x 1/2" (128 LF per gallon)	PA@.002	LF	.93	.11	—	1.04
1/2" x 1/2" (96 LF per gallon)	PA@.002	LF	1.23	.11	—	1.34
1/2" x 3/4" (68 LF per gallon)	PA@.003	LF	1.74	.16	—	1.90
1/2" x 1" (50 LF per gallon)	PA@.003	LF	2.37	.16	—	2.53
1/2" x 1-1/4" (40 LF per gallon)	PA@.004	LF	2.96	.21	—	3.17
1/2" x 1-1/2" (33 LF per gallon)	PA@.006	LF	3.59	.32	—	3.91
3/4" x 3/4" (46 LF per gallon)	PA@.004	LF	2.58	.21	—	2.79
3/4" x 1-1/4" (33 LF per gallon)	PA@.006	LF	3.59	.32	—	3.91
3/4" x 1-1/2" (27 LF per gallon)	PA@.007	LF	4.39	.37	—	4.76
3/4" x 2" (22 LF per gallon)	PA@.008	LF	5.39	.43	—	5.82
1" x 1" (25 LF per gallon)	PA@.008	LF	4.74	.43	—	5.17
Deduct for asphalt emulsion sealant	—	%	-86.20	—	—	—
Backer rod for joints in concrete pavement						
1/2" backer rod	PA@.002	LF	.14	.11	—	.25
3/4" backer rod	PA@.002	LF	.19	.11	—	.30
1" backer rod	PA@.002	LF	.49	.11	—	.60
Clean out old joint sealer in concrete pavement by sandblasting and reseal with PVC coal tar sealer, including new backer rod. Use $400 as a minimum job charge.						
1/2" x 1/2"	PA@.009	LF	.53	.48	.32	1.33
1/2" x 3/4"	PA@.013	LF	.68	.69	.47	1.84
1/2" x 1"	PA@.013	LF	.88	.69	.47	2.04
1/2" x 1-1/4"	PA@.018	LF	1.07	.96	.65	2.68
1/2" x 1-1/2"	PA@.022	LF	1.26	1.17	.79	3.22

	Craft@Hrs	Unit	Material	Labor	Total
Brick Paving Extruded hard red brick. These costs do not include site preparation. Material costs shown include 2% for waste. (Figures in parentheses show quantity of brick before allowance for waste.) For expanded coverage of brick paving, see the *National Concrete & Masonry Estimator*, http://CraftsmanSiteLicense.com					
Brick laid flat without mortar					
Using brick, per thousand	—	M	352.00	—	352.00
Running bond					
4" x 8" x 2-1/4" (4.5 per SF)	M1@.114	SF	1.59	5.44	7.03
4" x 8" x 1-5/8" (4.5 per SF)	M1@.112	SF	1.54	5.35	6.89
3-5/8" x 7-5/8" x 2-1/4" (5.2 per SF)	M1@.130	SF	1.78	6.21	7.99
3-5/8" x 7-5/8" x 1-5/8" (5.2 per SF)	M1@.127	SF	1.78	6.06	7.84
Add for herringbone pattern	M1@.033	SF	—	1.58	1.58
Basketweave					
4" x 8" x 2-1/4" (4.5 per SF)	M1@.133	SF	1.61	6.35	7.96
4" x 8" x 1-5/8" (4.5 per SF)	M1@.130	SF	1.56	6.21	7.77
Brick laid on edge without mortar					
Running bond					
4" x 8" x 2-1/4" (8 per SF)	M1@.251	SF	2.87	12.00	14.87
3-5/8" x 7-5/8" x 2-1/4" (8.4 per SF)	M1@.265	SF	2.92	12.70	15.62
Brick laid flat with 3/8" mortar joints and mortar setting bed. Mortar included in material cost.					
Running bond					
4" x 8" x 2-1/4" (3.9 per SF)	M1@.127	SF	2.25	6.06	8.31
4" x 8" x 1-5/8" (3.9 per SF)	M1@.124	SF	2.20	5.92	8.12

	Craft@Hrs	Unit	Material	Labor	Total
3-5/8" x 7-5/8" x 2-1/4" (4.5 per SF)	M1@.144	SF	2.46	6.87	9.33
3-5/8" x 7-5/8" x 1-5/8" (4.5 per SF)	M1@.140	SF	2.41	6.68	9.09
Add for herringbone pattern	M1@.033	SF	—	1.58	1.58
Basketweave					
4" x 8" x 2-1/4" (3.9 per SF)	M1@.147	SF	1.40	7.02	8.42
4" x 8" x 1-5/8" (3.9 per SF)	M1@.144	SF	1.35	6.87	8.22
3-5/8" x 7-5/8" x 2-1/4" (4.5 per SF)	M1@.147	SF	1.61	7.02	8.63
3-5/8" x 7-5/8" x 1-5/8" (4.5 per SF)	M1@.144	SF	1.56	6.87	8.43
Brick laid on edge with 3/8" mortar joints and setting bed, running bond, including mortar					
4" x 8" x 2-1/4" (6.5 per SF)	M1@.280	SF	3.18	13.40	16.58
3-5/8" x 7-5/8" x 2-1/4" (6.9 per SF)	M1@.314	SF	3.32	15.00	18.32
Mortar color for brick laid in mortar, add per SF of paved area					
Add for red or yellow	—	SF	.10	—	.10
Add for black or brown	—	SF	.15	—	.15
Add for green	—	SF	.39	—	.39
Base underlayment for paving brick					
Add for 2" sand base (124 SFper ton)	M1@.009	SF	.12	.43	.55
Add for 15 lb felt underlayment	M1@.002	SF	.05	.10	.15
Add for asphalt tack coat (80 SF per gallon)	M1@.005	SF	.04	.24	.28
Add for 2% neoprene tack coat (40 SF per gal.)	M1@.005	SF	.21	.24	.45
Brick edging, 8" deep, set in concrete with dry joints					
Using brick, per thousand	—	M	348.00	—	348.00
Headers 4" x 8" x 2-1/4" (3 per LF)	M1@.147	LF	1.08	7.02	8.10
Headers 3-5/8" x 7-5/8" x 2-1/4" (3.3 per LF)	M1@.159	LF	1.19	7.59	8.78
Rowlocks 3-5/8" x 7-5/8" x 2-1/4" (5.3 per LF)	M1@.251	LF	1.90	12.00	13.90
Rowlocks 4" x 8" x 2-1/4" (5.3 per LF)	M1@.265	LF	1.90	12.70	14.60
Brick edging, 8" deep, set in concrete with 3/8" mortar joints					
Using brick, per thousand	—	M	352.00	—	352.00
Headers 4" x 8" x 2-1/4" (2.75 per LF)	M1@.159	LF	.99	7.59	8.58
Headers 3-5/8" x 7-5/8" x 2-1/4" (3 per LF)	M1@.173	LF	1.08	8.26	9.34
Rowlocks 3-5/8" x 7-5/8" x 2-1/4" (4.6 per LF)	M1@.298	LF	1.65	14.20	15.85
Rowlocks 4" x 8" x 2-1/4" (4.6 per LF)	M1@.314	LF	1.65	15.00	16.65

Masonry, Stone and Slate Paving These costs do not include site preparation. Costs for stone and slate vary widely. (Quantities shown in parentheses are before waste allowance.) Use $500 as a minimum job charge.

	Craft@Hrs	Unit	Material	Labor	Total
Interlocking 9" x 4-1/2" concrete pavers, dry joints, natural gray					
2-3/8" thick (3.5 per SF)	M1@.058	SF	3.20	2.77	5.97
3-1/8" thick (3.5 per SF)	M1@.063	SF	3.45	3.01	6.46
Add for standard colors (3.5 per SF)	—	SF	.24	—	.24
Add for custom colors (3.5 per SF)	—	SF	.50	—	.50
Patio blocks, 8" x 16" x 2", dry joints					
Natural gray (1.125 per SF)	M1@.052	SF	1.68	2.48	4.16
Standard colors (1.125 per SF)	M1@.052	SF	1.87	2.48	4.35
Flagstone pavers in sand bed with dry joints					
Random ashlar, 1-1/4"	M1@.193	SF	3.91	9.21	13.12
Random ashlar, 2-1/2"	M1@.228	SF	5.89	10.90	16.79
Irregular fitted, 1-1/4"	M1@.208	SF	3.26	9.93	13.19
Irregular fitted, 2-1/2"	M1@.251	SF	5.01	12.00	17.01
Flagstone pavers in mortar bed with mortar joints. Add the cost of mortar below					
Random ashlar, 1-1/4"	M1@.208	SF	4.00	9.93	13.93
Random ashlar, 2-1/2"	M1@.251	SF	6.07	12.00	18.07
Irregular fitted, 1-1/4"	M1@.228	SF	3.36	10.90	14.26
Irregular fitted, 2-1/2"	M1@.277	SF	5.12	13.20	18.32

	Craft@Hrs	Unit	Material	Labor	Total
Granite pavers, gray, sawn, thermal finish, 3/4" joint. Add bedding costs from the section that follows					
4" x 4" x 2" thick	M1@.184	SF	30.60	8.78	39.38
4" x 4" x 3" thick	M1@.184	SF	36.70	8.78	45.48
4" x 4" x 4" thick	M1@.184	SF	41.60	8.78	50.38
4" x 8" x 2" thick	M1@.171	SF	26.60	8.16	34.76
4" x 8" x 3" thick	M1@.184	SF	30.10	8.78	38.88
4" x 8" x 4" thick	M1@.184	SF	33.10	8.78	41.88
8" x 8" x 2" thick	M1@.171	SF	21.80	8.16	29.96
8" x 8" x 3" thick	M1@.171	SF	23.50	8.16	31.66
8" x 8" x 4" thick	M1@.184	SF	25.50	8.78	34.28
12" x 12" x 2" thick	M1@.171	SF	10.70	8.16	18.86
12" x 12" x 3" thick	M1@.171	SF	12.60	8.16	20.76
12" x 12" x 4" thick	M1@.171	SF	13.50	8.16	21.66
Mortar bed, 1/2" thick, 24 SF per CF of mortar					
SF of bed	M1@.039	SF	.47	1.86	2.33
Sand bed, 2" thick, 150 SF per CY of sand					
Per SF of bed	M1@.024	SF	.12	1.15	1.27
Limestone flag paving					
Sand bed, dry joints					
Random ashlar, 1-1/4"	M1@.193	SF	4.25	9.21	13.46
Random ashlar, 2-1/2"	M1@.228	SF	8.11	10.90	19.01
Irregular fitted, 1-1/2"	M1@.208	SF	3.69	9.93	13.62
Irregular fitted, 2-1/2"	M1@.251	SF	6.26	12.00	18.26
Mortar bed and joints					
Random ashlar, 1"	M1@.208	SF	3.57	9.93	13.50
Random ashlar, 2-1/2"	M1@.251	SF	7.81	12.00	19.81
Irregular fitted, 1"	M1@.228	SF	3.21	10.90	14.11
Irregular fitted, 2-1/2"	M1@.277	SF	5.99	13.20	19.19
Slate flag paving, natural cleft					
Sand bed, dry joints					
Random ashlar, 1-1/4"	M1@.173	SF	12.90	8.26	21.16
Irregular fitted, 1-1/4"	M1@.193	SF	12.10	9.21	21.31
Mortar bed and joints					
Random ashlar, 3/4"	M1@.173	SF	9.95	8.26	18.21
Random ashlar, 1"	M1@.208	SF	11.60	9.93	21.53
Irregular fitted, 3/4"	M1@.193	SF	9.26	9.21	18.47
Irregular fitted, 1"	M1@.228	SF	10.80	10.90	21.70
Add for sand rubbed slate	—	SF	2.20	—	2.20

Curbs, Gutters and Driveway Aprons Costs assume 3 uses of the forms and 2,000 PSI concrete placed directly from the chute of a ready-mix truck. Concrete cast-in-place curb. Excavation or backfill not included. Use $750 as a minimum job charge.

	Craft@Hrs	Unit	Material	Labor	Equipment	Total
Curbs						
Using concrete, per cubic yard	—	CY	123.00	—	—	123.00
Vertical curb						
6" x 12" straight curb	P9@.109	LF	5.28	5.29	1.58	12.15
6" x 12" curved curb	P9@.150	LF	5.36	7.28	2.18	14.82
6" x 18" straight curb	P9@.119	LF	7.84	5.78	1.73	15.35
6" x 18" curved curb	P9@.166	LF	7.97	8.06	2.41	18.44
6" x 24" straight curb	P9@.123	LF	10.40	5.97	1.79	18.16
6" x 24" curved curb	P9@.179	LF	10.50	8.69	2.60	21.79

	Craft@Hrs	Unit	Material	Labor	Equipment	Total
Rolled curb and gutter, 6" roll						
6" x 18" base, straight curb	P9@.143	LF	10.40	6.94	2.08	19.42
6" x 18" base, curved curb	P9@.199	LF	10.50	9.66	2.89	23.05
6" x 24" base, straight curb	P9@.168	LF	13.10	8.15	2.44	23.69
6" x 24" base, curved curb	P9@.237	LF	13.30	11.50	3.44	28.24
Driveway aprons. Concrete cast-in-place driveway aprons, including 4% waste, wire mesh, forms and finishing. Per square foot of apron, no site preparation included. Use $200 as a minimum job charge.						
4" thick (80 SF per CY)	P9@.024	SF	3.27	1.16	.25	4.68
6" thick (54 SF per CY)	P9@.032	SF	4.07	1.55	.34	5.96
Walkways Concrete, 2,000 PSI placed directly from the chute of a ready-mix truck, vibrated, plain scored, and broom finished. Costs include 2% allowance for waste but no forms or reinforcing.						
4" thick (80 SF per CY)	P8@.013	SF	1.61	.60	.03	2.24
Add for integral colors, most pastels	—	SF	2.09	—	—	2.09
Add for 1/2" color top course	P8@.012	SF	2.09	.56	.03	2.68
Add for steel trowel finish	CM@.011	SF	—	.56	.05	.61
Add for seeded aggregate finish	CM@.011	SF	.18	.56	.05	.79
Add for exposed aggregate wash process	CM@.006	SF	.07	.31	.03	.41
Asphalt walkway, temporary, including installation and breakout, but no hauling. Use $500 as a minimum job charge.						
2" to 2-1/2" thick	P5@.015	SF	2.15	.68	.64	3.47
Headers and Dividers						
2" x 4", treated pine	C8@.027	LF	.78	1.27	—	2.05
2" x 6", treated pine	C8@.028	LF	1.02	1.32	—	2.34
2" x 6", redwood	C8@.028	LF	1.63	1.32	—	2.95
2" x 4", patio type dividers, untreated	C8@.030	LF	.52	1.41	—	1.93
Porous Paving Systems Thin-walled HDPE plastic rings connected by an interlocking geogrid structure, installed on a porous base course for commercial applications. Rings transfer loads from the surface to the grid structure to an engineered course base. Equipment includes a 1/2 CY backhoe. Installed on an existing prepared base.						
Porous paving system, grass. Rolled out over base course and seeded with grass mixture. Includes fertilizer and soil polymer mix for spreading over base.						
6.6' wide by 164' long rolls	S6@.100	CSF	314.00	4.66	1.93	320.59
Add for 1" sand fill	S6@.030	CSF	5.15	1.40	—	6.55
Porous paving system, gravel. Rolled out over base course and covered with decorative fill gravel.						
6.6' wide by 164' long rolls	S6@.110	CSF	314.00	5.12	2.12	321.24
Add for 1" gravel fill	S6@.030	CSF	11.10	1.40	—	12.50
Grass-stone pavers Open diamond pattern concrete block filled with grass or aggregate laid on a compacted sand base						
24" x 16" x 3-1/2" block	CL@.085	SF	5.19	3.51	—	8.70
Guardrails and Bumpers Equipment is a 4,000 lb forklift. Use $4,000 as a minimum job charge						
Steel guardrail, standard beam	H1@.250	LF	25.40	13.60	2.15	41.15
Posts, wood, treated, 4" x 4" x 36" high.	H1@1.00	Ea	7.98	54.40	8.59	70.97
Guardrail two sides,						
Channel rail and side blocks	H1@1.00	LF	43.20	54.40	8.59	106.19
Sight screen	H1@.025	LF	2.21	1.36	.21	3.78
Highway median barricade, precast concrete						
2'8" high x 10' long	H1@.500	Ea	445.00	27.20	4.30	476.50
Add for reflectors, 2 per 10' section	—	LS	17.50	—	—	17.50
Parking bumper, precast concrete, including dowels						
3' wide	CL@.381	Ea	35.50	15.70	6.55	57.75
6' wide	CL@.454	Ea	62.60	18.70	7.80	89.10
Remove and reset wheel stop	CL@.908	Ea	—	37.50	15.60	53.10

	Craft@Hrs	Unit	Material	Labor	Equipment	Total
Bollards Posts mounted in walkways to limit vehicle entry. Equipment is a 4,000 lb. capacity forklift. Add for concrete footings, if required, from costs shown at the end of this section. Use $1,000 as a minimum job charge.						
Cast iron bollards, ornamental, surface mounted						
12" diameter base, 42" high	S1@1.00	Ea	1,320.00	49.30	17.20	1,386.50
17" diameter base, 42" high	S1@1.00	Ea	2,220.00	49.30	17.20	2,286.50
Lighted, electrical work not included, 17" diameter base, 42" high	S1@1.00	Ea	2,480.00	49.30	17.20	2,546.50
Concrete bollards, precast, exposed aggregate, surface mounted						
Square, 12" x 12" x 30" high	S1@1.00	Ea	496.00	49.30	17.20	562.50
Round, 12" diameter x 30" high	S1@1.00	Ea	506.00	49.30	17.20	572.50
Granite bollards, doweled to concrete foundation or slab (foundation not included.) Costs will be higher when granite is not available locally.						
Square, smooth matte finish, flat top						
16" x 16" x 30", 756 lbs	S1@1.00	Ea	1,210.00	49.30	17.20	1,276.50
16" x 16" x 54", 1,320 lbs	S1@1.50	Ea	1,530.00	73.90	25.80	1,629.70
Square, rough finish, pyramid top						
12" x 12" x 24", 330 lbs	S1@1.00	Ea	543.00	49.30	17.20	609.50
Round, smooth matte finish, flat top						
12" diameter, 18" high	S1@1.00	Ea	1,160.00	49.30	17.20	1,226.50
Octagonal, smooth matte finish, flat top, 24" x 24" x 20", 740 lbs	S1@1.00	Ea	1,770.00	49.30	17.20	1,836.50
Pipe bollards, concrete filled steel pipe, painted yellow, 8' long, set 4' in concrete, includes digging hole						
6" diameter pipe	S1@.750	Ea	151.00	37.00	13.70	201.70
8" diameter pipe	S1@.750	Ea	252.00	37.00	13.70	302.70
12" diameter pipe	S1@.750	Ea	408.00	37.00	13.70	458.70
Wood bollards, pressure treated timber, includes hand-digging and backfill of hole but no disposal of excess soil. Length shown is the portion exposed. Costs include bury to 3' depth.						
6" x 6" x 36" high	S1@.750	Ea	35.10	37.00	12.90	85.00
8" x 8" x 30" high	S1@.750	Ea	57.30	37.00	12.90	107.20
8" x 8" x 36" high	S1@.750	Ea	62.40	37.00	12.90	112.30
8" x 8" x 42" high	S1@.750	Ea	67.80	37.00	12.90	117.70
12" x 12" x 24" high	S1@.750	Ea	116.00	37.00	12.90	165.90
12" x 12" x 36" high	S1@.750	Ea	142.00	37.00	12.90	191.90
12" x 12" x 42" high	S1@.750	Ea	154.00	37.00	12.90	203.90
Footings for bollards, add if required						
Permanent concrete footing	C8@.500	Ea	44.40	23.60	—	68.00
Footing for removable bollards	C8@.500	Ea	202.00	23.60	—	225.60
Pavement Striping and Marking Use $150 as a minimum job charge. Pavement line markings.						
Single line striping, 4" wide solid	PA@.005	LF	.13	.27	.04	.44
Single line striping, 4" wide skip	PA@.005	LF	.06	.27	.04	.37
Red curb painting	PA@.006	LF	.21	.32	.05	.58
Parking lot spaces. For estimating purposes, figure one space per 300 SF of parking pavement area.						
Single line striping, approximately 25 LF per space	PA@.115	Ea	3.23	6.12	.97	10.32
Dual line striping, approximately 45 LF per space	PA@.175	Ea	5.81	9.32	1.48	16.61
Traffic symbols						
Arrows	PA@.250	Ea	8.80	13.30	2.12	24.22
Lettering, 2' x 8' template	PA@.500	Ea	56.50	26.60	4.23	87.33
Handicapped symbol						
One color	PA@.250	Ea	7.23	13.30	2.12	22.65
Two color	PA@.500	Ea	9.31	26.60	4.23	40.14

	Craft@Hrs	Unit	Material	Labor	Total
Speed Bumps and Parking Blocks Prefabricated solid plastic, pre-drilled. Based on Super Saver Bumps or Super Saver Blocks as manufactured by The Traffic Safety Store (www.trafficsafetystore.com) Costs shown include installation hardware. Labor includes drilling holes in substrate for anchors. Available in yellow, gray, blue, white.					
Speed bumps, based on quantity of 16 bumps					
6' x 2" x 10" (25 lbs each)	CL@.750	Ea	98.50	30.90	129.40
10' x 2" x 10" (45 lbs each)	CL@1.00	Ea	189.00	41.30	230.30
Parking blocks, based on quantity of 25 blocks					
6' x 4" x 6" (16 lbs each)	CL@.750	Ea	77.00	30.90	107.90
Traffic Signs Reflectorized steel, with a high strength "U"-channel galvanized steel pipe post 10' long set 2' into the ground. Includes digging of hole with a manual auger and backfill.					
Stop, 24" x 24"	CL@1.25	Ea	107.00	51.60	158.60
Speed limit, Exit, etc., 18" x 24"	CL@1.25	Ea	144.00	51.60	195.60
Warning, 24" x 24"	CL@1.25	Ea	163.00	51.60	214.60
Yield, 30" triangle	CL@1.25	Ea	177.00	51.60	228.60
Handicapped parking, 12" x 18"	CL@1.25	Ea	95.80	51.60	147.40
Add for breakaway galvanized square sign post	—	Ea	30.50	—	30.50

	Craft@Hrs	Unit	Material	Labor	Equipment	Total
Post Holes Drilling 2' deep by 10" to 12" diameter fence post holes. Equipment is a gasoline powered 12" auger. Costs will be higher on slopes or where access is limited. These costs do not include layout, setting of fence posts or disposal of excavated material.						
Light to medium soil, laborer working with a hand auger						
4 holes per hour	CL@.250	Ea	—	10.30	3.51	13.81
Medium to heavy soil, laborer working with a breaking bar and hand auger						
2 holes per hour	CL@.500	Ea	—	20.60	7.02	27.62
Medium to heavy soil, 2 laborers working with a gas-powered auger						
15 holes per hour	CL@.133	Ea	—	5.49	1.87	7.36
Broken rock, laborer and equipment operator working with a compressor and jackhammer						
2 holes per hour	S1@1.00	Ea	—	49.30	13.40	62.70
Rock, laborer and an equipment operator working with a truck-mounted drill						
12 holes per hour	S1@.166	Ea	—	8.18	4.96	13.14
Fencing, Chain Link Fence, industrial grade 9 gauge 2" x 2" galvanized steel chain link fabric and framework, including 2" or 2-3/8" line posts, as indicated, set at 10' intervals, set in concrete in augured post holes and 1-5/8" top rail, tension panels at corners and abrupt grade changes. Add for gates, gate posts and corner posts as required. Equipment is a gasoline-powered 12" auger. Use $600 as a minimum job charge. For scheduling purposes, estimate that a 2-man crew will install 125 to 130 LF of fence per 8-hour day.						
4' high galvanized fence, 2" line posts	C4@.073	LF	7.09	3.13	.34	10.56
6' high galvanized fence, 2" line posts	C4@.106	LF	8.61	4.54	.50	13.65
6' high galvanized fence, 2-3/8" line posts	C4@.109	LF	9.91	4.67	.51	15.09
7' high galvanized fence, 2-3/8" line posts	C4@.127	LF	10.00	5.44	.59	16.03
8' high galvanized fence, 2-3/8" line posts	C4@.146	LF	11.80	6.25	.68	18.73
10' high galvanized fence, 2-3/8" line posts	C4@.182	LF	13.70	7.79	.85	22.34
12' high galvanized fence, 2-3/8" line posts	C4@.218	LF	15.90	9.33	1.02	26.25

	Craft@Hrs	Unit	Material	Labor	Equipment	Total
Add for vertical aluminum privacy slats	C4@.016	SF	2.24	.68	—	2.92
Add for vinyl coated fabric and posts	—	%	50.0	—	—	—
Add for under 200 LF quantities	C4@.006	LF	.97	.26	.03	1.26
Deduct for highway quantities	—	LF	−1.86	—	—	−1.86
Deduct for 11 gauge chain link fabric	—	SF	−1.75	—	—	−1.75
Deduct for "C"-section line posts	—	LF	−2.72	—	—	−2.72
Gates Driveway or walkway. 9 gauge 2" x 2" galvanized steel chain link with frame and tension bars. Costs shown are per square foot of frame area. Add for hardware and gate posts, from below.						
With 1-3/8" diameter pipe frame	C4@.025	SF	23.20	1.07	—	24.27
With 1-5/8" diameter pipe frame	C4@.025	SF	26.80	1.07	—	27.87
Gate hardware, per gate						
Walkway gate	C4@.250	Ea	10.90	10.70	—	21.60
Driveway gate	C4@.250	Ea	26.80	10.70	—	37.50
Add for vinyl-coated fabric and frame	—	SF	1.11	—	—	1.11
Corner, end or gate posts, complete, heavyweight, 2-1/2" outside diameter galvanized, with fittings and bracc. Costs include 2/3 CF sack of concrete per post.						
4' high	C4@.612	Ea	35.20	26.20	2.87	64.27
5' high	C4@.668	Ea	39.20	28.60	3.13	70.93
6' high	C4@.735	Ea	41.20	31.50	3.44	76.14
7' high	C4@.800	Ea	40.90	34.20	3.75	78.85
8' high	C4@.882	Ea	54.10	37.80	4.13	96.03
10' high	C4@.962	Ea	61.40	41.20	4.50	107.10
12' high, with middle rail	C4@1.00	Ea	67.70	42.80	4.68	115.18
Add for vinyl-coated posts						
Per vertical foot	—	VLF	.48	—	—	.48
Deduct for 2" outside diameter	—	VLF	−1.32	—	—	−1.32
Barbed wire topper for galvanized chain link fence						
Single strand barbed wire	C4@.004	LF	.12	.17	—	.29
3 strands on one side, with support arm	C4@.008	LF	.79	.34	—	1.13
3 strand on each side, with support arm	C4@.013	LF	1.47	.56	—	2.03
Double coil of 24" to 30" barbed tape	C4@.038	LF	.23	1.63	—	1.86
Baseball Backstops Galvanized 9 gauge mesh chain link backstop with 2-5/8" OD galvanized vertical end posts, 2-3/8" OD galvanized vertical back posts and 1-5/8" OD galvanized framing. Includes 4' deep overhang, 20 LF behind home plate, 16 LF on both first and third base lines, rear and wing planks 3' high and two 12' long benches. Equipment is a 4,000 lb forklift.						
Traditional, 20' H x 58' W x 14' D	S6@24.0	Ea	9,000.00	1,120.00	275.00	10,395.00
Traditional, 30' H x 68' W x 14' D	S6@24.0	Ea	13,200.00	1,120.00	275.00	14,595.00
Arched, 20' H x 62' W x 20' D	S6@44.0	Ea	10,200.00	2,050.00	504.00	12,754.00
Arched, 18' H x 62' W x 20' D	S6@44.0	Ea	9,450.00	2,050.00	504.00	12,004.00
Add for concrete footings, 12" diameter x 24" deep, includes digging by hand and spreading excavated material adjacent to hole, using fence post mix bagged concrete.						
Per footing	S6@4.00	Ea	6.89	186.00	—	192.89
Sprinkler Irrigation Systems Typical complete system costs, including PVC pipe, heads, valves, fittings, trenching and backfill. Per SF of area watered. Add 10% for irrigation systems installed in areas subject to freezing hazard. Equipment is a 55 HP pneumatic tired riding type trencher.						
Large areas using pop-up impact heads, 200 to 300 SF per head, manual system						
To 5,000 SF job	S4@.005	SF	.20	.21	.09	.50
Over 5,000 SF to 10,000 SF	S4@.004	SF	.17	.17	.07	.41
Over 10,000 SF	S4@.003	SF	.15	.12	.05	.32
Add for automatic controls	S4@.001	SF	.09	.04	.02	.15

	Craft@Hrs	Unit	Material	Labor	Equipment	Total
Small areas, under 5,000 SF, spray heads						
Strip, automatic, shrub type	S4@.008	SF	.31	.33	.14	.78
Commercial type, manual	S4@.007	SF	.30	.29	.12	.71
Residential type, manual	S4@.007	SF	.28	.29	.12	.69
Add for automatic controls	S4@.001	SF	.09	.04	.02	.15
Trenching for sprinkler systems, in normal non-compacted topsoil						
Main lines with a 55 HP riding type trencher, 18" wide						
12" deep, 143 LF per hour	S1@.007	LF	—	.34	.18	.52
18" deep, 125 LF per hour	S1@.008	LF	—	.39	.21	.60
24" deep, 100 LF per hour	S1@.010	LF	—	.49	.26	.75
Lateral lines with a 20 HP riding type trencher, 12" wide						
8" deep, 200 LF per hour	S1@.005	LF	—	.25	.10	.35
12" deep, 125 LF per hour	S1@.008	LF	—	.39	.17	.56
Add for hard soil (shelf, rock field, hardpan)	S1@.006	LF	—	.30	.12	.42
Boring under walkways and pavement.						
To 8' wide, by hand, 8 LF per hour	CL@.125	LF	—	5.16	—	5.16
Backfill and compact trench, by hand.						
Mains, to 24" deep, 125 LF per hour	CL@.008	LF	—	.33	—	.33
Laterals, to 12" deep, 190 LF per hour	CL@.005	LF	—	.21	—	.21

	Craft@Hrs	Unit	Material	Labor	Total
Restore turf above pipe after sprinkler installation					
Replace and roll sod	CL@.019	SY	6.16	.78	6.94
Reseed by hand, cover, water and mulch	CL@.010	SY	.29	.41	.70
Connection to existing water line					
Residential or small commercial tap	CL@.939	Ea	26.80	38.70	65.50
Residential or small commercial stub	CL@.683	Ea	20.80	28.20	49.00
Medium commercial stub	CL@1.25	Ea	56.20	51.60	107.80
Atmospheric vacuum breaker					
3/4"	CL@.470	Ea	18.60	19.40	38.00
1"	CL@.500	Ea	24.90	20.60	45.50
1-1/2"	CL@.575	Ea	63.00	23.70	86.70
2"	CL@.625	Ea	109.00	25.80	134.80
Pressure type vacuum breaker, with threaded ball valves					
3/4"	CL@.700	Ea	163.00	28.90	191.90
1"	CL@.750	Ea	185.00	30.90	215.90
1-1/2"	CL@.850	Ea	445.00	35.10	480.10
2"	CL@.939	Ea	510.00	38.70	548.70
Double check valve assembly with two ball valves					
1-1/2" valve	CL@.750	Ea	404.00	30.90	434.90
2" valve	CL@.939	Ea	483.00	38.70	521.70
3" valve	CL@1.25	Ea	1,660.00	51.60	1,711.60
4" valve	CL@1.50	Ea	2,590.00	61.90	2,651.90
Reduced pressure backflow preventer with gate valves					
1" backflow preventer	CL@.750	Ea	208.00	30.90	238.90
1-1/2" backflow preventer	CL@.939	Ea	389.00	38.70	427.70
2" backflow preventer	CL@.939	Ea	438.00	38.70	476.70
3" backflow preventer	CL@1.25	Ea	1,630.00	51.60	1,681.60
4" backflow preventer	CL@1.50	Ea	2,520.00	61.90	2,581.90
6" backflow preventer	CL@1.88	Ea	3,270.00	77.60	3,347.60
Valve boxes, plastic box with plastic lid					
7" round	CL@.314	Ea	9.85	13.00	22.85
10" round	CL@.375	Ea	13.60	15.50	29.10

Sprinkler controllers, solid state electronics, 115-volt/24-volt electric timer, add electrical connection and feeder wire to valves

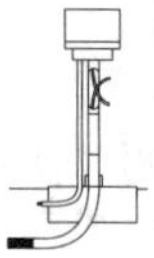

	Craft@Hrs	Unit	Material	Labor	Total
Indoor mount, 4 station	CL@.960	Ea	21.00	39.60	60.60
Indoor mount, 6 station	CL@.960	Ea	53.50	39.60	93.10
Indoor mount, 8 station	CL@1.10	Ea	57.40	45.40	102.80
Outdoor mount, 6-8 station, PC programmable	CL@1.10	Ea	114.00	45.40	159.40
Outdoor mount, 12 station	CL@1.10	Ea	68.80	45.40	114.20
Pedestal for outdoor units, set in concrete	CL@1.00	Ea	69.20	41.30	110.50

Underground control wire for automatic valves, includes waterproof connectors, wire laid in an open trench, common ground, one conductor per valve

	Craft@Hrs	Unit	Material	Labor	Total
4 conductors	CL@.001	LF	.26	.04	.30
5 conductors	CL@.001	LF	.31	.04	.35
7 conductors	CL@.002	LF	.35	.08	.43

Anti-siphon solenoid flow control valves, with atmospheric vacuum breaker. UV-resistant PVC, 24 volt. Add control wire as required.

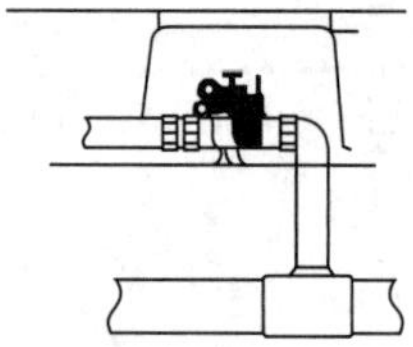

	Craft@Hrs	Unit	Material	Labor	Total
3/4", residential	CL@.341	Ea	15.10	14.10	29.20
1" residential	CL@.341	Ea	15.20	14.10	29.30
3/4", commercial	CL@.341	Ea	25.40	14.10	39.50
1" commercial	CL@.418	Ea	27.40	17.20	44.60
1-1/2" commercial	CL@.796	Ea	35.10	32.80	67.90
2" commercial	CL@.866	Ea	37.80	35.70	73.50

Manual sprinkler control valves, anti-siphon, brass, with union

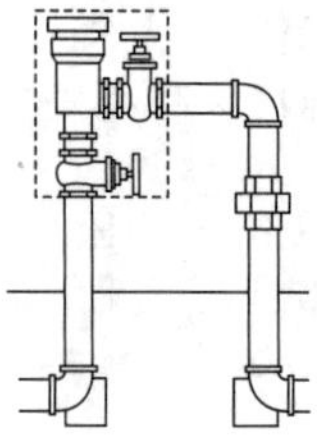

	Craft@Hrs	Unit	Material	Labor	Total
3/4" valve	CL@.518	Ea	45.20	21.40	66.60
1" valve	CL@.610	Ea	58.60	25.20	83.80
1-1/4" valve	CL@.677	Ea	92.30	27.90	120.20
1-1/2" valve	CL@.796	Ea	101.00	32.80	133.80
2" valve	CL@.866	Ea	147.00	35.70	182.70

Angle valves, brass, with union

	Craft@Hrs	Unit	Material	Labor	Total
3/4" valve	CL@.518	Ea	42.70	21.40	64.10
1" valve	CL@.610	Ea	53.80	25.20	79.00
1-1/4" valve	CL@.677	Ea	117.00	27.90	144.90
1-1/2" valve	CL@.796	Ea	128.00	32.80	160.80
2" valve	CL@.866	Ea	177.00	35.70	212.70

PVC Schedule 40 pipe and fittings, except as noted. Solvent welded. Plain end. Schedule 40 denotes wall thickness. Class 315, 200 and 160 identify the normal working pressure, 315, 200 or 160 PSI. Add the cost of excavation and backfill.

	Craft@Hrs	Unit	Material	Labor	Total
1/2" pipe	CL@.005	LF	.19	.21	.40
1/2" pipe, Class 315	CL@.005	LF	.14	.21	.35
1/2" ell	CL@.120	Ea	.38	4.95	5.33
1/2" tee	CL@.140	Ea	.44	5.78	6.22
3/4" pipe	CL@.005	LF	.23	.21	.44
3/4" pipe, Class 200	CL@.005	LF	.17	.21	.38
3/4" ell	CL@.160	Ea	.48	6.60	7.08
3/4" tee	CL@.180	Ea	.59	7.43	8.02
1" pipe	CL@.006	LF	.34	.25	.59
1" pipe, Class 200	CL@.006	LF	.20	.25	.45
1" ell	CL@.180	Ea	1.01	7.43	8.44
1" tee	CL@.220	Ea	1.24	9.08	10.32
1-1/4" pipe	CL@.006	LF	.56	.25	.81
1-1/4" pipe, Class 160	CL@.006	LF	.26	.25	.51
1-1/4" ell	CL@.180	Ea	1.50	7.43	8.93
1-1/4" tee	CL@.250	Ea	2.14	10.30	12.44

	Craft@Hrs	Unit	Material	Labor	Total
1-1/2" pipe	CL@.007	LF	.60	.29	.89
1-1/2" pipe, Class 160	CL@.007	LF	.33	.29	.62
1-1/2" ell	CL@.180	Ea	1.70	7.43	9.13
1-1/2" tee	CL@.250	Ea	2.26	10.30	12.56
2" pipe	CL@.008	LF	.83	.33	1.16
2" ell	CL@.200	Ea	2.56	8.25	10.81
2" tee	CL@.300	Ea	3.03	12.40	15.43
3" pipe	CL@.008	LF	1.83	.33	2.16
3" ell	CL@.240	Ea	9.83	9.90	19.73
3" tee	CL@.360	Ea	13.00	14.90	27.90
Polyethylene pipe, 80 PSI, black, flexible 100' rolls					
3/4" diameter	CL@.006	LF	.22	.25	.47
1" diameter	CL@.006	LF	.34	.25	.59
1-1/4" diameter	CL@.007	LF	.47	.29	.76
1-1/2" diameter	CL@.008	LF	.66	.33	.99
Polyethylene pipe, 100 PSI, black, flexible 100' rolls					
1-1/2" diameter	CL@.008	LF	1.48	.33	1.81
2" diameter	CL@.009	LF	.81	.37	1.18
Add for 125 PSI polyethylene pipe	—	%	25.0	—	—
Polyethylene pipe to male iron pipe thread adapter, brass					
3/4" male adapter	CL@.112	Ea	4.83	4.62	9.45
1" male adapter	CL@.172	Ea	6.55	7.10	13.65
1-1/4" male adapter	CL@.200	Ea	9.07	8.25	17.32

Shrub and Lawn Sprinkler Heads and Risers

	Craft@Hrs	Unit	Material	Labor	Total
Shrub bubbler, plastic nozzle, brass adjustment screw					
1/4 circle	P1@.120	Ea	1.20	4.43	5.63
1/2 circle	P1@.120	Ea	1.20	4.43	5.63
Full circle	P1@.120	Ea	.99	4.43	5.42
Mushroom spray	P1@.120	Ea	1.30	4.43	5.73
Flush head plastic lawn sprinkler, brass insert					
1/4 circle	P1@.120	Ea	1.30	4.43	5.73
1/2 circle	P1@.120	Ea	1.30	4.43	5.73
Full circle	P1@.120	Ea	1.30	4.43	5.73
Strip sprinkler	P1@.120	Ea	3.03	4.43	7.46
Brass 2" pop-up lawn sprinkler					
1/4 circle	P1@.120	Ea	3.35	4.43	7.78
1/2 circle	P1@.120	Ea	3.35	4.43	7.78
Full circle	P1@.120	Ea	3.35	4.43	7.78
Spring-loaded plastic 4" pop-up lawn sprinkler					
1/4 circle	P1@.120	Ea	3.20	4.43	7.63
1/2 circle	P1@.120	Ea	3.20	4.43	7.63
Full circle	P1@.120	Ea	3.20	4.43	7.63
Adjustable circle	P1@.120	Ea	4.06	4.43	8.49
Gear-driven rotating lawn sprinkler, 40 to 360 degrees					
15' to 30' circle	P1@.140	Ea	7.15	5.16	12.31
Pop-up impact sprinkler, adjustable, 40 to 360 degrees					
To 80' radius	P1@.140	Ea	13.20	5.16	18.36
Sprinkler riser nipples					
1/2" x close	P1@.030	Ea	.14	1.11	1.25
1/2" x 2"	P1@.030	Ea	.15	1.11	1.26
1/2" x 6" cut-off	P1@.030	Ea	.26	1.11	1.37
1/2" x 6" flexible cut-off	P1@.030	Ea	.26	1.11	1.37
1/2" x 6"	P1@.030	Ea	.28	1.11	1.39

	Craft@Hrs	Unit	Material	Labor	Total
1/2" x 12"	P1@.030	Ea	.41	1.11	1.52
1/2" threaded ell	P1@.030	Ea	1.22	1.11	2.33
1/2" and 3/4" x 6" cut off	P1@.030	Ea	.77	1.11	1.88
1/2" and 3/4" x 6" flexible cut-off	P1@.030	Ea	.77	1.11	1.88
3/4" x close	P1@.030	Ea	.22	1.11	1.33
3/4" x 2"	P1@.030	Ea	.23	1.11	1.34
3/4" x 6" cut off	P1@.030	Ea	.77	1.11	1.88
3/4" x 6" flexible cut-off	P1@.030	Ea	.77	1.11	1.88
3/4" threaded ell	P1@.030	Ea	.99	1.11	2.10
Quick coupling valves, add swing joint costs below					
3/4" regular	CL@.089	Ea	37.50	3.67	41.17
3/4" 2-piece	CL@.089	Ea	43.90	3.67	47.57
1" regular	CL@.094	Ea	52.00	3.88	55.88
1" 2-piece	CL@.094	Ea	63.70	3.88	67.58
1-1/4" regular	CL@.108	Ea	66.80	4.46	71.26
1-1/2" regular	CL@.124	Ea	80.60	5.12	85.72
Add for locking vinyl cover	—	Ea	16.20	—	16.20
Double swing sprinkler riser. Two close nipples, two PVC ells, one cut-off riser.					
1/2" pipe	P1@.150	Ea	2.97	5.53	8.50
3/4" pipe	P1@.150	Ea	3.21	5.53	8.74
Triple swing sprinkler riser. Three close nipples, three PVC ells, one cut-off riser.					
1/2" pipe	P1@.150	Ea	4.33	5.53	9.86
3/4" pipe	P1@.150	Ea	4.42	5.53	9.95
Hose bibb					
1/2" with 12" galvanized riser	CL@.041	Ea	13.50	1.69	15.19
3/4" with 12" galvanized riser	CL@.041	Ea	15.40	1.69	17.09
1/2" x 8" frost-proof with vacuum breaker	CL@.041	Ea	26.70	1.69	28.39
3/4" x 8" frost-proof with vacuum breaker	CL@.041	Ea	34.40	1.69	36.09

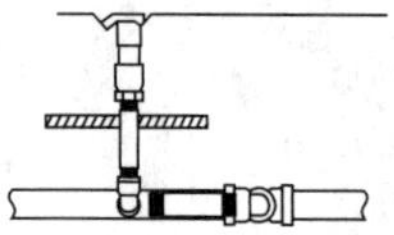

Planting Bed Preparation

	Craft@Hrs	Unit	Material	Labor	Equipment	Total
Spreading topsoil from piles on site, based on topsoil delivered to the site. Topsoil prices can be expected to vary widely.						
Hand work, 10 CY job, level site, 10' throw	CL@.500	CY	47.70	20.60	—	68.30
Move 25' in wheelbarrow	CL@1.00	CY	47.70	41.30	—	89.00
With 3/4 CY loader, 100 CY job, level site	T0@.080	CY	47.70	4.58	2.50	54.78
Spreading granular or powdered soil conditioners, based on fertilizer at $.26 per pound. Spread 20 pounds per 1,000 square feet (MSF). Add the cost of working fertilizer into the soil from below.						
By hand, 2,250 SF per hour	CL@.445	MSF	8.33	18.40	—	26.73
Hand broadcast spreader, 9,000 SF per hour	CL@.111	MSF	8.33	4.58	.42	13.33
Push gravity spreader, 3,000 SF per hour	CL@.333	MSF	8.33	13.70	1.83	23.86
Push broadcast spreader, 20,000 SF per hour	CL@.050	MSF	8.33	2.06	.28	10.67
Tractor drawn broadcast spreader, 87 MSF per hour	CL@.011	MSF	8.33	.45	.48	9.26
Spreading organic soil conditioners, based on peat humus at $.19 per pound. Spread 200 pounds per 1,000 square feet (MSF). Add the mixing cost from below						
By hand, 1,000 SF per hour	CL@1.00	MSF	62.40	41.30	—	103.70

	Craft@Hrs	Unit	Material	Labor	Equipment	Total
Push gravity spreader, 2,750 SF per hour	CL@.363	MSF	62.40	15.00	2.00	79.40
Manure spreader, 34,000 SF per hour	CL@.029	MSF	62.40	1.20	.14	63.74
Fertilizer and soil conditioners						
Most nitrate fertilizers, ammonium sulfate	—	Lb	.26	—	—	.26
Lawn and garden fertilizer, calcium nitrate	—	Lb	.28	—	—	.28
Hydrated lime sodium nitrate	—	Lb	.22	—	—	.22
Ground limestone	—	Ton	214.00	—	—	214.00
Ground dolomitic limestone	—	Ton	220.00	—	—	220.00
Composted manure	—	Lb	.04	—	—	.04
Peat humus	—	Lb	.04	—	—	.04
Vermiculite, perlite	—	CF	9.18	—	—	9.18

Spreading lime at 70 pounds per 1,000 SF. Based on an 8 acre job using a tractor-drawn spreader at $25.00 per hour and 1 acre per hour. Add mixing cost from below. Note: 1 acre equals 43,560 square feet.

	Craft@Hrs	Unit	Material	Labor	Equipment	Total
Lime	TO@1.00	Acre	468.00	57.30	41.70	567.00
Lime	TO@.656	Ton	268.00	37.60	27.30	332.90

Mixing soil and fertilizer in place. Medium soil. Light soil (sand or soft loam) will decrease costs shown by 20% to 30%. Heavy soil (clay, wet or rocky soil) will increase costs shown by 20% to 40%. Add soil conditioner cost from the preceding sections.

	Craft@Hrs	Unit	Material	Labor	Equipment	Total
Mixing by hand						
2" deep, 9 SY per hour	CL@.111	SY	—	4.58	—	4.58
4" deep, 7.5 SY per hour	CL@.133	SY	—	5.49	—	5.49
6" deep, 5.5 SY per hour	CL@.181	SY	—	7.47	—	7.47
Mixing with a 11 HP rear-tined hydraulic tiller						
2" deep, 110 SY per hour	CL@.009	SY	—	.37	.19	.56
4" deep, 90 SY per hour	CL@.011	SY	—	.45	.23	.68
6" deep, 65 SY per hour	CL@.015	SY	—	.62	.32	.94
8" deep, 45 SY per hour	CL@.022	SY	—	.91	.46	1.37
Mixing with a 3' wide, 20 HP tractor-driven tiller						
2" deep, 50,000 SF per hour	TO@.020	MSF	—	1.15	.63	1.78
4" deep, 40,000 SF per hour	TO@.025	MSF	—	1.43	.79	2.22
6" deep, 30,000 SF per hour	TO@.033	MSF	—	1.89	1.05	2.94
8" deep, 20,000 SF per hour	TO@.050	MSF	—	2.86	1.59	4.45
Mixing with a 6' wide, 40 HP tractor-driven tiller						
2" deep, 90,000 SF per hour	TO@.011	MSF	—	.63	.39	1.02
4" deep, 70,000 SF per hour	TO@.014	MSF	—	.80	.50	1.30
6" deep, 53,000 SF per hour	TO@.019	MSF	—	1.09	.68	1.77
8" deep, 35,000 SF per hour	TO@.028	MSF	—	1.60	1.00	2.60
Leveling the surface for lawn or planting bed						
By hand, 110 SY per hour	CL@.009	SY	—	.37	—	.37
With 6' drag harrow, at 60,000 SF per hour	TO@.017	MSF	—	.97	.60	1.57
With 12' drag harrow, at 115,000 SF per hour	TO@.009	MSF	—	.52	.47	.99
Plant bed preparation						
With a 3/4 CY wheel loader, at 12.5 CY per hour	TO@.080	CY	—	4.58	3.49	8.07
By hand to 18" deep, 8.35 SY per hour	CL@.118	SY	—	4.87	—	4.87

	Craft@Hrs	Unit	Material	Labor	Equipment	Total
Mixing planting soil						
By hand, .9 CY per hour	CL@1.11	CY	—	45.80	—	45.80
With 3/4 CY wheel loader, 7 CY per hour	T0@.143	CY	—	8.19	6.23	14.42
With a soil shredder, 11 CY per hour	T0@.090	CY	—	5.16	3.92	9.08
Seeding and Planting						
Seeding with a hand broadcast spreader, 10 pounds per 1,000 SF. The cost of grass seed will vary greatly depending on variety — see below.						
4,000 SF per hour, hand seeding	CL@.250	MSF	34.60	10.30	.94	45.84
Seeding with push broadcast spreader, 5 pounds per 1,000 SF						
10,000 SF per hour, Push spreader seeding	CL@.100	MSF	17.30	4.13	.55	21.98
Seeding with a mechanical seeder at 175 pounds per acre, 5 acre job						
Mechanical seeding	T0@13.1	Acre	605.00	750.00	576.00	1,931.00
Mechanical seeding	T0@.300	MSF	13.90	17.20	13.20	44.30
Hydroseeding subcontract (spray application of seed, binder and fertilizer slurry). Costs will vary with access restrictions and site requirements.						
Minimum charge	—	LS	—	—	—	500.00
2,000 to 10,000 SF job	—	MSF	—	—	—	180.00
10,001 SF to 1 acre job	—	MSF	—	—	—	150.00
1 to 4.99 acre job	—	MSF	—	—	—	120.00
5 to 9.99 acre job	—	Acre	—	—	—	4,790.00
10 to 19.99 acre job	—	Acre	—	—	—	4,360.00
20 to 49.99 acre job	—	Acre	—	—	—	3,920.00
50 to 99.99 acre job	—	Acre	—	—	—	3,480.00
Over 100 acre job	—	Acre	—	—	—	3,050.00
Sealing soil, application by a hydroseeding unit. Use $750 as a minimum job charge.						
Copolymer based liquid for erosion control	C4@.020	SY	1.50	.86	.21	2.57
Grass seed						
Annual ryegrass	—	Lb	2.87	—	—	2.87
Most fescue	—	Lb	2.46	—	—	2.46
Kentucky bluegrass	—	Lb	6.66	—	—	6.66
Bermuda	—	Lb	5.04	—	—	5.04
Heat-and drought-resistant premium blend	—	Lb	7.53	—	—	7.53
Dichondra	—	Lb	20.70	—	—	20.70
Centipede	—	Lb	48.50	—	—	48.50
Sodding, placed on level ground at 25 SY per hour. Add delivery cost below. Use 50 SY as a minimum job charge. Prices will vary by region and season.						
Bluegrass and bluegrass blends	CL@.040	SY	4.77	1.65	—	6.42
Fescue varieties	CL@.040	SY	6.88	1.65	—	8.53
Bermuda and centipedes	CL@.040	SY	6.22	1.65	—	7.87
Zoysias	CL@.040	SY	6.06	1.65	—	7.71
St. Augustine varieties	CL@.040	SY	6.79	1.65	—	8.44
Typical delivery cost, to 90 miles	—	SY	.75	—	—	.75
Add for staking sod on slopes	CL@.010	SY	.26	.41	—	.67
Deduct for 100 SY or greater jobs	—	%	-45.0	—	—	—
Work grass seed into soil, no seed included. Use $1,500 as a minimum job charge.						
By hand, 220 SY per hour	CL@.005	SY	—	.21	—	.21
6' harrow and 40 HP tractor 60 MSF per hour	T0@.017	MSF	—	.97	1.13	2.10
12' harrow and 60 HP tractor 100 MSF per hour	T0@.010	MSF	—	.57	.53	1.10

	Craft@Hrs	Unit	Material	Labor	Equipment	Total
Apply top dressing over seed or stolons.						
300 pounds per 1,000 SF (2.7 pounds per SY)						
By hand, 65 SY per hour	CL@.015	SY	.55	.62	—	1.17
With manure spreader						
10,000 SF per hour	CL@.125	MSF	61.00	5.16	—	66.16
Roll sod or soil surface with a roller.						
With a push roller, 400 SY per hour	CL@.015	SY	—	.62	—	.62
With a 20 HP tractor						
25,000 SF per hour	T0@.040	MSF	—	2.29	1.14	3.43
Sprigging, by hand.						
6" spacing, 50 SY per hour	CL@2.22	MSF	.64	91.60	—	92.24
9" spacing, 100 SY per hour	CL@1.11	MSF	.98	45.80	—	46.78
12" spacing, 150 SY per hour	CL@.778	MSF	1.30	32.10	—	33.40
Hybrid Bermuda grass stolons,						
Per bushel	—	Ea	3.00	—	—	3.00
Ground cover, large areas, no surface preparation						
Ice plant (80 SF per flat)	CL@.008	SF	.42	.33	—	.75
Strawberry (75 SF per flat)	CL@.008	SF	.47	.33	—	.80
Ivy and similar (70 SF per flat)	CL@.008	SF	.44	.33	—	.77
Gravel bed, pea gravel (1.4 tons per CY)						
Spread by hand	CL@.555	CY	43.40	22.90	—	66.30
Trees and shrubs						
Shrubs, most varieties						
1 gallon, 100 units	CL@.085	Ea	16.10	3.51	—	19.61
1 gallon, over 100 units	CL@.076	Ea	14.80	3.14	—	17.94
5 gallons, 100 units	CL@.443	Ea	41.70	18.30	—	60.00
Trees, most varieties, complete, staked, typical costs						
5 gallon, 4' to 6' high	CL@.716	Ea	62.20	29.50	—	91.70
15 gallon, 8' to 10' high	CL@1.37	Ea	164.00	56.50	—	220.50
20" x 24" box, 10' to 12' high	CL@4.54	Ea	857.00	187.00	—	1,044.00
Specimen size 36" box,						
14' to 20' high	CL@11.6	Ea	1,770.00	479.00	—	2,249.00
Guaranteed establishment of plants						
Add, as a % of total contract price	—	%	—	—	—	12.0
Edging						
Plastic benderboard,						
5" x 3/8", staked	CL@.013	LF	.87	.54	—	1.41
Redwood benderboard,						
4" x 5/16",	CL@.013	LF	.39	.54	—	.93
Redwood headerboard, 2" x 4", staked						
Construction Common grade	CL@.127	LF	1.35	5.24	—	6.59
Decomposed granite edging						
Saturated and rolled, 3" deep	CL@.011	SF	.63	.45	—	1.08
Landscape stepping stones (concrete pavers)						
Laid on level ground, 12" x 12",						
30 lb. each	CL@.024	SF	1.44	.99	—	2.43
Pressure-treated piles, in 2' to 5' sections,						
9" to 12" diameter	CL@.045	LF	4.32	1.86	—	6.18

32 Exterior Improvements

	Craft@Hrs	Unit	Material	Labor	Total
Tree Grates Two piece cast iron grates surrounding a tree trunk, set in concrete. Add for delivery.					
36" x 36" x 2-3/4" square (270 lbs.)	C4@4.00	Ea	352.00	171.00	523.00
48" x 48" x 2-3/4" square (512 lbs.)	C4@5.00	Ea	389.00	214.00	603.00
60" x 60" x 2-3/4" square (750 lbs.)	C4@6.50	Ea	438.00	278.00	716.00
36" diameter x 2-3/4" round (230 lbs.)	C4@4.00	Ea	358.00	171.00	529.00
48" diameter x 2-3/4" round (480 lbs.)	C4@5.00	Ea	413.00	214.00	627.00
Add for cast steel frame	—	%	45.0	20.0	—

33 Utilities

	Craft@Hrs	Unit	Material	Labor	Equipment	Total

Cast Iron Flanged Pipe AWWA C151 pipe with cast iron flanges on both ends. Pipe is laid and connected in an open trench. Equipment includes a wheel-mounted 1 CY backhoe for lifting and placing the pipe and fittings. Trench excavation, dewatering, backfill and compaction are not included. Use $3,000 as a minimum job charge. See next section for fittings, valves and accessories.

	Craft@Hrs	Unit	Material	Labor	Equipment	Total
4" pipe, 260 pounds per 18' section	U1@.057	LF	24.20	2.90	.79	27.89
6" pipe, 405 pounds per 18' section	U1@.075	LF	28.40	3.81	1.04	33.25
8" pipe, 570 pounds per 18' section	U1@.075	LF	40.60	3.81	1.04	45.45
10" pipe, 740 pounds per 18' section	U1@.094	LF	54.80	4.78	1.31	60.89
12" pipe, 930 pounds per 18' section	U1@.094	LF	74.50	4.78	1.31	80.59

Cast Iron Fittings, Valves and Accessories Based on type ASA A21, 10-A21-11-6 and 4C110-64, C111-64 fittings. Installed in an open trench and connected. Equipment includes a wheel-mounted 1 CY backhoe for lifting and placing. Trench excavation, dewatering, backfill and compaction are not included. These items are also suitable for use with the Ductile Iron Pipe in the section that follows. Costs estimated using this section may be combined with the costs estimated from the Cast Iron Flanged Pipe section or the Ductile Iron Pipe section for arriving at the minimum job charge shown in those sections.

	Craft@Hrs	Unit	Material	Labor	Equipment	Total
Cast iron mechanical joint 90 degree ells						
4" ell	U1@.808	Ea	182.00	41.10	11.30	234.40
6" ell	U1@1.06	Ea	272.00	53.90	14.80	340.70
8" ell	U1@1.06	Ea	396.00	53.90	14.80	464.70
10" ell	U1@1.32	Ea	598.00	67.10	18.40	683.50
12" ell	U1@1.32	Ea	747.00	67.10	18.40	832.50
14" ell	U1@1.32	Ea	1,700.00	67.10	18.40	1,785.50
16" ell	U1@1.65	Ea	1,960.00	83.90	23.00	2,066.90
Deduct for 1/8 or 1/16 bends	—	%	-20.0	—	—	—
Cast iron mechanical joint tees						
4" x 4"	U1@1.22	Ea	281.00	62.00	17.00	360.00
6" x 4"	U1@1.59	Ea	356.00	80.80	22.10	458.90
6" x 6"	U1@1.59	Ea	388.00	80.80	22.10	490.90
8" x 8"	U1@1.59	Ea	559.00	80.80	22.10	661.90
10" x 10"	U1@1.59	Ea	812.00	80.80	22.10	914.90
12" x 12"	U1@2.48	Ea	1,050.00	126.00	34.50	1,210.50
Add for wyes	—	%	40.0	—	—	—
Add for crosses	—	%	30.0	33.0	33.0	—
Cast iron mechanical joint reducers						
6" x 4"	U1@1.06	Ea	204.00	53.90	14.80	272.70
8" x 6"	U1@1.06	Ea	305.00	53.90	14.80	373.70
10" x 8"	U1@1.32	Ea	397.00	67.10	18.40	482.50
12" x 10"	U1@1.32	Ea	534.00	67.10	18.40	619.50

	Craft@Hrs	Unit	Material	Labor	Equipment	Total
AWWA mechanical joint gate valves						
3" valve	U1@3.10	Ea	575.00	158.00	43.20	776.20
4" valve	U1@4.04	Ea	814.00	205.00	56.30	1,075.30
6" valve	U1@4.80	Ea	1,290.00	244.00	66.80	1,600.80
8" valve	U1@5.14	Ea	2,210.00	261.00	71.60	2,542.60
10" valve	U1@5.67	Ea	3,460.00	288.00	78.90	3,826.90
12" valve	U1@6.19	Ea	5,880.00	315.00	86.20	6,281.20
Indicator post valve						
6" upright, adjustable	U1@6.50	Ea	911.00	330.00	90.50	1,331.50
Fire hydrant with spool						
6"	U1@5.00	Ea	1,570.00	254.00	69.60	1,893.60
Backflow preventers, installed at ground level						
3" backflow preventer	U1@3.50	Ea	2,680.00	178.00	48.70	2,906.70
4" backflow preventer	U1@4.00	Ea	3,650.00	203.00	55.70	3,908.70
6" backflow preventer	U1@5.00	Ea	6,160.00	254.00	69.60	6,483.60
8" backflow preventer	U1@6.00	Ea	8,690.00	305.00	83.50	9,078.50
Block structure for backflow preventer						
5' x 7' x 3'4"	M1@32.0	Ea	1,220.00	1,530.00	—	2,750.00
Shear gate						
8", with adjustable release handle	U1@2.44	Ea	2,130.00	124.00	34.00	2,288.00
Adjustable length valve boxes, for up to 20" valves						
5' depth	U1@1.75	Ea	191.00	89.00	24.40	304.40
Concrete thrust blocks, minimum formwork						
1/4 CY thrust block	C8@1.20	Ea	87.90	56.60	—	144.50
1/2 CY thrust block	C8@2.47	Ea	177.00	116.00	—	293.00
3/4 CY thrust block	C8@3.80	Ea	262.00	179.00	—	441.00
1 CY thrust block	C8@4.86	Ea	351.00	229.00	—	580.00
Tapping saddles, double strap, iron body, tap size to 2"						
Pipe to 4"	U1@2.38	Ea	57.00	121.00	33.10	211.10
8" pipe	U1@2.89	Ea	74.90	147.00	40.20	262.10
10" pipe	U1@3.15	Ea	76.40	160.00	43.90	280.30
12" pipe	U1@3.52	Ea	101.00	179.00	49.00	329.00
14" pipe, bronze body	U1@3.78	Ea	101.00	192.00	52.60	345.60
Tapping valves, mechanical joint						
4" valve	U1@6.93	Ea	928.00	352.00	96.50	1,376.50
6" valve	U1@8.66	Ea	1,240.00	440.00	121.00	1,801.00
8" valve	U1@9.32	Ea	1,860.00	474.00	130.00	2,464.00
10" valve	U1@10.4	Ea	2,810.00	529.00	145.00	3,484.00
12" valve	U1@11.5	Ea	4,250.00	585.00	160.00	4,995.00
Labor and equipment tapping pipe, by hole size. Add the cost of excavation and backfill.						
4" pipe	U1@5.90	Ea	—	300.00	82.10	382.10
6" pipe	U1@9.32	Ea	—	474.00	130.00	604.00
8" pipe	U1@11.7	Ea	—	595.00	163.00	758.00
10" pipe	U1@15.5	Ea	—	788.00	216.00	1,004.00
12" pipe	U1@23.4	Ea	—	1,190.00	326.00	1,516.00

	Craft@Hrs	Unit	Material	Labor	Equipment	Total
Ductile Iron Pressure Pipe Mechanical joint 150 lb Class 50 ductile iron pipe. Installed in an open trench to 5' deep. Equipment includes a wheel-mounted 1 CY backhoe for lifting and placing the pipe. Trench excavation, dewatering, backfill and compaction are not included. Cast iron fittings and valves appear in the preceding sections. Use $4,000 as a minimum job charge.						
4" pipe	U1@.140	LF	14.50	7.12	1.95	23.57
6" pipe	U1@.180	LF	23.20	9.15	2.51	34.86
8" pipe	U1@.200	LF	28.60	10.20	2.78	41.58
10" pipe	U1@.230	LF	36.90	11.70	3.20	51.80
12" pipe	U1@.260	LF	42.80	13.20	3.62	59.62
14" pipe	U1@.300	LF	64.10	15.20	4.18	83.48
16" pipe	U1@.340	LF	67.80	17.30	4.73	89.83
18" pipe	U1@.400	LF	76.00	20.30	5.57	101.87
20" pipe	U1@.500	LF	85.30	25.40	6.96	117.66
24" pipe	U1@.600	LF	93.30	30.50	8.35	132.15
PVC Water Pipe Installed in an open trench. Equipment includes a wheel-mounted 1 CY backhoe for lifting and placing the pipe. Trench excavation, bedding material and backfill are not included. Use $2,500 as a minimum job charge.						
Class 200 PVC cold water pressure pipe, bell end, SDR 21						
1-1/2" pipe	U1@.029	LF	.55	1.47	.40	2.42
2" pipe	U1@.036	LF	.83	1.83	.50	3.16
2-1/2" pipe	U1@.037	LF	1.24	1.88	.52	3.64
3" pipe	U1@.065	LF	1.75	3.30	.90	5.95
4" pipe	U1@.068	LF	2.94	3.46	.95	7.35
6" pipe	U1@.082	LF	6.42	4.17	1.14	11.73
90-degree ells Schedule 40						
1-1/2" ells	P6@.385	Ea	1.77	20.20	—	21.97
2" ells	P6@.489	Ea	2.89	25.60	—	28.49
2-1/2" ells	P6@.724	Ea	8.74	37.90	—	46.64
3" ells	P6@1.32	Ea	10.50	69.20	—	79.70
4" ells	P6@1.57	Ea	18.30	82.30	—	100.60
6" ells	P6@1.79	Ea	59.50	93.80	—	153.30
Deduct for 45-degree ells	—	%	-5.0	—	—	—
Tees						
1-1/2" tees	P6@.581	Ea	2.37	30.40	—	32.77
2" tees	P6@.724	Ea	3.59	37.90	—	41.49
2-1/2" tees	P6@.951	Ea	11.40	49.80	—	61.20
3" tees	P6@1.57	Ea	15.10	82.30	—	97.40
4" tees	P6@2.09	Ea	27.50	109.00	—	136.50
6" tees	P6@2.70	Ea	91.10	141.00	—	232.10
Polyethylene Pipe Belled ends with rubber ring joints. Installed in an open trench. Equipment includes a wheel-mounted 1/2 CY backhoe for lifting and placing the pipe. No excavation, bedding material, shoring, backfill or dewatering included. Use $2,000 as a minimum job charge. SDR is Standard Dimension Ratio, comparing pipe diameter with pipe wall thickness. The smaller the first number, the higher the pressure rating.						
160 PSI polyethylene pipe, SDR 11 to 1						
3" pipe	U1@.108	LF	9.06	5.49	1.18	15.73
4" pipe	U1@.108	LF	15.10	5.49	1.18	21.77
5" pipe	U1@.108	LF	23.50	5.49	1.18	30.17
6" pipe	U1@.108	LF	32.60	5.49	1.18	39.27
8" pipe	U1@.145	LF	55.10	7.37	1.59	64.06
10" pipe	U1@.145	LF	86.60	7.37	1.59	95.56
12" pipe	U1@.145	LF	122.00	7.37	1.59	130.96

	Craft@Hrs	Unit	Material	Labor	Equipment	Total
100 PSI polyethylene pipe, SDR 17 to 1						
4" pipe	U1@.108	LF	10.30	5.49	1.18	16.97
6" pipe	U1@.108	LF	22.00	5.49	1.18	28.67
8" pipe	U1@.145	LF	36.90	7.37	1.59	45.86
10" pipe	U1@.145	LF	56.90	7.37	1.59	65.86
12" pipe	U1@.145	LF	80.50	7.37	1.59	89.46
Low-pressure polyethylene pipe, SDR 21 to 1						
4" pipe	U1@.108	LF	8.45	5.49	1.18	15.12
5" pipe	U1@.108	LF	12.50	5.49	1.18	19.17
6" pipe	U1@.108	LF	18.40	5.49	1.18	25.07
7" pipe	U1@.145	LF	20.80	7.37	1.59	29.76
8" pipe	U1@.145	LF	30.60	7.37	1.59	39.56
10" pipe	U1@.145	LF	46.10	7.37	1.59	55.06
12" pipe	U1@.145	LF	66.50	7.37	1.59	75.46
14" pipe	U1@.169	LF	80.50	8.59	1.85	90.94
16" pipe	U1@.169	LF	106.00	8.59	1.85	116.44
18" pipe	U1@.169	LF	130.00	8.59	1.85	140.44
20" pipe	U1@.212	LF	162.00	10.80	2.32	175.12
22" pipe	U1@.212	LF	197.00	10.80	2.32	210.12
24" pipe	U1@.212	LF	234.00	10.80	2.32	247.12
Fittings, molded, bell ends						
4" 90-degree ell, 160 PSI	U1@2.00	Ea	205.00	102.00	21.90	328.90
4" 45-degree ell, 160 PSI	U1@2.00	Ea	205.00	102.00	21.90	328.90
6" 90-degree ell, 160 PSI	U1@2.00	Ea	419.00	102.00	21.90	542.90
6" 45-degree ell, 160 PSI	U1@2.00	Ea	419.00	102.00	21.90	542.90
4" to 3" reducer, 160 PSI	U1@2.00	Ea	121.00	102.00	21.90	244.90
6" to 4" reducer, 160 PSI	U1@2.00	Ea	293.00	102.00	21.90	416.90
3" transition section, 160 PSI	U1@2.00	Ea	257.00	102.00	21.90	380.90
6" transition section, 160 PSI	U1@2.00	Ea	1,150.00	102.00	21.90	1,273.90
10" by 4" branch saddle, 160 PSI	U1@3.00	Ea	372.00	152.00	32.90	556.90
3" flanged adapter, low pressure	U1@1.00	Ea	194.00	50.80	11.00	255.80
4" flanged adapter, low pressure	U1@1.00	Ea	277.00	50.80	11.00	338.80
6" flanged adapter, low pressure	U1@1.00	Ea	363.00	50.80	11.00	424.80
8" flanged adapter, low pressure	U1@1.50	Ea	525.00	76.20	16.50	617.70
10" flanged adapter, low pressure	U1@1.50	Ea	741.00	76.20	16.50	833.70
4" flanged adapter, 160 PSI	U1@1.00	Ea	302.00	50.80	11.00	363.80
6" flanged adapter, 160 PSI	U1@1.00	Ea	424.00	50.80	11.00	485.80
Fittings, fabricated, belled ends						
10" 90-degree ell, 100 PSI	U1@3.00	Ea	2,130.00	152.00	32.90	2,314.90
10" 45-degree ell, 100 PSI	U1@3.00	Ea	1,190.00	152.00	32.90	1,374.90
4" 30-degree ell, 100 PSI	U1@2.00	Ea	346.00	102.00	21.90	469.90
8" to 6" reducer, 100 PSI	U1@3.00	Ea	629.00	152.00	32.90	813.90
10" to 8" reducer, 100 PSI	U1@3.00	Ea	741.00	152.00	32.90	925.90
4" 45-degree wye, 100 PSI	U1@2.00	Ea	914.00	102.00	21.90	1,037.90

Water Main Sterilization Gas chlorination method, typical costs for sterilizing new water mains prior to inspection, includes operator and equipment. Add $200 to total costs for setting up and removing equipment. Minimum cost will be $500. These costs include the subcontractor's overhead and profit. Typical cost per 1,000 LF of main with diameter as shown.

	Craft@Hrs	Unit	Material	Labor	Equipment	Total
3" or 4" diameter	—	MLF	—	—	—	57.50
6" diameter	—	MLF	—	—	—	102.00
8" diameter	—	MLF	—	—	—	135.00

	Craft@Hrs	Unit	Material	Labor	Equipment	Total
10" diameter	—	MLF	—	—	—	155.00
12" diameter	—	MLF	—	—	—	191.00
14" diameter	—	MLF	—	—	—	226.00
16" diameter	—	MLF	—	—	—	240.00
18" diameter	—	MLF	—	—	—	299.00
24" diameter	—	MLF	—	—	—	394.00
36" diameter	—	MLF	—	—	—	567.00
48" diameter	—	MLF	—	—	—	769.00

Water Tanks, Elevated Typical subcontract prices for 100' high steel tanks, including design, fabrication and erection. Complete tank includes 36" pipe riser with access manhole, 8" overflow to ground, ladder with protective cage, vent, balcony catwalk, concrete foundation, painting and test. No well, pump, fencing, drainage or water distribution piping included. Costs are per tank with gallon capacity as shown. Tanks built in areas without earthquake or high wind risk may cost 15% to 25% less.

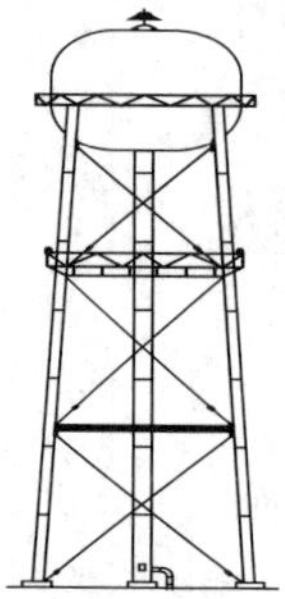

	Craft@Hrs	Unit	Material	Labor	Total
75,000 gallon	—	Ea	—	—	411,000.00
100,000 gallon	—	Ea	—	—	441,000.00
150,000 gallon	—	Ea	—	—	528,000.00
200,000 gallon	—	Ea	—	—	690,000.00
300,000 gallon	—	Ea	—	—	855,000.00
400,000 gallon	—	Ea	—	—	990,000.00
Add or subtract for each foot of height more or less than 100, per 100 gallons of capacity	—	Ea	—	—	.98
Cathodic protection system, per tank	—	LS	—	—	20,900.00
Electric service, including float switches, obstruction marker lighting system, and hookup of cathodic protection system					
Per tank	—	LS	—	—	16,300.00

PVC Sewer Pipe 13' lengths, bell and spigot ends with rubber ring gasket in bell. Installed in open trench. Equipment includes a wheel-mounted 1 CY backhoe for lifting and placing the pipe. Trench excavation, dewatering, backfill and compaction are not included. Use $2,500 as a minimum job charge.

	Craft@Hrs	Unit	Material	Labor	Equipment	Total
4" pipe	C5@.047	LF	1.86	2.18	.65	4.69
6" pipe	C5@.056	LF	4.04	2.60	.78	7.42
8" pipe	C5@.061	LF	7.21	2.83	.85	10.89
10" pipe	C5@.079	LF	11.30	3.67	1.10	16.07
12" pipe	C5@.114	LF	15.70	5.29	1.59	22.58

Sewer cleaning, ball method Typical costs for cleaning new sewer mains prior to inspection, includes operator and equipment. Add $200 to total costs for setting up and removing equipment. Minimum cost will be $500. These costs include the subcontractor's overhead and profit. Typical costs per 1,000 LF of main diameter listed.

	Craft@Hrs	Unit	Material	Labor	Equipment	Total
6" diameter	—	MLF	—	—	—	99.80
8" diameter	—	MLF	—	—	—	130.00
10" diameter	—	MLF	—	—	—	155.00
12" diameter	—	MLF	—	—	—	192.00
14" diameter	—	MLF	—	—	—	227.00
16" diameter	—	MLF	—	—	—	254.00
18" diameter	—	MLF	—	—	—	299.00
24" diameter	—	MLF	—	—	—	394.00
36" diameter	—	MLF	—	—	—	593.00
48" diameter	—	MLF	—	—	—	770.00

	Craft@Hrs	Unit	Material	Labor	Equipment	Total
Sewer cleaning, jet vac Jet-Vac 2,000 psi blast to remove sediment and debris from catch basins, sanitary or storm sewers, conduit, culvert or drain pipe 6" to 36" diameter. Includes truck and operator. Time starts at the shop. Typical production rate is 400 to 500 LF per hour.						
Full 8-hour day	—	LS	—	—	—	1,770.00
Half day (4 hours)	—	LS	—	—	—	1,040.00
Addition hours	—	Ea	—	—	—	285.00
Add for debris disposal, 800 gallon load	—	LS	—	—	—	388.00
Polyethylene flexible drainage tubing Corrugated drainage tubing, plain or perforated and snap-on ABS fittings. Installed in an open trench. Excavation, bedding material and backfill not included.						
3" (10' length)	CL@.009	LF	.86	.37	—	1.23
3" (100' coil)	CL@.009	LF	.54	.37	—	.91
4" (10' length)	CL@.011	LF	.73	.45	—	1.18
4" (100' coil)	CL@.011	LF	.65	.45	—	1.10
6" (100' coil)	CL@.014	LF	2.20	.58	—	2.78
8" (20' or 40' length)	CL@.017	LF	3.45	.70	—	4.15
10" (20' length)	CL@.021	LF	7.58	.87	—	8.45
12" (20' length)	CL@.022	LF	11.00	.91	—	11.91
Polyethylene tube snap fittings, elbows or tees						
3" fitting	CL@.025	Ea	6.59	1.03	—	7.62
4" fitting	CL@.025	Ea	7.87	1.03	—	8.90
6" fitting	CL@.025	Ea	13.10	1.03	—	14.13
Filter sock sieve. Keeps soil out of perforated pipe. Reduces need for aggregate filters. By pipe size. Per linear foot of sock.						
3", 10' length	CL@.006	LF	.56	.25	—	.81
4", 10' length	CL@.007	LF	.60	.29	—	.89
4", 100' length	CL@.007	LF	.22	.29	—	.51
Hi-Q drain pipe Corrugated high-density polyethylene drainage tubing and culvert pipe installed in an open trench. Excavation, bedding material and backfill not included. 20' lengths.						
4"	CL@.009	LF	1.54	.37	—	1.91
6"	CL@.014	LF	1.76	.58	—	2.34
12" culvert	CL@.022	LF	4.03	.91	—	4.94
15" culvert	CL@.026	LF	5.29	1.07	—	6.36
18" culvert	CL@.045	LF	6.80	1.86	—	8.66
24" culvert	CL@.090	LF	11.30	3.71	—	15.01
Corrugated drain pipe fittings						
4" snap adapter	CL@.025	Ea	3.96	1.03	—	4.99
6" snap adapter	CL@.025	Ea	13.00	1.03	—	14.03
6" x 4" reducer	CL@.025	Ea	8.30	1.03	—	9.33
6" snap coupling	CL@.025	Ea	4.43	1.03	—	5.46
6" wye	CL@.037	Ea	10.90	1.53	—	12.43
6" tee	CL@.037	Ea	19.50	1.53	—	21.03
6" blind tee	CL@.037	Ea	14.50	1.53	—	16.03
6" split end cap	CL@.025	Ea	8.54	1.03	—	9.57
12" split coupling	CL@.050	Ea	20.10	2.06	—	22.16
15" split coupling	CL@.090	Ea	20.10	3.71	—	23.81
Non-Reinforced Concrete Pipe Smooth wall, standard strength, with tongue-and-groove mortar joint ends. Installed in an open trench. Equipment includes a wheel-mounted 1 CY backhoe for lifting and placing the pipe. Trench excavation, bedding material and backfill are not included. Use $3,500 as a minimum job charge.						
6" pipe	C5@.152	LF	6.02	7.06	2.12	15.20
8" pipe	C5@.176	LF	9.12	8.17	2.45	19.74
10" pipe	C5@.176	LF	11.80	8.17	2.45	22.42
12" pipe	C5@.186	LF	13.40	8.64	2.59	24.63

	Craft@Hrs	Unit	Material	Labor	Equipment	Total
15" pipe	C5@.210	LF	18.00	9.75	2.92	30.67
18" pipe	C5@.234	LF	24.60	10.90	3.26	38.76
21" pipe	C5@.234	LF	28.50	10.90	3.26	42.66
24" pipe	C5@.260	LF	35.60	12.10	3.62	51.32
30" pipe	C5@.286	LF	58.50	13.30	3.98	75.78

Non-Reinforced Perforated Concrete Underdrain Pipe Perforated smooth wall, standard strength, 3' lengths with tongue and groove mortar joint ends. Installed in an open trench. Equipment includes a wheel-mounted 1 CY backhoe for lifting and placing the pipe. Trench excavation, bedding material and backfill are not included. Use $2,200 as a minimum job charge.

	Craft@Hrs	Unit	Material	Labor	Equipment	Total
6" pipe	C5@.152	LF	6.72	7.06	2.12	15.90
8" pipe	C5@.208	LF	9.07	9.66	2.90	21.63

Reinforced Concrete Pipe Class III, 1350 "D"-load, ASTM C-76, 8' lengths. Tongue-and-groove mortar joint ends. Installed in an open trench. Equipment cost shown is for a wheel-mounted 1 CY backhoe for lifting and placing the pipe. Trench excavation, dewatering, backfill and compaction are not included. Use $3,000 as a minimum job charge.

	Craft@Hrs	Unit	Material	Labor	Equipment	Total
18" pipe	C5@.272	LF	29.70	12.60	3.79	46.09
24" pipe	C5@.365	LF	44.00	16.90	5.08	65.98
30" pipe	C5@.426	LF	73.40	19.80	5.93	99.13
36" pipe	C5@.511	LF	99.40	22.90	7.11	110.36
42" pipe	C5@.567	LF	124.00	26.30	7.89	158.19
48" pipe	C5@.623	LF	162.00	28.90	8.67	199.57
54" pipe	C5@.707	LF	186.00	32.80	9.84	228.64
60" pipe	C5@.785	LF	224.00	36.40	10.90	271.30
66" pipe	C5@.914	LF	279.00	42.40	12.70	334.10
72" pipe	C5@.914	LF	316.00	42.40	12.70	371.10
78" pipe	C5@.914	LF	547.00	42.40	12.70	602.10
84" pipe	C5@1.04	LF	617.00	48.30	14.50	679.80
90" pipe	C5@1.04	LF	730.00	48.30	14.50	792.80
96" pipe	C5@1.18	LF	806.00	54.80	16.40	877.20

Reinforced Elliptical Concrete Pipe Class III, 1350 "D", C-502-72, 8' lengths, tongue-and-groove mortar joint ends. Installed in an open trench. Equipment includes a wheel-mounted 1 CY backhoe for lifting and placing the pipe. Trench excavation, dewatering, backfill and compaction are not included. Use $3,500 as a minimum job charge.

	Craft@Hrs	Unit	Material	Labor	Equipment	Total
19" x 30" pipe, 24" pipe equivalent	C5@.356	LF	55.10	16.50	4.96	76.56
24" x 38" pipe, 30" pipe equivalent	C5@.424	LF	72.90	19.70	5.90	98.50
29" x 45" pipe, 36" pipe equivalent	C5@.516	LF	100.00	24.00	7.18	131.18
34" x 53" pipe, 42" pipe equivalent	C5@.581	LF	161.00	27.00	8.09	196.09
38" x 60" pipe, 48" pipe equivalent	C5@.637	LF	203.00	29.60	8.87	241.47
48" x 76" pipe, 60" pipe equivalent	C5@.797	LF	269.00	37.00	11.10	317.10
53" x 83" pipe, 66" pipe equivalent	C5@.923	LF	321.00	42.90	12.90	376.80
58" x 91" pipe, 72" pipe equivalent	C5@.923	LF	380.00	42.90	12.90	435.80

Flared Concrete End Sections For round concrete drain pipe, precast. Equipment includes a wheel-mounted 1 CY backhoe for lifting and placing the items. Trench excavation, dewatering, backfill and compaction are not included. Use $2,500 as a minimum job charge.

	Craft@Hrs	Unit	Material	Labor	Equipment	Total
12" opening, 530 lbs	C5@2.41	Ea	349.00	112.00	33.60	494.60
15" opening, 740 lbs	C5@2.57	Ea	375.00	119.00	35.80	529.80
18" opening, 990 lbs	C5@3.45	Ea	416.00	160.00	48.00	624.00
24" opening, 1,520 lbs	C5@3.45	Ea	498.00	160.00	48.00	706.00
30" opening, 2,190 lbs	C5@3.96	Ea	595.00	184.00	55.10	834.10
36" opening, 4,100 lbs	C5@3.96	Ea	1,160.00	184.00	55.10	1,399.10
42" opening, 5,380 lbs	C5@4.80	Ea	1,260.00	223.00	66.80	1,549.80
48" opening, 6,550 lbs	C5@5.75	Ea	1,620.00	267.00	80.10	1,967.10
54" opening, 8,000 lbs	C5@7.10	Ea	2,700.00	330.00	98.90	3,128.90

	Craft@Hrs	Unit	Material	Labor	Equipment	Total

Precast Reinforced Concrete Box Culvert Pipe ASTM C-850 with tongue-and-groove mortar joint ends. Installed in an open trench. Equipment includes a wheel-mounted 1 CY backhoe for lifting and placing the pipe. Trench excavation, dewatering, backfill and compaction are not included. Laying length is 8' for smaller cross sections and 6' or 4' for larger cross sections. Use $8,500 as a minimum job charge.

	Craft@Hrs	Unit	Material	Labor	Equipment	Total
4' x 3'	C5@.273	LF	283.00	12.70	3.80	299.50
5' x 5'	C5@.336	LF	372.00	15.60	4.68	392.28
6' x 4'	C5@.365	LF	433.00	16.90	5.08	454.98
6' x 6'	C5@.425	LF	508.00	19.70	5.92	533.62
7' x 4'	C5@.442	LF	524.00	20.50	6.15	550.65
7' x 7'	C5@.547	LF	647.00	25.40	7.62	680.02
8' x 4'	C5@.579	LF	562.00	26.90	8.06	596.96
8' x 8'	C5@.613	LF	731.00	28.50	8.53	768.03
9' x 6'	C5@.658	LF	780.00	30.60	9.16	819.76
9' x 9'	C5@.773	LF	929.00	35.90	10.80	975.70
10' x 6'	C5@.787	LF	932.00	36.50	11.00	979.50
10' x 10'	C5@.961	LF	1,020.00	44.60	13.40	1,078.00

Corrugated Metal Pipe, Galvanized 20' lengths, installed in an open trench. Costs include couplers. Equipment includes a wheel-mounted 1 CY backhoe for lifting and placing the pipe. Trench excavation, dewatering, backfill and compaction are not included. Use $3,500 as a minimum job charge.

	Craft@Hrs	Unit	Material	Labor	Equipment	Total
Round pipe						
8", 16 gauge (.064)	C5@.102	LF	14.80	4.74	1.42	20.96
10", 16 gauge (.064)	C5@.102	LF	15.50	4.74	1.42	21.66
12", 16 gauge (.064)	C5@.120	LF	16.10	5.57	1.67	23.34
15", 16 gauge (.064)	C5@.120	LF	19.80	5.57	1.67	27.04
18", 16 gauge (.064)	C5@.152	LF	24.30	7.06	2.12	33.48
24", 14 gauge (.079)	C5@.196	LF	37.50	9.10	2.73	49.33
30", 14 gauge (.079)	C5@.196	LF	46.30	9.10	2.73	58.13
36", 14 gauge (.079)	C5@.231	LF	56.20	10.70	3.22	70.12
42", 14 gauge (.079)	C5@.231	LF	65.50	10.70	3.22	79.42
48", 14 gauge (.079)	C5@.272	LF	74.30	12.60	3.79	90.69
60", 12 gauge (.109)	C5@.311	LF	126.00	14.40	4.33	144.73
Oval pipe						
18" x 11", 16 gauge (.064)	C5@.133	LF	23.80	6.18	1.85	31.83
22" x 13", 16 gauge (.064)	C5@.167	LF	28.40	7.75	2.33	38.48
29" x 18", 14 gauge (.079)	C5@.222	LF	44.30	10.30	3.09	57.69
36" x 22", 14 gauge (.079)	C5@.228	LF	54.90	10.60	3.17	68.67
43" x 27", 14 gauge (.079)	C5@.284	LF	59.50	13.20	3.95	76.65
Flared end sections for oval pipe						
18" x 11"	C5@1.59	Ea	128.00	73.80	22.10	223.90
22" x 13"	C5@1.75	Ea	154.00	81.30	24.40	259.70
29" x 18"	C5@1.85	Ea	232.00	85.90	25.80	343.70
36" x 22"	C5@2.38	Ea	372.00	111.00	33.10	516.10
43" x 27"	C5@2.85	Ea	617.00	132.00	39.70	788.70
Add for bituminous coating, with paved invert						
On round pipe	—	%	20.0	—	—	—
On oval pipe or flared ends	—	%	24.0	—	—	—
Deduct for aluminum pipe, round, oval or flared ends	—	%	–12.0	—	—	—

	Craft@Hrs	Unit	Material	Labor	Equipment	Total
Corrugated Metal Nestable Pipe Split-in-half, Type I, 16 gauge. Trench excavation, backfill, compaction and grading are not included. Equipment includes a wheel-mounted 1 CY backhoe for lifting and placing the pipe. Use $5,500 as a minimum job charge.						
12" diameter, galvanized	C5@.056	LF	27.10	2.60	.78	30.48
18" diameter, galvanized	C5@.064	LF	35.10	2.97	.89	38.96
Add for bituminous coating, with paved invert	—	%	20.0	—	—	—

Fiberglass Trench Drain System System includes 16 sloped channels, each 6 feet long, 16 channel frames, 64 iron grates, each 18 inches long, 128 grate locking bolts, outlet and end caps. Neutral channels extend the system run beyond 96 feet. Corrosion resistant polyester or vinylester. Channel has 8" internal width and built-in slope of 1%. Installed in an open trench.

	Craft@Hrs	Unit	Material	Labor	Total
Typical 96' fiberglass drainage system	P6@10.0	Ea	7,180.00	524.00	7,704.00
Typical 96' fiberglass drainage system, per LF	P6@1.04	LF	74.70	54.50	129.20
System components					
6' sloped channel	—	Ea	223.00	—	223.00
6' channel frame	—	Ea	89.20	—	89.20
18" cast iron grate	—	Ea	41.70	—	41.70
6" grate locking bolt	—	Ea	1.15	—	1.15
6" outlet cap	—	Ea	31.90	—	31.90
6" closed end cap	—	Ea	32.30	—	32.30
Add for 6' neutral channels	—	Ea	224.00	—	224.00

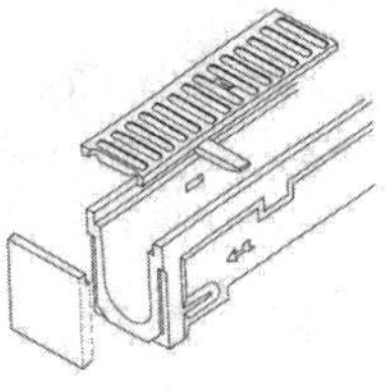

Precast Trench Drain System System includes 30 framed, interlocking tongue-and-groove connection channels, one meter long each, with integral cast-in metal rail edge, 30 snap-in galvanized steel slotted grates, 24" x 24" catch basin, 60 grate locking bolts, outlet and end caps. Channel has 4" internal width and built-in slope of .6%. All channels have preformed round and oval drillouts for vertical outlet connection with underground piping. Neutral channels extend the system run beyond 30 meters. Channel and grating combination certified to Load Class D (90,000 lbs). Installed in an open trench.

	Craft@Hrs	Unit	Material	Labor	Total
Typical 98' galvanized steel drainage system	P6@8.00	Ea	3,740.00	419.00	4,159.00
Typical 98' galvanized steel drainage system, per LF	P6@.082	LF	38.20	4.30	42.50
System components					
1 meter sloped channel with frame	—	Ea	89.10	—	89.10
1 meter galvanized steel grate	—	Ea	20.40	—	20.40
24" x 24" catch basin	—	Ea	143.00	—	143.00
Grate locking bolt	—	Ea	4.78	—	4.78
4" outlet cap	—	Ea	10.70	—	10.70
4" closed end cap	—	Ea	10.70	—	10.70
Add for 1 meter neutral channels	—	Ea	89.10	—	89.10

	Craft@Hrs	Unit	Material	Labor	Equipment	Total
Corrugated Polyethylene Culvert Pipe Heavy-duty, 20' lengths. Installed in an open trench. Equipment includes a wheel-mounted 1 CY backhoe for lifting and placing the pipe. Trench excavation, dewatering, backfill and compaction are not included. Based on 500' minimum job. Various sizes may be combined for total footage. Couplings are split type that snap onto the pipe. Use $2,500 as a minimum job charge.						
8" diameter pipe	C5@.035	LF	3.50	1.63	.49	5.62
10" diameter pipe	C5@.038	LF	7.75	1.76	.53	10.04
12" diameter pipe	C5@.053	LF	10.90	2.46	.74	14.10
18" diameter pipe	C5@.111	LF	22.30	5.15	1.55	29.00
8" coupling	C5@.105	Ea	9.39	4.88	1.46	15.73
10" coupling	C5@.114	Ea	9.09	5.29	1.59	15.97
18" coupling	C5@.331	Ea	29.20	15.40	4.61	49.21

	Craft@Hrs	Unit	Material	Labor	Equipment	Total
Vitrified Clay Pipe Extra strength, installed in open trench. 4" through 12" are 6'0" joint length, over 12" are either 7' or 7'6" joint length. Costs shown include one coupler per joint. Couplers consist of a rubber sleeve with stainless steel compression bands. Equipment includes a wheel-mounted 1 CY backhoe for lifting and placing the pipe. Trench excavation, dewatering, backfill and compaction are not included. Use $3,500 as a minimum job charge.						
4" pipe	C5@.081	LF	2.87	3.76	1.13	7.76
6" pipe	C5@.175	LF	6.21	8.13	2.44	16.78
8" pipe	C5@.183	LF	8.96	8.50	2.55	20.01
10" pipe	C5@.203	LF	14.30	9.43	2.83	26.56
12" pipe	C5@.225	LF	20.30	10.40	3.13	33.83
15" pipe	C5@.233	LF	19.10	10.80	3.24	33.14
18" pipe	C5@.254	LF	27.60	11.80	3.54	42.94
21" pipe	C5@.283	LF	37.70	13.10	3.94	54.74
24" pipe	C5@.334	LF	50.20	15.50	4.65	70.35
27" pipe	C5@.396	LF	57.40	18.40	5.51	81.31
30" pipe	C5@.452	LF	69.90	21.00	6.29	97.19
1/4 bends including couplers						
4" bend	C5@.494	Ea	19.10	22.90	7.88	49.88
6" bend	C5@.524	Ea	33.20	24.30	7.30	64.80
8" bend	C5@.549	Ea	44.40	25.50	7.64	77.54
10" bend	C5@.610	Ea	76.70	28.30	8.49	113.49
12" bend	C5@.677	Ea	98.20	31.40	9.43	139.03
15" bend	C5@.715	Ea	259.00	33.20	9.95	302.15
18" bend	C5@.844	Ea	356.00	39.20	11.80	407.00
21" bend	C5@.993	Ea	482.00	46.10	13.80	541.90
24" bend	C5@1.17	Ea	630.00	54.30	16.30	700.60
30" bend	C5@1.37	Ea	903.00	63.60	19.10	985.70
Wyes and tees including couplers						
4" wye or tee	C5@.744	Ea	24.70	34.50	10.40	69.60
6" wye or tee	C5@.787	Ea	42.10	36.50	11.00	89.60
8" wye or tee	C5@.823	Ea	62.20	38.20	11.50	111.90
10" wye or tee	C5@.915	Ea	134.00	42.50	12.70	189.20
12" wye or tee	C5@1.02	Ea	177.00	47.40	14.20	238.60
15" wye or tee	C5@1.10	Ea	288.00	51.10	15.30	354.40
18" wye or tee	C5@1.30	Ea	392.00	60.40	18.10	470.50
21" wye or tee	C5@1.53	Ea	514.00	71.00	21.30	606.30
24" wye or tee	C5@1.80	Ea	612.00	83.60	25.10	720.70
27" wye or tee	C5@2.13	Ea	746.00	98.90	29.70	874.60
30" wye or tee	C5@2.50	Ea	727.00	116.00	34.80	877.80
Catch Basins Catch basin including 6" concrete top and base. Equipment includes a wheel-mounted 1 CY backhoe for lifting and placing the items. Trench excavation, bedding material and backfill are not included. Use $3,000 as a minimum job charge.						
4' diameter precast concrete basin						
4' deep	S6@19.0	Ea	2,090.00	885.00	353.00	3,328.00
6' deep	S6@23.7	Ea	2,590.00	1,100.00	440.00	4,130.00
8' deep	S6@28.9	Ea	3,190.00	1,350.00	537.00	5,077.00
Light-duty grate, gray iron, asphalt coated						
Grate on pipe bell						
6" diameter, 13 lb	S6@.205	Ea	19.60	9.55	3.81	32.96
8" diameter, 25 lb	S6@.247	Ea	53.40	11.50	4.59	69.49
Frame and grate						
8" diameter, 55 lb	S6@.424	Ea	113.00	19.80	7.87	140.67
17" diameter, 135 lb	S6@.823	Ea	275.00	38.30	15.30	328.60

	Craft@Hrs	Unit	Material	Labor	Equipment	Total
Medium-duty, frame and grate						
11" diameter, 70 lb	S6@.441	Ea	138.00	20.50	8.19	166.69
15" diameter, 120 lb	S6@.770	Ea	248.00	35.90	14.30	298.20
Radial grate, 20" diameter, 140 lb	S6@1.68	Ea	284.00	78.30	31.20	393.50
Heavy-duty frame and grate						
Flat grate						
11-1/2" diameter, 85 lb	S6@.537	Ea	178.00	25.00	9.97	212.97
20" diameter, 235 lb	S6@2.01	Ea	484.00	93.60	37.30	614.90
21" diameter, 315 lb	S6@2.51	Ea	592.00	117.00	46.60	755.60
24" diameter, 350 lb	S6@2.51	Ea	655.00	117.00	46.60	818.60
30" diameter, 555 lb	S6@4.02	Ea	961.00	187.00	74.60	1,222.60
Convex or concave grate						
20" diameter, 200 lb	S6@1.83	Ea	343.00	85.30	34.00	462.30
20" diameter, 325 lb	S6@2.51	Ea	562.00	117.00	46.60	725.60
Beehive grate and frame						
11" diameter, 80 lb	S6@.495	Ea	248.00	23.10	9.19	280.29
15" diameter, 120 lb	S6@1.83	Ea	236.00	85.30	34.00	355.30
21" diameter, 285 lb	S6@2.51	Ea	492.00	117.00	46.60	655.60
24" diameter, 375 lb	S6@2.87	Ea	685.00	134.00	53.30	872.30

Manholes Equipment includes a wheel-mounted 1 CY backhoe for lifting and placing the items. Trench excavation, bedding material and backfill are not included. Use $3,000 as a minimum job charge. Precast concrete manholes, including concrete top and base. No excavation or backfill included. Add for steps, frames and lids from the costs listed below

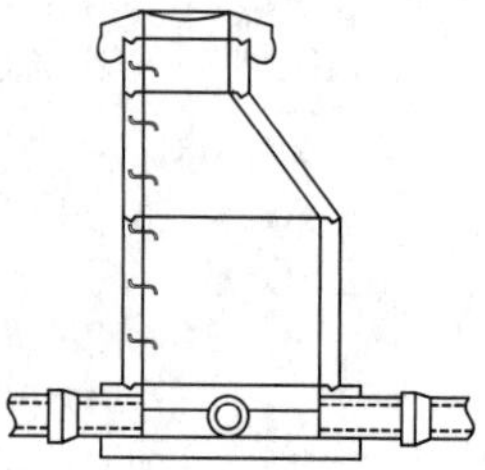

	Craft@Hrs	Unit	Material	Labor	Equipment	Total
3' x 6' to 8' deep	S6@17.5	Ea	2,440.00	815.00	325.00	3,580.00
3' x 9' to 12' deep	S6@19.4	Ea	2,860.00	904.00	360.00	4,124.00
3' x 13' to 16' deep	S6@23.1	Ea	3,690.00	1,080.00	429.00	5,199.00
3' diameter, 4' deep	S6@12.1	Ea	1,440.00	564.00	225.00	2,229.00
4' diameter, 5' deep	S6@22.8	Ea	1,740.00	1,060.00	423.00	3,223.00
4' diameter, 6' deep	S6@26.3	Ea	1,970.00	1,230.00	488.00	3,688.00
4' diameter, 7' deep	S6@30.3	Ea	2,140.00	1,410.00	563.00	4,113.00
4' diameter, 8' deep	S6@33.7	Ea	2,410.00	1,570.00	626.00	4,606.00
4' diameter, 9' deep	S6@38.2	Ea	2,550.00	1,780.00	709.00	5,039.00
4' diameter, 10' deep	S6@43.3	Ea	2,790.00	2,020.00	804.00	5,614.00
Concrete block radial manholes, 4' inside diameter, no excavation or backfill included						
4' deep	M1@8.01	Ea	582.00	382.00	—	964.00
6' deep	M1@13.4	Ea	854.00	640.00	—	1,494.00
8' deep	M1@20.0	Ea	1,240.00	955.00	—	2,195.00
10' deep	M1@26.7	Ea	1,280.00	1,270.00	—	2,550.00
Depth over 10', add per LF	M1@2.29	LF	160.00	109.00	—	269.00
2' depth cone block for 30" grate	M1@5.34	LF	243.00	255.00	—	498.00
2'6" depth cone block for 24" grate	M1@6.43	LF	315.00	307.00	—	622.00
Manhole steps, cast iron, heavy type, asphalt coated						
10" x 14-1/2" in job-built manhole	M1@.254	Ea	28.40	12.10	—	40.50
12" x 10" in precast manhole	—	Ea	26.00	—	—	26.00
Gray iron manhole frames, asphalt coated, standard sizes						
Light-duty frame and lid						
15" diameter, 65 lb	S6@.660	Ea	147.00	30.70	12.30	190.00
22" diameter, 140 lb	S6@1.42	Ea	324.00	66.20	26.40	416.60
Medium-duty frame and lid						
11" diameter, 75 lb	S6@1.51	Ea	173.00	70.40	28.00	271.40
20" diameter, 185 lb	S6@3.01	Ea	396.00	140.00	55.90	591.90

	Craft@Hrs	Unit	Material	Labor	Equipment	Total
Heavy-duty frame and lid						
17" diameter, 135 lb	S6@2.51	Ea	302.00	117.00	46.60	465.60
21" diameter, 315 lb	S6@3.77	Ea	669.00	176.00	70.00	915.00
24" diameter, 375 lb	S6@4.30	Ea	775.00	200.00	79.80	1,054.80
Connect new drain line to existing manhole, no excavation or backfill included.						
Per connection	S6@6.83	Ea	229.00	318.00	127.00	674.00
Connect existing drain line to new manhole, no excavation or backfill included.						
Per connection	S6@3.54	Ea	138.00	165.00	65.70	368.70
Manhole repairs and alterations, typical costs						
Repair manhole leak with grout	S6@15.8	Ea	645.00	736.00	293.00	1,674.00
Repair inlet leak with grout	S6@15.8	Ea	784.00	736.00	293.00	1,813.00
Grout under manhole frame	S6@1.29	Ea	13.40	60.10	24.00	97.50
Drill and grout pump setup cost	S6@17.4	LS	784.00	811.00	323.00	1,918.00
Grout for pressure grouting	—	Gal	13.30	—	—	13.30
Replace brick in manhole wall	M1@8.79	SF	19.30	420.00	—	439.30
Replace brick under manhole frame	M1@8.79	LS	63.70	420.00	—	483.70
Raise existing frame and cover 2"	CL@4.76	LS	353.00	196.00	—	549.00
Raise existing frame and cover more than 2", per each 1" added	CL@.250	LS	121.00	10.30	—	131.30
Grouting concrete pipe joints						
6" to 30" diameter	S6@.315	Ea	32.30	14.70	5.85	52.85
33" to 60" diameter	S6@1.12	Ea	63.60	52.20	20.80	136.60
66" to 72" diameter	S6@2.05	Ea	129.00	95.50	38.10	262.60

TV inspection of pipe interior, Robotic crawl camera inspecting 6" to 36" pipe. Report includes a DVD or VHS images and a plot of obstructions. Equipment is a video truck with operator. Time starts at the yard.

	Craft@Hrs	Unit	Material	Labor	Equipment	Total
Full 8-hour day	—	LS	—	—	—	1,450.00
Half day (4 hours)	—	LS	—	—	—	830.00
Addition hours	—	Ea	—	—	—	227.00
Pipe locator (2 hour minimum)	—	Hr	—	—	—	157.00

Accessories for Site Utilities Equipment includes a wheel-mounted 1 CY backhoe for lifting and placing the items. Trench excavation, bedding material and backfill are not included. Costs estimated using this section may be combined with costs estimated from other site work utility sections for arriving at a minimum job charge.

	Craft@Hrs	Unit	Material	Labor	Equipment	Total
Curb inlets, gray iron, asphalt coated, heavy-duty frame, grate and precast curb box						
20" x 11", 260 lb	S6@2.75	Ea	534.00	128.00	51.10	713.10
20" x 16.5", 300 lb	S6@3.04	Ea	581.00	142.00	56.40	779.40
20" x 17", 400 lb	S6@4.30	Ea	735.00	200.00	79.80	1,014.80
19" x 18", 500 lb	S6@5.06	Ea	881.00	236.00	93.90	1,210.90
30" x 17", 600 lb	S6@6.04	Ea	953.00	281.00	112.00	1,346.00
Gutter inlets, gray iron, asphalt coated, heavy-duty frame and grate						
8" x 11.5", 85 lb	S6@.444	Ea	178.00	20.70	8.24	206.94
22" x 17", 260 lb, concave	S6@1.84	Ea	510.00	85.70	34.20	629.90
22.3" x 22.3", 475 lb	S6@2.87	Ea	555.00	134.00	53.30	742.30
29.8" x 17.8", 750 lb	S6@3.37	Ea	850.00	157.00	62.60	1,069.60
Trench inlets, ductile iron, light-duty frame and grate for pedestrian traffic						
53.5" x 8.3", 100 lb	S6@.495	Ea	174.00	23.10	9.19	206.29
Trench inlets, gray iron, asphalt coated frame and grate or solid cover						
Light-duty, 1-1/4"						
8" wide grate	S6@.247	LF	73.50	11.50	4.59	89.59
12" wide grate	S6@.275	LF	106.00	12.80	5.10	123.90
8" wide solid cover	S6@.247	LF	81.50	11.50	4.59	97.59
12" wide solid cover	S6@.275	LF	115.00	12.80	5.10	132.90

	Craft@Hrs	Unit	Material	Labor	Equipment	Total
Heavy-duty, 1-3/4"						
8" wide grate	S6@.275	LF	79.80	12.80	5.10	97.70
12" wide grate	S6@.309	LF	117.00	14.40	5.74	137.14
8" wide solid cover	S6@.275	LF	92.20	12.80	5.10	110.10
12" wide solid cover	S6@.309	LF	127.00	14.40	5.74	147.14

Concrete headwalls By culvert drain pipe size. With 30-degree skewed wingwall. Add the cost of excavation, backfill and compaction.

	Craft@Hrs	Unit	Material	Labor	Equipment	Total
Cast in place concrete headwalls.						
12" pipe	P9@3.50	Ea	650.00	170.00	—	820.00
15" pipe	P9@3.80	Ea	478.00	184.00	—	662.00
18" pipe	P9@4.00	Ea	996.00	194.00	—	1,190.00
24" pipe	P9@4.50	Ea	1,480.00	218.00	—	1,698.00
30" pipe	P9@5.00	Ea	1,730.00	243.00	—	1,973.00
36" pipe	P9@7.50	Ea	1,960.00	364.00	—	2,324.00
42" pipe	P9@7.80	Ea	2,390.00	379.00	—	2,769.00
48" pipe	P9@9.90	Ea	2,510.00	481.00	—	2,991.00
54" pipe	P9@14.0	Ea	2,660.00	680.00	—	3,340.00
60" pipe	P9@15.5	Ea	3,450.00	752.00	—	4,202.00
Precast concrete headwalls, placed with a 1.38 CY wheel-loader backhoe						
12" pipe	S6@8.00	Ea	375.00	373.00	16.60	764.60
15" pipe	S6@8.00	Ea	375.00	373.00	16.60	764.60
18" pipe	S6@9.60	Ea	375.00	447.00	20.20	842.20
24" pipe	S6@9.60	Ea	455.00	447.00	20.20	922.20
30" pipe	S6@12.0	Ea	693.00	559.00	25.20	1,277.20
36" pipe	S6@12.0	Ea	693.00	559.00	25.20	1,277.20

Gas Distribution Lines Installed in an open trench. Equipment includes a wheel-mounted 1 CY backhoe for lifting and placing the pipe. No excavation, bedding material or backfill included. Use $2,000 as a minimum job charge.

	Craft@Hrs	Unit	Material	Labor	Equipment	Total
Polyethylene pipe, 60 PSI						
1-1/4" diameter, coils	U1@.064	LF	2.37	3.25	.89	6.51
1-1/2" diameter, coils	U1@.064	LF	1.70	3.25	.89	5.84
2" diameter, coils	U1@.071	LF	4.48	3.61	.99	9.08
3" diameter, coils	U1@.086	LF	4.30	4.37	1.20	9.87
3" diameter, 38' long with couplings	U1@.133	LF	5.31	6.76	1.85	13.92
4" diameter, 38' long with couplings	U1@.168	LF	9.49	8.54	2.34	20.37
6" diameter, 38' long with couplings	U1@.182	LF	32.80	9.25	2.53	44.58
8" diameter, 38' long with couplings	U1@.218	LF	39.50	11.10	3.04	53.64

Meters and pressure regulators Natural gas diaphragm meters, direct digital reading, not including temperature and pressure compensation. For use with pressure regulators below.

	Craft@Hrs	Unit	Material	Labor	Equipment	Total
425 CFH at 10 PSI	P6@4.38	Ea	358.00	229.00	—	587.00
425 CFH at 25 PSI	P6@4.38	Ea	474.00	229.00	—	703.00
Natural gas pressure regulators with screwed connections						
3/4" or 1" connection	P6@.772	Ea	36.50	40.40	—	76.90
1-1/4" or 1-1/2" connection	P6@1.04	Ea	194.00	54.50	—	248.50
2" connection	P6@1.55	Ea	1,590.00	81.20	—	1,671.20

Pipe Jacking Typical costs for jacking .50" thick wall pipe casing under an existing roadway. Costs assume casing is left in place. Add 15% when ground water is present. Add 100% for light rock conditions. Includes jacking pits on both sides. Equipment includes a 1 CY wheel-mounted backhoe plus a 2-ton truck equipped for this type of work. Size shown is casing diameter. Use $2,200 as a minimum job charge.

	Craft@Hrs	Unit	Material	Labor	Equipment	Total
2" casing	C5@.289	LF	8.43	13.40	6.15	27.98
3" casing	C5@.351	LF	9.89	16.30	7.47	33.66
4" casing	C5@.477	LF	13.00	22.10	10.20	45.30
6" casing	C5@.623	LF	16.80	28.90	13.30	59.00

	Craft@Hrs	Unit	Material	Labor	Equipment	Total
8" casing	C5@.847	LF	22.40	39.30	18.00	79.70
10" casing	C5@1.24	LF	32.90	57.60	26.40	116.90
12" casing	C5@1.49	LF	39.70	69.20	31.70	140.60
16" casing	C5@1.78	LF	47.30	82.60	37.90	167.80
17" casing	C5@2.09	LF	54.30	97.00	44.50	195.80
24" casing	C5@7.27	LF	193.00	338.00	155.00	686.00
30" casing	C5@7.88	LF	208.00	366.00	168.00	742.00
36" casing	C5@8.61	LF	231.00	400.00	183.00	814.00
42" casing	C5@9.29	LF	244.00	431.00	198.00	873.00
48" casing	C5@10.2	LF	269.00	474.00	217.00	960.00

Index

C

D

E

F

G

H

I

J

K

L

Q

R

S

T

U

X

Y

Z

Excavation & Grading Handbook Revised

The foreman's, superintendent's and operator's guide to highway, subdivision and pipeline jobs: how to read plans and survey stake markings, set grade, excavate, compact, pave and lay pipe on nearly any job. Includes hundreds of informative, on-the-job photos and diagrams that even experienced pros will find invaluable. This new edition has been completely revised to be current with state-of-the-art equipment usage and the most efficient excavating and grading techniques. You'll learn how to read topo maps, use a laser level, set crows feet, cut drainage channels, lay or remove asphaltic concrete, and use GPS and sonar for absolute precision. For those in training, each chapter has a set of self-test questions, and a Study Center CD-ROM included has all 250 questions in a simple interactive format to make learning easy and fun. **512 pages, 8½ x 11, $59.00**
Also available as an eBook (PDF), $29.50 at www.craftsman-book.com

Construction Contract Writer

Relying on a "one-size-fits-all" boilerplate construction contract to fit your jobs can be dangerous — almost as dangerous as a handshake agreement. *Construction Contract Writer* lets you draft a contract in minutes that precisely fits your needs and the particular job, and meets both state and federal requirements. You just answer a series of questions — like an interview — to construct a legal contract for each project you take on. Anticipate where disputes could arise and settle them in the contract before they happen. Include the warranty protection you intend, the payment schedule, and create subcontracts from the prime contract by just clicking a box. Includes a feedback button to an attorney on the Craftsman staff to help should you get stumped — *No extra charge.* **$149.95.**
Download the *Construction Contract Writer* at:
http://www.constructioncontractwriter.com

Markup & Profit: A Contractor's Guide, Revisited

In order to succeed in a construction business, you have to be able to price your jobs to cover all labor, material and overhead expenses, and make a decent profit. But calculating markup is only part of the picture. If you're going to beat the odds and stay in business — profitably, you also need to know how to write good contracts, manage your crews, work with subcontractors and collect on your work. This book covers the business basics of running a construction company, whether you're a general or specialty contractor working in remodeling, new construction or commercial work. The principles outlined here apply to all construction-related businesses. You'll find tried and tested formulas to guarantee profits, with step-by-step instructions and easy-to-follow examples to help you learn how to operate your business successfully. Includes a link to free downloads of blank forms and checklists used in this book. **336 pages, 8½ x 11, $52.50**
Also available as an eBook (ePub, mobi for Kindle), $39.95 at www.craftsman-book.com

Roofing Construction & Estimating

Installation, repair and estimating for nearly every type of roof covering available today in residential and commercial structures: asphalt shingles, roll roofing, wood shingles and shakes, clay tile, slate, metal, built-up, and elastomeric. Covers sheathing and underlayment techniques, as well as secrets for installing leakproof valleys. Many estimating tips help you minimize waste, as well as insure a profit on every job. Troubleshooting techniques help you identify the true source of most leaks. Over 300 large, clear illustrations help you find the answer to just about all your roofing questions. **448 pages, 8½ x 11, $38.00**
eBook (PDF) also available, $19.00 at www.craftsman-book.com

Concrete Construction

Just when you think you know all there is about concrete, many new innovations create faster, more efficient ways to do the work. This comprehensive concrete manual has both the tried-and-tested methods and materials, and more recent innovations. It covers everything you need to know about concrete, along with Styrofoam forming systems, fiber reinforcing adjuncts, and some architectural innovations, like architectural foam elements, that can help you offer more in the jobs you bid on. Every chapter provides detailed, step-by-step instructions for each task, with hundreds of photographs and drawings that show exactly how the work is done. To keep your jobs organized, there are checklists for each stage of the concrete work, from planning, to finishing and protecting your pours. Whether you're doing residential or commercial work, this manual has the instructions, illustrations, charts, estimating data, rules of thumb and examples every contractor can apply on their concrete jobs. **288 pages, 8½ x 11, $28.75**
Also available as an eBook (PDF), $14.38 at www.craftsman-book.com

Standard Estimating Practice, 10th edition

Estimating isn't always an easy job. Sometimes snap decisions can produce negative long-term effects. This book was designed by the American Society of Professional Estimators as a set of standards to guide professional estimators. It's intended to help every estimator develop estimates that are uniform and verifiable. Every step that should be included in the estimate is listed, as well as aspects in the plans to consider when you're estimating a job, and what you should look for that may not be included. The result should help you produce more consistently accurate estimates.
852 pages, 8½ x 11, $99.95

Craftsman's Construction Installation Encyclopedia

Step-by-step installation instructions for just about any residential construction, remodeling or repair task, arranged alphabetically, from *Acoustic tile to Wood flooring.* Includes hundreds of illustrations that show how to build, install, or remodel each part of the job, as well as manhour tables for each work item so you can estimate and bid with confidence. Also includes a CD-ROM with all the material in the book, handy look-up features, and the ability to capture and print out for your crew the instructions and diagrams for any job. **792 pages, 8½ x 11, $65.00**
Also available as an eBook (PDF), $32.50 at www.craftsman-book.com

National Building Cost Manual

Square-foot costs for residential, commercial, industrial, military, schools, greenhouses, churches and farm buildings. Includes important variables that can make any building unique from a cost standpoint. Quickly work up a reliable budget estimate based on actual materials and design features, area, shape, wall height, number of floors, and support requirements. Now includes free download of Craftsman's easy-to-use software that calculates total in-place cost estimates or appraisals. Use the regional cost adjustment factors provided to tailor the estimate to any jobsite in the U.S. Then view, print, email or save the detailed PDF report as needed.
280 pages, 8½ x 11, $88.00. Revised annually
Also available as an eBook (PDF), $44.00 at www.craftsman-book.com

National Electrical Estimator

This year's prices for installation of all common electrical work: conduit, wire, boxes, fixtures, switches, outlets, loadcenters, panelboards, raceway, duct, signal systems, and more. Provides material costs, manhours per unit, and total installed cost. Explains what you should know to estimate each part of an electrical system. Includes a free download of an electronic version of the book with *National Estimator*, a stand-alone *Windows*™ estimating program. Additional information and *National Estimator* ShowMe tutorial is available on our website under the "Support" drop-down tab. **552 pages, 8½ x 11, $97.75. Revised annually**
Also available as an eBook (PDF), $48.88 at www.craftsman-book.com

Estimating & Bidding for Builders & Remodelers

This 5th edition has all the information you need for estimating and bidding new construction and home improvement projects. It shows how to select jobs that will be profitable, do a labor and materials take-off from the plans, calculate overhead and figure your markup, and schedule the work. Includes a CD with an easy-to-use construction estimating program and a database of 50,000 current labor and material cost estimates for new construction and home improvement work, with area modifiers for every zip code. Price updates on the Web are free and automatic.
272 pages, 8½ x 11, $89.50
Also available as an eBook (PDF), $44.75 at www.craftsman-book.com

Estimating Home Building Costs, Revised

Estimate every phase of residential construction from site costs to the profit margin you include in your bid. Shows how to keep track of manhours and make accurate labor cost estimates for site clearing and excavation, footings, foundations, framing and sheathing finishes, electrical, plumbing, and more. Provides and explains sample cost estimate worksheets with complete instructions for each job phase. This practical guide to estimating home construction costs has been updated with digital *Excel* estimating forms and worksheets that ensure accurate and complete estimates for your residential projects. Enter your project information on the worksheets and *Excel* automatically totals each material and labor cost from every stage of construction to a final cost estimate worksheet. Load the enclosed CD-ROM into your computer and create your own estimate as you follow along with the step-by-step techniques in this book.
336 pages, 8½ x 11, $38.00
Also available as an eBook (PDF), $19.00 at www.craftsman-book.com

Builders Guide to Swimming Pool Construction

Break into the lucrative swimming pool construction business with this practical how-to guide. Here you'll learn how to get the permits and do the surveying, planning and layout for a typical pool, including how to read a soils report. You'll read about the excavation, backfill, soil compaction, sand and gravel bedding and drainage requirements, and mechanical systems such as pumps, heaters, filters, skimmers, and solar systems. Covers underground piping, including drain, supply, and gas; and electrical work, including grounding and supply to breaker, pump, underwater lighting, and heater. Shows wood and pre-fabricated metal forms for walls, steps, spas, equipment base and diving board base, and how to install bar and mesh steel reinforcement. Covers cast-in-place and sprayed concrete and modern pool finishes. Includes scheduling, and a section on estimating labor, material and equipment costs.
240 pages, 8½ x 11, $49.95. Published by Builder's Book, Inc.

National Home Improvement Estimator

Current labor and material prices for home improvement projects. Provides manhours for each job, recommended crew size, and the labor cost for removal and installation work. Material prices are current, with location adjustment factors and free monthly updates on the Web. Gives step-by-step instructions for the work, with helpful diagrams, and home improvement shortcuts and tips from experts. Includes a free download of an electronic version of the book, and *National Estimator*, a stand-alone *Windows*™ estimating program. Additional information and *National Estimator* ShowMe tutorial is available on our website under the "Support" dropdown tab.
568 pages, 8½ x 11, $98.75. Revised annually
Also available as an eBook (PDF), $49.38 at www.craftsman-book.com

Estimating Excavation Revised eBook

How to calculate the amount of dirt you'll have to move and the cost of owning and operating the machines you'll do it with. Detailed, step-by-step instructions on how to assign bid prices to each part of the job, including labor and equipment costs. Also, the best ways to set up an organized and logical estimating system, take off from contour maps, estimate quantities in irregular areas, and figure your overhead. This revised edition includes a chapter on earthwork estimating software. As with any tool, you have to pick the right one. Written by an experienced dirt contractor and instructor of computer estimating software, this chapter covers the program types, explains how they work, gives the basics of how to use them, and discusses what will work best for the type of work you handle. This e-Book is the download version of the book in text searchable, PDF format. Craftsman eBooks are for use in the freely distributed Adobe Reader and are compatible with Reader 6.0 or above. **550 pages**
eBook (PDF) also available, $21.75 at www.craftsman-book.com

Builder's Guide to Accounting Revised

Step-by-step, easy-to-follow guidelines for setting up and maintaining records for your building business. This practical guide to all accounting methods shows how to meet state and federal accounting requirements, explains the new depreciation rules, and describes how the Tax Reform Act can affect the way you keep records. Full of charts, diagrams, simple directions and examples to help you keep track of where your money is going. Recommended reading for many state contractor's exams. Each chapter ends with a set of test questions, and a CD-ROM included FREE has all the questions in interactive self-test software. Use the Study Mode to make studying for the exam much easier, and Exam Mode to practice your skills. **360 pages, 8½ x 11, $35.50**
Also available as an eBook (PDF), $17.75 at www.craftsman-book.com

Insurance Restoration Contracting: Startup to Success

Insurance restoration — the repair of buildings damaged by water, fire, smoke, storms, vandalism and other disasters — is an exciting field of construction that provides lucrative work that's immune to economic downturns. And, with insurance companies funding the repairs, your payment is virtually guaranteed. But this type of work requires special knowledge and equipment, and that's what you'll learn about in this book. It covers fire repairs and smoke damage, water losses and specialized drying methods, mold remediation, content restoration, even damage to mobile and manufactured homes. You'll also find information on equipment needs, training classes, estimating books and software, and how restoration leads to lucrative remodeling jobs. It covers all you need to know to start and succeed as the restoration contractor that both homeowners and insurance companies call on first for the best jobs. **640 pages, 8½ x 11, $69.00**
Also available as an eBook (PDF), $34.50 at www.craftsman-book.com

Building Code Compliance for Contractors & Inspectors

An answer book for both contractors and building inspectors, this manual explains what it takes to pass inspections under the 2009 *International Residential Code*. It includes a code checklist for every trade, covering some of the most common reasons why inspectors reject residential work — footings, foundations, slabs, framing, sheathing, plumbing, electrical, HVAC, energy conservation and final inspection. The requirement for each item on the checklist is explained, and the code section cited so you can look it up or show it to the inspector. Knowing in advance what the inspector wants to see gives you an (almost unfair) advantage. To pass inspection, do your own pre-inspection before the inspector arrives. If your work requires getting permits and passing inspections, put this manual to work on your next job. If you're considering a career in code enforcement, this can be your guidebook.
8½ x 11, 232 pages, $32.50
Also available as an eBook (PDF), $16.25 at www.craftsman-book.com

National Repair & Remodeling Estimator

The complete pricing guide for dwelling reconstruction costs. Reliable, specific data you can apply on every repair and remodeling job. Up-to-date material costs and labor figures based on thousands of jobs across the country. Provides recommended crew sizes; average production rates; exact material, equipment, and labor costs; a total unit cost and a total price including overhead and profit. Separate listings for high- and low-volume builders, so prices shown are specific for any size business. Estimating tips specific to repair and remodeling work to make your bids complete, realistic, and profitable. Includes a free download of an electronic version of the book with *National Estimator*, a stand-alone *Windows*™ estimating program. Additional information and *National Estimator* ShowMe tutorial is available on our website under the "Support" dropdown tab.
512 pages, 8½ x 11, $98.50. Revised annually
Also available as an eBook (PDF), $49.25 at www.craftsman-book.com

Pipe & Excavation Contracting Revised

This popular manual has been updated and improved to bring it more current with modern earthmoving and trenching equipment, refined excavation techniques, stricter safety rules, and improved materials. Shows how to read plans and compute quantities for both trench and surface excavation, figure crew and equipment productivity rates, estimate unit costs, bid the work, and get the bonds you need. Learn how to choose the right equipment for each job, use GPS, how to lay all types of water and sewer pipe, work on steep slopes or in high groundwater, efficiently remove asphalt and rock, and the various pipe, joints and fittings now available. Explains how to switch your business to excavation work when you don't have pipe contracts, and how to avoid the pitfalls that can wipe out your profits on any job. **328 pages, 8½ x 11, $35.00**
Also available as an eBook (PDF), $17.50 at www.craftsman-book.com

Moving to Commercial Construction

In commercial work, a single job can keep you and your crews busy for a year or more. The profit percentages are higher, but so is the risk involved. This book takes you step-by-step through the process of setting up a successful commercial business: finding work, estimating and bidding, value engineering, getting through the submittal and shop drawing process, keeping a stable work force, controlling costs, and promoting your business. Explains the design/build and partnering business concepts and their advantage over the competitive bid process. Includes sample letters, contracts, checklists and forms that you can use in your business, plus a CD-ROM with blank copies in several word-processing formats for both Mac™ and PC computers.
256 pages, 8½ x 11, $42.00
***Also available as an eBook (PDF), $21.00* at www.craftsman-book.com**

Profits in Buying & Renovating Homes

Step-by-step instructions for selecting, repairing, improving, and selling highly profitable "fixer-uppers." Shows which price ranges offer the highest profit-to-investment ratios, which neighborhoods offer the best return, practical directions for repairs, and tips on dealing with buyers, sellers, and real estate agents. Shows you how to determine your profit before you buy, what "bargains" to avoid, and how to make simple, profitable, inexpensive upgrades.
304 pages, 8½ x 11, $24.75

Craftsman eLibrary

Craftsman's eLibrary license gives you immediate access to 60+ PDF eBooks in our bookstore for 12 full months!
You pay only one low price. $129.99.
Visit www.craftsman-book.com for more details.

International Residential Code (IRC) 2018 Fast-Tabs

User-friendly International Residential Code (*IRC*) Tabs are a great way to organize the *IRC* 2018. These self-adhesive tabs can reduce the time spent searching to find key information. Tabs are durable and allow for positioning adjustments after being placed on the code paper. Affordable and time-saving, these are a must-have for IRC users. Can also be used with loose-leaf version.
8 x 5½, $15.95. Published by Builder's Book, Inc.

International Building Code (IBC) Quick-Card: Based on 2018 IBC

In this unique, 6-page laminated quick-reference guide, you get all the International Building Code (IBC) essentials you need to know based on the current 2018 IBC. The scope of the International Building Code (IBC) includes all buildings except detached one- and two-family dwellings and townhouses up to three stories. Featured sections: Foundations & Footings, Concrete, Floor Framing, Wall Framing, Roof Framing, Interior Dimensions, Means of Egress, Fire & Smoke Protection, Safety Glazing, Handrails, Stairways & Guards, Masonry.
6 pages, 8½ x 11, $9.95. Published by Builder's Book, Inc.

International Building Code (IBC) 2018 Fast-Tabs

User-friendly International Building Code (*IBC*) Tabs are a great way to organize the *IBC* 2018. These self-adhesive tabs can reduce the time spent searching to find key information. Tabs are durable and allow for positioning adjustments after being placed on the code paper. Affordable and time-saving, these are a must-have for IBC users. Can also be used with Loose-leaf version.
8 x 5½, $15.95. Published by Builder's Book, Inc.

Estimating Electrical Construction Revised

Estimating the cost of electrical work can be a very detailed and exacting discipline. It takes specialized skills and knowledge to create reliable estimates for electrical work. See how an expert estimates materials and labor for residential and commercial electrical construction. Learn how to use labor units, the plan take-off, and the bid summary to make an accurate estimate, how to deal with suppliers, use pricing sheets, and modify labor units. This book provides extensive labor unit tables and blank forms on a CD for estimating your next electrical job. **272 pages, 8½ x 11, $59.00**
***Also available as an eBook (PDF), $29.50* at www.craftsman-book.com**

National Electrical Code Quick-Card 2020 NEC (Bldrs Book)

In this unique, 6-page laminated quick-reference guide, you get all the National Electrical Code (*NEC*) essentials you need to know based on the current 2020 *NEC*. **6 pages, 8½ x 11, $9.95**

Contractor's Guide to QuickBooks by Online Accounting

This book is designed to help a contractor, bookkeeper and their accountant set up and use QuickBooks Desktop specifically for the construction industry. No use re-inventing the wheel, we have used this system with contractors for over 30 years. It works and is now the national standard. By following the steps we outlined in the book you, too, can set up a good system for job costing as well as financial reporting.
156 pages, 8½ x 11, $68.50

OSHA Construction Safety Essentials Quick-Card

This extended, 6-page guide covers the OSHA Construction Safety Essentials. Great for contractors, builders, architects and engineers... anyone who needs a quick overview of the basics involved in this key construction issue. Featured sections: Personal Protective Equipment (PPE), Construction Site — Fall Protection — Openings, Scaffolding Safety, Site Safety — Ladders & Stairways, Excavation & Trench Safety, Electrical Safety, Hazard Communication.
6 pages, 8½ x 11, $7.95. Published by Builder's Book, Inc.

Renovating & Restyling Older Homes

Any builder can turn a run-down old house into a showcase of perfection — if the customer has unlimited funds to spend. Unfortunately, most customers are on a tight budget. They usually want more improvements than they can afford — and they expect you to deliver. This book shows how to add economical improvements that can increase the property value by two, five or even ten times the cost of the remodel. Sound impossible? Here you'll find the secrets of a builder who has been putting these techniques to work on Victorian and Craftsman-style houses for twenty years. You'll see what to repair, what to replace and what to leave, so you can remodel or restyle older homes for the least amount of money and the greatest increase in value. **416 pages, 8½ x 11, $33.50**

National Appraisal Estimator

An Online Appraisal Estimating Service. Produce credible single-family residence appraisals – in as little as five minutes. A smart resource for appraisers using the cost approach. Reports consider all significant cost variables and both physical and functional depreciation. For more information, visit
www.craftsman-book.com/national-appraisal-estimator-online-software

Insurance Replacement Estimator

Insurance underwriters demand detailed, accurate valuation data. There's no better authority on replacement cost for single-family homes than the *Insurance Replacement Estimator*. In minutes you get an insurance-to-value report showing the cost of re-construction based on your specification. You can generate and save unlimited reports. For more details, visit
www.craftsman-book.com/insurance-replacement-estimator-online-software

National Plumbing & HVAC Estimator

Manhours, labor and material costs for all common plumbing and HVAC work in residential, commercial, and industrial buildings. You can quickly work up a reliable estimate based on the pipe, fittings and equipment required. Every plumbing and HVAC estimator can use the cost estimates in this practical manual. Sample estimating and bidding forms and contracts also included. Explains how to handle change orders, letters of intent, and warranties. Describes the right way to process submittals, deal with suppliers and subcontract specialty work. Includes a free download of an electronic version of the book with National Estimator, a stand-alone WindowsTM estimating program. Additional information and *National Estimator* ShowMe tutorial is available on our website under the "Support" dropdown tab.
480 pages, 8½ x 11, $98.25. Revised annually
***eBook (PDF) also available,* $49.13 at www.craftsman-book.com**

The Art of Roof Cutting Series DVD Library - Basic DVD

You don't have to climb the walls, to learn to raise a roof! Steve Peters has been a framing contractor in Southern California for 14 years as well as a framer for more than 20 years. In this 120-minute video, Steve will share with you his extensive knowledge on the art of cutting and assembling theses roofs. **$79.95**

The Art of Roof Cutting Series DVD Library - Advanced DVD

In this Advanced Edition DVD video, expert framing contractor Steve shares his extensive knowledge on the art of cutting and assembling roofs. Used in Technical Schools and highly recommended by Building Contractors. **$79.95**

Wood-Frame House Construction

Step-by-step construction details, from the layout of the outer walls, excavation and formwork, to finish carpentry and painting. Packed with clear illustrations and explanations updated for modern construction methods. Everything you need to know about framing, roofing, siding, interior finishings, floor covering and stairs — your complete book of wood-frame homebuilding.
320 pages, 8½ x 11, $25.50. Revised edition

How to Succeed With Your Own Construction Business

Everything you need to start your own construction business: setting up the paperwork, finding the jobs, advertising, using contracts, dealing with lenders, estimating, scheduling, finding and keeping good employees, keeping the books, and coping with success. If you're considering starting your own construction business, all the knowledge, tips, and blank forms you need are here. **336 pages, 8½ x 11, $28.50**
***eBook (PDF) also available,* $14.25 at www.craftsman-book.com**

Shear Walls & Sheathing Lateral Loads Quick-Card (Bldrs Book)

This 6-page card quickly covers the construction essentials you need in loads and shear walls based on the new 2018 International Residential Code (IRC) for loads, shear walls & sheathing. Special sections focus on specific essentials for each area of framing. **6 pages, 8½ x 11, $7.95**

Residential Wood Framing Const. Quick-Card (Bldrs Book)

This 6-page laminated card covers the construction essentials for wood framing based on the new 2018 International Residential Code (IRC).
6 pages, 8½ x 11, $9.95

Planning Drain, Waste & Vent Systems

How to design plumbing systems in residential, commercial, and industrial buildings. Covers designing systems that meet code requirements for homes, commercial buildings, private sewage disposal systems, and even mobile home parks. Includes relevant code sections and many illustrations to guide you through what the code requires in designing drainage, waste, and vent systems. **192 pages, 8½ x 11, $29.95**

Basic Engineering for Builders

This book is for you if you've ever been stumped by an engineering problem on the job, yet wanted to avoid the expense of hiring a qualified engineer. Here you'll find engineering principles explained in non-technical language and practical methods for applying them on the job. With the help of this book you'll be able to understand engineering functions in the plans and how to meet the requirements, how to get permits issued without the help of an engineer, and anticipate requirements for concrete, steel, wood and masonry. See why you sometimes have to hire an engineer and what you can undertake yourself: surveying, concrete, lumber loads and stresses, steel, masonry, plumbing, and HVAC systems. This book is designed to help you, the builder, save money by understanding engineering principles that you can incorporate into the jobs you bid.
400 pages, 8½ x 11, $39.50
***eBook (PDF) also available;* $19.75 at www.craftsman-book.com**

Home Building Mistakes & Fixes

This is an encyclopedia of practical fixes for real-world home building and repair problems. There's never an end to "surprises" when you're in the business of building and fixing homes, yet there's little published on how to deal with construction that went wrong - where out-of-square or non-standard or jerry-rigged turns what should be a simple job into a nightmare. This manual describes jaw-dropping building mistakes that actually occurred, from disastrous misunderstandings over property lines, through basement floors leveled with an out-of-level instrument, to a house collapse when a siding crew removed the old siding. You'll learn the pitfalls the painless way, and real-world working solutions for the problems every contractor finds in a home building or repair jobsite. Includes dozens of those "surprises" and the author's step-by-step, clearly illustrated tips, tricks and workarounds for dealing with them.
384 pages, 8½ x 11, $52.50
***eBook (PDF) also available,* $26.25 at www.craftsman-book.com**

Contractor's Math Short Cuts Quick-Cards

In this single, 4-page laminated card, you get all the math essentials you need in contracting. The formulas and rules of thumb for calculating dimensions, surface areas, volume, etc. **4 pages, 8½ x 11, $7.95**

Drywall Essentials Quick Cards

This extended, 6-page guide covers the basics of the Drywall. Great for contractors, property owners... anyone who needs a quick overview of the basics involved in this key building phase. **6 pages, 8½ x 11, $7.95**

Residential Construction Foundation 2018 Quick-Card

An improperly constructed foundation will adversely affect the entire structure. But there are far too many details, measurements and rules — all code-enforced — to trust to memory. This handy 6-page guide provides at a glance the precise details and code requirements of this critical phase in residential construction. Based on the 2018 *IRC*. **6 pages, 8½ x 11, $9.95**

NE NOV 2020